# THE WINE BIBLE

# THE WINE BIBLE

## BY KAREN MacNEIL

WORKMAN PUBLISHING • NEW YORK

*To Dennis*
*and to the lesson of red tulips . . .*

Library of Congress Cataloging-in-Publication Data
MacNeil, Karen
The wine bible / by Karen MacNeil.
p. cm.
Includes index.
ISBN 1-56305-434-5 (alk. paper)
1. Wine and wine making. I. Title.
TP548.M24 2001
641.2′2—dc21                                   2001026549

Cover design by Paul Gamarello
Book design by Janet Vicario
Cover photographs by Anthony Loew except: *front*/center left, by
The Image Bank/Berglund; *front*/bottom right, by CORBIS/Spiegel;
*spine*, by Karen MacNeil; *back*/right, by Rick Grossman

Page 31 excerpt: From *Proof*, by Dick Francis, copyright © 1984 by Dick Francis.
Used by permission of G.P. Putnam's Sons, a division of Penguin Putnam Inc.

Workman books are available at special discounts when purchased in bulk
for premiums and sales promotions as well as for fund-raising or educational use.
Special editions or book excerpts can be created to specification.
For details, contact the Special Sales Director at the address below.

Workman Publishing Company, Inc.
708 Broadway
New York, NY 10003-9555
www.workman.com

Printed in the U.S.A.
First printing September 2001
10 9 8 7 6 5

# Acknowledgments

One day in 1990, while I was sitting in my office (then in New York City), the phone rang. The voice on the other end of the line said, "This is Peter Workman. I read a piece you wrote in *The New York Times*. Want to have lunch?" I knew who Peter Workman was, but I certainly didn't know Peter Workman. Still there's only one response to a question like that. At lunch the next day Peter said, "So what book have you always wanted to write?" I was speechless. Books don't happen like that (not to normal writers anyway). And so, above all, I want to thank Peter Workman for believing in me, for knowing, even before I did, what was possible.

Also at that lunch was Suzanne Rafer, who would become my editor. The relationship of editor and writer deserves a book itself, for it is filled with twists and turns, ups and downs, intrigue and emotion. In the end, a writer prays for an editor who's smart and kind and wise—the sort of editor who does everything in her power to help you write the best book you possibly can. Suzanne is that kind of woman, and I can't thank her enough. While many books may involve a single editor, *The Wine Bible* was daunting enough to deserve two. Barbara Mateer went through the book line by line, word by word, checking and questioning and making me refine, explain, rewrite, and polish passages until I could barely see straight. I have never met a woman of more formidable intellectual discipline, and *The Wine Bible* is a vastly better book because of Barbara's unrelenting pursuit of perfection. In addition to Suzanne and Barbara, I'm also grateful for Janet Vicario, who took a formidably large manuscript and from it created a compelling design for this book.

Many people have provided encouragement over the years of writing *The Wine Bible* and have also helped me immeasurably by being loyal friends (new and old), wise advisors, and wonderful companions with whom to share the special gift that a great bottle of wine undoubtedly is. These include Susan and Ed Auler, Kathy and David Best, Barbara and Alston Boyd, Meredith Luce Billingsly and Rusty Billingsly, Bob and Irene Belknap, Bob Cappuccino, David Chalfant, Eileen Crane and Eric Murray, Nancy and Michael Daniels, Joyce Goldstein, Carl Doumani, Arlene and Smitty Kogan, Lori and Harvey Marshak, Susan and Jay Magazine, Jim Spingarn, and my three dearest friends—Debra Deininger, Pam Hunter, and Terry Theise.

I've also benefited from a core of excellent assistants whose tasks have been endless and to whom thanks would be not nearly sufficient, given all their hard work. To Madeleine Albert, Clover Chadwick, Marion Groetschel, Daylen Jones, Penny Nann, Emily Richer, and Kay Wilson—thank you for bearing with me through the long hours, months, and years of this manuscript.

In the course of writing this book I've needed the patience and understanding of my editors at magazines as well as that of my colleagues at the Culinary Institute of America. For their support over the years I thank Stacy Morrison, Sara Schneider, Rosalie Wright, Lisa Higgins, Donna Warner, Greg Drescher, Holly Briwa, Reuben Katz, Mark Erickson, Christina Adamson, Cathy Jorin, Max Duley, Doug Crichton, and John Buechsenstein.

With writing a book this large comes the fear (usually at three in the morning) that you've forgotten some essential piece of information or overlooked a critical concept or—worse—gotten something entirely wrong. And so, early on in the writing, I asked numerous colleagues and experts to read selected parts of the first draft, knowing that the book would be stronger for their input. For their generosity in doing this, I want to thank: Rory Callahan, of Wine and Food Associates, who read a substantial part of the book; winemakers Zelma Long, John Alban, and Bill Dyer, who read winemaking and viticulture sections; Margo True, editor at *Gourmet*, and viticulturist Daniel Roberts, who read Mastering Wine; winemaker Eileen Crane, who read sections on sparkling wines and Champagne; Robin O'Connor, of the Bordeaux Information Bureau, and Fiona Morrison, Master of Wine, of the Conseil Interprofessional du Vin de Bordeaux, who read the Bordeaux chapter; Jean-Louis Carbonnier, former director of the Champagne Information Bureau, who read the chapter on Champagne; wine merchant and writer Kermit Lynch, who read the chapters on Beaujolais, Alsace, and Languedoc-Roussillon; winemaker Craig Williams, who read sections on the Rhône and Rhône varietals; Christopher Cannan, of Europvin, and Patrice Monmousseau, *président directeur général* of Bouvet-Ladubay, who read the Loire chapter; Jean Trimbach, of F. E. Trimbach, and Eveline Beydon-Schlumberger, of Domaines Schlumberger, who read the Alsace chapter; Martin Sinkoff, of Val d'Orbieu Wines, who read the Languedoc-Roussillon chapter; Giorgio Lulli, Augusto Marchini, Hermolina Ressa, Fred Marrapodi, and Jim Johnson, all from the Italian Trade Commission, who, in different ways, each provided immeasurable help by reading and providing information for the Italian section; Katrin Naelapaa and Louis Broman, of Wines from Spain, who read the Spanish section; Bartholomew Broadbent, who read the Port section; James Symington, of Symington Port and Madeira Shippers, who read the Madeira section; Terry Theise, of Terry Theise Selections, Bill Mayer, of The Age of Riesling, and Carol Sullivan and Cindy Krebs, of the German Wine Information Bureau, all of whom read the German section; Willi Balanjuk and Fritz Ascher, of the Austrian Wine Marketing Board, who read the Austrian section; Ben Howkins, of Royal Tokaji Wine Company, Thomas Laszlo, of Château Pajzos, and George Lang, of Lauder/Lang Vineyards and Lang Gastronomia, all of whom read the Hungarian section; Larry Brooks, wine consultant, who read the Carneros section; Jim Trezise, of the New York Wine and Grape Foundation, who read the New York State chapter; Simon Siegl, formerly of the Washington Wine Commission, who read the Washington State chapter; winemakers Steve Carey and David Lett, who read the Oregon chapter; vintners Susan and Ed Auler, who read the Texas chapter; Tony Bieda, of Horton Vineyards and Montdomaine, and Peggy Law, of Linden Vineyards, who read the Virginia chapter; Joel Butler, Master of Wine, and Nick Bulleid, Master of Wine, of Southcorp Wines, who read the Australian section; Lauraine Jacobs, of *Cuisine* magazine, and Philip Gregan, of the Wine Institute of New

Zealand, who read the New Zealand section; South African writer and wine critic Allan Mullins, who read the South Africa section; and Agustin Huneeus, of Quintessa, who read the section on Chile.

Also *The Wine Bible* could never have been written without the generous and patient assistance of many people who were willing to constantly supply me with facts, data, and research. There were many times when this wasn't as easy as it sounds, and so for going to great lengths to help me get the information I needed, I thank: Nancy Light and the public relations team at Robert Mondavi; Nancy Rugus, formerly of Seagram Chateau & Estate Wine Company; Margaret Stern, of Margaret Stern Communications; Michelle Armour and Amy Basle, of Maisons Marques & Domaines, and Lisa Somogyi, formerly of that company; Odila Galer Noel, of Frederick Wildman; Jan Stuebing, of the Australian Wine Bureau; Mary Marshall, Sheila Nicholas, and Mary Ann Sullivan, from Paterno; Tor Kenward and the staff of Beringer; Philip di Belardino, of Banfi; Barbara Edelman, of Barbara Edelman Communications; Julie Ann Kodmur, public relations consultant; Glenn McGourty, viticulture advisor for Mendocino and Lake Counties; Linda Reiff and the staff of the Napa Valley Vintners Association; Robert Sawicki, of Tamalpais Wine Agency; Mireille Guiliano, Suzanne da Silva, and the staff of Clicquot, Inc.; Cathleen Burke, Mary Ann Dancisin, Sara Powers, and Donna White, of Kobrand; Kimberly Charles, formerly of Gallo; Shirley Alpert, of the House of Burgundy; Martine Saunier, of Martine's Wines; Mary Davis Barton, of the division of marketing of the Virginia Department of Agriculture; Steve Burns and the staff of the Washington Wine Commission; Tim Dodd, of the Texas Wine Marketing Institute; Marcya Bagnall, of the Oregon Wine Advisory Board; Jeff Pogash, media relations manager, Schieffelin and Somerset; Pasquale Iocca and the staff of the Portuguese Trade Commission; Marsha Palanci, of Cornerstone Communications; Megghen Driscol, of Southcorp Wines North America; Steve Metzler, of Classical Wines of Spain; Jorge Ordonez, of Fine Estates from Spain; Laura Catena, of Catena Winery; Johannes Selbach, of Selbach-Oster; Ed Schwartz, of Ed Schwartz Public Relations; John Gillespie, of the Wine Market Council; Lara Zahaba and Sally Congleton, of Winebow; Georg Riedel, of Riedel Glass; and Kathleen Talbert, of Talbert Communications. I would also like to express my gratitude to the staffs of the Wine Institute; Foods and Wines from France; the Italian Trade Commission; Wines from Spain; the German Wine Information Bureau; Balzac Communications; Old Bridge Cellars; and Kermit Lynch Wine Merchant.

Finally, I want to thank my American colleagues in wine writing who, by being incredibly good at what they do, have challenged me to work even harder. Especially Gerald Asher, Alex Bespaloff, Anthony Dias Blue, Gerald Boyd, Bruce Cass, Mary Ewing-Mulligan, Daniel Johnnes, Matt Kramer, Anthony Gismondi, Howard Goldberg, Evan Goldstein, Sid Goldstein, Jim Gordon, Josh Greene, Harriet Lembeck, Thomas Matthews, Ed McCarthy, Richard Nalley, Steve Olson, Robert M. Parker Jr., Frank Prial, Bill Rice, David Rosengarten, Charlie Rubenstein, Bill St. John, Rod Smith, Harvey Steiman, Lettie Teague, Bob Thompson, Josh Wesson, and Kevin Zraly.

# Contents

IX

# Introduction

What possesses a person to spend ten years writing a 900-page wine book, you might wonder. In all honesty, there have been times—especially on weekends or late at night—that I've sat here at the computer and wondered the same thing. On top of this, writing about wine brings with it a kind of agonizing temptation that's wonderful and cruel at the same time. Alas, *writing* about Champagne (or Côte-Rôtie or California cabernet or Australian shiraz) is definitely not the same as *drinking* it, and there were times when I really wanted to trade in the keyboard for a corkscrew.

So why write something as encompassing as *The Wine Bible*?

Because I wanted people like you and me—wine lovers—to have a single authoritative book that would bring the world of wine alive. I hoped to write a book that would be comprehensive not just in the sense that you could find chapters on virtually every wine region worldwide, but a book that would look at wine from the perspectives of history, culture, and cuisine. Because that's how I think about wine. To me, it's a way—quite possibly the most pleasurable way—of understanding history, experiencing culture, and exalting in cuisine. (This might be the first wine book with full sections on the cuisines of all those sensational regions known both for wine *and* food.) And then there's wine itself, an endless treasure trove of fascination. Wine is the only beverage in the world that draws us in intellectually, causes us to think about it, to ponder it, to question why it tastes the way it does. Wine, it seems to me, is compelling not solely because it tastes good (though it surely does that) but because it appeals to the mind.

Because of these beliefs, I wrote *The Wine Bible* in a way that's different from most other wine books. Throughout the text you'll find material featured in boxes that I hope will cause you to say to yourself, "Isn't that amazing [or odd, fascinating, funny, wacky, or wonderful]." To me, wine is too exciting to be portrayed in endless gray columns of print. And so from the very beginnings of my research, I went in search of what I've come to think of as the delicious details that give wine its place and meaning. Writing a book this way means something else, too: It means you don't have to begin on page 1 and read straight through to the end. You can dip in anywhere.

There's something else you should know. In addition to being a wine, food, and restaurant writer, I am a wine teacher. For more than ten years, I've been a private wine tutor for both individuals and corporations nationwide and, as the chairman of the wine department of the Culinary Institute of America's Greystone campus in the Napa Valley, I teach wine courses for professionals in the wine, restaurant, food, and hospitality industries. In other words, I think like a teacher. And as you'll see, this is pretty apparent in *The Wine Bible*. Wherever and whenever possible, I've tried to explain even the most complex wine concepts right down to the most elemental notions. In fact, all along in the writing of this book, I've imagined you sitting here asking those questions we all have. I hope I've been able to sense them accurately and answer them well.

Despite these teacherly leanings, I've tried not to be pedantic. And in point of fact, much of my research has been anything but archly academic. That research started more than twenty years ago (before I ever imagined *The Wine Bible*), and it has taken me to every major wine-producing country in the world and many of the not so major ones as well. During these times, I've tried to understand any given wine in the context of those people who live and breathe it every day. This has caused me to have more than a few memorable experiences. I've drunk amarone while eating horsemeat (a tradition) in the Veneto; sipped just-fermented wine from goatskin bags in northern Greece (much as the ancients would have); been strapped into a contraption that lowers pickers down into steep German vineyards that sometimes have a slope of more than 50 degrees (an experience that momentarily convinces you your life is over); shared wine and cigars with bullfighters in bodegas in Rioja; ridden

through the vineyards of Australia on top of gargantuan picking machines; ridden through the vineyards of Texas on horseback; eaten octopus and drunk assyrtiko with Greek fishermen in Santorini (considered by some to be the lost Atlantis); picked tiny oyster shells from among the remnants of fossilized sea creatures that make up the chalky moon-crater-like soil of Chablis; waltzed among wine barrels with winemakers in Vienna; and worked for two weeks with a Mexican harvest crew in California, one of the hardest and most rewarding experiences I've ever had. These encounters brought wine so vividly into my life that I ultimately moved from Manhattan and now live on the top of a mountain, surrounded by grapevines.

In the end, there are numerous good wine books, many of them written by my colleagues and friends. My office is filled with these books, and I am grateful to own them. To these, I hope *The Wine Bible* will make a solid contribution. If it doesn't, I'll have to give back the red wagon my husband gave me to wheel the manuscript around in.

*—Karen MacNeil,*
*The Napa Valley*

# How to Use This Book

very author writing about wine has to make decisions about what to include, what to exclude (a harder choice), and how to present information that can be technical, complex, or just plain messy in scope. Here are my decisions and the thinking behind them.

## Where to Begin

Acquiring knowledge about wine doesn't usually occur in a linear fashion and neither, I suspect, does reading about wine. So *The Wine Bible* is written in a way that allows you to begin anywhere. You can, of course, start on page 1 with the part I call Mastering Wine, but if you want to read about Spain first, by all means, go ahead. Some readers may read this work cover to cover, but you can also dip into it over time as your fascination with a given topic, country, or type of wine takes hold.

## The Countries and Their Most Important Wines

Authoritative wine books written in the 1950s covered two countries—France and Germany. Sometimes Spain, Italy, and Portugal would be lumped together in a smaller chapter. Places such as the United States and Australia usually weren't covered at all. We live in a different world today. Wine is now made everywhere from Canada to New Zealand, as well as in places that can cause you to do a double take—like Japan. Having to draw the line, I decided to include all those countries whose wines I thought you would be

likely to encounter. Regrettably, because of space, I did omit others. So if you wanted to know about the wines of Bulgaria, Israel, Japan, or Romania, my apologies; they are not included here.

For every country that is included, you'll find a Most Important Wines box. The wines listed are divided into Leading Wines and Wines of Note. For each type of wine, I'll then tell you whether it is red, white, and/or rosé, and whether it's dry, sweet, sparkling, and/or fortified. By a sweet wine, I mean one that is, or could be, dessert. Let me add that in a few rare instances, a type of wine may be leading or noteworthy as a red but not as a white or vice versa. So Port—as a red wine—is listed as a leading wine in Portugal; white Port, though it exists, is not.

My hope is that the Most Important Wines boxes will give you a quick idea of the wines that most deserve your attention. For example, if you're going to Tuscany, which wines should you be sure not to miss? Helpful as I thought boxes like this would be, writing them was just short of agony, and I know there will be readers who disagree with my choices. Is Rosso di Montalcino a leading type of Tuscan wine, a wine of note, or not worth listing at all? (I decided it was noteworthy.) For the record, if a given type of wine is made in significant amounts and is potentially remarkable in quality or is in some other way fascinating and worth going out of your way to find, then it's a candidate for the Leading Wines list. By comparison, Wines of Note are those certainly worth trying (and good examples of these wines do exist) but are generally not worth passing up a leading wine for if you have to make a choice.

## About the Wines to Know

For each country, there's a section called the Wines to Know. (In major wine-producing countries, there's a Wines to Know section for each significant region within that country.) The Wines to Know are highly personal descriptions of individual wines that I recommend you try because I think they'll tell you, within a few sips, the story of that place in a way that words never can. (Just as an aside, looking for the wines that tell the story of a place is slightly different from looking only for "great" wines that might score high in a critic's notebook.) In the case of every such list, I tasted dozens upon dozens and often hundreds of wines to come up with the four to twelve or so that I consider pivotal. That, too, was often a difficult decision, and I know I've left some deserving wines out.

Let me say right from the start that some (but no means all) of the Wines to Know may be a little hard to find. This may depend on where you live. European wines, in particular, have traditionally been hard to find in smaller American cities and towns, especially in the Midwest. Luckily, the ability to buy wines on the Internet is now helping to improve that situation. But there are other wines that may be hard to find because, quite frankly, they aren't made in the hundreds of thousands of cases and so can't show up everywhere. These wines end up being bought by the wine drinkers who take the time to search them out. If there's a Wine to Know you're especially interested in,

call the best wine shop in your area and ask them to try to track down a few bottles for you. Really good wine shops distinguish themselves by providing services like this. Finally, I know that there will be a couple of wines that will probably prove nearly impossible to locate in wine shops. Nonetheless, I've included them because you may very well encounter them on a restaurant wine list (many small wineries sell virtually all their production to restaurants) and because these wines are well worth keeping an eye out for if you travel to the place where they were made.

## About Vintages

You'll notice that the Wines to Know don't include vintages. Not because vintages of a given wine aren't different—of course they are—but my hope was to present wines that are worth your knowing about in *any* vintage. I also hope that the whole concept of vintages is something that you'll take in stride because most vintages aren't nearly as cut and dry, black or white, good or bad as they are often made out to be. In this spirit, I hope you'll find How Much Do Vintages Matter? (page 78) evocative and worth consideration. In the meantime, if you want specific recommendations on vintages, there are numerous wonderful newsletters and magazines that regularly supply such information. One caveat: Don't expect leading critics to agree on subjects like this; it's not unusual for one critic to think a vintage is pretty exemplary, while another pans it.

## About Cost

I haven't given prices in *The Wine Bible*. That sort of information often changes so rapidly that only newsletters, newspapers, and magazines can attempt to be accurate. But I have sometimes indicated that a wine is a steal, or moderately priced, or super-expensive, and so on. As of the beginning of 2001, here are my definitions of those categories (prices are for single bottles): A steal: a wine selling for less than $8 that tastes like it should cost more. An inexpensive wine: one that costs less than $12. A moderately priced wine: one that costs between $12 and $18. An expensive wine: one that costs $30 or more. A superexpensive wine: one that costs $75 or more.

## About Food

What would a wine book be without food—wine's ineluctable companion? Mastering Wine has a section outlining strategies for pairing wine and food (page 83) and for each country you'll find boxes on some-times traditional, sometimes whimsical, wine and food marriages. But most won-derful of all for me was writing entire sec-tions on the foods of different countries or wine regions, for in many places—espe-cially in the Old World—the two topics are intimately entwined. Again, however, deciding whether or not a country's or region's foods were compelling enough to write about here was, well, fun to research and, in the end, a subjective decision.

## About the Glossaries

Though I've used English throughout *The Wine Bible* (or given definitions for foreign words), there are many foreign terms you might encounter on wine labels or while visiting various wine regions. As a result,

I've included French, Italian, Spanish, German and Austrian, Portuguese, Hun-garian, and Greek wine glossaries along with the comprehensive general glossary of wine terms. All of these glossaries appear at the end of this book.

## A Personal Admission

In the course of writing this book, I mar-ried Dennis Fife, proprietor of Fife Vine-yards in the Napa Valley. I want you to know this because Fife Vineyards is listed among other top producers in the Cali-fornia chapter.

## And Finally—About Names, Spelling, and Punctuation

As seemingly prosaic as this topic is, it can galvanize you as you attempt to write a book of this scope. Grape varieties are called different things or spelled different ways in different countries. Throughout, I've tried to be as clear as possible, always tipping you off about synonyms and local spellings. As for punctuation, you'll find that I've capitalized all wines that are named after places (this is standard), and put all grape varieties (and wines named after grape varieties) in lowercase. Thus in Piedmont, Italy, two of the leading wines are Barolo and barbera; the first capped because it takes its name from a place, the second appearing in lowercase because it's named after the grape. The only exception to this practice is grapes named after people, such as Muller-Thurgau and Palomino, both of which are capitalized.

# Mastering Wine

# What Makes Great Wine Great?

Most wine books begin with what wine is, and we'll definitely get into that. But I decided to lead off the first section of *The Wine Bible* with something different: the bottom line, the big question, and the most important part for most of us, and that is: What makes great wine great? From there, we'll get down to the specifics, and I'll take you through the details of what wine is; why great wines don't come from just anywhere; the stunning role that place plays in making a wine taste as it does; the vast world of grape varieties and how to get to know them; how wine is made; plus everything you need to know before you taste, from how to feel comfortable in a wine shop to how to choose the best wineglasses to the differences between aerating and decanting. Finally, we'll end with a bang: how to taste wine like a professional. I've concluded with this, not to be archingly academic but because the better your tasting technique, the more taste sensations (and pleasure) you'll derive from wine. And pleasure, I think you'll agree, is the whole point.

A final thought: I know that some parts of this first section are, well, not exactly edge-of-your-seat reading. It's hard to make ideas like clones and malolactic fermentation sexy. But I think you'll find that understanding the big picture of wine

*More than any other beverage, wine—and the pleasure it evokes—is meant to be shared.*

in all of its magnificent, wacky, and elemental details will only enhance your awe and enjoyment of what is, after all, the world's most captivating beverage.

## ASSESSING YOUR ASSESSMENT

One of the most insidious myths in American wine culture is that a wine is good if you like it. Liking a wine has nothing to do with whether it is good. Liking a wine has to do with liking that wine, period.

Wine requires two assessments: one subjective, the other objective. In this it is like literature. You may not like reading Shakespeare but agree that Shakespeare was a great writer nonetheless.

Getting to the point where you are knowledgeable enough to have both a subjective and an objective opinion of a wine is one of the most rewarding stages in developing wine expertise. It allows you to separate your liking of something from its quality. For example, it's entirely possible to love a wine but know it's not a great wine in the big scheme of things. I can think of a dozen wines that, for me, fit this bill perfectly.

Each of us has a subjective opinion, of course. Having a valid objective opinion, however, requires experiencing a particular wine and understanding how it classically presents itself.

Achieving this sort of discernment is possible only if you expand your sphere of tasting beyond the wines you already know you like. It is only by drinking wines that are unfamiliar to you and tasting them in a focused way with an open mind that you vault your wine knowledge into a higher realm.

*In the late nineteenth and early twentieth centuries, some of the first wine advertising campaigns depicted wine drinking as sensual and sophisticated. The posters often featured well-endowed women in evocative poses—with, of course, the requisite glass of wine in hand.*

Drinking wines within a narrow range of preference has another problem. It skews your palate. If all of the red wine you drink is muscular, tannic California cabernet sauvignon, over time you begin to think that good red wine is supposed to taste muscular and tannic. Then when someone hands you a glass of pinot noir from Germany (of which the Germans are justifiably proud), you'll find it thin, meek, and watery. Scientists call this phenomenon "frame error"—coming to a wrong assessment because the entity was evaluated in an inappropriate or jaded context.

3

The goal is to consciously try to avoid superimposing your ideas of what a wine is supposed to taste like, and instead to listen first to what the wine is "saying." Only over time can a wine drinker sense what to look for in a certain type of wine and evaluate it in its correct context.

## WHAT TO LOOK FOR

There are five qualities a taster must assess in order to determine whether a wine is great: varietal character, integration, expressiveness, complexity, and connectedness.

**Distinct varietal character** is a good thing. The more Granny Smith-ish the Granny Smith apple is, the more it can be savored and appreciated. The same is true for grape varieties. Each variety of grape presents itself in a unique way (see Getting to Know the Grapes, page 48).

---

### NICE LEGS . . .

The rivulets of wine that roll down the inside of the glass after a wine has been swirled are called legs here and in Britain. The Spanish call them tears; the Germans, church windows. Some wine drinkers look for great legs, falsely believing that nicely shaped legs (and who knows what that means?) portend great flavor. In fact, legs are a complex phenomenon related to the rate at which liquids evaporate and the differences in surface tension between water and the wine's alcohol content. Legs have nothing to do with greatness.

With wine, as with women, there is very little meaningful information one can deduce by looking at the legs.

---

When a young wine that has been made from a single variety of grape presents its inherent grape aromas and flavors in a straightforward, clear, and focused way, it is said to have varietal character.

Not all varietal characteristics have mass appeal. Some wine drinkers think the assertive, tangy green herb, olive, and straw character of some sauvignon blancs is quite nasty, especially if the aromas go one step further and take on what is often described as a cat piss smell. "Cat piss," as long as it's not extreme, is a description used approvingly by some wine drinkers (including me) who *do* like sauvignon blanc. There's an obvious analogy here with cheese. Just because some people cannot bear smelly cheese, is blue cheese awful? Should every cheese be remade in the image of Kraft singles, just because these have widespread appeal? The idea is absurd.

In addition to varietal character, a wine taster looks for four other qualities in a great wine: integration; expressiveness; complexity; and connectedness.

**Integration** is a state whereby the components of a wine (acid, tannin, alcohol, and so forth—we'll look at these in Where It All Begins, starting on page 7) are so impeccably interwoven that no one characteristic or component stands out. Integration means more than just balance (a good tension of opposites). Integration implies that all the components have come together in a harmonious fusion.

No matter how seemingly amorphous a concept, integration is what we are specifically after in wine. It is the bedrock upon which all wine judgment rests. Wine that is not integrated is far easier to describe than wine that is. The first presents itself like a star in the mouth. One can taste and talk about the "points" of acidity or tannin or oak. By comparison, an

4

*Parisian waiters on their "coffee" break. Many French brasseries, bistros, and wine bars buy entire barrels of good, simple wines. When you order a carafe of wine, it's filled directly from the barrel.*

integrated wine presents itself like a sphere in the mouth. So round, so harmonious that one cannot easily grab onto any single component, sensorially or intellectually.

**Expressiveness** is the quality a wine possesses when its aromas and flavors are well-defined and clearly projected. While some wines seem muddled and diffused, others beam out their character with almost unreal clarity and focus. Imagine the image projected by an out-of-focus black-and-white television without a cable hook-up compared to the same image in high-density color. An expressive wine is like the latter.

Given two well-made wines from two above-average vineyards in the same good year, it is not clear why one wine might be less expressive than the other. There are many ways in which winemaking could be at fault (overhandling a wine, for example, can discombobulate it). But it is also well known that certain vineyards year in and year out—for reasons too complex to fathom—simply produce expressive wines.

• • •

"Great wine is about nuance, surprise, subtlety, expression, qualities that keep you coming back for another taste. Rejecting a wine because it is not big enough is like rejecting a book because it is not long enough, or a piece of music because it is not loud enough."

*—Kermit Lynch,*
Adventures on the Wine Route

• • •

**Complexity** is not a thing but a phenomenon. Unlike, say, jamminess or acidity, you cannot go looking for the thing called complexity. Complexity is more like a force that pulls you into a wine and impels you to repeatedly return for another smell and sip because each time you do, you find something new.

Movie critics say that the greatest films are those that continue to crop up in your consciousness days after you have seen them. Walking down the street, you are suddenly filled with the image of a certain scene. Art critics, similarly, make a distinction between art that evokes a simple, momentary response in us and art that we cannot stop looking at.

The wine writer Matt Kramer points out that complexity in wine is "more than multiplicity [of flavors]" and that for a wine to be "truly satisfying, especially after repeated exposure, it must continually surprise us and yet we must still be able to grasp these surprises as part of a larger and pleasing pattern."

Like an integrated wine, a complex wine almost defies you to describe it. Yet just as the pain of a sore muscle feels good after exercise, the frustratingly undefinable nature of a complex wine heightens its gratification.

**Connectedness** is perhaps the most elusive of these concepts and the most difficult quality to ascertain. It is the sense you get from the wine's aroma and flavor that it could not have come from just anywhere but rather is the embodiment of a single piece of earth. Connectedness is the bond between a wine and the plot of land it was born in.

Connectedness, like cultural identity, makes a thing different from other things and therefore worthy of appreciation. It was, for example, curiously satisfying when, not so long ago, Frenchmen still wore berets, when you could find only olive oil (not butter) in the south of Italy, when Spanish children were given wine-dipped bread sprinkled with sugar as a snack. Each of these things, small as they were, revealed the links between people and their cultures and homes. Wine without connectedness to the ground from which it came may be of good quality but, like a Ramada Inn in Pamplona, there is a limit to how deep one's aesthetic appreciation of it can be.

Admittedly, a wine's integration, expressiveness, complexity, and connectedness (or lack thereof) may not be immediately obvious. But if you taste the wine slowly and think about these concepts, they'll soon begin to make sense. It's also fun to get an even greater command of these traits through some practice. So here's your wine homework: To discover what integration means, buy a white Burgundy, such as a Meursault, and think about harmony. For expressiveness, try a New Zealand sauvignon blanc and consider its intensity. Go looking for complexity by drinking a mature (ten years old or more) top-notch Bordeaux or Napa Valley cabernet sauvignon. And connectedness, though hard to describe, is easy to find. Try a Côte-Rôtie from the northern Rhône, with its almost savage peppery flavors, or a shimmeringly tart riesling from the Mosel region of Germany. Neither of these wines could come from anywhere other than the place it did.

# Where It All Begins

*Merlot grapes gathering sunshine on the vine. In most parts of the world dappled sunlight is ideal. There's neither too much shade, which would impede photosynthesis, nor so much sun that the grapes become sunburned.*

For all of wine's complexity, it is born of something utterly simple: a grape. A grape berry is, by weight, 75 percent pulp, 20 percent skin, and 5 percent seeds (there are usually two to four of them). Pulp is the soft, juicy center of the grape and the thing that will become the wine. Mostly water and, after that, sugar, the pulp of a ripe grape contains minuscule amounts of acids, minerals, and pectin compounds, plus a trace of vitamins. It's the sugar in the pulp that's crucial to vinification, since it's the sugar that will be converted to alcohol. As for the skins, they get to play the sexy part. They're largely responsible for the wine's aroma and flavor, as well as its color and

tannin (those seeds contribute a little bit of tannin, too). But a bunch of grapes has a way to go before it can be called wine. And once it's transformed, there will be several essential attributes to consider: alcohol, acid, tannin, fruitiness, and sweetness or dryness.

## GETTING FROM THE GRAPES TO THE GLASS

Alcohol is what results when yeasts come in contact with the natural sugar in grape pulp. Alcohol is a critical constituent in wine, not because of the genial mood it can evoke (although that's surely part of its charm), but rather because of the complex role it plays in the wine's ultimate quality. And, the more ripe the grapes are, the more natural sugar they will contain and the higher the alcohol content will be. Why does this matter?

First, because alcohol affects the body of the wine as well as the texture. High-alcohol wines are full, round, and supple; sometimes they can even seem almost thick and chewy (think about ripe, rich, red zinfandel). By comparison, very low alcohol wines are so light they almost seem sheer (think about dry German rieslings).

Alcohol also influences aroma and flavor. An out-of-balance, high-alcohol wine has a "hot" smell. You can actually feel it as a slight burning sensation far up in the nose. Alcohol's flavor—somewhat mysteriously—is sweet. A solution made up of only water and a small bit of pure ethyl alcohol will taste sweet to any taster.

Of course, that alcohol in the wine doesn't exist in a vacuum. So a high level of alcohol (with that corresponding sweetness) allows a wine to support a high level of acidity and still taste balanced. Balance is critical. A high-alcohol wine without a good measure of acidity tastes flaccid and amorphous and is as unsatisfying as tasteless bread or weak coffee.

Compare two good wines from the same area side by side and often the wine with the higher alcohol content will be considered the better of the two. This has

*If you can bear to get up at 5 A.M., hot-air ballooning in the stillness of dawn is one of the most glorious ways to really see vineyards.*

nothing to do with the alcohol per se. The more mature grapes (which, because they were richer in sugar, made the higher level of alcohol possible in the first place) also brought other assets: softer and more developed tannin (we'll get to this) and fuller aromas and flavors.

• **Acid** is the most important element in the pulp other than water and sugar, even though, as I've said, there's not all that much present (relatively speaking). As a grape ripens its sugar content increases and its acid content decreases. The challenge is to harvest precisely when an optimal balance between the two is struck. Acidity gives wine vivacity and, to a certain extent, makes it thirst quenching. Without a sufficient amount of acidity, a dry wine seems languid, dull, and flat. A sweet wine that doesn't have enough acidity tastes flabby. Wines that lack acidity are also susceptible to spoilage and do not age well. (A low-acid jug wine turns brown and falls apart if you try to age it for a decade.) On the other hand, a wine that's too acidic tastes mean and biting. In the end, having just the right amount of acidity—no more and no less—is as pivotal in wine as it is in lemonade (actually more so).

In wine regions with hot climates, such as certain areas of California and Australia, where grapes quickly lose their natural acidity, winemakers commonly adjust the acid by adding 2 to 3 grams of acid per liter to the fermenting wine. Small as it is, this bit of acid can help a wine taste more focused.

One type of acidity, volatile acidity (sometimes called V.A.), is not an inherent part of the grape, but instead is acetic acid formed by bacteria during or after fermentation. A tiny amount of volatile acidity is neither harmful not perceptible. If, however, the bacteria are exposed to air and allowed to multiply, the resulting volatile acidity will make the wine smell vinegary and taste somewhat dank and sour. A wine with very noticeable volatile acidity is considered flawed.

• **Tannin,** which belongs to a class of compounds called phenols and comes, as I've said, from the skins and seeds, is among the most intellectually intriguing components in wine—especially red wine. Depending on the amount and nature of tannin and how it is balanced (or not) by those other constituents, it can add to a wine's greatness or augment its inferiority.

A friend of mine who is a wine professional once described tannin with the following parable: A woman who loves tea makes herself a cup. Just as she finishes pouring the boiling water over the tea bag, the telephone rings. It's her best friend who tearfully announces she's going to get a divorce. The woman consoles her friend for half an hour. When she goes back for her tea—which she is now craving—she finds she has left the tea bag (the last in the house) in the cup.

The bitterly astringent flavor of the tea brewed too long comes from tannin, found in the leaves. Tannin in tea is related to tannin in wine. If you can imagine the harshness of that cup of tea, you can imagine the harshness tannin can potentially (but not necessarily) bring to wine.

The question is: What can the woman do to make her cup of tea taste better? Adding more hot water will simply produce diluted bitterness. Adding sugar will disguise the bitterness momentarily, but then the harshness will kick back in with a vengeance after the sweet flavor disappears. Adding lemon will make the tea thoroughly intolerable, since acidity and bitterness reinforce each other. The only substance that could improve the tea's flavor is milk. Milk's fat and protein can effectively camouflage the bitterness and make the tea taste softer.

In wine drinking the same idea has been applied for centuries. Why, in all those nostalgic European travel posters, does the villager cradling a jug of wine hold a chunk of cheese in the other hand? Because after hundreds of years of unconscious trial and error, Europeans came to understand that cheese somehow made wine, especially cheap red wine, taste better. Like milk in strongly tannic tea, cheese tempers the harshness of the tannin in the wine. (There's an entertaining tip here. As clever caterers have always known, no one will notice the shortcomings of an inexpensive wine as long as enough cheese is served alongside.)

Although excessive tannin can make your mouth feel as if it has been sheathed in shrink-wrap, an appropriate amount, well balanced by other elements, will not. When in harmony, tannin is "sensed" as the wine's structure and backbone. With a well-defined structure, wine takes on a certain formidableness and beauty. Like the flying buttresses of a cathedral, tannin becomes a part of a wine's aesthetic and of its form.

Tannin is also a natural preservative. All other things being equal, wines with a powerful tannin profile live longer than wines without one. Hence red varietals with commanding tannin—such as cabernet sauvignon or nebbiolo—are those that can be aged the longest.

And, it should be added, need to be aged the longest. For the tannin, and the perception of it, changes over time—sometimes dramatically. Herein lies one of wine's conundrums. Until recently it was assumed that young wines had a certain amount of inevitably harsh tannin that would eventually mellow and soften as the wines aged. But several winemakers began to notice that sometimes severely bitter tannin in a young red wine never ameliorated. The wine simply became an old wine with bitter tannin. In the 1980s viticultural research on phenolic compounds began to paint a new picture. The new view suggested two types of tannin—good ripe tannin and bad unripe tannin. Ripe tannin resulted in richly colored, structured wines that did not taste bitingly astringent, even when the wines were young. Unripe tannin resulted in blunt wines with almost ragged dryness.

Determining the ripeness of tannin, however, is no piece of cake. Unlike the ripeness of sugar, which can easily be measured, tannin's ripeness eludes quantification. It can only be estimated by tasting the grape. You'd think this would be easy, but it isn't. Frustratingly for the taster, grapes can be fully ripe in terms of

*Grapes have traditionally been harvested by hand, as this man in Tuscany is doing. Technology notwithstanding, many vintners continue to believe that there is no substitute for so gentle and painstaking an approach.*

sugar and yet have unripe tannin. With practice winemakers can begin to sense tannin apart from the sweetness derived from sugar. As enigmatic as tasting for ripe tannin may be, it is now the method by which top winemakers and viticulturists decide when to harvest.

Just what is happening during the ripening of tannin is not fully understood. Viticulturists observe that leaving grapes to hang on the vine well after their sugar is ripe results in the more total physiological maturity of the grape. (However waiting to harvest means taking climatic risks.) Scientists speculate that as grapes reach full physiological maturity, small astringent tannins may polymerize, or group together, forming larger molecules. Although the number of tannins does not change, these larger molecules are perceived by the taste buds as softer.

*One of the satisfying coincidences of wine is that it literally reflects the earth from which it came.*

11

• **Fruitiness** is what the word suggests–the propensity of a wine to display fruitlike aromas and flavors. Fruitiness is most marked in young wines and rarely found in mature ones. Some varietals— gewürztraminer and gamay, for example—are characteristically very fruity. Gewürztraminer has effusive litchi aromas and flavors; drinking gamay is like diving into a pool of black cherries.

• **Sweetness and dryness** might seem like easy concepts, but they are often misunderstood. For example, many people say they prefer dry wines, even though the wines they commonly drink, such as chardonnay, may actually contain a little bit of sweetness. A finished wine may or may not contain some of the sugar that was there in the pulp of the ripe grapes. The presence of sugar does not necessarily make the wine a sweet dessert wine. A small amount of natural sugar may purposefully be left in to balance the tartness of the acidity or augment the wine's fruitiness.

Bringing us to the (sticky) questions: Can a wine be fruity and sweet? What about fruity and dry? Or sweet and dry? The answers are: yes, yes, no. Sweetness in wine is so often confused with fruitiness that the two terms are sometimes used interchangeably even though they mean entirely different things. We know what fruitiness is; as for sweetness and dryness, they refer to a different issue altogether, which is the original sugar content of the grapes. If all or virtually all of the sugar in the ripe grapes was converted to alcohol, the wine is considered dry. If only some of the sugar was converted to alcohol, the wine is said to have residual sugar—that is, leftover sugar, which the yeasts did not ferment. A fruity wine with 1 to 2 percent residual sugar, such as a California riesling or gewürztraminer, may still be perceived as dry by most people. At 3 percent residual sugar, a wine tastes off-dry or even slightly sweet. Dessert wines can range from 5 to 30 percent residual sugar or more. Some of the most stunning dessert wines in the world, German *trockenbeerenausleses*, for example, can broach the higher number. But once again, balance is everything. A wine that has 8 percent residual sugar can taste as sickeningly cloying as children's cough syrup or gorgeously honeyed and vivid, depending upon the amount of balancing acidity.

## GREAT WINES DON'T COME FROM JUST ANYWHERE

The Earth has her own erogenous zones—a few places of harmonic convergence, where every facet of the vineyard and every nuance of the grape fit together like chromosomes on a DNA helix. In these rare places, grapes and ground are transformed into thrilling wine.

*Vit, the Latin root of the word* viticulture, *is also the source of* vita—*life itself.*

During the last three decades of sweeping technological advancement, wine-making—not viticulture, the science of grape growing—has often claimed most of our attention. But if machines have sometimes seemed more sexy than dirt, it is only because in the history of wine, dirt has been a constant while machines are fascinatingly new. No thinking winemaker anywhere, however, would suggest that a vineyard plays any less important a role in wine than a mother does in the birth of her child.

*Twenty-eight-year-old cabernet sauvignon vines have gnarly, thick trunks. At about this age, a grapevine will usually slow down, producing far fewer clusters of what are often beautifully concentrated grapes.*

In fact, the beginning of the twenty-first century may come to be known as the Era of the Vineyard, a time when the spotlight is once again on the grapes and the land. Already by the early 1990s, notions such as "wine is made in the vineyard" and "flavors begin with farming" had become the norm at quality-oriented wine estates everywhere in the world (if they weren't already solidly entrenched). The focus on fine wine is important. Inexpensive quaffing wine is not so much a product of viticulture as it is a product of agriculture. On first consideration, viticulture might seem like a subset of agriculture, but at their philosophical cores, the two are quite different. Agriculture tends to seek standardization, uniformity, high yield, and consistency on as large a scale as possible. A jug wine fits neatly into an agricultural frame.

What makes fine wines compelling, however, are quirks of individuality. We are awed by the fact that two châteaux separated by no more than a gravel path can make wines that taste remarkably unalike—so much so that one wine can be twice as expensive as the other.

Let's consider wine from a viticulturist's perspective. Though a vineyard may appear passive and pastoral to the casual observer, to the viticulturist, it is a powerful, animate ecosphere full of complex factors. Independently and synergistically, such factors as climate, soil, grape variety and clone, rootstock, spacing, and many others push and pull wine in different directions. Like the colors in a kaleidoscope, these elements are swirled together in thousands of intricate patterns, profoundly influencing the aroma, flavor, body, and finish of a wine.

## Climate

Nature influences wine quality conspicuously and dauntlessly through climate. For starters, climate determines if grapes can exist at all. Grapevines thrive in temperate regions where long, warm, frost-free periods allow them to develop. Specifically, vines begin to grow when the ambient temperature reaches about 50°F (the precise temperature varies from one grape variety to another). Below 50°F, the vines remain dormant. When the average daily temperature reaches 63°F to 68°F, vines will flower. Flowering is critical, for only those flowers that become fertilized and "set" on the cluster become individual grape berries. As crucial as it is, set is an extremely fragile phenomenon. Even under favorable climatic conditions, up to 85 percent of a vine's flowers never set at all and are destined to die as "shatter." As

the temperature moves into the mid-80s, vines hit their growth stride and flourish. However, the optimal temperature for vine development is one thing; the optimal temperature necessary to grow grapes that will make great wine, quite another.

**Microclimates:** If you narrow your field of vision, you find progressively smaller and exceedingly different microclimates created by such factors as the proximity of oceans and bays; the presence of hills and mountains; the slope, orientation, and altitude of the vineyard; plus wind, cloudiness, and precipitation.

Take, as an example, the Napa Valley— a small wine region and one that is generally thought of as having a single climate. Yet the valley has three distinct temperature zones: cool Carneros, a moderately warm band running from Oakville to St. Helena, and the territory around Calistoga, only 30 miles from Carneros, but substantially warmer. These zones form an eco-reality that can initially seem to be at odds with logic. Calistoga—the warmest part of

13

### PHOTOSYNTHESIS

Photosynthesis is the process that produces the sugar—and hence, provides the energy— that vines need in order to grow. Sugar production has four requirements: the green chlorophyll molecules found in the vines' leaves, light, a small amount of water, and carbon dioxide from the surrounding air. When all of these components come together at the right temperature, the leaves become "photocells," capturing light energy and converting it to sugar.

*Spring Mountain Winery, a Victorian mansion built in the nineteenth century, is tucked into the stunning green foothills of the Spring Mountain District in the Napa Valley. Named for its numerous underground springs, the area boasts more than twenty wineries.*

the Napa Valley—is the farthest north; Carneros—the coolest part of this region— is the farthest south (its lower temperatures are caused by the adjacent San Pablo Bay). Another even more dramatic reversal of the expected: Several of the wine regions in Santa Barbara County, nearly 300 miles to the south of Napa, are some of the coolest in California. Those wine regions fall in valleys that run east-west, forming virtual wind tunnels for bracing breezes and fog drawn in off the Pacific.

Ironically, bodies of water can have a cooling effect or a warming effect or both at different times. Water tempers and stabilizes the climate. A marine breeze can cool down a hot vineyard, but it can also warm a vineyard where temperatures are dropping and frost threatens.

**Catching the Sun:** Perhaps the most intriguing aspect of any climate is the impact of hillsides and mountains. A mountain's creased face contains crevices, caverns, and canyons that become nichelike mini-microclimates on their own. Mountains can block cold winds, acting as shields behind which grapes can ripen. They can act as huge slides, causing frost and cold air to pool on the valley floor. But mountains also force clouds to give up their moisture as rain on one side, thus vineyards on the other side often require irrigation. A perfect example of this is found in Washington State where the Cascade mountain range causes the western part of the state to be extremely rainy, while in the eastern part, grapes—with the help of irrigation—

thrive in near desertlike conditions. Mountains also offer the possibility of different altitudes. A vineyard at 2,500 feet will be cooler than one at 500 feet on the same mountain. Not surprisingly, the wines will usually be strikingly different. In general, in cool regions, south-facing slopes (or, for wine regions in the Southern Hemisphere, north-facing slopes) are considered prime vineyard locations, for only good exposure to the sun can ensure ripeness. In Piedmont, Italy, the names of famous vineyards are often preceded by the words *bricco* or *sorì*, as in the Bricco Asili vineyard of the producer Ceretto or the Sorì Tildìn vineyard of Angelo Gaja. A *bricco* is the sun-catching crest of a hill; *sorì* in Piedmontese dialect means south-facing slope where the sun melts the snow first. Along the winding Mosel River in cold northern Germany, the most prized vineyards cover steep mountainous slopes precisely tilted and angled southward to snatch every ray of sun.

Too little sun, of course, is not the problem in many vineyards outside Europe. Too much is. Intense sun can bake acidity right out of the grapes, leading to flat, flabby wine, or cause hyperactive leaf growth, shading the grapes from the sun and possibly leading to vegetal and other off flavors in the wine. As heat becomes excessive, unprotected grapes begin to scorch and their leaves wither and burn. At about 104°F, sustained heat becomes intolerable for most grapevines, and the grapes start to shrivel into raisins. So, wine producers in warm, sunny climates often face hurdles that are the complete opposite of those faced by wine producers in cooler climates. While south-facing slopes are almost mandatory for great wine in parts of Germany, Italy, and

France, in parts of California, viticulturists prefer north-facing slopes so that the ripening process is slowed and lengthened and so the grapes do not get sunburned.

In the end, much the same way that a winemaker aims for balance in a wine, viticulturists everywhere are trying to find balance in the climate of a vineyard. When this is achieved, the vines strike a healthy medium between what viticulturists call vigor and fruitfulness. Vigor is the rate of growth of leaves and shoots, the vegetative green parts of vines. Fruitfulness refers to the number of grape clusters per vine and the number and size of berries on each cluster. Though it's tempting to concentrate solely on the grapes, leaves are critical because, as the main site of food production, they convert light energy to chemical energy (sugar) through the process called photosynthesis. Without enough leaves, a vine allowed to overcrop can produce more clusters than it can ripen. The results are grapes (and wines) that are weak and lackluster in flavor.

*The simple reality of viticulture is that there are very few monodimensional rules. Any given factor can be positive or negative, depending on the context.*

But leaves can also be too much of a good thing. High-vigor vines can have leaves that are so prolific and dominant they create a canopy that shades grapes from the sun. Grape clusters can have a hard time forming and ripening in competition with so much vegetation. But again, one must consider all other factors. In Portugal, for example, copious leaves can be a blessing, shading the grapes from sunburn and heat stress.

15

## HANG TIME

—◦◦◦—

Let's say a grape variety normally takes 120 days to ripen. In an especially hot year, it may ripen after only 110 days; in a cooler year, after 130 days. Would a viticulturist prefer one scenario over the other? This is a highly complex question, fraught with countless "it depends on" considerations. That said, viticulturists generally do want long growing seasons. Long ripening allows components in the grape other than sugar—tannin, for example—to reach greater physiological maturity. Fully developed grapes, of course, hold more promise for fully developed flavors and aromas. Historically, perfectly ripe (but not overripe) grapes with long "hang times" have often produced superior wines that age gracefully.

## Stress

One of the few monodimensional rules is one of wine's wonderful curiosities. In making fine wine, what is ideal is not a perfect environment but, rather, something less than consummate. A perfectly sunny, very warm climate augmented by moisture and nutrients may be good for many plants (as jungles testify) but it's too much for grapevines. All of the world's great vineyards are in climates that are in some way marginal. Assuming that the stress (lack of sun, water, and/or nutrients) is not so severe that the vines shut down, go into shock, or die, an endurable amount of adversity forces grapevines to struggle and adapt. When healthy vines work to grow and the plants are forced to concentrate their sugars in a limited number of grape clusters, the result is grapes and wine of greater character and concentration.

## Temperature Swings

Many growers believe that good stress can come in the form of wide temperature fluctuations, either from spring to fall or from day to night or both.

Temperature swings can help create balance. Wine regions that are extremely hot during the day (Ribera del Duero on the north-central plains of Spain, for example) benefit from cold nights, which effectively shut down the ripening process, helping grapes to preserve essential acidity. By delaying ripening, cool nights also extend the span of time from bud break to harvest, leading to a more developed physiological maturity in other components.

At least this is how it works in hot climates when certain grape varieties are present, the tinto fino grape in Ribera del Duero being one of them. This does not mean, however, that cool nights are universally favorable. If cabernet sauvignon is grown in an already coolish region, such as the Loire Valley of France, and the grapes then experience even cooler nights, the wine may end up with all the charm of a green bell pepper.

As for seasonal change, grapevines don't like ambiguity. Vines need precise temperature cues so that bud break and grape development and maturation proceed steadily and uniformly, assuring (all other things being equal) a good harvest.

Warmish winters can waken vines. With nutrients being pumped into their shoots, vines soon become confused and begin to bud in the wrong season. Uneven or untimely budding can wreak havoc on a vineyard, creating a patchwork quilt of schizophrenic vines, all maturing at different rates and different times. A definitively cold winter, followed by its opposite, a definitively warm spring and summer, is the optimal viticultural scenario.

Finally, days and hours of sun are not the same as average temperature. Thus, various combinations can lead to compensations. Although the summertime temperatures in northern German vineyards, say, do not approximate the temperatures in the Napa Valley, the farther north one moves from the equator, the longer the hours of sunshine per day—compensation.

**Frost:** Frost is an unconditional threat to grapes and grapevines. Early fall frosts ravage foliage, prevent the grapes from making their final push to full ripening, and may even kill the vines themselves, especially if they are young. Spring frosts may kill buds and shoots and thus destroy the potential for a crop. Even in winter, when the vine is dormant, an excessive cold snap can be ruinous. Below 25°F, the vine's trunk may split, leaving it open to infection. After prolonged below-freezing temperatures, the entire vine and root system can die.

The methods used to counter frost are often desperate and generally expensive, but vintners have no choice; the financial repercussions of losing an entire year's crop are too severe. Burning oil in smudge pots placed so that the wind will carry wisps of heat over the vineyard is one solution, although studies have shown it to be only marginally effective.

Giant windmills can be used to stir up the warm air hovering above the vineyard and to mix it with the colder air that has settled like a thick blanket over the vines. This method is also only partially effective. A more expensive takeoff on the windmill idea is to hire helicopters to fly low over the vineyards, zigzagging back and forth until the threat of frost has passed. By beating and churning the air, a helicopter can sometimes keep the ambient temperature a critical degree or two above freezing.

And last there's a solution that seems crazy, but works: spraying the vines with water, using overhead sprinklers. The water coats the leaves, shoots, and buds, forming a thin glove of ice that insulates the vines from windchill and traps the plant's natural heat. That incremental amount of insulation, coupled with the tiny amount of heat thrown off when water turns to ice, is enough to keep the leaves, shoots, and buds from freezing unless it gets significantly colder.

*Frost clings to the vines on the high plains of Ribera del Duero in winter. As long as the vines are completely dormant and the freezing temperatures are not too extreme, no harm will be done. But a frost such as this in late spring, when the vines are beginning to bud, could be devastating.*

## Water

Like sunlight, the water vines receive must be part of an overall balanced environment. There is no optimal amount. How much water vines need depends on a number of factors, including the age and size of the vines, the length of the growing season, the temperatures during the growing season, wind, humidity, the drainage and water-holding capacity of the soil, and the spacing of the vines, to name a few.

Vines are not arbitrary in the way they grow; they search for water. Dry soil encourages the roots to burrow deeper into the earth, where in turn, they find a more stable environment of moisture and nutrients. Vines with fully developed root systems can handle drought or other climatic difficulties better.

To help ensure the quality of the wines, many European wine regions forbid irrigation during the growing season. In Europe, natural rainfall and moisture is almost always sufficient to grow healthy vines. If the vines were irrigated in addition, they would undoubtedly produce fatter grapes and more bunches. A larger yield, however, would result in thinner, lower-quality wine, which is why irrigation is prohibited.

The water situation is not the same in the dry areas of California, Washington State, Australia, or Chile where lack of rainfall is often exacerbated by long drought-like summers. In New World wine-growing regions, irrigation is permitted, but it must be used judiciously. Again, too much water could cause the vines to produce too many bunches and to explode helter-skelter into a massive orb of leaves at the expense of a limited number of quality grapes.

Timing is everything. In the spring, right before flowering, vines need water as a jump start. Without water at this critical moment, the flowers will not set properly—and therefore will not create grape berries. Water is also critical during veraison—the time in early summer when the grapes begin to change color from pea green to yellow (for white wine) or to purple (for red). A lack of water then can lead to excessively small grapes that never achieve maturity.

The most important time to avoid water is just before harvest. Excessive irrigation or rain then swells the grapes with water, diluting them. Severe rain or hail can break open grapes or even tear off the bunches. If the rain or oversoaking of the soil is followed by warmth and no wind,

*The Greek island of Santorini, in the Aegean Sea, is bathed in the sort of brilliant sunlight that grapevines love. But the winds are so fierce that many grapevines must be trained extremely close to the ground, lest they be ripped apart.*

the resulting humidity can lead to rot or mildew. Also, trying to harvest vineyards a foot deep in mud is no picnic.

## Wind

In one of the most windswept wine regions of Greece, not even the mostly impervious to everything olive tree can grow. Vines survive only because they are trained so low that they look like large doughnuts lying flat on the ground with the grapes crouching even lower in the center hole. Each vine is called a *stefáni* (crown); it will grow that way for twenty years, after which time the trunk becomes strong enough to withstand the whipping wind, and the vine can be trained upright in the normal manner.

Most wine regions are not subject to such gales, but wind still torments grapevines in many parts of the world. Although a gentle breeze is almost always good (it cools the grapes and promotes air circulation as a guard against rot), a slashing wind is another story. Right after flowering, a severe wind can prevent vines from setting properly, scattering the flowers in the air so that they never get the chance to become grapes. Bludgeoning wind can break off tender parts of the vines, damage the canes, bruise the leaves, and even rip away the fruit. Wind can also bring with it the windchill factor—bad news if the vineyard is already in a borderline cold region. Finally, viticultural research suggests that a stiff wind may cause the vine to close its stomata, tiny microscopic holes in the undersides of the leaves that are responsible for evaporation. With the stomata closed, the vine ceases to draw water through its root tips. Eventually, without some amount of water flow within the plant, all growth comes to a halt.

## Soil

Dirt has always been seductive—the smell of it, the feel of it, the sight of it, and certainly the possession of it. The history of civilization is in large part a running commentary on man's relationship to the land. Soil's allure is very evident in the world of wine. There is something strangely beautiful about the white chalk of Champagne, the legacy of ancient seabeds and sea fossils; or the jet-black pitted stones of Santorini in Greece, the relics of a massive volcanic explosion; or the cool blue-gray slate shards of the Mosel in Germany, remnants of the path of glaciers. Remarkably, vines grow contentedly in all of these.

### PLUGGING THE DRAIN

Almost everywhere in the world, the best soils for vineyards are those that are well drained. Nothing about viticulture, however, is absolute. In the Sherry country of Spain, for example, the stark white *albariza* soil is a crumbly mixture of clays, carbonates, and prehistoric sea fossils. Light and soft as cake flour, the soil must be tilled to compact it and increase its water-holding capacity. Moisture in the soil helps prevent the vines from going into shock during the long, often drought-ridden summers.

Most viticulturalists today believe that the most important soil factor is its structure—especially its capacity to drain water. Nothing could seem less exciting, yet good drainage is critical in viticulture, ensuring that vines push their roots deep into the ground to find a stable source of water and nutrients. A soil's capability for

*The vineyards of Châteauneuf-du-Pape are planted in ancient stony riverbeds that were created millennia ago by the then larger Rhône River.*

water drainage is far more important than its fertility. Most of the world's best vineyards are not located on fertile land, and many are planted in places so barren almost nothing else will grow there.

There are countless types of soil. They are defined according to the size of the soil's particles. Sand and larger particles are important for good drainage. But smaller particles, such as silt, are also important, for these form loams and clays that hold just enough water to support the vine's growth. Other particles, such as rocks and organic matter, also help create the delicate balance of water drainage vs. water retention. In addition, rocks and organic matter aerate the soil and contribute minerals and nutrients.

The geologic formation of the land is another important element in drainage. Limestone and schist have large vertical planes sliced by fissures—perfect for vine roots tunneling in search of water. Conversely, dense subsoil or some sort of impenetrable horizontal formation may cause the roots to remain closer to the surface where they can drown in heavy rains.

One of the most important—if curious—aspects of soil is its color and ability to reflect sunlight. In the cool, northern region of Champagne, vines are trained low so that the ripening grapes can take advantage of the warm sun bouncing off the white chalky ground. In fact, at one time the thrifty Champenois used to accentuate this phenomenon by scattering unrecyclable bits of white plastic garbage in the vineyards, which like the chalky soil, reflected sun. Helpful as this was in ripening the grapes, the practice had a few public relations drawbacks and so was discontinued.

If you compare the chalk of Champagne, the black stones of Santorini, and the shards of slate from the Mosel and then think about how utterly different the white wines from those places are, it would seem almost self-evident that the soil profoundly affects flavor. Of course, those differences in flavor could have come from a score of factors besides soil. The wines, after all, come from different grape varieties, the climates of the regions are wildly different, and so on. So, suppose we look at two wines from two tiny vineyards, mere footsteps apart. The wines are made from the same grape, both vineyards experience the same sun and climate, the grapes are harvested and made in the exact same way by the same winemaker. Yet the wines *still* taste quite different. Small growers in Germany and Burgundy and other great regions throughout the world find themselves in this situation all the time. Two minuscule vineyards, barely a stone's throw apart, end up producing wines with distinctly different characters. And the only dissimilarity the grower can point to is the soil.

If soil does indeed influence flavor, however, it does so in an indirect way. While it's tempting to think of the soil as a kind of underground spice shop in which a vine can literally root around for flavors, that's not quite how a vine works. The roots of grapevines can only suck up molecules, ions, and minerals. These building blocks are then metabolized to promote vine and grape growth. Ultimately, the character of the grapes will be a springboard for the numerous chemical reactions that, during fermentation, will begin to shape the flavor of the wine.

**Terroir:** A distinction must also be made here between soil and *terroir*. Though the two are often used interchangeably, soil is just one aspect of *terroir*. This French word means the total impact of any given site—soil, slope, orientation to the sun, and elevation, plus every nuance of climate including rainfall, wind velocity, frequency of fog, cumulative hours of sunshine, average high temperature, average low temperature, and so forth. There is no single word in English that means quite the same thing. Generally viticulturists believe that soil indirectly bestows flavor (and relative quality) only insofar as it is one of the voices in the chorus of *terroir*.

## Matching the Right Grapes to the Right Ground

However omnipotent climate and soil may seem, they cannot be considered apart from the variety of the grape being grown. A climate too warm for successful pinot noir is one that can be perfect for syrah. Varieties respond differently to heat, hours of sun, water, wind, and every other facet of climate and soil. Great wine can only result when the grape variety is tuned in, like the signal on a radio dial, to the "channel" of its environment. To continue the metaphor, when a grape variety is less perfectly suited to its environment, you can still hear the music, but it doesn't have the same sound quality. This is why a vineyard that produces extraordinary riesling should not simply be pulled up and replanted with merlot just because merlot has become popular. Clearly, it *can* be pulled up and replanted, and some vintners do chase trends. However, mediocre merlot is not better than excellent riesling, even though it might very well make the vintner more money.

In general, certain grape varieties (cabernet sauvignon, zinfandel, sauvignon blanc) prefer relatively warm temperatures; others (pinot noir, riesling), cool ones. And some grapes can dance to almost any beat. Chardonnay is mind-boggling in its flexibility. It is as happy in the warm regions of Australia as it is in nippy Chablis, France. Miraculously, it can produce good wine in

## GRAPES IN FASHION

According to the Wine Institute, in 1978, California had 13,000 acres of chardonnay grapes; in 1998, 93,000. During the same time, other varieties started disappearing. Plantings of petite sirah, for example, dropped from 13,000 acres to about 2,700. By 1998, just two grapes— chardonnay and cabernet sauvignon— accounted for 33 percent of the value of all *vinifera* grapes crushed in California.

either climate, although admittedly, the style of the chardonnay will change. Great chardonnay, however, still appears to be the province of selected sites within cooler environments.

There is an old rule of thumb in Bordeaux that vines need one hundred critical days for proper ripening. In fact, different grape varieties may take as few as 90 days or nearly twice that to ripen. The time required dictates where certain varieties can successfully be planted. Clearly, it would make no sense to plant a variety that needs 150 days to ripen in a place with a growing season 120 days long. And obviously, how long a grape takes to ripen also depends on the amount and intensity of the sunlight where it is grown. Riesling takes longer to ripen in Germany than it does in California.

If grape varieties are sensitive to their sites, does that mean that every site is ideal for only one grape variety? It depends on the site and its size.

Many of the world's top wine-growing sites—for example, the Burgundy vineyard called Romanée-Conti where pinot noir is grown or the Mosel vineyard Bernkasteler Doctor, in Germany, where riesling is grown—are planted with the single variety that supremely expresses the uniqueness and inherent greatness of that plot of land. These wines become something more than just great tasting. They become legendary—masterpieces of Nature.

On the other hand, many sites the world over provide excellent environments for two or more grape varieties that are fairly similar in their needs. For example, in both Bordeaux and northern California cabernet sauvignon and merlot are often planted in adjoining vineyard blocks. If a site can support two or more similar varieties well, then planting those there can have advantages both in the vineyard and in the cellar. In the vineyard, multiple varieties can be an asset because grapes ripen at different rates. If the earlier-ripening grape is already picked when a devastating storm hits, the grower loses only a percentage of the crop. Many Old World vineyards, including the vineyards of Bordeaux, are planted with several varieties precisely as an economic hedge against bad weather. In the cellar, the winemaker now has more colors on the palette with which to paint. By blending two varietals together, he or she can often achieve a level of quality and complexity that was otherwise unattainable.

## Clones

When most of us think about wine flavors, we think about various grape varieties. Chardonnay tastes different from sauvignon blanc, zinfandel tastes different from merlot, and so forth. Moreover, we think about a grape variety as a single thing. Actually, grape varieties are not quite that simple.

Grapevines, it turns out, are not genetically stable; they spontaneously mutate slightly over time and as a result of viruses. Each grape variety, therefore, is made up of numerous subtypes called clones. A clone is a population of vines all of which were derived from a single vine called a mother vine. There are dozens of clones of pinot noir, for example, and each has different characteristics. A trained viticulturist can look at a vineyard of pinot noir and see small differences among the vines. Some vines might be larger or more robust, some might produce smaller berries. All of this is highly significant, for grapevines are not propagated from seed, but by cuttings. As a result, a viticulturist can choose a single superior plant and by taking cuttings from that plant, propagate new vines. Each of these vines will be identical to its mother, the single superior plant. Collectively, these vines are all the same clone.

Different clones taste different, which is why winemakers are so concerned about them. One clone of pinot noir may have a strong strawberry jam character; another clone may be suggestive of mushrooms. Some clones have more intensity of flavor in general, while others can be fairly neutral tasting. All of this is important for wine producers, for a wine's ultimate flavor and character will be affected by the clones or clone the producer chooses to plant. This said, clonal research is very new. The discovery of clones dates back just to the 1920s, and practically speaking, it has only been in the last couple of decades that producers have been able to request the specific clone they want when they purchase cuttings from a nursery. Most vineyards worldwide remain as they always have been, a mixture of clones. Often, this is a good thing. After all, by blending several clones of a given variety, a winemaker may have a better chance of producing a wine with nuance and complexity.

As clonal research continues, the quality of wine is expected to improve. Among other things, such research will allow producers to better match a clone or clones to a given site. For now, though, there is no way of knowing what clones of chardonnay are in producer X's wine. Such information is

not commonly listed on wine labels, and in any case, even the producers themselves may not know what clones are in their vineyards.

## *Rootstocks*

One of the simple but rather amazing facts about grapevines is that most of those growing in the world today are not growing from their own roots. Instead most grapevines are grafted onto one of a handful of different rootstocks bred to be tolerant of specific pests or soil conditions. This might not seem particularly compelling news but if it were not for rootstocks, the main species of grapes used for wine would have become extinct in most parts of the world about a century ago.

The rootstock is simply the root system beneath the soil. And that rootstock has nothing to do with the variety of grapes produced. The grapes come from the grape variety grafted on to the rootstock. The portion being grafted is called the scion or budwood. Varieties as dif-

23

*A baby vine already grafted onto a rootstock is ready to plant (left). The vine above is budding.*

## PHYLLOXERA

n the latter part of the nineteenth century, phylloxera—a tiny yellow aphid one-thirtieth of an inch long and one-sixtieth of an inch wide—spread throughout Europe destroying every vineyard in its path. From Europe, phylloxera moved around the world killing vineyards in South Africa, Australia, New Zealand, and California. So swift and sure was the annihilation that many vintners believed the world's vineyards were doomed and that wine would cease to exist.

Originally named *Phylloxera vastatrix* (the devastator) and now specifically identified as the insect *Dactylasphaera vitifoliae,* phylloxera feeds on a vine's roots, ultimately sucking life out of the vine. Although native to America, the bug remained harmless and unknown for centuries. The reason? Indigenous American vines belong to several species that are tolerant of the insect. Native European vines belong to the species *vinifera,* which is phylloxera susceptible.

In the 1860s, when native American vines were sent to southern France for experimentation, phylloxera, unbeknownst to anyone, hitched a ride on the roots. Within two decades, most of the vineyards of Europe were destroyed. If phylloxera was deadly, it was also eerie. Too minuscule to be seen, the insect wreaked havoc totally undetected. European growers watched in desperate frustration as their vines yellowed, shriveled, and then slowly perished. If the grapes managed to ripen at all, the wine made from them was often weak and watery. Eventually the vine would simply collapse.

Countless remedies were tried. French vineyards were doused with chemicals, flooded with water, and irrigated with white wine. By 1873 the French government even offered a prize—30,000 francs or about $60,000—to anyone who could come up with a solution. Nothing worked.

While phylloxera was waging war in Europe, the young California wine industry was unknowingly setting itself up to become phylloxera's next victim. California's first vintners busily began planting vineyards with European vines, considered superior to native American ones. Once phylloxera struck, some 17,000 acres of

ferent as chardonnay, sangiovese, and riesling can all be grafted onto the same type of rootstock. It's also possible to change the variety growing on a rootstock. If a grower who has planted sauvignon blanc on a rootstock later decides he would do better with chardonnay, he can usually scalp off the sauvignon blanc and graft chardonnay onto that same rootstock instead.

It might seem as though the roots are merely a channel through which water and nutrients flow. In actuality, rootstocks play a far more complex and important role. They have the power to affect a vine's vigor, fruitfulness, and resistance to drought and disease.

Let's backtrack a moment. Until the mid-1800s, most vines grew on their own original roots. However, when phylloxera, a root-eating aphid, began to ravage vineyards around the world, rootstocks took on new importance. The minuscule yellow aphid (see Phylloxera, above) is native to North America. Native American vines, which belong to several different species, are tolerant of the pest. Unfortunately, European vines, all of which belong to the single species *vinifera,* are not. In

California vineyard were ruined before the only known remedy was discovered. By grafting European vines onto the roots of American varieties, the aphid can be rendered powerless.

As the twentieth century approached, vineyards around the world were painstakingly uprooted vine by vine and replanted on American rootstocks. Today most wines worldwide come from vines growing from American roots.

Growers and winemakers undoubtedly thought they'd seen the last of phylloxera. But when the second wave of the pest spontaneously erupted in the Napa Valley in 1983, the wine industry knew it was up against an extremely formidable foe. Known as biotype B, the new phylloxera began moving at lightning speed through vineyards planted with a specific type of American rootstock called AxR1. Throughout the California wine boom of the 1960s and 1970s, AxR1 had been the rootstock of choice. By 1980 nearly two-thirds of Napa and Sonoma vineyards were planted with it.

The fatal flaw was genetic: AxR1, a hybrid, had one American species parent and one *vinifera* parent. California plant biologists knew this, but in early experimental trials, AxR1 had performed well against phylloxera—so well that Californian scientists felt safe in recommending it. (Interestingly, European scientists remained skeptical about AxR1 and suggested that European growers use other American rootstocks instead.) By 1995, biotype B had spread throughout much of California and into Washington State and Oregon. As of 1997 (the final year statistics were collected), replanting costs in California alone were estimated at 1.2 billion dollars as more than 16,000 acres of Napa and Sonoma vineyards were pulled up.

It takes an average of three years before new vines can be commercially harvested. For every California winery with vineyards planted on AxR1, the staggering financial burden of replanting was exacerbated by the loss of income from vineyards that were not fully productive for several years.

There is a small silver lining to the story, however. The replanting that's taken place has been done with the benefit of several decades worth of knowledge. As a result, vineyards have been replanted with varieties, clones, and rootstocks better suited to each site. Will even better California wines naturally follow? Most winemakers and viticulturists say yes.

the mid-1800s, when American vines were first brought to France for experimental purposes, phylloxera, clinging to the roots, rode along.

The American pest soon annihilated Europe's vineyards. Later, ironically, the roots of American grapevines proved to be their saviors. The great Texas vine expert T. V. Munson discovered that when European *vinifera* vines were grafted onto American rootstock, the grapes continued to be *vinifera*, but the roots were no longer vulnerable to the rapacious insect. Eventually, most vineyards worldwide were pulled out and the vines replanted on American rootstocks.

Today, most rootstocks can be traced back to three major native American grape species: *Vitis riparia*, *Vitis rupestris* (also known as St. George), and *Vitis berlandieri*. Many of the rootstocks used throughout the world are crosses or hybrids of these that were bred to tolerate certain vine pests or soil conditions. They have such exciting names as 3309, 110R, or SO4.

How does rootstock affect vine growth? Rootstocks can be high vigor or low vigor, can have shallow or deep roots, can be drought-resistant or tolerate wetter conditions, and can be more or less tolerant of certain soil pests or other soil conditions. Selecting the best rootstock for a given location can therefore be one of the most critical decisions the grower must make. Of all the subjects currently being aggressively researched, rootstock is considered by many viticulturists to be one of the next big keys to understanding why a given wine tastes the way it does.

## Vineyards and the Harvest

Americans traveling in Europe for the first time often drive past vineyards, having no idea what they are. Unlike something immediately recognizable no matter where you are—say, a rose bush—vines can come in a dizzying array of shapes and sizes. Vineyards in Burgundy in France, the Sonoma Valley of California, and the province of Galicia in Spain look about as similar as Abraham Lincoln,

*If the ground is flat and the vineyard has long rows with wide spacing between them, mechanical harvesters can be used. A mechanical harvester can pick up to 200 tons of grapes a day.*

26

Winston Churchill, and Elizabeth Taylor (not necessarily in that order).

The size and shape of the vine is the result primarily of the grape variety and the climate, but the way vines are pruned, trellised, and spaced is also critical. Pruning is the exhausting process of cutting back the vines while they are dormant during the winter. Although nothing might seem more boring, viticulturists consider pruning to be both an art and a science, and experienced pruners often adopt a zenlike contentment after spending several cold and rather solitary weeks in a starkly barren vineyard during the winter. What the pruner decides to leave becomes the basis for the next year's crop. If pruned too severely, the vines' fruitfulness and strength may be compromised. Conversely, if pruned too little, the vines will push out too many shoots and leaves

## A TON OF GRAPES

A ton of grapes can produce about 60 cases, or 720 bottles, of wine. That number, however, is extremely approximate since the amount of juice from a ton of grapes varies. Grape bunches made up of small berries will have less juice than grape bunches with large berries since with small berries, there is a correspondingly higher ratio of skins, stalks, and stems. The amount of juice obtained also depends, of course, on how firmly the grapes are pressed. The best estates barely press their grapes at all; much of the juice is simply natural "free run."

and produce too much fruit and become unbalanced. The overabundance of fruit will mean the crop will have a hard time ripening, and this in turn, could lead to fewer shoots and stunted growth in subsequent seasons.

In many parts of the world, especially where there are old vineyards, vines still grow out of the ground like short stubby bushes. In most modern vineyards, however, the vines are trellised up on wires. The rationale behind trellising is simple. By lifting the vines up and spreading the canopy along wires, the leaves get the sun they need for photosynthesis, but at the same time, the grapes hang freely in the air where, less shaded, they get more direct sunlight, for ripeness, and good air circulation, to mitigate against rot.

Like every other aspect of viticulture, trellising must be fine-tuned so that it is maximally suited to the site and to the grape variety. Low-vigor vines may get all the sunlight and air circulation they need if trained along a single vertical trellis. A more wildly vigorous vine may benefit from a trellising system that splits the prolific canopy into a V along two wires, allowing sunlight to penetrate into the middle.

The spacing of vines, like trellising, has become something of a mini science that must take into consideration the site. In the past vines were spaced with only one factor in mind: economics. In Europe, this often meant the space taken up by a man with a basket on his back or that taken up by a horse-drawn plough. In California, spacing at larger intervals, usually 8 feet between vines; 12 feet between rows, neatly accommodated all sorts of machines and tractors, including those pulling gondolas into which the harvested grapes would be dumped. But spacing has implications far beyond such simple economic issues as size or type of equipment. The closer vines are spaced, the more their roots may have to compete for the same soil, nutrients, and water. If the vines are too vigorous, this competition may be beneficial, acting to slow the vines' growth down, limit the number of grape clusters produced, and bring the vines into a better balance. The better balanced the vineyard, of course, the better the grapes and, all things being equal, the better the wine.

In California, the vines in many new and replanted vineyards are now placed more closely together. Twenty years ago

27

*In many parts of Europe, such as here in Bordeaux, picking baskets or tubs are strapped to workers' backs, giving literal poignancy to the idea of harvesting as backbreaking work.*

## CHINESE IN THE VINEYARDS

—⚬⚬⚬—

In *The University of California Book of California Wine*, Jack Chen, writing about the contributions of the Chinese, notes that in the 1880s, Chinese made up 80 to 85 percent of the vineyard workers in California. For the prior decade, however, anti-Chinese sentiment had been building as the economy worsened and unemployment rose. In 1882, Congress passed the Chinese Exclusion Act, banning further immigration. By the 1890s, Chinese who worked in vineyards were being taxed a punitive charge of $2.50 a month, and labor leaders had successfully forced several wineries to add the racist statement "Made with White Labor" to their bottles.

an acre of California vineyard typically contained four to six hundred or so vines. With closer planting, the range is now from six hundred to nearly three thousand vines per acre (and sometimes even more).

The romantic vision of grapes lovingly picked by hand is, in many cases, just that—a romantic vision. Mechanical harvesting is being used with increasing frequency throughout the world. It has both drawbacks and advantages over handpicking. First, a machine can never be as selective as a person. Second, even though modern mechanical harvesters are calibrated to distinguish between ripe and unripe grapes, some unripe grapes and material other than grapes (MOG) still get picked. Unripe grapes and MOG can cause vegetal and/or bitter flavors. A machine can also never be as careful as a person.

Mechanical harvesters can easily break and damage the skins of grapes, as well as the vines themselves if the plants are young.

On the other hand, mechanical harvesters have some very real assets. They can operate 24 hours a day, ensuring that large vineyards can be picked swiftly once the grapes reach ripeness. A mechanical harvester can pick an astounding 80 to 200 tons of grapes in an eight-hour day, compared to the 2 tons picked by the average California harvest worker (admittedly still a breathtaking amount for one person). Speed, of course, is critical if bad weather is about to break. With machines, large tracts of vineyard can also be harvested at night, a real advantage in very warm climates since cool temperatures help preserve the fruit's freshness. (Handpickers with appropriate lights can also work at night but on a smaller scale.) Finally, mechanical harvesting is usually less expensive than handpicking and is critical in wine regions with limited availability of labor, such as Australia.

## Quality vs. Quantity

When Johannes Selbach, of the Selbach Oster wine estate located on the Mosel River in Germany, asked his vineyard workers, most of whom were older women, to cut off developing bunches in order to decrease the yield, the women cried and went home, leaving Selbach to thin the vineyards himself. Cutting off some of the developing fruit that Nature worked so hard to foster can seem counterintuitive if not sacrilegious, which is what it seemed to the vineyard workers. Yet among winemakers and viticulturists the world over, the consensus has been that quality and quantity are often, but not always, mutually exclusive.

Virtually every great wine estate in the world limits the yield from its vineyards. This is because wine will generally be more concentrated and flavorful when the vine and the *terroir* bring everything they have to bear on ripening, say, twenty-four bunches of grapes rather than sixty. Conversely, producers of very inexpensive wines, for whom great quality is not an issue, want to pull the maximum production they can from any plot of land. In California a cabernet vineyard on the floor of the Napa Valley often yields about 5 tons of grapes; on the hillside 3 to 4 tons is more usual, and some vineyards may only yield 2. By comparison, in the hot central San Joaquin valley, the yield of grapes, used to make jug wine, is typically 8 to 12 tons or more per acre. One of the highest yields I know of occurs in Australia where the Spanish grape Pedro Ximénez, which the Australians use to make low-quality fortified wine, may achieve 20 tons per acre!

There is no one perfect yield, of course. With some grape varieties an above-average wine can be made from a fairly wide range of yields. Chardonnay and cabernet sauvignon are like this. Other grape varieties—pinot noir is the best example—quickly lose their "stuffing" and make innocuous wines if the yield broaches an even moderately high level.

Are quality and quantity mutually exclusive? Maverick viticulturists in Australia are looking more at berry size than at yield. As long as the grape variety can generate berries that are small (with a good ratio of skin to juice), they let the vines erupt into prolific masses of bunches. Yields reach three to four times what would be considered appropriate for good-to-great wine in France, without—the Australians say—a diminution in quality.

In the end, each vineyard must be viewed as its own entity and every factor must be considered before any specific assessments can be made of yield. How strong the vines are, how old the vineyard is, the characteristics of the vineyard's *terroir*, the intensity of prevailing stress factors, the type of grapes grown—all of these dramatically influence the quality that can be derived from any given yield. Despite all other contingencies, we do know this: For every vineyard, there is a breaking point—a point where too many grapes will cause the vineyard to be out of balance and where the subsequent quality of the wine will plummet.

29

*Since 1945, Chateau Mouton-Rothschild has had a famous artist design their labels each year. Clockwise from the top are Mouton-Rothschild labels by Keith Haring (1988), John Huston (1982), and Pablo Picasso (1973).*

# How Wine Is Made

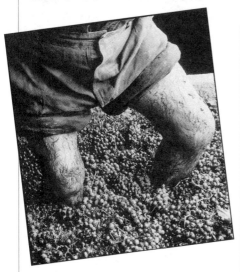

Wine has been with us for more than 5,000 years. Yet the natural, complex process by which it is made—fermentation—has been understood for only a little more than 150 years. It was not until the 1850s, when Louis Pasteur's research in microbiology linked sugar's conversion to alcohol (fermentation) to the living organisms called yeasts, that winemaking moved out of the realm of the occult and into the realm of science. More than a century more would pass before the next significant advances in winemaking occurred.

Up until World War II, most wines were made according to two classic methods, one for white wine, the other for red. The only exceptions were fortified wines, such as Sherry and Port, and sparkling wines, such as Champagne—all of which were made in specialized, complex ways of their own. By the 1960s, advances in winemaking around the world plus the advent of more sophisticated winemaking equipment—especially temperature-controlled stainless steel tanks—meant that winemakers possessed a far greater ability to sculpt a wine's aromas, flavors, texture, and finish.

A powerful new world of winemaking was born. Yet for the best wines in the world, the goal of winemaking remained unchanged: to protect and nurture those characteristics of wine that come from the vineyard. Winemaking always begins in the vineyard with the choice of the site, the selection of grape varieties and clones to plant, and the plans for both the way the vineyard will be laid out and the way the vines will be trellised and cared for.

*Treading grapes by foot (upper left) and punching them down with a paddlelike device are time-honored practices still carried out in several places around the world.*

31

## NO NEED FOR TOOTHPASTE

⟨∂⟩

He looked round the shop as if at a new world. "Is there anything you can't drink wine with?" he said. "As far as I'm concerned . . . grapefruit."

He made a face.

"And that's from one," I said, "who drinks wine with baked beans, who practically scrubs his teeth in it."

"You really love it?"

I nodded. "Nature's magical accident."

"What?"

"That the fungus on grapes turns the sugar in grape juice to alcohol. That the result is delicious."

"For heaven's sake . . ."

"No one could have invented it," I said. "It's just there. A gift to the plant. Elegant."

—Dick Francis, *Proof*

At harvest, the emphasis shifts to the cellar, where the aim is to help the wine make itself in the best possible way. How does mere grape juice become the stuff of poetry and legend? Just what are the steps a winemaker takes and what happens in the cellar? And, above all, why is white wine white and red wine red?

With very rare exceptions, the juice of all grapes, red and white, is almost colorless. The bold difference between red wine and white wine is this: For red wine, the juice is fermented with the red grape skins. Skins, it turns out, are like a packet of dye.

During fermentation, heat is generated as well as alcohol. Both help to leach out the reddish-purple color pigments from the skins, tinting the surrounding wine. In the case of white wine, the skins are quickly separated from the juice before the juice is fermented. This is also what happens with white wines made from red grapes. For example, in the case of Champagne, where two of the three grapes used are red, the juice is quickly separated from the red skins before any coloring can take place.

## MAKING RED WINE

Besides color pigments, grape skins contain tannin. Since red wines are fermented with the grape skins present, red wines contain substantially more tannin than white wines. As we've seen, tannin forms the structure or backbone of the wine and acts as a natural preservative. Because of tannin, red wines can be aged far longer than whites. That said, not all red grape varieties have the same amount of tannin in their skins. Some are genetically prone to have more; others, less. Cabernet sauvignon, for example, has a significant amount of tannin, while pinot noir has only a moderate amount.

Tannin is also found in grape seeds and stems, and this fact figures into the first decision that must be made in red winemaking. Should the stems be removed from the grapes before they are crushed or not? With naturally tannic varieties, such as cabernet sauvignon, stems can add excessive bitter tannin to the juice. As a result, the stems are usually removed by putting the grape bunches into a machine called a crusher-destemmer.

With less tannic varieties, such as grenache from the Rhône or pinot noir from Burgundy, winemakers may choose to leave the stems on precisely because they do add a soupçon of tannic strength. Also, by taking up space, the stems allow for better circulation of the wine in the fermenting vat, thereby aiding the extraction of color and tannin from the skins.

*The introduction of temperature-controlled stainless steel tanks revolutionized the wine business by giving winemakers far greater control over the fermentation. White wines, in particular, benefited from the new tanks, which, by keeping the wine cool, better preserve delicate aromas and flavors.*

The soupy mass of crushed grapes, juice, skins, pulp, seeds, and possibly stems is called the must. In the old days, this would be fermented in large wooden vats. Today, most red wine is fermented in stainless steel tanks, which are both easier to clean and easier to control in terms of temperature.

Like any place where regular fermentations occur, a cellar is full of yeasts. With the help of these ambient yeasts, a mass of crushed grapes left alone will turn itself into wine. A winemaker, however, may choose to use cultured yeasts, thereby gaining control over the onset and rate of fermentation. Something as simple as the speed at which fermentation proceeds can profoundly affect the flavor of the wine, with slower fermentations often producing more complex wines.

Fermentation is a furious chemical reaction, during which carbon dioxide gas and heat are thrown off. As the yeasts begin to convert the grape sugar into alcohol, carbon dioxide bubbles up from the fomenting mass and pushes the skins to the surface. Unattended, the skins will float like a shag carpet on top of the wine. But the winemaker does not want them to float there. This dense cap of skins is critical to the eventual character of the wine, for as we know, the skins contain the wine's potential color and tannin, as well as compounds that become aromas and flavors. The more the wine is in contact with the cap, the more color, tannin, flavor, and aroma can be extracted.

Winemakers, therefore, gently break up the cap and submerge it in the wine. Sometimes this is done by punching down—literally pushing the skins under the surface of the liquid using a rakelike pole or a mechanical plate that acts like a plunger. A similar technique, stripping off most of one's clothes, hopping in the tank, and using one's legs and arms as paddles, worked for centuries. The cap can also be loosened by pumping over. In this case a large hose is run from the bottom of the tank to the top and juice is sprayed over the thick mantle of skins, allowing the juice to trickle through the cap, picking up color, tannin, aroma, and flavor.

During the process of fermentation, the temperature of the must rises to between 60°F and 85°F. The winemaker does not want it to rise above 85°F, for at higher temperatures the delicate fruit flavors of the wine may be volatilized, or burned off.

After virtually all of the sugar has become alcohol (a process that can take from several days to a few weeks) the wine is said to be dry. Ripe grapes (white and red) contain an amount of sugar that will naturally result in a wine that is 8 to 15 percent alcohol. In any case, wine cannot, by natural methods, be much more than 16.5 percent alcohol. At about this concentration, the yeasts die by being poisoned by the very alcohol they created.

Red wine can also be made according to a second method called carbonic maceration. Light, supergrapey wines, such as Beaujolais, are made in this manner. During carbonic maceration, whole bunches of grapes are carefully put into a closed fermenting tank in which the oxygen has been replaced by carbon dioxide, creating an anaerobic environment. The weight of the grapes on top crushes the grapes below. With the help of yeasts naturally present on the grape skins, fermentation soon bursts into action, releasing even more carbon dioxide. Once the amount of carbon diox-

## NOT ROMANTIC BUT REVOLUTIONARY

No single entity has had a more profound impact on white wine than the temperature-controlled stainless steel tank. In such tanks fermentation can take place slowly and at a cool temperature, resulting in white wines with fruity aromas and great delicacy.

Before the tank's invention in the latter half of the twentieth century, many of the world's white wines tasted slightly oxidized and flat. The best white wines came, virtually without exception, from Germany and in France from Champagne and northern Burgundy, where the naturally cold climates preserved the wines' freshness and finesse.

In 1912 the giant German industrial conglomerate Krupp filed for a patent on the first chrome-nickel-steel-molybdenum tank. This stainless steel tank was not re-frigerated, but it resisted corrosion from acids far better than its predecessor, the simple chrome-steel tank. Still, it would be several decades before the technology to cool such huge tanks would be invented and the temperature-controlled stainless steel tank would become a common sight in European wineries.

In the United States, the first nonrefrigerated stainless steel tanks were probably those commissioned by Gallo after World War II. Finally in the 1950s, advanced rotary compressors capable of refrigerating 25,000-gallon tanks became commercially available (and affordable). By the late 1960s, temperature-controlled stainless steel tanks were a fixture in every American winery serious about white wine.

# WARNING: THIS LABEL IS MISLEADING

—◈◈◈—

"Contains Sulfites." With the initiation of that federally mandated warning label in 1988, wine drinkers began to worry. What were sulfites and why were they suddenly being put into wine? In the confusion that followed, wine was blamed for everything from headaches to rashes.

The facts are these: Wine has always contained sulfites. The compounds occur as a natural by-product of fermentation. Historically, winemakers have also added small, controlled amounts of sulfites to wine to prevent oxidation and spoilage.

Widespread concern over sulfites first occurred in the late 1970s and early 1980s with the dawning of the salad bar. Cut vegetables and fruits were routinely sprayed with large amounts of sulfites (up to 2,000 parts per million—ppm) to keep them from wilting and turning brown. The FDA received reports of cases of adverse reactions from several hundred people. In response, strict regulations were enacted to protect the estimated 0.4 to 0.8 percent of the population, most of them severe asthmatics, considered at risk.

*Wineries regularly test for the amount of sulfites in a wine; these are compounds that occur naturally as a result of fermentation.*

Historically, however, the regulations on sulfites in wine have been stricter than those applied to salad bars. In wine the upper limit is 350 ppm. In practice, most wines today contain 150 ppm or less. In wineries where the grapes are healthy and unbruised and where sterilized equipment is used, the amount of sulfites in the wine may be far less. Several California wines are now made entirely without added sulfites.

When sulphur is used in winemaking in small, judicious doses it cannot be smelled or tasted. Nor is it responsible for headaches, according to allergists. Current research suggests that wine-related headaches are more probably related to difficulties the individual may have in metabolizing wine.

In addition to wine, sulfites are found in beer, cocktail mixes, cookies, crackers, pizza crust, flour tortillas, pickles, relishes, salad dressings, olives, vinegar, sugar, shrimp, scallops, dried fruit, and fruit juice, among other foods and beverages.

---

ide gas is great enough, some begins to pass into the grape berries themselves causing them to ferment from the inside even though they are intact. The result is a soft, effusively fruity, grapey-flavored wine.

At the end of both regular fermentation and carbonic maceration, the wine is usually drained off the skins (this wine is known as free run) and then pumped or drained into barrels or possibly another tank to begin the aging process (which in the case of a wine like Beaujolais can be very brief). The remaining mixture of wine and solids is gently pressed to release additional wine. This gently pressed juice (called first press) may not be as virginal as free run, but it often contains valuable tannin as well as flavor and aroma components. Superpremium wines are made mainly from free-run juice. But in some cases a small amount of first-press added to free-run wine can act like a vitamin B shot, giving the wine oomph.

Fruity red wines meant to be happily quaffed but not thought about will usually be kept for a few months in a tank or vat, then bottled. More serious reds will go into a barrel for periods ranging from a few months to a few years, depending on the potential complexity and structure of the wine. The barrels are virtually always oak. In them, complex chemical interactions will take place that will gradually and subtly alter the wine's aroma, flavor, and texture (see What Oak Does, page 40).

An important part of barrel aging is the racking of the wine. Racking is simply the process of allowing solids to settle to the bottom of the vat or barrel, then pouring or drawing the clear wine off. A wine may be racked numerous times as various types of solids continue to precipitate out. Racking also aerates the wine, helping it mature.

**Malolactic fermentation** is another important process that most red wines and many white wines go through naturally during the barrel-aging process. This process is brought about by benign bacteria. During malolactic fermentation, tart malic acid (imagine the acid in a green apple) is converted into softer lactic acid (imagine the acid in milk), making the wine taste softer. Depending on the winemaker's preference and the cellar temperature, malolactic fermentation may occur during the yeast fermentation, almost immediately following it, or as late as the following spring when the winery warms a little.

A winemaking process that is sometimes utilized in the later stages of aging is fining. Fining clarifies a wine of minute solids still suspended in the liquid. Fining also helps precipitate out excessive tannin, thus helping to improve the wine's texture and balance. To fine a wine, bentonite, a granular clay coagulant, or some type of protein coagulant, such as egg whites, casein (a milk protein), gelatin, or—hardest of all to imagine—isinglass (a gelatinous substance derived from the air bladders of fish) is stirred into the wine. Like one half of a Velcro patch, the coagulant attaches itself (in this case, chemically) to the suspended haze of particles, which acts like the other piece of the Velcro. Together, the coagulant and the haze form molecules that are too heavy to remain in suspension and so fall to the bottom of the barrel. The clear wine can then be racked off the formerly suspended particles. (So, in case you might be wondering, no egg whites or worse, fish bladders, remain in the wine.)

After oak aging and before bottling, a wine may be filtered. No winemaking

## A FEAST OF YEASTS

Yeasts, 40,000 of which could fit on the head of a pin, exist naturally in vineyard soils, cling to grapes as they grow, and are present in the air of wine cellars. Some winemakers allow these ambient yeasts to carry out fermentation, believing that they impart desirable characteristics and more complexity to the final wine than cultured yeasts would. Ambient yeasts, however, are unpredictable in the alcohol levels they can achieve and in the aromatic components they form, some of which may be disagreeable. In addition, ambient yeasts can be slow, even sluggish, about getting the fermentation to begin. As a result of these factors, many winemakers prefer to use a strain of cultured yeast, which can be depended on to multiply actively at a given temperature. There are many strains of cultured yeasts. A winemaker's choice depends on how fast and intense he or she wants the fermentation to be. This in turn may subtly affect the flavors and aromas of the wine.

practice today is more controversial than filtering, which has generated so many invectives you'd think the subject was taxes. The facts are these: There are times when a wine must be filtered to avoid being spoiled by bacteria and other times when filtering is undesirable as it may result in a lesser wine. The real art is knowing when to filter if at all and exactly which method to use so that the wine is improved, not harmed. Filtering helps to stabilize a wine and helps clarify it by removing from suspension particles that are greater than a certain chosen size. Excessive filtering, however, also removes desirable particles and thus strips the wine of some of its flavor and aroma.

There are several types of filters, most of which work in a similar manner. In one commonly used type, the wine is pumped through a series of porous pads made of simple cellulose fibers. The pores of the pads may be wide or narrow. In what is called a loose polish filtration, wide-pore pads are used to clarify a wine without removing flavors and aromas. Pads with smaller pores remove smaller particles. Filtered tightly enough, a wine can be made to taste as bland and boring as sliced white bread.

Finally, after filtering (or not), the wine is bottled, often to be aged yet again. In a bottle, the water and alcohol can't evaporate and, assuming the cork is sound, oxygen cannot readily penetrate. The bottle itself, unlike a barrel, is sterile and chemically inert. In the bottle, the components in the wine interact alone, slowly coalescing into harmony. Together barrel and bottle aging work synergistically toward a level of optimal maturity. The greatest red wines in the world always experience both barrel (oxidative) and bottle (reductive) aging.

*Bottling, the final stage in a wine's life before it's ready to be sold and consumed, is a laborious, if essential, process.*

# MAKING DRY WHITE WINE

Although conscientious winemakers everywhere take enormous care to harvest all types of grapes quickly and as gently as possible, white grapes require special speed and handling. Accidentally crushing grapes on the way to the winery can cause the skins to leak tannin into the juice, which can make a white wine taste coarse. Bruised white grapes also risk losing their delicate range of aromas and flavors.

In making red wine, the color-packed skins remain with the juice during fermentation and are only removed when the fermentation is finished. With white wine, however, the juice is separated from its skins before fermentation begins. To obtain the juice, whole bunches of white grapes are either put into a crusher-destemmer that removes the stems or are put directly into the press. In wineries fanatic about freshness, the grapes may first be chilled, since chilling helps preserve the grapes' freshness and delicate fruit flavors. More commonly, though, the pressed juice may be chilled before fermentation.

In most modern wineries, bladder presses have replaced the old basket presses in which a metal or wooden plate attached to a screw mashed the pulp down against the bottom of the press. In a bladder press, a pliable air tube suspended in the center of the press (the bladder) is carefully inflated, slowly pushing the grapes against the fine screen inside the press. The grapes are squeezed so gently that the stems and seeds are not broken.

In the past, once a white wine was pressed, it was transferred to a settling tank so that particles in suspension (mostly minute pieces of grape pulp) could fall to the bottom. Today the settling process may be accomplished faster if the winemaker chooses to fine, filter, or centrifuge the juice instead. Regardless of the method used, once the settling process is finished the clean juice is ready to be fermented.

As is true of red wine, white wine will ferment on its own using ambient yeasts.

Some winemakers, however, prefer to manually introduce a yeast culture, making the process of fermentation easier to control.

White wines may be cooled in temperature-controlled fermentation tanks so they ferment at 50°F to 65°F (as opposed to 75°F to 85°F for red wines). With white wines, the goal is not to extract color (as is true with red wines) but to preserve the freshness and delicacy of the fruit, which happens best in a slow, cool environment. Temperature-controlled stainless steel tanks are usually double skinned, wrapped on the outside with a cooling jacket through which glycol runs. Or such tanks can be constructed so that cold water can be run down the outside, thereby cooling off the tank and lowering the temperature of the fermenting juice inside.

Although temperature-controlled stainless steel tanks preserve a white wine's freshness and delicacy and give the wine-

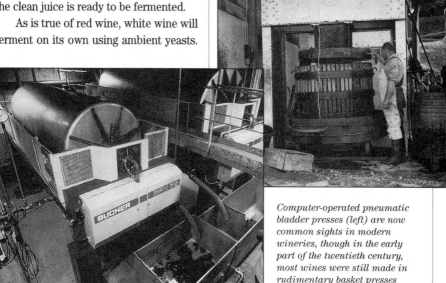

*Computer-operated pneumatic bladder presses (left) are now common sights in modern wineries, though in the early part of the twentieth century, most wines were still made in rudimentary basket presses (above).*

## WINEMAKING

# THE SHORTHAND METHOD

| RED WINES | WHITE WINES |
|---|---|
| • Grapes are picked | • Grapes are picked |
| • Grapes are crushed; stems are removed (or not) | • Grapes are crushed and stems are removed (or not) |
| • Crushed grapes, juice, skins, and seeds are put into a tank | • Grapes are pressed; skins are removed; juice is put into tank |
| • Yeasts are added, if the winemaker is not relying on ambient yeasts | • Yeasts are added, if the winemaker is not relying on ambient yeasts |
| • Fermentation begins (malolactic fermentation also begins or may occur later) | • Fermentation of juice begins (malolactic fermentation may also begin, may occur later, or may be prevented altogether) |
| • Cap of skins is pushed down or pumped over the fermenting liquid | • When fermentation is complete, wine is left to sit in contact with lees (or not) |
| • When fermentation is complete, wine is pressed off the skins | • Wine is racked off the lees if necessary |
| • Wine is put in barrels to age | • Wine is possibly cold stabilized |
| • Wine is periodically racked | • Wine is possibly put into barrels to age |
| • Wine is possibly fined and/or filtered | • Wine is possibly fined and/or filtered |
| • Wine is bottled | • Wine is bottled |

maker a measure of control over fermentation, some potentially full-bodied grapes—notably chardonnay—can benefit from being fermented in small oak barrels. Hardy and full-bodied are key qualifications, for a more fragile variety like riesling tastes disgustingly like liquid wood when it's barrel fermented.

During barrel fermentation the barrel is filled three-quarters full to prevent the wine from foaming over. As the wine ferments, the temperature rises to 70°F or more. In the warm tango of fermentation, the yeasts help pull toasty, vanillin flavors from the wood. Fresh fruit aromas and flavors are sacrificed but, if the winemaker is skilled, the wine can gain complexity in their place.

At first thought, it might seem as though a barrel-fermented white wine would also take on an undesirable amount of tannin from the barrel itself. Curiously, this is not the case. During fermentation the developing wine does extract tannin lodged in the staves. But when fermentation is complete and the spent yeast cells (lees) are removed from the wine, many of the wood tannins cling to them and are removed as well.

In addition to being barrel-fermented, full-bodied white wines, such as chardonnay, may also be left *sur lie*, on their lees or spent yeast cells. Rather than racking the juice off the yeast cells, these wines are allowed to rest in contact with them. In effect the wines are marinating with the yeasts. This adds a slightly richer texture and sometimes more complexity to the wines. In Burgundy and frequently in California, the lees are regularly stirred up to accentuate the effect. (Continuing the culinary metaphor, this would be like basting.) A white wine such as chardonnay typically spends four to twelve months in contact with its lees. Finally, the wine is racked off the lees.

Winemakers do not put white wines through malolactic fermentation as routinely as they do reds. With red wines, crisp acidity is not really a goal so malolactic fermentation (converting very tart acid to softer acid; see page 35) makes sense. But with white wines, winemakers often prevent malolactic fermentation from occurring precisely because they want to preserve the tart, thirst-quenching acidity in the wine. Many sauvignon blancs, rieslings, and pinot grigios, for example, do not undergo malolactic fermentation. Chardonnay, on the other hand, almost always does and, as a result, chardonnay has a soft texture. During malolactic fermentation, a buttery-flavored compound called diacetyl may be produced. It is diacetyl that gives many chardonnays their butteriness. (Note: Diacetyl is regularly added to margarine to make it taste more like butter.)

To prevent a white wine from spontaneously undergoing malolactic fermentation, a winemaker can fine and then filter out the remaining yeast cells, proteins, and bacteria or chill the wine sharply or stun the bacteria with a small dose of sulphur dioxide.

At this point, most white wines are cold stabilized—chilled down to a point slightly above freezing for a period of several days. Cold stabilization precipitates tartrate crystals (the solid form of tartaric acid) out of the wine and thus prevents them from sud-

denly appearing later on in the bottle. If you've ever chilled a wine that wasn't stabilized, you probably noticed that small snowflakelike crystals—tartrates—formed. Before modern winemaking, white wines were usually left for a year or more in cold cellars where the tartrates would precipitate out naturally and form a thick crust on the inside of barrels. In wine regions such as Germany, it is still possible to see old barrels lined 6 inches thick with what looks like white stalactites and stalagmites.

After cold stabilization, some white wines, like red wines, are aged in oak, though for considerably shorter periods. Oak aging (especially when the barrels are new) can profoundly change the flavor of white wines (see What Oak Does, which follows). When aged in wood too long, a white wine loses delicacy and the purity of its fruit and instead takes on the brazen

*Because they maintain fairly constant cool temperatures and high humidity, underground cellars or caves are perfect for aging wine. Most were dug by hand, though large machines now exist that can bore underground and into hillsides in a fraction of the time hand digging took.*

39

flavor of wood and candied vanilla. In anthropomorphic terms, such a wine can seem like the equivalent of a small-built woman wearing tons of makeup and a huge fur coat. Conversely, when oak-aged with care and restraint, such full-fruit grapes as chardonnay can acquire greater lushness and complexity.

Finally, white wine, like red, may be filtered or fined to stabilize and further clarify it. It is then bottled and, again like red wine, may be given further aging in bottle.

## WHAT OAK DOES

Without oak, many wines as we know them would not exist. They would not taste the same, smell the same, or have the same texture. Nor are there substitutes for oak. Cherry, walnut, chestnut, pine, and many other woods can all be made into barrels; none, however, enhances wine the way oak does. Nor has technology devised an oak alternative. In short, wine and oak—inseparable for the last two millennia of winemaking—show every sign of remaining married.

Why is there a special affinity between oak and wine? Oak has the ability to transform wine, to coax it out of the genre of simple fermented fruit juice and give it depth, length, complexity, and intensity.

Which is not to say that every wine is enhanced by time in a barrel. Some—light-bodied white wines in particular—have a structure too small to shoulder the weighty sweet vanilla and oak flavors wood imparts. Immersing such wines in new wood barrels robs them of varietal character in much the way that slathering a steamed lettuce leaf in cream sauce would obliterate the flavor of the lettuce. The opposite is true of certain full-bodied white and red wines. For these, oak, used judiciously, can be an asset.

Although open wooden buckets were used to hold and transport wine more than two thousand years before Christ, closed oak barrels first came into use during the Roman Empire. Oak, plentiful in the forests of Europe, had many desirable qualities: It was strong enough to withstand considerable wear and tear yet sufficiently lightweight and malleable to be shaped into barrels that could be rolled and moved. And oak was leakproof.

Lastly, oak had a desirable effect on the wine itself. Early winemakers discerned that wine grew softer and in many cases tasted better after oak aging, even though they were not sure why. During the last third of the twentieth century, research on oak aging has begun to unravel the enigma. Enologists now speculate that two processes may be responsible for the transformation.

The first is evaporation. Both water and alcohol diffuse outward through the staves of a closed oak barrel. A 50-gallon barrel of cabernet sauvignon, for example, may lose as much as 5 to 6 gallons of liquid per year. If the barrel is sound, the wine will age in a slow, reductive manner. Yeast cells still in the wine may marry with other components, helping to influence the course of maturation as well.

At the same time, minute amounts of oxygen from outside are seeping through the grain and into the barrel, helping to weave together the elements of the wine and giving it a softer dimension. Oxygen also becomes a factor in the equation each time the winemaker removes the bung (stopper) from the barrel and tops up the wine or partially clarifies it by racking it into another barrel.

Oak wood is composed of several classes of complex chemical compounds, which also leave their mark on a wine's aroma, flavor, and texture. The most noticeable of these are phenols, some of which impart vanilla-like flavors, notes of tea and tobacco, and impressions of sweetness. One of the most important classes of phenols are the substances commonly called tannin.

The impact oak has on wine depends, among other things, on the type of oak used and the way the barrel was made (see How Barrels Are Made, page 42). Of the four hundred species of oak trees that grow around the world, three main types are used in winemaking: the American oak *Quercus alba* (mainly from the Midwest) and the French oaks *Quercus robur* and *Quercus sessiliflora* (from central and eastern France). The flavor American oak imparts to wine is quite different from the flavor French oak imparts to wine; American oak tends to be more pronounced and vanillin; French oak, more subtle. Neither is necessarily better than the other in the same way that basil isn't necessarily better than rosemary. The idea is to find a type of oak that will best show off the fruit flavors in a given wine. To determine this, winemakers age small lots of their wines in several different oaks from different forests and a variety of coopers in both countries and then see which ones work best.

A winemaker can choose to put a wine into new barrels, used barrels, or a combination of new and used barrels. Although the extraction rate of vanilla and oak flavors differs based on the grain of the wood, most barrels impart little flavor after four to six years of use. Also, some wines leave layers of natural deposits on the insides of the barrels, which, over time, shield a wine from any wood contact whatsoever.

*The barrel-aging cellar at Châteaux Margaux: Resting in barrels in a cool, humid cellar, wine ages slowly, becoming more harmonious and developing a softer texture.*

# HOW BARRELS ARE MADE

The story of an oak barrel ultimately begins with the tree from which the wood came. A tree, like a grapevine, is affected by climate. In cold, dry climates, a tree grows slowly, forming a narrow growth ring for that year. In wetter, warmer climates, a tree grows more quickly and the growth ring is wider. The widths of all the rings together become the wood's grain. A tree with mostly wide rings is loosely grained; a tree with mostly narrow rings is tightly grained.

*French oak trees near the village of Cognac await their fate.*

Because the wood inside a narrow ring is more dense than that inside a wide ring, flavor is extracted from a narrow ring more gradually. Winemakers generally prefer this, for in wines aged in barrels made from narrow-ring, tight-grained oak, the oak character is usually better integrated into the wine and the overall flavor of oak is more mellow. This is why barrels made from trees that grow in the French forests of Tronçais, Vosges, and Nevers are so sought after. All three forests are cool and dry and thus are known for their narrow-ring, tight-grained oaks. The forest of Tronçais, in particular, was planted in the late 1600s as a source of superior ship masts for the French navy. Though American oak is not designated by the forest from which it came, the best American oak also comes from cool places, such as Minnesota and Iowa.

In addition to the species of oak used (French or American), the manner in which a barrel is made significantly affects the flavor of a wine. An oak tree is generally harvested when it is one hundred years old or more. For centuries, the traditional European practice—still used today by the best coopers—has been to hand split the oak into staves along natural grain lines, then air-dry and season the staves by leaving them stacked outdoors, exposed to sun and rain for two or three years. During this period when the wood is unprotected, the harshest tannin is gradually leached out—ultimately to the benefit of the wine.

The next step is to fit the staves together as tightly as possible. An imperfect seam could result in a leaky barrel or one that allows considerable oxygen to seep between the staves, oxidizing and spoiling the wine. To form a barrel, a cooper using the traditional European method heats the staves over an open fire to make them pliable enough to bend into shape. This is still done entirely by hand with only the help of winches and chains, as well as iron rings that must be hammered into place and act like belts holding the staves together. It is backbreaking work. A top cooper working swiftly can make just one barrel a day. The fire that helps bend the staves also "toasts" them, caramelizing the wood's natural sugar into toasty, spicy, vanilla flavors, which are ultimately imparted to the wine. Like breakfast toast in a coffee shop, winemakers can order their barrels lightly, moderately, or well-toasted, depending on the degree of toasty flavor they want to impart.

In addition to this traditional European method, there is a second method—one

43

*Barrel making is practiced today in much the same way it has been for centuries. The oak is hand split (with a little mechanical help) along the grain (left). Staves are carefully placed into position (right) using nothing but an iron hoop and a lot of skill.*

which, while sharply criticized today, has been used extensively, especially in the past for American oak barrels. In this method, the staves are quickly dried in a kiln rather than outdoors over the course of years. Although expeditious, kiln drying does not have the tannin-leaching or seasoning effect that air drying has. As a result, kiln-dried barrels tend to impart coarse flavors. This doesn't matter too much if the liquid inside is bourbon, but if it's chardonnay, the result can taste terrible.

The staves for American barrels have usually been bent over steam rather than fire. Barrels with steam-bent staves impart a far less complex, less toasty character to wine than barrels made from fire-bent staves.

*The staves of a partially made barrel can be slowly bent into place when heated over an open fire. With multiple fires going constantly, temperatures inside the cooperage can reach 120°F.*

(Think of the difference between boiled beef and grilled beef.) The world of American oak barrel making is changing, however. Since the mid-1990s, the best American oak barrels have been made according to the traditional European method.

## BOTTLES AND BARRELS

# HOLD EVERYTHING

From the time it came into being thousands of centuries ago, wine has been stored in a variety of vessels. Precisely how much wine any one ancient vessel held, however, is difficult to determine. Often wine vessels might be called by the same name in different countries, but the amount of liquid each held would be different. According to Tim Unwin in *Wine and the Vine: An Historical Geography of Viticulture and the Wine Trade,* it was not until the Middle Ages, when governments began to regulate the wine trade more closely, that some of the more common measures came to be standardized. Even then, barrels could vary in size from country to country or even region to region, depending on local customs. This is still somewhat the case. Here however, are the capacities of various containers used to store and age wine today.

### Bottle

Initially, the amount glass bottles held was not consistent. From the fifteenth to the seventeenth century bottles held anywhere from 16 to 52 ounces. Today a standard wine bottle holds 25.36 ounces (750 milliliters). Restaurants generally pour five to six glasses of wine from a single bottle.

### Small Barrel

Although first used as a general term to describe any wooden container, barrels are now used as specific measures. The small medieval *barile* of Florence held 10.01 gallons, and the small fifteenth-century English wine barrel held 31.5 gallons. Today three types of small barrels are standard around the world. French oak Bordeaux barrels, used for many types of wine, including cabernet sauvignon, merlot, and Bordeaux wines, hold 59.43 gallons (225 liters). French oak Burgundy barrels, generally used for pinot noirs worldwide, including Burgundies, hold 60.2 gallons (228 liters). And American oak barrels, used for all types of wine, are made in both sizes.

### Hogshead

Although the volume of the medieval hogshead was not consistent, by the fifteenth century the English hogshead held 63 gallons. A modern hogshead, quite a bit larger than a small barrel, holds 79.25 gallons (300 liters). Winemakers use hogsheads when they want the wine to be less stamped by oak, as may be the case with such delicate varieties as sangiovese and pinot noir. Hogsheads are used for many types of wine, however.

### Puncheon

Like a hogshead, the volume a puncheon holds has varied over history. Modern puncheons, commonly used for wines like sangiovese that don't benefit from a lot of wood contact, come in two sizes: 79.25 gallons and 132.08 gallons (300 and 500 liters respectively).

### Pipe

In fifteenth-century England a pipe held 126 gallons, but in Spain it ranged from 100 to 105 gallons. In Victorian England, where a pipe of Port was commonly given to a newborn child as a gift, a pipe held 141.13 gallons (534.24 liters). Today the volume pipes hold ranges from 145.29 gallons (550 liters) to 166.42 gallons (630 liters), depending on the country they come from and whether they are used for maturing or shipping a wine. Pipes commonly contain Port, Sherry, Madeira, Marsala, or Cognac.

Finally, there is no one perfect length of time a wine should spend in oak. A California pinot noir may begin to soften and come into focus after a year in oak; a Bordeaux made mostly from cabernet sauvignon may require two; a Barolo, made from nebbiolo, four. It is a question not only of the grape variety but also of the intensity and strength of the wine itself.

Cultural preferences in flavor also dictate how long a wine will be aged in oak. In Spain, winemakers in Rioja have traditionally aged their best red wines, made principally from tempranillo grapes, for as long as ten years in used American oak barrels because they like the soft, earthy vanilla character that results.

Aging in oak is not the same as fermenting in oak. The two distinctly different processes have different consequences. Imagine, for example, a batch of chardonnay that is fermented in oak and then aged in oak for six months. Imagine a second batch that is fermented in stainless steel and then aged in oak for the same period. Although you might expect that the wine receiving two doses of oak (during fermentation and aging) would have the most pronounced oak and vanilla flavors and the strongest impression of tannin, the opposite is usually true. When a wine is fermented in oak, the yeasts also interact with the wood. When the spent yeast cells (lees) are ultimately removed from the wine, a measure of the wood tannin may be removed with them.

By comparison, a white wine fermented in stainless steel and then put without the lees into oak barrels readily absorbs the wood flavors and tannins to which it is exposed. If the wine is delicate and the oak is new, the winemaker must be exceedingly careful, otherwise the result will be something that tastes more like a vanilla-coated two-by-four than like grapes.

For the last three decades, many California chardonnays have been given considerable exposure to oak. Some wine drinkers—especially those who embarked on wine drinking during the 1970s and 1980s—came to love the toasty, oaky flavors and to think of them as the flavor of the varietal itself. More experienced wine drinkers knew better. What is the point of drinking chardonnay, they argued, if you cannot taste chardonnay in the "chardonnay"?

In using oak judiciously, a winemaker can opt to: ferment the wine in oak but not age it in it; age the wine in oak but not ferment it in it; use a little of both; or use none of either.

# MAKING OFF-DRY WINE

Slightly sweet wines, sometimes called off-dry, are made just a bit differently from dry white wines. During the fermentation of dry white wines, yeasts convert virtually all of the sugar in the grapes to alcohol. However, for slightly sweet wines the process of fermentation is stopped before the yeasts can convert all the sugar. This leaves a wine with a touch of natural sweetness and a lower level of alcohol. In this scenario, the wine is not sweet enough to be a dessert wine; the tiny bit of residual sugar may be barely perceptible. The goal is not so much to create a sweet taste as it is to enhance the fruitiness of the wine. Many California chenin blancs, gewürztraminers, rieslings, and rosés are made in this way.

How is the fermentation stopped? Either by giving the wine a small dose of $SO_2$ (sulfur dioxide), which will kill the yeasts before they have converted all the sugar, or by chilling the wine and then filtering out the yeasts.

## KOSHER WINE

—⟨∞⟩—

Until the 1980s many kosher wines tasted like a cross between Kool-Aid and ground up St. Joseph's aspirin for children. Today, however, kosher wines are in an entirely different league. Made by winemakers with good credentials from such classic varieties as chardonnay and cabernet sauvignon, kosher wines now compete with fine wines made anywhere in the world.

To be kosher, a wine must be made under rabbinical supervision and must be handled throughout vinification by a Sabbath-observant Jew. Wine handled or served by a nonobserver is considered unfit for sacramental use.

Historically, of course, Jewish religious authorities knew that wine was used not just for sacramental purposes but also socially. Wine eased and encouraged social interaction. Religious scholars speculate that rabbis and Jewish intellectuals may have feared such socializing, viewing it as the first step toward the disintegration of Jewish culture and the assimilation of Jews into other cultures. To mitigate against this, two versions of kosher wine were made. The first, *mevushal* (literally, cooked) wine, would be boiled, making it in a sense morally sterilized. Though *mevushal* wine would therefore be less palatable than regular wine, it could be shared by non-Jews and nonobservant Jews with observant Jews.

The other type of kosher wine would be non-*mevushal* and, as a result, generally better tasting. Non-*mevushal* wine could be drunk and served only by Sabbath-obser-

46

# MAKING SWEET WINE

How does a wine come to be sweet enough to be dessert in itself? The process starts with grapes that are very high in sugar because they were:

**1.** Picked after the regular harvest when their sugar content is very high; or

**2.** Picked, laid out on mats, and allowed to raisinate, thereby concentrating their sugar; or

**3.** Permitted to freeze on the vine (as in *eiswein*) so that water can be separated from the sugary juice; or

**4.** Attacked by the fungus *Botrytis cinerea* (the noble rot of French Sauternes), which consumes some of the water in the grapes and helps more to evaporate, again concentrating the sugar.

All of these processes are extremely risky—animals may eat the sweet grapes, the grapes may be attacked by unfavorable molds or diseases, weather may destroy the grapes before the crop can be picked, and so on. Moreover, each of these processes is very labor intensive. Sweet wines, as a result, are almost universally rare and expensive.

No matter which of the four methods is used, the resulting grape juice has a higher sugar content than usual. Before the yeasts can convert all this sugar to alcohol, either the winemaker stops the fermentation early, as with an off-dry wine, or the yeasts' action is halted by the very alcohol they have produced. Once the alcohol level has reached about 16 percent, most yeasts can no longer function; whatever natural sugar is left remains.

vant Jews. If a non-Jew or a non-Sabbath-observant Jew touched a non-*mevushal* wine, even accidentally, it could not be consumed by someone who strictly followed kosher dietary law. As of the mid-1990s, only 10 percent of kosher wines in the United States were non-*mevushal*.

Initially, *mevushal* wines were quite literally boiled. Today the unfermented grape juice or wine is flash pasteurized—a more modern method of sterilization—and the wine is then aged. Flash pasteurization is also kinder than boiling when it comes to preserving the wine's aroma and flavor.

In both Europe and Israel, kosher wine has always been made from classic European grape varieties, such as cabernet sauvignon, chardonnay, chenin blanc, and merlot. While that is now true in the United States as well, in the past most American-made kosher wines were produced from foxy-tasting native grapes, such as Concord, which were also used for jelly. These grapes thrived along the East Coast, where the largest centers of Jewish population were to be found. Over time, American-made kosher wine became inextricably linked with syrupy sweet wine, such as Manischevitz.

The largest United States importer and distributor of kosher wines is the New York-based Royal Kedem, which annually markets more than a million cases of upscale kosher wine made in Europe and the United States. As for specific producers of kosher wine, the best in California include Weinstock, Hagafen, Gan Eden, and Baron Herzog. The most famous French kosher wine is the one called Baron Rothschild, an expensive kosher Bordeaux produced by Baron Edmund Rothschild of the Lafite-Rothschild family. And from Israel, the producers to look for are Yarden and Golan. The bottles of most kosher wines will indicate on the back labels whether the wine is *mevushel* or non-*mevushel*.

## CHAPTALIZATION

Chaptalization (named after Jean-Antoine Chaptal, minister of agriculture under Napoleon, who first sanctioned the process) is the act of adding sugar to a low-alcohol wine before and/or during fermentation so the yeasts will have more sugar to convert and the alcohol level will be increased. Don't confuse chaptalization with the making of slightly sweet or dessert wines.

You cannot taste sugar in the chaptalized wine; the process does not increase the wine's sweetness; it increases its alcohol. Critics, however, contend that chaptalized wines take on a blowsy, out-of-balance character, since the final alcohol has been artificially jacked up.

Many wines in northern Europe are routinely chaptalized since the grapes may not be ripe enough to produce sufficient alcohol. Conversely, wines made in such sunny places as California and Australia are rarely chaptalized because grapes in those places virtually always get ripe enough to produce a substantial amount of alcohol.

*Kosher wines have come a long way in quality as this delicious Baron Herzog Chenin Blanc attests.*

# Getting to Know the Grapes

Airén is a good place to begin. Recognize the name? What about rkatsiteli? They are respectively the grape variety thought to cover the most acreage of vineyards in the world and the most widely planted grape in the former Soviet Union (it also grows in New York State). But you've probably never drunk wine made from airén or rkatsiteli. And, in fact, neither is a classic.

What defines a classic variety? First, it must have manifested considerable quality over a long period of time and, second, have done so in more than one place. Cabernet sauvignon and chardonnay, for instance, are made into good (and occasionally great) wines everywhere from France to Chile. Each of the classic grape varieties discussed here is also discussed in depth in the sections devoted to wine regions around the world. From the classic grapes, I'll move on to briefer profiles of what I call the important grapes, and finally, you'll find at the end of this chapter a glossary of virtually every other grape you're likely to encounter worldwide.

## THE CLASSIC WHITES

There are five white grape varieties that are considered classic. These range from the extremely popular char-

48

*Though there are numerous species and thousands of varieties of grapes, all of the top grape varieties used for wine belong to just one species—vinifera.*

## AMPELOGRAPHY

———

Ampelography is the science of vine identification and description. By studying and measuring a vine's shoots, canes, buds, flowers, clusters, seeds, and grapes, an ampelographer can tell chardonnay from chenin blanc, pinot gris from pinot blanc. Vines are also now being identified by DNA fingerprinting.

donnay to the less familiar but no less fascinating sémillon.

## Chardonnay

For several decades, chardonnay has been one of the most successful white wines in the world. The wine's appealing, big flavors—vanilla, butter, butterscotch, buttered toast, custard, green apple, tropical fruit, lemon, pineapple—are matched by equally effusive textures—creamy, lush, and full-bodied. (I sometimes think of chardonnay as Marilyn Monroe.)

In much of the world—and almost always in the United States, Australia, and the famous Côte d'Or villages of Burgundy, France—chardonnay is both fermented and aged briefly in oak barrels. Why is this significant? Because barrel fermentation and aging transforms chardonnay, helping it to take on rich notes, develop a creamier body, lengthen its finish, and possibly, but not always, give it more complexity.

There is a hitch. Left just a little too long in contact with wood, chardonnay can taste diffused, flabby, and overdone. When all you can taste in a chardonnay is oak and toast, the wine has been ruined by the very process that was supposed to enhance it.

To be truly great and to work well with food, chardonnay must taste like the fruit from which it came and must have a good core of acidity. Oak must be used judiciously. Just as a cream sauce is supposed to complement the flavor of a vegetable, not disguise it, so too, the flavor of oak should be the seasoning, not the main dish.

Chardonnay is grown and made all over the world. Important chardonnay-producing countries and states include: Argentina; Australia; California; Chile; France, especially in Burgundy, Champagne (where it is a component of Champagne), and the Languedoc-Roussillon; Italy, in the Tre Venezie and Tuscany; New York State, especially on Long Island; New Zealand; Oregon; South Africa; Texas; Virginia; and Washington State.

49

## THE GRAPE WORLD

• There are some 24,000 names for varieties of wine grapes.

• Ampelographers believe these represent about 5,000 truly different varieties, since most varieties have numerous names, depending on where they are grown.

• Of those 5,000 grape varieties, only 150 are planted in commercially significant amounts.

• And of the 150 varieties, only the following nine are considered classic:

| WHITE GRAPES | RED GRAPES |
|---|---|
| • chardonnay | • cabernet sauvignon |
| • chenin blanc | • merlot |
| • riesling | • pinot noir |
| • sauvignon blanc | • syrah |
| • sémillon | |

*Cabernet sauvignon grapes*

*Riesling grapes*

*Pinot gris grapes*

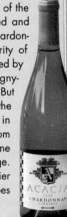

*Sauvignon blanc grapes*

## TASTING FOR INTEGRITY

A varietal is a wine made entirely from one particular variety of grape. The grapes, whether they're chardonnay, riesling, cabernet sauvignon, or any other variety, can each be turned into wines that have distinctly individual flavors.

Just as you can imagine the different tastes of lamb chops, steak, and pork chops without actually eating them, you can learn to "mind-taste" zinfandel, pinot noir, merlot, and a dozen other varietal wines.

Why bother? Because understanding the differences among varietals tells you what to look for in any given wine. Once you know what to be looking for, evaluating a wine (and remembering it) is far easier. Great wine must always taste true to the inherent flavor of the grape from which it was made. Part of a wine's beauty, part of its deliciousness, is derived from the purity of its intrinsic flavors.

In the past a wine couldn't help but taste like the grapes from which it came. That is not true today. Advanced technology allows winemakers and viticulturists to act like plastic surgeons, changing the wine's acidity, making it taste bigger than it really is, altering the impression of tannin, adjusting the amount of alcohol; even the wine's basic flavor—its very soul—can be modified. This can be good for jug wines—their deficiencies can be mollified with the right technological help. But for better-than-good wines, dabbling has its downside. Winemakers who muck around too much with the integrity of a grape end up making overworked wines that taste muddled. Wise, talented winemakers on the other hand are like wise, talented chefs: reductionists at heart. They want the intrinsic personality of the thing, be it syrah or salmon, to show through.

A final point: In the United States and most of the rest of the New World, most wines are named and labeled according to grape variety. Acacia chardonnay is precisely what it says it is. The majority of European wines, however, are named and labeled by geographic origin. Domaine Leflaive Puligny-Montrachet, for example, is also chardonnay. But the only way you'd know that is by memorizing the fact that Puligny-Montrachet is a village in Burgundy, France, and that all white wines from there are chardonnay. I know that European wine can seem daunting in this regard. Have courage. Linking geography with a given grape gets easier as you go along (see Matching the Right Grapes to the Right Ground, page 21).

## Chenin Blanc

Before chardonnay began to grow in popularity in the 1970s, chenin blanc was the most widely planted classic white grape in California. That it is found there now in a smaller amount is not a reflection of chenin blanc's merits but evidence of chardonnay's easy likability and successful promotion.

The most famous, vibrant chenin blancs in the world come from the Loire Valley of France, specifically from the appellations Vouvray, Savennières, Anjou, and Saumur. In particular, the great Vouvrays and Savennières are stunningly complex, long-lived wines with shimmering acidity. In the Loire chenin blanc is made in a variety of degrees of sweetness from bone-dry to quite sweet. Many have a touch of sweetness that is barely perceptible, the result of leaving a tiny bit of natural grape sugar (residual sugar) in the wines to accentuate roundness and balance the acidity. Fully sweet chenin blancs can be phenomenal. The most legendary of all is Quarts de Chaume, from a tiny area in the middle of the Loire Valley.

Chenin blanc is also the leading white grape of South Africa, where it is known as steen. There, however, it is unfortunately made mostly into a simple, innocuous quaffing wine. In California, chenin blanc becomes a wine that is effortless to drink, with soft, round flavors reminiscent of pears, melons, apricots, red apples, peaches, and fruit-cocktail syrup. Although riesling in California can seem similar to chenin blanc, chenin is usually a fuller wine. If modern life allowed for such seemingly lost pleasures as sitting in a field of wildflowers and reading *Madame Bovary* or *The Age of Innocence*, chenin blanc would be the fitting wine to drink.

Chenin Blanc is grown and made principally in: California; France, in the Loire Valley (where it is used in Vouvray, Savennières, and other wines); South Africa; Texas, and Washington State.

The Savennières from Clos de la Coulée de Serrant is one of the most famous—and delicious—chenin blancs in the world.

## Riesling

Despite its neglect in the United States, riesling is considered by many wine experts to be the most noble and unique white grape variety in the world. Great riesling has soaring acidity and considerable extract (the nonsoluble substances in wine that add to its flavor). Yet the wine is often low in alcohol and thus light in body. Riesling can have an alcohol level as low as 8 percent; by comparison, most chardonnays are 13 percent alcohol or more.

Given the right soil and winemaking methods, the triad of high acidity, high extract, and low alcohol leads to intensely flavorful wines of ravishing delicacy, transparency, and lightness. Riesling's refined structure is complemented by the mouthwateringly delicate flavors of fresh ripe peaches, apricots, and melons, sometimes pierced with a vibrant mineral quality, like the taste of water running over stones in a mountain stream.

More than almost any other white grape, riesling is temperamental about where it is planted. It doesn't grow well in very warm places, and even in cooler sites, the quality and character of the wine can vary enormously. The most elegant and precise rieslings come from cool to cold climates—Germany, the Alsace region of France, northern Austria, and upstate New York. Rieslings from a slightly warmer climate, such as California's, are usually softer, slightly fuller, and can have more diffuse flavors.

Rieslings can be dry or have various levels of sweetness. Dry and sweeter examples are found in Germany, Alsace, and virtually everywhere else the grape is grown. At its sweetest, riesling becomes lavish and honeyed. German riesling

*Rieslings the world over are commonly bottled in tall, tapered bottles.*

TBAs (*trockenbeerenauslesen*) can have up to 30 percent residual sugar.

In the United States riesling is sometimes called Johannisberg riesling, after the German city of Johannisberg, which is famous for its riesling. Australians sometimes refer to riesling as Rhine riesling.

Riesling is grown and made principally in: Australia; Austria; California; France, in Alsace; Germany; New York State; New Zealand; South Africa; Virginia; and Washington State.

## Sauvignon Blanc

The polar opposite of chardonnay—where chardonnay is all buttery roundness, sauvignon blanc is taut, lithe, and herbal, with a keen stiletto of acidity that vibrates through the center of the wine. If chardonnay is Marilyn Monroe, sauvignon blanc is Jamie Lee Curtis.

The name sauvignon comes from the French *sauvage*, meaning wild. It's a fitting name for a vine that, if left to its own devices, would grow with riotous abandon. Riotous can also describe sauvignon's flavors. These are not nicely tamed tastes. Instead, straw, hay, grass, meadow, smoke, green tea, green herbs, and gunflint charge around in your mouth with wonderful intensity. Some sauvignons push the envelope even further, taking on a character described as cat pee. Unless the pee quality is extreme, this is often considered a positive attribute.

The best, most outrageous sauvignons come from the Loire Valley of France (Sancerre and Pouilly-Fumé) and from New Zealand. On the heels of these come the sauvignons from Austria and South Africa. In Bordeaux virtually all white wines are made from a blend of sauvignon blanc plus sémillon. In blending the two, sauvignon's tart herbalness is mellowed by sémillon's broad, honeyed character. Blending the two is also a common practice in California and Australia.

Many California winemakers go out of their way to downplay sauvignon's herbalness. Often the wine is barrel fermented and otherwise made like chardonnay. These sauvignons frequently take on a soft fig and melon character. Some California vintners use the term fumé blanc for their sauvignon blanc. This is purely a marketing decision, for both fumé blanc and sauvignon blanc wines are made from sauvignon blanc grapes. It is not necessarily true that wines labeled fumé blanc have a smoky character.

As for Chilean sauvignon blancs, know that some wines so labeled are actually made from sauvignon vert, a different grape. Sauvignon vert makes likeable wine, but it's usually considerably less dramatic and herbal than sauvignon blanc. In many of Chile's newest vineyards, however, true sauvignon blanc is now being planted.

When sauvignon blanc is poorly made, it tastes vegetal. This is different from herbal. Vegetal wines taste like the water that artichokes have been boiled in. Sauvignon blanc can become vegetal for a variety of reasons, including being planted in wet, poorly drained soil or being allowed to grow out of control.

Sauvignon Blanc is grown and made principally in: Austria; California; Chile; France, in the Loire Valley (where it is used in Sancerre and Pouilly-Fumé) and in Bordeaux; Italy, in the Tre Venezie; New Zealand; South Africa; Texas; and Washington State.

*Sauvignon blanc is so treasured in New Zealand that it is honored on stamps.*

## Sémillon

A friend once told me that sémillon always brought back his childhood memories of the smell and taste of cotton sheets as he ran under the clothesline on a summer day. Whimsical as that description might seem, there can indeed be something broad, pure, and yes, cottony about many sémillons when they are young.

*Come harvest time in Bordeaux, everyone in the family pitches in.*

In Bordeaux and California, sémillon is often blended with a bit of sauvignon blanc. Sauvignon, with its lean tartness, is the mirror opposite of big-elbowed sémillon. Together, the two are like the odd couple—so completely different that they make for a consummate partnership. Both dry white Bordeaux and the sweet wines from the Sauternes region are principally sémillon, blended with a smaller amount of sauvignon blanc. Sémillon is, in fact, ideal for Sauternes; the grapes' thin skins are readily attacked by the noble rot, *Botrytis cinerea* (see page 136).

Outside of Bordeaux, sémillon's most famous home is Australia, where it can be made into magnificent dry white wines. Many of these are straight sémillon, but Australia is also known for sémillon-chardonnay and sémillon-sauvignon blanc blends.

Age often transforms sémillon. Older sémillons develop a rich, honeyed flavor and a lush, almost lanolin-like texture.

Only a small amount of aged sémillon is produced, mostly in Bordeaux and Australia.

Sémillon is grown and made principally in: Australia and France, in Bordeaux (including Sauternes).

# THE CLASSIC REDS

The four red varieties considered classic—cabernet sauvignon, merlot, pinot noir, and syrah—are used to make the majority of the world's greatest red wines.

## *Cabernet Sauvignon*

The preeminent classic red grape variety is cabernet sauvignon. More than any other, cabernet has vast ranges of quality, of structure, and of maturity. It is astounding that a wine so often a bit angular and introverted when young can meta-

---

### TOP TEN DESCRIPTORS A WINEMAKER HATES TO HEAR

10. Wet rodent
9. Labrador breath
8. Mace
7. Moist navel lint
6. '63 Chevy Nova exhaust
5. A men's room at a baseball park during a game
4. Mustard gas
3. Velveeta
2. Old running shoes
1. Old running shorts

—John Cunin,
*owner of the Cypress Club,
San Francisco*

morphose into a satiny, rich, and complex wine with several years' aging. Cabernet can be like the awkward, seemingly unremarkable kid who grows up to be a Fullbright Scholar and sexy to boot.

Not all cabernet sauvignons have this ability, of course. Many moderately priced versions, such as those from Chile or France's Languedoc-Roussillon, are made in a style that is intentionally modest. Relatively soft and easy drinking, these cabernets lack the structure, depth, and intense concentration of, say, Château Latour from Bordeaux, Sassicaia from Italy, or Shafer Vineyards Hillside Select from California, but they can still possess cabernet charm.

Cabernet sauvignon's aromas and flavors are so compelling that we've come to think of them as the cynosures of red wine: blackberry, black currant, cassis, mint, eucalyptus, cedarwood, leather, and plum. These elements are then swirled into a delicious amalgam as the wine ages. In fact, because of the grape's powerful fruit and linear structure, great cabernet needs both oak and bottle aging to pull it into harmony. Poorly made cabernet sauvignon, like poorly made sauvignon blanc, usually tastes vegetal, like a dank mixture of bell peppers and the water cabbage has been boiled in.

Historically, the world's most prized cabernets came from the Médoc communes of Margaux, St.-Julien, Pauillac, and St.-Estèphe in Bordeaux, where the wines were (and still are) ranked into growths, from First Growth, the most renowned, down to Fifth Growth. However, world-class cabernets are now regularly being made in California (where it

leads in vineyard acreage for red grapes), Italy, and Australia; Washington State is poised to join this group soon, too.

Cabernet Sauvignon is grown and made principally in: Argentina; Australia; California; Chile; France, in Bordeaux and Languedoc-Roussillon; Hungary; Italy, in the Tre Venezie and Tuscany; New York State, on Long Island; New Zealand; South Africa; Texas; Virginia; and Washington State.

---

## LOOKING FOR CABERNET

This "wet dog" business caused a somewhat embarrassing scene only last week. My Irish setter had just come into the office out of the rain. After the usual shake, distributing the surplus raindrops onto the wall, curtains, and important documents filed temporarily on the floor, she went obediently to her basket. The temptation was too great. I knelt down beside her and started sniffing. At that moment my daughter walked in. She is used to my doing odd things in the office (there is often not much else to do), but she had never seen me with my nose tucked in behind the Irish setter's left ear, my eyes closed, and my breathing irregular.

"What on earth are you doing?" she asked.

"Looking for cabernet sauvignon," I told her.

—Anthony Barton,
"A Wet Chihuahua"

*Anthony Barton, proprietor of Château Langoa-Barton and Château Léoville-Barton, both in Bordeaux, with his daughter Lillian.*

55

*Château Pétrus, from the Bordeaux subdistrict Pomerol, the most famous merlot in the world.*

## Merlot

Very similar in flavor to cabernet sauvignon, merlot—the name means little blackbird—is easily confused with it in blind tastings. Its aromas and flavors include blackberry, cassis, baked cherries, plums, chocolate, mocha, and sometimes, leather.

Like cabernet sauvignon, the most famous region for merlot has historically been the Bordeaux region of France, where merlot (not cabernet sauvignon) is the leading grape in terms of total production. Merlot in Bordeaux is planted mostly outside of the Médoc; it is, for example, the leading grape in the wines of Pomerol and St.-Emilion. Nonetheless, merlot is almost always blended with cabernet sauvignon, cabernet franc, and possibly malbec and/ or petit verdot. There is one extremely famous exception—Château Pétrus (from Pomerol), one of the most expensive wines in the world, is 99 percent merlot.

In Bordeaux and California, merlot is often said to be more soft, fleshy, and plump than cabernet sauvignon. And that can be true—sometimes. Softness in wine is a complex phenomenon, dependent on many factors, including the ripeness of the grapes. When merlot grapes from great vineyards fully ripen, the tannin in them can come across as relatively soft and round on the palate. That said, merlot has no exclusivity when it comes to softness, and there are many examples of merlots that are anything but soft. Certain regions, notably northern Italy and Long Island in New York State, are known for a lean, sleek style of merlot.

While California is seen as merlot's home base in the New World, this distinction is one it should share with Washington State. The sheer number of exciting, deeply concentrated merlots coming from Washington State is astounding and growing larger year after year.

In Chile, however, merlot, like the sauvignon blanc in that country, may not be entirely the real thing. Many Chilean wines labeled merlot turn out, after scientific testing, to be merlot interplanted with carmenère, a variety once well known in Bordeaux but now virtually extinct there. In some of Chile's newest merlot vineyards, however, merlot *is* planted exclusively.

Merlot is grown and made principally in: California; Chile; France, in Bordeaux and Languedoc-Roussillon; Italy, in the Tre Venezie; New York State, on Long Island; Virginia; and Washington State.

## Pinot Noir

If a computer search were conducted on the words and phrases used to describe pinot noir, this detail would emerge: More than any other wine, pinot is described in sensual terms. Pinot noir's association with sensuality derives from the remarkably supple, silky textures and erotically earthy aromas that great pinot noirs display. In your mouth the best pinots exude warm baked cherries, plums, damp earth, mushrooms, cedar, cigars, chocolate, worn leather, sweat, and dry leaves.

Pinot noir is lighter in body and far less tannic than cabernet sauvignon, merlot, or zinfandel. It is lighter in color, too, leading beginning wine drinkers to assume that pinot noir's flavors are feeble. For the great pinots just the reverse is true.

Of all the classic grapes, pinot noir is the most difficult to make into wine. It mutates easily in the vineyard (a large number of clones have already been identified), is highly sensitive to climate changes and variations in soil composition, and is unstable during winemaking. All this makes pinot noir a riskier (and more expensive) proposition for the winegrower, the winemaker, and the wine drinker than, say, cabernet sauvignon. But it's precisely this enological gamble that makes pinot noir all the more fascinating and irresistible.

The region of Burgundy, in France, where all the red wines, except Beaujolais, are made from pinot noir, is the most legendary area for the variety. Superexpensive and limited in production, red Burgundies are described as some of the earthiest wines in the world.

In the New World, Oregon specializes in pinot noir, and the grape also does well in certain parts of California, especially in the Santa Maria Valley and the Santa Ynez Valley in central-southern California and in Carneros, Anderson Valley, Sonoma Coast, and the Russian River Valley in the north.

Pinot Noir is grown and made principally in: California; France, in Burgundy and Champagne (where, with chardonnay and pinot meunier, it is a component of Champagne); New Zealand; and Oregon.

## Syrah

Syrah reminds me of the kind of guy who wears cowboy boots with a tuxedo. Rustic, manly, and yet elegant—that's syrah. In fact, at the turn of the twentieth century, the British scholar and wine writer George Saintsbury described the famous Rhône wine Hermitage (made exclusively from syrah) as the "manliest wine" he'd ever drunk.

The village of Vosne-Romanée, in Burgundy's Côte d'Or, is encircled by some of the most treasured pinot noir vines in the world.

*The old sloped vineyards of Chapoutier in the Côte-Rôtie, in the northern Rhône Valley, are home to some of the most intense syrah in the world.*

In France, syrah's potent and exuberant aromas and flavors lean toward leather, damp earth, wild blackberries, smoke, roasted meats, and especially pepper and spice. The best wines have a kinetic mouthfeel with flavors that detonate on the palate like tiny grenades. The most dramatic syrahs in the world come from the northern Rhône Valley. There, in exclusive, small wine districts, such as Hermitage and Côte-Rôtie, the only red grape allowed is syrah. In the southern Rhône Valley, syrah is usually part of the blends that make up Châteauneuf-du-Pape and Gigondas. In Australia and California, syrah takes on a softer, thicker, more syrupy boysenberry-spice character.

In the seventeenth century, French Huguenots brought syrah from France to South Africa's Cape of Good Hope, where it was rechristened shiraz. From South Africa, it was brought to Australia, which also calls syrah shiraz and now produces delicious gobs of the wine. Australia's most renowned shiraz is Grange (formerly called Grange Hermitage). Australia also produces numerous blends of shiraz and cabernet.

Why syrah's name was changed to shiraz in South Africa and Australia isn't quite clear, although a popular if highly unlikely legend has it that syrah may have originated near the Persian city of Shiraz and later traveled to France by way of Greece. Still, this does not explain why a grape known as syrah in France would be given a Persian name once it was brought to South Africa and Australia in the seventeenth and eighteenth centuries.

In the early 1980s, syrah and other Rhône grapes began to grip the imaginations of maverick California winemakers. The Rhône Rangers, as they came to be called, went on to make some surprisingly rich syrahs that were so copiously imbued with ripe, spicy fruit that California quickly became a promising new frontier for the grape.

What Californians call petite sirah (sometimes spelled petite syrah) is not exactly the same as syrah, but the histories of the two are interwoven in what can seem like a confusing manner. Briefly, here's the story. Vines called petite sirah have grown in California since the 1880s. In the early days some of those vines were probably a type of syrah that had small—petite—grapes. (All things being equal, winemakers prefer small grapes because there's a high ratio of skin to juice. Since color, flavor, and tannin come primarily from a grape's skin, small grapes yield the most concentrated, flavorful wines.) Over the course of many decades, however, other wines were mixed in with these petite sirah vines, creating what are known as field blends in the same vineyard. As more and different varieties found their way into California, and as new vineyards were begun with unidentified cuttings from older vineyards, petite sirah's true identity grew more and more obscure.

## IT'S ALL ABOUT SPECIES

All grapevines belong to the genus *Vitis*. Sometime in the late Tertiary Period, climatic changes caused the genus to split into a number of separate species. The two most important species for wine drinkers are *vinifera* and *labrusca*.

Today 99.99 percent of the wines in the world are made from grapes from *Vitis vinifera*, a vine native to Europe and Asia. Chardonnay, cabernet sauvignon, merlot, riesling, sauvignon blanc, and zinfandel, for example, are all *Vitis vinifera* grapes.

*Vitis labrusca*, by comparison, is the native vine of New England and Canada. Concord is the best-known *Vitis labrusca* grape. It was probably *labrusca* vines that inspired Leif Eriksson to name North America Vinland in 1001. Wines are still made from this species, especially in upper New York State.

Then in the 1990s groundbreaking DNA fingerprinting of many of California's petite sirah vineyards revealed that wines labeled petite sirah are one of three different possibilities. First, it can be a field blend of many varieties, including true syrah, carignan, zinfandel, barbera, and grenache. Second, the wine may be made from peloursin, an ancient Rhône grape. Finally, and this is the most likely scenario, the wine may be Durif, a cross of peloursin and syrah created in France in the 1880s. None of this information shows up on the labels of wines called petite sirah, but maybe that just adds to the wine's mysteriousness and cultlike appeal. What is clear is that petite sirah is not the same as syrah even though both can be massive, rich, rustic wines.

Syrah is grown and made principally in: Australia (where it is known as shiraz); California; France, in the Rhône and Languedoc-Roussillon; and South Africa (where, again, it is known as shiraz).

# IMPORTANT GRAPES

From the classic varieties, we move on to the important ones. Admittedly, five wine writers asked to name the individual varieties they considered important would undoubtedly come up with five somewhat different lists. This is my list and, clearly, it's subjective. These ten grapes may not have the cachet of the classic ones, but each can be irresistibly delicious. Many of these grape varieties are also intimately tied to a single place where they excel. I can't think about gewürztraminer without thinking about Alsace or consider nebbiolo without seeing Piedmont in my mind, and is any variety more inextricably tied to a place than gamay is to Beaujolais?

## Important Whites

The four important white varietals fall into two camps: Gewürztraminer and viognier are exotically flavored, fairly full-bodied wines that are heady with aroma. Pinot blanc and pinot gris on the other hand are usually lighter in body and more subtle in aroma and flavor. All four have precise personalities and offer satisfying drinking.

### GEWÜRZTRAMINER

Like Lucille Ball or Goldie Hawn, gewürztraminer is a little eccentric in a lovable way. The prefix *gewürz* means spice in German, and though most professionals describe the wine as spicy, the kitchen spice rack is not what they have in mind. Rather, gewürztraminer is spicy in the sense that its aromas are perfumed and its flavors are saucy, bold, kinetic, and extroverted. Litchi nuts, gingerbread, vanilla, fruit-cocktail syrup, grapefruit, smoke, stones, minerals, and honeysuckle do not simply rest in the glass—they rage about in it. Such massive fruitiness is sometimes mistaken for sweetness, but many gewürztraminers are bone-dry.

The world's most complex and breathtaking dry gewürztraminers are made in France in Alsace. Germany, with a cold climate like Alsace, also makes delicious examples. And, you'll find gewürztraminers from California and New York State.

### PINOT BLANC

Pinot blanc generally makes good, not great, wines. Many California versions taste like modest versions of chardon-

According to *The Wine Regions of America*, by John J. Baxevanis, for most of history, in nearly every wine-producing country, red wines have been more popular than whites. Reds were easier to make in most parts of the world and seemed better suited to hearty meals and the hard physical labor that agriculturally based economies required. Between the end of World War II and the early 1990s, however, white wine consumption in America increased thirty-four times. Changing lifestyles, the drastic reduction in agricultural employment, the rise in economic activity, central air-conditioning, refrigeration, and the dietary shift away from red meat to lighter meats, fish, and vegetables all helped transform the United States into a white-wine drinking country by the last two decades of the century. Many industry experts, however, predict that in the twenty-first century, red wine will again become more popular than white.

nay. They fit the bill precisely when you want a soft, easy-drinking white.

A few extremely good pinot blancs do exist, however. Small producers in the Tre Venezie in Italy and in Alsace can make fantastic stuff from the grape, as do a handful of producers in California (notably Chalone and Byron) and in Oregon. Like pinot gris, pinot blanc is an ancient mutation of pinot noir. The Italians refer to it as pinot bianco.

### PINOT GRIS

Depending on where it is grown, pinot gris can taste strikingly different. In the Tre Venezie in Italy, pinot gris—pinot grigio—is often a simple, light, crisp wine; however, some small producers make versions that are so intense and dramatic, they might appear to come from an entirely different grape. Then there's the fact that Italian pinot grigio bears no resemblance to the majestic, opulent, sometimes spicy pinot gris of Alsace, formerly known as tokay-pinot gris. In Germany, pinot gris (called grauburgunder or ruländer) can be something else again—broad, even Rubenesque (by German wine standards).

In Oregon, where pinot gris became wildly popular in the 1990s, the best are very tasty wines with pear and spice-cake flavors. As for California pinot gris (some of which are called pinot grigio), most are crisp, fresh wines, sometimes with an intriguing edge of pepperyness or arugula-like bitterness.

Pinot gris, like pinot blanc, is an ancient, natural mutation of pinot noir. In the vineyard, pinot gris (gray pinot) grapes can be any color from bluish-silver to mauve-pink to ashen-yellow. As a result, this white wine varies in color, too, although subtly.

## VIOGNIER

A Los Angeles restaurateur once described viognier this way: "If a good German riesling is like an ice skater (fast, racy, with a cutting edge), and chardonnay is like a middle-heavyweight boxer (punchy, solid, powerful), then viognier would have to be described as a female gymnast—beautiful and perfectly shaped, with muscle but superb agility and elegance."

Viognier is one of the finest but rarest French white grapes. Less than 300 acres are planted in the grape's home, the northern Rhône. There viognier makes the prestigious wines Condrieu and Château-Grillet, and a small amount is also planted

in among the syrah vines of Côte-Rôtie. These white viognier grapes are harvested, crushed, and fermented along with the syrah grapes giving Côte-Rôtie (which is a red wine after all) a slightly more exotic aroma than it might otherwise have.

Viognier exploded in popularity in the United States in the 1990s. In half a decade, the number of California producers went from a mere few to more than thirty. By 1998 there were more than a thousand acres of this variety planted in California.

Viognier's appeal is its exotic, honeysuckle, musky fruit, its round body, and—most of all—its mesmerizingly lanolinish texture.

Besides in France's Rhône Valley and in California, viognier is also grown and made in France's Languedoc-Roussillon region and in the United States in Virginia. There are promising experimental plantings in Australia and Italy.

## Important Reds

The six important red varietals represent an enormous range of textures and flavors. From gamay with its exuberant Popsicle-like fruitiness to dark, black, almost menacingly serious nebbiolo, these are some of my favorites. They are also some of the best all-around reds for food. Three of these grapes—sangiovese, nebbiolo, and barbera—are among the leading grape varieties of Italy and so have been partnered to a dizzyingly vast number of Italian dishes. And no red variety beats California's zinfandel when it comes to accompanying the grilled and barbecued foods of summertime.

## BARBERA

Barbera is the Eliza Doolittle of red grapes. For decades, it was a rather coarse, unsophisticated quaff. Then in the 1980s several winemakers in the Piedmont region of northwestern Italy gave barbera the *My Fair Lady* treatment. By planting it in better sites, limiting the yield, and aging the wine, they discovered that barbera could be a mouthfilling, rich wine packed with just about every black fruit flavor imaginable: blackberry, black cherry, black raspberry, and black plum. The wine also has a vivacity, a vibrancy that comes from the grapes' high natural acidity.

Barbera is the most widely planted red in Piedmont, even though the nebbiolo grape (which makes Barolo and Barbaresco) is more renowned. It is barbera, not nebbiolo, that Piedmontese winemakers invariably drink with dinner.

Barbera has a long history in California—and a promising future. The grape was planted a century ago in fairly poor, usually hot areas by Italian immigrants looking for an easy to make hearty red wine. But in the early 1990s, several of the state's best winemakers began practicing a few Professor Higgins tricks of their own, planting barbera in far better sites and making it as a serious wine. Italy and California remain the major areas for barbera; little is planted elsewhere in the world.

## GAMAY

The gamay grape is the source of the French wine Beaujolais (and Beaujolais Nouveau), oceans of which are washed down in Parisian bistros every year. Of all the important red grapes, gamay is utterly the simplest. Its blatant fruity flavor is a dead ringer for melted black cherry Jell-O. Because of its uninhibited fresh fruitiness and lack of tannin, gamay is meant to be served slightly chilled.

Outside France, gamay is virtually nonexistent. In California the wine called Napa gamay is not made from true gamay but from a grape called valdiguié. The California wine called gamay Beaujolais is also not true gamay but rather a somewhat undistinguished clone of pinot noir. California jug wine producers make Napa gamay and gamay Beaujolais blush wines similar to white zinfandel.

## NEBBIOLO

If any one grape has a physical effect on the mouth, it is nebbiolo. Massively structured and adamantly tannic when young, nebbiolo can simply close your palate down and cause your taste buds to shrink away. There's a reward for being patient with this young brute, however. With age, nebbiolo becomes a delicious combination of suppleness and power.

In the minds of Italians, nebbiolo holds a place equal to that of cabernet sauvignon in France. It is the king. The grape grows virtually exclusively in Piedmont, in Italy's northwest corner, where it makes the exalted wines Barolo and Barbaresco. (There is another precious commodity that grows in this area: the white truffle.)

Nebbiolo, from *nebbia*, the thick fog that envelops the hills in the late fall when the grapes are picked, has very particular flavors and aromas reminiscent of tar, violets, and often a rich, espresso-like bitterness. With the exception of some small plantings in California, very little nebbiolo is planted outside Italy.

## SANGIOVESE

Italy's most famous grape, sangiovese is responsible for the three great wines of Tuscany: Chianti, Vino Nobile di Montepulciano, and the magnificent and expensive brunello di Montalcino. And along with cabernet sauvignon, it is also a major grape in many of the prestigious wines known as the Super Tuscans. Outside Tuscany, sangiovese is used to make red wines in the neighboring regions of Umbria and Emilia-Romagna.

The sangiovese vine has many genetic variations, or clones. The differences among these clones coupled with differences in the sites where sangiovese is planted mean that the wines made from the grape vary widely in style and quality. Some sangioveses are as thin and dreary as red-stained, watery alcohol; some are as earthy, rich, and complex as a great sauce. In flavor and structure, sangiovese is closer to pinot noir than it is to cabernet sauvignon. When it's young, sangiovese has the wonderful appeal of a fresh warm cherry pie. As it ages, sangiovese can take on dried leaf, dried orange peel, tea, mocha, and earthy flavors.

In addition to Tuscany, sangiovese is increasingly successful in California. Dozens of California wineries now make it.

## TEMPRANILLO

Everything about Spain seems hot—music, machismo, flamenco, religion, passion. Little surprise then that we imagine vines growing on the hot plains over which Don Quixote once rode. But Spain's most famous red grape, tempranillo, is not the heavy-footed blockbuster one associates with hot climates. Tempranillo, in

*Nowhere do nebbiolo grapes make more stunning wine than they do in Piedmont, Italy, where they are the source of Barolo and Barbaresco.*

fact, is usually a fairly refined red wine. When young, it bursts with cherries. After being aged—commonly for two years or more, usually in old American oak—tempranillo takes on an earthy sweet vanillin flavor.

Tempranillo grows in Spain's north-central region of Rioja, next door in Ribera del Duero where it is called tinto fino, and in the eastern Penedès region, where they refer to it as *ull de llebre* (eye of the hare). In Portugal, tempranillo, known as tinta roriz, is one of the grapes that make up Port. The grape is also grown in Argentina, where they spell it tempranilla.

### ZINFANDEL

For decades, zinfandel was the most widely planted red grape in California until cabernet sauvignon surpassed it in 1998. Now number two in acreage, zinfandel is a chameleon. It can be (and is) made into everything from white wine to sweet port-style wine. But the zinfandel knowledgeable wine drinkers rave about—true zinfandel—is a mouthfilling dry red wine

crammed with jammy blackberry, boysenberry, and plummy fruit. Made in this traditional style it can be thick, chewy, and notorious for (temporarily) staining one's teeth the color of cherry Kool-Aid.

Until 1972 zinfandel was always a hearty, rustic red wine. But in that year, the large California winery Sutter Home made the first "white zinfandel"—actually light pink—by quickly removing zinfandel's red skins before much color was imparted to the wine. Today, white zinfandel outsells true (red) zinfandel. Yet because it is often slightly sweet and almost always mass produced from less than top-quality grapes, white zinfandel is considered a beginner's wine by serious wine drinkers.

The zinfandel grape has a long history in California and since almost no other wine region in the world has plantings, it is often thought of as an indigenous American variety. It is not. Zinfandel belongs, as do cabernet sauvignon, merlot, and pinot noir, to the European species *vinifera*. As a result of DNA testing, it is now thought that zinfandel probably originated in Croatia. It is identical to the Italian grape primitivo.

Red zinfandel vineyards are some of the oldest in California. These prized vineyards produce zinfandels of such concentration that vintners often use the term *old vines* on their labels. Although the term has no legal definition, generally wines are labeled old vines only if the vines are at least forty years old.

Several different zinfandel vineyards in Amador County and Sonoma vie for the title oldest in California. While it's difficult to determine precisely when these vineyards were planted, they are all well over a hundred years old, and one—the Grandpère vineyard in Amador County's Shenandoah Valley—is thought to have been planted in 1866.

# A GLOSSARY OF
# OTHER GRAPE VARIETIES WORLDWIDE

Most of the wines we drink are based on classic varieties (see page 48 for whites and page 54 for reds) or on what I've called important varieties (see page 59). But with roughly 5,000 grape varieties in the world, there are dozens of others a wine lover is bound to encounter. Following are the most noteworthy of those. While some of these grape varieties are usually the sources of wines on their own—Spain's albariño and Italy's dolcetto, for example—others, such as France's carignan, are very important as grapes used in blends.

## *Whites*

### A

**Airén:** The most widely planted grape of Spain, grown mainly on the central plains of La Mancha, immortalized by Don Quixote. Used in blending and on its own, where it makes simple, rustic, high-alcohol whites.

**Albana:** Ancient variety grown in the region of Emilia-Romagna, Italy.

**Albariño:** Grown in the far northeastern province of Galicia, Spain, and just below that in northern Portugal, where it is spelled alvarinho. Makes a delicious, light, lemony, often slightly spritzy wine. Spanish albariño generally has considerably more character than Portugese alvarinho.

**Aligoté:** Fairly rare grape of Burgundy, France. The light, tart, white wine made from it is used with crème de cassis in the Kir cocktail.

**Alvarinho:** See ALBARIÑO.

**Arneis:** One of the three top white grapes of Italy's Piedmont region, the other two being cortese and moscato (muscat). Makes refreshing dry wines.

**Assyrtiko:** Greek grape with lively acidity. Specialty of the volcanic island of Santorini in the Aegean.

**Auxerrois:** Fairly common grape in Alsace, France, where it is often blended into pinot blanc. Confusingly, there is also a red grape named auxerrois, which is the same as the Bordeaux variety malbec.

### B

**Baco Blanc:** A French-American hybrid, also known as Baco 22A, it was developed in 1898 by French nurseryman François Baco.

Used as the basis for Armagnac until the 1970s, it continues to be used in that distilled spirit, although to a lesser extent.

**Bourboulenc:** Ancient, simple-tasting, and now relatively rare blending grape used primarily in southern France, in particular in such wines as white Châteauneuf-du-Pape and white Côtes-du-Rhône.

**Bual:** Cultivated on the island of Madeira, this rare grape makes a fairly rich wine.

### C

**Cape Riesling:** A widely planted grape in South Africa, where it is used mostly in cheap blends. Not the same as true riesling, Cape riesling is thought to be related to the obscure French grape crouchen blanc.

**Catarratto Bianco:** One of two grapes used in making Italian Marsala; the other is grillo.

**Cayuga:** An important French-American hybrid especially in New York State, where it is made into off-dry and sweet wines.

**Cereza:** Widely planted in Argentina, this pink-skinned grape variety is a major source of neutral white jug wines in that country.

**Chasselas:** Ancient, low-acid variety also known as fendant. Best known in the French-speaking part of Switzerland. Also cultivated to a smaller extent in Alsace. In Germany it is referred to as gutedel.

**Clairette:** At low yields this variety is beautifully fresh and aromatic. A common blending component in many white wines of southern France, including those of Provence, Châteauneuf-du-Pape, and Côtes-du-Rhône.

**Colombard:** See FRENCH COLOMBARD.

**Cortese:** Northwestern Italian grape that makes the medium-bodied wine Gavi, historically the most prized white wine of Piedmont, Italy.

**Criolla:** A pink-skinned variety grown widely in Argentina for use in white jug wines.

# E

**Ehrenfelser:** A German cross of riesling and silvaner now popular in Canada.

**Emerald Riesling:** Cross of muscadelle and riesling. Cultivated in California and Texas.

**Encruzado:** Important grape in the dry white wines of Portugal's Dão region.

# F

**Fendant:** See CHASSELAS.

**Fiano:** A famous grape of ancient Rome now grown primarily around the town of Avellino in the southern Italian region of Campania.

**Folle Blanche:** Once, but no longer, a leading grape in Cognac and Armagnac. Today used mostly in the western Loire to produce the extremely tart, thin Gros Plant.

**French Colombard:** Widely planted grape for California jug wines. In France, distilled into eaux-de-vie. Known as colombar in South Africa, where it also is made into jug wines.

**Furmint:** The major grape in the famous Hungarian sweet wine Tokay Aszú, furmint is also used for dry wine. Also grown in Austria.

# G

**Garganega:** Major grape of Soave. Grown in the northern Italian region of the Veneto.

**Gouveio:** One of the grapes used to make the dry white wines of the Douro in Portugal and also used in the making of white Port.

**Grauburgunder:** See RULÄNDER.

**Grechetto:** Grown in the central Italian province of Umbria, it is one of the grapes that make the medium-bodied Italian wine Orvieto.

**Greco:** An ancient Greek variety now grown primarily in the southern Italian region of Campania, where it is made into distinctive white wines, the most famous of which is greco di Tufo.

**Grenache Blanc:** A white-berried form of the red grape grenache, grenache blanc is a leading blending grape in the white wines of southern France, including the whites of Provence, the Languedoc-Roussillon, and the southern Rhône.

**Grillo:** Along with catarratto bianco, one of the two grapes used in making Italian Marsala.

**Grüner Veltliner:** Austrian grape packed with a spicy and musky personality. Often has an intriguing peppery finish.

**Gutedel:** German name for the Swiss grape chasselas. In Germany, planted mostly in the Baden region, where it makes basic wines.

# H

**Hanepoot:** See MUSCAT.

**Hárslevelü:** Aromatic Hungarian grape that lends a smooth spicy character to the renowned sweet wine Tokay Aszú.

**Huxelrebe:** Developed in Germany, this unusual cross of gutedel and the obscure grape courtillier musque makes aromatic wines, especially in Germany's Pfalz and Rheinhessen regions.

# K

**Kerner:** Successful German cross of the red grape trollinger with the white grape riesling.

# L

**Loureira:** Grown in the northwestern Spanish province of Galicia, loureira is sometimes added in small amounts to albariño. Also grown in Portugal where it is known as loureiro and forms part of the blend in Vinho Verde.

# M

**Macabeo:** Northern Spanish grape also known as viura. One of the three grapes used in *cava*, Spanish sparkling wine, and the primary grape in the white wines of Rioja. A small amount is grown in the Rhône, in France, where it is used in the appellation of Lirac; it is also used to a small extent in the Languedoc-Roussillon.

**Madeleine Angevine:** Pleasantly floral grape variety grown principally (amazingly) in England, although small amounts are also grown in the United States in Washington State.

**Malmsey:** See MALVASIA.

**Malvasia:** Ancient grape of Greek origin planted in Greece, Italy, France, Spain, Madeira, and Portugal, but on the decline. In Spain, a component in white Rioja and, formerly, in red as well. In Italy, made into the famous Sicilian dessert wine malvasia delle

Lipari. Also used in Frascati and in the famous Tuscan dessert wine, *vin santo*. Historically, small amounts of malvasia were also added to Chianti for fragrance. In Portugal, where it is known as malmsey, it is used to make a sweet style of Madeira. Malvasia is also thought to be the same as or similar to vermentino in Italy and on the French island of Corsica.

**Marsanne:** The workhorse white grape of the northern Rhône in France. Makes big-bodied, usually rustic wines. Often blended with the aromatic and elegant grape roussanne. It is also grown in the Languedoc-Roussillon, as well as in California.

**Mauzac:** In the Languedoc-Roussillon, in France, the grape used to make sparkling Crémant de Limoux.

**Melon de Bourgogne:** The grape that makes the light, tart, dry French wine Muscadet, considered the working man's accompaniment to oysters.

**Morio-Muskat:** Found mostly in Germany's Pfalz and Rheinhessen regions, this grape of minor importance is a cross of silvaner and weissburgunder.

**Moscatel:** A minor grape in Jerez, Spain, where it is made into a sweet wine that is used in blending and also drunk on its own.

**Moscofilero:** Highly aromatic grape that is the source of the Greek Peloponnesian wine Mantinia.

**Müller-Thurgau:** Famous cross of uncertain parentage, although many believe it to be a cross of two different clones of riesling. Germany's most widely planted grape.

**Muscadelle:** Perfumed grape blended in small amounts with sémillon and sauvignon blanc to make many white Bordeaux. In Australia, used to make the Australian fortified wine tokay. Not the same as South African muscadel, which is a member of the muscat family (see MUSCAT).

**Muscadet:** The name sometimes used for the grape that is the source of the sharp, light, dry French wine Muscadet, although the grape's correct name is melon de Bourgogne.

**Muscat:** A prolific family of ancient grapes, including muscat of Alexandria, muscat blanc à petits grains, and muscat de Frontignan. Usually very perfumed and fruity. Grown all over the

world and made into everything from dry wines to sparkling wines (Italy's Asti) to sweet fortified wines (France's muscat de Beaumes-de-Venise, South Africa's hanepoot, and Portugal's Setúbal). In Italy, known as moscato.

**N**

**Neuburger:** Austrian grape known to make simple dry wines and some good sweet wines.

**Niagara:** An American cross, best known in New York State, where it is the source of off-dry and sweet wines.

**P**

**Palomino:** Major grape of Sherry, grown in southern and central Spain.

**Parellada:** The most refined of the three grapes from which *cava*, Spanish sparkling wine, is made.

**Pederña:** One of the minor grapes sometimes included in the blend to make the Portuguese wine Vinho Verde.

**Pedro Ximénez:** Cultivated throughout the south of Spain. Nicknamed PX, it's the second most important grape for Sherry. Unblended, it makes a supersweet style of cream Sherry.

**Petit Manseng:** Primarily used in the sweet wine Jurançon, a rare specialty of southwestern France. Commonly, the grapes are left on the vine until they are shriveled and their sugar is concentrated, although the noble mold botrytis may also take hold.

**Picardan:** One of the minor white grapes sometimes used in the wines of France's southern Rhône, especially in Côtes-du-Rhône and white Châteauneuf-du-Pape. On its own picardan makes neutral-tasting, fairly uninteresting wine.

**Picolit:** Highly regarded, rare grape native to the Friuli-Venezia Giulia region of northeast Italy, where it is the source of the prized dessert wine also known as picolit.

**Picpoul:** One of the minor grapes of southern France, where it is used in the southern Rhône as part of the blend in Côtes-du-Rhône, Tavel, and Châteauneuf-du-Pape. In the Languedoc-Roussillon, the red version of this grape, picpoul noir, is a minor ingredient in some basic-quality blends. Also spelled piquepoul.

**Prosecco:** Northeastern Italian grape, grown especially in the Veneto, where it is turned into the soft, bubbly Italian sparkling wine also known as prosecco.

### R

**Ravat Blanc:** See VIGNOLES.

**Ribolla Gialla:** Well known in the Friuli-Venezia Giulia region of Italy for making lemony white wines of good character.

**Rieslaner:** A German cross of riesling and silvaner, which is the source of good zesty wines, especially in Germany's Pfalz and Rheinhessen regions.

**Rkatsiteli:** Most widely planted grape of the former Soviet Union and a specialty of the Republic of Georgia. Also well known in eastern Europe, and there are even plantings in New York State. Made into fascinating spicy, floral dry wines as well as sweet and fortified wines.

**Robola:** Grown principally on several Greek islands; may be related to Italy's ribolla.

**Roditis:** The source of the simple white wine Patras, which is made on the Peloponnese peninsula of Greece.

**Rolle:** Used primarily for blending in southern France, in particular in the Languedoc-Roussillon. Known in Italy as vermentino; may be the same as malvasia though this has not been conclusively proven.

**Roussanne:** A variety of the French Rhône, appreciated for its greater elegance in comparison to its sister marsanne, with which it is often blended. Also grown in the Languedoc-Roussillon and in California.

**Ruländer:** One of the German names for the grape pinot gris, which is also known as grauburgunder.

### S

**St.-Emilion:** Name used in the Cognac region for the grape ugni blanc. Has nothing to do with the town St.-Emilion in Bordeaux.

**Sämling:** Fairly obscure cross of silvaner and riesling. Grown in Austria where, on occasion, it makes very good *eiswein.*

**Sauvignonasse:** See SAUVIGNON VERT.

**Sauvignon Vert:** A lightly floral grape planted mostly in Chile, where it is also known as sauvignonasse. Confusingly, Chilean wines labeled sauvignon blanc may be true sauvignon blanc or sauvignon vert.

**Savatiano:** Widely planted in Greece, it is the grape most frequently used to make retsina.

**Scheurebe:** Germany's best-kept secret, scheurebe has an unusual spicy, rich flavor. A cross of riesling and silvaner, it doesn't taste like either.

**Scuppernong:** A native American grape, scuppernong grows prolifically along the Eastern seaboard of the United States. Around 1607 the Jamestown colonists made wine from scuppernong grapes they found growing in Virginia.

**Sercial:** Esteemed Madeira grape, even more rare than bual. Makes the lightest, driest Madeiras.

**Seyval Blanc:** The most popular French-American hybrid. Widely planted in England, Canada, and the eastern United States, particularly New York State and Virginia.

**Silvaner:** German variety, mostly neutral in character. Also grown in Alsace, France, and Switzerland, where it is spelled sylvaner.

**Sultana:** See THOMPSON SEEDLESS.

### T

**Thompson Seedless:** This is the California name for the grape variety sultana, a variety frequently dried for raisins. A prolific grower, it is also fermented into bland jug wines.

**Tocai Friulano:** Planted mostly in the northeastern Italian region of Friuli-Venezia Giulia, this grape, also called simply tocai, is the source of somewhat spicy, full-bodied wines that are considered among the region's best.

**Torrontés:** Perfumed grape that is the source of one of Argentina's most interesting white wines.

**Trajadura:** See TREIXADURA.

**ABBAZIA
DI ROSAZZO
COLLI ORIENTALI
DEL FRIULI**
DENOMINAZIONE DI ORIGINE CONTROLLATA

**TOCAI FRIULANO**

WHITE WINE
Net contents   ESTATE BOTTLED BY AZIENDA AGRICOLA
e 750 ml   ZAMÒ & PALAZZOLO sas - ROSAZZO - ITALIA
   CONTAINS SULFITES - PRODUCT OF ITALY
Alc. 13%   IMPORTED BY WINEBOW INC. NEW YORK
by volume   SHIPPED BY LEONARDO LO CASCIO
   AND PETER MATT, ROME, ITALY

**Traminer:** The perfumed ancestor of gewürztraminer. In the northern Italian region of Trentino-Alto Adige, it is the source of delicious, exotically aromatic wines. It is also grown in Austria.

**Trebbiano:** Thought to be the most prolific vine in the world, yielding more gallons of neutral, bland wine than any other grape. (Though it produces the most wine, it does not cover the most vineyard area.) Grown principally in Italy and France. In Italy, it is part of the blend that makes Soave as well as other wines. In France it is known as ugni blanc and St.-Emilion. Cognac is made from distilled trebbiano.

**Treixadura:** Along with loureira, a grape grown in Rías Baixas, in the Spanish province of Galicia, where it is sometimes blended in small amounts into albariño. In Portugal, it is known as trajadura and is part of the blend in Vinho Verde.

### U

**Ugni Blanc:** One of the leading grapes of France in terms of production, it is the same as the variety known in Italy as trebbiano. Makes a thin neutral-tasting wine that is the basis for Cognac and is one of the grapes used to make Armagnac. Also known as St.-Emilion.

### V

**Verdejo:** Grown in the north-central Spanish province of Rueda. Makes one of Spain's top dry whites.

**Verdelho:** Madeira's most planted white. The name is used on the label to indicate a medium-dry, nutty style of Madeira. Verdelho is also grown in Australia.

**Verdello:** One of the minor blending grapes in the Italian wine Orvieto.

**Verdicchio:** Simple, clean Italian white of no particular distinction. Cultivated principally in central Italy.

**Verduzzo:** Grown in northeastern Italy, primarily in Friuli, where it makes both dry and deliciously honeyed sweet wines. The latter are better known.

**Vermentino:** Well known along the Italian Riviera, where it is the source of dry, floral white wines considered indispensable partners for Ligurian fish soups. Also grown on the islands of Corsica and Sardinia and in southern France, where it's known as rolle. Thought to be the same as (or related to) malvasia.

**Vernaccia:** Lively light Italian wine grape grown around the charming Tuscan hilltop town of San Gimignano, as well as on the island of Sardinia.

**Vespaiola:** Native grape of the Veneto region of Italy where it is the source primarily of sweet wines.

**Vidal:** French-American hybrid planted in Virginia, New York State, and Canada. In the latter two places it is made not only into dry wines but also into some terrific ice wines. Also known as vidal blanc.

**Vignoles:** Major French-American hybrid also known as Ravat blanc. In New York State, it is the source of both dry and sweet wines.

**Viosinho:** One of the grapes used in white Port and in the dry table wines of Portugal's Douro region.

**Viura:** The leading white variety in Spain's Rioja region, where it is the source of simple, dry whites. Also known as macabeo.

### W

**Weissburgunder:** In Germany and Austria, the name for pinot blanc.

**Welschriesling:** Not a riesling, despite its name. Common grape variety of eastern Europe and northern Italy.

### X

**Xarel-lo:** Spanish grape cultivated in the Penedès for its fruity contribution to *cava*, Spanish sparkling wine.

69

# Reds

## A

**Agiorgitiko:** Important Greek grape, it is the source of Nemea, a spicy, earthy wine from the Peloponnese peninsula. Also known as St. George.

**Aglianico:** Ancient grape brought to southern Italy by the Greeks. Makes the famous wine called Taurasi.

**Alfrocheiro Preto:** One of the important grapes in the red wines of Portugal's Dão region.

**Alicante Bouschet:** A characterless, neutral-tasting, high-yielding grape once planted extensively in southern France and now on the decline. In the United States, this was also the most popular grape with home winemakers during Prohibition.

**Aragonez:** One of the Portuguese names for tempranillo. Grown primarily in southern Portugal where it is used in the red wines of the Alentejo region.

**Auxerrois:** Leading variety in Cahors, France. Also known in Cahors as cot. Same as the Bordeaux variety malbec. Confusingly, auxerrois is also the name of a white grape grown in Alsace, France.

**Azal Tinto:** One of the grapes that are used to make the strident, rare red version of Portugal's Vinho Verde.

## B

**Baco Noir:** One of the most famous French-American hybrids, created in 1894 by French nurseryman François Baco. Once cultivated in Burgundy and the Loire Valley, Baco Noir is now principally found in New York State and Canada.

**Baga:** Possibly Portugal's most widely planted red grape. Leading grape of the region of Bairrada.

**Bastardo:** Common workhorse grape for dry Portuguese reds, including those made in the Dão and in Bairrada.

**Blauburgunder:** In Austria, blauburgunder is the name for pinot noir.

**Blauer Portugieser:** Prolific vine that has nothing to do with Portugal. Very widely planted in Austria and elsewhere in eastern Europe. Also makes up a lot of Germany's red wine.

**Blaufränkisch:** Highly esteemed Austrian variety. Makes a hearty, earthy wine. Also grown in Hungary.

**Brachetto:** Found primarily in Piedmont, Italy, where it is used to make brachetto d'Acqui, a deep-red colored and delicious, if somewhat soda-poplike, sparkling wine.

## C

**Cabernet Franc:** Third most important red Bordeaux grape after cabernet sauvignon and merlot. Château Cheval Blanc, one of the world's greatest red wines, is made mostly from cabernet franc. Also grown extensively in the Loire, in France, where it is the source of Chinon and Bourgueil.

**Calitor:** One of the lesser red grapes used in France's southern Rhône. Calitor is virtually always blended.

**Canaiolo:** An important blending grape in Tuscany and throughout central Italy. Among other wines, canaiolo is used as part of the blend in making Chianti. A rare white variety, canaiolo bianco, is often used in making the wine Orvieto.

**Cannonau:** The famous grape of the Italian island Sardinia. Known in Spain as garnacha and in France as grenache.

**Carignan:** Generally used as a blending grape in the Languedoc-Roussillon, Provence, and Rhône regions of southern France, as well as in Rioja, Spain, where it's known as mazuelo, and in Priorato, where it is known as cariñena. In Italy, on the island of Sardinia, it's known as carignano. Also grown in California where it is spelled carignane and is often a part of blends.

**Carmenère:** Ancient Bordeaux variety now virtually extinct in that region but widespread in Chile. Confusingly, Chilean wines labeled merlot are often actually made in part from carmenère.

**Catawba:** American cross, it is made into light red and rosé wines, especially in New York State.

**Chambourcin:** A French-American hybrid grown principally in Virginia where it makes good, aromatic red wine.

**Cinsaut:** French grape grown all over the south and in the southern Rhône; most frequently used in blends, where it adds a slight spiciness. It can also be found in Algeria and South Africa. Sometimes spelled cinsault.

**Concord:** The most well-known New York State grape, of *labrusca* parentage. Makes distinctly flavored but not very highly esteemed wines with brazen, candylike aromas and flavors that are often described as foxy. Concord is much more appreciated as jelly than wine.

**Cornalin:** Indigenous Swiss variety, considered the top red in a country better known for its whites.

**Corvina:** Most important grape in the well-known Italian wines amarone and Valpolicella; usually blended with rondinella and molinara.

**Cot:** Somewhat ordinary workhorse grape of Bordeaux, also known as malbec. Does better farther south in Cahors, where it has a third name: auxerrois.

**Counoise:** One of the common, if lesser, red grapes in France's southern Rhône Valley. Used in Gigondas and sometimes in Châteauneuf-du-Pape. Also grown in California.

**Criolla:** Brought by the Spaniards in the sixteenth century, this is one of the first varieties planted in Argentina. Makes undistinguished, crude wine.

### D

**Delaware:** More pink skinned than truly red, this American cross is grown primarily in the Lake Erie region of New York State, where it is used to make soda-popish wine-cooler type wines. Curiously, Delaware is also grown in Japan.

**Dolcetto:** Fruity grape producing a delicious everyday wine—the quaffing wine of northern Italy's Piedmont region.

**Dornfelder:** Promising German variety, similar in flavor to Beaujolais. A cross of two rare grapes, helfensteiner and heroldrebe, both of which are crosses themselves.

**Durif:** A Rhône cross of syrah and the now obscure grape peloursin. Though Durif has virtually disappeared in France, it lives on in California, where it is the source of most of the wines known as petite sirah.

### G

**Gaglioppo:** An ancient grape variety, gaglioppo is the source of the grapey red Italian wine Cirò in the province of Calabria.

**Garnacha:** Native Spanish grape and the most widely planted red grape in that country. An important part of the blend in the wines of Rioja, Priorato, and Navarra, Spain. In France it is called grenache. Often used in blending because of its high alcohol, big body, and jammy, spicy flavors.

**Girò:** An ancient grape variety that is grown in Sardinia, in Italy. Girò is probably of Spanish origin.

**Graciano:** High-quality but not widely planted Spanish grape, with delicate, slightly spicy flavors. Used primarily in Rioja as part of traditional Rioja blends. Also found to a small extent in the Languedoc-Roussillon, where it is called morrastel.

**Grenache:** The French name for the Spanish grape garnacha. In France, it grows throughout most of the southern wine regions, including Provence, the Languedoc-Roussillon, and the southern Rhône, where it is a critical presence in Châteauneuf-du-Pape and Gigondas, as well as in most Côtes-du-Rhône. In the Languedoc-Roussillon grenache is the principal grape in the sweet fortified wine Banyuls. It is also prolific in Australia and in the United States.

71

**Grignolino:** Native to Piedmont, Italy, where it is the source of light-reddish colored, frothy, delicate wines.

**Grolleau:** A mostly uninspired grape used primarily in France's Loire Valley in the red and rosé wines of Anjou.

## CALIFORNIA'S FIRST EUROPEAN GRAPES

—◦◦◦—

The first European (*vinifera*) grape variety planted in California was mission, named for the early Franciscan missions where it was initially grown. A coarse, high-yielding red grape, mission came from Spain and arrived in southern California via Mexico. The same grape (or a close sibling) was also brought to Chile and Argentina, where it became known as pais and criolla respectively. Precisely when the grape was first planted in Californian soil is not known. In the beginning, the California missions relied on wine brought up from Mexico. But difficulties and mishaps along the supply route eventually led the California missionaries to plant vineyards of their own. The first reference to grape growing at the missions was in 1779 at the Mission San Juan Capistrano in southern California.

The mission grape remained the backbone of the California wine industry until the 1870s. The grape is still grown in California, mostly in the hot San Joaquin Valley. As of the mid-1990s, 5,000 tons of it were crushed annually and made into wine that is bland at best.

**J**

**Jaen:** Important blending grape in the red wines of Portugal's Dão region.

**K**

**Kotsifali:** Unique to the Greek island of Crete, it is the most important grape in the wine Acharnes.

**L**

**Lambrusco:** Makes a light, low-alcohol, slightly sweet fizzy wine. Specialty of the Emilia-Romagna region of Italy.

**Lemberger:** Traditionally grown in Austria where it is known as blaufränkisch, this dark, spicy grape is also made into wine in the United States in Washington State.

**Limnio:** Greek variety appreciated by Aristotle. Native to the island of Lemnos.

**M**

**Malbec:** Soft, juicy low-acid grape famous in Argentina, where it is the source of most of the best red wines. In Bordeaux, its home, it is now on the decline. Also known farther south in France in Cahors as cot and auxerrois.

**Mandelari:** Native to Crete, where it is blended in small amounts with kotsifali to make the wine Archanes.

**Mavrodaphne:** The leading grape in the famous Greek wine mavrodaphne de Patras, a long-aged, sweet fortified wine made in Patras on the Peloponnese peninsula.

**Mazuelo:** Used as a blending grape in Rioja, Spain, as well as in the Languedoc-Roussillon, Provence, and Rhône regions of southern France, where it's known as carignan.

**Mission:** The first *vinifera* variety planted in California. Brought by Franciscan missionaries from Mexico sometime in the 1600s or 1700s. Remained the mainstay of the California wine industry until about 1870.

**Molinara:** With corvina and rondinella, used to make Italy's amarone and Valpolicella.

**Monastrell:** Widely planted rustic Spanish grape used to make *rosados* (rosés) and light red wines. The Spanish name for what the French call mourvèdre.

**Montepulciano:** Confusingly, this is not the grape of Vino Nobile di Montepulciano, which is made from sangiovese. Instead, the grape montepulciano is widespread throughout central and southern Italy and is especially well known in Abruzzi, where it makes the good, but rustic montepulciano d'Abruzzo.

**Mourvèdre:** One of the four important grapes in Châteauneuf-du-Pape, along with grenache, syrah, and cinsaut. Also a major blending grape in other Rhône, Provence, and Languedoc-Roussillon wines. In Spain, known as monastrell.

**Muscardin:** Relatively rare, fairly neutral grape used in France's southern Rhône in such wines as Châteauneuf-du-Pape and Gigondas.

### N

**Negoska:** A Greek variety used with xynomavro to make the popular Greek wine Goumenissa.

**Negrara:** A minor blending grape in the Italian wines amarone and Valpolicella.

**Negroamaro:** *Negro* (black) and *amaro* (bitter) tell it all. Appealing southern Italian grape with slight bitter espresso-like flavors. Widely grown in the Apulia region, especially in the hot, dry Salento peninsula, the spur of the Italian boot.

**Nero d'Avola:** The aristocratic red grape of Sicily, making wines that are mouthfilling and often complex. Sometimes called calabrese.

**Norton:** An American cross grown in Virginia where it is the source of some surprisingly good zinfandel-like wines.

### P

**Pais:** Prolific variety in Chile, where it is the source of common undistinguished table wine. Thought to be the same as, or closely related to, California's mission grape and Argentina's pink grape criolla.

**Peloursin:** Ancient Rhône variety now grown primarily in California, where it is the source of some wines commonly called petite sirah.

**Periquita:** The parakeet; a hearty grape that is grown all over southern Portugal. Periquita is also the brand name of a popular Portuguese red wine.

**Petite Sirah/Petite Syrah:** The name is a curiosity, for nothing is petite about the wines that come from it. Makes a blockbuster blackish, peppery, spicy, tannic wine. Recent DNA research indicates that wines labeled petite sirah are most often the Rhône grape Durif (a cross of peloursin and syrah), but they may also be the Rhône grape peloursin or a field blend of many varieties, including syrah, zinfandel, and several varieties common to southern France.

**Petit Verdot:** Important Bordeaux grape, traditionally blended with cabernet sauvignon and merlot. Added in small amounts for spice, depth, and color.

**Pinotage:** South African cross of pinot noir and cinsaut. Makes a very popular red wine.

**Pinot Meunier:** The most extensively planted of the three Champagne grapes. The other two are pinot noir and chardonnay. Fruity.

**Plavac Mali:** Most highly regarded red grape native to Croatia; a specialty of the Dalmatian coast, as well as other parts of the former Yugoslavia. Zinfandel, which bears some flavor resemblance to plavac mali, may be genetically related to it.

### R

**Refosco:** Also known as mondeuse noire and once grown all over eastern France. Now grown in and associated primarily with the Friuli-Venezia Giulia region of northeastern Italy, where it makes tasty everyday red wines.

**Rondinella:** With corvina and molinara, used to make the Italian wines amarone and Valpolicella.

**Rossese:** The leading red grape of Liguria, in Italy, where it makes the wine Dolceacqua.

**Ruby Cabernet:** One of the oldest California crossings, in this case of cabernet sauvignon and carignan. Has few of cabernet's attributes, however. Makes good jug wine.

### S

**Sagrantino:** In Italy, the delicious, bold-tasting grape used in one of Umbria's top wines, sagrantino di Montefalco.

**St. George:** See AGIORGITIKO.

**St. Laurent:** Fruity and simple grape used to make one of Austria's hearty reds.

**Schioppettino:** Fascinating though fairly rare grape native to northeastern Italy; a specialty of the region of Friuli-Venezia Giulia, where it makes spicy, aromatic wines.

**Spätburgunder:** German name for the grape variety pinot noir.

## T

**Tannat:** One of the leading grapes in southwest France, particularly used in the wine Madiran. Robust and deeply colored.

**Tazzelenghe:** In Italian the name means cut the tongue—a reference to the sharp acidity of the wine made from this grape. A specialty of Italy's Friuli-Venezia Giulia region.

**Teroldego:** One of the leading red grapes of Trentino-Alto Adige, the northernmost region in Italy. The grape makes fascinating, highly structured wines with blackberry fruit and tar characters.

**Terret Noir:** Grown in southern France in the Languedoc-Roussillon and in the southern Rhône. Of good but rarely great quality, terret noir is often a minor part of the blend in Côtes-du-Rhône and Châteauneuf-du-Pape.

**Tinta Barroca:** One of the grapes commonly used as part of the blend of Port as well as in the dry table wines of Portugal's Douro region.

**Tinta Negra Mole:** Grape most often used for basic Madeiras of modest quality.

**Tinta Roriz:** Also known as tempranillo. One of the grapes commonly used as part of the blend in Port as well as in the dry table wines of Portugal's Douro region.

**Tinto Cão:** Another grape commonly used as part of the blend in Port as well as in the dry table wines of Portugal's Douro region.

**Touriga Francesa:** Lighter than touriga nacional but an important component in the Port blend for its refined aroma. Also used in the dry table wines of Portugal's Douro region.

**Touriga Nacional:** The most esteemed and richest of the several grapes that make up Port. Also used in the dry wines of the Douro.

**Trincadeira Preta:** A grape grown all over southern Portugal, where it makes appealing rustic wines.

**Trollinger:** Common German variety making mostly undistinguished wines, especially in the Württemberg area.

## V

**Vaccarèse:** One of the common red grapes in France's southern Rhône Valley. Frequently used in Châteauneuf-du-Pape.

**Valdiguié:** Old French variety now virtually extinct there but growing in California, where it is the source of wines known confusingly as Napa gamay.

**Vinhão:** Along with azal tinto, a strident Portuguese variety used in the rare red versions of Vinho Verde.

## X

**Xynomavro:** From *xyno*, acid, and *mavro*, black. Greece's most intense, well-respected red grape. Makes Naoussa, one of the best Greek wines.

## Z

**Zweigelt:** Austrian cross of blaufränkisch and St. Laurent, it is the source of grapey, fruity red wines in that country.

# Before You Taste

What makes wine continually fascinating is that, apart from the hedonistic pleasure it provides, it appeals to the intellect in a way that, say, root beer or vodka do not. And because wine entices the mind, wine lovers are always beset by questions: Should you let a wine breathe? How much do vintages matter? How long does wine need to age? Even simple issues like choosing good wineglasses or knowing the right temperatures at which different wines should be served present questions.

I hope this section will provide you with answers. I'll begin with what ought to be the simplest issue of all: feeling comfortable in a wine shop. Trepidation was my early-on reaction to wine shopping (is there anyone for whom that isn't true?). Let's tackle it first.

## SHOP TALK—HOW TO BUY WINE COMFORTABLY

In so complex a world, buying a bottle of wine for dinner should be one of life's easier (and happier) tasks. Unfortunately, it often doesn't seem that way. When I first started buying wine, I was so overwhelmed by the sheer number of bottles in my local wine shop that for a good six months, I simply chose from a cache of assorted wines on sale all sitting in a bin positioned near the cash register (allowing at the very least for a quick getaway should embarrassment set in). I was about twenty-one and, as I recall, I wound up drinking a lot of cheap Bulgarian wine, which was (somewhat inexplicably) what the bin usually contained. The fact is, navigating a wine shop isn't a snap. Even a

*A wall of wine bottles can seem daunting at first, especially since even a moderate-size wine shop may offer more than 700 selections. But think of all the delicious discoveries to be made!*

medium-size wine shop might have 700 or so different wines and a large store, 4,000 or more. So how do you make buying wine a comfortable experience? Here's some insider's advice:

**1. Choose the right wine shop.** Forget those stuffy places that make you feel like a dunce. At the same time don't necessarily opt for a big impersonal discount store. It's true that discount stores are less likely to be staffed by clerks with nose-in-the-air attitudes, but it's also true (regrettably) that some discount stores employ people who know next to nothing about wine. You want someplace different from either of these—a place that lets you browse around, ask questions (and get answers)—a place where, over time, you can get to know one or two of the clerks well enough to trust them to point out new and exciting wines. In my experience, the best wine shops are those with newsletters. By a newsletter, I don't mean a price list. I mean a real newsletter that describes wines well enough so that you have a pretty good idea of what they taste like. Reading a shop's newsletter is not only a painless way to make new wine discoveries, but just reading the thing will give you a sense of the personality of the shop and whether or not it has a style and an approach you like.

**2. Don't let yourself be intimidated.** Sometimes intimidation is external— somebody acts in a way that makes you feel inadequate. But a lot of wine intimidation is internal. A little voice in your head says, "You'll never understand this." That's complete nonsense. You learned about food, didn't you? Don't forget that there was a time when you didn't know what avocados, sushi, or peach ice cream tasted like either. But you decided to give

*A wine shop in Bordeaux advertises a little Château Margaux to entice you in.*

each of them a try anyway, and in so doing, you expanded your knowledge about different foods and their flavors. Trying a wine you don't yet know is really the same thing.

**3. Make a plan.** Corny as it might seem, one way to go about conquering intimidation is to make a six-month plan; three months devoted to white wine, three months to red. Over the course of the white wine months, plan to try four different white varietals, sampling three examples of each. For instance, say you start with chardonnay. The first three times you go to the wine shop, buy a differernt chardonnay each time. The next three times, try different sauvignon blancs. The three times after that, bring home gewürztraminers or maybe pinot grigios. After you've experienced four white varietals, move on to reds. Remember, it doesn't matter what you choose as long as it's different each time. The goal here is to get your feet wet and to build up a reservoir of wine experiences so that you begin to know the flavors you love, the flavors you like, and the flavors you'd just as soon let somebody else have.

**4. Realize that no price is too little.** You don't have to spend a fortune to drink good wine. If you are going to a friend's house for lasagna, a $60 bottle of wine is not only unnecessary, one could argue it's out of place. One of the discoveries I made during the early part of my career is that wine professionals often buy very reasonably priced wines. Wine pros care about what's inside the bottle and the cheaper the price, the better. It's often people who don't know a lot about wine who pay enormous amounts for it, hoping that price will be some sort of assurance. It doesn't really work that way. Unlike cars and stereo systems, there are very good wines at all prices.

**5. That said, don't be afraid to treat yourself.** There are extraordinary wine experiences to be had, and for many of these the wines are expensive. While you don't have to spend a lot on wine on a regular basis, occasionally springing for a special bottle enriches your wine knowledge and can be very satisfying.

**6. Think of wine as a way to travel.** You may not be able to get to Tuscany or the south of France next summer but you can certainly have a lot of fun experimenting with Tuscan or southern French wines anyway. Again, it doesn't matter where you begin. If you're fascinated by Australia, start there. If you've never tried a wine from Spain, try one now. Ask the wine

shop clerk (your new friend) to point out a couple of wines that are classic examples from the place you've chosen, then ask him or her to tell you as much as possible about those wines.

**7. Be endlessly curious.** Remember, you are not the only one who doesn't know what's inside all those bottles. Most people don't. The wine drinkers who have the most fun and learn the most are those who have the courage to be curious. And being curious means being willing to ask questions. What does this wine taste like? is the most natural and reasonable question you can ask.

## BUT NONE FROM FAT

One 5-ounce glass of typical white wine contains about 104 calories; a typical red contains about 110. Wines that have a small touch of sweetness, such as some rieslings, may have an additional 5 to 10 calories. By comparison, the same amount of grape juice has about the same number of calories—102.

**8. Finally, use food as a language.** If you're trying to describe to the clerk the kinds of wines you like and you're at a loss for words, think about foods. Wines can be big and juicy like a steak; fresh and light like a salad; or spicy and bold like a Mexican sauce. It isn't necessary to use technical wine terms; in fact, they can get in the way. One day, wanting an adventure, I asked a wine clerk to give me a wine like Robin Williams. Amazingly enough, and without a minute's hesitation, he did just that.

# How Much Do Vintages Matter?

I magine this scenario: A waiter comes back to a group of diners and explains that the restaurant is out of the 1996 Château Pavie, but has the 1997; would the customers like that? Eyebrows furrow. A slight uneasiness comes over the table. No one wants to make a mistake. People begin rummaging through their wallets for crumpled vintage charts.

Should vintages be so troubling? Consider the reason behind giving wines vintage dates in the first place. Part of the premise of vintage dating is that, as a rule (especially in the Old World), weather is not on a grapevine's side. Historically, listing the vintage was a way of alerting consumers to certain years when very bad weather led to wines that were disappointingly thin. Such wines would generally be priced cheaply. People would drink the poor vintage until a better vintage came along, but no one would buy up cases of the wine and cellar it away to age.

And, of course, there would always be many vintages that weren't exactly poor—but were not stellar either. In these years, quite good wines might be made—wines that would be perfectly fine for, say, drinking over dinner, though they might not make anyone stop in his or her tracks.

Winemakers played a very small role in this yearly drama. No matter how talented they were, Nature had the upper hand and the final say. From both the winemakers' and the wine drinkers' standpoints, vintages had to be accepted for what they were. Some were poor, some were good, most were somewhere in between.

In the last twenty plus years, however, the picture has changed. Both winemaking technology and viticultural science have advanced to such a degree that talented winemakers can sometimes turn out fairly delicious wines even when Nature is working against them. The fact is, climate can now have a less detrimental impact on the final wine than it once did. This is not to say that vintages do not matter; they do. Or that wines taste the same every year; they clearly do not. But given the extraordinary knowledge, skill, and access to technology winemakers now have, vintage differences are often differences of character. For example, in a hot year many wines will be packed with big jammy fruit flavors. In a cool year they will be more austere, lighter in body, and possibly more elegant. Are any of these qualities terrible? Isn't it at least theoretically possible to like both kinds of wine? Unfortunately, vintage

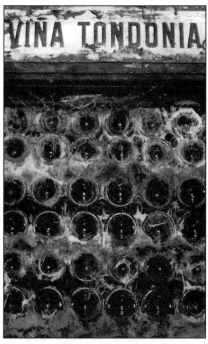

*In the cellars of R. Lopez de Heredia in Rioja, Spain, top vintages of the bodega's most famous wine, Viña Tondonia, rest amid the mold and cobwebs.*

assessments assume that for all wines and all wine drinkers everywhere, greatness comes in one form: bigness. But that is simply not true.

There is another problem: Vintages are categorized by the media once—when the new wine is tasted in the spring following the harvest. Wine, however, changes over time. There are many examples of vintages deemed magnificent at first, only to be later declared not as good as originally thought, as well as the opposite—vintages proclaimed average at first and then later awarded praise. From a wine drinker's standpoint, what is the point of memorizing the pluses and minuses of vintages if the pluses and minuses change? The final sensible approach can only be to have an open mind. Take the vintage charts with a big grain of salt. Remember that wines evolve and that one-shot vintage proclamations are entirely too superficial. Remember that talented winemakers can surprise us even when Nature has worked against them.

## WHERE TO STORE WINE AND WHERE NOT TO

K eeping wine in a way that keeps it wine, rather than transforming it into vinegar, has been a challenge for thousands of years. The ancient Greeks, for example, mixed wine with honey (sugar acts as a preservative), poured olive oil on top of it (as a barrier to air), and stored it in large ceramic amphorae buried in the ground to keep the wine cool.

By the sixteenth century, much of the wine traded throughout Europe was heavy, heady, and potently fortified with brandy to preserve it. The base wine itself may have come from any warm place along the Mediterranean, from southern Spain to

*My cellar—not fancy, but very functional. I plan to drink every one of these wines.*

Crete. In many cases, the origin did not matter; what was important was that the raw wine be fortified sufficiently so that it would still be drinkable when it reached England, Ireland, or northern Europe. Shakespeare wrote fondly of these formidable wines; he called them simply sacke.

Any wine that was not fortified was drunk immediately. These young fresh wines were highly desirable. For most of history, in fact, young wine was always more expensive than old. Intentionally storing wine to age it came into practice only after the eighteenth century when bottles and corks came into use. When aged in a bottle with a tight-fitting cork, wine not only did not turn to vinegar, some of it actually improved—sometimes markedly so, especially if it was red. For the first time, certain older wines began to command a higher price than young. And "laying a wine down" to better it began to take on romantic and sophisticated connotations.

The legacy remains. Aging a wine still seems like the correct thing to do, despite the fact that most modern wine is actually not meant to be aged for long periods of time. Virtually all white wines and rosé wines are made to be drunk fresh and young. Even among red wines, only those with generous fruit and firm structures are meant for the long haul. The French make a distinction between wines intended for current drinking and the far smaller universe of wines they call *vins de garde*— wines to save.

In reality, many a *vin de garde* is "saved" just about as long as it takes to get it home from the store. Still, despite the pull of immediate gratification, most of us will eventually be faced with the issue of wine storage. First, we sometimes find ourselves in possession of an especially fine wine that should be kept. Second, it generally makes economic sense to buy more than one bottle at a time. Thus, even novice wine drinkers can easily find that they've accumulated say, thirty or more assorted bottles of every-night dinner wines. How and where should they be stored?

Wine doesn't care if it's stored in a $10,000 custom-built cellar, in a damp basement, or between shoes in the closet, as long as three things are true:

**1.** The environment is cool.

**2.** The bottle is lying on its side or upside down (but not standing upright).

**3.** There is no direct sunlight.

Temperature matters because it affects the rate at which various chemical changes will take place as the wine matures. According to research conducted at the Department of Viticulture and Enology at the University of California at Davis, the rate of chemical reactions in wine can double with each 18°F increase in temperature. Thus, a wine stored at 75°F may change twice as fast as a wine stored at 57°F.

Couldn't that be a good thing? Instead of waiting ten years for a great wine to mature, why not put it in a warmer room and wait five? The idea is good all right—too good to be true. Unfortunately, evolution that is fast is not the same as evolution that is beneficial. Wines forced to mature too quickly show a sharp, exaggerated curve of awkward development, followed by dramatic deterioration. In a hot room, a fine wine can be shoved so quickly through the stages of aging that it begins to unravel. In order to develop properly and with stability, a fine wine must mature slowly over a long period of time. Scientists say this happens best when wines are kept at about 55°F. But what about less expensive wines? Scientists suggest that all wines, regardless of cost, be stored at temperatures under 70°F. Stored implies something more than a week. Professor Cornelius Ough of the Davis Department of Viticulture and Enology notes that most wines of average quality could be heated to 120°F for a few hours (as in the trunk of a car in summer) and remain unscathed. However, several days at such temperatures would cause the wines to taste stewed. It's important to note that we're talking here about wines of modest quality and cost. Speaking personally, I wouldn't leave a rare, older, or truly great wine in a hot trunk for even 10 minutes.

Scientists also insist that violent swings of temperature are detrimental—as, for example, when a wine is alternatively taken out of a hot closet and put into a cold refrigerator several times because plans to drink it have changed. Extreme fluctuations in temperature can affect both how the wine matures and the pressure inside the bottle, which in turn shifts the cork and thus may allow air to enter, oxidizing the wine. So once you've chilled that bottle of white or sparkling wine, drink it!

Similarly, when a wine is stored upright, the cork begins to dry out and shrink. After a few months, air may begin to slip between the cork and the neck of the bottle, oxidizing the wine. A bottle is best kept on its side or upside down, so that the cork, moist with the wine, stays swollen against the neck of the bottle.

Sunlight is harmful because ultraviolet light in particular causes free radicals to develop in wine, resulting in rapid oxidation. This is why the best wine stores don't display wine in the windows, unless those bottles are dummies that are not going to be sold.

Finally, vibration may be detrimental, although scientists have not seen conclusive evidence for this. Before Les Caves Taillevent, one of the most famous wine shops in central Paris, was built, the owners embarked on an extensive and nearly impossible search to find a neighborhood location far away from all metros. Although the rumble of Parisian trains is barely discernible anywhere beyond the train platform itself, the owners decided not to take any chances with their multimillion-dollar inventory.

*A good cellar can be as small and inexpensive as a cool closet or as elaborate and expensive as this one. In either case, it's important to remember that collecting wine is only one part of the equation—drinking is the best part.*

# WHEN IS IT READY?

While it may not make them fascinating dinner companions, experienced wine drinkers can spend hours discussing the wines—often the cabernet sauvignons—they have drunk and whether or not such wines were ready at the time. The question of readiness is a valid, if frustrating, one. Drinking a wine when its most interesting flavors are being fully expressed is clearly preferable to drinking a wine that's too young to have anything much to say. Saddest of all is to open a bottle you have patiently saved only to find the wine has wizened and dried up in old age.

I am speaking here primarily of red wines. Only they go from being somewhat difficult to charming. Tannin in red wine acts as a preservative, giving the wine a potentially long life. White wines, which have very little tannin, have a correspondingly shorter life and a more narrow window of drinkability. There are two exceptions, however. White wines that are high in acid, such as German rieslings, can age for long periods (acid is also a preservative), as can sweet wines, such as French Sauternes (sugar is also a preservative).

Let's suppose you were given a bottle of Château Latour (current vintage) as a birthday present. How would you know when to drink it? The first important realization is this: There is no one magic moment when the wine spontaneously metamorphoses into a supple, perfect drink. Most red wines evolve and soften progressively. They start out with rather tight, berry-flavored fruit and, bit by bit, slowly become softer and potentially more complex. Where a wine is along this spectrum at any point in time is a matter of conjecture.

## TOPPING UP WINE AND CHAMPAGNE

The time to top up a wine is when there are about two sips left in the glass. If you top up more frequently, you never get to experience how the wine evolves in the glass. With Champagne, there's another menace—temperature. Just as the constant topping up of coffee means you never have a really hot cup, constantly topping up Champagne leaves you with a quasi-chilled glass of bubbly.

Interestingly, a wine somewhere in its midlife can also go into what winemakers call a dumb phase where it may actually taste almost blank—without charm, without depth. In Bordeaux, this is called the wine's *age ingrat*, difficult age. Like adolescence, it is not permanent. And some wines never go through it. At some unknown point, however, every wine turns its own corner and begins to move toward maturity.

Predicting the arrival of that maturation remains anything but easy. Each wine is a living substance that changes according to its own rhythms. This should not be disillusioning. In fact, it is just the opposite. The unpredictability of wine makes it all the more compelling. Never truly knowing what to expect is part of the attraction; it is why wine appeals to the intellect in a way that, say, vodka does not. Best of all, the incontrovertibly inexact nature of readiness is a good excuse for buying more than one bottle of a fine wine, then trying these at several stages to see how it's developing.

I know. You *still* want a specific idea of when that bottle of Château Latour

82

might be ready, right? Use this as a bold-stroke guiding principle: The firmer and more structured the wine, the longer it can be kept. With a very expensive, high-quality cabernet sauvignon, merlot, nebbiolo, or other wine that is highly structured and full of fruit when young, the simplest rule of thumb is to wait at least five years. This sort of wine may have decades of staying power. Tuck it away someplace cool and wait that five years before drinking it. If you drink it in ten, that's great. If you want to get a sneak peak and drink it in three years, you'll probably still have a terrific experience (even though you will have knowingly decided to forgo whatever additional nuances the wine might have slipped into given more time).

## HOW MUCH WINE DO YOU NEED FOR A PARTY?

—◦◦◦—

Caterers—who as a group, it should be noted, love parties—work on the formula of one bottle per person. That figure is based on the assumption that it is better to have unopened bottles of wine leftover than it is to run out. (It's also based on the assumption that you've got plenty of designated drivers.) Since it is impossible to predict precisely how much (or how little) each guest may drink, a bottle per person allows for quite a comfortable margin of error. If the party will take place over several hours and is especially celebratory (like a wedding), and if you know everyone will be having wine, you should plan for somewhat more. One bottle of wine will yield about five standard glasses of wine when each glass is filled halfway.

Reds that are better than average but not extremely pricey may need three years or so before reaching their full expression. But again, there is no way to know for sure and, in any case, a wine that may be ideal after three years can still be delicious two months after the wine appears on the market. Moderately priced everyday reds are generally in good drinking shape as soon as they are released.

Recommendations like these can only be loose guidelines at best. The type of varietal, the powerfulness of the vintage, and the tannin/acid/fruit structure of the wine are only three of the multiple factors that dictate how long a wine can and should be kept.

## PAIRING WINE WITH FOOD

Wine and food, as we all undoubtedly agree, belong together. At the very least they can make each other taste better; and in the best of circumstances, when certain wines are paired with certain foods the result can be downright thrilling. Despite this, I have an admission to make: I don't think every wine always needs to be perfectly matched to a food or vice versa. And I don't say this because I lack passion for food. I started out as a food (not a wine) writer, I love to cook, and as you will perhaps deduce from the many food sections scattered throughout the chapters of this book, I have a deep appreciation for the historic connection between the foods of a place and the wines of a place. Together the two allow us, however briefly, to actually participate in the culture of a place. And that, it seems to me, is one of the true gifts wine and food offer us.

*The rich sweetness of scallops and fresh corn in a butter sauce is beautifully mirrored by a rich, buttery chardonnay.*

84

Wine and food matching is a bit different. Beginning in the 1980s, wine and food pairing became something of a national sport. Restaurants offered wine and food dinners; food magazines began to suggest wines with certain recipes; the back labels on bottles of American wines began to suggest accompanying dishes. It was all very exciting.

But as time went on, what started out as an exploration meant to heighten enjoyment began to border on the neurotic. I remember reading a magazine article by a famous food and wine writer who described in great detail why a steak should never be paired with zinfandel unless the steak was cooked rare and was liberally seasoned with black pepper. Medium-done steak minus black pepper, he said, married best with cabernet sauvignon. Continuing, he explained why Champagne and caviar were an awful match. And so

the article went. Acidity contrasts with salt. Salt fights with fat, and on and on. By the end of the piece, I was dizzy from so many new "rules."

The problem with this sort of approach is that it has very little connection—today or historically—to how we actually behave when we cook, eat, and drink. A hundred years ago, did an Italian grandmother stop to consider the acidity level in her pasta sauce before choosing a wine for dinner? I doubt it. Admitedly, she had very little choice; only a limited selection of wines would have been available to her. But it's also true that both then and now, we sometimes choose wines as much to match the mood as the food. Sometimes maybe more so. All of this is simply to point out that wine and food don't always have to be technically perfect together to be delicious anyway.

That said, it's certainly true that extraordinary flavor affinities do exist, and that

*Lamb is one of the most versatile meats with wine. Bordeaux, Riojas, and California cabernet sauvignons are all terrific partners.*

most of us have had at least a few of those "wow" moments when the wine and food combination was unbelievably good. How do you create those moments? It isn't easy. A meal, after all, rarely highlights the flavor of a single food, and many dishes present countless variables. Say you were trying to choose a wine to go with grilled chicken breasts with spicy coconut sauce. What exactly would you be matching? The chicken? The coconut milk? The spices and chiles in the sauce? And what if those chicken breasts were just one part of the dish? What if they were accompanied by a rice pilaf seasoned with coriander, cumin, and toasted almonds?

There's simply no absolute way to predict what might happen when all these flavors plus the multiple flavors in a wine are all swirled together like in a giant kaleidoscope. And even if you could predict the result, would we really all agree on whether it was delicious or not? Ultimately, taste preferences are highly individual.

So where does that leave us? To me, it leaves us squarely in the realm of instinct. People who pair wine and food together well don't have a set of rules as much as they have good instincts. And good instincts can be acquired. It's simply a matter of drinking lots of different kinds of wines with different kinds of dishes and paying attention to the principles that emerge. After years of doing precisely that, here's what I've discovered:

• This might seem like the most elemental of ideas, but for me, the first important principle is simply: Pair great with great, humble with humble. A hot turkey sandwich doesn't need a pricey merlot to accompany it. On the other hand, an expensive crown rib roast may just present

the perfect moment for opening that powerful, opulent Napa Valley cabernet sauvignon you've been saving.

• Second, match delicate to delicate, robust to robust. It only makes sense that a delicate wine like a red Burgundy will end up tasting like water if you serve it with a dramatically spiced dish like curry. Dishes with bold, piquant, spicy, and hot flavors are perfectly cut out for bold, spicy, big-flavored wines. Which is why various zinfandels are terrific with many Mexican dishes.

*The earthy flavors of a goat cheese and vegetable terrine are just waiting for a crisp, herbal sauvignon blanc.*

• Decide if you want to mirror a given flavor or set up a contrast. Chardonnay with lobster in cream sauce would be an example of mirroring. Both the lobster and the chardonnay are opulent, rich, and creamy. But delicious matches also happen when you go in exactly the opposite direction and create contrast and juxtaposition. That lobster in cream sauce would

## COOKING WITH WINE

Anywhere wine is made, it is used, usually liberally, in cooking. And for good reason. Wine obviously layers in more flavor and richness than water. Used this way, wine becomes another seasoning. The wine's flavors marry with other flavors in a dish, so that in the end, you can't taste the actual wine itself. In addition, wine is often included as a final splash of flavor in sauces and various dishes. In this scenario, wine is added at the end precisely so that you *can* taste some of it in the dish.

Before exploring ways to maximize wine's flavors in cooking, let's talk about the alcohol. The conventional wisdom of the past has been that after a few minutes of cooking, the alcohol in wine evaporates and is therefore eliminated. That's not exactly the case. Research conducted by the U.S. Department of Agriculture in the mid-1990s showed that 85 percent of the alcohol

*Mussels steamed in white wine . . . a delicious classic.*

remained when alcohol was added to a boiling liquid that was then removed from the heat. The longer something is cooked, however, the less alcohol will remain. If a food is baked or simmered for 15 minutes, about 40 percent of the alcohol will remain. After one hour, only 25 percent will remain and after 2½ hours, just 5 percent will be present. Remember that wine does not have huge amounts of alcohol to begin with—most wines are between 12 and 14 percent alcohol by volume—so for most people, the final amount of alcohol remaining in a dish is usually not a problem.

As for cooking with wine, here is a rundown of the important guidelines:

• Never use poor-quality wine. If you wouldn't drink it, don't pour it into the stew. A poor-quality wine with sour or bitter flavors will only contribute those flavors to the dish.

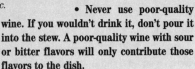

also be fascinating with Champagne, which is sleek, crisp, and sharply tingling because of the bubbles.

• Think about flexibility. Ironically enough and lobster notwithstanding, though chardonnay is wildly popular, it's one of the least flexible white wines with food. Especially if it's a chardonnay from California. These wines often have so much toasty oak and high alcohol that they are very hard to pair. For maximum flexibility, go with a sauvignon blanc or a dry German or Alsace riesling, both of which have cleansing acidity. Wines with high

acidity leave you wanting to take a bite of food, and after taking a bite of food, you'll want a sip of wine. The perfect seesaw.

• The most flexible red wines either have good acidity, such as Chianti, red Burgundy, and California and Oregon pinot noir, or they have loads of fruit and not a lot of tannin. For this latter reason, zinfandel, lots of simple Italian reds, and southern Rhône wines, such as Châteauneuf-du-Pape, are naturals with a wide range of dishes from such simple comfort foods as grilled chicken to more complex dishes like pasta *bolognese*.

- Never use cooking "sherry" or other wines billed for cooking. These wretched liquids are horrible tasting, cheap, thin base wines to which salt and food coloring have been added.

- If a recipe calls for dry white wine, many whites from all over the world will work, but among American wines, the best and easiest choice is a good-quality sauvignon blanc. Not only is sauvignon blanc moderately priced, but it has a fresh, light herbal tilt to it that works well for a broad spectrum of dishes.

- If the dish has bold or spicy flavors, try a white wine that's powerfully fruity and aromatic. Gewürztraminer, riesling, and viognier, for example, can all have dynamic, exotic floral and fruity flavors and aromas.

- If the recipe calls for dry red wine, think about the heartiness of the dish. A rustic, long-cooked casserole of lamb shanks or a substantial beef stew needs a correspondingly hearty wine. Use a big-bodied red zinfandel or petite sirah, both of which are also packed with fruit flavor.

- When you can, match the wine's flavor to the food's flavor. Every time I sauté mushrooms, I can't help but add a little pinot noir, which, like mushrooms, has an earthy flavor.

- Don't pass up Port, Madeira, Marsala, and the nutty styles of Sherry, such as amontillado. I could not cook without these scrumptious wines. All four are fortified, which means they have slightly more alcohol, but they all pack a bigger wallop of flavor too. Plus, opened, they can be used for cooking for several months or more. Just remember to taste them occasionally to make sure they are still full of flavor. Be sure to use the real thing. Port from Portugal, Sherry from Spain, and so on. The ersatz California versions are very weak. Port has a rich, sweet, winey flavor, a real plus in meat casseroles. The styles known as ruby Port and late bottled vintage Port give the most flavor for the lowest cost. Sherry's complex roasted nutty flavors can transform just about any soup, stew, or sautéed dish; use amontillado as mentioned or the even richer oloroso. Madeira can be mesmerizingly lush, with toffee and caramel flavors; use the medium-rich style known as bual. And Marsala's light caramel-like fruitiness is incomparable in Mediterranean sautés. I like to use dry Marsala.

- Not surprisingly, dishes with fruit in them or a fruit component to them—pork with sautéed apples, roasted chicken with apricot glaze, duck with figs, and so forth—often pair beautifully with very fruit-driven wines that have superfruity aromas. Gewürztraminer, muscat, viognier, and riesling are in this camp.

- Saltiness in food is a great contrast to acidity in wine. Think about smoked salmon and Champagne or Parmigiano-Reggiano cheese and Chianti. Asian dishes that have soy sauce in them often pair well with high-acid wines like German rieslings.

- Saltiness is also a stunning contrast to sweetness. Try that Asian dish seasoned with soy sauce with an American riesling that's slightly sweet, and watch both the food and the wine pull together in a new way. This is the principle behind that great old European custom of serving Stilton cheese (something salty) with Port (something sweet).

- A high-fat food, something with a lot of animal fat, butter, or cream, usually calls out for an equally rich, intense, structured, and concentrated wine. Here's where a well-balanced red wine with tannin, such as a good-quality cabernet sauvignon or merlot, works wonders. A powerful California cabernet sauvignon with a grilled steak is pretty hard to beat. This same principle is at work when a Bordeaux wine (made primarily from cabernet sauvignon and merlot) is served with roasted lamb. And pairing richness with richness is also the principle behind what is perhaps the most decadent wine and food marriage of all: Sauternes and foie gras.

• With desserts, consider sweetness carefully. Desserts that are sweeter than the wine they accompany make the wine taste dull and blank. In effect, the sweetness of the dessert can knock out the character of the wine. Wedding cake, for example, can ruin just about anything in a glass, though happily, no one's paying attention anyway. The best dessert and dessert wine marriages are usually based on pairing a not-too-sweet dessert, such as a fruit or nut tart, with a fairly sweet wine.

So there they are, a group of fairly simple principles, meant only as a guide. The real excitement is in the experimentation and only you can do that.

## TEMPERATURE

On the first day of my wine classes, I serve two red wines blind and ask the participants to pick the one they like better and describe why. Invariably most people like B, but there are always votes for both wines and a lively discussion of how different the two wines are. In fact, wines A

### CHILLING WINE QUICKLY

The fastest method of chilling wine is to put it in an ice bucket filled half with ice and half with cold water. Chilling wine this way takes about half the time of chilling it in a bucket full of ice alone. To chill the wine as quickly as possible, the bucket must be deep enough so that the bottle can be submerged up to its neck in the ice water bath.

Here are some guidelines for chilling wines that are at a warm room temperature using an ice water bath:

• Chill red wines for about 5 minutes.

• Chill superfruity red wines, such as Beaujolais, for about 15 minutes.

• Chill white wines for 15 to 25 minutes.

• Chill Champagne and sparkling wines for about 30 minutes.

and B are the same red wine—with one difference: B is about 3 degrees cooler than A.

The class is always stunned that so small a difference in temperature could have so major an effect. But it does. The perception of alcohol, acidity, fruitiness, and balance are all influenced by a wine's temperature. Temperature, in fact, can make the difference between enthusiasm and apathy for the same wine.

At cool temperatures a white wine's acidity is highlighted and the wine seems to taste lighter and fresher. It is also possible, however, to chill a white down to the point where it is so cold, it can barely be tasted at all. Bartenders sometimes serve cheap white house wines much colder than fine white wines precisely so you don't taste them. Increases in temperature have a different effect. As the temperature of a white wine rises, its alcohol becomes more obvious and the wine begins to taste coarse. An already high-alcohol chardonnay can taste almost caustic at too warm a temperature.

Red wines are more tricky. While a red wine served too warm can also taste alcoholic and coarse, the same wine over-chilled can taste thin. Historically, the solution for red wines has been simple: Serve them at room temperature—European room temperature prior to central heating, that is. In other words, about 60°F to 65°F. Often these wines would be brought up from an even cooler cellar.

Room temperature in the United States is, of course, far warmer, and many red wines don't taste their best as a result. You can easily demonstrate this for yourself. Pour a glass of good red wine from a bottle that has been kept in a warm room. Now chill the rest of the bottle in a bucket of ice and water for five to ten minutes. The idea is not to make the red wine cold but simply to bring its temperature down to about 65°F. At that temperature good red wines taste balanced, focused, and full of fruit.

There's one exception to the rule above. Extremely fruity, low-tannin red wines—Beaujolais, for example—should be cooled almost as much as white wines so that their fruitiness is magnified.

In restaurants, I often ask for a red wine to be put in an ice bucket for a few minutes (much to the dismay of waiters who think they know better).

### B.Y.O.B. Alert

Corkage is the price per bottle a restaurant or hotel will charge you for bringing your own wine. The fee is somewhat euphemistically said to cover the cost of opening the wine and providing glassware. But neither of those factors addresses the real basis of corkage, which is to recover money from a lost sale. In the 1990s the corkage fee in many top restaurants in New York City was equal to the cost of a moderately expensive wine on the establishment's list. Thus the corkage on a wine you bring to the restaurant can be twice the cost of the wine itself, especially if the restaurant has a high markup on its wines and you've brought along a modest bottle.

## UNCORKING THE BOTTLE

Canines aside, man's best friend is surely an obliging corkscrew—one that does not require the user to have bell-shaped biceps; one that does not shred the cork to smithereens half the time. Decent corkscrews now exist. For most of history, however, they have been frustrating, imperfectly designed tools.

Originally called bottle-screws, corkscrews were invented in England between 1630 and 1675, where they were used not for wine but for beer and cider. Both sparklers required tight-fitting corks (often tied on) capable of trapping fermenting gas. Such corks, forced deep into the necks of bottles, often proved impossible to extract without the help of some kind of tool.

The first tool took its inspiration from a gun. Manufacturing records from the 1630s describe a bullet-extracting "worm" supplied with muskets and pistols. By the 1800s several English firms that manufactured steel worms for muzzle-loaded firearms also made corkscrews.

Corkscrews went from being helpful to being essential with the discovery that wine matures favorably in bottles, as well as in casks. New cylindrical aging bottles, meant to be laid on their side and stacked for long periods of time, were designed. Corks now had to be fully driven into the neck of the bottle for a leakproof fit. Corkscrews became necessities.

The early T-shaped corkscrew with its simple handle and worm spawned thousands of design variations. Double-wormed, folding, left-handed, brush-tipped, and combination corkscrews (walking stick cork-

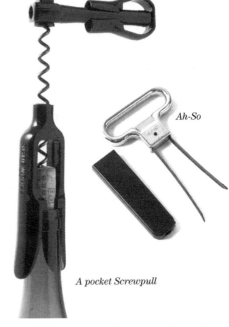

*Ah-So*

*A pocket Screwpull*

screws, cigar cutter corkscrews, and so on) were made of a variety of materials: silver, gold, bronze, steel, gilt on copper, wood, mother-of-pearl, ivory, horn, teeth, tusks, seashells, bone, and later, plastic. Handle shapes knew no bounds, from a cardinal's cap to a woman's legs.

The flat, lever-type waiter's corkscrew was invented in Germany in 1883 by Carl Wienke, a civil engineer. Its convenient fold-up design and concealed knife has made it an artifact of virtually every restaurant in the world.

A somewhat less popular corkscrew— actually more of a cork puller—is the Ah-So, patented in 1879. Originally named the Magic Cork Extractor, the Ah-So has been so called since the 1960s. The derivation of the name is unclear although some speculate that it describes the user's surprise at how the devise works. The Ah-So has no worm but rather two flat metal blades that are inserted down the side of the cork. In England this cork

*Why wrestle with a bottle of wine? A good corkscrew makes life easier. The lever Screwpull is effortless to use.*

*Screwpull*

puller was nicknamed the butler's friend because it enabled a disaffected butler to remove a cork, sample some of his master's best, replace that with inferior wine, and then recork the bottle with no telltale hole as evidence.

The most important advance in corkscrew design occurred in 1979 with the birth of the Screwpull, the first nearly infallible corkscrew. Invented by the late Herbert Allen, a Texas oil field equipment engineer, the Screwpull's extremely long worm is coated with Teflon so it glides without friction through the cork. As the worm descends, the cork is forced to climb up it and out of the bottle, requiring no effort (or expertise) on the part of the puller.

All good corkscrews, including the Screwpull, have a helical worm with a thin, needle-sharp point. A helix is a straight line wrapped around an imaginary cylinder. Thus, the center of a good corkscrew is not its worm but the space framed by the worm. You can drop a toothpick into a helix-shaped worm. Such a design means that as the point spirals down through the cork the rest of the worm follows the exact same path, minimizing damage to the surrounding cork cells. Because the cork is basically intact, it does not shred as you pull up. By comparison, a worm that is the central shaft of the corkscrew (as is true of most "rabbit ears" corkscrews) plows a hole through the belly of the cork, ripping apart cells and causing the cork to disintegrate into bits.

## Using a Waiter's Corkscrew

It takes between 50 and 100 pounds of pulling force to extract a cork using a waiter's corkscrew. Here's the correct technique: Place the bottle on a flat surface. Using the knife attached to the corkscrew, cut the foil capsule under the second rim at the top of the bottle neck and remove the top part of the capsule. Hold the corkscrew so that the worm's point is curved down toward the bottle and, using a good amount of pressure, insert the worm into the cork slightly off center. Slowly spiral the corkscrew down through the cork. The worm's point should pierce through the bottom of the cork, assuring a firm hold. (It is a myth that cork will fall into the wine; cork's physical properties prevent this.) Position the lever against the rim of the bottle neck and ease the cork straight upward; don't bend it over the side. Screw the worm down again; ease the cork upward again. When the cork is mostly but not entirely out, grasp it and gently pull it the rest of the way up and out.

*Waiter's Corkscrews*

*Classic waiter's corkscrews like these were invented in 1883 in Germany. Expensive versions like the Laguiole (center) have bone or ebony handles and a worm coated with a Teflon-like substance to ensure an easy glide through the cork.*

# CORKS: BACK TO THE FUTURE

In a technologically advanced civilization, sealing wine with a hunk of bark may seem hopelessly archaic. Indeed, cork has its critics. Yet the promising *thwack* as a cork leaves a bottle, a familiar sound for centuries, will probably be heard for many decades to come.

Cork, the bark of the cork oak tree, is native to the poor rocky soil of southern Portugal and Spain, as well as to Sardinia, Algeria, Tunisia, and Morocco. Most of the corks used in the United States come from Portuguese trees.

Cork's structural composition is remarkable. A 1-inch cube contains roughly 200 million fourteen-sided cells filled with air. With a specific gravity of 0.25, cork is four times lighter than water, yet highly elastic, capable of snapping back to its original shape after withstanding 14,000 pounds of pressure per cubic inch. Cork is impervious to air, almost impermeable by water, difficult to burn, resistant to temperature changes and vibration, does not rot, and has the ability to mold itself to the contour of the container it is put into (such as the neck of a wine bottle).

A cork tree is harvested or stripped for the first time when it is twenty-five years old, and thereafter once every nine years. Although stripping does no permanent damage, the tree will need two years or more to recover its vitality. A cork tree will be stripped fifteen times in its life.

The stripping itself is grueling work. Using special wedge-shape axes, workers peel 4-foot planks from the bark during the intense summer heat when the tree's sap is circulating, making it possible to pry off the bark. Once the bark is stripped off, it is left outdoors to season and dry for up to a year. After it has dried, the bark is then boiled or steamed to improve its elasticity and flatten it and then is dried again. Finally the bark is trimmed into planks and separated according to quality. Wine corks are machine-punched from the planks, graded, and washed in a mild hydrogen peroxide solution to remove dust and to sanitize them.

Washing has proven problematic. Before 1995 most corks were washed in a chlorine solution. It is now known that chlorine can react with moisture and fungi inside the cork to facilitate the growth of 2,4,6-trichloranisole (TCA), the chemical responsible for the "wet newspaper" musty aroma wine can pick up from corks. A wine tainted with TCA is said to be corked. (Corked wine, therefore, does not smell like cork.)

Though chlorine is no longer used in cleaning corks, the problem of corked wines has remained. As it turns out, TCA can be generated by a variety of means. Sometimes the compound exists naturally in raw cork bark. Sometimes it has been found on cardboard boxes and wooden pallets and from there, it has contaminated corks, which in turn have tainted wine. All this said, the incidence of corked wines is not high (most estimates range from 2 to 5 percent), and drinking a corked wine is not harmful, just unpleasant.

Not long ago cork's future looked bleak. Prior to 1974, cork forests in Portugal were neglected and reforestation was haphazard or nonexistent. Threatened by the loss of a valuable industry, the Portuguese government ultimately passed laws to encourage cork reforestation and improvements in cork manufacture. By the late 1990s, 13 billion wine corks were being produced each year, enough to meet world demand.

## Smelling the Cork

You order wine in a restaurant and the waiter puts the cork down beside you. You are supposed to:

1. Smell it?
2. Feel it?
3. Glance at it, then ignore it?

The answer is number 3. The practice of placing the cork on the table dates from the eighteenth century when wineries began branding corks to prevent unscrupulous restaurateurs from filling an empty bottle of Château Expensive with inferior wine, recorking it, then reselling it as Château Expensive. In honest restaurants, the cork was placed on the table so the diner could see that the name on it matched that on the label, a guarantee that the wine had not been tampered with. Admittedly, feeling the cork tells you if the wine was stored on its side and that can be a clue to its soundness. But a moist cork is no guarantee that the wine is in good condition; similarly, a dry cork does not necessarily portend a wine gone awry.

*From ancient times, wine has been poured from decorative wine vessels such as this one from the Lungarotti wine museum in Torgiano, Italy.*

# AERATING WINE

What is often called breathing—the idea that many wines soften and open up after exposure to air—is true. However, simply pulling the cork out of a bottle and letting the bottle sit, opened, for a few minutes is meaningless, despite the fact that you see this done in restaurants all the time. The amount of air in the tiny space of the neck of an opened bottle is simply much too small relative to the volume of wine to have an effect—unless, perhaps, you left it open for nearly a day.

To effectively aerate a wine, you have to pour it into a decanter, carafe, or pitcher so that it mixes with oxygen as it pours from the bottle. Allowed to breathe in this way, the flavors of many wines—especially young, tannic reds, such as cabernet sauvignon, merlot, nebbiolo, and petite sirah—will almost seem to unfurl. White wines, too, will open up as a result of exposure to oxygen, though the effect is less pronounced and it may be more important to keep a white wine chilled by leaving it in its original bottle.

Delicate reds need special attention in this regard. Splashing an older fragile pinot noir into a decanter, for example, could blunt its flavor and make it taste dull. As a result, older red Burgundies, along with older Riojas (made from tempranillo) and older Chiantis (made from sangiovese), are rarely poured out to aerate them.

# DECANTING

A more complex procedure than aerating, decanting a wine involves pouring the clear wine off any sediment that may have precipitated out of it. Sediment—mostly residues of color and other particulate matter—generally is present only in older red wines that were once deeply colored, such as cabernet sauvignon, and in vintage Ports. If you carefully take an older cabernet out of its resting place and hold it up to a light, you'll often see a sort of crusty material clinging to the inside of the bottle. That's sediment. It's more difficult to see the sediment in an old vintage Port since many Port bottles are traditionally made from dark, opaque glass. Of course, you could drink an old wine that has thrown some sediment without decanting it; the sediment is not harmful, just slightly gritty.

When is a wine old enough to possibly need decanting? Though there's no absolute rule, wines ten years old or more are generally considered in that range.

## LEAD CRYSTAL

An English glassmaker named George Ravenscroft discovered in 1674 that adding lead oxide to molten glass made it softer and easier to work. As a result, lead crystal could be cut into elaborate designs. But even more important, lead made glass more durable and more brilliant.

In 1991 researchers at Columbia University found that wine and other acidic beverages left in lead crystal decanters *for several months* could absorb possibly dangerous amounts of lead. Subsequently, the FDA recommended against storing acidic foods and beverages for long periods of time in lead-glazed pottery or lead crystal decanters. The specific health hazards, however, are still not known. Since wine does not stay in a crystal glass long enough to leach lead from it, drinking wine from lead crystal glasses is considered safe.

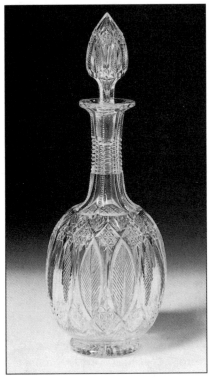

*The Rare Wine Company specializes not just in rare wine but also in antique crystal decanters such as this one.*

Just because a wine is older, however, doesn't necessarily mean it has thrown a sediment. And if it has not thrown a sediment, it does not need to be decanted.

Decanting a wine is not difficult. First, the wine bottle must be placed standing upright for a day or two to let all the sediment gently settle to the bottom of the bottle. Without picking the bottle up or turning it around, remove the cork slowly (a Screwpull works best for this). Now pick the bottle up carefully and with a light source behind it (a candle, small light, or flashlight will do), begin pouring the clear wine slowly into a decanter. When less than 2 inches of wine is left, you should begin to see sediment coming into the neck of the bottle. That's when to stop.

*The Austrian glass manufacturer Riedel makes what many wine lovers consider the best wine-glasses in the world. Riedel has designed a different glass for every major type of wine. Though the uninitiated are usually skeptical of the idea that a glass can make that much difference, try a Bordeaux in the Riedel Bordeaux glass, then compare it to the same wine in any other glass (including any other Riedel glass) and you'll be won over, too.*

The clear wine is now all in the decanter; the sediment remains in the bottle.

Old wines are often unpredictable and usually somewhat frail. In the presence of oxygen, some will throw off their aromas and flavors and immediately begin to slide toward their death. The general rule of thumb is to decant older tannic wines—Port, cabernet sauvignon, Bordeaux, Barolo, and Rhône wines, for example—less than an hour before serving. More fragile wines that were never strongly tannic or deeply colored in the first place—pinot noir, Rioja, or Chianti, for example—may never need decanting at all, but if you see sediment, decant them just before serving.

## WINEGLASSES

Although wine can be happily drunk from just about anything from Flint-stones jelly glasses to Baccarat crystal, most wine drinkers would agree that a good wineglass can heighten the pleasure of wine drinking and actually enhance the aroma and flavor of wines. This is easy to prove to yourself. Pour the same wine into a tumbler and into a good, ample size wineglass. From which glass does the wine taste better?

How do you go about buying good wineglasses when there are dozens of glass manufacturers to choose from and prices for wineglasses can range from five to a hundred dollars a glass? Here are some guidelines:

• Only buy wineglasses you can afford to break. If spending fifty dollars per glass means you'd never use them, buy ones that are less expensive.

• Buy more glasses than you think you'll need. Glasses do break. And besides, there may be times when you want to serve two different zinfandels side by side for comparison.

• Consider buying one great style of wineglass that can be used for both red and white wines. It's simply nonsense that white wines should be served in smaller glasses. A well-designed good wineglass—whether it will eventually hold red or white wine—should have a generous bowl. An ample bowl gives the wine's flavors room in which to evolve. Closer to the rim, however, the bowl should narrow, forcing the aromas to be focused toward your nose.

• Buy glasses that are absolutely clear and smooth, not faceted, to show off the depth and richness of the wine's color. Colored and/or cut glass may be beautiful, but you cannot see the wine.

• Make sure the glass has a thin rim so that the wine glides over it easily and so that you don't feel like you have to chew on the glass to get to the wine.

• Choose a glass with a stem long enough to give you something to hold other than the bowl. Holding the glass around the bowl can warm the wine.

## CLEANING WINEGLASSES

A wine that smells or tastes strange, or off, may be perfectly fine. The culprit could be the glass. Invisible soapy residue inside a wineglass can react with the components in the wine, making it smell stinky and taste odd. Soapy flutes will make the bubbles in Champagne fizzle and go flat. Often in restaurants the wines sent back are, in fact, perfectly fine; it's the glasses that are in poor condition.

The best way to wash crystal wineglasses is by hand, using your hand (not a sponge) and a small amount of diluted soap and lukewarm water. Crystal glasses should be rinsed several times in hot, but not scalding, water. Very hot water can cause the glass to expand rapidly and crack. Drain crystal briefly upside down, then turn the glasses upright and let them dry in the air. Any drops or spots can be finished off with a clean soft cloth. Crystal should not be put in a dishwasher, where it can be easily done in by the intensity of the heat and the abrasiveness of the dishwasher soap. And once it's dry, a wineglass should be stored right side up, standing on its foot, not on its more fragile rim.

Interestingly, in Italy, in many homes and virtually all top restaurants, a perfectly clean wineglass is not yet considered ready for use. The Italians always pour a small amount of wine in the glass, swirl it around, then throw this wine rinse out. When asked about this, Italians will say that they are preparing the glass to receive the wine—a baptism of sorts. Is it any wonder that most of us, on our first trip to Italy, fall in love with Italian wine, Italian food, and Italian sensibility?

## THE COAST BEFORE THE TOAST

During the eighteenth century, the wine "slide," known now as a coaster, became popular. Originally coasters served to facilitate the passing of wine from one man to another. Bottles would be brought out for serious drinking after the women had been dismissed to the drawing room and the table cleared of its covering and impediments. Coasters were constructed of smoothly polished wooden or fabric-covered plinths that glided across a table without scratching the mahogany surface. Each coaster was also fitted with a gallery (often of silver) that held the bottle more or less upright while it was "coasted" from one person to another. When leaving the tablecloth on the table after the meal became commonplace, the coaster went from being a handy serving device to a simple protection against wine spills on the linen.

• Never buy small glasses. Drinking wine out of a small glass feels as awkward as sitting on a chair that's too small or eating dinner off a bread plate.

• In addition to regular wineglasses, buy flutes for serving Champagne and sparkling wines. The long tapered shape of a flute encourages a steady stream of bubbles, and with these wines, bubbles are part of the pleasure.

*Elaborately designed wineglasses show just how advanced glassmaking technology has become. Alas, the more ornate the glass, the less effective it usually is when it comes to wine tasting.*

## Pouring

Wineglasses should only be filled halfway. That leaves plenty of room to swirl the wine so that its aromas and flavors come alive as they mix with oxygen. The exception is when serving Champagne and sparkling wine. Flutes can be filled slightly more since the goal is to encourage a long bead of bubbles streaming to the surface. However, flutes should not be filled to the absolute brim. Some air space will help to focus the aromas.

# Tasting Wine Like a Professional

*"To know is to be able to name."*

—Emile Peynaud, Le Goût du Vin (The Taste of Wine)

S uppose you were asked to write a ten-word description of a wine you drank three nights ago. Could you? Unfortunately, it is possible (easy, in fact) to go for years drinking wine without tasting it in a way that helps you understand and remember it. Most of us—even those of us who are committed food lovers—don't really taste with conscious intent, nor do we take time to concentrate on what we smell. Tasting and smelling are often virtually mindless tasks. Yet without sensory focus and without a systematic method of smelling and tasting, it's just about impossible to develop a taste memory and, ultimately, impossible to understand anything significant about wine.

Let me carry this idea one step further. What do you suppose distinguishes wine experts from most other people who enjoy wine? Better taste buds? More extensive tasting experiences? We can eliminate better taste buds as a possibility right away. Unless you have had an illness that has physiologically or neurologically dam-

*The author at work: Each year I taste and evaluate 2,500 to 3,000 wines.*

aged your ability to taste and smell, you bring to wine tasting all of the sensory equipment necessary to make a professional evaluation. As for the number of

## A WHOLE MOUTH EXPERIENCE

———∽∾∽———

Taste research in the 1980s and 1990s suggests that some supertasters may experience bitter compounds, such as caffeine, or sweet compounds, such as sucrose, more intensely than other individuals. However, the effect is greatest when small, localized areas of the tongue are stimulated. Interestingly and inexplicably, when the whole mouth is stimulated (as would be the case in drinking a glass of wine), individuals—regardless of the acuity of their taste sensitivity—experience many stimuli the same way.

tasting experiences, if that made one an expert, then a wine drinker who was sixty might reasonably be expected to know more about wine than someone who was, say, thirty-five. However, no such direct correlation between number of wines tasted and expertise exists. Many wine experts, including individuals who have passed difficult wine exams (like the one given for a Master of Wine diploma) are actually fairly young. What makes wine experts expert is something remarkably basic: They smell and taste in a consistent, logical way, and they always pay attention.

Most experts did not begin to develop sensory focus as soon as they started drinking wine. Years of drinking wine—however enjoyable—do not automatically lead to an increase in knowledge. To gain expertise, you must learn to be a deliberate taster. And beyond that, you must be able to describe what you taste.

Whether at backyard picnics or in the tasting rooms of Château Margaux, experts always spend a concentrated minute smelling, tasting, and accessing the wines—thereby taking mental snapshots of them. Unfortunately, many wine drinkers remain at the "I know what I like and I know what I don't like when I taste it; but I can't describe either one" stage their entire lives. It's entirely possible, however, to learn to use the techniques of the experts. Frankly, wine drinking gets even more pleasurable when you do. Here are the basics you must know to become a deliberate taster, a thoughtful evaluator, and a person who can describe and recall wines.

## SETTING THE SCENE

The circumstances in which you taste, including the time of day, affect your judgment. Professionals often taste before lunch when they are alert and their mouths are not recovering from a meal of calamari with garlic mayonnaise, followed by an espresso sweetened with saccharin. Though it is unlikely that many of us will do most of our wine tasting in pristine conditions at 11 A.M., being aware of factors that may skew your perceptions is nonetheless valid.

There is another important point: The first few sips of any wine often taste abrupt because your mouth has not yet adapted to the acidity and the alcohol. Thus, your judgment of a wine may be, initially anyway, flawed. In professional judgings, wine jurors often go back to a wine one or two more times during a tasting to make sure they are evaluating it correctly.

## GET IN THERE AND SNIFF

At the turn of the twentieth century, only a handful of elements in wine were known. Today, hundreds are. Most of these identified elements can be smelled. Yet, currently, the taste of a wine remains largely confined to just three well-known concepts, sweet, sour, and bitter. (The fourth taste—salt—is rarely found in wine, though there are exceptions.) Some chemists have suggested that wine is a virtually tasteless liquid that happens to be deeply fragrant. Indeed, smelling a wine is critical to tasting it.

Importantly, you continue to smell a wine once it is in your mouth. You actually smell it better at that point. As the wine is mixed with your saliva and warmed, volatile compounds are released and waft back through your mouth and up to the cavity behind the bridge of your nose. There, they are absorbed by receptor nerve cells five million of which flash information to the olfactory bulb of the brain. These cells, stimulated by everything you breathe in and out, are the most exposed nerves in the body.

If you do not smell a wine or simply take a brief cursory whiff, very little information goes to the brain, and not surprisingly, you have trouble deciding what the wine tastes like.

How do you smell correctly? Start by swirling the wine in the glass. Swirling aerates wine. The best way to do this is to rest the glass on a table, and holding it by the stem, rapidly move it as if you were drawing small circles.

*In Britain, smelling a wine is often referred to as nosing it.*

As for actually sniffing the wine, nothing is achieved by holding your nose 2 inches above the glass and taking a polite whiff. You must get your nose (a big one is an asset) *into* the glass near the liquid. Then take a series of short quick sniffs.

*Georg Riedel tasting wine from one of his glasses—aroma is key.*

## BOTTLE SICKNESS

Much to the agony of winemakers, wines that have recently been bottled occasionally develop bottle sickness—a temporary condition wherein the wine tastes lifeless, as though it has lost its aromas and flavors. Bottle sickness can happen to any wine. It is thought to be the result of the agitation and, possibly, exposure to oxygen that happens during bottling.

Winemakers, of course, easily recognize this condition since they have also tasted the wine before it was bottled and therefore have a point of comparison. Wine drinkers, however, may misinterpret a bottle-sick wine as one that's of poor quality. That said, to experience what a wine with bottle sickness tastes like, you'd have to open it within a few days or perhaps a week of it having been bottled, since after the wine rests for a few weeks more, the bottle sickness goes away and the wine tastes again as it originally did. Luckily, most wines for sale in shops and restaurants were bottled months if not years before, so the chances of encountering bottle sickness are fairly slim.

Why not one long inhale? Imagine putting a grilled steak at one end of the room, and tying up a dog at the other. The dog wouldn't take one long deep breath, but instead, would sniff rapidly and repeatedly, to maximize the impression of the aroma.

Sniffing, the corollary to swirling, creates tiny air currents in the nose that carry aroma molecules up to the nerve receptors and ultimately to the brain for interpretation.

Since the nose fatigues quickly—in about six seconds—you must try to assess the aromas in the glass immediately. This requires considerable mental focus. Although the "nose knows" and can distinguish thousands of smells, most people, when presented with many aromas, can actually name only a handful. Scientists call this the "tip of the nose phenomenon." Smell, they hypothesize, is elusive because it is the most primitive of the senses. Having evolved millions of years ago as a survival mechanism for guiding eating and sexual behavior, smell is not easily grasped by the verbal-semantic parts of the brain. If you give someone a list of multiple choices, however, their ability to name aromas improves dramatically.

There's a wine lesson in this. Rather than tasting a wine and then trying to think of what it smells like, run lists of possibilities through your mind. By suggesting ideas to yourself, you'll often have an easier time hitting upon the aroma you're searching for.

Not everything has a pronounced smell, of course. Substances such as glass and sugar, for example, are made up of molecules that do not easily volatilize, or throw off aroma molecules. However, heating a substance—forcing it to become more volatile—makes it smell stronger. Sautéed garlic, for example, has a more poignant aroma than uncooked garlic. For the same reason, a wine that is very cold may seem to have little aroma. But if you cup the glass in your hands and warm it, the aroma will appear.

Finally, the smell of a wine may be called its nose, aroma, or bouquet. Today, these words are used virtually interchangeably, although aroma and bouquet actually refer to two different things. Technically, aroma is used to describe smells associated with the grape. A young wine, for example,

# SAUERKRAUT, SKUNKS, AND SWEATY SOCKS

You bought a bottle of wine that you'd been wanting to try. The reviews were terrific and finding the wine had been difficult. Finally, the big moment arrived and you pulled the cork. What greeted you was a smell one step away from sweaty socks. What on earth had gone wrong with the wine?

Wines can develop foul odors and tastes for a wide variety of reasons ranging from the presence of offensive-smelling bacteria to overexposure to oxygen to unclean barrels. A full understanding of these aromas would require mastery of organic chemistry, but that's not our purpose here. Instead, the simple explanations below are provided for those wine drinkers who have ever encountered a wine that smelled, well, not like anything they'd want to drink. Keep in mind that the number of wines with off-putting aromas is a small fraction of the total number of wines produced each year. Also, individuals vary greatly in their sensitivities to different odors, and certain off odors can actually seem attractive when present in tiny amounts.

BANANA AROMAS:
A by-product of malolactic fermentation, a process during which malic acid, which has a sharp mouthfeel, is converted to lactic acid, which is softer. While a small amount of banana aroma and flavor is not objectionable, a signficant amount tastes odd, especially in red wines.

BAND-AID AROMAS:
One of the manifestations of *Brettanomyces* (spoilage yeasts; see Horse Blanket).

BURNING MATCH AROMAS:
A sign of excessive sulfur dioxide. Sulfur has been used as a preservative for centuries. It is used in the vineyard to protect vines from mildew and mold and in the winery to protect grapes and grape juice from oxygen, unwanted yeasts, and bacteria that may cause them to spoil. It is impossible to produce a wine entirely without sulfur dioxide since, even when it is not added by winemakers, the compound is a natural by-product of fermentation.

CANNED ASPARAGUS AROMAS:
Found most commonly in poor-quality sauvignon blancs. Often a sign that the vines were not carefully cultivated and that the grapes were picked when underripe.

DIRTY SOCK AROMAS:
Could be the result of a myriad of problems, anything from bacterial contamination to unclean barrels.

FAKE BUTTER/OILY AROMAS:
The result of excessive diacetyl, the buttery compound formed during the primary fermentation, when sugar in the grapes is converted into alcohol, and also during malolactic fermentation, when the wine's sharp tasting malic acid is converted to softer tasting lactic acid. Although a small amount of diacetyl can be attractive, a large amount tastes very offensive.

HORSE BLANKET/MANURE AROMAS:
A sign of *Brettanomyces,* sometimes called Brett, a yeast that causes wine to spoil. While many winemakers abhor even the faintest aroma of *Brettanomyces,* other winemakers find a faint suggestion of the aroma attractive. In particular, *Brettanomyces* aromas are often found in California syrahs and French red Burgundies.

MOLDY AROMAS:
Bacterial spoilage, moldy grapes, or unclean barrels can all produce a moldy aroma.

MUSTY/DANK AROMAS:
Indicates use of unclean barrels or a slight corkiness (see Wet Cardboard).

NAIL POLISH REMOVER/
PAINT THINNER AROMAS:
A sign of ethyl acetate, a harsh smelling compound that can be formed when acetic acid, a common acid in wine, combines with ethanol, the most common type of alcohol in wine.

ROTTEN EGG AROMAS:
Hydrogen sulfide, a foul-smelling gas that can be created during or at the end of fermentation, lends the odor of rotten eggs. Hydrogen sulfide can be the result of an excessive amount of sulfur applied late to grapevines, usually to prevent mildew or rot. The formation of hydrogen sulfide is exacerbated when the grape juice is deficient in nitrogen. Some varieties, such as riesling, chardonnay, and syrah, are especially vulnerable since they are low in nitrogen.

RUBBING ALCOHOL AROMAS:
Usually experienced as a hit high up in the nostrils, the aroma of rubbing alcohol indicates that the wine's alcohol is out of balance with such other compounds in the wine as its fruit and acidity. A wine that is too high in alcohol feels caustic in the mouth and is described as "hot."

SAUERKRAUT/CABBAGE WATER AROMAS:
Another possible by-product of malolactic fermentation. Alternatively, bacteria that cause wine to go bad can also create sauerkraut-like aromas.

SHERRYLIKE AROMAS:
A sign that the wine—unless it's Sherry—has been excessively exposed to oxygen. In the winery, oxidation can be minimized by careful and quick handling of both the grapes and the wine. At home, oxidation can be prevented by storing bottles on their sides so that the corks remain moist and form a tight seal with the necks of the bottles. Oxidized wines take on a brownish or burnt orange color, which is especially no-

ticeable in whites. While oxidation is a fault in most table wines, some wines, such as Sherry and tawny Port, take on their special character by controlled oxidation.

SKUNKY AROMAS:
A sign of mercaptan compounds. These horrible smelling sulfer compounds can be created after fermentation when hydrogen sulfide and other basic sulfur compounds combine to create larger compounds.

VINEGARY AROMAS:
A sign of acetic acid bacteria, which can begin to grow in wines where the fermentation is not handled properly or at any time when alcohol, oxygen, and acetic acid bacteria find themselves together.

WET CARDBOARD/SHEEP DOG AROMAS:
A sign that wine is corked, meaning that the cork and subsequently the wine have been contaminated by the compound trichloranisole, noticeable even when present in only a few parts per trillion. Though the wine and cork industries are working aggressively to combat the problem, there have been no perfect solutions. Unlike natural corks, plastic and synthetic corks do not contribute to corkiness, but many plastic and synthetic corks have unattractive aromas of their own. In addition, preliminary research indicates that wines stoppered with plastic and synthetic corks do not age as well as wines stoppered with natural corks.

*Professionals often taste wine together—a fault that one person may not detect will almost certainly be noticed by someone else.*

## THE TALE OF TASTE BUDS

⟶ ⟞⟝ ⟵

Taste buds were first detected in the nineteenth century by two German scientists, Georg Meissner and Rudolf Wagner. We now know that these buds—which are shaped like onions—each contain between fifty and one hundred taste cells. The top of each taste bud has an opening called a taste pore. When we taste something, it's because chemicals from that food have dissolved in our saliva and then come in contact with the taste cells by slipping through the taste pores. Taste buds, incidentally, can be found not only on the tongue, but on the soft palate, pharynx, larynx, and epiglottis as well.

The discovery of taste buds paved the way for the next step in taste research—determining the mechanisms by which taste cells carry out their work. From the 1940s through the 1970s, virtually every basic biology textbook—and certainly every wine book—perpetuated the myth that taste buds were grouped in the mouth according to specialty. Correspondingly, the tongue was diagramed into separate areas where certain tastes were registered: sweetness at the tip; sourness on the sides, and bitterness at the back of the mouth.

In the 1980s and 1990s, however, research at Yale University, Monell Chemical Senses Center, in Philadelphia, and the University of Connecticut, as well as elsewhere, demonstrated that the tongue map explanation of how we taste was, in fact, false. As it turns out, the map was a misinterpretation and mistranslation of research conducted in Germany at the turn of the twentieth century.

Today, leading taste researchers, such as Dr. Linda Bartoshuk of the Yale University School of Medicine, believe that taste buds are not specialized and are not grouped according to specialty. According to Bartoshuk's research, sweetness, saltiness, bitterness, and sourness can be tasted everywhere in the mouth, although they may be perceived at slightly different intensities at different sites.

can have a cherry aroma. Bouquet is the part of a wine's smell derived from its development while it was in the bottle. A mature red wine, for example, can have a complex bouquet made up of many scents that have evolved over time.

## WHAT IS TASTE?

Taken together, aroma, body, texture, and flavor comprise what we commonly experience as taste. We've already talked about smell, now let's look at the other elements.

A wine's *body* is described as light, medium, full, or some permutation in between. How do you decide? Imagine the relative weights of skim milk, whole milk, and half-and-half in your mouth. A light-bodied wine, like skim milk, slides easily down your throat. A medium-bodied wine has more viscosity, like whole milk. A full-bodied wine seems to coat your palate, like half-and-half. Body, in other words, is only about the weight of the wine. It has nothing to do with:

1. **Quality.** Full-bodied wines aren't necessarily better.

2. **Intensity of flavor.** Full-bodied wines aren't necessarily more intense in flavor. Like a great sorbet, a wine can be light and intense.

**3. Finish.** Full-bodied wines don't necessarily have flavors that last long in the mouth, what is called the wine's finish.

Closely related to body is *texture* or *mouthfeel*. A wine's mouthfeel is the tactile impression it leaves in your mouth. Fabrics are often used as metaphors. A wine can be as richly soft as flannel (an Australian shiraz for example), as seamlessly smooth as silk (a pinot noir), or as coarse and scratchy as wool (some southern French reds feel this way). It can also feel syrupy, gritty, or have any of dozens of other textures. In order to assess a wine's texture, you must roll it around in your mouth and literally feel it. Swallow too quickly and you'll miss this aspect of wine altogether.

## TASTEVINS

Silver, shallow-sided *tastevins* (tasting cups), often ridiculed as the supercilious adornment of officious sommeliers, were invented for tasting in dark cellars. The cups are more portable and less fragile than glass would be. More important, they have circular indentations in their sides that reflect candlelight across the metal base of the cup and make it possible to determine, in a dark cellar, the clarity of a wine just drawn from the barrel.

*Small silver* tastevins—*the necklace so often seen on sommeliers in the past— were originally intended for tasting small amounts of wine from barrels in a dark cellar.*

As a side note, it can be fascinating when a wine seems to go beyond mere texture and actually suggests a three-dimensional form. For example, one wine might bring to mind Arnold Schwarzenegger, another, Audrey Hepburn. In form, wine can be gargantuan, buxom, hollow, linear, airy, spherical, loose. In my wine classes, I frequently ask beginners who cannot describe a given wine to draw a picture of it. Amazingly, they often can.

*Flavor* is much more complex and difficult to describe than body and texture. We commonly describe our flavor world as being composed of four basic tastes: sweet, sour, bitter, and salty (this last one being a flavor that, as I've said, does not usually occur in wine). Scientists, however, continue to debate whether these four cover all experiences. A growing body of data suggests that taste is far more complicated than the basic four would imply. And, in fact, to these, scientists may soon add *umami* (Japanese for meaty or savory). Curiously, ancient philosophers had their own lists, which include urinous, acrid, and putrid—words that occasionally come in handy as wine descriptors, even if they aren't tastes.

For the wine taster, the basic tastes only take us so far. What's important with wine is to describe the flavors as specifically as possible, thereby increasing your chances of remembering the wine. This is easier said than done. Sometimes you taste a wine and flavorwise, absolutely nothing occurs to you. The wine just tastes like, well, wine.

One of the ways out of this frustration is to suggest flavors as well as aromas to yourself as you are tasting. In other words, as you taste, imagine as many different potential flavors and aromas as you can and then find those that fit the wine. And don't forget to hold the wine in your mouth for a few seconds. If you swallow too quickly (the way you would a bad-tasting medicine), you won't pick up much flavor at all.

When I taste wine, I find myself running the following flavors and aromas through my mind. Though some of these, like geranium or rubber boot, may seem odd—even off-putting—characteristics to find in a wine, a tiny note of flavors or aromas like these often makes a wine all the more intriguing. The following flavor/aroma schools, as I think of them, are simply the ones I use. Start here. Once you get the hang of it, you'll probably want to create categories of your own.

## Flavors and Aromas of White Wines

**Fruits:** Fresh—apple, apricot, banana, coconut, fig, grapefruit, lemon, lime, litchi, melon, dried orange peel, peach, pear, pineapple; cooked—baked apple, baked pear

**Butter and Cream:** Butter, butterscotch, caramel, cream, custard

**Vegetables:** Asparagus, bell pepper, green beans, olives

**Grains and Nuts:** Almond, biscuit, bread dough, brioche, hazelnut, roasted nut, yeast

**Spices:** Cinnamon, cloves, ginger, white pepper

**Flowers:** Gardenia, geranium, honeysuckle, rose

**Earth:** Chalk, flint, grass, hay, minerals, stone, straw

**Barrel Aromas and Flavors:** Oak, toast, vanilla

**Other Aromas and Flavors:** Honey, gasoline, rubber boot

*Sharing the fruits of one's labor with colleagues is part of the joy of winemaking.*

## THE WHITE WINE WITH FISH RULE

—◦◦◦—

The old rule "white wine with fish; red wine with meat" is based on matching body (the weight of the wine in the mouth) and color. The adage dates from the days when many white wines were light in body and whitish in color (like fish), and many red wines were weighty and, obviously, red (like meat). It is, however, the body and components of the wine—not its color—that are important in matching wine with food. Today many red wines, such as Oregon pinot noirs and northern Italian merlots, are far lighter in body than, for example, barrel-fermented and barrel-aged California and Australian chardonnays. In the 1980s many of us realized this (or at least sensed it unconsciously), abandoned the old rule, and began drinking red wine with fish and white wine with meat. By the mid-1980s top American steak houses were selling almost as much chardonnay as cabernet sauvignon.

## Flavors and Aromas of Red Wines

**Fruits:** Fresh—blackberry, black currant, blueberry, boysenberry, cherry, cranberry, dried orange peel, plum, pomegranate, raspberry, strawberry; cooked—baked blackberry, baked cherry, baked raspberry, jam, prunes

**Vegetables:** Asparagus, bell pepper, green beans, mushrooms, olives, truffle

**Chocolate and Coffee:** Bitter chocolate, cocoa, milk chocolate, mocha, coffee, espresso

**Spices and Herbs:** Black pepper, cinnamon, cloves, licorice, mint, spiced tea

**Tobacco:** Cigar box, pipe tobacco, smoke

**Flowers:** Geranium, rose, violet

**Earth:** Cedar, damp earth, dried leaves, eucalyptus, forest floor, gravel, pine, stone

**Animal:** Barnyard, horse blanket, manure, sweat

**Barrel Aromas and Flavors:** Oak, toast, vanilla

**Other Aromas and Flavors:** Cola, game, leather, tar, tea, worn boot

## GOOD WINES FINISH LAST

Suppose you were trying to determine which of two wines was the higher quality, more complex wine. You liked both wines equally well and had decided that they were both very good, even though they were different. How would you decide which one was better?

Assuming both wines were well-balanced, good examples of their kind, and generous in flavor, you would look at what is called a wine's finish. This is the extent to which a wine's aromas and flavors persist in your mouth even after you've swallowed. The better the wine, the longer the finish. All truly great wines of every varietal type have a long finish. By contrast, the flavor of, say, a jug wine disappears almost as soon as you swallow it.

You can prove it to yourself. The way to "get a finish" is by retro nasal breathing the wine (it sounds more complicated than it is). To do this: Take a sip, hold the wine in your mouth, swirl it around, and swallow it, keeping your mouth closed. With your mouth still closed, breathe out forcefully through your nose. (Make sure you swallow before breathing out or you'll be in for a dry cleaning bill.) Now notice the sensation. If the wine has a long finish, you'll still be able to taste and smell it even though you've swallowed. If it has a short finish, you'll sense very little, if any, flavor or aroma.

What retro nasal breathing does is force the wine's aromas back up through the nasal passages at the back of your throat. This allows you to get a more fully developed sense of the wine's aroma and flavor and to see how long they last. How long *can* they last? Up to a minute and occasionally even longer.

## Color, Sediment, and Crystals

Most wine books deal with color first, but in my experience, if you don't taste the wine correctly to begin with, color is somewhat beside the point. So I've chosen to place it last in this section on tasting and to include with it two other potential aspects of a wine's appearance, crystals and sediment.

The color of a wine comes from a group of pigments in grape skins called anthocyanins. Red wine is red because of the skins (the juice of red grapes is actually the same color as the juice of white grapes: clear).

The correct way to look at color is not to hold the glass up in the air, but rather to look down and across the wine-filled glass while holding it at a 45 degree angle against a white backdrop. Different grape varieties have different hues. Pinot noir makes a wine that is light vermillion. Gamay is cherry Jell-O red; zinfandel can be electric purple; nebbiolo, almost black. When an experienced taster is given an unidentified wine, color gives the first hint of which varietal is in the glass.

A common mistake is thinking that the intensity of a wine's color is related to the intensity of its flavor. Deeply red wines (like cabernet sauvignon) are not necessarily more flavorful than pale red wines (like pinot noir).

Color is also a clue to age. White and red wines behave inversely:

- **White wines** get darker as they get older.
- **Red wines** get lighter as they get older.

For white wines, clarity of color—often called limpidity—is also important. Today, improved winemaking means that virtually all white wines have clarity. A murky, cloudy white may mean the wine has problems.

For red wine, clarity is neither wholly good or bad. Many great reds have perfect clarity, others (those that have not been filtered, for example) may seem more opaque. Being opaque is not the same as having sediment. As red wine ages, color pigments in the wine combine with tannin to form long chains of molecules too heavy to stay in solution. These sometimes precipitate out, forming a sediment. Sediment is harmless.

So are potassium bitartrate crystals, more commonly called tartrates. These are the snowflakelike crystals that are sometimes found floating in white wine or sticking to the bottom of the cork. These tasteless, harmless crystals (which are the same as cream of tartar) are bits of natural tartaric acid that have precipitated out of the wine, usually because of a quick and extreme drop in temperature. This

---

### TWELVE TRUTHS WINE PROS KNOW

- A systematic approach to tasting is critical to understanding wine and being able to remember what you tasted.

- Perceptions of a wine can be skewed by outside influences as innocent as eating a bag of M&M's.

- The first sip is not always reliable.

- At least 80 percent of taste is smell.

- Swirling the wine in the glass helps you smell and therefore taste it better.

- You continue to smell a wine once it is in your mouth.

- Light, medium, and full-bodied wines feel in the mouth like skim milk, whole milk, and half-and-half, respectively.

- A full body is no guarantee of an intense flavor.

- To get the total impact of flavor, you must hold the wine in your mouth for a few seconds.

- The world's best wines all have long finishes.

- White wines get darker in color as they get older.

- Red wines get lighter as they get older.

---

can happen when, for example, you take a wine that was in a hot car and put it immediately in a very cold refrigerator.

## CHARTING FLAVOR

What can you expect once you've taken these first sips of wine? Here are some of the common ways a wine might present itself. Given the vast number that exist worldwide, however, you may encounter wines that don't fit any of the descriptions below.

**1.** Good wines begin with simple fruit flavors that expand quickly in your mouth then fade.

**2.** Slightly better wines begin with more pronounced fruit flavors that are sustained longer in your mouth.

**3.** Some above-average wines begin with exciting flavors and have long, evocative finishes. Wines at this level make you take notice of them.

**4.** Sometimes a wine begins with a bang of flavor, has a "doughnut" or hole of

little or no flavor in the middle, then finishes with an abrupt halt.

**5.** In some complex, relatively young wines, powerful layers of flavor burst open and rush over the palate in one long continuous wave.

**6.** In a complex, relatively young red, a mantle of tannin may also temporarily cover the fruit. The initial big arc is mostly a power surge of tannin, behind which the wine seems to drop off. In time, if the tannin is subdued as the wine ages, the wine will resume a long, graceful curve.

**7.** In a complex, old red wine, the initial big arc of tannin and fresh fruit is subdued. The wine is almost erotically subtle, opening with concentrated but tranquil fruit and ending with a finish that does not seem to want to end.

Winemakers can, to a degree, affect the shape and length of a wine's curve. For example, by aging a simple white wine in new oak, the winemaker can build up the front and back ends of the wine, giving it a greater impact of flavor and texture.

Blending in a different grape can also smooth out bumps and holes in a wine. Thus the flavor of one kind of red grape might be fleshed out and made more complete by blending in another red grape variety. Cabernet sauvignon and merlot, for example, enhance each other in this synergistic manner.

## THE END . . . BUT REALLY THE BEGINNING

Whether you read Mastering Wine in its entirety or flipped back and forth between sections, I want you to know that you've just finished what I think is the most important part of *The Wine Bible*. I knew when I wrote Master-

ing Wine that many readers might breeze by it and get right to the juicy parts of France or Italy. But the truth is that a really intimate knowledge of anything necessarily begins with the fundamentals of that thing. With wine, I'd even go one step further and say that the capacity for pleasure—the capacity to be thrilled by wine—is ineluctably tied to understanding it in all its most basic naked details. Anyone can drink good wines and anyone wealthy enough can drink rare, superexpensive wines. But without knowledge, the soulful, satisfying part of the experience is lost. All of this is by way of saying, Bravo! You did it. This may be the last section of Mastering Wine, but it's the beginning of many delicious things to come.

And now for the world of wine . . .

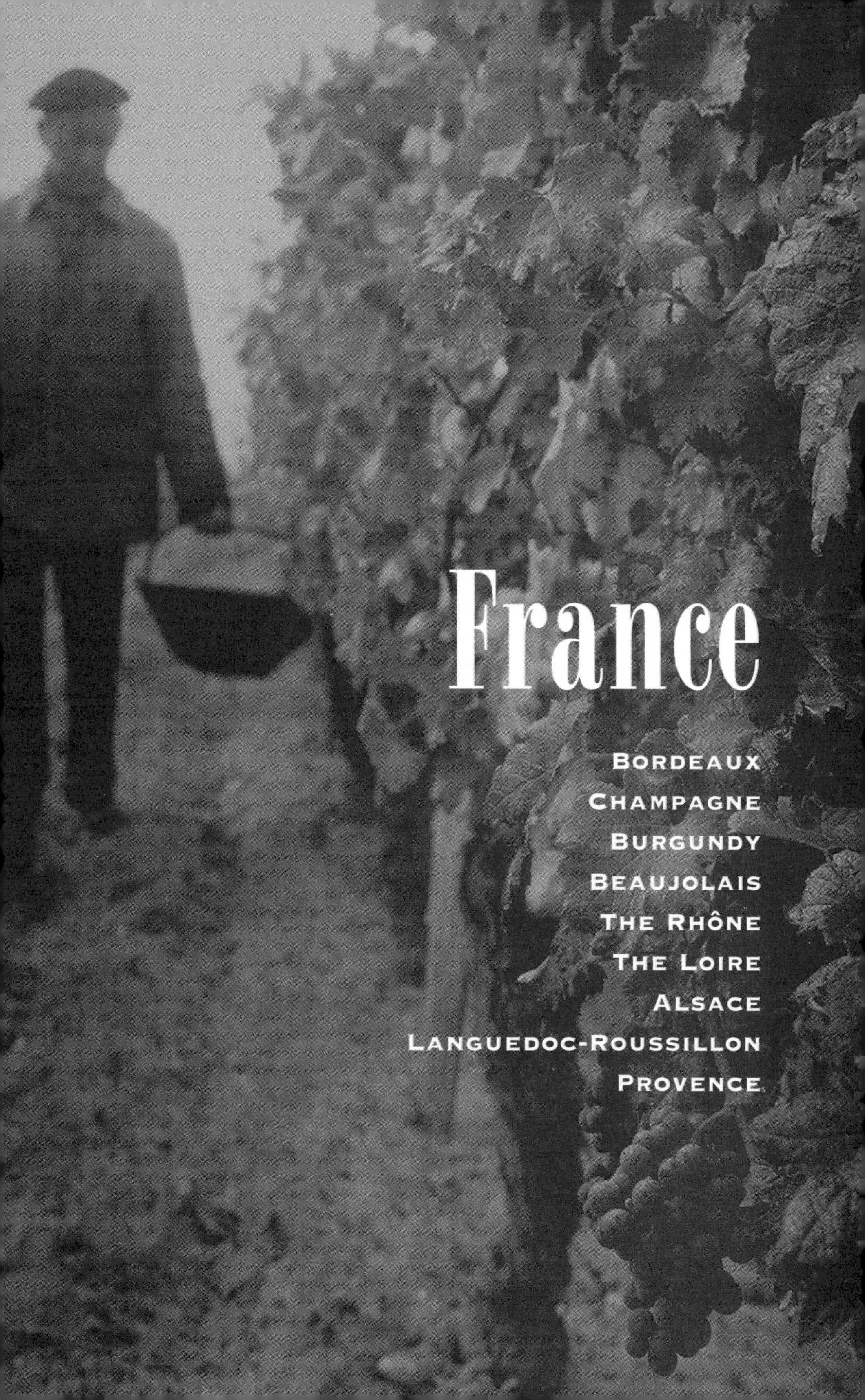

# France

BORDEAUX
CHAMPAGNE
BURGUNDY
BEAUJOLAIS
THE RHÔNE
THE LOIRE
ALSACE
LANGUEDOC-ROUSSILLON
PROVENCE

*Laissez le vin de se faire:*
*Let the wine make itself.*
—*Burgundian saying*

France produces more *fine* wines than any other country in the world. This fact alone has elevated some French wines to almost mythic status. Indeed, French winemaking techniques, viticultural practices, even French grape varieties have been adopted by wine regions around the world. Like French food, French wine has been (and largely remains) the benchmark against which greatness elsewhere is judged.

But France's impact extends even further. The country has molded the very way we think about great wine. It was in France that the fundamental concept of *terroir* (the idea that the site determines the quality of the wine) became pervasive and flourished. Traditionally the French have been so convinced that nature and geography make the wine that there has never been a French word for winemaker. Instead, the term commonly used, *vigneron*, portrays man's role as more humble. *Vigneron* means grape grower.

France's near obsession with geography (plus numerous episodes of wine fraud) resulted, in the 1930s, in the development of a detailed system of regulations known as the *Appellation d'Origine Contrôlée* (AOC). This system designated those places where today most of the best wines in France are made and then went on to define how those wines must be made. Given the emphasis on

place of origin, most AOC wines are logically known by their geographic names (Sancerre, Côte-Rôtie, Volnay, and so on), not by the names of the grape varieties from which they were made (see France's Wine Laws, page 116).

Luckily for the French, their homeland is blessed with numerous locations in which fine wines can be made. The first of these areas was established by the Greeks in 600 B.C. at Massalia, now Marseilles. From there, with Greek and later Roman

| KEY TO FRANCE'S WINE REGIONS | |
|---|---|
| **CHAMPAGNE** | **THE RHONE** |
| **ALSACE** | **NORTHERN** |
| **THE LOIRE** | 11 Côte-Rotie |
| **MUSCADET** | 12 Château-Grillet |
| **ANJOU-SAUMUR** | 13 Condrieu |
|  | 14 St. Joseph |
| 1 Savennières | 15 Crozes-Hermitage |
| 2 Quarts de Chaume | 16 Hermitage |
| 3 Coteaux de l'Aubance | 17 Cornas |
| 4 Bonnezeaux | |
| 5 Coteaux du Layon | **SOUTHERN** |
|  | 18 Gigondas |
| **TOURAINE** | 19 Vacqueyras |
| 6 St.-Nicholas-de- | 20 Beaumes-de-Venise |
| Bourgueil | 21 Châteauneuf-du-Pape |
| 7 Bourgueil | 22 Tavel |
| 8 Vouvray | **LANGUEDOC-** |
| 9 Montlouis | **ROUSSILLON** |
| 10 Chinon | 23 Faugères |
| **SANCERRE** | 24 St.-Chinian |
| **POUILLY-FUMÉ** | 25 Frontignan |
| **MENETOU-SALON** | 26 Minervois |
| **QUINCY** | 27 Corbières |
| **REUILLY** | 28 Rivesaltes |
|  | 29 Banyuls |
| **BURGUNDY** | |
| *(see page 189 for* | **PROVENCE** |
| *detailed map)* | 30 Coteaux d'Aix-en- |
|  | Provence |
| **BORDEAUX** | 31 Côtes de Provence |
| *(see page 119 for* | 32 Cassis |
| *detailed map)* | 33 Bandol |

GREAT
BRITAIN

*English Channel*

Strait of Dover

NETHERLANDS

GERMANY

BELGIUM

Roubaix

LUXEMBOURG

*Guernsey* *Sark*
*Channel
Islands
(Br.)* *Jersey*
*Gulf of
Saint-Malo*

Lille

NORD-
PAS-DE-
CALAIS

Le Havre

Amiens

*Somme*

PICARDIE

*Aisne R.*

Reims

*Oise R.*

Epernay

CHAMPAGNE

Metz

LORRAINE

Nancy

Strasbourg

ALSACE

Colmar

*Vosges Mts.*

*Meuse River*

HAUTE-
NORMANDIE

Rouen

*Seine R.*

Caen

BASSE-NORMANDIE

*Orne B.*

Paris

ILE-DE-
FRANCE

NORMANDY

*Marne River*

CHAMPAGNE-
ARDENNE

BRETAGNE

Rennes

*Vilaine River*

*Rance R.*

*Moselle R.*

*Ill R.*

*Rhine R.*

FRANCHE-
COMTÉ

Besançon

SWITZERLAND

L. Geneva

Le Mans

PAYS DE LA LOIRE

Orléans

*Yonne R.*

Dijon

BOURGOGNE

Beaune

*Aube R.*

*Loire R.*

THE LOIRE

Angers

**7** TOURAINE

**6**

**8**

Tours

SANCERRE
MENETOU-
SALON

Pouilly-Fumé

BURGUNDY

*Ile d'Yeu*

Nantes

**1**

**2**

**3**

Saumur

**9**

QUINCY
REUILLY

*Allier River*

Mâcon

*Saône River*

*JURA*

*Ile de Ré*

**4** **5** **10** Chinon

ANJOU-
SAUMUR

MUSCADET

*Vienne River*

CENTRE

RHONE-ALPES

**11**

Lyon

*Ile d'Oléron*

POITOU-
CHARENTES

LIMOUSIN

**12**

**13**

**14** **15**

**16**

COGNAC

Limoges

Clermont-
Ferrand

AUVERGNE

St.-
Etienne

Grenoble

*Isère River*

**17**

Valence

*ALPS*

Cognac

Jarnac

*Charente R.*

*Gironde*

Blaye

BORDEAUX

Bergerac

*Dordogne River*

THE RHONE

ITALY

*Bay
of
Biscay*

Bordeaux

Monbazillac

Duras

*Garonne River*

*Lot River*

Cahors

*Massif
Central*

*CÉVENNES*

Nyons

**19** **18**
**20**

**21**

PROVENCE-ALPES-
COTE-D'AZUR

AQUITAINE

ARMAGNAC

Condom

Auch

MIDI-PYRENEES

**22**

Nîmes

Avignon

*Rhône River*

*Durance River*

Nice

Toulouse

**23**

Montpellier

PROVENCE

**30**

Aix-en-Provence

**31**

Cannes

*St.-Tropez*

*PYRENEES*

Limoux

**24** **25**

**26**

**27**

Béziers

*Gulf of
Lion*

Marseille

**32**

Bandol

**33**

Toulon

**28**

Perpignan

LANGUEDOC-
ROUSSILLON

**29**

ANDORRA

SPAIN

*Mediterranean
Sea*

France ranks second
among wine-producing
countries worldwide.
The French drink an
average of 16.4 gal-
lons of wine per person
each year; only the
people of Luxembourg
drink more.

N

0        50        100 mi
0    50    100 km

© MapQuest.com

*Mediterranean
Sea*

Bastia

*CORSICA
CORSE*

Ajaccio

## FRANCE'S NATIONAL TREASURES

———

The French take their food and wine very seriously. For one week each year, French schoolchildren, under the auspices of the Ministry of Culture, go on field trips to three-star restaurants in order to taste foie gras, Bresse chickens, Roquefort cheese, and other famous French products, including, sometimes, wines.

help, viticulture spread throughout what is now southern France. Indeed, Provence gets its name from the Romans, who called it *nostra provincia*—our province. However, by the fifth century A.D., with the collapse of the Roman Empire, the vineyards of France increasingly fell under the control of the Catholic church. In particular, such powerful monastic orders as the Benedictines painstakingly and systematically planted vineyard after vineyard until vines stretched beyond Paris. To the ancient Greeks this would have been a startling achievement, for the wisdom of antiquity held that grapevines would survive only as far north as olive and fig trees grew.

Perhaps the most dramatic period in France's wine history is the era it would most like to forget. Sometime between 1860 and 1866, the deadly, root-eating phylloxera arrived from America. The subsequent epidemic it unleashed is thought to have begun in the southern Rhône Valley. From there, the microscopic aphid spread throughout the country, throughout Europe, and eventually throughout much of the world (see page 24).

*In France, food and wine are officially recognized as national cultural treasures. When it comes to enjoying both, rushing is unheard of. The French think nothing of sitting for hours in a café while sharing some wine and conversation.*

The French are a proud, individualistic people. Many of them spend their entire lives drinking wine from their local area alone. (The word *chauvinism*, perhaps not surprisingly, comes from the French.) It seems rather ironic that, in an otherwise sophisticated country, you find Burgundians who have never tasted Bordeaux or Bordelais who have never tasted a wine from Alsace. And it's not as though France is that big; the whole country would fit inside Texas. Nonetheless, even at that size, France, with more than 2.2 million acres planted with grapevines, produces more wine than any other country except Italy.

Climatically and geographically, France can be thought of as being divided into three parts. In the north, such regions as Champagne and Burgundy have a continental climate, with severe winters and cool, often rainy falls, meaning that grapes may not fully ripen and thus produce wines that can be delicate, even fragile. By comparison, southern France has a Mediterranean climate. Achieving ripeness presents little problem, and the wines are fleshier, fuller, more "sunny" in the mouth. Lastly, on the Atlantic coast the wine regions of Bordeaux and the western Loire have a maritime climate. Here the Gulf Stream tempers what might otherwise be too harsh an environment, but again, rain and humidity can present problems. There are some silver linings. Bordeaux's muggy summers, for example, make the great sweet wine Sauternes possible.

About 90 percent of French wine is based on thirty-six grapes. The wines made from these varieties span the full gamut from dry to sweet, from still to sparkling. And in addition to wine, of course, two of the world's most famous grape-based spirits are French: Cognac and Armagnac (see page 157 and page 228, respectively).

Notwithstanding the worldwide prestige of several French white wines, about two thirds of the country's wine production is red. Walk into any restaurant or wine bar and it's clear that red wine is also, by far, what the French prefer to drink. More than two thirds of all wine sales are red, although in the summer copious amounts of rosé are tossed down (slightly more rosé wine is sold than white).

## SEPARATING THE GREAT FROM THE NOT SO GREAT

More than any other country in the world, France loves to rate her vineyards and her wines. Several of the major French wine regions have their own powerful and often complex classification systems that rank vineyards and/or wines. Bordeaux alone has four separate regional classification systems. Though the classifications are controversial and the rankings are usually fiercely debated, no one in France, it seems, thinks of doing away with them.

Unlike the wines of most other European countries, French wine is known in virtually every corner of the globe. A thirsty traveler in Fiji, Nairobi, or Taipei can usually hunt down a bottle of Champagne, even when all other wine possibilities seem exhausted. Of course, the quality of French wine accounts for a good measure of its appeal, but so do various historic and geographic considerations. France was the first European country to develop significant international trade for its wines. This was possible thanks to the proximity of most

French wine regions to large navigable rivers. As early as the twelfth century, Bordeaux wines were being shipped down the Gironde River and out to sea headed for England and Scotland.

But France has given the world more than just her wine. From the seventeenth to the nineteenth centuries, as the New World began to take shape, French vine cuttings—often from revered estates and châteaux—were shipped, smuggled, or lugged in suitcases to South Africa, South America, and North America. For the settlers of those territories, including our own, French vines held out the hope that one day they too might bring into the world a great wine.

We'll look at France's most important wine regions in the order that, I believe, reflects their importance and prestige, although Bordeaux, Champagne, and Burgundy could arguably all be first in line.

# FRANCE'S WINE LAWS

Maybe you'd like to pour yourself a glass of wine—French, of course—and get comfortable before we start in on this. French wine laws are a bit complicated. In 1935 the Institut National des Appellations d'Origine (INAO) was created with the mission of setting up the French *Appellation d'Origine Contrôlée* (AOC) system. Today the AOC system is still administered and periodically revised by the INAO. The system sets standards for specific categories of wine as well as various foods, including Grenoble walnuts, Bresse chickens, Isigny butter, Nyons olive oil, and Brie, Cantal, Roquefort, and Reblochon cheeses. While the system has become a model for wine-producing countries around the world, it

has also been criticized for being too rigid and a major barrier to creativity.

Here's what you need to know—under the AOC system, the three main categories of wine are in descending order of quality:

## VINS D'APPELLATION D'ORIGINE CONTRÔLÉE

The category Vins d'Appellation d'Origine Contrôlée—AOC—includes the finest wines of France. Each wine must abide by a strict set of regulations. These cover:

*Area of Production:* Each area is precisely defined. Only wines made from vines growing within the borders of the appellation have the right to use that appellation.

*Variety of Grape:* Each area has permissible grape varieties, which may be used only in given proportions. If a producer makes wine from grapes other than those permitted or uses a ratio of grapes that is not permitted, he or she must forfeit the appellation.

*Yield per Hectare:* The basic yield allowed is set, though in some years it may be increased. In Bordeaux, for example, the yield permitted for red wine is 55 hectoliters per hectare, or 1,452 gallons of wine for every 2.47 acres. The legal yield for white wine is slightly higher.

*Vineyard Practices:* How and when the vines can be pruned, the type of trellising system, and whether the use of irrigation is permitted are regulated.

*Degree of Alcohol:* All AOC wines have a minimum level of alcohol content and some have a maximum level.

*Winemaking Practices:* Winemaking practices, such as chaptalization (see page 47) are regulated, as are, in some cases, aging requirements.

## READING A FRENCH WINE LABEL

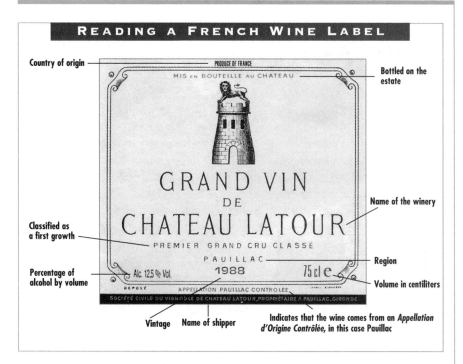

Country of origin — PRODUCE OF FRANCE

MIS EN BOUTEILLE AU CHATEAU — Bottled on the estate

GRAND VIN

DE

Name of the winery

Classified as a first growth — CHATEAU LATOUR

PREMIER GRAND CRU CLASSÉ

PAUILLAC — Region

Percentage of alcohol by volume — Alc. 12.5 % Vol. 1988 75 cl e

Volume in centiliters

DÉPOSÉ APPELLATION PAUILLAC CONTROLEE

SOCIÉTÉ CIVILE DU VIGNOBLE DE CHATEAU LATOUR, PROPRIÉTAIRE À PAUILLAC, GIRONDE

Vintage    Name of shipper

Indicates that the wine comes from an *Appellation d'Origine Contrôlée*, in this case Pauillac

*Tasting and Analysis:* All AOC wines must go through a chemical analysis and pass a taste test for typicity—that is, they must taste true to their kind. Those wines that fail must be declassified.

*Varietal Labeling:* The laws governing varietal labeling are beginning to change, but in general, putting the name of the grape variety on the label is forbidden unless the producer has been given special permission. This law does not apply in areas, such as Alsace, where varietal labeling is traditional. In some areas if producers choose to use the name of the grape variety, they must forfeit the right to use any appellation except the most basic one. For example, if a Burgundian producer with a vineyard in Pouilly-Fuissé wants to put chardonnay on his label, he can but he forfeits the right to use the appel-

lation Pouilly-Fuissé and instead must declassify the wine to the most basic appellation, Bourgogne Blanc.

### VINS DÉLIMITÉS DE QUALITÉ SUPÉRIEURE

The group of wines in the category Vins Délimités de Qualité Supérieure—VDQS—falls slightly below those of the AOC in quality. Yields may be higher and alcohol levels may be lower.

### VINS DE PAYS

France's so-called country wines—*vins de pays*—are defined by region. Like AOC wines, they must meet certain rules, though these rules are usually far less strict than for AOC wines. Permissible yields are higher, and the rules concerning grape varieties are more flexible. You can nonetheless find *vins de pays* that are very drinkable, and one region—the Languedoc-Roussillon—is famous for them as you'll see.

# Bordeaux

Bordeaux—the word alone fires the mind with the anticipation of greatness. No other wine region is more powerful, more commercially clever, or more important as a source of profoundly complex, ageworthy wines. The challenge is to comprehend it all, for Bordeaux is the largest fine-wine vineyard on the globe. This single region covers more territory than all of the vineyard areas of Germany put together and is ten times larger than the vineyard acreage of New Zealand. In Bordeaux some 15,000 growers and dozens of top-class estates—plus thousands more of lesser standing—produce a daunting 700 million bottles of wine every year, including many of the priciest wines in the world.

Just about halfway between the North Pole and the equator, Bordeaux lies along the path of three important rivers—the mighty Gironde, plus the two rivers that feed it, the Dordogne and the Garonne. To the immediate west is the Atlantic Ocean, and everywhere the region is crisscrossed by small streams. As we shall see, all of this water plays a critical role in shaping this region and ultimately the wines it produces.

Both literally and psychologically, Bordeaux is a red-wine region. More than 80 percent of the wine made is red. Five red grapes are used and they are almost always blended together. The two most important grapes are merlot and cabernet sauvignon. The range of red Bordeaux is

*The Place de la Bourse (the Bourse is France's stock exchange) in Bordeaux, France's fifth largest city. Having a commercially successful major city in their midst has helped Bordeaux's wine regions thrive.*

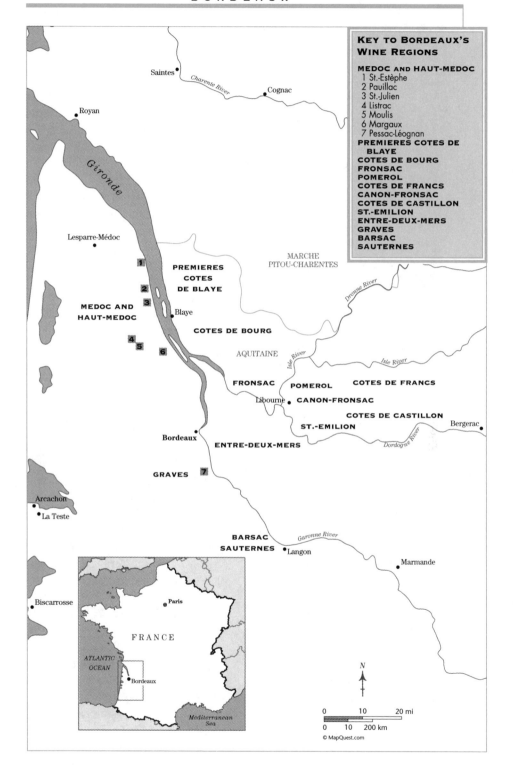

BORDEAUX

**KEY TO BORDEAUX'S WINE REGIONS**

**MEDOC AND HAUT-MEDOC**
1 St.-Estèphe
2 Pauillac
3 St.-Julien
4 Listrac
5 Moulis
6 Margaux
7 Pessac-Léognan
**PREMIERES COTES DE BLAYE**
**COTES DE BOURG**
**FRONSAC**
**POMEROL**
**COTES DE FRANCS**
**CANON-FRONSAC**
**COTES DE CASTILLON**
**ST.-EMILION**
**ENTRE-DEUX-MERS**
**GRAVES**
**BARSAC**
**SAUTERNES**

Saintes

*Charente River*

Cognac

Royan

*Gironde*

Lesparre-Médoc

MARCHE
PITOU-CHARENTES

**1**

**PREMIERES COTES DE BLAYE**

*Dronne River*

**2**

**3**

**MEDOC AND HAUT-MEDOC**

Blaye

**COTES DE BOURG**

**4 5**

**6**

AQUITAINE

*Isle River*

*Isle River*

**FRONSAC**

**POMEROL**

**COTES DE FRANCS**

Libourne

**CANON-FRONSAC**

**COTES DE CASTILLON**

Bergerac

**ST.-EMILION**

Bordeaux

**ENTRE-DEUX-MERS**

*Dordogne River*

**GRAVES**

**7**

Arcachon

La Teste

**BARSAC**

*Garonne River*

**SAUTERNES**

Langon

Marmande

Biscarrosse

Paris

FRANCE

ATLANTIC
OCEAN

Bordeaux

Mediterranean
Sea

N

0    10    20 mi
0    10    200 km

© MapQuest.com

## THE QUICK SIP ON BORDEAUX

• Although the very top Bordeaux wines are renowned worldwide, these constitute but a small percentage of the region's total output. Most Bordeaux are neither famous nor expensive but, instead, are good, every-night dinner wines.

• Bordeaux wines are about elegance and intensity of flavor; they are rarely massive or powerful.

• Both red and white Bordeaux are almost always blends of two or more varieties. In Bordeaux blending is used to achieve more complex flavors.

astounding. At the most basic level there are scores of utterly simple Bordeaux, such as Mouton Cadet, one of the most well-known wine brands in the world, even if it is pretty innocuous. At the most rarefied level, however, the famous Bordeaux we all hear about can be the apotheosis of refinement.

Monumental wines, of course, do not happen everywhere. Given the vast and variable climatic and geologic forces that must come together to make a wine what it is, why is it that so many Bordeaux are considered great? When you ask Bordelais winemakers that question, chances are they will answer with a single word: *terroir*. The most renowned Bordeaux wines—wines such as Château Latour, Château Margaux, Château Pétrus, Château Cheval Blanc, Château Haut-Brion, and so on—are said to be wines of *terroir*, that is, they derive their characters from singular plots of land. In addition, such wines are usually made with state-of-the-art equipment, the latest technology, and new oak barrels each year.

Bordeaux's famous wines represent just a small fraction of all of the Bordeaux produced. Most Bordeaux wines are *not* wines of *terroir* nor are they made by ultraexpensive means. Rather, the vast majority are modest dinner wines. Wines labeled simply Bordeaux or Bordeaux Supérieur fall into this category. Still, when most of us think about Bordeaux, we are in fact imagining those wines at the top, the cream of the crop. The complexity of these Bordeaux is often what most amazes wine drinkers. To an almost mesmerizing degree, a first-rate Bordeaux lures you back over and over again, each time revealing something new. This phenomenon has, over centuries, established the very best Bordeaux as among the most prized wines in the world.

# THE LAND, THE GRAPES, AND THE VINEYARDS

As I've said, Bordeaux's vineyards are all in close proximity to large bodies of water. In addition to the three major rivers that dominate the region, the huge Gironde plus the two smaller but still substantial rivers, the Dordogne and Garonne, the Atlantic Ocean itself is only a one hour drive away. These nearby waterways are partially responsible for Bordeaux's early success. As of the thirteenth and fourteenth centuries, barges would dock along the wharves of the Gironde, ever ready to ferry wine to and fro between merchants and ultimately to ships headed for England. This, at a time when most other wine regions in France were relatively unknown beyond their own borders.

Most important, the rivers and adjacent sea (warmed by the Gulf Stream) act to temper the region's climate, thereby providing the vineyards with a milder and more stable environment than would otherwise be the case. In addition, Bordeaux is edged on the south and west by vast pine forests that also help to shield the region from extreme weather. Were it not for the maritime climate and the presence of these forests, Bordeaux's vineyards would be at even greater risk of damage by severe cold snaps, potentially devastating frosts, and/or summer storms.

*The name Bordeaux derives from*
au bord de l'eau,
*meaning along the waters.*

Sometimes, of course, the proximity to water and the protection afforded by forests isn't enough. In April of 1991 Bordeaux was whipped by a terrible frost that left the vineyards bedraggled and dotted with frostbitten bald spots a quarter mile wide. In some areas 80 percent of the grapes were destroyed. In a year like this the quantity of Bordeaux can plummet, though the quality—surprisingly enough—may still be good. It all depends on the character of the growing season as a whole plus, of course, the skill of the winemaker.

Many of the vineyards of Bordeaux—and especially of the Médoc, including Margaux, Pauillac, St.-Emilion, and St.-Estèphe—appear quite flat. And they are, if one compares them to, say, the steeply sloped vineyards of the northern Rhône, those of northern Portugal, or most precipitous of all, the vineyards of Germany's Mosel region. The vineyards of the Médoc are spread over gentle hillocks. In Pomerol and St.-Emilion these hills sometimes rise and fall a bit more. The variations in topography, combined with the specific composition of the soil, create multiple drainage

## THE GRAPES OF
# BORDEAUX

### WHITES

**Muscadelle:** A minor grape sometimes incorporated into blends for its light floral character.

**Sauvignon Blanc:** Major grape. Crisp, austere, lively. Has an herbal freshness. Usually blended with sémillon.

**Sémillon:** Major grape. Dry and clean. Provides weight and depth. Usually blended with sauvignon blanc. The primary grape for Sauternes.

**Ugni Blanc:** A neutral blending grape used for the most part in inexpensive white wines.

### REDS

**Cabernet Franc:** A minor grape, but used in most blends. Valuable for the violet and spice aromas it can contribute.

**Cabernet Sauvignon:** Major grape. Highly structured, intense, and deeply flavored. The racehorse.

**Malbec:** A minor grape, used in blends in very small amounts if at all. Contributes a soft character.

**Merlot:** A major grape and the most widely planted one. Round and supple. The flesh on cabernet sauvignon's bones.

**Petit Verdot:** A minor grape used, like malbec, in very small amounts if at all. Helps add alcohol and backbone.

patterns. And drainage is key. The best vineyards tend to be on well-drained soil of gravel and stone. In the Médoc these deep gravel beds are frequently near the Gironde River. An old Bordeaux saying has it that the best vineyards "can see the river," and not surprisingly, if you stand in the middle of the vines at Château Latour, at Château Pichon Longueville Comtesse de Lalande, or at many of the other top estates, you can indeed watch the boats moving up and down the Gironde.

It was precisely such gravelly soil that gave Graves its name. Graves (pronounced grahv), one of the important subregions within Bordeaux, produces wines that at their pinnacle evoke the subtle aroma and flavor of the gravel and stones from which they come.

If the gods had been generous, every square inch of Bordeaux would have been gravel and stone. Unfortunately they were not, and it is not. The soil of many vineyards includes clay. Since water drains poorly from clay, this is usually not ideal. But, as we know, in the world of wine, no one factor can be considered out of relationship to all others. A good slope can even generally improve the drainage of a clay-based vineyard.

By law, red Bordeaux wines must be made from one or more of five red grapes: merlot, cabernet sauvignon, cabernet franc, petit verdot, and malbec. Merlot, the most widely planted of these, is often described in Bordeaux as fleshy and round. Cabernet sauvignon, by comparison, is frequently credited with giving red Bordeaux

*An urn depicting Bacchus at Château Margaux.*

its structure. Structure, which can be thought of as the architecture or framework of the wine, comes principally from tannin, and tannin is something cabernet sauvignon has in spades. Tannin also acts as a preservative in wine, which is why so many top Bordeaux can be aged for such long periods of time. Together, merlot and cabernet sauvignon make up the lion's share of most red Bordeaux.

Cabernet franc, petit verdot, and malbec all play a much smaller role. In a Bordeaux blend they are the seasonings. Of the three, cabernet franc is the most well regarded for the enticing violet aroma it can contribute.

## HONEY WAITING TO HAPPEN

Sémillon is the leading grape in Sauternes, Bordeaux's famous sweet wine, in part because it's very susceptible to *Botrytis cinerea,* the beneficial mold (fondly called noble rot) that must envelope the grapes for Sauternes to be produced. But sémillon, when aged, is also prone to developing a rich honeyed flavor, a fitting characteristic for Sauternes.

For white Bordeaux wines, four grapes are permitted: sémillon, sauvignon blanc, muscadelle, and ugni blanc. Sémillon, considered the soul of white Bordeaux, is the most widely planted. With age, sémillon takes on a wonderful honey flavor and a creamy, almost lanolinlike texture.

Sémillon is typically blended with sauvignon blanc, a wine that is its complete opposite. While sémillon is usually creamy, sauvignon blanc virtually vibrates with

*The close spacing of vines in Bordeaux has necessitated small tractors that straddle the vines, rather than travel between rows. Some work, however, continues to be done by hand.*

zesty acidity. The root of the word *sauvignon* is *sauvage* (wild, as in wild vigorous growth). Even the flavor of sauvignon blanc can seem untamed, with a wild herb tilt to it. Only a few top white Bordeaux are exclusively sauvignon blanc, notably Pavillon Blanc from Château Margaux. As for muscadelle and ugni blanc, the first provides floral hints; the latter is pretty neutral and used almost exclusively in very inexpensive white Bordeaux.

Over generations, these nine grapes have not only proved themselves well suited to Bordeaux's climate but they also have been found to enhance one another when blended (not all grapes do). The fact that nine grape varieties are planted in Bordeaux makes the practice and philosophy of winemaking extremely different from that in Burgundy, Bordeaux's northern neighbor and rival, where there is just one leading red grape, pinot noir, and one white, chardonnay. For the Bordelais winemaker blending is critical; it is one of the methods by which complexity in wine is achieved.

The grapes of Bordeaux were not arrived at solely because they create good flavor synergy, however. Equally important was the fact that they ripen at different times. In Bordeaux's rain- and frost-prone climate, planting several grape varieties was one of the ways growers could mini-mize the risk of losing entire crops to bad weather. According to the English wine writer David Peppercorn in his comprehensive book *Bordeaux*, the process of matching grape to ground occurred most rapidly during the last two centuries. As of 1784 thirty-four red varieties and twenty-nine white varieties could still be found in parts of St.-Emilion and Pomerol.

# MAKING BORDEAUX

In the last decades of the twentieth century, winemaking changed considerably in Bordeaux. For white wine, the changes were monumental. Great white wine, more fragile and less structured than red, is extremely sensitive to every element of its creation: the precise moment of the harvest, the conditions under which the grapes are picked, the length of time the juice is in contact with the skins, the temperature at which the wine is fermented, and crucially, whether or not the wine is fermented and/or aged in small oak barrels. In Bordeaux, wide-

123

## BORDEAUX

**LEADING APPELLATIONS**

**Barsac** white (dry and sweet)

**Graves** white and red

**Margaux\*** red

**Pauillac\*** red

**Pessac-Léognan** white and red

**Pomerol** red

**St.-Emilion** red

**St.-Estèphe\*** red

**St.-Julien\*** red

**Sauternes** white (dry and sweet)

**APPELLATIONS OF NOTE**

**Canon-Fronsac** red

**Côtes de Bourg** red

**Côtes de Castillon** red

**Côtes de Francs** red

**Entre-Deux-Mers** white

**Fronsac** red

**Listrac\*** red

**Moulis\*** red

**Premières Côtes de Blaye** red

*\*These appellations are within the region known as Haut-Médoc, itself within an even larger region called the Médoc. See Bordeaux's Subregions, on opposite page.*

One of the most important advances was a new understanding of what it meant for a grape to be ripe. In the past in Bordeaux (and everywhere else in the world) grapes were picked when the sugars in them reached a certain density. By the 1980s, however, all of the top Bordeaux estates had begun to pick based not just on sugar ripeness but on a new concept called tannin ripeness. Although the ripeness of tannin is difficult to quantify scientifically, winemakers can, by repeatedly tasting the grapes, sense when the tannin in them is mature and when it is immature, or "green." Since a wine with green tannin usually tastes bitter and hard edged (even after aging), the new focus on ripeness of tannin was pivotal. It has, in short, led to more supple-tasting wines that additionally seem to age more smoothly.

Bordeaux was also the first wine region to implement advanced—and often controversial—techniques for concentrating a wine's flavor, body, and, in the case of sweet wines, sweetness. Among these techniques is one called reverse osmosis, an expensive process used by the very top châteaux for red wine. Essentially the wine is passed under pressure through a membrane that separates water molecules from alcohol. By then removing some of the water, a more densely concentrated wine can be made. Depending on who you talk to, altering the concentration and body of a wine by removing water from it is either cheating or a smart business practice. If nothing else, using reverse osmosis would seem inconsistent with the philosophy that *terroir* makes the wine. The châteaux owners who use the technique, however, defend it, maintaining that the end (denser wine) justifies the means.

spread changes in these methods have resulted in fresher, creamier, richer, more deeply flavored white wines.

As far as red winemaking is concerned, Bordeaux is a mecca of sophistication. From the mid-1970s onward, repeated advances led to wines that are less harshly tannic, easier to drink at a younger age, and yet still capable of aging.

# BORDEAUX'S SUBREGIONS

Bordeaux is divided into multiple smaller subregions. I've listed below the ones I consider most important; you'll find sections on each of these in this chapter. Keep in mind, however, that Bordeaux has many less well known subregions from which come numerous delicious wines that represent good value. These include Listrac and Moulis, Entre-Deux-Mers, Fronsac and Canon-Fronsac, and the outlying districts known collectively as the Côtes. We'll look at each of these though in less detail, later.

Starting on the left bank of the Gironde River and then moving southward in a big U to end on the right bank, the most important subregions are:

- **Médoc** and **Haut-Médoc:** together referred to as the Médoc. Inside the Haut-Médoc are six communes— even smaller appellations. Four are famous. Starting from the city of Bordeaux and going northwest along the Gironde River toward the Atlantic Ocean, they are: Margaux, St.-Julien, Pauillac, and St.-Estèphe.
- **Graves:** Inside Graves is one famous smaller appellation, Pessac-Léognan.
- **Sauternes** and **Barsac**
- **St.-Emilion**
- **Pomerol**

Generally speaking, the smaller the appellation, the finer the wine. Think of appellations as a series of progressively smaller boxes, one within the next. The biggest box of all is the appellation Bordeaux. A wine labeled simply as Bordeaux can be made from grapes grown any place in Bordeaux, and it will almost always be a very basic wine.

Within Bordeaux, however, a somewhat better wine might come from the smaller appellation Haut-Médoc. Even better still will be wines from a smaller prestigious appellation within the Haut-Médoc, such as Pauillac or Margaux. Let's use Château Mouton-Rothschild as an example. Mouton-Rothschild is:

- A Bordeaux and more specifically,
- An Haut-Médoc and even more specifically,
- A Pauillac (which is what will appear on the label as the wine's appellation).

In the past Bordeaux's different regional appellations were a tip-off to flavor and texture. For example, the wines of Pauillac, as a group, shared certain characteristics of soil and climate that made them taste different from Pomerol wines. Though this is still somewhat true today, distinctions among the regions have been largely blurred by modern winemaking.

*Since 1946, Château Mouton-Rothschild has commissioned a different artist every year to design the label for that year's vintage. This label, by the Danish artist Per Kirkeby, depicts a giant glass overflowing with dark red wine. It was created for the 1992 Mouton-Rothschild.*

A look at each appellation will follow. But first, let's look at how Bordeaux wines are classified.

# THE
# CLASSIFICATIONS

F asten your seat belt. Bordeaux is a baffling amalgam of regional classifications that can seem insanely complicated. To begin with, the classifications are different from one region to the next, even though the terms used may be the same or similar. Thus the words *Grand Cru Classé* mean one thing in St.-Emilion, nothing at all a few miles away in Pomerol, and in Graves a similar-sounding designation, *Cru Classé*, means something different yet again.

Just what are the classifications referring to? Two of the most important—those that apply in the Médoc and in Graves—are based on the estate not on the land. Thus, when a famous grand château in either of these regions buys a neighboring lesser château, the lesser château could be elevated to the higher rank. This is quite at odds with the Bordeaux philosophy that *terroir* makes the wine, but it is nonetheless the way the Médoc and Graves classifications are legally structured.

The classification of the Médoc was the first and remains the most famous classification. It occurred in 1855 and is called, logically enough, the 1855 Classification. It ranked sixty top châteaux in the Médoc, plus one, Château Haut-Brion, in Graves. The châteaux were categorized as *Premier Cru*, or First Growth,

*Deuxième Cru*, or Second Growth, and so on, down to *Cinquième Cru*, or Fifth Growth.

*In Bordeaux, the French word* cru, *or growth, is used to indicate a wine estate, vineyard, or* château. *Thus a* Premier Cru, *or First Growth, is a wine estate of the top (first) rank.*

The châteaux of Sauternes and Barsac were also part of the 1855 Classification, though they were categorized differently. Here, the best château (there was only one—Château d'Yquem) was called *Premier Cru Supérieur Classé*, First Great Classified Growth. The second best châteaux were called First Growths and the third best, Second Growths.

If you're on the verge of skipping the next couple of pages, I understand. Unfortunately, though, there's no good way to tackle this information other than to dive straight in.

The wines of Graves (including Haut-Brion, although it had already been classified as part of the Médoc's 1855 Classification) were classified in 1953 and revised in 1959. In both the original and revised classifications, no hierarchical order was established. The thirteen reds and eight whites considered best were simply given the legal right to call themselves *Cru Classé*, Classified Growth.

St.-Emilion was first classified in 1954, with the provision that the classification be revised every ten years (not true for the Médoc or Graves classifications). In St.-Emilion, the best wines were termed *Premier Grand Cru Classé*, First Great Classified Growth. The second best were named *Grand Cru Classé*, Great Classified Growth. Below that came *Grand Cru*, Great Growth. The top level, *Premier Grand Cru Classé*, was further divided into an "A" group and a "B" group. Only two wines made the "A" notch; all other *Premiers Grands Crus Classés* were designated "B," although these were still, of course, considered above the *Grands Crus Classés*.

In the midst of so much potentially confusing information, Pomerol, sanely enough, was never classified. For a complete list of the Bordeaux châteaux classified in 1855, see page 885.

Finally, it's interesting and a little startling to realize that even in those regions with classifications, most of the wines within those regions were never classified. Which brings us to the *Cru Bourgeois*.

## The Crus Bourgeois

In the Médoc, there's a collective name for approximately 200 châteaux that were not classified. They are called the *Crus Bourgeois*. For the most part, *Cru Bourgeois* cost considerably less than the classified growths. In general, a well-regarded *Cru Bourgeois*, such as Château Fourcas-Hosten, costs one fifth of the price of a First Growth, such as Château Lafite-Rothschild. *Cru Bourgeois* are clearly the Médoc wines meant for casual drinking.

Although the *Cru Bourgeois* was once divided into three levels, with the top wines carrying the title *Crus Bourgeois Exceptionnel*, recent European Union legislation allows only the term *Cru Bourgeois*. At one end of the spectrum *Cru Bourgeois*

## CLASSIFICATIONS: THE CHEAT SHEET

Here's a quick take on the confusing world of Bordeaux classifications. Each area has its own system as well as its own terminology. Unfortunately wine labels don't always indicate a wine's classification.

- The Médoc: In 1855, the châteaux of the Médoc and one château in Graves were classified into four *Premiers Crus* (First Growths), fourteen *Deuxièmes Crus* (Second Growths), fourteen *Troisièmes Crus* (Third Growths), ten *Quatrièmes Crus* (Fourth Growths), and eighteen *Cinqièmes Crus* (Fifth Growths). In 1973 Château Mouton-Rothschild was raised from a Second Growth to a First, bringing the total of First Growths to five. For a list of all the Médoc châteaux classified in 1855, see page 885.

- Sauternes and Barsac: Also in 1855, the châteaux of Sauternes and Barsac were classified. One château was designated as *Premier Cru Supérieur Classé*, eleven as *Premiers Crus Classés*, and twelve as *Deuxièmes Crus Classés*. Some châteaux in the *Premiers Crus Classés* category have since been broken into smaller estates, so the total number of *Premiers Crus Classés* is now fifteen. For a list of all the châteaux in the 1855 classification, see page 885.

- Graves: In 1953, sixteen châteaux in Graves were classified as *Crus Classés*. The classification was revised in 1959.

- St.-Emilion: In 1954, the châteaux of St.-Emilion were classified into eleven *Premiers Grands Crus Classés* and fifty-three *Grands Crus Classés*. The classification, which is revised every decade, was last updated in 1996.

- Never classified: Pomerol, as well as Entre-Deux-Mers, Fronsac, Canon-Fronsac, and other outlying areas.

127

can be merely ordinary, but at the other end, the best wines often surpass Fourth and Fifth Growths in quality.

---

*Some Favorite Cru Bourgeois*

**CHÂTEAU CHASSE-SPLEEN**

**CHÂTEAU D'ANGLUDET**

**CHÂTEAU DU BREUIL**

**CHÂTEAU FOURCAS-HOSTEN**

**CHÂTEAU HAUT-MARBUZET**

**CHÂTEAU LES ORMES-SORBET**

**CHÂTEAU MAUCAILLOU**

**CHÂTEAU MEYNEY**

**CHÂTEAU POTENSAC**

**CHÂTEAU POUJEAUX**

**CHÂTEAU SOCIANDO-MALLET**

---

## The First Growths and the Super Seconds

The First Growths come from specific *terroirs* considered to be the best in Bordeaux. No expense is spared making these wines. This is also true for the so-called Super Seconds, a loosely defined, unofficial grouping of the wines that a large number of discerning consumers consider to be in the same ballpark with Château Latour, Château Lafite, and the other First Growths (see Classifications: The Cheat Sheet, page 127).

In general, a First Growth and a Super Second cost two to three times more to make than a merely good Bordeaux. In the vineyard each vine is doted on and nurtured like a child. Only the best grape clusters are picked. The châteaux also thin the crop by cutting off as much as 35 to 50 percent of the clusters to concentrate the sugar in the remaining grapes (a practice common in many of the world's greatest wine

regions). First Growths and Super Seconds will be aged in a large percentage of, if not entirely in, expensive new oak barrels in a *chais* (cellar) that is usually immaculate and solemn (some Bordelais refer to their cellars as cathedrals). The wines will reach their pinnacles of complexity, flavor, and texture only after aging both in the barrel and bottle. At five to ten years of age, such wines are just beginning their descent (or perhaps the word is ascent) into harmony and refinement.

*Among the First Growths, Margaux and Lafite-Rothschild are often the most elegant and subtle; Haut-Brion, the most earthy; and Mouton-Rothschild and Latour, the most powerful.*

*Built in Pauillac in the sixteenth century, Château Lafite-Rothschild experienced a long succession of owners until it was purchased in 1868 by Baron James Rothschild. Rothschild, an old man at the time of the purchase, died before he saw the château and its vineyards.*

128

# THE 1855 CLASSIFICATION

—◁◦◦◦▷—

The legendary treatise known as the 1855 Classification laid the foundation for the way we think about and evaluate many of the top Bordeaux châteaux today. What happened was this:

In 1855, Napoleon III asked Bordeaux's top château owners to rate their wines from best to worst for the Paris Exhibition, a fair. One imagines that the château owners cringed. The prospect was nightmarish. Rating the wines, one against the other, could only turn neighbors into enemies.

The château owners stalled. Eventually, the Bordeaux Chamber of Commerce was invested with the job. The Chamber of Commerce members grouped the châteaux into five categories based on the selling price of the wines. The *Premiers Crus,* or First Growths, were those wines that sold for the most. The *Deuxièmes Crus,* Second Growths, sold for a little less. The system continued down to Fifth Growths. In all, sixty-one châteaux were classified. The hundreds of châteaux whose wines cost less than the Fifth Growths were not classified at all.

Curiously, as I've said, the classified châteaux were not from all over Bordeaux. In fact, they were located only in the Médoc and in Sauternes and Barsac. There was one exception, Château Haut-Brion in Graves.

Unveiling a first-time-ever classification of important wines may have made the Paris Exhibition more exciting, but it also started a political and ideological battle that continues to this day.

Those opposed to the classification wonder why a wine that sold for the most money in 1855 should still be rated one of the best wines in Bordeaux today? Châteaux, after all, go through changes in ownership. Some owners are more quality conscious than others. Should a château now producing ordinary wines have the right to retain its original high ranking? Conversely, what if an estate originally ranked as a Fourth Growth undergoes dramatic improvement?

The logical solution would have been to periodically review the ratings and adjust them up or down, like adding or subtracting stars to or from a restaurant review.

The Médoc château owners have often considered doing just that. But each time lack of consensus has led to even more argument. In the end, proposals to readjust the ratings have only worked salt into the wound. So the château owners live with the 1855 Classification as it stands. Wine drinkers, they reason, will find their way to the best wines no matter what.

One man did challenge and ultimately change the classification of his château: Baron Philippe de Rothschild. Originally, there were four First Growths: Château Margaux, Château Latour, Château Haut-Brion, and Château Lafite-Rothschild. Mouton-Rothschild was ranked a Second Growth. The Baron would have none of it. Obstinate and relentless, he petitioned the government for twenty years to upgrade Mouton. His persistence paid off in 1973; Château Mouton-Rothschild was moved up to First Growth rank. The classification was thereby changed for the first and last time.

129

## How Much Do the Rankings Matter?

How much should you care about a wine's classification? Before tackling that question, let me point out that for most of us it would be a waste of time and brain space to memorize all of the rankings of Bordeaux wines. This is the kind of wine information that can and should be looked up whenever you are curious. And besides, no one (at least I hope no one) comes home from work and says, "Honey,

I'm in the mood for a Third Growth with dinner tonight."

Nonetheless the classifications can be helpful as a very general guide to quality. A majority of the First and Second Growth wines can be truly extraordinary. Part of the reason for this is the price those wines command. Clearly, châteaux with strong cash flows can afford to keep their vineyards and equipment in top form, as well as attract the best professional talent.

But there are countless wines that, today, are either better or worse than when they were first ranked, and many very good Bordeaux were never part of any official classification at all. The prime example is Château Pétrus, one of the most expensive Bordeaux of all, but not classified because it is a Pomerol.

In the end, rankings and ratings are fragile and temporal things. They tend to close the door on wine experience rather than open it, narrow the sphere of pleas-

ure instead of expand it. Rankings, in other words, are no substitute for the best evaluation method of all—tasting.

# THE MÉDOC

The largest of the famous regions of Bordeaux, the Médoc starts at the city of Bordeaux and stretches northward like a snake for 50 miles along the left bank of the Gironde River. The Médoc is made up of two smaller appellations. One is, confusingly, also called the Médoc (the top northern third), and the other is called the Haut-Médoc (the bottom, southern two thirds). It is in the Haut-Médoc that you find the famous communes (villages) of Margaux, St.-Julien, Pauillac, and St.-Estèphe. These four, all at the river's gravelly edge, have the best *terroir*. Virtually all the châteaux rated in the 1855 Classification are scattered through these four communes. (For a list of the châteaux in the 1855 Classification, see page 885.) Farther inland are the Haut-Médoc's two less important communes, Listrac and Moulis. Here, away from the river, the heavier, less well drained soils often result in somewhat coarser wines.

Almost all the Médoc's wines are red. The dominant grape is cabernet sauvignon (forming up to 60 to 70 percent of all blends), followed by merlot. Both do well in the Médoc's stony soil, which, here and there, is interspersed with clay.

Amazingly, the flat plateaus of the Médoc were originally marshlands—low-lying semiswamps badly suited to making any wine at all, never mind great wine. In the seventeenth century, however, the Bordeaux nobility brought in Dutch engineers to cut huge drains in the land, effectively lowering the water table and creating riverside gravel banks. With the

## THE SUPER SECONDS

—◈—

Not to be confused with the Second Growths, the Super Seconds are an unofficial group of highly sought after Médoc wines considered approximate in quality to the First Growths. Though the term is commonly used by wine merchants, there is no absolute consensus as to which wines belong among the Super Seconds. The following châteaux, however, are almost always named: Château Pichon Longueville Comtesse de Lalande; Château Pichon Longueville Baron; Château Cos d'Estournel; Château Ducru-Beaucaillou; Château Léoville-Las Cases; and Château Palmer.

*The nineteenth-century Château Palmer in Margaux is named for its second owner, Charles Palmer, an English general under Wellington. When he purchased the property in 1814 from the widow Marie Brunet de Ferrière she insisted that she be given 500 liters of wine a year, for life.*

marshes drained, Bordeaux's emerging class of wealthy lawyers and merchants saw their chance to become landowners. Huge parcels of land along the banks of the Gironde were purchased, grand estates were built, and a vine-growing "revolution" ensued. During the seventeenth and eighteenth centuries, many of the most prestigious châteaux and vineyards were established, including Lafite, Latour, and Mouton.

## Margaux

The southernmost and largest commune of the Médoc, Margaux has more classified estates than St.-Estèphe, Pauillac, or St.-Julien. The aristocratic Château Margaux is here, of course, plus twenty other well-known properties.

The soil in Margaux is among the lightest and most gravelly in the Médoc, giving the best wines in the best years a sort of soaring elegance and refinement plus wonderful generous aromas. Margaux are often described as being like an iron fist in a velvet glove. It has been this combination of power with delicacy that has given these wines their vaunted reputation.

The two most renowned Margaux are the First Growth Château Margaux and the Third Growth (considered a Super Second) Château Palmer. In top years these wines can be superbly elegant, with long, silky, hedonistic flavors. Château Margaux also makes one of the leading dry white wines in the Médoc, Pavillon Blanc du Château Margaux.

Two other exceptional Margaux to consider: Château Rausan-Ségla (a Second Growth), one of the oldest properties in the Médoc, known for its silky, black currant-packed wines; and those from Château Angludet (a *Cru Bourgeois*), the wines of which can be full of lovely berry and chocolate flavors.

*Château Margaux was built between 1802 and 1816. In addition to its red wine of the same name, the estate makes Pavillon Blanc, one of the few whites that come from the Médoc.*

Other top Margaux to try include Château Brane-Cantenac, Château Lascombes, Château Labégorce-Zédé, Château Prieuré-Lichine, Château Siran, and Château Monbrison.

## St.-Julien

Just north of the largest commune, Margaux, is the smallest, St.-Julien. It's easy to drive right through it and not realize you've been there. Of all the communes, St.-Julien has the highest percentage of classified growths—about 95 percent of the wines here are Second, Third, or Fourth Growths, although there are no Firsts and no Fifths. If you were to drink only the wines from this commune for the rest of your life, you could be very happy.

Among St.-Julien's most well-known wines are the three Léovilles: Léoville-Barton, Léoville-Las Cases, and Léoville-Poyferré. All are classified as Second Growths, although in many years, Léoville-Las Cases in particular can broach First Growth status. Wonderfully structured

and intense, Las Cases is the true lion among the Léovilles.

Like those of Margaux, the leading wines of St.-Julien are known for their precision and refinement. Three others to consider: Château Ducru-Beaucaillou (a Second Growth), as classic as an ancient Greek statue; Château Gruaud-Larose (a Second Growth), the sort of earthy, lavishly ripe wine that rarely lets you down; and Château Gloria, a delicious, easy-drinking favorite for Bordeaux lovers who want to drink well at a moderate price.

Other top St.-Juliens to try include Château Beychevelle, Château Branaire-Ducru, Château Lagrange, Château Talbot, and Château Lalande Borie.

## Pauillac

This word is music to the ears of Bordeaux lovers. Pauillac (POY-yack), just north of St.-Julien, is where much of the excitement in Bordeaux is centered. Three of the five First Growths are born in this soil: Château Lafite-Rothschild, Château Mouton-Rothschild, and Château Latour. In all, Pauillac has eighteen of the sixty-one classified wines, including many of the best.

Pauillac wines can lean several ways. Some have a sort of full-bodied luxuriousness; others, a bold structure; still others, a subtle, precise refinement. The best are always complex with rich black currant and cranberry flavors, often overlaid with cedary notes. The range of styles within this commune is due to variable *terroir* and marked differences among the châteaux in the composition of their blends. In the north Lafite-Rothschild sits on bits of limestone scattered through the gravel. The wine is generally about 70 percent cabernet sauvignon and 20 percent merlot, with the remainder composed of one or more of Bordeaux's three other red grapes. Further south, Pichon Longueville Comtesse de Lalande (often called simply Pichon Lalande) sits on soil that is more gravel and clay. The wine is usually about 45 percent cabernet sauvignon and 35 percent merlot. Compared to Lafite, it is often a rounder, fleshier, more supple wine.

If money is no object, then drinking one of the Pauillac First Growths is certainly a nice introduction to Pauillac flavors, especially if the wine has been aged eight years or more. But also consider these others: Pichon Longueville Comtesse de Lalande's neighbor Pichon Longueville, Baron (also a Second Growth), which can have the same soaring structure robed in voluptuousness; Château Lynch-Bages (a Fifth Growth), a scrumptious, lively Pauillac; and Château Haut-Batailley (a Fifth Growth), a velvety Pauillac with ripe berry flavors.

Still other top wines to try include Château Grand-Puy-Lacoste, Château Pontet-Canet, and Château Haut-Bages-Libéral.

## St.-Estèphe

Stacked on top of Pauillac is the northernmost Médoc commune of St.-Estèphe, known for wines that, at least by Bordeaux standards, have the staunchness of an army general. The best also have a totally captivating, racy intensity. St.-Estèphe's more rugged style comes from its heavier soil, closer to the mouth of the Gironde River. Châteaux here tend to use a high percentage of merlot. Yet, the wines are not so much soft and supple as they are dense, almost chewy.

The leading estate is Cos d'Estournel, which, in the great years, makes a blatantly sensuous wine (about 38 percent merlot), with waves of chocolaty, earthy black currant fruit that often seem to be bursting at the seams. Even in less great years, Cos d'Estournel always seems com-

133

*Each year, 240,000 bottles of Château Latour are painstakingly hand wrapped to protect the labels from scratches and smudges in transit.*

## CHÂTEAU, CUVIER, AND CHAI

—⦿⦿⦿—

Three of the most important words in Bordeaux are *château, cuvier,* and *chai.* Though we think of a château as a palatial estate, anything can be a château in Bordeaux—from a farmhouse to a garage. The word simply refers to a building attached to vineyards with winemaking and storage facilities on the property. Within the château is the *cuvier,* the building where the wine will be made, and the *chai,* the cellar where it will be stored and aged.

paratively rich and expressive. The château itself, with its copper pagoda roof and massive carved door, is one of the most intriguing in Bordeaux.

Some of the best *Crus Bourgeois* and nonclassified wines also come from St.-Estèphe, including Château de Pez, with its good grip and jammy flavors, and Château Meyney, full of saddle leather aromas and grilled mushroom flavors.

Other St.-Estèphes to look for include Château Calon-Ségur, Château Montrose, Château Lafon-Rochet, Château Phélan-Ségur, Château Haut-Marbuzet, and Château Les-Ormes-de-Pez.

## GRAVES

South of the city of Bordeaux, Graves extends like a sleeve dangling off the arm of the Médoc. It is named for its famous gravelly soil, the gift of Ice Age glaciers. The glaciers also deposited tiny white quartz pebbles easily found in all the best vineyards.

Graves holds the distinction of being the only part of Bordeaux where both red and white wines are made by most châteaux. The vineyards, some of the most ancient in the region, were the first to be known internationally. Casks of wine were shipped to England as early as the twelfth century and by the sixteenth century several important estates were already established, including Graves' most famous château, Haut-Brion. Spelled Ho Bryan, the wine it produced was praised by the seventeenth-century British. A century later, Thomas Jefferson wrote about how delicious "Obrion" was and purchased six cases to be sent from the château to Virginia.

*Graves is the only region of Bordeaux where almost every château produces both a red and a white wine.*

So stunning was Château Haut-Brion that it was the sole Graves wine to be included in the 1855 Classification. Powerful yet hauntingly supple, Haut-Brion has an almost primordial earthy character. The other top wines of Graves were first

*Footmen and butlers used* rafraîchissoirs *to prevent glasses from breaking en route to and from the dining room. To chill glasses for white wine (to compensate for the lack of refrigeration) the* rafraîchissoir *was filled with ice water so that the bowls of the glasses were submerged.*

134

*Every other year Bordeaux hosts Vinexpo, one of the world's largest wine trade fairs and certainly the most prestigious. Dozens of elaborate parties are thrown, but the one invitation everybody wants is to the black-tie Fête de la Fleur. The Commanderie du Bontemps de Médoc et des Graves (above) sport their velvet robes.*

classified in 1953 and the classification was later revised in 1959.

Graves includes the subappellation Pessac-Léognan. Many of the best red and white Graves come from this area of ten tiny communes, grouped together by the French government in 1987. Thus, many of the wines once considered the best of Graves are now the best of Pessac-Léognan.

Although many wine drinkers think of dry white wines when they think of Graves, slightly more red wine than white comes from here, and in fact, about a dozen of the region's most stunning wines, all of which, incidentally, carry the Pessac-Léognan appellation, are red. Cabernet Sauvignon is the dominant red grape, but not by much. Merlot and cabernet franc are also used extensively. Château Haut-Brion has by far the most merlot (about 30 percent) and the most cabernet franc (about 20 percent) of any of the First Growths.

In addition to the voluptuous Haut-Brion, Château La Mission-Haut Brion, Château Pape-Clément, Château Haut-Bailly, and Château La Louvière all make outstanding red wines, with rich, almost roasted, earthy, chocolaty, plummy, spicy elements and, sometimes, a very appealing animal quality. Other red Graves not to miss include Domaine de Chevalier, a gorgeous wine—the embodiment of chocolate cherries jumping out of a glass—and Château Bouscaut, with its cassis jam flavors.

White Graves—well loved since the turn of the twentieth century—underwent an enormous revolution in quality in the late 1980s and 1990s. Thanks to new viticultural and winemaking practices, many white Graves are creamier, more intense, and more complex than ever. And a number of them—notably the whites of Château La Mission-Haut-Brion, Château Laville-Haut-Brion, and Domaine de Chevalier—can be mind-boggling in their complexity.

All three carry the appellation Pessac-Léognan and all three are among the most delicious white wines in the region.

Classically, all white Graves are blends of sémillon and sauvignon blanc. From sémillon comes richness, body, depth, and the ability to age with honeyed overtones. From sauvignon comes sprightly acidity and a fresh snap of flavor, characteristics that are terrific assets when pairing white wine with food. One of the best illustrations of the harmony between the two white grapes comes from Château Carbonnieux. The wine has a bright, minerally vibrancy and a satiny mouthfilling texture when young and develops a rich lanolinish, honeyed character after several years of aging.

Among the other top Graves and Pessac-Léognan wines to try are the white wines of Château La Louvière and Château Couhins-Lurton, as well as the red and white wines of Château de Fieuzal and Château Pape-Clément.

## SAUTERNES AND BARSAC

Quite a bit south of Graves along the Garonne River are Bordeaux's sweet-wine-producing communes, the most important of which are Sauternes and Barsac. Sauternes and Barsac are not simply two unique small places within Bordeaux; they are among the few regions in the world devoted to sweet wines. Sauternes, the more famous of the two, is about four times larger than tiny Barsac, but the wines from each can be extraordinary. At their best, these are wines with an apricotish opulence that detonates in your mouth and then spreads over your taste buds like liquefied honey. Their leading rivals are Germany's and Austria's ultraluxurious *beerenauslesen* and *trockenbeerenauslesen* and Alsace's superb *sélection de grains nobles*.

It takes merely a sip of a great Sauternes or Barsac to create a convert.

*Château Haut-Brion in Graves is the only First Growth owned by Americans. In 1935 it was purchased by the financier Clarence Dillon and remains in his family.*

After the first taste, the expression on the lucky taster's face says: "Where has this wine been all my life?" The great examples are wonderful not because of their sweetness, however, but because of their extraordinary balance. The best are luscious without being cloying; richly honeyed, without tasting like cheap candy. To achieve this, the wines must have just the right acidity and alcohol and must be complex.

How is this done? Sauternes and Barsac are made mostly from sémillon and, to a lesser extent, sauvignon blanc grapes left on the vine well into the fall, whereupon they become infected with the benevolent fungus *Botrytis cinerea*, also known as *pourriture noble* or noble rot. Sémillon, the leading grape in the area, is especially susceptible to the fungus because of its large bunches of thin-skinned grapes with a high sugar content.

Though it seems unlikely that grapes left to decay into furry, moldy raisins will become magnificent wine, they can. In Sauternes and Barsac the process occurs naturally though erratically, by virtue of the region's singular climate. For the botrytis fungus to take hold on healthy, ripe grapes, the region must have just the right amount of humidity and warmth (too little or too much can produce problems). Sauternes and Barsac, the farthest south of all the important regions of Bordeaux, are ideally situated. Here, the Ciron River meets the Garonne River, creating gentle morning mists. If all goes well, nearby forests will help to hold the moisture in the air. When the day warms up and grows drier, a perfect stage is set for botrytis to appear.

As the beneficial mold punctures the grapes' skins in search of water to germinate its spores, the water begins to evaporate and the grapes dehydrate. Inside the

## THE UNLIKELY DISCOVERY THAT ROT COULD BE NOBLE

ince the sight of moldy grapes is not exactly appealing, the discovery that rotten grapes could ultimately be turned into great wine was most probably an accident born of necessity. The first written account of a sweet wine made from grapes infected with noble rot occurred in the mid-1600s—not in France, but in the Tokay region of Hungary when a priest/winemaker delayed the harvest because of an impending attack by the Turks.

shriveled berries, the sugar in the juice becomes progressively more concentrated. The botrytis also alters the structure of the grapes' acids, but the amount of acidity in the wine is not diminished.

The process begins in late September, but the rate at which botrytis takes hold is unpredictable. In great years, the berries will begin to desiccate, forming a tiny amount of liquorous sweet juice by late October. In other years, the process may be painfully slower. Throughout, the château owner is sitting on pins and needles. First, he or she hopes for a good warm growing season so that as fall approaches, the grape bunches are healthy and ripe. Next he prays for just the right balance of moisture, dryness, and warmth so that the bunches will become botrytized as evenly and uniformly as possible. But the most nerve-racking part is the race against winter. Day by day as winter approaches the risks of losing the crop increase. One cold snap, one heavy rain, one winter storm could knock the fragile berries off the vine, swell them with water, or freeze them before the botrytis has taken hold. In each case the crop could be ruined, and the château could conceivably be left with nothing.

As the botrytis spreads through the vineyard, the château owner is keenly aware of its growth pattern. Botrytis that takes hold sporadically means a difficult, laborious harvest, for only perfectly rotted berries with concentrated juice can be picked and pressed. Grapes only partially infected by the mold can give diluted juice or juice with funky off flavors.

Unfortunately, botrytis rarely reaches readiness at one moment throughout an entire vineyard. To harvest each bunch at perfect "rottenness," therefore, pickers must go into the vineyards four to ten times over the course of several weeks in October and November. The cost of such painstaking repetition is considerable. In the end, for the greatest of estates like Château d'Yquem, the grapes picked from one vine may ultimately yield not much more than one glass of wine.

The individually handpicked grapes and whole bunches are brought into the cellar. There, they are pressed with great difficulty since the grapes are so dehydrated, and the must is transferred into oak barrels where it will ferment. Because of the concentration of sugar in the must, fermentation is difficult and takes a long time—up to a year (by comparison, a dry white wine generally ferments in two weeks to a month).

During fermentation yeasts convert the sugar in the must into alcohol (see How Wine Is Made, page 30). As you know, a dry wine is dry because the yeasts convert all but the merest trace of sugar into alcohol. With Sauternes and Barsac the yeasts begin to convert the sugar as usual. At a certain point, however, the concentration of alcohol is so great, it kills the yeasts. Fermentation stops, even though there is unconverted natural grape sugar left in the must. What remains, in other words, is a wine with leftover or residual sugar—a naturally sweet wine. Sauternes and Barsac usually have 8 to 12 percent residual sugar.

These are not feeble wines. The sensory impact of a wine with 14 percent alcohol and 10 percent residual sugar is formidable. Plus, another factor comes into play: the botrytis itself. When the grapes being pressed have been perfectly infected, the mold, as well as the alcohol, can help kill the yeasts. As a result, the fermenting must may only reach 13 percent alcohol before the mold and alcohol working in tandem destroy the yeasts and cause fermentation to stop. At 13 percent alcohol, a sweet wine tastes more refined, elegant, and in balance than it does at a higher level of alcohol. Thus, with Sauternes and Barsac the finesse and complexity of the wines is directly related to how thoroughly and uniformly the botrytis takes hold in the vineyard.

Can you taste botrytis in the wine? An experienced taster can. The mold is not washed off or in any other way removed from the grapes and bunches, and it does contribute to the flavor. That flavor, however, is not like something that was left too long in the back of the refrigerator. Botrytis adds an extra dimension, sometimes described as being faintly like sweet corn, to the overall complexity of the wines.

Botrytis is, in all circumstances, a fragile phenomenon, highly susceptible to the climatic vagaries of an approaching winter. In poor years when rain has swelled the grapes with water, some châteaux use a concentration method called cryoextraction. The grapes are put into a machine that

## SAD BUT TRUE

———❦❦❦———

I n years with very bad weather, a top château in Sauternes may decide to make no sweet wine rather than lower its standards. Salvaged grapes will be sold to lesser châteaux, and the top château will take the enormous financial loss of having no product for the year. So, about twice a decade Château d'Yquem may choose not to make any sweet wine.

slowly freezes the water in them. When they are removed, they begin to warm slightly. The change in temperature causes the ice crystals to separate out from the thick sweet juice. In this way the diluting water can be removed and the sweet juice can be fermented as usual.

After a Sauternes or Barsac has completed fermentation, it remains in a cask for at least two years of aging. (At Château d'Yquem it is aged for three years.) It then goes on to age in the bottle. After thirty or more years, a top Sauternes or Barsac can still be remarkably alive. Which is

not to say you *have* to age these wines for three decades. The wines' honeyed apricot flavors are almost irresistible when they are young, say, five years after the vintage date. But it's only after about ten years, once the obvious hit of sweetness has passed and the flavors have totally coalesced, that the wines' mesmerizing opulence comes into full force.

The term Sauternes is often used to refer to all sweet wines from Bordeaux. However, there are actually five small communes that produce it. Sauternes and Barsac are the most renowned; Bommes, Fargues, and Preignac are less important communes producing generally lower-quality sweet wines.

The wines of Sauternes and Barsac were the only ones rated, along with the Médoc, in the famous 1855 Classification. One Sauternes was singled out and given the highest rating of *Premier Cru Supérieur Classé:* Château d'Yquem (pronounced E-kem). Yquem is still the ultimate, richest, most perfectly balanced Sauternes. After Yquem, fifteen châteaux are classified as *Premier Cru* and twelve as *Deuxième Cru* (see page 885 for lists of these châteaux).

Dry white wines are also made in Sauternes and Barsac, although they are not well known in the United States. Château d'Yquem named their dry wine Y (*ygrec*, pronounced Egrek, the French name for the next to last letter of the alphabet). This set off a trend. Now most dry Sauternes are named after the first letter of the château's name. Château Rieussec's is called R; Château Guiraud makes G. Dry Sauternes

*The wine of Château d'Yquem (above), the most magnificent Sauternes of all, is predictably expensive and often sold in half-bottles.*

have an unusual bold flavor. Made principally from sémillon, they are very full-bodied, thick textured, and relatively high in alcohol. A few red wines are also made in Sauternes and Barsac. They carry the appellation Graves and are rarely shipped outside the region.

Among the most exceptional Sauternes and Barsac to try in addition to Château d'Yquem are Château Suduiraut (Sauternes) Château Rieussec (Sauternes), Château Climens (Barsac), Château Lafaurie-Peyraguey (Sauternes), and Château Guiraud (Sauternes).

# St.-Emilion

Like its soul mate nearby, Pomerol, St.-Emilion is not a part of the Médoc or Graves but, instead, is on the other side of the Gironde River, on Bordeaux's less well-known Right Bank. It is a region that, in every way, is as different from the Médoc as it can be. The vineyards of St.-Emilion tend to be smaller than those in the Médoc; the châteaux far more modest. Often much of the work, both in the vineyard and in the cellar, is done by the proprietor and his family.

The first thing that strikes most visitors is the village of St.-Emilion itself. A small, fortresslike medieval town carved out of limestone, it is by far the most stunning Old World village in the Bordeaux region. Nothing in the Médoc or Graves comes close. In the center of the village is the twelfth-century Eglise Monolithe, one of Europe's only underground churches, carved by Benedictine monks, by hand, out of one massive block of limestone.

*The steeple of the Eglise Monolithe in the center of the medieval town of St.-Emilion.*

## THE MODERN JURADE

In 1948 the Jurade was revived as a wine fraternity dedicated to the advancement and promotion of St.-Emilion wines. Twice a year, during the first flowering of the vines in spring and again during the autumn harvest, the Jurade conducts a majestic pageant. Members, wearing flowing red robes trimmed in white and puffy red caps, proceed through the streets of St.-Emilion to a solemn candlelit mass in the cloister of the town's monolithic church. As part of the pageant, visiting dignitaries—princes, ambassadors, politicians, famous artists—are inducted into the Jurade. Alan Shepard, the first American astronaut in space, has been made a member, as has the cellist Mstislav Rostropovich. The Jurade tries not to take itself too seriously, however. It has also inducted Mel Brooks.

The church, which is quite large, is built on the site of a hollowed-out cave said to be the hermitage of an eighth-century saint. Visitors to the church can see two blocks of stone, each with shallow indentations, said to be the saint's chair and bed. (A local superstition has it that women who sit on the saint's chair will become pregnant.)

From the Middle Ages on, St.-Emilion was the home of several monastic orders. Community life was extremely religious. All governing power was exercised by the Jurade, a coterie of men given complete authority through a charter granted them in

*St.-Emilion (the wine) is inescapable in St.-Emilion (the place). The town's tiny cobblestone streets are home to nearly a hundred wine shops.*

1199 by King John of England. Part of the Jurade's mandate was insuring the quality and prominence of St.-Emilion wine.

Only red wines are made in St.-Emilion, and the wine community is extremely chauvinistic about them—there are ninety-eight wine shops in the village! This pride is justified; in very good years, the best wines, Château Cheval Blanc, Château Magdelaine, and Château Ausone, to name three, can be positively riveting.

Unlike the long, flat stretch of the Médoc or the long, gently rolling landscape of Graves, St.-Emilion has hillsides (the *côtes*)—limestone outcroppings and plateaus, plus gravelly terraces. Over centuries of geologic upheaval, clay, sand, quartz, and chalk have been intermixed there. The twists and turns and different soil compositions make St.-Emilion, small as it is, a patchwork quilt of varying *terroir*. A fairly wide range in the style and quality of the wines is the result. Merlot and cabernet franc are the dominant grape varieties.

Arguably, the very best St.-Emilion is the superelegant Château Cheval Blanc, with Château Ausone a close second. Cheval Blanc and Ausone are the only two wines designated as "A" among St.-Emilion's *Premier Grand Cru Classé*.

Cheval Blanc has the highest percentage of cabernet franc of any well-known Bordeaux estate—almost 70 percent, with the remainder of the blend being merlot. In great years the wine can have an almost unnerving texture—it is, all at the same time deep, luxuriant, and kinetically alive in the mouth. When young, the wine fairly oozes with decadent blackberry fruit laced with vanilla, rather like eating a bowl of squashed ripe blackberries drizzled with crème anglaise. (One of the greatest Bordeaux—indeed, one of the greatest wines—I have ever drunk was a 1947 Cheval Blanc, considered among the most majestic wines Bordeaux produced in the entire twentieth century.)

The vineyard of Cheval Blanc is on a mostly gravelly terrace several miles north of St.-Emilion, almost in Pomerol. However, many of the châteaux producing the best St.-Emilion are those on the southwestern limestone hillsides hugging the village. Château Ausone, Château Canon, Château Magdelaine, and Château Pavie are all here. In addition to wines from these vineyards some others to try include Château Angélus, Château Domi-

Pomerol and St.-Emilion remained far less well-known than the Médoc even after the first bridges over the Garonne and Dordogne Rivers were built in the mid-1800s. Wine estates in the two regions were small; no château had an established, bankable reputation; and for Bordeaux's wine brokers it was difficult to get to these inland vineyards and even harder to transport the wine out. It made much more sense for the brokers to do business with the larger, well-known Médoc châteaux, which were also far more accessible thanks to their proximity to the Gironde River just north of the city of Bordeaux. Over time, of course, this only made the Médoc châteaux more well known, and the Pomerol and St.-Emilion châteaux less well known.

nique, Château Figeac, Château Trottevielle, and Château l'Arrosée.

## POMEROL

The tiniest of all the major Bordeaux wine regions, Pomerol is also the one that today has the most cachet. This wasn't always so. At the turn of the twentieth century, the wines of Pomerol were considered merely average. The region's current fame is based, in part, on the fact that Pomerol is the home of Château Pétrus. Year in and year out, Pétrus is one of Bordeaux's most expensive and sought-after wines. Often ravishing, opulent, and complex, it sets the esthetic criteria for other Pomerols.

Like its neighbor St.-Emilion, Pomerol is on the Right Bank of the Gironde River. The wines here are exclusively red, and the majority are based on merlot and cabernet franc. Merlot alone accounts for more than 70 percent of all the grapes planted in Pomerol, and not surprisingly, it is extremely well suited to the region's gravel and clay beds. Cabernet sauvignon is rarely part of a Pomerol blend.

Pomerols from the best sites stand out with a velvetlike texture and a plum/cocoa/violet richness. This is Bordeaux's harmonic convergence of intensity and elegance at its best. Their relative softness make Pomerols fairly easy to drink young. As is true with the wines of St.-Emilion, Pomerols are a good choice in a restaurant when the Bordeaux on the wine list are all from recent vintages.

Historically, the estates of Pomerol, isolated inland from the Gironde River, were virtually unknown compared to the wines of the Médoc. As a result, they were left out of the 1855 Classification and have remained unclassified since.

Pomerol began to emerge from its obscurity in the 1940s and 1950s. It was then that Jean-Pierre Moueix, a talented *négociant* with a keen palate, began buying exclusive sales and marketing rights to Pomerol's best châteaux. In 1964, he bought a 50 percent share of what was to become the most prized property of all, Pétrus.

Improving quality was an obsession for Moueix. Soon, news of the newly supple, rich, plummy character of the wines under his direction spread by word of mouth. By the mid-1960s, Pomerols in general began to develop a cult following in the United States.

Jean-Pierre Moueix was followed by his son Christian, an equally driven, quality-conscious man. In addition to the portfolio of Moueix wines in Pomerol and the neighboring region, Fronsac, Christian Moueix owns Dominus, a top estate in the Napa Valley of California.

The tiny town of Pomerol encompasses the square around the small church and not much more. Similarly, most Pomerol properties are small, especially compared to those in the Médoc. In general, a proprietor here owns a vineyard that's less than 10 acres in size and eighty Pomerol châteaux have fewer than 2 acres. By comparison, vineyards in the Médoc span dozens and sometimes hundreds of acres. Finally, Pomerol châteaux are extremely modest; there are no breathtaking mansions. Even Pétrus, with its turquoise shutters, looks more like a

*Château Pétrus—compared to the grand estates of the Médoc, it's rather humble.*

farmhouse than one of the world's most famous wine estates.

If price and availability were indeed no object, the Pomerol we should all experience would be this legendary Pétrus. In the best vintages the wine's exotic licori-

143

## IF MONEY WERE NO OBJECT

Let's say you were willing to pay $5,000 to $12,000 per case for Château Pétrus (the cost for top contemporary vintages), how would you go about buying it? Alas, the process wouldn't be easy. Pétrus is rarely available to the average consumer. Here's why:

Each year around 3,000 cases of Pétrus are made, 500 to 700 of which are allocated to Pétrus' United States importer. The importer, in turn, offers the wine to a small, select group of wholesalers around the country who have consistently bought Pétrus in the past. These wholesalers in turn offer their limited allotments only to a small, select group of their best customers—exclusive wine shops and prestigious restaurants that have seniority based on their past record of purchases.

A wine shop will offer the wine, often personally by telephone, to a select group of customers, mostly collectors who buy Pétrus every year from the shop regardless of the cost. As for restaurants, with their tiny allocations, they may include the wine on their wine lists only for a short period of time (or at an outrageously expensive price), after which it will be offered verbally only to certain customers.

For average wine drinkers who are not wealthy collectors, it can be next to impossible to break into this loop.

cey and jammy aroma leaps out of the glass, after which, a creamy, black raspberry explosion fills your mouth. It is hard to imagine a more luxurious red wine, where each of the components is so seamlessly integrated into the whole.

But Pétrus aside, there are a number of other terrific Pomerols. Unfortunately, many of these are, like Pétrus, made in small quantities. Nonetheless, among the ones to seek out are: Château Le Pin, very, very hard to find but a wonderfully seductive Pomerol; Château La Fleur du Gay, another lush, hedonistic wine; Château Lafleur, with its rich, supple, and explosive fruit; Château L'Evangile, situated between Cheval Blanc and Pétrus and a meaty, opulent, powerhouse of a wine; and Château Le Bon Pasteur, in the best vintages, a delicious wine howling with toast, plum, and mocha flavors. Also keep an eye out for Château La Conseillante, Château Certan de May, Château Trotanoy, and Vieux-Château-Certan.

## OTHER REGIONS OF BORDEAUX

The less-important wine districts of Bordeaux are less important for a good reason. Much of the wine made there is simply simplistic. Lacking the best *terroir*, winemakers in these regions must be especially gifted, able to overcome many of the obstacles that less than ideal soil and climate present. Despite the odds, some delicious wines are indeed made. Think of the regions that follow as good hunting grounds for little-known, inexpensive wines that are potentially diamonds in the rough.

I'll begin with Listrac and Moulis, which are the other regions of the Médoc,

### CLARET

The British often call red Bordeaux claret. The word comes from the French *clairet*, which originally referred to a light red wine. Today, of course, the top red Bordeaux are anything but light in color or in body.

and then move on to Entre-Deux-Mers east and south of the city of Bordeaux, over to Fronsac and Canon-Fronsac near Pomerol and finally to the Côtes, the most well regarded of Bordeaux's farthest outlying districts.

## Listrac and Moulis

The Médoc's less prestigious communes, Listrac and Moulis, are the source of wines that don't exactly rival their sister wines from Margaux, St.-Julien, Pauillac, and St.-Estèphe. That said, some surprisingly good wines do come from these two communes. Bargain hunters can have a field day. The wines are virtually all red. Like Médocs in general, they are built on a foundation of cabernet sauvignon, with merlot and cabernet franc added for roundness and nuance and petit verdot sometimes added as a spice note.

Listrac and Moulis are inland communes of the Médoc, that is, they are not positioned on the gravelly banks of the Gironde River, as are the more famous communes. Away from the riverbanks, the soil tends to be heavier and to hold more water. As a result, the wines of Listrac and Moulis are generally rougher textured and less polished. They can sometimes seem straitjacketed by tannin and short on fruit. There are exceptions, especially in Moulis. Several of the best *Crus Bourgeois*, for example, carry the Moulis appellation, including Château Poujeaux and Château Chasse-Spleen. Both are wines of jammy, earthy richness; both have a mountain of tannin. Both are relative bargains.

Some other top Moulis and Listrac wines to consider include Château Maucaillou (Moulis), Château Fourcas-Hosten (Listrac), and Château Gressier Grand-Poujeaux (Moulis).

## Entre-Deux-Mers

Entre-Deux-Mers (literally between two seas) is the vast expanse of forested land between the Dordogne and Garonne tributaries of the Gironde River. Although a large wine region and a picturesque one, it is considered less important than the Médoc, Graves, Pomerol, or St.-Emilion for two reasons. First, while Entre-Deux-Mers has patches of good *terroir*, the soil and climate here never produce wines that on the whole equal the quality of wines in the other regions. Second, the appellation Entre-Deux-Mers applies to dry white wines only. Thus, for wine drinkers who believe a region is only as good as its reds, Entre-Deux-Mers doesn't count. Red wines actually are made here, but because they are generally lower in quality than the region's whites, they must carry the appellation Bordeaux or Bordeaux Supérieur, not Entre-Deux-Mers.

Yet this charming, pastoral region of rolling woods and tiny, family-owned vineyards should not be written off easily.

145

## BON APERITIF

The word *aperitif* comes from the Latin *aperire,* meaning to open, and indeed, a variety of fresh, slightly bitter drinks have traditionally been used to open both meals and appetites. More than mere cocktail-hour stimulants, however, wine aperitifs are also thought to be healthful because many contain small amounts of quinine, an ingredient originally added to protect French soldiers from malaria.

Currently, the best-selling French aperitif in the United States is Lillet, first created in 1887 when two French brothers blended white Bordeaux wine with a mixture of macerated fruits and a small amount of quinine.

Today, ten different fruits—eight of which are a well-kept secret—along with sweet and bitter orange peel and quinine are cold-macerated in French brandy for four to six months before they are mixed with wine and aged.

Two types of Lillet are made: nonvintage, also called classic, and vintage, making it the only vintaged aperitif in the world. Vintage Lillet is aged in newer oak barrels than nonvintage. Lillet Blanc, both vintage and nonvintage, is produced from Bordeaux-grown sauvignon blanc, sémillon, and muscadelle grapes. Lillet Rouge, whether vintage or nonvintage, is a blend of merlot and cabernet sauvignon.

Since the late 1980s and early 1990s wine-makers have been on a determined quality campaign—especially for low and moderately priced white wines. Today, many Entre-Deux-Mers whites are zesty wines that buzz with refreshing lemon, vanilla, and almond flavors. For simple pleasure, these wines take the cake.

Entre-Deux-Mers whites are blends of sémillon, sauvignon blanc, and usually a small amount of muscadelle, which adds a faint spicy-flowery quality. They are rarely barrel fermented, which means they are fresh and light—perfect for pairing with fish and shellfish.

Entre-Deux-Mers wines have never been classified. Among the Entre-Deux-Mers worth seeking out are Château Bonnet, Château Turcaud, Château Nardique la Gravière, Château de Camarsac, and Château Peyrebon.

146

## Fronsac and Canon-Fronsac

If any areas are now on the fast track out of "lesser-dom" and into prominence, they are Fronsac and Canon-Fronsac. These two communes, spread over the hillsides just north and slightly west of Pomerol and St.-Emilion, are turning out a handful of dazzlers—wines full of ripe black raspberry flavors; wines with a kind of edgy power.

The wines are all red; the best sites are clay and sand interlaced with limestone. Merlot is the dominant grape followed by cabernet franc with a bit of cabernet sauvignon sometimes blended in for strength and balance. This is similar to the grape profile found in Pomerol and St.-Emilion, yet the wines of Fronsac and Canon-Fronsac tend to be a little darker, more rustic, and bolder. They are the Heathcliffs.

## FUTURES

The most expensive red Bordeaux wines are frequently sold as futures. Under this system, customers buy the wine from retailers up to two years before it is actually released from the château. The customers base their decisions (a gamble, really) on the reputation of the château and on early assessments of the vintage. Buying futures is, in effect, buying on speculation. In return for taking the risk and for paying cash in advance, these customers are assured of securing what is usually a highly sought after wine and they get to buy that wine at a price lower than the eventual release price.

Some of Bordeaux's most gifted enologists are working on properties in Fronsac and Canon-Fronsac, and this in part, is why both regions are moving forward so quickly. For example, Michel Rolland (considered one of the world's top consulting enologists for red wines) owns Château Fontenil and has consulted with many Fronsac properties. In general, Fronsac and Canon-Fronsac wines sell for half the price of St.-Emilion and Pomerol wines.

Among the wines worth seeking out, in addition to those from the château already mentioned, are Château La Vielle-Cure (Canon-Fronsac) and Château Dalem (Canon-Fronsac).

## The Côtes

Outlying the four communes of Pomerol, St.-Emilion, Fronsac, and Canon-Fronsac are a handful of satellite regions called the *côtes* (hillsides): the

Côtes de Bourg, Côtes de Castillon, Côtes de Francs, and Premières Côtes de Blaye.

The rural, hilly *côtes* are some of the oldest wine regions in Bordeaux. Vines were planted here by the Romans. The wines are mostly reds for everyday drinking—light and juicy when they are good, shallow and thin when they are not. Merlot is the leading grape variety, but *côtes* wines very rarely have the plummy depth and lushness of merlot planted in, say, Pomerol or St.-Emilion. Often, this is due to the fact that the grapes are planted in more fertile soil and harvested at higher yields.

Among the best red *côtes* are Château Puygeraud (Côtes de Francs), Château Roc des Cambes (Côtes de Bourg), Château Les Jonqueyres (Côtes de Blaye), and Château de Francs (Côtes de Francs).

## Other Lesser Appellations

There are several other appellations you will find on bottles of dry Bordeaux, including Bordeaux, Bordeaux Supérieur, Graves de Vayre, Entre-Deux-Mers-Haut-Benauge, Lussac-St.-Emilion, Montagne-St.-Emilion, Lalande de Pomerol, Puisseguin-St.-Emilion, Ste.-Foy-Bordeaux, and St.-Georges-St.-Emilion. Wines from these areas can be quite decent; many are uninspired.

This is also true of the outlying appellations producing mostly sweet wines. Cadillac, Cérons, Côtes de Bordeaux-Saint-Macaire, Loupiac, and Ste.-Croix-du-Mont each make sweet wines, though the quality is generally well below the quality of the wines from Sauternes and Barsac.

One final note about the appellations Bordeaux and Bordeaux Supérieur. These are the two most basic appellations Bordeaux wines can carry. Any château can use these appellations as long as the wine

in question meets certain baseline requirements for alcohol and grape yield. Most Bordeaux and Bordeaux Supérieur are simple, ordinary wines.

# BORDEAUX VINTAGES AND THE QUESTION OF READINESS

Wine drinkers worry more about the vintages and readiness of Bordeaux than of any other wine, with the possible exception of Burgundy. Is such great concern warranted? In Bordeaux itself, châteaux owners often feel that Americans are rash and hyperjudgmental concerning vintages. Further, they suggest that this tendency causes us to miss out on many delicious wines since vintages and wines not given immediate high marks tend not to be imported. One might

*Château Ausone's cellar holds bottles of past vintages that are definitely ready to drink.*

## SECOND IN LINE

To make the best possible wine, a top château will blend together only its very finest lots of wine. These generally come from the most mature and well-sited vineyard plots. What happens to all the other, lesser lots of wine? In many cases, the château makes a second wine, which will have its own name and its own distinct label. (A second wine has nothing to do with a Second Growth or the Super Seconds.)

A second wine is usually made by the same winemaker in essentially the same manner as the famous wine, and it will usually come from the same vineyard, although the age of the vines will generally be younger. Though it may have hints of the famous wine's character, the second wine will be less polished, less structured, less complex, and less intense. And a lot less expensive. The second label of a wine such as Château Latour or Château Margaux, for example, can be a relative bargain.

Châteaux rarely promote their second wines, preferring to be known for their famous ones. Often, the label on a second wine does not reveal the château it came from, but the name may be close enough to tell.

### SOME OF THE BEST SECOND WINES

**Bahans Haut-Brion**
Château Haut-Brion

**Carillon de L'Angélus**
Château L'Angélus

**Carruades de Lafite-Rothschild**
Château Lafite-Rothschild

**Château Haut-Bages-Averous**
Château Lynch-Bages

**Clos du Marquis**
Château Léoville-Las Cases

**De Marbuzet**
Château Cos d'Estournel

**La Croix**
Château Ducru-Beaucaillou

**La Tour-Léognan**
Château Carbonnieux

**Le Petit Cheval**
Château Cheval Blanc

**Les Forts de Latour**
Château Latour

**Les Pensées de Lafleur**
Château Lafleur

**Pavillon Rouge du Château Margaux**
Château Margaux

**Reserve de la Comtesse**
Château Pichon Longueville
Comtesse de Lalande

argue that of course châteaux owners feel this way. Clearly, their best interests are served if all vintages sell well regardless of the character of each vintage.

Let's try to sort things out. If you intend to buy Bordeaux for drinking (as opposed to buying it for investment and reselling), there are indeed problems inherent in rushing to judgment or slavishly following vintage pronouncements.

The first problem is that vintages today are rarely categorically horrendous. A vintage may, because the grapes received less sun over the course of the growing season, produce a lighter style wine. You might not prefer light wines, but lightness, in and of itself, is not bad. What if the wine were, in all other ways, perfectly balanced? What if it had beautiful, delicate flavors? Would these traits make it a bad wine? Was it, then, a bad vintage? The fact of the matter is that modern viticulture and winemaking allow the winemaker to compensate as never before for nature. Undeniably, nature still rules, and undeniably, vintages are different and the taste of a wine varies year to year. But why not celebrate that fact?

In Bordeaux today vintages are only considered a total washout in the most extreme cases, and even then, the most talented winemakers believe they still make very good wine. Let's take a dramatic example—the 1991 vintage. In April of that year, Bordeaux was thrashed by a devastating frost that severely damaged the vines. In some areas, 80 percent of the crop was lost. Châteaux owners salvaged what they could. The extremely reduced crop ripened throughout the summer. Then on the eve of the harvest, Bordeaux was hit by torrential rains. It is hard to imagine a worse scenario than severe frost in the spring and rain in the fall. Yet by mid-December,

after the wines were made, the winemakers at Château Ausone and Château Margaux were quoted in a leading wine publication as saying they believed that they had made beautiful and very good wines in 1991, despite the climatic conditions.

As it turned out, both winemakers attempted to select only berries undamaged by the initial frost. They also cut off all clusters that subsequently grew back on the vine, since these would mature at a different rate and taint the final wine with unripe flavors. At harvest, both winemakers were able to work quickly, so that the grapes were not allowed to bloat with rainwater. Finally, both winemakers were extremely strict in selecting only their best vats for blending. As a result of all these factors, both estates made only a tiny quantity of wine, but it was good. Not great admittedly, but also not dishwater.

There is another problem. Bordeaux is so important a wine region that when vintages are first categorized in the press

*An almost reverential sense of quiet and calm pervades Château Mouton-Rothschild's chai, where the newest vintages rest in French oak until they are bottled.*

that assessment tends to live on forever. Wine, however, changes over time. There are many examples of Bordeaux vintages deemed magnificent at first, only to be later declared not as good as originally thought, and vice versa, vintages at first thought average that seemed to come into their own over time.

The sensible approach to Bordeaux vintages then, can only be to have an open mind. Remember above all that Bordeaux wines evolve and that one-shot vintage proclamations are often superficial. Remember, too, that talented winemakers can surprise us even when Nature has worked against them.

As for the question of when a Bordeaux is ready, we need to put this in perspective. Readiness was somewhat easier to assess in times past when most serious Bordeaux were made so that they were not ready to be drunk any time soon, meaning within ten years of bottling. People bought good wines every year and put them away. Thus some wines, purchased many years earlier, were always coming into maturity.

Today, life rarely involves walking into a well-stocked cellar and pulling out something that's been maturing for a decade. Every top château now wants to make wine that's both capable of long aging yet drinkable soon after it's released. Admittedly, the two ideas do seem mutually exclusive. But they're not. A top Bordeaux can be drinkable—even delicious—when it's fairly young if the grapes were fully ripe when picked, if the tannin was physiologically mature, and if the wine is loaded with a lot of expressive fruit. At the same time, if that foundation of mature tannin is substantial enough and if it's balanced with good acidity and alcohol, the wine should age well for a long time.

Of course, no matter how delicious a top young Bordeaux is, it will almost always be more thrilling when it's older, after it's had a chance to evolve, become more complex, and reveal other facets and nuances of its personality. How much older? No one can say for sure. There is never one magic moment when a wine is ready. Most Bordeaux—most structured red wines—evolve and soften progressively. They usually go from being slightly tight to being supple and having a wider range of more complex flavors. But where a wine is along this spectrum at any point in time is a matter of conjecture. And no matter where it stands in this spectrum, it will have its positive points.

Generally, the tighter and more structured the wine when young, the more slowly it will evolve. Since most top Bordeaux are very structured wines, they usually take at least eight or ten years of aging before beginning to soften and show more complex nuances. (This is not the case with medium-quality everyday Bordeaux, of course.) For the very best, however, eight to ten years of aging is probably a minimum. These are not the kinds of wines that will be over the hill in fifteen years. Many will continue to grow more fascinating for decades.

In the end, perhaps the best way to gauge readiness is philosophically. A wine is ready when you can't bear to wait for it any longer.

# THE FOODS OF BORDEAUX

Bordeaux may have many of France's most impressive wines but, on the whole, it comes nowhere close to having France's most impressive food. Admittedly, describing French food, any morsel

# SWEET SUCCESS: MACARONS AND CANELÉS

Who would imagine that two of the most famous food specialties in the world's most prestigious wine region are a chewy cookie and a miniature cakelike sweet? What's more, no one seems to know how these two simple items became so legendary. Nonetheless, you have not truly experienced Bordeaux until you go on a tasting expedition in search of the ultimate example of each.

*Macarons* won't present a problem. These chewy almond cookies, thought to date from the early 1600s, are a specialty of just one place: the ancient walled village of St.-Emilion. Virtually every pâtisserie in the village sells them.

Then there are *canelés,* small confections that are often eaten with a glass of red wine on a Sunday afternoon. If anything can drive a Bordeaux pastry chef to fits of fanaticism, these homey, much-loved confections can, for they are a challenge to make perfectly (and easy to make poorly). Nonetheless, virtually all top Bordelais pastry chefs are members of the *Confrérie du Canelé de Bordeaux,* an organization of pâtissiers devoted to the tradition of baking this unusual local specialty.

A *canelé* is difficult to describe. It looks like a molded cream puff. The center is sort of custardy; the outside, crunchy and caramelly. But a *canelé* is not a pastry per se, not a cookie, and not really a cake either. If they weren't French, *canelés* would be perfect as part of English afternoon tea. The origin of this sweet is not clear, though one historical account suggests that the first *canelé* may have been baked by a nun who accidentally overcooked her pastry cream sometime in the thirteenth century.

*Madame Blanchez and her famous macarons.*

of it, as less than stellar seems gastronomically sacrilegious. After all, French food at its lowest ebb is *still* French food. And so goes the cooking in Bordeaux. It is French; it is good. Yet, the paradox is nagging. How can a region of France produce wine so incredibly inspired and food that, for the most part, is so incredibly "un"?

My first suspicion that Bordeaux might not be as electrifying culinarily as enologically came while dining at a renowned château. The regal eighteenth-century dining room was dominated by a 20-foot-long table on which rested heir-

## BORDEAUX'S CLASSIC MARRIAGES

The red, white, and sweet wines of Bordeaux all have classic food matches. Red Bordeaux and lamb are considered an exemplary and historic match. Before the 1970s, sheep were often taken from the rural areas ringing Bordeaux to graze over the winter in the vineyards of Pauillac, St.-Julien, St.-Estèphe, and Margaux. Here they would feed on the grasses that grew between the rows of vines—grasses said to give their meat an especially delicious flavor. And here, too, among the dormant vines, lambs would be born.

Bordeaux's renowned sweet wine Sauternes also has a famous partner, or in this case, two: foie gras and Roquefort. Sauternes and foie gras, usually served as an appetizer, must be one of the most hedonistic marriages of food and wine in the world. Sauternes and Roquefort cheese is a fascinating pairing. While the bold salty pungency of the blue cheese would deaden most red wines, with Sauternes the match is brilliant.

As for Bordeaux's refreshingly crisp, dry, minerally white Graves, these are some of the best wines in the world for fresh briny oysters.

loom silver and three antique crystal decanters containing some of the château's older vintages. Dinner consisted of potatoes, green beans, and chicken.

Potatoes, green beans, and chicken? The holy trinity of my grandmother's Irish-Scottish kitchen was the last thing I expected to be eating in one of the world's most famous châteaux. And it wasn't the last time. Again and again in other châteaux the food served was, well, plain compared to other regions of France. To be sure, these were delicious waxy French potatoes, pencil-thin *haricots verts*, and chicken that was scrumptious. But still.

When I asked why Bordeaux had such simple food compared to other parts of France, several hypotheses were suggested. The first was that cooking in Bordeaux is partly Anglo-Saxon in orientation thanks to the long-standing deep ties between the Bordelais and the British. In fact for three centuries, beginning with the marriage of Eleanor of Acquitaine to Henry II in 1152, the people of Bordeaux considered themselves citizens of England, not France. The bonds that formed were so strong that to this day Britain is Bordeaux's most important market, and a large percentage of château owners speak flawless English.

Several Bordelais, however, rejected this theory. The simple cooking of Bordeaux, they said, reflected the region's close-knit, hardworking conservative families who prefer modest, unadorned cooking. By way of evidence, they pointed out that many of the best restaurants in the region are the simplest ones that, like the legendary Le Lion d'Or in Margaux, serve local specialties. Among these:

**Entrecôte Bordelaise:** A juicy steak topped with a heap of caramelized shallots.

**Oysters and Sausage:** Local oysters served raw on the half shell accompanied by homemade sausage patties on the side.

**Lamprey:** Large, fatty, eel-like fish caught from local rivers and usually baked in casseroles, often with red wine.

**Roasted Lamb:** Lamb was once a specialty of the Haut-Médoc. Today it is raised mostly in other parts of Bordeaux.

**Canelés Bordelaise:** Unusual and delicious, not-too-sweet miniature cake-like affairs, very particular to Bordeaux and found in every good pastry shop. Eaten with wine or coffee (see page 151).

**Macarons:** Sweet almond cookies; these are the specialty of the village of St.-Emilion (see page 151).

# VISITING BORDEAUX CHÂTEAUX

Today, you can visit almost all the Bordeaux châteaux, although many are not open to the public for drop-in tastings or tours in the way that most California wineries are. In order to visit a château, you need to write or fax the estate well ahead of time to make an appointment. Specify the number of people in your group and the language(s) you speak. Once you arrive in France, call the château to confirm your visit.

Each region in Bordeaux has a *syndicat viticole*, which publishes a guide to touring vineyards in the area. These guides list the châteaux, the languages spoken, potential visiting hours, addresses, and

## BORDEAUX'S WINE BARS & BRASSERIES

The city of Bordeaux has a number of classic spots for a great glass of wine and a simple meal.

**BISTROT DES QUINCONCES**
4 Place des Quinconces
011-33-5-56-52-84-56

**BISTROT DU SOMMELIER**
167 Rue Georges Bonnac
011-33-5-56-96-71-78

**CELLIER BORDELAIS**
30 Quai de la Monnaie
011-33-5-56-31-30-30

**LE CLARET**
46 Rue Pas-St.-Georges
011-33-5-56-01-21-21

**LES NOAILLES**
12 Allée de Tourny
011-33-5-56-81-94-45

153

*Leoville Barton, in St.-Julien, is owned by the Barton family, who came to Bordeaux from Ireland early in the eighteenth century and founded a successful négociant business. France and Ireland enjoyed a thriving wine and wool trade at the time.*

# LE ST.-MARTIN

Bordeaux is France's fifth largest city and very industrial. Though modern hotels are ubiquitous, what is not so easy to find is a place like Le St.-Martin— a small inn that makes you feel as though you're inside a Hemingway novel.

Le St.-Martin is in the hamlet of Langoiran, about twenty minutes south of Bordeaux. The hotel is on the banks of the Garonne River; standing in the dining room, you could throw your wineglass into the water. Built in 1850, the hotel was recommended in the 1914 *Michelin* guide for its full-course dinner, which cost the equivalent of 10 cents. Back then, Langoiran was a port village bustling with river traffic and boats hauling wine casks to the coast for trade. In time, roads and trucks took over the local commerce, people moved away to bigger cities, and Le St. Martin became a forgotten hotel.

In 1990, three wine-loving businessmen restored and renovated Le St.-Martin back

*Le St.-Martin is known for its home cooking (top) and lovely river views (above).*

to its former simple elegance. Jean Michel and Marie Helene Rechard, a husband and wife team, were installed as chef and manager respectively. When Jean Michel started cooking, eyebrows were raised and lips were smacked. Langoiran had not had such sensational food for decades.

Though it is now a secret the Bordelais like to keep to themselves, you will eat better (and much less expensively) at Le St.-Martin than at most of the fancy restaurants in the city of Bordeaux. The upstairs dining room, filled with bouquets of wildflowers, overlooks the old wood and steel bridge built by Alexandre-Gustave Eiffel (of Tower fame) that connects Entre-Deux-Mers on one side of the river with Graves on the other.

Reservations are needed both to dine and stay at the hotel.

*Le St.-Martin, Langoiran, Bordeaux; 011-33-5-56-67-02-67; fax 011-33-5-56-67-15-75.*

telephone and fax numbers. To obtain copies, contact the Bordeaux wine council—the Conseil Interprofessionnel du Vin de Bordeaux (C.I.V.B.)—and specify the regions in which you are interested.

**Conseil Interprofessionnel du Vin de Bordeaux,** Maison du Vin, 3 Cours du XXX Juillet, 33075 Bordeaux-Cedex; 011-33-5-56-00-22-66.

For other useful advice, as well as for maps, brochures, and so forth, contact the Bordeaux Wine Bureau in New York or the office of tourism in Bordeaux.

**Bordeaux Wine Bureau,** c/o SOPE-XA-Food and Wines from France, 215 Park Avenue South, Suite 1600, New York, New York 10003; (212) 477-9800.

**Bordeaux Office de Tourisme,** 12 Cours du XXX Juillet, 33000 Bordeaux-Cedex; 011-33-5-56-00-66-00.

# THE BORDEAUX WINES TO KNOW

There are lots of delicious, moderately priced Bordeaux wines available in the United States—wines you can discover simply by talking to a good wine merchant. And of course it's always intriguing, if expensive, to taste one of the great First Growths (Château Latour, Château Margaux, Château Lafite-Rothschild, Château Mouton-Rothschild, and Château Haut-Brion). In addition, here are some of the wines that, for me, have come to capture and symbolize the spirit of Bordeaux.

## *Whites*

### CHATEAU CARBONNIEUX

Pessac-Léognan

*Cru Classé*

approximately 60% sauvignon blanc, 35% sémillon

This is one of the great classic white Graves—Carbonnieux, unlike many other châteaux, has been serious about making fine white wine for decades. Lots of minerally, citrusy pizzazz here; drunk with oysters in wine bars all over Bordeaux.

### CHATEAU LA LOUVIERE

Pessac-Léognan

unclassified

approximately 85% sauvignon blanc, 15% sémillon

One of the delicious, snappy, new-style white Graves with fresh, citrus and almond flavors, plus a streak of minerals. La Louvière is made by the very innovative André Lurton, owner of several other top châteaux.

### CHATEAU LAVILLE HAUT-BRION

Pessac-Léognan

*Cru Classé*

approximately 70% sémillon, 30% sauvignon blanc

Bordeaux has but a handful of stunning, regal, elegant white wines. This is my vote for the best of them. Complex yet racy, Laville Haut-Brion is one of the world's most  stunning examples of the mesmerizing richness that can be achieved by blending sémillon and sauvignon blanc. The château is owned by the Dillon family (Americans), who also own Château Haut-Brion.

*Château Pichon Longueville Comtesse de Lalande, in Pauillac, was built in the 1840s by the widow Marie Laure Pichon-Longueville, the Comtesse de Lalande, whose lover, Comte de Beaumont, then owner of Château Latour next door, gave her the land so that she might live close by.*

# Reds

## CHATEAU DE PEZ

St.-Estèphe

*Cru Bourgeois*

approximately 70% cabernet sauvignon, plus merlot and cabernet franc

De Pez falls into that blessed category of delicious wines that do not require you to be rich to drink them—just smart. Considered one of the best *Cru Bourgeois* of St.-Estèphe, de Pez can be a rugged, tannic blockbuster when young, a tamed lion when aged.

## CHATEAU GRUAUD LAROSE

St.-Julien

Second Growth

approximately 65% cabernet sauvignon, 25% merlot, plus cabernet franc and petit verdot

156

The earthy, smoky flavors of Gruaud Larose seem almost primordial, and though the flavors are somewhat old-fashioned (no bouncy up-front fruit), the wine is considered one of Bordeaux's fabulous standbys. The château is run by the large, prestigious *négociant* firm of Cordier, which has a reputation for making easily drinkable wines at easy to handle prices.

## CHATEAU PETRUS

Pomerol

unclassified

99% merlot, 1% cabernet franc

I know I've mentioned how difficult it is to get Pétrus, but I include it here in the hope that somehow, you'll get the chance to try it anyway. Universally considered to be the equivalent of a First Growth, Pétrus is the kind of wine that can send quivers of excitement down the spine of any experienced wine lover. In great years Pétrus is ravishing, elegant, and rich—Ingrid Bergman in red satin.

## CHATEAU PICHON LONGUEVILLE COMTESSE DE LALANDE

Pauillac

Second Growth

approximately 45% cabernet sauvignon, 35% merlot, plus cabernet franc and petit verdot

Pichon Lalande, as it is simply called, is located beside Château Latour and deserves to share Latour's First Growth status. In great years, the wine smells as if an entire forest of pine trees was dipped in black cherry—chocolate sauce. Pichon Lalande has a higher proportion of merlot than most Pauillac wines, giving it a particular silky lushness. The château is owned and run by dynamic, forward-thinking May Eliane de Lencquesaing.

# Sweet Wine

## CHATEAU D'YQUEM

Sauternes

*Premier Grand Cru*

approximately 80% sémillon, 20% sauvignon blanc

Mesmerizingly luscious, Yquem is indisputably France's most exalted dessert wine. Few other wines come close in dazzling richness, finesse, and depth of flavor. For each perfect grape that is individually hand-selected, hundreds of others may be passed over. In great years 5,000 to 6,000 cases of Yquem may be made; in poor years, none. Foie gras and Yquem are a consecrated marriage in France. The wine, made mostly from sémillon, is wildly expensive and worth it for every nectar-like drop.

# COGNAC

'm not sure I knew what to expect the first time I visited the Cognac region, but the throttling potency of the (not very high quality) Cognacs I had drunk up until then certainly did not prepare me for so gentle, so pastoral, so enchanting a landscape. This is France at her most timeless—rolling green vineyards, thick cornfields, and meadows noisy with birds are dotted here and there with stone farmhouses and unassuming hamlets. The region, almost 200,000 acres of vines, is about 70 miles north of Bordeaux and worlds apart in character.

Technically, the Cognac region falls into two French administrative *départements* (the rough equivalent of states): Charente-Maritime on the Atlantic coast and, just inland from that, Charente. (Besides Cognac, this part of France is renowned for the excellence of its butter, snails, and *fleur de sel*, the finest type of natural sea salt.) Both *départements* take their names from the Charente River, which meaders through them. The two important towns Cognac and Jarnac are situated on the river. Cognac, of course, has given Cognac, the brandy, its name, and about 10 miles away, Jarnac, the other hub of Cognac activity, is home to such prestigious firms as Courvoisier, Hine, and Delamain.

An old chestnut has it that all Cognac is brandy, but not all brandy is Cognac. Price alone testifies to this. In the year 2000 many of the top Cognacs cost $100 to $200 or more a bottle, and the most expensive of all, Courvoisier's Succession JL, cost about $3,700. What makes Cognac Cognac is the uniqueness of its region and the ancient, artisanal process by which it is made and aged.

Poised between the ocean and the Massif Central, where oceanic and continental climates collide, Cognac also straddles a northern French climate and a southern one. These factors combined with wide variations in the soil mean that Cognac is really made up of six smaller subdistricts or *crus,* each of which produces a Cognac of a different character and quality. (The name of the subdistrict usually appears on the label; if there is no subdistrict name, then the Cognac is a blend of different *crus.*) The top three *crus* in descending order of quality are Grande Champagne, Petite Champagne, and Borderies. The word *champagne* here has no relationship to the wine of the same name. Rather, Champagne in Cognac derives from the Latin *campagna,* meaning open fields, as distinguished from the French *bois,* woods. Cognac's three less highly regarded subdistricts, Fins Bois, Bons Bois, and Bois Ordinaires (fine woods, good woods, and ordinary woods, respectively) were all once forests. Grande Champagne is indisputably the most renowned of the districts and its porous chalky soil is thought to produce the richest tasting Cognacs with the most elegance and finesse. But we're not done yet. Just to upset this tidy scheme, there's one more designation: Fine Champagne. Not a subdistrict itself, Fine Champagne is Cognac distilled from wines made exclusively in Grande and Petite Champagne; at least 50 percent of the blend must come from the Grande Champagne.

Cognac is made from the most innocuous of grape varieties. The leading one by far is ugni blanc, which in the Cognac region is inexplicably called St.-Emilion, even though it has nothing to do with the wine district of that name in Bordeaux.

Colombard and folle blanche are used in much smaller amounts. (By law, five other varieties, all very obscure, may also be included, but together they must account for no more than 10 percent of the grapes used.) All of these grapes are grown to produce enormous yields, resulting in a thin, high-acid wine barely palatable on its own. Distillation changes everything, and a high-acid wine is ideal for distillation for acidity contributes to the brandy's structure.

Distillation (in a nutshell) involves boiling a liquid and then condensing the vapors that form. These condensed vapors are a highly concentrated form of the original liquid. The first distillers were Egyptians who as early as 3000 B.C. used crude stills to make perfumes. But in the Cognac region, distillation—and the birth of Cognac as we know it today—was the result of Dutch intervention. From the end of the Roman Empire until the sixteenth century the area surrounding the Charente River was known for neutral-tasting wine, most of it white and low in alcohol. The Dutch traded in the area, primarily for salt, and despite their disappointment with the wine's proclivity to deteriorate during the sea voyage, they began to purchase and ship it to England and other northern countries. The solution they eventually found to the deterioration was to distill the wine in the Netherlands and then sell the more durable result, which they called burnt wine—*brandewijn*. By the seventeenth century the Dutch began to install stills in the Charente region itself. Today more than 200 firms distill Cognac, though just four—Hennessy, Martell, Rémy Martin, and Courvoisier—account for about 90 percent of the sales.

Cognac is distilled twice (unlike most of the world's other brandies) in small copper pot stills, known as *alambics charentais* and heated by gas. The first distillation produces a cloudy liquid that is roughly 30 percent alcohol (the *brouillis*). This is distilled a second time (*la bonne chauffe,* literally, the good heating) to produce a clear Cognac that is 70 percent alcohol, or 140 proof, about twice what it will be once it's bottled. During each distillation the distiller must expertly make *la coupe,* the cut, separating the "heads," the liquid distilled first, and the "tails," what is distilled last, from the *coeur* or heart. The heads and tails contain off odors and flavors; only the heart is used to make Cognac.

The heart at this point is a clear, rather harsh brandy traditionally called *eau-de-vie*—water of life. What transforms this into Cognac is long aging in moderately large barrels that hold between 270 and 450 liters and that are made of oak from one of two famous French forests, Tronçais or Limousin. Immediately as it leaves the still, the brandy is put into barrels (either new or old depending on the firm's preference for intense or delicate flavors). Left in these barrels for years, the water in the brandy gradually evaporates, as does the alcohol. Between 2 and 5 percent of pure alcohol, called the angels' share, evaporates from each barrel each year. (Given the vast number of barrels in the region, it's estimated that about 20 million bottles' worth of brandy evaporates yearly.) During this process the level of humidity in a firm's

*Small copper pot stills called* alambics charentais *are traditional for distilling* Cognac.

huge barrel-holding warehouse, or *chai,* is crucially important. Too little humidity and the brandy loses its alcohol more slowly because more water evaporates. This hardens and dries out the brandy. Too much humidity and the Cognac will be flabby and lack structure. The perfect level of humidity is found right beside the Charente River, where many of the old warehouses are located. Throughout the process of evaporation and concentration, the brandy is also acted on by oxygen, which through numerous natural chemical reactions causes the brandy to soften and become more fragrant. All the while it is also absorbing the subtle vanilla and crème brûléelike flavors of the oak and taking on a rich brownish amber color.

*1800 Cognac aging in glass*

Though the brandy progressively loses alcohol as it rests in the barrel, it does so slowly. Its strength must still be brought down to the level stipulated by law for bottling, 40 percent alcohol, or 80 proof. This is done by gradually adding distilled water to the brandy as it ages in barrel or by adding *faible,* a weak mixture of distilled water and Cognac that have been aged together.

Unlike most wines, most Cognacs are expected to be consistent year after year, and so most don't carry a vintage date. Courvoisier XO, for example, has a certain style, aroma, and flavor that customers expect whether they buy a bottle today or ten years from now. Each Cognac firm achieves consistency by a complex and continual process of blending different lots of brandy from different harvests. Theoretically a brandy that has aged two and a half years could be a candidate for blending. In practice, brandies are aged in barrels far longer, generally twenty-five to sixty years. (After sixty years, the brandy is thought to decline rather than improve.) It's said that

no truly great Cognac can be produced without including a proportion of very old brandy, which contributes a pungent earthy character known as *rancio.*

When a Cognac firm advertises that its Cognac has been aged thirty-five years, that figure is the average age of all the brandies that went into the blend. This is not, however, what you will see on the label. Such label designations as XO or VSOP refer to the *youngest* eau-de-vie in the blend, not the average age of all of them. In Courvoisier XO, for example, the youngest eau-de-vie must be aged six and a half years. (The average age of the eaux-de-vie in this Cognac, however, is thirty-five to fifty years. The average age of the eaux-de-vie in any Cognac blend does not appear on the label.)

Cognac labels use a code to indicate the age of the youngest eau-de-vie in the blends. Here's how to decipher it.

- VS (very superior) or three star (***) indicates that the youngest eau-de-vie in the blend is not less than two and a half years old.

- VSOP (very superior old pale), VO (very old), and Réserve denote that the youngest eau-de-vie in the blend is at least four and a half years old.

- XO (extra old), Napoléon, Extra, Vieux, Vieille Réserve, and Hors d'Age describe a blend of eaux-de-vie in which the youngest is at least six and a half years old.

As for vintage Cognacs, though a rarity, they do exist. Their story is a bit convoluted. Even though for much of French history *appellation contrôlée* laws have prohibited the production of vintage-dated Cognacs, many of the top Cognac houses have set aside casks of brandy from particularly good years anyway. This allowed the houses to watch the evolution of brandy from those years and besides, in special cases, the laws could be bent to allow a small amount of a particularly spectacular vintage Cognac to be released. In addition, to avoid French bureaucratic red tape altogether, a Cognac firm could always send a barrel to Britain (where it would be known as "early landed"), then let the British bottle it as a vintage Cognac. In 1987 French law changed, and vintage Cognac is now legal. To prevent fraud, barrels of vintage Cognac must be aged in special locked cellars, which can only be opened with two keys, one of which is kept by the government, the other by the Cognac firm. Since most firms believe that a vintage Cognac requires at least fifteen years aging, we can expect to see more of them appearing on shelves from 2003 onward.

*The United States is now the leading market in the world for Cognac. In 1999, 35.8 million bottles were sold there.*

At its best, Cognac should taste complex, balanced, and smooth and have long-lasting aromas and flavors that subtly suggest flowers, citrus, honey, vanilla, smoke, and earth. Among the top Cognacs (their average age is noted in parentheses) are: A. de Fussigny Fine Champagne Vieille Réserve (thirty years); A. E. Dor X.O. (twenty-five years); Courvoisier XO (thirty-five to fifty years); Delamain Très Vénérable (forty-five to fifty years); Martell Extra (forty to fifty years); Rémy Martin X.O. (twenty-two years); and Hine Triomphe (forty to fifty years).

## STORING, SERVING, AND TASTING

Cognac, Armagnac, and Calvados are very different from wine when it comes to storing, serving, and drinking. First, none of them improve with age; each is ready to drink when you buy it. Not drinking the entire bottle immediately however presents no problem. An open bottle of Cognac or Armagnac will remain in good condition for about a year if the bottle is essentially full. Calvados, in this scenario, will last two to three years. If there's only a small amount left, your best bet is to finish it off within a couple of months for Cognac and Armagnac; within a year for Calvados.

Bottles of Cognac, Armagnac, and Calvados need to be stored upright, not on their side. The high alcohol content in the spirits can rot the corks, causing unpleasant aromas to form inside the bottles.

As for giant balloon snifters, forget them. Impressive as they may appear, such snifters dissipate brandy's aroma, meanwhile propelling alcohol vapors toward you so forcefully that you may feel like you've been smacked between the eyes. In the regions of Cognac, Armagnac, and Calvados, the preferred glass is a relatively small (it should be easy to cradle in your hand), chimney-shaped glass with a thin rim. And all the Hollywood portrayals to the contrary, neither the glass nor the spirit should be warmed over a flame; direct heating discombobulates the brandy's aroma and flavors. (Gently warming these spirits by cupping the glass in your hands is harmless.) Generally speaking a 1- to 2-ounce serving is customary.

Wine tasters commonly plunge their noses into wineglasses and inhale deeply. Not a good idea with any of these spirits. They are meant to be sniffed gently and at a slight distance. Similarly, taking tiny, not large, sips accentuates the spirits' smoothness. Finally, don't assume that a deep rich color indicates that the spirit has been aged a long time. Caramel is allowed as a coloring agent, enabling some Cognacs, Armagnacs, and Calvados to appear far older than they really are.

# Champagne

*". . . the one thing that gives me zest when I feel tired."*
—*Brigitte Bardot, in 1984, six months before her fiftieth birthday*

Legend has it that Marilyn Monroe once took a bath in 350 bottles of Champagne. According to her biographer George Barris, she drank and breathed Champagne as if it were oxygen. Marilyn Monroe was certainly not alone in her fascination with Champagne. Few wines captivate us to the extent Champagne does. But then Champagne is not simply a wine; it is also a state of mind.

Champagne's story begins 65 million years ago, when a vast prehistoric sea covered northern France and Britain. As the waters receded, they left behind a great crescent of chalk, rich with minerals and fossils. From this geologic legacy would eventually emerge the vineyards of Champagne. Its wines have become the ones we use to mark the most important moments in life. When we marry; when a child is

161

At Veuve Clicquot, grapes are sometimes ceremoniously picked in the traditional dress of the Champenois. Today, typical harvesting garb is decidedly less prim.

## THE QUICK SIP ON CHAMPAGNE

- True Champagne comes from only one region, also called Champagne, about 90 miles northeast of Paris.

- All Champagnes are blends of thirty to sixty separate still wines.

- The complex process by which Champagnes are made involves a secondary fermentation during which natural carbon dioxide gas is trapped inside each bottle. The trapped $CO_2$ will eventually become Champagne's bubbles.

born; when we land a new job. Champagnes have a celebratory status no other wine has. That status is also dizzyingly powerful. Handed a glass of Champagne, we simply abandon ourselves to its implied pleasure. No thought required. More than any other wine, Champagne unlocks wine's archetypal promise: joy.

*The name Champagne
is derived from* campagnia,
*a Latin term for the countryside
north of Rome.*

The wine Champagne comes from the region Champagne—about 90 miles northeast of Paris. Here, 15,000 growers raise the grapes that 110 wine firms, known as houses, make into sparkling wines recognized in every corner of the world.

Although wine has been made in the Champagne region since Roman times, the bubbly wine we call Champagne was first made as the seventeenth century drew to a close. The story goes that Dom Pierre Pérignon, a Benedictine monk and

the cellarmaster at the Abbey of Hautvillers, invented Champagne. That the world's most notorious "seduction wine" should have been the brainchild of a monk is described by the British wine writer Nicholas Faith as "an agreeable paradox."

However agreeable the tale, Champagne was not created by Dom Pérignon (although he was important in its development) nor by any one person. Champagne was the curious result of both the work of many Champenois and the happenstance of nature.

The region of Champagne is one of the coolest wine-producing areas in the world. In the past, wines would be made in the fall and left to settle over the winter. The cold temperatures would generally paralyze the yeasts, halting the fermentation before all of the grape sugar had been turned into alcohol. Once spring arrived and the wines (and yeasts) warmed up, they would begin to referment—or sparkle.

The Champenois were not amused. Wines that foamed were frightening. Worse, it seemed that only the wines of Champagne behaved so strangely. Wines

*Harvesting Champagne grapes in the vineyards of Veuve Clicquot.*

## DOM PÉRIGNON

Although no one person invented Champagne as such, Dom Pérignon was among a handful of innovative clerics whose techniques furthered Champagne's evolution.

According to Nicholas Faith in *The Story of Champagne,* Pérignon was sent, at the age of twenty-nine, to the Abbey of Hautvillers (property now owned by Moët & Chandon). Soon thereafter, he became its *procureur,* the administrator in charge of all the goods that provided a living for the monks, including wine.

Though he never drank wine himself, Pérignon was an avid winemaker and savvy businessman. He increased both the size of the abbey's vineyard holdings and the value of the wine produced. By 1700 the wines of Hautvillers were worth four times that of basic Champagne.

Pérignon and his monk/winemaker colleagues were the first to master the art of making white wine from red grapes. Although this is easily done today, all white wine made at the turn of the seventeenth century came necessarily from white grapes.

Pérignon was fanatical about consistency, precision, and discipline in grape growing and winemaking. He insisted that vines be pruned severely and only sparingly fertilized, thus lowering the yield of each grapevine and improving the concentration of the wine.

He mandated that grapes be picked before ten in the morning so that their delicate aromas and flavors would not be compromised by the hot afternoon sun. He had *pressoirs* (winepresses) built in the vineyards, so that the grapes could be pressed as quickly as possible.

Pérignon was also the first to keep the wines from different vineyard lots separate and the first to realize that blending several still wines ultimately leads to a more interesting Champagne. Most important, he was the first to insist that Champagne should be put in glass flasks to preserve the color and freshness, instead of leaving it in wooden barrels.

All of these innovations made Champagne a vastly better wine. But for Pérignon, one goal remained frustratingly elusive. He was never able to prevent Champagne's sparkle, and like every other winemaker of his time, Dom Pérignon knew that if a wine erupted into frothy bubbles, there was something wrong with it.

163

made in Burgundy—Champagne's arch rival—never bubbled.

Frustrated by Champagne's petulant foam, thin body, and tart flavor, many clerical winemakers, including Dom Pérignon and Dom Ruinart (working at what would become the house of Ruinart), strove painstakingly to develop techniques that would tame the fizziness, improve the taste, and establish Champagnes as superior to other French wines. By today's standards, their Champagnes would have been unrecognizable (and mostly unpalatable). They were cloudy, gritty, coarse, frothy pinkish wines, often heavily sweetened to disguise their tartness.

Champagne's seventeenth-century winemakers began to give up hope of ever making anything different. Decades of trying to make red wines that would outclass Burgundy had come to no avail. The Champenois did the only thing they could. They began to look at their wine differently. Maybe Champagne's sparkle wasn't so bad after all; maybe that's what made the wine special.

## THE CATHEDRAL OF KINGS—
## THE WINE OF KINGS

Champagne's characterization as the wine of Kings is based on its association with the Cathedral of Reims, the coronation site of virtually every French king. Built in the thirteenth century, known as the century of cathedrals since eighty were constructed during that period, the cathedral marks the site of the baptism of Clovis I, King of the Franks in 496. Modern Christian France takes as its date of birth Clovis' baptism.

Construction of the cathedral began in 1225 on the site of two former Romanesque cathedrals. By the time it was completed almost one hundred years later, the cathedral, with its dramatic great rose stained glass window and its 2,300 statues, was considered among the most stunning Gothic cathedrals of all time.

The cathedral's vibrant stained glass windows rank with those at Chartres and Bourges. They have remained under the care of one family of glassmakers—the Simon family—since the seventeenth century. In 1954 Jacques Simon was commissioned by the Champagne producers to create three tryptic windows portraying the art of vine growing and winemaking in Champagne.

The facade's portals contain some of the most impressive statuary to be seen in any Gothic cathedral, including figures representing David and Goliath, the coronation of the Virgin, the kings of France, and the famous, Smiling Angel, *l'Ange au Sourire*. The local Champenois expression for joy, the smile of Reims, is based on the statue's beaming countenance.

Especially if you could actually watch the lively bubbles. But by 1815, Champagnes were sometimes being decanted from bottle to bottle to remove the cloudy sediment of spent yeast cells. If you wanted to keep the bubbles, this caused a problem—the more a Champagne was decanted, the more likely it was to go flat. The solution was a process called *rémuage*, or riddling, which allowed the yeasts to be removed from the wine in one frozen clump. The process was developed in 1818 by an employee of the widow (*veuve* in French) Clicquot of the Champagne house Veuve Clicquot.

Slowly, more improvements ensued. The flavor of Champagne was getting better and, as a result, there was less need to camouflage it with sweetness. Champagnes began to get drier. First came half-dry Champagnes—demi-sec. When these proved successful, producers began making sec, or dry, Champagnes (these were actually lightly sweet by today's standards). Next came extra dry, and finally an even drier brut (which is how extra dry turns out to be in effect slightly sweeter than brut).

In 1846 in a radical move at the time, Perrier-Jouët made a Champagne without any sugar at all

*Perrier-Jouët's prestige* cuvée *in its Belle Epoch-style flower bottle.*

(possibly the first commercial brut). But Champagne drinkers found it too severe—too brutelike. It took another generation before a brut wine gained widespread acclaim. In 1874 the Pommery wine called Nature was the first to establish Champagne as a dry wine.

# THE LAND, THE GRAPES, AND THE VINEYARDS

Everywhere sparkling wine is made (and it's made just about everywhere in the wine-producing world, from South Africa to Italy to Texas), it is always distinguished from Champagne. This is true even though all of the best sparkling wines are made in a virtually identical manner. The reason Champagne is held apart from, if not above, all other bubblies is not necessarily because it's better (sometimes it isn't), but because the region is unique. Mapped out by the Institut National des Appellations d'Origine (INAO) in 1927, the Champagne region covers some 85,000 acres. Of this, about 75,000 acres are now in production and less than 80,000 acres may legally be used to grow Champagne grapes. Thus, all the vines of Champagne would easily fit into, say, the city limits of Denver, Colorado.

The region has two great assets: its iffy, northerly climate and its chalky soil. Because of both, Champagne ends up being unique. Climatically, Champagne lives

## CHALK IMMORTALIZED

In order to have enough stone to construct the city of Reims in what was then Gaul in the third century, the Romans dug 250 immense quarries in the chalky rock. These same deep chalk pits, called *crayères*, are used today by the Champagne houses to age Champagne. Les Crayères is also the name of a sensational three-star restaurant in Reims, Champagne.

165

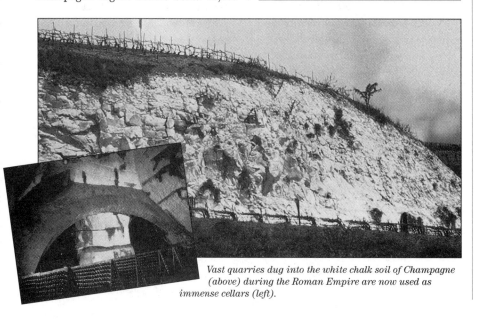

*Vast quarries dug into the white chalk soil of Champagne (above) during the Roman Empire are now used as immense cellars (left).*

## THE GRAPES OF

# CHAMPAGNE

## WHITE

**Chardonnay:** Major grape and the only white grape grown in the region. Used in virtually all Champagnes generally for its finesse. Champagnes called *blanc de blancs* are based exclusively on chardonnay.

## REDS

**Pinot Meunier:** Major grape, though some houses consider it the least important of Champagne's three grapes. A common ingredient in nonvintage Champagnes, it usually contributes fruitiness and body.

**Pinot Noir:** The more revered of Champagne's two red grapes. Pinot noir is used in most Champagnes (not, of course, in *blanc de blancs*). It often contributes body, texture, and aroma.

cliffs of Dover. Like a great chalk crescent, the area that spans from the British cliffs to Champagne was the basin of a vast prehistoric sea some 65 million years ago. When the waters receded, they left behind minerals, such as quartz and zircon, plus fossils of sea urchins, sea sponges, and other sea animals. These fossils helped form the chalk. Millions of years later, violent earthquakes erupted, mixing the chalk with material from within the earth and creating the sloping hills over which the best Champagne vineyards now lie.

Walking in the countryside, it is not unusual to see stark white outcroppings, bare slices of earth pierced by the tips of deeply burrowed grapevine roots. The soft and porous chalk encourages the roots to delve deeply into the earth in search of water. Chalk drains well but also stores just enough moisture so that the vines are rarely parched.

All other things being equal, grapes grown in poor soil generally make better wine than grapes grown in rich soil. In Champagne, the soil is fairly barren and so natural compost must be used as a fertilizer.

Champagne may only be made from three grapes: chardonnay, pinot noir, and pinot meunier. Conventional wisdom has it that chardonnay contributes finesse and elegance; pinot noir, body and texture; and pinot meunier, fruitiness and earthiness, but this is a simplistic assessment. Much depends on the vintage and the location of the vineyards. In certain vintages and from less perfect vineyards, chardonnay can lack finesse and pinot noir lack body.

Champagne is divided into five main vineyard areas:

**1.** The Montagne de Reims, the mountain of Reims; mostly planted with pinot noir and pinot meunier.

life on the edge. It can be wet and rainy at the worst possible time—in late summer when rot can erupt and the grapes themselves can become waterlogged. It's also very cold in the winter, and spring frosts are not unusual. In short, the grapes often have a difficult time surviving and then ripening evenly and fully. In fact, the vines are intentionally trained low to the ground so that they can absorb whatever warmth might be reflected off the white soil. (In times past the Champenois—ever the pragmatists—used to spread bits of white plastic garbage bags in the vineyards to reflect even more sun. Seeing some of Europe's most famous vineyards strewn with trash bags was, if nothing else, a remarkable sight. The practice is now forbidden.)

The famous white chalk soil of Champagne is the geologic sister of the white

2. The Côte des Blancs, the hillside of whites; named for the chardonnay vines that grow there almost exclusively.

3. The Vallée de la Marne, valley of the Marne River; mostly planted with pinot meunier.

4. Côtes de Sézanne, planted with chardonnay.

5. The Aube, mostly planted with pinot noir.

Of these areas, the Montagne de Reims, the Côte des Blancs, and the Vallée de la Marne are the three most important. The first two between them share all seventeen villages considered extraordinary (historically rated 100 percent). Some thirty-eight more villages are considered good to great (rated 89 to 99 percent); and the remainder are judged good (rated 80 to 90 percent). Unfortunately, the quality status of villages is rarely listed on a Champagne label. In 1994 Bollinger was the first house to disclose such information on the label, and it remains one of the few.

The vineyards of Champagne are not owned primarily by the 110 Champagne houses but rather by approximately 15,000 growers who have long-term contracts with the houses. Growers may sell their wine to one or several houses and, some 5,000 growers also keep some of their grapes and make Champagne themselves. These Champagnes, now coming into the United States more often, can be fantastic.

From the houses' standpoint, of course, it would be ideal to own at least some vineyards, over which the house would have more complete control.

## THE GRANDES MARQUES

The words *Grandes Marques* do not refer to a quality level of Champagne but rather to an organization of approximately thirty well-established and highly renowned houses. The Syndicat de Grandes Marques de Champagne has in fact been in existence for more than a century and is one of the oldest French unions.

*Champagne's serene vineyards are the most northern in France.*

Several houses do own significant acreage. At Roederer, 75 percent of the house's grape needs can be fulfilled from the house's own vineyards; at Bollinger, 70 percent; at Krug, 40 percent.

# MAKING CHAMPAGNE

Champagne, along with Sherry and Port, is one of the world's most complicated wines to make. Not only are the steps involved numerous and demanding, but the winemaking itself requires a specific type of intellectual dexterity that can be daunting.

The Champagne maker makes not one or even five wines but as many as sixty. These are based on three grapes: chardonnay (white), pinot noir, and pinot meunier (both red; in Champagne, red grapes are usually referred to as black grapes). All will eventually be blended. And that is where the plot thickens.

The Champagne maker's goal is *not* to make a blend of wines that immediately tastes good. This, in any case, would be difficult, for the base wines used to make Champagne are screechingly high in acidity, low in alcohol, and generally taste rather meager. Instead, the Champagne maker blends these still, base wines with an idea, a notion, an imagining of what the blended wine will taste like years later once it has undergone a second fermentation, has developed bubbles, and has a bit of sweetened reserve wine in it. Years of skill, guess work, experimentation, experi-

*Wooden basket presses were formerly the norm in Champagne. Most of these presses were not ideal since grapes in them could be easily bruised and abraided, leading to coarse wine. Modern pneumatic presses are much more gentle.*

ence, and flying by the seat of one's pants are needed to understand what a given blend might taste like post-transformation.

The process begins with the harvest. Because two of the three grapes used in making Champagne are red, they must be harvested gently by hand so that the juice doesn't pick up any reddish highlights or tannic coarseness from the skins. The grapes are then pressed in some 2,000 pressing houses scattered throughout the vineyards. Each lot of grapes is kept separate. The reason for this is straightforward. The 312 Champagne villages, or *crus*, have different reputations for the quality and characteristics of the grapes they produce. Long ago, each village was given a rating from 80 percent (the lowest) to 100 percent (the highest). (The village's rating determined how much growers in that village would be paid for their grapes.) Since each house buys grapes from many different villages, they have multiple wines of varying characteristics—aromas, acidity, degree of alcohol, and so on—to work with.

In most cases, grapes are fermented in stainless steel vats, which allows the winemaker to control the temperature and pace of the fermentation. A few houses, however, still ferment the wines in wood as was historically done. Krug ferments all of its wines in cask and Bollinger, all of its vintaged wines. Other houses that ferment some of their wines in wood include Taittinger, Louis Roederer, Gratien, and Jacquesson.

The casks are not brand-new, for new oak barrels would impart such significant toasted oak flavors and tannin that the delicacy of the wines would easily be compromised. Even with used oak, however, the Champagne maker must be cautious. Elegance can be easily erased.

*The old cellars at the house of Roederer: Large oak barrels such as these were once common throughout Champagne.*

Besides the thirty to sixty or so separate lots of still wine a Champagne house makes each year, it will also have reserve wines held back from former years. This is a critical, if little realized, fact for even a small amount of reserve wine can give a Champagne blend extra depth and richness. As a matter of law, a minimum of 20 percent of the vintage *must* be held in reserve for future blending. The practice of setting aside some wines for use in future years is traditional and eminently sane. In a climate as cold and marginal as Champagne's, no winemaker could ever rest assured that the next harvest would bring enough good grapes. But even that's not the whole story. These reserve wines will also be the reservoir from which wine is drawn to top up the bottles after the secondary fermentation. (This will make sense in a minute.)

In the spring after the harvest, the head winemaker for each house, his assistants,

169

and an enologist begin to make the house's basic nonvintage (multivintage would be a more exact term) wine by blending dozens of still wines from different years. This is called the *assemblage*. If the weather has been particularly good, certain lots of wine will be set aside as blending material for the house's vintage Champagne and for a prestige *cuvée*. However, no house will use up all of its great lots making a vintage or a prestige *cuvée* wine at the expense of turning out a mediocre nonvintage. Since the lion's share of what every house makes every year is nonvintage, making an inferior one would make no sense.

Next, the nonvintage blend will be mixed with a small amount of yeasts plus a *liqueur de tirage*—a combination of sugar and wine—and then bottled and capped. The predictable happens. The yeasts eat the sugar (this constitutes a second fermentation), forming a bit more alcohol and throwing off carbon dioxide gas. Or trying to. Because the bottles are capped, the $CO_2$ has no place to go. It becomes physically trapped in the wine as dissolved gas. When the bottles are eventually opened, this trapped gas will explode and become bubbles.

The bottles rest in the cellars for at least a year at this point. Because the spent yeasts (lees) are still inside the bottles, the wine is said to be resting *sur lie* (on the lees). Though seemingly neutral, these spent yeast cells enhance the complexity and texture of the wine through a process called autolysis.

If the Champagne was sold at this point, it would be cloudy and a little gritty with spent yeasts. To remove the yeasts, the bottles are inserted in A-frames called *pupitres*. There, each day, the bottles are riddled—turned slightly and upended a fraction. Traditionally, this was done completely by hand by a person called a *rémueur*. A good *rémueur* can riddle

*In a typical Champagne cellar, there will be miles of caverns where bottles, resting in A-shaped frames, wait to be riddled. A bike is helpful for getting around.*

## HOW DRY IS THAT CHAMPAGNE?

Afer the yeasts are removed from each bottle, Champagnes are topped up with sweetened reserve wine, or liqueur d'expédition. The level of sweetness of this wine determines the category of Champagne that will be made. As you will see, categories overlap. A Champagne that is 1.4 percent sugar might be deemed a brut by one house but an extra dry by another.

Despite its beginnings as a fairly sweet beverage, most of the Champagnes now produced are brut. Brut Champagne is best drunk as an aperitif or with a meal. Champagne that is slightly sweet generally works better than brut after a meal. Extra dry is a good example. The wine is not truly sweet in the conventional sense but, rather, simply more round and creamy than brut. Moët & Chandon's wildly popular White Star Champagne is not brut, as many believe. It's extra dry.

Dry and demi-sec (half dry) Champagnes, slightly sweeter than extra dry, are extraordinary wines to end a meal with and also unbeatable with fruit desserts. Only a few houses make dry and demi-sec Champagne: Veuve Clicquot, Moët & Chandon, and Mumm are the top three.

Here are the categories of Champagne based on their sweetness:

**Extra Brut**
Very, very dry: O to 0.6% sugar
(0 to 6 grams of sugar per liter)

**Brut**
Very dry: less than 1.5% sugar
(less than 15 grams of sugar per liter)

**Extra Dry**
Off-dry: 1.2 to 2% sugar
(12 to 20 grams of sugar per liter)

**Sec**
Lightly sweet: 1.7 to 3.5% sugar
(17 to 35 grams of sugar per liter)

**Demi-Sec**
Sweet: 3.3 to 5% sugar
(33 to 50 grams of sugar per liter)

**Doux**
Quite sweet: more than 5% sugar
(more than 50 grams of sugar per liter)

171

30,000 to 40,000 bottles a day. Today about 25 percent of Champagne is hand-riddled. The rest is riddled equally effectively, but more efficiently, by large machines called gyropalettes.

Slowly, as the bottles are riddled, the yeast cells slide down the inside walls of the bottles. By the time the bottles are completely upside down, all of the yeasts will be collected in the bottle necks. Now removal is easy. In a process called *dégorgement*, each bottle is placed, still upside-down, in a brine solution, which freezes the entire length of the neck and its contents. When the bottle is then quickly turned upright and the cap removed, the frozen plug of yeasts shoots out. This leaves a clear, bone-dry wine. But it also leaves about a ¼ inch of space. Immediately, the Champagne is topped up with a *liqueur d'expédition*, a combination of wine—specifically some of the reserve wine—and sugar. The sweetness level of the *liqueur d'expédition*, also known as the *dosage*, determines how dry or sweet the Champagne will be.

The vast majority of Champagne is brut, although a number of houses make extra dry, which is a shade sweeter. Extra dry is not the same as extra brut, the newest category relatively speaking. Extra dry Champagnes are slightly sweet; extra brut are almost or entirely bone-dry. Some wines that are entirely bone-dry are Piper-Heidsieck's Brut Sauvage, Laurent-Perrier's Ultra Brut, and LeClerc Briant's Brut Zéro.

## Why Blend?

Champagne cannot be divorced from the art of blending. The very soul of a Champagne rests on the quality of the wines to be blended and the blending skills of the winemaker. The complexity of the Champagne, in fact, hinges on the success of the blend. The goal is to marry wines in such a way that they do not cancel each other out but, rather, coalesce into a compelling, synergistic whole.

*Krug's renowned vineyard Clos du Mesnil.*

Nonvintage Champagnes require the greatest artistry and skill on the part of the winemaker. First, because the wines from which they are made may be of varying qualities. Second, the wines might span up to ten different vintages. Whatever blend the Champagne maker settles on, *that* blend will be further blended by the addition of the *dosage*. Of course, in simplistic terms, if it were not for blending, there would be no need for Champagne houses. If Champagne were unblended, then the wine would reflect an individual vineyard more than it did the blending talents of its maker.

Among the well-known houses, only a few do not blend some of their wines. Krug and Philipponnat make unblended Champagnes from single vineyards called Clos du Mesnil and Clos des Goisses respectively. Krug's Clos du Mesnil is a 4½-acre vineyard in the highly regarded village of Le Mesnil-sur-Oger. Clos du Mesnil has been enclosed by a private wall since 1698. The vineyard produces wines of such unique and extraordinary flavor that Krug feels it would be almost sacrilegious to blend it with other wines. Indeed, the house treats the *clos* with painstaking care. Even though the vineyard is small and could be picked in a day, pickers go through it again and again over several days, picking only perfectly ripe bunches each time. About 15,000 bottles are made annually.

## STYLES OF CHAMPAGNE

Champagne is really not one wine, but a range of wines that span a spectrum of flavors and textures. At one end are the light-bodied Champagnes, with fine citrusy acidity and delicate creamy flavors. At the other are opulent, full-bodied Champagnes with toasty, biscuity, vanilla flavors and dense, custardy textures.

It is entirely possible that wine drinkers who love spiky, light, vibrant Champagnes with lots of zing will find the fuller styles overwrought. Similarly, people who love toasty, rich, creamy Champagnes wonder if there's any there there in lighter-style Champagnes. Style preferences, in other words, are subjective.

Every producer blends in such a way as to achieve the same style year after year. Houses that make full-bodied Champagnes often use a larger percentage of pinot noir grapes and rely on vineyards known to yield fuller-bodied wines. Houses that lean toward a lighter-bodied style frequently use a higher proportion of chardonnay grapes and rely on vineyards known to yield delicate-bodied wines. These statements are, of course, generalizations, for chardonnay can certainly be robust, just as pinot noir can be delicate. I have grouped the Champagnes in the chart on this page according to how I would describe their styles.

# THE BUBBLES

For starters, how many bubbles does a bottle of Champagne have? The answer is 56 million, give or take a few. But that's only if the bottle is open; an unopened bottle only has the potential for bubbles. The figure comes from the house of Bollinger, which has studied bubbles seriously.

A bubble is a thin film of liquid filled with gas. Bubbles, however, are not all created equal: Just compare Coke with Champagne. The fat bubbles in Coke are created by injecting carbon dioxide into the liquid with a machine called a carbonator. Champagne's tiny bubbles, on the other hand, emerge from their dissolved state in the liquid.

One of the axioms of Champagne has always been: The smaller the bubbles; the finer the wine. Bubble size is affected both by the length of time a Champagne ages (the longer, the smaller) and by the temperature of the aging cellar (the cooler, the smaller).

---

## CHAMPAGNE BY STYLE

Various Champagne houses are known for producing either lighter- or fuller-style Champagnes. Remember that the categories light, light to medium, and so on, refer to the body or weight of the wine—how light or full it is in the mouth—not to the sweetness level of the wine.

### LIGHT
Abelé, Besserat de Bellefon, Bricout, Charbaut, Jacquesson, Lanson, Taillevent

### LIGHT TO MEDIUM
Ayala, Billecart-Salmon, De Venoge, Laurent-Perrier, Nicolas Feuillatte, Perrier-Jouët, Pommery, Taittinger

### MEDIUM
Charles Heidsieck, Delamotte, Deutz, Heidsieck-Monopole, Jacquart, Joseph Perrier, Moët & Chandon, Mumm, Philipponnat, Piper-Heidsieck, Pol Roger, Salon

### MEDIUM TO FULL
Alfred Gratien, Gosset, Henriot, J. Sélosse, Ruinart, Veuve Clicquot Ponsardin

### FULL
Bollinger, Krug, Louis Roederer

## COMPARING NONVINTAGE, VINTAGE, AND PRESTIGE CUVÉES

Nonvintage Champagne, the least expensive type, should really be called multivintage. Vintage Champagnes, on the other hand, are made only in years when the harvest is considered exemplary. One house may declare a vintage when another does not. On average, vintages are declared three times a decade. Prestige *cuvées* are also made at the house's discretion. They are generally, but not always, vintage dated.

Four factors help to determine the differences among nonvintage, vintage, and prestige *cuvées*. They are: the vineyards, the grapes, the blending, and the aging.

| | Nonvintage Champagne | Vintage Champagne | Prestige Cuvée |
|---|---|---|---|
| **VINEYARDS** In the past, the vineyards of Champagne were given ratings from 80 to 100 percent, and growers were paid accordingly. (To make the math simple, if for instance a kilo of grapes cost $10, then a grower who owned a vineyard rated 100 percent would be paid $10 for each kilo. The owner of a vineyard rated 80 percent would be paid $8 per kilo.) Today, although the system of grape pricing has been modified, the vineyard ratings are still used to set a reference price for the grapes. | Grapes come mostly from good vineyards, historically rated 80 to 90 percent, with a tiny amount of superior wine blended in. | Grapes come from good to great vineyards, historically rated 90 to 100 percent. | Grapes come from the greatest vineyards, historically rated 100 percent. |
| **GRAPES** Most Champagnes are a blend of chardonnay, pinot noir, and pinot meunier. However, because pinot meunier has fruity, earthy flavors, some houses prefer to use it only in small amounts. Nonetheless, virtually every house uses it to some extent. | Pinot meunier is almost always included in blend. | Pinot meunier is sometimes included in blend. | For most—but not all—houses, pinot meunier is rarely included in blend. |
| **BLENDING** All Champagnes are blends. Blending, in fact, is considered the most critical skill a Champagne maker must possess. | As many as 30 to 60 still wines from several years. | As many as 30 to 60 still wines from a single year considered exceptional. | Blend of only the best wines from the best vineyards to which the producer has access. |
| **AGING** These are the legal minimums; most houses exceed them considerably. | 15 months in the bottle. | 3 years in the bottle. | No requirement; common practice: 4 to 7 years. |

174

The quantity of Champagne bubbles and their persistence are primarily due to the holding power of colloids (extremely tiny particles that are not easily filtered out of the wine) and the amount of protein found in various grape varieties. The amount of protein can vary by vintage year and certain strains of yeast liberate more colloids than others. Chardonnay, in general, is higher in proteins than pinot noir and as a result, creates more bubbles.

To determine how many bubbles a standard bottle of Champagne has, Bollinger first computed the diameter and the volume of a bubble. (The math is intense.) Next, they determined the potential size of the area the bubbles could fill (essentially the space occupied by the dissolved $CO_2$). Finally, the size of the bubbles was divided into the area, yielding the figure 56 million.

## TYPES OF CHAMPAGNE

By far, most Champagne produced is golden in color and made from all three Champagne grapes: chardonnay, pinot noir, and pinot meunier. However, there are two fairly rare types of Champagne that can be quite special: *blanc de blancs* and rosé.

### Blanc de Blancs Champagnes

Literally white from whites, *blanc de blancs* Champagne is made entirely from chardonnay grapes. It was created in 1921 by Eugène-Aimé Salon, founder of the Champagne house Salon, whose intention was to create a Champagne with maximum finesse, lightness, and elegance. Easier said than done. Today, although a number of houses make a small amount of *blanc de blancs*, only

a few (Taittinger, Salon, Krug) make consistently delicious *blanc de blancs*.

The best *blanc de blancs* come from the chalky slopes of the Côte des Blancs, one of the three premier grape-growing regions in Champagne and the one planted almost exclusively with chardonnay. Within the Côte des Blancs is the village of Le Mesnil-sur-Oger, rated 100 percent and home to two of the most extraordinary *blanc de blancs* Champagnes in the world: Krug's Clos du Mesnil and Salon's Le Mesnil. *Blanc de blancs* Champagnes may be nonvintage or vintage. They are generally more expensive than brut nonvintage Champagnes.

*Krug's expensive Champagne Clos du Mesnil comes entirely from grapes grown in a vineyard by the same name.*

## THE FINE PRINT

A Champagne bottle always carries one of the following designations in small print on its label:

**NM:** *Négociant-manipulant*, refers to houses that buy grapes to make their wines.

**RM:** *Récoltant-manipulant*, refers to growers that make and sell Champagnes from their own grapes. They can buy only 5 percent of their needs for additional grapes.

**RC:** *Récoltant coopérateur*, refers to growers that make and sell Champagnes with the help of cooperatives.

**CM:** *Coopérative-manipulant*, a gathering of growers that make and sell Champagnes on behalf of its members.

**MA:** *Marque d'acheteur*, a brand that is owned by a third party and not by the maker of the wine.

*Blanc de blancs* is the opposite of *blanc de noirs* (white from reds), an ever so slightly pink-tinged golden Champagne made entirely from red grapes. *Blanc de noirs* Champagnes are extremely rare in Champagne itself. Champagne makers seem to like definitiveness when it comes to color; if they're not making a golden Champagne, then they're making an un-apologetically rosy pink rosé. Curiously, just the opposite is true in California. Very few sparkling wine producers there make a rosé sparkler, perhaps because rosés have always had an image problem in the United States. Yet many California sparkling wine makers produce *blanc de noirs*.

### Rosé Champagnes

Among wine drinkers who know their Champagne, rosé Champagnes are considered the crème de la crème. They are more expensive than golden Champagnes, a reflection of the fact that they are more difficult to produce, and they're far more rare, forming 3 to 5 percent of all exports. There are two methods for making them. The first—and historical—method involves letting some of the base wine sit in contact with pinot noir skins until it picks up enough color to tint the wine pink. The other method, more modern and more common, involves adding a small bit of still pinot noir wine into each Champagne bottle before the second fermentation. This method is preferred for several reasons, among them the fact that such rosés seem to age better. Both processes are complex, and achieving a certain exact coloration is difficult, as a lineup of rosé Champagnes will attest. The colors range from baby pink to deep coppery salmon.

Though often mistakenly thought of as light and fairly simple, rosé Champagne can be richer and fuller than golden. The basic blend counts for a lot. The rosé might be a blend of 80 percent pinot noir and 20 percent chardonnay—or just the opposite, 80 percent chardonnay and only 20

## BIBLICAL BOTTLES

———〜〜〜———

The smallest Champagne bottles hold about one glass of bubbly; the largest, about one hundred glasses. There are, in total, nine different sizes. Large Champagne bottles are rarities and are seldom shipped from France, where they are individually hand blown. For unknown reasons, in the late 1800s, such bottles were given the names of biblical kings.

| Size | Equivalent |
| --- | --- |
| Split | 187.5 milliliters, about 1½ glasses |
| Half-bottle | 375 milliliters, about 2½ glasses |
| Bottle | 750 milliliters, about 5 glasses |
| Magnum | 2 bottles, about 10 glasses |
| Jeroboam | 4 bottles, about 20 glasses |
| Methuselah | 8 bottles, about 40 glasses |
| Salmanazar | 12 bottles, about 60 glasses |
| Balthazar | 16 bottles, about 80 glasses |
| Nebuchadnezzar | 20 bottles, about 100 glasses |

Jeroboam was king of the newly formed northern kingdom of Israel. Methuselah, not an ancient king, was distinguished by his incredible longevity, living 969 years. The Assyrian king Salmanazar ruled over the Judean kingdom. Balthazar was the name of one of the Three Wise Men, known as the Lord of the Treasury and also considered to be a grandson of Nebuchadnezzar. The king of Babylon, Nebuchadnezzar was a prominent and powerful ruler who destroyed Jerusalem.

percent pinot noir. A rosé can be made either way, but when you drink them the impressions the two wines make will be quite different.

## NOT WITH A BANG BUT A WHISPER

Before opening and serving Champagne, the first important step, of course, is to chill it. Because Champagne bottles are made with thicker glass than regular wine bottles, the time required to chill them is longer. Allow twenty to forty minutes (depending on the original temperature of the bottle) in a bucket of ice and water—which is the fastest way.

Opening Champagne is not difficult, but it is different—and far more exciting—than opening a bottle of still wine. Each Champagne bottle is under 6 atmospheres of pressure, about the same as a truck tire. With so much pressure behind it, a cork can fly an astounding distance. But that's only if you open the bottle incorrectly. The correct, safe, and controlled way to open and serve Champagne is:

**1.** Break and remove the foil, not the wire cage, from around the cork.

**2.** Place your thumb firmly on top of the cork to keep the cork from flying.

**3.** With your other hand, unscrew the wire (it takes about six turns) and loosen the cage. You actually don't have to take the cage off completely.

**4.** Holding the cork firmly, begin to twist it in one direction as, from the bottom, you twist the bottle in the other direction. Contrary to popular opinion, a Champagne cork should not make a loud

*thwock!* You're supposed to ease the cork out, so that it makes just a light hissing sound. Unbidden, more than one older Frenchman has advised me that a Champagne bottle, correctly opened, should make a sound no greater than that of a contented woman's sigh. Frenchmen are French men after all.

**5.** Holding the bottle around the base, pour. Fill each glass with about 2 inches of Champagne. Then go back and top them all up.

**6.** If there's Champagne left, seal the bottle using a Champagne stopper and place it back in the ice bucket or refrigerator.

**7.** Do not immediately top up glasses with fresh Champagne every time a sip has been taken. Just as topping up a half-filled cup of coffee ensures that you'll never have the satisfaction of a fresh, steaming hot cup, so too, frequent topping up of Champagne can mean the wine is never nicely chilled. Wait until there's only about one sip remaining to top it up.

**8.** In Champagne, it's considered rude to turn an empty bottle upside down in an ice bucket.

## THE PUNT

t's often seemed to me that 99 percent of all the waiters in the world pour Champagne by holding the bottles with their thumbs inserted in the punts, or indentations in the bottoms of the bottles. As chic as this looks, the punt was never intended for such a purpose. Originally, punts were a way of preventing the jagged pontil mark—the point left over after a glass bottle was blown and shaped—from scratching the surface of a table. By pushing the pontil up into the interior of the bottle, a punt was formed and the table was saved. When mold-made wine bottles were introduced, the punt remained, since it adds stability to the bottle when upright. With Champagne bottles, however, the punt has quite a different purpose. During the second fermentation, which ultimately gives Champagne its bubbles, considerable pressure is built up inside the fragile glass wall of the bottle. The Champagne bottle's prominent punt allowed for a more even distribution of pressure inside the bottle, preventing the disastrous explosions that were a common and serious problem for early Champagne makers.

## BUBBLE WRAP

Ever watch people being handed flutes of Champagne? At least half of them immediately stand up straighter and adopt a sexier tone of voice. The flute—elegant, sleek, and long-lined—is about as sophisticated as glassware gets.

Flute-shaped glasses were already in use for beer and ale by the time Champagne made its debut in the late seventeenth century. The basic shape evolved from conical-shaped glasses made between 1300 and 1500 in Venice. These in turn were inspired by some of the earliest drinking vessels, such as animal horns.

Serendipitously, the art of glassmaking was reaching its apex just as Champagne making was beginning. By the late seventeenth century, Venetian glassmakers were capable of creating fragile goblets that possessed remarkable clarity. Historians theorize that the transparent beauty of such glass may have been one of the considerations that ultimately led winemakers to develop techniques for making crystal-clear, sediment-free Champagne.

As Champagne vessels, the flute and its cousin, the tulip glass, proved to be eminently practical. When Champagne is poured into either, the $CO_2$ gas dissolved in the liquid rubs against microscopic points on the glasses' seemingly smooth inside surface. The friction causes the gas to burst into bubbles. But there's more: Bubbles in any liquid vary in size depending on the pressure of the surrounding liquid. By virtue of the increased pressure at their bases, the flute and tulip encourage long beaded lines of especially tiny bubbles.

As for the saucer-shaped Champagne coupe (often used at weddings), legend has it that the first was a porcelain version invented by Marie Antoinette, who used her breast (reportedly the left breast because it was closer to her heart) as the mold. Notwithstanding so compelling a beginning, the coupe is terrible for Champagne. In it, bubbles dissipate quickly, the Champagne is easily warmed by the drinker's hand, and the vessel itself is so

*The house of Veuve Clicquot (then simply named Clicquot) was founded in 1772 by Philippe Clicquot-Muiron. When his son died, his son's twenty-seven-year-old widow, Nicole Barbe Ponsardin, took over, becoming one of the most enterprising and powerful women in Champagne. A relief (inset) carved into the wall in Clicquot's chalk cellars dates from the nineteenth century.*

## MATCHING LUXURY

Champagne and caviar have always been perceived as a classic match, perhaps because of the special occasion, celebratory aura they share. Yet from the perspective of flavor, the two don't always work together, especially if the caviar is very salty and the Champagne delicate. To enhance the match, be sure to choose a high-quality, subtly flavored, very fresh caviar—osetra is wonderful—and serve it with a rather full-bodied Champagne (see page 173 for the styles of Champagne). Another extraordinary, though admittedly not classic, match for Champagne is sushi. In particular, extra dry Champagne, with its faint touch of sweetness, is a perfect foil when the sushi is gently seasoned with ginger, wasabi, and soy sauce.

frustratingly shallow, it hardly holds more than two sips.

Not surprisingly, in the region of Champagne, coupes are never seen. But remarkably, there aren't many flutes either. At most Champagne houses, the slightly wider tulip or a deep white-wine glass with a generous round bowl is preferred. According to Rémi Krug, managing director of the Champagne firm that bears his family name, a generous tulip glass is better than a flute

180

for appreciating the Champagne's aroma. Being able to watch a long train of bubbles isn't particularly important to Krug either. Bubbles, he maintains, are simply meant to be discreetly felt "dancing in the mouth."

# VISITING THE CHAMPAGNE HOUSES

From Paris, the Champagne region is just an hour-and-a-half train ride or a morning's drive (about 90 miles) away. The tours given by most of the large houses are a step-by-step education in how Champagne is made and may last up to two hours. English is almost always spoken. Appointments are usually necessary, and it is best to make them at least a month in advance, especially if you are traveling during the summer.

Champagne's two most important cities are Reims, full of churches, palaces, abbeys, and great cafés, and Epernay, which is smaller, more like a charming village. Just outside Epernay is the Benedictine Abbey of Hautvillers, where Dom Pérignon lived and worked. Now owned by Moët & Chandon, it has been rebuilt into a small museum that re-creates monastic life and houses many antique Champagne presses and tools.

The roads of Champagne have been mapped into three itineraries, which together form the Route Touristique du Champagne. For more information, contact Foods and Wines from France, 215 Park Avenue South, New York, New York 10003; (212) 477-8492. The telephone numbers that follow here include the dialing code you'll need when calling from the United States. If you're calling from within France, eliminate the 011-33 and add a zero before the next number.

## FLATTERY— OHIO STYLE

———

Moët & Chandon's White Star (an extra dry) is the largest selling Champagne in the United States. In the 1870s, one of the most infamous sparkling wines in the country copied the name. White Star Champagne was made in Ohio —probably from native catawba grapes—by Michel Hommel, a winemaker who had been born and trained in Epernay. Hommel's pseudo "champagne" became the wine of choice for christening ships built in shipyards along the Great Lakes.

**A. CHARBAUT & FILS**
17 Avenue de Champagne
51205 Epernay Cedex
011-33-3-26-54-37-55

**AYALA & CO.**
Château d'Aÿ
2 Boulevard du Nord
51160 Aÿ
011-33-3-26-55-15-44

**LOUIS ROEDERER**
21 Boulevard Lundy
51053 Reims Cedex
011-33-3-26-40-42-11

**MOËT & CHANDON**
20 Avenue de Champagne
51333 Epernay
011-33-3-26-54-71-11
Visiting the museum at the Abbey of Hautvillers requires an appointment.

**PERRIER-JOUËT**
26 Avenue de Champagne
51200 Epernay
011-33-3-26-55-20-53

**POL ROGER**
1 Rue Henri-Lelarge
51206 Epernay
011-33-3-26-55-41-95

**RUINART**
4 Rue des Crayères
51100 Reims
011-33-3-26-85-40-29

**TAITTINGER**
9 Place Saint-Niçaise
51100 Reims
011-33-3-26-85-45-35

**VEUVE CLICQUOT PONSARDIN**
12 Rue du Temple
51100 Reims
011-33-3-26-40-25-42
To make an appointment, call Veuve Clicquot headquarters in New York; (212) 888-7575.

*Claude Taittinger in Taittinger's underground chalk cellars in Reims.*  **181**

# THE STARS AMONG THE CHAMPAGNES

Prestige *cuvées*, also known as *cuvées spéciales*, are the most expensive and highest-quality category of Champagnes. The first prestige *cuvée* was made in 1876 by the house of Roederer for Czar Alexander II of Russia, who wanted an exclusive Champagne not available to the lower aristocracy. The czar further dictated that it be shipped in leaded crystal bottles. Roederer's prestige *cuvée* was hence named Cristal. The second prestige *cuvée* was Dom Pérignon, first made by Moët & Chandon in 1921 and shipped to the United States for the first time in 1936. Here are some of the others, listed below the house that makes them. I've also indicated if the prestige *cuvée* comes as golden, rosé, or both. (Some houses make two prestige *cuvées*.)

**A. Charbaut & Fils**
Certificate, *golden and rosé*

**Billecart-Salmon**
Cuvée N. F. Billecart, *golden*

**Bollinger**
Année Rare R. D., *golden and rosé*
Grand Année, *golden and rosé*

**Deutz**
Cuvée William Deutz, *golden and rosé*

**Gosset**
Grand Millésime, *golden and rosé*

**Heidsieck Monopole**
Diamant Bleu, *golden*

**Henriot**
Baccarat, *golden*

**Jacquart**
Cuvée Nominée, *golden*

**Jacquesson**
Signature, *golden*

**Joseph Perrier**
Cuvée Joséphine, *golden*

**Krug**
Clos du Mesnil, *golden*
Grande Cuvée NV, *golden and rosé*
Krug Vintage, *golden*

**Lanson**
Special Cuvée 225, *golden*

**Laurent-Perrier**
Grand Siècle, *golden and rosé*

**Louis Roederer**
Cristal, *golden and rosé*

**Moët & Chandon**
Dom Pérignon, *golden and rosé*

**Mumm**
Grand Cordon, *golden and rosé*
René Lalou, *golden*

**Perrier-Jouët**
Blason de France, *golden and rosé*
Fleur de Champagne, *golden and rosé*

**Philipponnat**
Clos des Goisses, *golden*

**Piper-Heidsieck**
Rare, *golden*

**Pol Roger**
Cuvée Sir Winston Churchill, *golden*

**Pommery**
Cuvée Louise Pommery, *golden and rosé*

**Ruinart**
Dom Ruinart, *golden and rosé*

**Salon**
Le Mesnil, *golden*

**Taittinger**
Comtes de Champagne, *golden and rosé*

**Veuve Clicquot Ponsardin**
La Grande Dame, *golden*

# THE CHAMPAGNES TO KNOW

Most of us are happy being handed a glass of any Champagne whatsoever. But as with other wines, there are both better and worse Champagnes, so it's wise to experiment. For me a great Champagne is like whipped cream wrapped around a sword. The whipped cream is the wine's hedonistic flavor; the sword is the wine's unmistakable and dramatic acidity. There are many wonderful Champagnes from established houses—some of my favorites are listed below. In addition, a number of small growers are now exporting their Champagnes to the United States.

## *Whites*

### AYALA

nonvintage brut

approximately 65% pinot noir,
30% chardonnay, and 5% pinot meunier

Ayala may be less well known than many Champagne houses, but it is a solid winner. The bruts are always bright, snappy, and focused, with gorgeous straw, lemon, green apple, pear, and gingery flavors that ride on a jet stream of little bubbles.

### BOLLINGER

Special Cuvée

nonvintage brut

60% pinot noir, 25% chardonnay,
and 15% pinot meunier

Founded in 1829, Bollinger is one of the best-known *Grandes Marques*—and one with a distinct philosophy. Namely, to leave a Champagne in contact with its yeasts for as long as possible. What this means is that Bollinger wines, even this nonvintage brut called Special Cuvée, are disgorged only when there is market demand. Does this affect flavor? Yes. Extended contact with the yeasts preserves a Champagne's freshness at the same time that it contributes a wonderful yeastiness. Special Cuvée is a great example: dramatic, sleek, citrusy. With an aroma that's as fresh as a lemon grove, it's also beautifully evocative of warm brioche—altogether very satisfying.

### DELAMOTTE

blanc de blancs

nonvintage brut

100% chardonnay

The first time I tasted Delamotte (their regular brut nonvintage, not a *blanc de blancs*), I thought: three cases of this, a few months, and a desert island is all I need. Well, the part about three months and a desert island is, alas, a fantasy, but (luckily) what I *can* have is Delamotte. And I'll take this *blanc de blancs,* for it's appealing, rich, and totally satisfying. The flavors lean toward lemon tart, crème anglaise, and ginger, but what's really stunning is the way the wine's ultracreamy body is wrapped around a core of incisive acidity. The finish is wonderfully long. Delamotte is not very well known, but this small house is completely focused on quality.

**183**

### DEUTZ

Cuvée William Deutz

prestige *cuvée*

vintage brut

30% chardonnay, 60% pinot noir,
and 10% pinot meunier

Deutz (pronounced Deuhtz) may not be a household name in the United States, but Champagne lovers know this house produces dependably luscious Champagnes of great finesse. Deutz's prestige *cuvée,* Cuvée William Deutz (named after the founder, who established the house in 1838), while expensive, reminds you of what you're paying top dollar for—namely, utter refinement and subtlety. The wine begins with rich biscuity aromas and then teasingly opens up into flavors that are at once creamy and crisp. Because the balance and elegance here are impeccable, Cuvée William Deutz could easily win over even the toughest Champagne snob.

## KRUG

Grande Cuvée

prestige *cuvée*

nonvintage brut

approximately 50% pinot noir,
30% chardonnay, and 20% pinot meunier

One of the most legendary Champagnes, Krug is not for everyone. Not because it's palm-sweatingly expensive, which it is, but because it's the polar opposite of what many love about Champagne—namely, its zesty, lively kineticness. Krug, on the other hand, is broodingly rich; as supple as lanolin and positively Rubenesque in its fullness. Every molecule aches with density and intensity.

## LOUIS ROEDERER

*blanc de blancs*

vintage brut

100% chardonnay

While many Champagne houses in the nineteenth century counted the Russian nobility among their

best customers, the firm of Louis Roederer was especially successful, for the czar himself was its best customer. In 1876 at the request of Alexander II, Louis Roederer's eponymous son created Cristal, then a sweet Champagne (it's now dry) presented in a custom-designed crystal bottle. Cristal became the first prestige *cuvée*, and it is still the house's most famous and expensive wine. While Cristal is certainly a Champagne not to be missed, Louis Roederer's vintage *blanc de blancs*, with its beautifully refined creamy, yeasty, and rich *tarte Tatin* flavors is (comparatively anyway) a steal. Champagne connoisseurs know it to be one of the best deals in the world of bubbles.

## POL ROGER

Cuvée Sir Winston Churchill

prestige *cuvée*

vintage brut

mostly pinot noir

The warm biscuity aroma of Pol Roger's prestige *cuvée* lulls you in, then, a split second later, vibrant, rich citrusy flavors start vibrating on your tongue. The elegance here is impeccable. Cuvée Sir Winston Churchill was named in honor of the great statesman. He returned the favor and named his racehorse Pol Roger.

## POMMERY

Louise

prestige *cuvée*

vintage brut

60% chardonnay, 40% pinot noir

Louise, Pommery's prestige *cuvée*, is named after Jeanne Alexandrine Louise Pommery, widow of the founder, who in 1858 went on to run the company, building it into a house more successful than even her husband could have (probably) imagined. The wine is exquisite with a fine filigreed frothy *mousse* that is ethereally light on the palate. At the same time, the flavors are rich, creamy, and concentrated. An expensive Champagne to be sure, but one that ensures a sensational experience.

## SALON

Le Mesnil

*blanc de blancs*

prestige *cuvée*

vintage brut

100% chardonnay

Rare, exquisite, and singular, Salon is considered by many to be the apotheosis of Champagne. It was first produced in the early part of the twentieth century and, unusual at the time, was made entirely from chardonnay. It was also made, again atypically, from the grapes of a single vineyard, the famous Le Mesnil. Today only a scrumptious pittance is made from that same vineyard—and only in the most remarkable of years (about three every decade). The sensation of drinking this wine is both electrifying, due to the stilettos of acidity, and soothing, a result of the rushes of creaminess, at the same time.

## VEUVE CLICQUOT PONSARDIN

nonvintage brut

approximately 55% pinot noir,
30% chardonnay, and 15% pinot meunier

From this simple brut up to the prestige *cuvée* La Grande Dame, Veuve Clicquot Champagnes have a shimmering elegance on the palate and a richness that is irresistible. The brut, with its balletlike balance, is creamy yet zesty. Consistently one of the best bruts made.

*Nicole Barbe Ponsardin, better known as Veuve (widow) Clicquot, was a formidable businesswoman. In fact, from the turn of the nineteenth century onward, the women of Champagne were highly instrumental in the wine's evolution and the region's success.*

## THE LITTLE GUYS

So accustomed are we to hearing about and buying Champagnes from the well-known and well-established houses (Veuve Clicquot, Taittinger, Moët & Chandon, and so on), that it's easy to miss the fact that scores of delicious Champagnes are made by small growers. These growers, often family firms, make what might be called artisanal Champagnes from the grapes they grow. As a result, a small grower's Champagne is usually based on a very much smaller number of base wines that are blended together before the wine undergoes the second, bubble-inducing fermentation. Fewer wines in the blend mean that a small grower has less flexibility in creating the flavor of its Champagnes; rather its Champagne will necessarily reflect the *terroir* where the grapes were grown. In the past, many small growers sold their Champagnes exclusively in France, but a number are now being exported (albeit in small amounts) and they are fascinating to taste. Among the producers to look for: René Geoffroy, Jean Milan, and Pierre Peters.

185

## *Rosé*

## TAITTINGER

Comtes de Champagne

prestige *cuvée*

vintage brut

mostly pinot noir with a small amount of chardonnay

Luxuriously creamy, Taittinger's stellar prestige *cuvée* rosé has a core of acidity that's kinetic. The wine's delicious berry flavors explode in the mouth then linger endlessly. A powerhouse of a rosé, yet perfectly elegant.

# CALVADOS

Unlike its cousins Cognac and Armagnac, both of which are distilled from grapes, Calvados is distilled from apples—but not just any apples. By law, the varieties used for Calvados include Clos Renaux, Petit Jaune, Rouge Buret, and more than 115 others. These fall into four flavor categories: sweet, bittersweet, bitter, and acidic. By distilling different kinds of apples in different proportions, the Calvados maker crafts a subtle, complex apple spirit. About 17 pounds of apples are needed to make one bottle of Calvados.

By law, Calvados can be made only in Normandy. It's a staunch tradition for diners in the region to imbibe a shot of Calvados in the middle of a long, rich meal. The shot, called a *trou Normand* (Norman hole), supposedly creates a hole in the stomach, temporarily halting digestion and allowing even more food to be eaten!

The most famous district within the Calvados region is the Pays d'Auge, known for its chalky soil and superior apples. All

Pays d'Auge Calvados is double-distilled and aged in oak casks for a minimum of twenty-four months, although some of the finest spirits may be aged in oak for more than six years. (For a discussion of how to store and serve Calvados, see page 160 of the Cognac box.)

*Calvados is distilled twice in small alembic stills (above). Apple trees (left) are inescapable in the countryside of Normandy.*

# Burgundy

To the proverbial question, If you could take just one wine to a desert island, what would it be? many zealous wine lovers answer instantaneously: Burgundy. It's not just that the best Burgundies—Bourgognes in French—are extraordinary wines (which they are) or that they taste phenomenally good (which they do). It's that a great Burgundy elicits two things most other wines don't: emotion and intrigue. If it were economically feasible to drink great Burgundy for a lifetime, most people would probably never be bored. Burgundy, after all, has multiple adventures up its sleeve.

What is it about this wine from a small, almost secluded region that makes it so compelling? Above all, the great white Burgundies are stunningly complex. Drinking them can be an exercise in delicious patience as layer of flavor after layer of flavor reveals itself. The great red Burgundies are indisputably sensual. For

## THE QUICK SIP ON BURGUNDY

- Burgundy, a fairly small wine region in central eastern France, makes some of the world's most sought-after, expensive, and exquisite wines.

- The system of land ownership is complex. Burgundy has thousands of tiny vineyards, each of which has multiple owners.

- Two grape varieties dominate. All top white Burgundies are made from chardonnay. All top reds come from pinot noir.

centuries they have been described in the most erotic of ways, and sipping them has been compared, among other things, to falling in love. This sensuality extends beyond the wines' provocatively earthy aromas and flavors. The top Burgundies, white and red, have beguiling textures

*The château of Clos de Vougeot sits on one of Burgundy's most famous vineyards. Built in the sixteenth century as a place where visiting abbots could spend the night, it is now owned by the promotional wine fraternity the Confrérie des Chevaliers du Tastevin.*

## BURGUNDY'S DOMAINES

—◁∅∅▷—

In Burgundy, the term *domaine* is not precisely equivalent to that of *château* in Bordeaux. In Bordeaux a château is a single estate composed of vineyards surrounding a building or house that is sometimes quite palatial. In Burgundy a domaine is a collection of vineyard parcels, often extremely small, owned by the same person or entity. Usually these parcels are scattered throughout many villages and appellations, and the domaine will make a separate wine from each. A typical Burgundian domaine produces many wines, all in small quantities.

that melt over or dance upon or explode against the palate in unforgettable ways. Unlike many types of wine, Burgundy's physicality is trenchant. Great ones can send shivers up your spine.

Burgundy's vineyards are mainly planted with just two grape varieties: chardonnay and pinot noir. Both grapes achieve their greatest elegance when planted in a relatively cool climate, and that Burgundy has. Of all the wine regions in the world famous for red wine, Burgundy is the coolest and most northern. The downside of this is that there are years when the lack of sun and/or the frequency of rain results in grapes that are not fully ripened and mature, leading to considerably leaner, less flavorful wines. These less than ideal years are not uncommon, and as a result, there are very apparent differences among vintages of Burgundy.

Given such vintage variation, Burgundies and the exalted experiences they

can evoke are anything but dependable. Drinking Burgundy is, in fact, wine's ultimate crapshoot. For reasons described later in this chapter, even the most pedigreed and priciest Burgundies can turn out disappointing. As spellbinding as a great Burgundy is, a poor one is almost depressing. Burgundy keeps you guessing, keeps you on the edge. But then this, too, is part of its seductive strategy.

## TERROIR, MONKS, AND THE FRENCH REVOLUTION

Its small size not withstanding, Burgundy is one of the world's most intricate and complex wine regions. For more than ten centuries much of the land and most of its wines were under the powerful command of Benedictine and Cistercian monks. Through their painstaking labor, the monks began to establish and define countless tiny parcels that would ultimately become Burgundy's best vineyards and yield its greatest wines.

The top Burgundies are, along with the top wines of Germany, the best examples in the world of wines that reflect their *terroir;* that is, in a thoroughly holistic way they reflect the individual site and unique environment—from sun and soil to shade and slope—in which the vines grew. In fact, the very idea of *terroir* is a kind of mental construct that, at least in Burgundy, is inescapable. You cannot think of the region simply in terms of pinot noir and chardonnay, for in the most elemental sense, Burgundy is not about pinot noir and chardonnay. Burgundy is about what a particular site has to say. Pinot noir and chardonnay are the voices through which the message is expressed.

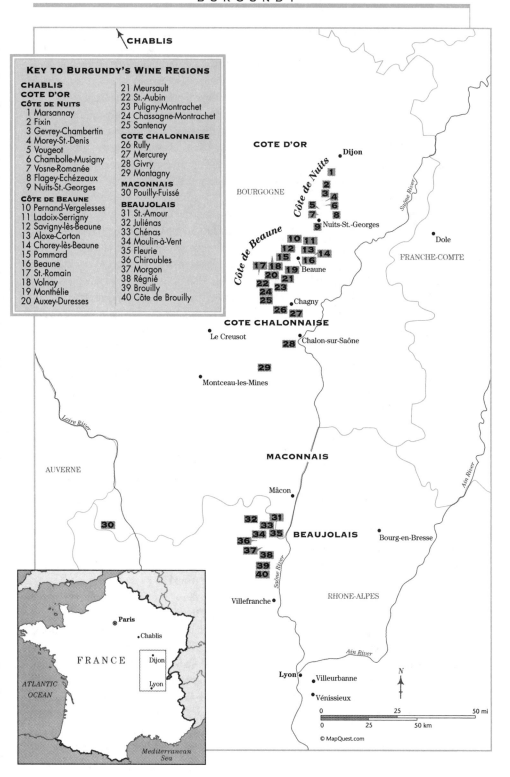

BURGUNDY

CHABLIS

**KEY TO BURGUNDY'S WINE REGIONS**

**CHABLIS**
**COTE D'OR**
**CÔTE DE NUITS**
1 Marsannay
2 Fixin
3 Gevrey-Chambertin
4 Morey-St.-Denis
5 Vougeot
6 Chambolle-Musigny
7 Vosne-Romanée
8 Flagey-Echézeaux
9 Nuits-St.-Georges
**CÔTE DE BEAUNE**
10 Pernand-Vergelesses
11 Ladoix-Serrigny
12 Savigny-lès-Beaune
13 Aloxe-Corton
14 Chorey-lès-Beaune
15 Pommard
16 Beaune
17 St.-Romain
18 Volnay
19 Monthélie
20 Auxey-Duresses

21 Meursault
22 St.-Aubin
23 Puligny-Montrachet
24 Chassagne-Montrachet
25 Santenay
**COTE CHALONNAISE**
26 Rully
27 Mercurey
28 Givry
29 Montagny
**MACONNAIS**
30 Pouilly-Fuissé
**BEAUJOLAIS**
31 St.-Amour
32 Juliénas
33 Chénas
34 Moulin-à-Vent
35 Fleurie
36 Chiroubles
37 Morgon
38 Régnié
39 Brouilly
40 Côte de Brouilly

COTE D'OR

Dijon

Côte de Nuits

BOURGOGNE

Nuits-St.-Georges

Côte de Beaune

Dole

FRANCHE-COMTE

Beaune

Chagny

COTE CHALONNAISE

Le Creusot

Chalon-sur-Saône

Montceau-les-Mines

MACONNAIS

Mâcon

BEAUJOLAIS

Bourg-en-Bresse

RHONE-ALPES

Villefranche

AUVERNE

Loire River

Saône River

Ain River

Ain River

Villeurbanne

Lyon

Vénissieux

N

FRANCE

Paris

Chablis

Dijon

Lyon

ATLANTIC
OCEAN

Mediterranean
Sea

0          25          50 mi

0     25     50 km

© MapQuest.com

## TERROIR AND THE VIGNERON

—⟨φ/φ⟩—

No single word exists in English for *terroir*, the sum entity and effect of soil, slope, orientation to the sun, and elevation, plus every nuance of climate: rainfall, wind velocity, frequency of fog, cumulative hours of sunshine, average high temperature, average low temperature, and so on. In Burgundy a wine is thought to taste the way it does first because of its *terroir* and second because of the way the winemaker made it. Curiously, though, there is no word in French that corresponds exactly to winemaker. Historically, the idea was considered inappropriate. Man, after all, did not make wine; Nature did. In France the person who helped guide the process along has been called by a variety of names, including the one most often used in Burgundy, today, *vigneron*, which means vine grower.

To some this distinction might seem awfully precious. Yet *terroir*—and, in Burgundy, the incredible specificity of *terroir*—cannot be easily dismissed or avoided. Taste two wines from the same domaine and you may find enormous differences between them. How can these be explained when both wines were made by the same person, in the same exact manner, from the same variety of grapes grown in the same way? The clearly apparent variable and the factor that reasonably seems responsible for those differences is place.

Of course, the idea that certain sites give rise to special wines is not new. Far back into antiquity, writings on wine vessels and amphorae suggested this. But it wasn't until the Middle Ages when the monks of Burgundy began to delineate and codify the region's vineyards that *terroir* became the critical core of viticulture. Patient in temperament, systematic in approach, well bestowed with land, and most important, literate, the monks were uniquely prepared for their mission. Plot by plot, they studiously compared vineyards and the wines made from them, recording their impressions over centuries.

The first monastic order to do this was the Benedictines, who for 500 years, from the fifth to the eleventh centuries, were the only order in western Europe and, as such, the keepers of knowledge. At the height of their dominance, the Benedictines controlled more than 1,500 monasteries, including Burgundy's magnificent Abbey of Cluny, the largest cathedral in Europe until St. Peter's in Rome was built and surpassed it.

Each monastery, of course, came with considerable landholdings, buttressing the church's already immense power. In Burgundy, which at the time covered a large area, including parts of what are today northern France, Belgium, and the Netherlands, the church shared its power with a series of flamboyant and wealthy dukes who, in return for religious approbation, bestowed even more land upon the monks. When the pious among the nobility began donating land to the monks as well, it seemed as though the fortunes of the church would know no bounds.

At the end of the eleventh century a reform movement within the Benedictines resulted in the formation of a second order, the Cistercians. Ascetic and uncompromising, the Cistercians found their joy in physically grueling labor. It was they who cleared and cultivated the most difficult limestone slopes of the Côte d'Or, establishing many of what would ultimately become Burgundy's greatest vineyards.

## THE MOST IMPORTANT

## VILLAGES OF BURGUNDY

*To name every important appellation in Burgundy would take pages because, in addition to all the villages, there are no fewer than 562 Premier Cru vineyards and 33 Grand Cru (see The Grand Cru Vineyards of the Côte d'Or, page 204). Here's a list of the most significant villages only. The subregion to which the village belongs appears in capital letters. The subregions and villages within these are listed from north to south.*

### LEADING VILLAGES

CHABLIS
**Chablis** *white*

CÔTE DE NUITS
**Gevrey-Chambertin** *red*
**Morey-St.-Denis** *red*
**Chambolle-Musigny** *red*
**Vougeot** *red*
**Flagey-Echézeaux** *red*
**Vosne-Romanée** *red*
**Nuits-St.-Georges** *red*

CÔTE DE BEAUNE
**Pernand-Vergelesses** *white and red*
**Ladoix-Serrigny** *red*
**Aloxe-Corton** *white and red*
**Savigny-lès-Beaune** *red*
**Beaune** *white and red*
**Pommard** *red*
**Volnay** *red*
**Meursault** *white*
**Puligny-Montrachet** *white*
**Chassagne-Montrachet** *white and red*

### VILLAGES OF NOTE

CÔTE DE NUITS
**Marsannay** *red*
**Fixin** *red*

CÔTE DE BEAUNE
**Chorey-lès-Beaune** *red*
**Monthélie** *red*
**St.-Romain** *white and red*
**Auxey-Duresses** *white and red*
**St.-Aubin** *white and red*
**Santenay** *red*

CÔTE CHALONNAISE
**Rully** *white and red*
**Mercurey** *white and red*
**Givry** *white and red*
**Montagny** *white*

MÂCONNAIS
**Vergisson\*** *white*
**Solutré-Pouilly\*** *white*
**Fuissé\*** *white*
**Chaintré\*** *white*
**St.-Vérand\*\*** *white*

*\*One of the villages that produces the well-known wine Pouilly-Fuissé.*
*\*\*The village that produces the popular wine St.-Véran.*

191

In 1789 the French Revolution ended forever the hegemony of the church and Burgundy's infamous dukes. Immense tracts of land were split into parcels and sold off. Later, these smaller plots were further fragmented as a result of the Napoleonic Code, which stipulated that upon the death of a parent, all children must inherit equally. As a result of this successive fragmentation, it's not unusual

*The village of Rochepot and its stunning castle sit sleepily in the hills of the Côte de Beaune, just a fifteen-minute drive from Burgundy's epicenter of commerce: Beaune.*

today for a Burgundian to own just a few scant rows of vines.

Despite the combined power of the dukes and the monks during the Middle Ages, the wines of Burgundy were never as well known as those of Bordeaux. It's probably safe to say that even today, most wine drinkers find it easier to name a famous Bordeaux château than a famous Burgundy domaine.

Burgundy's comparative obscurity was largely due to its inland location. For most of history, wine has been transported over water—that is, if it hasn't been completely consumed by the population at hand. As early as the thirteenth century barrels of Bordeaux were being shipped down the Gironde River, then out to sea, headed for England. But Burgundy, deep in France's interior, was without a great waterway. Transporting its wines meant hauling heavy loads over potholed dirt roads. It wasn't until the fourteenth century when the papal court and resi-

dence moved from Rome to Avignon in southern France that Burgundy began to achieve recognition.

Not surprisingly, the newly arrived clerics were keen to drink the wines so intimately cared for by Burgundy's monks. Demand soared. Later, as towns grew and roads got somewhat better, Burgundy's fame spread. Its reputation as a great wine was solidified when Louis XIV's personal physician prescribed aged Burgundy as being even better for the sovereign's health than Champagne.

# UNDERSTANDING HOW BURGUNDY WORKS

Burgundy is often thought of as one of the world's most difficult wine regions to understand (a distinction it shares with Germany). And it *is* complicated—especially when compared to, say, California or Australia. But Burgundy is by no means incomprehensible. Here are six key points essential to understanding Burgundy.

**1.** White Burgundy is virtually synonymous with chardonnay; chardonnay accounts for the vast majority of all of Burgundy's white grapes. Red Burgundy is virtually synonymous with pinot noir; again, pinot accounts for just about all of Burgundy's red grapes. (This does not include gamay, the red grape of Beaujolais. Though Beaujolais is legally and geographically a subregion within Burgundy, it is so different from Burgundy in every way that I have given it a separate chapter. See page 219.) In Burgundy, at least with the top wines, chardonnay and pinot noir are never blended. (This is the opposite of Bordeaux where most wines are blends of several grape varieties.)

**2.** Of Burgundy's five major subregions (discussed later in this chapter), the most important and renowned is the Côte d'Or. The wines of the Côte d'Or are grouped into four levels. Starting with the most basic (least expensive) wine and moving to the most sophisticated, the levels are:

- *Burgundy Red and White*—Bourgogne Rouge and Blanc to the French— are simple, basic regional wines, generally blends of various lots of wine made from grapes of the same variety grown anywhere in the entire region of Burgundy. These basic regional wines account for 52 percent of Burgundy's total production.

- *Village Wine* This is where Burgundy begins to get interesting. As the name implies, a village wine is made entirely from grapes grown in and/or around that village. This is a step up in price (and presumably quality) from a regional

wine because the grapes come from a smaller, more well-defined place. The name of the village—Beaune, Volnay, Gevrey-Chambertin, Pommard, Meursault, Nuits-St.-Georges, Chambolle-Musigny, and so on—will appear on the label. Village wines account for 35 percent of Burgundy's total production.

- *Premier Cru* The smallest, most well-defined place of all is a vineyard. In 1861 the top vineyards of Burgundy were classified as either *Premier Cru*—First Growth—or given an even higher designation, *Grand Cru*. There are 562 *Premier Cru* vineyards. Wines from these vineyards are invariably expensive. The name of the vineyard will appear on the label, after the name of the village; for example, Beaune Clos de la Mousse or Gevrey-Chambertin aux Combottes. *Premier Cru* wines account for 11 percent of Burgundy's total production.

*Le Musigny is one of two* Grand Cru *vineyards in the village of Chambolle-Musigny (the other is Bonnes Mares).*

- **Grand Cru** The highest designation a Burgundian vineyard can hold is *Grand Cru*—Great Growth. Wines made from *Grand Cru* vineyards are the most treasured and expensive wines in Burgundy and rank among the most costly wines in the world. Only thirty-three vineyards are designated as *Grand Cru*. The *Grands Crus* are so famous that their names alone appear on the labels. For example: La Tâche, Le Montrachet, and Le Chambertin are all *Grands Crus* (see The *Grand Cru* Vineyards of the Côte d'Or, page 204). Wines from *Grand Cru* vineyards account for just 2 percent of Burgundy's total production.

Now, since wine from a *Grand Cru* vineyard is far more prestigious than wine from a village, how does the wine drinker who has limited experience of Burgundies tell the vineyard names apart

194

## PAPAL PERK

—◅◦∞◦▻—

Long before the French appellation system was established in the twentieth century, the Benedictine and Cistercian monks of Burgundy had already begun to define, differentiate, and characterize the region's vineyards and the wines that came from them. Even within the single vineyard known as Clos de Vougeot, for example, the monks specified three levels of wine quality. The wines from the lower part of the slope were known as the *cuvées des moines* (wines for the monks), wines from the preferred middle of the slope were called the *cuvées des rois* (wines for the kings), and the very best wines from the top of the slope were the *cuvées des papes* (wines for the popes).

from the village names? There is no foolproof method. However, a fairly good way of guessing is to know that vineyards are often (but admittedly not always) preceded by a definite article. Thus, La Tâche, Le Montrachet, and Le Chambertin are all vineyards, but Pommard, Beaune, and Volnay are all villages. It's also helpful if you remember that many Burgundian villages have hyphenated names because the village has annexed the name of its top vineyard in order to benefit from the prestige of that vineyard. The village Chambolle-Musigny used to be called just Chambolle until it appended the name of its most famous vineyard, Le Musigny, to its own name. Similarly, the village Aloxe added the name of its renowned vineyard Le Corton to become the village of Aloxe-Corton, and the village of Gevrey became Gevrey-Chambertin by incorporating the vineyard Le Chambertin into its name. Nonetheless, when you see these hyphenated names on bottles, you are still looking at village wines.

**3.** You probably think of a vineyard as that piece of land owned by a single vintner. In other words, from an American viewpoint, vineyards are defined by the legal construct of ownership. Even though the property within a vineyard may contain highly variable *terroir*, it is still considered one vineyard when it's owned by one person. The opposite holds true in Burgundy. There, the boundaries of most vineyards were established centuries ago by monks attempting to define parcels of ground solely on the basis of geography and *terroir*. To the monks, what in the United States would be considered one vineyard could be two, four, or even ten parcels, depending upon the number of different *terroirs* the monks observed. Each of those parcels would have been considered a distinct vineyard, an entity unto itself, and different—sometimes decidedly so—from neighboring vineyards.

4. Since vineyards in Burgundy are defined by their *terroirs*, not necessarily by who owns them, ownership itself takes on a different spin. Though it's a bit hard to picture at first, most vineyards in Burgundy, even the tiniest ones, have more than one owner. Perhaps the most well-known example is the vineyard Clos de Vougeot. At 125 acres, Clos de Vougeot has about eighty owners, all of whom make a wine called Clos de Vougeot. By way of a simple analogy, a Burgundian vineyard is like a condominium. There are several owners, all of whom own distinct parts of the condominium and do as they please with their parts. Still, each of the separate parts is a portion of the same condominium. As for that small number of

---

### PASSE-TOUT-GRAINS

～⁂～

Not widely exported, *passe-tout-grains* are inexpensive, rough-and-ready quaffing Burgundies that are made from a blend of pinot noir and gamay.

---

vineyards that do have only one owner, these vineyards are known as *monopoles*.

5. Now you can begin to see why the conventional tidy image of a wine estate surrounded by vineyards isn't really applicable to Burgundy. Instead, most growers own many small parcels of many different vineyards in many different villages. For the top wines, though not for the basic ones, the grapes from those parcels will almost never be blended together even though they

195

*Harvesting pinot noir in the vineyards of Louis Jadot in 1900 and circa 1950 (inset).*

might all be the same variety—say, pinot noir. Instead, the grower will make a separate pinot noir from each village and/or vineyard. Growers often own parcels of several different vineyards within the same village. The grower Domaine Roumier, for example, makes three wines from the village of Chambolle-Musigny: a village wine—Domaine Roumier Chambolle-Musigny; a *Premier Cru*—Domaine Roumier Chambolle-Musigny Les Amoureuses; and a *Grand Cru*—Domaine Roumier Le Musigny. And those are just the wines the domaine makes from one village. Domaine Roumier also has vineyard holdings in several other villages.

Why go to the added trouble and expense of making, aging, bottling, marketing, and selling multiple pinot noirs when you could blend them together and make just one pinot noir as much of the rest of the world does? It's a matter of philosophy and purpose. For wines above the level of basic Bourgogne, the Burgundian grower's goal is to express the *terroir* of each individual site, to let the personality of the

place emanate through the wine. Making one large blend would obliterate the differences in flavor and aroma derived from place. Still, it's a decision not without practical consequences, for vineyard parcels can be tiny. It is not unusual for a grower to own just a few rows of vines, enough perhaps to make but a single barrel (twenty-five cases) of wine from that appellation.

**6.** Until the 1980s most of the commerce in Burgundian wine was controlled by powerful brokers known as *négociants*. The *négociants* rose to power after the French Revolution, when fragmented ownership of small parcels of land in Burgundy made it economically and physically difficult for small growers to bottle, market, and sell their own wine.

Traditionally, *négociants* bought (negotiated for) dozens if not hundreds of small lots of wine from numerous growers, then blended these lots into several wines, bottled them, and sold them under their own labels. A *négociant* house, such as Labouré-Roi, would buy many tiny lots of Gevrey-Chambertin to bottle a Labouré-Roi Gevrey-Chambertin and many lots of Pouilly-Fuissé to bottle a Labouré-Roi Pouilly-Fuissé. The *négociant* could even buy many lots of a *Premier Cru* vineyard. For example, Labouré-Roi might buy several lots of the *Premier Cru* vineyard Les Amoureuses and make a Labouré-Roi Chambolle-Musigny Les Amoureuses. Generally speaking, the *négociants* of the past owned few—if any—vineyards themselves.

By the 1960s and 1970s, however, the *négociant* business began to change. Many small growers—even the tiniest ones—decided to bottle their wines under their own labels, leaving fewer available sources of grapes for *négociants* to buy. The wines many *négociants* produced began to suffer in quality. To remedy this, *négociant* houses increasingly became growers themselves. The *négociant* house Louis Jadot, for example, owned one small vineyard when it was founded in 1859. Today the firm has 300 acres of vineyards and makes wines from more than ninety appellations. However, with the exception of a few top *négociant* houses, such as Jadot, *négociant* wines are often considered far less exciting than the wines from small domaines.

# THE GRAPES AND THE WINEMAKING

As we'll see, trying to remember the vineyards and appellations of Burgundy may be a little exasperating, but remembering the grape varieties is a cinch. There are just two main ones: the white grape chardonnay and the red grape pinot noir. A few other grapes are also grown, the two most significant of which are aligoté and gamay. Aligoté, a neutral-tasting, high-acid white grape, is grown in small amounts and used as part of the blend to make the sparkling wine Crémant de Bourgogne. In addition, the traditional Kir cocktail is aligoté mixed with a bit of crème de cassis. Gamay, a fruity red grape, made mostly into simple and nouveau wines, is grown predominantly in the subregion Beaujolais. (Beaujolais has its own chapter following this one.)

But chardonnay and pinot noir don't merely happen to grow in Burgundy. Rather, of all the wine regions in the world, it is in Burgundy that chardonnay and pinot noir reach their apogees.

Though it's hard to imagine now, until the modern wine revolution of the 1950s

## THE GRAPES OF BURGUNDY

### WHITES

**Aligoté:** Very minor grape. Grown principally in the Mâconnais, where it is used to make inexpensive neutral-tasting quaffing wines, although some surprising examples can be found. Also a frequent component in the sparkling wine Crémant de Bourgogne.

**Chardonnay:** Major grape. Used to make everything from simple wines like Pouilly-Fuissé and St.-Véran to Burgundy's most profound and lush whites, including the wines of Chassagne-Montrachet, Puligny-Montrachet, and Meursault.

### RED

**Pinot Noir:** Major grape. All of the red wines discussed in this chapter are made from this variety, including humble reds, such as Montagny and Givry, as well as the world-renowned wines from such places as Chambolle-Musigny, Aloxe-Corton, Vougeot, and Vosne-Romanée.

and 1960s, chardonnay was hardly heard of outside France. Just a smattering of acres existed in the entire New World. But as Californians, Australians, and others discovered how enticing white Burgundy could be, chardonnay plantings soared. There are now more than 100,000 acres of chardonnay in California alone. This is more than the total vineyard acreage in Burgundy, where chardonnay and pinot noir combined cover not quite 62,000 acres.

Still, if chardonnay and pinot noir reach their greatest heights in Burgundy, they do so only when the yields of a given vineyard are low. In a relatively cool northern climate, where achieving ripeness is a concern, it's no surprise that vineyards maxed out by trying to ripen too much fruit end up not ripening any of it very well. Thus, the potential successes of winemaking always begin in the vineyard.

Another concern is deciding when to pick. In Burgundy, where it often rains in early fall, this can be the most critical wine-making decision of all. Growers who pick early in the season might avoid rain, but the slightly underripe grapes they harvest might also produce thin, bland wines that no amount of winemaking wizardry will substantially improve. Growers who pick late are gambling that they can dodge the rain, thus letting the grapes benefit from a longer ripening time, with richer wines as the result. But such growers are also gambling that if it does indeed rain, they'll be able to harvest the crop before the grapes get waterlogged or before a serious rot sets in.

In the past, picking early (the less nerve-racking of the two scenarios) was often the choice of growers for whom top quality was not necessarily paramount. Besides, if it seemed as though the wine was going to be a bit weak, the grower could employ a practice still legal in Burgundy—chaptalization. Chaptalization involves adding plain old sugar to the fermenting vat. This, in turn, gives the yeasts more material to ferment. And the more sugar the yeasts have to ferment, the higher the alcohol level of the wine will be. It's safe to say that top producers avoid chaptalization, since wines with high alcohol but meek flavors can often taste out of balance and discombobulated.

There are several other important facets of Burgundian winemaking, two of the most important of which are whether or not to use new oak barrels to lengthen and deepen the wine's flavor and if so, to what extent, and whether or not to fine and/or filter to clarify the wine.

It's difficult to generalize when it comes to these issues, because all Burgundian growers have opinions and strategies that have been formed based on the individual character of their wines. That said, it is true that more new oak is being used in Burgundy today than at any other time in recent history. Very few domaines, however, use only new oak every year as is frequently done in California.

As for fining and filtration, whether or not to use these processes is a decision winemakers all over the world must make. The relative fragility of pinot noir means that Burgundian growers—at least the top growers—are used to having to handle their wines with extreme care. In particular, filtration done carelessly can easily strip pinot noir or chardonnay of aroma and flavor, so many of the best Burgundian growers try to avoid it. As with every winemaking procedure, however, the decisions to do something or not always depend on the character of that year's wines.

In the end, making a great Burgundy—red or white—is an extremely difficult process fraught with anxiety. Making red Burgundy is especially daunting, for pinot noir is more fickle and less hardy and requires far more delicate handling than chardonnay.

# THE LAND AND THE VINEYARDS

Just driving down a road in the Côte d'Or reveals how intimately connected growers are to the land and portends just how site specific the wines can be. Instead of vast, amorphous tracts of vineyards, vines are grown in small paddocklike areas, often enclosed by fieldstone walls. Since growers plant their rows in different directions and tend their vines in different ways, the visual effect, even from a short distance, is that of a loopy patchwork quilt of green. Together all of these tiny vineyards amount to just under 62,000 acres of vines. By comparison, Bordeaux with about 280,000 acres is four-and-a-half-times larger.

Though many wine drinkers think of just one or two small areas when they use the term Burgundy, the region is composed of five main subregions. We'll look at these individually beginning on page 201, but for now, here's a brief overview:

• **Chablis** This is the most northern subregion of Burgundy, just 100 or so miles southeast of Paris. Chablis is entirely devoted to growing chardonnay grapes.

• **Côte d'Or** Most of Burgundy's legendary wines come from the Côte d'Or, the collective name for the Côte de Nuits and the Côte de Beaune. The Côte d'Or is a 30-mile-long limestone escarpment, or ridge, with villages on the eastern side of the slope. Because the vines face east, they are perfectly oriented to catch the morning sun each day. The Côte de Nuits (the northern half of the escarpment) is planted virtually entirely with pinot noir and hence makes red wines only. The Côte de Beaune (the southern half) is planted both with pinot noir and chardonnay and makes both red and white wines.

• **Côte Chalonnaise** Just south of the Côte d'Or is the Côte Chalonnaise, which while not as famous as its sisters, nonetheless produces some quite good red and white wines, and these almost always cost less than the wines of Chablis, the Côte de Nuits, or the Côte de Beaune. The most famous red wine here is from the village of Mercurey.

---

## LOOKING EAST

━━◈◈◈━━

The name Côte d'Or is often translated as golden slope, perhaps because the wines from here cost a ransom or perhaps because the vineyards turn golden in autumn. However, the term is actually a contraction of Côte d'Orient, eastern-facing slope—a reference to the fact that the vineyards are perfectly oriented to catch each day's morning sun.

---

• **Mâconnais** Moving south from the Côte Chalonnaise, you come next to the Mâconnais, a fairly large region mainly devoted to white wine. Oceans of good, everyday chardonnay are made here. The three most well-known wines are Mâcon Villages, Pouilly-Fuissé, and St.-Véran. In addition, many simple Bourgognes Blanc and Rouge are also produced.

• **Beaujolais** The southernmost subregion of Burgundy, Beaujolais, is devoted to fruity red wines made from the gamay grape. Because Beaujolais has little in common with the rest of Burgundy, it has its own chapter, beginning on page 219.

Each of these subregions has many specific characteristics of climate and soil that define it. But in general, what makes Burgundy Burgundy are two enormously important realities. First, it is a cool place. As I mentioned earlier, of all the regions in the world famous for red wine, Burgundy is the most northern. Summers here are generally cooler than in Bordeaux and much cooler than in most of California. And because Burgundy is a cool place, its wines are usually not massive, syrupy, and overtly fruity. Instead, at their best they are intensely flavored but have a light to medium body and an almost gossamer gracefulness.

Burgundy's cool climate also means that the region is well suited to pinot noir and chardonnay. Being as tempermental as it is, pinot noir will produce wines that possess finesse, nuance, and complexity only when it is planted in a cool place so that the grapes are allowed to ripen slowly and methodically over a relatively long period of time. When pinot noir is planted in a hot,

sun-drenched site, the grapes virtually explode with ripeness, leading to wines that are often oafish, monodimensional, and dull. As for white Burgundies, while chardonnay can be and is planted in quite warm places around the world, many knowledgeable chardonnay lovers would argue that the most nuanced and elegant wines come from grapes that are grown in cooler spots.

The problem in Burgundy therefore is never too much sun but the threat of too little. A rainy September can mean the grapes will never experience that final push of ripeness just before the harvest season. Not surprisingly, wine made from grapes that are not completely ripe can taste hollow and lacking, just as an unripe peach can. Thus, years that are not very sunny overall can result in many weakly flavored wines. One of the reasons the best vineyards are considered the best is because they tend to lie in the sunniest spots. So even in what

*The village of Nuits-St.-Georges is considered the gateway to the northern half of the Côte d'Or, the Côte de Nuits. Large compared to most villages in Burgundy, it is known for relatively robust pinot noirs.*

are, for the most part, cloudy, rainy years, the wines from certain sunnily sited vineyards often turn out better than wines from neighboring vineyards.

There's another consideration. Lots of rain falling intermittently throughout the summer brings with it the risk of rot, which in turn, brings with it the potential for strange flavors in the wine. There are many interrelated precautions Burgundian growers take to guard against rot and the resulting off flavors. The final precaution is to be extremely selective when the grapes are harvested, so that all rotten bunches and even rotten berries are sorted out.

What else makes Burgundy Burgundy? Limestone. No one describes it more vividly than Anthony Hanson in his authoritative book *Burgundy:*

> During the Jurassic period (135-195 million years ago), the whole of Burgundy sank beneath shallow seas. Archaeopteryx, or some other ancestral bird, took wing, great dinosaurs roamed the land, while on the sea bed, marine sediments were slowly laid down. The shells of myriads of baby oysters piled one on another, while the skeletons of countless crinoids or sea lilies were compacted together; from such petrified remains, limestone is formed. Jurassic limestone rocks, interspersed with marlstones, are fundamental keys to the excellence and variety of Burgundy's wines.

Burgundy's subregions are laced with limestone—some more so, some less. Chablis is like a small chalky island of the stuff. Pick up a handful of the cratery whitish soil, and you'll actually find tiny seashells. The Côte d'Or is a long ridge of limestone, and in the Côte Chalonnaise and Mâconnais, many of the best vineyards sit atop limestone outcroppings.

# CHABLIS

The northernmost subregion of Burgundy, Chablis sits like an isolated island far north of the Côte d'Or and the rest of Burgundy. In fact, the vineyards of Chablis are closer to Champagne, about 20 miles away, than they are to the rest of Burgundy, more than 60 miles away.

Chablis is an amazing looking place. Vineyards roll this way and that, as if they grew on ocean waves. The whitish crusty limestone soil is so stark that at twilight you feel as though you're on the moon. The little town of Chablis itself is deathly quiet.

This subregion is famous for the only wine it makes: chardonnay. In fact, Chablis was so famous that from the late nineteenth century onward, its name was usurped by American and Australian jug winemakers who proceeded to label any cheap generic white wine "chablis." (Nevermind that there wasn't a chardonnay grape in any of those wines.)

Today, two realities make Chablis less well known than it once was. First, there's been an extraordinary proliferation of chardonnays from a dozen other countries around the world (California alone produces more than 700). Second, Chablis is no longer the all-around favorite brasserie wine of Paris. This is precisely what it *once* was. The vineyards of Chablis are some of the closest to Paris, and thus the wines were easily transported there. Today dozens of wines, many shipped by rail from the south of France, compete for the thirsty Parisian market.

Sadly, Chablis is not just less well-known than it once was, it's maybe even less well understood. That's because for many wine drinkers Chablis is not as immediately lovable as countless New World chardonnays. The climate of the region is harsh, wet, and cold, leading to wines that can have daggers of crisp acidity. This climate, coupled with Chablis' dramatic limestone and clay soil (the best vineyards are chockful of tiny fossilized oyster shells) makes for wines that are more steely, minerally, and stony than chardonnays grown elsewhere. The French often call the unique flavors of a good Chablis *goût de pierre à fusil*—gunflint. When, with a great *Premier* or *Grand Cru* Chablis, these gunflint flavors are draped with light honey, the effect can be sensational.

Many basic Chablis are made entirely in stainless steel or in neutral wood, so they have little of the pronounced oaky, vanilla flavors we have become accustomed to assuming are the flavors of chardonnay. Some domaines, however, ferment in stainless steel but go on to briefly age their Chablis in small oak barrels in order to deepen the wine's flavors and add to its complexity. Still other producers (a small number) barrel ferment as well as barrel age their Chablis, especially their *Grands Crus*, which are thought to be intense enough to stand up to the oak's impact. In every case, the decision is individual, for the delicate flavors of Chablis are easily camouflaged by too much contact with wood.

Chablis has seven *Grand Cru* vineyards: Blanchot, Bougros, Grenouilles, Les Clos, Les Preuses, Valmur, and Vaudésir; and seventeen well-known *Premier Crus*. These are the wines to concentrate on, for many basic Chablis are so lean, they're almost mean.

*Some of the Best Producers of Chablis*

**CHÂTEAU GRENOUILLE**

**DOMAINE DE LA MALADIÈRE**

**DOMAINE LAROCHE**

**FRANÇOIS RAVENEAU**

**GUY ROBIN**

**JEAN DAUVISSAT**

**LONG-DEPAQUIT**

**LOUIS MICHEL**

**RENÉ ET VINCENT DAUVISSAT**

**R. VOCORET**

*The sleepy village of Chablis and its vineyards are closer to Champagne than they are to the rest of Burgundy. The cool, limestone-laced vineyards produce some of the world's purest, sleekest, most austere chardonnays.*

# THE CÔTE D'OR

The 30-mile-long escarpment known as the Côte d'Or is Burgundy's most-renowned wine region. When wine drinkers talk about being left spellbound by Burgundy, they are almost assuredly talking about wines from here.

The Côte d'Or runs north-south, starting near the city of Dijon and traveling down to the city of Santenay. It's actually a narrow ridge of limestone, divided almost equally in half. The northern part, known as the Côte de Nuits, produces red wines almost exclusively. Starting with the northernmost village and moving south, the appellations of the Côte de Nuits are: Marsannay, Fixin, Gevrey-Chambertin, Morey-St.-Denis, Chambolle-Musigny, Vougeot, Flagey-Echézeaux, Vosne-Romanée, and Nuits-St.-Georges.

The southern half, the Côte de Beaune, produces both red and white wines, though whites dominate. Starting with the northernmost village and moving south, the appellations of the Côte de Beaune are: Pernand-Vergelesses, Ladoix-Serrigny, Aloxe-Corton, Savigny-lès-Beaune, Chorey-lès-Beaune, Beaune, Pommard, Volnay, Monthélie, St.-Romain, Auxey-Duresses, Meursault, Puligny-Montrachet, St.-Aubin, Chassagne-Montrachet, and Santenay.

Every village in the Côte d'Or is said to have its own character—the wines of Chambolle-Musigny, for example, are frequently considered elegant while the wines of Nuits-St.-Georges are thought to be more sturdy and rustic. But the character of any given wine will always be individual, based on the *terroir* of the vineyard as interpreted by the producer.

There is one broad generalization that can be made concerning red wines: The top reds from the Côte de Nuits (Gevrey-Chambertin, Flagey-Echézeaux, Vosne-Romanée, Nuits-St.-Georges, and others) often have more grip, greater intensity, and a firmer structure than red wines from the Côte de Beaune (Aloxe-Corton, Beaune, Volnay, Pommard, and so on). By contrast, the top Côte de Beaune reds are frequently softer and sometimes more lush. In general reds from all over the Côte d'Or are prized for their soaring earthy and gamy flavors sometimes laced with exotic spices, licorice, chocolate, or truffles. Of all the red wines in the world,

## SOME OF THE BEST PRODUCERS OF THE CÔTE D'OR

Most producers make many Côte d'Or wines, all of which are not necessarily equally great in every year. A domaine that in one year makes a great Gevrey-Chambertin might produce a merely good Meursault. But with the next vintage, the situation could be different.

There are hundreds of producers in the Côte d'Or alone. Here are some of my favorites: Albert Morot, Antonin Rodet, Armand Rousseau, Bertrand Ambroise, Christian Sérafin, Coche-Dury, Comte de Vogüé, Comtes Armand, Comtes Lafon, Daniel Rion, Domaine de la Romanée-Conti, Domaine Dujac, Domaine Jean Grivot, Domaine Leroy, Etienne Sauzet, Georges Roumier, Gros Frère et Soeur, Henri Jayer, J. Confuron-Cotetidot, J. F. Mugnier, Jean Boillot, Jean-Noel Gagnard, Jean-Marc Morey, Joseph Drouhin, Leflaive, Louis Jadot, Méo-Camuzet, Michel Lafarge, Mongeard-Mugneret, Paul Pernot, Philippe Leclerc, Ramonet, René Leclerc, Robert Chevillon, Robert Jayer-Gilles, and Tollot-Beaut et Fils.

## THE GRAND CRU VINEYARDS OF THE CÔTE D'OR

*There are thirty* Grand Cru *vineyards in the Côte d'Or. The villages in which they are found are listed here in* **boldface,** *ranging from north to south.*

### CÔTE DE NUITS*

**Gevrey-Chambertin**
Chambertin Clos-de-Bèze
Chapelle-Chambertin
Charmes-Chambertin
Griotte-Chambertin
Latricières-Chambertin
Le Chambertin
Mazis-Chambertin
Ruchottes-Chambertin

**Morey-St.-Denis**
Bonnes Mares
*(Only part of Bonnes Mares is located within Morey-St.-Denis.)*
Clos de la Roche
Clos des Lambrays
Clos de Tart
Clos St.-Denis

**Chambolle-Musigny**
Bonnes Mares
*(Most of Bonnes Mares is located within Chambolle-Musigny.)*
Le Musigny
*(Produces some white wine.)*

**Vougeot**
Clos de Vougeot

**Flagey-Echézeaux**
Echézeaux
Grands Echézeaux

**Vosne-Romanée**
La Romanée
La Tâche
La Grande Rue
Richebourg
Romanée-Conti
Romanée-St.-Vivant

### CÔTE DE BEAUNE†

**Pernand-Vergelesses**
Corton-Charlemagne
*(This vineyard is shared with two other villages.)*

**Ladoix-Serrigny**
Corton-Charlemagne
*(This vineyard is shared with two other villages.)*

**Aloxe-Corton**
Corton-Charlemagne
*(This vineyard is shared with two other villages.)*
Le Corton
*(Almost all its wines are red.)*

**Puligny-Montrachet**
Bâtard-Montrachet
*(The vineyard is divided between two villages, Puligny-Montrachet and Chassagne-Montrachet.)*
Bienvenues-Bâtard-Montrachet
Chevalier-Montrachet
Le Montrachet
*(The vineyard is divided between two villages, Puligny-Montrachet and Chassagne-Montrachet.)*

**Chassagne-Montrachet**
Bâtard-Montrachet
*(The vineyard is divided between two villages, Puligny-Montrachet and Chassagne-Montrachet.)*
Criots-Bâtard-Montrachet
Le Montrachet
*(The vineyard is divided between two villages, Puligny-Montrachet and Chassagne-Montrachet.)*

---

* All of the Grand Cru vineyards of the Côte de Nuits produce only red wine unless otherwise indicated.
† All of the Grand Cru vineyards of the Côte de Beaune produce only white wine unless otherwise indicated.

*The tiny village of Vosne-Romanée has almost mythic status, for in the surrounding vineyards are found eight prestigious* Grands Crus, *including the vineyard Romanée-Conti, which gives rise to the famous wine by the same name (inset).*

these are some of the most heady in aroma and long in the mouth.

As for white wines (again, all of which come from the Côte de Beaune), the most famous villages are Meursault, Puligny-Montrachet, Chassagne-Montrachet, Ladoix-Serrigny, and Beaune. The top *Premier* and *Grand Cru* wines from these villages can be amazingly rich and concentrated without being heavy or ponderous. Their tightly woven flavors are dripping with honey, toasted nuts, truffles, and vanilla. A wine such as the *Grand Cru* Corton-Charlemagne from the Domaine Bonneau du Martray, for example, can have such exquisite elegance, it's toe curling.

The word *côte* is translated as slope, and where a vineyard is located on the slope of the Côte d'Or is usually a clue to its rank. Village wines generally come from vineyards on the bottom of the slope or on the flatlands, where the soil is heaviest,

## DOMAINE DE LA ROMANÉE-CONTI

The most-renowned estate in Burgundy, perhaps in all of France, the Domaine de la Romanée-Conti, has been the subject of entire books. The DRC, as it is referred to, is owned by the de Villaine and Leroy families and comprises parcels of seven vineyards, all of which are *Grands Crus* and all of which have been considered exemplary for centuries. These include one vineyard devoted to white wine, Le Montrachet, and six devoted to red, Romanée-Conti and La Tâche (both of which are *monopoles* owned exclusively by the domaine), as well as Richebourg, Romanée-St.-Vivant, Echézeaux, and Grands Echézeaux. Together these seven holdings make up just a little more than 62 acres of vines. Because the yields from these vineyards are kept extremely low, production is minuscule and prices astronomic. The entire production of Romanée-Conti is a mere 400 to 500 cases a year. This is about ¹⁄₁₀₀ the production of Château Lafite-Rothschild in Bordeaux. As for cost, year in and year out the wines of the DRC are the most expensive in Burgundy. The 1998 Romanée-Conti cost $1,100 a *bottle*.

least well drained, and most full of clay. As you move up the slope, the soil is thinner, better drained, and is increasingly based on limestone. Vineyards on the slope also tend to have the best exposure to sun throughout the day. All of the *Premier Cru* and *Grand Cru* vineyards are up here. At the very top of the slope are woodlands that protect the vines from wet winds coming out of the west.

## CÔTE CHALONNAISE

A few miles south of the Côte d'Or is the Côte Chalonnaise. There are five main wine villages here: Mercurey, Bouzeron, Rully, Givry, and Montagny. In addition to wines from these villages, much basic Bourgogne is also produced here. There are no *Grand Cru* vineyards in the Côte Chalonnaise. There are, however, numerous *Premiers Crus*.

The wines of the Côte Chalonnaise are almost always less expensive than the wines of the Côte d'Or, so this is the subregion bargain hunters love to explore. Of course, Chalonnaise wines generally don't match the Côte d'Or in quality either. But delicious surprises can crop up, especially from the top producers.

The area's best-known and largest village, Mercurey, can produce very good reds with lots of spicy cherry character. You have to hunt for good Mercureys; unfortunately, there are also countless examples that are watery and weak. One of the reasons for these poorer quality wines may be vineyard expansion. All over the Côte Chalonnaise the amount of land planted with vineyards has skyrocketed. Not all of these new vineyards are exactly ideal. Finally, while Mercurey is thought of as a red-wine village, it also produces a small amount of lovely, appley, minerally white wine.

Bouzeron is the northernmost village of the Côte Chalonnaise. It is known primarily for aligoté. In fact, perhaps the best wine made from aligoté in France is produced here by Aubert de Villaine, codirector of the prestigious Domaine de la Romanée-Conti in the Côte d'Or.

The village of Rully used to be one of the centers of sparkling wine production in Burgundy, and a fair amount of Cré-

*The rolling vineyards of the Côte Chalonnaise, just south of the Côte d'Or, produce wines that, by standards for Burgundy, are relative bargains.*

mant de Bourgogne (a sparkling wine produced using the Champagne method) is still produced there. Otherwise, the village is known mostly for its simple reds and somewhat better whites, which can be crisp and lemony with nutty overtones.

Givry is better known for its red wines, though whites also come from there. Again, quality depends on the producer, but there are some very good wines with earthy and cherry flavors.

And Montagny, the small southernmost village of the Côte Chalonnaise, is exclusively devoted to chardonnay. Many Burgundy insiders consider Montagnys the best value white Burgundies going.

---

*Some of the Best Producers*
*of the Côte Chalonnaise*

A. & P. DE VILLAINE

ANTONIN RODET

CHARTON ET TRÉBUCHET

DOMAINE DE LA FOLIE

DOMAINE DE RULLY
ST.-MICHEL

DOMAINE DE SUREMAIN

DOMAINE JOBLOT

DOMAINE THENARD

DOMAINE VEUVE
STEINMAIER

FAIVELEY

LOUIS LATOUR

MICHEL JUILLOT

---

# MÂCONNAIS

South of the Côte Chalonnaise is the Mâconnais, a large area of low-lying hills, woodlands, farmland, and meadows. The Mâconnais is principally a white wine region, producing oceans of basic, fairly cheap Bourgogne Blanc, much of it at

## CRÉMANT DE BOURGOGNE

≈≈≈

Crémants are sparkling wines made by the Champagne method outside of Champagne, and Burgundy has its share. By law, 30 percent of the blend called Crémant de Bourgogne must come from pinot noir, chardonnay, pinot gris, or pinot blanc grapes; the rest may come from lesser varieties, such as aligoté. Most Crémant de Bourgogne is consumed in France.

cooperatives. A step above these utterly simple quaffing wines are the Mâconnais' best-known wines—Mâcon, Pouilly-Fuissé, and St.-Véran. There are no *Grands Crus* or *Premiers Crus* in the Mâconnais.

Mâcon, Pouilly-Fuissé, and St.-Véran are all made from chardonnay. Curiously, there is also a tiny Mâconnais village called Chardonnay, but its wines are passable at best. Historians aren't sure if Chardonnay the village is the actual birthplace of chardonnay the grape or if the village was named after the grape. Of all white Burgundies, Mâcon, Pouilly-Fuissé, and St.-Véran are three of the most widely available and affordable. Unfortunately, quality swings widely.

Mâcon is found as either simple Mâcon, slightly better Mâcon Supérior, or even better Mâcon Villages, which can come from any one of forty-three villages. There are also Mâcons that actually name specific villages, such as Mâcon Lugny. Even the finest Mâcons are still fairly straightforward, simple wines. More than 75 percent of Mâcons come from cooperatives.

Pouilly-Fuissé, from the area around the four small hamlets of Vergisson, Solutré-

Pouilly, Fuissé, and Chaintré can be dreadful and overpriced or delicious and overpriced. In general, however, Pouilly-Fuissés are rather stout whites that lack the elegance of whites from the Côte d'Or. (Don't confuse Pouilly-Fuissé with Pouilly-Fumé. The latter is a sauvignon blanc from France's Loire Valley.) And last, from the village of St.-Vérand comes the wine St.-Véran (minus the d in its name), which is usually less expensive than Pouilly-Fuissé and often better.

*Some of the Best Producers*
*of the Mâconnais*

**ANDRÉ BESSON**

**CHÂTEAU FUISSÉ**

**DOMAINE CHENEVIÈRE**

**DOMAINE CORSIN**

**DOMAINE DE LA MAISON**

**DOMAINE MANCIAT-PONCET**

**GEORGES DUBOEUF**

**GUFFENS-HEYNEN**

**J. A. FERRET**

**JOSEPH DROUHIN**

**LOUIS JADOT**

**LOUIS LATOUR**

**ROGER LASSERAT**

**THIERY GUÉRIN**

*Some of Burgundy's most inexpensive every-night chardonnays come from big stretches of vineyards in the Mâconnais.*

# WHAT TO EXPECT FROM WHITE AND RED BURGUNDIES

A lifetime of experience with California chardonnay (or chardonnay from other parts of the New World) would give you little idea of what to expect from a white Burgundy, for these wines are completely different, even while they span an enormous range of styles and flavors. At a fairly simple level there are crisp appley-lemony wines from such Mâconnais and Côte Chalonnaise villages as Mâcon, St.-Vérand, Rully, and Montagny. These everyday drinking wines are almost never going to be called opulent, buttery, butterscotchy, oaky, bursting with tropical fruit, or any other descriptor commonly applied to California chardonnays. Even Pouilly-Fuissé, which can have some weight to it, is far less conspicuous and less bosomy than most New World chardonnays.

Then there are the wines of Chablis, all of which are chardonnay. As the northernmost subregion of Burgundy, Chablis produces wines that are austere and snappy, with what can feel like lightning bolts of acidity. Often the wines have a penetrating steeliness or mineraliness overlaid by a drizzle of honey flavors. Chardonnay doesn't get any sleeker than in Chablis.

The wines of the Mâconnais, Côte Chalonnaise, and Chablis, however, are in sharp contrast to most *Premier Cru* or *Grand Cru* white Burgundies of the Côte d'Or. The legendary wines from such villages as Meursault, Puligny-Montrachet, and Chassagne-Montrachet can be hauntingly complex and refined, with rich but not overwrought honey, toasted nut, and vanilla flavors.

## SERVING BURGUNDY—A FEW SPECIAL CONSIDERATIONS

—⟶⟋⟋⟋⟵—

Serving a great Burgundy, white or red, in too small a glass should be considered a crime. Burgundies are, by their nature, highly aromatic wines. The only way to experience the full impact of these wines is to drink them from generous size glasses with ample bowls that taper toward the top.

More than any other type of wine, Burgundy tends to change in the glass. In fact, it's almost impossible to accurately assess a great Burgundy after the first one or two sips. In twenty minutes the wine may be transformed substantially, offering a whole new world of flavors and aromas. For many wine drinkers, this propensity to evolve in the glass is part of what makes Burgundy intellectually intriguing. (Note that a simple Burgundy probably won't do this; I'm talking here of top-quality wines.)

Precisely because a great Burgundy does evolve in the glass, it's best *not* to top off the glass after just a few sips. Instead, pour and slowly drink an entire glass, so you can experience the different flavors and aromas as they emerge. When the glass is almost empty, then pour some more.

With a fine red Burgundy, the wine's inclination to evolve and the relative fragility of the pinot noir grape mean that, in general, you should not open the bottle many hours before dinner or, worse, decant it. Pinot noir is the complete opposite of cabernet sauvignon in this regard. When pinot noir, especially a pinot that is fifteen years old or more, is given too much oxygen, its flavors can seem to fade and fall apart. So remember: Pour red Burgundy from the bottle and drink it soon after it's opened.

As for red Burgundies, don't believe your eyes: The intensity of the wine's color is not necessarily a reflection of the intensity of its flavor. Many wine drinkers wrongly assume that a red Burgundy that is pale will be weak in flavor and that a darker-colored red Burgundy will be richer and more nuanced. Not necessarily the case.

With that in mind, the flavor range of Burgundian red wines is even greater than that of whites. At a fairly modest level, though well above basic Bourgogne Rouge, are such wines as Mercurey, Fixin, Marsannay, and Santenay. At their best, they are lovely wines with good plummy fruit sometimes laced with spice, citrus, or mocha flavors.

But the most fabled wines are great reds from such villages as Gevrey-

Chambertin, Vougeot, Vosne-Romanée, Flagey-Echézeaux, and Nuits-St.-Georges. Especially after several years of aging, these can be so primordially earthy, so rich and gamy, so sensual, so aromatic, so nuanced with flavor, and so long in the mouth that they are, in a word, mesmerizing.

The adjective *earthy* deserves a few words more, for while it is the term most often used to describe great red Burgundy, it can mean several things, at least one of which is controversial. When a wine is earthy, it is often, quite simply, reminiscent of the earth, of soil, or of things that grow in the earth, such as moss, mushrooms, or truffles. But the term can also be used to describe the pleasantly sensual smell of the human body. And, for many wine drinkers, earthy is almost synonymous with the more graphic term *barn-yard*, the odors that arise from animals confined in a small space. A pronounced barnyard stinkiness is, in fact, more often associated with red Burgundy than with any other wine in the world. It's interesting that while legions of wine drinkers love a little barnyard in their Burgundy, the trait is often highly criticized by New World winemakers who attribute it to spoilage by *Brettanomyces* yeasts.

## BUYING BURGUNDY AND THE QUESTION OF VINTAGES

Depending on your viewpoint (and the amount of money you can afford to lose on wines that prove disappointing), buying Burgundy is either frightening or exciting for there are almost no absolutes that can be counted on, and many assumptions you might think would be safe prove otherwise. In the end, buying Burgundy is a matter of trial and error, luck, intuition, and you hope, some good advice. Actually, there *is* one absolute: Bargain Burgundies do not exist. Like caviar, the top Burgundies are expensive, whether they taste extraordinary or humdrum. Beyond that there's little to go on.

You might logically think that *Grands Crus* are dependably better than *Premiers Crus* and that *Premiers Crus* are dependably better than village wines. Not necessarily true. Red Burgundies in particular can belie this presumption, since of all the world's top grape varieties, pinot noir is decidedly the most temperamental. Pinot noir that is planted in a humble site can sometimes be cajoled into a surprisingly delicious wine, and pinot noir planted in one of the best sites sometimes ends up becoming a lackluster wine.

### THE HOSPICES DE BEAUNE

One of the most prestigious wine events anywhere is the Hospices de Beaune, a charity auction held each November in Beaune's stunning Hôtel Dieu. Built in 1451 as perhaps the most magnificent home ever created for the sick and the poor, the Hôtel Dieu owns almost 150 acres of vineyards, which were donated to it over centuries. The wines made from these vineyards are sold in a highly publicized auction that brings in considerable sums to benefit the collective hospitals of Beaune.

Can you buy Burgundy based on tasting a bottle? Even this has limitations. Burgundy—and again, especially red Burgundy—can take on remarkably different qualities as it ages. The Burgundy that tasted simplistic and boring when you bought it might (no one can predict for sure) taste scrumptious at some time in the future. That said, there is no good rule of thumb for knowing when a given Burgundy will move into the scrumptious zone (or even if it will), for Burgundy rarely ages in a linear, predictable way. Given two different wines stored for ten years under the same conditions, one might be full of flavor, the other, rather tired and faded. Finally, although conventional wisdom has it that red Burgundy does not age as long as Bordeaux, tastings of Burgundies fifty to one hundred years old prove that old Burgundy sometimes has more staying power than it's given credit for.

And of course buying Burgundy encourages you to consider the place as much as the producer. A wine from the village of Chambolle-Musigny traditionally tastes quite different from a wine from the village of Nuits-St.-Georges. It's fascinating to try to taste these "flavors of place" and to see if you can recognize the commonalities among, say, three Pommards from three different producers. On the other hand, it is also critical to consider the producer. Producer X's Nuits-St.-Georges is bound to be different from Producer Y's in much the same way that lamb given to two different chefs emerges as two different-tasting dishes.

Alas, in Burgundy, remembering which producer is which can be daunting since many growers are siblings with the same last name. For example, in the small sleepy village of Chassagne-Montrachet alone, there are three producers with the last name Morey (Domaine Bernard Morey, Domaine Jean-Marc Morey, and Domaine Marc Morey), three producers with Ramonet in their name (Domaine Ramonet, Domaine Ramonet-Prudhon, and Domaine

Bachelet-Ramonet), and four producers with the name Gagnard—and that's just in Chassagne-Montrachet! It's easy to see why taking exact notes on the name of a Burgundy is essential if you ever want to find it again.

As for vintages, Burgundy—unlike, say, California, Chile, or Australia—is a place where the differences among vintages are clearly apparent. The region's coolish continental climate, the variations in sites, and the exigencies of growing pinot noir and chardonnay in such a place mean that harvest conditions and wines can vary considerably. But, it's best to be cautious about blanket proclamations. The fact that a given year was declared a vintage of the century is never a guarantee of every wine produced in that vintage. In *every* vintage, both good and poor wines are produced.

Still all this misses the most important truth of all: Most vintages are neither great nor poor. They are someplace in between. It doesn't make sense to think

**211**

*The magnificent tiled roof of the Hôtel Dieu, best known as the site of the Hospices de Beaune, one of the world's most famous wine auctions.*

about Burgundian vintages in such black-or-white terms when, in fact, that sort of thinking has little basis in reality.

Not surprisingly, Burgundians don't always agree with the assessments the press in the United States makes of a given vintage. And those initial assessments of a vintage are only that—first impressions. After a few years a vintage may and often does show itself quite differently.

In the end, it all comes down to the unavoidable question of what you are looking for. Sun-drenched years are usually proclaimed the best vintages and sun-drenched years tend to yield the biggest, ripest wines. But what if you're not after a blockbuster pinot noir or a fleshy chardonnay? What if you're after grace, elegance, an unearthly lightness of being? Vintages are intriguing to ponder, but to be ruled by them is misguided.

# THE FOODS OF BURGUNDY

If any one dish epitomizes the intimate connection of wine and food in Burgundy it is coq au vin (hen or rooster cooked in Burgundy wine). Rustic, hearty, and slow cooked, it is soulful, humble fare that speaks of the earth not of artifice. Burgundian cooking may not be cutting edge or elaborate, but it is honest and true to centuries of good home cooks who knew how to take snails, rabbits, and guinea hens and make them irresistible.

Burgundy's most famous vineyards are bracketed by two of the legendary food capitals of France—Dijon and Lyon. Dijon calls itself the mustard capital of the world, and mustard, simple as it is, is France's best-loved condiment. You can find a little pot on every table of virtually every bistro in the country. About 70 percent of France's mustard is *moutarde de Dijon*, which refers to the style—a creamy, smooth, especially pungent mustard—originally developed in Dijon. Today, many Burgundian villages have their own *moutarderie*, or mustard shop, where artisanal mustards are made, sometimes with slightly fermented white grape juice rather than vinegar.

Though snails are cooked and eaten all over France, no snail preparation is more well known than *escargots à la bourguignonne*, snails cooked Burgundy

## FOOD AND WINE

## WHERE'S THE BOEUF?

Burgundy's famous *boeuf bourguignon* is a slowly braised beef stew made with beef, pearl onions, mushrooms, bits of fried bacon, and a whole bottle of Burgundy wine. Needless to say, no sane cook—and certainly no Burgundian cook, since most of them are known for their thriftiness—would pour a *Premier Cru* or *Grand Cru* into the pot. No, the stew is made with a basic Burgundy, something that won't require the cook to hock the family jewels. The Burgundy you drink with the stew, well, that's a different story. In the end, however, it's the combination that counts, and a rich, winey stew of slowly braised beef is one of the most stunning partners a bottle of great Burgundy could have.

## WHITE BURGUNDY AND LOBSTER

M ove over Champagne and caviar. Among the world's most indulgent and sensational food and wine combinations is surely a *Premier Cru* or *Grand Cru* white Burgundy, especially an opulent Puligny-Montrachet or Chassagne-Montrachet, with lobster drizzled with butter. When the sweet, rich creaminess of the wine meets the sweet, rich meatiness of the lobster, well, if you don't die of poverty first, you'll die from the pleasure.

style. Today canned and frozen snails from Turkey and Algeria show up in many restaurants worldwide, but in Burgundy, wild snails can still be collected in the vineyards. Traditionally these are stuffed with garlic butter, cooked, and served piping hot from their shells.

The beef dishes of Burgundy are also much acclaimed, especially the slowly braised beef stew known as *boeuf bourguignon*. But the most exciting beef of all is Charolais, named for the town of Charoles in southwestern Burgundy and one of Europe's finest breeds. These massive cattle have meat that is tender and succulent, with an incomparable full, rich flavor. A hunk of roasted Charolais and a glass of Pommard or Volnay is Burgundy gift wrapped. With Charolais, meat is just the beginning, however. From the Charolais' milk come cylinders of rich Charolais cheese, which are also prized.

But the most legendary Burgundian cheese of all must be the pungent, runny Epoisses de Bourgogne, named after the village of the same name. Sought after all over the world, Epoisses is aged slowly and given a daily washing with *marc de Bourgogne*, the local eau-de-vie made from pomace (the grape skins, seeds, and stems that are left after pressing).

Finally, there's *pain d'épice*, Burgundy's spice bread. In Gallo-Roman times, Burgundy was one of the corridors of the spice trade to the northern countries. Dijon's love of mustard resulted from this propitious positioning and so did spice bread. The dense loaves, made with honey, cinnamon, cloves, nutmeg, coriander, aniseed, and orange peel are not exactly sweet, they're more of a hearty snack. Who knows how many generations of *vignerons*, come winter, have devoured an entire *pain d'épice* after a day spent pruning in the damp, cold vineyards of Burgundy.

213

## VISITING THE WINERIES OF BURGUNDY

B urgundy is filled with quiet, charming villages, many of which surround impressive medieval churches or cathedrals. There are scores of fabulous tiny restaurants specializing in the region's humble, delicious cooking, and dozens of small comfortable hotels. Even just driving down the narrow country roads can be thrilling as you pass one world-famous village or vineyard after another. No visit to Burgundy, however, would be complete without seeing two magnificent, historic buildings: the first, in Vougeot, the château of Clos de Vougeot, sitting like a jewel in the middle of the walled vineyard, and the second, in Beaune, the impressive fifteenth-century

Hôtel Dieu with its colorful tiled roof and breathtaking grand hall. Each year, this is where the prestigious Hospices de Beaune wine auction is held.

All of this notwithstanding, Burgundian domaines can be very difficult to visit since they are so tiny. Small producers are simply not set up to receive visitors, and even if you call in advance, your request may be refused. This is not necessarily the result of meanness or snobbishness. With small Burgundian producers, there is nothing that resembles a winery in the Californian sense. Rather, if you're lucky, you'll end up going with the proprietor down into a cold damp cellar, where perhaps a dozen barrels are crowded together, and if you're super lucky, the proprietor will draw some wine out of a barrel to taste. There's no state-of-the-art equipment, no slide show, and no gift shop selling T-shirts that say Puligny-Montrachet. Speaking French is almost obligatory, and so are appointments in advance. It is somewhat easier to visit the larger *négociants*, such as Domaine Joseph Drouhin, Maison Louis Jadot, and Maison Moreau (all listed here). The telephone numbers include the dialing code you'll need when calling from the United States. If you're calling from within France, eliminate the 011-33 and add a zero before the next number.

Given that estates are difficult to get into, there's another way to "visit" Burgundy, which is to take a class that focuses on top producers, with several of those producers in attendance. Possibly the best such classes in the United States are given in New York City by the Burgundy Wine Company, which once a year organizes an all-day seminar during which you "travel" around Burgundy by tasting the wines of different villages and vineyards. Several top Burgundians act as guides. For more information, contact the Burgundy Wine Company, 323 West 11 Street, New York, New York 10014; (212) 691-9092.

*Maison Louis Jadot's logo: a sculpted head of Bacchus.*

**CHÂTEAU DU CLOS DE VOUGEOT**
21640 Vougeot
011-33-3-80-62-86-09

**DOMAINE COMTE GEORGES DE VOGÜÉ**
Rue Sainte Barbe
21220 Chambolle-Musigny
011-33-3-80-62-86-25

**DOMAINE COMTES LAFON**
5 Rue Pierre Joigneaux
Clos de la Barre
21190 Meursault
011-33-3-80-21-22-17

**DOMAINE DUJAC**
7 Rue La Bussière
21220 Morey-St.-Denis
011-33-3-80-34-01-00

**DOMAINE LEFLAIVE**
Place des Marronniers
21190 Puligny-Montrachet
011-33-3-80-21-30-13

**DOMAINE ROBERT CHEVILLON**
68 Rue Félix Tisserand
21700 Nuits-St.-Georges
011-33-3-80-62-34-88

**MAISON JOSEPH DROUHIN**
7 Rue d'Enfer
21220 Beaune Cedex
011-33-3-80-24-68-88

**MAISON LOUIS JADOT**
5 Rue Samuel-Legay
21220 Beaune
011-33-3-80-22-10-57

**MAISON MOREAU J. ET FILS**
Route d'Auxerre
89800 Chablis
011-33-3-86-42-88-00

# THE BURGUNDIES TO KNOW

When I approached the writing of this section, I had all the enthusiasm of a woman going to have a root canal. Frankly, recommending Burgundies is fraught with problems, chief among them the knowledge that you probably won't have an easy time getting your hands on these (which doesn't mean you shouldn't try). Made mostly in minuscule quantities, great Burgundies are immediately snapped up in wine shops, and some may never appear on the shelf at all since the wine shop owner may have standing orders from good customers. That said, if I know a wine is completely inaccessible, I have not included it here.

Then there's the worry over the wines themselves—the wines of Burgundy are fragile creatures. Vintages, the age of the wine, and how the wine was handled all dramatically leave their stamp. Despite these hesitations and more, the wines here have all provided me with stellar experiences, and I've loved them to the very last drop. I offer them in the hope that you too will one day taste them and be equally pleased.

## *Whites*

### BERNARD MOREY ET FILS

Chassagne-Montrachet

Morgeot

*Premier Cru*

100% chardonnay

From Morgeot, one of the top *Premier Cru* vineyards in the village (and white wine haven) of Chassagne-Montrachet, comes Bernard Morey's silky and densely rich but ever so elegant wine. This is no mean feat, producing a wine that is powerfully concentrated but doesn't feel ponderous on the palate. In top years the Morey Chassagne-Montrachet Morgeot begins with beguilingly subtle honey aromas and then explodes in a shower of honeyed flavors. Woven through these are suggestions of crème brûlée, chalk, minerals, and flowers.

### BONNEAU DU MARTRAY

Corton-Charlemagne

*Grand Cru*

100% chardonnay

Possibly the most sought-after white Burgundy of all, Corton-Charlemagne is the world's greatest chardonnay. The centuries-old vineyard is thought to have been owned in the late 700s by Charlemagne himself. With the vineyard's perfect exposure and soil, Corton-Charlemagne is a wine that ought to be mind-blowing, and it is. This one, from Bonneau du Martray, is honeyed, peachy, minerally, utterly refined, and yet profoundly sensual. White wine doesn't get more dreamlike, more poetic, more ethereal than this.

215

### DOMAINE HENRI CLERC & FILS

Bienvenues-Bâtard-Montrachet

*Grand Cru*

100% chardonnay

One of the four prestigious *Grands Crus* of the village of Puligny-Montrachet, Bienvenues-Bâtard-Montrachet, the smallest, is just 9.1 acres in size. It nonetheless has fifteen owners, including the Domaine Henri Clerc, which, in warm years, makes an enticingly virile and powerful example. Many top white Burgundies have flavors that can be described as earthy, but few wines give you as stunning, surprising—and not unpleasant—a sensation of soil, herbs, and chalk as this. What makes it work are the honey and caramel flavors, which seem like a welcome topping on a strangely irresistible ice cream sundae. The texture of Bienvenues-Bâtard-Montrachet can be sublimely creamy, a characteristic that is accentuated after the wine has seen eight or ten years of aging.

## DOMAINE ROBERT-DENOGENT
Mâcon-Solutré-Pouilly

Clos des Bertillonnes

100% chardonnay

The Mâconnis region makes oceans of rather washed-out, screechingly tart wine, all of which is appropriately cheap. Then there are the gems—wines that usually cost a bit more but have quadruple the character. This is one of those. Mâcon-Solutré-Pouilly is one of the forty-three villages entitled to the designation Mâcon Villages (a step up from basic Mâcon). With its bursting lemon and apple flavors, Robert-Denogent's refreshing wine has something that is rare in the chardonnay world: snappiness. The wine comes from the Clos des Bertillonnes, a hillside vineyard near Pouilly-Fuissé.

## FRANCOIS JOBARD
Meursault

Poruzot

Premier Cru

100% chardonnay

Meursault—the very word makes me think of the seductive smell of the earth. One of the best villages for whites, Meursault is the source of ripe, hedonistic wines (especially *Premiers Crus* and *Grands Crus*) that have what the French call *gout de terroir*, literally taste of the place. And so it is with François Jobard's Meursault from the *Premier Cru* vineyard known as Poruzot. At its best it is a massively endowed, beautifully honeyed wine that is also fascinatingly laden with aromas of stones, minerals, truffles, and soil. Poruzot, a well-kept secret as far as vineyards go, is adjacent to one of Meursault's most famous *Premier Cru* vineyards, Les Genevrières, and the wines are often like sisters. François Jobard, a small domaine of just 11 acres, is a star among Meursault producers and is known for beautifully delineated, classic wines.

## OLIVIER LEFLAIVE
Corton-Charlemagne

Grand Cru

100% chardonnay

The sheer drama of a wine such as Corton-Charlemagne compels me to include it twice (see Bonneau du Martray on page 215), and indeed Olivier Leflaive's interpretation—full of ripe guava, minerals, crème brûlée, and honey aromas and flavors—is magnificent to its core. But I admit, I'm generally knocked out by all of Olivier Leflaive's top white Burgundies: his Chassagne-Montrachets, Meursaults, Puligny-Montrachets, and Bâtard-Montrachets. They have a vivid opulence, a tangible passionate streak to them that just doesn't seem possible given the wines' utter finesse. Maybe Olivier Leflaive is just trying harder than a lot of people. Having left the family firm, which is known simply as Domaine Leflaive, in the 1980s (not exactly commonplace in a region as tradition-bound as Burgundy), Olivier seems to have had something to prove. Could he, within a mere decade, begin to make some of the most stunning wines in the world? Just one sip of his Corton-Charlemagne holds the answer.

## PAUL PERNOT
Puligny-Montrachet

Les Pucelles

Premier Cru

100% chardonnay

One of the most exciting, if little known, producers of white Burgundies, Paul Pernot and his two sons make Puligny-Montrachets that, when they're young, have a creaminess and fatness (by Burgundy standards anyway) that is positively hedonistic. The sweet nutty flavor of toasted new oak barrels is obvious in the wines' youth; with some age this melts into a sort of caramely, crème brûlée–like character that is hard to resist. For all this richness, Pernot's wine are beautifully laced with acidity that, like a ribbon, draws together the lush flavors beautifully.

## RENE ET VINCENT DAUVISSAT

Chablis

Vaillons

*Premier Cru*

100% chardonnay

Shiveringly vibrant with acidity, René and Vincent Dauvissat's Chablis seems to personify the stark cold white landscape that is Burgundy's most northern enclave. As with sushi knives, Chablis should never be dull, and this one from the *Premier Cru* vineyard known as Vaillons certainly isn't. Though the wine can have a honey-peach aroma that sets you up for something mellow and lush, watch out. Once they're in your mouth, top examples of this wine are almost savagely focused, pure, and cleansing. Vaillons is one of the finest *Premier Cru* vineyards, and no one makes better wines from this small parcel than the Dauvissat family.

## *Reds*

### DOMAINE DANIEL RION & FILS

Chambolle-Musigny

Les Charmes

*Premier Cru*

100% pinot noir

Great Burgundy is often the equivalent of quiet music. The wine is not flashy, not fleshy, not extroverted, and not obvious. Yet something about it pulls you back again and again—the mystery factor. Daniel Rion's Chambolle-Musigny from the *Premier Cru* vineyard Les Charmes can be like this. Seamless and supple, it often displays a beautiful juicy core of grenadine, citrus, and earth. And all so impeccably balanced, silky, and understated, it's unnerving. In general, Chambolle-Musignys are more about grace than power, as Rion's Les Charmes charmingly shows. The Rion family, considered to be among Burgundy's top-ranking producers, is also known for their sumptuous Nuits-St.-Georges.

### DOMAINE DUJAC

Chambolle-Musigny

Les Gruenchers

*Premier Cru*

100% pinot noir

I may be trampling on my own introductory comments here because Domaine Dujac is indeed very hard to find—but the search is worth it. This domaine, owned by the influential, highly praised winemaker Jacques Seysses, has been garnering nothing but accolades for more than a decade. Deservedly so, for the domaine's wines are among the most sublime from Burgundy. As a village, Chambolle-Musigny is known for the almost lacy elegance of its wines. Add to that a top *Premier Cru* vineyard like Les Gruenchers and an artist like Seysses and you have the makings of magic. When I have tasted it, Les Gruenchers has been the epitome of sensuality, with long, creamy mocha and earth flavors.

217

### DOMAINE MEO-CAMUZET

Nuits-St.-Georges

Aux Boudots

*Premier Cru*

100% pinot noir

Known for its outstanding holdings in many extraordinary vineyards (Clos de Vougeot for example), Méo-Camuzet is a name that electrifies red Burgundy lovers. Exotic, supple, and intense, the wines from this domaine have immediate sex appeal. The Nuits-St.-Georges from Aux Boudots, one of the best of forty *Premier Cru* vineyards, is one of its simpler wines (simple being a relative proposition in this case). At its best, this sweetly ripe wine, with its not so subtle hints of proscuitto, leather, and cigar, is mouthfilling, dazzling, and complex. Then after it has been aged, somewhere between five and ten years, Aux Boudots turns the corner of youth, becoming a wine of depth and almost unbearable tenderness.

## DOMAINE MICHEL LAFARGE

Volnay

100% pinot noir

Finding a simple village wine (priced like a simple village wine) that tastes like a *Premier Cru* is sweet revenge. Enter the Lafarge Volnay, at its best a hedonistic wine that intriguingly possesses a rich meaty quality at the same time that it hints irresistibly of raspberry or boysenberry pie. The texture is pure silk. As a group, Volnays are rather hard to pin down, some leaning toward delicacy, others toward heft. Michel Lafarge's Volnay strikes a perfect balance. Drinking it immediately inspires a craving for something as comforting: beef *bourguigon* maybe?

## DOMAINE PONSOT

Latricières-Chambertin

*Grand Cru*

100% pinot noir

The wine that changed the way I thought about wine forever after was a Latricières-Chambertin. I had never experienced anything (well anything in the world of beverages) quite so tantalizing. It was a wine that appealed as much to the head as to the senses. I couldn't stop drinking it. I still love Latricières-Chambertin, one of the eight *Grands Crus* of the village of Gevry-Chambertin. Domaine Ponsot's Latricières is classic red Burgundy: supple and earthy with the magical, if not oxymoronic, ability to seem both powerful and fragile at the same time. After aging for, say, ten years or more, mature examples of this wine from top vintages have sensual aromas and sensationally long finishes.

## DOMAINE ROSSIGNOL-TRAPET

Chambertin

*Grand Cru*

100% pinot noir

Chambertin, the best-known *Grand Cru* from the village of Gevrey-Chambertin, can often produce sensational wines that are untamed in their wild earthiness, silky, and mouth-filling. A relatively new domaine formed by the partnership of two families, Domaine Rossignol-Trapet makes Chambertins that can be among the spiciest, with hints of sandalwood, cedar, pine, and moss, richly set off against the background aromas of damp earth. If any wine could be said to be the adult equivalent of the Enchanted Forest, this is it.

## MONGEARD-MUGNERET

Grands-Echézeaux

*Grand Cru*

100% pinot noir

The otherwise unremarkable village of Flagey-Echézeaux has two stars: the *Grand Cru* vineyards of Grands-Echézeaux and Echézeaux. As its name implies, Grands-Echézeaux is the more majestic of the two and is often grouped for purposes of comparison with three world-famous vineyards very close by: Romanée-Conti, Richebourg, and La Tâche. (Unless you're head of a Fortune 500 company, the price of these wines will make your palms sweaty, but for the record, Grands-Echézeaux is the least expensive of the four by far.) The wines from Grands-Echézeaux are usually superbly concentrated and, in the best vintages, none more so than Mongeard-Mugneret, which makes a lush, generous wine so seductively earthy, leathery, meaty, and rich that a sip can only be followed by spellbound silence.

# Beaujolais

The vineyards of Beaujolais extend north to south for some 35 miles over low granite hills in the southernmost reaches of Burgundy. For French administrative purposes, Beaujolais is considered part of Burgundy even though, aside from proximity, the two regions have almost nothing in common. The climates are dissimilar; the grapes are different; the way the wines are made varies radically. Even the spirit of each place is singular. Beaujolais is as lighthearted as Burgundy is serious.

Beaujolais is both the name of the place and the wine made there. The sad misconception about the wine Beaujolais is that it's solely a once a year wine experience, drunk around the end of November when signs in restaurants and wine shops from Paris to Tokyo scream *Le Beaujolais Est Arrivé!* (The Beaujolais Has Arrived!) What has arrived, to be exact, is Beaujolais Nouveau, a grapey young wine made immediately after the harvest in celebration. Beaujolais Nouveau is great fun, but as wines go, regular Beaujolais is so much better. We'll look at Beaujolais Nouveau later in this chapter (see page 225).

> ## THE QUICK SIP ON BEAUJOLAIS
>
>
>
> • Beaujolais and Beaujolais Nouveau are distinctly different. The first is a straightforward and fruity wine, the second, a cheerful, young version meant for celebrating the harvest.
>
> • All Beaujolais is made from gamay, a soft, fruity grape.
>
> • Most Beaujolais is made by a special fermentation technique—carbonic maceration—that maximizes the wine's inherent fruitiness.

**219**

*The grand Château de la Chaize is one of the largest producers in Brouilly, which itself is the largest of the Beaujolais Crus.*

## THE GRAPES OF
## BEAUJOLAIS

The only grape used in red Beaujolais is gamay, more correctly called gamay noir à jus blanc (literally, black gamay with white juice). A very small amount of white Beaujolais is also produced. It's made from chardonnay and aligoté grapes.

Beaujolais has been called the only white wine that happens to be red. An apt reference, for despite its vivid magenta color, Beaujolais is quite like white wine in its expressiveness and thirst-quenching qualities. The wine's personality begins with the gamay grape, the only one used in Beaujolais' production. Gamay's flavors are virtually unmistakable: a rush of sweet black cherry and black raspberry, then a hint of peaches, violets, and roses, followed by a smidgen of peppery spiciness at the end. In many reds a tight rasp of tannin acts as a cloak over the fruit flavors. Not so in Beaujolais. Because gamay is naturally low in tannin, its already profuse fruitiness seems even more dramatic.

Beaujolais' character comes, however, not solely from gamay, but also from the unusual manner in which the wine is made. The process, long a tradition, is called carbonic maceration. During it, clusters of grapes are put whole into the fermenting tank and fermentation literally takes place inside each grape. Carbonic maceration could theoretically be used with any grape, but it happens to be particularly successful with ultrafruity grapes, such as gamay.

After Beaujolais is fermented, it rests in tanks (a few growers also put it briefly in small, relatively new oak) for five to nine months before being sold. Though five months may not seem long, it's just enough to take the grapey newborn edge off the wine and allow it to evolve more fruit, flower, and spice flavors.

# COMMERCIAL VS. OLD-STYLE BEAUJOLAIS

As far as regular Beaujolais goes, the distinction between what is commercial and what might be called old-style Beaujolais is important for anyone who cares about flavor. Several decades ago all Beaujolais was old-style. Unfortunately, Beaujolais' commercial success, fueled by the wild popularity of Beaujolais Nouveau, has led most growers and producers to take shortcuts. Vine yields are now often stretched to the maximum allowed by law,

*Making Beaujolais the very old way, in a wooden basket press.*

## THE BEAUJOLAIS CRUS

From north to south, here are the ten villages—*crus*—that produce some of the most distinctive Beaujolais and a brief description of the wines that bear their names. The labels on bottles of Beaujolais Cru will often only name the producer and the *cru*. The word *Beaujolais* will not appear.

### St.-Amour
Rich, silky, and sometimes spicy wines; the aroma can suggest peaches. St.-Amour means holy love. One theory suggests the name is derived from a Roman soldier who, after escaping death, converted to Christianity and set up a mission. He was canonized as St. Amour.

### Juliénas
Rich and relatively powerful, the flavor of Juliénas is spicy. Its bouquet may make you think of peonies. Named after Julius Caesar.

### Chénas
A supple and graceful wine, with a subtle bouquet of wild roses. Chénas is the smallest Beaujolais Cru.

### Moulin-à-Vent
Hearty, rich, and well-balanced in texture, bouquet, and flavor. With Fleurie and Morgon, Moulin-à-Vent is one of the *crus* said to age the best. The name means windmill, in honor of a 300-year-old stone one that rises above the vines.

### Fleurie
Velvety in texture, with a bouquet both floral and fruity. Fleurie is considered the most feminine and delicate of the Beaujolais Crus.

### Chiroubles
Grapes for Chiroubles come from some of the vineyards located at the highest altitudes in Beaujolais. The wines are very low in tannin and light bodied, often with a bouquet of violets.

### Morgon
With a personality that stands apart from all the other *crus*, Morgan is rich, masculine, deep purple in color, and rather full in body for a Beaujolais. It tastes of apricots, peaches, and the earth.

### Régnié
Has relatively full-bodied, round, red currant and raspberry flavors. The newest *cru*, Régnié was added in 1988.

### Brouilly
The wines of Brouilly are fruity and grapey, with aromas of raspberries, cherries, blueberries, and currants. Relatively light bodied. This is the largest *cru*.

### Côte de Brouilly
Wines from the Côte de Brouilly are heady and lively, with a deep fruity quality and light body. Located on the slopes of Mont Brouilly, an extinct volcano.

and the grapes are picked early, before they are fully mature and ripe with sugar. Using a technique called chaptalization (see page 47), a quick fix of cane sugar is added to the fermenting tank to compensate for the low natural sugar. This legal but controversial process allows the winemaker to get a high-alcohol wine, even from grapes insufficiently ripe. Critics consider this akin to cheating.

The final step in making a commercial Beaujolais is to filter it severely so that it will be completely stable. Unfortunately, severe filtering can also strip a wine of its true flavor and body. Beaujolais made in this large-scale, commercial way tastes more tutti-frutti than truly fruity. Its flavor is often a dead ringer for Jell-O. The artificially high alcohol gives the wine a swollen body rather than a natural roundness.

By comparison, old-style Beaujolais is made by a very small percentage of growers, who are often considered fanatics. These traditional growers keep yields 20

*Old gamay vines, solidly entrenched in Beaujolais' stony, granitic soil.*

to 30 percent below the amount allowed, do not chaptalize, filter lightly if at all, and hold the wine up to ten months before bottling it as an estate wine.

How can you tell traditionally made Beaujolais from commercially made? There is no foolproof way; however, traditionally made Beaujolais most often costs more, is generally bottled by an individual estate, and is usually imported into the United States by a handful of selected importers who specialize in small estates (the name of the importer will be on the label). The importers who specialize in top-notch, old-style Beaujolais include Alain Jugenet, Kermit Lynch, Louis/Dressner, Martine's Wines, and Weygandt-Metzler.

## To Chill or Not to Chill?

◆━◆◆◆━◆

Chill it. When Beaujolais is served cool—not cold—to the touch, after about fifteen minutes in the refrigerator, its flavors explode with fruit and spice. Chilling the wine is customary in the region. On Sundays jugs of Beaujolais are still set in buckets of cold water and placed under the shade of a tree in the center of the village so that men playing *boules* will have something to slake their thirst.

## THE LAND AND THE VINEYARDS

The Beaujolais vineyards carpet a corridor 35 miles long and about 9 miles wide. On the east is the Saône river valley, on the west, the Monts de Beaujolais, a mountainous spur of the Massif Central. The climate is continental, with cold winters and hot, mostly dry summers. The soil is largely decomposed granite in the north and, farther south, sedimentary rock, clay, and bits of limestone. In all, there are ninety-six villages, ten of which are recognized as producing superior wine. These ten are known as the *crus* of Beaujolais (see page 221).

## CATEGORIES OF BEAUJOLAIS

Regardless of whether the wine is made in a traditional or commercial way, the law defines three categories of Beaujolais. In ascending quality (and price), they are:

- Beaujolais

- Beaujolais-Villages

- Beaujolais Cru

The basic stuff is labeled simply Beaujolais. The grapes come mainly from less distinguished vineyards in the south. Soil there is more fertile and the land is flatter. As a result, the wines tend to be lighter, with less concentration of fruit flavors, though there are exceptions.

Beaujolais-Villages, which is a notch better in quality, comes from thirty-nine villages in the hilly midsection of the region.

Soil here is poorer, composed of granite and sand, forcing the vines to struggle more and ultimately yield better grapes. Beaujolais-Villages wines are generally a blend of grapes or wines from several villages.

Better still are the Beaujolais Cru. In Beaujolais the word *cru* does not indicate a vineyard as it does in other French regions, but, instead, refers to ten special villages. Beaujolais Cru wines come from these villages, all of which are located on steep granite hills (about 1,000 feet in elevation) in the northern part of Beaujolais. The *crus*, looking more or less from north to south, are: St.-Amour, Juliénas, Chénas, Moulin-à-Vent, Fleurie, Chiroubles, Morgon, Régnié, Brouilly, and Côte de Brouilly. *Cru* wines tend to be denser and more expressive (display more dramatic flavors) than basic Beaujolais. They also can be aged longer since they have more structure, tannin, and acidity. While Beaujolais Cru can be kept five years or even more,

### A BEAUJOLAIS BY ANY OTHER NAME . . .

The red wine known in California (at least until 2007) as gamay Beaujolais does not come from the gamay grape nor is it related to Beaujolais. Instead, it is made from a clone of pinot noir. Gamay Beaujolais first became popular in California in the 1960s as a blending grape. Today it is still used in blends, some of which are labeled pinot noir, while others are called gamay Beaujolais.

To muddy the waters still further, gamay Beaujolais is not the same as yet another grape, Napa gamay. Napa gamay is actually the French grape valdiguié, although the wines it produces in California are more often called gamay Beaujolais than Napa

gamay (and rarely valdiguié). Got it?

For their part, French vintners have insisted that the term Beaujolais should be reserved exclusively for wines produced in the Beaujolais region of France. This eventually prompted the United States government to enact legislation stipulating that the terms gamay Beaujolais or Napa gamay be phased out. California producers may legally use these terms until 2007; after that it's all over.

The least perplexing thing about Beaujolais in California is the way it is made: Almost all winemakers use carbonic maceration, the fermentation technique used to make true Beaujolais.

many wine drinkers prefer to drink them soon after they are released, when the fruit is still young and vivid. Moulin-à-Vent, Fleurie, and Morgon are generally considered the *crus* with the most aging potential, but it depends on how the wine is made. Traditionally made Beaujolais wines age the best and often take on earthy, pinot noir–like characteristics as they get older.

## WHO MAKES BEAUJOLAIS?

Most Beaujolais are blended, bottled, and sold by *négociants*. These are individuals or firms that buy separate lots of wine from the more than 4,000 growers and some 19 cooperatives that actually vinify the wine. The final blended wine is always labeled with the name of the *négociant*.

*Georges Duboeuf (right) and his son Franck make some of Beaujolais' most popular wines. Many are about as exuberant, bouncy, and fruit-packed as wine gets.*

There are about thirty *négociants* in Beaujolais. Among the best known are Bouchard Père et Fils, Prosper Maufoux, and Louis Jadot. The most famous Beaujolais *négociant*, however, is Georges Duboeuf, known for wines that seem almost to bounce with sweet fruit. Duboeuf's wines are well loved by many, although purists find some of them over manipulated. The man himself is a legend in the region, both for his commercial success and for his extraordinary palate (he has been known to taste up to 300 wines a day).

A fraction of Beaujolais is not bought and blended by *négociants* but is made at small estates that grow their own grapes. These wines are often made by traditional methods and brought to the United States by specialty importers.

## WHITE BEAUJOLAIS

Beaujolais Blanc exists, although it represents only a minuscule amount (about 2 percent) of the total Beaujolais production and virtually none is imported into the United States. Beaujolais Blanc and Beaujolais-Villages Blanc are generally made from either chardonnay or aligoté grapes.

# BEAUJOLAIS NOUVEAU

Beaujolais Nouveau (also called *vin primeur*—first wine) is regular Beaujolais, generally from the lesser districts, that is seven to nine weeks old. Like Thanksgiving, it's meant to be enjoyed as a harvest celebration.

Nearly a century ago, casks of the just-made grapey wine would be shipped by paddleboat down the Saône River to the bars and bistros of Lyon (and later, Paris) so that city people would have something with which to celebrate. By the 1960s, almost half a million cases of Nouveau were being sold. Today Beaujolais Nouveau accounts for about a third of all Beaujolais production.

Grapes destined to be Nouveau may come from the Beaujolais appellation or the better Beaujolais-Villages appellation. Beaujolais Cru grapes from the ten top northern villages, however, are never used.

In 1985 the Institut National des Appellations d'Origine (INAO) established the third Thursday in November as the wine's uniform release date. Nouveaus destined for export can be shipped earlier than the third Thursday, but they must be held in bonded warehouses until 12:01 A.M., whereupon the wines can be drunk.

Or more likely, gulped. Most Nouveau is joyfully consumed within a month of its release while the fresh, raw, grapey flavors are in full tilt. Drunk, say, a year later, Nouveau won't have gone bad; it will simply taste less vibrant.

Like regular Beaujolais, there is better and worse Nouveau. Overmanipulated, cheap, commercial Nouveau can taste like melted purple Popsicles. Top-quality Nouveau has a kind of exuberant berryness. Its charm is its innocent, not-quite-wine char-

## BISTRO LESSONS

The vineyards of Beaujolais lie just north of France's gastronomic capital Lyon, and in many ways the city offers the perfect lesson in matching Beaujolais with food. Despite its lofty title, Lyon's approach to eating is decidedly roll up your sleeves. It's no surprise that France's first bistros are thought to have originated here, and even today, no-frills hearty dishes remain the city's signature. As does Beaujolais, a bottle of which seems to appear on just about every bistro table. And what better way to wash down poached country-style pork sausages with warm potatoes bathed in olive oil and shallots, grilled paper-thin calf's liver, frisée salad with bacon and croutons, or a winey coq au vin? Beaujolais—bursting with fruitiness—is not a shy wine. And among all the world's reds, it is one of the least tannic. This, coupled with Beaujolais' easy quaffability, makes it a great match for humble meats, roasts, stews, and other down-to-earth dishes that many food and wine lovers (including this one) find irresistible.

acter. Drinking it gives you the same kind of silly pleasure as eating cookie dough.

# VISITING BEAUJOLAIS WINERIES

Winemakers and grape growers in Beaujolais are warm and welcoming. To arrange for a tour and tasting, it is best to call ahead and make an appointment. While many speak English, it's helpful if you speak some French.

Being part of greater Burgundy, the Beaujolais region is full of terrific country restaurants specializing in earthy home cooking. In addition, Lyon—considered the gastronomic capital of France—is less than 15 miles from the southern part of Beaujolais.

The telephone numbers include the dialing code you'll need when calling from the United States. If you're calling from within France, eliminate the 011-33 and add a zero before the next number.

---

## BEAUJOLAIS AS DESSERT

———

According to the famous French chef Paul Bocuse, one of the favorite traditional desserts of wine-growers in Beaujolais is freshly picked wild peaches sliced into a glass and topped with black currants drenched in cool Beaujolais.

---

**CHÂTEAU THIVIN**
Brouilly
69460 Odeans
011-33-4-74-03-47-53
A Côte de Brouilly producer.

**DOMAINE BERNARD DIOCHON**
La Passerelle
71570 Romanèche-Thorins
011-33-3-85-35-52-42
A Moulin-à-Vent producer.

**DUBOEUF EN BEAUJOLAIS**
Route Nationale 6
between Belleville and Mâcon
011-33-3-85-35-20-75
Beaujolais' largest *négociant*, Georges Duboeuf, has created this virtual "village of wine" in Romanèche-Thorins. Duboeuf en Beaujolais provides an extensive tour of both cellars and a small vineyard, plus

multiple exhibits, a wine museum, and film presentations, as well as a wine tasting room and a retail shop. There is a small admission charge.

**JANIN PAUL ET FILS**
La Chevillère
71720 Romanèche-Thorins
011-33-3-85-35-52-80
A Moulin-à-Vent and Beaujolais-Villages producer.

**MARCEL LAPIERRE**
Les Chênes
69910 Le Pré Jourdain
011-33-4-74-04-23-89
A Morgon producer.

**MICHEL CHIGNARD**
Le Point du Jour
69820 Fleurie
011-33-4-74-04-11-87
A Fleurie producer.

**PATRICK ET NATHALIE BRUNET**
Le Champagne
69820 Fleurie
011-33-4-74-04-12-11
A Morgon and Fleurie producer.

*Duboeuf en Beaujolais, a favorite destination for visitors.*

# THE BEAUJOLAIS TO KNOW

Wine shops are full of simple, tasty Beaujolais that would cheer up any situation. The Beaujolais below, however, are more serious red wines that in good vintages have a greater range of flavors plus better focus and structure.

## BRUNET

Fleurie

Domaine de Robert

100% gamay

The panoply of fruit flavors in Brunet's Fleurie is entrancing. There's every ripe red and black berry imaginable, plus loads of spice, vanilla, coconut, and a bracing touch of citrus. The fruit rolls like waves in your mouth.

## GEORGES DUBOEUF

Beaujolais-Villages

Domaine du Granit Bleu

100% gamay

This single estate wine from *négociant* superman Georges Duboeuf is about as playful and childlike as wine gets. With aromas and flavors reminiscent of blueberry pancake syrup, peach jam, and strawberry milk shakes, it's a great wine for unapologetic, hedonistic gulping.

## GEORGES DUBOEUF

Fleurie

Domaine des Quatre Vents

100% gamay

Georges Duboeuf specializes in crafting wines that roar with sweet cherry flavor—usually. Not so this Fleurie, a lovely wine with berry, peach, and ginger flavors that seem to tap-dance softly in your mouth. Duboeuf makes hundreds of different wines, but those that carry the name of the original domaine, as in this case, are always the most interesting.

## JANIN

Moulin-à-Vent

Domaine des Vignes du Tremblay

100% gamay

One of the most elegant and structured Beaujolais around. When a bottle from a good vintage is first opened, the fruit is so encapsulated by the tannin that the wine just sits there like a stubborn child. Within about ten minutes, however, there's an uncanny explosion of saturated berry fruit flavor. A real mouthfiller of a wine.

## KERMIT LYNCH

Beaujolais

100% gamay

It's a basic Beaujolais, but this traditionally made wine is leagues more delicious than you might expect. Year after year, the aroma is so heady, you'd think you'd just stuck your nose into a basket filled with roses and just-picked black raspberries. The wine is personally selected and bottled by Kermit Lynch, a well-known importer who specializes in French wines.

227

## ARMAGNAC

Deep in France's southwest corner, about 100 miles south of Bordeaux, lies Gascony, a bucolic farming region and an enclave for perhaps the most sensual, rich, rustic cooking in France. Indulgences elsewhere, foie gras and confit of duck are virtually daily fare here, and the propensity to sauté the accompanying potatoes (or just about any other vegetable) in duck fat, too, leaves French nutritionists wondering why the local population isn't keeling over. But in Gascony, eating well *matters*. Not surprisingly, so does drinking well.

As the local desserts—soufflé of prunes in Armagnac and fruit strudel laced with Armagnac—reveal, this is the home of one of France's most well-loved brandies. Armagnac is far less famous than its sister Cognac (see page 157) and the two are usually assumed to be quite similar since both are distilled from grapes. Not so. In everything from how it tastes to how it is made, Armagnac is distinct and unique. It is decidedly not Cognac, and when you're in Gascony, you get the feeling that the Armagnacais, as the people of the region are called, like it that way. Proud and somewhat stubborn, they quickly remind you that this, after all, is the home of d'Artagnan, the most famed of the king's musketeers who, in the nineteenth century, were immortalized by Alexandre Dumas.

Armagnac has the longest history of any French brandy. By the thirteenth century, simple distilling techniques first used in the Arab world (primarily for perfumes) had spread into Spain and over the Pyrenees into southwest France. Like distillations of local herbs and flowers, the first distillations of the region's grapes, thought to have occurred in the early fifteenth century, were for medical purposes. The clear brandies that resulted—the seminal Armagnacs—were said to inspire a sense of well-being, relieve toothaches, diminish mental anguish, and promote courage. (Joan of Arc, although not from the region, came to be known as l'Armagnacaise, because of her courage.)

Being first didn't guarantee Armagnac the prominence you might expect. Unlike the region of Cognac, Armagnac was isolated inland with no navigable river that could serve as an easy means of promoting commerce. Nonetheless, by the seventeenth century Dutch traders installed themselves in Gascony, as they did in Cognac, and the production of Armagnac increased, even though it had to be transported overland before it could be loaded on ships destined for northern markets. By the middle of the nineteenth century a canal built on a local river connected Armagnac to Bordeaux, and for the first time its brandy became readily accessible.

The Armagnac region covers some 86,500 acres and is divided into three subdistricts: the Bas Armagnac, Ténarèze, and the Haut Armagnac. Of the three, the Bas Armagnac (lower Armagnac, so named for

*Armagnac, Cognac's less well-known cousin, is the older of the two famous spirits.*

*Florence Castarède, head of Castarède cellars in Lavardac.*

its lesser altitude) not only produces the most wine for distillation (almost 60 percent), but it's also home to most of the top producers and best Armagnacs. Situated in western Gascony near the pine forests of the Landes, the Bas Armagnac is noted for its sand-based soil, often with a high iron content plus small pieces of clay. The Armagnacs from this subdistrict are the most elegant, with the most pronounced flavor of prunes and plums. Armagnacs from Ténarèze can be more floral, lively, and sharp when young, though they develop finesse with age. About 40 percent of the wine destined for distillation is made in this subregion. As for the Haut Armagnac, few brandies are produced there today, with most grapes made into wine instead.

The top Armagnacs are more rustic, robust, fragrant, and full-bodied than the top Cognacs, and the reason begins with the grapes. In Cognac the neutral-tasting grape ugni blanc makes up most of the blend. In Armagnac ugni blanc is only about 55 percent of the blend to be distilled. The rest comes from up to eleven other white grapes, though just three—folle blanc, colombard, and Baco blanc—are of primary importance. Folle blanche contributes elegance plus floral and fruity notes, and colombard is said to add a slightly herbal note. Most important of all is Baco blanc, or Baco 22A as it is more technically known, a hybrid. It was developed after the phylloxera epidemic and was well appreciated for its resistence to rot and mildew. In Armagnac it adds such fullness and character to the blend that the resulting eau-de-vie is almost fat. Armagnacs made with a significant amount of Baco are instantly loved for their rich fruitness, even if they do lack a little elegance. Alas, Baco will soon be no more—in Armagnac anyway. The French government has stipulated that wines and brandies that have *Appellation d'Origine Controlée* status (and Armagnac does) must, as of 2010, be made only from *vinifera* varieties; no hybrids allowed.

Armagnac is distilled in a way that accentuates its already bold character. Rather than being double distilled as Cognacs are, most (but not all) Armagnacs are distilled only once. Single distillation results in a more gutsy, aromatic, and less polished eau-de-vie when it is young. The distillation takes place in what is known as a continuous still. The process goes like this: The wine enters a gas-fired still and is heated in a chamber. From there it passes into the main column of the still, where it cascades over a number of hot plates. When it reaches the bottom, it begins to evaporate. The alcoholic vapors then rise back up through the incoming wine, causing the eau-de-vie to take on more flavors and aromas. Finally the vapors exit through the top of the column into a condensing coil, where they become liquid as they cool. There are numerous variations on this basic traditional method, but the goal for Armagnac producers who use it remains the same: to attain an eau-de-vie that retains a lot of its original "stuffing"—strong aromas and rustic flavors that would be pretty much eliminated by double distillation.

Since Cognac's double distillation results in a more polished, elegant brandy that can ultimately be drunk younger, you might wonder why single distillation is appealing to most Armagnac producers. The answer is historic. Armagnac producers tend to be tiny (there are no large firms equivalent to Cognac's Courvoisier, Martell, or Hennessy) and comparatively poor. Many never had the capital

required to own their own stills. Producers traditionally relied on distillers who, with movable stills (*alambics ambulants*) went from farm to farm from November to January. The continuous still was and is both easier to transport and cheaper to run.

The eau-de-vie that emerges from the still in precious drops is not yet an Armagnac, however. What turns the eau-de-vie into brandy is aging in oak barrels, in this case, 400- to 420-liter casks, often from the black oak of the Monlezun forest in Bas Armagnac. While the Armagnac-to-be is left in wood to mature, evaporation concentrates the alcohol. As a result Armagnacs, like Cognacs, are gradually cut with water or *petites eaux*, a weak mixture of water and Armagnac, to bring their final alcohol level down to 40 percent or 80 proof.

If an Armagnac is from the Bas Armagnac, it will say so on the label. Armagnacs from Ténarèze are sometimes labeled as such, but more often the label will simply read Armaganc.

Armagnacs are sold in three ways: by such terms as VSOP and XO, by age designations, and by vintage. Armagnacs that carry designations like VSOP are blends of a variety of eau-de-vie of different ages. As in Cognac, the designations indicate the age of the youngest eau-de-vie in the blend, but the average age of the Armagnac is usually older. Confusingly, although the same terms are used to designate Armagnacs as Cognacs, the minimum ages differ. In Armagnac:

- VS (very superior) or three star (***) indicates that the youngest eau-de-vie used in the blend is not less than three years old.
- VSOP (very superior old pale), VO (very old), and Réserve denote that the youngest eau-de-vie in the blend is at least five years old.

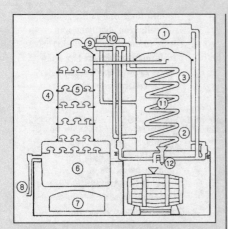

*Armagnac is distilled in what is known as a continuous still. Though it looks like a complex contraption, this still operates on the very simple idea of creating vapors and then capturing them as condensed liquid.*

- XO (extra old), Napoleon, Extra, and Vieille Réserve, describe blends of eau-de-vie in which the youngest is at least six years old.
- Hors d'Age means the youngest eau-de-vie in the blend is at least ten years old.

Some Armagnac makers, however, dispense with letters like XO and names like Napoleon and simply indicate the age of the brandy, as in an Armagnac labeled *vingt ans d'age,* twenty years of age.

Finally, Armagnacs are often labeled according to vintage, something that's rare in Cognac. The eau-de-vie in a vintage Armagnac must come entirely from that vintage. And the bottle must indicate a bottling date so that you know when the Armagnac was taken out of the barrel. (Armagnacs don't really age once they are removed from the barrel and are put in glass bottles where they're protected from oxygen.) A 1947 Armagnac that stayed in the barrel for twenty years, for example, is different from a 1947 Armagnac that stayed

in the barrel for forty years before being bottled. But a 1947 Armagnac taken out of the barrel and put in bottles in 1975 and one distilled in 1970 and bottled in 1998 are equally mature—twenty-eight years—even though they bear different vintage dates.

A great Armagnac has a complex flavor reminiscent of prunes, quince, dried apricots, vanilla, earth, caramel, roasted walnuts, and toffee, and it should be well aged, which is to say fifteen years old or older. Younger Armagnacs have not developed any of the extraordinary nuances of older ones, and they often taste too blatantly fiery. It's easy to tell how old a vintage Armagnac is; ditto for an Armagnac labeled *trente ans d'age* (thirty years old). But it's not so easy to tell when the Armagnac is labeled with letters or names, such as Extra or Napoleon, since those letters and names tell you only the minimum age of the youngest eau-de-vie in the blend, not the avarage age of blend as a whole. The best advice here is to let price be your guide. There's no such thing as a cheap well-aged Armagnac.

Among the top producers of Armagnac are: Sempé, Larressingle, Samalens, de Montal, Cerbois, and Marquis de Caussade. (For a discussion of how to store and serve Armagnac, see page 160 of the Cognac box.)

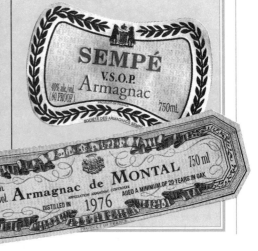

# The Rhône

Not long ago, Rhône wines were viewed as good, sturdy country wines—blue collar compared to aristocratic Bordeaux, plebeian compared to elegant Burgundies. The Rhône's second-class status was, however, not without a touch of irony. For centuries, the wines of Bordeaux and Burgundy were given fairly hefty (usually secret) doses of Rhône wine to flesh them out, color them, and deepen their flavors. The reputation of Rhône wines changed completely in the late 1980s. The wines' generous, dramatic appeal, highlighted by increases in quality, was never more apparent. Price—always a good barometer—told the story best: The top Rhône wines began to sell for more and disappear faster than some of the best Bordeaux.

Among the world's great reds, Rhônes are the most untamed. Flavors dart around in them like shooting stars. There are

## THE QUICK SIP ON THE RHÔNE

- The Rhône Valley in southeast France is divided into two parts: the northern Rhône and the southern Rhône. Wines from each are distinctly different.

- Red wines dominate the region, although whites and rosés are made in the Rhône. The most famous northern Rhône reds are Côte-Rôtie and Hermitage; the most famous southern red is Châteauneuf-du-Pape.

- Syrah is the sole red grape in the north. Southern Rhône reds are usually blends of many grapes, the most important of which are grenache and mourvèdre.

*whooshes* of sweet earthiness and surges of smoky black fruit. The wines' howling spiciness has no parallel. Rhônes are the wine equivalent of a primal scream.

*In the Rhône, the age of the vines is a critical factor in producing rich, concentrated wines. The best are virtually always the product of old, gnarled, dwarflike vines, such as these sixty-year-old vines in Vacqueyras in the southern Rhône.*

The Rhône Valley takes its name from the Rhône River, which begins high in the Swiss Alps and flows into France through the canyons of the Jura Mountains. South of Lyon and just north of Ampuis where the vineyards begin, the river makes a sharp turn and plunges southward for 250 miles until it washes into the Mediterranean, just west of Marseille.

The valley is divided into two parts: the northern Rhône, smaller and a bit more prestigious, and the southern Rhône, larger and more well known. It takes about an hour to drive between the two, and along the way, you see only patches of isolated vineyards. In fact, the northern and southern Rhône are so distinct and different that, were it not for the river that connects them, they would almost certainly be considered separate wine regions.

In both the north and the south there are multiple wine districts, or appellations. The most renowned northern reds are Côte-Rôtie and Hermitage; the most famous southern red is Châteauneuf-du-Pape. The popular, well-priced wines known as Côtes-du-Rhône—staples in French cafés and many cafés in the United States, too—can come from either part of the valley, although most come from large tracts of vineyards in the south.

Though twenty-three varieties of grapes are grown in the Rhône Valley, only a handful of these are truly important. The others—many of them grapes that have grown in the Rhône for centuries—are today used almost nostalgically to add nuance and what winemakers sometimes call the flavors of tradition. As a matter of law, each appellation specifies which of the twenty-three grapes can be used within its borders (see the charts: The Major Appellations, Wines, and Principal Grapes of the Northern Rhône, page 236, and The Major Appellations, Wines, and Principal Grapes of the Southern Rhône, page 247). Winemakers are then free to create their personal "recipe blend" from the permissible varieties.

The grapes of the northern Rhône are the easiest to remember. All red wines come from only one red grape—syrah. All white wines are made from either viognier or a blend of marsanne and roussanne.

The southern Rhône is just the opposite. In such appellations as Châteauneuf-du-Pape, Gigondas, and Vacqueyras, a

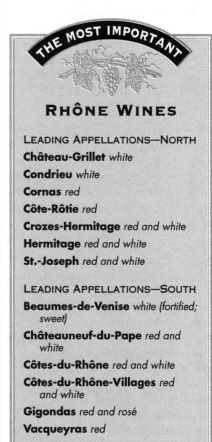

## THE MOST IMPORTANT

## RHÔNE WINES

LEADING APPELLATIONS—NORTH

**Château-Grillet** *white*

**Condrieu** *white*

**Cornas** *red*

**Côte-Rôtie** *red*

**Crozes-Hermitage** *red and white*

**Hermitage** *red and white*

**St.-Joseph** *red and white*

LEADING APPELLATIONS—SOUTH

**Beaumes-de-Venise** *white (fortified; sweet)*

**Châteauneuf-du-Pape** *red and white*

**Côtes-du-Rhône** *red and white*

**Côtes-du-Rhône-Villages** *red and white*

**Gigondas** *red and rosé*

**Vacqueyras** *red*

APPELLATION OF NOTE—SOUTH

**Tavel** *rosé*

# THE GRAPES OF
# THE RHÔNE

## WHITES

**Bourboulenc:** A common component in southern Rhône blends, especially in white Côtes-du-Rhône, where it adds acidity.

**Clairette:** Fresh and beautifully aromatic when grown at low yields, clairette plays a leading role in virtually all of the white Côtes-du-Rhône.

**Grenache Blanc:** The white form of grenache and the workhorse white grape of the southern Rhône. Has high alcohol and low acidity. Can make coarse wines unless grown at low yields and blended skillfully.

**Marsanne:** Important white grape of the northern Rhône. Makes up the majority percentage in Hermitage Blanc, Crozes-Hermitage Blanc, and St.-Joseph Blanc. Also used widely in the south. Usually blended with roussanne and/or grenache blanc and other white grapes.

**Muscat Blanc à Petits Grains:** The deeply aromatic grape that makes the Rhône's famous fortified dessert wine, muscat de Beaumes-de-Venise.

**Picardan** and **Picpoul:** Blending grapes of modest quality that are used in southern Rhône blends.

**Roussanne:** Elegant, aromatic white of the northern Rhône, though also grown by top estates in the south. Often added to marsanne to improve the latter.

**Ugni Blanc:** Prolific white grape grown all over southern and central France. Used as filler in inexpensive southern blends.

**Viognier:** The most voluptuous white of the Rhône. Grown in small quantities in the north where it becomes Condrieu and Château-Grillet. Small amounts of viognier are also grown in the southern Rhône, where it makes its way into some of the top Côtes-du-Rhône.

## REDS

**Calitor** and **Carignan:** Used mostly in Côtes-du-Rhône and rosé wines. In particular, carignan from old vines can add real character to blends.

**Cinsaut:** Blending grape in southern Rhônes. Adds finesse and cherry nuances and can make especially lovely rosés.

**Counoise, Muscardin, Terret Noir,** and **Vaccarèse:** Minor blending grapes used in many southern Rhônes for aromatic and flavor nuances.

**Grenache:** Leading grape of the southern Rhône. Makes up the dominant percentage of virtually all red blends. Has elegant, expressive cherry and raspberry confiture flavors. Although chauvinistically claimed by the French, grenache originated in Spain, where it is known as garnacha.

**Mourvèdre:** Major blending grape in southern Rhônes. Gives structure, acidity, and leather and game flavors.

**Syrah:** Star grape of the northern Rhône, where it is used alone to make bold, spicy, peppery wines. In the south, it is an important part of such blends as Châteauneuf-du-Pape, Gigondas, and Côtes-du-Rhône.

small chorus of red and white grapes come out to sing, including grenache and syrah, as well as mourvèdre. As we'll see, there is a good reason northern Rhône reds are the expression of one grape and southern Rhônes the expression of many.

The Rhône Valley is one of the oldest wine regions in France. When the Romans arrived some two thousand years ago, the inhabitants of what was then Gaul were drinking wines that the Roman writer Pliny described as excellent. Keep in mind, however, that Rhône wines are not cut from a single cloth. The large number of small growers here, plus the huge differences in the *terroirs*, plus the wide range of grape varieties, all add up to a mountain of highly individual, exciting wines.

## THE NORTHERN RHÔNE

The northern Rhône is where many of the Rhône Valley's rarest and most expensive, reds and whites are made. The region begins with Côte-Rôtie, the northernmost appellation, and extends about 50 miles south, as far as Cornas and the small, inconsequential St.-Péray. In between are the five appellations: Condrieu, Château-Grillet, St.-Joseph, Hermitage, and Crozes-Hermitage.

The best vineyards cling to narrow, rocky terraces on the steep slopes that loom over the river. The ancient, shallow granite and slate soil there is poor. Erosion is such a threat that, were it not for the terraces and the hand-built stone walls that wearifully hold them in place, the vines would slide down the hillsides. Even so, some of this weathered, crumbly soil usually does wash down the slopes in the winter rain, and when it does, Rhône winemakers do what they've always done: haul the precious stuff back up in small buckets.

The climate in the northern Rhône is continental, entirely unlike the climate in the south, which is Mediterranean. In the north, the winters are hard, cold, and wet; the summers hot. Late spring and early fall fog make the southern orientation of the vineyards critical. Without this good southern exposure the grapes would not receive enough sunlight and heat to ripen properly. It helps that the well-drained granite soil retains heat, for the howling, icy northern wind known as *le mistral* can quickly cool the vines.

The only red grape permitted in the northern Rhône is syrah. Divine enological wisdom must have been operating when that decision was made, for syrah planted there makes what are unquestionably some of the world's most exotic, intense wines. Wild and dramatic, they almost pant with gamy, meaty, animal flavors.

Plus the flavor that tips you off that you're in the northern Rhône—white pepper, which is evident in virtually every wine here. But pepper is just the beginning. From there, the wines explode with aromas of incense, forest, and leather, while the flavors of black plums, blackberries, and blueberries pile on. The fervor of these flavors is due in part to the age of the vines. Many are at least forty years old and some broach a hundred. These oldsters don't produce many bunches of grapes, but the grapes they do produce are packed with power and concentration.

## THE MAJOR APPELLATIONS, WINES, AND PRINCIPAL GRAPES OF THE NORTHERN RHÔNE

The appellations are listed following the Rhône River north to south. All of the red wines of the northern Rhône are made from one red grape exclusively—syrah. While the region is primarily devoted to red wine, the two small appellations Condrieu and Château-Grillet are both devoted entirely to white wines made from viognier. (No rosés are made in the northern Rhône.) The white grapes listed first tend to make up the greater percentage of the blend.

| Appellation | Wine(s) Made | Principal Red Grape | Principal White Grape(s) |
|---|---|---|---|
| Côte-Rôtie | red | syrah | none |
| Condrieu | white | none | viognier |
| Château-Grillet | white | none | viognier |
| St.-Joseph | red and white | syrah | marsanne roussanne |
| Hermitage | red and white | syrah | marsanne roussanne |
| Crozes-Hermitage | red and white | syrah | marsanne roussanne |
| Cornas | red | syrah | none |

There are several theories—a truer word might be fables—concerning how syrah got to the northern Rhône. One suggests that syrah came from and is named after the Persian city, Shiraz. Indeed, the grape syrah is called shiraz in both South Africa and Australia. Just why syrah would be called shiraz in Africa and Australia but not in France—which, after all, gave those two continents the grape—is never made clear. Another fable concerns the Roman emperor Probus who allegedly brought syrah to France from the city of Syracuse, in Sicily. The most logical and realistic theory is that syrah may be indigenous to the northern Rhône.

As for white wine, only a small amount is made here. Condrieu and Château-Grillet are the most renowned and expensive northern whites. Both are made exclusively from the decadently lush white grape, viognier. All other northern Rhône whites—Hermitage Blanc, Crozes-Hermitage Blanc, St.-Joseph Blanc, and so on—are made from two other white grapes: marsanne, the heartbeat of the blend, and roussanne, added for its finesse and exotic aromas and flavors of quince, peaches, and lime blossoms.

*Although the southern Rhône is well known for rosé wines, no rosés are made in the north.*

Northern Rhône wines are made by small, family-owned estates, by larger producers, by *négociants* who buy wine, blend it, and then bottle it under their own brand label, and by cooperatives (which make the least interesting wines). The small estates are very small. Many Côte-

Rôtie producers own fewer than 10 acres of vineyards. The larger family-owned firms, such as M. Chapoutier, E. Guigal, and Paul Jaboulet Aîné, own more land and, for certain appellations, buy wine from small growers as well.

It will come as no surprise that winemaking styles in the northern Rhône continue to move (slowly) in a modern direction. Yet a steadfast maintenance of certain traditional methods is also evident. Key among these is the old custom of including the stems along with the grapes during fermentation. You might wonder why this seemingly simple practice is worthy of attention. The fact is stems profoundly affect a wine's flavor. Including them gives northern Rhône wines their distinctive spicy, briary aroma, somewhat like that of cedar or sandalwood. In addition, since stems as well as grape skins contain tannin, not removing the stems increases the tannin and gives the wines more edge, more grip.

Because the production of most northern Rhônes is limited and because many vineyards are extremely difficult to work, the wines—especially the top Côte-Rôtie and Hermitage—are expensive.

## Côte-Rôtie

Some of the most thrilling wines of the Rhône carry the appellation Côte-Rôtie (literally, roasted hillside). They are dramatic wines with incisive, earthy, and gamy flavors. Pepper seems to pace back and forth in the glass like a caged animal. All are 100 percent syrah. No white wine is made in this appellation.

There are slightly less than 500 acres of Côte-Rôtie vineyards, the best of which are on precipitous granite slopes with grades of up to 60 degrees, facing due south. On these hillsides the grapes do not exactly roast, but they do sunbathe.

There are other Côte-Rôtie vineyards on the plateaus above the slopes (the

*The steep terraced hillsides of the Côte-Rôtie make harvesting exhausting work. Men pick the grapes, put them in wooden containers, and carry the containers down the hills on their shoulders. In the steepest vineyards, human chains are formed to pass the containers from man to man down the hill.*

ironic "non-*côtes*" Côtes). These newer vineyards were permitted to be established when the original appellation was expanded. But when syrah is removed from its tenuous, terrace-clinging perch, it does not make as fine a Côte-Rôtie.

Wherever they are found, steep vineyards that happen to fall in direct sun are coveted, for the grapes are drenched in light (for ripeness) but cooled by the altitude and breezes (preserving acidity and finesse). Syrah, in particular, needs this yin and yang of warmth and coolness. When it is grown in the hotter, southern Rhône, syrah can be fatter, even richer on the palate, but it loses the savage precision and striking ferocity of a great Côte-Rôtie.

Within the Côte-Rôtie are two famous slopes: the Côte Brune and the Côte Blonde. According to a predictable legend, these were named after the daughters— one brunette, one blond—of an aristocratic feudal lord. The wines are just what the stereotypes suggest. Côte Brunes are generally more tannic and powerful; Côte Blondes, more elegant and racy. If a Côte-Rôtie comes from one of these slopes or is a blend of the two, the label will say so.

Producers in Côte-Rôtie, and in the Rhône in general, commonly blend grapes from different vineyard sites to achieve complexity. Occasionally, if the vineyard is extraordinary, grapes from it may be vinified separately and made into a wine labeled with the name of the vineyard. Such wines are frequently expensive and ravishing. Among the top vineyards are La Mouline, La Landonne, La Chatillone, La Garde, La Chevalière, and La Turque.

Côte-Rôtie is one of only two top French red wines that, by law, may be made with a small quantity of white grapes blended in (the other being Hermitage). The reason for this is largely practical since in Côte-Rôtie viognier vines are scattered in among the syrah vines in many vineyards. Viognier's creamy texture was historically thought to soften the sometimes blunt edges of syrah. Today viognier is included more for its exotic aroma, making Côte-Rôtie more fascinating. Though up to 20 percent viognier can, by law, be included in red Côte-Rôtie, most producers include less than 5 percent.

The most famous producer of Côte-Rôtie is the family-owned firm of E. Guigal. In the 1980s Guigal pushed the envelope on winemaking in the Rhône by employing techniques that were either entirely new or so old they had not been

*The old terraced vineyards of E. Guigal produce wines of dramatic depth and personality.*

practiced for nearly a century. The most well known of these techniques is using small, new oak barrels for aging. Many thought this the height of modernity. In fact, it was a step into the past. According to several vintners who have researched the region's history, northern Rhône wines such as Côte-Rôtie and Hermitage were being aged in small, new oak barrels before phylloxera arrived in the Rhône in the mid-nineteenth century.

The vanilla-y, toasty flavors of new oak took to Guigal's wines like cream to coffee. They were so richly flavored and successful that the wines received rave reviews from critics, and ultimately other producers followed Guigal's example. Yet if there is one truth about winemaking, it is that almost nothing is universally good. Though new-oak aging worked well for Guigal's wines, for other Côte-Rôties the flavors of new oak masked the nuances of the wines. Today aging in small, new oak is not standard but, instead, varies with the producer.

There are two other fairly large, well-known names in Côte-Rôtie, M. Chapoutier and Paul Jaboulet Aîné. In the 1990s Chapoutier wines soared in quality as the family firm was taken over by the ambitious son, Michel Chapoutier, who made major changes in both winemaking and viticulture. And in addition to these three firms, some of the most exciting Côte-Rôties are made by such tiny producers as René Rostaing, Robert Jasmin, Henri Gallet, Jamet, Michel Ogier, and Bernard Burgaud.

## Condrieu and Château-Grillet

Condrieu and Château-Grillet are the Rhône's most famous white wines. These two appellations—one tiny, one microscopic—are located just south of Côte-Rôtie. Château-Grillet, of course,

*The tiny appellation Condrieu is the source of France's most renowned viogniers.*

sounds as though it is one producer, not an appellation. It is both. Within the appellation Château-Grillet there is but one producer: Château-Grillet. At 8.6 acres it is the smallest appellation in France and sits like an enclave within Condrieu.

Both Condrieu and Château-Grillet are made from viognier, possibly the most drippingly sensual white grape in the world. This is chardonnay's ravishing, exotic sister. In great years and when it's perfectly made, viognier explodes with lush flavors and heady aromas. Honeysuckle, ripe peaches, white melons, litchis, fresh orange peel, and sometimes gardenias mesmerize one's senses. The wine's texture is as soothing as fresh whipped cream. But viogniers like this are hardly a dime a dozen. The grape is notoriously fickle, sensitive to its site, and difficult to grow. Its naturally low acidity means that if the producer isn't careful, the wine can wind up tasting bleak. The grape's graceful flavors are also easily overwhelmed by aging the wine too long in wood. All in all, making great viognier is no piece of cake.

There is very little viognier in France. In addition to the 250 or so acres in Condrieu and the 8.6 acres in Château-Grillet, there are smatterings in other parts of the Rhône, as well as a small but growing amount in the Languedoc-Roussillon. Outside of France, California is the leading grower of viognier. As of the late 1990s, there were more than 1,000 acres or about four times as much viognier in California as in the Rhône.

*The village of Condrieu sits at a curve in the Rhône River. The name comes from the French* coin de ruisseau, *corner of the brook.*

Condrieu and Château-Grillet are both very expensive wines. This is the result not only of their rarity but also of the low yields from viognier planted in ancient, impoverished soils.

The most well-known, top producer of Condrieu is Georges Vernay. Look also for excellent Condrieu from E. Guigal, René Rostaing, Dumazet, Yves Cuilleron, Philippe Faury, and Robert Niero. As for Château-Grillet, the quality of the wines from this prestigious estate has been slipping for several years.

## St.-Joseph

When it was first established in 1956, St.-Joseph was a small appellation directly across the river from Hermitage. The vineyards covered low hills. The wines had a very good reputation. Today, while some St.-Josephs are dynamite, many others lack stuffing, seeming coarse and thin. One reason for this is the appellation's expansion. St.-Joseph has grown into a long corridor stretching from Con-

### THE RHÔNE RANGERS

By the end of the 1970s in California, chardonnay and cabernet sauvignon dominated the wine landscape. Even more portentously, these grapes molded the very way California winemakers thought about great wine.

Then in the mid-1980s, about a dozen maverick winemakers cracked the mold. These supercreative winemakers—independently and nearly simultaneously—had heard a muse. She whispered a single suggestion: "Think Rhône."

Rhône grapes were not new in California. Mourvèdre (known to Californians as mataro), syrah, and grenache had all been planted in the nineteenth century. However, only small patches of these grapes remained throughout the state, mostly in obscure or forgotten vineyards. The Rhône Rangers, as they were dubbed, searched them out and, in addition, began planting other Rhône varieties, such as viognier, marsanne, and roussanne. By the late 1990s, more than eighty wineries in California produced Rhône-style wines, and Rhône varieties accounted for more than 20,000 acres of the state's 440,000 plus acres of grapes.

drieu to the bottom tip of the northern Rhône. Vineyards are now planted on plateaus and where the exposure to the sun is less ideal.

The reds are made from syrah, of course, and St.-Joseph Blanc (white St. Joseph) from marsanne, with touches of roussanne. Like the reds, the white wines range in quality from quite good to ho-hum. One of the best, Roger Blachon's, has, in great years, the ethereal flavor and texture of the finest honey.

Among the top producers of white and red St.-Joseph are M. Chapoutier, Jean-Louis Chave, Yves Cuilleron, Jean-Louis Grippat, Alain Graillot, and André Perret.

## Hermitage

In the eighteenth and nineteenth centuries, Hermitage was France's costliest red wine. Not only was it more expensive than the best Bordeaux, but the best Bordeaux were usually "hermitaged," meaning that Hermitage was secretly blended in to give the Bordeaux extra depth, color, and richness. Even First Growths, such as Château Lafite and Château Margaux, were occasionally hermitaged, though the châteaux's owners would have denied it.

The appellation Hermitage is actually a single 1,000-foot-high granite hill, with vineyards clinging to its mostly southern-facing slope. There is room for only about 300 acres of vines, making the whole of Hermitage smaller than some wine properties in California.

Predictably, there are many legends concerning hermits who supposedly gave Hermitage its name. The one most often told concerns a medieval crusader, Gaspard de Sterimberg, who, after being wounded in war, was granted, by Queen Blanche de Castille, the right to establish a sanctuary on top of the hill. A small, ancient stone chapel still marks the spot. It is for this chapel that La Chapelle, the top wine of Paul Jaboulet Aîné, is named.

Red Hermitage is probably the most revered wine of the northern Rhône, though Côte-Rôtie is certainly right on Hermitage's heels. In great years, Hermitage is a leathery, meaty red, packed with blackberry and black cherry fruits and smoky, damp earth flavors. The famous English scholar and wine writer George Saintsbury once described Hermitage as "the manliest wine" he'd ever drunk. And

241

*On the hill of Hermitage, surrounded by old syrah vines, stands a medieval stone chapel, overlooking the Rhône River. This is the chapel for which Paul Jaboulet Aîné's Hermitage La Chapelle is named.*

Saintsbury was right. The wine has that kind of salty, almost sweaty allure of a man's body.

Like Côte-Rôtie, the only red grape in Hermitage is syrah. It is generally vinified in a traditional manner and aged for up to three years in large casks. Some producers age Hermitage wholly or partly in small, new-oak barrels. Up to 15 percent white grapes (marsanne and/or roussanne) are allowed in red Hermitage, but few producers add them.

The impoverished soil that covers the hill of Hermitage varies depending on the site, ranging from sandy gravel to flint, limestone, and chalk. To achieve the maximum complexity and nuance of flavors, most producers blend grapes from several vineyard blocks at different locations on the slope.

Hermitage Blanc (white Hermitage) can be made from two grapes: marsanne and roussanne. Marsanne, the more common and plentiful one, can have all the subtlety of a bull in a china shop. It tends to be a big, bold-tasting grape, sometimes with an oily texture and an unusual aroma that Rhône winemakers describe as being like cosmetic products. The wine writer Jancis Robinson writes in *Vines, Grapes and Wines* that marsanne has "a very definite smell, slightly but not unpleasantly reminiscent of glue." Yet marsanne, it seems, is a chameleon. Just when one is ready to write the grape off, along comes a beautiful example that is rich, earthy, and vanilla-y, without a whiff of Elmer's or Revlon. For the best wines, marsanne is most often blended with a bit of roussanne, a rarer grape with the sensual aromas and flavors of peaches, quince, almonds, honeysuckle, and lime. Roussanne's job is to add complexity to marsanne, and it does.

White Hermitage is an acquired taste. The wine isn't fruity exactly, but instead is oily, resiny, and earthy. It's fairly common to think the first few sips a bit odd, only to find you can't put the glass down (at least some of us can't). In fact, these wines can be so expressive of their home, you feel as though you're swallowing the *terroir* itself. Their whopping levels of alcohol immediately mark them as the powerhouses they are. The two best in this big gun style are Jean-Louis Chave's Hermitage Blanc and M. Chapoutier's Chante Alouette Hermitage Blanc. Both are massive wines with swaths of flavor so bold they seem like brushstrokes on an impressionist painting.

The top Hermitage producers, some of whom make both red and white wine, include Albert Belle, E. Guigal, Jean-Louis Chave, Marc Sorrel, and M. Chapoutier. Paul Jaboulet Aîné keeps you guessing, sometimes making wines that live up to their reputation and price but, sadly, at other times, not.

## Crozes-Hermitage

Following Hermitage tradition, Crozes-Hermitage makes red wines from syrah and white wines from marsanne and a bit of roussanne. The Crozes-Hermitage vineyards, however, are mostly on the flatlands that spread out south and east of the hill of Hermitage. The area they cover is ten times larger than Hermitage.

Because Crozes-Hermitage comes from less distinguished, higher-yielding vineyards, it is usually lighter and less exciting than either Côte-Rôtie or Hermitage. There are notable exceptions. The red Crozes-Hermitage of Alain Graillot, for example, comes from syrah planted in

*The precipitous rocky vineyards of Cornas (left) produce black-colored wines with gripping power. The steep terraces (right) have been built by hand from local stones.*

very poor soil and that is harvested at very low yields. A vibrant, complex, peppery wine, packed with delicious black currant flavors, it's easily the equal of many Hermitages—at less than half the price.

White Crozes-Hermitages are broad, straightforward, tasty wines, generally with pronounced fruity aromas and lanolin or oily textures. There aren't many of them, however.

The Crozes-Hermitage producers to know are Alain Graillot, Albert Belle, M. Chapoutier, and Domaine Combier.

## Cornas

The tiny region of Cornas sits at the bottom of the northern Rhône. Only red wines are made here, all of them exclusively from syrah. At their best, Cornas are dense, edgy, masculine wines with a phalanx of white pepper that hits you in the teeth. A split second later, a briary character explodes on your palate, and, if the Cornas is especially untamed, that may be followed by what can only be described as the sense that your tongue is

being lashed by strips of black leather. Cornas is not everyone's cup of tea, but those of us who love it, love it madly.

*The word* cornas
*is thought to be derived from
the old Celtic word
for burnt or scorched earth.*

Aging is a critical factor. In the Rhône Valley, Cornas is generally drunk after it has been aged for seven to ten years. The wine changes substantially, taking on a fine leatheriness and earthiness.

As in Côte-Rôtie and Hermitage, Cornas' best vineyards are on dangerously steep hillsides precariously held in place by ancient terraces with stone walls. The vineyards, interspersed by patches of oak and juniper forest, face due south. The hills above block cool winds from the north. Both the light and the heat of the sun are intense. It's a perfect equation for powerful wine. Top Cornas producers include Auguste Clape, Jean-Luc Colombo, and Noël Verset.

# The Northern Rhône Wines to Know

## Whites

### DOMAINE GEORGES VERNAY
Condrieu
L'Enfer
100% viognier

Vernay is considered the master of viognier in Condrieu, and this wine, from the vineyard called L'Enfer (French for *hell*), is one of the most elegant in the region. It has such incredible clarity, it reminds me of the lucidity of light very early in the morning. The lime, pear, almond, and mineral flavors are so rich yet refined they seem suspended in the wine.

### M. CHAPOUTIER
St.-Joseph Blanc
Les Granits
100% marsanne

Michel Chapoutier makes wines in virtually every major Rhône appellation, and so many of them are stunning that it's hard to choose among them. Without a doubt, however, Chapoutier's Les Granits St.-Joseph Blanc, made from old vines planted in a small hillside vineyard, comes as close to riveting as St.-Joseph gets. Minerally, honeyed, and massive, it is a fascinating and irresistible wine. Chapoutier's regular St.-Joseph Blanc, called Les Deschants, is also delicious.

### YVES CUILLERON
Condrieu
Les Chaillets
100% viognier

Yves Cuilleron is one of the Rhône's shining lights. His exquisite Condrieu fills your mouth as opulently as a

spoonful of whipped cream. The incredible honeysuckle and soft vanilla flavors are utterly refined yet rich. More than many other producers, Cuilleron has enormous talent when it comes to weaving lushness together with elegance.

## Reds

### ALAIN GRAILLOT
Crozes-Hermitage
La Guiraude
100% syrah

Graillot makes one of the few great Crozes-Hermitages, a wine so good many believe it the equal of Hermitage—at less than half

the cost. This is a dark, brooding, edgy, Clint Eastwood of a wine, with flavors that wrestle each other in the glass. Spices, pepper, earth, blackberries, and violets all collide in a delicious explosion.

La Guiraude, a special selection of the best lots of wine, is made only in very good years. Not to worry. Graillot's regular Crozes-Hermitage is also pretty wonderful.

## DOMAINE JEAN-LOUIS CHAVE

Hermitage

100% syrah

Hermitage has been called the manliest of wines, and this one has the sort of sensual darkness that fills the bill precisely. At first the huge, mesmerizing aromas and flavors suggest smoking meat, leather, sweat, and damp earth. But Chave's wines are so complex, they can pour forth new flavors by the minute. The Chave family has been making Hermitage since the fifteenth century, and over those centuries very little about the winemaking has changed.

## E. GUIGAL

Côte-Rôtie

La Mouline

almost entirely syrah with a trace of viognier

Guigal is one of the most outstanding producers in the Rhône, year in and year out making sensuous wines of profound depth and concentration. When I was just beginning my wine career, it was a Guigal Côte-Rôtie, known as Brune et Blonde (a blend of grapes from two vineyards evocatively named the brunette and the blond), that convinced me that nothing on earth was quite as mesmerizing, as intellectually riveting as a great wine. I still love Brune et Blonde, but if one of Guigal's stars shines just a little bit brighter than all the others, it is its Côte-Rôtie known as La Mouline, one of three esteemed single-vineyard wines in the Guigal portfolio (the other two are La Turque and La Landonne). Sweetly rich and ripe, a great La Mouline is fat with velvety-textured boysenberry/cassis fruit interwoven with violets and exotic spices, and buttressed against a dramatic, almost primal gaminess. The heady aroma alone is enough to stop you in your tracks. But don't stop . . . not that you could.

## JEAN-LUC COLOMBO

Cornas

Les Ruchets

100% syrah

Here it is—quintessential Cornas: brooding, black, massive, earthy, leathery, and yet somehow voluptuous at the same time. Jean-Luc Colombo, restless, driven, and impatient, is one of the young turks turning out some of the most sensational Cornas today. In Colombo's hands, Les Ruchets (the beehives) sacrifices none of its power, but

there's an elegance, a sweet ripeness here, too, that's seductive. Colombo's mother was a chef, and he makes all of his wines, he says, with food in mind. So what did he have in mind with this? Wild hare.

## MICHEL OGIER

Côte-Rôtie

100% syrah

Not everyone immediately loves Michel Ogier's wines, so packed are they with gamy aromas and flavors. Citrus and earth also hurl themselves out of the glass with real severity. Full of grip and personality, Ogier's wines are not for gentle souls.

## R. ROSTAING

Côte-Rôtie

100% syrah

The flavors in Rostaing's Côte-Rôties usually begin quietly, like a whisper, then crash in wave after wave of delicious intensity. Taste buds need seat belts for this wine. All of the quintessen-

tial northern Rhône flavors and aromas are here: white pepper and exotic spices; incense, roasted meat; gaminess; plowed earth, blueberries, and blackberries. Rostaing, a small producer, is known for wines full of energy and personality.

# THE SOUTHERN RHÔNE

For Americans traveling in France for the first time in the 1960s and 1970s, Châteauneuf-du-Pape was a wine so delicious to drink, so charmingly named, and so evocative of the bucolic countryside that virtually overnight it became the Rhône's best-known wine. Châteauneuf, however, is just one of several wine regions in the southern Rhône. The other two major ones are Gigondas and Vacqueyras, followed by southern France's self-styled capital of rosé, Tavel. In addition, most of the Côtes-du-Rhône and Côtes-du-Rhône-Villages wines come from southern vineyards.

The southern Rhône does not begin where the north leaves off but about an hour's drive farther south. In between only a few patches of vineyards can be found. The gulf of separation is significant. The southern and northern Rhône have little in common, except the river that gives them their names. The differences in climate are major. The southern Rhône is part of the sunny, herb-scented, lavender-strewn, olive-growing Mediterranean. Hot days are pierced by *le mistral*, the savage, cold wind that blows down from the Alps and through the Rhône River valley, gathering speed and ferocity as it goes. Though you can barely stand up when the mistral is blowing hard, it nonetheless is a grape grower's friend. During the growing season it cools down the vines, helping the grapes retain acidity. Even more important, near harvesttime it acts like a giant blow-dryer, making sure the grapes are free of humidity and mold. Many winemakers also believe that the mistral causes substantial evaporation, which then concentrates the sugar and acid inside the grapes. The mistral can be so violent, however, that it can rip apart the vines. As a result, the best vineyards are found in partly sheltered pockets of land, and the vines are pruned low to the ground. The older gnarled ones look like twisted black dwarfs in the glaring sun.

There are significant differences between northern and southern Rhône in the proximity and orientation of the vineyards to the river. In the north vineyards are poised above and so close to the river they almost seem as though they could fall into it. In the south they spread out from the river for 20 to 30 miles over flatter land and gentler hillocks.

Soil in the south is also fundamentally different from that in the north. Most is either clay, sandy limestone, gravel, or just plain stones, compared to the north's slate and granite. In many places, what we think of as dirt is almost nonexistent, and the vines are planted in what looks like a vast carpet of riverbed rocks, some the size of a cantaloupe.

Grenache, not syrah, is the leading red grape of the south. But what is even more significant is that, unlike northern Rhône wines, which are based on a single grape variety, southern Rhône wines are always, like rainbows, combinations of many different varieties. There is a reason for blending. In the southern Rhône's hot, dry climate, such classic grapes as syrah can lose their focus and intensity. Other, less noble grapes may adapt well to the heat, but they rarely possess enough character on their own to make a satisfactory wine. Blending is a way of creating a whole wine that is more than the sum of its parts.

The twelve grapes permitted in red wines are a casting call of familiar and obscure varieties: grenache, mourvèdre,

## THE MAJOR APPELLATIONS, WINES, AND PRINCIPAL GRAPES OF THE SOUTHERN RHÔNE

Twenty-three grape varieties are permitted in the southern Rhône, though not all of them are legal in all appellations. The twenty-three fall into two groups: principal varieties and secondary varieties. The principal varieties are listed below. Today many of the secondary varieties are used only in tiny amounts, if they are used at all. These secondary varieties include for red wines: calitor, carignan, counoise, gamay, muscardin, pinot noir, terret noir, and vaccarèse; and for white wines: marsanne, roussanne, picardan, picpoul, viognier, ugni blanc, macabeo, and muscat blanc à petits grains. Rosé wines can be made from a combination of any of the grapes, red and white. As always with wine, however, there are some notable exceptions. Roussanne, for example, is the grape on which Château Beaucastel's famous white Châteauneuf-du-Pape Vieilles Vignes is based. There are also interesting peculiarities. Muscat is grown only in Beaumes-de-Venise. And only Châteauneuf-du-Pape allows slightly more than half of all the twenty-three varieties (see the Châteauneuf "Thirteen," page 249).

| Appellation | Wine(s) Made | Principal Red Grape(s) | Principal White Grape(s) |
|---|---|---|---|
| Châteauneuf-du-Pape | red and white | grenache syrah mourvèdre cinsaut | grenache blanc clairette bourboulenc |
| Gigondas | red and rosé | grenache syrah mourvèdre cinsaut | none |
| Vacqueyras | red, white, and rosé | grenache syrah mourvèdre cinsaut | grenache blanc clairette bourboulenc |
| Tavel | rosé | grenache cinsaut syrah mourvèdre | clairette bourboulenc |
| Côtes-du-Rhône and Côtes-du-Rhône-Villages | red, white, and rosé | grenache syrah mourvèdre cinsaut carignan | grenache blanc clairette bourboulenc roussanne viognier |
| Beaumes-de-Venise | white (fortified; sweet) | none | muscat |

247

cinsaut, syrah, counoise, muscardin, terret noir, vaccarèse, carignan, calitor, gamay, and pinot noir. Each appellation specifies which of these grapes can be used. Gamay and pinot noir, for example, are used hardly at all and only in Côtes-du-Rhône.

Another eleven grapes are grown for white wine, including grenache blanc (the white form of grenache), clairette, bourboulenc, picardan, picpoul, and ugni blanc, along with the northern Rhône whites marsanne, roussanne, and a small amount of viognier, plus muscat, which is used primarily in the fortified dessert wine Beaumes-de-Venise, and macabeo, used only in the small uneventful appellation of Lirac. Again, not all grapes are permitted in all appellations.

While there are only five cooperatives in the northern Rhône, there are almost sixty in the south. These make 70 percent of southern Rhône wine. The cooperatives have amazing clout. They make dozens—sometimes hundreds—of different blends that they bottle under scores of brand names, some of which, cleverly, seem like the names of estates. In addition, the cooperatives sell to dozens of *négociants* who do the same thing on a smaller scale.

Two additional types of wine are made in the south that, with minor exceptions, cannot be found in the north: rosés and sweet wines. Tavel, the leading rosé of the southern Rhône, is also (thanks to tourism in southern France) one of the most well-known rosés in the world. The south's sweet wine is equally famous: muscat de Beaumes-de-Venise.

Of all the southern Rhône's important wine appellations, the one that can rival the north's Côte-Rôtie or Hermitage is Châteauneuf-du-Pape, so it leads off our exploration of the southern Rhône.

• • •

"The inseparable connection in southern France between wine, food, and the earth reminds me that wine is a gift from God. People have been making it forever. In a visceral sense, drinking Châteauneuf-du-Pape and eating local sausages becomes a way of transcending time, of experiencing that which, though it may seem temporal, is, in fact, timeless."

—*Steve Edmunds,*
*co-owner, Edmunds St. John*
*Winery, which specializes*
*in Rhône wines made*
*in California*

## Châteauneuf-du-Pape

The most southern of the major southern Rhône wine appellations, Châteauneuf-du-Pape is just a fifteen-minute drive from the historic city of Avignon. The region, which encompasses the plateaus and slopes around the town of Châteauneuf-du-Pape plus four adjacent villages, is large by Rhône standards—slightly more than 8,000 acres (Hermitage has only about 300 acres). More wine is made in this one place than in all of the northern Rhône. To put Châteauneuf in perspective, however, the Napa Valley is more than four times larger, and Bordeaux is thirty-four times larger.

## THE CHÂTEAUNEUF "THIRTEEN"

There are actually fourteen grape varieties permitted to be used in Châteauneuf-du-Pape if the white form of grenache is counted independently from the red. The most important grapes are listed first.

| Red | White |
|-----|-------|
| Grenache | Grenache Blanc |
| Syrah | Clairette |
| Mourvèdre | Bourboulenc |
| Cinsaut | Roussanne |
| Muscardin | Picpoul |
| Counoise | Picardan |
| Vaccarèse | |
| Terret Noir | |

Before World War I much of the Châteauneuf-du-Pape harvest was sold in bulk to Burgundy, to be used as *vin de médecine*—a quick fix of alcohol to boost Burgundy's strength. Decades later the practice was still commonplace. Only since the 1970s has the number of quality-minded southern Rhône producers increased significantly, and today more than any other wines, the top reds of Châteauneuf-du-Pape define the southern Rhône. They are often not the big, blowsy, easygoing wines you might expect from a warm Mediterranean region. Just the opposite. These are penetrating, dense, sassy wines that can come at you with a dagger of earthy, gamy flavors. They have a wildness to them, a fascinating edge of tar, leather, and rough stone. They beg for a hot night, chewy bread, and a dish loaded with garlic, black olives, and wild herbs. The wines of Châteauneuf-du-Pape, in other words, are memorable. So is the

name. Châteauneuf-du-Pape, new castle of the pope, refers to the time in the fourteenth century when the pope resided not in Rome but in the walled city of Avignon, just south of these vineyards. The pope who instigated this startling change in residence was the Frenchman Clement V (in Bordeaux, Château Pape-Clément is named after him). Later, his successor, John XXII, built a new papal summer home out among the vineyards. Châteauneuf-du-Pape was then, and continued to be for the next six centuries, called Châteauneuf-Calcernier, after a nearby village and its limestone quarry. It wasn't until the twentieth century, after vast improvements were made in the vineyards and winemaking, that the new name Châteauneuf-du-Pape took hold.

## CHÂTEAUNEUF-DU-EXTRATERRESTRIAL

The vintners of Châteauneuf-du-Pape have always been fastidious when it comes to creating laws that will protect their vineyards. In a legendary 1954 municipal decree they mandated the following:

Article 1. The flying overhead, landing, and taking off of aeronautical machines called "flying saucers" or "flying cigars," of whatever nationality they may be, is strictly forbidden on the territory of the commune of Châteauneuf-du-Pape.

Article 2. Any aeronautical machine—"flying saucer" or "flying cigar"—that lands on the territory of the commune will be immediately taken off to the jail.

(No joke.)

*Some of the Best Producers of*
*Châteauneuf-du-Pape*

**CHÂTEAU BEAUCASTEL**

**CHÂTEAU DE LA GARDINE**

**CHÂTEAU LA NERTHE**

**CHÂTEAU RAYAS**

**CLOS DES PAPES**

**CLOS DU MONT OLIVET**

**DOMAINE DE BEAURENARD**

**DOMAINE DE CHANTE-PERDRIX**

**DOMAINE DE LA CHARBONNIÈRE**

**DOMAINE DE LA JANASSE**

**DOMAINE DU PÉGAU**

**DOMAINE DU VIEUX TÉLÉGRAPHE**

**FONT DE MICHELLE**

**LE BOSQUET DES PAPES**

**LE VIEUX DONJON**

**LES CAILLOUX**

**M. CHAPOUTIER**

250

## THE PROTOTYPE

━━◌◌◌━━

Regulations enacted in the early 1920s to improve Châteauneuf-du-Pape later became the basis for France's monumental *Appellation d'Origine Contrôlée* laws. The rules in Châteauneuf were proposed by a leading vintner and lawyer, Baron Pierre le Roy of Château Fortia, who had grown concerned about the decline in quality of Châteauneuf-du-Pape, especially after the phylloxera scourge and the First World War. His rules for Châteauneuf were the first in France to set strict limits on where the grapes could be grown and to specify the minimum alcohol level of the wine (12.5 percent). The rules also mandated that a percentage of all picked grapes had to be culled out and discarded. This clever way of forcing vintners to remove unripe and rotten bunches was unheard of at the time.

Of all the things that set Châteauneuf apart, the most startling are its smooth, rolled stones. They are everywhere. Many vineyards are simply vast rock beds with no visible soil whatsoever. The stones and rocks (which range from fist size to the size of a small pumpkin) are the remnants of ancient Alpine glaciers. The withdrawal of these glaciers, along with temperature rises, ripped quartzite off the flanks of the Alps. Over many millennia these chunks of quartzite were rolled, broken, and rounded by the tumultuous waters of the then larger Rhône River. As the river receded the stones were left scattered over the plateaus and terraces. Although there *is* soil underneath the stones, varying from clay to sandy limestone to gravel, the land is extremely difficult to work, and tending the vineyards is a painstakingly slow process.

What southern Rhône vineyards do not lack is heat. Yet, in a coals-to-Newcastle manner, the stones retain this heat and therefore hasten ripening. At the same time, however, the stones protect the ground from becoming parched and dry and help hold moisture in the soil, a boon for the vines, especially as summer proceeds.

More than 90 percent of Châteauneuf-du-Pape is red, although there are white and rosé wines. The grapes that can be used are the so-called Châteauneuf Thirteen (actually fourteen)—eight reds and six whites. Almost no producer other than Château Beaucastel grows and makes wine from the whole gamut. The majority of Châteauneufs are based on grenache grown until it is sweetly ripe and tasting like homemade jam. Blended into the grenache are syrah, to deepen the color and add spice, as well as mourvèdre, which adds structure and elegance. Other red grapes may play a role, too, but none are as important as these three.

A small amount of white wine is produced (about 7 percent of total production). Much of it is shapeless, fairly flavorless stuff, but there are delicious exceptions. Among the top Châteauneuf-du-Pape whites are two from Château Beaucastel, their leading wine, known as Cuvée Classique, and the rarer Vieilles Vignes (remarkably made solely from roussanne), as well as those from Château Rayas, Clos des Papes, Château La Nerthe, Château de la Gardine, Les Cailloux, and Domaine du Vieux Télégraphe.

With Châteauneuf-du-Pape, the most critical winemaking factors are yield and oak (actually the absence of oak). Yield is pivotal because at high yields, the grapes that make up Châteauneuf all taste terrible and thin. It's only at very low yields that these grapes move into the realm of the extraordinary, and so it's perhaps not surprising that by law, Châteauneuf-du-Pape is required to have the lowest yields in France—35 hectoliters per hectare (368 gallons per acre). This is about half the yield at most Bordeaux estates, for example.

As for oak, you don't see many small, new-oak barrels in the southern Rhône, and there's a reason for that. Grenache is usually vinified in large cement tanks (grenache is easily susceptible to oxidation, so wooden barrels, which are porous, are not ideal). Wines made from other grapes like syrah and mourvèdre are usually made in large old barrels called *foudres*. Because the wines are generally not put in small, new-oak barrels, they don't have that unmistakable toasty, vanilla-y character. Instead you taste what Châteauneuf-du-Papes (as well as Gigondas and Vacqueyras) are truly about: stones and soil—the naked flavors of their *terroir*.

---

## MADE FOR FROMAGE

~⦿~

Maybe it's their dark intensity or the way they evoke an almost primordial earthiness, but Châteauneuf-du-Papes, Vacqueyras, and Gigondas all beg for a good—a really sensual—cheese. If you visit these wine regions, there is no better place to find one (or several) than La Fromagerie du Comtat, in the center of the old walled city of Carpentras, which is about ten minutes from Châteauneuf-du-Pape. The aroma that hits you as you open the door of the fromagerie assures you that you're in the right place, for it's unmistakably the sort of aroma that would make a U.S. health department inspector blanche. The cheeses, all handmade raw milk cheeses from local small farms, are sensational. Don't miss the tiny chevres (goat's milk cheese) wrapped in chestnut leaves or the utterly amazing sheep's milk cheese wrapped in crushed white wine grapes that have been affected by *Botrytis cinerea*, France's noble rot.

*La Fromagerie du Comtat, 23 Place de l'Hôtel de Ville, 84200 Carpentras; 011-33-4-90-60-00-17.*

## Gigondas

The Gigondas vineyards cover a series of hills just below the jagged spurs of rock known as the Dentelles de Montmirail. This is the most northern of the important southern Rhône appellations. A few miles below it is Vacqueyras and below that and to the west is Châteauneuf-du-Pape.

Maybe Gigondas took its cue from the rugged Dentelles, for its wines are as strong and appealing as a firm handshake. The best have explosive raspberry, leather, and spice aromas and flavors and chewy textures. They are often characterized as robust versions of Châteauneuf, but the truth is they have an altogether different personality. To drink Gigondas is to go back to a time when great red wines were muscular and rough—a time before winemakers knew how to soften up wine and give it polish.

Only red and rosé Gigondas are made. By law, the reds must be no more than 80 percent grenache, with no less than 15 percent syrah and/or mourvèdre blended in.

The remaining fraction is often cinsaut but may be made up of any other red Rhône grape except carignan.

All of Gigondas was once simply Côtes-du-Rhône-Villages. But in 1971 the reds and rosés of the area were given a new, higher status and the appellation Gigondas, named after the nearby village, was born. Its top producers include Domaine de Cayron, Domaine de la Garrigue, Les Hauts de Montmirail, Grand Bourjassot, Domaine Santa Duc, St. Cosme, and Domaine les Pallières.

## Vacqueyras

Just south of Gigondas, Vacqueyras became an appellation in 1990. Before that, like Gigondas, wines from this area were labeled Côtes-du-Rhône-Villages. Vacqueyras are sturdy, bold red wines—rather like even more rustic versions of Gigondas. The best smell and taste like the land itself; there's the aroma of sun on the hot stony ground, of scrappy dried

*Rising above Gigondas is the rugged outcropping known as the Dentelles de Montmirail. From a distance the rocky spurs look rather like teeth, leading many visitors to assume that that is how they got their name (*dents *in French means teeth). Dentelle, however, means lace, and these mountains were named for what the local populace insists is their lacy look.*

brush and wild herbs. Charging through this is the flavor of black currants, blueberries, and pepper.

Grenache, syrah, mourvèdre, and cinsaut are the dominant grapes. But whereas Gigondas are weighted toward grenache, most Vacqueyras have significantly higher percentages of syrah. A minuscule number of white wines and rosés are also made.

Among the producers to try are Domaine de la Charbonnière, Tardieu-Laurent, Domaine le Sang des Cailloux, and, most especially, the sensational Domaine des Amouriers (which seems like it ought to mean the domain of lovers, but *amouriers* are actually mulberry trees).

## Tavel

Tavel is precisely the kind of wine you fall in love with on some wonderful vacation, even though you might never have bought it at home. And why? Because it is a rosé. Pink wines taste delicious if you're on a beach in St.-Tropez, but they have never played all that well in the United States, where the collective memory of Boones Farm, Riunite, and White Zinfandel has created a wicked mental block.

Tavels, in any case, taste nothing like those innocuous, mass-produced wines. Despite their pretty pink colors, most Tavels are rugged wines with robust, spicy, berry flavors. Bone-dry, they have an appealing roughness, an edge that makes them perfect for washing down southern French dishes laden with garlic, olive oil, and fresh, wild herbs.

Tavel rosés are made in the tiny, sleepy village of the same name, less than 10 miles southwest and across the river from Châteauneuf-du-Pape. No red or white wines come from here. Nine Rhône grapes, both red and white, can be used, but

### ONE OF THE PLACES WHERE PHYLLOXERA BEGAN

Just north of Tavel is Lirac, a modest place that makes even more modest wines. But Lirac does have one claim to fame: It's thought to be one of the areas where the European phylloxera epidemic began. According to John Livingstone-Learmonth in *The Wines of the Rhône*, sometime around 1863 the innovative owner of Château de Clary decided to plant a few California vine cuttings to see how they'd fare in the south of France. The cuttings, unable to adapt, died. The microscopic aphids (phylloxera) clinging to the cuttings' roots survived. Phylloxera destroyed the vineyards at Château de Clary and from there spread through neighboring vineyards. But phylloxera's presence already extended beyond the southern Rhône, for at that time Europe permitted extensive importation of living plants. Also in 1863, a professor at Oxford University reported finding phylloxera in plants growing outside London. Within a few years there were several reports of the pest in the Languedoc and by 1869, evidence of phylloxera in Bordeaux.

253

grenache is generally the leader. As is true in Châteauneuf-du-Pape, each winemaker in Tavel creates his or her own blend.

The wine is usually made by putting whole red and white grapes together in a single tank. The weight of the grapes on top begins to crush the ones below. The pink color comes as the juice sits in contact with the red skins. As seemingly straightforward as Tavel rosé is, it is not easy to make a good one—one that has freshness and bright flavors.

Tavel should be drunk young and chilled, so that its exuberant flavors explode in your mouth. A good one to try: the rosé from Château d'Aqueria, one of the largest and oldest estates in the region.

## Côtes-du-Rhône, Including Côtes-du-Rhône-Villages

Awhopping 77 percent of all Rhône wines are Côtes-du-Rhône and Côtes-du-Rhône-Villages. Unlike Côte-Rôtie, Hermitage, or Châteauneuf-du-Pape, however, wines with these two designations do not come from a single place. Instead, the terms refer to wines made from grapes that, in the case of Côtes-du-Rhône specifically, are grown on vast noncontiguous tracts of less prestigious vineyards totaling more than 140,000 acres. You'll find both appellations all over the Rhône Valley, although most vineyards are in the south. Here's the key part, however. Despite the fact that virtually all Côtes-du-Rhône and Côtes-du-Rhône-Villages are extremely reasonable in price, the quality of these wines ranges all over the board from wines that have little going for them other than the fact that they're wet (most of these are made by cooperatives) to sensational juicy, spicy wines with real character.

The relatively large reputable Rhône producers like E. Guigal, M. Chapoutier, and Beaucastel all make delicious Côtes-du-Rhône. But the real story here is all the small producers who in the 1990s began making fabulous wines. Part of the reason for this is that for a new generation of French winemakers, Côtes-du-Rhône and Côtes-du-Rhône-Villages offer a lot of freedom. The appellations are large, so there are numerous *terroirs* to choose from. The

### RASTEAU

—◦◦◦—

In addition to some terrific, rustic and gutsy dry wines, sweet fortified wines (*vins doux naturel*) are also made in the village of Rasteau, one of the sixteen best villages of the appellation Côtes-du-Rhône-Villages. Sweet fortified Rasteau is made from just-fermented grenache grapes mixed with grape spirits. By leaving the wine in old casks and allowing it to be exposed to air, it becomes Rasteau *rancio*, a thick, slightly oxidized, sweet fortified wine that is an acquired taste.

rules governing the two appellations are comparatively flexible, and any of the Rhône grapes can be used. For a talented winemaker wanting to prove his (or her) stuff, it's just what the doctor ordered. Most of the best of these modern Côtes-du-Rhône and Côtes-du-Rhône-Villages are red, although a few very good whites and some mostly serviceable rosés are also made.

So just what are the differences between Côtes-du-Rhône and Côtes-du-Rhône-Villages? Côtes-du-Rhône is the basic appellation; theoretically, Côtes-du-Rhône-Villages is a step up in quality. Generally speaking, this is true. However, several of the very best wines of all are Côtes-du-Rhône, so no hard-and-fast rules can be made. You should know this, however: Of the ninety-six tiny villages legally entitled to make Côtes-du-Rhône-Villages, sixteen are considered superior, and in recognition of that fact, they are allowed to append their name as, for example, with Rasteau Côtes-du-Rhône-Villages. Of the sixteen villages, the five best are Cairanne, Beaumes-de-Venise, Rasteau, Sablet, and

Séguret, all within about a fifteen-minute drive of each other, near Gigondas.

Who are the best producers of Côtes-du-Rhône and Côtes-du-Rhône-Villages? These are the wines not to miss, especially since many of them are a steal: Cru de Coudoulet de Beaucastel (made by Château Beaucastel), Château de Fonsalette (made by Château Rayas), Domaine Gramenon (especially its wine called Cuvée de Laurentides), St.-Cosme, Domaine Santa Duc, Domaine de Trignon (especially its Côtes-du-Rhône-Villages, Rasteau, and Sablet), Jean-Luc Colombo (especially the red Les Forots and white Les Figuières), and Domaine de la Renjarde.

## Beaumes-de-Venise

Beaumes-de-Venise, one of the sixteen top villages making Côtes-du-Rhône-Villages, is famous for its fortified sweet wine (*vin doux naturel*), muscat de Beaumes-de-Venise, made from the brazenly aromatic muscat grape.

Drinking a glass of muscat de Beaumes-de-Venise is as mindlessly hedonistic as drinking a piña colada. Peach, apricot, ripe melon, and orange flavors dance in the glass, but the wine is not sugary sweet. One sip simply makes you want to take another. Though we think of muscat de Beaumes-de-Venise as a dessert (or in place of dessert) wine, in the southern Rhône locals often drink it as an aperitif.

Muscat is actually a large family of closely related grapes. The one used for muscat de Beaumes-de-Venise is specifically muscat blanc à petits grains, the same gor-

## AN ANCIENT MEDITERRANEAN MARRIAGE

Throughout the Mediterranean the affinity between lamb and wine is centuries old. And for good reason. Historically, much of the Mediterranean's ancient, arid, impoverished soil could support only the least demanding crops and livestock. And thus in regions as diverse as Bordeaux, Greece, north-central Spain (Rioja and Ribera del Duero), and southern France (the Rhône and Provence), grazing sheep and planting vineyards became a way of life. Today in each of those wine regions, lamb is considered the quintessential accompaniment for the local wine. Which brings us to the provocative question: Which wine is best with lamb? And the answer, as someone who's eaten lamb in Bordeaux, Greece, Spain, and southern France will quickly attest, can only be: all of them. That said, there is something especially satisfying about the rich, wild, gamy flavors of lamb fed on the wild herbs and grasses of southern France when it is mirrored by the Rhône's rich, wild, gamy wines made from syrah, grenache, and mourvèdre.

geously aromatic grape that makes sparkling Asti and that is a component in the best dry muscats of Alsace.

Among the best muscats de Beaumes-de-Venise are those from Paul Jaboulet Aîné, Domaine Durban, Domaine Coyeux, and Vidal Fleury.

## VISITING RHÔNE WINE ESTATES— NORTH AND SOUTH

Your first visit to a famous Rhône wine estate may be a little shocking. The old cellars are often decrepit and more than a little dirty; the tasting table may be an old board balanced between two barrels. Don't expect a spiffy tour and video presentation. What you may end up having, however, is an extraordinarily memorable wine experience. Tasting a great Rhône in the humble cellar from which it comes is like eating a great meal in the kitchen of a restaurant. The flavors seem somehow more primal and more profound. Many Rhône wine estates are so small you will probably be taken around by the owner. It is almost always necessary to have an appointment. It is greatly helpful to speak French. The telephone numbers include the dialing code you'll need when calling from the United States. If you're calling from within France, eliminate the 011-33 and add a zero before the next number.

256

*The tiny village of Châteauneuf-du-Pape is full of little cellars (caveaux) where you can taste and buy wine.*

### NORTHERN RHÔNE

**BERNARD BURGAUD** (Côte-Rôtie)
Le Champin
69420 Ampuis
011-33-4-74-56-11-86

**DOMAINE JEAN-LOUIS GRIPPAT**
(St.-Joseph)
La Sauva
07300 Tournon-sur-Rhône
011-33-4-75-08-15-51

**GEORGES VERNAY** (Condrieu)
Rue National
69420 Condrieu
011-33-4-74-59-52-22

**M. CHAPOUTIER** (Hermitage)
18 Avenue du Docteur-Paul-Durand
26600 Tain l'Hermitage
011-33-4-75-08-28-65

**PAUL JABOULET AÎNÉ** (Hermitage)
Les Jalets
26600 Roche de Glun
011-33-4-75-84-68-93

**RENÉ ROSTAING** (Côte-Rôtie)
Le Port
69420 Ampuis
011-33-4-74-56-12-00

### SOUTHERN RHÔNE

**CHÂTEAU LA NERTHE**
(Châteauneuf-du-Pape)
Route de Sorgues
84230 Châteauneuf-du-Pape
011-33-4-90-83-70-11

**DOMAINE DE CAYRON** (Gigondas)
84190 Gigondas
011-33-4-90-65-87-46

**DOMAINE DU VIEUX TÉLÉGRAPHE**
(Châteauneuf-du-Pape)
Route de Châteauneuf-du-Pape
84370 Bedarrides
011-33-4-90-33-00-31

# THE SOUTHERN RHÔNE WINES TO KNOW

## *White*

### CHATEAU DE BEAUCASTEL

Châteauneuf-du-Pape Blanc

Vielles Vignes

100% roussanne

If ever there was a wine that you'd like to smell for eternity, this is it. The utterly refined, totally sensual top white from Château Beaucastel has no equal in Châteauneuf-du-Pape (and maybe few equals in all of France). Made entirely from roussanne from a patch of eighty-year-old vines, it's unearthly in its complexity and in the way the flavors of honey, roasted nuts, and crème brûlée embrace your tongue. And this is a dry wine! When young it's a show-stopper, but with ten years of age or more, the wine is so good it defies description. The Perrin family who own Château Beaucastel drink this with another southern Rhône masterpiece: buttery scrambled eggs cooked with the local black truffles.

## *Reds*

### CHATEAU DE SAINT COSME

Gigondas

80% grenache, 15% syrah, and 5% cinsaut

In medieval times, when doctors regularly prescribed wine for various ailments, Saint Cosme (pronounced comb) was the patron saint of medicine. I'm not sure if this wine is healing, but it's wonderfully hedonistic and very evocative of its *terroir*. Imagine leather and cherry jam somehow combined and then poured over minerals and black earth, and you've got this gripping Gigondas.

### CHATEAU LA NERTHE

Châteauneuf-du-Pape

approximately 50% grenache, 20% mourvèdre, 20% syrah, 5% cinsaut, and 5% other

Château la Nerthe (pronounced nairt) was built in 1760, and it is unquestionably one of the most majestic sites in Châteauneuf-du-Pape. The precious old vineyards ring the graceful, grand château, which also houses immaculate (rather rare in France) wine-making cellars. And the wine is stupendous. Long and saturated on the palate, it is suffused with the flavors of chocolate, espresso, grenadine, game, and stones. As with all top Châteauneufs, there's real grip here but also real elegance. In addition, La Nerthe makes a special (more expensive) Châteauneuf called Cuvée des Cadettes. One of the rare Châteauneufs to see 100 percent new oak, it's a massive wine that requires about a decade of aging before it becomes expressive and well integrated.

## DOMAINE DU CAYRON

Gigondas

approximately 75% grenache, 15% syrah, and 10% cinsaut

The Faraud family, owners of Domaine du Cayron, make what is possibly the wildest, most intense, and most sophisticated of all Gigondas. Usually massively structured and dramatically flavored, the Domaine du Cayron has an exotic sort of pepperiness and primordial gaminess that you just don't find in an average Gigondas. It's also so packed with ripe raspberry and boysenberry flavors that it could easily pass for a more expensive Châteauneuf-du-Pape. While I would happily drink the Domaine du Cayron Gigondas anytime, there's no question that a rich, long-simmered meat stew has no better partner.

## DOMAINE DU VIEUX TELEGRAPHE

Châteauneuf-du-Pape

approximately 70% grenache, 15% syrah, and 15% mourvèdre

Known for wines with grip, complexity, and elegance, Vieux Télégraphe (old telegraph) is one of the great historic estates of Châteauneuf. When first poured, the wine seems almost biting with its sharp tar, earth, and spice aromas and flavors. But after a short time in the glass, the texture begins to turn to cashmere and a wealth of other gamy and boysenberry jam flavors emerge. The grapes from which this wine comes grow out of a bed of stones.

## DOMAINE LE SANG DES CAILLOUX

Vacqueyras

approximately 65% grenache, 20% syrah, 10% mourvèdre, and 5% cinsaut

Translated, the name of the domaine is the blood of stones. No title could be more perfect, for while juicy and sensual, this Vacqueyras nonetheless smells and tastes like hard stone. At first. Then right behind the stoniness comes a mouthful of what the southern French call garigue—that flavor of the Rhône and Provence, reminiscent of wild thyme and rosemary, dry scrub brush, dead leaves, and warm earth. Did I forget to mention blueberries? This is one of the most complex, satisfying Vacqueyras around.

## DOMAINE LES PALLIERES

Gigondas

80% grenache, 10% syrah, 5% mourvèdre, and 5% other

On the beautiful sloping hills of Gigondas sits the old estate Les Pallières. In 1998 just about the best thing possible happened to this estate: It was bought by the Brunier family (owners of Vieux Télégraphe) and the American wine importer Kermit Lynch. Under their direction, the wines have become stunning. Gamy, peppery, sweetly rich, explosively fruity, and with a soaring structure, Pallières is once again one of the top Gigondas.

# The Loire

The Loire is the most diverse wine region in France. Just about every style of wine is made here, from dry still wines to snappy sparkling wines to elegant, long-lived sweet wines. In the United States the most familiar of these are the white still wines Muscadet, Vouvray, Sancerre, and Pouilly-Fumé. Yet the Loire is also well known for reds, rosés, and sparkling wines. Although such rosés as Cabernet d'Anjou and such reds as Chinon do not crowd the shelves of most wine stores in the United States, they are very popular in France, especially in Parisian bistros and wine bars, where they are virtual fixtures, served slightly chilled with everything from roast chicken to onion soup.

The Loire is defined by the Loire River, France's longest, and the pastoral valley that extends along its banks, which is known as the garden of France. Although because of silt the river is now too shallow to be navigated, it once provided an easy means of transport. Thus even as early as the Middle Ages, Loire Valley wines were being shipped north to Flanders and Britain, where they were quickly snapped

## THE QUICK SIP ON THE LOIRE

- The Loire is one of the largest and most diverse wine regions in France. Virtually every type of wine is made there—still and sparkling, dry and sweet, red, white, and rosé.

- The signature characteristic of all Loire wines is their zesty acidity.

- The leading white grapes of the Loire—chenin blanc and sauvignon blanc—make wines that are so extraordinary, they are the world's standard-bearers for these grapes.

259

*From medieval times onward, the Loire River valley was one of the richest regions in France and home to some of the country's most impressive castles, such as this one, the Château d'Amboise.*

up by a new and growing market of wine drinkers. The river's source is deep within the volcanic peaks of the Massif Central. From there it flows north for about 300 miles, makes a left turn, and then flows from east to west for another 300 miles until it empties into the Atlantic. It is in this east/west part of the Loire that all of the best wine regions are found. Farthest east is Sancerre and its neighbor Pouilly-Fumé. Farthest west is Muscadet, bordering on the Atlantic Ocean. In between are more than fifty appellations, including a number of celebrated ones, perhaps the best known of which are Vouvray and Chinon.

*Gamay grapes are grown primarily in the middle Loire.*

The Loire is one of France's larger wine regions. Slightly more than 185,000 acres are planted with vines, making the region about two thirds the size of Bordeaux. Of France's wine regions, however, the Loire is the least easy to characterize. Those fifty appellations produce wines that, in almost every way, are more different than they are similar. Except for one thing: All of the wine districts of the Loire share the region's cool, northern climate. Like Champagne, the Loire exists on the fringe of the lowest temperatures at which grapes can ripen. This is a plus in warm years. When the grapes get enough heat and sunlight to ripen, the cool climate gives the wines of the Loire their elegance and haunting precision (the result of high acidity). In great years the best wines can have such dynamic tension they seem poised on a tightrope. In French, their refreshing vigor is described as *nervosité*.

But such a climate can also mean nail-biting worry for Loire grape growers. If the year is especially cool or rainy, the wines can be thin. In these years winemakers often add cane or beet sugar to the fermenting wine to increase its alcohol and give it more body (see Chaptalization, page 47). Though controversial, chaptalization is widely practiced in the Loire, as it is in several other northern French wine regions. The Loire's top producers use the technique sparingly and only in the poorest, coolest years.

Wine estates in the Loire Valley are generally small and often family owned. In the past little capital was available for expansion or major improvements. This opened the door for the creation of cooperatives, as well as a widespread network of *négociants* who buy wines, blend them, and then bottle them under their own label. As of the mid-1990s, there were more than two hundred *négociants* and some twenty cooperatives in the Loire. Still, in most appellations the best wines are usually produced by growers who make and bottle their own wines. In Sancerre about half the total production is made and bottled by small growers. In Muscadet, however, wines made by individual growers are much more difficult to find. There 80 percent of the wines are sold by *négociants*.

The Loire has historically been a region committed to making wines that are pure expressions of *terroir* and of the grape varieties' inherent flavors. The winemaking is, for the most part, minimalist, straightforward, and low-tech. Preserving the inherent beauty of the fruit's flavors and the natural crisp acidity in the grapes is still the goal of most top producers. Yet important changes came about in the late 1980s as a widespread spirit of experimentation gripped the region. For the first time in the history of the Loire, numerous white wines began to be fermented and aged in small barrels. The result has been a new, controversial style of Loire whites—soft, fuller bodied, toasty—that bears little resemblance to the classic version.

As I've said, the wines of the Loire can be divided into three broad areas: the western Loire near the Atlantic coast, which produces Muscadet; the eastern Loire far inland, the source of Sancerre and Pouilly-Fumé; and the middle Loire, where a vast number of different wines are made, including Savennières, Vouvray, Quarts de Chaume, Chinon, and Bourgueil. Dry white wines are produced at both ends of the valley, east and west. In the middle Loire, both dry and sweeter wines are made, including some stunning wines made from botrytized grapes, plus most of the Loire's best rosés, reds, and sparkling wines.

The two leading white grapes of the Loire are sauvignon blanc and chenin blanc. (Both are grapes that produce truly stunning wines in only a few other places in the world.) Sancerre and Pouilly-Fumé, both made from sauvignon blanc, set the

## THE GRAPES OF
## THE LOIRE

### WHITES

**Arbois:** Minor grape. Native to the Loire, the use of arbois in small amounts in blends is declining.

**Chardonnay:** Minor grape. Found in blends for both white and sparkling wines of the middle Loire.

**Chenin Blanc:** Major grape, also called pineau de la Loire. Historically, the most important grape of the middle Loire, used for numerous wines including Savennières and Vouvray. Wines made from it may be still or sparkling, dry or sweet.

**Folle Blanche:** Minor grape. Used to make the wine called Gros Plant in the Muscadet region of the western Loire.

**Melon de Bourgogne:** The source of Muscadet in the western Loire.

**Sauvignon Blanc:** Major grape. Used to make the famous wines Sancerre and Pouilly-Fumé, as well as Menetou-Salon, Reuilly, and Quincy, plus many simple whites from the middle Loire.

### REDS

**Cabernet Franc:** Major grape. The source of the best Loire reds, Chinon, Bourgueil, and St.-Nicolas-de-Bourgueil. Also used as a blending grape in the reds, rosés, and sparkling wines of the middle Loire.

**Cabernet Sauvignon, Côt (Malbec), Pineau d'Aunis,** and **Pinot Meunier:** Minor grapes. Used as blending components in the red, rosé, and sparkling wines of the middle Loire.

**Gamay:** The grape that makes Anjou and Touraine gamay. Also a blending grape for red, rosé, and sparkling wines of the middle and eastern Loire.

**Grolleau:** Native grape. Usually the dominant grape in Rosé d'Anjou. Also blended into other rosé, red, and sparkling wines of the middle Loire.

**Pinot Noir:** Used for the red wines of Sancerre and the eastern Loire and as a blending grape in the reds, rosés, and sparkling wines of the middle Loire.

world standard for that grape, just as the wines Vouvray, Coteaux du Layon, and Quarts de Chaume epitomize the complexity that chenin blanc, planted in the right place, can achieve.

Most of the best Loire reds and rosés are made from cabernet franc, although seven other red grapes are grown, including cabernet sauvignon, pinot noir, gamay, and native varieties, such as grolleau. Loire reds are unmistakably stamped by their northern climate. These are zesty, light wines that are appreciated precisely because they are *not* fleshy and full-bodied.

What follows is a look at the major appellations of the Loire, starting at the mouth of the river and moving inland.

## LOIRE WINES

LEADING APPELLATIONS

**Bourgueil** red

**Chinon** red

**Crémant de Loire** white (sparkling)

**Menetou-Salon** white

**Montlouis** white (dry and sweet)

**Muscadet** white

**Pouilly-Fumé** white

**Quarts de Chaume** white (sweet)

**Sancerre** white

**Savennières** white

**Vouvray** white (dry and sweet)

APPELLATIONS OF NOTE

**Anjou-Villages** red

**Bonnezeaux** white (sweet)

**Coteaux de l'Aubance** white (sweet)

**Coteaux du Layon** white (sweet)

**Quincy** white

**Reuilly** white, red, and rosé

**Rosé d'Anjou** rosé

**St.-Nicolas-de-Bourgueil** red

**Saumur-Champigny** red

**Sparkling Saumur** white

**Sparkling Touraine** white

**Sparkling Vouvray** white

**Touraine** white and red

## MUSCADET

The most western part of the Loire, the part that borders on the Atlantic coast, is well-known for one wine alone: Muscadet. A dry, fairly neutral-tasting white, Muscadet's claim to fame has always been its easy partnership with seafood. More Muscadet is produced than any other Loire wine. It is made from the melon de Bourgogne grape, often referred to simply as melon. Melon was introduced to the area in the seventeenth century by Dutch traders in need of base material for their *brandewijn*, distilled wine later known as brandy. Muscadet, so easily accessible by river and sea, was an ideal place to plant the grape.

The Muscadet area is a sea of vines, some 32,000 acres of them, spread over gently rolling terrain (the vineyards of Sancerre, by comparison, cover about 5,600 acres). Like an upside-down fan, the region spreads in a vast arc west, south, east, and northeast of the city of Nantes. The soil here is highly variable, but the best vineyards tend to be planted on mixtures of granite, gneiss, and/or schist. Within this area is one important subzone: Muscadet de Sèvre-et-Maine, named for the small Sèvre and Maine Rivers that flow through the district. Virtually all of the tastiest Muscadet wines come from Muscadet de Sèvre-et-Maine.

*Old melon de Bourgogne vines in the Grand Mouton vineyard of Louis Métaireau et ses Vignerons d'Art. Métaireau may be a bit pretentious (*vignerons d'art *roughly translated means vine growers who are artists), but few would argue that he makes one of the most steely, precise, dramatic Muscadets around.*

The labels of most of the top Muscadets read *sur lie*, on the lees, meaning that the wine was left in contact with the yeast lees for several months before it was bottled. A Muscadet made this way takes on an extra bit of flavor and a finer structure from the yeasts, plus a slight refreshing spritz. The practice dates from the beginning of the twentieth century, when producers would put aside an especially good barrel of Muscadet for family celebrations. Over time, they noticed that the wine in this barrel, known as the honeymoon barrel, got even better thanks to its longer contact with the yeasts. In the 1970s and 1980s many low-quality Muscadets carried the designation *sur lie*, even though the flavor of the wine could not have been more innocuous and whatever spritz it had was probably the result of being injected with $CO_2$. With the new, stricter regulations that were enacted in 1994, however, the term *sur lie* has again begun to have significance. For most

Muscadet, fermentation in stainless steel tanks is standard, although some barrel-fermented Muscadets have been made, especially for restaurants, which can sell them at high prices.

Muscadet is made by more than 2,500 small farmers, most of whom sell their wines to some forty *négociants* who blend and bottle the wines under their own labels. Many Muscadets from *négociants* are serviceable at best. But there are a handful of *négociants* as well as many small producers who make considerably higher quality, more delicious wines. These can take some searching for. Should you ever encounter them, here are the Muscadets to buy: Domaine de l'Ecu, Louis Métaireau, Chéreau-Carré, and Château du Cléray.

Another wine produced in the Muscadet area is a white called Gros Plant—a tart, somewhat watery cousin of Muscadet. Gros Plant is made from the folle blanche grape.

# ANJOU-SAUMUR AND TOURAINE

The middle Loire is probably the most fascinating and least well-known part of the valley. This is where the Loire's best sweet and medium-sweet wines, sparkling wines, and red wines are all made, along with many terrific dry wines and rosés. While several grape varieties are grown, the leading white grape is chenin blanc, the leading red, cabernet franc.

The middle Loire is divided into two parts: Anjou-Saumur and Touraine. Anjou-Saumur, in the west near the city of Angers, includes the appellations Savennières, Quarts de Chaume, Bonnezeaux, Coteaux du Layon, and Coteaux de l'Aubance, all of which produce white wines. Other white wines are made in Anjou-Saumur, though they are several notches below the wines from these appellations in quality. These other white wines, most of which are vaguely sweet, carry the generic appellation Anjou-Blanc. Touraine, in the east near the city of Tours, includes the appellations Chinon, Bourgueil, and St.-Nicolas-de-Bourgueil, which produce red wines, and Vouvray and Montlouis, which produce white wines.

## *Savennières*

Anjou-Saumur's most extraordinary dry white wine, Savennières, is possibly the greatest dry chenin blanc in the world. Made in a tiny area just southwest of the city of Angers, Savennières are densely flavored wines with such intensity, grip, minerality, and taut acidity that they can be aged for decades. The vineyards are spread over steep, south-facing slopes of

*Many old vineyards in Anjou-Saumur are planted with grolleau and other red grapes used for making rosés.*

volcanic schist. Yields from these vineyards are among the lowest in the Loire, which accounts, in part, for Savennières' concentration and depth of flavor. The Loire wine expert Jacqueline Friedrich calls Savennières the most cerebral wine in the world. But sheer hedonistic flavors are operating here, too, for Savennières tastes like nothing else. It's a whirlwind of quince, chamomile, honey, and cream, all pierced by a lightning bolt of citrus.

Among the great producers of Savennières are Domaine des Baumard, Château d'Epiré, and Domaine du Closel. But the most famous of all Savennières is Clos de la Coulée de Serrant, considered one of the greatest white wines in the world. Coulée de Serrant is made on the single estate also called Coulée de Serrant. The

## COULÉE DE SERRANT—MODEL BIODYNAMICS

O ne of the Loire's most famous and longest-lived whites, Clos de la Coulée de Serrant, comes from a 17-acre vineyard that is farmed according to the principles of biodynamics. First propounded by the Austrian philosopher Rudolf Steiner in the 1920s, biodynamics is a holistic system of "living agriculture" whereby the soil is nurtured through the natural forces and rhythms of the cosmos. The Coulée de Serrant vineyards are not exposed to chemicals. Planting, harvesting, and bottling take place only at certain times according to the positions of planets, as well as the intensity of light and heat. Natural animal and vegetable matter is applied to the soil to strengthen it, and various herbal and mineral preparations may be added to help the soil maximize light and heat for photosynthesis. The Joly family, owners of the vineyard since 1959, believe that modern agricultural methods have thoroughly ravaged the soil, creating inferior wines as a result. Though many consider the Joly ideas eccentric, a number of famous French wine producers, including Domaine Leroy in Vosne-Romanée and M. Chapoutier in the Rhône, also follow the principles of biodynamics.

*Nicolas Joly, France's apostle for biodynamics.*

prized vineyards are owned by the Joly family, which farms them according to the principles of biodynamics. At only 17 acres, Coulée de Serrant is so special it has its own appellation. (Only two other appellations in France are made up of a single property: Romanée-Conti in Burgundy and Château-Grillet in the Rhône.)

### The Sweet Wines of Anjou-Saumur

A number of the best wines of Anjou-Saumur are medium-sweet or fully sweet whites that carry the appellations Quarts de Chaume, Bonnezeaux, Coteaux du Layon, or Coteaux de l'Aubance. The smallest and most prestigious of these appellations is Quarts de Chaume, and its wines can be absolute masterpieces, with soaring elegance, lightness, and a real purity of fruit. In all four appellations the wines are always made from chenin blanc, which in this part of the world exudes gorgeous floral, peachy, apricoty flavors. Yet the naturally high acidity in the northern-climate grapes plus a certain flintiness from the soil keep the wines from being overwrought or saccharine.

The vineyards spread out along the fairly steep slate, schist, and clay slopes that form the banks of the Layon River, a tributary of the Loire. In good years, the sheltered open slopes receive just the right combination of morning moisture from the river followed by afternoon sun for *Botrytis cinerea*, or noble rot, to form. (This is the same beneficial fungus that makes France's most famous sweet wine, Sauternes.)

Among the wonderful wines to try from this part of the Loire are the Quarts de Chaume from Domaine des Baumard and Château de Bellerive, as well as the Bonnezeaux from Domaine de la Sansonnière.

## SIDETRACKED BY TARTE TATIN

One of the most famous rustic desserts of France, *tarte Tatin*, originated in the Touraine region of the Loire in the tiny village of Lamotte-Beuvron. An upside-down caramelized apple tart, it was created in the nineteenth century by two sisters, Stephanie and Caroline Tatin, owners of the Hôtel-Terminus Tatin, a wayside stop for travelers across from the train station. *Tarte Tatin* is the perfect accompaniment for one of the Loire's other prizes—Quarts de Chaume, the gorgeously sweet, lightly honeyed dessert wine made from chenin blanc grapes.

## The Rosés of Anjou

Most of the wine produced in Anjou is not white but rosé. Rosé d'Anjou, simple and medium sweet, is usually made primarily from the local red grolleau grape, although five other red grapes can be part of the blend: cabernet franc, cabernet sauvignon, côt (the local name for malbec), pineau d'aunis, and gamay.

Rosé cabernet d'Anjou—made from cabernet franc or cabernet sauvignon—is somewhat better than Rosé d'Anjou, although it, too, is medium sweet.

There is a third type of rosé, this one dry: Rosé de Loire. By law, Rosé de Loire can be made anywhere in the middle Loire, though most are made in Anjou. The best Rosés de Loire are good, fruity quaffing wines with light cherry flavors and a hint of acidity. Rosés de Loire are made from the same roster of red grapes as Rosés d'Anjou, except that côt is not allowed but pinot noir is.

## The Red Wines of Anjou-Saumur

Rarely imported to the United States, the red wines of Anjou-Saumur are popular on their home turf. Anjou Rouge, a passable but unexciting red, is the basic generic appellation. Anjou Rouge can be made from cabernet franc and/or cabernet sauvignon. A sister wine, Anjou gamay, is made from gamay. Far better than these are red wines that carry the appellations Anjou-Villages and Saumur-Champigny. Usually made from cabernet franc with cabernet sauvignon blended in, both must be aged at least a year.

## Saumur: The Loire's Top Sparkling Wines

Although sparkling wines are made throughout much of the middle Loire, most of the best come from a large area surrounding the town of Saumur, which is located near the boundary between Anjou-Saumur and Touraine. Here the especially cool climate and calcareous rock create an ideal environment for making the kind of low-alcohol, high-acid base wines necessary to make crisp sparkling wines. The three top Loire sparkling-wine producers are all located in Saumur, and all are owned by or related

*Windmills in the countryside near Savennières, one of the best places in the world for dry chenin blanc.*

to Champagne firms. Bouvet-Ladubay is owned by Taittinger; Gratien et Meyer is a sister company of the house of Alfred Gratien; and Langlois-Château is owned by Bollinger. As in Champagne, these sparkling-wine firms buy most of their grapes from small growers.

*Outside Champagne,
the Loire is France's main source
of sparkling wines.*

Loire sparkling wines fall into two categories: sparkling wines with a specific appellation (sparkling Saumur, sparkling Vouvray, sparkling Touraine, and so forth) and Crémant de Loire. A sparkling wine that carries an appellation can be white or rosé. They are made by the *méthode traditionelle*—that is, in exactly the same way Champagne is.

A grab bag of different grape varieties can be used for these sparklers. Sparkling Saumur is usually a blend of chenin blanc plus chardonnay and cabernet franc. By law, seven other grapes may also be used (sauvignon blanc, cabernet sauvignon, côt, gamay, pinot noir, pineau d'aunis, and grolleau), but in practice their inclusion is rare.

The appellation Crémant de Loire is a slightly different category of Loire sparkling wine. *Crémants*, too, can be white or rosé and, like sparkling wines with an appellation, they must be made according to the *méthode traditionelle*. But instead of coming from a specific small appellation, such as Saumur or Vouvray, the grapes for a *crémant* can come from anywhere in the Loire (most still come from the middle Loire). To make a *crémant*, by law the grapes must be harvested by hand, yields

267

## IT TAKES TWO
## TO BE TANGY

Though many of us immediately think of red wine when we think of cheese, the tangy, creamy, chalky, salty, and fatty flavors of most goat cheeses can neutralize the flavor of many red wines. Sancerre and Pouilly-Fumé, on the other hand, are perfect counterpoints in part because they are so tangy themselves. In particular, the combination of Sancerre and Crottin de Chavignol, a small disk of goat cheese from the nearby village of Chavignol, is considered to be a French classic.

## GOOSEBERRIES AND CAT PEE

—⁓—

Gooseberries and—yes, you read it right—cat pee are terms commonly used by wine experts to describe, usually favorably, the aromas and flavors of some sauvignon blancs, especially those from the Loire. Gooseberries are tart green berries that grow all over northern Europe (but rarely in the United States). Cat pee is, well, cat pee; when used in the context of sauvignon blanc, the term usually refers to a strident, wild, tangy smell.

must be lower than those for wines labeled sparkling, and the wine must be aged for one year. In practice, however, most of the top sparkling-wine producers are as conscientious as the *crémant* producers.

Crémant de Loire is often made from a more Champagne-like blend of grapes than are other sparkling wines. More chardonnay and less chenin blanc is used. Unlike Champagne, many blends contain some cabernet franc. The greatest proportion—95 percent—of Loire sparkling wines (both those with an appellation and *crémants*) are dry, or brut. However, as in Champagne, sweeter styles—extra dry and demi-sec—are also made.

While such large sparkling-wine firms as Bouvet-Ladubay concentrate solely on sparkling wine, small producers in the Loire often make varying amounts depending on the year. In cooler years, when the grapes are higher in acidity, more sparkling wine will be produced; in warmer years more still and sweet wines will be made.

## Touraine, Chinon, Bourgueil, and St.-Nicolas-de-Bourgueil

Touraine, a fairly large area due east of Anjou-Saumur, surrounds the city of Tours, extending both east and west. It is a wine region befitting Cinderella. Centuries-old storybook châteaux, replete with turrets, moats, and drawbridges, rise up from verdant rolling fields and vineyards. The châteaux were built by seventeenth- and eighteenth-century aristocrats attracted by the agricultural wealth and abundance of the region. Unlike those in Bordeaux, few of these châteaux are wine-producing estates today.

Touraine is where the climate shifts from the milder western Loire, influenced by the Atlantic, to the eastern Loire, with its hot summers and extremely cold winters. The top vineyards in Touraine seem to have gotten the best of both worlds—

*The diversity of Loire wines (and their modest prices) plus the region's proximity to Paris have meant that these wines have always been favorites in that city's bistros.*

mildness as well as warmth, a situation ideal for red wines.

The three most famous red wine appellations of the Loire are found here: Chinon, Bourgueil, and St.-Nicolas-de-Bourgueil. Each is a small appellation within the larger appellation Touraine. All three types of wine are almost always made entirely from cabernet franc. Of the three, Chinon is generally the softest and most elegant. No Paris bistro is ever without red wines from at least one of these three places, especially in summer when they are served cool to the touch. Among the most delicious of these reds are the Chinons from Charles Joguet and the Bourgueils from Pierre-Jacques Druet.

Chinon, Bourgueil, and St.-Nicolas-de-Bourgueil can vary tremendously with the vintage. In good years when the cabernet franc grapes ripen fully, the wines fairly burst with raspberry, violet, cassis, and briary/spicy flavors, but in poor years, they can be on the thin side.

Not all Touraine reds are Paris bistro classics, however. Much of what is produced is simple, fruity Touraine Rouge made from one or any combination of the following: gamay, cabernet franc, cabernet sauvignon, côt, pineau d'aunis, and grolleau. Many Touraine Rouges are simply made from gamay alone in a super-fruity style resulting from carbonic maceration, the same technique used to make Beaujolais. Touraine Primeur is Touraine Rouge bottled immediately after the harvest when it is fresh and grapey (like Beaujolais Nouveau).

## *Vouvray and Montlouis*

One white wine appellation of Touraine is well known the world over: Vouvray. Just across the Loire River is Montlouis, although the wines here are not as well recognized nor, in most instances, are they as exciting. By law, both Vouvray and Montlouis must be made of 100 percent chenin blanc. In the case of Vouvray, that perhaps states the case too simplistically, for the best Vouvrays are absolutely exquisite and exceptional examples of the grape. No other place in the world produces

---

### VOUVRAY—DRY TO SWEET

Vouvray is divided into four levels of sweetness: sec, demi-sec, moelleux, and doux, according to the amount of residual sugar in the wine. The impression of sweetness for any given wine, however, is based not only on the quantity of residual sugar present but also on the degree of acidity. A demi-sec Vouvray can actually taste quite dry if the wine's sweetness is counterbalanced by a high level of acidity. A Vouvray label will usually, but not always, indicate the level of sweetness of the wine.

**Sec**
Dry: 0 to 0.4% sugar
(less than 4 grams of sugar per liter)
Very dry wines are called sec-sec, dry dry, and less severe wines are called sec-tendres, gently dry.

**Demi-Sec**
Medium dry, sometimes called off-dry: 0.4 to 1.2% sugar
(4 to 12 grams of sugar per liter)

**Moelleux**
Medium sweet, literally mellow: 1.2 to 4.5% sugar
(12 to 45 grams of sugar per liter)

**Doux**
Quite sweet: more than 4.5% sugar
(more than 45 grams of sugar per liter)
Sometimes described as liquoreux, syrupy sweet.

chenin blancs that are so gossamer, richly flavored, and honeyed—even when dry.

Most astonishing of all is how long a great Vouvray lasts. It would seem counterintuitive that a white wine could taste vibrant and luxurious after half a century or more, but the top Vouvrays can and do. Not surprisingly, these have always been collectors' wines. Truly great Vouvray is rare, however. Far more Vouvray today is simply nice tasting commercial wine made by *négociants*. Not particularly expensive, it is meant to be drunk right away.

Vouvray can be almost any kind of wine—dry (sec), medium dry (demi-sec), medium sweet (*moelleux*), or totally sweet (doux) (see page 269). In addition, a share of the total production is sometimes, but not always, made into sparkling Vouvray. The amount of sparkling wine depends on the weather. Vouvray has one of the coolest climates in the Loire. Harvests here are as late as many in Germany, often well into November. Thus, in extremely cool years when the acidity in the grapes remains high, such top producers as Huet, Champalou, Prince Poniatowski, and the *négociant* house of Marc Brédif may make twice as much

For the vigneron, *everything depends on the quality of the grapes; in this case they have been attacked by the noble rot*, Botrytis cinerea.

sparkling wine as still. In warmer years with riper grapes, the situation flip-flops. And in warm years sweet wines can be made, but in very cool years it is almost never possible to make these by natural means.

The best naturally sweet Vouvrays are always the product of *Botrytis cinerea*, the beneficial fungus that also produces Sauternes. As in many areas of the middle Loire, the vineyards of Vouvray get just the right proportion and progression of sun, moisture, and dryness to be infected with the noble rot.

Because they are also full of daggerlike acidity, Vouvray's greatest sweet wines are an extraordinary taste sensation. When the tension of opposites—sweetness and acidity—is perfectly balanced in these wines, they can be otherworldly in their vibrancy and richness. Often they must be aged for three to seven years before the counterpoint tastes harmonious. Sweet (*moelleux*) and medium-dry (demi-sec) Vouvrays are traditionally drunk with rich dishes, especially those with complex sauces.

Many of Vouvray's cellars were chiseled into caves left behind after the local stone was quarried to build châteaux.

Some of the vineyards and cellars of Vouvray almost defy existence. Vineyards cling to the top of cliffs, with cellars and houses below them, cut into the soft, *tuffeau* rock, a type of limestone, that forms the face of the cliff. Many cellars were chiseled into the caves left behind long ago after the *tuffeau* was quarried for building materials for châteaux.

As for Montlouis, in general it tends to be softer and less dramatically focused than Vouvray. That said, certain producers, such as Domaine Deletang, make extraordinary Montlouis that is every bit the equal of Vouvray.

In addition to Vouvray and Montlouis, Touraine is also home to simple whites that can come from anywhere in the region. These can be made from a variety of grapes, including chenin blanc, sauvignon blanc, and chardonnay, as long as the latter makes up no more than 20 percent of the blend. The most popular of the Touraine whites is Touraine sauvignon, which is made from the sauvignon blanc grape. The best Touraine sauvignons taste like very simple versions of Sancerre and are good carafe wines.

## SANCERRE, POUILLY-FUMÉ, MENETOU-SALON, QUINCY, AND REUILLY

The eastern Loire is some 300 miles from Muscadet and the Atlantic coast but less than half that distance from Paris. The famous dry white wines Sancerre and Pouilly-Fumé come from this easternmost part of the Loire Valley, as well as the dry whites from Menetou-Salon, Reuilly, and Quincy. All are made from sauvignon blanc.

What chenin blanc is to the middle Loire, sauvignon blanc is to the eastern Loire—the quintessential expression of the grape. With their racy gunflint, herbal, and smoky flavors, the best of these wines are true to the word *sauvignon*'s root, *sauvage*, meaning wild. They are the world's model

271

*France's most tangy, crisp, and outrageous sauvignon blancs come from vines near the village of Sancerre, in the eastern Loire.*

for crisp, focused, full-throttle sauvignon blanc and are considered some of the best white wine matches for food. Most of the finest wines in this part of the Loire carry the appellation Sancerre or Pouilly-Fumé. Numerous producers in these two locations are maniacal about quality, and the soil and climate are ideal for producing wines with elegance, precision, and focus.

The vineyards of Sancerre are spread over chalky limestone and flint hills near the town of the same name on the western bank of the river. There are a number of excellent vineyards here, but the three called Le Grand Chemarin, Chêne Marchand, and Clos de la Poussie are especially exemplary. As of the mid-1990s, however, a curious Sancerre ruling prevented wine producers from ever using the name of vineyards on their labels. Wine producers therefore resorted to "creative" ways of letting consumers know where the grapes came from. The great producer Jean-Max Roger, for example, calls his top Sancerre Cuvée GC (meaning Grand Chemarin).

Opposite Sancerre, on the eastern bank of the Loire, is the town of Pouilly-sur-Loire. In Pouilly the landscape is more gentle and the soil contains slightly more limestone and flint. This soil, it was believed, gave the wine a more pronounced gunflint or smoky flavor, hence the name of the wine—Pouilly-Fumé. The word *fumé* means smoke. In truth, few people except local experts can tell Pouilly-Fumé and Sancerre apart in a blind tasting.

The philosophy of winemaking in both Sancerre and Pouilly-Fumé has traditionally focused on preserving the pure,

uninhibited flavors of sauvignon blanc and the grape's naturally high acidity. To this end, most wines have always been made in inert large casks or stainless steel tanks. Such top producers as Henri Bourgeois, Cotat Frères, Lucien Crochet, Domaine Laporte, and de Ladoucette remain staunchly traditional in their winemaking practices.

A small number of New Wave Sancerres and Pouilly-Fumés, made in small oak barrels, have appeared since the 1980s. The best producer of this style is Didier Dagueneau, called the wild man of Pouilly, a renegade winemaker whose expensive barrel-fermented and barrel-aged Pouilly-Fumés set off a quiet storm of controversy in the Loire. Complex, lush, superrich, full-bodied, and expensive, the Dagueneau wines—especially the one called Pur Sang—are considered delicious by many, though few would say they taste traditionally of the Loire.

Although the very word *Sancerre* brings to mind white wine, red and rosé Sancerres are also made. Red Sancerre, in fact, accounts for about 20 percent of total production. Both red and rosé Sancerres are made from pinot noir with some gamay. Finding the red grapes of Burgundy here is not surprising; Burgundy's vineyards begin about a hundred miles to the southeast.

The eastern Loire has three other appellations that are less well known in the United States but very appreciated in France. Menetou-Salon, just west of Sancerre, can make sauvignon blanc with all the fire and brimstone of the best Sancerre and Pouilly-Fumé. The two top producers are Henri Pellé and Domaine de Chatenoy.

Quincy and Reuilly are two tiny appellations near the river Cher, a tributary of the Loire. Again, the sauvignons can be quite crisp and delicious—and less expensive than Sancerre or Pouilly-Fumé. Look especially for the Quincy from Domaine Mardon.

# VISITING LOIRE WINE ESTATES

The middle of the Loire Valley can be reached in about two hours by car from Paris. The region is beautiful, full of forests and fields, plus stunning châteaux. The eastern part of the Loire, around Sancerre, is known for its artisanal goat cheeses; the western part of the Loire, where Muscadet is made, is known for oysters and fish dishes. With the exception of the sparkling wine houses Bouvet-Ladubay and Gratien-Meyer, the producers listed below are fairly small. It's best to call well ahead for an appointment. Knowledge of French is helpful. The telephone numbers include the dialing code you'll need when calling from the United States. If you're calling from within France, eliminate the 011-33 and add a zero before the next number.

**BOUVET-LADUBAY**
St.-Hilaire St.-Florent, 49400 Saumur
011-33-2-41-83-83-83

**DOMAINE BOURILLON-DORLÉANS**
4 Rue du Chalateau
37210 Vouvray
011-33-2-47-52-83-07

**DOMAINE DELÉTANG ET FILS**
19 Route d'Ambroise
37270 Saint Martin Le Beau Montlouis
011-33-2-47-50-67-25

## THE SECRET TO MARRIAGE: ACIDITY

Two of the Loire's most famous wines, Sancerre and Pouilly-Fumé, are among the world's most flexible when it comes to pairing wine with food. And the reason is: acid. Bone-dry and refreshing, both Sancerre and Pouilly-Fumé possess the kind of clean, bracing acidity that can counterbalance a surprising array of dishes from Chinese chicken salad to roast duck to grilled salmon with mango salsa. At the same time, both of these sauvignon blanc–based wines are dramatic enough so that their own flavors are not subdued by most foods. As for a time-honored partnership, Sancerre or Pouilly-Fumé with seafood is certainly one. (The Loire boasts a number of seafood festivals including an oyster fair, a crayfish fair, and even a deep-fried fish fair.)

273

**DOMAINE HENRI BOURGEOIS**
18300 Chavignol-Sancerre
011-33-2-48-54-21-67

**DOMAINE LAPORTE**
Saint Satur
18300 Sancerre
011-33-2-48-54-04-07

**GRATIEN-MEYER**
Route de Montsoreau-B.P.22
49401 Saumur
011-33-2-41-51-01-54

**PRINCE PONIATOWSKI**
Le Clos Baudoin
Vallée de Nouy
37210 Vouvray
011-33-2-47-52-71-02

# THE LOIRE WINES TO KNOW

*Whites*

### CHATEAU D'EPIRE
Savennières

100% chenin blanc

Among all the extraordinary dry chenin blancs made in the Loire, those from Savennières can have the most outrageous personalities. Château d'Epiré is the perfect example. The Savennières from this distinguished estate can be fascinating, with a whirlwind of flavors ranging from apple cider and quince to licorice and curry powder. The importer Kermit Lynch personally selects special lots of this wine to be bottled and imported into the United States.

*The de Ladoucette family estate, Château de Nozet: Fairy tale-like châteaux such as this one are common in the Loire.*

### CLOS DE LA COULEE DE SERRANT
Savennières

100% chenin blanc

The most famous Savennières, Coulée de Serrant, is also one of the most famous white wines in the world. In great years, it is chenin blanc from another galaxy. The wine can be so suffused with apple-caramel flavors, you feel as though you're inside a *tarte Tatin*. The finesse, the nuance, the incisive focus, the gripping flavors that melt into a silky, honeyed body—it's all here for the hedonist. The 17-acre Coulée de Serrant vineyard is cared for by the Joly family, the world's leading proponents of the biodynamic approach to viticulture (see page 265).

### DE LADOUCETTE
Baron de L

Pouilly-Fumé

100% sauvignon blanc

A stunning, and stunningly expensive, wine, full of mineral, lime, grapefruit, herbal tea, cream, and vanilla flavors, with a kind of vividness and elegance that make your spine tingle. De Ladoucette is one of the largest and most famous wine producers in Pouilly-Fumé, and the Baron de L is the estate's most prestigious wine. (The regular Pouilly-Fumé, pictured at left, is delicious as well.) The de Ladoucette family also owns a considerable number of vineyards in Sancerre, where it makes the wine called Comte Lafon.

## DIDIER DAGUENEAU

En Chailloux

Pouilly-Fumé

100% sauvignon blanc

DIDIER DAGUENEAU
EN CHAILLOUX

The first Pouilly vintner to make big-style, oak-fermented Pouilly-Fumé, Didier Dagueneau is considered both a renegade and a genius in the Loire. His wines, which some criticize as being too "international," are dramatic and sophisticated, with fruit so alive it dances in your mouth. Of Dagueneau's several wines, the En Chailloux is the most refined, elegant, and focused, though for pure opulent hedonism (and price) the Pur Sang has few competitors.

## DOMAINE DES AUBUISIERES

Le Bouchet

Vouvray

demi-sec

100% chenin blanc

The Vouvrays of Bernard Fouquet at the small Domaine des Aubuisières are among the most elegant, delicate, and precise in the Loire. Their almost haunting clarity, creamy apple-pear flavors, and soaring lightness are mesmerizing. Though medium-dry, this wine is pierced with such a lightning bolt of acidity that it seems bone-dry. Another from the Domaine des Aubuisières, the sweet (moelleux) wine called Le Marigny is so phenomenal it has developed cult status in Europe. Fouquet, like the Joly family of Coulée de Serrant, uses strict biodynamic methods in his vineyards, which are all top-notch.

## DOMAINE HENRI BOURGEOIS

Grande Réserve

Sancerre

100% sauvignon blanc

The wine estate Domaine Henri Bourgeois makes some of the loveliest Sancerres around. They are slightly creamy wines with generous ripe fruit and a spinal cord of acidity. Among Bourgeois' several Sancerres, the Grande Réserve has gorgeous flavors of lime, ginger, gooseberry, and baked apple. Its body is as streamlined as a 1940s woman's suit.

## DOMAINE HENRI PELLE

La Croix au Garde

Sancerre

100% sauvignon blanc

This is the Ingrid Bergman of Sancerres—ravishing, polished, and effortlessly elegant. In great years, besides having perfect tension between acidity and fruit, the wine has a unique kind of purity and clarity, with absolutely vivid smoky/minerally flavors. Pellé himself was considered one of the legendary masters of the sauvignon blanc grape, and now his family carries on, making wines that are widely admired. The Pellé estate is perhaps best known for its extraordinary rich, dramatic Menetou-Salon, which is also where the estate is located.

## LAPORTE

Domaine du Rochoy

Sancerre

100% sauvignon blanc

Nothing soft or mellow going on here. Laporte's Domaine du Rochoy is a firecracker of a Sancerre. Spicy, edgy, zingy, and cat pissy (in a good way), it's invariably loaded with all the wild green, flinty flavors hard-core sauvignon blanc drinkers love. Not for the timid. Domaine du Rochoy, a single vineyard owned by the Laporte family, is one of the vineyards closest to the Loire River.

## PRINCE PONIATOWSKI

Aigle Blanc

Vouvray

sec

100% chenin blanc

At their best, the Vouvrays of Prince Poniatowski are a cascade of rich honey on the one hand, vibrant acidity on the other. So perfectly juxtaposed are these two components that Poniatowski's

wines often take at least a decade to grow into themselves. When aged this long, they taste not the least bit faded but precisely the opposite: opulent, vivid, elegant, and extremely complex. Prince Philippe Poniatowski, a descendent of the last royal family of Poland, is the third generation to run the estate. The Aigle Blanc (white eagle) vineyard is contiguous with another famous Poniatowski vineyard, Clos Baudoin.

# Red

## CHARLES JOGUET

Les Varennes du Grand Clos

Chinon

100% cabernet franc

Here's a cabernet franc that comes into your mouth like a raspberry/violet bullet train—all speed, grace, and power. Raspberries, violets, and spicy cassis are signature flavors of the best Chinon in the top years, and no wine has more of these flavors than Joguet's. It's simply explosive, especially so when drunk with food. Les Varennes du Grand Clos is a quintessential bistro wine if ever there was one.

# Sweet Wine

## DOMAINE DELETANG

Les Petits Boulay

Montlouis

moelleux

100% chenin blanc

The greatest *moelleux* wines of Montlouis and Vouvray rate among the finest sweet wines of the world, and this one from Domaine Deletang shows why. At its best, the wine, with its honey cream beginning and citrusy vibrant finish, has impeccable balance and polish. Made entirely from chenin blanc, it is nearly rapturous.

# Alsace

Alsace is one of the rare wine regions in the world devoted almost exclusively to white wine. More than seven different varieties are common and, with few exceptions, they are whites rarely made in other parts of France. Although by law (and in spirit), Alsace is a French wine region, it has also at various times in its past belonged to Germany. The two powers have repeatedly battled each other over this small strip of land, for Alsace is one of Europe's strategic geopolitical crossroads.

It is also a wine region so charming it may as well have emerged straight out of a fairy tale. The vineyards are sun dappled, the half-timbered houses are cheerfully adorned with flower boxes, the 118 villages—centuries old—are immaculate. All are set against the grand backdrop of the Vosges Mountains.

The most important grapes are riesling, gewürztraminer, pinot gris (formerly called tokay), muscat, and pinot blanc. All are white. The lone red grape, of which only a tiny amount is grown, is pinot noir.

The great unsung heroes of France, Alsace whites are not the placid, demure wines that you might imagine. Nor are they slightly sweet, a common misconception. The best among them are powerful, bold, and dramatic. They

277

*Alsace is the second most northern wine region in France (after Champagne), but the Vosges Mountains offer shelter and harvests usually take place in dry, sunny weather.*

## THE QUICK SIP ON ALSACE

• The wines of Alsace are predominantly dry whites. That said, there are two types of late harvest wine: *vendange tardive* and *sélection de grains nobles*.

• A single, passionate philosophy pervades Alsace winemaking: to create wines with pure fruit flavors. New oak is almost never used.

• Thanks to the unique northern but sunny climate, Alsace wines are massively bodied, superconcentrated wines, often with a dramatic streak of acidity.

virtually always taste dry (unless a sweet late harvest wine is intentionally being made). Moreover, they are made according to a single, deeply held philosophy—namely that great wine should be the purest possible expression of two factors, the grapes it is made from and the ground it is grown in. An Alsace winemaker's goal is not to craft a wine with certain flavors, it's to showcase the inherent character of the grape itself when grown in a certain plot of earth. The emphasis on the grape is so strong that blending is (almost) unthinkable. The most highly regarded wines are almost always 100 percent of the variety named on the label.

For wines to be truly expressive of grape and ground the winemaking must be hands-off. In Alsace, indigenous yeasts are usually used instead of commercial yeasts, and the wines are made in neutral containers—either stainless steel or cement tanks, or older, inert casks called *foudres*. The lightning bolt of natural acid-ity in the wines is never mollified by letting them go through malolactic fermentation, a process that would soften the impression of acid. The combination of lively acidity, dryness, and unhampered, uninhibited, unleashed fruit is what defines Alsace wines and makes them some of the best all-around marriage partners for food.

There is one thorn in the otherwise purist philosophy of winemaking in Alsace. Some producers add cane sugar to the grape must before or during fermentation to raise the final alcohol level. This technique, called chaptalization, is legal—though controversial—in the region. The purpose of chaptalization—which is widely practiced in northern Europe—is to help assure that there is enough alcohol in the wine, even if it's made from insufficiently ripe grapes. Unfortunately, winemakers more interested in high yields than quality can let their vines produce gargantuan crops, knowing full well that the vines cannot possibly ripen so many bunches. Chaptalizing then becomes a quick alcohol fix for a large but poor-quality crop. There is no way of knowing which producers chaptalize and which do not. The top estates are least likely to, since the quality of their wines is based, to begin with, on low yields and well-situated, sunny vineyards.

Not every Alsace wine is dry; two extremely rare types are exceptions. *Vendange tardive* wines are made from superripe, late-harvested grapes. Powerful and concentrated, VT wines, as they are known, can be dry or slightly sweet. The second category, even more rare than VT, is *sélection de grains nobles* (SGN). These are ravishingly unctuous wines made from superconcentrated, late-harvested, botrytis-affected grapes. Curiously, the final taste impression of both VT and SGN wines is *not* of sugary sweetness but of hauntingly dense concentration.

Alsace was one of the first regions in the modern world to label its wines according to the grape variety, for example pinot blanc or pinot gris, rather than by the place where the grapes grow, as is done in other parts of France.

As luck (or marketing) would have it, the vast majority of Alsace wines exported to the United States are wines of very high quality. Average and mediocre wines are either drunk locally or are shipped to other markets. This makes buying Alsace wines a good bet, even if you don't know the producer.

## TYPES OF WINE

Amazingly, most leading Alsace producers—even small producers—make twenty to thirty different wines. The majority of these can be broken down into three types: regular, reserve, and late harvest. The regular bottlings are the producer's standard bread-and-butter wines. A typical producer will make regular bottlings of all five leading grapes—riesling, gewürztraminer, pinot gris, pinot blanc, and muscat.

Next are the reserve bottlings. Though the word *reserve* might cause you to imagine a single special wine, in Alsace producers usually make multiple reserve wines. There can be three reserve rieslings, four reserve gewürztraminers, and so on, all from the same producer. Alas, reserve wines may be labeled in a number of ways. The label may carry the name of a special, well-known vineyard, such as Zind Humbrecht's Clos St.-Urbain. Or, if the reserve wine happens to come from a

*Grand Cru* vineyard (not all do), it may be labeled with the words *Grand Cru* plus the name of the vineyard. And finally, a reserve wine may be given a title such as *réserve personelle* or *réserve exceptionnelle*. Such designations, however, have no legal definition.

The third type of wine—late harvest wine—is made when the harvest permits. A producer may make up to six of the rare specialties *vendange tardive* and *sélection de grains nobles*. They will be among the estate's most precious and expensive offerings.

On top of all this, just for the fun of it, many producers also make a pinot noir or a sparkling wine or an inexpensive blended quaffing wine—or all three. And so it's easy to see how all these wines add up. From the perspective of an Alsace producer, more wines mean the ability to show off how distinctly different the flavors derived from different sites can be.

279

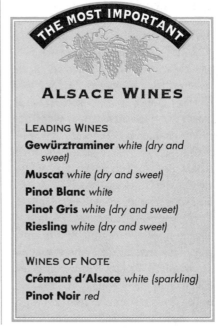

### THE MOST IMPORTANT

## ALSACE WINES

LEADING WINES

**Gewürztraminer** white (dry and sweet)

**Muscat** white (dry and sweet)

**Pinot Blanc** white

**Pinot Gris** white (dry and sweet)

**Riesling** white (dry and sweet)

WINES OF NOTE

**Crémant d'Alsace** white (sparkling)

**Pinot Noir** red

*Hillside vineyards poised above the small, sleepy village of Rouffach. Since the twelfth century this village has had a reputation for being the home of especially feisty and independent-minded women.*

280

## CRÉMANT D'ALSACE

All of the sparkling wine made in Alsace is called Crémant d'Alsace, and like all *crémants*, it is made in the same painstaking way as Champagne. A blend of grapes is used, including pinot blanc, auxerrois, pinot noir, pinot gris, and/or chardonnay. These are harvested earlier than grapes for Alsace still wines so that their acidity is pronounced. It's this vivid acidity, of course, that will give the final wine its snap, crackle, and pop.

A word on chardonnay. So little is planted in Alsace that the first time the grape appeared in official harvest statistics was 1990. By law, chardonnay is permitted only in Crémant d'Alsace. In reality, producers have been known to take poetic license with this rule. In any case, whether in *crémant* or surreptitiously in other wines, chardonnay is used mostly in small amounts to add nuance and body to a blend.

Crémant d'Alsace, which is an official appellation, accounts for about 10 percent of the total production of Alsace wine. It's generally made by the larger firms.

## THE LAND AND THE VINEYARDS

Alsace lies about 300 miles due east of Paris. The vineyards run north to south in one long, thin strip over the foothills along the eastern flank of the Vosges Mountains. Germany's Rhine River is about 12 miles to the east, and even closer (about 6 miles to the east) is Alsace's river Ill.

After Champagne, this is France's most northern wine region, yet it is not generally overcast and cool as one might presume but surprisingly sunny and dry. Thanks to the protective mantle of the Vosges Mountains, less rain falls on the vineyards here than on vineyards elsewhere in France.

### CRÉMANT COCKTAILS

The Alsatians often use Crémant d'Alsace in cocktails. When Crémant d'Alsace is mixed with curaçao, it is called a blue *crémant;* mixed with tangerine juice, it's a *crémant mandarine;* with orange juice, a *crémant orange;* and finally, with iced verbena tea, it's a *crémant verveine.*

About two dozen estates account for the vast majority of top-quality wine in Alsace. Many of these estates are family owned firms. Some own all of their own vineyards, others supplement their grapes with those bought from the region's 7,000 small growers. The properties of many of these growers are so small, however, that they make wine almost entirely for personal use.

The best vineyards are south facing for maximum sun, and most are located in the southern part of the region, known as the Haut Rhin or upper Rhine. The growing season is long, assuring that even at this northern latitude grapes growing in the best, sunniest sites develop full physiological maturity. The harvest generally takes place in mid-October.

Soil in Alsace is varied enough to be a geologist's dream. Wide variations in soil often mean wide variations in the flavor and quality of the wines. And in fact, there is an enormous difference in flavor between an average wine from a nondescript vineyard and a wine from an extraordinary vineyard, such as Trimbach's Clos Ste.-Hune, which year in and year out produces one of the greatest rieslings in the world.

The checkerboard of soil types in Alsace includes chalk combined with clay, limestone, granite, schist, volcanic rock sediment, and sandstone. Alsace's pinkish-colored sandstone, called *grès de Vosges*, is a favorite building material for local cathedrals.

*In Alsace all wines—even red ones—must, by law, be bottled in long tapered bottles, called flûtes d'Alsace.*

# THE GRAND CRU

In 1983 twenty-five of the very best vineyard sites in Alsace were for the first time legally recognized as superior. They were designated the *Grand Cru*. The act, however, was wildly controversial. For two decades prior to this designation, Alsace producers and growers had not only debated which vineyards were indeed the crème de la crème but also what the boundaries of those vineyards should be and what, if any, limits should be set on a *Grand Cru*'s yield. Clearly, the stricter the requirements, the more impact and validity the designation Alsace *Grand Cru* would have.

As it turned out, the standards set were not as stringent as many producers would have liked. To add fuel to the fire, twenty-five more vineyards were later added to the original twenty-five, bringing the total number of *Grand Cru* vineyards to fifty. That's far too many to suit a number of producers. Moreover, the yield set for *Grand Cru* vineyards (65 hectoliters per hectare or more than 4 tons of grapes to the acre) is generally recognized as much too high for the production of great wine.

On the other hand, just because the regulations could be stricter does not mean that no great *Grand Cru* wines are being made. They are. In fact, most wines labeled *Grand Cru* are far more intense, elegant, complex, and structured than the producers' regular bottlings. But, some top producers, as a quiet form of protest, refuse to use the term *Grand Cru* even though they own *Grand Cru* vineyards. Instead, they call their best wines by a vineyard name or a proprietary name. The producer Hugel simply uses the word *Jubilee* (as in Hugel Riesling Jubilee) to designate wines that come from *Grand Cru* vineyards.

By law, only wines made from four grape varieties are allowed to be called *Grand Cru,* and they are the varieties that, over many decades, producers have deemed capable of greatness: riesling, gewürztraminer, pinot gris, and muscat. If a producer chooses to label his wine *Grand Cru,* the label must also state the specific *Grand Cru* vineyard from which the wine came. *Grand Cru* wines are two to three times more expensive than regular bottlings.

# THE WINES (AND GRAPES) OF ALSACE

Alsace wines are based on and named after the grapes from which they've come. Here are the main wines.

## *Riesling*

Alsace's most prestigious grape, riesling is the source of its leading wine. Alsace riesling, however, is as thoroughly different from German riesling as a wine can be and still come from the same grape—grown virtually next door to boot! The best German rieslings are finely etched, exquisitely nuanced wines, low in alcohol, vibrating with acidity, and usually balanced with a softening pinch of sweetness.

Alsace rieslings are not nearly as dainty. These are mostly very dry, broad wines with palate-coating, full-throttle flavors that lean toward gunflint, steel, and minerals, all drizzled with peaches, green

---

## SURPRISING AGING POTENTIAL

—◦◦◦—

Only exceptional white grapes can be made into wines that will stand up to long aging—say, twenty years or more. Riesling is the world's preeminent white grape in this regard, followed by (in no particular order) chardonnay, sémillon, pinot gris, and gewürztraminer. In general, for a white wine to age, it must have an impeccable balance of fruit and alcohol, and it helps if the wine has high acidity.

When made by the best producers, three of the most important Alsace whites—riesling, gewürztraminer, and pinot gris—all age remarkably well. Alsace rieslings, in particular, have an amazing ability to become graceful and honeyed, the older they get.

---

plums, and a limey sort of citrus. Tight and austere when young, the wines begin to come out of their closets after two to three years. With a decade or more of age, they take on a ripe, fruity richness, as well as a viscosity and flavor that is often referred to (positively) as petrolly.

Riesling in Alsace—and virtually every place else—is more sensitive to its *terroir* than most other white grapes. Grown in a merely decent vineyard, it makes dull wine. Extraordinary riesling requires near perfect vineyard conditions. Which is why it is, necessarily, a rare commodity. On the other hand, when you do find it, great riesling is so outrageously good, it's mind-boggling.

There are scores of truly great Alsace rieslings, so singling out a few is anything but satisfying. Still, no discussion of great Alsace riesling could fail to include two from Trimbach: Clos Ste.-Hune and Cuvée Frédéric Emile, as well as Domaine Zind Humbrecht's Rangen, Domaine Weinbach's Cuvée Ste.-Cathérine, and Domaine Marcel Deiss' Altenberg de Bergheim.

## Gewürztraminer

It's often said that gewürztraminer (or, gewurztraminer without the umlaut, as you'll almost always see it, this being France) is something you either really like or can't stand. This seems especially true of average-quality gewürztraminers, which, like average-quality anchovies, are not easy to fall in love with, although some people manage to. Great gewürztraminer, it seems to me, is a whole different ball game. The first time you taste a truly fine one, you almost can't believe it *is* gewürztraminer.

The problem is that great gewürztraminer does not come from just any place. In fact you'll find it almost nowhere outside of Alsace. Whatever it is about the Alsace *terroir*, gewürztraminer here takes on a range of gripping flavors, a finesse, and a complexity not seen elsewhere.

The aromas and flavors are extroverted. Litchi nuts, gingerbread, vanilla, fruit-cocktail syrup, grapefruit, smoke, spice, stones, minerals, and honeysuckle do not simply rest in the glass—they rage about in it. Such massive fruitiness is sometimes mistaken for sweetness, but most Alsace gewürztraminers are dry or nearly so (unless a late harvest wine like a *vendange tardive* is being made).

To go along with their big Technicolor fruit, Alsace gewürztraminers have an

# THE GRAPES OF
# ALSACE

## WHITES

**Auxerrois:** An important grape, though rarely made into wine on its own. Broad and full-bodied, auxerrois is usually blended with pinot blanc.

**Chardonnay:** A minor grape legally permitted to be used only in Crémant d'Alsace, a sparkling wine.

**Gewürztraminer:** A major grape. Makes flamboyant dry wines full of personality, plus extraordinary late-harvest wines.

**Muscat:** Two types grow in Alsace. These are often blended to make stunningly aromatic wines usually drunk as aperitifs.

**Pinot Blanc:** A major grape. Makes creamy, medium-bodied wines of good, not usually great, character.

**Pinot Gris:** A major grape. The source of unique full-bodied wines, totally unlike pinot gris planted elsewhere in the world. Older vintages may still carry pinot gris' former name, tokay or tokay-pinot gris.

**Riesling:** A major grape and the most prestigious one. Alsace rieslings can have remarkable complexity and aging potential. Also used for late harvest wines.

**Sylvaner:** A minor grape. Usually turns into bland wine. Often used in inexpensive blends. Sylvaner is also a common grape in Germany, where it is spelled silvaner.

## RED

**Pinot Noir:** A minor grape but noteworthy because it is Alsace's only red. Occasionally makes fascinating wine.

enormous body and low natural acidity. If the existing acidity is not carefully protected, therefore, the wine can end up tasting flabby. With age, Alsace gewürztraminer seems—if this is possible—even bigger flavored. Made as a *vendange tardive*, it can be a knockout.

Many Alsace producers make excellent gewürztraminers. Some of my favorites: Domaines Schlumberger Kessler *Grand Cru*, Kuentz-Bas Pfersigberg *Grand Cru*, Domaine Zind Humbrecht Goldert *Grand Cru*, Domaine Weinbach Altenberg *Grand Cru* Cuvée Laurence, Hugel et Fils Hommage à Jean Hugel, and Domaine Marcel Deiss Altenberg *Grand Cru*.

## Pinot Gris

Riesling may be the most prestigious grape in Alsace, but pinot gris is the well-loved hometown girl. In Alsace pinot gris has such depth and richness it's reminiscent of white Burgundy. What it is generally *not* like, however, is pinot gris from Oregon or from Italy (pinot grigio). Both of those are usually lighter in body and somewhat more subtle in flavor. Alsace pinot gris, on the other hand, is a high-impact wine, with a full body and bold, concentrated flavors of bitter almonds, peach, ginger, smoke, vanilla, and earth.

In the past Alsatians called pinot gris tokay or they hyphenated the name to tokay-pinot gris. The grape, however, is not related to Hungary's Tokay wine (spelled Tokaji in Hungarian and made principally from the white grape furmint) nor is it related to the tocai grape of Friuli

in Italy. So how would pinot gris acquire the unlikely name tokay? Tom Stevenson in *The Wines of Alsace* suggests that pinot gris originated in Burgundy, as did its siblings pinot noir and pinot blanc. Sometime during the Middle Ages, pinot gris was brought from Burgundy to Hungary and from Hungary, the grape traveled back to France, to Alsace.

Once in Alsace, it was rather confusingly given the name of the famous Hungarian dessert wine Tokay, which, at the time, was one of the most sought-after wines in Europe. In 1980, however, the European Economic Community prohibited Alsace pinot gris from being called tokay and mandated that after a period of transition, it be called by its correct name.

Among the great pinot gris are those from Kuentz-Bas, Léon Beyer, Domaine

---

## THE STATUE OF LIBERTY AND NEW WAVE BLENDS

In 1986 the Domaines Schlumberger was asked by the French American Committee for the Restoration of the Statue of Liberty to create a commemorative wine to celebrate the restoration. Ms. Liberty, a gift from France to the United States, had been created one hundred years earlier by the Alsatian sculptor Frédéric-Auguste Bartholdi. The wine the Domaines created, called Schlumberger Réserve, was the first New Wave, high-quality Alsace blend (rather than a single varietal). Schlumberger Réserve is a combination of pinot blanc, riesling, and gewürztraminer.

Marcel Deiss, Domaine Ernest Burn (especially the Clos St.-Imer), and Zind Humbrecht. Pinot gris is often made into lush *vendange tardive* wines.

## Muscat

Thought to be one of the oldest varieties of grapes, muscat is actually an enormous extended family of vines with members living all over the world. Ampelographers think there may be hundreds of genetic variations.

Two types of muscat grow in Alsace, muscat blanc à petits grains—called muscat d'Alsace—and muscat ottonel. Muscat d'Alsace, considered the star of the muscat family, is the fuller bodied of the two, with outrageously floral and citrus flavors. Muscat ottonel is lighter, fresher, and more aromatic. The two are so eminently complementary that they are usually blended together. The result is a dry, dramatically aromatic wine redolent of peaches, orange peel, tangerine, and musk. It is one of the world's most evocative aperitifs. Alsace is one of the few places where dry muscat is made. Far more often, the grape is made into a sweet or sweetish wine. (The French dessert wine muscat de Beaumes-de-Venise and Italy's semisweet sparkler Asti are both made from muscat.)

The muscats to search out? Those from Domaine Albert Boxler, Domaine Ernest Burn, Léon Beyer, Domaine Ostertag, and Zind Humbrecht.

## Pinot Blanc

Alsace's chardonnay, pinot blanc is easy to like, dependable, and safe. It's never as thrilling as riesling, as zany as gewürztraminer, or as novel as pinot gris;

*The tiny, storybook village of Eguisheim, which dates from the sixth century, is surrounded by some of Alsace's greatest gewürztraminer vineyards.*

nonetheless the top Alsace pinot blancs are tasty wines with baked-apple flavors and light, creamy textures. Unfortunately, there are also many bland versions.

Pinot blanc is the genetic cousin of pinot gris and pinot noir. It is often blended with auxerrois, even though this goes against the Alsace "rule" of 100 percent varietal wine. Auxerrois, a well-established Alsace grape, is somewhat fatter and broader than pinot blanc, and some winemakers prefer it, believing it to be slightly richer. The label will not usually indicate whether or not the pinot blanc has auxerrois blended into it. Top producers of pinot blanc include Domaine Albert Boxler, Josmeyer, and Domaine Weinbach.

## Pinot Noir

The only red wine made in Alsace is pinot noir. In the past the quality was so variable that much of it ended up looking like rosé. One got the feeling that pinot noir was made not because it was very good but because Alsatian winemakers had some sort of psychological need to break out of their whiteness. Then in the 1990s, a few of the top wineries began rethinking their approach to pinot noir. They began planting it in better sites, lowering the yields, buying special equipment that could extract more color, flavor, and aroma from the grape, and aging it in new barrels.

As expected, the wine got better. What no one expected, however, was just how much better it became. In good vintages Marcel Deiss' Bergheim Burlenberg pinot noir and Hugel's Jubilee pinot noir show earthy, complex, almost Burgundy-like flavors.

Like all other Alsace wines, pinot noir must, by law, be bottled in tall, Germanic flute bottles. Because it's surprising, if not a little unnerving, to see red wine flow from what looks like a bottle of riesling, several producers are battling the bottle law, in hopes of having the rule rescinded.

This fountain in Colmar is dedicated to Baron Lazare de Schwendi, who, as the story goes, led an expedition to Hungary in the mid-sixteenth century to fight the Turks and returned to Alsace with vines (possibly pinot gris) that he'd found growing in the Tokay region. As a result, Alsace pinot gris became known as tokay-pinot gris.

### NOT SO NOBLE

Edelzwicker is the collective term for inexpensive Alsace quaffing wines made up from a hodge-podge blend of whatever Alsace grapes the producer has on hand or can buy cheaply. Ironically, the name literally means noble blend.

## Vendange Tardive and Sélection de Grains Nobles

Two sensational types of late harvest wines, *vendange tardive* and *sélection de grains nobles*, can be made only in certain favorable years (sometimes only once or twice a decade). But sensational isn't nearly adequate as an adjective. These wines can be liquid ecstasy. By law, only the four grape varieties allowed for *Grand Cru* wines may be used: riesling, gewürztraminer, pinot gris, and muscat. *Vendange tardive* and *sélection de grains nobles* wines are so rare that even in the best of years, they generally make up less than 1 percent of the entire region's production.

*Vendange tardive,* or VT, wines are not exactly dessert wines but, rather, wines of such profound concentration they seem to have atomic density not to mention strapping lushness, all underscored by exuberant acidity. They may be a touch sweet or dry; unfortunately, there's no way to tell from the label. VTs are so spellbinding, they are generally drunk by themselves or with something utterly simple. (I always drink them as the finale to Thanksgiving dinner.)

To achieve such concentration, the grapes must be picked at a stage of advanced physiological maturity—simple sugar ripeness is not enough. Generally this means picking about two weeks after the regular harvest. VT wines may also be infected with *Botrytis cinerea,* the noble rot responsible for Sauternes.

*Sélection de grains nobles,* or SGN, are late-harvested wines that are always sweet and always infected with botrytis. To say that the wines are sweet, however, doesn't even begin to scratch the surface of their characters. SGN wines can make Sauternes seem shy. Wines of ravishing unctuousness, SGNs are balanced by such soaring acidity, profound alcohol, and huge extract that they actually finish in a way that seems almost dry. The right descriptor for SGN might be seductive.

Because a significant amount of botrytis does not appear in Alsace vineyards every year (or even very easily in any year), the production of SGNs can range from nothing to a barely commercial amount.

A producer's VTs and SGNs will often come from the same vineyard, usually one of the best. First, the pickers will go through the vineyard choosing, berry by

berry, only the botrytis-infected grapes for SGN. Then, they'll go back and pick the remaining superripe grapes for VT.

VT and SGN wines are governed by extremely strict regulations. Producers must officially declare their intentions to produce them, and governmental authorities must then test the grapes as they are being pressed. The wines cannot be chaptalized. Once they are made, they are subjected to a tasting test before they can be sold. In some years, up to 35 percent of the wines fail to pass the test! VT and SGN wines are expensive, but they are unequaled in the world. If you can get your hands on any VT or SGN from any of the following producers, do! Léon Beyer, Domaine Albert Boxler, Domaine Marcel Deiss, Hugel et Fils, Kuentz-Bas, Trimbach, Domaines Schlumberger, Domaine Weinbach, or Domaine Zind Humbrecht.

287

# No
# Substitutions
# Please

From April until June in Alsace, small specialized restaurants open that serve only one food: asparagus. Serious asparagus aficionados believe there to be only one perfect accompaniment to the vegetable: a glass of dry muscat. After a long winter, the most sensational way to celebrate the arrival of spring may well be with a huge platter of asparagus drizzled with hollandaise sauce and accompanied by a bottle of Domaine Zind Humbrecht Goldert Grand Cru Muscat.

## FRUIT BRANDIES

—◄◦◦◦►—

Alsace is famous for eaux-de-vie—clear fruit brandies—distilled not just from the region's extraordinary fruits (wild plums, elderberries, blackberries, pears, mirabelles) but also from things like wild mint, rose hips, juniper, pine, and wild holly berries. No hearty country meal is truly complete without a little glass of the potent stuff, considered a *digestif*. Less courageous souls (or those with more delicate constitutions), forgo tasting and just sniff. Among the top distillers: Windholtz, Metté, Miclo, Massenez, and Theo Preiss.

## THE FOODS OF ALSACE

After a few days in Alsace, even the most insatiable food and wine lover is ready to beg for mercy. The sheer number of delicious regional dishes is daunting, and the number of great restaurants—both humble and grand—is second only to Paris, which, of course, does not have world-class wine estates.

*Kugelhopf* is a good example of the irresistibility of Alsace specialties. These turban-shaped rolls, rich with eggs and butter, are dusted with sugar or flecked with walnut pieces and sometimes diced bacon. In every bakery, they line the shelves like perfect soldiers, along with *pains paysans*, golden, crusty loaves studded with raisins and almonds, and *petits pains au lait*, soft doughy milk rolls.

Kugelhopf—the pride of Alsace.

Alsace's most stunning "bread," however, is *flammekueche*, also known as *tarte flambée*—best described as pizza meets the onion tart. First a thin layer of bread dough is stretched across a chopping board; it's then smeared with *fromage blanc*, a fresh white cheese, and heavy cream. Next it's topped with smoked bacon and onions, and finally it's baked in a fiery, wood-burning oven until blistered. In *winstubs* (wine bars) all over Alsace, *flammekuechen* can't be baked fast enough for the hoards of happy families and friends who come to share it.

Since roughly the tenth century, Alsace has been the capital of Munster, a creamy, pungent cheese. Almost as important as driving along the Route du Vin is driving along a smaller side road, the so-called Route du Fromage (cheese route), where country restaurants and inns offer homemade Munster, baked with potatoes and onions and served with bacon and cured ham.

With due respect to the Romans, who fattened snails on choice tidbits and housed them in special snail boxes, the French, and especially the Alsatians, have raised the eating of escargots to a fine art. Drizzling snails with garlic butter is merely the tip of the iceberg. There are dozens of ways of preparing snails, including a famous one in which the mollusks are simmered with wild chanterelle mushrooms, garlic, and shallots in a wine and whipped cream stock, then served with a chilled riesling.

In Alsace, April is not the cruelest month; it is the time for unrestrained asparagus madness. The vegetable inspires such devotion that there are restaurants open only from mid-April until the end of June that serve nothing but. Connoisseurs sit with napkins tucked under their chins, devouring the thick spears after dipping them in one of three traditional sauces: vinaigrette, homemade mayonnaise, or hollandaise. Alsatians say there's only one wine that's perfectly compatible with asparagus: dry muscat.

Alsace is one of the two great capitals of foie gras (the other is southwestern France). Geese are force-fattened until their livers are large and rich. The livers are then seasoned with salt, pepper, and a touch of Cognac and coddled in a *bain-marie*. In pâté de foie gras, the liver is flecked with truffles and wrapped in a rich pastry crust, then cooked. But Alsatian chefs never miss an opportunity when it comes to foie gras. They also stuff game birds with it, sauté it in gewürztraminer, even top plebeian sauerkraut with it!

Speaking of cabbage, although its exact origins are not known, *choucroute* is so undeniably Alsatian that locals are often referred to as *choucroute*-eaters by the rest of France. *Choucroute* is prepared by shredding young white cabbage and layering it with salt in large crocks until it ferments. The fermented cabbage is then cooked in wine—usually a riesling—and served with a stunning array of potatoes, several cuts of pork, and sausages. If the *choucroute* is fancy, pieces of suckling pig will be added.

Given the heartiness of Alsace cooking, it might seem as though only the lightest of sorbets should be in order for dessert. Fat chance. Dense, creamy cheesecakes are common, as are apple tarts, plum pies, and soufflés made with the local kirsch (cherry brandy). One thing never shows up with dessert, however. That is a *vendange tardive* or *sélection de grains nobles*. These rare late-harvest wines are so extraordinary and complex that dessert only seems to get in the way.

## WHITE WINE AND THE OTHER WHITE MEAT

Among all the world's rieslings, pinot blancs, pinot gris, and gewürztraminers, those of Alsace are usually the most full-bodied and concentrated. This makes them great choices when you're having meat but want to drink a white wine. Which is what happens in Alsace all the time. The region's robust, down-to-earth, cold-weather food revolves around pork and game that are often cooked with hearty vegetables, such as potatoes, onions, and cabbages. The region's specialty, *choucroute garni*, a dish of sauerkraut, pork, sausages, bacon, and potatoes, is stellar with riesling. But *choucroute* aside, even a simple pork roast is raised to new heights when it's served with a powerfully fruit-packed, crisp Alsace riesling.

*Cabbage as high art*, choucroute *is one of Alsace's best-loved dishes. It is usually served with multiple cuts of pork and sausages.*

# THE ALSACE WINES TO KNOW

*Whether dry or sweet, all these Alsace wines are whites. And, this being France,
you won't see an umlaut on the u in gewürztraminer on most labels.*

## *Whites*

### DOMAINE MARCEL DEISS

Riesling

Altenberg de Bergheim

*Grand Cru*

100% riesling

All of the best Alsace rieslings have lift. They are like Gothic arches, soaring in their elegance, never heavy, never weighted down. Marcel Deiss' rieslings are a prime example. These are wines of impeccable elegance. In the best years they are thoroughly concentrated with fruit but so carefully balanced by a tight rope of acidity that the overall impression is not of fruit or acid but simply of beauty and delicacy.

### DOMAINE WEINBACH

Cuvée Laurence

Tokay-Pinot Gris

100% pinot gris

Built in the early eighteenth century as a Capucin monastery, Domaine Weinbach is now owned and run by three women, Madame Faller and her daughters Catherine (in charge of marketing) and Laurence (the winemaker). The wines from this estate are among the most expressive, powerful, and elegant in all of Alsace. They have a purity to them that can seem absolutely regal. The domaine's tokay-pinot gris Cuvée Laurence is a stunning example. Rich, minerally, spicy, creamy, and utterly dense with flavor, it is nonetheless a wine with a long, refined finish that ends like a slow fading whisper. In upcoming years the label of this highly sought-after wine will read simply pinot gris.

### DOMAINE ZIND HUMBRECHT

Gewürztraminer

Goldert

*Grand Cru*

100% gewürztraminer

From the *Grand Cru* vineyard Goldert comes this richly dense and opulent yet refined and intriguing gewürztraminer, evocative of tropical fruits fused with roses and exotic spices. Few white grapes are more expressive and powerful than gewürztraminer, and gewürztraminer is nowhere more expressive or powerful than in Alsace, especially from a top *Grand Cru* vineyard. To make matters even more irresistible, few Alsace producers make gewürztraminers more expressive and powerful than those of Zind Humbrecht. In other words, this wine has it all. But then virtually all Zind Humbrecht wines are massively lush and fleshy with bold, extroverted flavors. Not for the faint of heart.

### HUGEL ET FILS

Gentil

mostly sylvaner, with some gewürztraminer, riesling, pinot gris, and muscat

Hugel's inexpensive, aromatic, zesty, bone-dry wine is a good introduction if you've never tasted Alsace wines before, and it's a new twist on an old idea. After  the First World War several producers made *gentil* blends (in Alsace the word means noble). By the 1960s the practice was abandoned; quality wines were increasingly 100 percent varietal. In 1994 the family-owned firm of Hugel et Fils released this New Wave blend. This *gentil* is the essence of Alsace wrapped up in one delicious ball.

## KUENTZ-BAS

Gewürztraminer

Pfersigberg

*Grand Cru*

100% gewürztraminer

Kuentz-Bas makes some of the most stunning gewürztraminers in the world. This one, from the *Grand Cru* vineyard Pfersigberg (hill of peach trees), is so taut, hard, and sleek, the sensation is akin to running your hand over the biceps of a bodybuilder. In great years, the creamy, spicy flavors are massively concentrated, and yet the wine is also ravishingly elegant. The aroma is so heady, you'd swear you're lying in a bed of acacia and honeysuckle blossoms.

## TRIMBACH

Riesling

Cuvée Frédéric Emile

100% riesling

A family-owned estate, Trimbach makes scrumptious gewürztraminer and pinot gris, but their rieslings (they make four) can be simply devastating in their elegance and concentration. The Cuvée Frédéric Emile, named after an ancestor, was first made in the 1960s and comes from old vines in two *Grand Cru* vineyards: Osterberg and Geisberg. At its best, the aroma of this wine is quintessential riesling—somewhat like cold stone that has been rubbed with peaches and apricots.

*Trimbach, one of Alsace's top wine producers, was founded in 1626. Today the firm is headquartered in the picturesque village of Ribeauvillé.*

# *Sweet Wines*

## DOMAINES SCHLUMBERGER

Gewürztraminer

*sélection de grains nobles*

Cuvée Anne

100% gewürztraminer

The largest of the top producers, Domaines Schlumberger has 350 contiguous acres, half of which are classified *Grand Cru*. The rieslings from this family-owned estate are delicious, but the gewürztraminers truly leave you dazzled. For sheer intrigue, try Cuvée Anne, a rare, late harvest gewürztraminer SGN, produced on average only twice a decade. The wine is so opulent and powerful it tastes as though every molecule of water has been siphoned out of it, leaving only the utter essence of fruit. The flavors and aromas zigzag among ginger, apricots, and wet granite, with flying sparks of acidity. The estate considers Cuvée Anne one of its greatest wines.

## DOMAINE WEINBACH

Tokay-Pinot Gris

*vendange tardive*

100% pinot gris

One of the best wineries in Alsace, Domaine Weinbach is an extraordinary producer of VTs and SGNs. This is the domaine's simplest and least expensive (though still pricey) *vendange tardive*, yet it is a masterpiece. Sensationally pure and deep aromas and flavors of orange marmalade and dried peaches predominate. The texture is like cool silk. Though sweet, the wine does not come off sugary but has a refinement that is both beautiful and memorable. Future labels will refer to the wine as pinot gris, omitting the tokay.

# VISITING ALSACE WINERIES

The best way to visit the wineries of Alsace is simply to follow the wine route of Alsace, which winds for 75 miles along the eastern side of the Vosges Mountains, over the vineyard-covered hillsides and along the floors of deep valleys. The walled towns tucked away in the shadow of the mountains are charming, with their bell towers, ramparts, storybook inns, churches, and roadside crucifixes. Castles overlook the plain, paths run through the vineyards, and everywhere, wine taverns and cellars provide a close to poetic atmosphere.

In the heart of the vineyards, a few kilometers from Colmar, is the Kientzheim castle, headquarters of the Confrérie Saint-Etienne, a society dating from the 1400s, which now acts as a promotional organization hosting, among other events, some of the most lavish banquets in France. Kientzheim castle also houses the Alsace wine museum. The museum re-creates

*You can eat and drink well throughout France, but no region is more renowned for both its restaurants and its wines than Alsace.*

wine cellars of the past and includes a valuable collection of Alsatian wineglasses, bottles, flagons, and jugs dating from the fifteenth century.

Advance appointments are not always necessary at wineries but are advised. Although many people speak English, it's helpful to understand some French. The telephone numbers include the dialing code you'll need when calling from the United States. If you're calling from within France, eliminate the 011-33 and add a zero before the next number.

**CONFRÉRIE SAINT-ETIENNE**
Château de Kientzheim
68240 Kayserberg
011-33-3-89-78-23-84

**DOMAINES SCHLUMBERGER**
100 Rue Théodore Deck
68500 Guebwiller
011-33-3-89-74-27-00

**DOMAINE ZIND-HUMBRECHT**
2 Route de Colmar
68230 Turckheim
011-33-3-89-27-02-05

**F. E. TRIMBACH**
15 Route de Bergheim
68150 Ribeauvillé
011-33-3-89-73-60-30

**HUGEL ET FILS**
3 Rue de la Première Armée
68340 Riquewihr
011-33-3-89-47-92-15

**LÉON BEYER**
2 Rue de la Première Armée
68420 Eguisheim
011-33-3-89-41-41-05

**MAISON KUENTZ-BAS**
14 Route du Vin
68420 Husseren-les-Châteaux
011-33-3-89-49-30-21

# Languedoc-Roussillon

emarkably, the wine region today considered to be one of the most exciting and innovative in France, the Languedoc-Roussillon, was a place that until the 1990s few wine drinkers in the United States had ever even heard of. This seemingly improbable fact is made even more surprising by the region's size. With more than 700,000 acres of vines spanning the vast curving arc of France's western Mediterranean coast, the Languedoc-Roussillon is thought to be the single largest wine-producing area in the whole world. A century ago almost half of all French wine was made in this one place. Today more than a third still is.

So how come wine drinkers have been hearing about the wines only since the early 1990s or so? Because only since then have a significant number of them been any good. In the past the Languedoc (as it is often called) produced mostly the sort of no-name, no-frills *vin ordinaire*—very *ordinaire*—that was bought in bulk and cost less than water. (During the world wars, the ration of wine given daily to French soldiers usually came from here.) In fairness, there were small enclaves where making fine wine had always been important, but they were just that—small enclaves.

Undistinguished quaffing wine, however, was not to be the Languedoc's legacy

*In the rugged landscape between the Pyrenees and the Massif Canigou lie old vineyards that time seems to have forgotten. Before the mid-seventeenth century, this area, now part of the Languedoc-Roussillon, belonged to Spain.*

## THE QUICK SIP ON LANGUEDOC-ROUSSILLON

• The wines of Languedoc-Roussillon are among the most exciting best-value wines in France.

• The Languedoc is the largest wine-producing region in France. More wine is produced in this one area than in the entire United States.

• A wide variety of grapes are grown, from Mediterranean varieties, such as syrah and grenache, to international varieties, such as cabernet sauvignon and chardonnay.

forever. With a climate and terrain similar to neighboring Provence and the southern Rhône, the Languedoc as a whole was waiting to be tapped by quality-minded producers. When that happened in the 1980s, a whirlwind transformation of the local wine industry ensued. Year after year, wine quality increased by leaps and bounds while prices stayed low. The Languedoc quickly became, and has largely remained, a paradise for bargain hunters seeking easy-to-drink French wines that go well with Mediterranean foods.

Languedoc wines cover a broad spectrum, from white to red; dry to sweet; still to sparkling—but the most distinctive wines are generally the soft, rustic red blends based on several of the same traditional Mediterranean grapes used in the southern Rhône Valley: syrah, mourvèdre, grenache, and carignan. These wines are known, as are most wines in France, by their appellations—Corbières, Faugères, St.-Chinian, and so on. However, the Languedoc is also one of the few regions in France where

wines can be named after a grape variety. Thus you find a plethora of modern-style cabernets, merlots, chardonnays, and so forth that bear little resemblance to the region's more traditional wines. These are known as Vin de Pays d'Oc.

The Languedoc-Roussillon is spread over the immense crescent of land west of Provence, along the coast of the Mediterranean Sea. The region stretches from the Rhône River in the east to the Pyrenees and the Spanish border in the west, a distance of about 150 miles. The vineyards, considered some of the oldest in France, date back to the early Greeks.

The Languedoc and the Roussillon were two separate provinces for most of history. The Languedoc became part of France in the late thirteenth century, but the Roussillon belonged to Spain until the mid-seventeenth century. Nonetheless, the regions have always been entwined culturally and financially; they were finally joined administratively in the late 1980s. Today threads of Spanish culture and language are still evident in this French province. The Languedoc-Roussillon, for example, is passionate about bullfighting.

*The Languedoc-Roussillon is sometimes called le Midi, loosely translated as the land of the midday sun.*

Like Provence and the southern Rhône, the Languedoc is warm, arid, and so luminously full of light it can seem as though the sky itself is somehow bigger there. Compared to the vineyards of northern France, it is a blissfully easy place in which to grow grapes. The landscape is dominated by the scratchy patchwork of low bushes, resinous plants, and wild herbs known as garigue. In fact, the best Languedoc wines exude garigue, as though the heady scents and earthy flavors of wild thyme, rosemary, and lavender have insinuated themselves into the wine itself.

The wines of the Languedoc have had a mercurial history. During the Middle Ages, when most vineyards were in the care of monks, the wines were prized. In the fourteenth century wines from the area of St.-Chinian had achieved such fame that the hospitals of Paris prescribed them for their healing powers. By the twentieth century, however, the quality and reputation of the wines had plummeted. Wine books published as recently as the 1970s bluntly described the Languedoc, if they mentioned it at all, as France's biggest producer of characterless plonk. It took numerous small producers—Château des Estanilles, Gilbert Alquier, Domaine d'Aupilhac, Mas de Daumas Gassac, and others—plus large companies, such as Fortant de France, and quality-oriented cooperatives, such as Val d'Orbieu, to initiate in the 1980s what would become a remarkable transformation of the region's wines.

*The Languedoc region is named after a group of languages and dialects spoken in southern France during the Middle Ages, known collectively as the* langue *(language)* d'oc *(of* oc, *then the common word for* yes).

Although today there are virtually no wines that might be considered majestic, there are nonetheless scores of delicious mouthfilling ones that are full of personality. The vibrant lusty fruit these wines possess makes them perfect for pairing with the bright Mediterranean flavors of garlic, tomatoes, and olive oil.

## THE TWO CATEGORIES OF LANGUEDOC WINE

295

In most French wine regions, wines are labeled according to the *Appellation d'Origine Contrôlée* (AOC) from which they come, not the grape variety (or vari-

*The walled medieval village of Carcassonne is one of the most stunning in the Languedoc-Roussillon. Up in the foothills just southwest of here is the tiny village of Limoux, where the Languedoc's sparkling wines Blanquette de Limoux and Crémant de Limoux are made.*

eties) from which they are made. Sancerre, St.-Emilion, and Meursault, for example, are all appellations—specific, delimited areas where wines are made in a traditional way according to strict regulations. Appellation wines are meant to reflect their *terroir*; to taste of their place.

The Languedoc-Roussillon can be confusing because while some wines *are* labeled according to their appellation (Corbières, Faugères, Minervois, and so on), others are labeled according to the variety of grape from which they are made (chardonnay, merlot, and the like) or are sometimes labeled with a proprietary name (like Le Jaja de Jau). Languedoc-Roussillon wines that are labeled varietally or with proprietary names fall into a category known as Vin de Pays d'Oc. Vin de Pays d'Oc is just one example of wines that come under the *vins de pays* category of French wines (see page 117).

There are often big differences between AOC wines and Vins de Pays d'Oc. In general, the Languedoc's appellation wines—there are some twenty-five different appellations—are traditional Mediterranean blends. The best of them can be downright sensational. Like all the top wines of France, these wines strive to reflect the *terroir* from which the grapes came. Usually they are made from three or more grape varieties, most often including, if the wine is red, syrah, mourvèdre, grenache, and/or carignan. By comparison, Vins de Pays d'Oc are generally far less traditional and the rules for making them are far more flexible. Most are made from a single variety of grape, but the grapes used usually will have been grown in more than one location. A Vin de Pays d'Oc chardonnay can be made from a blend of chardonnay grapes grown all over the region—in other words, place is a far less important

*Grenache grapes grow to be superripe in the Languedoc's abundant sun. Some of these are used in the exotic, and fairly rare, red versions of the sweet fortified wines known as* vins doux naturels.

## LANGUEDOC-ROUSSILLON WINES

### LEADING APPELLATION-DESIGNATED WINES

**Banyuls** red (fortified; sweet)

**Corbières** red

**Coteaux du Languedoc**
white, red, and rosé

**Faugères** red

**Minervois** red

**Muscat de Frontignan** white
(fortified; sweet)

**Muscat de Rivesaltes**
white (fortified; sweet)

**Muscat de St.-Jean-de-Minervois** white
(fortified; sweet)

**St.-Chinian** red

### LEADING VARIETALLY DESIGNATED WINES— VINS DE PAYS D'OC

**Cabernet Sauvignon** red

**Chardonnay** white

**Merlot** red

**Sauvignon Blanc** white

**Syrah** red

**Viognier** white

### APPELLATIONS OF NOTE

**Blanquette de Limoux**
white (sparkling)

**Collioure** red

**Côtes de Roussillon-Villages** red

**Crémant de Limoux**
white (sparkling)

**Fitou** red

**Limoux** white

factor. Many Vins de Pays d'Oc are merely average in quality, with decent flavors and small price tags. On the other hand, a few of the most creative and personality-driven wines of the region are also Vins de Pays d'Oc. Among the most famous are the single most renowned wines of the Languedoc-Roussillon: those from the estate Mas de Daumas Gassac, some of which cost as much as top Bordeaux.

## THE LAND, THE GRAPES, AND THE VINEYARDS

The majority of the vineyards of the Languedoc are planted on a curved plain that forms a giant, sunny semicircle facing the Mediterranean Sea. In so dependably warm a climate the best wines generally come from vineyards where the yields are kept low. Many of the top vineyards, however, are not on the plain but are planted on higher, cooler plateaus or along the foothills of the Pyrenees or the Cévennes Mountains.

le p'tit Grain de Sauvignon

Vin de Pays d'Oc
Mis en bouteille au Domaine de Gourgazaud
34210 La Livinière - France
e 75 cl    PRODUCE DE FRANCE  12 % alc./vol.

297

The soil of the Languedoc varies. Near the sea it tends to be alluvial; farther inland, there's more chalk, gravel, and limestone. Some of the best vineyards are filled with round, ancient riverbed stones, similar to those in Châteauneuf-du-Pape.

Before phylloxera invaded southern France in the latter part of the nineteenth century, the Languedoc-Roussillon was home to more than 150 different varieties of grapes. Today more than thirty grape varieties still grow here, but the lesser grapes that once dominated production—aramon, macabeo, and the like—have been in a free-

## THE GRAPES OF
# LANGUEDOC-ROUSSILLON

### WHITES

**Bourboulenc, Clairette, Grenache Blanc, Picpoul, Marsanne, Rolle,** and **Roussanne:** Used in numerous traditional white wines throughout the region. When yields are low and winemaking is skillful, blends of these grapes can be delicious.

**Chardonnay:** Major grape for international style Vin de Pays d'Oc. Also used in the traditional sparkling wine Crémant de Limoux.

**Chenin Blanc:** Minor grape used primarily in the traditional sparkling wine Crémant de Limoux.

**Mauzac:** Native Languedoc grape used mainly in the sparkling wines Blanquette de Limoux and Crémant de Limoux.

**Muscat Blanc à Petits Grains:** Considered the greatest of the muscat grapes in terms of quality. Used to make the sweet fortified wines muscat de Frontignan and muscat de St.-Jean-de-Minervois.

**Muscat of Alexandria:** Part of the family of muscat grapes. Considered less prestigious than muscat blanc à petits grains. Used to make the popular sweet fortified wine muscat de Rivesaltes.

**Sauvignon Blanc:** Used for international style Vin de Pays d'Oc.

**Viognier:** Major grape. Source of some of the best white Vin de Pays d'Oc.

### REDS

**Cabernet Sauvignon:** Major grape. Used for high-quality Vin de Pays d'Oc.

**Carignan:** Major grape. Used in numerous traditional red wines including Corbières, Faugères, Fitou, Minervois, and others.

**Cinsaut:** Workhorse grape used in inexpensive traditional red table wines and rosés.

**Grenache:** Major grape. Used for blending in traditional dry red wines but also famous as the principal grape in the renowned sweet fortified red wine Banyuls.

**Lladoner Pelut, Picpoul Noir,** and **Terret Noir:** Minor grapes. Used in small amounts in traditional reds and rosés, though plantings are on the decline.

**Merlot:** Major grape for international style Vin de Pays d'Oc.

**Mourvèdre:** Major grape. Used in numerous traditional red wines, including Corbières, Faugères, Fitou, Minervois, and others.

**Syrah:** Major grape. Used in numerous modern and traditional red wines, including those of Corbières, Faugères, Fitou, Minervois, and others.

fall decline for more than a decade. Meanwhile, well-regarded Mediterranean varieties, such as syrah, mourvèdre, and grenache, are on a dramatic rise, and international varieties, such as chardonnay, cabernet sauvignon, and merlot, are being planted with furious speed. In 1968 there was no merlot in the Languedoc. By 1999, there were more than 8,400 acres of it.

One of the best of the newly planted varieties is viognier, the traditional white grape of Condrieu in the northern Rhône and a fashionable grape in California. In comparison to Condrieu and California viognier, Languedoc viogniers have flavors that are far less concentrated. Their light honeysuckle and cream flavors, however, make them effortless to drink and at prices about a third of viogniers from elsewhere in the world, they are pretty effortless to buy.

# THE TRADITIONAL DRY WINES OF THE LANGUEDOC

If you go into a simple neighborhood wine shop in Paris, chances are you'll see quite a few shelves sporting wines with the names Corbières, Faugères, Minervois, St.-Chinian, and the large area known as Coteaux de Languedoc. These are the Languedoc's five best-known appellations for dry wines, and because all are relative steals, the shop's proprietor will usually be doing a brisk business in them. Many of these wines will be the products of cooperatives (which the Languedoc has in spades), and they won't be much more than serviceable. The wines from the small producers are generally infinitely better, and more wines from small producers are coming into the United States. (It's worth noting that while the three minor appellations Collioure, Côtes de Roussillon-Villages, and Fitou produce mostly unremarkable wines, you can occasionally uncover some that are real gems.)

As for the major appellations themselves, Corbières, traditionally the highest regarded of the four AOCs, is spread over the undulating northern foothills of the Pyrenees in the western part of the Languedoc-Roussillon. This fairly large region (about 34,000 acres) specializes in dense, juicy, slightly spicy, rustic red blends that often possess that warm sunbaked earth and dried resinous herb quality known as garigue. For most of these wines, carignan is the dominant red variety, followed by syrah and mourvèdre, although many wines will also contain southern France's other usual suspects—grenache, cinsaut, terret noir, and so forth. Using the same grapes, Corbières is also made as a rosé wine, although only a small amount is produced. As for white Corbières, of which there's even less than rosé, it's dry, refreshing, and gets the job done. Top small Corbières producers include Domaine de Grand Cres and Château Mansenoble.

Faugères is about one eighth the size of Corbières and makes only red wines. The wine-growing area itself is in the hills north of the little town of Béziers, more or less in the center of the Languedoc-Roussillon. Here carignan is again typically the leading grape, and it can produce great results if the vines are old and the yields low. With it syrah, mourvèdre, and/or grenache are blended to make wines that at their best taste spicy, earthy, and powerful. Faugères' top producer is Gilbert Alquier.

North of Corbières in the hilly western Languedoc, Minervois (about 12,000 acres)

*Though many white grapes are grown in the Languedoc-Roussillon (and made into some surprisingly good wines), the region is still best known for its traditional rustic red wines.*

## COOPERATIVE CLOUT

———⚜———

There are some five hundred cooperatives in the Languedoc (one in every village), and their winemaking standards vary from quite high to pathetically low. One of the largest (and best) of these is the "super-co-op" Les Vignerons du Val d'Orbieu, a collective of smaller co-ops plus 190 growers. The collective produces well over half a billion bottles of wine a year, making it one of the largest producers in France.

is known for reasonably priced red wines that can be little more than soft and juicy or can be totally outrageous. The outrageous ones come from a subdistrict called La Livinière, which is up in the rocky hills above the flat plateau. (The words *La Livinière* will appear on the labels of these fantastic wines.) Here, old low-yield vines of carignan, along with grenache, syrah, and other southern French varieties are made

into wines that are dense, rich, and for all the world, taste like blackberry syrup poured over stones. Some basic, serviceable rosés and whites are also made, but red is where the action is. Among the best producers here are Château de Gourgazaud, Château Massamier la Mignarde, and Domaine la Combe Blanche.

Between Minervois and Faugères lies the small (about 6,000 acres) red wine appellation of St.-Chinian. From the northern part of the region come gutsy red wines with sharp-edged grip, while wines from the southern part are far softer and less well defined. As in Minervois, the reason is related to altitude, yield, and, here, soil. The north's higher vineyards grow on schist, while the vineyards in the south, lower in altitude, grow in clay. As is true in Corbières, Faugères, and Minervois, carignan is still a major player in the blends here, but increasingly it is being supplanted by syrah, grenache, and mourvèdre. Look for the producers Canet Valette and Château Maurel Fonsalade.

Finally, there's Coteaux de Languedoc, an extensive appellation covering more

*Grapes for the Languedoc's* vins doux naturels *remain on the vine until they are so ripe they almost threaten to become raisins.*

than 20,000 acres. A lot of pretty wishy-washy *vin ordinaire* is made here, but nonetheless the Coteaux de Languedoc deserves your attention because there are real gems here, too. These come from a number of subdistricts that (as of this writing) haven't yet received their own appellations, but they undoubtedly will. The wines from these subdistricts can be packed with dense blackberryish fruit and suffused with licorcey, gamy, stony aromas and flavors. The subdistricts to look for (their names will appear on the label) are, above all, Pic St.-Loup, plus La Clape, Picpoul de Pinet, Montpeyroux, and St.-Saturnin. If you come across a Pic St.-Loup from Clos Marie, Château de la Lancyre, or Château la Roque, buy it.

## THE SWEET FORTIFIED WINES OF THE LANGUEDOC

The Languedoc has a long tradition of producing sweet fortified wines, which are known collectively as *vins doux naturels*—naturally sweet wines. The term, however, is somewhat inexplicable since these "naturally sweet" wines actually achieve their sweetness by being fortified with clear brandy (grape spirits) in order to stop fermentation early, thereby leaving the sweetness in the wines.

Several of the best-known *vins doux naturels* are based on muscat grapes, including the locally famous wines muscat de Frontignan, muscat de Rivesaltes, and muscat de St.-Jean-de-Minervois. Muscat is actually not a single grape but a large family of related grapes that have grown throughout the Mediterranean since ancient times. The oldest and most renowned of these is muscat blanc à petits grains, which was cultivated by the

Romans around the historic cities of Narbonne and Frontignan on the Languedoc coast. Muscat de Frontignan and muscat de St.-Jean-de-Minervois are made with muscat blanc à petits grains, but muscat de Rivesaltes, the muscat wine produced in the largest quantities, is made with the somewhat less distinguished grape muscat of Alexandria.

Although the muscats are the most pervasive of the Languedoc's *vins doux naturels*, the most exciting sweet fortified wine is Banyuls, a reddish-colored wine made principally from grenache. Port might spring to mind when you think about sweet fortified reds, but Banyuls is anything but portly. Neither massive in size nor dense in texture, it's deceptively (even dangerously) easy to drink thanks to its heady flavors of coffee, chestnut, mocha, and tea, which can be irresistible.

Most *vins doux naturels* taste both more alcoholic and less sweet than they really are. They tend to have an alcohol content of 16 to 17 percent and usually have 8 to 10 percent residual sugar. (Sauternes has about the same residual sugar: 8 to 12 percent.) In the past, *vins doux naturels* were often drunk as hearty aperitifs; today they are more commonly drunk with (or as) dessert. *Vins doux naturels* are not widely or consistently available in the United States. You may come across one from any of a number of different producers; they are all fun to try.

## CRÉMANT DE LIMOUX

The word *crémant* is used to describe a French sparkling wine that is made outside the Champagne district but according to the Champagne method. *Crémants* come from all over France; some of the best

## THE CAPITAL OF
## MUSSELS

Culinarily speaking, the Languedoc is not as famous as its next-
door neighbor Provence with perhaps
one exception: mussels. The Languedoc's tiny hamlet of Bouzigues near the
town of Sète is considered the unofficial
mussel capital of France. Bouzigues, in
fact, is really just a string of no-frills
seafood cafés that jut out over the glistening blue saltwater lagoon called
Bassin de Thau. Here in the lagoon's
slow-moving current, fat juicy mussels
are cultivated in special nets or clinging
to wooden frames. In just about every
café, the mussels show up, often strewn
with bits of grilled sausage, along with
bottles of red Corbières, Faugères,
Minervois, and St.-Chinian. While on
first consideration mussels may seem
exclusively white wine fare, the cafés of
Bouzigues prove otherwise. Juicy, rustic
Languedoc reds, with their supple,
earthy, slightly spicy flavors, can be real
winners in this combination.

known include Crémant d'Alsace, Crémant
de Bourgogne, Crémant de Loire, *and*
Crémant de Limoux.

Crémants de Limoux are simple, tasty
sparkling wines made in some forty-one
small villages surrounding the town of
Limoux. The wines are made from the local
grape mauzac, which can constitute up to
70 percent of the wine and chardonnay or
chenin blanc, which form no less than 30
percent. Crémant de Limoux must spend at
least a year aging on the yeast lees.

A more traditional style of sparkling
Limoux is called Blanquette de Limoux. It
is made by the Champagne method but
consists entirely of mauzac and is aged
three months less than *crémant*. I wish
that, instead of describing vinification
details, I could simply say go out and buy
this or that Crémant or Blanquette, but it
isn't that easy. These wines are made by
scores of small producers whose wines
are imported, but erratically. It's simply
best to give the wines a try—whatever
producers you come across—and if you
find one you like, buy several bottles.
Lastly, the appellation Limoux (not
Crémant de or Blanquette de) is a still, not
sparkling, white wine made from chardonnay. It's not particularly moving.

## VISITING THE
## WINERIES OF
## THE LANGUEDOC-
## ROUSSILLON

The Languedoc-Roussillon is, like its
neighbor Provence, an ancient, rural
region that piques one's wanderlust.
There are no grand châteaux with polished equipment and formal tasting
rooms. Most wineries are small, humble
affairs where, chances are, you'll be taken
into the cellar by the owner and handed a
glass of wine straight from the barrel. I've
included some wineries here that are particularly fun to visit. The Languedoc is
also packed with cooperatives. Virtually
every village has one, and visiting it is
important for a balanced sense of winemaking in the region. For small wineries,
appointments are necessary. At some
only French is spoken. The telephone
numbers include the dialing code you'll
need when calling from the United States.
If you're calling from within France, eliminate the 011-33 and add a zero before the
next number.

**CHÂTEAU LASTOURS**
Portels des Corbières
011-33-4-68-48-29-17

**CHÂTEAU VILLERAMBERT-JULIEN**
Caunes Minervois
011-33-4-68-78-00-01

**DOMAINE DE GOURGAZAUD**
La Livinière
011-33-4-68-78-30-24

**DOMAINE DE L'ARJOLLE**
Pouzolles
011-33-4-67-24-81-18

**FORTANT DE FRANCE**
278 Avenue Marechal Juin
Sète
011-33-4-67-46-70-23

Above all, no trip to the Languedoc would be complete without visiting the ancient Mediterranean cities of Narbonne, Carcassonne, Béziers, Collioure, Céret, and Nîmes. And another must: visiting the tiny coastal village of Bouzigues near Sète, where extraordinary oysters and mussels are farmed in saltwater lagoons. The only establishments in Bouzigues are no-frills seafood cafés where the platters of shellfish are incomparable.

*Unabashedly modern, Fortant de France is one of the leading wine companies making international-style Vins de Pays d'Oc.*

**CHÂTEAU DE L'ENGARRAN**
Laverune
011-33-4-67-47-00-02

**CHÂTEAU DE L'HOSPITALET**
Route de Narbonne Plage
Narbonne
011-33-4-68-45-34-47

**GILBERT ALQUIER**
4 Route de Pezenes les Mines
Faugères
011-33-4-67-95-00-87

**LES VIGNERONS DU VAL D'ORBIEU**
This astoundingly large, progressive cooperative is made up of many facilities, several of which can be visited. For information, call 011-33-4-68-42-38-77.

# THE LANGUEDOC-ROUSSILLON
## WINES TO KNOW

The appellation Vin de Pays d'Oc is a regional appellation that contains dozens of smaller appellations, including Vin de Pays de l'Hérault, Vin de Pays des Côtes de Thongue, and Vin de Pays du Mont Baudile, examples of each of which you'll find here.

## *Whites*

### CHAIS BAUMIERE

Sauvignon Blanc

La Baume

Vin de Pays d'Oc

100% sauvignon blanc

This is the kind of zingy sauvignon blanc that sauvignon purists love. Packed with snappy hay and grapefruit flavors, it ends in a terrific crescendo of wild herbs. Just waiting to be drunk with the herb-and-garlic-infused dishes of the south of France.

### DOMAINE DE GOURGAZAUD

Viognier

Vin de Pays d'Oc

100% viognier

Domaine de Gourgazaud makes intense wines, including the plushest viognier in the Languedoc. In good and great vintages this wine oozes with exotic honey flavors and is easy on the pocketbook besides. The old domaine, which dates from the seventeenth century, is set in the foothills of the Montagne Noire above Minervois.

### MAS DE DAUMAS GASSAC

Blanc

Vin de Pays de l'Hérault

approximately a third each chardonnay, viognier, and petit manseng, plus muscat, marsanne, and roussanne

One of the most remarkable Mediterranean white wines. The richness of chardonnay and the exoticness of viognier make a powerful duo, yet the wine possesses an uncanny elegance. The vibrant fruit flavors are classy and the finish is usually hauntingly long.

## *Reds*

### CHATEAU MASSAMIER LA MIGNARDE

Domus Maximus

Minervois La Livinière

80% syrah, 20% grenache

One sip of this incredibly long-on-the-palate wine with its saturated, ripe boysenberry and chocolate-like flavors, soaring structure, and aroma of black earth and stones makes you realize that the tiny area of Minervois called La Livinière is one of the best-kept secrets of the Languedoc. With one sip, the taste buds reel and the mind leaps to lamb shanks or long-simmered stew made with a bottle of this wine. Domus Maximus is made by Château Massamier la Mignarde, a producer to watch.

### DOMAINE D'AUPILHAC

Carignan

Vin de Pays du Mont Baudile

100% carignan

Here's what a supposedly less distinguished grape—namely, carignan—can do in the hands of the right producer. Made entirely from very old carignan vines grown at low yields, Domaine d'Aupilhac's wine has the classic suppleness of traditional southern French reds. The soft licoricey and menthol flavors are beautifully mellow and full of garigue.

## DOMAINE DE L'ARJOLLE

Cabernet de l'Arjolle

Vin de Pays des Côtes de Thongue

100% cabernet sauvignon

If you didn't see the label that reads Languedoc, you'd swear it's a Bordeaux for its great structure, gorgeous balance, rich minty and cassis flavors. Domaine de l'Arjolle is a good example of one of the small, dynamic, family-run estates now making some of the best wines in the Languedoc.

## DOMAINE DE L'HORTUS

Classique

Coteaux du Languedoc

approximately 50% syrah, 30% grenache, and 20% mourvèdre

Domaine de l'Hortus is known for soft, thick, minty reds with waves of garigue and the scent of woodlands floating through them. Their wine comes into your mouth with a big arc of flavor and finishes with a licoricey bang. The domaine is a family estate lying in a valley between two facing limestone cliffs near the village of Pic-St.-Loup. The word *hortus* is Latin for garden.

## GILBERT ALQUIER & FILS

Faugères

approximately one third each syrah, mourvèdre, and grenache

Some of the most elegant, beautifully focused red wines in the Languedoc come from the schist hillsides of Faugères, inland from the coast. Gilbert Alquier's Faugères is full of graceful black currant, violet, and mint flavors, all laced with spicy garigue. Perfect to go with a Mediterranean dish full of garlic, tomatoes, and olive oil.

## LES VIGNERONS DU VAL D'ORBIEU

La Cuvée Mythique

Vin de Pays d'Oc

approximately one quarter each syrah, mourvèdre, grenache, and carignan, plus a tiny amount of cabernet sauvignon

305

A very good southern French wine from a century ago might very well have tasted like La Cuvée Mythique, a deliciously rustic wine indelibly stamped with wild hints of garigue plus warm berries, violets, cedar, and licorice. This is the top wine of the Val d'Orbieu cooperative. To make it, more than a hundred separate wines are considered before the final blend is drawn from only the best small lots.

## *Sweet Wine*

## LA CAVE DES VIGNERONS DE ST.-JEAN-DE-MINERVOIS

Muscat de St.-Jean-de-Minervois

100% muscat blanc à petits grains

A hedonistic sweet *vin doux naturel*— light, sweet peaches leap out of the glass. Excellent dessert wines such as this are common in the Languedoc, but most are not, as this one is, made by a cooperative, nor are they as easy on the pocketbook.

# Provence

Les Apilles (the little Alps), a chain of rocky limestone outcroppings, protect vineyards in Les Baux de Provence from fierce northern winds.

The word *Provence* induces hunger, not thirst. One hardly thinks of wine at all, except as something to brace you for the oncoming wave of a great, garlicky aioli. It's not that the wines of Provence do not deserve attention. The problem is getting sidetracked by bouillabaisse—or by landscapes so beautiful that van Gogh, Renoir, Matisse, Picasso, and Cézanne could not stop painting them. Yet Provence's wines are both special and delicious. Provençal rosés (what everyone drinks with the local cuisine) are famous for their refreshing slash of flavor. The region's reds—bold, concentrated, and distinctive—are creating a surge of new excitement. And although the quality of the white wines ranges across the

Roman artifacts, some of them—like this ancient amphora—beautifully intact, are found all over the Provençal countryside.

board, the best of them are perfect with a plate of grilled fish.

Provence encompasses the vast, rambling countryside of far southeastern France. In fact, one can't get any farther south, for Provence dead-ends on the beaches of the French Riviera. From the coast with its famous seaside towns of Marseille, Bandol, and St.-Tropez, Provence extends inland. How far is hard to say. The French often define the region by its remarkable landscape—which is to say, by the presence of garigue. The word describes the character of the land: parched, low rolling limestone hills covered in dry scrub with tough, resiny plants: wild rosemary, wild thyme, lavender, and half-decayed green oaks. Even the sunbaked earth seems to have a perfume of its own.

It's a landscape that extends far enough north that parts of the southern Rhône are sometimes also considered *en Provence*. Most important of all, the landscape seems, in a surreal way, to reverberate through the wines themselves. The best Provençal wines are said to smell and taste of garique.

*The Romans called this region* nostra provincia, *our province, hence Provence.*

Provence's four most important wine appellations all fall in the far south, with some bordering on the Mediterranean. They are: Bandol, Cassis, Coteaux d'Aix-en-Provence (and its terrific tiny subregion Les Baux de Provence), and Côtes de Provence. Bandol is the most prestigious; Côtes de Provence, the largest.

Provence is a candy store of grape varieties. The eclectic hodgepodge of grapes reflects the region's rich history and political affiliations with just about every Mediterranean power, large and small. Most of the Rhône grapes are grown, as well as traditional Provençal grapes and even Italian grapes, such as vermentino, and northern grapes, such as cabernet sauvignon.

The climate of Provence is dramatic. The sun (3,000 hours of sunlight a year!) bounces off the land and sea, creating an almost relentless light—no wonder painters love it. As in the Rhône, the aggressive wind from the north, *le mistral*, cools the vines and helps prevent rot, but it can also tear the vines apart. The best vineyards are therefore located in protected pockets, mostly facing south toward the Mediterranean, with the hills at their backs.

In this ancient, impoverished soil, many crops would fare badly. But grapevines and olive trees thrive. Patches of limestone, schist, and quartz are scattered throughout the thin, rocky soil along the coast. Farther inland the soil also contains clay and pebbly sand.

Provence's wines have always played a supporting role to the mesmerizingly delicious local dishes. In fact, until recently, wine more or less took a backseat. Food was the real (and only) star. This is now changing, but there's another phenomenon at work, too: Provençal food has a startling effect on Provençal wine.

## TOUJOURS AIOLI

In Provence, aioli—a velvety, super-garlicky, homemade mayonnaise—is the traditional focus of holiday feasts. It is made with so much fresh garlic that around holidays local dentists have been known to hang signs on their doors reading *Fermé à Cause d'Aïoli,* Closed Due to Aioli.

Over and over again wine professionals report being unimpressed by Provençal wines, only to change their minds when they have had those same wines with local dishes. Just romance? Maybe. Or maybe the wild herb garigue flavors in the food are a catalyst for those flavors in the wine. Whatever the reason, Provençal foods do throw the switch that makes Provençal wines come alive.

## BANDOL

The best appellation in Provence, Bandol is a relatively small seaside region about a 30-mile drive southeast from the center of Marseille. The best Bandol rosés usually have a higher percentage of spicy, structured mourvèdre than less well favored examples. Such rosés as Domaines Ott's Cuvée Marine, for example, are so vibrant and so full of powerful, earthy, strawberry flavors that they easily rival the Tavels of the Rhône. But red wines are where the real action is. These are deep, wild, leathery, spicy wines. By law, they must be 50 percent mourvèdre, and some producers use as much as 100 percent.

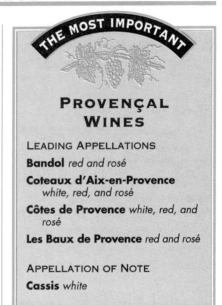

### THE MOST IMPORTANT

## PROVENÇAL WINES

**LEADING APPELLATIONS**

**Bandol** red and rosé

**Coteaux d'Aix-en-Provence**
white, red, and rosé

**Côtes de Provence** white, red, and rosé

**Les Baux de Provence** red and rosé

**APPELLATION OF NOTE**

**Cassis** white

There are dozens of small producers in Bandol, as well as cooperatives. The most famous producer is Domaine Tempier, owned by the ebullient Peyraud family. Like characters out of a novel, the Peyrauds not only make some of Provence's most ravishing red and rosé wines but they are also among the region's best cooks. The matriarch of the family, Lulu Peyraud, was a mentor for the famous California chef Alice Waters.

*Lulu Peyraud of Domaine Tempier, one of the legendary cooks of Provence, in her kitchen in Bandol (left). Grilling baskets are lined up over Peyraud's fireplace, ready for use.*

## COTEAUX D'AIX-EN-PROVENCE

The old town of Aix, in the heart of Provence, has always been a favorite home base for tourists, since making day trips from here is easy. North and west of Aix is the wine region of Coteaux d'Aix-en-Provence. At about 8,000 acres, it's roughly twenty times larger than Cassis. Within this large appellation is a smaller, renowned subappellation known as Les Baux de Provence. Here the limestone soils and hot days are perfect for red grapes (the surrounding valley is known as the Val d'Enfer—valley of hell).

The best wines are indeed red and are made, remarkably, from cabernet sauvignon, plus syrah, cinsaut, mourvèdre, and grenache. Cabernet is a big surprise for it's not a Mediterranean grape and is extremely rare in other parts of Provence and nonexistent in the Rhône. Less white and rosé wine is made in Coteaux d'Aix. What is, is made from Rhône varieties plus chardonnay, sauvignon blanc, and sémillon. There are some surprisingly good ones.

*The mixture sold as herbes de Provence varies with the packager although it almost always includes the popular Provençal herbs thyme, rosemary, bay leaf, savory, and marjoram.*

The top producers here are Mas de la Dame, Domaine de Trévallon, and Château

## THE PROVENÇAL KITCHEN

**Aioli:** A thick, very garlicky homemade mayonnaise.

**Bouillabaisse:** A heady, saffron-infused fish stew, traditionally containing rockfish, John Dory, conger eel, lotte de mer, red mullet, whiting, sea perch, and spiny lobster, crabs, and other shellfish and served with aioli and rouille.

**Bourride:** A thick, white-wine based fish soup, pungent wth garlic, onions, orange peel, and sometimes saffron.

**Brandade:** A purée of salt cod, olive oil, milk, garlic, and cream.

**Fougasse:** Flat bread baked with herbs.

**Glace de Lavande:** Vanilla ice cream flavored with lavender.

**Lotte de Mer:** Monkfish.

**Loup:** Sea bass.

**Pan-bagnat:** A large sandwich of tomatoes, anchovies, and olives.

**Pieds Paquets:** Sheep's tripe stuffed with sheep's feet and simmered in white wine.

**Pissaladière:** An anchovy, tomato, olive, and onion tart that bears a strong resemblance to pizza.

**Pistou:** A vegetable and basil soup.

**Ratatouille:** A stewlike mixture of zucchini, peppers, eggplant, and garlic.

**Rouget:** Red mullet.

**Rouille:** Aioli flavored with Spanish peppers to make it piquant.

**Tapenade:** A thick purée of black olives, anchovies, and capers.

## THE GRAPES OF
# PROVENCE

Provençal wines have historically been blends of many grape varieties that on their own would be undistinguished.

### WHITES

**Bourboulenc** and **Rolle:** Grapes commonly used in blending. Rustic and undistinguished on their own.

**Chardonnay, Marsanne, Sauvignon Blanc, Sémillon,** and **Viognier:** Commonly used in blends, especially in more modern avant-garde wines.

**Clairette** and **Grenache Blanc:** Very common blending grapes in traditional white wines.

**Ugni Blanc:** Very common, if undistinguished, blending grape.

### REDS

**Braquet, Calitor, Carignan, Cinsaut, Folle Noire,** and **Tibouren:** Grapes used in blending. At low yields, carignan can have real character and cinsault is a major force in many rosés.

**Cabernet Sauvignon:** Used in some of the best reds and rosés, especially in the appellations Coteaux d'Aix-en-Provence and Côtes de Provence.

**Grenache:** Common blending grape used in many reds and most rosés. Can add delicious jammy flavors.

**Mourvèdre:** Major grape, used in many of the top reds and rosés for structure.

**Syrah:** Fairly minor grape in Provence but used in some of the very best reds.

Vignelaure. It was the former owner of Château Vignelaure, Georges Brunet, who, among others, brought cabernet sauvignon to Provence from Bordeaux in the 1960s. Brunet had once owned Château La Lagune.

# CÔTES DE PROVENCE

Like Côtes-du-Rhône, the appellation Côtes de Provence is not a single place but rather many vast tracts (about 44,000 acres in all) of noncontiguous vineyards. These are found in every part of Provence except the west. Côtes de Provence wines are therefore the product of numerous small individual climates and terrains. Not surprisingly, they range a lot in quality.

About three quarters of the wine is dry rosé, based on grenache, cinsaut, and the local red grape tibouren. A lion's share of this is simply chugalug co-op pink. But there are also a few fine estates concentrating on making serious rosés, as well as full-bodied reds, based increasingly on cabernet sauvignon or syrah.

The most famous and largest of the top estates is the family-owned firm of Domaines Ott, the wines of which are sold in unique amphora-shaped (some say bowling-pin-shaped) bottles. The Otts own several properties in the Côtes de Provence, plus one in Bandol. Though white wines are fairly rare in the Côtes de Provence, the Otts make three, as well as two earthy, spicy reds. But most famous are the Ott rosés. The regular one, called Clair de Noirs, is a wine you could easily drink all summer long, and the sharper, more bracing one, called La Déesse, is just waiting for any food slathered in aioli. Widely available in the United States, the Domaines Ott rosés have become favorites among Americans who need a south-of-France fix.

## CASSIS

The cassis most of us first knew is a black currant liqueur, which, when added to white wine, makes an aperitif called a Kir. Though the names are the same, Cassis, the wine region, has nothing to do with the liqueur. A popular (but not major) appellation of Provence, Cassis is a charming small fishing village, a few miles southeast of Marseille. Stories are told about the prostitutes of Marseille who, in times past, helped pick the grapes at harvest. Surrounding the fishing village are the vineyards, fewer than 400 acres in all.

The white wine of Cassis, made principally from clairette and marsanne grapes, is much more prevalent and popular than its red or rosé usually made from mourvèdre and grenache. The best whites are broad, dry wines that don't have a lot to say on their own but manage to be perfect for washing down whatever *fruits de mer* the local fishermen caught that day, no matter with how much garlic they're cooked.

## VISITING PROVENÇAL WINE ESTATES

Provence is undoubtedly one of the world's most charming wine regions. Wine lovers have been known to take weeks simply crisscrossing the countryside, visiting wine estates and feasting in local restaurants. Though this is a small chapter, I've suggested quite a few wineries so you'll be ready should wanderlust strike. Most Provençal wine estates are small and fairly humble. Sometimes the owner himself or a member of the family will take you around. It's necessary to make an appointment in advance and very helpful to speak French. The telephone numbers include the dialing code you'll need when calling from the United States. If you're calling from within France, eliminate the 011-33 and add a zero before the next number.

### BANDOL

**CHÂTEAU DE PIBARNON**
83740 La Cadière-d'Azur
011-33-4-94-90-12-73

**DOMAINE RAY-JANE**
83330 Le Plan-du-Castellet
011-33-4-94-98-64-08

**DOMAINE TEMPIER**
83330 Le Plan-du-Castellet
011-33-4-94-98-70-21

**DOMAINES OTT CHÂTEAU ROMASSAN**
83330 Le Plan-du-Castellet
011-33-4-94-98-71-91

### CASSIS

**CLOS SAINTE-MAGDELEINE**
Avenue du Revestel
13620 Cassis
011-33-4-42-01-70-28

### CÔTES DE PROVENCE

**DOMAINE RICHEAUME**
13114 Puyloubier
011-33-4-42-66-31-27

**DOMAINE SAINT-ANDRÉ-DE-FIGUIÈRE**
Quartier Saint-Honoré
83250 La Londe-les-Maures
011-33-4-94-66-92-10

**DOMAINES OTT CHÂTEAU DE SELLE**
Route Departementale 73
83460 Taradeaux
011-33-4-94-68-86-86

### LES BAUX DE PROVENCE

**MAS DE LA DAME**
13520 Les Baux de Provence
011-33-4-90-54-32-24

# THE PROVENÇAL WINES TO KNOW

## White

### ROUTAS

Coquelicot

Vin de Pays du Var

approximately 50% viognier, 50% chardonnay

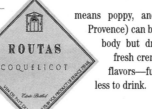

At its best, Routas' Coquelicot is summer in a glass. Coquelicot (the name means poppy, and poppies abound in Provence) can be as light as a feather in body but dripping with delicious, fresh crenshaw melon and lemon flavors—full of charm and effortless to drink.

## Rosés

### DOMAINES OTT

Château de Selle, La Déesse Rosé

Côtes de Provence

approximately 65% cinsaut, 35% cabernet sauvignon

The family-owned firm of Domaines Ott is undoubtedly the best-known producer in Provence. From three separate estates the firm makes earthy, spicy reds; full-bodied whites that pair well with local seafood dishes; and best of all, three delicious dry rosés. The most elegant of the bunch, La Déesse, is a bracing, spicy wine that has hints of *herbes de Provence*.

### DOMAINE TEMPIER

Bandol

approximately 40% mourvèdre, 25% grenache, 30% cinsaut

The color of this wine—almost copper—is the first tip-off that it's not going to be your standard cotton-candyish, flaccid, high-alcohol rosé. No, this boldly focused wine smells and tastes so much of warm earth, haystacks, and dried wild herbs that your mind leaps to images of paintings by Vincent van Gogh.

---

## RETHINKING ROSÉ

If there's a lesson in matching wine and food to learn from Provence, it's the amazing versatility of snappy, boldly fruity rosés in complementing countless Mediterranean dishes. In particular, Provençal rosés are delicious with the region's seafood dishes, seasoned as they usually are with generous amounts of olive oil, garlic, herbs, and spices. The supreme example is bouillabaisse, the traditional Provençal fish stew flavored with olive oil, saffron, and dried orange peel and then usually served with croutons and rouille, a supergarlicky, pepper-spiked mayonnaise. The flavor of many wines would disappear or be distorted by such dramatic ingredients. Not so with Provençal rosés. Boldly fruity and substantial in body, they are tailor-made for bouillabaisse and other hearty seafood dishes.

# *Reds*

## DOMAINE DE TREVALLON

Vin de Pays des Bouches du Rhône

approximately 50% cabernet sauvignon,
50% syrah

This absolutely scrumptious and legendary wine is not to be missed. Black, thick, and silky, in most years it's got an almost hauntingly masculine, sweaty, earthy aroma. The flavors all suggest wildness—wild blackberries and brambles; wild resiny herbs; wild tangles of dried brush; wild exotic spices. Domaine de Trévallon's vineyards are surrounded by the eerie desolate landscape of the Val d'Enfer. The domaine specializes in cabernet sauvignon, which here turns into wines as startling and dramatic as the land itself.

## DOMAINE TEMPIER

Classique

Bandol

approximately 50% mourvèdre,
35% grenache, plus small amounts of cinsaut
and carignan

The flagship red wine of the famous Domaine Tempier in Bandol reminds you of how full of vibrant flavor Provençal reds can be. Were cinnamon, mint, and chocolate-covered cherries accidentally dropped into the fermenting vat? Often there's also a scrumptious bolt of licorice and black pepper running through the wine. The Peyraud family, which owns Domaine Tempier, was the original driving force behind the making of high-quality wines—especially reds—in Provence.

## MAS DE LA DAME

Coin Caché

Les Baux de Provence

80% grenache, 20% syrah

From the centuries-old Mas de la Dame (farm of the woman) comes this sensational, juicy, full-bodied, full-blooded wine suggestive of leather, bitter chocolate, and ripe blackberries. Coin Caché (hidden corner in French) comes from vineyards that lie sheltered in the protective arc created by Les Apilles (little Alps), a range of small chalky mountains. It's a serene spot. In fact, according to the sixteenth-century French physician and astrologer Nostradamus, when the world ends, the water that will cover the earth will stop at Mas de la Dame.

## PASTIS

The most well-loved aperitif in Provence is pastis, a greenish-yellow licorice-flavored liqueur served with a carafe of ice water. When the water is added to the pastis, the drink immediately turns ominously cloudy. The licoricey forerunner of pastis, absinthe, was outlawed by the French government in 1915 because of the toxicity of the wormwood leaves from which it was made. Pastis, which is not toxic, is made by infusing either licorice or aniseed in a distilled spirit.

# SOMMELIERS

During the French Renaissance, a sommelier bought the title and paid to become part of the retinue of the king or a nobleman. The sommelier, responsible for stocking food and wine for journeys, kept the provisions in a carriage called a *somme*. Simply stocking provisions, however, was not the sommelier's most important job; ensuring the condition of the perishables was. He did this rather riskily by taking a bite of each food and a sip of each wine before it was presented to his lord. If the food or wine had been poisoned by an enemy, the sommelier was the first to know.

Today in the United States, the word *sommelier* sometimes evokes caricatures of tuxedo-clad, *tastevin*-necklaced, arch-eyebrowed wine advisors who skillfully intimidate restaurant customers into buying superexpensive wines. By the 1980s this image had become so offensive that most American sommeliers refused to wear tuxedoes, abandoned *tastevins,* and began calling themselves wine buyers or wine stewards, rather than using the French term.

A modern American wine buyer/sommelier chooses the wines, stocks the restaurant's cellar, monitors the inventory, conducts wine training sessions for other members of the staff, and works in the dining room recommending wines.

Wine buyers/sommeliers are paid a salary by the restaurant and sometimes get a small percentage of the revenue derived from wine sales. They generally do not expect to be tipped, although tipping (5 to 10 percent of the bottle price) may be in order if the sommelier has introduced you to an especially remarkable wine that you would not have otherwise discovered.

Although increasingly restaurants all over the world employ sommeliers, it's no surprise that Italy, where the passion for wine and food borders on religious, has more than any other country (including France)—some 8,000 individuals, according to the Italian Trade Commission. In the United States and Great Britain sommeliers often aspire to attain the prestigious Master Sommelier degree awarded by the Court of Master Sommeliers headquartered in London. To earn the title Master Sommelier (which has been awarded in the United States only since 1987), sommeliers must pass a daunting three-day tasting and written exam. As of 2000, there were forty-two Master Sommeliers in the United States, ten of them women.

# Italy

*The ancient Greeks called Italy Oenotria,
the land of wine.*

I n Italy, making wine—like eating or breathing—is so utterly natural it almost seems instinctive. Grapevines grow everywhere; they are Italy's version of the American lawn. There is simply no region, no district, virtually no cranny of the country that does not produce wine. The numbers are astonishing: 900,000 registered vineyards are scattered throughout Italy's twenty regions. From these vineyards come a dizzying number of wines (no one knows precisely how many) based on more than a thousand documented grape varieties.

Wine at this order of magnitude can seem unfathomable—especially if your experience revolves around, say, a half dozen chardonnays and cabernets. Of course, not all of these wines are considered of major importance. Many Italian wines are just simple quaffing wines and scores of others are consumed almost entirely in or near the villages where they are made.

The Italian wines that knowledgeable wine drinkers get excited about come predominantly from a few major areas. These include Piedmont, Tuscany, and the three northeastern regions known collectively as the Tre Venezie: Friuli-Venezia Giulia, Trentino-Alto Adige, and the Veneto.

Lovers of Italian wines will also want to know about several other wine regions. These include Lombardy, the source of

| KEY TO ITALY'S WINE REGIONS | |
|---|---|
| **PIEDMONT** | 22 Brunello di |
| 1 Gattinara | Montalcino |
| 2 Ghemme | 23 Vino Nobile di |
| 3 Barbera | Montepulciano |
| 4 Arneis | **UMBRIA** |
| 5 Barbaresco | 24 Torgiano |
| 6 Barolo | 25 Montefalco |
| 7 Dolcetto | 26 Orvieto |
| 8 Asti | **ABRUZZI** |
| 9 Gavi | 27 Montepulciano |
| **LOMBARDY** | d'Abruzzo |
| 10 Valtellina | **APULIA** |
| 11 Franciacorta | **CAMPANIA** |
| 12 Oltrepò Pavese | 28 Greco di Tufo |
| **THE TRE VENEZIE** | 29 Taurasi |
| **TRENTINO-ALTO ADIGE** | 30 Fiano di Avellino |
| **THE VENETO** | **BASILICATA** |
| 13 Prosecco | 31 Aglianico del |
| 14 Bardolino | Vulture |
| 15 Valpolicella | **CALABRIA** |
| 16 Soave | 32 Cirò |
| **FRIULI-VENEZIA GIULIA** | **SICILY** |
| **LIGURIA** | 33 Malvasia delle |
| **EMILIA-ROMAGNA** | Lipari |
| 17 Lambrusco | 34 Marsala |
| 18 Albana di | 35 Moscato di |
| Romagna | Pantelleria |
| **TUSCANY** | **SARDINIA** |
| 19 Carmignano | 36 Vermentino di |
| 20 Chianti | Gallura |
| 21 Vernaccia di San | 37 Vernaccia di |
| Gimignano | Oristano |

some of Italy's best *spumante*; Liguria, the crescent-shaped region known as the Italian Riviera, home to white wines historically paired with fish dishes; and Emilia-Romagna, one of the greatest regions in the world for food and the birthplace of cheerful, fizzy lambrusco. Umbria is home of dry, refreshing Orvietos. Abruzzi is memorable for such soft, thick, mouth-filling reds as montepulciano d'Abruzzo, a wine just waiting to be paired with rustic

AUSTRIA

HUNGARY

SWITZERLAND

THE TRE VENEZIE

Bolzano

N

0       75      150 mi

0    75    150 km

Trentino-
Alto Adige

San
Daniele

Trento

Friuli-
Venezia Giulia

SLOVENIA

ALPS

10

Valdobbiadene

13

Conegliano

CROATIA

VALLE
D'AOSTA

LOMBARDY

11

L.
Garda

14

Mt. Lessini

THE
VENETO

Milan

Adige R.

15 16

Vicenza

Trieste

Verona

Venice

PIEDMONT

1  2

BOSNIA
AND
HERZEGOVINA

Turin

Asti

3

12

Po River

Po   River

4

Alessandria

5

Alba

7 8

9

Parma

17

Modena

6

Dogliani

Genoa

Bologna

EMILIA-ROMAGNA

LIGURIA

18

FRANCE

SAN MARINO

19

Florence

Ligurian
Sea

TUSCANY

20

21

MARCHES

Siena

22 23

UMBRIA

Montalcino

24

Perugia

Montefalco

CORSICA
(Fr.)

26

25

Orvieto

27

Pescara

LATIUM

ABRUZZI

Rome

Adriatic
Sea

APENNINES

Frascati

MOLISE

CAMPANIA

APULIA

Bari

28  29

31

Salento
Peninsula

SARDINIA

36

Naples

30

Mt. Vesuvius

Amalfi
Coast

BASILICATA

37

Capri

Oristano

Tyrrhenian Sea

CALABRIA

32

Cagliari

Ionian
Sea

33

Lipari Is.

Palermo

34

Strait of Sicily

SICILY

TRAPANI

Mediterranean
Sea

TUNISIA

35

Pantelleria
Island

pasta dishes. Finally, there are Italy's most southern regions: Campania, Apulia, Basilicata, and Calabria, plus the islands of Sicily and Sardinia. All are sources for delicious wines that are good values, and several make wines from rare, ancient grape varieties as well.

Though wine and food are inextricably linked in most parts of the world, in Italy they are fervently wedded. Wines that seem slightly lean, tart, or tannic to some Americans are highly appreciated by the Italians precisely because they have the grip and edge to slice through the dauntless flavors of Italian food. But it goes even farther than that. Wine *is* food in Italy. Not so long ago a daily supply of basic village wine cost Italians less than their daily supply of bread, according to Burton Anderson in his authoritative *The Wine Atlas of Italy*. Wine and bread are as essential to an Italian diner as a fork and knife (probably more so). Along with olive oil, they make up what the Italians call the *Santa Trinità Mediterranea*—the Mediterranean Holy Trinity. An Italian friend once summed up the special affinity between Italian wine and food this way: "If someone drinks a little too much wine, the Italians don't say he has drunk too much; they say he hasn't eaten enough food yet."

Italian wines can vary substantially in flavor, texture, and body—even when the wines being compared are the same type. Two Chiantis from estates less than a half mile apart can taste remarkably dissimilar. Some of this variability is due to differences in winemaking, for Italy is a country of fiercely maintained ancient traditions

*Ancient wine vessels, some dating from pre-Roman times, have been found throughout Italy.*

and, at the same time, extremely sophisticated modern methods. But an equally compelling reason is this: Italy is a tangle of different, tiny microclimates that powerfully influence the character of any given wine. As Burton Anderson points out, you can stand on Italian soil and look at the Alps, but you can also stand on Italian soil and look at North Africa.

What creates those microclimates? First, the geography of the land itself. Italy is about 40 percent mountains (even Sicily has them!) and another 40 percent hills. As any drive from one village to the next proves, straight lines don't seem to exist in this country. The combined zigzagging slopes of hills and mountains, plus the close proximity of four seas (the Tyrrhenian, Adriatic, Ligurian, and Mediterranean), plus the geologic impact of numerous earthquakes has produced an almost pointillistic profusion of environments in which grapes grow.

*Of all the wine made worldwide each year, Italy and France together produce more than 30 percent.*

Although Italy's most revered wines are known worldwide, the grape varieties that constitute them are rarely found outside the country. You won't find sangiovese, the leading grape of Chianti, or nebbiolo, the grape that makes Barolo, growing in France, Spain, or Australia. In fact, one of the few countries to embrace Italian varietals has been the United

318

## IS IT A GRAPE OR A PLACE?
## THE ITALIAN CONUNDRUM

O ne of the difficult and somewhat confusing aspects of Italian wine is this: In many regions, wines are sometimes named after the grape variety used to make them and at other times named after the place where the grapes grew. Two of the most important wines in Piedmont, for example, are barbera and Barolo. The wine barbera is named for bar- bera, the grape from which it's made, while the wine Barolo is named after the village of Barolo, its home. To make matters even more complex, the names of some Italian wines (and even some grapes) combine both grape and place. The wine named monte- pulciano d'Abruzzo, for example, pairs montepulciano, the grape, with Abruzzo, the place.

States. There in the late 1980s and early 1990s the so-called Cal/Ital movement took off when dozens of top California vintners began successfully planting some of Italy's best-loved grapes.

The Italians, however, adopted caber- net sauvignon and other international varieties with lightning speed and total confidence. The first wave of cabernet sauvignon plantings in Italy actually occurred in the late eighteenth century, though the appeal of this *uva francesca*— French grape, as the Italians called it— was initially found to be limited. Taste shifted and almost two hundred years later in the 1970s and early 1980s, many of the country's best winemakers spoke more often, more highly, and more enthu- siastically of cabernet than of just about any other grape. Native grapes, by compar- ison, sometimes took on the aura of mis- fits. For a number of sophisticated Italians, the wines made from such grapes lacked worldliness; their old-fashioned flavors seemed out of sync with the times.

Then, right in the midst of Italy's caber- netization, opinions changed. It seemed as though every avant-garde winemaker came to the same conclusion, namely that ancient Italian wine traditions were too valuable to be allowed to fade. By 1990 many Italian winemakers had decided that they liked the idea of making two styles of wine, one ancestral, the other contemporary.

# ITALY'S REGULATIONS AND THE FINE WINE REVOLUTION

T o gain insight into Italian wine today and to understand the revolution in quality that Italian wine underwent in the latter part of the twentieth century, it's important to understand something of the history of Italy's wine laws. Admittedly, gov- ernmental regulations usually make for pretty dry reading but, in Italy's case, it's almost impossible to comprehend the coun- try's wines without first getting a grasp of how they are categorized by the Italian gov- ernment and by the Italians themselves.

Italy's wine revolution was provoked by a set of governmental regulations defin- ing the areas where specific wines can be made. These laws—*Denominazione di Origine Controllata, Denominazione di Origine Controllata e Garantita,* and *Indicazione Geografica Tipica*—are known by their acronyms, DOC, DOCG, and IGT (see Italy's Wine Laws, page 323). More than three hundred wine zones have been designated as DOCs and twenty-one as DOCGs, yet the wines from these zones, widely regarded as many of the best wines in the country, represent only about 15 percent of all the Italian wines produced. More than 120 wine areas have been named IGTs, a more humble designation.

The story behind these pivotal if sometimes confusing regulations begins in the 1960s. Although great wine families, such as the Antinoris, Frescobaldis, Contini-Bonacossis, and Boscainis, had all been making fine wine for centuries, many Italian wines were still the product of peasant winemaking. But with the enact-

## THE ULTIMATE GIFT

⟿⟿

In ancient Rome wine was linked with authority. Of all the pleasures and privileges of power, none was rated more highly than the possession of a vineyard. The highest favor bestowed by the Roman emperor Julian was the gift of a vineyard prepared—actually planted and pruned—by his own hands.

ment of the DOC laws in 1963, for the first time in Italian history an official regulation stipulated standards for certain types of wine. The first wine given DOC status was the Tuscan white vernaccia di San Gimignano in 1966. The course of Italian wine changed dramatically.

No sooner had the DOC commandments been handed down than innovative Italian winemakers began to chafe against them. The vintners' frustration was this: As comprehensive and protective as the DOC laws sought to be, they failed to take into consideration a basic fact—advances in quality often come through creativity, innovation, and the introduction of new techniques. The DOC stipulations for any given type of wine were formed around what was traditional practice in that region. Traditional practice reflected traditional taste. And traditional taste was, in many cases, that of palates rarely exposed to anything more than the wine from vineyards within a twenty-mile radius.

In the 1970s Italian winemakers got restless. They tasted their way through France, noting how the French used small new-oak barrels to give depth and complexity to their wines. They went to California and watched as their colleagues

*In many parts of southern Italy vines were trained off the ground on overhead pergolas, allowing farmers to get huge yields. Today, old practices such as this are rapidly dying out.*

there made wines in ways and styles limited only by their imaginations.

Piero Antinori, head of a centuries-old Tuscan winemaking family and a prominent force within the Italian wine industry, made the first well-publicized break with DOC regulations in 1971. Antinori's wine, called Tignanello, was modeled after a wine that virtually no one had ever heard of or tasted: Sassicaia. Though Sassicaia was made in Tuscany, it was not a Chianti, not a brunello, nor was it any other familiar type of Tuscan wine. Moreover, it wasn't even based on the traditional Tuscan grape sangiovese. Sassicaia was a cabernet sauvignon modeled, unusually enough, on French Bordeaux. Sassicaia was made in extremely limited amounts; Antinori knew about it because his cousins were its creators (see the chapter on Tuscany, page 372).

Antinori's Tignanello was made in the Chianti region, but it was not—as far as the Italian government was concerned—a true Chianti since it had not been made according to the DOC regulations. Therefore, like Sassicaia, it could be officially considered only a *vino da tavola* (table wine), the lowest status an Italian wine can hold. Tignanello and Sassicaia thus became the first two *vini da tavola* to cost a small fortune in an ocean of *vini da tavola* that cost peanuts. None of this seemed to bother wine drinkers or the wine press, who bestowed on these wines (and the others like them that followed) their lasting nickname, the Super Tuscans.

Then in 1980, just as the first steps toward better-quality wine were being taken in many parts of Italy, the government enacted the DOCG—*Denominazione di Origine Controllata e Garantita*—for wines of exceptional quality and renown. The DOCG regulations were even more strict than the DOC. The first DOCGs were brunello di Montalcino and Vino Nobile di Montepulciano in Tuscany and Barolo and Barbaresco in Piedmont, all designated in 1980. By 1999, there were twenty-one DOCGs, thirteen of which were red. In addition to the first four, these include Carmignano, Chianti, Chianti Classico, Gattinara, Ghemme, sagrantino di Montefalco, Taurasi, Torgiano Rosso Riserva, and Valtellina Superiore.

The remaining DOCGs include the white and sparkling wines albana di Romagna, Asti (*spumante*), brachetto d'Acqui, Franciacorta, Gavi, recioto di Soave, vermentino di Gallura, and vernaccia di San Gimignano, which was elevated from DOC status. The first of the white DOCGs, albana di Romagna, granted in 1987, made the government look silly. Albana, a fairly neutral wine from the Emilia-Romagna region, comes nowhere close to being one of Italy's top white wines. Albana's status as the first white DOCG threw a cloak of suspicion over the whole system.

A more serious flaw in the DOCG, however, is the way the word *garantita* in its title misleads consumers by implying that the quality of the wine is guaranteed. It isn't. The DOCG is applied to an entire region. Both the greatest wine in that region and the most plebeian get to say they are DOCG. And, although the DOCG was intended as a further step toward improving quality, it still did not address the growing number of creative, nonconformist wines, many of which came from places outside DOC and DOCG wine areas and

321

all of which continued to be officially considered mere *vini da tavola*. Therefore, in 1992 the third designation, *Indicazione Geografica Tipica*, was created. While IGT wine zones include many places that make good, even great, wines, they are places that historically have never been considered as prestigious as the areas awarded DOC and DOCG status. Most IGT wines are the equivalent of French *vins de pays*, or country wines.

The DOC, DOCG, and IGT regulations continue to evolve, allowing not only for more wines but also for more creativity in how wines are made. The overall result of these regulations has been a tremendous rise in the quality of Italian wine across the board. So what does all this mean in the end? From a practical standpoint, knowing that a wine has IGT, DOC, or DOCG status doesn't guarantee that that particular wine will be exemplary. But these designations are a tip-off to the places that are recognized for the quality or prestige of their wines. Think of the designations as forming a pyramid of Italy's best wines. *Vini da tavola* constitute the broad base; IGT are next, in the middle; DOC wines are nearer the top; and DOCG wines are at the apex.

## HOW THE ITALIANS EAT PASTA

Pasta became commonplace in Italy in the thirteenth and fourteenth centuries. Early pasta dishes all had a similar sauce: melted butter and some type of hard cheese, such as Parmigiano-Reggiano. To make the dish even more special, the pasta would often be sprinkled with sugar and spices as well. (Tomato sauces did not appear until sometime after the tomato was brought from the New World in the sixteenth century.) The difficulty of eating buttery pasta with the fingers may have contributed to the early use of the fork in Italy.

Watch Italians eat slender pasta, such as spaghetti, and you will not see them twirling the strands around forks set into the bowls of spoons. Italians eat pasta with forks only. The correct technique involves stabbing some pasta near the edge of the bowl, usually at the twelve o'clock position (*not* in the center of the mound), and then twirling the fork while bracing it against the inside rim of the bowl. It's considered appropriate to have a few strands hanging down from the fork as you lift it to your mouth.

The American habit of twirling the fork against a soupspoon is thought to have originated around the turn of the twentieth century when poor Italian immigrants came to the United States and found bountiful supplies of affordable food. As the ratio of sauce to pasta increased, a spoon became necessary to scoop it all up. Inevitably, someone got the cunning idea of using the spoon to assist in eating the pasta as well.

## READING AN ITALIAN WINE LABEL

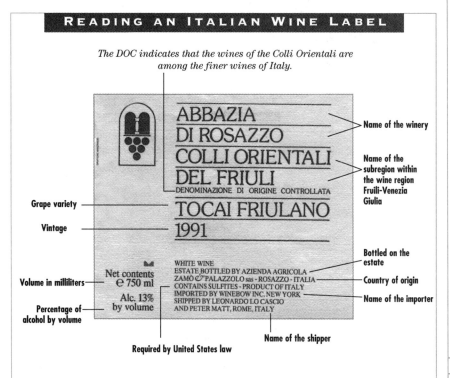

*The DOC indicates that the wines of the Colli Orientali are among the finer wines of Italy.*

**ABBAZIA DI ROSAZZO** — Name of the winery

**COLLI ORIENTALI DEL FRIULI** — Name of the subregion within the wine region Fruili-Venezia Giulia

DENOMINAZIONE DI ORIGINE CONTROLLATA

**TOCAI FRIULANO** — Grape variety

**1991** — Vintage

Volume in milliliters — Net contents ℮ 750 ml

Percentage of alcohol by volume — Alc. 13% by volume

WHITE WINE
ESTATE BOTTLED BY AZIENDA AGRICOLA — Bottled on the estate
ZAMÒ & PALAZZOLO sas - ROSAZZO - ITALIA — Country of origin
CONTAINS SULFITES - PRODUCT OF ITALY
IMPORTED BY WINEBOW INC. NEW YORK — Name of the importer
SHIPPED BY LEONARDO LO CASCIO
AND PETER MATT, ROME, ITALY

Name of the shipper

Required by United States law

323

# ITALY'S WINE LAWS

Italian wine regulations are roughly similar to the French *Appellation d'Origine Contrôlée* laws (see France's Wine Laws, page 116). The Italian Ministry of Agriculture and Forestry oversees the regulations. There are three main categories: DOC, DOCG, and IGT:

• *Denominazione di Origine Controllata* and *Denominazione di Origine Controllata e Garantita:* There are more than three hundred areas where wine is produced that have been given *Denominazione di Origine Controllata* (DOC) status and twenty-one have *Denominazione di Origine Controllata e Garantita* (DOCG) status. In these regions the DOC and DOCG laws govern the area of production, the permissible grape varieties, the maximum yield of grapes per hectare, the minimum degree of alcohol the wines must possess, such vineyard practices as pruning and trellising systems, winemaking practices, and the requirements for aging. In addition all wines must pass chemical analysis and taste tests for typicity. The rules for DOCG wines are somewhat stricter than those for DOC wines.

• *Indicazione Geografica Tipica:* Roughly equal to the French designation *vin de pays, Indicazione Geografica Tipica* (IGT) wines must also meet certain rules regarding the area of production, the permissible grape varieties, the maximum yield of grapes per hectare, and so forth, but these rules are generally much less stringent than for DOC or DOCG wines. There are more than 120 IGTs.

# Piedmont

L ying in a remote white amphitheater created by the Alps, Piedmont is Italy's preeminent wine region. Barolo and Barbaresco—two of the country's most legendary reds—are born here. So is the world's easiest to drink sparkling wine, the former Asti Spumante, now officially referred to simply as Asti.

If Italy is sometimes thought of as the cradle of Bacchanalian frivolity, you'd never know it in Piedmont. Winemakers here are serious, prudent, and diligent about their work. Their winemaking style, as well as the culinary traditions of the region, has strong links to that of their closest neighbor, France. If Piedmont has an enological soul mate, it is not Tuscany, as one might expect, but France's Burgundy. In both regions wine estates are mostly small and meticulously cared for. The wine traditions of both were firmly molded by

## THE QUICK SIP ON PIEDMONT

• Two of Italy's most majestic, powerful red wines—Barolo and Barbaresco— come from Piedmont. Like great red Bordeaux, they can be and often are aged a decade or more before being drunk.

• Barolo and Barbaresco are made from the nebbiolo grape, a highly site-specific variety known for its forceful tannin.

• Piedmont's other major wine is Asti, a semisweet sparkler known the world over for its provocative, fruity-musky flavor.

centuries of Benedictine rule. Most important of all, Piedmont and Burgundy share the philosophic belief that great wine is the progeny of a single, perfectly adapted grape variety (nebbiolo in Piedmont; pinot

324

*Surrounded by gently rolling vineyards of nebbiolo grapes, the sleepy village of Barbaresco is home to the wine of the same name.*

noir in Burgundy). This is in complete opposition to most of the rest of Italy, and indeed most of France, where wines tend to be made from a blend of grapes rather than a single variety.

It's difficult to describe just how important Piedmont's leading wines Barolo and Barbaresco are not just in Piedmont but in Italy as a whole. In the last few decades of the twentieth century, the wines of Tuscany, especially the Super Tuscans, often stole the limelight and received more press, but Barolo and Barbaresco remain Italy's most esteemed traditional wines. One reason for this has to do with their quality. Equally important is the fact that nebbiolo is one of the world's most site-specific grape varieties and, in terms of winemaking, one of the most difficult to master. As the twenty-first century begins, it can be safely said that no place in the world has succeeded with this complicated, demanding, challenging grape— no place, that is, except Piedmont.

Like the great red Bordeaux, Barolo and Barbaresco are highly structured wines that can be aged for years, even decades. Until the 1990s, Piedmontese winemakers routinely advised waiting no less than ten years and sometimes as many as twenty years before drinking them. Today most Barolos and Barbarescos are made in a way that renders them softer at a younger age and thus enjoyable earlier. Still, as we'll see in the section on Barolo and Barbaresco (see page 327), even these modern versions are often massive and tannic enough to need at least several years of aging.

The fact that Barolo and Barbaresco are among the most long lived of all Italian wines plus the fact that they're expensive has meant that these two kings of the Italian wine world are decidedly not what the Piedmontese drink with dinner every night. That distinction goes to two other red wines that stand next in the hierarchy of importance: barbera and dolcetto. Barbera, made from the barbera grape, is a vibrant, sometimes rustic wine, oozing with a wealth of fruit flavors. The grape is Piedmont's most widely planted variety. Dolcetto is a juicy quaffing wine and often has an attractive, bitter edge. It's made from the dolcetto grape.

In addition to these important wines, there are a number of others that, like Barolo and Barbaresco, are made from nebbiolo, although they are usually less polished, less complex, and generally more rough and lean. The best known and most important of these wines is Gattinara, followed by Ghemme, nebbiolo d'Alba, and spanna.

Piedmont is also home to four principal white wines: the dry whites Gavi and arneis; the slightly sweet, refined, and rare moscato d'Asti; and as already mentioned, the irrepressibly popular semisweet sparkler Asti.

## THE LAND, THE GRAPES, AND THE VINEYARDS

Piedmont, meaning foot of the mountain, is the largest region of the Italian mainland. As its name suggests, Piedmont comprises mountains and rolling foothills. Since much of this land is too steep or cold for vines, Piedmont, despite its size, is not Italy's leading producer of wine. If only

325

## IN VINEYARDS VERITAS

—⟶∘∘∘⟵—

Today's Piedmontese vintners are as obsessed with the individual characteristics of vineyards as are their Burgundian counterparts. Rather than making a single Barolo or Barbaresco most top producers now make multiple versions of both, designating each according to the specific vineyard from which it came.

Vineyard-designated wines are almost always expensive. Among the most famous Barolo vineyards are Rocche, Cannubi, Brunate, and Bussia-Soprana. Top Barbaresco vineyards include Rabajà, Sorì Tildìn, and Asili.

fine wines are considered, however, it excels. More than 17 percent of all the DOC and DOCG wines in Italy are made there. This is more than any other region except for the Veneto, which also produces about 17 percent.

While there are vineyards in the more Alpine, colder parts of northern Piedmont, the wines produced there, including the two best known—Gattinara and Ghemme —can have a leanness and hard edge to them. Nearly all of Piedmont's best vineyards are located in warmer areas farther south, especially along the two hilly southeastern ranges known as the Langhe and Monferrato. Here are found the important wine towns of Alba, Asti, and Alessandria, the most treasured of which is Alba.

The tiny villages of Barolo and Barbaresco (from which the wines take their names) lie about a dozen miles apart on either side of Alba, which, despite its being a rather humble town, holds an almost

mythic place in the minds of food and wine lovers. Not solely for mighty Barolo and Barbaresco, alas, but also because this is where the world's most astonishing white truffles are unearthed each fall. Just imagining autumn in Alba—drinking sumptuous Barolos and dining on homemade pasta generously mounded (this is Piedmont after all) with white truffles—is enough to send shivers up my spine.

The soil around Alba is clay, limestone, and sand. The best vineyards, most of which are planted with nebbiolo, are located on the domes of hills that are tilted south, resulting in maximum exposure to the sun and hence ripeness. The names of the vineyards underscore the sun's importance. The producer Ceretto, for example, makes a famous Barolo from a vineyard called Bricco Rocche; in Piedmontese dialect a *bricco* is the sun-catching crest of a hill. Similarly the producer Angelo Gaja makes an extraordinary Barbaresco from a vineyard called Sorì Tildìn; a *sorì* is the south-facing part of a slope where in winter the snow melts first. The hills around Alba are also home to a considerable number of barbera and

*Bruno Ceretto has spent a lifetime positioning and promoting Piedmontese wines—especially Barolo—as among the greatest in the world.*

dolcetto vines, as well as arneis, which makes a stylish dry white wine.

Piedmont's most important and most traditional white grape, however, is moscato, the Italian name for the ancient variety muscat blanc à petits grains. The town that will forever be linked with moscato is Asti, northeast of Alba. Two moscato-based wines take their names from Asti: the gorgeously refined low-alcohol wine moscato d'Asti, which the Piedmontese adore, and the widely popular, though not always praised, slightly sweet sparkling wine once known as Asti Spumante and now officially called simply Asti.

The vineyards that surround Asti and the town of Alessandria to its east lie in the Monferrato range of limestone-laced hills. This is a region also well-known for the red wines barbera and dolcetto. At the southeastern edge of these hills is the town of Gavi where the white grape cortese is the source of the dry, straightforward, traditional wine that bears the town's name.

The producers in Piedmont tend to be relatively small; the average landholding is about three acres. Nonetheless, most producers make multiple wines.

# BAROLO AND BARBARESCO

Close your eyes and imagine it is evening in the dark foothills of the Alps: A fire crackles in the hearth of a stone farmhouse; game is being roasted slowly in the oven. Wine in this setting becomes more than a beverage. It is solace.

Barolo and Barbaresco are sometimes accused of being *too* powerful. But in their cultural context the wines make utter sense. These big, soul-warming, almost black-red wines are meant to be drunk with the region's substantial meats,

formidable pastas, and rich risottos. If you take them to the beach or try pairing them with steamed vegetables, they'll just taste disappointing.

Barolo and Barbaresco are located in the Langhe hills of southeastern Piedmont. Although both wines can be powerful and although both must be made solely from nebbiolo grapes, their personalities are quite different. Grown on steeper, cooler sites, Barolo is generally the more robust, austere, and masculine of the two. Barbaresco tends to be slightly more graceful, even though it, too, is often described as having brooding power. Another important difference concerns supply. Each year, less than half as much Barbaresco is produced as Barolo. While Barbaresco is made in three tiny villages—Barbaresco itself plus Neive and

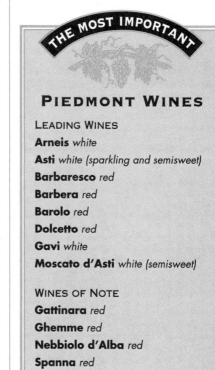

### THE MOST IMPORTANT

## PIEDMONT WINES

LEADING WINES

**Arneis** white

**Asti** white (sparkling and semisweet)

**Barbaresco** red

**Barbera** red

**Barolo** red

**Dolcetto** red

**Gavi** white

**Moscato d'Asti** white (semisweet)

WINES OF NOTE

**Gattinara** red

**Ghemme** red

**Nebbiolo d'Alba** red

**Spanna** red

Treiso—Barolo is made in eleven, the most important of which are Barolo, La Morra, Castiglione Falletto, Monforte d'Alba, and Serralunga d'Alba. Because Barolo spans a larger number of microclimates, it is said to be more variable in quality and style, producer to producer, than Barbaresco.

---

## THE GRAPES OF

## PIEDMONT

### WHITES

**Arneis:** Makes a bold, fresh wine of the same name.

**Cortese:** Source of the dry, delicately flavored wine Gavi.

**Moscato:** The same grape as the French muscat blanc à petits grains, an ancient variety with extremely fruity, floral, and musky aromas and flavors. Used to make sparkling Asti and moscato d'Asti. Sometimes called moscato bianco (white muscat) or moscato Canelli (Canelli muscat, a reference to the village south of Asti, which is famous for the grape).

### REDS

**Barbera:** Most widely planted grape in Piedmont; the source of a vibrant, mouth-filling, often slightly rustic wine by the same name; it's a favorite local dinner wine.

**Bonarda** and **Vespolina:** Two minor blending grapes used with nebbiolo in the wines Gattinara and Ghemme.

**Dolcetto:** Makes a simple, fruity quaffing wine also called dolcetto.

**Nebbiolo:** Piedmont's star grape and one of the most renowned red grapes in all of Italy. Known for power, structure, and tannin; makes the legendary reds Barolo and Barbaresco and is the primary grape in Gattinara and Ghemme.

---

Until recently, Barolo and Barbaresco were almost unpalatable unless they had been aged ten to fifteen years, whereupon the wines' fierce tannin might begin to mellow. Truly supple Barolo or Barbaresco often required a twenty-year wait. Daring drinkers who opened the wines earlier often ended up with tongues that felt as though they'd been sheathed in shrink-wrap.

Why were Barolo and Barbaresco so severe? First, because the nebbiolo grape is genetically high in tannin compounds. To make matters worse, it is a late-ripening variety, often harvested on the brink of winter when the ambient temperature is cold. In the past this meant that fermentation choked along in fits and starts, often for months before it got rolling effectively. Piedmontese winemakers were forced to stand by and let nebbiolo run its long course, even though in the process, hard, bitter tannins were extracted from the grape skins. Many winemakers then inadvertently exacerbated that harshness by leaving the wine for years in large oak or chestnut casks, often desiccating its fruitiness and sometimes oxidizing the wine in the process.

*The name nebbiolo comes from nebbia, the fog that often settles over Piedmont in late October, during the harvest.*

As modern tastes swung toward soft, flavorful wines that could be drunk the night they were bought, consumers began bypassing Barolo and Barbaresco. The two were on their way to becoming the dinosaurs of red wine. Then in the 1980s winemakers using modern technology discovered that the punishing tannin could be ameliorated.

# GAJA

No man has heralded the virtues of Piedmont more than the dynamic, ambitious, and inventive Angelo Gaja. For decades he has traveled around the world, talking about Barbaresco and Barolo to every journalist and restaurateur who would listen (and making converts of most of them).

Gaja's wines can have spellbinding intensity and power. The best seem not simply great but virtually unreal in their ability to be massively opulent and yet finely etched at the same time. They are also gaspingly expensive.

Gaja made his mark with his estate-grown Barbarescos, especially his intense single-vineyard Barbarescos called Sorì Tildìn and Sorì San Lorenzo. Later, he bought a famous but rundown property outside Alba and began making the now legendary Barolo Sperss.

For all of his inventive vineyard and cellar practices, Gaja is a traditionalist in his devotion to nebbiolo. When he made Piedmont's first cabernet sauvignon in 1978, he called it Darmagi in honor of his father. In the local dialect,

*darmagi* means what a pity; this was what Gaja's father mumbled every time he passed the cabernet vineyard and thought about the nebbiolo vines that had been pulled out to plant the cabernet. Though Darmagi was highly praised internationally (as were Gaja's two chardonnays, Rossj Bass and Gaia & Rey), Gaja maintains that it was merely a marketing ploy. Making a cabernet that could rival the great Bordeaux, he says, was just a clever way of drawing the world's attention to Barbaresco and Barolo and to Piedmont.

*A powerhouse of energy, Angelo Gaja has been one of Italy's most innovative producers.*

Barolo and Barbaresco were born again, this time as monolithic wines that nonetheless were neither savage nor completely inaccessible.

Introducing temperature-controlled tanks meant that fermentation could be immediately warmer, quicker, and more stable, thereby avoiding the most astringent tannin. Juice could be pumped over the grape skins in a way that imparted maximum color to the wine but, again, minimized harsh tannin. Finally, winemakers began to understand

how to divide the aging of nebbiolo between small French barrels and bottles so that the lush fruit quality of the wine would not be sacrificed.

There continue to be legal minimums for aging, which many producers exceed by at least a year. By law, Barolo must be aged a total of three years between barrel and bottle, and the total is five years for Barolo *riserva*.

## BAROLO CHINATO

━━◁∿∿▷━━

A rare Piedmontese *digestivo* (*digestif*), Barolo Chinato is made by steeping the bark of the cinchona tree (quinine) in aged Barolo. Each producer then flavors his *digestivo* with secret ingredients, including iris flowers, vanilla, coriander, cinnamon, and mint. Usually served after dinner, Barolo Chinato is soft, silky, and mellow—the very opposite of that other favorite Piedmontese after-dinner drink, grappa.

Barbaresco must be aged a total of two years between barrel and bottle, with four years for Barbaresco *riserva*.

## Emerging Tastes

Wines made from nebbiolo have very specific aromas and flavors. Tar is one of the favorite descriptions used by Italian wine experts, along with licorice, violets, leather, chocolate, prunes, and figs. None of these characteristics emerges gently and in an orderly fashion from the wines. With most Barolos and Barbarescos, flavors hurl themselves over you like an ocean wave. Though most are now made to be drunk sooner, sooner is a relative term. A Barolo or Barbaresco less than five years old may still be imprisoned by a fortress of tannin and may taste monochromatic, closed, and not particularly complex, none of which may be true once it is aged. With these wines, you simply must wait. If that statement seems broad, keep in mind that it's impossible to know exactly how long to age any wine. First of all, aging wine is not like baking a cake—wine is not ready at one precise moment. It has a range of readiness since it is changing subtly all the time. Moreover, each wine's readiness is influenced by a myriad of factors, including how it was made and what the vintage was like (see When Is It Ready? page 82). With such masterful wines as Barolo and Barbaresco, the most important proviso is this: Do not drink them in the first few years after the vintage date. At this stage the wines have not yet evolved into themselves.

---

*Some of the Best Producers of Barolo*

**ALDO CONTERNO**

**BRUNO GIACOSA**

**CERETTO**

**GAJA**

**GIACOMO CONTERNO**

**GIUSEPPE MASCARELLO**

**LUCIANO SANDRONE**

**LUIGI EINAUDI**

**MARCARINI**

**PAOLO SCAVINO**

**PRUNOTTO**

**ROBERTO VOERZIO**

---

*Some of the Best Producers of Barbaresco*

**BRUNO GIACOSA**

**CIGLIUTTI**

**GAJA**

**MARCHESI DI GRESY**

**MOCCAGATTA**

**PRUNOTTO**

**RENATO RATTI**

---

*Old wine bottles and wine pitchers line the shelves in the kitchen of a Piedmontese farmhouse.*

## GATTINARA, GHEMME, NEBBIOLO D'ALBA, AND SPANNA

A slew of wines besides Barolo and Barbaresco are made from nebbiolo, including Gattinara, Ghemme, nebbiolo d'Alba, and spanna. Nebbiolo d'Alba is slightly different from the others in that, like Barolo and Barbaresco, it too is produced in the famous Langhe foothills near the town of Alba. But the grapes that go into nebbiolo d'Alba come from outlying areas and don't quite have the finesse and power that nebbiolo intended for Barolo and Barbaresco possesses. Still, nebbiolo d'Alba is a good lower-priced alternative to Barolo and Barbaresco, and because it's less powerful, it doesn't require the same aging that its more famous sisters do.

Gattinara and Ghemme are produced far north of Alba, in colder Alpine foothills with glacial soil and terrain. Though Gattinara in particular can occasionally seem like a mini Barolo with fairly powerful flavors, both Gattinara and Ghemme are generally leaner than Barolo or Barbaresco, with simpler flavors and tannin that is sometimes aggressive. Often harsh by themselves, these wines can taste entirely transformed if drunk with a juicy roast or creamy risotto. Gattinara and Ghemme are frequently combined with a small percentage of bonarda or vespolina, two minor blending grapes that help tone down and soften the northern-grown nebbiolo. The best known of these wines in the United States is the Gattinara made by Travaglini, shipped in an almost square-shaped black bottle.

Curiously, in northern Piedmont nebbiolo is called spanna. Thus, both Gattinara and Ghemme are usually said to be made from spanna, not nebbiolo. Wines labeled simply with the word *spanna* are basic wines made from nebbiolo grown in northern Piedmont. Rustic defines them best.

## BARBERA

The word *barbera* may sound as though it could be related to barbaric, but in reality, this is Piedmont's most juicy, straightforwardly delicious red wine. Scan any Piedmontese restaurant around dinnertime; a bottle of barbera will be on most tables. In many ways, barbera is the antithesis of Barolo and Barbaresco. It usually does not have hard, tannic edges, nor does it require superlong aging. Instead of Barolo's blackish hue, barbera is almost shockingly magenta. And unlike Barolo and Barbaresco, it is not considered a classic. Barbera, at its best, is simply a captivating wine with lots of flavor muscle.

*Some of the Best Producers
of Barbera*

ALDO CONTERNO

COPPO CAMP DU ROUSS

ELIO ALTARE

GAJA

GIACOMO BOLOGNA

GIUSEPPE MASCARELLO

MARCARINI

PAOLO SCAVINO

PIO CESARE

PRUNOTTO

RENATO RATTI

VIETTI

The barbera grape is Piedmont's most widely planted variety. Historically it was grown almost everywhere—everywhere, that is, except in the best soil on the best south-facing slopes. Those went to Barolo or Barbaresco. In the winery, barbera received stepsister treatment as well. The best barrels were reserved for Barolo and Barbaresco, which also got more winemaking attention. Worst of all, barbera was often cultivated for quantity. Instead of limiting yields, producers stretched them. Given barbera's second-class treatment in the past, it's surprising that the wine was as good as it was.

In the 1980s, however, such forward-thinking producers as Giacomo Bologna and Renato Ratti began to view barbera as a diamond in the rough. Planting it on better sites, they limited yields, vinified it more carefully, and began aging it in small new-French-oak barrels. Quality jumped.

Although there are many decent, one-dimensional barberas, a remarkable number of the ones being made today are more stunning wines, with supple, feltlike tex-

tures, and mouthfilling chocolaty, licoricey, cherry, figgy fruit. And because the barbera grape is naturally high in acid, the wines also have a kind of vibrancy and zip that make them great counterpoints to food.

Barbera is grown everywhere in Piedmont, though the two places that produce most of the outstanding wines are the area around the town of Alba (barbera d'Alba) and near Asti (barbera d'Asti). A small number of producers have begun to blend barbera and nebbiolo in the hopes of fusing barbera's blackberry fruit vibrancy with nebbiolo's structure and complexity. Some of these blends, like Conterno Fantino's Mon Pra, are delicious.

## DOLCETTO

The appealing simplicity of dolcetto has caused it to be misleadingly pegged as Italy's Beaujolais. In fact, the two wines taste quite different. Dolcetto, made from dolcetto grapes, has firm grapey-spicy fruit set off against a subtle bitter-chocolate background. Beaujolais, made from gamay, has a grapey fruitness, almost like the flavor of melted black cherry Jell-O.

Dolcetto has relatively little acid, not much tannin, and is lighter in body than barbera, making it so easy to drink it becomes almost gulpable. It, too, is a favorite every-night wine in Piedmont and is often served with the gargantuan Piedmontese *antipasto misto*. Though most dolcetto is made to be merely easy-drinking stuff, a few producers make serious versions—wines with such forthright grip, structure, and depth that they hardly seem like dolcetto. These producers include Chionetti, Marcarini, and Vietti.

Dolcetto is made in selected spots all around Piedmont, but the best wines generally come from near Alba (dolcetto d'Alba) and from around the small village of Dogliani (dolcetto di Dogliani), which calls itself the birthplace of dolcetto.

## GAVI AND ARNEIS

In Piedmont red wine has always been a religion, white wine, something of an afterthought. Nonetheless, a small number of good (and expensive) white wines are being made, notably those called Gavi and arneis. Gavi, the wine made in and around the village of the same name, has more than a Piedmontese reputation. During the 1960s and 1970s, many wine experts considered it the best dry white wine in all Italy. (By the 1980s, the stunning whites of Friuli-Venezia Giulia began to challenge Gavi's standing.) In particular, the Gavi from the estate of La Scolca was known in the United States and around Europe as a paragon of Italian white winemaking. La Scolca, not modest about the fact, called its wine Gavi dei Gavi (*the Gavi of Gavi*). Later, new laws forced the

*Displaying the coat of arms of the order of men devoted to the truffles and wines of Alba, this wine bar promises good things to eat and drink.*

estate to rename the wine Gavi di Gavi (Gavi of Gavi).

Gavi is made from cortese, a grape native to Piedmont. At its best the wine is bone-dry and crisp, with citrus and mineral notes—pleasant enough to be sure but probably not as grand as its former reputation would suggest. About thirty estates specialize in Gavi (and many more make at least a decent version). Most of the specialists are located in and around the small village, in the southeast corner of Piedmont near Liguria. The area's proximity to the Ligurian coast, the Italian Riviera, has made Gavi a natural partner for seafood.

Arneis, which means rascal in the Piedmontese dialect, has gone through several fashion cycles. For decades plantings were in decline, but in the mid-1980s arneis began to acquire underground cult status as another chic match for seafood in fashionable restaurants along the Ligurian coast. More and more producers began making arneis, although by the mid-1990s excitement about the wine, as well as demand for it, seemed to level off. Despite the vagaries of fashion, this can be a delicious wine—dry, lively (like that rascal), and fairly full in body with light pear and apricot flavors. Arneis is made mostly in the hills of Roero northwest of Alba. The best producers include Vietti, Ceretto, Bruno Giacosa, and Castello di Neive.

333

## ASTI

Italy produces more sparkling wines from more different grape varieties than any other country in the world. The best known is Asti, commonly called Asti Spumante, an aromatic semisweet sparkler made from moscato grapes grown all over southeastern Piedmont but especially around the famous wine towns of Asti and

## VERMOUTH

The indispensable ingredient in a martini, vermouth was first created and commercially sold in Piedmont in the 1700s. Vermouth is red or white wine that has been infused with a secret blend of more than a hundred aromatic spices, barks, bitter herbs, and flavorings, among them angelica, anise, bitter almond, chamomile, cinnamon, coriander, ginger, nutmeg, peach, quinine, rhubarb, and saffron. Until it was banned because of its toxicity, absinthe was also included. In fact, the word *vermouth* comes from the German *wermut*, wormwood, or absinthe. Historically, the Piedmontese used muscat grapes as their base

wine and thus most vermouth was white. Today, cheap red or white bulk wine from the south of Italy is usually used as the base and as a result, the quality of vermouth is not as high as it once was. After the wine has been infused, it is then fortified to raise the alcohol content to 15 to 21 percent (table wine is usually 12 to 14 percent). Red vermouth is generally sweet; white vermouth may be dry or semisweet. Both are consumed solo as aperitifs or mixed into various cocktails. The leading vermouth firms, such as Cinzano, Martini & Rossi, and Punt e Mes, are all headquartered around Turin, the capital of Piedmont.

Alba. South of Asti and east of Alba is the tiny village of Canelli, where Asti production began in the latter part of the 1800s. The village is such a hub of Asti production that the grape moscato is sometimes called moscato Canelli. As if that weren't enough, the grape has a third name, too: moscato bianco, white muscat. All of these names refer to the same grape that in French is known as muscat blanc à petits grains.

If everyone in the world were sitting down together for one immense lunch party and only one wine could be served, a top Asti might be a good choice. The frothy sparkler (*spumante* means foaming) is as irresistible as chilled peaches on a hot day. Yet the wine has anything but a good public relations image. Lots of poorly made, com-

mercial Asti Spumante exported to the United States after World War II gave it a cheap fizz reputation that has been slow to die. Many wine drinkers still dismiss Asti as a noxiously sweet poor man's Champagne. The best modern Astis are far from that. They are not sugary sweet like candy but, rather, dizzyingly fruity and evocative of perfectly ripe peaches and apricots. Plus there's the wine's intriguing muskiness—a hallmark of moscato grapes. Asti is also quite light—7 to 9 percent alcohol (standard wines are 12 to 14 percent). It should be served exactly like Champagne—chilled and in a tall narrow glass.

Moscato belongs to the prolific family of muscat grapes grown the world over and thought to be the oldest vines known to man. Moscato may well have been the first grape cultivated in Piedmont, although nebbiolo, too, is an ancient variety. Despite moscato's long sojourn in Piedmont, its use in sparkling wine is relatively recent. The first Asti is attributed to Carlo Gancia who introduced the Champagne method to the region around 1870 and applied it to the local grapes.

Today most Asti is not made according to the *méthode champenoise* (with secondary fermentation in the bottle) but by the Charmat or tank method. In this type of fermentation, the grapes are crushed and the must is put in large vats and chilled to near freezing, preventing immediate fermentation. The wine is then fermented in batches as needed, preserving the sensational fruitiness of the grapes. The process takes place in enormous, pressurized sealed tanks that trap the natural carbon dioxide gas and cause it to dissolve back into the wine (the trapped carbon dioxide will become the wine's bubbles). When the wine has reached about 7 to 9 percent alcohol and about 3 to 5 percent of the natural grape sugar remains, it is chilled down to stabilize it, centrifuged to remove all remaining yeasts, and bottled. At that point the sparkler is immediately shipped so that it can be consumed at its freshest and liveliest. Asti producers do not generally put vintage dates on bottles, since the wines for sale should always (you hope) be from the immediate past harvest.

Each year, copious amounts of Asti are made by a handful of giant companies including Cinzano, Contratto, Gancia, Fontanafredda, and Martini & Rossi. In fact, more than ten times as much Asti is made yearly than Barolo. The sweetness level of each producer's Asti will vary slightly according to the preferences of the producer.

## MOSCATO D'ASTI

Asti's more prestigious cousin, moscato d'Asti is generally made in tiny batches and in limited quantities by small Piedmontese producers using selected grapes. Delicate, lightly sweet, and gorgeously fruity, moscato d'Asti is particularly low in alcohol—no more than 5.5 percent by law (Asti is usually 7 to 9 percent alcohol). This makes moscato d'Asti a fairly fragile wine, which in turn, has made it highly desirable among Italian wine connoisseurs.

Moscato d'Asti is also less effervescent than Asti. It is not considered *spumante* (foaming) at all, just a bit *frizzante* (fizzy). Since it is under less pressure than Asti, it is stoppered with a regular cork, not a Champagne cork and wire. Moscato d'Asti is vintage dated and is served chilled, generally in regular wineglasses, not Champagne flutes. It should be drunk while fresh, soon after release. In Piedmont it's traditional to drink a glass at Christmas.

### RED SPUMANTE?

Though Asti is the most famous *spumante* in Piedmont, it's not the only one. Some of the most intriguing Piedmontese sparklers are, surprisingly enough, the bright red *spumantes* that are usually made from barbera or nebbiolo grapes. One particularly renowned crimson-colored *spumante* is brachetto, made from the grape of the same name. Brachetto is dramatic and fruity with just a touch of strawberrylike sweetness. Often it's served with fruit, though sausages are another traditional match. Brachetto from the area around Acqui (brachetto d'Acqui) is especially good.

## PIEDMONT'S OTHER TREASURE: WHITE TRUFFLES

ozens of foods all over the world, from oysters to chocolate, can make a food lover shiver with anticipation. But no food is more riveting than the Piedmontese white truffle. Its aroma and flavor could be described as narcotic. Of the more than seventy species of truffles that can be found throughout the world, white truffles are the most prized. They grow in unpredictable spots a foot or more underground, generally near oak, chestnut, or beech trees. They ripen throughout the late fall; their harvest corresponds with that of Piedmont's grapes.

No one knows why white truffles grow mainly in Piedmont or why the Piedmontese sort is superior in flavor to the small quantity that can be unearthed in Tuscany, Umbria, Emilia-Romagna, and the former Yugoslavia. White truffles have never been successfully cultivated.

Because white truffles cannot be detected by humans, mongrel dogs (or sometimes pigs) are trained to sniff them out. The truffle hunter (*trifalao*) must be careful to yank the animal away at just the right moment lest the truffle become pet chow. White truffles are always hunted under the cover of night so that the location of the truffle bed remains secret.

According to research conducted in Germany and England, truffles are profoundly and appealingly aromatic because they contain a special substance that is also

---

*Some of the Best Producers of Moscato d'Asti*

**CASCINA LA SPINETTA-RIVETTI**
**ICARDI**
**I VIGNAIOLI DI SANTO STEFANO**
**MARCHESI DI GRESY**
**VIETTI CASCINETTA D'ASTI**

# THE FOODS OF PIEDMONT

Northern Italian food, including the food of Piedmont, is not what many people imagine it to be—and for a good historical reason. The great wave of Italian immigrants who arrived in the United States at the beginning of the twentieth century consisted mostly of extremely poor people from southern villages. They brought with them a modest repertoire of regional peasant dishes that revolved around pasta, olive oil, tomatoes, and vegetables. From this humble base grew "American Italian" food—a motley assemblage of southern Italian recipes adapted to American ingredients. By the 1960s, many of the well-loved dishes served in "red sauce" Italian restaurants (including spaghetti with meatballs) bore little resemblance to what was being cooked and eaten in Italy itself.

The stage was set for the inevitable. As the 1970s progressed, a new generation of sophisticated diners in the United States found themselves looking for something other than the gloppy, garlicky dishes served in old-style American/Italian

found in the testes of men and boars. This substance is secreted by the sweat glands in a man's armpit and can be detected in the urine of women. Researchers report that the substance has a powerful psychological effect on human beings.

White truffles are ugly things—gray knobbed balls that look as though they have been deformed by some especially evil bit of witchcraft. They range in size from that of a marble to that of a baseball, though the larger ones are exceedingly rare. They are breathtakingly expensive. But only a tiny amount is needed to transform a dish. In Piedmont white truffles are shaved raw over homemade pasta, risotto, polenta, soft scrambled eggs, veal carpaccio, or veal *tartare*. The earthy pungency of

*When asked to reveal their favorite hunting locations, truffle gatherers are anything but loquacious.*

the truffle seems to intensify the earthiness of the Barbaresco or Barolo that is usually served alongside.

Each autumn in Alba a truffle market is held under a long medieval arcade. Truffle hunters with scales at their sides display their finds. The air is heady with the collective aroma of thousands of truffles. Restaurateurs, buying in quantity, have sometimes been accompanied by bodyguards.

A final note: Tartufi Ponzio in the center of Alba is a tiny shop that sells products related exclusively to truffles and wine. There are white-truffle oils, pâtés with truffles, truffle sauces, truffle slicers, and so forth, plus a small but stunning collection of Piedmontese wines.

*Tartufi Ponzio, 26 Via Emanuele, Alba.*

restaurants. All of a sudden, so-called northern Italian cuisine—which was viewed as lighter, more pristine, and more simple—was in.

Here's the ironic fact. Northern Italian food is precisely the opposite of its stereotype in the United States; it often *is* rich and heavy. The hearty, copious dishes of Piedmont evolved as the logical sustenance of people who lived in the cold shadow of the Alps and drank robust red wines to keep warm.

Moreover, Piedmont, on the border of France, was once part of the Kingdom of Savoy. As the cuisines clanged together, Piedmont adopted the most luxurious French ingredients. Butter, cream, and eggs are used more extensively here than in any other region of Italy, with the possible exception of Emilia-Romagna.

Perhaps the most startling difference between the cooking of Piedmont and that of the rest of Italy is the prominence of meat. In no other region are diners presented with such he-man-size hunks of roasted game, veal, and lamb. Remarkably, the carnivorous feast is usually preceded by a herculean Piedmontese *antipasto misto*—a series of up to twenty dishes (egg frittatas, sausages with beans, veal *tartare*, and so on) that could feed at least a dozen people more than those to whom it's served. A Piedmontese waiter, hearing me groan over the abundance of dishes, once quipped, "In Piedmont you have to eat. If you want to diet go to France."

One of the single most compelling Piedmontese appetizers is *bagna cauda*, literally hot bath, a hearty fall specialty

## FOOD AND WINE

# TAGLIATELLE AND BAROLO

In the United States a plate of pasta—any pasta—seems immediately to call for a bottle of Chianti. Not so in Italy, where each region has its own traditions of pairing certain pastas with certain wines. In Piedmont the most renowned of pastas is tagliatelle, long thin handmade egg noodles lavishly but simply dressed with nothing more than melted butter and sage. In the fall, white truffles will be shaved over the pasta, falling like snowflakes on top of the glistening yellow strands. Though a good Gavi can be delicious with this dish, such is the renown (and richness) of great tagliatelle that the Piedmontese often drink Barolo with it. The wine's brooding dark flavors and tannic grip glide through the richness of the pasta like a hot knife through butter.

The two famous Piedmontese pasta dishes are tagliatelle and agnolotti. Tagliatelle are thin strips of homemade egg pasta, often sauced simply with melted butter and sage. Agnolotti are small half-moon shaped ravioli, frequently stuffed with veal and sage or such vegetables as pumpkin or spinach and, again, drizzled lightly with melted butter.

Stretching across the north of Italy is a vast corn and rice belt, and so polenta and risotto are as customary as pasta. Piedmontese risottos, made with rich meat broths and the region's earthy wild mushrooms, are irresistible. Polenta (cornmeal as art) is often pan sautéed in butter and served (like our mashed potatoes) as a foil for roasts.

In Piedmontese restaurants, large breadsticks—*grissini*—are immediately brought to the table lest anyone go hungry in the first few seconds after arrival. These impressive specimens can be as long as the width of the table or just big and fat. Baking in general is more significant in the north thanks to both French and Austrian influences.

always served during the grape harvest. Extra-virgin olive oil, butter, anchovies, and garlic are whisked together, heated to near boiling and served with a variety of vegetables that you dip in the hot oil. These include cardoons (a member of the artichoke family), red peppers, fennel, leeks, radishes, onions, cabbage, beets, and bitter lettuces. Bread is put to use as an edible plate, helping to convey the vegetables from the pot to the mouth without dripping oil all over the tablecloth.

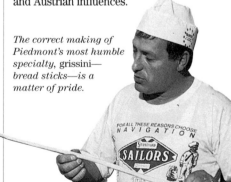

*The correct making of Piedmont's most humble specialty, grissini— bread sticks—is a matter of pride.*

Above all else, however, the food that immortalizes Piedmont is the white truffle—one of the world's most rarified specialties and a tribute to Italian hedonism.

# VISITING PIEDMONTESE WINE ESTATES

The best wine estates in Piedmont are all within easy driving distance from Alba, a charming small town as famous for white truffles as it is for wine. Conveniently, many of Piedmont's best restaurants, such as Guido, are also located in this part of the wine country. Piedmontese wine estates are generally small and often family run. Visiting them is strictly by appointment. It helps to speak Italian or French, though many Piedmontese are fluent in English. The telephone numbers include the dialing code you'll need when calling from the United States. If you're calling from within Italy, eliminate the 011-39.

**BRAIDA DI GIACOMO BOLOGNA**
94 Via Roma
14030 Rocchetta Tanaro, Asti
011-39-0141-64-41-13

**CERETTO**
34 Località San Cassiano
12051 Alba
011-39-0173-28-25-82

**FONTANAFREDDA**
15 Via Alba
12050 Serralunga d'Alba
011-39-0173-61-31-61
Fontanafredda is the largest and one of the oldest wineries in the Barolo area.

**GAJA**
36/A Via Torino
12050 Barbaresco
011-39-0173-63-51-58

**PODERI ALDO CONTERNO**
48 Località Bussia
12065 Monforte d'Alba
011-39-0173-781-50

**PRUNOTTO**
4/G Regione San Cassiano
12051 Alba
011-39-0173-28-00-17

**RENATO RATTI**
7 Fraz. Annunziata
12064 La Morra
011-39-0173-50-18-5

**VIETTI**
5 Piazza Vittorio Veneto
12060 Castiglione Falletto
011-39-0173-628-25

# THE BEST RESTAURANTS IN PIEDMONT

**BOCCONDIVINO**
14 Via Mendicità Istruita, Bra

**CACCIATORI**
30 Via Moreno, Cartosio
(a village 10 miles southwest of Acqui Terme)

**DA DIRCE**
53 Via Valleversa, Caniglie
(a *località* 5 miles northeast of Asti)

**GUIDO**
1 Piazza Umberto, Costigliole d'Asti

**IL GIARDINO DA FELICÌN**
18 Via Vallada, Monforte d'Alba

**TORNAVENTO**
7 Piazza Baracco, Treiso

# THE PIEDMONTESE WINES TO KNOW

## *Whites*

### CERETTO

Arneis

Blangé

100% arneis

As befits a wine made from arneis (which means rascal in the Piedmontese dialect), Ceretto's Blangé is impish and lively. No arneis is profound exactly, but Ceretto's is certainly appealing with its light almond and wildflower aromas and vanilla, citrusy flavors. A delicious aperitif.

### GAJA

Chardonnay

Rossj-Bass

100% chardonnay

Angelo Gaja makes two mind-blowing chardonnays: Rossj-Bass and Gaia & Rey. Though the latter is more famous and more intensely voluptuous, the Rossj-Bass is the more pure, high-toned, elegant wine. There's just enough oak to enrich the fruit yet not so much that the wine is overwrought with buttered toast flavors. Rossj-Bass possesses the essence of sheer chardonnay fruit. There's a dense, creamy pear-nectar quality, always spiked with jazzy appley acidity. The grapes come from two vineyards, one in Barbaresco, one in Barolo.

## *Reds*

### BRAIDA DI GIACOMO BOLOGNA

Barbera

Bricco dell'Uccellone

100% barbera

In dialect, *uccellone* are women witches with big, hooked noses. If such creatures exist, they've infused this barbera with the power to cast a spell over those who drink it, for the wine is nothing short of hypnotic. In the best vintages, the aroma is like walking into a chocolate factory crossed with a winery. Exuberant aromas and flavors of ripe figs, tar, and even (like Barolo) violets fill the senses. The wine can be so thick, rich, and satisfying it's like a bear hug. The late Giacomo Bologna was a driving force in establishing barbera as one of northern Italy's best reds, and it shows in this wine. A longer-aged *riserva* version of the wine, called Bricco della Bigotta, is utterly stunning and supple. A *bigotta* is a woman who goes to church and gossips.

### CERETTO

Barolo

Bricco Rocche

100% nebbiolo

Bricco Rocche Bricco Rocche (the name of the wine and the name of the tiny 3.7 acre vineyard are the same) is above all an elegant wine of intense concentration with a flawless suede-like texture. The irresistible musky, earthy, almost body scent this wine sometimes has can stop you in your tracks. This is the most expensive and refined of the three Ceretto single-vineyard Barolos. Ceretto only produces Bricco Rocche Bricco Rocche four or five times a decade.

## GAJA

Barbaresco

Sorì Tildìn

100% nebbiolo

Gaja makes a number of stunning Piedmontese wines, including his four Barbarescos, which are the heart and soul of the winery. Though all are richly flavored, complex wines with soaring structures, the single-vineyard Sorì Tildìn is utterly incomparable. The sensation of sipping this wine is rather like coming in from the cold and being wrapped up in a warm blanket. The wine gushes with violets, chocolate, and figs and the tannin broaches silk in its ability to be strong and soft at the same time.

## MARCARINI

Dolcetto d'Alba

Boschi di Berri

100% dolcetto

Dolcetto doesn't get better than Marcarini. The wine is a vibrating bowl full of burstingly ripe, maddeningly red cherries laced with vanilla cream sauce. The fruit is so dense it seems muscular. The balance is also perfect and the finish is remarkably long. Crave inducing.

## PODERI ALDO CONTERNO

Barbera d'Alba

100% barbera

It's true that Aldo Conterno and his family make some of the most majestic Barolos in Piedmont, but their barbera is a show stealer. If barbera occasionally has rustic edges, you don't sense them here. The flavors of chocolate, mocha, and figs open up into a juicy, almost syrupy wine with velvet-soft tannin. Conterno captures barbera's natural acidity in the wine's zippy finish.

## PODERI LUIGI EINAUDI

Barolo

100% nebbiolo

Italy's first president, Luigi Einaudi, was the man who held the country together after the collapse of Fascism during World War II. His fervent love of the land, and especially of Piedmont, led him to create a wine estate, which is today run by his descendants. Piedmont's affinity with Burgundy is evident in every sip of this Barolo, for it seems almost unctuous, with sexy-earthy aromas and a seamless texture. There's usually a boatload of tannin here, but the tar, violets, vanilla, and fruit are often so potent that the wine is poised in terrific balance. Einaudi is a traditionalist estate, but the wines always have flashy personalities.

## VIETTI

Barbera d'Alba

Pian Romualdo

100% barbera

341

The spirited Vietti family is intensely hardworking, and their passion shows through in their wines. They make three single-vineyard barberas (Bussia, Scarrone, and Pian Romualdo), and each has explosive, rich fruit. Yet the

*barrique*-aged Pian Romualdo, from a very high altitude vineyard, is the one that will stop you in your tracks. This is a wine that can seem so kinetic it actually seems alive. The citrus, leather, and vanilla flavors rage around tempestlike in the glass.

# The Tre Venezie

Friuli-Venezia Giulia, Trentino-Alto Adige, and the Veneto, the three northeastern regions of Italy, are known collectively as the Tre Venezie—Three Venices—because of their historical relationship to the Republic of Venice. Today they are united by more than history alone. With only a handful of exceptions, Italy's most stylish, highest quality white wines, including some of the raciest sparkling wines, now come from this area. In addition, the Tre Venezie boasts a slew of fascinating reds. Though the three regions produce only about 15 percent of all Italian wines, they account for about 30 percent of DOC—that is premium—wines.

Bordered on the north by the majestic Alps, the regions share a northern climate and a way of doing things that doesn't quite seem Mediterranean in spirit. Germanic, Austrian, Swiss, and Slovenian influences go back centuries. The cultural ties crop up in local dialects, local dishes, and even in the precise and decisive way winemakers go about making their wines. Not surprisingly, two of the best wine schools in Italy are located in the Tre Venezie, and one of Europe's largest vine nurseries is in Friuli-Venezia Giulia. More than half the vines planted in Italy originated there.

The Tre Venezie is known internationally for several popular wines named for the places where they are made, notably Soave and Valpolicella. But many other wines from these regions are labeled varietally, making them very easy to under-

342

*The Grand Canal in Venice: The city's extensive waterways and direct access to the sea made it one of the most commercially successful in Italy.*

stand. Virtually all of Italy's top pinot grigios (pinot gris), pinot biancos (pinot blancs), sauvignon blancs, and chardonnays come from here. It's tempting to imagine that varieties of grapes such as these were imported relatively recently. However, most of the so-called international varieties have been grown in the Tre Venezie since the nineteenth century. In addition to these, native varieties, such as teroldego, tocai friulano, schioppettino, and lagrein, make very exciting wines. Although for centuries they were consumed almost exclusively locally or in nearby Germany and Austria, these wines are now being exported more widely. The Tre Venezie is also home to many of Italy's best dessert wines, all of which are made from native grapes, including verduzzo, picolit, nosiola, and vespaiolo.

# FRIULI-VENEZIA GIULIA

Usually just called Friuli, Friuli-Venezia Giulia sticks out like a small ear from the northeastern top of Italy. Psychologically, the region seems much closer to Austria and Germany than, say, to Rome. One can almost taste the proximity. The wines of Friuli have precision, focus, and grip. They, among all the wines of the Tre Venezie, may well be the most Teutonic.

In a country where "real" wine generally means red wine, Friuli is acclaimed as one of the top places in the world for snappy whites. In particular, Friulian pinot grigios, pinot biancos, and sauvignon blancs can be stunning, as can its chardonnays. But if any white wine has captured the Friulian heart, it is one that is theirs alone: tocai (officially called tocai friulano). Tocai, which rhymes with high, is the Slavic word for here. Though it may seem odd for an important Italian grape to have a Slavic name, over centuries this part of the world has changed hands frequently as its neighbors jockeyed for power. And on the heels of tocai is another indigenous white-wine favorite: ribolla gialla. Each of these varieties is used on its own and in the region's numerous blends.

> ## THE QUICK SIP ON FRIULI
>
>
>
> • Many of Italy's most vibrant, racy white wines are produced here.
>
> • Some of the best whites are intriguing blends of such native varieties as tocai friulano and ribolla gialla with international varieties like pinot grigio (pinot gris), sauvignon blanc, pinot bianco (pinot blanc), and chardonnay.
>
> • Despite the renown accorded the region's whites, red wines account for almost half of the total production in Friuli. The most prestigious red grapes are merlot, cabernet sauvignon, and cabernet franc, as well as the native grape schioppettino.

The popularity and success of Friuli's white wines, however, doesn't mean that the region lacks good reds. Nearly half of the region's wines are red. Most of this is merlot, which, grown in Friuli's warmer pockets, can be surprisingly good. But the most fascinating, boldly flavored reds by far are such indigenous varieties as schioppettino and tazzelenghe.

Friuli is often characterized as one of the most ambitious and successful wine-making regions of Italy. Premium wines (those with DOC status) constitute more than 40 percent of its total production. Moreover, in less than two decades Friuli's white wines have gained an international following. No other region of Italy has moved so quickly from near obscurity to distinction.

## THE NAME FRIULI-VENEZIA GIULIA

Friuli and Venezia Giulia were once two separate provinces. According to Burton Anderson in *The Wine Atlas of Italy,* the Giulia of Venezia Giulia refers to Julius Caesar. So does Friuli, which is derived from the Latin Forum Julii, now the city of Cividale, in the renowned eastern wine district of Colli Orientali.

Culturally and historically, Friuli is rich. For centuries, northern European and Near Eastern tribes moved through the region on their way to the Mediterranean. The overland spice routes ran through Friuli from the markets of the Byzantine Empire to Venice. Much later—before it became part of the newly formed country of Italy in 1866—Friuli was the strategic Mediterranean port province of the Austro-Hungarian Empire.

Thus, after centuries of exposure to eclectic ethnic influences, cultural diversity, political jockeying, and mercantile bustle, the Friulians have been left with a sense of dynamism, a can-do spirit, and a healthy attitude when it comes to change.

The wines reflect this. As a group, Friulian wines are spirited, creative, highly varied, and wholly individualistic.

# THE LAND, THE GRAPES, AND THE VINEYARDS

The Alps form Friuli's northern border, and the northern half of the region is extremely mountainous. As a result, nearly all of the vineyards are located in the southern half. The best are situated on sloping Alpine foothills, but the vast majority of Friulian vineyards are on the plains stretching inland from the Adriatic Sea. It is this juxtaposition of mountains and sea that creates the cool nights and warm days that contribute to the exhilaratingly taut structure and pinpoint balance of Friuli's best wines. It is important that the vineyards lie across hillsides and plains on the sunny side of the Alps. Here, exposed to the heat and light of the sun, the grapes have time to ripen fully. As a result, Friulian whites are not fragile; they are whites with body and a determined grip.

Although the region's fine wine reputation was built on white wines—especially those made from tocai, pinot grigio, pinot bianco, ribolla gialla, chardonnay, and sauvignon blanc—about half of total production is red. Merlot is the leading variety, with cabernet franc and cabernet sauvignon in pursuit, plus terrific indigenous red grapes, such as schioppettino and refosco. In all, more than thirty grape varieties are commonly planted, with about a dozen dominating. (If this seems like a lot for a region just two thirds the size of Connecticut, consider that before phylloxera arrived in Friuli at the end of the nineteenth century, more than 350 varieties were grown!)

## THE GRAPES OF
# FRIULI-VENEZIA GIULIA

### WHITES

**Chardonnay:** An increasingly important grape. Can make monodimensional wines or lush, highly complex ones, depending on the producer and the site.

**Picolit:** A native grape used to make interesting, rare dessert wines. Only a tiny amount is produced due to the vines' genetic abnormalities.

**Pinot Bianco:** Also known as pinot blanc. Wines from it are round, and fairly lush. Often blended with chardonnay.

**Pinot Grigio:** Also known as pinot gris. A popular variety. Makes light- to medium-bodied wines that range from decent to delicious.

**Ribolla Gialla:** Native variety. Makes very attractive wines with delicious citrusy, peachy flavors.

**Sauvignon Blanc:** Popular variety. Turned into zesty, wild, dramatic wines, the best of which are reminiscent of French Sancerre.

**Tocai Friulano:** Also called simply tocai. A local favorite and a native grape. The wines made from it are medium-bodied and creamy with herbal hints.

**Verduzzo:** A special native grape that is used to make Friuli's most stunning dessert wine, verduzzo di Ramandolo.

### REDS

**Cabernet Franc:** The second most popular red variety. First planted in Friuli in the late nineteenth century. Often high in acidity and lean in body but can make good cranberry-flavored wines.

**Cabernet Sauvignon:** While less widespread than cabernet franc, cabernet sauvignon was planted in Friuli even earlier. The wines are usually lean and tight.

**Merlot:** Most widely planted red. Makes wines that range in quality from lean and austere to rich and silky.

**Refosco:** Popular native red. Turned into zesty, inky, easy-drinking wines.

**Schioppettino:** Most sophisticated native red variety. Wines made from it are sharp and concentrated with multiple fruit and spice flavors.

**Tazzelenghe:** Translates literally as cuts the tongue. Native variety. Makes unusually bold, high-acid wines.

Although wines based on a single variety are common, Friuli is also where some of the most compelling Italian white blends are to be found. The two most famous are Vintage Tunina, a blend of four or five grapes by the producer Jermann, and Ronco delle Acacie (which means hilltop of the acacias), a blend of four grapes by the producer Abbazia di Rosazzo (the abbey of roses). Finally, two of Italy's most exquisite dessert wines, verduzzo di Ramandolo and picolit, are both made in Friuli.

The two most prestigious wine districts in Friuli are the Colli Orientali del Friuli and the Collio (technically known as the Collio Goriziano). Both are in the far east, just short of the Slovenian border. Here the best hilly vineyards are located on terraces, where the well-drained, crumbly, calcium-rich marl and sandstone soil is known as flysch. The soil in the valleys tends more toward clay, sand, and gravel.

In the local Friulian dialect, the tops of the terraced hillsides are called *ronchi*. The

## THE MOST IMPORTANT

# FRIULIAN WINES

### LEADING WINES

**Cabernet Franc** red
**Cabernet Sauvignon** red
**Chardonnay** white
**Merlot** red
**Pinot Bianco** white
**Pinot Grigio** white
**Refosco** red
**Ribolla Gialla** white
**Sauvignon Blanc** white
**Schioppettino** red
**Tocai Friulano** white

### WINES OF NOTE

**Picolit** white (sweet)
**Tazzelenghe** red
**Verduzzo di Ramandolo**
white (sweet)

Although there are a growing number of oaky chardonnays made in Friuli, they are not the region's signature. For the most part, its whites do not have the dominant toasty, vanilla cloak of flavor that comes from being fermented and/or aged in wood, nor do they undergo the acid-flattening effects of malolactic fermentation. For Friulian winemakers, the flavor of the fruit and the natural acidity is everything. This devotion to purity is a fairly rare philosophy in the world of white wine. The other places that share it are Alsace and the Loire Valley in France and the wine regions of Germany, Austria, and to a slightly lesser extent, New Zealand.

*Some of the Best Producers of*
*Friulian Pinot Grigio*

ABBAZIA DI ROSAZZO

ENOFRIULIA

JERMANN

MARCO FELLUGA

PIERPAOLO PECORARI

RENATO KEBER

RONCO DEL GNEMIZ

RONCO DEI TASSI

STEVERJAN

word *ronchi*—or the singular *ronco*—is often the first word of the name of a vineyard or wine estate, such as Ronco dei Tassi (hilltop of the badgers). As for the word *colli*, it means small hills in Friulian dialect. Colli Orientali refers to eastern hills.

## *Friulian Whites*

Sophisticated white wine was Friuli's toe up in the world, but characteristically, the Friulians took their own atypical approach to making it. During the 1970s and 1980s, while almost every up-and-coming wine region in the world was focused on creating unctuous, barrel-fermented, oak-aged wines, especially chardonnays, Friuli was making the opposite—taut, kinetic whites with stiletto acidity.

## THE PINOT FAMILY

The pinot grigio grape, grown throughout the Tre Venezie, is the same as the French pinot gris. The pinot family, native to Burgundy, also includes the white grape pinot blanc and two reds, pinot noir and pinot meunier. Wines made in the United States from pinot gris grapes may be called pinot gris or pinot grigio.

*Unlike their French colleagues, many sommeliers in Italy are women.*

Above all, Friulian whites have presence. They are rarely plain-Jane, rarely frail. Instead, these are concentrated whites with pronounced fruity-spicy-earthy flavors. While many pinot grigios are about as exciting as tap water, the top Friulian pinot grigios can soar with delicate peach, almond, and green apple flavors (Steverjan's, for example) or be so voluptuous and rich they seem descended from ice cream (Jermann's).

Tocai, the local favorite, is probably the hardest Friulian wine to describe. It ranges from smoky, peppery, and sharp to lush and vanilla-y to being spiked with minerals and exotic spices. Because of its bold personality, many Friulian winemakers refer to it as the most masculine of the white grapes. (Tocai, an ancient indigenous variety in Friuli pronounced toe-KI, is *not* related to the Alsace wine nicknamed tokay, pronounced toe-KAY, which is

really pinot gris. Nor is it related to the famous Hungarian dessert wine Tokay, also toe-KAY, which is made principally from the grape furmint.)

Wines made from ribolla gialla can be so pretty, so delightfully peachy and lightly citrusy, and so simply satisfying that it's amazing this grape is not grown anywhere else except Slovenia and Greece. The sauvignon blancs (the name is usually shortened to just sauvignon) can be lean and smoky with all the herbal character of a Sancerre or creamy and dripping with delicate honey and hazelnut flavors. As for Friulian chardonnays, their quality and style vary greatly, but from a master like Jermann, chardonnay—even in a voluptuous style—is utter elegance.

347

*Some of the Best Producers of Tocai Friulano*

**ABBAZIA DI ROSAZZO**

**ENOFRIULIA**

**FRANCESCO PECORARI**

**JERMANN**

**LIVIO FELLUGA**

**PIERPAOLO PECORARI**

**RONCO DEI TASSI**

**STEVERJAN**

**ZAMÓ & ZAMÓ**

## JERMANN

—◦◦◦—

Among the most legendary Friulian wines are those of the shy, artistic winemaker Silvio Jermann. In 1977 at the age of twenty-one, Jermann created Vintage Tunina, a blend of chardonnay, sauvignon blanc, ribolla gialla plus other grapes. Vintage Tunina was so voluptuous and nuanced, it set off the modern trend for making sophisticated Friulian white blends. (Tunina was the name of the old woman who originally owned the vineyard from which the grapes came. Later, the Jermann family bought it.) Jermann's genius is the ability to pull deep facets of personality from each grape.

*Where the Dreams have no end ....*

FRIULIAN WHITE TABLE WINE - PRODUCT OF ITALY - NET CONT. 750 ML - ALC. 13% BY VOL.

Every Jermann wine, from sauvignon blanc and ribolla gialla to tocai and chardonnay, is clearly focused, powerfully flavored, and impeccably balanced. Until 1987 no Jermann wine was made or aged in new oak. In that year Jermann created a 100 percent barrel-fermented chardonnay called Where the Dreams Have No End. The name, a take-off on the song "Where the Streets Have No Name" by the Irish rock group U2, was later changed to just Were Dreams. Jermann maintains that his dreams are very important in helping him with winemaking and viticultural decisions.

## *Friulian Reds*

It would seem counterintuitive that a relatively cool region known for vivacious white wines would also produce a significant number of reds. Yet about 40 percent of Friulian wine is red, and much of that is merlot. Cabernet franc, cabernet sauvignon, the fascinating native grapes schioppettino, refosco, and tazzelenghe, plus a small number of other varieties round out the rest.

Many of the most dynamic reds are made from the indigenous grape varieties. Schioppettino can be startling—hauntingly dry with sharp peppery, spicy, black cherry flavors and a tight, angular body. The word *schioppettino* means gunshot, a reference to the intensity of the wine's flavor and texture. Refosco is a great everyday drinking wine with dense blueberry and blackberry flavors and vivid acidity. The wine tazzelenghe is dagger sharp.

Merlot and cabernet have been made in Friuli for more than a century. In the past, these were austere, light, and lean wines. But as winemakers have begun to better understand the nuances of making red wines in fairly cool climates, Friuli's merlots and cabernets have become more flavorful and concentrated. In great vintages, Schiopetto's merlot, for example, is a wine not to be missed. And the same can be said of Zamo & Zamo's fabulous cabernet, a wine that often possesses remarkably lively menthol and mint flavors. Like several producers, Zamo & Zamo labels its blend of cabernet franc and cabernet sauvignon simply with the word cabernet.

As is true of the white wines, the reds of Friuli are often unpredictably intriguing blends. Abbazia di Rosazzo's Ronco dei Rosetti, for example, takes on a sharply spicy forest-floor character thanks to the tazzelenghe and refosco that are added to the standard blend of cabernet sauvignon, merlot, and cabernet franc.

## *Friuli's Sweet Wines*

Italy makes more diverse, fascinating dessert wines than any other country in the world, and two of the most intriguing are Friulian—verduzzo di Ramandolo,

## THE FAMOUS PROSCIUTTO OF FRIULI

On September 6, 1989, 6,000 haunches of prosciutto were cradled aboard jets and flown to the United States. It was the first time in two decades (the hams had been banned since 1968) that true Italian prosciutto was legally available in the United States.

Prosciutto is made all over Italy, but the best comes from just one type of pig: the massive (350 pound) Lambrea pig raised either in Friuli near the town of San Daniele (for *prosciutto di San Daniele*) or in Emilia-Romagna near the town of Parma

(for *prosciutto di Parma*). The pigs are fed natural grains and the rich whey from such famous cheeses as Parmigiano-Reggiano.

The raw ham is cured without smoke or heat over the course of 400 days. (Some American hams are processed in *one* day.) First the meat is thickly salted, then the hams are massaged, pounded, rubbed, and eventually washed with water and a stiff wire brush. The haunches are hung to slowly air-cure in specially designed buildings with long vertical windows. In Friuli it is said that the warm, salty sea air mixed with the cold Alpine air is a perfect combination—the result is a coral pink ham with a silky texture and a sweet, meaty taste that is exceedingly complex. In Friuli, prosciutto combined with melon or figs is served with a fruity, floral white wine, often a glass of tocai or ribolla gialla.

*Prosciutti are cured naturally and very slowly by hanging them so that they are well exposed to air. The art of slicing a prosciutto correctly so that it is paper-thin takes years of practice (and a special knife).*

made from verduzzo grapes, and picolit, made from picolit grapes. Both grape varieties are grown on the Alpine hillsides of the Colli Orientali. Verduzzo di Ramandolo is made near the tiny village of Ramandolo. This is one of the lightest-bodied, most exquisite dessert wines made anywhere. Often it has a beautiful coppery sheen and a touch of herbal flavors. The best producers are Giovanni Dri, Russiz Superiore, and Ronchi di Cialla.

Picolit probably shouldn't even exist. The grape variety has a genetic mutation that causes it to spontaneously abort the flowers on its newly formed clusters (flowers ultimately become grapes). Even in good years, less than half of picolit's flowers survive to become grapes. The wine, as a result, is very expensive. The best picolits are gossamer in their light, delicate honeyedness. Top producers vary considerably from vintage to vintage depending on who has had success with the grapes.

*Grape pickers in northern Italy are often students and frequently women.*

## VISITING FRIULIAN WINE ESTATES

Friuli-Venezia Giulia is not a large region. Most wineries in the Collio and Colli Orientali districts are an easy drive from the ancient port city of Trieste. Farther inland, the wine town of Udine with its Venetian Renaissance-style piazza serves as an unofficial headquarters for traveling wine lovers who want to make day trips in all directions. When visiting Friulian wineries, it's necessary to make appointments in advance and helpful, though not critical, to speak Italian. The telephone numbers include the dialing code you'll need when calling from the United States. If you're calling from within Italy, eliminate the 011-39.

**ABBAZIA DI ROSAZZO**
Località Rosazzo
33044 Manzano, Udine
011-39-0432-75-90-91

**AZIENDA FRATELLI PIGHIN**
1 Viale Grando, Fraz. Risano
33050 Pavia di Udine, Udine
011-39-0432-67-54-44

**PIERPAOLO PECORARI**
36/C Via Tommaseao
34070 S. Lorenzo Isontino, Gorizia
011-39-0481-80-87-75

**RONCO DEL GNEMIZ**
5 Via Ronchi
33048 San Giovanni al Natisone, Udine
011-39-0432-75-62-38

**STEVERJAN**
S. Floriano del Collio
Steverjan, Bukuje 6, 34070, Gorizia
011-39-0481-88-41-92

**VIGNE DAL LEON**
Località Rocca Bernarda
33040 Ipplisoli Premariacco, Udine
011-39-0432-75-96-93

# THE FRIULIAN WINES TO KNOW

## *Whites*

### ABBAZIA DI ROSAZZO

Ronco delle Acacie

chardonnay, tocai, and pinot blanc;
percentages not disclosed

Long regarded as one of the most beautifully structured, densely flavored wines of Friuli, Abbazia di Rosazzo's Ronco delle Acacie is often extraordinary. In top vintages, this rich, lush white is so precise and balanced that it seems utterly elegant. The creamy, hazelnut, and honey flavors that surge through the wine give it dizzying liveliness.

### ABBAZIA DI ROSAZZO

Tocai Friulano

Colli Orientali del Friuli

100% tocai friulano

If a wine could prance, this tocai would. Exuberant fresh apple and spice flavors spring around with such energy that the wine cannot help but be refreshing. Abbazia di Rosazzo is one of the top Friuli producers committed to preserving such ancient indigenous grape varieties as tocai.

### JERMANN

Tocai Italico

100% tocai friulano

The producer Jermann (the *j* is pronounced like a *y*) is legendary for wines of impeccable elegance and unmatched richness. The tocai is as peachy and vanilla-y as fresh peach shortcake drizzled with crème anglaise. Hints of ginger, pepper, and minerals make it exotic. Once tasted, the wine, as oxymoronic as it may sound, explodes slowly.

### JERMANN

Vintage Tunina

chardonnay and sauvignon blanc with small amounts of ribolla gialla, malvasia, and sometimes picolit; percentages not disclosed

One of the greatest Italian white wines from one of the greatest Friulian winemakers, Vintage Tunina proved early on that the sky was the limit for Friulian whites. The wine—a blend of multiple grapes—is a huge, voluptuous riot of juicy flavors, the equivalent of an impressionist painting.

### MARCO FELLUGA

Pinot Bianco

100% pinot bianco

Many of the best pinot biancos in northern Italy come from Friuli. These are wines that are not pale imitations of chardonnay, as many pinot biancos are, but rather wines of real personality. Often, one of the finest is Marco Felluga's, a wine that can be beautifully focused,  with flavors of peach and apple and a fresh streak of crispness. Perfect with a platter of grilled fish.

### STEVERJAN

Pinot Grigio

100% pinot grigio

Too many pinot grigios are disappointingly innocuous, but this is not the case with Steverjan's, which is extremely focused and bone-dry. The wine has almost razor-sharp acidity and a hint of sparkle. The flavors of ginger, almonds, and peaches seem to tiptoe around—lightly and pristinely—in the glass.

351

## VENICA

Vignis di Venica

approximately 50% tocai friulano, 40% chardonnay, and 10% sauvignon blanc

In a world where so many white wines have all the individuality of Kleenex, wines like Vignis di Venica—a fascinating

VIGNIS DI VENICA
VINO DA TAVOLA
- FRIULI WHITE TABLE WINE -
PRODUCED AND BOTTLED
BY AZIENDA AGRICOLA
VENICA & VENICA
DOLEGNA DEL COLLIO - ITALY
PRODUCT OF ITALY
750 ML - ALCOHOL 12.50% BY VOLUME

combination of tocai, chardonnay, and sauvignon blanc—prove just how distinctive and delicious Friulian blends can be. The pure smoky, fruit-hay-meadow aromas and flavors of Venica's sharply focused wine are dazzling. And they all derive from the grapes themselves—no new oak is used. The grapes come from a family-owned estate in the Collio.

## Reds

### RONCHI DI CIALLA

Schioppettino di Cialla

100% schioppettino

One of the best, Ronchi di Cialla's schioppettino fairly quivers with vibrant spiciness. In addition, in top vintages, leathery, earthy, and gamy aromas and flavors stream through the wine as though conducted by electric current. Around these is wrapped a robe of bright sweet cherry. One of Friuli's most lip-smacking reds, like all good schioppettinos, it begs for food.

### SCHIOPETTO

Merlot

100% merlot

Mario Schiopetto was one of the early pioneers committed to making world-class Friulian wines. Schiopetto's pinot bianco and tocai can be stunning, but he also makes more than a dozen other wines and all are snapped up almost immediately after release. In top vintages, the Schiopetto merlot, oozing with warm blackberry and black cherry flavors, is one of the best in Italy. After a few minutes exposure to air, the wine's complexity reveals itself as hints of mint, game, bark, black pepper, and exotic spices begin to emerge. The texture is tantalizing: as langorous as cough syrup, yet with a racy edge.

### VIGNE DAL LEON

Schioppettino

100% schioppettino

The word *schioppettino* means gunshot and, in good vintages, there's no better term to describe the mouthfeel of this wine. First there's the bullet of spiciness, then the long, scratchy trail of peppery

black cherry flavors. Wines from the schioppettino grape are naturally angular and sharp. That edge makes them a perfect counterpoint to any dish with lots of olive oil.

### ZAMO & ZAMO

Cabernet

50% cabernet franc, 50% cabernet sauvignon

Le Vigne di Zamó—known to most wine drinkers as Zamó & Zamó—makes a wine called simply cabernet. It's a great example of the raw intensity the reds of Friuli possess at their best. Some might pass this

wine up as too severe, but careful tasting reveals a sensational core of ripe, minty, menthol-y fruit. If you like wines with bracing grip and drive, this red's for you.

# TRENTINO-ALTO ADIGE

No Italian wine region extends farther north than Trentino-Alto Adige, where pristine vineyards carpet narrow Alpine valleys as high as 3,600 feet in elevation. The sheer rock faces of the foreboding Alps rise up majestically and virtually perpendicularly behind the vines. These are some of the most breathtaking vineyards in the world.

Trentino-Alto Adige, despite its hyphen, is really two distinct places. Trentino in the south is primarily Italian speaking. But in Alto Adige, nestled beneath Austria in the north, German, not Italian, is the primary language. Once known as the South Tyrol, Alto Adige was ceded to Italy by Austria after World War I. Politics, however, don't always amend the ideology of a place, and for many residents of Alto Adige the Südtirol is still the name of the place where they live.

While cultural differences between Trentino and Alto Adige can run deep, the two provinces share a common ideology

## THE QUICK SIP ON TRENTINO-ALTO ADIGE

• The top Trentino-Alto Adige wines, including chardonnays, pinot biancos, pinot grigios, traminers, and sparkling wines, have precision, grip, and focus.

• Trentino-Alto Adige boasts a large number of grape varieties, including fascinating indigenous varieties, such as teroldego and lagrein, as well as international varieties, such as cabernet sauvignon and merlot.

• Encompassing what was once known as the South Tyrol and enveloped by the Alps, Trentino-Alto Adige is one of the most beautiful wine regions in Europe.

353

when it comes to wine. Like Friuli-Venezia Giulia, Trentino-Alto Adige brings a northern, even Teutonic sensibility to winemaking. Here again, the best wines have focus and solid presence. And here again, the

*Trento, the capital of Trentino, is breathtakingly poised in front of the Dolomite Alps.*

ranks of premium wines are growing. Although the number of top estates is admittedly smaller in Trentino-Alto Adige than in Friuli-Venezia Giulia, the best producers—such wineries as Alois Lageder, J. Hofstätter, Pojer e Sandri, and Zeni to name a few—make wines of ravishing beauty.

As is true for the rest of the Tre Venezie, Trentino-Alto Adige is home to a vast range of indigenous and international grape varieties. Among the most important white grapes are pinot grigio, pinot bianco, traminer, and chardonnay, the last having been grown in the region since the mid-nineteenth century. Given the availability of chardonnay, plus the penchant for precision among top winemakers, it's no surprise that the Trentino-Alto Adige has also developed a thriving sparkling wine industry.

Amazingly, despite the success of its white wines, and as unexpected as it might seem for a northern region, Trentino-Alto Adige produces more red wine than white. Cabernet franc, cabernet sauvignon, and merlot are widely planted along with lagrein, schiava, and teroldego. While some of this is drunk locally, much also goes to satisfy the red wine cravings of the nearby Germans, Austrians, and Swiss.

## THE LAND, THE GRAPES, AND THE VINEYARDS

Unlike Friuli-Venezia Giulia and the Veneto, both of which open onto the Adriatic Sea, Trentino-Alto Adige is landlocked. The Alps virtually surround the region in the north, the Veneto borders it on the south and east, Lombardy on the south and west. Running through the middle of the region is the river Adige, the second longest in Italy, from which the district of Alto Adige takes its name.

It seems almost miraculous that vineyards can exist in Trentino-Alto Adige's high narrow valleys, which have been sculpted over eons by ancient glaciers and streams. Yet vines appear to cover every square inch of valley floor, and vineyards also perch on ancient terraces built by hand into the hillsides. None of this is a new phenomenon. Vineyards have filled these valleys since Roman times.

*Grapes trained high up on a pergola.*

One of the vestiges of traditional viticulture here is an old system of trellising in which vines are trained up on poles and across wires, creating an overhead arbor. Known as a *pergola trentina*, this trellising system looks quite charming and Old World, and it does have the advantage of keeping the grapes far above the ground, thereby minimizing dew and, potentially, rot. But a great disadvantage of the system is that the vines tend to grow profusely, creating high yields that often lead to thin, bitter wines. As a result most of the best vineyards are planted in a standard manner, not on pergolas.

This is the sunny, south-facing side of the Alps and so despite Trentino-Alto Adige's northern latitude, the vineyard-covered valleys are warm enough during summer to ripen grapes. The soil is also pretty ideal. Well drained and laced with limestone, it was created by glacial and

## THE GRAPES OF
## TRENTINO-ALTO ADIGE

### WHITES

**Chardonnay:** An important variety. Can make light innocuous wines or lively intense wines with creamy, apple-vanilla flavors. Also the leading varietal in the region's dry *spumantes* (sparkling wines).

**Müller-Thurgau:** A surprisingly successful variety, especially in the Alto Adige where it is turned into some lovely, floral, vibrant wines.

**Nosiola:** Fairly rare native grape used in the production of *vino santo*, an opulent dessert wine.

**Pinot Bianco:** Also known as pinot blanc. Can make lovely light, citrusy-peachy wines.

**Pinot Grigio:** Also known as pinot gris. An important variety, it is the source of wines that range from light and crisp to richly floral with citrus and mineral notes.

**Sauvignon Blanc:** Shows promise. At its best makes smoky, spicy herbal wines.

**Traminer:** The progenitor of the better-known grape gewürztraminer. Although traminer can be very aromatic and concentrated, it is usually light in body.

### REDS

**Cabernet Franc:** First planted in Trentino-Alto Adige in the late nineteenth century. The wines are frequently high in acidity and lean in body but with good leathery aromas.

**Cabernet Sauvignon:** Leading international variety planted here in the nineteenth century. The wines are often sleek, with herbal and leathery notes, but the best vineyards can produce wines of greater depth and intensity.

**Lagrein:** Important native variety. Makes fascinating, tasty, sharp wines.

**Lambrusco:** Widely planted for inexpensive blends, this grape is not the same as the grape also called lambrusco in Emilia-Romagna.

**Marzemino:** A native grape. Wines made from it are rustic and juicy.

**Merlot:** Generally a source of simple, lean, everyday reds.

**Schiava** or **Vernatsch:** Productive and important native variety. Makes light, sometimes spicy wines with a bitter almond flavor. It's the leading grape in Santa Maddalena and Caldaro.

**Teroldego:** Important native variety and a specialty of Trentino. Makes dark, smoky, spicy, minerally wines with bitter chocolate and dried cherry flavors.

355

alluvial deposits of gravel, sand, and clay.

Some twenty different grape varieties are planted here. These are made into wines named after the variety of grape (teroldego, pinot grigio, and so forth) or named for their place (Santa Maddalena, for example). Moreover, though it can make a wine label look crowded, wines from Alto Adige will usually carry both Italian and German designations. A bottle of Santa Maddalena therefore will also note its German name, St. Magdalener.

Chardonnay, the most important white, is made into wines that run the gamut from innocuous quaffers to sassy, fresh, lime-scented wines to more modern, toasty, oaky examples. It's also the base for a small ocean of good dry *spumante*. Sparkling wines were pioneered in the region in the early twentieth century by Giulio Ferrari, and Ferrari is still

## THE MOST IMPORTANT

## TRENTINO-ALTO ADIGE WINES

### LEADING WINES

**Cabernet Franc** red
**Cabernet Sauvignon** red
**Chardonnay** white
**Lagrein** red
**Merlot** red
**Pinot Bianco** white
**Pinot Grigio** white
**Schiava** or **Vernatsch** red
**Sparkling Wines** white
**Teroldego** red
**Traminer** white

### WINES OF NOTE

**Lambrusco** red
**Marzemino** red
**Müller-Thurgau** white
**Sauvignon Blanc** white
**Vino Santo** white (sweet)

ALOIS LAGEDER

BENEFIZIUM PORER

PINOT GRIGIO ALTO ADIGE

Thurgau, usually a pretty unexciting grape. The most fascinating of these is Pojer e Sandri's sensationally spicy, minerally Müller-Thurgau. The most famous is Tiefenbrunner's Feldmarschall von Fenner zu Fennberg Müller-Thurgau, named after a disciple of Kaiser Wilhelm II. It comes from the vineyard thought to have the highest elevation in Italy.

As for reds, the leading international varieties are cabernet sauvignon, cabernet franc, and merlot, and like chardonnay, they have been planted here since the nineteenth century. For anyone accustomed to drinking California versions of these varieties, many Trentino-Alto Adige cabernets and merlots can seem sleek and even slightly bitter. But the top examples, such as the cabernet sauvignons from Alois Lageder, can be surprisingly powerful, deep, and intense.

The adventurous will find Trentino-Alto Adige's indigenous reds to be captivating. One of the specialties of Trentino is a brooding, superspicy, tannic wine made from teroldego, a grape that grows best in the gravelly glacial soil of the Rotaliano plain. Another Trentino specialty, schiava (which in Alto Adige is called vernatsch), is turned into light, spicy wines with a slight bitter almond character. Schiava is used for everything from inexpensive blends to such extremely popular wines as Santa Maddalena and Caldaro (in German, Kalterersee).

Two other important native red grapes are lagrein and marzemino. Fascinating, dark, sharp, robust wines are what result from lagrein, but marzemino seems capable of becoming little more than a grapey rustic quaffing wine.

one of Trentino-Alto Adige's, indeed one of Italy's, top sparkling wine houses and the best known from the region.

The grape variety called traminer is a specialty here. Gorgeously floral, intensely flavorful, and yet light as a feather in body, traminer is the progenitor of gewürztraminer, a grape more familiar to most wine lovers. In the hands of a producer like Pojer e Sandri, traminer is irresistible for its purity, liveliness, and brilliance.

Pinot grigio (pinot gris), and pinot bianco (pinot blanc) are also the sources of tasty wines. And there are a number of very classy sauvignon blancs and even a number of vibrant wines made from Müller-

The most widely planted red grape however is lambrusco, which forms the base of many inexpensive reds.

The most important wine districts in Trentino-Alto Adige cluster around the cities of Bolzano and Trento, which are respectively the main cities of Alto Adige in the north and Trentino in the south.

---

*Some of the Best Producers of Trentino-Alto Adige Wines*

ALOIS LAGEDER

FORADORI

HIRSCHPRUNN

J. HOFSTÄTTER

LA CADALORA

POJER E SANDRI

TIEFENBRUNNER

ZENI

---

## VINO SANTO

⋙⋙⋙

Trentino-Alto Adige's highly prized dessert wine is *vino santo* (holy wine; probably a reference to its historic use as part of the Mass). A specialty of the Valle dei Laghi near the northern end of Lake Garda and also of the hills west of Trento, *vino santo* is traditionally made by leaving native nosiola grapes on trays to dry for several months, thereby concentrating the sugar in them. After the juice from the grapes is fermented and aged in the barrel, often for two or three years, the wine that emerges is amber colored, silky, and irresistibly sweet. Despite the similarity in their names, Trentino-Alto Adige's *vino santo* is not the same as Tuscany's *vin santo*, which is generally made from trebbiano and/or malvasia grapes.

## VISITING THE WINE ESTATES OF TRENTINO-ALTO ADIGE

Few wine regions are as stunning as Trentino-Alto Adige, with the Alps for a backdrop, majestic lakes dotting the countryside, and castles, churches, and vineyards that are simply immaculate. Not surprisingly the region is a hotbed of tourism. For driving alone, the Südtiroler Weinstrasse (South Tyrol wine road) in Alto Adige is one of the most charming roads in Italy. Many of the top wine estates here are family run. It's best to have an appointment and helpful to speak Italian or German, though English is widely understood. The telephone numbers include the dialing code you'll need when calling from the United States. If you're calling from within Italy, eliminate the 011-39.

**ALOIS LAGEDER**
Tenuta Löwengang
39040 Magre, Bolzano
011-39-0471-80-95-00

**FORADORI**
1 Via Damiano Chiesa
38017 Mezzolombardo, Trento
011-39-0461-60-10-46

**POJER E SANDRI**
6 Località Molini
Faedo, Trentino
011-39-0461-65-03-42

**TIEFENBRUNNER**
Località Niclara
4 Via Castello
39040 Cortaccia, Bolzano
011-39-0471-88-01-22

**ZENI FRAZ. GRUMOS**
2 Via Stretta
38010 Grumo San Michele All'Adige
Trento
011-39-0461-65-04-56

357

# THE TRENTINO-ALTO ADIGE WINES TO KNOW

## *Whites*

### ALOIS LAGEDER

Pinot Grigio

100% pinot grigio

Some of Trentino-Alto Adige's most brilliant and bracing wines come from Alois Lageder. While Lageder's single-vineyard pinot biancos and chardonnays have deservedly impressive reputations, a more humble variety like pinot grigio demonstrates just how masterful Lageder truly is. Talk about intensity! Here's a pinto grigio that zooms into focus with penetrating acidity and delicious ginger and lime flavors laced with hints of mineral.

### J. HOFSTATTER

Gewürztraminer

Kolbenhof

100% gewürztraminer

At its best, J. Hofstätter's gewürztraminer ranks as one of the most impressive in Europe, easily as penetrating and mouthfilling as the great gewürztraminers of France's Alsace region. What's especially appealing here is the wine's full-throttle spicy, rich litchi flavors and aromas, which are wrapped around a core of vibrant acidity. In Trentino-Alto Adige a powerful gewürztraminer like this would be drunk with roasted meat—especially pork—but this is also the sort of wine that's perfect served with Asian-inspired dishes.

### POJER E SANDRI

Müller-Thurgau

100% Müller-Thurgau

You could probably count on one hand the number of wineries in the world that take Müller-Thurgau seriously, and it's a testament to Pojer e Sandri's creativity and passion for excellence that they are one of them. In this case, however, what's amazing is not just the winery's determination with a Cinderella-like grape but the fact that the wine itself is fabulous. Spicy, sharp, and long on the palate, Pojer e Sandri's Müller-Thurgau is a liquid onslaught of ginger, lime, lemongrass, and mineral flavors.

### POJER E SANDRI

Traminer

mostly traminer with a tiny amount of gewürztraminer

Traminer, like its close relative gewürztraminer, is a variety that can be monumentally aromatic, and none more so than Pojer e Sandri's completely seductive version. If this wine's

mesmerizingly intense aromas of marzipan, litchi, minerals, and roses don't get you, then the purity and richness of its flavors will. To be both ethereally light in body but hauntingly intense in flavor at the same time is a feat not many wines manage, but such wines are Pojer e Sandri's hallmark. Admittedly, there aren't many traminers made in the world, but this well may be the best.

# *Reds*

## VIGNETO SGARZON

Teroldego Rotaliano

100% teroldego

Possibly even more sassy and dagger sharp than the Zeni teroldego that follows, this one from Vigneto Sgarzon is not for the faint of heart (or palate). The wine's slightly biting tannin is part of its rugged appeal, and the cocoa, pomegranate, bitter chocolate, espresso, and smoky flavors are terrific. This is exactly the kind of incisive red that works perfectly with rich pastas.

## ZENI

Teroldego Rotaliano

100% teroldego

In a world where softness is considered a virtue among red wines in general, the top reds of Trentino-Alto Adige stand in stark opposition. Renegade in style, they are sharp, edgy, sleek reds that often possess the liveliness of great whites. Zeni's sensational teroldego from the gravelly plain known as Rotaliano is a perfect example. Flamboyant and packed with black raspberry, black cherry cassis, and bitter chocolate flavors, here's a rustic, dramatic red just waiting for a creamy pasta or rich mushroom risotto.

# GRAPPA

You can always tell when Italians don't want the night to end. Out comes the grappa. This, in turn, causes everyone to recount their most infamous grappa-drinking stories—which leads to the pouring of more grappa—which leads to more stories. Though today grappa is made and drunk all over Italy, historically it was a specialty of the northern part of the country, where a small shot in the morning coffee helped one get going on a freezing day.

Grappa is the clear brandy that results when grape pomace (the pulpy mash of stems, seeds, and skins left over from winemaking) is refermented and distilled. Depending on the quality of raw material and the method of distillation, the final product can taste as though a grenade has just ignited in your throat or it can taste smooth, winey, and powerful. *Ue,* a softer, lighter type of grappa, is a distillate of actual grapes rather than pomace. And *grappa di monovitigno* is a grappa from a single grape variety, such as riesling, moscato, gewürztraminer, or picolit. These grappas are considered superior because the result carries a faint suggestion of the aroma and flavor of the original grapes. Expensive and rare, such grappas incite cult worship. In fact, grappa fans are called *tifosi di grappa,* a phrase that implies almost feverish allegiance (the word *tifosi* also means people suffering from typhoid).

The bottles are part of the attraction. Since the late 1980s, the dazzling, avantgarde designs of grappa bottles have been nothing less than astounding. No northern Italian *enoteca* is without an astonishing display of these elegant bottles, each holding a grappa that looks far more innocent than it tastes.

# THE VENETO

O f the three regions that make up the Tre Venezie, the Veneto is by far the best known, although probably for the wrong reasons. In terms of volume, this is the leading wine-producing region of the north and, in some years, the most prolific region in all of Italy, beating out even Sicily and Apulia, the south's two megaproducers. Unfortunately, oceans of Veneto wine are entirely forgettable, obscuring the fact that the region is also home to a few great classics, such as amarone, considered by many Italian wine experts to be the greatest traditional red wine in the Tre Venezie, as well as some top-notch contemporary wines made by avant-garde producers. The Veneto is also somewhat less similar to Friuli-Venezia Giulia and Trentino-Alto Adige than either of those regions is to the other.

In the Veneto, starting in the 1960s and 1970s, a big-business philosophy began to prevail as the region geared up to produce industrial amounts of the white Soave and the reds Valpolicella and Bardolino, much of these intended for the United States and Great Britain, where easy-drinking, inexpensive Italian wines had begun to sell like hotcakes. It's only when you look past the commercial versions of these wines that you begin to see what makes the Veneto compelling.

Both the Veneto and its beloved city of Venice take their names from the Veneti, the tribe that settled in the area around 1000 B.C. As one of the leading ports and commercial centers of the medieval world, Venice was a link between the Byzantine Empire in the east and the emerging countries of northern Europe. Its extensive trade in wines, spices, and food, as well as its wealth and accomplishments in art, architecture, and glass production laid the groundwork for

*Verona, the city of Romeo and Juliet, is the unofficial wine capital of the Veneto.*

## THE QUICK SIP ON THE VENETO

- Two of Italy's most well-known and widely exported wines come from the Veneto: Soave, a white, and Valpolicella, a red. Both are available as low- and high-quality wines.

- Some Veneto wines, both dry and sweet, are made by a special process known as *recioto*, which concentrates the sugars in the grapes. The best known of these is the dry red amarone.

- The Veneto's most celebratory wine is prosecco, one of Italy's most popular *spumantes* and the sparkling wine behind the legendary cocktail the Bellini.

Venice to become one of the most sophisticated cities in all of Italy.

From Venice and the Adriatic coast the plains of the Veneto stretch inland through fairly flat farmland until they come to the lower foothills of the Alps and the border with Trentino-Alto Adige in the northwest. Much of this land is fertile and extremely productive, which helped set the scene for the ambitious scale of viticulture that has ensued.

Many millions of cases of the popular threesome Soave, Valpolicella, and Bardolino are made every year along with a good amount of pinot grigio, merlot, and Bianco di Custoza, a white wine not unlike simple Soave. But that doesn't mean that all of these wines can be dismissed out of hand. A perfect example is Soave; while most of it is a mass-produced liquid with only slightly more flavor than water, there are a number of quite extraordinary Soaves—wines many of us might never guess were Soave if we didn't know. This is also true

for Valpolicella (though not for Bardolino). It would be incorrect then to stereotype Soave and Valpolicella as merely commonplace. With these wines you can either drink very casually or take a giant step up in quality (and a good step up in price) and drink some really stellar examples.

The Veneto also produces several sweet wines made by a method called *recioto*. The word *recioto* derives from *recie*, dialect for ears, in this case referring to the protruding lobes or "ears" of a bunch of grapes. Since they are the part of the bunch that is most exposed to the sun, the ears often have the ripest grapes. To make a *recioto* wine either the ears or, if they are ripe enough, entire bunches of grapes are dried until the sugar is very concentrated. The wine that results can be rich indeed. Opulent yet elegant sweet versions of both Soave and Valpolicella are made in this way. The Veneto's great dry red, amarone (see page 364), is also made by the *recioto* method.

Against the backdrop of such extremely well-known wines as Soave and Valpolicella you'll find several Veneto wines with almost cultlike followings. Among these are those of the producer Maculan, made near the village of Breganze. Maculan was one of the first to approach chardonnay and cabernet sauvignon with quality (and higher prices) in mind. But Maculan's most renowned wine is Torcolato, the most famous dessert wine of the Veneto. Made primarily from native vespaiolo grapes that have been allowed to dry out in a special drying loft (in the manner of *recioto* wines), Torcolato is a gorgeously balanced wine with striking raisin, orange, vanilla, green tea, and roasted nut flavors. The name Torcolato (twisted in Italian) refers to the special way the winery's workers tie bunches of grapes with twine, twisting them so that each bunch hangs freely, completely surrounded by air, assuring perfect drying.

Lastly, the Veneto is home to prosecco, the *spumante* (sparkling wine) traditionally blended with the juice of fresh white peaches to make Venice's most famous cocktail, the Bellini, but eminently drinkable on its own.

## THE LAND, THE GRAPES, AND THE VINEYARDS

Though the northern and western parts of the Veneto can be quite mountainous, the region is farther south, warmer, more maritime, and less thoroughly influenced by the Alps than either of its neighbors, Trentino-Alto Adige in the northwest and Friuli-Venezia Giulia in the northeast. Both the Adige and Po rivers, on their way to the Adriatic Sea, flow across the broad plains of the Veneto creating large expanses of rich farmland where vegetables and fruits, including grapes, grow profusely. Since great wines in general come not from fertile soil but from the opposite, the Veneto's best vines tend to be planted near hills on well-drained volcanic soil interspersed with sand, clay, and gravel.

The Veneto can be divided into three zones. In the far west near Lake Garda and the volcanic mountain range of Monte Lessini, the traditional wines Soave, Valpolicella, Bardolino, and amarone are produced, as well as Bianco di Custoza, one of those simple sorts of white wines that taste best when drunk in the region where they're made. Verona, the major city, is one of Italy's wine capitals; each year the country's largest wine fair, Vinitaly, is held here.

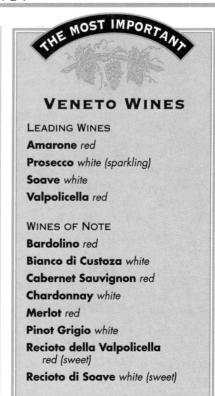

### VENETO WINES

LEADING WINES

**Amarone** red

**Prosecco** white (sparkling)

**Soave** white

**Valpolicella** red

WINES OF NOTE

**Bardolino** red

**Bianco di Custoza** white

**Cabernet Sauvignon** red

**Chardonnay** white

**Merlot** red

**Pinot Grigio** white

**Recioto della Valpolicella** red (sweet)

**Recioto di Soave** white (sweet)

(Spread over five or more coliseum-size buildings, the fair includes so many thousands of wines that tasting them all could take weeks.) In the Veneto's northern hills above Treviso (held to be the radicchio capital of Italy), prosecco is made. What is considered more or less the center of the Veneto, from Venice to Vicenza, is the source of several different types of wine, ranging from easy-drinking merlots, cabernet sauvignons, chardonnays, and pinot grigios of no particular distinction (the well-known pinot grigio Santa Margherita comes from here) to more exciting wines, especially from around Breganze, Colli Berici, and Colli Euganei.

As with the other two regions that make up the Tre Venezie, the Veneto was once home to dozens of grape varieties and many of them are still grown today, though

## THE GRAPES OF
# THE VENETO

## WHITES

**Chardonnay:** Can make some attractive New World-style wines but more often they are merely decent.

**Garganega:** Leading grape, probably of Greek origin but grown in the Veneto since the Rennaissance. The dominant grape in Soave, where it is blended with trebbiano.

**Pinot Bianco:** A minor grape in terms of production, but when pinot bianco (pinot blanc) is used, as it often is, as part of a blend, it contributes good body and character. Sometimes forms part of the blend in the sparkling wine prosecco.

**Pinot Grigio:** Also known as pinot gris, pinot grigio makes volumes of decent light wine (with a few exceptions, most are not usually as good as the pinot grigios of Friuli-Venezia Giulia or Trentino-Alto Adige). Sometimes used in the blend for prosecco.

**Prosecco:** Probably originally native to Friuli-Venezia Giulia but now grown almost exclusively in the Veneto. The prinicpal grape in the well-loved *spumante* (sparkling wine) that is also known as prosecco.

**Tocai Friulano:** Not as popular or as widespread in the Veneto as it is in Friuli-Venezia Giulia, but this fascinating white grape occasionally shows up, especially in high-quality blends.

**Trebbiano:** Leading grape. Blended with garganega to make Soave and Bianco di Custoza. The type known as trebbiano di Soave is of a better quality than a second type, trebbiano Toscano.

**Vespaiola:** Native grape. The source of some interesting dry white wines and more famous sweet ones.

## REDS

**Cabernet Sauvignon:** With a few notable exceptions, made into relatively insubstantial wines.

**Corvina:** Leading red grape. Thanks to its good structure, it's the lion's share of the blend in amarone, Valpolicella, and most Bardolinos.

**Merlot:** Mostly made into simple, serviceable, but uninspired wines.

**Molinara:** A key blending component in the wines amarone, Valpolicella, and Bardolino.

**Negrara:** A minor blending component in the wines amarone, Valpolicella, and Bardolino.

**Rondinella:** The second most important grape after corvina in amarone, Valpolicella, and Bardolino.

363

in smaller amounts. In addition to the international varieties already mentioned, several native grapes are key. The leading native red grape by far is corvina, sometimes called corvina veronese, the major grape in amarone, Valpolicella, and Bardolino. Corvina is usually blended with smaller amounts of rondinella, molinara, and sometimes negrara. The leading white grape for the traditional wine Soave is garganega, almost always blended with a type of trebbiano called trebbiano di Soave. Vespaiola is far more rare than garganega or trebbiano but it can make some fascinating wines, especially sweet wines. The grape owes its name to the word *vespa* (Italian for wasp) because when ripe, the grapes attract large numbers of these insects.

## Soave

Italy's best-known exported white wine, Soave comes from the castle-topped hillside town of the same name, just east of Verona in the western part of the Veneto. Traditionally, Soaves—made from garganega and trebbiano—were light, fresh, and at their best, smooth and *soave* (suave in Italian). Since the early 1970s, however, a lot of the Soave produced has been commercial, bland, cheap jug wine produced from vineyards that have enormous yields. Much of this neutral wine is made from trebbiano Toscano (Tuscan trebbiano), a rather flavorless trebbiano compared to the higher-quality trebbiano di Soave.

Basic featherweight Soave is never aged and can come from anywhere in the Soave denomination, which was greatly expanded in the 1970s. A step up in quality is Soave Classico, wine that comes from the original, smaller Soave zone on the steep hills above the towns of Soave and Monteforte d'Alpone. An even greater step up in quality is Soave Classico Superiore, which must be aged eight months before release.

Finally, each year a tiny amount of sweet Soave is made by the *recioto* method. Like amarone and recioto della Valpolicella, recioto di Soave is made from very ripe grapes that have been put in special drying rooms, allowing the grapes to dry out and their sugar to concentrate. Since fermentation is halted before all of the sugar is converted into alcohol, recioto di Soave is sweet. Though made in small amounts, it is one of the true specialties of the Veneto and can be a stunningly delicious wine.

The three absolute champions when it comes to Soave are the producers Anselmi (which labels its Soaves with such proprietary names as Capitel Croce), Gini, and Leonildo Pieropan. Other top producers to

look for include Bertani and Guerrieri Rizzardi. Bolla, a name virtually synonymous with Soave, produces 400,000 cases a year of straightforward stuff but also has a special single-vineyard Soave called Tufaie.

## Prosecco

The Veneto's ubiquitous *spumante*, prosecco is made principally from prosecco grapes, sometimes with small amounts of pinot bianco and pinot grigio added. The best of the prosecco grapes undoubtedly come from vineyards just north of Venice in the rambling hills between the villages of Conegliano and Valdobbiadene. Traditionally, the sparkler was rather soft, slightly sweet, and only slightly fizzy. Today most examples are dry and fully *spumante*, though still more fruity and less dramatically crisp than Champagne. Prosecco is not made by the Champagne method, but rather by the Charmat process, in which the wine undergoes a second fermentation in pressurized tanks rather than in individual bottles. In the late afternoon virtually every bar in Venice pours glass after glass of prosecco, which the civilized Venetians consider an *ombrette*, a pick-me-up. Such is the fame of prosecco that it is now the second leading *spumante* in Italy after Asti. Top producers include Adriano Adami, Desiderio Bisol & Figli, Cardinal, Carpenè Malvolti, Nino Franco, and Zardetto.

## Amarone

Big, dense red wines the world over are unquestionably the product of very ripe grapes, and very ripe grapes in turn are the product of warm, sunny places. Historically this simple fact meant that most relatively cool regions, and the Veneto is one, learned to be satisfied making lighter reds or settling for whites. How

## AMARONE:
## SAY CHEESE

Despite the rather common assumption that all red wines taste good with cheese, many cheeses can make red wines taste flat and hollow. A wine that truly stands up to even dramatic cheeses is amarone. At 15 to 16 percent alcohol and with a Portlike body and deep bitter chocolate, mocha, dried fig, and earthy flavors, amarone is a powerhouse. The Italian wine expert Victor Hazan (husband of famed cookbook author Marcella Hazan) suggests that amarone is the perfect wine to drink with a roast, being careful to save the last glasses to sip during the finale: a plate of walnuts and bite-size chunks of Parmigiano-Reggiano.

then did the Veneto get to be famous for amarone, an intense wine with a syrupy thickness? By the special style of winemaking called *recioto*. Here's what happens.

Amarone (the name means big, bitter one) is made in the Valpolicella region near Verona from the same grapes as Valpolicella: mainly corvina, with rondinella, molinara, and sometimes negrara. But while the grapes for Valpolicella are picked during the regular harvest, the grapes for amarone are left to hang on the vine a little longer, achieving extra ripeness before they are picked. Next whole bunches of grapes are spread on bamboo shelving or mats and left in cool drying lofts for three to four months, although the exact amount of time varies from producer to producer. This causes the grapes to shrivel, further concentrating

their sugar and flavors. As they dry and raisinate, the grapes lose up to a third of their weight, mostly water. When the grapes are finally crushed and fermented, the resulting wine is opulent, full-bodied, and, at 15 to 16 percent alcohol, significantly higher in alcohol than a regular Valpolicella, which averages around 11 percent. Many amarones are then aged for five years or more before release. Today some of that aging may take place in small, new-oak barrels, giving the wine even broader and more powerful flavors. The labor-intensive method of concentrating grape sugar not only adds to the wine's cost, but the process itself is also fairly risky. Even a small amount of wet autumn weather can cause the bunches to rot rather than dry out. As a result, producers who are less than scrupulously careful and clean in their winemaking can end up with amarones with flavors that seem to hint of mold and a certain dankness. But when the winemaking is above reproach and the grapes come from a good vineyard, an amarone can be spellbinding—powerful almost to the point of Port-like concentration and packed with mocha and earthy flavors at the same time.

*Some of the Best Producers*
*of Amarone*

**ALLEGRINI**

**BERTANI**

**BOLLA**

**BOSCAINI**

**FRATELLI TEDESCHI**

**MASI**

**QUINTARELLI**

**SERÈGO ALIGHIERI**

**TOMMASI**

**ZENATO**

# A HISTORY OF WINEGLASSES AND A BIT ABOUT BOTTLES

From the beginning of time, drinking vessels have taken their inspiration from natural forms: hands cupped together, the conical horn of an animal, a gourd split into two bowls, a flower and its stem. Such simple images as these have given rise to an incredible number of objects used throughout history from which to drink wine. These range from the animal skins of the ancient world to the plastic tumblers of today.

But if any one substance was meant to carry wine, it is glass. Wineglasses are not a modern invention. In the first century before Christ, mouth-blown goblets, beakers, and bottles were being made in the Mediterranean and Near East. These early vessels were extremely precious and rare.

Remarkably, modern glasses are made in essentially the same way ancient ones were. Basically, common sand—which contains silica—is combined with ashes from trees—potash. The mixture is then fired at intense heat—up to 2,500° F—causing the substances to melt together. After firing, the molten blob is blown by mouth and shaped.

Glassmaking reached its zenith in the sixteenth and seventeenth centuries on the island of Murano near Venice, Italy. There, glassmakers were held as virtual captives of their guild. Any glassblower caught trying to escape from the island or revealing the secret of Venetian glassmaking was punished by death. (Murano glass is still considered among the finest in Europe.)

*During the sixteenth and seventeenth centuries, advances in glassmaking led to stunning, often ornate glasses affordable by only the wealthiest Europeans. The graceful beauty of these glasses inspired winemakers to make more refined wines.*

Meanwhile in England, perhaps the single greatest innovation in glassmaking had been stumbled upon. In 1674 a glassblower named George Ravenscroft discovered that adding a small amount of lead oxide to molten glass made it more malleable. Elaborate designs could now be etched and cut into the lead crystal. Moreover, after being formed, lead crystal was more brilliant and durable than simple glass.

In propitious yin-yang fashion, more beautiful glasses became an incentive to create better wines and beverages. These, in turn, inspired ever more beautiful glasses. One of the best examples is Champagne. First made in the late 1600s, Champagne was hazy with sediment, viscous, and sweet. When advances in glassmaking led to glasses with a transparent brilliance and elegance never before thought possible, the new, graceful glasses inspired improvements in Champagne making. In turn, improvements in the clarity of Champagne inspired ever more stunning glasses into which beautiful Champagne could be poured.

From their invention until the beginning of the nineteenth century, glasses were used mainly by royalty and principally on special occasions. The purchase of a single wineglass was considered a serious investment, and at the most prestigious banquets, one glass might be shared by several dinner guests. If the host was especially wealthy, the banquet glasses might include some intentionally designed with a rounded bottom and no stem. Such glasses made the party livelier since only cups that had been drained of their contents could be put down lest the liquid tumble out. These glass cups were the forerunners of our tumblers.

In the nineteenth century glass production soared as blowing techniques improved. Glass houses capable of large-scale manufacture began to emerge. The process of making glasses in molds was invented. Glassmaking quickly achieved a scale of production that allowed sets to become affordable. Glasses became status symbols. At all of the best dinner parties, each guest's place would be set with numerous goblets: one for Champagne, one for red wine, one for white, one for Sherry, and so on.

Modern molds and techniques also allowed greater variation in bottle shapes and colors. Glass houses throughout Europe began producing signature bottles meant to be identified with certain wines. Bottles with sloping shoulders were used for Burgundy; extremely tapered bottles held German wines. High-shouldered bottles (helpful in blocking sediment while decanting) were used for Bordeaux.

*The delicacy of grappa bottles does not portend the power of what's inside.*

As the twentieth century drew to a close, a renewed sense of creativity gripped the world of glassmaking. Wineglass design ranged from dramatically whimsical to almost exaggeratedly classic. And for the first time in decades, wine bottles again became a vehicle for avant-garde design. Witness the utterly fragile, delicately curved modern shapes of grappa bottles. As much as the liquid inside, the beauty of these bottles has inspired a whole new generation to at least buy (if not to drink) grappa.

## Valpolicella and Bardolino

Like amarone, valpolicella is made mainly from corvina with rondinella, molinara, and sometimes negrara grapes. But there the similarity ends—or at least it used to. In the 1980s the power and richness of amarone led producers to reconsider basic Valpolicella, which was nothing if not amarone's opposite. Today, five distinct styles of Valpolicella are made. First is the basic lightweight grapey stuff, which is usually not aged and can come from anywhere in the Valpolicella denomination. Like Soave, this area was greatly expanded in the 1970s to meet increasing demand. Better quality is Valpolicella Classico, which refers to wines that come from the original, smaller Valpolicella zone. Much better still is Valpolicella Classico Superiore, which must be aged a year before release and in practice commands better grapes. In the hands of a great producer like Allegrini, Valpolicella Classico Superiore can be a sensational wine with rich, smoky, dried cherry and licorice flavors.

But there's an even higher-quality, more intensely flavored and thicker textured kind of Valpolicella yet. Called Valpolicella *ripasso*, it is made by taking the newly fermented Valpolicella wine and adding it to amarone pomace, which is the pulpy mass of seeds and skins leftover after the amarone has fermented. The Valpolicella is left in contact with the amarone pomace for a couple of weeks, during which time the wine picks up extra color, tannin, flavor, and structure. In the end the wine can possess an almost zinfandel-like jamminess. The process is called *ripasso* from the verb *ripassare*—to pass over or do something again. In particular the producer Masi has been at the forefront of making Valpolicella *ripasso*. Theirs, which was the first, is called Campo Fiorin.

Finally, there's the fifth kind of Valpolicella, recioto della Valpolicella. Like amarone, recioto della Valpolicella is made from the ripest grapes that have been put in special drying rooms, allowing the grapes to raisinate and their sugar to concentrate. But while in the case of amarone all that sugar is converted into

*Beautifully sited on the crest of a hill, the vineyard La Poja belongs to Allegrini, one of the Veneto's star producers.*

alcohol, thereby making the wine dry, fermentation is halted in recioto della Valpolicella before all of the sugar is converted into alcohol and so the wine is sweet. Only a tiny amount of recioto della Valpolicella is made, and it can be utterly sensational—a rich, sweet, but not saccharine red wine that is supple and complex and just waiting for an oozingly creamy Italian cheese like a ripe Taleggio.

The top producers of Valpolicella in addition to Allegrini and Masi are Bertani, Boscaini, Fratelli Tedeschi, Quintarelli, and Tommasi.

Though often thought of as a stand-in for Valpolicella and though made from the same grapes, Bardolino is quite different. Named after the town of Bardolino on Lake Garda, the wine—more pink than red—is very light bodied with faint cherry flavors and sometimes, a nice edge of spiciness. Bardolino Classicos from the original district surrounding the town are often more interesting wines than simple Bardolinos. When turned into an inexpensive sparkling wine, Bardolino is called *chiaretto*, which is a popular summertime quaff. In the fall Bardolino is also made as a *novello* wine, a takeoff on Beaujolais Nouveau. Both *chiaretto* and *novello* are drunk chilled, and even regular Bardolino is best with an edge of coolness. The top producer of Bardolino is Guerrieri-Rizzardi.

# VISITING THE WINE ESTATES OF THE VENETO

M ost visitors to the Veneto start out in Venice, and though it's tempting to stay happily ensconced within the boundaries of that magical city, those who venture out into wine country are in for a treat. The Veneto's vine-covered hills stretch from the Austrian border through the *spumante* country around Treviso to the eastern shores of Lake Garda. The landscape is beautiful; the food stellar. Lovers of sparkling wine should not miss the Strada del Vino Prosecco (Prosecco wine route) that winds through the Treviso hills. For most wineries appointments are necessary, and it helps to have a working knowledge of Italian. The telephone numbers include the dialing code you'll need when calling from the United States. If you're calling from within Italy, eliminate the 011-39.

**ALLEGRINI**
7 Corte Giare
37022 Fumane, Verona
011-39-045-770-11-38

**ANSELMI**
46 Via S. Carlo
37032 Monteforte d'Alpone, Verona
011-39-045-761-14-88

**BOSCAINI PAOLO E FIGLI**
Via Cà de Loi 2
37020 Marano di Valpolicella, Verona
011-39-045-680-08-40

**CAV. G. B. BERTANI**
Località Novare, Fraz. Arbizzano
37020 Negrar, Verona
011-39-045-601-12-11

**FRATELLI BOLLA**
3 Piazza Cittadella
37122 Verona
011-39-045-867-09-11

**LEONILDO PIEROPAN**
3 Via Camuzzoni
37038 Soave, Verona
011-39-045-619-01-71

**MASI**
Via Monteleone, Fraz. Gargagnago
37010 S. Ambroggio di Valpolicella
Verona
011-39-045-680-05-88

# THE VENETO WINES TO KNOW

## Whites

### ANSELMI

Capitel Croce

100% garganega

Made in the Soave district but not called a Soave, Capitel Croce is a surprising experience—a wine that's nutty, lemony, and vanilla tinged, with a pleasingly fat round body, and great vivacity. Roberto Anselmi is one of a handful of producers who take garganega very seriously.

### MACULAN

Breganze di Breganze

85% tocai friulano, 15% pinot bianco

Breganze is both the name of this famous wine and the name of a village and the vineyards that surround it, located in the hills northwest of Venice (hence *Breganze di Breganze,* Breganze of Breganze). The man who makes this wine, Fausto Maculan, is something of a legend. When so many other producers in the central hills of the Veneto were making lackluster wines at best, Maculan was pushing the envelope with stylish dry white blends, intriguing sweet wines, and expensive single-vineyard cabernet sauvignons. This wine clearly shows Maculan in top form. Its sassy mint, lime, and sage flavors are made even more dramatic by a prickly sense of spiciness and minerality. Fresh, thirst-quenching, and long in the finish, Breganze is (not surprisingly) a favorite with Venetian fish dishes.

### ZENATO

Pinot Grigio

100% pinot grigio

Gertrude Stein's infamous quip about Oakland ("There is no there there") could equally be applied to most pinot grigios. But not the one grigio from the Zenato family. Floral and creamy, this finely etched wine is laced with light peach, almond, and herbal notes.

## Reds

### ALLEGRINI

Valpolicella Classico Superiore

La Grola

approximately 70% corvina, 20% rondinella, 5% syrah, and 5% sangiovese

If I could drink only one Veneto wine for the rest of my life, it would be a red wine from the Allegrini family. Whether it's their regular Valpolicella, their single-vineyard Valpolicellas like this La Grola, their amarone, or their sweet recioto, these wines never seem to miss the mark. La Grola, in particular, is a star and the opposite of so many thin, rather washed out versions of Valpolicella. Smoke, spice, and licorice, with dried cherry, violet, vanilla, and mocha flavors and aromas—it's a wine that's sweetly ripe, creamy, and full.

### MASI

Amarone della Valpolicella

70% corvina, 20% rondinella, and 10% molinara

If you don't know amarone, Masi is a good place to begin for its big, ripe, almost Port-like character. Plus, among all the amarones, this is probably the easiest to find. At its best, this is a wine that is utterly fascinating, with flavors and aromas suggestive of leather, grenadine, and black licorice. In the small restaurants of northern Italy, amarones like Masi's are drunk with hearty slabs of roasted meat.

## ZENATO

Amarone della Valpolicella

70% corvina, 20% rondinella, and 10% molinara

No wine is more perfect during the long, raw, cold winters in northern Italy (or anywhere, for that matter) than amarone. Big, lustful, and earthy, amarone is warming and satisfying. Zenato's amarone fits this bill exactly, but in great years, it's also among the softest and most hedonistic of amarones. Think chocolate-covered cherries with brandy liqueur inside.

# *Sweet Wines*

## ALLEGRINI

Recioto Classico della Valpolicella

Giovanni Allegrini

75% corvina, 20% rondinella, and 5% molinara

Take out Port and other fortified wines and there aren't that many red sweet wines in the world, so curious wine drinkers should definitely not miss this. Named for the late Giovanni Allegrini, who founded the Allegrini wine estate in the 1950s, this recioto della Valpolicella is superb. Waves of intense blackberry fruit flavors are punctuated with eucalyptus and licorice. And the texture is mind-blowingly creamy. There's sweetness here to be sure, but it's very modest, very elegantly presented. Italians drink recioto della Valpolicellas with ripe creamy cheeses like Taleggio, though a slice of rich ricotta cheesecake could have no better partner than this.

## MACULAN

Torcolato

85% vespaiolo, 10% tocai friulano, and 5% garganega

Italian desserts and sweet wines are generally not as sweet as their French counterparts. Torcolato is a great example of this. Concentrated and creamy, it's only faintly sweet, and it's certainly not syrupy or voluptuous. Instead, this forceful wine is packed with flavors (bitter walnut skin, dried orange peel, apricot, honey) that mingled together taste strangely beautiful and refined. In Italy, Torcolato is called a wine for meditation, and while it is often drunk (meditatively) on its own, other Italians apparently like to meditate when there's a nut cake or fruit tart in the vicinity.

371

# THE BELLINI

Italy's legendary summertime cocktail, the Bellini is a combination of icy cold sparkling prosecco and fresh white peach juice. The drink was invented in the 1930s at Harry's Bar in Venice, which employed one man each summer—when peaches were ripe—to do nothing but cut and pit small, fragile Italian white peaches (never the yellow variety) and then squeeze them by hand to extract the juice. Today, many Bellinis are made with frozen white peach juice exported from France and any sort of sparkling wine, but in the Veneto, every Bellini is the real thing.

# Tuscany

*From the Tuscan standpoint the first duty of a good grape is to be red. Come fall, entire families participate in the harvest, a time of hard work and plenty of celebration.*

Toscana to the Italians, Tuscany is the quintessential Italian wine region. Here, where the Renaissance was born and where the church has reigned with near omnipotent power, wine has strong ties to both art and religion. Yet at the same time, wine has always been the most humble of Tuscan comforts—on the table at every meal (breakfast excepted); sometimes, with a piece of bread, a meal in itself.

Tuscany is also the birthplace of three of Italy's most important red wines: Chianti, brunello di Montalcino, and Vino Nobile di Montepulciano. Though all are made from the sangiovese grape, the wines taste remarkably different. The reasons? Sangiovese, a finicky and demanding grape, has begotten many genetic variations of itself. Over time these variations (each of which is referred to as a different clone) have taken on distinct flavor characteristics. But another cause for the differences among Chianti, brunello, and Vino Nobile is this: Tuscany is a virtual kingdom of distinct microclimates. These are created by an endless succession of twisting, turning, undulating hills.

For wine drinkers and food lovers in the 1960s Tuscany seemed to symbolize a kind of cultural chic. Chianti, in particular, was romantic, earthy, "European," and fit the bohemian esthetic (and budget). But the old Chianti of red checkered tablecloths and amorous evenings was, for the most part, not very good wine. By the 1970s the market for Chianti—and the wine's reputation—had reached an all-time low. As

# THE LAND, THE GRAPES, AND THE VINEYARDS

A s visitors to Tuscany quickly discover, there doesn't seem to be a straight line in the entire region. Winding back and forth and up and down along Tuscany's rural roads, it's impossible not to fall in love with the patchwork of vineyards that cover a landscape undulating so magically. To any driver, it comes as no surprise that the region is roughly 68 percent hills. The paucity of flat land means that nearly every vineyard is on a slope of some kind, gentle or steep, and that even two vineyards that are only a stone's throw apart often produce wines of very different character.

Tuscany stretches from the Tyrrhenian Sea in the west to the low mountains that separate the region from Emilia-Romagna, the Marches, and Umbria, its neighbors in

*The undulating countryside of Tuscany supports a profusion of diverse microclimates in which grapes grow.*

the full impact of this realization began to sink in, Tuscans were shocked into action. With the help of new wine laws (see Italy's Regulations and the Fine Wine Revolution, page 319), the Tuscan wine industry has bounced back with what is considered one of the most dramatic revolutions in the world of modern wine. The result is vastly superior, exciting wines, including a slew of internationally acclaimed, expensive Super Tuscans.

So much good red wine has always been made in Tuscany that, with the exception of the famous dessert wine *vin santo*, white wine has been mostly an afterthought for both wine producers and wine drinkers. Yet the production of high-quality Tuscan dry white wine, while still minuscule, is slowly growing. Most of the new, modern-style whites are substantial, bold-flavored sauvignon blancs and chardonnays. And even Tuscany's standby traditional dry white, vernaccia di San Gimignano, is now being made with a new emphasis on quality.

**THE MOST IMPORTANT**

## TUSCAN WINES

### LEADING WINES

**Brunello di Montalcino** red

**Chianti** red

**Super Tuscans** red

**Vino Nobile di Montepulciano** red

### WINES OF NOTE

**Carmignano** red

**Chardonnay** white

**Rosso di Montalcino** red

**Rosso di Montepulciano** red

**Sauvignon Blanc** white

**Vernaccia di San Gimignano** white

**Vin Santo** white (sweet)

recognized). But in modern times, the region has been identified almost exclusively with two grapes: the indigenous variety sangiovese, for centuries Tuscany's single greatest grape, and cabernet sauvignon, the international variety that since the 1980s has been responsible for making up in whole, or as part of the blend, numerous famous Super Tuscan wines (see page 376).

Sangiovese is an exacting, troublesome grape. It doesn't ripen easily or uniformly. In sites that are not consistently sunny or in rainy, overcast years, it's common around harvesttime to see bunches with soft, purple, ripe grapes as well as slightly green, underripe ones. Unevenly ripe bunches can lead to thin or unbalanced wines. This is just one of the challenges sangiovese presents.

There's another vexing issue: sangiovese's genetic predisposition to reinvent itself as different variations known as clones (see page 22). Central Italy is literally strewn with multiple clones of sangiovese. Though no one knows precisely how many different clones there are, winemakers are convinced that the main ones vary enormously in flavor and that the future of Tuscan wine lies in clonal research. (The world's most ambitious study of grape clones was begun in Chianti in 1987; as of 2001, the research was not yet complete.) With the knowledge derived from such research, wine producers (at least the quality-oriented ones) can pull out sangiovese vines that belong to inferior, poor-tasting clonal types and plant superior clones in their place. Among the top clones are sangioveto, one of the clones found in the best Chianti Classicos; brunello, the clone used for brunello di Montalcino; and prugnolo, the primary clone used for Vino Nobile di Montepulciano.

the east. At nearly 9,000 square miles, it is the fifth largest region in Italy. Yet most of the important wine zones are more or less in the middle of the region, from Florence in the north to Siena in the center and then south to the tiny hill town of Montalcino (famous for brunello). The climate in this central zone is warm, though not as warm or humid as along the Tyrrhenian coast. Nights are cool, helping to preserve the natural acidity of the grapes, particularly sangiovese. Soil varies considerably, but the well-drained slopes of the central hills tend to be sandy or stony, calcareous, and interspersed with schist and *galestro* (a crumbly stony marl).

Like many Italian wine regions, Tuscany was once home to dozens of grape varieties (in the mid-eighteenth century, more than two hundred were officially

As for cabernet sauvignon, though it was brought to Tuscany in the eighteenth century, reportedly by Grand Duke Cosimo de' Medici III, the variety was largely unimportant for centuries except as a component in Carmignano (see page 386). In the late 1970s and 1980s, however, cabernet soared into prominence as one of the varieties of (or in some cases, the only) grapes used in the Super Tuscans.

White grapes have never been very important in Tuscany, although an enormous number of neutral trebbiano and somewhat more interesting malvasia vines were planted in the past. The best of these grapes were (and still are) used to make *vin santo*, while the remainder were mostly used in red wines—in particular, Chianti and Vino Nobile di Montepulciano.

Even vernaccia, the grape of vernaccia di San Gimignano and the only white grape of any character, still makes what most Italian experts consider a serviceable, occasionally charming, white at best.

As for chardonnay and other international whites, there are far fewer examples in Tuscany than there are in Friuli-Venezia Giulia or Trentino-Alto Adige. That said, unlike those regions, chardonnay is relatively new in Tuscany. Beginning in the 1980s, several Tuscan winemakers decided to make what they called "serious" white wines, which turned out to mean big-bodied, oaky, buttery chardonnays and fruit-packed sauvignon blancs. These wines are not made on a large scale. The most impressive of them include the absolutely stunning and rich Capannelle chardonnay,

## THE GRAPES OF
# TUSCANY

375

## WHITES

**Chardonnay:** Increasingly grown in Tuscany and made into the region's most expensive white.

**Malvasia:** In the past the white grape blended into Chianti in small amounts to lighten it. Now the grape best known for *vin santo*, the famous Tuscan dessert wine.

**Sauvignon Blanc:** Limited amounts are grown, but wines made from this grape show real promise.

**Trebbiano:** Formerly used with malvasia in Chianti. Now used for *vin santo* as well as for dry white wines generally of neutral character.

**Vernaccia:** Makes Tuscany's most traditional, refreshing white wine; grown around the hill town of San Gimignano.

## REDS

**Cabernet Sauvignon:** Often blended in very small amounts with sangiovese to make contemporary Chianti. The sole grape variety or a component in many Super Tuscan wines.

**Canaiolo:** Historically the other red grape besides sangiovese in the traditional Chianti blend. Declining in use.

**Merlot:** Sometimes blended in small amounts with sangiovese to make contemporary Chianti. Also used in a limited number of Super Tuscans.

**Sangiovese:** Major Tuscan grape used for all the important traditional red wines of the region. Important clones include sangioveto (used in Chianti Classico), brunello (used in brunello di Montalcino), and prugnolo (used in Vino Nobile di Montepulciano).

as well as Torniello, the sauvignon blanc from Castello di Volpaia (castle where the foxes live), and Poggio alle Gazze (hill of the magpies), the sauvignon blanc from Ornellaia (magpies *do* live in the vineyard).

# CHIANTI AND THE SUPER TUSCANS

C hianti has come a long way from its role as companion to spaghetti and meatballs. Not that this association in the United States was always pejorative. After World War II, being cheap and gulpable was pretty ideal. Chianti implied neither snobbism nor wealth; it was just plain easy to drink. But as time went on the wine grew increasingly disappointing. Part of the problem was the Chianti formula.

*The word* sangiovese *is thought to derive from* sangue di Giove—*the blood of Jove.*

Traditionally Chianti was a blend of grapes: red—sangiovese and canaiolo—and white—malvasia and/or trebbiano. The formula was developed in the mid-1800s by Baron Bettino Ricasoli, whose family had been making Tuscan wine since the twelfth century. Ricasoli posited that adding a small amount of white malvasia to Chianti would heighten its vivacity, boost its flavor, and make it more drinkable when young. Imbedded in this notion were the beginnings of disaster.

The more popular Chianti became the more it was lightened with white grapes—and not just malvasia as Ricasoli had intended but also with the fairly dull type of trebbiano known as trebbiano Toscano (which in France was, and still is, used as neutral distilling material for Cognac). Far

from adding character to Chianti, trebbiano turned it into an anorexic red, gaunt, hollow, and unbalanced. Yet by World War II trebbiano made up more than 30 percent of some Chiantis.

Even more trouble lay ahead. In the economic aftermath of the war, wine-growers were given agricultural development funds by the government. Responding to increased demands for affordable Chianti, they planted new vineyards, and not just in the small hilly *classico* region between Florence and Siena that had historically defined the Chianti zone but throughout Tuscany. Worst of all, the nurseries that the growers relied on to provide them with new planting material were so pressed to keep up with demand that they began selling a different type of sangiovese, a clone called sangiovese di Romagna brought in from the nearby region of Emilia-Romagna and less well suited to Tuscany. Given overproduction, poorly situated vineyards, ill-suited clonal types, and dilution with white grapes, the quality of Chianti collapsed. By the late 1960s, Italian romance notwithstanding, Chianti was bought as much for its straw-covered bottle (the candleholder of the era) as for the liquid inside.

Faced with the possibility of the industry's demise, a handful of innovative, iconoclastic producers in the mid-1970s began taking the first steps toward making wines that would be the polar opposites of "spaghetti Chianti." Their inspiration was Sassicaia, made by Marchese Mario Incisa della Rocchetta at his estate Tenuta San Guido near the coast in Bolgheri. An artisanal wine that broke every rule, Sassicaia did not have a drop of sangiovese in it but, instead, was made from cabernet sauvignon from vines that had come indirectly from Château Lafite.

## SOME OF THE TOP SUPER TUSCANS

M any of what are considered Italy's superstar wines were first made in Tuscany in the 1970s and 1980s. Unique and stylized, they are wines that try to be what many wine professionals once considered impossible—Italian yet international at the same time. The collective name for these wines, the Super Tuscans, is a consumer term, not an official designation. Each wine listed below has its own proprietary name; the words *Super Tuscan* never appear on the label. The primary grape in each wine is noted since this information also rarely appears on the label.

| Proprietary Name | Producer | Primary Grape |
|---|---|---|
| Cepparello | Isole e Olena | sangiovese |
| Coltassala | Castello di Volpaia | sangiovese |
| Flaccianello | Fontodi | sangiovese |
| Fontalloro | Felsina | sangiovese |
| Grosso Senese | Il Palazzino | sangiovese |
| Il Sodaccio | Montevertine | sangiovese |
| I Sodi di San Niccolò | Castellare | sangiovese |
| Le Pergole Torte | Montevertine | sangiovese |
| Masseto | Ornellaia | merlot |
| Monte Antico | Monte Antico | sangiovese |
| Olmaia | Col d'Orcia | cabernet sauvignon |
| Ornellaia | Ornellaia | cabernet sauvignon |
| Percarlo | San Giusto | sangiovese |
| Sammarco | Castello dei Rampolla | cabernet sauvignon |
| Sassicaia | Marchesi Incisa della Rocchetta | cabernet sauvignon |
| Solaia | Antinori | cabernet sauvignon |
| Solatio Basilica | Villa Cafaggio | sangiovese |
| Summus | Castello Banfi | sangiovese |
| Terrine | Castello della Paneretta | canaiolo |
| Tignanello | Antinori | sangiovese |
| Tinscvil | Monsanto | sangiovese |
| Vigna d'Alceo | Castello dei Rampolla | cabernet sauvignon |

The Sassicaia vineyards were planted in what was considered just about the worst possible location in Tuscany. And the wine was aged in *barriques*—small, new French-oak barrels—when every other wine in Tuscany was aged in large old barrels, mostly made of Slavonian oak.

The first Sassicaias made in the 1940s were awkward, even coarse wines. But by the 1960s Incisa della Rocchetta had refined his techniques considerably and the wine, defying expectation, turned out to be very impressive. Not that anyone knew it; the Incisa della Rocchetta family made barely enough for themselves and friends. Piero Antinori knew about it, however; the Incisa della Rocchettas were his cousins. Antinori himself was the head of a centuries-old Tuscan winemaking family. Thus, Sassicaia became the catalyst for Antinori's Tignanello—the first well-known non-Chianti Chianti.

Made in 1971, Tignanello had no white grapes, was based almost entirely on sangiovese (later, cabernet sauvignon and cabernet franc were added), and was aged in *barriques*. Tignanello was like a flashlight in the dark. Other top producers immediately followed suit, making expensive proprietary wines of their own, sometimes from sangiovese blended with cabernet sauvignon, sometimes from either grape alone. What unified these wines was what they were not: They were not made according to the traditional Chianti formula specified at that time in the DOC laws (see Italy's Wine Laws, page 323). As a result the government considered them mere *vini da tavola;* the press nicknamed them the Super Tuscans.

The eclectic group of Super Tuscans motivated winemakers to further improve

the quality of Chianti. In 1984 Chianti was elevated from DOC to DOCG status, paving the way for additional improvements commensurate with the region's enhanced status. There have been more changes since then. The DOCG laws for Chianti have been revised and made more liberal. No longer are white grapes a mandatory part of the Chianti formula, and cabernet sauvignon, merlot, and selected other red grapes may constitute up to 15 percent of the blend. For producers of Super Tuscan wines this change in the law presents an intriguing dilemma. Since some (though by no means all) Super Tuscans can now qualify as, and be labeled as, regular Chiantis, should the producer abandon the wine's proprietary name and relabel the wine as Chianti? Many have decided not to. The Super Tuscan concept has such marketing cachet that it is undoubtedly here to stay. And besides, most wines considered Super Tuscans aren't really traditional no matter how close they come to fitting into the

## ORNELLAIA: PLACE OF ASH TREES

Tignanello was not the only legendary wine inspired by Sassicaia. When the Sassicaia (dialect for place of stones) vineyard was planted at Bolgheri on the Tuscan coast, few believed that a wine from that area would have even a remote chance of success. Bolgheri, full of marshes and woodland, was hotter in many spots than the central hills of Chianti. Only a small amount of wine had ever been produced there and that, by general consensus, was barely drinkable. Sassicaia, of course, went on to defy all expectations. A legendary fluke, it was Tuscany's first dramatic cabernet.

Bolgheri might have remained ignoble,

and Sassicaia a quirk, if it was not for Ornellaia, a second stunning red first made in 1985 by Lodovico Antinori, Piero Antinori's younger brother. Planted literally next door to Sassicaia on relatively steep, south-facing slopes, Ornellaia (dialect for place of the ash trees) was also based on cabernet sauvignon, this time with a small amount of merlot blended in. Together the wines proved that certain sites planted with the right grape varieties could produce great wine, even if those sites were in an unlikely and off-the-beaten-track part of Tuscany. Sassicaia and Ornellaia remain two of the most intense Tuscan wines, with fruit that seems to explode in your mouth.

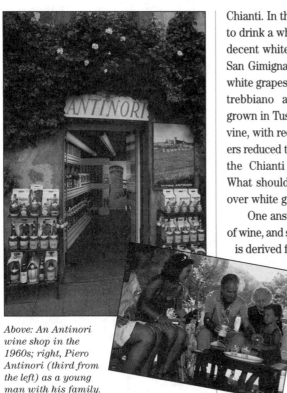

*Above: An Antinori wine shop in the 1960s; right, Piero Antinori (third from the left) as a young man with his family.*

Chianti. In the past when Tuscans wanted to drink a white wine, they drank the only decent white in the region—vernaccia di San Gimignano (see page 387). Of course white grapes other than vernaccia (mostly trebbiano and malvasia) have always grown in Tuscany, often mixed in, vine by vine, with red varieties. When wine producers reduced the amount of white grapes in the Chianti blend, the question arose: What should be done with all those leftover white grapes?

One answer was to invent a new type of wine, and so they did. Galestro (the name is derived from the fragmented stones of crumbly marl found in Tuscan soil) is a featherweight, low-alcohol, inexpensive white quaffing wine. It is definitely not a Chianti. Tuscans consider it somewhere above water and below wine in the hierarchy of beverages.

379

DOCG laws. Super Tuscans are made in an international style; generally flamboyant, dense, and powerful, they are wines packed with tannin and wrapped in the vanilla robe of flavor new oak imparts.

Traditional Chianti is something quite different. Sangiovese is a grape the entire flavor profile of which seems built for food. It's more supple and less tannic than cabernet sauvignon; more elegant and lighter in body than syrah or zinfandel. Most important of all, wines made from sangiovese often possess a fascinating suggestion of saltiness (this is just an illusion; salt is not an actual component of the wine) and a good bit of acidity, the kind of acidity that clears your palate and makes you want to take another bite of food.

Finally, by definition Chianti is a red wine. There is no such thing as white

## Chianti Classico

Chianti is made in seven subzones that span roughly half the land of Tuscany. While a number of very good wines can now be found in several of those zones (see Other Chianti Zones, page 381), the area that historically yielded the richest, fullest Chianti was the original small hilly central region known as Chianti Classico. In 1984 the uniqueness of Chianti Classico was underscored when it was given a DOCG of its own.

This is a place of inspiring beauty. Vineyards share the hillsides with olive groves, cypresses, umbrella pines, castles, and centuries-old stone farmhouses. From ancient times, artists and poets have been captivated by the lucid softness of the daylight, which seems as though it has been brushed onto the sky with a feather.

The microclimates of the Chianti Classico are multiple and diverse thanks to the undulating hills and the variations in geology. The ancient communes of Panzano, Radda, Gaiole, and Castellina, for example, slope toward the basin of Siena—once a prehistoric lake. The Tyrrhenian Sea is close enough to bring cooling, dry breezes that help minimize the humidity. The grapes, the best of which are planted on south and southwest facing slopes, mature gradually over a long summer of warm Mediterranean days and cool nights.

By law, Chianti Classico can be composed of 75 to 100 percent sangiovese, up to 10 percent canaiolo, up to 15 percent other red grapes, including cabernet sauvignon and merlot, and up to 6 percent of the white grapes trebbiano or malvasia. Chianti Classico Riservas must abide by these percentages as well, except that no white grapes are allowed. In practice, most estates now omit white grapes altogether for both their regular and *riserva* wines, and many estates minimize the amount of canaiolo they use.

As for the other red grapes allowed, cabernet sauvignon is the most common choice for distinct practical and economic reasons. Unlike sangiovese, cabernet is relatively easy to grow and make into wine, and it's a known commodity in the international marketplace. But from a flavor standpoint, the two might seem to be odd bedfellows. Sangiovese, after all, tends to be delicate and high in acidity; cabernet, more dense, bold, and tannic. In some wines even amounts of cabernet well

## A FIASCO BY ANY OTHER NAME . . .

The round, straw-covered bottle nearly every Chianti used to come in is called a *fiasco*. The word, probably of medieval Italian origin, described a glass bottle or flask with a long neck and a bulbous body usually covered in wicker or straw for protection. Historically both wine and olive oil came in *fiaschi*. According to the *Oxford English Dictionary*, our word *fiasco*—meaning a failure or complete breakdown—comes from the Italian expression *fare fiasco*, to make a bottle. How this Italian expression came to mean a foul up is unknown. Some wine experts have speculated that the poor quality of past Chianti may be the reason. Today in Tuscany one still finds old trattorias called *fiaschetterias*—workingmen's taverns known initially for cheap, hearty Tuscan wines and later for the homey Tuscan specialties that went with them.

under the allowable 15 percent have overwhelmed the sangiovese, making them taste unbalanced and odd. Tuscan winemakers are very aware of the challenge. In every wine where cabernet is part of the blend, the goal is to allow the flavors of sangiovese to somehow shine through.

The best basic Chianti Classicos have plum and dried cherry flavors and sometimes a touch of salt and spice. The more structured, complex, and elegant Chiantis are the Chianti Classico Riservas—aged, by law, at least two years in wood and three months in bottle. Many are aged longer and most are aged, at least partially, in small, new-French-oak barrels. *Riservas* are generally made only in the best vintage years from grapes that come from selected vineyard sites. Produced in these great years, *riservas* can develop mesmerizing waves of refined aromas and flavors: fig, chocolate, cedarwood, dried orange, earth, smoke, saddle leather, prune, minerals, salt, and exotic spices. Paradoxically, these flavors can seem both supple and explosive at the same time. They are flavors that linger long after you've swallowed.

*Some of the Best Producers of*
*Chianti Classico Riserva*

ANTINORI

BADIA A COLTIBUONO

CASTELLARE

CASTELLO DELLA PANERETTA

CASTELLO DI AMA

CASTELLO DI VOLPAIA

FATTORIA DI FELSINA

FATTORIA SELVAPIANA

FONTERUTOLI

FONTODI

MONSANTO

ROCCA DI COSTAGNOLI

RUFFINO

SAN FELICE

VILLA CAFAGGIO

## Other Chianti Zones

Although the most famous Chiantis are made in Chianti Classico, more Chianti is produced outside the *classico* subzone than inside it. There are six other subzones: Chianti Rufina, Colli Fiorentini, Colli Aretini, Colli Senesi, Colline Pisane, and Chianti Montalbano.

While many Chiantis from these subzones are simpler and less expensive than most Chianti Classicos, the best wines easily rival *classicos.* In particular, wines from Chianti Rufina can be stunning. Among the best Rufinas are those produced by Castello di Nipozzano, the estate owned by the Frescobaldi family (one such Frescobaldi wine, Montesodi, is renowned), as well as those produced by Selvapiana.

## THE CHIANTIGIANA

One of the most beautiful roads in Italy is the Chiantigiana, the country road that twists and turns, rises and falls through the vineyards and woodlands that connect Florence with Siena.

381

# BRUNELLO DI MONTALCINO

Brunello (dialect for the nice dark one) is Tuscany's most revered wine. It is also Tuscany's rarest, most expensive, and longest lived. It is made in Montalcino, a walled medieval village clinging to a rocky hilltop, about an hour's drive south of Chianti Classico. This southern region is warmer and as a result, the wines have historically been bigger bodied than Chiantis. The extra bit of warmth provides winemakers here with more assurance that each year sangiovese grapes will indeed ripen and produce wines of nuance and complexity. As a result, from the beginning brunello di Montalcino has been based on sangiovese alone. Unlike Chianti and Vino Nobile di Montepulciano, other grape varieties have not been blended with the sangiovese to layer in more flavor.

The vineyards of brunello di Montalcino cover a modest area, some 3,000 acres. (Chianti, by comparison, covers more than 41,000 acres.) The best vineyards, as well as the village, are some 1,800 feet above sea level, where they are blanketed by a luminous swatch of sunshine. In the spring the light in Montalcino is unlike any in the rest of Tuscany. There is more limestone in the soil than there is in Chianti, and there are strips of clay, schist, volcanic soil, and plots of the crumbly marl called *galestro*. The best vineyards are planted on slopes facing south and southwest. Like a giant rock curtain, the Monte Amiata range to the southeast helps to protect the vineyards from sudden rain and hail.

*Some of the Best Producers of Brunello di Montalcino*

ALTESINO

ARGIANO

BIONDI-SANTI

CASANOVA DEI NERI

CASANUOVO DELLA CERBAIE

CASSE BASSE

CERBAIONA DI DIEGO MOLINARI

CIACCI PICCOLOMINI D'ARAGONA

CONTI COSTANTI

FERRO DI BURONI CARLO

GORELLI

I DUE CIPRESSI

IL POGGIONE

LA FORTUNA

LA SERENA

PIEVE DI SANTA RESTITUTA

POGGIO ANTICO

Brunello di Montalcino is not made from the clones of sangiovese that are the source of Chianti but, instead, from a special clone called brunello. In good years the brunello clone yields a lavish wine, fleshier in texture than Chianti, with complex aromas and flavors of blackberry, black cherry, and black raspberry fruit, and chocolate, violet, and leather. By law, brunello di Montalcino must be aged longer than most other Italian wines—for four years, two of which must be in oak, for regular brunello di Montalcino; for five years, two and a half years of which must be in oak, for the *riserva*.

The kinds of barrels used for aging vary, resulting in two extremely different

## THE LAW OF MEZZADRIA

As late as 1960, the relationship of land owners to land workers in Tuscany was governed by a law known as the Law of the Mezzadria. Tuscany was divided into many *fattorie* (large farms) owned by wealthy landowners. Each *fattoria* was made up of ten to twelve *poderi* (small farms). Each *podere* covered about 20 acres and was worked by one family (the *mezzadri*). The agriculture of the *podere* was *promiscuo*—a mixture of olives, corn, wheat, wine grapes, vegetables, fruit trees, sheep, and chickens—virtually everything the working family needed to survive. Of the total production, 51 percent went to the landowner; the *mezzadri* kept 49 percent as payment for their labor.

Though the system of *mezzadria* is gone and land workers are now paid salaries, many Tuscan wine estates are still known as either *fattoria* or *podere* (Fattoria di Felsina; Fattoria di Montevertine; Podere Il Palazzino). And some small Tuscan vineyards remain as they have been for decades, planted not only with several varieties of grapes but also with fruit and olive trees scattered among the vines.

*The old stone farmhouse of Poderi Castellare, known for its excellent Chianti.*

383

styles of wine. Traditional producers still use large old Slavonian oak casks, which allow the wine to age and evolve but which do not impart significant character themselves. More modern producers use small, new-French-oak barrels, which give the wine more structure and an unmistakable note of sweet vanilla. And many producers, creating a third style, use a combination of both so that oak flavors, if apparent at all, are more subtle.

In great vintages brunello can take on stunning elegance, suppleness, and concentration. The flavors seem almost animate as they somersault over themselves and out of the glass. The texture can be as unctuous as chocolate syrup. Still, like the best Chiantis, the top brunello di Montalcinos are not about raw power.

Brunello di Montalcino has a reputation for longevity. One of the most legendary wines in this regard—not just in Tuscany, but in Italy—is the Biondi-Santi brunello di Montalcino. After a hundred years it can still be remarkable, with fragile but complex flavors that almost tremble in the mouth. Brunello di Montalcino was initially the vision and creation of Ferruccio Biondi-Santi who, in the 1870s, isolated the brunello clone of sangiovese and planted it throughout the vineyards at his estate Il Greppo, some 1,790 feet above sea level. Biondi-Santi's brunello could not have been more unconventional. At the time, most of the wine made in Montalcino was sweet and white. Those who preferred red drank Chianti, much of which was light in style and not very ageworthy. Biondi-Santi's brunello di Montalcino was the exact opposite: ample in body, packed with flavor, intensely colored, and capable of being cellared for decades. Having isolated the clone, Biondi-Santi went on to limit the yields of his vines and then, during fermentation, to let the grape skins sit with the juice for maximum color extraction. He aged the resulting wines for years before releasing them. Though common today, each of these practices was virtually unheard of in the mid-nineteenth century, especially in a rural village in agrarian central Italy. (The first paved road to Montalcino was completed in 1960!) In 1980 brunello di Montalcino was awarded DOCG status; it was one of the first Italian reds to be given the designation.

Today slightly more than one hundred producers continue to shape and improve what has been considered a venerable wine for the last hundred years. Most of these producers are small. However, one producer—the American-owned firm of Banfi—is colossal. The estate, spread over more than 7,000 acres, includes a state-of-the-art winery that makes several wines including a good brunello.

## Rosso di Montalcino

Sometimes thought of as brunello di Montalcino's younger sibling, Rosso di Montalcino is a lighter, fruitier, less complex wine than brunello di Montalcino; it's also a lot less expensive. Rosso di Montalcino is usually made from grapes from the younger and/or less ideal vineyards in Montalcino; the older and better ones being reserved for brunello di Montalcino. The yields of Rosso are not as limited as those for brunello di Montalcino. And by law Rosso di Montalcino must be

### A TASTING LIBRARY

Roughly midway between Rome and Florence is the dramatic walled city of Siena, home of Italy's most famous *enoteca* (wine library), visited by more than 100,000 people every year. Housed within the imposing Cosimo de' Medici fortress, the Enoteca Italiana holds more than 1,000 different wines from about 500 producers representing every region of Italy. Tastings are held regularly; there is a small fee.

*30 Piazza Matteotti, 53100 Siena; 011-39-0577-46-091.*

aged one year compared to brunello di Montalcino's four. In poor vintages, however, Rosso di Montalcino can be a smart choice since many brunello di Montalcino producers declassify their brunello grapes and make Rosso di Montalcino with them instead.

Only a few producers consistently make truly exciting Rosso di Montalcino. In many cases, these producers give brunello-like treatment to their Rosso, leaving the juice in contact with the skins for a longer period than usual and aging the wine in small oak barrels. Among the best producers of Rosso di Montalcino are Argiano, Casse Basse, Conti Costanti, I Due Cipressi, and Poggio Antico.

## VINO NOBILE DI MONTEPULCIANO

Wine has been made in and around the town of Montepulciano since Etruscan times. It was not until the eighteenth century, however, that the wine was given the name Vino Nobile, a reference not to the nobleness of the wine but rather to the noblemen, poets, and popes who regularly drank it. Today Vino Nobile does not necessarily live up to so lofty a name. Ask any number of Italian sommeliers what they think of Vino Nobile and invariably they will pause or shrug a bit, then meekly suggest that there are some good ones. Admittedly, there *are* some good ones—Vino Nobiles with spicy concentration and ultrasharp yet balanced acidity. But too many are just plain thin and tart, without sufficient structure, fruit, or flavor. In all fairness, proponents contend that a golden period for Vino Nobile may dawn once producers get a firmer grasp on clones, limit the yields, and begin to understand better how to tame Vino Nobile's often strident acidity and tannin.

Like brunello di Montalcino and Chianti, Vino Nobile is made primarily from its own clone of sangiovese, this one called prugnolo (the word means little prune, a reference to the prunelike shape, color, and aroma of the grapes). Often the grapes are, as they are in Chianti, blended with a small amount of canaiolo, malvasia, and/or trebbiano.

The vineyards of Montepulciano ring the city of Siena, near the southern end of the Valley of Chiana. Curiously enough, Chiana may partly explain Vino Nobile's prestige. The valley is famous for a special breed of white cattle, Chianina, which is the source of Tuscany's renowned specialty: mammoth T-bone steaks called *bistecca alla fiorentina*. Maybe the perfection of the steaks led people to assume that the accompanying wine had to be pretty incredible, too.

Montepulciano's vineyards are planted on broad open slopes. At about 600 feet above sea level, they stand at less than half the altitude of the brunello di Montalcino vineyards. The soil is mostly sandy clay. By law, the wines must be aged for two years in wood; *riservas* must be aged for three years. Vino Nobile di Montepulciano was granted DOCG status in 1980. Avignonesi, Poderi Boscarelli, and Terre di Bindella are among the best producers.

Finally, don't confuse Vino Nobile di Montepulciano, made principally from the prugnolo clone of sangiovese, with the grape montepulciano, which is planted throughout central and southern Italy and is a specialty of the region of Abruzzi.

385

*Vino Nobile de Montepulciano takes its name from the ancient hill town of Montepulciano, about 75 miles southeast of Florence.*

### *Rosso di Montepulciano*

Like Vino Nobile, Rosso di Montepulciano is made from the prugnolo clone of sangiovese, but the two wines generally come from separate vineyards: Rosso di Montepulciano from the younger vineyards, Vino Nobile from the older. The yields of Rosso are not as limited as those for Vino Nobile, and Rosso di Montepulciano is generally aged a shorter period of time. All of this would seem to make Rosso di Montepulciano pale in comparison to Vino Nobile, but the quality is entirely dependent on the producer. The immediate splash of fruit in some Rossos can make them taste a lot better than some thin, tired Vino Nobiles. A bottle of Gattavecchi's Rosso di Montepulciano served with a juicy *bistecca alla fiorentina* will prove the point.

*From the medieval towers of San Gimignano, once used to store grain in the thirteenth century, you can take in the panorama of Tuscany's undulating green hills.*

## CARMIGNANO

It may lack the prestige of brunello di Montalcino, the popularity of Chianti, and the lucky name of Vino Nobile, but Carmignano nonetheless has an important claim to fame: cabernet sauvignon. Not an imported international upstart here, in this tiny wine region just west of Florence,

## THE ETRUSCANS

From 800 to 300 B.C., the Etruscans, an ancient civilization of highly cultured people, lived in what is now Tuscany. Many of the hilltops where they built their flourishing villages are now blanketed by a pastoral carpet of vines. Some historians believe the Etruscans to be the first purely indigenous Italic race. But their almond-shaped eyes and slanting eyebrows lead others to suggest that they may have migrated from Asia Minor. Elaborate Etruscan tombs, funerary drawings, and grave artifacts depict a vibrant society of aristocrats and slaves that formed a culture that was both obsessed with ceremony and superstitious. Divination, for example, was performed by "reading" the entrails of freshly slaughtered animals, the flight of birds, or flashes of lightning during thunderstorms. Tomb murals portray sybaritic banquets, full of wine drinking, dancing, and athletic contests. Later this hedonism, along with Etruscan military pageantry, would profoundly affect the Romans who, by the end of the third century B.C., defeated and dissolved the Etruscan world.

cabernet sauvignon has been a part of the Carmignano blend since the eighteenth century. Today by law Carmignano must be composed of a minimum of 50 percent sangiovese with 10 to 20 percent cabernet sauvignon and/or cabernet franc, plus a maximum of 20 percent canaiolo, a maximum of 10 percent trebbiano or malvasia, and a maximum of 10 percent other allowable reds.

Carmignano, which has a reputation for finesse and structure, comes from a tiny area. There are fewer than a dozen producers, most of them minuscule. In fact, the wine drinker is likely to encounter only one or two producers, and most probably the first will be the famous estate of Villa de Cappezana, which makes what many Italian wine lovers consider the very best Carmignano. The estate was originally a Medici villa.

## VERNACCIA DI SAN GIMIGNANO

Although everything about Tuscany seems to put a person in the mood to drink red wine, there is a historic white wine to consider: vernaccia di San Gimignano, traditionally referred to as the wine that kisses, licks, bites, and stings. Actually, only the best vernaccia di San Gimignanos do that; plenty of others are just about as innocuous and coarse as white wine gets.

As its name suggests, vernaccia di San Gimignano is made from vernaccia grapes grown on the slopes surrounding the storybook medieval hill town of San Gimignano, roughly an hour's drive southwest of Florence. Though historically vernaccia di San Gimignano was made and aged in large old wood casks, the best modern

versions owe much of their charm to the high-tech treatment they get. Vinification generally takes place in temperature-controlled stainless-steel tanks, after which the wine is usually bottled young and fresh. There are about 500 small producers. The best of these include Il Cipressino, Riccardo Falchini, Montenidoli, Pietrafitta, La Quercia di Racciano, San Quirico, and Teruzzi e Puthod.

## VIN SANTO

Of the hundreds of different sweet wines produced in Italy, the best known may be *vin santo*, holy wine, so named because priests have drunk it during the Mass for centuries. Unlike many sweet wines, however, *vin santo* is not served solely on ceremonious occasions. It is the customary finale to even the humblest Tuscan meal, served after espresso,

*Malvasia and trebbiano grapes must be dried for three to six months before they can be made into* vin santo.

almost always with a plate of small *biscotti* called *cantucci*, stubby, twice-baked cookies meant for dunking.

Most *vin santo* does not taste as sweet as, say, Sauternes. The wine has a delicate, creamy, honey-roasted flavor, and the color can be unreal, from radiant amber to neon orange. The sweetness level, however, is entirely up to the producer, and there are even some rare *vin santos* that are bone-dry.

True *vin santo* is expensive because the ancient process of making it remains artisanal and labor intensive. First the grapes (generally malvasia or trebbiano) are partially dried for three to six months. Though there are several ways this can be accomplished, the preferred method is to hang them from rafters in an airy, dry attic or room. During the drying period nearly half of the liquid (mostly water) in the grapes evaporates, concentrating the remaining sugar. The grapes are crushed, combined with a *madre*, or mother (a small remnant of the thick residue from a former batch), and then the must is left to ferment slowly for three to five years in small, sealed barrels placed in a warm attic or loft called a *vinsantaia*. The barrels are commonly oak, but some producers give the wine greater complexity by using juniper, cherry, and chestnut as well, then blending the final lots. (This idea of using several different types of wood to contribute to the complexity of flavor is also used in neighboring Emilia-Romagna to make the best balsamic vinegars, and indeed, if everything does not go right, a Tuscan winemaker can end up with some very delicious vinegar rather than *vin santo*.)

Typically families make their own *vin santo* for home use and as a proud offering to guests. In addition, there are several dozen small commercial producers. Of them, these seven make the most stunning *vin santos:* Avignonesi, Badia a Coltibuono, Fontodi, Isole e Olena, San Giusto a Rentennano, Selvapiana, and I Selvatici.

In addition, the large producers Antinori, Barone Ricasoli, Frescobaldi, and Lungarotti make very good *vin santos* that are not as limited in production and so are more easily found.

## STEAK ITALIAN STYLE

If the wine lists in most steak houses in the United States are any evidence, a thick grilled steak tastes delicious with a powerful cabernet sauvignon. But when it comes to steak's perfect marriage partner, Tuscany offers a different idea. Tuscany's specialty *bistecca alla fiorentina*, the huge slab of grilled beef that is thicker than the thickest steak in the United States, is always served with a wine made principally from sangiovese—especially a top Chianti Classico Riserva, brunello di Montalcino, or Vino Nobile di Montepulciano. Sangiovese, with its underlying bright acidity and hint of saltiness, is stunning when set off by the richness and fat of the beef.

# THE FOODS OF TUSCANY

Perhaps because it was the birthplace of the Renaissance, Tuscany is often associated with refinement, wealth, even ostentation. And so we assume that Tuscan cooking will exhibit these characteristics as well and that the cuisine will be both sumptuous and elaborate.

## OLIVES AND GRAPES

For centuries around the Mediterranean, vines and olive trees have grown side by side (sometimes literally entwined), often in soil so arid little else will grow there. The bond between the two crops is especially strong in Tuscany, where many wine estates double as top olive-oil producers. Grapes and olives here seem connected not just agriculturally and gastronomically but also spiritually. In fact, in 1985 when a blast of cold weather killed 90 percent of the region's ancient olive trees, Tuscan winemakers reportedly wept as they listened to the eerie sound of treasured old olive trees rupturing from frozen sap.

Tuscan extra-virgin olive oil is considered by many experts to be the world's finest. The first reason: the olives themselves. The three varieties used—*frantoio, maraiolo,* and *lecciono*—are known respectively for their fruitiness, spiciness, and richness. The second factor has to do with harvesting. Because Tuscany is cold in the fall, olives are harvested early, before potential frosts—so early that Tuscan olives are picked green, before they are fully ripe (most other olives worldwide are harvested after they ripen, when they are black). Olives that are not fully ripe give Tuscan oil its classic lime green color, an almost herbal freshness, an explosive fruitiness, and a kind of peppery bite. Among the finest producers of Tuscan extra-virgin olive oil are Antinori, Avignonesi, Caparzo, Castellare, Castello di Ama, Castello di Fonterutoli, Castello di Volpaia, and Fattoria di Felsina.

Sumptuous it can be. Elaborate, almost never. Tuscan cooking is some of the humblest in Italy. It is quite definitively poor people's cuisine. In contrast to special-occasion dishes, such as *bistecca alla fiorentina* (mammoth slabs of grilled Chianina beef), everyday meals are more likely to be dominated by beans and bread. When other Italians want to be derogatory, they call the Tuscans by their age-old nickname: *mangiafagioli*, bean eaters.

But if beans are commonplace in the region's culinary repertoire, bread is even more so. The entire *cucina* of Tuscany is said to revolve around this one essential food, and in no other region of Italy does bread seem more intimately tied to everyday life. The Tuscans may have been among the first people to regularly use forks, but bread is a Tuscan's oldest and most treasured utensil. At every meal it is enlisted to help transport one thing or another to the mouth.

Tuscan bread, *pane toscano*, tastes like no other bread in Italy, mostly because it is made without salt. In restaurants and trattorias this bread is the first thing whisked to the table, even though great examples are, sadly enough, increasingly hard to find. Many trattorias serve a cardboardlike version that discriminating pigeons would reject. Butter is never served alongside, nor is olive oil for dipping. (The latter is a United States restaurant custom begun in California in the 1980s.) Generally, and without regard for its quality, a small cover charge for *pane toscano* appears on the bill.

Tuscan children walking to school often munch on *schiacciata*, a piece of flat bread baked with olive oil and sometimes sweetened with sugar or wine grapes. Before lunch or dinner there are always *crostini*, thin slices of Tuscan bread traditionally spread with an earthy paste of chopped liver but sometimes, in more creative cases, covered with grilled wild mushrooms or a purée of olives and garlic. *Crostini* are not the same as *bruschetta*—which, in any case, is not a Tuscan term but the Roman one for peasant bread that has been grilled over a fire, brushed with olive oil, rubbed with garlic, and then possibly topped with chopped fresh tomatoes.

But perhaps the most glorious way to serve bread is as *fettunta*, a piece of toasted *pane toscano* swathed with just-pressed, ripe, green, unfiltered Tuscan extra-virgin olive oil. Technically you can only eat *fettunta* in the late fall right after the olives have been harvested and the oil is at its apex. The name *fettunta* comes from *fetta*, the name workers used to describe the hunk of bread that they anointed with intensely flavorful extra-virgin oil as it ran fresh from the press.

In Tuscany, bread is also constantly used in cooking, especially good bread gone stale. The homiest Tuscan soup is *ribollita* made with stale bread, black Tuscan cabbage, and beans. *Panzanella*, the humble and irresistibly delicious Tuscan salad, is made of stale bread moistened with a little water and then tossed with fresh tomatoes, chopped basil, onions, celery, and olive oil. A classic Tuscan cookbook, *Con Poco o Nulla, With Little or*

## CANTINETTA ANTINORI

An elegant trattoria beside the fifteenth-century Antinori palace in the center of Florence, the Cantinetta Antinori began as a small shop from which the family sold their wine. Historically Tuscan wine was often sold in this manner. Wealthy noblemen would bring wine made on their country estates to their city palaces and sell it from there. Sometimes bits of food would be offered to wine purchasers. Over time some of these shops evolved into small *cantinetti*, where simple pastas and soups would be served.

From this forthright start the Cantinetta Antinori has metamorphosed into one of the most vibrant trattorias in Florence. The lusty Tuscan dishes it features are thoroughly traditional, starting with the ubiquitous *crostini*. Its stellar *carpaccio di bresaola* (paper-thin slices of dried beef) is drizzled with Antinori-estate extra-virgin olive oil and a squeeze of fresh lemon juice, sprinkled with coarsely grated Parmigiano-Reggiano cheese, and then set off against peppery arugula.

The Cantinetta's thick *ribollita*, a soul-warming soup of vegetables and beans thickened with bread, evokes images of clever Italian grandmothers creating magic at their stoves. This is the place to eat bowls of *fagioli* (white beans), *finocchiona* (sausage flavored with fennel seeds), and osso buco (slowly simmered veal shank). Chestnut flour is a Tuscan specialty, and the *cantinetta*'s chestnut flour cake (*castagnaccio*) is the perfect light, not too sweet ending to a hearty meal.

Though one would assume that there would be countless places in Italy serving wine by the glass, there are not. Cantinetta Antinori is an exception, making even such an expensive Super Tuscan wine as Solaia a lunchtime possibility.

*Cantinetta Antinori, 3 Piazza degli Antinori, 50123 Florence; 011-39-055-29-22-34.*

solid. What more could be asked for? Then again, perhaps this small but admirable bit of culinary compatibility was the result of more mundane considerations. Culinary historians point out that salt was always a precious, expensive commodity in Tuscany and that often it was heavily taxed. *Pane toscano*, it seems, could also have been the legacy of a tax revolt.

## VISITING TUSCAN WINE ESTATES

Central Tuscany is one of the most romantic and culturally vibrant wine regions in the world. It was in Florence, after all, that the Renaissance was born, and the area is still a haven for every sort of artisan—cabinetmakers, sculptors, silversmiths, gilders, and of course, winemakers.

From Florence south to Siena and then south again to Montalcino are small villages and hill towns that, in most respects, seem untouched by time. The twisting country roads are more suited to horses and scooters than to high-speed cars. No road even remotely

*Nothing*, opens with ten suggestions for using day-old bread.

Bread made without salt has a muted, almost bland flavor.

*Florence has been symbolized for centuries by the Duomo, built by the early Renaissance architect Brunelleschi.*

That Tuscan bakers would intentionally choose to make their bread this way seems surprising, until you consider that bread alone is not the issue. In the Tuscan triumvirate of bread, olive oil, and wine, the plain *pane toscano* is the perfect backdrop for the pepperyness of Tuscan olive oil, and both are delicious juxtaposed with the slight perception of saltiness in many wines made from sangiovese grapes. Salt and pepper. Wine and bread. Liquid and

resembles a straight line.

Wine estates vary tremendously in size, from small farms that have been converted into working wine villas to large wineries. Whether large or small, a Tuscan wine estate is almost always a challenge to find. There are rarely any signs or street addresses on the properties themselves. You simply have to meander around the commune (small hamlet or rural principality usually attached to a village) or go into the local bar or café and ask for directions (not a guarantee either). On the other hand, it's hard to get truly lost in central Tuscany: Dirt paths off the main road almost always end at some wine estate.

English is often spoken, but it is extremely helpful to have a command of basic Italian. Some wineries have small shops where you can buy the estate's wine, as well as its olive oil, and sometimes honey. Appointments are suggested.

Before visiting any wine estate, however, it's very helpful to visit the local *consorzio*, or governing body, for that wine region. There is a *consorzio* for Chianti Classico, and one each for brunello di Montalcino and Vino Nobile di Montepulciano. The *consorzio* can give you an overview of winemaking in the region, provide you with maps, answer questions, and suggest producers to visit.

Above all, no wine trip to Tuscany would be complete without a visit to the *enoteca* (see page 384) in Siena. Hundreds of wines from all over the country are available there for tasting.

The telephone numbers include the dialing code you'll need when calling from the United States. If you're calling from within Italy, eliminate the 011-39. Don't worry if you notice that some of the phone numbers are longer than others; Italian telephone numbers aren't standardized the way they are in the United States.

**AVIGNONESI**
91 Via di Gracciano nel Corso
53040 Montepulciano
011-39-0578-75-78-72 or
011-39-0578-75-78-73

**BADIA A COLTIBUONO**
Località Badia a Coltibuono
53013 Gaiole, Chianti
011-39-0577-74-94-98
Has a wonderful restaurant.

**BARONE RICASOLI**
Gaiole, Chianti
011-39-0577-74-90-66
Brolio castle, part of the Barone Ricasoli estate, offers several beautiful guest apartments for visitors interested in renting accommodations by the week.

**CASTELLARE DI CASTELLINA**
Località Castellare
53011 Castellina, Chianti
011-39-0577-74-04-90

**CASTELLO BANFI**
53024 Montalcino
011-39-0577-84-01-11

**CASTELLO DI VOLPAIA**
Località Volpaia
1 Piazza della Cisterna
53017 Radda, Chianti
011-39-0577-73-80-66

**CONSORZIO BRUNELLO DI MONTALCINO**
1 Costa del Municipio
53024 Montalcino
011-39-0577-84-82-46

**CONSORZIO CHIANTI CLASSICO**
155 Via degli Scopeti
50026 San Casciano
Val di Pesa, Florence
011-39-055-822-81-73

**FATTORIA DI FELSINA**
484 Strada Chiantigiana
53019 Castelnuovo Berardenga
011-39-0577-35-51-17

**MARCHESI ANTINORI**
3 Piazza degli Antinori
50123 Florence
011-39-055-235-95

**RUFFINO**
42/44 Via Aretina
50065 Pontassieve
011-39-055-836-05

**VILLA CAFAGGIO**
5 Via S. Martino in Cecione
50020 Panzano, Chianti
011-39-055-854-90-94

# THE TUSCAN WINES TO KNOW

*While white wines are made in Tuscany, the wines of most importance,*
*including the ones below, are all red.*

## ANTINORI

Tignanello

approximately 80% sangiovese, 20% cabernet
sauvignon

Tignanello, the first well-known Super Tuscan, is the red wine that carved out a radically new direction for Tuscan winemaking and, in the process, galvanized the creative spirit of winemakers throughout Italy. When it was first made in 1971 Tignanello contained no cabernet, but from the beginning, it was aged in small, French-oak barrels. By the early 1990s, after a few slight changes in the blend and winemaking method, some of the best Tignanellos ever were being made. In the finest vintages Tignanello can possess that rare character of being both refined and powerful, a richly berried wine with tannin that is as soft as felt.

## BIONDI-SANTI

Brunello di Montalcino

riserva

100% brunello

The brunello clone was first isolated and propagated by the Biondi-Santi family around 1870. They were the only estate to produce brunello di Montalcino until after the Second World War when several other producers joined the ranks. This is the most legendary estate in Montalcino and also the most traditional. Wines here have been made in essentially the same manner for nearly a century and the grapes come from a perfect high-altitude vineyard. The Biondi-Santi wines age in large, old, Slavonian-oak casks, where they evolve painstakingly slowly. When they emerge, however, they are fascinating, complex wines with stunning elegance and balance.

393

## AZIENDA AGRICOLA FONTODI

Flaccianello della Pieve

100% sangiovese

Flaccianello della Pieve, Fontodi's Super Tuscan, is named for a Christian cross in the nearby village of Pieve. In great vintages this is the sort of wine you can drink once and remember forever. It's often one of the most exotic sangioveses made—syrupy in texture, tooth-stainingly rich, exceptionally complex, and dappled with uncommon flavors, such as ginger, black licorice, persimmon, and grapefruit. Most impressive of all is the way the wine explodes with sappy juiciness. Fontodi, a small producer, also makes wonderful Chianti Classico Riserva.

## CASTELLARE

I Sodi di San Niccolò

mostly sangiovese

This Super Tuscan has a large international following, and it deserves it. In Tuscan dialect, the word *sodi* indicates a hard vineyard, one with stones and rocks, as opposed to a *campo*, a vineyard that is easy to work with a hoe. In great years Castellare's I Sodi di San Niccolò is a wine of immense complexity, intensity, and elegance—the sort of wine that takes over your mouth (and mind) with its suppleness and opulence. The aromas and flavors are racy and thick: black figs, rich earth, truffles, mocha, tar, spices, and orange. The finish is hauntingly long.

## CONTI COSTANTI
Rosso di Montalcino

100% brunello

Imagine bittersweet chocolates, purple plums, and black figs buried under rich dark earth. Costi Costanti's is an uncommon Rosso di Montalcino from a great vineyard. Most Rosso di Montalcinos are a far cry from their older sibling, brunello di Montalcino. Not this one, which is aged in small, French-oak barrels. In top years it is complex and refined, with suedelike smoothness.

## FATTORIA DI FELSINA
Chianti Classico

Berardenga

mostly sangiovese

While many basic (that is non-*riserva*) Chianti Classicos lack personality and flair, this one from Felsina can positively dance with black cherry, blackberry, and spice flavors. Basic *classicos* also often lack any finish, but again, the Felsina is often just the opposite, with flavors that seem to linger on and on. Felsina's Chianti Classico Riservas are also delicious. The one called Rancia—ranch—can be a knockout.

## MARCHESI INCISA DELLA ROCCHETTA
Sassicaia

Tenuta San Guido

100% cabernet sauvignon

Sassicaia (the word means place of stones) was the limited-production wine that inspired the revolutionary Super Tuscan wines, such as Tignanello, I Sodi di San Niccolò, and Sammarco. It was the first Tuscan wine to be made entirely from cabernet sauvignon, the first to be aged in new French *barriques,* and the first to challenge the assumption that great Tuscan wines could only be made in the central Chianti hills. The wine now ranks as one of Italy's top cabernets and has become the standard against which other cabernets are judged. In great vintages Sassicaia is highly structured yet utterly supple, with intense and lingering blackberry and chocolate flavors.

## MONTEVERTINE
Le Pergole Torte

100% sangiovese

The small estate of Montevertine makes three Super Tuscan wines, all of which are based on sangiovese and all of which have pinpoint clarity and focus. Le Pergole Torte is perhaps the most dramatic, but only by a sliver. At its best, it's a rich-textured wine packed full of high-toned black cherry and black fig flavors, with spicy notes of vanilla, violets, and orange peel thrown in. Like I Sodi di San Niccolò, Le Pergole Torte is a stop-you-in-your-tracks, world-class sangiovese.

## POGGIO ANTICO

Brunello di Montalcino Riserva

100% brunello

Poggio Antico (the name means ancient small hill) is the source for one of the most dense, explosive, and complex of all the brunellos made in a modern style. The estate's vineyards are the highest in Montalcino, which is thought, in part, to account for the elegance and concentration of the wine. For all of the blackberry fruit, chocolate, tar, leather, mushroom, truffle, and gamy aromas and flavors, this *riserva* can be as graceful as a Gothic arch. In great vintages, Poggio Antico is also renowned for its thick, silky texture.

## RUFFINO

Chianti Classico

Riserva Ducale

riserva

mostly sangiovese

One of the leading producers of traditional Chianti, Ruffino makes a terrific flavor-packed basic Chianti. But it's Ruffino's Chianti Classico *riserva* called Riserva Ducale that is the jewel in the crown. The wine is a template for traditional sangiovese aromas and flavors: dried orange, earth, prune, plum, and dark chocolate, and often has a salty flip at the end. In the best vintages, it is velvet textured and bursting with fruit flavor. There are actually two Riserva Ducales, the regular and a Riserva Ducale Oro, or gold label. The latter, more expensive, is made only from grapes from selected vineyards and only in the best vintages.

## VILLA CAFAGGIO

Chianti Classico

riserva

100% sangiovese

Villa Cafaggio's vineyards roll over steep, stony hills in Greve, one of the top communes of Chianti Classico. In very good vintages, Villa Cafaggio produces a *riserva* that is compact, vigorous, and precise. The wine opens with complex herbal and chocolate aromas, then vaults into vivid mocha, mint, cherry, and dried orange flavors. No muddled flavors in this wine; it's all laser-sharp focus and bright fruit intensity. The *riservas* are made only in the best years—usually four to six times a decade.

*For centuries oak has been the preferred wood for barrels because of its durability. Here workers move new barrels by rolling them.*

# Wine Regions of Note

From a wine standpoint, Italy is so diverse that the major areas alone can't tell the whole story. Here are some of the lesser-known wine regions. While not as prominent as the big three (Piedmont, the Tre Venezie, and Tuscany), these regions are nonetheless significant for the popular and often fascinating wines that are made in them. I'll start in the north, in Lombardy, home to many of Italy's top sparkling wines and then, zigzagging south through Liguria, Emilia-Romagna, Umbria, Abruzzi, and the southern penninsula (Campania, Apulia, Basilicata, and Calabria), eventually end up on the islands of Sicily and Sardinia, where intriguing wines, many from quite ancient grape varieties, continue to be made.

## LOMBARDY

The north central region of Lombardy—Lombardia in Italian—is Italy's most populous region and the country's leading industrial zone. Nowhere is the region's commercial flair more evident than in Milan, Lombardy's most important city and Italy's fast-paced capital of fashion and finance. With business so preeminent, there hardly seems room for a wine industry. But there is one; this is Italy after all.

Unlike Piedmont or Tuscany, Lombardy is not associated with a grape variety, and there is no well-known, esteemed

*The impressive Gothic cathedral (Duomo) of Milan: Its ornate facade is a reflection of the city's power and wealth.*

wine zone, such as Barolo or Chianti. Wine here is made in three principal areas located far from its center, along the region's borders. In the north just a short drive from Switzerland is the Valtellina; in the southwest corner near Emilia-Romagna is the Oltrepò Pavese; and in the far east near Lake Garda and the Veneto is the most important of all three areas: Franciacorta. Both sparkling Franciacorta and Valtellina Superiore have DOCG status.

Though *spumante* (sparkling wine) is made in virtually every region of northern Italy, Lombardy's Franciacorta is the country's leading area for sophisticated dry sparkling wines made by the Champagne method. Historically a fairly bucolic place and home to many convents and monasteries, Franciacorta became Italy's premier "Champagne" zone in the 1970s largely because of the pioneering success of the producer Berlucchi. Today a number of prestigious sparkling wine firms are located there, including Bellavista, Ca' del Bosco, and Cavalleri. Like Champagne, Franciacorta's sparkling wines are made from chardonnay and pinot noir, although here pinot grigio and pinot bianco are also allowed. To distinguish them from *spumantes*, such as Asti, that are made by the Charmat method, these sparklers are labeled *metodo tradizionale* or *metodo classico*. Like Champagne, they can be austerely elegant with a fine, creamy *mousse* of bubbles. By law, nonvintage *metodo tradizionale spumantes* must be aged at least eighteen months in the bottle; vintaged *spumantes* must be aged for thirty months.

In the same general area as Franciacorta but farther east near Lake Garda is the home of Lugana, a dry Italian white wine based on trebbiano di Lugana, considered one of the most tasty, aromatic types of trebbiano. Though most trebbiano-based wines are innocuous, Lugana can be nicely refreshing. Some of its appeal may be related to the fact that it's the wine usually served with the region's other specialty: trout from Lake Garda.

The Oltrepò Pavese, of all three areas the closest to Milan, is the source of the major share of Lombardian wine. Most of it is of quaffing quality or just slightly better. Many rustic red wines are based on barbera or croatina (a simple indigenous red); humble whites are based on riesling italico (a grape also grown in Austria and eastern Europe and not the same as true riesling). Quite a bit of easy-drinking well-priced *spumante* also comes from here, most of which in quality is not up to *spumante* from Franciacorta, but then you're paying less for it, too.

Lombardy's third wine-producing area is the Valtellina in the far north on the precipitous, cold yet sunny foothills of the Alps. Vineyards here are on slopes so steep they must be terraced, and in some cases, as in Germany's Mosel region, harvested grapes are relayed down the mountainside in buckets attached to cables. This is the most northern wine-growing region in the world for nebbiolo. Regular Valtellina is a simple, rough-edged, lean red made principally from that grape. A notch higher in quality is Valtellina Superiore made exclusively from nebbiolo

397

and aged at least two years (compared to regular Valtellina's one). There are four subdistricts where Valtellina Superiore can be made: Grumello, Sassella, Inferno, and Valgella. Of the four, Inferno is where the tastiest and the biggest bodied wines are made. The name Inferno, hell in Italian, does not describe what the wine tastes like but, rather, refers to the summer sun, which beats down on the terraced mountainside vineyards, ripening the grapes.

## LIGURIA

Known as the Italian Riviera, Liguria is the crescent-shaped region arcing from the French border down to Tuscany. Virtually in the center is Genoa, Liguria's capital and one of Italy's most historic and busiest ports. In this small, hilly region perched on the ridges of the Apennine mountain range as they descend into the Ligurian Sea, wine is little more than a basic commodity. Pesto and olive oil, both Ligurian specialties, are far more famous.

Four easy-drinking types of wine are important in the region. To Genoa's east is found the wine known as Cinqueterre, five lands (so called because the wine is made near five fishing villages). Cinqueterre, a neutral tasting but nonetheless popular white, is made from bosco and albarola, two fairly innocuous varieties, plus vermentino, which has more character. More impressive than Cinqueterre itself are the vineyards from which the grapes come. It's stunning to see vineyards clinging to cliffs so close to the sea.

West of Genoa, ormeasco, vermentino, and Dolceacqua are made. Ormeasco is Liguria's name for dolcetto; it is turned into fruity quaffing reds. Vermentino grapes were probably brought to Italy from Spain via Corsica in the fourteenth century. The variety is the source of the dry, floral white wine also known as vermentino, a classic with Ligurian fish soups. Dolceacqua, sometimes known by its more

*The vineyards of Liguria back up against the ridges of the Apennine mountain range.*

formal name, rossese di Dolceacqua, comes from rossese, the leading red grape of the Italian Riviera. Reportedly a favorite of Napoleon, this wine is commonly used as an ingredient in one of the specialties of the region, rabbit braised with olives.

Estates in Liguria are small, many of them just local family operations, and often the smaller the property, the more interesting the wine. It's impossible to recommend producers under these circumstances and, in any case, the number of Ligurian wines exported to the United States is tiny. When in Liguria, the best strategy is an old European one: Find a great chef and ask what he or she drinks.

# EMILIA-ROMAGNA

"Ask an Italian where to eat only one meal in Italy and, after recommending his mother's house, it is more than likely he will send you to the region of Emilia-Romagna." With this declaration Lynne Rosetto Kasper opens her authoritative cookbook *The Splendid Table*, and Kasper is right. Emilia-Romagna is Italy's ultimate food region and a place so consumed by its passion for gastronomy that even the name of its capital is telling: Bologna means the fat one. Here in the land that gives the world such serious delicacies as Parmigiano-Reggiano, balsamic vinegar, and *prosciutto di Parma*, wine is, well, playful might be the best word. There are no wines of renown, nothing on a par with Chianti, brunello di Montalcino, Barolo, or Barbaresco. What there is, however, is a seemingly endless sea of fizzy grapey lambrusco. Lambrusco, in fact, is the leading Italian wine in the United States. The cooperative Riunite alone exports to the United States two million cases a year in three versions: white, pink, and purple-red. Cooperatives in general make a large part of Emilia-Romagna's wines.

What makes Emilia-Romagna so culinarily rich is also what makes much of the wine so comparatively poor. Running across the width of the region is the fertile Po river basin. Readily available water and nutrients may be great for food crops but for grapes it's a worrisome equation that results in high yields and thin, simple wines. The citizenry of Emilia-Romagna doesn't seem to mind. Go into any good restaurant and lambrusco is being gulped down with pride and abandon. Surprisingly, the fizzy purplish wine (only for foreign markets is it made into white and pink versions) often tastes quite good with the region's hearty sausages and pastas. Moreover, the people of Emilia-Romagna insist that the light, frothy, fairly high acid wine is the perfect aid to digestion in a region that lives for its stomach.

Emilia-Romagna spans nearly the entire width of Italy, from its border with Liguria in the west to the Adriatic Sea in the east. As its name suggests, Emilia-Romagna is actually two regions. Emilia to the west of Bologna is the definitive home of lambrusco. In Romagna to the east, most red wines are still, dry, and based on sangiovese. Romagna's leading white wine, albana di Romagna, is a fairly characterless white, though it does have the major claim to fame of being (illogically) the first Italian white wine granted DOCG status.

Lambrusco is made from the grape variety also known as lambrusco and can be a dry or slightly sweet wine. As noted, it is usually what the Italians call *frizzante*, slightly fizzy, not quite sparkling

*Indisputably one of the world's greatest cheeses, Parmigiano-Reggiano is made only in the region of Emilia-Romagna.*

## BALSAMIC VINEGAR

Wine's "other self" is vinegar. And the best vinegar in the world is widely acknowledged to be Italy's balsamic vinegar. In fact, balsamic is so utterly unlike everything else called vinegar that some producers don't call it vinegar. They call it a "sauce from wine grapes."

Standard vinegar (the word comes from the French *vin aigre,* sour wine) is created when bacteria convert a fermented liquid into acetic acid. The process is quick; the final liquid is blunt and sharp. Traditional balsamic vinegar, on the other hand, is an exquisitely mellow, deeply concentrated, syruplike liquid, sweet enough to drink on its own. In Italy it's often sipped from a small glass like a dessert wine. The adjective *traditional* is critical. There are countless inexpensive supermarket "balsamic vinegars" that are just ordinary red wine vinegar that has been sweetened and colored with caramel. They could come from Kansas.

Real balsamic vinegar is made only in Emilia-Romagna, just north of Tuscany, around the towns of Modena and Reggio. It's labeled *aceto balsamico tradizionale di Modena* or *di Reggio,* and recognizing its unique origin and authenticity, the Italian government grants it a DOP, Denomination of Protected Origin, equivalent to DOC status for wines. Price is always a tip-off: A small 3-ounce vial of *balsamico tradizionale* can be three to five times the cost of a moderately expensive bottle of wine. The price reflects the painstaking artisanal process by which traditional balsamic vinegar is made. First, the unfermented must of crushed grapes (usually trebbiano, but three others are also allowed) is boiled down to a sweet syrup, which then ferments and turns to vinegar. To condense the vinegar even more, the rich liquid is then aged a minimum of twelve years (it may be even decades) in a series of progressively smaller barrels made from different woods—oak, chestnut, cherry, linden, mulberry, juniper, ash, and so forth. As the water component of the liquid evaporates through the grain in the wood, the remaining liquid grows ever more dense and lush. Meanwhile, each wood imparts a different nuance to the final flavor of the vinegar. Although handcrafted, long-aged vinegars have been revered in Italian homes for centuries, the name balsamic was first used in the eighteenth century to refer to the "balmy" wood odors that would emanate from country farmhouses where the vinegar was patiently being made, usually in the attic.

Traditional balsamic vinegar is used very selectively in Italy. It is dribbled (too expensive to be poured) into a small amount of olive oil or butter and drizzled over cooked vegetables or fish. In the summer, it is dripped over fresh strawberries; in the fall, over fresh, thinly shaved raw porcini mushrooms. For many Italians, however, the most godly of all culinary combinations is Parmigiano-Reggiano moistened with a few drops of an especially lush, old, traditional balsamic vinegar.

enough to be considered *spumante.* Lambrusco is not made like Champagne or the top Italian *spumantes,* where each individual bottle undergoes a second, bubble-inducing fermentation. Lambrusco gets its fizz in pressurized tanks. Only if you are in Emilia itself is it possible to find zesty, good-tasting artisanal lambruscos from the four distinct zones that specialize in it. The majority of the commercially available lambruscos are far less exciting and are based on big blends with the grapes coming from all over the region. In either case, lambrusco is meant to be drunk young and indeed tastes best when consumed soon after release.

As for the wines of Romagna, albana di Romagna can be a soft and pleasant if unremarkable white. Most versions are dry but in Romagna you will come across slightly sweet versions as well as *spumantes* made from the albana grape. The most popular red wine is sangiovese di Romagna, based on a clone of sangiovese, and usually considered simple at best. With some searching it is possible to find more compelling versions made by small producers, including Fattoria Paradiso, Ferrucci, and Tenuta Zerbina.

# UMBRIA

Compared to its neighbor Tuscany, the small region of Umbria is a serene, bucolic, understated sort of place. Here, smack in the center of Italy, the landscape is gentle and rolling, and the sunlight is almost as arrestingly gossamer as it is in Tuscany. It seems fitting that Saint Francis of Assisi, Umbria's most beloved son, would have lived here.

Umbria's best-known wine is Orvieto, a stylish, crisp, slightly peachy white wine produced around the medieval hill town of the same name in the southern part of the region. Orvieto, the best versions of which can have real character, is made from trebbiano (here called procanico), along with verdello, grechetto, drupeggio, and sometimes malvasia. A step up in quality from basic Orvietos are the Orvieto Classicos, wines that come from the original, smaller Orvieto zone. Though most Orvietos encountered today are dry, the wine was originally slightly sweet. While produc tion is now limited, some of the most fascinating Orvietos are sweet versions known as *amabile* or even sweeter still, *dolce*. Several large important Tuscan firms, such as Antinori, Ruffino, and Barone Ricasoli make dry Orvieto, and there are a number of very good smaller Umbrian producers, including Barberani, Conte Vaselli, and Decugnano dei Barbi.

Umbria's well-known red wines are mostly made in the hills that surround Perugia. Two types in particular are considered among Umbria's best: Torgiano Rosso Riserva and sagrantino di Montefalco, both of which have DOCG status. Torgiano (from Torre di Giano, tower of Janus, the Roman god of gates and the namesake of January) is a tiny village where the wine Torgiano is made from three of the same grapes permitted for Chianti: sangiovese, canaiolo, and trebbiano. The village and surrounding area are dominated by the family-run winery Lungarotti, whose *museo del vino* (wine museum) houses one of the most impressive personal collections of wine artifacts in Italy. Lungarotti's wines, especially the Torgiano Rosso Riserva called Rubesco, can be stunning and long lived.

401

*One of the treasures to be found in Torgiano is the* museo del vino, *with its striking collection of ancient ceramics.*

Sagrantino di Montefalco wines are quite the opposite of Torgiano wines. While most Torgiano reds have the medium weight and relative delicacy of Chianti Classicos, sagrantino di Montefalcos are powerhouses—big, bold, gripping wines that have been compared to amarones. The wines are made from sagrantino grapes, and though the majority of examples today are dry, sweet versions made from dried grapes were far more common in the past. There aren't many producers of sagrantino di Montefalco; the top one is Adanti.

## ABRUZZI

With its ample sunshine, dry climate, hilly terrain, and coastal breezes off the Adriatic Sea, Abruzzi appears tailor-made for vineyards, and indeed, this region in central Italy is one of the most productive in the country. Unfortunately, almost all of the production is simple characterless red and white table wines based on grapes grown at staggeringly high yields. But this is perhaps not truly surprising. As one moves farther south into Italy's poorer and more rural regions, quantity not quality is the central theme of winemaking. The situation might not be so regrettable if it were not for the fact that Abruzzi certainly *could* produce higher-quality wines (all the physical requirements of climate and soil are there), and besides, the region has a wonderfully vivid and hearty local cuisine that begs for something delicious to drink.

That said, one of Abruzzi's wines can be pretty delicious and that's montepulciano d'Abruzzo. Lots of this mouthfilling red is now being exported, and it's among the country's top good-value wines. Unlike, say, a superinexpensive Chianti, which will tend to be thin and hollow, or an inexpensive nebbiolo, which will tend to be thin and tannic, montepulciano d'Abruzzo is solidly built with a soft texture and good, thick fruit flavors in the middle. Rustic it is, but the price is right, so don't be afraid to try whatever you see on the shelf.

Montepulciano d'Abruzzo is made from the grape variety also known as montepulciano. It should not be confused with Vino Nobile de Montepulciano, one of the leading wines of Tuscany and a wine made primarily from sangiovese grapes. The wine montepulciano d'Abruzzo is made throughout Abruzzi, and though montepulciano grapes also grow in all the neighboring regions, it is in Abruzzi that

the grape variety is turned into the most notable and robust wines.

The best-known white wine of Abruzzi is trebbiano d'Abruzzo, a bland dry inexpensive quaffer that is drunk liberally with the region's many fish dishes. Trebbiano d'Abruzzo, despite its name, is not made from trebbiano but rather from a neutral-tasting grape variety called (not onomatopoeically) bombino.

## CAMPANIA, APULIA, BASILICATA, AND CALABRIA

When the ancient Greeks admiringly called Italy *Oenotria*, the land of wine, they were referring specifically to the southern peninsula—the toe, heel, and ankle of the Italian boot. In this rugged, sunny, mountainous land they found scores of fascinating grape varieties. To these they contributed many of their own, establishing an even richer foundation of viticulture. By the time of the ancient Romans, the south was a treasure trove of wines including the wine the Romans esteemed most: *falernian* (also called *falernum*), a white wine produced on the slopes of Monte Massico in Campania.

As in Greece itself, however, this auspicious beginning never evolved into the kind of future it seemed to promise. Today the four regions of the southern peninsula—Campania, Apulia, Basilicata, and Calabria—make comparatively few wines of high quality and only one truly famous wine. Admittedly, these regions are among Italy's poorest and most rural. The combination of poverty and a hot

climate conducive to high yields has meant that quantity rather than quality has been the driving force behind the wines. In virtually every region of the south most of the wines are made by cooperatives, and unlike northern and central Italy, there are very few prestigious individual producers. Moreover, a lot of the wine here is not even bottled but is sold directly from the cask to local customers toting their own jugs.

Still, the southern peninsula can't be completely dismissed. Revolutions in quality have happened elsewhere, and there's at least some reason to believe one may happen here. Already stirrings in that direction have begun, and more and more delicious southern Italian wines—many of them great values—are being exported.

### CAMPANIA

Campania is certainly better known for Naples, the Amalfi Coast, and Capri than it is for wine, even though this is the most exciting of the four southern regions. It was here that the Greeks introduced three of the south's most impressive grape varieties: aglianico, fiano, and greco. All three varieties thrive in the volcanic soils of Avellino northeast of Mount Vesuvius, a still active volcano that erupted violently in A.D. 79, destroying the nearby city of Pompeii. Preserving these three varieties—often called the archeological varieties—has been the mission of the south's most famous and important producer: Mastroberardino. In the late 1990s the Mastroberardino family, working with Italian archeologists, developed a project to replant the slopes of Mount Vesuvius with vineyards devoted to these ancient grape varieties much as such vineyards might have existed in antiquity.

Aglianico, a red variety, is the basis for the south's most famous red wine, Taurasi. It's the sole wine in any of the four regions with DOCG status. Almost blackish in color and with fascinating bitter chocolate, leather, and tar aromas and flavors, Taurasi is also one of the only wines in the south noted for its capacity to age. Mastroberardino's most famous Taurasi is called *Radici*, roots, a reference to the family's having made wine since the early 1700s. The name was first used in 1980 after the Mastroberardino winery was destroyed in the earthquake that occurred that year.

Because summers can be fiercely hot and because most southern Italian wineries lack modern equipment, including temperature-controlled tanks, the south is not known for white wines, which suffer more than reds under such conditions. The two exceptions are Campania's fiano di Avellino and greco di Tufo, made respectively from fiano and greco grapes. Both wines have a bitter almond character and an intriguing ashy aroma. Mastroberardino is again the leading producer of both.

## APULIA

The long fertile strip of land across the Adriatic Sea from Greece, Apulia stretches from the spur of the Italian boot to its heel. Apulia usually vies with Sicily as the most productive region in southern Italy, although like its sister regions, much of this is basic, cheap table wine. Nonetheless there are some very good everyday red wines, the sort that would make perfect bargain-priced house reds.

The leading grape varieties are negroamaro (the name means black bitter), uva di troia, and primitivo. All three can be rustic, juicy, and very tasty. Negroamaro is the primary grape in Apulia's hot, arid, and most famous wine district, the Salento peninsula. Here it is made into the wine Salice Salentino, one of the most popular low-priced wines on Italian restaurant wine lists in the United States, especially the dependably tasty Salice Salentino made by Cosimo Taurino. Uva di troia, thought to have been named after the city of Troy in Asia Minor, was brought to Italy by the Greeks and is the source of the robust red wine Castel del Monte. Primitivo is the same as California's zinfandel, though the grape was brought (probably from Croatia) to California in the early 1800s before it was brought to Italy. In Apulia, primitivo is often used as a blending grape but it's also made into a wine on its own, with some creative producers now even labeling it zinfandel!

RISERVA

SALICE SALENTINO

DENOMINAZIONE DI ORIGINE CONTROLLATA

ROSSO

RED WINE - PRODUCT OF ITALY

Produced and Bottled by: Azienda Agricola
TAURINO Dr. Cosimo
GUAGNANO - ITALIA

Alcohol 13% by Vol.          Net. cont. 750 ML ℮
Selected and Shipped by LEONARDO LO CASCIO & PETER MATT, ROME, ITALY
Imported by: WINEBOW Inc. NEW YORK, N.Y. 10010

## BASILICATA

Nearly landlocked and extremely poor, Basilicata has but one important wine, the red aglianico del Vulture. As it was in Campania, the aglianico grape variety was brought to Basilicata by the Greeks who planted it in the volcanic soil of Mount Vulture. The most highly regarded producer of aglianico del Vulture is Fratelli d'Angelo.

## CALABRIA

The toe of Italy's boot, Calabria was a favorite place among ancient Greek adventurers. The arid, mountainous terrain makes grape growing a challenge; nonetheless good wines are made. The most important of these is Cirò, a medium-bodied grapey, spicy red made from the ancient variety gaglioppo. The two top producers are Librandi and Fattoria di San Francesco. Just east of Calabria's, and the country's, southernmost point is the remote seaside town of Bianco. This is the source of Calabria's other notable wine, greco di Bianco. A dessert wine made from partially dried greco grapes, it has a fascinating herbal, citrus flavor. The two best producers are Umberto Ceratti and Ferdinando Messino.

# SICILY AND SARDINIA

The Mediterranean's two largest and most centrally located islands, Sicily and Sardinia, have been the prized acquisitions of virtually every Mediterranean power in antiquity from the Phoenicians, Byzantines, and Arabs to the Romans and Catalans. Though the two islands epitomize the sunny Mediterranean climate and share a long history of producing sweet, fortified wines, in many other ways each is unique.

## SICILY

In the country that ranks first in the world in wine production, Sicily is often the most productive region (only in some years does the Veneto surpass it). It is also Italy's largest region—10,000 square miles, 1,000 more than in Tuscany, itself a fairly large region. Viticulture first flourished in Sicily under the Greeks, and the island's wines soon became some of the most famous of the ancient world. By the time of the Roman Empire, the sweet Sicilian wine known as *mamertine* was highly admired by the ruling class and is said to have been the favorite wine of Julius Caesar.

In no place is the *Santa Trinità Mediterranea*—Mediterranean Holy Trinity—of wine, olive oil, and bread more evident than in Sicily. The island's hilly terrain, poor soil, and unfaltering sunlight are tailor-made for the production of all three Italian necessities. Moreover, Sicily's

405

*Eating, drinking, and (playfully) arguing:*
*Sicilian national sports.*

strategically located port cities have made the trading of all three relatively easy both today and in the past.

For much of the twentieth century Sicily suffered from the same southern mentality that handicapped Apulia, Campania, Basilicata, and Calabria—namely that quantity mattered more than quality. As in those regions, the yields in Sicilian vineyards were pushed to the limit and winemaking was haphazard at best; Sicilian wine grew predictably worse. Ironically, the island so famous for its wines in antiquity became, in the twentieth century, infamous for ultracheap *vino da tavola*. In the 1970s and 1980s the decline of the reputation of Sicilian wines caused the top producers to launch a mini revolution oriented toward quality. Today more fascinating wines are coming out of Sicily than ever before, and though the best of these are still not widely known, many of them could one day rank with the best wines produced in the entire country.

Sicily's most famous wine is Marsala, a sweet fortified wine that, despite numerous cheap supermarket examples, can be extremely delicious when made by a first-rate producer. In addition to Marsala, two of Italy's most fabulous dessert wines come from Sicily: moscato di Pantelleria and malvasia delle Lipari. Maybe best of all, however, are Sicily's juicy, robust, concentrated reds, many of which are based on the grape variety nero d'Avola, also known as calabrese.

Marsala, which takes its name from the ancient port city, is made principally from grillo and catarratto bianco grapes grown on the plains and low hills of Sicily's prolific Trapani province in the far western part of the island. Though well regarded wines have been made in this region from classical times, Marsala as we know it today was invented in the 1770s by an Englishman, John Woodhouse, who predicted that the sweet and fortified wine would be an immediate hit in cold, rainy Britain where the market for such warming wines as Port, cream Sherry, and Madeira had already proven gargantuan. Woodhouse was right; almost immediately several large Marsala firms sprang up and the fortunes of the city escalated. Over most of the subsequent two centuries, however, the quality of Marsala dropped to the point where it was relegated more to cooking than to collecting. In the 1980s Marsala production experienced a small but significant turnaround and today, high-quality Marsalas are again being made, though in minuscule amounts.

Marsala comes in three colors—*oro* (golden), *ambra* (amber), and *rubino* (ruby). *Rubino* is extremely rare. Each type can be made at three levels of sweetness: fairly dry, noticeably sweet, or very sweet, and each is fortified to 17 or 18 percent alcohol. Within each category, there is a hierarchy based on how long the wine is aged. *Fine* Marsala is aged one year; *superiore* is aged two years; *superiore riserva* is aged four years; *vergine* is aged five years; and the oldest, *vergine stravecchio*, is aged ten years.

The multiple and intricate ways in which Marsalas are made could easily take up a book in itself, since different production techniques are used depending on the type of Marsala being made. That said, many of the best versions are made by a method similar to the solera process of fractional blending used for Sherry (see page 441). In that process, older wines are blended with younger wines, using a complex system of a hierarchy of barrels. The least aged (and least expensive) Marsalas are those that sell the best, but the most stunning Marsalas are the *vergines* and *vergine stravecchios*, which in finesse and richness equal the best tawny Ports and oloroso Sherries.

The largest producer of Marsala is Florio & Co., owned by the drinks giant Cinzano. But the single producer widely recognized as making a Marsala in a league of its own is Marco de Bartoli, whose Marsala is called Vecchio Samperi.

Sicily's two renowned dessert wines are so wickedly hedonistic they make everyone who has ever tasted them sit up and take notice. Moscato di Pantelleria is made on the volcanic island of Pantelleria between Sicily and Tunisia. The wine is made from the grape variety zibibbo (also known as muscat of Alexandria), said to have been brought to the island by Phoenicians who dedicated the wines made from it to Tanit, the Phoenician goddess of love. In the sun-drenched vineyards of Pantelleria, zibibbo grapes have no trouble growing fat with sugar, but to make the wine even more luxurious, the sugar is further concentrated when the ripe grapes are spread out on mats in the sun to dry before they are fermented.

*Sicily's most famous wine, Marsala, has seen its fortunes decline, but when it is made by top producers, the sweet, fortified wine can be delicious.*

The best producer of moscato di Pantelleria is Marco de Bartoli, who makes the wine called Bukkuram.

Halfway around Sicily from Marsala, off the northeastern coast, is the tiny volcanic island of Lipari. This is where malvasia delle Lipari, Sicily's other stunning dessert wine, is made from malvasia grapes. Quantities of Lipari are minuscule. There is only one small producer of note—Carlo Hauner. Nonetheless, Hauner's hauntingly orange-amber malvasia delle Lipari, with its gorgeous apricot and citrus flavors, is an experience no wine lover should miss.

Sicily also makes some surprising reds. Many of these come from the grape variety nero d'Avola (also called calabrese), a variety that can produce intensely black colored wines of real depth, juiciness, and charm. The best examples are the wine called Duca Enrico, from the leading producer Duca di Salaparuta, a company owned by the Sicilian regional government, and the wine Rosso del Conte, from the other leading producer, the family-owned Regaleali. Duca di Salaparuta also makes the well-known, well-priced brand Corvo.

## SARDINIA

Compared to the friendly welcoming aura of Sicily's vineyards, vegetable markets, hill towns, and fishing villages, Sardinia (Sardegna in Italian) seems remote, even austere. At 125 miles from the mainland, the island is far more isolated and its people more insular. Sardo, the local language, is a curious mix of Italian, Spanish, Basque, and Arabic. And despite the island's extensive coastline, the local inhabitants are far more likely to be descended from a long line of shepherds than from fishermen. Grazing animals, not making wine, is still the dominant activity on this rugged, sparse, mountainous island.

Like Sicily, Sardinia was ruled by a succession of Mediterranean peoples, although the Spanish had more influence here than they did in Sicily. As a result, several of the grape varieties grown in Sardinia today are Spanish in origin, including cannonau (related to Spain's garnacha), carignano (cariñena or carignan), and the ancient variety girò. Planted all over the island, cannonau is Sardinia's most important red grape. Though sometimes made as a sweet wine (as it was in centuries past), modern cannonau is a basic dry red that is solid and serviceable but not particularly exciting. Girò, planted mostly near Sardinia's major city Cagliari, makes an interesting Port-like wine though not a lot is produced. And carignano, grown in what was once known as Sulcis in the far south of the island, makes a decent grapey red.

As for white wines, two are worth noting. Vernaccia di Oristano is a fascinating bone-dry, bitter white made in a way that allows the wine to partially oxidize so that it tastes rather like a simple Sherry. Confusingly, Sardinia's vernaccia is not the same grape as the vernaccia in Tuscany's vernaccia di San Gimignano. The other white is vermentino di Gallura, a strong dry wine made in the far northern part of the island near the neighboring island of Corsica, where vermentino is also the leading white grape variety.

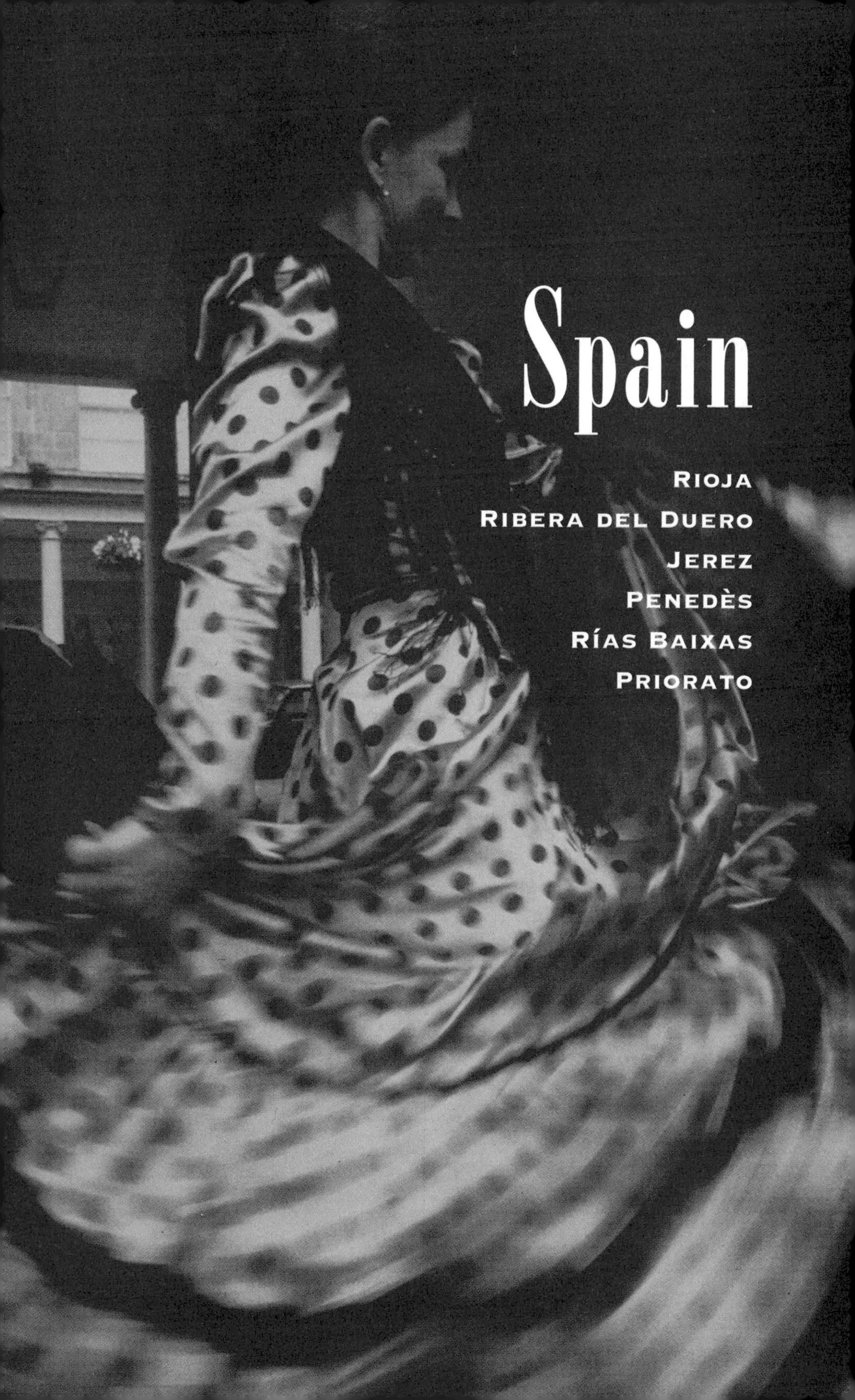

# Spain

RIOJA
RIBERA DEL DUERO
JEREZ
PENEDÈS
RÍAS BAIXAS
PRIORATO

*"In Spain, no matter if you make screwdrivers,
at some point after you have saved a little money,
the first thing you want to do is own a bodega.
It is very important to the Spanish soul."*

—Yolanda Garcia, winemaker, Bodegas Valduero

Spaniards talking about making wine use the verb *elaborar*, to elaborate, not *fabricar*, to produce or manufacture. To elaborate something, Spain's winemakers say, implies consciousness, time, and the labor of creation and nurturance. It is different from mere production. More than at any other time in recent history, Spanish wines truly are being elaborated. After decades of passivity during which many of Spain's wines seemed mired in mediocrity, the top Spanish winemakers have catapulted themselves to a new level of quality. A new golden age has begun.

Spain is a country in love with its bittersweet past; the land itself seems to quicken with the collective spirit of Cervantes, Ferdinand and Isabella, Goya, Franco, Picasso, El Cid, Dalí, and Saint Teresa. And so, to understand Spain you must consider history and tradition.

For many Spanish vintners now making wine with shiny high-tech equipment, it seems as though it was just yesterday when they were stripping off their clothes, hopping into the vats and crushing the grapes by foot. For all of the modernization that the country has experienced, Spanish winemakers continue to respect the wisdom of old ways—and the flavors that result from them.

One of the greatest flavors of tradition in Spanish wines is the flavor

*Though the Bay of Biscay and the Atlantic Ocean are just sixty miles north, Rioja and its vineyards are sheltered from cold maritime winds by the Cantabrian Mountains.*

ATLANTIC
OCEAN

*Bay of Biscay*

Spain ranks third in wine-
producing countries worldwide. The Spanish drink an
average of 10.06 gallons
of wine per person each
year; they're ninth in world
wine consumption.

FRANCE

*Cape of
Ortegal*

La Coruña

Santiago de
Compostela

*Cape of
Fisterre*

GALICIA

Vigo    *Miño River*

**RIAS BAIXAS**

Gijón

Oviedo

Santander

ASTURIAS

CANTABRIA

León

*Esla River*

Burgos

CANTABRIAN MOUNTAINS

Bilbao

BASQUE
COUNTRY

Vitoria

Haro

NAVARRE

Pamplona

ANDORRA

PYRENEES

CASTILE and LEON

**1**

**2** Logroño

*Ebro River*

**3**

**RIOJA**

CATALONIA

Barcelona

Palencia

Valladolid

*Duero R.*

Aranda
de Duero

Soria

**RIBERA DEL DUERO**

Medina
del Campo

Salamanca

*Tormes R.*

Zaragoza

ARAGON

SISTEMA IBERICO

**PENEDES**

**PRIORATO**

Tarragona

*Cape of
Tortosa*

*Balearic
Sea*

MADRID

⊙ Madrid

M E S E T A

*Tagus River*

LA MANCHA

ESTREMADURA

*Guadiana River*

Badajoz

SIERRA MORENA

Córdoba

*Guadalquivir River*

ANDALUSIA

Huelva

Seville

*Júcar River*

VALENCIA

Valencia

*Gulf of
Valencia*

BALEARIC ISLANDS

*Majorca*

*Ibiza*

*Formentera*

Castellón de la Plana

*Cape
of la
Nao*

Alicante

*Segura River*

MURCIA

Murcia

Cartagena    *Cabo de Palos*

Granada

B E T I C O S

*Bay of Cádiz*

Sanlúcar de Barrameda

Puerto de Santa María

Cádiz

**JEREZ**

Jerez de la
Frontera

S I S T E M A S

Málaga

*Costa    del    Sol*

*Strait of Gibraltar*

*Alboran
Sea*

Almeria

*Cabo
de Gata*

M E D I T E R R A N E A N   S E A

ALGERIA

MOROCCO

N

0        50        100 mi
0    50    100 km

© MapQuest.com

**KEY TO SPAIN'S
WINE REGIONS**

**RIOJA**
1 Rioja Alavesa
2 Rioja Alta
3 Rioja Baja

**RIAS BAIXAS**

**RIBERA DEL DUERO**

**PENEDÈS** (source of *cava*)

**PRIORATO**

**JEREZ** (source of Sherry)

PORTUGAL

imparted by long aging in barrels. In the past, Spanish reds and whites were aged in barrels longer than any other wines in the world. That could mean twenty-five years—a remarkable period of time. Spanish wines are no longer kept in barrels for over two decades (though many continue to be aged longer than their counterparts elsewhere in the world). Modern tastes have changed, and even in Spain where tastes change slowly, there is a new appreciation for younger, fresher wines with more pronounced fruit flavors.

*When they think a wine is extraordinary, Spaniards say "Beber este vino es como hablar con Dios"—tasting this wine is like talking with God.*

The singular image of Spain as a blisteringly hot country has given rise to the assumption that all of its wines are big and coarse, possessing all the finesse of an orangutan. This is patently not true in the top wine regions where the best wines can be breathtaking in their complexity and refinement.

According to European Economic Community statistics, Spain has more land planted with grapes than any other nation in the world—some 2.9 million acres. It does not, however, produce the most wine. Spain ranks third in production, after Italy and France, due to the large number of old, low-yielding vines planted on extremely dry, infertile land.

There are more than six hundred varieties of native Spanish grapes, twenty of which account for 80 percent of production. Surprisingly, in a country associated with red wine, the most widely planted grape by far is the white airén. Grown on the torrid, central plains of Don Quixote's La Mancha, airén makes a neutral-tasting carafe wine mostly drunk in bars. Spain's top grape varieties, by comparison, have personality in spades. Such grapes as albariño and parellada (the white grapes of Rías Baixas and the Penedès respectively) are revered for their regional character. But the country's best-loved and most-prized grape is decidedly tempranillo—the red grape that is the source of the legendary wines of Rioja and Ribera del Duero plus numerous other wines made throughout the country. Tempranillo is to Spain what cabernet sauvignon is to Bordeaux or sangiovese is to Italy.

The five most important wine regions are Rioja, Ribera del Duero, Jerez (the region that produces Sherry), the Penedès, and Rías Baixas. Following these in importance is Spain's most exciting up-

*Aging wines in oak barrels for long periods is a Spanish tradition. As a result, the cellars of even modest-size bodegas are often crammed with thousands of barrels.*

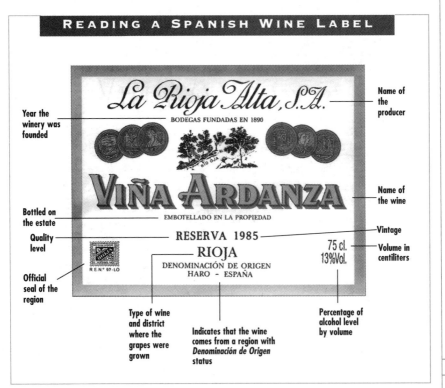

**READING A SPANISH WINE LABEL**

*La Rioja Alta, S.A.* — Name of the producer

BODEGAS FUNDADAS EN 1890

Year the winery was founded

VIÑA ARDANZA — Name of the wine

EMBOTELLADO EN LA PROPIEDAD — Bottled on the estate

RESERVA 1985 — Vintage

Quality level

RIOJA — 75 cl. — Volume in centiliters

DENOMINACIÓN DE ORIGEN — 13%Vol.

HARO - ESPAÑA

Official seal of the region — R.E.N.° 97-LO

Type of wine and district where the grapes were grown

Indicates that the wine comes from a region with *Denominación de Origen* status

Percentage of alcohol level by volume

and-coming region, the Priorato. Wines from bodegas (wineries) located in these six regions are the ones to seek out, although in a country with about a fifth of all the vineyard land in Europe, it is certainly possible to come across engaging wines outside the major regions.

## SPAIN'S WINE LAWS

The Spanish *Denominación de Origen* (DO) laws, first enacted in 1932 and revised in 1970, are similar to France's *Appellation d'Origine Contrôlée* laws, which define and protect wines from specific geographic areas.

There are fifty-four DOs, or officially recognized and geographically defined wine regions, in Spain. In addition, Rioja is the only *Denominación de Origen*

*Calificada* (DOC), or Qualified Denomination of Origin. To qualify for DO or DOC status a wine region must meet rigid requirements. These are set forth by the National Institute of Denominations of Origin. However, each DO and DOC also has its own *Consejo Regulador*, a governing control board that enforces specific viticultural and winemaking standards and regulates the total acreage that may be planted, the types of grapes planted, the maximum yield, the minimum length of time wines must be aged, plus the information that may be given on the label.

In addition, each *Consejo Regulador* maintains a laboratory and tasting panel. Every wine awarded DO or DOC status must be tasted, evaluated, and found to be true to type.

# Rioja

For more than a century, Rioja has been considered Spain's preeminent wine region. The vineyards, running for 75 miles along both banks of the Ebro River, cover more than 123,000 acres in the remote interior of northern Spain. Behind them, craggy mountains stand in desolation. While white and rosé wines are made here, the region's fabled reputation is built almost exclusively on reds, all of which are based primarily on tempranillo grapes. Rioja is often referred to as Spain's Bordeaux, despite the fact that its supple, earthy, often refined red wines more closely resemble Burgundies. The region's ties to France are multiple, beginning in the Middle Ages with the *camino*

414

## THE NAME RIOJA

The region of Rioja, so called since the eleventh century, probably derived its name from the tiny Rio Oja, one of the seven tributaries of the Ebro River, which flows through the region. Other theories, however, suggest that the name comes from theRuccones, a pre-Roman tribe that inhabited the region; or *roja,* red in Spanish and a possible reference to the rose-colored soil; or the Basque words *ería ogia,* meaning land of bread, since the region is also known for cereal crops.

*It may be small as towns go, but Haro, the unofficial wine capital of Rioja, is full of congenial bars where Rioja flows like water.*

*Frances*, the French road, a route through Rioja named for French pilgrims who, with millions of other devout Europeans, walked across northern Spain to the shrine of the apostle James in Santiago de Compostela, in the far western province of Galicia.

The signature of Rioja wines—long aging in oak barrels—was also inspired by French practice. In 1780 a Rioja winemaker named Manuel Quintano adopted the Bordelaise method of aging wine and began successfully maturing his wine in wood. Unlike the French, however, Quintano used large barrels. By the 1850s the Marqués de Murrieta and the Marqués de Riscal (founders of two bodegas that are still considered among the region's best producers) were both using oak—this time, small barrels—to age their wines.

The 1850s and 1860s were difficult times for French vintners, and the winemakers of both Rioja and the Penedès profited from the distress of their French counterparts. First oidium, a parasitic fungus, attacked French vineyards. In its wake came the fatal plant louse phylloxera. To satisfy the demand for wine, French merchant/*négociants*, called *comisionados* in Spanish, traveled to Rioja. Wine sales there boomed. Within a single generation the vineyard area in Rioja grew by 40,000 acres.

Some of the French who came to buy wine stayed and began bodegas of their own. By buying grapes (rather than wine) from small local vineyard owners, then vinifying the grapes and aging the wine in traditional small Bordeaux oak barrels, the newcomers were able to create wines that tasted as close as possible to the French wines they were used to.

In 1880, with the first railroad link between the rural Rioja village of Haro and the village of Bilbao on the northern coast,

Rioja wines became far easier to ship into France. Two years later, Haro got its first telephone; eight years later, its first electric light. Haro became the nerve center of the wine community (which it remains), and Rioja wine became essential to the French market. Commerce flourished.

The party ended as the twentieth century dawned. Phylloxera crept into Rioja in 1901 and destroyed 70 percent of the vineyards. Meanwhile, the antidote—grafting native European vines onto tolerant American rootstock—had been discovered. French vintners quickly went about reestablishing their vineyards. Many of the French in Rioja returned home, and the booming market for Rioja wine collapsed.

Rioja vintners also began to graft their vines onto American rootstock. But left without a major market the industry stagnated. A number of growers, financially destitute, simply sold their vineyards and left. World War I, and later the Spanish Civil War and World War II, further impeded progress. Widespread hunger in Spain caused the government to decree that vines be torn out and vineyard land

415

## THE OLD MAN AND THE WINE

━━━━◦◦◦◦━━━━

No American expatriot has loved Spain more than Ernest Hemingway. Though a legendary hard spirits drinker, Hemingway visited the famous old Rioja bodega Paternina every year for twenty-five years, generally with a bullfighter in tow. During his last visit in 1959, the novelist was accompanied by the bullfighter Antonio Ordoñez, who became the inspiration for *Death in the Afternoon.*

replanted with wheat. It was not until the 1960s that Rioja began to regain its footing. The year 1970, heralded as a major vintage of the century, was a turning point for its wine industry. With the return of Spain's financial stability, investors turned their sights on the extraordinary wines coming out of Rioja. In half a decade the region had more than a dozen new, well-capitalized bodegas. Many of the old bodegas modernized and expanded. By this time, the technique of aging wine for long periods of time in small oak barrels had been used for more than a century. The technique was not only ubiquitous, it had become the region's trademark.

Though the barrels used were always oak, each bodega was free to choose whatever type of oak it preferred. During the first financially difficult decades of the nineteenth century, many bodegas found that rather than import French oak barrels, it was more economical to buy American oak wood and make the barrels themselves in the traditional (French) manner. That meant hand splitting the wood into staves, allowing the staves to air

dry, then bending the wood over an open flame (for more on barrel making, see page 42). Today, the majority of barrels used in Rioja are still crafted by Spanish coopers using American oak. But that is beginning to change. While many bodegas consider the pronounced vanilla flavor of American oak to be the perfect complement to the intrinsic flavor of Rioja wines, other bodegas are turning to French oak or even aging their wines for a period of time in each type of barrel.

As a group, Riojas are aged longer before release than any other wines in the world. For red wines four to ten years is common. As long as this is by modern standards (the best French wines, for example, are aged two to three years before release), it is far shorter than in the past when the top Rioja reds were often aged at the bodega for fifteen to twenty years or more before they were sold to consumers. In an example that is almost unbelievable today but was quite common in Rioja not so many years ago, the renowned estate of Marqués de Murrieta released their 1942 *gran reserva* in 1983—forty-one years after it was made! Ideas about the benefits of long aging are changing in Rioja, however. Some bodegas have veered away from tradition and are now aging their wines for shorter periods. Thus for wine drinkers today two Riojas exist: an old world of well-aged, mellowed earthy wines laced with notes of vanilla and a new world of fresher, berry-fruit wines made more in what might be called an extroverted California-like style.

Finally, Rioja is the only wine region in Spain that carries the designation *Denominación de Origen Calificada*, a status awarded it in 1988. To be granted DOC status, a wine region must meet the highest standards in its winemaking and viticultural practices. The most significant of the rules that apply to Rioja is the one that stipulates that the price of the grapes used to make Rioja wines must exceed 200 percent of the average national price for wine grapes.

## THE LAND, THE GRAPES, AND THE VINEYARDS

Although it is only 60 miles south of the Bay of Biscay and the coastal cities of San Sebastián and Bilbao, Rioja does not have a maritime climate. Several small mountain ranges and the outlying ridges of the Cantabrian Mountains isolate the region from the moderating effects of the ocean, and they also help act as a shield, shutting out the harshest northern winds.

Though Spanish vineyards are often imagined to be at about sea level, Rioja rests on a vast plateau at an elevation of more than 1,500 feet. The region is divided into three subregions: the Rioja Alta, the Rioja Alavesa, and the Rioja Baja. The finest grapes come from the Rioja Alta and Rioja Alavesa, which, being higher and farther north and west toward the Atlantic, experience a cooler climate. The land then slopes downward to the warmer, lower, drier Rioja Baja in the southeast. Grapes here make wines that are higher in alcohol, lower in acidity, and generally have a coarser character than grapes from the Rioja Alta and Rioja Alavesa. The best Rioja wines rarely contain any significant percentage of Baja grapes.

Three types of soil dominate: clay mixed with limestone and sandstone, iron-rich clay, and loamy soil with alluvial silt from the Ebro. The best vineyards are planted in clay/limestone/sandstone soils found mostly in the Rioja Alavesa and Rioja Alta. Many of these vineyards are forty years old or more. Though not very productive, old vines are treasured because their grapes usually have more concentrated flavors.

Like Bordeaux, after which they were modeled, Rioja wines have traditionally been a blend of grapes. For reds the finest grape, and the one that accounted for a lion's share of the blend, was tempranillo. Three other grapes could be added to it:

*Marqués de Murrieta, one of the oldest and most prestigious bodegas in Rioja, dates from around 1860. Among the bodega's most prized possessions is the estate (above) known as Ygay, acquired in 1872. Today all of the bodega's wines come from approximately 750 acres of vines surrounding the estate.*

## THE GRAPES OF
# RIOJA

### WHITES

**Garnacha Blanca:** Minor blending grape added for body.

**Malvasia:** Minor blending grape added for aroma.

**Viura:** Major grape in all Rioja white wines. Contributes aroma, mild fruit flavors, and good acidity. Same as macabeo in the Penedès.

### REDS

**Garnacha:** Seasoning grape used to contribute alcohol and body. Known in France as grenache.

**Graciano:** Minor grape used in some red Riojas to add grace notes of aroma and flavor to tempranillo.

**Mazuelo:** Robust seasoning grape used in some red Riojas. Known in France as carignan.

**Tempranillo:** Major grape in all red Riojas. Contributes aroma, flavor, delicacy, and aging potential.

the native Spanish varieties garnacha (which the French call grenache) and mazuelo (which the French call carignan), plus graciano. Today, while many Riojas continue to be blends, a growing number are made up entirely of tempranillo.

In flavor, tempranillo grown in Rioja is often compared to France's pinot noir and Italy's sangiovese. Like these grapes, tempranillo has not, at least thus far, been made into wines that are massive or powerful but, rather, wines that are elegant, earthy, and can seem almost fragile when aged. It has even been suggested that tempranillo could have evolved as a locally

adapted variant of pinot noir vines brought to northern Spain by Burgundian monks making pilgrimages to the tomb of the apostle James in Santiago de Compostela. Ampelographers have dismissed this theory as more romantic than probable.

The tempranillo-cabernet sauvignon blends are a new but still rare phenomenon in Rioja. In the 1980s such bodegas as Marqués de Riscal and Martinez Bujanda led the way with these special proprietary wines that taste almost nothing like classical Rioja but can be delicious. Martinez Bujanda's Vendimia Seleccionada, for example, can be a powerhouse of vibrant raspberry and eucalyptus flavors. And Marqués de Riscal's Baron de Chirel Reserva with its smoky, cocoa flavors is totally delicious.

Rioja's major white grape is viura (known as macabeo in other regions of Spain), which makes up the largest proportion of the blend in any white wine. Viura has good acidity and an almost viscous texture. A tiny amount was often added to Rioja red wines to increase their acidity. Viura is sometimes blended with malvasia, which adds extra aroma and crispness, and garnacha blanca, blended in for body.

*Compared to many other grape varieties, tempranillo ripens early. In fact, the name tempranillo comes from* temprano, *Spanish for early.*

In the past, most of Rioja's 150 or so bodegas owned no land at all but, instead, bought grapes and/or wine from the region's 14,000 small growers, most of whom owned fewer than 10 acres of land. Today, while the majority of bodegas still buy some grapes and wine from growers, as well as from the region's cooperatives, there is a strong movement toward ownership of vineyards. When a winery owns its vineyards, of course, it has far more control over the quality of the grapes it receives. As of the 1990s about twenty bodegas had bought sufficient land to make wines entirely from their own estates, including Barón de Ley, Contino, Granja Nuestra Señora de Remelluri, Marqués de Murrieta, and Martinez Bujanda.

## THE ORIGINAL WINE COOLER

Spain's first bottled sangria did not originate in the scorchingly hot south, as might be expected, but rather in Rioja. In the 1960s, Bodegas Rioja Santiago developed the technology to stabilize and bottle what, until then, had been a typical homemade Spanish punch of wine and citrus juice. Called Sant'gria (Santiago sangria), the new beverage was shown at a trade fair in New York, where it piqued the interest of the importing company Monsieur Henri Wines, a subsidiary of Pepsi-Cola. Renamed Yago Sant'gria, the wine/citrus combination was such a success that Pepsi ultimately bought the entire Rioja Santiago bodega.

# CRIANZA, RESERVA, AND GRAN RESERVA

Rioja wines are classified according to the quality of the grapes used and how long the wines are aged. The hierarchy includes *crianza* (the youngest; in Spanish the word refers to something that is raised or nursed), *reserva*, and *gran reserva*. When visiting Rioja you might also encounter very basic wines known as *vinos joven* or *sin crianzas*. Younger than crianzas and from grapes of a lower quality, they are usually not exported.

Red *crianzas* have the most vibrant flavors. They are easy-drinking wines full of earth, spice, cherry, and vanilla. *Crianzas*, the bread-and-butter wines of every bodega, are generally made with grapes from good but not exceptional vineyards.

Made from superior grapes from prime sites, *reservas* are more than just simple fruity wines, and though they are far more lush and concentrated than *crianzas*, they are not necessarily powerhouses. In fact, just the opposite can be true. *Reservas* can be subtle, supple wines with quiet but intense echoes of earth, old saddle leather, and dried leaves. *Reservas* are only made in exceptional years.

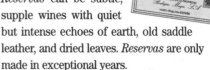

*Gran reservas*, also made only in exceptional years, come from the very best vineyards of all and are extremely rare. In most years, *gran reservas* represent just 1 to 10 percent of the wines produced. In particular, white *gran reservas* are very uncommon and are now made only by a handful of bodegas.

Red *gran reservas* are the most elegant, silky, and refined Riojas of all and the ones given the longest aging in the old-

419

## RED ALERT

Rioja wine bottles are sometimes wrapped in a protective lattice of thin wire called a *red* (net) or *malla* (mesh). The practice dates from the nineteenth century, prior to the establishment of the *Consejo Regulador,* when bodegas sought to prevent unscrupulous people from refilling Rioja bottles with inferior wine, recorking the bottles, and then reselling them as premium Rioja. Today, the *red* is solely decorative.

est, most neutral barrels. In fact, though five years of aging is required by law, in reality *gran reservas* are aged an average of eight and a half years.

The bottle's front label does not always indicate whether the wine is a *crianza, reserva,* or *gran reserva.* However, the back label or neck label will carry a *Consejo* stamp indicating its designation.

# THE EFFECTS OF LONG OAK AGING

Although it is still true that aging red wines for four or more years is common in Rioja, the practice is controversial. Modern critics say that Riojas are aged so long that the wine's fruit vibrancy is lost. Traditionalists believe that wines made from tempranillo—like wines made from pinot noir—only begin to develop their range of earthy, sophisticated flavors after they have been aged.

The issue is important, for oak has an almost magical ability to transform wine, to lift it out of simple berryness and give it depth, length, complexity, and intensity (see What Oak Does, page 40). The length of aging time is key since a wine kept in poor conditions or too long does not become mellow and complex but, instead, becomes dried out and thin—a shadow of its former self.

The type of oak is also critical. The use of American oak has been traditional in Rioja for decades, although French oak

*To visit a Rioja bodega such as R. López de Heredia is to go back in time. Besides cobwebs, the damp, black, moldy underground cellar of this bodega contains more than 15,000 oak barrels and almost nothing else. As is true of many traditional bodegas, all work is done by hand.*

is on the rise. The American oak barrels employed are almost never brand-new. Used oak has a far softer impact on the flavor of the wine than new oak, which can be dramatic and overtly vanilla-y. For traditional, family-owned bodegas such as Marqués de Murrieta and R. López de Heredia, this gentle vanilla earthiness is what makes Rioja Rioja.

Modernists, such as the bodegas Marqués de Cáceres, Martinez Bujanda, and Palacio y Hermanos, see Rioja wines differently. For them, a more vivid, up-front fruit character plus a dollop of oak flavor is what counts. The ranks of the modernists are growing, fueled by younger wine drinkers with contemporary palates who associate great wine with the full-throttle jamminess and oakiness of California, Australian, and certain in-vogue Rhône and Italian wines.

It is unlikely, however, that any of Rioja's winemakers will ever fully abandon the practice of significant wood aging. Maturing a wine is almost a moral imperative for Spaniards. The sheer number of barrels in Rioja is a testimony to this; most bodegas have 10,000 to 40,000.

If the concern that Riojas were sometimes aged so long they lost their spirited edge had validity for reds, the criticism had special poignancy for whites. Though only a small amount of white wine is made in Rioja, the majority of the traditional bodegas do make at least some. And for most of the twentieth century, this was aged in oak for two to five years and then for several more years in the bottle. In excellent vintages, dramatic wines often

## AGING REQUIREMENTS FOR RIOJA

~~~

While the law dictates the minimum length of time a Rioja must be aged, in practice, many are aged far longer.

**Crianzas**
- Reds: Must be aged for at least two years, one of which must be in oak barrels.
- Whites: Must be aged for six months in oak barrels.

**Reservas**
- Reds: Must be aged for at least three years, one of which must be in oak barrels.
- Whites: Must be aged for one year, six months of which must be in oak barrels.

**Gran Reservas**
- Reds: Must be aged for at least five years, two of which must be in oak barrels and the remaining three of which must be in bottles.
- Whites: Must be aged for four years, six months of which must be in oak barrels.

resulted—mature whites with slightly oxidized coffee, honey, caramel, and roasted nut flavors. Admittedly, these aged white Riojas were—and still are—an acquired taste.

And, unfortunately, another sort of wine resulted as well. Unable to support the heavy

*R. López de Heredia's most renowned wine, Viña Tondonia, from the legendary vintage of 1970.*

cloak of oak, some white Riojas ended up tasting like musty liquid with odd rubber boot and petrol aromas. Wines such as these became the nails in the coffin of traditional white Rioja. As the 1980s unfolded, long-aged whites—both well made and not—were increasingly regarded as examples of what a great white wine was *not* supposed to taste like.

Most bodegas today no longer age their whites for long periods in the barrel, and some do not age their whites in barrel at all. But as long as there are enough experienced palates to appreciate them, long-aged white Riojas will continue to be made by many bodegas. Two of the finest aged white Riojas are made by Marqués de Murrieta and R. López de Heredia.

*Some of the Best Producers of Rioja*

**BODEGAS ARTADI**

**BODEGAS BRETON**

**BODEGAS FERNANDO REMIREZ DE GANUZA**

**BODEGAS MARQUÉS DE MURRIETA**

**BODEGAS MONTECILLO**

**COMPAÑÍA DE VINO TELMO RODRIGUEZ**

**CONTINO**

**CUNE**

**FINCA ALLENDE**

**LA GRANJA NUESTRA SEÑORA DE REMELLURI**

**LA RIOJA ALTA**

**MARQUÉS DE CÁCERES**

**MARQUÉS DE RISCAL**

**MARTINEZ BUJANDA**

**MUGA**

**R. LÓPEZ DE HEREDIA**

# THE FOODS OF RIOJA

If you are not vigilant, you can find yourself craving—and eating—roasted baby lamb and, if it's spring, fresh white asparagus every day in Rioja, a testimony to just how addictive these two specialties can be. Lamb and white asparagus, however, are just the beginning.

## WET AND WILD

Though wild mushrooms (*setas*) are more abundant and varied in Catalonia, they somehow seem more decadent in Rioja where a glass of red wine and a huge plate of them sizzling in hot, garlicky extra-virgin olive oil is often the way a meal begins. The combination, straightforward as it is, can be magic. No wines accentuate the rich earthiness of wild mushrooms better than red Riojas, which are among the world's most beautifully earthy wines.

Rioja is a region of basic foodstuffs, straightforward cooking techniques, and hearty dishes. The success of any given dish is based solely on the integrity and freshness of the ingredients. Herbs and spices are rarely used. The simple homeyness of the food is beautifully in tune with the elegant, sweetly ripe flavors and silky textures of Rioja wines.

The fertile Ebro River valley is planted with a panoply of vegetables and fruits; the surrounding hills and mountains are home to goats, lambs, rabbits, quail, and large wild game. Rioja's goat cheeses are renowned. As is true of many

## CASA EMILIO

—◦◦◦—

If you ask where to eat in Logroño, the major city of Rioja, you will be guided to a handful of respectable dining rooms. The one place you will probably not be told about is exactly where you should eat. Asador Casa Emilio is a spare, no-nonsense restaurant off an unremarkable side street. You would walk right by the place, but for the alluring aroma of roasting meats that wafts out the front door.

*Cabrito* (baby goat), the restaurant's specialty, is slowly roasted over acorns and maple wood in an old brick oven until it is as tender and succulent as butter. The must-have starter is *setas*—wild mushrooms, each the size of a compact disk, that have been sautéed in ripe olive oil and a welter of garlic. These are followed by *pimientos rellenos espinacas y gambas,* roasted sweet red peppers stuffed with creamy spinach and shrimp, or garlicky *almejas,* thumb-nail-size baby clams cooked in a light broth strewn with serrano ham.

Because so many bodega owners and winemakers come to Casa Emilio, the wine list is excellent and wine is priced extremely low. This is the place to dine if you want to spring for a *gran reserva* or two.

*Asador Casa Emilio, 18 Perez Galdos, Logroño, Rioja; 011-34-941-25-88-44.*

---

inland regions of Spain, the local *embutido* (charcuterie) is irresistible.

The names of many dishes include the words *a la riojana*—in the Riojan style. Generally, this means that tomatoes and fresh or dried sweet red peppers are part of the preparation. Rioja's classics include:

**Chuletas al sarmiento:** Lamb chops grilled over an open fire of vine shoots.

**Menestra de verduras:** A vegetable casserole that, depending on the season, includes artichokes, asparagus, Swiss chard, peas, carrots, leeks, or green beans tossed together with diced, cured ham and sautéed in olive oil.

**Patatas a la riojana:** Potatoes that are cooked in meat stock with spicy chorizo sausage.

**Pochas a la riojana:** A stew of young white beans, chorizo, peppers, and tomatoes, sometimes with roasted quail added.

**Pimientos rellenos:** Small local red peppers stuffed with minced meat or puréed vegetables, then dipped in batter, fried, and cooked in a wine and tomato sauce. Sometimes shrimp, cod, hake, or pig's feet are added to the stuffing.

423

*Stuffed red peppers, pimientos rellenos, baked in a wood-burning oven are a Rioja specialty.*

# THE RIOJA WINES TO KNOW

## Whites

### MARQUES DE MURRIETA
Castillo Ygay

*reserva*

approximately 95% viura, 5% malvasia

No white wine in Rioja, with the possible exception of R. López de Heredia's Viña Tondonia (at right), is more expressive in every facet than Murrieta's white Ygay. In the best vintages its aroma is so earthy it is positively subterranean. The acidity has the precision of a sushi knife. And the racy flavors of almonds, crème brûlée, roasted nuts, honey, buttered toast, cloves, and cinnamon drape over the acidity like the folds of a velvet curtain.

### R. LOPEZ DE HEREDIA
Viña Tondonia

*crianza*

approximately 90% viura, 10% malvasia

Complex and multifaceted, the white Viña Tondonia is one of the two best traditional-style whites in Rioja (the other is Murrieta's Castillo Ygay, at left), and a wine that brilliantly captures the regional character. Everything about it from the color (like honey) to the finish (extremely long) is mesmerizing. In top years the aroma is all butter, hazelnuts, and earth; the flavor, lemony and fresh. The texture feels as though it's made up of ribbons of cream.

424

## Reds

### CUNE
*reserva*

approximately 80% tempranillo, with mazuelo, garnacha, graciano, and viura

Founded in 1879, CUNE (the abbreviation for Compañía Vinicola del Norte de España, pronounced coon-ay) makes *reservas* that perfectly demonstrate aged Rioja's delicacy. Subtle aromas and flavors of truffles, dried leaves, spices, cassis, rose petals, and old saddle leather seem to peek out from the wine. CUNE's Imperial *gran reservas* are also stunners—as irresistible in flavor as chocolate-covered cherries, as smooth in texture as homemade ice cream.

### LA GRANJA NUESTRA SENORA DE REMELLURI
*reserva*

mostly tempranillo

Known simply as Remelluri, the family-owned estate is one of the most creative bodegas in Rioja. The small company grows all of its own grapes, makes only *reservas*, and is impeccable in every detail of its winemaking, including the fact that the grapes are hand sorted for perfection before they are pressed. The wines are aged mostly in used French oak and the result is delicious New Wave *reservas* that can taste like baskets of oozingly ripe cherries warmed in the sun.

## LA RIOJA ALTA, S.A.

Viña Alberdi

*crianza*

approximately 80% tempranillo, 20% graciano

Even though they are simple *crianzas*, the top Viña Alberdis seem to possess every classic Rioja aroma and flavor—from saddle leather, prunes, and orange peel to spiced tea, vanilla, and earth. These swirl around in the wine with wonderful focus. The long, earthy finish is bracing.

## LA RIOJA ALTA, S.A.

Viña Arana

*reserva*

approximately 75% tempranillo, with graciano, mazuelo, and viura

In great Rioja vintages drinking this wine is so comforting, it's like being wrapped up in a cashmere blanket. The aromas are rich and earthy—suggestive of saddle leather. There are elegant, complex flavors of vanilla, plum, chocolate, and spiced tea, and the texture is lanolin soft. All of the grapes come from the Rioja Alta.

*A traditional stone hut known as a guardavinas at Marques de Riscal.*

## MARQUES DE MURRIETA

Ygay

*reserva*

approximately 75% tempranillo, with mazuelo, garnacha, and graciano

When the vintages are at their best, Murrieta's red Ygay, like a top Bordeaux, has a core of opulent fruit. Opening with mesmerizing aromas—bitter chocolate, menthol, smoke, leather, and cocoa—it segues into flavors that are unearthly in their earthiness. The long, smoky, blackberry finish fades as gradually as a sunset. Murrieta, a prestigious old bodega, is the passion of its owners, the Cebrian family, who have spent a large fortune caring for the impressive estate.

## MUGA

Prado Enea

*gran reserva*

approximately 80% tempranillo, with smaller amounts of garnacha, mazuelo, and graciano

425

Dating from 1932, Muga is a family-owned bodega making some of the top traditional-style wines in Rioja. Like the best red Burgundies, these are Riojas with magnificent and complex aromas and long finishes. In the middle are sublime, if subtle, layers of earthy flavor. Prado Enea is the name of the winery's refined *gran reserva*, generally aged eight years, four of them in barrels that the Muga family makes themselves, using oak they import from the United States. In the 1990s Muga also began making small quantities of what is now a highly sought after wine, Torre Muga. Big, concentrated, and super-oaky (it's aged in both American and French oak), Torre Muga is New World in style and very much the opposite of Prado Enea.

## MARQUES DE RISCAL

*reserva*

mostly tempranillo, with some graciano

Dating from the mid-nineteenth century, Marqués de Riscal is one of the oldest bodegas in Rioja, with 2½ miles of eerily beautiful undergound cellars, most of them draped with cobwebs and grayish white mold. After some uninspiring wines in the late 1980s and early 1990s, this bodega is back making superb traditional-style Riojas that could not be more refined. In great years the wine is amazingly complex with briary currant, mushroom, and sweet chocolate flavors and a stunningly silky texture.

## R. LOPEZ DE HEREDIA

Viña Tondonia

*gran reserva*

approximately 75% tempranillo, with garnacha, mazuelo, and graciano

The red Viña Tondonia *gran reservas* can be mind-altering. In great vintages drinking them is like being in that state before waking up when all sensations seem dreamlike. Both the aromas and flavors are exceedingly complex, with hints of exotic spices, forests, and earth. Viña Tondonia is a quiet, refined wine, not a powerhouse. It's renowned in Spain for its harmony and finesse—a great classic.

# VISITING RIOJA BODEGAS

426

Many Rioja bodegas conduct tours that include a tasting of the bodegas' wines. It's necessary to make an appointment in advance, and a knowledge of Spanish is helpful although not necessary at every bodega.

Visiting a Spanish bodega is often like taking a trip back in time. Some of the most impressive of them are a century or more old and have dark, damp cellars covered with mold and cobwebs and filled with bottles of decades-old Rioja. Marqués de Riscal, López de Heredia, and Federico Paternina are good examples. Another interesting bodega to visit is Martinez Bujanda, which has a small wine museum. The telephone numbers include the dialing code you'll need when calling from the United States. If you're calling from within Spain, eliminate the 011-34 and add a zero before the next number.

**BODEGAS LA RIOJA ALTA**
Avenida Vizcaya, s/n
26200 Haro
011-34-941-31-03-46

**BODEGAS MUGA**
B. de la Estación, s/n
26200 Haro
011-34-941-31-18-25

**FEDERICO PATERNINA**
11 Avenida Santo Domingo
26200 Haro
011-34-941-31-05-50

**MARQUÉS DE RISCAL**
1 Torrea
01340 Elciego, Alava
011-34-941-10-60-00

**MARTINEZ BUJANDA**
Camino Viejo, s/n
01320 Oyón, Alava
011-34-941-12-21-88

**R. LÓPEZ DE HEREDIA**
3 Avenida Vizcaya
26200 Haro
011-34-941-31-02-44

# Ribera del Duero

About 80 miles north of Madrid, Ribera del Duero is in the province of Castile and León, a severe, dramatic land of rough mesas and rocky plateaus that stretch as far as the eye can see. Massive stone castles stand as fortresses atop the highest ridges. The masculine power and glory of medieval Spain is palpable.

On these ocher plains where Cervantes began to write *Don Quixote*, the vineyards, too, have a severity. Old vines, gnarled as if in agony, protrude from the rough ground. If the ground holds vines in place everywhere else in the world, in Ribera del Duero the opposite seems true. The Earth herself clings to the muscular vines.

Ribera del Duero is almost exclusively a red wine region, although simple rosés are made for local consumption. The best reds are deeply concentrated, fleshy, ripe, and structured, without being

> ## THE QUICK SIP ON RIBERA DEL DUERO
>
> • Ribera del Duero is the poster image of Don Quixote's Spain, a land of rugged ocher mesas. All of its top wines are red. No whites of importance are produced.
>
> • The most legendary and expensive red wine in Spain, Vega-Sicilia's Unico, is made here.
>
> • At their best, Ribera del Duero wines are deeply concentrated, richly textured, and among the longest lived of all Spanish red wines.

aggressive, tannic, or alcoholic. The ability of Ribera del Duero wines to be both packed with fruit yet refined places them among the greatest wines of Spain. In fact, two Ribera del Duero wines—Unico and

427

*From medieval times, the province of Segovia in southern Ribera del Duero was home to numerous Castilian kings who built impressive alcazárs—castles—such as this one built in the thirteenth century.*

north central Spain, ultimately plunging downward into Portugal where it becomes the Douro (linked famously to Port) and finally empties into the Atlantic. The river forms a wide valley with flat-topped mountains on either side. Vineyards, interspersed among fields of sugar beets, are scattered along a 60-mile strip on the north and south sides of the valley. Still, the actual acreage planted with vines is fairly modest. Ribera de Duero has about 30,000 acres of vineyards; Rioja, 123,000 acres. The entire *Denominación de Origen* spans four districts within Castile and León: Burgos, with the vast majority of vineyard land; Soria; Segovia; and Valladolid, where many of the top estates are located.

During much of the Middle Ages, Castile was the battleground on which the Catholic kings fought the Moors, the Islamic conquerors who invaded Spain in 711. The stark, ponderous fortresses and castles along the Duero date from this time. Although grapes were grown throughout the upheavals, it was not until Spain was completely reconquered by the Catholic

*For centuries Ribera del Duero formed the border between Spain's Catholic kings and the Moors. Today massive fortified castles still dot the region.*

Pesquera—are among the most outstanding red wines anywhere in the world.

There are about one hundred wine estates in Ribera del Duero, plus several cooperatives. The major grape is tinto fino, also known as tinta del país, a genetic variation of tempranillo. After centuries of adaptation to Ribera del Duero's harsh, dramatic climate, the clone tinto fino makes thicker textured and bolder, more rustic flavored wines than does tempranillo grown in Rioja.

That said, one thing Ribera del Duero and Rioja have in common is the practice of aging for fairly long periods in oak. As in Rioja, most of the barrels are used, not brand-new, so that the flavors they impart are more subtle. In addition, and again like Rioja, the majority of the barrels have been made from American, not French, oak.

Ribera del Duero is named for the river Duero, which crosses the high plateaus of

*Aging wine for a considerable period of time in used oak barrels is a signature of Ribera del Duero, just as it is of Rioja.*

monarchs in the fifteenth century that Ribera del Duero, free of political conflict, could come into its own as a wine region. The city of Valladolid became the capital of Spain; Ferdinand and Isabella were married there in the late fifteenth century.

From the beginning of the twentieth century until the 1980s, Ribera del Duero was a wine region known primarily for cheap, gruff reds churned out by cooperatives that had been built after the 1950s with government subsidies. Mediocrity reigned. Most wines, even as late as 1970, were made in unclean barrels and left unattended to ferment at will. The wines were seldom racked off their lees, never filtered, and rarely bottled commercially. Customers simply arrived at the bodega with reusable containers and bought what they needed directly from the barrel.

An enormous turnaround came in the 1980s. The success of two exceptional wineries, Vega-Sicilia and Pesquera, inspired an influx of capital and technical skill plus a new passion for quality. By the mid-1990s the wines coming out of the region were so shockingly good that some Spanish wine lovers suggested Ribera del Duero—rather than Rioja—might just be the finest wine region in Spain.

# THE LAND, THE GRAPES, AND THE VINEYARDS

Despite its gentle-sounding name, Ribera del Duero is a region of harsh intensity; bodega owners call it the land of extremes. Summers are blistering, with temperatures often exceeding 100°F. Winters are fiercely cold, frequently below zero. On any given day during the grapes' ripening cycle, the temperature may fluctuate from scorchingly hot in the afternoon

## THE GRAPES OF
# RIBERA DEL DUERO

Ribera del Duero is planted almost exclusively with red grape varieties. The lone white variety, albillo, is planted in tiny amounts and is not commercially significant.

**Cabernet Sauvignon:** Only a tiny amount of cabernet sauvignon is planted mainly by the bodega Vega-Sicilia. The bodega also has minuscule plantings of merlot and malbec.

**Garnacha:** Minor grape made into locally consumed, inexpensive rosés.

**Tinto Fino:** Major grape used almost exclusively in virtually all red wines. Thought to be a genetic variation of tempranillo, the main grape of Rioja.

429

to quite cool at night. Certain grape varieties manage to thrive on such stress, and Ribera del Duero's tinto fino is one.

Except for the bodegas built since the late 1980s, Ribera del Duero seems unchanged by passing centuries. For much of the year this is a brown, almost desolate place. Above ground, dirt fields stretch endlessly, hiding crops of sugar beets below. Villages appear subdued and turned inward away from travelers. In some parts of the region, the only signs of life come from the flocks of sheep that roam the countryside.

Then there are the vines, which seem imbued with a life force all their own. Planted on low hills about 2,500 feet above sea level, the vines look like small stunted arms protruding no more than a foot or two out of the earth. Most are still planted in the traditional manner, without posts, wires, or trellising of any sort. Many vines are thirty to fifty years old or more and thus produce grapes with concentrated flavor. The best soil is laced with sand, limestone, and gravel, and much is heavily strewn with ancient riverbed stones.

As for the Duero River itself, though it is neither wide nor deep nor particularly grand (at least as it flows through Ribera del Duero), it does help temper the region's dry, harsh climate. The river adds moisture to the air, and in summer, the riverbanks buffer the hot dry winds that sweep through the valley. In fall and spring the river's stabilizing warmth helps protect against frost.

In Ribera del Duero, tinto fino accounts for more than 85 percent of all plantings. All the top wines are made almost entirely from it but it is not necessarily the sole grape. Some wines also include a fraction of white albillo grapes. Blending a tiny amount of white grapes into red has been traditional in Europe for centuries and is still done to a small extent in Rioja, Chianti, and the Rhône, among other places.

Tinto fino can make absolutely delicious wines full of licorice, leather, mocha, plum, and dark berry aromas and flavors. At their best, they are full, robust, and mouthfilling, with loads of amazingly soft, supple tannin.

## THE BODEGAS THAT SPARKED A REVOLUTION

Made in a remote and rocky part of the Duero, Vega-Sicilia is Spain's most legendary and expensive wine. Even Spanish schoolchildren know its name. While most other bodegas in Ribera

## VEGA-SICILIA

The name Vega-Sicilia originated several centuries ago, although its precise etiology remains a mystery. *Vega* is the word for the green part of a riverbank. *Sicilia* evolved from St. Cecilia and is not, as is commonly thought, a reference to the Italian island of Sicily. It is not known precisely why the two words became the name of the wine.

del Duero were making innocuous wine throughout the 1950s, 1960s, and 1970s, Vega-Sicilia had embarked on making one of the finest wines in the world. This early commitment to quality in a region that was untested at the time—at least for fine wine—established Vega-Sicilia as an extremely serious estate. The fact that the wines were stunning only cemented the winery's reputation further.

The estate was first planted in 1864 by Don Eloy Lecanda, a winemaker who had studied in Bordeaux and returned to Castile bringing cabernet sauvignon, merlot, and malbec vines with him. These grapes were combined with tinto fino to become the first Vega-Sicilia wines; a blend that has continued to the present. Today, about 25 percent of Vega-Sicilia's 250 acres of vineyards are planted with cabernet. Most of the estate, however, is planted with the region's traditional grape variety, tinto fino. For both cabernet sauvignon and tinto fino, vines—some more than a century old—predominate. Carefully nurtured, these old vines yield just a little more than one ton of grapes per acre.

Vega-Sicilia makes three wines: Valbuena 5, so named because it is sold after five years of aging, the very prestigious Unico (Spanish for unique), and the utterly rare Reserva Especial. According to its winemaker, Unico is aged in barrel and bottle "as long as it takes." That is, until the winemaker *feels* it is perfectly ready to drink, which as it happens, is rarely in less than ten years and not according to any regular marketing schedule. Amazingly, the bodega released both its 1982 and 1968 Unicos at the same time—in 1991. That's after nine and twenty-three years of aging, respectively. This practice makes Unico one of the world's longest-aged reds before release. Moreover, in poorer vintages, two to three times a decade, no Unico is made at all; the grapes are usually sold off instead.

Made exclusively for private customers, Reserva Especial is a blend of three to five vintages, each of which has been aged

separately for up to thirty years! Fewer than 500 cases are produced for the world annually. Finally, Vega-Sicilia also owns Alion, another bodega nearby. The red wine from Alion couldn't be more different from Unico. Modern in style, it is aged for a far shorter period of time and almost entirely in new oak.

Vega-Sicilia wines would be exceptional in most contexts, but against the backdrop of what was happening (or not happening) in Ribera del Duero for decades, they were otherworldly.

Then in the 1970s, a second bodega, Pesquera, also began to build a reputation for remarkable wines. Pesquera is owned by Alejandro Fernández, an energetic maverick who is convinced that Ribera del Duero is potentially one of the world's best wine regions. After a full career making agricultural equipment, Fernández built

431

*The broad, brown, vine-covered plateau of Ribera del Duero with mesas rising in the background. In 1972, using the money he earned inventing agricultural machinery, Alejandro Fernández (inset) founded a modest bodega outside the sleepy hamlet of Pesquera de Duero. By the late 1980s, his dense, sensual Pesquera had become one of the most sought after of all Spanish wines.*

Pesquera, planted vineyards, and started making what he called "masculine" wines. Tiny lot by tiny lot, he pressed the grapes in an old wooden press (used until 1982). The wines were put into barrels immediately after pressing and left to age. They were never filtered. Filtering a wine, Fernández said, was like "pushing a fat man through a keyhole." The body invariably got damaged.

Like Vega-Sicilia, Pesquera turned out to be a profoundly rich and complex wine. After both bodegas began to receive world attention in the 1980s, new capital flooded into Ribera del Duero. Serious bodega owners hired ambitious, quality-driven winemakers with enology degrees. A new era for Ribera del Duero was born.

## CRIANZA, RESERVA, AND GRAN RESERVA

As is true in Rioja, Ribera del Duero wines are classified according to the quality of the grapes and how long the wines are aged. Wines fall into the categories *crianza*, the youngest; *reserva;* and *gran reserva*. While you may find the simple, grapey wines known as *tintos joven*

**GROWING UP WITH WINE**

For centuries in Spain, as in all Mediterranean countries, wine has been considered a food and, as such, it is a facet of everyday life. Children are taught early on to appreciate wine in moderate amounts for its flavor, never for its alcohol content. Many Spaniards remember being given a childhood snack of bread dipped in wine and sprinkled with sugar. Today, the inescapable presence of packaged snacks and fast food means that fewer Spanish children munch on wine-and-sugar-sprinkled bread after school. Still, wine remains deeply rooted in Spanish culture, and children are often allowed small amounts of it with meals.

(young reds) in Ribera del Duero itself, these are never exported.

Ribera del Duero *crianzas* are good, easy-drinking wines with cherry pie, spice, earth, and vanilla flavors and aromas. These wines generally come from good but not exceptional vineyards, and must be aged a minimum of two years.

Made from superior grapes grown at better sites, *reservas* have fuller, fleshier textures and greater overall depth, concentration, and intensity. *Reservas* must be aged a minimum of three years. Coming from the very best vineyards, *gran reservas* and are the most polished and refined wines of all. Matured at least five years before release, their extended aging gives them a special harmony and subtlety that only aged wines possess. *Reservas* and *gran reservas* are usually made only in above-average years. They represent just a small percent of all the wine made in the region.

In Ribera del Duero, the bottle's front label usually does not indicate whether the wine is a *crianza, reserva,* or *gran reserva.* A *Consejo*'s stamp on the back or neck label of the wine will indicate its designation.

---

*Some of the Best Producers of Ribera del Duero*

**ABADIA RETUERTA**

**BODEGAS ALEJANDRO FERNÁNDEZ**

**BODEGAS ARZUAGA**

**BODEGAS HNOS. PÉREZ PASCUAS**

**BODEGAS ISMAEL ARROYO**

**BODEGAS MAURO**

**BODEGAS REYES**

**BODEGAS Y VIÑEDOS ALION**

**CONDADO DE HAZA**

**DOMINIO DE PINGUS**

**PROTOS**

**VEGA-SICILIA**

---

## THE FOODS OF RIBERA DEL DUERO

The legendary dish of Ribera del Duero is *lechazo,* a baby lamb fed only mother's milk and weighing less than 15 pounds. In fact, *lechazo* is sometimes the only dish to be found in the best *asadores*—simple, tavernlike roast houses, which can be found throughout the region. The heavenly aroma of roast baby lamb can be smelled several blocks away from an *asador,* and it is hard to pass up.

The chef of each *asador,* who is usually also the owner, buys his lamb directly from shepherds and butchers it himself. He seasons it with only a sprinkle of salt and pepper, then slowly roasts it in a *cuenco* (a ceramic roasting dish) over a hardwood fire in an old brick oven until the meat is seared crackling crisp on the outside and so meltingly tender on the inside that it falls off the bone.

Eating *lechazo* is an experience in pure carnivorousness. In rustic *asadores,* nothing is served with the central attraction except a sharp knife and a fork, a bottle or carafe of Ribera del Duero, and a small salad of lettuce and tomatoes. At slightly more upscale *asadores,* you might begin with a plate of garlicky grilled *setas* (wild mushrooms) or grilled *morcilla* (blood sausage stuffed with rice). Finally, there will be *Páramo de Guzmán,* an artisanal cheese made from the milk of a special breed of Churra sheep, and *cuajada,* creamy, tangy sheep's milk yogurt served in an earthenware jar. Into it, you spoon the local honey.

433

## A SENSUOUS COMBINATION

Nowhere else in Spain are sheep more omnipresent than in Ribera del Duero, where drivers must repeatedly stop for huge flocks of long-legged, black-eared Churra sheep crossing the road. And nowhere else in Spain, save perhaps for Rioja, is roast lamb so well loved with the local red wine. The combination is winning. The ripe bold flavors and supple textures of red wines from Ribera del Duero are neither too powerful nor too frail but uncannily perfect for the sweet bold meatiness of roast lamb.

# THE RIBERA DEL DUERO
# WINES TO KNOW

*The extremes of Ribera del Duero's climate mean that for fine wines, only reds are produced here.*

## ABADIA RETUERTA

Pago Negralada

Sardon de Duero

100% tempranillo

Although technically it is just outside the borders of Ribera del Duero, Abadia Retuerta is nonetheless considered a Ribera del Duero bodega—and not just any bodega, but one of the largest, most elaborate and expensive bodegas ever built in the region. The 500-acre estate includes the *abadia* (abbey) Santa Maria de Retuerta, which dates from 1146, plus a state-of-the-art winery. Heading the winery is the famous Bordeaux winemaker Pascal Delbeck, who also makes the wines at Château Ausone. Pago Negralada, the bodega's top wine, is priced like a top-flight Bordeaux and tastes as saturated and dense as a California cabernet sauvignon, even though it's made entirely from tempranillo. Utterly hedonistic, the wine is packed with the aromas and flavors of cocoa, licorice, dried figs, leather, and sweet pipe tobacco.

*Abadia Retuerta's eponymous Abadia Retuerta, a blend of tempranillo, cabernet sauvignon, and merlot, is the little sister of (and less expensive than) the estate's luxury tempranillo called Pago Negralada (described above).*

## BODEGAS ALEJANDRO FERNANDEZ

Pesquera

*reserva*

100% tinto fino

"A wine is not created; a wine *is*." With his Zenlike philosophy and old-fashioned style, Alejandro Fernández makes one of Ribera del Duero's most intense, personality-driven wines. In great years the Pesquera *crianzas* are positively lip smacking and the estate's *reservas* are nothing short of huge, ripe, and jammy with aromas and flavors that ring of pine, menthol, earth, tar, chocolate, and vanilla. And the finish! Just when you think the flavors should end, Pesquera's intensity unfolds even more. Fernández's other estate, Condado de Haza, also in Ribera del Duero, makes equally delicious wines that are earthy and gripping.

## BODEGAS Y VINEDOS ALION

*reserva*

100% tinto fino

The sister winery of Vega-Sicilia is much smaller and devoted to making big, powerful modern-style wines that, like most California and Bordeaux reds, are aged only for two to three years, with much of that time in new oak. In great vintages Alion is stunning. Beautifully balanced, it nonetheless surges with brooding power. Alion tastes almost nothing like Ribera del Duero's traditional wines; however, it may well be a taste of things to come.

## BODEGAS ISMAEL ARROYO

ValSotillo

*reserva*

100% tinto fino

This small bodega, run by a father and son team, makes some of Ribera del Duero's most suave, silky wines. In great years, they are vibrantly alive with cherry, earth, and cranberry fruit, and the perfect balance is mesmerizing. Ismael Arroyo is one of the few small, family-owned bodegas that has been passed down through the generations in Ribera del Duero.

## BODEGAS HNOS. PEREZ PASCUAS

Viña Pedrosa

*crianza*

100% tinto fino

Expressiveness is everything in a *crianza,* and in top years Viña Pedrosa positively jumps with the immediately attractive aromas and flavors of cherries jubilee. The texture is as soft and generous as flannel. The *reservas* and *gran reservas* from this bodega can be wonderful.

*Manuel Pérez Pascuas, one of the three Pérez Pascuas brothers, creators of Viña Pedrosa.*

## PROTOS

*crianza*

100% tinto fino

Driving along the stalwart mesas that soar upward on each side of the Duero, there is one special bend that must be rounded. The sight on the other side takes your breath away. Above looms the massive walled fortress/castle of Peñafiel perched menacingly atop the mesa, looking every bit as fearsome as it must have eight centuries ago. At the foot of the castle is Bodegas Protos. The *crianzas* here often have bursts of cherries tied with a satin ribbon of vanilla.

## VEGA-SICILIA

Unico

*gran reserva*

approximately 60% tinto fino, 25% cabernet sauvignon, with tiny amounts of merlot, malbec, and albillo

Considered one of the most majestic red wines of Spain, Vega-Sicilia's Unico was the first to demonstrate that the forbidding, desolate land of Ribera del Duero held surprising promise. Unico is aged longer before release than most other wines anywhere. Yet beguilingly, as well aged as it always is, the wine can soar with fruit. Cassis, black plums, earth, violets, truffles, blackberries, and leather all pour out of the glass like smoke from a chimney, but considering its age, the flavors and aromas remain intriguingly elusive. As one might expect, the texture of this wine is utterly silky.

435

## THE WHITE WINES OF RUEDA

⟨⟨⟨⟨⟨⟩⟩⟩⟩

Although Ribera del Duero produces virtually no white wine, its close neighbor, Rueda, is considered one of the important if small white wine regions of Spain. Slightly southwest of Ribera del Duero, Rueda is also spread over dramatic plateaus slashed by the river Duero before it flows into Portugal.

Like Ribera del Duero, this is a region of extremely cold winters and scorchingly hot summers. For centuries the principal grape was Palomino, the heat-tolerant grape of Sherry. The ponderous, high-alcohol Rueda wines that resulted were turned into rather innocuous fortified wines.

Then in the early 1970s, the historic Rioja firm Marqués de Riscal consulted with the legendary French enologist Emile Peynaud and came to the startling conclusion that Rueda (more than Rioja) had the potential to make lively white wines. Riscal built a modern white wine bodega in Rueda called Vinos Blancos de Castilla. By using verdejo, a native Rueda grape; making the wine in temperature-controlled stainless steel tanks; and bottling it young without wood aging, Riscal produced a fresh, fruity, nutty, full-bodied wine that did, indeed, put Rueda on the map as an important Spanish white wine region.

By the 1990s there were twenty-four bodegas in Rueda making fresh-style whites. The best wines are deemed Rueda Superior and must contain at least 85 percent verdejo. Viura, the white grape of Rioja, and sometimes Palomino make up the rest of the blend. Although it has not been as successful as verdejo, sauvignon blanc is also made in Rueda, and chardonnay has been planted. In addition to Marqués de Riscal, other top producers include Compañía de Vinos de la Granja, Marqués de Griñon, and Bodegas Angel Lorenzo Cachazo.

# VISITING RIBERA DEL DUERO BODEGAS

Many of the bodegas in Ribera del Duero are accustomed to wine drinkers stopping by to buy their wine. If you want a tour of the winery and a tasting, however, you must call in advance. It is difficult to arrange a tour of Vega-Sicilia or Pesquera unless you have business with those bodegas. At all bodegas it helps to speak Spanish. The telephone numbers include the dialing code you'll need when calling from the United States. If you're calling from within Spain, eliminate the 011-34 and add a zero before the next number.

**BODEGAS ARZUAGA**
Ctra. Valladolid-Soria, km. 325
47359 Quintanilla de Onésimo, Valladolid
011-34-983-68-11-46

**BODEGAS ISMAEL ARROYO**
71 Los Lagares
09441 Sotillo de la Ribera, Burgos
011-34-947-53-23-09

**BODEGAS HNOS. PÉREZ PASCUAS**
09314 Pedrosa de Duero, Burgos
011-34-947-54-04-99

**BODEGAS PROTOS**
64 Avenida General Sanjuro
47300 Peñafiel, Valladolid
011-34-983-88-12-72

**BODEGAS VALDUERO**
Ctra. Aronda, s/n
09440 Gumiel del Mercado, Burgos
011-34-947-54-54-59

# Jerez

The three words *Jerez*, *Xérès*, and *Sherry* that appear on bottles of Sherry are a testament to the diverse names for Spain's most glorious fortified wine. Sherry is an English word, and Xérès a French one, for the wines made in Jerez. But no matter what you call it, if there were justice in the wine cosmos, which there is not, Sherry would be one of the world's best-loved and oft-sipped wines. As it stands, Sherry, the unsung hero of the great wine classics, is misunderstood, underappreciated, and wrongly cast as the libation of old ladies. This last idea strikes southern Spanish men—known for their machismo, love of bullfights, and predilection for cigars—as quite amusing; Sherry is, after all, their daily drink.

As a fortified wine, Sherry's alcoholic strength has been raised to between 15½ and 22 percent. (A standard table wine is usually 12 to 14 percent alcohol.) In addition to being fortified, Sherries are also slowly and carefully allowed to oxidize to varying degrees depending on the type being made. This helps contribute to the fact that Sherry has a flavor unlike any other in the world. Or rather, flavors. Sherries come in styles that run from the driest of the dry to the sweetest of the sweet.

Although vineyards and beaches would seem to make strange bedfellows, Sherry comes from a small wedge of land along the sea in southwest Spain in the province of Andalusia. This is the Spain of a Cecil B. De Mille movie—a land of flamenco, prized horses, bullfighting, whitewashed villages, and perhaps the world's most mouthwatering array of shellfish. It was from these stark, chalky-white shores

*Pride isn't lacking in the Spanish temperament. Nowhere is this more true than in Andalusia, the ancestral home of bullfighting and flamenco dancing, and of Spain's most renowned fortified wine—Sherry.*

that Columbus began his westward sail. If he brought wine with him (which he probably did), Sherry was the first European wine drunk in America.

# THE LAND, THE GRAPES, AND THE VINEYARDS

Sherry comes from an eerie, barren moonscape of blinding whiteness along Spain's southwestern Andalusian coast. The vineyards spread in triangular fashion from an inland point north of the town of Jerez de la Frontera to the small towns of Puerto de Santa María on the Bay of Cádiz and Sanlúcar de Barrameda on the Atlantic shore at the mouth of the Guadalquivir River.

The best vineyards lie in the heart of this triangle, a region designated as Jerez Superior by Sherry's *Consejo Regulador*,

or governing body. Within the Superior region, the vineyards of highest regard roll like waves over low hillocks that arc slightly north and west of the town of Jerez. Here the verdant vines glisten like emeralds in the glaring summer sun.

Three soil types are found in this region: *albariza*, a stark white, light marl (a crumbly mixture of clays, calcium, magnesium carbonates, and prehistoric sea fossils); *barro*, a brownish, more fertile clay; and *arena*, sand. Of these, *albariza*, found mostly on the hill tops, is the most prized. The *albariza* soil reflects sunlight up to the vines, helping to ripen the grapes. Because it is as light and soft as cake mix, *albariza* must be tilled and compacted by rollers attached to tractors. Working the soil this way helps it hold just enough water to prevent the vines from going into shock during long, often drought-ridden summers.

Jerez is horse country as well as wine country. Appropriately, the most widely planted grape is named Palomino; 95 percent of Sherry is made from it. The name Palomino, however, refers not to horses but to Fernán Yanes Palomino, a thirteenth-century knight to King Alfonso X. Until recently, the Palomino family was a Sherry producer. Palomino grapes please growers because they are disease resistant and vigorous. But in terms of aroma, flavor, and character, Palomino won't turn any heads.

As it happens, that very neutrality is sought after. With a relatively bland grape as a blank canvas, a Sherry's individuality comes from the *albariza* soil in which its grapes are grown and the solera in which it is made. About twelve bodegas make white table wine from Palomino, the best of which by far is made by the bodega Antonio Barbadillo. The wines are generally not found outside the region.

---

## THE QUICK SIP ON SHERRY

- As Champagne is in France or Port is in Portugal, Sherry is Spain's most complex and labor intensive wine. The immense difficulty of producing this handcrafted wine has earned it its exceptional reputation.

- Sherry is made in multiple styles. These range from hauntingly bone-dry to teeth-achingly sweet. The dry Sherries, like white wines, should be consumed within a few days of being opened.

- Sherry country is also one of Spain's most thrilling food regions and the place where the small dishes known as tapas were first created. Sherry is their quintessential accompaniment.

Jerez is planted exclusively with white grape varieties.

**Moscatel:** Minor grape made into a wine on its own and used as a sweet blending wine.

**Palomino:** Major grape for all styles of Sherry. Its neutral flavors are good raw material for the solera process.

**Pedro Ximénez:** Minor grape best known for making the supersweet dessert Sherry also called Pedro Ximénez.

There are two other grapes—both white—found in Jerez. Moscatel is used to make a sweet wine for blending and occasionally, a stunning dessert wine on its own. Each year, however, it accounts for less acreage. Pedro Ximénez, PX, is used to make the style of sweet Sherry called, eponomously, Pedro Ximénez, and it's also used as a sweet blending wine. Because PX is disease prone and gives a low yield, it too is increasingly rare. That said, if you ever come across a PX—especially an old one—don't pass up the opportunity to try it. Dense, syrupy, and almost black in color, PX is a dessert wine like no other.

## MAKING SHERRY

Sherries range along a spectrum from dry to sweet. At one end are the manzanillas and finos, with their tangy, crisp, green earthiness; in the middle are the amontillados, palo cortados, and olorosos, with their lusty, roasted, nutty flavors; and finally come the creams with their sweet, lush, toffee, and fig flavors. None of these Sherry flavors, textures, and aromas ever

quite falls into what we might think of as the galaxy of white or red wine. The flavor of Sherry forms a world unto itself.

This is because of the unique way the wine is made. Sherry is a fortified wine progressively blended and aged in a complex network of old barrels, called a solera. Depending on how the wine moves through the solera, different styles of Sherry can be made.

## The Seven Styles of Sherry

Sherry falls into two broad categories: the fino-type sherries, which are light, dry, and crisp, and the oloroso-type sherries, which are fuller bodied, darker in color, nutty, and sometimes sweet. Under these two banners come seven specific styles. Within these styles, however, Sherries are crafted differently from bodega to

*Holding the* venencia *(a unique long-handled utensil used to withdraw Sherry from a cask) high over his head, the* venenciador *(the person responsible for sampling and assessing a Sherry) pours it into traditional* copitas—*glasses.*

## HOW SHERRY GOT ITS NAME

—⚬⚬⚬—

The name Sherry has a long pedigree. The Greeks called the region Xera, the Romans, Ceret. By the early Middle Ages the Arabs called the region Sekeris and northern Spanish Castillians called it Xeres, and later Xerez. By the late nineteenth century, Xerez had become Jerez, and the town that marked the frontier between the Arabs and the northern Spanish was called Jerez de la Frontera. The Spanish pronunciation of Jerez—hare-ETH—was corrupted by British importers of the wine who pronounced it JER-rez, then JER-ee, and finally Sherry.

bodega. An amontillado from one bodega may be significantly sweeter than the amontillado from another and still another's amontillado may be bone-dry. What may seem like anarchy is actually a reflection of the near limitless possibilities Sherry offers.

FINO-TYPE SHERRIES

MANZANILLA
FINO
AMONTILLADO
PALO CORTADO

OLOROSO-TYPE SHERRIES

OLOROSO
CREAM
PEDRO XIMÉNEZ

### MANZANILLA

A highly revered, light, elegant style of Sherry that comes only from the tiny seaside town of Sanlúcar de Barrameda. There, the wet ocean air gives manzanilla a salty tang as well as a sea spray aroma, similar to the aroma of a freshly shucked oyster.

Manzanilla has a delicate, slightly crisp edge to it. It's entirely dependent on the bloom of flor, the curious yellow foam of yeasts that forms on the surface of the wine as it develops. Because manzanillas are ultrafragile, most bodegas bottle and ship them to order. They must be drunk chilled and fresh; opened bottles last no more than one or two days.

### FINO

Fino is Sherry at the apex of refinement and complexity. Fino is pale in color and low in alcohol. Its unforgettable dry tang and aroma, reminiscent of a garden after a rain, make it one of the world's great seafood wines. Like manzanillas, finos are also dependent on flor. And though they are not quite as delicate as manzanillas, finos are still fragile and must be served well chilled and at peak freshness. An open bottle should be drunk, like most white wines, within two to three days.

### AMONTILLADO

An aged fino. After this wine has moved through its solera, it is then fortified so that its alcohol content is slightly higher than that of manzanilla or fino and it is put into another series of barrels where it will no longer be protected by flor. As a result, it will oxidize a bit more, taking on a deeper color as well as rich, nutty flavors. A few producers make dry amontillados; most others blend in a small percentage of sweet Pedro Ximénez to make a medium-dry wine. The label may or may not indicate the level of sweetness.

### PALO CORTADO

A rare, eccentric type of dry amontillado. Sometimes an amontillado aged an especially long time begins to take on the body, lushness, and concentration of an oloroso. This duplicitous curiosity, with the fragrance and finesse of a dry amontillado and the voluptuous body and concentration of a dry oloroso, is called a palo cortado. Amusingly, amontillados in the process of turning themselves into palo cortados often escape notice by the cellar master who, on a day-to-day basis, checks the developing wines by smelling them, not tasting them.

## OLOROSO

A gorgeously aromatic long-aged Sherry that traditionally has not been protected or influenced by flor. More than any other type of dry Sherry, olorosos are exposed to oxygen. This darkens the wine and imparts a profoundly nutty flavor. The initial raw material for an oloroso is pressed juice, which is slightly coarser than the free-run juice used to make fino. The wine is also more heavily fortified with grape spirits (18 to 20 percent) before it enters the oloroso solera. As a result, olorosos are richer, meatier, denser Sherries. Dry olorosos are a rare and remarkable treat. Most producers today sweeten them by blending in varying amounts of Pedro Ximénez.

## CREAM

Originally created for the British export market, cream Sherries are made by sweetening olorosos with substantial amounts of Pedro Ximénez. There is no legally mandated sweetness level, however. Some bodegas make a cautiously sweet cream Sherry; others make sugar syrup to the tenth power. Cream Sherries also range all over the board in quality—from inexpensive, mud-thick, saccharine quaffs to elegant, almost racy wines redolent of chocolate, licorice, figs, and roasted nuts. A vibrant and delicious Spanish cocktail calls for mixing good cream Sherry with Campari and red vermouth and then serving it over ice with a twist of lemon.

## PEDRO XIMÉNEZ

A sweet sherry that is often as dark and dense as blackstrap molasses. Pedro Ximénez is made from the Pedro Ximénez grape, unlike the vast majority of all other Sherries, which are made from the Palomino grape. Pedro Ximénez is generally used to sweeten dry Sherries. In small amounts it's also served on its own as a dessert wine or, as is often done in Spain, it can be slathered over vanilla ice cream.

## *How the Solera Works*

Each style of Sherry has its own separate solera. Precisely how does the solera system work and how do these styles come to be? The process, at its most simplistic, goes like this: White Palomino grapes are crushed, and the juice is fermented in stainless steel or cement tanks, very much the way any other white wine might be made. At this point the wine is lightly fortified with grape spirits. The fortified wine is then poured into barrels and set aside for a year or more to develop a bit of initial complexity. This wine, called *añada* (wine of the current year), will next enter the solera where it will be progressively blended and aged until it eventually emerges as Sherry.

To form the solera, multiple rows of 600-liter old American oak barrels, called butts, are lined

## THE SHERRY-CHAMPAGNE CONNECTION

—⚡—

Sherry is often compared to Champagne, and in fact, the two wines are almost like one subject looked at through different ends of the binoculars:

- Both are homages to white soil.
- Both are born in temperature extremes: Champagne in the northern cold, Sherry in the southern heat.
- Both are the epitome of refinement when very good; clunkers when poorly made.
- Both achieve their complexity through blending.
- Both come to be as a result of winemaking processes so intricate and painstaking, it is amazing that they were ever conceived in the first place and once conceived, that they weren't immediately abandoned as too troublesome.
- Both Champagne and Sherry taste best when drunk from special glasses engineered to highlight their flavors—a flute or a *copita* (see Serving Sherry, page 446) respectively.
- Both provide an experience beyond the realm of mere white wine.
- And finally, each is considered, with all due respect to the other, one of the most miraculous wines in the world.

up. Often these rows are stacked one row on top of the other, like children's building blocks. Generally the stack will be four or five rows of barrels high, but the solera may contain as many as fourteen rows of barrels. In the case of fourteen rows, the barrels would not all be stacked one on top of the other, otherwise the bottom barrels would burst from the weight. Even at five barrels high, a solera is an impressive sight. Sherry bodegas are locally referred to as cathedrals because of their soaring vaulted ceilings, which arch over the towering barrels.

The barrels on the bottom row contain the oldest sherry; from these barrels small amounts will be drawn off and bottled when an order is placed. This row is also called the solera row (from *suelo*, Spanish for floor). Each time Sherry is drawn off from the bottom row, bottled, and sent to market, the barrel is replenished with an equal quantity of wine from a barrel in the row above it. That row, second from the bottom, is called *criadera* #1, or the first nursery. It contains the second-oldest wine. When wine from the *criadera* #1 is drawn off, it, in turn, is replenished with wine from a barrel in the row above it, called *criadera* #2. *Criadera* #2 will be replenished with wine from the row above it, *criadera* #3, and so on. Thus a tiny amount of wine is constantly being drawn off and added to older wine, moving progressively down through lower and lower barrels. At the very top, the solera is fed with the wine of the current year, the *añada*.

*Each bottle of Sherry is a complex molecular kaleidoscope with what can only be an estimated age.*

As a result of the constant fractional blending of younger wines into older wines, Sherry is not the product of any one year. By law, it never carries a vintage date, although it is not uncommon for a Sherry label to designate the year the solera was formed. Also by law, only 30 percent of a solera can be drawn off each year.

The labyrinthine solera process is especially remarkable because it is impossible to determine just how old a Sherry is when it finally emerges from the bottom row. The reason is twofold. First, once the solera is set up the barrels are never completely emptied. Currently, Sherry barrels are on the average one hundred years old. Second, the small amount of wine drawn off and added to the wine in the barrel below is not stirred into that wine. The wine is therefore not truly blended in a homogenized sense. Each barrel will contain molecules of wine that were never drawn off and thus date from when the solera was begun, as much as two centuries earlier.

For Sherry to become Sherry requires more than simply the physical movement of wine through a solera, however. Why does fino become fino and oloroso become oloroso? That metamorphosis is fairly well understood today. For most of history, however, Sherry was inexplicably supernatural.

## Making Fino and Manzanilla

To make a fino, the Sherry maker crushes, but does not press, Palomino grapes. The free-run juice is fermented and then fortified only slightly with spirits. The wine is transferred into a Sherry butt, but instead of being filled to the top, the butt is filled only three-fourths full. Then a remarkable occurrence takes place. Though it is in no way technologically induced, a foamy mass of yellow-white matter called flor appears on the surface of the wine. In a month's time, the flor will completely blanket the wine.

Horrified by the foul-looking flor, Sherry makers a century ago

---

### THE KIND OF MANZANILLA YOU DID NOT HAVE IN MIND

In Spain, if you order a manzanilla just about anywhere outside Andalusia, you will invariably be brought a pot of hot chamomile tea. The word *manzanilla* also means chamomile. To be served manzanilla Sherry in Barcelona or Madrid you must order *manzanilla de Sanlúcar* or a *copita de manzanilla*.

---

believed that certain barrels of wine simply got "sick." Slowly, opinion changed. The flor-covered wines, they noticed, emerged from the solera light, fresh, and very dry. This came to be seen as a blessing, for such a wine was, in fact, well suited to the sultry local climate. Enologists now know that flor is a complex wild strain of *Saccharomyces* yeasts that bloom spontaneously in the region's humid air. The word *flor* itself means flower—a reference to its ability to bloom. Interestingly, flor taken from Sherry to other parts of the world quickly mutates or dies, conveniently assuring that true Sherry will never be made in California, Chile, Italy, or even anywhere else in Spain.

Flor is critical to a fino-to-be. Resting on the wine like a lace tablecloth, the flor yeasts protect the developing fino from oxidizing by consuming the surrounding oxygen (remember the barrel contents are one quarter air). Flor's shield is not absolutely impermeable, however. A small amount of oxidation will

443

occur—just enough to impart further complexity. The flor also gives the fino a subtle, yeasty aroma and flavor not unlike bread dough.

Flor is also critical to manzanilla, the rare, revered subset of fino. Of all Sherries, manzanilla is the most vulnerable to climate. By virtue of Nature's remarkable particularity, manzanilla can only be made by bodegas situated along the beach in the seaside town of Sanlúcar de Barrameda, where the salty air and humidity create a unique microclimate. So dependent is manzanilla on this oceanic microclimate that developing manzanillas taken to another bodega in the Sherry region (or even a bodega too far from the wet breezes off the beach) will turn into finos!

*A layer of yellow flor rests on the top of a fino. The barrel's head has been replaced with glass to make viewing the contents possible.*

In the humid conditions under which manzanilla is made, flor will blanket the developing wine throughout the year. Fino's case is slightly different. Fino is made in areas slightly more inland, less humid, and warmer than Sanlúcar. Around the town of Jerez where fino is made, the relative humidity throughout the year is 69 percent. In Sanlúcar, it is 78 percent.

With less humidity in which to flourish, the flor that covers fino comes and goes cyclically with the seasons. Manzanilla's keenly etched delicacy and lightness is thought to be the result of its thorough, uninterrupted covering of flor.

As for amontillados, they are made by taking fino sherries, fortifying them a bit more to a higher alcohol content, and then putting them through another solera where they will not be protected by flor. The amontillado that results is an aged, nutty, rich wine that has more alcohol and is more oxidized than a fino. If during this process the amontillado is aged for a considerable period of time, it will sometimes begin to take on the even fuller body of an oloroso. These rare super-amontillados are the palo cortados.

## Making Oloroso, Cream Sherry, and Pedro Ximénez

Until quite recently the mystical and unpredictable appearance of flor told Sherry makers whether they had emerging finos or manzanillas on their hands. If flor did not form in the butts, the Sherry makers knew the wines were destined to become olorosos and they would care for and age them accordingly.

Today an oloroso is usually made intentionally. Instead of taking the free-run juice and fortifying it only slightly, Sherry makers lightly press some of the juice from the grapes and fortify it enough so that flor cannot form. (Flor yeasts, like all yeasts, die in an environment that is greater than about 16.4 percent alcohol.) The extra bit of alcohol and tannin from the grape skins means that an oloroso will always have a rounder, fuller texture than the lighter, more elegant fino or manzanilla.

A Sherry maker moves the developing oloroso through its solera more slowly than fino or manzanilla go through theirs. By holding the oloroso longer in the solera, the sherry maker allows it to take on a deep, caramel-toffee richness.

When the oloroso is removed from the solera it is ready to be bottled as a dry

# THE ARABIC THREADS OF SHERRY HISTORY

For almost 800 years during the Middle Ages, while the rest of Europe was shrouded in cultural and intellectual darkness, the Moors controlled most of Spain. Progressive, powerful, and enlightened, they were not one people, but a group of Middle Eastern and North African Moslem tribes that entered through Andalusia. Their capital became the white-walled village of Córdoba, which under their caliphate became the most important city in Western Europe. By the tenth century, Córdoba had half a million people and was the first city in Europe with street lighting, a sewage system, and public fountains. There were fifty hospitals, three hundred public baths, sixty schools, twenty libraries, and over a thousand mosques. Despite brief waves of religious fanaticism, the caliphate of Córdoba was remarkably secular. For centuries, Moslems, Christians, and Jews lived in harmony under its rule. Such was the atmosphere of liberalness, open-mindedness, and tolerance, in fact, that the Moslems largely ignored the Koranic prohibition against drinking. By the end of Arabic hegemony, Sherry was a well-established beverage—one that scholars believe was decidedly present at the caliph's table.

wine. Or it may be lightly sweetened with a bit of ultrasweet juice from Pedro Ximénez grapes, making it a medium-sweet oloroso. If the oloroso is sweetened to the extent that Pedro Ximénez makes up about 15 percent of the final blend, the oloroso becomes a cream Sherry.

The first cream Sherries were made at the turn of the twentieth century for the British export market. They were lush, warming wines perfectly suited to bitter, raw English winters. Such was the popularity of cream Sherries that shortcuts were sometimes taken to meet the demand for them. Today many cream Sherries on the market are little more than dull base wines that have been quickly passed through a few barrels and then so heavily sweetened that they have virtually no character or complexity.

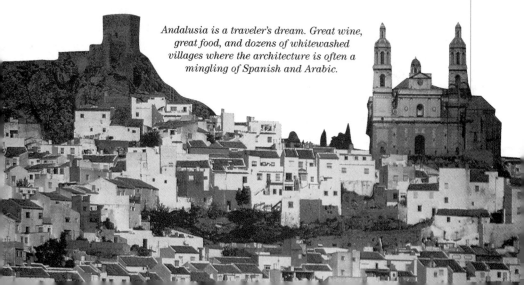

*Andalusia is a traveler's dream. Great wine, great food, and dozens of whitewashed villages where the architecture is often a mingling of Spanish and Arabic.*

As we've seen, Pedro Ximénez is more than just a sweetener; the grape variety is also made into a rare Sherry of its own. Most Pedro Ximénez Sherries are nearly black in color and have a texture thicker than cough syrup. A thimbleful is more than dessert wine, it's dessert. To achieve this degree of sweetness and intensity the grapes are picked and then laid out under the scorching sun for two to three weeks to dry and shrivel. Only when the sugar in them becomes very concentrated are the grapes slowly fermented into wine.

---

### SERVING SHERRY

⟨∽∾∾⟩

Sherry is traditionally served in a *copita*—a small stemmed glass with a narrow tulip-shape body. It is poured three-quarters full. The best *copita* substitute is a small, slender white-wine glass.

Finos, manzanillas, and amontillados are served chilled; serve palo cortados, olorosos, creams, and Pedro Ximénez at a coolish room temperature.

---

## The Almacenistas

Sherry is made predominantly by several large prestigious firms, including Domecq, Osborne, Gonzalez Byass, Sandeman, and Harveys. But it is also made by smaller firms with stellar reputations: Valdespino, Emilio Lustau, and Hidalgo, to name three. Then there are the *almacenistas*.

*Almacenistas* are individuals—often doctors, lawyers, and businessmen—with small, usually inherited, family soleras. Today there are about fifty of them, although their numbers are dwindling. *Almacenistas* do not actually produce finished Sherries, but rather mature them in their soleras and then sell them to larger bodegas. Generally, the bodega will blend the *almacenista*'s Sherry into its own Sherries as a way of further heightening complexity.

In the late 1970s the bodega Emilio Lustau (once an *almacenista* itself) decided that many *almacenista* Sherries had fascinating individual characters and deserved to be bottled individually. Lustau trademarked the name *almacenista* and began bringing these singular and costly Sherries onto the market. From the standpoint of flavor and complexity, an *almacenista* Sherry is not necessarily better than an established bodega's Sherry—in fact, quite the opposite is sometimes true. Nonetheless, Sherry made by an *almacenista* is always full of personality and intriguing to taste.

The *almacenista*'s name will be printed on the label along with Lustau's. Among the best are Lustau Almacenista Amontillado El Puerto, matured by José Luis Gonzalez Obregón, which is as dry and crisp as autumn leaves and has a fine lightly roasted nuttiness, and Lustau Almacenista Oloroso Viejo de Jerez, matured by Viudo de Antonio Borrego, which has real verve on the palate. Both are extremely refined, elegant, and intense wines.

## THE IMPORTANCE OF FRESHNESS

Freshness is as critical to the flavor of Sherry as it is to bread. Yet in many restaurants and bars outside of Spain it is not uncommon to be served from a bottle

446

that's been open for months. Such Sherry—especially if it's a fino or a manzanilla—will have an almost rancid flavor.

In Jerez an opened bottle of fino or manzanilla is kept no longer than a single day. More typically, the bottle is finished with the meal, which is why in Spain both types of Sherry are most often sold in half bottles. By comparison, amontillados, olorosos, and creams will last several months after the bottle has been opened with only a slight diminution of flavor. Immediate consumption is not as critical with these Sherries because they are less fragile and slightly more oxidized to begin with. If they contain some Pedro Ximénez, their sugar content also acts as a preservative.

Freshness, however, is not solely a question of how long you keep an opened bottle. Both fino and manzanilla begin to lose their zesty character six months after they leave the solera. Clearly, this presents a problem. Since Sherry, by law, cannot carry a bottled-on or drink-by date, there is no way of knowing whether any given bottle has been on the wine shop shelf ten weeks or ten months. The solution is to buy only top Sherries and only from the best wine shops. Producers of the highest-quality Sherries cannot afford to have their reputations sunk by stale bottles in the marketplace. Such producers bottle only when they receive an order from their importers, who, in turn, only place an order when wine shops and restaurants make their requests. As further insurance of freshness, the most fanatically conscientious producers sometimes ship their manzanillas by air (rather than by sea) at extra cost. Cleverly, the producer Hildago makes a "by air" version of their La Gitana manzanilla. Right on the label, it reads *Por Avión.*

*Some of the Best
Sherry Producers*

EMILIO LUSTAU

GONZALEZ BYASS

HIDALGO

OSBORNE

PEDRO DOMECQ

SANDEMAN

VALDESPINO

# THE FOODS OF SHERRY

Andalusia's pulsating drama of bullfights and flamenco, of cathedrals and mosques, of fino and fiestas, whispers the promise of good things to eat. This is,

## COOKING "SHERRY" AND SHERRY VINEGAR

So-called cooking "sherry"—the kind found in every supermarket in the United States—is not true Sherry but rather cheap American base wine that has been heated to give it a baked, caramel flavor, then had salt added to it. Wretched stuff, it does nothing for the flavor of a dish but it does, sadly, tarnish the image of Sherry.

Sherry vinegar is a whole other story. Made in its own separate bodegas in Jerez, Sherry vinegar is expensive and prized for its faintly sweet, nutty taste, not unlike Italy's balsamic vinegar. Sherry vinegar is aged from five to twenty-five years; with longer aging, the flavor becomes more complex.

## SHERRY AND SHRIMP

In Jerez, there is no more traditional pairing than a glass of bone-dry fino along with a small plate of thinly sliced *serrano* ham or, better yet, *jamón de jabugo*. It's an unbeatable match. Until you consider *gambas al ajillo* (garlic shrimp) and a glass of manzanilla, which together just might constitute the single most satisfying appetizer/aperitif combination in the world. The salty, briny, olive-scented tang of a great manzanilla is the perfect dramatic counterpoint to fresh shrimp that have been quickly sautéed in a pool of ripe olive oil with a sprinkle of dried red chile and more garlic than you want to know.

first and foremost, the home of a huge, sensual, movable feast of seafood. *Not* the sort that is neat and tidy, either. No, this is the roll-up-your-sleeves, peel-crack-and-pull-apart, eat-the-heads, eat-the-tails, slurp-the-juice, lick-your-fingers sort of seafood eating.

The love affair with gutsy seafood occurs throughout the region, but it is especially poignant in the seaside towns of Sanlúcar de Barrameda and Puerto de Santa María, where the heady aroma of the ocean air puts everyone in the mood to eat fish. Sanlúcar is best experienced first around twilight when the approach of evening brings cool air and the light over the sea fades to silver. The thing to do is eat platters of langoustines and drink Sanlúcar's famous manzanilla at a bar, such as Casa Bigote on the Bajo de Guía beach.

Later, go to Puerto de Santa María, where fishermen's bars, open-air café/markets, and *tascas* (taverns) are strung together as tightly as pearls along the waterfront roads Ribera del Marisco and Ribero del Rio. The idea is to stroll from place to place, drinking icy, fresh fino and eating a different assortment of fish at each: *langostinos, gambas,* and *cigalas* (spiny lobsters, prawns, and crayfish); then *boquerones* (fried fresh baby anchovies) and *percebes* (grotesque-looking, goose-necked barnacles that are remarkably delicious and virtually worshipped by Spanish seafood lovers); next *merluza* (ocean-sweet hake that's served dipped in semolina flour and fried) and baby *salmonetes* (red mullet); then *calamares rellenos* (stuffed squid with fresh mayonnaise); and, if you are lucky, *angulas* (baby white eels, no longer than a matchstick, sautéed for mere seconds in sizzling, garlic-strewn olive oil).

Between bites of seafood and sips of Sherry, you nibble spicy green olives that have been gently cracked and then marinated in freshly pressed olive oil, garlic, and Sherry vinegar.

Jerezanos begin their nightly culinary pilgrimage through the taverns around 10 P.M., and by midnight the seafood and Sherry feast is in full swing. Before 10 P.M. the streets are as quiet as convents. If bars and cafés offer such compelling food, you might imagine the restaurants to be thrilling. Not exactly. Over centuries, the hot climate, the proximity to the beach, the southern spirit of sensuality, and the open, relaxed lifestyle of the Jerezanos all came together in a way that was more suited to the vitality and conviviality of cafés and bars than to the formality of restaurants. Sherry country *is* its bars.

Eating in bars is different from eating in restaurants. Small dishes of many

448

*Tapas—a colorful array of dishes consumed standing up at a bar with a glass of wine alongside—are thought to have originated in Jerez.*

different simple foods (tapas)—most of which can be picked up with the fingers and eaten standing up—make more sense than full plates requiring correct utensils. Food historians suggest that the custom of eating tapas, which can be found throughout Spain today, probably began in Jerez. The ambience, the attitude, and the fact that people were drinking a stronger fortified wine and thus needed something to nibble on, all would have encouraged consuming many little dishes while at the bar.

As for restaurants, some of the best are *ventas*—casual places that began as inns for travelers. In *ventas* and restaurants you can sometimes find special Andalusian dishes that emerged from the mingling of Christian and Arab culinary traditions. Local roasted game, such as duck, partridge, and quail, for example, might first be marinated in Sherry, then seasoned and/or combined with spices and foods introduced by the Arabs: saffron, cumin, coriander, almonds, honey, figs, dates, and raisins.

The precursor to gazpacho, one of the most famous Andalusian dishes, was most probably the humble Arabic-influenced cold soup called *ajo blanco* (white garlic). For *ajo blanco*, almonds (brought to Spain from Jordan by the Arabs) are pounded and puréed together with garlic plus vinegar, bread, water, and olive oil. Centuries later, after Columbus brought tomatoes back to Spain from the Americas, gazpacho would be made using the same simple technique, with tomatoes in place of the almonds.

Soups, in general, are an important part of the cooking of southwest Spain, and they are always accompanied by a glass of Sherry. Some of the most traditional include *sopa al almejas y pinóns* (soup made with black clams, garlic, and pine nuts), *caldo de perro gaditano* (Cádiz-style fish soup with the juice of bitter oranges), and *sopa de mariscos* (shellfish soup).

In Andalusia overall, and Jerez in particular, no eating establishment is without its haunch of *jamón*. The finest Spanish

## BULL'S MEAT

—⊰◈◈◈⊱—

**T**oro, a bull raised for bullfighting, is an Andalusian culinary specialty. In particular, the tenderloin, the tail, and the testicles are prized. Historically, the poor and uneducated believed that eating the meat of an especially powerful bullfighting bull would imbue the eater with the bull's strength, courage, and virility.

Small slaughterhouses were built just outside bullrings where you could (and still can) buy such meat. *Toro* is also sold in Andalusian markets, although this is usually the meat of bulls deemed too passive to fight well. While the meat of a bull that has fought is more expensive, the meat of a nonfighter is considered more tender since the animal did not die under stress.

*jamón*, like fine Italian prosciutto, is the result of a long, painstaking process, during which the ham is rubbed with sea salt, then hung up to "sweat," first in rooms with long vertical windows that allow mountain breezes to mature and cure the ham and later in underground cellars. Eventually the salt is washed off, resulting

*In Sherry country, where bulls have almost mythic status, bullfighting is a passionate rite that honors the bull's power, courage, and virility.*

in a ham that is sweet and almost silky smooth in the mouth. No chemicals are involved. The entire natural aging process can take up to eighteen months.

Spanish *jamón* comes from two different strains of pig—*ibérico* and *serrano*. The black-hoofed *ibéricos*, thought to be related to a particular type of wild boar that once roamed the Iberian peninsula, have a somewhat more complex, sweet, nutty, and profound flavor than the *serranos* thanks to their diet of wild roots, bulbs, corn, wheat, and especially acorns, which the animals gorge themselves on. The most prized *ibéricos* come from the village of Jabugo, in the province of Huelva, just north of Sherry country. Many European connoisseurs consider *jamón de jabugo* the world's ultimate cured ham, surpassing even the finest prosciutto. In the best restaurants, taverns, and bars of Jerez, *jamón de jabugo* is sliced paper thin, fanned out on a plate, and eaten at room temperature. Purists accompany it with one thing only: a glass of Sherry.

# VISITING SHERRY BODEGAS

**S**everal bodegas have tours in English which include a tasting of their Sherries. There is no fee. Tours should be arranged in advance by letter or telephone. The telephone numbers include the dialing code you'll need when calling from the United States. If you're calling from within Spain, eliminate the 011-34 and add a zero before the next number. All bodegas are closed in the month of August.

**EMILIO LUSTAU**
4 Plaza del Cubo
11403 Jerez de la Frontera, Cádiz
011-34-956-34-15-97

**GONZALEZ BYASS**
12 Manuel María Gonzalez
11403 Jerez de la Frontera, Cádiz
011-34-956-34-00-00

**HIDALGO**
24 Banda de la Playa
11540 Sanlúcar de Barrameda, Cádiz
011-34-956-36-38-44

**OSBORNE**
3 Fernán Caballero
11500 El Puerto de Santa María, Cádiz
011-34-956-85-52-11

**PEDRO DOMECQ**
3 San Ildefonso
11404 Jerez de la Frontera, Cádiz
011-34-956-15-15-00

**SANDEMAN**
10 Pizarro
11402 Jerez de la Frontera, Cádiz
011-34-956-30-11-00

**VALDESPINO**
16 Pozo del Olivar
11403 Jerez de la Frontera, Cádiz
011-34-956-33-14-50

## BRANDY DE JEREZ

Spain makes more brandy than any other country in the world, and most of it is made in Jerez. Every Jerez bodega that makes Sherry also makes brandy. All brandies, including Cognac, which is the type of brandy made in the region of the same name in France, are spirits distilled from grapes. This distinguishes them from, say, scotch or vodka, which are distillates of grain.

Alembics, or pot stills, necessary for the process of distillation, were brought to Jerez in the early Middle Ages by Moslem tribes as they began their conquest of the Iberian peninsula. The Arabs used alembics to distill fruit and plant essences for the making of medicines and perfumes. The Christians soon adopted the Arabic technique, applying it to grapes in particular. The result was a white distillate used first to fortify the local wine (the precursor of Sherry) and later to make a stronger beverage on its own. From southern Spain stills and the technique for making brandy spread northward to France and ultimately to the rest of western Europe.

Top Jerez brandies, like Sherry, are handcrafted, complex, and made in a solera (not true of Cognac, Armagnac, or brandies made elsewhere in the world). Since the solera is made up of oak casks that once held Sherry, brandy de Jerez takes on unique flavors that tend to be deep, rich, mellow, and less acidic than other brandies. Moreover, brandy makers in Jerez use different types of used Sherry barrels to steer the flavor of their brandies in different directions. The top brandy of Gonzalez Byass, Lepanto, is matured in fino and dry oloroso barrels, resulting in a subtly nuanced, dry brandy. Cardenal Mendoza from the bodega Sanchez Romate uses sweet oloroso barrels, and the brandy that they produce is correspondingly more honeyed and vanilla-like.

Brandy de Jerez must be aged a minimum of one and a half years in a solera. The top brandies, however, far exceed this minimum and are aged in a solera ten to fifteen years. They are designated on the bottle as Brandy de Jerez Solera Gran Reserva. As a group, Solera *gran reserva* brandies are considerably less expensive than their cousins, the top Cognacs.

Among the most renowned *gran reservas,* in addition to the Gonzalez Byass Lepanto and the Sanchez Romate Cardenal Mendoza, are Carlos I by Pedro Domecq, Conde de Osborne by Osborne, and Gran Duque d'Alba by Diez Merito.

451

# THE SHERRIES TO KNOW

*The Sherries are listed from the driest, lightest style, manzanilla, to the sweetest and fullest, Pedro Ximénez.*

## HIDALGO, S.A.

Manzanilla

La Gitana Manzanilla Guadalquivir Especial

100% Palomino

More than any other style of Sherry, manzanilla has cachet. And more than any other manzanilla, Hidalgo's La Gitana (the gypsy) demonstrates why. The wine's gossamer-like complexity is evident every second you drink it—from the multi-aromatic nose of green moss, straw, almonds, and vanilla to the crisp, sea-fresh snap of flavor to the wine's shimmering nutty, minty finish. Manzanillas simply do not get more inspiring.

## PEDRO DOMECQ

Fino

La Ina

100% Palomino

Salty, minerally, and evocative of cucumbers with its fresh snappiness, La Ina is always considered one of the great classic finos and a must with seafood tapas. It has wonderful, deep penetrating flavors with a distinctive finish that is almost varnishlike and actually very appealing.

## VALDESPINO

Fino

Inocente

100% Palomino

A ballet dancer of a fino—on its toes and twirling with effortless grace. The wine starts out with a mossy, almondy nose that draws you in with its elegance and complexity. On the palate Inocente tastes like vanilla, almonds, apples, and honey dipped in cream and sprinkled with sea spray. There's not a trace of the bitterness sometimes apparent in other finos. Before it is moved through the solera, the base wine is fermented in wood to give the flavors additional nuance. The Valdespino bodega is one of the oldest in Jerez and is still family owned and operated. This is a single vineyard fino, a rarity in Spain.

## OSBORNE Y CA.

Amontillado

Amontillado AOS

100% Palomino

One of the top large sherry bodegas, Osborne makes classic dependable sherries in every style, but their Amontillado AOS is a real winner. With rich, round flavors of crème brûlée and roasted nuts coated in butter and some fine toffee and coffee notes, it's a great example of an amontillado that is both intense and refined. Just begging for a plate of *serrano* ham or Spain's ultimate—*jamón de jabugo.* AOS stands for Antonio Osborne Solera, a small amontillado solera founded in 1903 by Tomas Osborne Guezala, then Count of Osborne, to commemorate the birth of his son Antonio.

## SANDEMAN
Oloroso
Royal Corregidor Rare Oloroso
mostly Palomino with some Pedro Ximénez

The best olorosos lift you off your seat with their profoundly deep, lush flavors, and the Royal Corregidor is the perfect example. A combination of two rare oloroso soleras begun in the 1800s, this Sherry simply exudes nuttiness. Although very sweet in taste (cream Sherry lovers try this), the sweetness is intense without being sugary, rather like the elegance of expensive Belgian chocolate. In Jerez a glass of oloroso is often served with a piece of almond cake.

## EMILIO LUSTAU
Cream Sherry
Solera Reserva Superior Rare Cream
mostly Palomino with some Pedro Ximénez

The words *superior* and *rare* are apt here. There are countless undistinguished cream Sherries on the market but few great ones. The Lustau is certainly one of the latter. Not viscous, not heavy, not coarse, and not saccharin, this cream Sherry has distinct, finely etched, toffee and caramel flavors and a luxurious finish reminiscent of roasted nuts.

## PEDRO DOMECQ
Pedro Ximénez
Venerable Very Rare Pedro Ximénez
100% Pedro Ximénez

Pedro Ximénez is the sweetest style of Sherry, and Domecq's Venerable is the apotheosis of the style—as rich as velvet, powerfully sweet, almost explosive with deep licorice flavors. Sherry makers blend PX into other Sherries to sweeten them, but a great PX like this one can be sipped on its own. In Jerez, it's not unusual to find men smoking cigars and eating ice cream over which a great Pedro Ximénez like this one has been poured.

453

---

# ALVEAR MONTILLA

East and north of Jerez is the wine region Montilla-Moriles, near the old Moorish capital Córdoba. Here, under the blazing summer sun, Pedro Ximénez grapes achieve such sugar-loaded ripeness that they result in wines that are 15½ percent alcohol naturally. Montillas are not Sherries, but like them, they develop flor, are aged in a solera, and are made in such similar styles as fino, amontillado, and so forth. Unlike Sherry, however, the naturally higher alcohol means that Montilla wines do not have to be fortified with grape spirits. As a result, they are slightly lighter and sometimes more delicate than Sherry, though they are drunk in much the same way. Montillas are fermented in tall clay vessels called *tinajas*.

The best producer of Montilla is the legendary bodega Alvear, established in 1729. In particular, the Alvear fino seems to embody the intense and vibrant pulse of southern Spain. Despite its delicate body, the wine fairly bursts at the seams with the flavors of lemon, chalk, olives, pepper, spices, almond cake, and roasted nuts. Intriguingly, almond and olive trees line the vineyards. The wine is amazingly inexpensive.

# Penedès

*Barcelona, the capital of Catalonia, is the most vibrant city in Spain. About thirty miles away is a rolling landscape of vines whose grapes go to make Spain's top* cavas.

The Penedès wine region is in Catalonia, arguably the most dynamic province in Spain and the epicenter of Spanish art, literature, philosophy, gastronomy, finance, and culture. Catalonia is a province fervent about politics and religion; a province where everyone speaks Catalan first, Spanish second; a province that cultivates creativity and genius. The painters Joan Miró, Salvador Dalí, and Pablo Picasso are Catalans—as are the architect Antonio Gaudí, the cellist Pablo Casals, and the opera singers Monserrat Caballé and José Carreras. Catalonian artistry and exuberance is evident in the region's wines as well.

The region is not far from one of the most spirited cities of the Mediterranean—

Barcelona. Driving southwest out of the city, you pass through several miles of ugly industrial sprawl, but soon the sway of pine- and orchard-covered hills takes hold. Farther along, a patchwork quilt of vineyards unfolds across the rolling landscape. From the warm coastal land the vineyards progress upward to higher and cooler elevations inland. Although relatively small in surface area, the Penedès has a wide variety of climatic conditions and soil types.

The Penedès is only one of several *Denominaciónes de Origen* within Catalonia, but it continues to be the most important (a distinction that may one day change if the Priorato, its tiny but fast emerging sister region, becomes more famous).

Winemaking in the Penedès has deep roots. Amphorae and Egyptian wine jars uncovered at archaeological sites suggest that wine was introduced to the Penedès by the Phoenicians some seven centuries before Christ. For more than two and a half millennia, the production of these still wines continued.

When the very first *cava* (sparkling wine made in the same way as Champagne) was produced here in 1872, the course of Penedès winemaking changed forever. By the early part of the twentieth century, a handful of family bodegas had begun to specialize in it. Today, *cava* is the Penedès' best-loved specialty, and there are about 175 *cava* producers, including the two largest sparkling wine firms in the world, Freixenet and Codorníu. During harvest each of these bodegas presses more than a thousand tons of grapes every day.

Ironically, the period during which *cava* was born was also a golden age for

Catalonian still wines. Between 1868 and 1886 Catalonia produced nearly half of all the simple table wine in Spain. The best still wines were exported throughout Europe and as far away as Latin America. But it was French misfortune that catapulted Catalonian wines to their greatest recognition. As the vineyards of France were ravaged by oidium, a parasitic fungus, and phylloxera, a louse that destroys vines by attacking their roots, the production of Penedès and Rioja wines surged to accommodate French thirst. In particular, a number of very productive grape varieties were planted in the Penedès. According to Hubrecht Duijker in *The Wine Atlas of Spain*, these grapes were given nicknames, such as *afarta pobles*, people filler, and *quebranta-tinajas*, barrel buster.

The Penedès bodegas that specialize in still wines today have a reputation for creativity and have been quick to embrace interna-

*No firm has done more for Penedès still wines than Torres, today one of the largest and best-known wineries in Spain. Under the direction of the ever restless Miguel Torres, the winery has been at the forefront of numerous innovations. Seen here is Miguel Torres' Catalan estate, Agulladolc, in the stunning Sierra de Montserrat.*

## THE GRAPES OF
## THE PENEDÈS

### WHITES

**Chardonnay:** Increasingly used for *cava*, along with the native grapes listed below. Contributes finesse and aroma. Also used for still wines.

**Macabeo:** Major grape for *cava* and still wines; contributes fruity flavors and acidity. This is the grape known as viura in Rioja.

**Parellada:** Major grape for *cava* and still wines; contributes delicacy and aroma.

**Xarel-lo:** Major grape for *cava* and still wines; xarel-lo contributes alcohol, body, and acidity.

### REDS

**Cabernet Sauvignon:** Used alone and in blending to add depth, structure, complexity, and aging potential.

**Cariñena:** Major grape; in blends, contributes alcohol, body, and tannin. Known as mazuelo in Rioja and as carignan in France.

**Garnacha:** Minor grape. Contributes body and spiciness to still wines and rosé *cava*. Known as grenache in France.

**Merlot:** Minor grape generally used in blending to add depth, complexity, and aging potential.

**Monastrell:** Minor grape. Adds substantial body to still wines and rosé *cava*. Known as mourvèdre in France.

**Ull de Llebre:** Catalan for eye of the hare; local name for tempranillo. Major grape; contributes finesse, acidity, and aging potential.

tional varieties. Most make wines that are quite modern in style. Leading the way have been two family firms—Torres, a large producer, and the smaller Jean León. In 1979 world attention focused on Torres when its 1970 Gran Coronas Black Label (a wine composed of 70 percent cabernet sauvignon, 20 percent tempranillo, and 10 percent monastrell) was surreptitiously slipped into the Gault Millau French Wine Olympiad blind tasting of classified red Bordeaux. The Torres came out on top.

## THE LAND, THE GRAPES, AND THE VINEYARDS

The Penedès region is set off by striking natural boundaries. To the north is the Montserrat Massif, an awe-inspiring geological formation of mountains that from a distance resemble the teeth of a saw. To the east and south is the Mediterranean Sea. The terrain rises in a rugged steplike fashion from warm coastal land (the Low Penedès) to cooler high plateaus more than 2,000 feet above sea level (the High Penedès). A great many different microclimates are wedged into this modestly sized area of some 57,500 acres.

The Montserrat mountain range acts as an umbrella against harsh northern winds, and the Mediterranean Sea warms and tempers the climate. The diverse geology means that soil varies considerably. Much of it is calcareous on top, with alluvium and clay beneath. Small deposits of limestone are scattered throughout the region.

The production of white wines far outnumbers the production of red wines in the Penedès, and sparkling wines greatly outnumber still. As a result the three leading grapes are the native white grapes parellada, macabeo, and xarel-lo. Increasingly, chardonnay is also used for *cava*, either on its own or blended with the native varieties. These four grape varieties are also blended together or used on their own to make white still wines. This is also true of muscat, gewürztraminer, riesling, and sauvignon blanc, although these varieties represent only a tiny fraction of the grapes planted.

As for grapes used to make red and rosé wines, ull de llebre (the local Catalan name for tempranillo) and cariñena are the most important traditional varieties— ull de llebre for its balance, good acidity, and aging potential; cariñena for its alcohol, body, and tannin. Among international varieties, cabernet sauvignon leads in importance. Again, all of these varieties are used together in blends as well as on their own. Other red varieties used mostly for blending include the native grapes garnacha (which the French call grenache) and monastrell (mourvèdre to the French) and the international variety merlot.

# CAVA

Cava was the brainchild of Don José Raventós, head of the bodega Codorníu, who traveled throughout Europe during the 1860s selling red and white still wines, which the firm had been making since 1551. On one such mission, Raventós found himself in Champagne, where he was fascinated by the local sparkling wine. He returned to the Penedès keen to attempt his own sparkler. Using imported Champagne equipment and the three local white grapes still used in most *cava* today, Raventós produced Spain's first *méthode*

*champenoise* sparkler in 1872. The new wine was considered an intriguing triumph.

About this time, a small group of successful, forward-thinking winemaking families, including the Raventós family, began meeting every Sunday after the ten o'clock mass to discuss wine and share information. From these gatherings, an ambitious notion began to take shape.

## CAVA— DRY TO SWEET

After the yeasts are removed from each bottle, *cavas* are topped up with sweetened reserve wine. Depending on the level of sweetness in this wine (the *dosage*), a different category of *cava* can be made. The sweetness levels of *cava* are the same as those for Champagne. A brut *cava*, for example, has the same degree of sweetness as brut Champagne.

**Brut Nature**
Virtually bone-dry: 0 to .3% sugar
(0 to 3 grams of sugar per liter)

**Extra Brut**
Very, very dry: 0 to .6% sugar
(0 to 6 grams of sugar per liter)

**Brut**
Very dry: less than 1.5% sugar
(less than 15 grams of sugar per liter)

**Extra Dry—Extra Seco in Spanish**
Off-dry: 1.2 to 2% sugar
(12 to 20 grams of sugar per liter)

**Dry—Seco in Spanish**
Lightly sweet: 1.7 to 3.5% sugar
(17 to 35 grams of sugar per liter)

**Demi-Sec—Semiseco in Spanish**
Quite sweet: 3.3 to 5% sugar
(33 to 50 grams of sugar per liter)

**Sweet**
Very sweet: more than 5% sugar
(more than 50 grams of sugar per liter)

*Codorníu, one of the two largest sparkling wine firms in Spain, was founded in 1551 (it made still wines then) by the Raventós family, who remain its owners. In 1872, Don José Raventós (inset) made the first sparkling wine in Spain using the traditional Champagne method.*

458

Why not convert all of the local still wines to sparkling and establish the Penedès as Spain's Champagne region?

*When* cava *was first produced, it was called* champán *or* xampany. *Penedès winemakers, however, later decided that the sparkler was different enough from Champagne to deserve its own name. They agreed on* cava, *Catalan for cave or cellar.*

The nascent Penedès sparkling wine industry had barely begun, however, before it was ravaged by phylloxera in 1887. Luckily, several *cava* firms were able to survive until the antidote to phylloxera—replanting European vines on American rootstock that can tolerate the plant louse—was discovered. Today, by law *cava* can be made in any of six wine

## BILLIONS OF BUBBLES

〰️

More than 220 million bottles of *cava* are sold each year. Small bodegas such as Kripta make about 4,000 bottles a year. By contrast, a large firm such as Codorníu makes 44 million, and Freixenet makes 53 million (the Freixenet-owned firms Segura Viudas and Castellblanch make another 20 million). This makes Codorníu and Freixenet the two largest sparkling wine producers in the world. In addition to being rivals in Spain, the firms also compete in California. Freixenet owns the sparkling wine winery Gloria Ferrer; Codorníu owns Artesa Winery, which makes sparkling wine under the labels Cordoníu Napa and Joia (joy).

regions, however, 95 percent of all *cava*—and the best of it—is made in the Penedès. Indeed, the heart and soul of its production is the sleepy town of Sant Sadurní d'Anoia (in Catalan, or San Sadurní de Noya in Spanish) about 27 miles southwest of Barcelona.

To be called *cava*, a Spanish sparkling wine must be made by the same process employed in making French Champagne, in which the secondary fermentation (which creates the bubbles) takes place in each individual bottle (see page 168). (Lower-quality Spanish sparkling wines are made by the tank or bulk process method and cannot be called *cava*.)

*Less than 1 percent of all* cava *is rosé. Rosé* cava *tends to be fuller bodied than golden. The pink tinge may come from the addition of cabernet sauvignon, garnacha, or monastrell.*

Like Champagne, *cava* ranges in sweetness from brut nature, which is virtually bone-dry, to sweet (see page 457). The three driest categories (brut nature, extra brut, and brut) are the most popular. Also like Champagne, a *cava* can be either a nonvintage or a vintage wine. In nonvintage *cava* the wines that constitute the blend may come from several different years. In vintage *cava*, all of the wines in the blend come from the same year.

*Cava* must, by law, be made from one or more of five grape varieties: parellada, xarel-lo, and macabeo, plus chardonnay and the native variety subirat (malvasia), which has declined in impor-

## THE GYROPALETTE

In the early 1970s, Freixenet invented the gyropalette, sometimes called a *girasol,* Spanish for sunflower—a spherical steel frame that mimics *rémuage,* the process of gradually moving the sediment down into the downturned neck of the bottle. For more than two centuries, *rémuage* was done by hand, bottle by bottle, a process that is extremely time-consuming and costly. A typical gyropalette, by comparison, holds about 500 bottles of sparkling wine, and the entire frame is tilted and rotated incrementally by computer. Many studies have shown that gyropalettes are as effective at moving the spent yeasts down into the neck as traditional *rémuage.* Gyropalettes are now widely used throughout Spain and in California and France.

tance and is now rarely used. The first three are the most common and are used in widely varying proportions depending on the bodega, but rarely is one included to the exclusion of the others. Xarel-lo contributes a generous round body and good acidity. Macabeo is fruity and aromatic and also has good acidity. Parellada is the finest, most delicate of the three grapes and is grown in the higher, cooler vineyards. When chardonnay is added to these three varieties the resulting *cava* often has more finesse. The first *cava* to include chardonnay was Codorníu's Anna de Codorníu in 1981. Despite the success and high regard of *cavas* made in part from chardonnay, such wines are still limited in production.

## PAN CON COMFORT

Nothing could be more different than the behavior of the Spanish drinking *cava* and the behavior of the French drinking Champagne. Champagne is clearly a luxury often accompanied by that comparable indulgence, caviar. *Cava*, on the other hand, is comfort wine, the perfect way to begin a summer evening, especially when the *cava* is accompanied by a humble appetizer like *pan con tomate*, the Catalonian specialty of thick slices of warm grilled country bread, rubbed on both sides with the cut side of a juicy ripe tomato and then drizzled with extra-virgin olive oil. *Cava* and *pan con tomate* is any night fare—no special occasion required. Price, of course, has something to do with this, but then *cava* is nothing if not a steal.

In the end, the most important point is this: Even though Champagne was the inspiration behind it, *cava* is not sparkling wine trying to be Champagne. There are numerous things they do not have in common. Most of the grape varieties are different, with unique flavors and aromas. *Cava*, moreover, is the product of all white grapes, unlike most Champagne, which is a marriage of white and red grapes. The number of separate still wines blended to create *cava* is far smaller than the number of still wines in a Champagne blend. Vineyards in the Penedès are not rated for quality as they are in Champagne. Although certain vineyards are known to be better than others, the grapes from them are often simply mixed into a larger overall batch of grapes. Most *cava* is aged in contact with the yeasts for nine months, the legal minimum, while many Champagnes are aged at least fifteen months and usually far longer. Finally, there is the critical issue of *terroir*. Climatically and geologically, the Penedès and Champagne have almost nothing in common. How conceivable is it that the two wines could mirror one another in flavor?

All of this comes down to the fact that most *cava* tends to be fairly simple. Lemony and earthy, it's fruitier and has less frothy foam than Champagne or sparkling wine from California. In the past *cavas* were often described as having a rubbery or petrol quality, but that style is in decline. Today, the best *cavas* have a bright, citrusy streak of acidity running through them.

## WHO WOULDN'T LIKE TO BE THE BABY?

Since its beginnings at the turn of the twentieth century, *cava* has been readily consumed by the middle classes. Barcelona has dozens of *xampanyeria*, wine bars specializing in Spanish sparklers. It is a Catalonian family tradition to drive to Sant Sadurní on Saturdays for a picnic of *cava* and grilled lamb. Bodegas sell locally raised lamb and rent outdoor stone fireplaces. Of course, the sparkler is also sipped ceremoniously. At a baptism everyone drinks *cava*, even the baby, whose pacifier is dipped in the bubbly. Not to be left out (*cava* is a wine for everyone after all) and possibly more important, as a way of keeping them quiet in church, other babies may be given the same treat.

460

# THE CAVAS TO KNOW

## CODORNIU

Anna de Codorníu

vintage brut

approximately 90% chardonnay, 10% parellada

The first chardonnay-based *cava* made in Spain, this is a wine with wonderful finesse. A light custardy bouquet springs forth from the glass. The nice, biscuity finish is reminiscent of Champagne.

## HUGUET

*gran reserva*

vintage brut nature

approximately 75% parellada, with macabeo and chardonnay

Complex is a word not often heard in relation to *cava*, but the Huguet cannot be described any other way. It manages to be both breathtakingly dry, taut, and focused and, at the same time, creamy, generous, and supple. The wine comes from parellada grapes grown in select vineyards above 1,200 feet, and only when an importer or wine shop orders the wine is it riddled to remove the yeasts and disgorged, thereby giving the wine as much aging time in contact with the yeasts as possible.

## MIRO

nonvintage brut nature

approximately 50% parellada, 30% macabeo, and 20% xarel-lo

Lean, refined, and as distinct as the sound of two crystal glasses coming together, the Miro is another great example of the bracing quality contemporary *cava* aims for.

## MONT-MARCAL

vintage brut

approximately 30% parellada, 30% xarel-lo, and 30% macabeo

A *cava* with all the clean freshness of Irish air after a rain shower, the wine begins with a snappy lemon, ginger, and lime bouquet and finishes with a vibrant, lemony buzz. Mont-Marçal makes high definition *cavas* that have pinpoint acidity.

## SEGURA VIUDAS

Aria

nonvintage brut

approximately 60% macabeo, 20% xarel-lo, and 20% parellada

Aria is as alive, vibrant, and distinct as a saxophone solo. The usual earthiness and sometimes heavy fruitiness of *cava* is nowhere in evidence. Instead, there's a shower of lemon and the tart snap at the end could challenge a Granny Smith apple.

## SEGURA VIUDAS

Heredad

*reserva*

nonvintage brut

approximately 50% macabeo, 40% parellada, and 10% xarel-lo

The Earth Mother of *cavas*, the Segura Viudas Heredad (Spanish for estate) is the most satisying example of the creamy/earthy/spicy/almondy style of *cava*. The wine's copious flavors reverberate in your mouth. Its texture is both effervescent and silky. Heredad comes in what are surely the most expensive custom-made bottles in the Penedès. Labeled with metal crests, they are anchored by carved metal bases.

461

# PENEDÈS STILL WINES

A s the *cava* industry began to take serious form, Penedès still wines continued to evolve. The leading winery, Torres, was established in 1870. More than ever, this large (producing 2 million cases each year), family-owned bodega epitomizes the maverick streak for which Catalans are known.

Torres has experimental plantings of an astounding 170 different non-Penedès varieties, including roussanne, syrah, and chenin blanc from France; riesling and Müller-Thurgau from Germany; nebbiolo from Italy; and zinfandel from the United States. In 1970, when virtually all other Spanish whites were flat, soft, and even partially oxidized from being made and aged in wood, Torres produced Viña Sol, a snappy, aromatic, fresh white, made from 100 percent parellada and the first white wine in the country to be fermented in temperature-controlled, stainless steel tanks.

Torres went on to a number of other firsts, but their greatest achievement has always been the bodega's most prestigious wine, formerly called Gran Coronas Black Label (now known as Mas La Plana), made from 100 percent cabernet sauvignon. In 1979 when that wine (then a cabernet/tempranillo/monastrell blend) was slipped into a French blind tasting and came out on top over a field of renowned classified Bordeaux, Torres' reputation for quality was sealed. The Torres family also owns a winery in Chile plus Marimar Torres Estate, a prominent small winery in Sonoma, California, where

they have planted parellada to see what a native Spanish grape can achieve there. This is the only documented instance of parellada being grown in California.

The impulse to be avant-garde and the penchant for experimentation is not, however, limited to such a large bodega as Torres. The medium-size bodega Jean León was the first to plant and then produce chardonnay and cabernet sauvignon in the late 1960s. Cuttings for the chardonnay came from the Corton-Charlemagne holdings of Louis Jadot, and the cabernet came from Château Lafite-Rothschild. No Spanish varieties are grown on the estate.

Besides Torres and Jean León, there are many other excellent producers of still wines (see the list below), including Segura Viudas, primarily a *cava* producer.

---

*Some of the Best Producers of the Penedès*

### CAVA

CASTELLBLANCH

CAVAS HILL

CODORNÍU

FREIXENET

HUGUET

MIRO

MONT-MARÇAL

SEGURA VIUDAS

### STILL WINES

CAN FEIXES

CAN RÀFOLS DELS CAUS

JAUME SERRA

JEAN LEÓN

MASIA BACH

RAMON BALADA

SEGURA VIUDAS

TORRES

# THE FOODS
## OF THE PENEDÈS

Catalonian cuisine is the most complex and richly seasoned in Spain. The province's proximity to France, as well as Barcelona's longstanding role as a pivotal Mediterranean port, have given Catalonian food a depth, dimension, and sophistication not found in the other, more provincial regions of Spain. Though it is sometimes suggested that Catalonian cooking is similar to the cooking of Provence and various regions of Italy, something closer to the reverse is true. During the twelfth and thirteenth centuries, before Spain financed the exploration of the Americas, the kingdom of Aragon, including what is now Catalonia, ruled part of France as well as the kingdoms of Sicily and Naples. The cuisine that flourished within these regions, was a fertile mingling of Mediterranean ideas. Early on, Catalonian cooking was infused with a certain worldliness.

If cooking can be thought of as the voice of a given land, then Catalonian cooking tells the story of seacoast, farmland, and mountains. The larder includes shellfish, fish, lamb, wild game, veal, and pork, plus olive oil, garlic, tomatoes, onions, peppers, saffron, herbs, almonds, hazelnuts, fruits, and wine. Intriguingly, seafood is often combined with meat (spiny lobster and chicken in hazelnut sauce; baby squid stuffed with pork in chocolate sauce) as is meat with fruit (baby goose baked with pears; rabbit with quince and honey).

Four all-important sauces act as ties binding individual foods together. They are: *alioli, sofrito, picada,* and *romesco.* These are not truly sauces in the classic sense, however, but bold seasonings, unmasked by butter or cream. *Alioli* (or *allioli* in the Catalan spelling) is a mayonnaise-like emul-

sion of garlic and olive oil used as a condiment; *sofrito* (*sofregit* in Catalan), tomatoes and onion cooked in olive oil, is used as a flavor base; *picada,* a paste of garlic, almonds, olive oil, and possibly parsley, chocolate, saffron, and hazelnuts, is used as a seasoning and thickener; and *romesco* (*samfaina* in Catalan) is made from finely chopped almonds or hazelnuts combined with dried sweet peppers and tomatoes and is used both as a base and as a sauce.

Though it is often dramatic, Catalonian food is never fussy. The best-loved traditional dish of all is *pan con tomate,* called in Catalan *pa amb tomàquet*—bread with tomato—grilled country bread rubbed with ripe tomato, then drizzled with olive oil and sprinkled with salt. *Pan con tomate,* along with a few grilled fresh anchovies or slices of mountain ham, often begins a meal.

Other Catalonian classics include: *canalones,* the Catalonian version of Italian cannelloni, which are stuffed with ground pork, ground duck, spinach, veal, game, or fish; *zarzuela* (*sarsuela* in Catalan), a full-blown stew of shellfish and seafood, rather like bouillabaisse; *bacalao* (*bacalla*), dried salt cod that is made into many dishes including *brandade* (*brandada*), salt cod that has been desalted and whipped with potatoes, olive oil, and lots of garlic into a dish resembling mashed potatoes; and *mar i mutanya,* Catalan for sea and mountain, a homey ragout of fish and meat—sometimes chicken and prawns, sometimes rabbit, monkfish, and snails.

Finally, there is *crema catalana,* the Catalonian version of the French dessert crème brûlée, a rich creamy custard with a sheet of caramelized sugar on top. Catalans would wince to hear *crema catalana* thus described. The French dessert, they say, was inspired by theirs, not the other way around. Several food historians agree.

## MALVASIA FROM SITGES

＝⬥⬥⬥＝

A grape of ancient origin, malvasia is made into a tiny coterie of extraordinary dessert wines, including malmsey from the island of Madeira, malvasia delle Lipari from the island of Lipari off the Sicilian coast, and a malvasia made from grapes grown in the chalky soils of the seaside town of Sitges, south of Barcelona.

In the early part of the twentieth century, before the Spanish Civil War, the much sought-after malvasias of Sitges appeared on the finest upper-class dining tables of Europe. After the war, as Sitges increasingly became an affluent beach side hideaway, the vineyards disappeared. Today, one old bodega—Cellers J. Robert—remains, obstinately holding on to tradition. Its handcrafted malvasias have a cult following.

Both the regular Malvasia de Sitges and the *reserva* are made from grapes left to partially raisinate in the sun. The wines are extremely elegant, with gentle, gossamer-like notes of apricots, cream, and roasted nuts. Perfectly balanced, they hardly seem sweet.

# VISITING PENEDÈS BODEGAS

The *cava* giants, Freixenet and Codorníu, have sophisticated educational tours offered in several languages. In addition to a full tasting, visitors ride on tramcars through each bodega's underground aging cellars and watch films explaining *cava* production. Codorníu also has a striking wine museum.

By comparison, at a small *cava* bodega visitors are generally taken around by the owner/winemaker, and appointments must be made in advance. At small bodegas it helps to speak Spanish.

For still wines, Torres offers a complete tour, film, and tasting. Once again, visiting a small producer will make an interesting juxtaposition.

The telephone numbers include the dialing code you'll need when calling from the United States. If you're calling from within Spain, eliminate the 011-34 and add a zero before the next number.

### CAVA

**CASTELLBLANCH**
Avenida Casetas Mir, s/n
08770 Sant Sadurní de Noya,
Barcelona
011-34-93-818-30-01

**CODORNÍU**
Avenida Jaume Codorníu, s/n
08770 Sant Sadurní de Noya,
Barcelona
011-34-93-818-32-32

**FREIXENET**
2 Joan Sala
08790 Sant Sadurní de
Noya, Barcelona
011-34-93-818-32-00

### STILL WINES

**CAN RÀFOLS DELS CAUS**
s/n, 08739 Aviyonet del Penedès,
Barcelona
011-34-93-897-03-70

**JEAN LEÓN**
Mas Dén Rovira, Afueras, s/n
08775 Torrelavid, Barcelona
011-34-93-899-50-33

**MASIA BACH**
Ctra. Martorell—Capellades, km. 20.5
08781 Sant Esteve Sesrovires, Barcelona
011-34-93-771-40-52

**MIGUEL TORRES**
22 Commercio
08720 Villafranca del Penedès, Barcelona
011-34-93-817-74-00

# THE PENEDÈS STILL WINES TO KNOW

## Whites

### CAN RAFOLS DELS CAUS

Gran Caus

approximately 55% chardonnay,
40% xarel-lo, and 5% chenin blanc

The fish on the label suggest the right idea. This beautifully crafted, country white, with its fresh, lemony zip, begs for seafood. Many Catalans, including the owner of this family estate, believe that generously bodied, intensely fruity xarel-lo is the best native grape in the Penedès.

### SEGURA VIUDAS

Creu de Lavit

Xarel-lo

100% xarel-lo

Xarel-lo isn't often turned into a wine on its own, but the Creu de Lavit from Segura Viudas makes a very convincing case that it ought to be. If you're looking for a white wine unlike almost anything else you've tasted, this could be it. Aromas of pine forests open up into flavors that suggest lemons, mandarin oranges, and ripe peaches. Best of all, the wine manages to be creamy and incisively crisp at the same time. A great bet for seafood.

### TORRES

Viña Sol

100% parellada

The white wine that inspired winemakers all over Spain, Viña Sol was the first in the country to be made in temperature-controlled stainless steel

tanks, and rather than being aged, it was bottled soon after production. The result was—and today still is—a vibrant fresh wine that smells like a rain-drenched forest, while tart, appley flavors spring around in the glass. The wine's big sister is Gran Viña Sol, a blend of parellada and chardonnay briefly aged in French oak.

## Reds

### JAUME SERRA

reserva

approximately 60% cabernet sauvignon,
40% tempranillo

Jaume Serra reds are a beautiful expression of the delicious compatability of cabernet sauvignon and tempranillo. In good vintages the aromas and flavors are a collision of smoke, saddle leather, worn boots, damp earth, and roasted nuts—all wrapped in an easy-drinking silky textured wine.

### JEAN LEON

Cabernet Sauvignon

100% cabernet sauvignon

A wine with the posture, polish, and precision of a West Point cadet. Compact meaty, cranberry, and earth flavors wrap themselves around a nugget of ripe tannin and structure. There are bursts of eucalyptus and mint. The cuttings for the vineyard came from Château Lafite-Rothschild and the wine—unlike most cabernet sauvignon in

the Penedès—bears an unmistakable resemblance to top Bordeaux.

## TORRES

Mas La Plana

100% cabernet sauvignon

Known as Gran Cornas Black Label when it garnered world attention in 1979 by besting a group of classified Bordeaux in a blind tasting, Torres has renamed its wine Mas La Plana. In great years it does not so much command your attention as draw you in and make you want to listen to it. The texture is almost too svelte to suggest cabernet sauvignon, and the deep earth flavors are very satisfying.

## TORRES

Sangre de Toro

approximately 65% garnacha, 35% cariñena

Sangre de Toro (blood of a bull) has been one of the world's greatest wine values for decades. The name says it all—it's a masculine, structured wine, chock-full of simple, red cherry, earthy fruit.

## A MUST VISIT:
## THE MONASTERY OF MONTSERRAT

Built into the jagged peaks of one of the most awesome mountain ranges in the world is the monastery of Montserrat, poised like a guardian angel over the vineyards of the Penedès. Some say the mountains, which are shaped more like cylinders than pyramids, resemble contorted human forms; others, the ragged teeth of a saw. In fact, the words *mont serrat* in Catalan mean sawtooth mountain. The monks say the range was sawn by God.

The large Benedictine order living at Montserrat is devoted to preserving Catalonian culture —a mission that endears them to the Catalans. (So much so, that in tribute, thousands of Catalonian girls are named Montserrat—Montse for short.)

In the past Montserrat served as a political refuge. Under Franco's rule, scholars, artists, politicians, and students went there to meet in rooms that the monks rented out for a small fee. It was not unusual for the military police to be waiting a few miles down the mountainside. The monks still rent rooms, mostly now to poets in need of solitude or students who want to paint.

The monastery includes a museum of Catalonian art and a 200,000 volume library of rare manuscripts and engravings. There is also Montserrat's music school, Escolania, which dates from the thirteenth century, making it one of the oldest music schools in Europe. The fifty choir boys, who live and study with the monks, sing daily for visitors.

It is said that no Catalonian couple is ever truly married until they have come together to Montserrat, and so the monastery is always full of wedding parties. On Sundays these parties often break into the *sardana*, a gentle, rhythmic Catalonian round dance thought to be of Greek origin. Though it starts off as a small group of people holding hands, within minutes, the *sardana* is being danced by hundreds of people as everyone around joins in.

Montserrat is dedicated to La Moreneta, "the little dark one"—a sculpted black Virgin dating from the twelfth century.

# Rías Baixas

When the small white wine region of Rías Baixas (REE-ez BUY-shez) in far northwestern Spain came to prominence in the 1990s, a new era in Spanish white wine history was born. With the exception of Sherry, which is fortified, and *cava*, which is sparkling, the Spanish wines that have commanded world attention have always, almost exclusively, been red—not white. And with good reason. In the not so distant past, a typical Spanish white was made from grapes grown to produce big yields in a warm region and then left in a barrel where the fruit would dry out and the wine would begin to oxidize. To suggest

## THE QUICK SIP ON RÍAS BAIXAS

• Spain's most exciting whites are produced in this tiny northwest wine region.

• The best Rías Baixas whites are made from the albariño grape. The word *albariño* appears on every bottle. By comparison, most other Spanish wines are referred to by their geographic region.

• Albariño is a racy, refreshing wine considered one of the best matches in the world for seafood. It's meant to be drunk young.

467

*The cathedral of Santiago de Compostela is in the far western province of Galicia, where it was once thought the world ended. The vineyards of the Rías Baixas are not far from the "edge"—the Atlantic Ocean.*

that such baked, flat whites were an acquired regional taste would be charitable.

By the late 1980s and early 1990s, however, modern technology, including the use of temperature-controlled stainless-steel tanks, could be found in virtually all of the top wineries making white wine in Spain. Quality skyrocketed. Leading the way were the wines of Rías Baixas, a remote wine region poised on the Atlantic just above Portugal, in the southern part of the province of Galicia. Here, along the wind cooled coast, white grapes had been grown for centuries. But it wasn't until the technological revolution that the wines of Rías Baixas, referred to in Spain as wines of the sea, began to be considered among the best white wines in Spain.

*Galicia's ancient Celtic heritage is apparent in its music. The traditional local instrument is a* gaita, *similar in appearance and sound to a Scottish bagpipe.*

468

## THE GALEGOS

~~~

Rías Baixas is in the province of Galicia, which in numerous ways seems a world apart from Spain. The Galegos, as the people of Galicia are called, drink more wine and eat more seafood than any other Spaniards. They are hardworking, rural people of Celtic origin who, until the recent building of modern transportation routes, were geographically isolated from the rest of the country.

Like the Basques and the Catalans, the Galegos reinforced their separation and individuality by speaking their own distinct language, Galician. A Celtic sounding quasi-marriage of Spanish and Portuguese, Galician is an officially recognized language in the province and is taught, along with Spanish, in the schools.

Rías Baixas takes its name from the Galician words *rías*, sharp, fjordlike estuaries that slice like cobalt swords into the *baixas*, or lower part of southern Galicia. This is one of the world's most breathtaking wine regions and definitely one of the most unusual looking in Spain. It would be easy to think you were in Ireland or Wales—until you take note of the eucalyptus forests that cover the steep hills and deep ravines. Wild scarlet roses grow out of ancient Roman stone walls. Orange trees dance in the breeze. The mountainous air is pristine; the sun is like a scoop of lemon sorbet moving in and out of the thick coastal clouds. To find vineyards in the middle of this feels as though you've just uncovered a secret no one else knows.

PAZO DE SEÑORANS

Albariño

RIAS BAIXAS
DENOMINACION DE ORIGEN

12% vol.

Embotellado por R.E.N. N.º 6938/PO pat
Paradela-Mei

75 cl.

12,5% vol.

RIAS BAIXAS
DENOMINACION DE ORIGEN

*Fillaboa*

*Albariño*

VINO ELABORADO CON UVA DE NUESTROS VIÑEDOS DE LA VARIEDAD

ELABORADO Y EMBOTELLADO EN LA PROPIEDAD
GRANJA FILLABOA, S.A.- SALVATERRA (PONTEVEDRA)
R.E N.5467 - B.E M 003408 - PO
ESPAÑA

The best Rías Baixas wines are made principally from the white albariño grape. In fact, albariño, not Rías Baixas, is the name by which the wines are commonly known and labeled. This is in complete contrast to other Spanish wine regions where wines are typically referred to by region (i.e., Rioja), not according to the grape planted (i.e., tempranillo).

Albariño has a unique flavor profile. Not as zaftig as chardonnay, nor as minerally as riesling, nor as wild and herbal as sauvignon blanc, its flavors range from zingy citrus-peach to almond-honeysuckle. In texture, albariños are supple and lightly creamy. Yet because generally the wines are neither fermented nor aged in wood, the best of them are as light as gossamer on the palate.

Albariño's history is not entirely known nor is it well understood how the grape came to Galicia and northern Portugal, where known as alvarinho it is one of the grapes that is made into the Portuguese wine known as Vinho Verde. Curiously, the grape is not found in any other part of Spain, except for recent plantings in experimental vineyards. There is folkloric speculation that albariño is Germanic in origin and may have been brought from the Rhine in the twelfth century by Cistercian monks on their long pilgrimages to the tomb of the apostle James in the holy city of Santiago de Compostela in far west Spain. During the Middle Ages it was thought that that was where the world ended. However, like other native grapes along the Atlantic coast, albariño may simply have evolved over centuries through the miscegenation of grape species.

While grapes have been planted in Galicia for centuries, the hodgepodge of local varieties (plus inferior but high-yielding hybrids planted after phylloxera devastated the vineyards in the late nineteenth century) were, for the most part,

469

*In the 1980s, a mini wine revolution in Rías Baixas spawned scores of small, modern wineries producing sensational albariños. Until that point most wineries operated as they had for centuries, including using old wooden presses.*

haphazardly made into wine by families for private use. The Galegos, provincial and poor, spent very little money on making their wine. Because they drank every drop, there was never any commercial impetus to improve it. At the bodega Santiago Ruiz, for example, the old wooden presses and primitive winemaking tools now displayed in the bodega's museum look as though they were used more than a century ago. They were. And they were still being used up until the 1980s.

Other modern winemaking techniques also came late here, long after such practices had been established for decades in parts of Europe and in the United States. It was not until the late 1970s that a process as fundamental as racking, or filtering the sediment out of wine, was used. Self-taught Galego winemakers simply stored their wines standing up so that the particles that precipitated out would settle to the bottom of the bottle.

Statistics portray the radical turnaround best of all. In 1986, there were only five commercial wineries in Rías Baixas.

Two years later, there were eighty-eight. The exhilarating boom was driven by an emerging class of wealthy, well-educated Galegos with a profound sense of regional pride. Small consortiums of lawyers, doctors, and businessmen formed, buying and replanting family vineyards, building state-of-the-art wineries, investing huge sums in modern equipment, and most important, hiring young, well-trained enologists from Europe's enology schools.

# THE LAND, THE GRAPES, AND THE VINEYARDS

The western coast of Galicia is a wet place. Rainfall is heavy, some 50 or more inches each year. Yet critically, the rains usually occur in winter when the vines are dormant, not during early fall around harvest. Moisture, nonetheless, is a problem. Because mildew, mold, and fungal diseases are all threats, the vines are sometimes trained on *parras*. These are canopies of support wires attached to 8 to 10 foot high granite columns. At harvest, tractors run under the *parras* and pickers, working from stepladders, pick grapes that are over their heads. Lifted far above the land in this manner, not only are the grapes less affected by ground moisture but the increased air circulation also helps keep them dry. Dew and moisture notwithstanding, the presence of the ocean nearby is a positive force (as it is in Bordeaux), mitigating wide swings in temperature and otherwise extreme climatic conditions.

Though a small *Denominación de Origen*, Rías Baixas is spread over three

## THE GRAPES OF
## RÍAS BAIXAS

Rías Baixas is known exclusively for white wines.

**Albariño:** Major grape. Extremely aromatic and flavorful.

**Loureira:** Minor grape. Sometimes blended in for added aroma.

**Treixadura:** Minor grape. Sometimes blended in for body and added aroma.

noncontiguous areas. The northernmost zone is Val do Salnés; the most inland and more mountainous zone is Condado de Tea; and O Rosal, named for the roses that grow everywhere, is just over the border from Portugal. Each zone has its share of very good wines and top producers. The best vineyards have well-draining sandy/granitic soil, some of which has clay and limestone mixed in. They are planted on southwest-facing slopes to ensure the maximum number of hours of sun for ripening.

*Because of the great demand for it, albariño is one of the most expensive white grapes in Spain.*

Albariño is full of personality. Beautifully aromatic, it's a potpourri of citrus, lime, vanilla, peach, honey, and kiwi smells. The irresistible flavors range from almond-vanilla to ginger-spice. To underscore the freshness of these flavors, winemakers handle the grapes as little as possible. And because albariños are almost never barrel fermented, the flavors ring pure and vibrant.

Virtually all Rías Baixas bodegas make only one albariño. Such categories as *reserva* or *gran reserva* do not exist. There are a few plantings of red grapes in Rías Baixas, but no superior red wines have been made.

*Some of the Best Producers
of Albariño*

**AS LAXAS**

**BODEGA MORGADÍO**

**BODEGAS DE
VILARIÑO-CAMBADOS**

**BODEGAS SALNESUR**

**LAGAR DE CERVERA**

**LUSCO DO MIÑO**

**MAR DE FRADES**

**PAZO DE SEÑORANS**

**PAZO SAN MAURO**

**TERRAS GAUDA**

**VIONTA**

*Along the western coast of Galicia the grapes of Rías Baixas grow in a wet maritime climate. For centuries vines have been trained canopy style on overhead trellises called* parras, *which minimize the risk of mildew and rot.*

## THE BEST SEASIDE TAVERN IN SPAIN?

After countless pilgrimages (what else can they be called?) to the world's wine regions, I keep coming back to a final ineluctable truth: The most blissful experiences with food and wine are utterly, nakedly simple. They are experiences so pure they leave you helpless, speechless, and nearly mindless with joy—capable only of licking your fingers.

Tasca Xeito, a humble tavern across the road from the sea in the village of La Guardia in the southernmost corner of Galicia, may be the best seaside tavern in Spain. The word *xeito* refers to the local art of fishing for sardines. And as could only be true in a place where fish are revered, the word also means beauty or charm.

*Chus Castro, the sensational self-taught chef of Tasca Xeito.*

You walk through the bar to a small back room with no-nonsense red tablecloths, heavy wooden chairs, and Spanish ceramics on the walls. Nothing about the place prepares you for the fact that this is unquestionably one of the greatest seafood restaurants in Spain.

The chef, Chus Castro, is self-taught, and she has never cooked any place else. Each morning she walks across the street to the sea and buys the day's fish directly off boats that have just returned with their catch.

Señora Castro asks how hungry you are and then proceeds to cook for you as though you were sitting at her kitchen table. She might begin by making miniature *croquetas de bueyes de mar,* sweet creamy crab croquettes or *pimientos del piquillo rellenos,* peppers stuffed with wild mushrooms, prawns, and salmon. Next comes a huge *langosta*—spiny lobster—with sweet, juicy, snow-white meat, and then *lenguado a la plancha,* a pristine fresh sole broiled with a touch of ripe olive oil. Each fish is simply cooked and served. There are no adornments, no garnishes, and no sauces—just waves of oceanic flavor, so pure you could faint.

*Tasca Xeito, 19 Rúa Dr. Fernández Albor, La Guardia, Galicia; 011-34-986-61-04-74.*

## THE FOODS OF RÍAS BAIXAS

Seafood lovers go mad in Rías Baixas—in fact, anywhere in Galicia—for this is the single greatest seafood region in a country legendary for its fish. In the north, along the Cantabrian coast and in the west, along the Atlantic coast, Galicia is splintered by deep estuaries (the Rías Altas and Rías Baixas respectively). These fjord-like channels act as enormous funnels for fish. The seafood catch in Galicia is one of the largest in Europe.

Shellfish is pristine and dizzying in its variety: scallops, mussels, prawns, shrimp, lobster, crayfish, crabs, clams, spiny lobster, sea snails, oysters, cockles, barnacles, and more. Galicia is also famous for one of the most ugly and delicious seafoods imaginable: *percebes.* Goosenecked gray barnacles the size of a man's thumb, *percebes* are harvested by divers who, wearing protective helmets, lower themselves into the

## A HINT OF KIWI

—⁓⁓—

**M**any wine drinkers find an intriguing kiwi aroma in albariño. Just happenstance? In fact, kiwi is a major agricultural crop in Rías Baixas, and many bodegas have orchards. In the last several years, however, numerous kiwi orchards have been pulled out in order to plant more albariño, a more remunerative crop.

crashing waves off the treacherous cliffs of Costa de la Muerte, Death's Coast. Each year several divers die in their pursuit of *percebes*. The barnacle is, needless to say, expensive.

Grilled *pulpo* (octopus), sweet and tender, is another Galician specialty. On Sundays after church, the bars and tavernas are full of families eating *pulpo* drizzled with emerald olive oil served with wondrously crusty country bread. Glasses of chilled albariño are found on every table.

For centuries the Galegos have been renowned as particularly fearless fishermen who not only fish the *rías* but also venture far out into the ocean. Thus, the seafood kaleidoscope here also includes deep-sea fish, such as cod, hake, sardines, turbot, sole, and angler.

Fresh seafood lends itself to utterly simple cooking techniques. Over time, the simplicity afforded seafood came to define virtually every aspect of Galician cooking. The most complex Galician specialty, empanadas, is not particularly complicated at all. Empanadas are double-crusted pies usually filled with scallops, eel, potatoes, sardines, tuna, or pork. The filling is sautéed in olive oil with peppers, tomatoes, onions, and garlic. The crust is made from wheat flour or cornmeal. Empanadas are served in the humblest bars as well as in Galicia's best restaurants.

Finally, Galician cookery is also influenced by the region's Celtic roots. The potato is revered. In *caldo gallego*, the

473

*The Galician coast is one of Europe's greatest fisheries and the Galegos are among the continent's most renowned fishermen. The sheer range of delicious fresh fish is mind-boggling and begs to be washed down with albariño.*

## A BLESSED MARRIAGE

It hardly seems coincidental that Galicia, renowned in all of Europe for the abundance and variety of its seafood, would specialize in a wine considered one of the most compatible in the world with seafood, and albariño is. The wine's capacity to seem both crisp and creamy at the same time, plus its pure, clean flavors reminiscent of quince, almonds, ginger, and lemons make it a stunning partner for all sorts of simply prepared seafood dishes. But if there's one type of seafood just made for albariño, it's scallops. The sweet purity of scallops, often overwhelmed by other whites, is perfectly underscored by Spain's most famous white wine. In Galicia itself scallops have been treasured for centuries. For more than a thousand years the travelers who have walked across northern Spain on religious pilgrimages to the tomb of the apostle James in Galicia's Santiago de Compostela have taken the scallop shell as their religious symbol. The stone walls of Santiago's stunning cathedral are covered with carved scallop shells, and during the Middle Ages the millions who made the pilgrimage each year decorated their cloaks and hats with badges in the shape of scallop shells.

region's most famous peasant stew, potatoes are combined with kale, beans, pieces of pork (ear and tail), spicy sausage, and sometimes veal and chicken. Every Galician loves his or her mother's *caldo gallego*.

## VISITING RÍAS BAIXAS BODEGAS

It is possible to visit the bodegas of Rías Baixas, but you must call in advance. The bodegas are small, and chances are you will be shown around by the owner or winemaker. It helps to speak Spanish. The telephone numbers include the dialing code you'll need when calling from the United States. If you're calling from within Spain, eliminate the 011-34 and add a zero before the next number.

**BODEGAS MORGADÍO**
arrangements can be made through its business office at
18-20 Maria Berdiales
36203 Vigo, Pontevedra
011-34-986-43-42-33

**GRANJA FILLABOA**
La Fillaboa
36459 Salvaterra de Miño, Pontevedra
011-34-986-65-81-32

**PAZO DE SEÑORANS**
Vilanoviña
36616 Meis, Pontevedra
011-34-986-71-53-73

**PAZO SAN MAURO**
8 Travesía Alcalde Portanet
36210 Vigo, Pontevedra
011-34-986-20-41-20

**SANTIAGO RUIZ**
San Miguel de Tabagón
36770 O Rosal, Pontevedra
011-34-986-61-40-83

# THE RÍAS BAIXAS WINES TO KNOW

*The cool, relatively wet coastal region of Rías Baixas specializes
in only one white wine, albariño.*

## BODEGAS DE VILARINO-CAMBADOS

Albariño

Martin Codax

100% albariño

Albariño can be dramatically creamy, as the crème-brûlée-like texture of this wine proves, and the flavor can be a swirl of honeysuckle and marzipan. Martin Codax, named after a twelfth-century Galego poet, was the first albariño to be exported to the United States in 1988.

## BODEGAS SALNESUR

Albariño

Condes de Albarei

100% albariño

Like a young colt, Bodegas Salnesur's albariño exudes energy. There is an almost minerally, slatelike flavor to the wine plus heaps of lemony intensity and a slight zesty spritz. Condes de Albarei is one of the better-known albariños, easily found in Galicia's best seafood bars.

## LUSCO DO MINO

Albariño

100% albariño

With albariño, purity and intensity of flavor is everything. Lusco (the word means twilight in Galician) possesses both. The wine's gorgeously concentrated quince, ginger, and almond flavors and bright focused acidity make it irresistible. Best of all, there's an elegance and creaminess here that elevates this albariño to top rank.

## MAR DE FRADES

Albariño

100% albariño

Mar de Frades' striking royal blue bottle suggests a kind of sea freshness—which is just what you get. The flavors of the wine seesaw back and forth between fresh, vibrant ginger, spice, and citrus fruit and vanilla marzipan creaminess. Extremely light, with a finish that calls to mind cream soda and ginger ale.

## MORGADIO

Albariño

100% albariño

It is a rare wine that manages to be both lightly etched and deeply profound in flavor at the same time, but the Morgadío pulls it off. It's as though every elegant molecule were singing at the top of its lungs. In most years, wonderful splashes of ginger and almond plus a creamy body and a light tropical fruit and vanilla finish give the wine real zing and complexity.

## PAZO SAN MAURO

Albariño

100% albariño

In an almost Dolly Parton-like fashion, the Pazo San Mauro is tight and fleshy at the same time. In good years, the wine virtually bursts forward with seductive, lush vanillaness, yet it is so refreshing, crisp, and focused that the flavors seem magnified. The vineyard, which dates from 1591, rests on small rolling hills along a tiny tributary of the Miño River. On the other side of the river is Portugal. For centuries the Portuguese and Galegos have fought over the vineyard.

475

# Priorato

Often called by its Catalan name Priorat, Priorato is a tiny isolated wine region just west of Tarragona in Catalonia, but it is also Spain's brightest new star. Barely heard of in the early 1990s, the region has recently emerged on the international scene with a handful of exciting and highly sought after wines, some of which have upstaged even the most prestigious Riojas by costing four times as much. If all of this seems improbable, what makes it more surprising still is that this is happening in Spain, a country so enamored of tradition that it has rarely found itself on the vinous cutting edge. If Priorato is any evidence, perhaps that has begun to change.

Like Penedès, Priorato is an ancient wine region where vines grew centuries before the Romans arrived to mine lead and silver. It acquired its name during the Middle Ages when, as the story goes, a villager had a vision of angels ascending and descending a stairway to heaven. As a result, in 1163 Alfonso II of Aragón founded a Carthusian monastery on the spot. The monastery became known as Scala Dei (God's stairway) and given the important presence of the monks, the region was called Priorato, from the Spanish word for priory. Today, though the monastery has been long abandoned, the little hamlet nearby is still known as Scala Dei, and one of the region's bodegas, Cellars de Scala

*In the rugged, rocky, rural landscape of Priorato, little besides vines and olive trees grow. A Carthusian monastery founded here in the twelfth century led to the name Priorato, from the Spanish word for priory.*

Dei, operates in some of the old buildings that once belonged to the monastery.

The region's most famous wines are all red, and they are some of the most intense, inky, and powerful red wines in Spain (and as I said before, some of the most pricey). Massively structured and high in alcohol and tannin, they have thick Port-like textures and are loaded with ripe blackberry fruit, chocolate, and licorice flavors. The wines' concentration is a result of painfully low yielding old vines, which protrude, gnarled and contorted, from the poor, rocky, slate-laced soil called *llicorella* (licorice) because of its blackish color. Days here are intensely hot; nights, very cool. In this dry, infertile, unforgiving landscape, few crops other than grapevines and olive trees have ever survived.

The vineyards are scattered over a valley and up slopes more than 3,000 feet in elevation. Since much of the terrain is mountainous, many of these old vineyards are planted on terraces built centuries ago. Though the slate slopes are slippery and the heat in summer can be blistering, the vineyards are still worked by hand with only mules and horses for assistance. Tractors haven't been invented that could negotiate such vineyards as these.

Priorato's wines are based primarily on two native red grapes, garnacha and cariñena (known in France as grenache and carignan respectively). This is a bit surprising since almost everywhere else, with the notable exception of Châteauneuf-du-Pape and the rest of the southern Rhône, garnacha and cariñena are not considered particularly capable of producing great wines. In Priorato they have found a place to excel. In addition to these two varieties, some wines also contain smaller amounts of cabernet sauvignon, merlot, syrah, and tempranillo.

## THE GRAPES OF PRIORATO

Priorato is home to red grapes almost exclusively.

**Cabernet Sauvignon:** Used as an important blending grape though usually in small amounts in wines based primarily on cariñena and garnacha. Contributes structure.

**Cariñena:** Native Spanish grape and one of the two major grapes in Priorato, the other being garnacha, with which cariñena is blended. Known as carignan in France, where the grape sometimes makes undistinguished wine. Here, just the opposite is true; cariñena contributes intensity, depth, and concentrated fruit flavors.

**Garnacha:** Along with cariñena, with which it is usually blended, one of the two major grapes in the region. Contributes richness, juiciness, body, and density. Though a native Spanish grape, garnacha is better known in France where it is called grenache.

**Merlot:** Minor grape. Used as part of the blend in wines based on cariñena and garnacha. Adds structure and roundness.

**Syrah:** Minor grape. Like merlot, used as part of the blend in wines based primarily on cariñena and garnacha. Adds depth and earthiness.

**Tempranillo:** Minor grape used as a blender. Contributes aroma and acidity.

Unlike the wines of Rioja or Ribera del Duero, the wines of Priorato are not categorized according to the hierarchy of *crianza*, *reserva*, and *gran reserva*. And Priorato wines are much more likely to be aged in new French oak than used American oak. France has also inspired many of the wines' names. Clos Mogador, Clos de l'Obac, Clos Erasmus, and Clos Martinet all borrow the French concept of a *clos*, or a small defined vineyard where, by inference, special high-quality wines are made. Not all the wine is dry; several Priorato bodegas also make sweet, fortified red wines called *vis dolçes* (Catalan for sweet wines). These sweet bombs, with their syrupy textures and flavors of chocolate-covered cherries, can be simply extraordinary and are priced accordingly.

Until the 1990s there were very few independent bodegas in Priorato. Because the vineyards were difficult to work and the region was isolated and poor, most vineyards were just small plots tended by owners who sold their grapes to the local cooperatives. The cooperatives in turn made high-octane reds that were appealing in their rusticity but short on finesse. While cooperatives still dominate and the number of independent estates remains small, the situation is rapidly changing. Beginning in the early 1990s a few ambitious growers as well as visionary winemakers from elsewhere in Spain decided that the region's potential for producing

truly fine wine was just too great to ignore. Among the first independent bodegas to be founded were Costers del Siurana and Alvaro Palacios, two that remain among the best. Costers del Siurana makes the rich, deeply fruity wine Clos de l'Obac from garnacha and cariñena and the big, soft, chocolatey, plummy Miserere from garnacha, cariñena, cabernet sauvignon, tempranillo, and merlot. From Alvaro Palacios come what have become the two leading collector's wines from Priorato: the super-expensive, hugely concentrated, and lush L'Ermita, made from 100 percent garnacha, and its (theoretically) less powerful little sister Finca Dofi, though Finca Dofi, a blend of garnacha, cariñena, cabernet sauvignon, syrah, and merlot, is massive and supercomplex itself. In addition to Alvaro Palacios and Costers del Siurana, other top bodegas include Clos Erasmus, Clos Martinet, Morlanda, and Clos Mogador. The wines from Cellers de Scala Dei, while not quite as close to the top of God's staircase as the others, are also good. You'll frequently find all these wines labeled with the Catalan Priorat rather than the Spanish Priorato.

# Portugal

PORT
MADEIRA
PORTUGUESE TABLE WINES

More than any other European country, Portugal has remained steeped in tradition even as it has modernized. The grapes for certain wines are still painstakingly trodden by foot in ancient *lagares*, and in the hilly wine regions of the northeast, vineyards must still be worked by hand. The persistence of tradition is due in large part to the importance of Port, Portugal's most famous wine and a wine that, like Spanish Sherry and French Champagne, is still meticulously handcrafted using methods that are centuries old.

Port is a lusciously sweet, powerfully fortified wine, the drinking of which can only be described as a turbocharged experience. Since its evolution from the 1700s onward, it has been considered one of the most remarkable wines in the world. Because it is indeed Portugal's most extraordinary wine, Port leads off the chapter, followed by Madeira, Portugal's other sensational fortified wine. But

Portugal ranks fourteenth in wine-producing countries worldwide. The Portuguese drink an average of 12.51 gallons of wine per person each year; they're sixth in world wine consumption.

*If it looks exhausting but fun, it is. At Quinta do Noval, treading grapes by foot in the shallow stone troughs known as* lagares *is still practiced, though generally only for the quinta's best wines.*

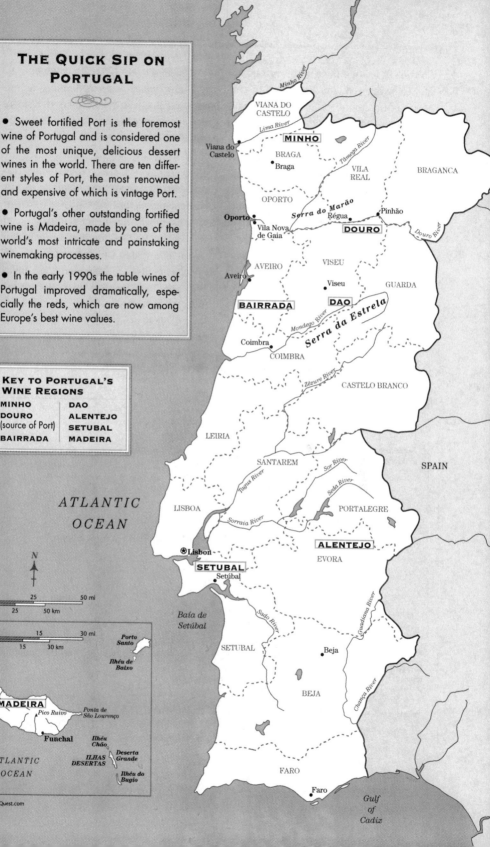

# THE QUICK SIP ON PORTUGAL

- Sweet fortified Port is the foremost wine of Portugal and is considered one of the most unique, delicious dessert wines in the world. There are ten different styles of Port, the most renowned and expensive of which is vintage Port.

- Portugal's other outstanding fortified wine is Madeira, made by one of the world's most intricate and painstaking winemaking processes.

- In the early 1990s the table wines of Portugal improved dramatically, especially the reds, which are now among Europe's best wine values.

## KEY TO PORTUGAL'S WINE REGIONS

| | |
|---|---|
| **MINHO** | **DAO** |
| **DOURO** | **ALENTEJO** |
| (source of Port) | **SETUBAL** |
| **BAIRRADA** | **MADEIRA** |

*ATLANTIC OCEAN*

N

0   25   50 mi
0   25   50 km

0   15   30 mi
0   15   30 km

Porto Santo

Ilhéu de Baixo

**MADEIRA**
Pico Ruivo
**Funchal**
Ponta de São Lourenço

Ilhéu Chão
**ILHAS DESERTAS**
Deserta Grande
Ilhéu do Bugio

*ATLANTIC OCEAN*

© MapQuest.com

Minho River

VIANA DO CASTELO

Lima River

Viana do Castelo

**MINHO**

BRAGA
• Braga

Tâmega River

VILA REAL

BRAGANCA

OPORTO

**Oporto**
• Vila Nova de Gaia

Serra do Marão
Régua
• Pinhão

**DOURO**

Douro River

AVEIRO

VISEU

Aveiro

• Viseu

GUARDA

**BAIRRADA**

**DAO**

Serra da Estrela

Mondego River

Coimbra
•

**COIMBRA**

Zêzure River

CASTELO BRANCO

LEIRIA

SANTAREM

Sor River

SPAIN

Seda River

LISBOA

Sorraia River

PORTALEGRE

Tagus River

**ALENTEJO**

⊛ Lisbon

**SETUBAL**
Setúbal

EVORA

Baía de Setúbal

Sado River

Guadiana River

SETUBAL

• Beja

BEJA

Chanca River

FARO

• Faro

Gulf of Cadiz

Portugal's leading table wine regions are not to be ignored. You'll also find discussions of the Minho, source of Portugal's most noteworthy white wine, Vinho Verde; Douro, home to table wines as well as to Port; Dão; Bairrada; and, at the end of this section, Alentejo.

Historically, there have been two Portugals—the Portugal that made Port and the Portugal that made dry table wines. The two worlds rarely overlapped, and the vast majority of producers made either one style of wine or the other, not both. Port was renowned but, with one or two exceptions, the country's table wines were cloaked in obscurity. Change came swiftly in the late 1980s. As wineries making table wines were modernized and as new capital was invested in equipment and in improving vineyards, Portugal's table wines, especially its reds, began to soar in quality. Today wine estates are increasingly making fine wine (as opposed to inexpensive quaffing wine), and the prestigious Port firms are moving into the table wine business, too.

Portugal, like its Iberian neighbor Spain, is carpeted with vineyards. A country that is just 370 miles long, 125 miles wide, and smaller than the state of Kentucky, it nonetheless ranks fourteenth in world wine production. An astounding

482

## READING A PORT WINE LABEL

Proprietary name of the wine

Average age of the blend

Type of Port

Bottling date

Name of the producer and bottler

Name of the producer

Date company was founded

Percentage of alcohol by volume

Volume in milliliters

Required by United States law

Country of origin

Name of the importer

230 different grape varieties grow there, more than 80 of which can be found in the Douro alone. Many of these are ancient, rare varieties and were probably brought to Portugal by the Phoenicians directly from the Middle East. Since those early times, Portuguese vines have had to struggle formidably to survive. Much of the land is impoverished, the summers can be unbearably hot, and in the northeast, the land is often so rugged, steep, and impassable that dynamite must be used to help clear narrow terraces for vineyards.

# PORTUGAL'S WINE LAWS

Portugal's wine industry was dramatically modernized after the country joined the European Union in 1986. The Douro was first delimited more than two centuries earlier—in 1756—but today, it plus another thirty-nine of Portugal's fifty-five wine regions are considered *Denom-*inação de Origem Controlada* or DOCs (denominations of controlled origin). Portugal's DOC laws are similar to France's *Appellation d'Origine Contrôlée* laws. Wines with DOC status must meet stringent requirements as set forth by the Instituto da Vinha e do Vinho (Institute of Vines and Wines), as well as by numerous local commissions. In addition, the DOCs Port and Madeira have separate governing bodies of their own.

The requirements for wine regions stipulate the total acreage that may be planted, the types of grapes and their maximum yield, the methods of vinification, the minimum length of time wines must be aged, and the information given on the label. As for labeling, most Portuguese table wines are named according to the geographic area from which they come: Douro, Dão, Alentejo, and so forth. However, some wines are also labeled according to grape variety. If the grape variety is given, at least 85 percent of the grapes for that wine must be of that variety.

# PORT

If Portugal is the mother of Port, Britain is certainly its father. The famous Port firms were, for the most part, begun by men with such properly British names as Sandeman, Croft, Graham, Cockburn, Dow, and Warre. British men, in fact, were not only Port's founders but also its most ardent, if exclusionistic, advocates. In fact, until recently Port might have been described as the most sexist beverage on earth. The quintessential man's drink, it was historically brought out (with great celebration and obligatory cigars) only after women had left the room. Women don't leave the room anymore, of course, and Port sales are probably the better for it.

Although the ancient Greeks and Romans prized the juicy red wines from the steep banks of the Douro River in northeastern Portugal, centuries passed before the ingenious British transformed these wines from simple tasty quaffs into Port, Britain's early version of central heating. There is a fable about Port's birth, even though in reality the wine's "invention" was more like a series of discoveries than a single creative act. As the apocryphal story goes, two young English wine merchants were traveling through Portugal in the late 1670s, looking for wines that would be saleable on the British market. For centuries the English had drunk mostly French wines. But from the mid-fifteenth century onward, escalating rivalry between the two nations had led to punitive import duties not to mention war. As the amount of French wine exported to Britain dwindled, Portuguese and Spanish wines increasingly made up the difference. The two young merchants supposedly found themselves at a monastery outside the town of Lamego near the Douro River. The abbot there served them a wine that was smoother, sweeter, and more interesting than any they'd tasted. When the young men pressed the abbot to tell them more, he confided that he'd added brandy to the wine as it fermented.

*The name Port is derived from the city of Oporto, a major port on the Atlantic at the mouth of the Douro River—the river of gold. Oporto is the second largest city in Portugal after Lisbon.*

What actually happened was far less fanciful. By the seventeenth century, wine was regularly being fortified with grape spirits simply to make it more stable during the voyage to England. At first the amount was small, about 3 percent. But then an incredible vintage in the year of 1820 caused Port shippers to rethink their product. That year the wine was remarkably rich, ripe, and naturally sweet. Sales soared. The next year, hoping to re-create their success, Port shippers added a greater amount of brandy and added it

## PORT SHIPPERS

〜〜〜

Most Port firms are called shippers because they originally shipped wine, still in casks, from Portugal to importers in England, who would then bottle and label the wine with their own name or brand. Today, although almost all styles of Port must by law be bottled in Portugal, the practice of referring to Port companies as shippers remains. There are slightly more than a hundred Port shippers in Portugal today.

*The legendary Factory House in Oporto, the historic British meetinghouse cum gentleman's club used by Port shippers for business and social purposes.*

*Barcos (above and left)—flat-bottomed, open boats that transport barrels of Port on the Douro River.*

sooner in order to arrest fermentation earlier and leave more sweetness in the wine. The idea worked. Gradually, over the course of many decades, the amount of grape spirits was incrementally increased, producing a sweet wine that is substantially fortified at the same time.

Port comes from only one place in the world, the 70-mile-long demarcated Port region in the Douro river valley. The Rio Douro begins in Spain (where it's known as the Duero River), northeast of Madrid, then carves a westward path through the rugged plains until it finally forges its way across the border. In Portugal the river cuts a gorgelike valley through the arid, rocky, unforgiving land, ultimately crossing the entire country and washing into the Atlantic at the town of Oporto.

# THE LAND, THE GRAPES, AND THE VINEYARDS

That vineyards are planted in the Douro is a testament to human will, for this is one of the most unmerciful environments in which grapes manage to grow. The hillsides of the river valley are extremely steep banks of schist and granite. These hardened rock slopes originally contained so little soil that more had to be carried there or created through generations of human labor. In many places the rock was chipped by hand with hammers and pointed iron poles (or later blasted with dynamite) and then mixed with organic matter. As the hillsides relented, thousands upon thousands of narrow terraces were built by hand and planted with vines.

The presence of schist and granite is extremely important. Both drain water well, and so the vines' roots must tunnel deeply (as much as 65 feet down) within the rocky crevices for nourishment. Roots that burrow deep into the earth find a stable environment there and thus become more stable themselves. This is critical in the Douro where the vines must be sturdy in order to survive the blazingly hot daytime temperatures.

*The forebodingly steep hillsides of the Douro valley range from 35 to 70 degrees in inclination. Terrace walls can be 15 feet high. These are some of the cruelest vineyards to work in Portugal's furnacelike summers.*

The Douro's long summers are infamous. Often the temperatures rise so high the vines temporarily shut down and wait until night to transport nutrients from the leaves to the grapes. The heat, luckily, is dry thanks to the Serra do Marão moun-

485

## THE MOST IMPORTANT

# PORTUGUESE WINES

LEADING WINES

**Alentejo** red

**Bairrada** red

**Dão** red

**Douro** red

**Madeira** white (fortified; dry and sweet)

**Port** red (fortified; sweet)

**Vinho Verde** white

WINE OF NOTE

**Setúbal** white (fortified; sweet)

*The harvest in the Douro is back-breaking work. The extremely steep vineyards are worked entirely by hand, often in blistering heat.*

tain range, which separates the Douro from western Portugal's cooler, more humid Atlantic climate.

The hot climate and difficult terrain also meant that in the past—in fact, until the 1950s—young wines (Ports to be) were made in the Douro by the growers but then transported down the river on flat-bottomed boats (*barcos*) to Oporto and its sister city Vila Nova de Gaia. There they would be blended and matured by the shippers. Today most Port is still blended, aged, and bottled in the shippers' large warehouses, known as lodges, although the Port itself is brought down from the Douro by tanker trucks, a feat that hardly seems possible given the extremely narrow roads, hairpin turns, lack of guardrails, and general absence of shoulders on roads that, in some places, barely cling to the cliffs.

Until the mid-1980s, maturing wines in the lodges was not just standard practice, it was the law. In 1986 new regulations allowed Port to be aged, bottled, and shipped directly from the farm estate (the *quinta*). As a result, several growers who had formerly sold to large shippers—Quinta do Infantado, for example—began marketing their own Ports.

There are more than 83,000 vineyard properties in the Douro. These are owned by the region's roughly 28,500 growers. The region is divided into three subzones, and vineyards are planted in all three. From west to east, they are the Lower Corgo, the Upper Corgo, and the Douro Superior.

The Lower Corgo, about 60 miles upriver from Oporto, is where basic quality Ports are made. Better-quality Ports, including all vintage Ports, come from either the Upper Corgo or the Douro Superior, which extends to the Spanish border.

Despite these generalizations, the Douro remains difficult to categorize. Countless microclimates, each independent from the next, are created by the twisting and turning of the river, the changes in orientation to the sun, the variations in elevation (between 1,200 and 1,700 feet), and numerous other factors. Vineyards may be close as the crow flies but vastly different in terms of the quality of grapes they produce.

In an attempt to make sense of all this, the Casa do Douro, an official regulating body, actually rated the vineyards in the early 1930s. These vineyards remain the most intricately rated in the world. Each is given points based on a myriad of factors, including altitude, nature of soil, shelter from wind, orientation to the sun, climate, age of vines, varieties planted, density of planting, and yield.

As for grapes, Port is almost always a blend of different varieties. Blending, in fact, is what gives Port part of its complexity. There are an astounding thirty-eight white grape varieties and fifty-one red grape varieties grown in the Douro. Five of these—all red—are considered the most important grapes for making Port. These may be blended together in any combination, using any proportions.

In the past the blend was made in the field—that is, the different vines themselves were interplanted in each vineyard. Field blends, still common in Portugal, make harvesting difficult since grape varieties ripen at different times. As a result, newly replanted Portuguese vineyards are planted with a single grape variety, and the wines made from those varieties are later blended in the winery.

The five leading grapes are touriga nacional, tinta barroca, tinto cão, touriga francesa, and tinta roriz. Touriga nacional is the preeminent variety because of its intense color, flavor, and aroma. Of all of the Douro grapes, it makes wines with the best balance and greatest longevity. The other grapes all add varying nuances of flavor, aroma, or body. Grapes are harvested by hand from the end of September through October.

## THE GRAPES OF PORT

### WHITES

**Códega, Gouveio, Malvasia Fina, Rabigato,** and **Viosinho:** Obscure grapes used for only one style of Port—white. Also used for table wines.

### REDS*

**Tinta Barroca:** Contributes alcohol, body, and aroma. Tinta barroca is also used for table wines.

**Tinta Roriz:** Contributes body, flavor, and aroma. Tinta roriz is also used for table wines. This grape is known in Spain as tempranillo.

**Tinto Cão:** Has a delicate character. Sometimes contributes spiciness. Tinta cão is also used for table wines.

**Touriga Francesa:** Contributes floral aromas. Despite its name, the touriga francesca has no French parentage. Also used for table wines.

**Touriga Nacional:** The most important grape variety used in Port and considered the best grape in the Douro. Contributes intense color, flavor, and aroma. Also used for table wines.

* The most important styles of Port are all red.

487

## MAKING PORT

The condensed version would go like this: Add one part grape spirits to four parts red wine while it's fermenting. In truth, however, making Port is quite a bit more involved. First, red grapes are crushed and put in a special automated tank to macerate. Until the 1960s, with ample farm labor available, the crushing was done exclusively by hand—or rather, by foot—in *lagares*, shallow stone or cement troughs large enough to hold between 1,300 and 2,000 gallons of wine. The process almost reads too cliché-like to be true, but it is. After an exhausting day of picking, men and women vineyard workers would don shorts, hop into the *lagar*, and tread the soupy purple mass of grapes for several hours. In the early part of the evening the workers would link arms and march in military-style lines. But as the night wore on, the time would come for the *liberdade* when everyone would break into free-style dancing, usually accompanied by musicians to spur them on.

The human foot is ideally suited to crushing grapes. Treading breaks the grapes, crushes the skins, and then mixes the skins with the juice for good flavor and color extraction—all without smashing the pips (tiny seeds), which contain bitter-tasting tannin. Several Port shippers still have some of their best grapes crushed in this traditional manner.

After the grapes have been trodden and have macerated in a tank for about twenty-four hours, fermentation begins and the grapes' sugar begins to be turned

*Beginning in the 1890s, the Port firm Adriano Ramos Pinto (known today as Ramos-Pinto) began a boldly risqué and highly effective advertising campaign composed of erotic posters, many of them created by leading European artists. The poster on the left, by an unknown artist, evokes the decadence of ancient Roman banquets. The poster on the right, by the Italian commercial artist Leopoldo Metlicovitz, shows a curvaceous, innocent-looking Eve entwined by a serpent holding a cup of wine between his fangs, as Adam looks on from the background.*

into alcohol. At the point when about half the natural sugar has been converted, fermentation must be stopped. To do this, the wine is poured off into a vat containing neutral grape spirits (clear brandy) with an alcoholic strength of 77 percent (150 proof). The alcohol in the spirits causes the yeasts in the wine to die, and fermentation subsides. The result is a sweet wine with about 10 percent residual sugar, fortified to about 20 percent alcohol.

Although this is the initial process by which all Port is made, it is only phase one. Phase two—maturing and aging the Port—is just as, if not more, critical. Each of the separate styles of Port are matured and aged differently.

---

*The Top Port Shippers*

**A. A. FERREIRA**

**COCKBURN**

**DOW'S**

**FONSECA**

**FONSECA GUIMARAENS**

**GRAHAM'S**

**NIEPOORT**

**QUINTA DO INFANTADO**

**QUINTA DO NOVAL**

**RAMOS-PINTO**

**SANDEMAN**

**SMITH WOODHOUSE**

**TAYLOR FLADGATE & YEATMAN**

**WARRE'S**

---

# THE STYLES OF PORT

There are ten different styles of Port, each one unique, though their similar-sounding names make it difficult to remember them all. Before examining the different styles, it's important to note that all Port falls into one of two major categories: those that are aged predominantly in wood (or in a tank) and those that are aged predominantly in bottles. Predominantly wood-aged Ports are ready to drink right after they're bottled and shipped. They should be consumed within a year and a half to two years after bottling. These Ports do not need to be decanted. Predominantly bottle-aged Ports, on the other hand, start out in barrels for a brief period of time but then mature and age for a longer, and sometimes very long, period inside a bottle. Vintage Port is the most famous type of bottle-aged Port. After this long aging, bottle-aged Ports throw a sediment, which, of course, should remain in the bottle. Most bottle-aged Ports therefore need to be decanted.

The ten styles of Port are described beginning, as much as possible, with the simplest styles. Regrettably, organizing the styles of Port into a logical progression isn't as easy as it might seem since many styles of Port are interdependent in the sense that the prerequisite for understanding one style is understanding another.

## "PORTS" AROUND THE WORLD

So-called Ports are made in the United States, South Africa, and Australia, among other places. These fortified wines, while they may be quite extraordinary (as they are particularly in Australia), are not true Ports. Like authentic Champagne or Sherry, real Port comes only from its historic demarcated region.

## *White Port*

White Port is the simplest type of Port—so simple, it's barely considered Port by many Port lovers. It's also a bit of an aberration, being made from indigenous but fairly obscure white grapes, including códega, gouveio, malvasia fina, rabigato, and viosinho. It represents only a small amount of the total production of Port.

While the most basic white Ports are aged only in tanks before being bottled and sold, the better ones are aged briefly in wood and so have a slightly nutty streak of flavor running through them. The majority of white Ports also have a little twang of sweetness, but extremely sweet white Ports, called *lagrima* (teardrops), are also made and are very popular in Portugal. Additionally, there is a more austere style of white Port called light dry (*leve seco*).

White Ports are usually drunk chilled and straight up, on the rocks with a twist of lime, or mixed with soda.

## Ruby Port

This is the least complex style of the red Ports, and it's inexpensive. It receives almost no bottle age before release. Fruity and straightforward, ruby Port is a blend of young wines from different years, all of which have been in barrels or tanks for two to three years. The grapes come from the less prestigious western end of the Douro. A good ruby Port is always a simple wine, but it can have—just as the name suggests—very tasty red fruit flavors. Some producers label their ruby Port "fine ruby."

## Young Tawny Port

There are two widely different types of tawny Port: young (unaged) tawny and aged tawny. Young tawny Port, like ruby Port, is basic and uncomplicated. It is less than three years old. It, too, is made from grapes that come from the less prestigious western end of the Douro. But in the case of a young tawny, the grapes yield a lighter-colored wine. The wine may then be made even lighter by minimizing the time the juice stays on the skins during fermentation. Sometimes, especially for

---

## THE BIRTH PRESENT

It is an old tradition among the wealthy British upper classes to give a newborn child a pipe (about sixty-one cases, clearly a lifetime's supply) of Port from the newborn's birth year. In the past, only vintage Port and single *quinta* vintage Port would be given. These would be shipped in cask to a British wine merchant who would bottle the Port, after which it would be stored in the parents' cellar. By the time the child was old enough to drink, the Port would be matured and ready. Today the Port is bottled in Portugal, not Britain, but the tradition remains essentially the same.

---

undistinguished young tawnies, white Port may be added to the blend as well. Young tawnies, as a result, have a pale, onionskin color. They are often drunk straight up or on the rocks as an aperitif. Young tawnies are also referred to as tawnies without an indication of age.

## Aged Tawny Port

Usually designated on the label as either ten, twenty, thirty, or more-than-forty years old, aged tawny Ports are among the best-loved Ports in Portugal, Britain, and France. They are drunk both as apertifs and at the close of a meal.

Aged tawny Ports are blends of Ports from several years left in the barrel until they take on nutty, brown sugar, and vanilla flavors and a soft, silky texture. Long barrel aging also changes the color of the wine from deep ruby red to, well, tawny. The designation ten-year-old and so on is an average age of the wines by *flavor*. In other words, a ten-year-old tawny tastes like it is made up of wines that are about ten years old (to an experienced taster at least).

The wines used for aged tawnies are of the highest quality. In fact, these wines often go into vintage Port in the years when a vintage is declared (see page 493). However, because they are made in completely different ways, aged tawnies and vintage Ports taste nothing alike. Aged tawnies are about finesse; vintage Ports, about power.

A rare special type of aged tawny is called a reserve aged tawny or *colheita* (col-YATE-ah) Port. A reserve or *colheita* (the word *colheita* means harvest) is a tawny from a single harvest. It must be aged a minimum of seven years, although there is no maximum. In practice many shippers release *colheitas* after they are ten, twenty, or even fifty years old. *Colheitas* are the rarest of all Ports; they account for less than 1 percent of production.

## *Vintage Character Port*

This is an especially confusing term, for many of these round, juicy Ports do not really resemble vintage Ports at all, and they don't come from a single vintage! A better name for them would be super rubies. Vintage character Ports are not very expensive, and their quality and bold flavors make them popular in both the United States and Britain. They are made up of wines of good but not great quality that on the average have spent four to six years aging in barrels, although some may have small amounts of even older wines blended in for extra richness and elegance. Generally, the shippers producing the best vintage Ports also produce the best vintage character Ports.

Many vintage character Ports have proprietary names. Cockburn's Special Reserve, Dow's AJS, Fonseca's Bin 27, Graham's Six Grapes, Quinta do Noval's LB, Ramos-Pinto's Quinta da Urtiga, Sande-

491

*Two of the most renowned* quintas *in the Douro, Dow's Quinta do Bomfim and Graham's Quinta dos Malevedos (inset), have an unparalled rugged beauty and are perfectly sited facing the river.*

## PORTUGAL'S NATIONAL DISH

—◈◈◈—

Dried salted cod—*bacalhau*—is Portugal's national dish. Although the fish is also popular in Spain and the south of France, no place is more passionate about *bacalhau* than Portugal where, it is said, there are at least a year's worth of different recipes for it.

By the time Columbus journeyed to America, the Portuguese were fishing for cod as far away as the Grand Banks of Newfoundland. The cod was salted with sea salt from the area south of Lisbon around Setúbal (also famous for its dessert wine).

*Bacalhau* is salted at sea and then dried onshore. The large, white, almost mummified fish can be seen hanging in *bacalerias*, shops that specialize in the fish. To prepare it, the fish is soaked for one to two days in several changes of water. This removes the salt and rehydrates the flesh. The fish is then cooked in any of a number of ways. In a very popular version, it's flaked, then whipped and cooked with olive oil, potatoes, and sometimes eggs, until it has a thick, creamy texture somewhere between that of scrambled eggs and mashed potatoes.

man's Founder's Reserve, Taylor Fladgate & Yeatman's First Estate and Warre's Warrior are all vintage character Ports.

## *Late Bottled Vintage Port*

Late bottled vintage Ports—LBVs—are also somewhat confusingly named. These are Ports from a single vintage that have been aged in the barrel for four to six years and then bottled. They are ready to drink when the shipper releases them. Though LBVs have been barrel aged for four years (as opposed to vintage Port's two), they are usually not substantial enough wines to have the potential to age for decades more in the bottle (which vintage Port can).

LBVs are made every year and are about half the cost of vintage Port. Unlike vintage Port, LBVs have usually been filtered before being bottled and therefore don't throw a sediment and don't require decanting. Their affordability and the fact that they don't have to be decanted make LBVs popular in restaurants.

But don't be misled. Late bottled vintage Ports, despite their impressive-sounding name, are not the equal of vintage Ports. They are wines of very good quality from good, not great years, but they lack the richness, complexity, and sophistication of vintage Port.

## *Traditional Late Bottled Vintage Port*

Only a few Port shippers, notably Ramos-Pinto, Warre's, Smith Woodhouse, and Quinta do Infantado, still make a traditional late bottled vintage Port, which is closer to vintage Port than to the standard LBV. Traditional late bottled vintage Ports are made like vintage Ports, but they come from good, not great (declared) years. They are aged in wood four years, two years longer than vintage Port.

Traditional late bottled vintage Ports are aged by the shippers in their lodges and then released when they are mature enough to drink. However, these Ports will continue to age well for two decades. Tra-

## DECLARING A VINTAGE

Vintages may be automatic for most wines, but for Port declaring one is a formal procedure. The shipper must submit its intention and samples of the wine to the Port Wine Institute. Only after approval is received from the institute can the vintage be considered declared and only then can the shipper put the words *vintage Port* on the label.

Each shipper decides independently whether or not it wants to declare a vintage Port year. Some shippers, such as Taylor Fladgate & Yeatman, Fonseca, and Graham's, declare virtually every year. Their small holdings of especially excellent vineyards allow them to make small quantities of vintage Port often. However, the truly great years for vintage Port are usually those declared by a significant percentage (50 percent or more) of all shippers. These happen about three times a decade.

The great Port years in the second half of the twentieth century have been 1955, 1958, 1960, 1963, 1966, 1970, 1975, 1977, 1980, 1983, 1985, 1991, 1992, 1994, 1995, and 1997.

only in very good years when Port shippers declare a vintage. All of the grapes in the blend will come only from that vintage and from top vineyards in the best parts of the Douro.

Vintage Ports are first aged two years in barrel, to round off their powerful edges, and then can age a long time in bottle. During bottle aging the Port matures slowly, becoming progressively more refined and integrated. A decade's worth of aging is standard, and several decades used to be fairly common. But this is changing. Thanks to improved viticultural and wine-making practices in the Douro, even very bold, young vintage Ports can be lip smackingly delicious. In fact, a growing number of wine drinkers prefer them when they have this sort of exuberance and power.

To maintain the intensity and richness of vintage Port, it is neither fined nor filtered. It therefore throws a great deal of sediment as it matures in the bottle and must be decanted.

493

*The United States is the largest market in the world for one style of Port: vintage Port.*

Vintage Port can only be made in exceptional years when the young wines show near perfect balance. In these years the shipper must first declare a vintage. In years not declared for vintage Port, Port shippers take the grapes they might have used for vintage Port and blend them into other styles.

According to historical record, the first Ports from a single vintage were made around 1734.

ditional late bottled vintage Ports are not filtered, so they do throw a sediment and need to be decanted. If the Port is a traditional LBV, the label will say so.

## Vintage Port

No Port is more sought after—or expensive. Vintage Port represents only 2 to 3 percent of the total production of Port. It is made

*Quinta Do Noval's 1985 Vintage Port, a particularly good year.*

They were aged in barrel for several years and then drunk as soon as the barrel was opened. Once bottles and corks came into use for vintage Port around 1775, the wines were aged for less time in the barrel and more time in the bottle.

## Single Quinta Vintage Port

The word *quinta* means farm, but in the Douro most *quintas* would be more accurately described as renowned vineyard estates. They range in size from a dozen to several hundred acres and usually include a house and sometimes gardens, in the manner of a French château. The grapes for a single *quinta* vintage Port come from a given *quinta* in a single year. The idea behind these Ports is that the very best vineyard estates are often located in special microclimates that allow exceptional wines to be made even in years when the vintage as a whole may not be declared.

Some single *quinta* vintage Ports are made by small independent firms, such as Quinta do Infantado, that own their own vineyards and do not buy grapes apart from those grown at the *quinta*. However, single *quinta* vintage Ports are also made by traditional shippers that keep the grapes from a given *quinta* separate and make a single wine from those grapes. The Port shipper Taylor Fladgate & Yeatman, for example, owns and makes wine from

---

### HOW LONG WILL AN OPENED BOTTLE OF PORT LAST?

Because Port is both fortified and sweet, an opened bottle generally lasts longer than an opened bottle of regular table wine. Precisely how long any Port will last is based on three factors:

1. How fragile or sturdy the wine is to begin with.

2. How you store the Port—in the refrigerator, or at least in a cool place, is recommended.

3. Your taste. Some wine drinkers like Port at its freshest; others like the flavor Port takes on after it's been exposed to oxygen.

*The following timetable is meant not to be a rule but a guideline.*

| Type of Port | Will Last |
| --- | --- |
| White | Several weeks to several months, when refrigerated |
| Ruby and Young Tawny | 2 weeks to 3 months |
| Aged Tawny | 1 month to 1 year |
| Colheita | 1 to 6 months |
| Vintage Character | 2 weeks to 4 months |
| Late Bottled Vintage and Crusted | 1 week to 2 months |
| Traditional Late Bottled Vintage | 1 day to 2 weeks |
| Vintage, Single Quinta Vintage, and Garrafeira | Depends on its age and delicacy: from 1 day for an old, delicate Port to 2 weeks or more for a younger, robust one |

## PORT TONGS

ottles of vintage Port that are more than thirty years old can sometimes have fragile, difficult to remove corks. Traditionally such bottles would be opened using a pair of Port tongs instead of a corkscrew. This is ceremony indeed. The tongs are heated until red hot, then clamped around the bottle neck below the cork. After about ten seconds, the tongs are removed and cool water is poured over the neck, causing a single dramatic crack that severs the neck from the bottle. The bottle neck with the cork still inside can then be lifted off the bottle—usually with great flourish—and discarded. Port tongs are not the easiest tools to find, but several good mail-order wine accessory companies carry them.

the prestigious Quinta de Vargellas. Shippers (as opposed to small firms) usually do not make single *quinta* vintage Ports in the same years they declare for vintage Ports. In years declared for vintage Port, the *quinta*'s grapes will be blended into the vintage Port and thus cannot be made into a wine of their own.

Apart from blending, single *quinta* vintage Ports are made in the same manner as vintage Ports. They are not filtered, require significant bottle aging, and throw a sediment, so that the wine must eventually be decanted. Single *quinta* vintage Ports are usually released after two years, just like vintage Ports. The wines are then aged a decade or more by the buyer. Single *quinta* vintage Ports are generally slightly less expensive than vintage Ports.

## Crusted Port

So evocatively well named, crusted Port is designated as such because it leaves a heavy crust, or sediment, in the bottle. This is simply a basic good hearty Port, made from a blend of several different years (the average age of the wines in the blend is three to four years), that has been bottled unfiltered. As a result, it throws a sediment and must be decanted. Gutsy, full-bodied, and moderately priced, it's sometimes described as the working man's vintage Port.

## Garrafeira Port

*Garrafeira* (garra-FAY-ra) Ports are not truly a separate style, but like *colheitas*, they are specialty Ports made in tiny amounts. The leading producer is Niepoort. *Garrafeiras* usually come from a single exceptional year and are aged briefly in wood and then a long time—as many as twenty to forty years—in large glass bottles called *bonbonnes*. After aging the *garrafeira* is decanted and transferred into standard 750-milliliter bottles and sold. This type of Port has the richness of a vintage Port yet the suppleness of an aged tawny. The word *garrafeira*

*Port was originally shipped to England in barrels and then bottled to order by English wine merchants, who used bottles like these.*

means wine cellar or bottle cellar (from the Portuguese *garrafa*—bottle). The term *garrafeira* is also used to designate Portuguese still wines of especially high quality.

## PORT'S CLASSIC PARTNERS

Whether it's drunk as an aperitif or after a meal, Port has two classic companions: roasted nuts and cheese. The cheese is invariably blue—especially Stilton and Gorgonzola—but mountain cheeses from Portugal (called *serra*) are also extraordinary. Hedonists pair vintage Ports (as well as LBVs and vintage character Ports) with anything containing bittersweet chocolate. As for tawnies, these Ports are explosively scrumptious when paired with almond or walnut cakes.

## DECANTING, DRINKING, AGING, AND STORING PORT

Decanting—which is not difficult (see page 93)—is only necessary for those Ports that throw a sediment. These include vintage Port, single *quinta* vintage Port, traditional late bottled vintage Port, and crusted Port. Depending on how old and delicate the wine is, it should be decanted from three to twelve hours before being served. If the wine is fairly young and robust you can decant it ten to twelve hours ahead; a more fragile wine should be decanted closer to the time when it will be drunk.

Ports that do not throw a sediment and so do not need to be decanted include ruby, young and aged tawny, vintage character, *colheita*, regular late bottled vintage, and white Port. These may be poured straight into the glass.

One of the oldest and most curious Port traditions concerns the direction in which a bottle is passed. By custom, Port is always supposed to be passed from the right to the left, in a clockwise direction. Although the origins of the custom are obscure, research by the house of Sandeman suggests the practice might be based on the old Celtic superstition that all circular motions should be *deiseal*, that is, turning in a way such that a person moving in a circle would have his right hand toward the center.

Drinking Port is the easiest part. Any good-size wineglass will do. (As with all wines, the glass should be large enough to allow the Port to be swirled.) Generally about 2½ to 3½ ounces of Port is poured in the glass—a slightly smaller amount, in other words, than you would pour of a regular wine.

As for aging, some Ports are made so that they can be drunk right away; others will mature and improve if stored well. The Ports that improve with age include vintage Port, single *quinta* vintage Port, traditional late bottled vintage Port, and crusted Port. These can be stored a long time. Most vintage Port is best after it has been aged at least ten years, and some will continue to mature well for three decades or more.

All other Ports—white, ruby, tawny, vintage character, and late bottled vintage—are ready to drink when released, although they can also be stored for about two years (or sometimes more) without any significant loss of quality. Ports that can be drunk right away generally have a stopper-type cork (a cork with a cap on top of it). These Ports should be stored standing up until you open the bottle.

Ports that improve with age, such as vintage Port, are sealed with regular corks (the kind that require a corkscrew). These should be stored lying down. The ideal storage place is cool, about 55°F, and dark, so that ultraviolet light does not instigate chemical reactions that, in turn, might cause the wine to oxidize. Port bottles themselves are generally black to help preserve the freshness of the liquid inside.

# VISITING PORT SHIPPERS

Virtually all of the Port shippers have lodges in Vila Nova de Gaia, across the river from Oporto. Most offer tours in English plus tastings, which may involve a modest fee. Appointments are generally not necessary, and bottles of Port are always available for purchase.

Visiting the *quintas* far inland where the grapes are grown is more difficult. Generally only members of the wine industry who have made special arrangements are allowed to do so. However, it might be preferable to stay in the city anyway. The nightmarishly narrow, steep roads of the inner Douro can cause even the most fearless drivers (and passengers) to have knots in their stomachs.

The telephone numbers include the dialing code you'll need when calling from the United States. If you're calling from within Portugal, eliminate the 011-351. Don't worry that some of the phone numbers are longer than others; Portuguese telephone numbers are not standardized the way they are in the United States.

**A. A. FERREIRA**
19 Rua da Carvalhosa
Apartado 1309
4400-501 Vila Nova de Gaia
011-351-22-374-5292

**ADRIANO RAMOS-PINTO**
380 Avenue Ramos-Pinto
Apartado 1320
4401-997 Vila Nova de Gaia
011-351-22-370-7000

**COCKBURN**
13 Rua as Coradas
Apartado 20
4431-951 Vila Nova de Gaia
011-351-22-377-6500

**SANDEMAN**
3 Largo de Miguel Bombarda
Apartado 1308
4401-501 Vila Nova de Gaia
011-351-22-374-0599

**SMITH WOODHOUSE**
85 Travessa Barão de Forrester
Apartado 26
4401-997 Vila Nova de Gaia
011-351-22-377-6300

**TAYLOR FLADGATE & YEATMAN**
250 Rua do Choupelo
Apartado 1311
4401-501 Vila Nova de Gaia
011-351-22-371-9999

**W. & J. GRAHAM'S**
514 Rua Rei Ramiro
Apartado 19
4400-281 Vila Nova de Gaia
011-351-22-377-6330

**WARRE'S**
85 Travessa Barão de Forrester
Apartado 26
4401-997 Vila Nova de Gaia
011-351-22-377-6300

# THE PORTS TO KNOW

*Tawny Ports, youngest to oldest, are listed first here. The other styles appear in order of increasing levels of complexity and intensity. Note that the labels on Port bottles always refer to Porto, the Portuguese word for Port.*

## DOW'S

### Tawny Port
### Boardroom

With its mellow, dry, caramel flavors, Dow's Boardroom tawny is one of the finest inexpensive Ports around and perfect as an aperitif. The wine is aged eight years, longer than for a young tawny but not quite as long as an aged tawny's ten or more years. Also sensational: Dow's reserve (*colheita*) tawny.

## TAYLOR FLADGATE

### 10-Year-Old Tawny Port

A scrumptious aged tawny, full of walnut, brown sugar, and vanilla flavors, yet still young enough to have hints of spicy berry flavors as well. Ten-year-old tawnies are generally less complex than twenty-year-olds, but they make up for it, as this one does, with zesty flavors. Taylor is also renowned for its rich, powerful vintage Ports and the stunningly delicious single *quinta* Port, Quinta de Vargellas.

## W. & J. GRAHAM'S

### 20-Year-Old Tawny Port

Of all the multiple styles of Port, nothing matches a great twenty-year-old tawny when it comes to finesse, elegance, and mesmerizing complexity. One sip of the Graham's is proof. Hauntingly delicious flavors of roasted nuts, brown sugar, exotic spices, and crème brûlée will entice you. The finish is so long, it might make your toes curl.

*Blue and white ceramic tiles known as* azulejos *are a signature design element in Portugal. These* azulejos *depicting the harvest festoon the wall of an old train station.*

## SMITH WOODHOUSE
### Vintage Character Port
### Lodge Reserve

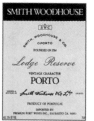

Surrender—it's the only logical reaction to a Port so voluptuous, plump, and syrupy. Chocolate, toffee, mocha, and baked cherry flavors ooze out of the glass. Smith Woodhouse is known for making scrumptious Ports at bargain prices. Though this is only a vintage character Port, it tastes like a baby vintage Port.

## ADRIANO RAMOS-PINTO
### Late Bottled Vintage Port

One of the top Portuguese-owned Port firms, Ramos-Pinto makes some of the richest, raciest LBVs in the Douro. A typical Ramos-Pinto LBV is very elegant, yet has remarkable tensile strength and torrents of plum, spice, and mocha flavors. The firm's vintage Ports are getting more stellar by the vintage.

## W. & J. GRAHAM'S
### Vintage Port

Graham's is usually among the most sensuous of all vintage Ports. Typically, sweet berry fruit soars in your mouth and then explodes over and over again—like a brilliant rush of fireworks. In great vintages, the combination of ultrarich fruit plus supple, powerful tannin and the wine's impeccable balance is unbeatable.

## NIEPOORT
### Vintage Port

Niepoort is a small, family-owned firm producing what are usually thrilling vintage Ports. Rich and beautifully balanced, they are full of sweet, powerful fruit. The firm is known as well for its legendary *colheita* Ports, reserve aged tawnies with absolutely mesmerizing syrupy brown sugar and vanilla flavors.

## QUINTA DO INFANTADO
### Single *Quinta* Vintage Port

The vintage Ports from the tiny firm Quinta do Infantado (*quinta* of the prince) have a unique personality. These are dry, chocolaty/spicy Ports with briary anise and nutmeg flavors. The fruit is lush, nuanced, almost feminine in its elegance. For years the wine made at Quinta do Infantado was sold to larger Port shippers such as Taylor Fladgate & Yeatman and Graham's. Today the firm's production is estate bottled. Remarkably, *every* grape used at the *quinta* is trodden by foot. Also not to be missed: Quinta do Infantado's estate reserve, a terrific, mouthfilling vintage character Port and one of the best Port values around.

499

## TAYLOR FLADGATE
### Vintage Port

Highly sought after, Taylor's vintage Ports are always among the most expensive. They're also among the most difficult to drink young. Unlike, say, Graham's vintage Ports, Taylors are hard-edged, powerful, and cloaked by a dense curtain of tannin. But give them fifteen or so years of maturation and the top Taylor vintage Ports undergo a transformation that defies prediction. Elegant and sophisticated, they exude finesse and richness.

# MADEIRA

The wine drunk by our founding fathers to toast the signing of the Declaration of Independence is reported to have been Madeira. During the eighteenth century, the American colonies imported a fourth of all the Madeira made, and no wine was considered more prestigious.

Madeira—from *ilha da madeira*, island of the woods—comes from the small, rugged, volcanic island of the same name. Though the island is geographically part of Africa (about 375 miles west of the Moroccan coast), it is nonetheless a province of Portugal, some 530 miles to the northeast. The island's subtropical climate is atypical for grape growing, but then almost everything about Madeira is unique, including the intricate and painstaking manner by which the wine is made.

Like Port, Madeira is a fortified wine (17 to 20 percent alcohol by volume) that started out unfortified. In the late 1500s unfortified Madeira was part of the provisions picked up by merchant ships traveling to Africa, India, and later, South America. Jostled and baked in a sweltering hold, the unfortified wine spoiled quickly.

By the late seventeenth century, brandy was being added to the wine to stabilize and preserve it. Fortified Madeira turned out to be a wholly different story. Aged over long months on a rolling ship in the equatorial heat, this Madeira became a deliciously rich wine. In time, the most prized Madeiras of all were the so-called *vinhos da roda*, Madeiras that had made a round-trip.

Today Madeira is easily misunderstood, for its quality ranges all across the board. At the lowest level, Madeira can be a cheap, bulk-processed wine that most consign to cooking rather than drinking. At the

*Madeira may be more than 500 miles from its mother country, Portugal, but the two have at least one thing in common. Harvesting grapes in hot, steep terrain is exhausting work.*

*Casks of vintage Madeira slowly mature in Blandy's hot attic loft (the exterior is seen in the inset). To achieve the finest, smoothest, most deeply complex Madeiras, the wines may be left to mature this way for twenty years or more.*

highest level, however, fine Madeira (the subject of this text) is a handcrafted wine of breathtaking complexity and longevity.

To make Madeira, clear brandy (neutral grape spirits) is added to the wine before it has completely finished fermenting. This neutralizes the yeasts, halts fermentation, and leaves a fortified wine that can have just a touch of sweetness—or more—depending on when the fermentation is stopped, which in turn, is based on the style of Madeira being made.

Madeira's toffee-caramel-like character comes as a result of heating the wine, a process called *estufagem*. There are several methods, depending on the quality of the Madeira being produced. The most basic of these involves placing the fortified base wines in containers (casks, large vats, or cement tanks) that are then heated to an average temperature of 105°F for three to six months.

However, for the very finest Madeiras (a minuscule 3 percent of all Madeiras made) the heating process is carried out naturally. Casks of the best wines are placed in the attics of the producers' lodges (warehouses), which, sitting under the hot Madeiran sun, build up tremendous heat. There the casks remain undisturbed usually for about twenty years although sometimes for longer. After the heating process is complete, the wine is carefully cooled and allowed to rest for a year or more to recover from the shock. When the wine is deemed ready, it is further aged.

For the best Madeiras, this aging process is also lengthy and involved. The wines are put into casks made from various woods—usually American oak, but sometimes chestnut, Brazilian satinwood, or even mahogany. The casks are not filled to the top; instead, a head space is delib-

502

## THE GRAPES OF MADEIRA

### WHITES

**Bual:** One of the four top grape varieties of Madeira. Used to make the medium-rich style also known as bual.

**Malmsey:** Known elsewhere as malvasia. One of the four top grape varieties of Madeira. Used to make the sweetest style also known as malmsey.

**Sercial:** One of the four top grape varieties of Madeira. Used to make the dry style also known as sercial.

**Verdelho:** One of the four top grape varieties of Madeira. Used to make the medium-dry style also known as verdelho.

### RED

**Tinta Negra Mole:** Important grape used for all basic, fairly low-quality Madeiras.

as noble by the Madeira Wine Institute. These are sercial, verdelho, bual, and malmsey (known elsewhere as malvasia). Their names are also used to designate various styles of Madeira.

# THE STYLES OF MADEIRA

**Sercial:** The driest style. Sercial grapes are grown in the coolest vineyards at the highest altitudes. The difficulties they encounter ripening make for tart base wines. These in turn lead to tangy, elegant Madeiras with a bracing grip.

**Verdelho:** The medium-dry style. Verdelho grapes, grown in slightly warmer vineyards, ripen more easily, making for Madeiras that are somewhat more full-bodied than sercials.

**Bual:** The medium-rich style. Bual grapes are grown in warm vineyards, producing concentrated Madeiras with sweet richness. Bual was a great favorite in English officers' clubs in India because it was a lighter wine than either malmsey or Port.

**Malmsey:** The richest, sweetest style. Malvasia grapes are grown in the warmest locations closest to sea level, usually on the south side of the island, producing superripe grapes and ultimately Madeiras of astonishing richness.

## *Quality Levels*

In addition to styles of Madeira, there are also quality levels. In ascending order they are bulk, three-year-old and rainwater, five-year-old, ten-year-old, fifteen-year-old, solera, and vintage Madeiras.

erately left so that the wine slowly oxidizes, mellowing the flavors even more.

Unbelievable as it may be, a Madeira may be aged anywhere from three to twenty years or more after the heating process but before blending and bottling. If a vintage Madeira is being made (rather than a blended one), the wine will be aged further, usually for two more years after bottling. Thus, some great Madeiras are more than forty years in the making!

Most basic-quality Madeiras are made from the versatile red grape tinta negra mole (the name means black, soft). The very best Madeiras, however, are made from one of four white grapes designated

**Bulk Madeira:** These are basic, low-quality blended Madeiras made from tinta negra mole grapes. They are heated quickly and aged for only a short time, usually about eighteen months. Their color is often not natural but the result of added caramel coloring.

**Three-Year-Old Madeira:** The next step up are Madeiras that are also made from tinta negra mole grapes and that also undergo a fairly quick heating process but that then must be aged three years, usually in tanks, not casks. These are sometimes labeled finest or choice.

The special type of light Madeira known as rainwater falls into this tier. These gentle Madeiras were first made for the southern Colonial American market in the mid-eighteenth century. They were given the name rainwater because the first ones were accidentally produced when rain seeped into casks left on the beach overnight before being loaded onto ships the next morning.

**Five-Year-Old Madeira:** These are blended Madeiras in which the youngest component in the blend is aged at least five years in casks. If a noble Madeira grape is listed on the label (sercial, bual, and so forth), the wine must be made from 85 percent of that variety. These are sometimes called reserve.

**Ten-Year-Old Madeira:** Higher still in quality are Madeiras often made from noble grapes where the youngest component in the blend is aged at least ten years in casks. Another name for them is special reserve.

**Fifteen-Year-Old Madeira:** Even better yet. The youngest component must be aged at least fifteen years. These wines are aged in casks (not in tanks) and are made mostly from noble grape varieties. Sometimes called extra reserve.

**Solera Madeira:** These wines can still be found, although they are no longer being made by the top firms. Like Sherry, solera Madeiras are made by an intricate process of fractional blending (see How the Solera Works, page 441).

**Vintage Madeira:** This is the ultimate-quality level. Unlike virtually all other Madeiras (which are blended), vintage Madeiras are wines of a single year. Remarkably, vintage Madeira must be aged

*The small, ancient, steep terraces of Madeira (facing page) were handcarved in steplike fashion out of the rugged volcanic rock. Madeira's mountainous terrain (below) rises to nearly 6,000 feet in altitude. Terraced vineyards, some of which seem to barely cling to the rocky slopes, must be worked by hand.*

at least twenty years in cask *after* the period of *estufagem*, or heating, and then an additional two years in the bottle. Vintage Madeira must be made from the grapes sercial, verdelho, bual, or malmsey.

## Producers

Although there were more than two dozen producers exporting Madeira at the time of the American Revolution, by the 1990s fewer than ten remained. Today the largest and most distinguished firm is the Madeira Wine Company, which owns most of the top brands, including Blandy's, Cossart Gordon, Leacock's, and Miles. The Madeira Wine Company is partly owned by the Symington family, which also owns many top Port firms including Warre's, Dow's, Graham's, and Smith Woodhouse. On the island of Madeira, you can visit the Madeira Wine Company at their visitors' facility, *São Francisco Lodge, 10 Rua de São Francisco, Funchal, Madeira; 011-351-291-740-110.*

## SERVING MADEIRA

Fine Madeira rarely, but sometimes, needs to be decanted before serving. In any case, you'll be able to see the sediment if it does. That said, it's generally a good idea to uncork the bottle and pour the wine into a carafe or decanter several hours ahead to let it open up (see aeration, page 93).

Madeira is best served in a good-size white wine glass so that there's enough room to swirl the wine. Sercials and verdelhos are usually served cool; the sweeter styles—buals and malmseys—at room temperature.

## COOKING WITH MADEIRA

Madeira is a fabulous wine to cook with, giving just about anything (roasts, soups, sauces, and so on) extra depth and richness. However, don't use the cheap California jug wines labeled "madeira" or other pseudomadeiras not from the island of Madeira. They have terrible flavors. The best Madeira for cooking is a simple but genuine Madeira, such as rainwater or a five-year-old reserve Madeira.

All styles of Madeira have a gripping backbone of natural acidity, making them refreshing to drink on their own but also exquisite counterpoints to food. Sercial and verdelho are dramatic aperitifs and delicious with first-course salads or soups. Bual and luscious malmsey can be desserts in themselves, but their acidity also means they are among the world's best juxtapositions to the richness of desserts made with cream or chocolate.

Finally, an opened bottle of Madeira lasts nearly forever. After everything it's been through—fortification, extreme heat, long aging in the presence of oxygen—Madeira is pretty indestructible.

*A century-old bottle of Madeira from the author's cellar. The grape variety moscatel is very rarely used for Madeira today.*

504

## SETÚBAL

ccording to legend, Setúbal was settled by one of Noah's sons—Tubal—hence the region's name. The small peninsula, about 20 miles south of Lisbon, is known for only one wine, the famous dessert wine also known as Setúbal. A sweet fortified wine like Port, Setúbal is made principally from two types of muscat grapes: moscatel de Setúbal (muscat of Alexandria) and moscatel roxo (purple muscat). Up to 30 percent of five other indigenous grapes may be blended in.

The best Setúbals are almost hauntingly aromatic, thanks to the extraordinarily long time the grape skins are left macerating in the wine—up to six months. The wine's flavor is outrageously irresistible, a rich, exotic mingling of mandarin oranges, caramel, molasses, and wild herbs. And the color can be mesmerizing, from vivid orange-red to rich chestnut. Setúbal is usually drunk with cakes made with nuts, such as a walnut cake.

Setúbal may be vintage dated or may be a blend of wines of different ages. A Setúbal labeled twenty years old, for example, will be a blend of several wines, the *youngest* of which will be twenty years old. Only twelve companies make Setúbal, including the well-respected firm J. M. da Fonseca. Located in the village of Vila Noguerira de Azeitão, J. M. da Fonseca is worth visiting not only for its wines and state of the art winery, but also for its fascinating wine museum, one of the best in Portugal (011-351-21-219-7500).

# PORTUGUESE TABLE WINES

S ome of the most underrated, good-value, dry table wines in Europe come from Portugal. Most of the best are bold, rustic, plummy reds, although some good white quaffing wines—notably Vinho Verde—are also made. Portuguese table wines are almost always blends of different grape varieties, most of which are thought to be Phoenician in origin and today are rarely found outside Portugal. There are a dizzying number of such varieties—more than 230. Some of the more commonly used grapes include jaén, alfrocheiro preto, periquita, and baga. There are new though still very limited plantings of such international varieties as cabernet sauvignon, merlot, syrah, and chardonnay as well. As is true almost everywhere in Europe, Portuguese wines are named not by grape variety, but by region.

Until the mid-1980s, cooperatives controlled most, if not all, wine production in many of Portugal's fifty-five wine regions. Vast amounts of poor-quality wine were made. The situation changed radically when Portugal joined the European Union, and today the number of independent estates making good wine is on the rise.

One term to be familiar with is *garrafeira*. This Portuguese word is sometimes used on wine labels to denote a table wine of especially high quality. In general, red wines designated *garrafeira* have been aged in any type of tank or barrel at least two years before bottling and have spent one year in the bottle. White wines designated *garrafeira* must be aged six months prior to bottling and six months in the bottle afterward.

Although table wines are made virtually everywhere in Portugal, you'll find the following five wine regions—going from north to south—to be the most important.

## The Minho

In the far northwest, just below the Spanish border, the fertile rolling green hills are crammed with orchards and farm crops (corn, potatoes, and beans). This is the Minho, one of the most agriculturally productive regions of the country, and the region where most of Portugal's popular white wine—Vinho Verde—is made.

Vinho Verde (literally, green wine) is a basic, light, low-alcohol white with a touch of spritz. The word *green* refers not to the wine's color but to the fact that it's a young wine meant to be drunk soon after it's made. So immediate is the consumption of Vinho Verde that most producers don't even bother to put a vintage date on the bottle.

Although much Vinho Verde is simply neutral wine made for washing down humble fish dishes, there are also Vinho Verdes with good forthright grip and light peachy and floral characters. The leading pro-

## THE GRAPES OF

# PORTUGAL—TABLE WINES

*Portugal has more than 230 grape varieties, and most table wines are blends of several of them. Below are the major grapes.*

## WHITES

**Alvarinho:** The grape used to make the best Vinho Verdes, although more than twenty other white grapes are also permitted to be used.

**Encruzado:** The leading grape in the crisp white wines of the Dão.

**Gouveio, Malvasia Fina,** and **Viosinho:** Commonly blended together to make white table wines in the Douro. Also used for white Port.

**Loureiro, Pedernã,** and **Trajadura:** Frequently used in the making of average to good-quality Vinho Verde, usually blended with each other.

## REDS

**Alfrocheiro Preto, Bastardo,** and **Jaén:** Important grapes in the Dão where they contribute spice and acidity.

**Aragonez:** Like tinta roriz, a name for tempranillo. One of the leading grapes used to make wines in the Alentejo.

**Azal Tinto** and **Vinhão:** Two of the leading grapes commonly blended together to make biting, strident, red Vinho Verde.

**Baga:** Grown in almost all regions but especially important in Bairrada. Baga is tannic and acidic.

**Periquita:** One of the leading grapes used to make wines in the Alentejo and grown in other regions as well.

**Tinta Barroca, Tinta da Barca, Tinta Roriz, Tinto Cão,** and **Touriga Francesa:** Common grapes, often blended together to make table wines in the Douro. All but tinta da barca are also used in the making of Port.

**Touriga Nacional:** Considered the best grape in Portugal. Rich and well balanced. Used to make the top table wines of the Douro and Dão. Also the leading grape used in Port.

**Trincadeira Preta:** One of the leading grapes used to make wines in the Alentejo.

ducer is Quinta da Aveleda and quality wines are also made by Quinta Villa Beatriz, Quinta de Pedra, Paço do Cardido, Paço de Teixeiró, and Palácio da Brejoeira.

Vinho Verde can be made from any or a combination of twenty-five white grapes. The best wines, however, come from four: alvarinho, trajadura, and loureiro (these three correspond to grapes with similarly spelled names—albariño, treixadura, and loureira—found in the Spanish province of Galicia next door) plus pedernã. The wine's slight fizzyness comes from a dose of carbon dioxide, which is added right before bottling.

A large percentage of Vinho Verde is not white but red. Red "green" wine is not exported, but when you're in Portugal, don't pass up a chance to try it. A shocking magenta in color, red Vinho Verde is also as bitingly acidic as red wine gets. This is considered a plus given the region's rustic bean, pork, and oily codfish dishes. In bars, red Vinho Verde is what is in the shallow white ceramic bowls (called *malgas*) that most men seem to be holding. Red Vinho Verde is usually a blend of several otherwise obscure grape varieties such as azal tinto and vinhão.

## *Douro*

While the Douro is famous for Port (see page 483), extremely good table wines are also made in the region. Many Portuguese wine experts consider the Douro the best region in Portugal for dry red wines. Portugal's most famous dry, nonfortified wine is made here, A. A. Ferreira's Barca Velha—the old barge—a wonderful wine with delicious minty-

---

### THERE REALLY WAS A QUEEN

The borough of Queens, part of New York City, was named after the Princess of Portugal Catherine of Braganza who became Queen of England in 1662. It was during the reign of her husband, King Charles II, that the colony of New Amsterdam became New York and Queens was named to honor Catherine.

---

chocolate flavors and a texture as soft as cashmere. Barca Velha's success has served as an inspiration, and today many other wine firms are beginning to make fine table wines here.

The vineyards for Douro table wines are, like the vineyards for Port, on rocky hillsides of schist. Of the nearly forty grapes allowed, the principal red grapes are the same as those used for Port, touriga nacional, tinta roriz (tempranillo), tinta barroca, tinto cão, touriga francesa, plus the spicy grape tinta da barca.

Douro reds range from light and fruity to supple and spicy wines full of dense plum and black raspberry flavors. Among the best: Quinta do Côtto—especially the Quinta do Côtto *cuvée* called Grande Escolha—from the producer Champalimaud, plus Duas Quintas from the Port producer Ramos-Pinto and Redoma from the Port producer Niepoort.

The Douro's white table wines are not particularly impressive. The principal white grapes are gouveio, malvasia fina, and viosinho.

507

## Dão

Another one of Portugal's most promising regions for table wines, the Dão began to produce markedly better wines in the late 1980s after the government rescinded the law requiring that all grapes grown in the region be sold to cooperatives. The region lies about 30 miles south of the Douro River. It is enclosed on three sides by mountains, which shelter the region from the chill and moisture of the Atlantic and give it a Mediterranean climate. Red wine predominates; it makes up 80 percent of the Dão's wine. The top wines may carry the designation *Dão nobre*—noble Dão.

Nearly fifty grapes are authorized for use in the region. The best of them is the red grape touriga nacional, which is also grown in the Douro and is considered the finest of the Port grapes. Other good quality grapes include tinta roriz (tempranillo), alfrocheiro preto, jaén, and bastardo for reds; encruzado is the leading grape for whites.

Two leading Dão wines, Grão Vasco and Duque de Viseu—both reds—are made by the large firm Sogrape. Other top producers from this region include Casal da Tonda, Quinta das Maias, Casa de Santar, Quinta dos Roques, and Quinta dos Carvalhais.

## Bairrada

Bairrada derives its name from *barro*, the Portuguese word for clay, which constitutes a large percentage of the soil in the region. Bairrada is just west of the Dão in central Portugal and is not far from the Atlantic Ocean. The leading grape is the juicy, acidic baga, which by law must make up 50 percent of the blend of any red wine made there. Some fifteen other grapes are grown.

*Stunningly well preserved, these ancient six-foot-high amphorae stand outside Lancers' cellars today. From Roman times until quite recently, many producers in southern Portugal made wine in amphorae rather than barrels.*

## ROMANCE—SIXTIES STYLE

——⋙✦⋘——

Although most Americans are unfamiliar with Portuguese table wines, two of them—both rosés—were once among the most recognized imported wine brands in this country: Lancers and Mateus. Considered wines for romance, both were known for their soft, tasty flavors and their memorable bottles: Lancers came in a ceramic carafe, Mateus in an oval-shaped glass flask. Although both brands continue to be made (and in fact, are better tasting than ever), their sales in the United States have dwindled as the sales of other soft pink wines, especially white zinfandels, have risen. As the chronicles of romantic dinners may one day show, however, white zinfandels can't hold a candle to Portuguese rosés when it comes to setting the mood.

About 60 percent of Portugal's sparkling wines are made here, including rustic, grapey red sparkling wines that are often paired with the region's specialty, roast suckling pig. Among the top Bairrada wines are those made by the producers Luis Pato, Caves São João, and Quinta do Carvalinho.

## Alentejo

The biggest wine region in Portugal, the Alentejo covers virtually all of the southeastern part of the country. The hot, dry rolling plains produce, in addition to wine, olive oil, and cereal grains, more than half of the world's supply of cork.

The soil here is mostly volcanic in origin and includes granite, quartz, schist, and chalk. As in most of Portugal's other top regions, the finest wines are red and there are dozens of grape varieties. Among the best grapes are periquita (the name means parakeet), aragonez (another name for tempranillo), and trincadeira preta. The Alentejo has historically been a poor region. Since Roman times, the lack of forests here meant that wines were made in huge earthenware amphorae. A handful of producers continue to make wine this way today.

The top Alentejo red wines have a plummy character and come from around several small towns near the Spanish border. Among the best are José de Sousa and Periquita, both from the producer J. M. da Fonseca; Tinto da Anfora from the J. P. Vinhos winery; and Quinta do Carmo, which is owned in part by Château Lafite-Rothschild.

509

## VISITING THE TABLE WINE PRODUCERS OF PORTUGAL

Visiting Portugal's table wine producers isn't quite as easy as visiting Port shippers. Conveniently, the lodges of most Port shippers are clustered around the town of Vila Nova de Gaia, near Oporto, while table wine producers are scattered throughout the country. Also unlike Port shippers, Portugal's table wine producers are generally not equipped to offer tours in English. Visiting these producers, in other words, is altogether a more rustic experience, and it's very helpful (though not always essential) to speak Portuguese. That said, some of the estates listed here—Casa de Santar for example—are not only interesting for their wines, but also include beautiful gardens and stately homes built as early as the seventeenth century.

The producers are organized by region, north to south. You'll notice that many of the addresses are pretty sketchy. You may wonder about some of these, but take it from someone who's been there. Many of the estates are out in the country; they may have been there for a century, and they don't have a formal address like you'd see in the United States.

The telephone numbers include the dialing code you'll need when calling from the United States. If you're calling from within Portugal, eliminate the 011-351. Don't worry if you notice that some of the phone numbers are longer than others; Portuguese telephone numbers are not standardized the way they are in the United States.

### MINHO

**PALÁCIO DA BREJOEIRA**
Pinheiros
4950 Moncão
011-351-251-666-129

**QUINTA DA AVELEDA**
Apartado 77
4560 Penafiel
011-351-255-718-200

### DOURO

**A. A. FERREIRA**
19 Rua da Carvalhosa
Apartado 1309
4400-501 Vila Nova de Gaia
011-351-223-745-292

### DAO

**CASA DE SANTAR**
3520 Santar
011-351-232-940-653

**SOGRAPE**
Aldeia Nova
4430 Avintes
011-351-22-785-0300

### BAIRRADA

**CAVES SÃO JOÃO**
São João de Anadia
3780 Anadia
011-351-234-743-118

**LUIS PATO**
Ois do Bairro
3780 Anadia
011-351-231-528-156

**QUINTA DO CARVALHINHO**
Ventosa do Bairro
3050 Mealhada
011-351-231-29-343

### ALENTEJO

**J. P. VINHOS**
59 Rua Infante D. Henrique
2925 Pinhal Novo
011-351-21-219-8660

# Germany

Until the twentieth century there were only two great wine-producing countries: France, of course, but the other may come as a surprise—Germany. While outstanding wines could occasionally be found elsewhere, no other country came close to these two for the supremacy of their wines. Today, Germany still produces some of the world's most majestic wines, a fact unaltered by the slings and arrows of politics and fashion.

What is most remarkable about Germany, however, is that *any* wine at all—never mind great wine—can be made there, for the country's vineyards lie at the northernmost extreme of where grapes can ripen. At latitudes of 49 to 51 degrees, these vineyards are as far north as Mongolia and Newfoundland. Insane as it might seem to attempt grape growing so far from the security of ample sun, it's precisely the tenuous existence of German vineyards that makes the wines unlike all other wines

512

*Behind the village of Bernkastel is the Doctor vineyard, so named because, as the story goes, an archbishop was cured of a terminal illness after drinking its wine.*

Germany ranks sixth in wine-producing countries worldwide. Germans drink an average of 6.16 gallons of wine per person each year; they're seventeenth in world wine consumption.

BERNKASTEL

• Germany is considered one of the world's top producers of elegant white wines, the best of which have almost ravishing delicacy and clarity.

• The vineyards are at the northernmost extreme of where grapes can ripen.

• The majority of fine German wines are *not* sweet. The exceptions are the expensive late harvest dessert wines *beerenauslesen* and *trockenbeerenauslesen*, which are crafted to be sweet.

in the world. If the top German wines were *not* as rarefied and extraordinary as they are, winemakers here would surely have thrown in the towel long ago (probably becoming *brewmeisters* and leading far less nerve-racking lives).

Of course, generic wines of no particular distinction are made in Germany, just as they are everyplace else. Fairly cheap, sweetish, and pleasant at best, these wines (sadly) constitute many wine drinkers' entire experience with German wines. The generic stuff, however, is about as similar to fine German wine as bargain clothing is to haute couture.

# THE TERRORS OF TERROIR

At northern extremes every nuance of *terroir* is magnified. Something as simple as being in the shadow of a ridge can ruin all hopes for ripeness and hence all hopes of producing a wine with depth and intensity. As a result, Germany's vineyards are the most precisely sited of any

in the world. The best are always planted on south-facing slopes to catch the light and warmth of every available sunbeam. (Northern slopes are easy to identify; they're always vineless.) Most of the vineyards are planted in the river valleys of the Rhine and Mosel or their tributaries, since bodies of water act to moderate the severe climate. Even the tiny amount of warmth that can be gleaned from the reflection of sunlight off the river is critical, which is why on any slope the best plots of vineyards are generally those closest to the river.

*The German word for vineyard is* weinberg, *literally wine hill. Many of the country's best vineyards are in fact on slopes, some of them as steep as 70 percent.*

Soil, too, must do its share. All of Germany's good vineyards are planted in places with heat-retaining soil and rocks, such as slate and basalt. For all this, full ripeness (a fact of life in most wine regions in the world) remains elusive in Germany. Most years the grapes achieve only varying degrees of semiripeness and are brimming— if not shimmering—with acidity.

What does this mean in wine terms? First of all, German wines are light in alcohol. They usually have a third less alcohol by volume (7 to 11 percent) than the standard California chardonnay (13 to 14 percent). Moreover, German wines have a singular quality known as transparency. Rarely found in wines elsewhere, transparency is not so much a thing as a sense that the wines' flavors are utterly naked. A transparent wine doesn't exactly have an essence; it is its essence. (The best way to understand transparency is by tasting a top

*The vineyards of the Mosel (left) are always found on steep slopes slanted perfectly to catch every ray of sun. In fact, the slopes are so steep that some are outfitted with monorails (right) that can be used to help haul grapes down to the bottom of the hill.*

German riesling and a California chardonnay side by side. The riesling will have real clarity of flavor; the flavors in the chardonnay, by comparison, will seem more diffused. If riesling is like sheer silk stockings, chardonnay is opaque tights.) The notion of transparency is the aesthetic underpinning of German wines.

## ROMAN ROOTS

German winemaking began with the ancient Romans, who conquered the region about 100 B.C. Later, during the Middle Ages, monks painstakingly planted and cultivated what are today considered the most famous vineyards. Church ownership of the vineyards ended in 1803 when Napoleon conquered the Rhine and vineyard land was divided up and auctioned off.

The naturally high acidity of German wines also plays a role in this drama. Instead of weight, most wines have tension, a dynamic energy coursing between the wine's acidity and fruit. So it's almost impossible to think about (or evaluate) a German wine in the same way you would, say, a California wine. Big and powerful may be desirable adjectives when applied to wines from California, but German winemakers' mind-sets are entirely different. What they hope to achieve are precision and finesse. Unlike in most other wine regions in the world, in Germany bigger isn't better.

*The top German wines are often described as transparent, indicating that the wines' flavors seem utterly naked.*

Transparency and tension are discernible in fine German wine only because the best winemakers are adamant

## THE MOST IMPORTANT

### GERMAN WINES

**LEADING WINE**
**Riesling** *white (dry and sweet)*

**WINES OF NOTE**
**Gewürztraminer** *white (dry and sweet)*
**Müller-Thurgau** *white*
**Rieslaner** *white (dry and sweet)*
**Ruländer\*** *white*
**Scheurebe** *white (dry and sweet)*
**Sekt** *white (sparkling)*
**Silvaner** *white*
**Spätburgunder\*\*** *red*
**Weissburgunder\*\*\*** *white*

*\*pinot gris*
*\*\*pinot noir*
*\*\*\*pinot blanc*

purists. They do nothing that would alter or mold the inherent flavor of the grapes. They do not: use commercial yeasts, alter the acidity in the grapes, ferment or age in new oak. And many do not even fine the wines to clarify them. Of course, the idea that winemaking should be more like midwifery than manufacture has been touted throughout the wine-producing world. But at the top estates in Germany, it's a reality.

Because of the overall coolness of the climate, grapes in Germany are only beginning to form in mid- to late June—considerably later than grapes in most other parts of the world. Harvest takes place from late September to late November, and some grapes will be left to hang still longer, even into January. Over this period the grapes mature gradually, almost incrementally. Blasts of heat and high temperatures are

rare. As a result, great grapes, such as riesling, have little trouble retaining elegance.

# THE LAND, THE GRAPES, AND THE VINEYARDS

Let's talk about grapes first. Germany is overwhelmingly a producer of white wines, although red wines account for about 18 percent of production and rosés (called *weissherbst*) are also made. Of the nearly sixty grapes grown, riesling is the most prestigious. Virtually all of the best wines are made from it, and in the finest wines it is never blended with another grape. Like pinot noir in Burgundy, fine riesling is too perfect on its own to diffuse its character by blending it.

In terms of production, however, the predominent grape is Müller-Thurgau, which usually makes decent, but rarely memorable, wines. Müller-Thurgau's parentage is cloudy. Invented at the Geisenheim viticultural station in 1882, it was

*In terms of production (but not quality) Müller-Thurgau is Germany's leading grape.*

originally said to be a cross of riesling and silvaner (which the French spell sylvaner), later defined as a cross of two clones of riesling, and even later said to have no riesling at all in its makeup. Today the grape's parentage remains a mystery.

Müller-Thurgau is not the only cross in Germany. In the late nineteenth and early twentieth centuries, plant scientists there developed a slew of them. The goal was to come up with a new variety that would be less fragile than riesling, ripen earlier, give higher yields, and at the same time, have riesling's complexity and flavor. Even for the best plant breeders this was a little too much to bite off. Today such crosses as kerner, Morio-muskat, huxelrebe, and the two best of them, scheurebe and rieslaner, make good and sometimes excellent wines, but they are rarely matches for riesling.

Germany's red wines are well loved— mostly by the Germans. It is such a triumph to make red wines this far north that almost regardless of quality, German reds are expensive and are immediately snapped up on the home turf. Spätburgunder (pinot noir), blauer portugieser (a variety which has nothing to do with Portugal), and trollinger (the same as the Italian variety schiava) are the most popular red grapes. While the best spätburgunders can have a spicy/earthy charm, most German red wine is lean, light, and rather un-red-like.

As for the land and the vineyards, while Germany's entire wine production amounts to just 3 percent of the world's total, there are more than 77,000 grape growers. The best estates are minuscule. A top Bordeaux château produces more wine in a vintage than a top German estate produces in a decade! And, the estates considered top-notch are changing. Many of the great old wineries no longer produce the kind of wines that made them legendary. A whole new set of wine estates is now among the stars of Germany. These include Müller-Catoir, Fritz Haag, Willi Schaefer, Lingenfelder, Gunderloch, Karlsmühle, and Dönnhoff.

Wineries are usually located in small villages at the edge of the vineyards. German wine labels (epitomes of precision) give not only the winery name, but also the town and vineyard names. This is not just

## ARE THESE VINEYARDS?

Though Germany would seem like the last country to give its vineyards whimsical names, there are dozens of them. Here are the names of a few well-known vineyards.

**Eselshaut:** Donkey hide

**Goldtröpfchen:** Little raindrops of gold

**Himmelreich:** Kingdom of heaven

**Honigsäckel:** Honey pot, with a sexual connotation

**Jesuitengarten:** Garden of the Jesuits

**Juffermauer:** Wall of the virgins

**Kalb:** Veal

**Katzenbeisser:** The biter of cats

**Lump:** Dope; idiot

**Nonnengarten:** Nun's garden

**Saumagen:** Pig's stomach

**Schneckenhof:** Home of the snails

**Sieben Jungfrauen:** Seven virgins

**Spinnennetz:** Spiderweb

**Ungeheur:** Monster

**Würzhölle:** Spice hell

**Zweifelberg:** Place of doubt

## A WOMAN'S TOUCH

In contrast to California's lightning-fast crews of Mexican harvest workers who are mostly young, strong, and male, many of Germany's harvest workers are middle-aged or elderly women, who often climb treacherously steep slate slopes in bitterly cold weather, carrying harvest baskets on their backs.

miscellaneous extra data. In the past, knowledgeable German wine drinkers (like Burgundy drinkers) bought wines based first on the reputation of the vineyard, *then* on the producer's name. And, of course, the wines' prices were based largely on the attributes of the vineyards. But consider: Until 1971, there were more than 30,000 individual vineyard names a

wine drinker might encounter! These were reorganized in 1971 and pared down to about 2,600—still a mind-boggling number. Yet, over time any wine drinker who loves German wines—just like any wine drinker who loves Burgundy—simply learns the names of a half-dozen great vineyards in the same way we all learn the names of a half-dozen great producers.

Germany is divided into thirteen wine regions. Two of these, Saale Unstrut and Sachsen, formerly in East Germany, were added after reunification in 1989. Of the thirteen, four are the most important—the Mosel-Saar-Ruwer, the Rheingau, the Pfalz, and the Rheinhessen.

Germany's thirteen wine regions are divided into forty districts called *bereiche*, which themselves are divided into 163 so-called collections of vineyards, each called a *grosslage*. Every *grosslage*, in turn, is made up of individual vineyard sites, each called an *einzellage*. There are now more than 2,500 *einzellagen*.

*In Germany, much of the work in the vineyards, exhausting as it is, is done by middle-aged and elderly women.*

518

## READING A GERMAN WINE LABEL

*Those seemingly daunting German labels are actually easy, logical, and hugely informative once you grasp some basics. What admittedly is difficult is reading the Gothic script that some wineries still use. There is a significant movement away from the use of that typeface, as in this case. Here is the information the typical German label conveys:*

Wine region

Name of the producer

Vintage

Grape variety

Official *Amtiche Prüfungsnummer* (*AP*), or testing number, proof that the wine has passed the analytical and sensory testing required for all QmP wines

Volume in milliliters

Name of the village, in this case Brauneberg, to which the suffix *er* is added and which is followed by the name of the vineyard from which the grapes came, here Juffer-Sonnenuhr

Level of ripeness of the grapes

Percentage of alcohol by volume

Winery's address

*Qualitätswein mit Prädikat,* literally quality wine with special attributes, indicating that this is a QmP wine

Bottled on the estate

**MOSEL·SAAR·RUWER**

**FRITZ HAAG**
1994
Brauneberger Juffer-Sonnenuhr
Riesling - Auslese

750 ml    A. P. Nr. 2 577 059 21 95    Alc. 7.0 % / Vol.
Qualitätswein mit Prädikat - Gutsabfüllung
WEINGUT FRITZ HAAG · DUSEMONDER HOF · D-54472 BRAUNEBERG/MOSEL

519

Why do we care? Because of one thing that can totally mislead consumers. Certain *bereiche* (districts) have the same name as the principal town in that district. Bernkastel is a good example. The vineyard area right around Bernkastel is famous, and wines such as Bernkasteler Doctor are legendary. However, since Bernkastel is also a *bereich* name, it can also be used on the labels of neutral wines made anywhere in the large surrounding area. So, recognizing the word *Bernkastel* on a label doesn't tell you if the wine is extraordinary—or mediocre. You'd have to know the vineyard name to figure out the wine's quality. The same is true of Johannisberg and Nierstein. The easiest solution to avoiding this confusion is price. If you find a supercheap Bernkastel

wine, despite its name, it will inevitably *not* be one of the great Bernkastels.

*In the Gothic script still often found on wine labels, the single German letter β (which almost looks like a capital B) is an s set, or* scharfeses, *and is pronounced like an English s.*

## GERMANY'S WINE LAWS

The vineyards and wines of Germany are governed by a monumental set of laws that took effect in 1971 and were aimed at simplifying German wine. It estab-

## LIEBFRAUMILCH

—◦◦◦—

The first Liebfraumilch (literally, milk of Our Blessed Lady) wines were produced several centuries ago, probably from vineyards surrounding the Liebfrauenkirche (Church of Our Blessed Lady). The church was founded by Capuchin monks in 1296 just outside the city of Worms. Liebfraumilch is a pleasant, basic, slightly sweetish, inexpensive wine of the QbA level. It is made from a blend of any combination of Müller-Thurgau, riesling, silvaner, and kerner, plus no more than 30 percent other grapes. These can be grown in one of four wine regions: Nahe, Rheingau, Rheinhessen, or Pfalz. The two most famous brands are Blue Nun and Madonna.

# RIPENESS: THE HEART OF THE GERMAN WINE HIERARCHY

German wines are organized in a hierarchy based on how ripe the grapes were at harvest. This is not an arbitrary methodology. In a country as far north as Germany the ripeness of grapes varies tremendously and profoundly affects the types of wine that can be produced.

Consider a typical vineyard in an average year. Grapes that are picked during the normal harvesttime may be somewhat unripe, resulting in a very light wine. The vineyard's owner, however, may decide to let certain bunches of grapes continue to hang, despite the risk of worsening weather. Days or weeks later, the owner goes through the vineyard and picks again. These riper grapes will be made into a separate wine, which will be fuller and richer than the first. During this second go through, the owner may leave certain bunches to hang even longer. Assuming that the weather doesn't harm them, these quite ripe bunches will be made into a third wine, fuller and richer than the second. And so the process goes. There are six degrees of ripeness, and a vintner in a good year may make wines at all of them from the same vineyard. These categories of ripeness appear on the labels. Thus, you can always anticipate how lean or full the wine will be. Among all of the world's wines, only those from Germany and Austria give consumers this kind of detailed information.

The ripeness categories of German wines are usually referred to as "quality categories." This is a misnomer; although ripeness is always a clue to the wine's body, it is not necessarily a predictor of its quality.

lished the eleven original German wine regions (which, in 1989, with the reunification of East Germany, became thirteen) and their subdivisions, the *bereiche* (districts) and *grosslagen* (collections of vineyards).

For the highest level of wine, *Qualitätswein mit Prädikat* (QmP), Germany's detailed wine laws also regulate where the grapes can be grown, the maximum yield of wine per hectare, whether chaptalization is permissable, what methods of fermentation may be used, and what information must appear on the label. The law requires that each wine be examined, tasted, and found to be true to type (more about QmP wines begins on the facing page).

Finally, the specific requirements for ripeness, which determine whether a wine falls into the category of *tafelwein*, QbA, or QmP and its subdivisions of *kabinett*, *spätlese*, *auslese*, and so on were all established in the 1971 regulations.

Also, remember that ripeness is determined by the grapes' sugar content when harvested and does not reflect the sugar content in the final wine. Thus a wine in almost any of the German categories can be dry (*trocken*) or fairly dry (*halbtrocken*).

Exactly how is ripeness measured? In Germany the procedure is based on the weight of the must, the thick, pulpy liquid of crushed grapes, and is called an Oechsle (ERKS-leh) rating, after the physicist Ferdinand Oechsle, who invented it in the 1830s.

There are two major categories: table wine and "quality" wine. Table wine includes the designations *tafelwein* and *landwein*. These are the rock bottom categories of inexpensive, neutral, light wine. Production levels are not high, and these wines are almost never imported into the United States. So-called quality wine, the other category, is very important; 95 percent of all German wine falls into this cat-

egory. Quality wine is divided by law into two types, known for obvious reasons by their acronyms QbA (*Qualitätswein bestimmter Anbaugebiete*) and QmP (*Qualitätswein mit Prädikat*).

**QbA or Qualitätswein bestimmter Anbaugebiete:** This is wine from one of Germany's thirteen official winegrowing regions. It is the basic level of everyday, mostly inexpensive, quaffing wines. The grapes used are at a fairly low level of ripeness. QbA wines may be (and usually are) chaptalized—that is, sugar may be added to the unfermented grape juice to boost the final alcohol, a process that in no way alters the sweetness (or lack thereof) of the wines. (Chaptalization is common in France as well as Germany; see page 47.)

**QmP or Qualitätswein mit Prädikat:** Translated as quality wine with specific attributes, this is the highest class of

**521**

*Where wine traditions are ancient, vintners rarely live far from their vines.*

German wines. But the Germans were not content to leave it at that. QmP wines have six levels, based on ascending degrees of ripeness of the grapes from which they are made. These wines all must be made naturally; no sugar may be added (no chaptalization employed) to increase the final alcohol level.

Within the designation QmP, wines made from grapes picked at each degree of ripeness *can* be made from any variety of grape. For such top expensive sweet wines as *beerenauslesen* and *trockenbeerenauslesen,* however, riesling is considered the classic. *Eiswein,* on the other hand, is a playful category. German vintners make *eiswein* with just about every good grape from riesling to scheurebe to weissburgunder. *Eisweins* have even been made from pinot noir.

The QmP categories are listed here beginning with the one that is based on the least ripe grapes and progressing to the one that is based on the ripest.

**Kabinett:** A wine made from grapes picked during the normal harvest; typically a light-bodied wine, low in alcohol, and usually dry. A *kabinett* is generally more polished than a simple QbA. *Kabinetts* are

---

## THE INCREDIBLE TBAS

—◦◦◦—

Though Germany's *trockenbeerenauslesen* are made in much the same way as French Sauternes, the two styles of wine taste remarkably different. Because TBAs generally contain only half as much alcohol, they are far lighter on the palate. And though TBAs are often twice as sweet as Sauternes, they also have far greater acidity, making them the more beautifully balanced of the two.

---

perhaps the most food friendly of German wines. German wine lovers typically drink them as casual dinner wines.

**Spätlese:** Literally, late harvest, made from late-picked, fully ripened grapes, *spätlesen* have greater intensity and strength than *kabinett* wines. A *spätlese* may be dry or have a touch of sweetness. Even those with some sweetness, however, usually do not taste overtly sweet because of the corresponding high level of acidity in the grapes.

*Superripe grapes for* beerenauslese *are often partially affected by* Botrytis cinerea. *One by one, the botrytized grapes are painstakingly picked by hand (inset). They are messy to press and difficult to ferment, but the wine will be extraordinary.*

*Harvesting frozen grapes, one by one, for* eiswein *is a labor of love. Working in thick gloves, pickers must be careful not to drop the fragile grapes in the snow, where they can be lost.*

**Auslese:** Literally, selected harvest, *auslesen* are made from very ripe grapes harvested in select bunches—another step upward in richness and intensity. Generally, *auslesen* can only be made in the best years that have been sufficiently warm. Picking individual bunches means that the wines are expensive. Most *auslesen* are lush with some sweetness.

**Beerenauslese:** Literally, berry selected harvest, *beerenauslesen* are rare and costly wines made from individual grapes selected by hand. Usually *beerenauslese* (called, thank goodness, BA for short) grapes have been affected by the noble rot, *Botrytis cinerea*, giving them a deep honeyed richness.

**Trockenbeerenauslese:** Literally, dry berry selected harvest, *trockenbeerenauslesen* (TBAs) are the richest, sweetest, rarest, and most expensive of all German wines. TBAs, produced only in exceptional years, are made from individual grapes shriveled almost to raisins by botrytis. It takes one person a full day to select and pick enough grapes for just one bottle. Because of the enormously concentrated sugar, the grapes have difficulty fermenting. As a result, many TBA wines are no more than 6 percent alcohol. TBAs are absolutely mesmerizing in their intensity and heart stopping in price.

**Eiswein:** Literally, ice wine, so called because it is made from very ripe frozen grapes that have been picked, often at daybreak, by workers wearing gloves so that their hands don't warm the grapes. As the frozen grapes are pressed, the sweet, high-acid, concentrated juice is separated from the ice (the water in the grapes). The wine,

## THE GRAPES OF
# GERMANY

## WHITES

**Bacchus:** Heavy yielding cross of silvaner and riesling with Müller-Thurgau. Minor grape. A source for soft, low-acid wines, made throughout much of Germany.

**Elbling:** Once the chief grape of the Mosel; now a minor grape rarely used except in sparkling wines.

**Gewürztraminer:** Very good quality grape, though not widely planted. Can make excellent wines, especially in the Pfalz.

**Gutedel:** The same as chasselas in Switzerland. Minor grape made into simple wines. Mostly found in Baden.

**Huxelrebe:** Relatively new cross of gutedel and courtillier musqué. Minor grape. Can produce aromatic and honeyed wines, especially when grown at low yields in the Pfalz and the Rheinhessen.

**Kerner:** A cross of riesling and the red grape trollinger. Makes a lively wine. Plantings are in decline.

**Morio-Muskat:** Cross of silvaner and weissburgunder. Minor grape. Its wines can be strong tasting. Found mostly in the Pfalz and Rheinhessen.

**Müller-Thurgau:** The most widely planted grape. A cross of unknown parentage. The vines produce larger yields than riesling, but the quality of the wine comes nowhere close.

**Rieslaner:** A cross of riesling and silvaner. Can make good, zesty wines, especially in the Pfalz and Franken regions.

**Riesling:** Considered Germany's greatest grape, though second in terms of production. Has remarkable finesse, elegance, and aging potential. Grown on all the best sites.

**Ruländer:** The same as pinot gris. Makes big wines with good flavor, especially in Baden. Also known as grauerburgunder.

**Scheurebe:** Like rieslaner, a cross of silvaner and riesling. A fascinating grape, wines made from it have grapefruit overtones. Increasingly used by top estates, especially in the Pfalz.

**Silvaner:** Major grape, the same as sylvaner in the Alsace region of France. A source of dependably good wines. Rarely great. The leading grape in Franken.

**Weissburgunder:** The same as pinot blanc. Minor grape, makes neutral to good, likeable wines. The best are often from Baden, the Pfalz, and the Nahe.

## REDS

**Blauer Portugieser:** Among reds, second in importance after spätburgunder. Makes light, acidic wines.

**Dornfelder:** A grape producing increasingly well-made and popular wines, fruity and grapey. Germany's Beaujolais.

**Spätburgunder:** The same as pinot noir. Germany's leading and best red grape. Makes light, spicy, expensive wines.

**Trollinger:** Minor grape, known as schiava in Italy. Makes light, sharp wines.

---

made solely from the concentrated juice (the ice is thrown away), is miraculously high in both sweetness and acidity, making drinking it an ethereal sensation. *Eiswein*

grapes are usually at the ripeness level of a *beerenauslese*. They must be frozen naturally on the vine. (Austria and Canada, two other countries famous for *eiswein*, also make it in this manner. In other countries, what is called "*eiswein*" is sometimes produced by freezing grapes in a commercial freezer. As far as purists are concerned, the freezer method is definitely cheating.)

# HOW SWEET IT ISN'T

As a group, German wines are falsely thought to be sweet. In actuality, most fine German wines are dry or at least taste that way. The origins of the sweetness myth are intricate, but several German wine writers contend that the fallacy stems from the period after World War II. At that time enormous quantities of inexpensive German wines were intentionally made sweet, both to appeal to American GIs stationed in the country and to appeal to the Germans themselves who, economically destitute and suffering from poor diets, craved sweetness—especially if it could be gotten cheaply. (Sugar had been severely rationed during the war.)

The sales of sugary-tasting table wines soared. By the mid-1960s, the idea that German wine was sweet was pervasive among all but the most erudite wine drinkers. Not surprisingly, modern Germans have become determined to put the war—and everything associated with it—behind them. The pendulum has swung back. By the late 1980s the taste in Germany was for wines so dry the acidity threatened to vaporize one's taste buds on impact.

Severe dryness has a problem—the same problem presented by mindless sweetness. Neither takes balance into account and balance is the linchpin of greatness. This is unconditionally true of German wines. A German wine without balance is immediately recognizable as out of whack (too acidic, too thin, too flat, and so on). So, to fine-tune the balance of certain wines, German winemakers leave a little bit of sweetness in them or add a touch of *süssreserve*—juice from the harvested grapes that has been held back, clarified, and left unfermented, so it's naturally sweet. Winemakers can add tiny amounts of *süssreserve* to wines that otherwise would be teeth-throbbingly acidic. The goal is *not* to make the wine taste sweet—in fact, the best don't taste at all sweet. The goal is to bring the wine into focus—to make its taste

---

## KEYS TO CHOOSING A GERMAN WINE

~~~

In selecting a German wine, you must decide on two things: ripeness and sweetness. Ripeness is under nature's control; sweetness, under the winemaker's.

### RIPENESS

The wine will fall into one of the following categories, listed by the ascending degrees of ripeness of the grapes used to make it.

- *Qualitätswein bestimmter Anbaugebiete* (QbA)
- *Kabinett*
- *Spätlese*
- *Auslese*
- *Beerenauslese* (BA)
- *Eiswein*
- *Trockenbeerenauslese* (TBA)

### SWEETNESS

The wine can be:
- Bone-dry (*trocken*)
- Dry to the taste but containing up to 1.8 percent residual sugar per liter (*halbtrocken*)
- Sweet, from a little bit to a lot

clearer and more distinct. Some wines, of course, have balance from the beginning. In good years the fruit, acidity, and alcohol may all be in dynamic equilibrium, eliminating the need for a touch of *süssreserve*.

Dry German wines can be labeled either *trocken* or *halbtrocken*. These terms are defined as follows:

*Trocken:* Very dry; can be almost biting. The wine must have fewer than 9 grams (0.9 percent) of residual sugar per liter.

*Halbtrocken:* Literally half dry; however, because of the high level of acidity in German wines, even *halbtrocken* wines taste practically dry. Technically they must have fewer than 18 grams (1.8 percent) residual sugar per liter.

Starting with the 2000 vintage, you may find two new words on German labels in place of *trocken* and *halbtrocken*—*classic* and *selection*. Classic can be used for regional/varietal wines (see opposite page) with less than 1.5 percent residual sugar. A wine labeled Rheinhessen Riesling Classic is a dry riesling from that region. Selection will appear on a wine where the name of the village and vineyard are given and there is less than 1.2 percent residual sugar. So, instead of Selbach-Oster Zeltinger Sonnenuhr Riesling *trocken*, you may see Selbach-Oster Riesling Selection Zeltinger Sonnenuhr.

When none of these terms appear on the label, the wine probably has some sweetness. Sometimes that will be perceptible when you taste it; often, not, since the wine's acidity may disguise the sweetness. Whether winemakers stop fermentation early or add *süssreserve* or use neither method is up to them; there are no governmental rules.

## TINY PRODUCERS, MULTIPLE WINES

A first-rate German winery will, despite its tiny size, produce a dozen or more wines. Even thirty is not uncommon. This is because most vintners are working with a number of different grape varieties and then making multiple wines from each of them. A vintner may make separate rieslings from different vineyards. Each of these will be made into several wines at various levels of ripeness, from *kabinett* up to TBA. Grapes of some ripeness levels may be turned into two different wines— one bone-dry (*trocken*), the other not. The same vintner may also grow silvaner and scheurebe. Each of these grapes, too, will be made into multiple wines with differing levels of ripeness and sweetness.

# VINTAGES

German wines live on the edge of ripeness and that ripeness can be erratic. As a result, vintages usually vary far more in Germany than in, say, California, Chile, or Australia. In less sunny years, German wines will be destined to become lighter and sharper and have shorter finishes. German winemakers, for their part, will make more simple QbAs and *kabinetts* in these years.

In years with more sun, the potential depth and fruitiness will be greater; wines will develop a more profound taste. Winemakers will make more *spätlesen*, *auselesen*, BAs, and TBAs in these years. The years of greatest ripeness will become prized vintages. Usually, lean, cool years outweigh sunny years, but miraculously, virtually the entire decade of the 1990s was stunning in Germany. No winemaker living in this

## GOLD CAPS

———

Some German estates use special capsules around the necks of the bottles of their best wines to distinguish them. If an estate produces three different riesling *auslesen* from the same vineyard in the same year, each at a slightly higher level of ripeness, the winemaker may bottle one in the normal manner, bottle the second with a gold capsule, and bottle the third with a long gold capsule. The color, size, and use of capsules to distinguish different wines is solely up to the wine estate; there are no governmental regulations.

period has previously experienced such a string of fabulous vintages.

## AGING

One of the fringe benefits of acidity is that it acts to preserve flavor. Thus, German wines, among the most acidic in the world, are also among the longest lived. If the wine in question also happens to be slightly sweet (sugar, too, is a preservative), it will age even longer.

While young German wines from the best estates have irresistible sizzle and freshness, many connoisseurs drink them when they are five to ten years old. Indeed, very special wines may be held and aged for twenty years or more.

At ten to twenty years of age a top German riesling does not fade but, rather, becomes richer and more harmonious. Individual flavor sensations (peaches, apricots, stones, and so on) are no longer discernible. Every component coalesces into the greater whole.

## SERVING GERMAN WINE

The cliché about German wines is that they're perfect for picnics or dessert. While this may be true, it certainly understates reality. The fact is that German wines, because of their high acidity and focused flavors, are among the most food-flexible and vibrant dinner wines in the world.

When serving German wines, use a good-size wineglass, just as you would for other white wines. The traditional small, squat wineglasses sometimes called riesling glasses are actually terrible for riesling (or any wine) since they dissipate the bouquet, and you can't swirl the wine.

When you first open the bottle of some German wines, they have a slight aroma of fermentation or sulfur dioxide, $SO_2$, suggestive of the scent of a match that's just been blown out. The aroma is in no way harmful and does *not* mean the wine is bad. Moreover, it will vanish after the wine spends a few seconds in the glass. Sulfur can sometimes be smelled because $SO_2$ molecules bind easily with fructose (natural grape sugar), and some German wines contain traces of fructose. Like winemakers everywhere in the world, German winemakers use small amounts of sulfur to preserve freshness and prevent spoilage of white wines. The minimal amounts used are usually undetectable.

## GERMANY'S REGIONAL/VARIETAL WINES

A relatively new category of wine that continues to gain in popularity is made up of so-called regional/varietal wines. These are good, casual, everyday wines—a step up from basic generics but

## BLUE NUN

―∿∿―

The largest-selling German wine in the English-speaking world got its name by accident. When the Sichel family began producing the wine in the early part of the twentieth century, it was called simply Sichel Liebfraumilch. By 1925 the wine had become so popular that the Sichels decided to create a more compelling label. It pictured a bunch of no-nonsense nuns in brown habits against a blue sky. (Nuns were used because of the close association in Germany of the church with wine; until the early part of the nineteenth century the church owned most German vineyard land.) Consumers began referring to the wine as the one with the blue label and the nuns. Soon afterward, the name was changed to Blue Nun. But it was not until 1958 that the nuns were clothed in blue habits. Over the 1970s and 1980s, the number of nuns was progressively reduced in order to make the label more striking. Today there is just one blue nun who, unlike the earlier nuns pictured on the labels, is smiling.

*The current label (near left) for Germany's most widely known wine with its smiling nun. A 1929 label depicted nuns with serious countenances.*

not as high in quality (nor as expensive) as fine German wines.

To make a regional/varietal wine, the producers of a given region get together and decide on a kind of wine. Criteria for the wine are developed, and an easy-to-read label is created. *All* producers will use that label, and it will list only the most basic information; for example, it might read Rheinhessen Silvaner. Gone are village names; gone are vineyard names; gone are ripeness categories, such as *kabinett* or *spätlese*. The only other information provided is whether the wine is bone-dry (*trocken*) or nearly dry (*halbtrocken* or a newer term, classic) and then, in smaller letters, the producer's name.

The goal of these regional/varietal wines is to make casual drinking less complicated. If you're choosing a wine for a modest dinner you may not want to know anything more than that it's a silvaner from the Rheinhessen. Certain estates, such as Gunderloch in the Rheinhessen, are now making excellent wines of this type.

## SEKT

Possibly the most easily pronounceable word in the German language, *sekt* is the term for sparkling wine. Although all sparkling wine in Germany is called *sekt*, there are two distinct types—the bargain stuff and fine *sekt*.

Bargain *sekt*—more than 95 percent of total *sekt* production—is light, clean, and uncomplicated. Germans drink it by the bucketful (no special occasion needed). Its fizziness is the result of the bulk process (the second fermentation takes place in large pressurized tanks, not in each individual bottle). The best of the bargain *sekte* are made entirely from German grapes and are labeled *Deutscher sekt*. A top example is Deinhard's Lila Brut, which has strong sales in the United States. More basic bargain *sekte* are usually made using grapes from other European countries— commonly Italy, Spain, or France. In general, all bargain *sekte* are labeled very simply. No villages, vineyards, or vintages are indicated.

Fine German *sekt*—a tiny portion of the German sparkling wine market—is different from the bargain stuff in every conceivable way. These top-notch *sekte* are made in modest lots by many small estates. The grapes used, generally riesling, weissburgunder (pinot blanc), or ruländer (pinot gris), are from distinguished vineyards, and the bubbles come as a result of the Champagne method. Fine *sekt* is usually vintage dated, and the village and vineyard the grapes come from will always be listed on the label.

These great German *sekte* are sparklers with bite. Their crisp, streamlined flavors are vividly clear. The goal in making them is not to achieve the custardy, creamy roundness of Champagne but to make a wine that has the clarity and purity of flute music. Many are so racy with acidity they're almost shocking in their refreshingness. In poor vintages, when grapes remain very high in acidity, the production of these handcrafted, high-quality *sekte* increases.

Most of the best fine *sekt* is very limited in production and easier to find in Germany than in the United States. In general, a *sekt* from a top producer of still wines is almost always a good bet. Here are some producers whose *sekte* should be snapped up if you run across them: Kurt Darting, Theo Minges, Pfeffingen, and Bürklin-Wolf, from the Pfalz; Hubert Gänz, from the Rheinhessen;

Schlossgut Diel, from the Nahe; and von Schleinitz and Kerpen, from the Mosel.

# THE FOODS OF GERMANY

Maybe it's the proximity of France and Italy, maybe it's the irresistible romantism the cuisines of both those countries possess, but somehow, Germany has been overshadowed and undervalued as one of the great food cultures of Europe. A definite mistake, for food is Germany's best-kept secret.

There are really two culinary worlds there. First, there's old-fashioned Germany, where meals can resemble a medieval feast of wursts (sausages), pig's knuckles, dumplings, potato salad, spaetzle, sauerkraut, and black bread. This is solid, sturdy fare, a straightforward response to the bodily needs imposed by a cold, damp northern climate. But there's also contemporary Germany, a land rich with game birds, wild mushrooms, a huge repertoire of river fish (including delicate pike and trout), the sweetest cherries, raspberries, and strawberries, plus bright green, tender garden cresses, mâche, and lettuces that simply have no equal anywhere. The German penchant for perfection doesn't stop with Porsches and Mercedes. You can bet that a country that prides itself on high tech prides itself on haute cuisine.

To travel in Germany is to experience how deliciously and often these two worlds collide. Still, some things—German breads, for example—remain steadfastly traditional. As they should, for with the exception of Austria, there is no better bread in Europe. Before I tasted German *brot* (bread), I used to wonder how so many Europeans in centuries past supposedly lived on bread alone. One bite of *brot* was evidence enough.

529

Dark, chewy, heavy, nutritious, and so packed with flavor it's easily a meal in itself, German bread has muscle. The most well known is pumpernickel, which historically in Germany is leaden in weight, spicy-sour in flavor, and nearly black in color thanks to the high percentage of dark rye flour used, plus a long slow baking, during which the flour's starches caramelize. The bread most capable of inducing a nostalgia attack, however, is undoubtedly stollen, German Christmas bread, a yeast bread lavishly strewn with nuts and candied fruits and then generously topped after baking with butter and confectioners' sugar. Every region of Germany has its own version of stollen, including the fabulous *mohnstollen*, poppy seed stollen, a specialty of Bavaria.

From bread to soup seems only a short distance (culinarily if not philosophically), and Germany is a land of soups. There are the expected and sensational *kartoffelsuppen* (potato soups) and many sturdy meat-and-vegetable based soups (pheasant and lentil soup, for example, or *gulaschsuppe*, Germany's equivalent of Hungarian goulash), but most surprising perhaps are the wealth of fish soups including *Hamburger aalsuppe* (eel soup from Hamburg) and Black Forest trout soup.

The first time I visited Germany, I imagined that vegetarians would find the

*Traditional foods like these are only one part of the German culinary experience.*

so-called land of wursts to be their worst nightmare. Not true. Germany's passion for vegetables and fruits has the intensity that only a culture where sun is scarce can possess. Among vegetables, cabbage (called *kraut* or *kohl* depending on the region) and asparagus (*spargel*) stand out in such classic dishes as sauerkraut, the laborious authentic version (as in neighboring Alsace) where cabbages are shredded, salted, and fermented until they are sweetly sour; braised red cabbage with onions and apples in wine sauce; and asparagus, green or white, sautéed with morels, for which many Germans forage. Each May at the height of asparagus season (and the height of asparagus mania), many chefs around Germany temporarily give up their regular menus to focus entirely on asparagus. Dozens of different asparagus dishes pop up on asparagus-only menus.

As for the humble potato (*kartoffel*), the number of compelling German potato dishes could make an Irish person (including this one) genuflect. There are infinite versions of *kartoffelklössen*, potato dumplings, the classic accompaniment to Germany's national dish—sauerbraten, a "sour" pot roast in which the beef marinates in wine for up to four days before being slowly braised until meltingly tender. Other homey potato standbys include *kartoffelpuffern*, potato pancakes, and *kartoffelsalat*, potato salad (usually served hot, often with bacon). When potatoes are not the accompaniment to a meal, *spätzle* (spaetzle) often is. Germany's equivalent of gnocchi, these little squiggles of egg and flour batter are pressed through a *spätzle*-maker (which looks like a potato ricer) and then, like pasta, briefly boiled. Soft and rich, they are the perfect tool for sopping up sauces.

And those sauces often surround meat. It would be a bit of a shame not to indulge in meat in Germany for the pork and beef are sumptuous. In addition to sauerbrauten, there are numerous hearty interpretations of beef stew, veal dishes simmered in riesling, and Wiener schnitzel (an Austrian dish, very popular in Germany, of pounded, breaded, and sautéed veal medallions). And wursts are so much a part of the German psyche that they figure into everyday language. (When a difficult decision must be made, the Germans say *Es geht um die Wurst*—the wurst is at stake.) German wurst is rather like French cheese, a way of defining regions culinarily. There are reportedly more than 1,500 different kinds of wursts in Germany, the most famous of which are frankfurters (authentic versions are still made in the city of Frankfurt entirely from pork leg meat and are served with hearty mustard), *leberwurst* (liverwurst; made from pork or beef with a texture that ranges from coarse to as smooth and silky as pâté), and bratwurst (spicy, coarsely textured pork sausages seasoned with caraway).

Germany, a country of immense forests, is known for the quality of its game as well, and Germans use it to create venison with chestnuts, wild rabbit braised in wine, pheasant with red currant gravy, and on and on.

Desserts would seem to be a German birthright, as the number and scope of *bäckereien* and *konditorein* (bakeries and pastry shops) attest. Many of the best desserts are based on fruits, for stone fruits such as cherries, orchard fruits like apples, and all manner of berries—*himbeeren* (wild raspberries), *johannisbeeren* (fresh currants), and *preiselbeeren* (similar to cranberries) in particular—excel in Germany. Among the classic desserts are *apfelstrudel*, apple strudel, often made more like a cobbler than rolled in the Hun-

---

## NOT MUTUALLY EXCLUSIVE

⟿

The German passion for wine is paralleled by an equally strong passion for beer. The average German drinks 39 gallons of beer each year, the highest per capita consumption in the world (Americans, by comparison, drink 33 gallons). In the past, beer making in Germany, like winemaking, was carried out by monks who used the revenue from both to support their monasteries. German monks made many of the most important discoveries in brewing, including the fact that hops could be used to add zestiness to beer and preserve its freshness. Today there are some 1,170 breweries in Germany—about 40 percent of the world total.

---

garian manner; *apfelpfannkuchen*, apple pancakes, and *zwetschgenkuchen*, a plum "cake" that looks like an open-faced pie, oozing with ripe purple plums. Quark, often served with peaches or cherries, brings back childhood memories for virtually every German. Something like a cross between cream cheese and ricotta, quark is thick and tart, quintessential comfort food. Finally there are cherries—*kirschen*—harvested from the cherry orchards that flourish along the Rhine river. Distilled into a clear brandy or eau-de-vie, cherries become kirschwasser, a favorite after-dinner digestif as well as an integral component in Germany's hedonistic chocolate dessert Black Forest cake. But cherries and kirschwasser know few limits. The Germans use them in everything from cherry tortes to cherry puddings to cherry pancakes served warm with whipped cream infused with, what else? Kirschwasser.

# Mosel-Saar-Ruwer

If one of Germany's wine regions could be considered greater than all others, many wine drinkers (including this one) would argue for the Mosel-Saar-Ruwer. This is where Germany's most evanescent, most transparent, most ravishing wines are made. The wine region is defined by the hauntingly beautiful and eerily still Mosel River, which cuts a deep, snakelike gorge through the land. The river enters Germany where Luxembourg, France, and Germany converge, then winds back and forth for about 145 miles northeast until it empties into the Rhine near the town of Koblenz. The Saar and Ruwer are small tributaries of the Mosel.

*The* grape of the Mosel (as the region is commonly called) is riesling. But that states the case too simplistically for along the Mosel riesling becomes wines that have such crystalline clarity, they are like sunlight on a subzero day. They are the most sheer of all German wines.

## THE STEEPEST VINEYARD IN THE WORLD

The steepest vineyard in Germany—and in the world—is Calmont near the village of Eller on the Mosel. Calmont's 76-degree incline makes it look like a vertical wall of vines, all tenaciously gripping the slaty cliff.

The reasons are several. The vineyards of the Mosel are the steepest in Germany and among the steepest in the world. This would be one thing if they were located someplace warm and sunny. But the vineyards of the Mosel are also among the most northern in Germany. Steepness in a cold, northern wine region means that the sun is in contact with the

*In vineyards like Calmont, vines must cling to the hillsides.*

vines for limited precious hours each day. And, of course, the total number of sunlight hours during the growing season is also modest (the Mosel gets, in a good year, about a third of the sunlight hours that Provence does).

If fine wine is to be made then, vineyards must be nothing short of perfectly sited so that each ray of light and warmth is maximized. As a result, the Mosel's vineyards hug only south-facing slopes. At each turn of the river where the banks face north, the slopes have no vines. In addition, the best vineyards are quite close to the river itself, for even the reflection of light off the water becomes one more increment in the quest for ripeness.

Nonetheless, in the best vineyards full ripeness remains elusive most years. With sugar low and acidity high, you would logically conclude that Mosel wines would be tart and thin. There are (miraculously) two compensating factors. First is the riesling grape itself. Unlike, say, chardonnay, riesling can produce wines of great finesse—precisely when it is not fully ripe. This atypical trait is the heart of its greatness.

Second is slate. The famous gunmetal-gray slate of the Mosel is highly porous and both heat retaining and heat reflecting. These qualities help riesling to ripen. But, in ways that remain chemically and biologically mysterious, slate also appears to contribute to flavor. Wine drinkers throughout history have cherished Mosel wines specifically for their slatey, minerally, wet-stone flavors. No other wines in Germany taste quite the same.

Slate is slippery. (Picture the typical vineyard worker, a woman about sixty years old, who climbs these perilously steep, slick slate slopes in the middle of November!) Each year during winter rains, some slate washes down the slopes.

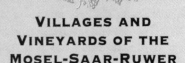

## VILLAGES AND VINEYARDS OF THE MOSEL-SAAR-RUWER

Wine labels for Mosel wines list both the village and the vineyard from which the grapes come. Here are some to look for; the village names appear in **boldface type**. More than one village may have a vineyard with the same name.

**Ayl:** Kupp

**Bernkastel:** Bratenhöfchen, Doctor, Graben, Lay, and Matheisbildchen

**Brauneberg:** Juffer and Juffer-Sonnenuhr

**Erden:** Prälat and Treppchen

**Graach:** Domprobst and Himmelreich

**Mertesdorf/Maximin Grünhaus:** Abstberg and Herrenberg

**Ockfen:** Bockstein and Herrenberg

**Piesport:** Goldtröpfchen

**Ürzig:** Würzgarten

**Wehlen:** Sonnenuhr

**Wiltingen:** Braune Kupp, Braunfels, and Gottesfuss

**Zeltingen:** Himmelreich, Scharzhofberg, Schlossberg, and Sonnenuhr

533

But not for long. The precious flat rocks, so necessary for ripeness, are immediately carried back up the hill in buckets.

Nowhere else in the world is there so great a concentration of top-notch wine producers in so small a place. The number of excellent wine estates on the Mosel is mind-boggling. Many of these producers are clustered together in the middle section, known as the Mittelmosel (middle Mosel). Here is where the famous villages of Bernkastel, Piesport, Brauneberg, and Wehlen are found. Wines such as Piesporter Goldtröpfchen and Bernkasteler Doctor are just two of the renowned examples from this tiny stretch of the Mosel. (The vineyard that rises up behind the town of Bernkastel received its "title" of Doctor from an archbishop from Trier who recovered from a terminal illness after drinking its wine.)

> *By tradition, not by law, Mosel wines are generally packaged in green bottles, Rhine wines in brown bottles.*

The three renowned *sonnenuhr*—sundial—vineyards are also in the Mittelmosel. They are the Wehlener Sonnenuhr, Brauneberger Juffer-Sonnenuhr, and Zeltinger Sonnenuhr. The huge sundials that give them their names were built more than a century ago in the sunniest part of three excellent slopes so that vineyard workers would know when to stop for lunch or for the day. Because the vines in the vicinity of the sundial also got the most sun (and made the richest wine), the areas around the sundials soon came to be considered separate vineyards. Today the *sonnenuhr* vineyards are among the best along the Mosel. Each has multiple owners who possess tiny plots. Some 200 wine estates own pieces of the Wehlener Sonnenuhr.

Müller-Thurgau and elbling are also grown on the Mosel. The first makes up about 20 percent of production and is turned into basic quaffing wine; the second, which forms

about 9 percent of production, is made mostly into inexpensive *sekt*.

The smaller Saar and Ruwer river valleys are more open and exposed than the Mosel. They are therefore colder and more windswept. If grape growing is hard on the Mosel, it's a nearly insurmountable proposition in these two little valleys. Nonetheless, a small amount of very fine, extremely austere wine is made in the Saar and Ruwer, and it is highly sought after.

*Some of the Best Mosel-Saar-Ruwer Producers*

**ALFRED MERKELBACH**

**CARL SCHMITT-WAGNER**

**C. VON SCHUBERT'SCHEN SCHLOSSKELLEREI**

**DR. H. THANISCH**

**DR. LOOSEN**

**EGON MÜLLER**

**FRITZ HAAG**

**JAKOBY-MATHY**

**JOH. JOS. CHRISTOFFEL**

**JOH. JOS. PRÜM**

**KARLSMÜHLE**

**KARP-SCHREIBER**

**KARTHÄUSERHOF**

**KERPEN**

**MILZ-LAURENTIUSHOF**

**REICHSGRAF VON KESSELSTATT**

**REINHOLD HAART**

**SCHLOSS SAARSTEIN**

**SELBACH-OSTER**

**VON HEDDESDORFF**

**VON SCHLEINITZ**

**WILLI HAAG**

**WILLI SCHAEFER**

**ZILLIKEN**

KERPEN

BERNKASTELER JOHANNISBRÜNNCHEN
RIESLING EISWEIN

MOSEL · SAAR · RUWER
alc. 7.5% by vol · 375 ml e

## SOME OF THE MOST EXTRAORDINARY EISWEINS IN THE WORLD

*iswein* is one of the greatest (and rarest) specialties of Germany. No other sweet wine has such high acidity. The magnetic juxtaposition of sweetness and acidity gives *eiswein* an electrified intensity. *Eiswein*, made from frozen grapes picked in the dead of winter, tastes quite different from *beerenauslesen* and *trockenbeerenauslesen*. And unlike BAs and TBAs, *eiswein* is not necessarily made from grapes affected by *Botrytis cinerea*.

Among the best German *eisweins* are those made by Darting, Eugen Müller, and Müller-Catoir, from the Pfalz; Gysler, from the Rheinhessen; Hermann Dönnhoff and Schlossgut Diel, from the Nahe; and Joh. Jos. Prüm, Karlsmühle, Kerpen, C. von Schubert'schen Schlosskellerei, and Zilliken, from the Mosel.

## VISITING THE WINE ESTATES OF THE MOSEL-SAAR-RUWER

There are impressive wine estates all along the Moselweinstrasse (Mosel wine route), which runs the entire length of the winding river. The best of them and the most spectacular vineyards are concentrated in the middle stretch. Bernkastel, the main village, is spellbinding and justifiably full of tourists. However, just standing in some of the smaller villages and letting your eyes take in the towering wall of vineyards above you can be a thrilling experience. Mosel estates are generally so small it's extremely important to call well in advance to make an appointment to visit. It helps immensely to speak German.

The telephone numbers include the dialing code you'll need when calling from the United States. If you're calling from within Germany, eliminate the 011-49 and add a zero before the next number. Don't worry if you notice that some of the phone numbers are longer than others; German

telephone numbers are not standardized the way they are in the United States. In mailing addresses, Bernkastel is linked with Kues, the village on the other side of the river.

**WEINGUT DR. LOOSEN**
St. Johannishof
54470 Bernkastel-Kues
011-49-65-31-3426

**WEINGUT JOH. JOS. PRÜM**
19 Uferallee
54470 Bernkastel-Kues
011-49-65-31-3091

**WEINGUT KARLSMÜHLE**
1 Im Mühlengrund
54318 Mertesdorf
011-49-651-5124

**WEINGUT SELBACH OSTER**
23 Uferallee
54492 Zeltingen
011-49-65-32-2081

**WEINGUT ZILLIKEN**
20 Heckingstrasse
54439 Saarburg
011-49-65-81-2456

535

# THE MOSEL-SAAR-RUWER
# WINES TO KNOW

You'll find the wines here, all of which are white, listed according to the category of the degree of ripeness of the grapes from which they were made, beginning with kabinett and continuing up to eiswein (for a full description of these categories, see page 522).

## Whites

### FRITZ HAAG

Riesling

Brauneberger Juffer-Sonnenuhr

kabinett

100% riesling

The wines that Fritz Haag makes from the incredible sundial—*sonnenuhr*—vineyard located above the village of Brauneberg are, year in and year out, classic examples of perfect Mosel riesling. The *kabinett* is sheer, gossamer elegance. In great years slate and minerals are spellbinding and intense. The Haag *spätlesen* and *auslesen* can be like pure thrusts of deliciousness—icy peaches drizzled with crème anglaise.

### WEINGUT ALFRED MERKELBACH

Riesling

Urziger Würzgarten

kabinett

100% riesling

The bachelor Merkelbach brothers seem like the elves of the Mosel. Small in stature and always grinning from ear to ear, they are devoted to making rieslings that are easy to love. The Merkelbach rieslings from the Würzgarten—spice garden—vineyard are indeed spicy and exuberant, with lots of slate and lacy peach flavors.

### WEINGUT KARLSMUHLE

Riesling

Lorenzhöfer Mäuerchen

kabinett

100% riesling

Nestled in meadowy mountains near the Ruwer River, the Karlsmühle estate makes wines that are as explosive as their location is pastoral. In good and great years the gingery, appley fruit of this *kabinett* is unstoppable. Acidity dances across your palate and doesn't pause to take a breath. The estate also makes phenomenal, high-impact riesling from the Kaseler Nies'chen vineyard. Drinking the *spätlese* from that spot is like being buried in ripe cantaloupes.

### CARL SCHMITT-WAGNER

Riesling

Longuicher Maximiner Herrenberg

spätlese

100% riesling

Like some wild peppermint-nectarine-lime sorbet, Schmitt-Wagner's rieslings from the Herrenberg vineyard are full of bracing, blazing, icy fruit. (Even the *kabinetts* are crackling crisp.) If acidity can be beautiful (I think it can), this is it.

## WEINGUT WILLI SCHAEFER

Riesling

Graacher Domprobst

*spätlese*

100% riesling

Schaeffer's wines from the Graacher Domprobst can be like crushed minerals experienced at ground zero. All of which is followed by an avalanche of ripe nectarine flavors. The finish can be so long and penetrating, it's ridiculous. The *beerenauslese* version makes you want to roll around on the carpet.

## JOH. JOS. PRÜM

Riesling

Wehlener Sonnenuhr

*auslese*

100% riesling

The estate of Joh. Jos. Prüm makes some of the most rarefied and delicate wines in Germany, hence their considerable fame. This *auslese* from the renowned sundial vineyard in Wehlen is like crystalline pear drops—mesmerizing in its transparency. Can wine actually be this elegant? Even in the weakest vintages, the Prüm wines are unmistakably filigreed and graceful.

# *Sweet Wines*

## SELBACH-OSTER

Riesling

Zeltinger Sonnenuhr

*beerenauslese*

100% riesling

Beerenauslesen (plural of *beerenauslese*) and *trockenbeerenauslesen* are rare along the Mosel, where cool temperatures and a far northern latitude generally prevent grapes from achieving such advanced ripeness and hamper the formation of botrytis. But in stellar vintages, when botrytis and superripeness do occur, the BAs and TBAs that result are simply astonishing. The magnificent riesling *beerenauslese* from the family firm of Selbach-Oster is a perfect example. Unctuously apricotish and utterly hedonistic, it nonetheless possesses sweeping elegance. Then there's the finish, which goes on for so long that you almost feel as if time has somehow been gloriously suspended. Few other wine experiences are so deeply rich yet so refined.

## DR. LOOSEN

Riesling

Bernkasteler Lay

*eiswein*

100% riesling

The fact that *eiswein* exists at all seems almost miraculous. Stories abound in Germany about the immense difficulty involved not just in picking the grapes but also in pressing them ever so gently. When it all works perfectly, the results can be an utterly outrageous wine, with honeyed opulence counterbalanced by icicle-sharp acidity. Dr. Loosen's riesling *eiswein* is a stunning, shimmering example.

# The Rheingau

Germany's reputation as the greatest white-wine producing nation in the world was historically based largely on the Rheingau. Today the supremacy of this small region is challenged by the gallons of delicious wine coming out of the Mosel and the Pfalz. And quite sadly, some of the most famous old Rheingau estates have been resting on their laurels in recent years and now make wines below the quality their reputations would suggest. Nonetheless, the Rheingau has, as the expert on German wine Stuart Pigott points out, the longest history of quality winemaking of any region in Germany.

The Rheingau is a serene, aristocratic wine region—one long, virtually continuous slope, a rolling carpet of vines, with the densely forested Taunus Mountains rising up behind. In a sense the mountains created the wine region, for they abruptly halted the Rhine's northward flow and

## HOCK

The British name for Rhine wine, hock, is a reference to the famous village of Hochheim in the Rheingau. At first hock implied a wine from Hochheim; later, it came to mean any Rheingau wine; and later still, any Rhine wine. Queen Victoria is credited with the line "A bottle of hock keeps off the doc."

*Rheingau's 1982 harvest (seen here) was considered one of Germany's rare great vintages—but in the 1990s, Germany experienced extraordinary vintage after extraordinary vintage, leaving vintners reeling with delight.*

forced it to veer straight west for 20 miles until it could again proceed north. The result was a nearly ideal south-facing bank backed by protective forests that block cold northern winds.

The leading grape of the Rheingau is riesling. Of all the German wine regions, the Rheingau has the highest percentage of riesling—more than 80 percent of its acreage. The rieslings here, however, are almost entirely different from Mosel rieslings. They are richer, rounder, earthier, and more voluptuous. Absent are the Mosel's icicle-like sharpness and slate flavors, and in their place is a near perfect gripping expression of fruit. The best Rheingau wines have amazing breadth; in a sip they can suggest everything from violets and cassis to apricots and honey. (All of this is, of course, easier tasted than it is expressed in words.)

Sun, soil, and latitude make the difference. To begin with, the Rheingau is farther south than the Mosel. Its long, south-facing bank rises up gently from the river, which for its part, acts like a giant sunlight reflector. The vineyards here are more reminiscent of a bunny slope than a course for downhill racers. And the soil is not solely slate but a vast mixture, including loess, loam, and quartzite.

The slightly stronger sun, of course, leads to greater—or at least more reliable—ripeness, which in turn gives Rheingau wines their fuller body and fruit. At the same time, high acidity in the grapes acts as a counterpoint, providing the wines with a kind of arching elegance. The potential for greater ripeness here bodes well for Rheingau *auslesen, beerenauslesen,* and *trockenbeerenauslesen.* These wines are legendary—the sort that make you want to lick the glass after swallowing the last drop. Yet for many wine drinkers, the less

extroverted Rheingau *kabinetts* are the truly mesmerizing wines, for they seem to have it all: elegance, transparency, richness, and profound fruit.

The most famous villages in the Rheingau include one that has become almost infamous: Johannisberg, named

## VILLAGES AND VINEYARDS OF THE RHEINGAU

Wine labels for Rheingau wines list both the village and the vineyard from which the grapes come. Here are some to look for; the village names appear in **boldface type.** More than one village may have a vineyard with the same name.

**Assmannshausen:** Frankenthal, Hinterkirch, and Höllenberg

**Eltville:** Langenstück, Rheinberg, and Sonnenberg

**Erbach:** Marcobrunn, Schlossberg, and Siegelsberg

**Geisenheim:** Kläuserweg, Mönchspfad, and Rothenberg

**Hallgarten:** Jungfer and Schönhell

**Hattenheim:** Nussbrunnen, Pfaffenberg, and Wisselbrunnen

**Hochheim:** Herrnberg, Hölle, and Königin Victoriaberg

**Johannisberg:** Goldatzel, Hölle, Klaus, and Vogelsang

**Kiedrich:** Gräfenberg and Wasseros

**Rauenthal:** Baiken, Gehrn, and Rothenberg

**Rüdesheim:** Berg Roseneck, Berg Rottland, Berg Schlossberg, and Bischofsberg

**Winkel:** Hasensprung and Jesuitengarten

539

## THE FIRST BOTRYTIZED WINES

⟨⟨⟩⟩

The discovery that grapes covered with the rather repulsive-looking mold *Botrytis cinerea* could actually lead to delicious wine probably occurred independently in three different wine regions. In Germany the first such wine, a *spätlese,* was made in the Rheingau at Schloss Johannisberg in 1775. Botrytized wines in Hungary predate those in Germany; they were made in the early 1600s in Tokay. In Bordeaux evidence is more sketchy, but the earliest accounts of botrytized wine supposedly date from 1847 at the famous Sauternes estate Château d'Yquem.

with a kind of bitter-almond flavor. The most famous come from the village of Assmannshausen and are expensive.

The Rheingau is the only German wine region that has a vineyard classification system. Starting with the 1999 vintage, it awards the designation *Erstes Gewachs* (literally first growth) to the top vineyards, rather like the way vineyards in Burgundy are designated *Grand Cru*. To be classified as *Erstes Gewachs* a vineyard must grow only riesling or spätburgunder and must meet a set of stringent requirements. Its wine must also meet exacting standards, including passing a sensory test, before it can be labeled *Erstes Gewachs* and bear the logo, three double Romanesque arches.

for Saint John the Baptist. Historically, such was the reputation of Johannisberg that in the nineteenth century, German immigrants to the United States renamed the riesling vine cuttings they brought with them Johannisberg riesling. By doing so they hoped to underscore the grape's authenticity and differentiate it from the inferior so-called rieslings brought from other parts of Europe. The new name stuck. Today many rieslings in the United States are labeled Johannisberg riesling.

Several dozen producers in this region are members of Charta, an association in the Rheingau devoted to making dry rieslings. Charta rieslings must pass a series of stringent quality tests. These wines all share a common bottle and capsule and display the Charta logo—a double Romanesque arch.

The other important grape of the Rheingau is spätburgunder (pinot noir), which here makes a pale but spicy red

*Some of the Best
Rheingau Producers*

**ALEXANDER FREIMUTH**

**AUGUST ESER**

**AUGUST KESSELER**

**BALTHASAR RESS**

**FRANZ KÜNSTLER**

**FRITZ ALLENDORF**

**GEORG MÜLLER STIFTUNG**

**H. H. ESER**

**JAKOB RIEDEL**

**JOSEF LEITZ**

**LANGWERTH VON SIMMERN**

**ROBERT WEIL**

**SCHLOSS JOHANNISBERG**

**SCHLOSS REINHARTSHAUSEN**

**SCHLOSS SCHÖNBORN**

**STAATSWEIN DOMAINE ELTVILLE**

**STAATSWEINGUT ASSMANNSHAUSEN**

## VISITING RHEINGAU WINE ESTATES

The Rheingau is a visitor's dream. Fine wine estates are numerous, welcoming, and easily spotted because of the identifying logo—a green and white sign displaying a riesling glass. This sign pops up all along the Rheingauer Riesling Route.

Not to be missed is the Kloster Eberbach, a monastery founded in 1135 by Cistercian monks. It was one of the most successful, creative wine estates of the Middle Ages, a reputation it held for the subsequent seven centuries. Located in Eltville, today it is the cultural wine center of the Rheingau and home of the German Wine Academy, which offers tastings and classes there.

Also worth seeing (though their wines are not as stellar as they once were) are two very famous, beautiful old castle/wine estates, Schloss Johannisberg and Schloss Vollrads. Schloss Vollrads has an excellent restaurant, the Graues Haus—gray house. There are excellent taverns and *weinstuben* in the Rheingau, plus inns, wine museums, vineyard hiking trails, and numerous wine festivals.

To visit, it's best to call the wine estate and make an appointment in advance.

*The Cistercian monastery Kloster Eberbach.*

Because the top estates are generally small and family run, it's considered good manners to buy a few bottles. It is very helpful to speak German. The telephone numbers include the dialing code you'll need when calling from the United States. If you're calling from within Germany, eliminate the 011-49 and add a zero before the next number. Don't worry if you notice that some of the phone numbers are longer than others; German telephone numbers are not standardized the way they are in the United States.

**SCHLOSS JOHANNISBERG**
65366 Geisenheim-Johannisberg
011-49-67-22-70090

**SCHLOSS VOLLRADS**
65375 Oestrich-Winkel
011-49-67-23-660

**STAATSWEINGUT ASSMANNSHAUSEN**
10 Höllenbergstrasse
65385 Assmannshausen
011-49-67-22-2273

**WEINGUT ALEXANDER FREIMUTH**
25 Am Rosengärtchen
65366 Geisenheim-Marienthal
011-49-67-22-981070

**WEINGUT AUGUST ESER**
19 Friedensplatz
65375 Oestrich-Winkel
011-49-67-23-5032

**WEINGUT FRANZ KÜNSTLER**
3 Freiherr-vom-Stein-Ring
65239 Hochheim
011-49-61-46-82570

**WEINGUT JOSEF LEITZ**
5 Theodor Heuss-Strasse
65385 Rüdesheim
011-49-67-22-4871

**WEINGUT ROBERT WEIL**
5 Mühlberg
65399 Kiedrich
011-49-61-23-2308

# THE RHEINGAU WINES TO KNOW

*You'll find the wines here, all of which are white, listed according to the category of the degree of ripeness of the grapes from which they were made, from* kabinett *to* spätlese *to* auslese *(for a full description of these categories, see page 522).*

## WEINGUT ABTEIHOF ST. NICOLAUS

Riesling

Hattenheimer Wisselbrunnen

*kabinett*

100% riesling

A laser beam. A sheet of ice. A great crackling bolt of lightning. And all of this precision drives wonderful rushes of apricots, peaches, and nectarines. The wines from Abteihof St. Nicolaus are always intense, lip-smacking Rheingau classics.

## WEINGUT ALEXANDER FREIMUTH

Riesling

Geisenheimer Mönchspfad

*kabinett*

100% riesling

One of the beauties of German wines is their ability to be delicate yet dynamic, and at its best the Geisenheimer Mönchspfad riesling is every bit the example. Rose and wildflower aromas fly out of the glass. The crystalline pure flavors of lime, melon, and apricot are so lively they seem to hover over your tongue. The family-owned Alexander Freimuth winery makes cutting-edge, New Wave Rheingau wines.

## AUGUST ESER

Riesling

Rauenthaler Rothenberg

*spätlese*

100% riesling

In a word: *exotic.* In top years, spicy, tropical, and menthol flavors collide like smashed atoms. Rushess of apricot nectar, melon, and a shimmering sense of minerals give the wine a haunting beauty. August Eser makes some of the most compelling, personality-driven wines of the Rheingau.

## WEINGUT GRIMM

Riesling

Rüdesheimer Berg Roseneck

*spätlese*

100% riesling

Like the perfect sorbet—intensely flavored, delicate, pure, clean, and charming. Grimm's rieslings also have wonderful surges of stoniness, though they are not a whit blunt. Is there such a thing as fairy-tale stoniness? The full name of the winery is Gebrüder Grimm, which does indeed mean the Brothers Grimm.

## WEINGUT JOSEF LEITZ

Riesling

Rüdesheimer Kirchenpfad

*spätlese*

100% riesling

Josef Leitz makes some of the most exciting contemporary-style wines in the Rheingau. They are wines that are simply more profound, more beautiful, more crammed with fruit than almost any others. The lush, glistening flavors of peaches, apricots, and marizipan are suffused with minerality. You don't just drink this wine, this wine compels you to drink it.

## FRANZ KUNSTLER

Riesling

Hochheimer Hölle

*auslese*

100% riesling

A great *auslese* is not clumsily sweet like candy but more sophisticated and nuanced. A great *auslese* is also not monodimensional; numerous entrancing flavors of minerals, fruits, and soil are woven together within the wine's sweetness. In the best years Künstler's *auslesen* exemplify this, revealing layer upon layer of fascinating sweetness.

# The Pfalz

The Pfalz is the most exciting, inventive wine region in Germany today. Like Texans, Pfalzers have an irrepressible spirit and their own irreverent way of doing things. The buttoned up (buttoned down?) image of German winemaking doesn't hold here. Individuality and creativity are prized above all. Not surprisingly, Pfalz winemakers make more great wines from more different types of grapes than winemakers anyplace else in Germany.

Although it is technically part of Germany's Rhineland, the Pfalz does not take its climatic cues from the Rhine River, as the other regions do. The river is a couple of miles east; no important vineyards border it. The dominant influence instead is the Haardt mountain range, the northern flank of France's Vosges Mountains. Just as the Vosges create a sunny, dry climate for Alsace wines, so the forested mountains of the Haardt create a protected environment for the vineyards of the Pfalz.

Given its more southerly latitude and more generous sun, ripeness is rarely a

*South of the Rheingau and the Mosel, the Pfalz is sunnier, warmer, and its vineyards are far less steep.*

problem. Pfalz wines, as a result, are almost bouncy with fruit. Among all German wines, they are the extroverts. Acidity, the soul of German wine, comes across differently here, too. It's not piercing; it doesn't howl. It doesn't even really seem like acidity. Instead, the best Pfalz wines have a tensile energy that's palpable. The sunniness of the Pfalz climate also means that the riper categories of wines—*auslesen, beerenauslesen,* and *trockenbeerenauslesen*— are found with a frequency (and intensity) not always shared by other regions. These lush, tangy, honeyed Godzillas, especially those from such producers as Müller-Catoir, Lingenfelder, and Koehler-Ruprecht, are some of Germany's most sensational wines.

The Pfalz has, after the Mosel, the most vineyard area planted with riesling. But unlike Mosel riesling, which has a definitive, brilliant slate character, Pfalz riesling is eccentric and variable. Some are real Creamsicles, full of vanilla, tangerine, and exotic citrus flavors; others taste like tropical fruit crème brûlée; and still others

543

## PFALZ

The name Pfalz derives from the Latin *palatium,* meaning palace. A palatine was a lord with royal privileges and the palatinate was the area he ruled. Today in Britain the Pfalz is often called the Palatinate because it was once controlled by palantine counts.

## VILLAGES AND VINEYARDS IN THE PFALZ

Wine labels for Pfalz wines list both the village and the vineyard from which the grapes come. Here are some to look for; the village names appear in **boldface type.**

**Deidesheim:** Grainhübel, Hohenmorgen, Kieselberg, and Leinhöhle

**Forst:** Freundstück, Jesuitengarten, Kirchenstück, Musenhang, and Ungeheuer

**Kallstadt:** Saumagen

**Mussbach:** Eselshaut

**Ruppertsberg:** Hoheburg, Nussbien, and Reiterpfad

**Ungstein:** Bettelhaus and Herrenberg

**Wachenheim:** Böhlig, Gerümpel, Goldbächel, and Rechbächel

muskat, and so on are grown in the Pfalz, too. For the most part these become simple, carafe-style wines. Except for one. Scheurebe (SHOY-ray-beh), a cross of silvaner and riesling, is one of the most exciting grapes in the Pfalz. With its zany grapefruity-vanilla tang, scheurebe is something you either really like (it has almost a cult following) or really don't. The best producers of scheurebe are Müller-Catoir, Lingenfelder, and Pfeffingen.

Although there are a number of merely good wine estates in the Pfalz, one is considered by many to be Germany's single best wine estate: Müller-Catoir. Words do not describe how fiercely vivid Müller-Catoir wines can be. They are among those rare wines in the world that—instead of *you* drinking *them*—seem to seize you, shake you, and make you surrender body and brain. But it's not vividness alone. There's a precision in every Müller-Catoir wine that is breathtaking. Like flashing sushi knives. Like sunlight bouncing off icicles.

are so gingery-peppery you want to grab a bottle and dash off to the nearest Thai restaurant. Pfalz (wickedly false) riesling keeps you guessing.

The wide variability of soil here is a key to the diversity of flavors. There is little slate and instead, limestone, loess, and light, well-drained sand.

Riesling is only one of several successful grapes in the Pfalz. The top estates make small lots of many others including gewürztraminer, weissburgunder (pinot blanc), ruländer (pinot gris), and spätburgunder (pinot noir). These can make very good to remarkably delicious wines, depending on the vintage and the knack of the winemaker.

Silvaner and all the workhorse crosses—Müller-Thurgau, kerner, Morio-

*Some of the Best Producers in the Pfalz*

BASSERMAN-JORDAN

DR. BÜRKLIN-WOLF

EUGEN MÜLLER

GEORG MOSBACHER

HERBERT MESSMER

JOSEF BIFFAR

JULIUS KIMMICH

KLAUS NECKERAUER

KOEHLER-RUPRECHT

KURT DARTING

LINGENFELDER

MÜLLER-CATOIR

PFEFFINGEN

THEO MINGES

## SAUMAGEN

❦

No visit to the Pfalz is complete without tasting the region's specialty, *saumagen,* the belly of a pig stuffed with pork, potatoes, and spices. For fun, *saumagen* should be accompanied by a riesling from the Karlstadter Saumagen, a famous—if strangely named—Pfalz vineyard owned by the Koehler-Ruprecht estate.

# VISITING THE PFALZ WINE ESTATES

A visit to the Pfalz is sure to be laden with discovery and extraordinary taste experiences. The Deutsche Weinstrasse (German wine route) runs through the region, with top estates strung all along it. The immaculate villages are full of cobbled streets and charming old houses. There are numerous good taverns, inns, and restaurants, including Weincastell Zum Weissen Ross, a charming inn and restaurant specializing in regional dishes. It's next door to the wine estate Koehler-Ruprecht and owned by the same family.

As in the rest of Germany, estates here are mostly small, so appointments to visit should be made in advance. Knowledge of German is useful. The telephone numbers include the dialing code you'll need when calling from the United States. If you're calling from within Germany, eliminate the 011-49 and add a zero before the next number.

Don't worry if you notice some of the phone numbers are longer than others; German telephone numbers are not standardized the way they are in the United States.

**WEINGUT DR. BÜRKLIN-WOLF**
65 Weinstrasse
67157 Wachenheim
011-49-63-22-95330

**WEINGUT JOSEF BIFFAR**
13/15 Niederkirchener Strasse
67146 Deidesheim/Weinstrasse
011-49-63-26-5029

**WEINGUT KOEHLER-RUPRECHT**
84 Weinstrasse
67169 Kallstadt
011-49-63-22-1829

**WEINGUT KURT DARTING**
2 Am Falltor
67098 Bad Dürkheim
011-49-63-22-2983

**WEINGUT LINGENFELDER**
27 Hauptstrasse
67229 Grosskarlbach
011-49-62-38-754

**WEINGUT PFEFFINGEN**
67098 Bad Dürkheim
011-49-63-22-8607

545

*Müller-Catoir is one of the great estates in the Pfalz, indeed, in all Germany.*

# THE PFALZ WINES TO KNOW

*You'll find the still wines here, all of which are white, listed according to the category of the degree of ripeness of the grapes from which they were made, from* spätlese *up to* beerenauslese *(for a full description of these categories, see page 522).*

## Sparkling Wine

**KURT DARTING**

Sekt

Riesling

*extra trocken*

100% riesling

Darting's wines are onomatopoetic—flavors dart around in your mouth with whirlwind crispness. Glimmers of pear, mint, earth, and spice come together in this sparkling wine with shimmering clarity.

## Whites

**LINGENFELDER**

Riesling

Freinsheimer Goldberg

*spätlese*

100% riesling

No one makes more beautiful, more nuanced, more refined wines in the Pfalz than Rainer Lingenfelder. Even in the least-great vintages, this wine from the Goldberg vineyard can be a masterpiece of complexity, full of mysterious tropical flavors wrapped up in a texture that coats your mouth like cream. Lingenfelder also makes one of the most compelling, trance-inducing scheurebes in Germany (if you only ever drink one scheurebe, Lingenfelder's scheurebe *beerenauslese* should be it).

**WEINGUT JOSEF BIFFAR**

Riesling

Wachenheimer Altenberg

*spätlese*

100% riesling

Like Müller-Catoir's wines, those of Josef Biffar are thoroughly captivating. In top vintages Biffar's seductive riesling *spätlese* from the Altenberg vineyard, for example, has jewel-like brilliance plus a vibrancy that's irrepressible. Fruit blazes out of the glass. The *auslese* version—riper, richer, more mesmerizing yet—has astonishing complexity and impact.

**WEINGUT MULLER-CATOIR**

Riesling

Haardter Bürgergarten

*spätlese trocken*

100% riesling

Most fans of German riesling would happily drink anything from Müller-Catoir; the wines are sensational across the board. But if forced to choose just one, this ultradry (*trocken*) riesling *spätlese* from the Bürgergarten vineyard would be

a must. The flavor comes at you like sheets of rain against a window pane—dramatic, bold splashes of fruit and minerals. The *kabinett* version of this wine is like some exotic melding of quince and buttermilk. Weingut Müller-Catoir makes dozens of wines, including devastating rieslaners, scheurebes, and gewürztraminers. Don't ever miss the chance to taste an *eiswein* from this estate; it's like drinking the platonic ideal of intensity itself.

## WEINGUT THEO MINGES

Riesling

Flemlinger Zechpeter

*spätlese halbtrocken*

100% riesling

Great riesling is never diffuse but always bright and focused. And so it is with the elegant, delicious rieslings Minges makes from the Zechpeter vineyard near the unfortunately named village of Flemlingen. The wine is high-toned, classic, gripping. Apricots and minerals, ginger and musk, earth and cream all come together in perfect balance.

## KOEHLER-RUPRECHT

Riesling

Kallstadter Saumagen

*auslese*

100% riesling

Koehler-Ruprecht makes rieslings that think they're Mae West—fleshy, forward wines oozing with creamy, luscious fruit. Classic, delicate, and sleek they are not. (Even the *kabinetts* from this estate are as juicy and rich as riesling gets.) Koehler-Ruprecht has an underground following in Germany for its hedonistically styled wines—especially those from the rocky Saumagen vineyard, which was once a Roman quarry.

## WEINGUT EUGEN MULLER

Riesling

Forster Kirchenstück

*auslese*

100% riesling

From the extraordinary Kirchenstück vineyard (considered one of the best not

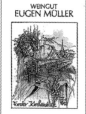

just in the Pfalz but in all Germany) Eugen Müller makes rieslings that are simply otherworldly. In great years the *auslese*'s apricot/ginger fruit is molten in intensity. Exotic spices unfold on the palate with seductive slowness. Acidity and mineral flavors slice through the wine like a saber. Drama is the wine's middle name.

**547**

## *Sweet Wine*

## KURT DARTING

Rieslaner

Ungsteiner Bettelhaus

*beerenauslese*

100% rieslaner

At its most stunning, a German sweet wine possesses pinpoint balance between sweetness and acidity, giving it almost unreal elegance. Such a wine should never descend into the gloppy, viscous, sugary world of so many dessert wines. Rather, a great German sweet wine should be sweet in a very pure, graceful manner and utterly light on the palate at the same time. Kurt Darting's rieslaner (the grape is a cross of riesling and silvaner) is a stellar example. The gorgeous burst of apricot sorbet, peach nectar, and

orange marmalade flavors is poised in breathtaking balance with the wine's tightrope of acidity. Top *beerenauslesen* should stop you in your tracks, and this one does just that.

*Dedicated and hardworking, the Darting family makes some of the most delicious wines in the Pfalz.*

# The Rheinhessen

Germany's largest wine area, the Rheinhessen, spreads out over 65,000 acres south of the Rheingau. Most of it is rather flat, fertile farmland, good for asparagus, orchards, corn, and sugar beets. As for wine, everything depends on precisely where you are. Most parts of the region make wine that is merely okay. Much of it is Liebfraumilch, a pleasant, mild, inexpensive generic wine that is also, alas, the best-known German wine in the world (see page 520). Buckets of bland, sweetish wines are also produced. Usually made by cooperatives from Müller-Thurgau grapes or one of the German crosses (bacchus, kerner, Moriomuskat, huxelrebe, and so on), these carafe wines are sold at bargain prices in European supermarkets.

Most of the truly interesting wine is made from the tiny amount of riesling grown in the region (about 10 percent of production). The majority of this riesling comes from vineyards in one concentrated area, from Bodenheim to Mettenheim, along the steep west bank of the Rhine. Known as the Rheinterrasse (Rhine terrace), this brief stretch includes the well-known wine villages of Nackenheim, Oppenheim, and Nierstein. The soil here is unlike any in Germany—a reddish sandstone mixed with slate. The rieslings that come from this soil are earthy and juicy, with the kind of up-front fruit that catapults out of the glass and smacks you on the lips. There are only a handful of top producers, including Gunderloch, J. und H. A. Strub, and Freiherr Heyl zu Herrnsheim.

One caveat about the village name Nierstein. A wine such as Niersteiner Hipping from the great Hipping vineyard is usually an extraordinary wine. But the word *Nierstein* is also a *bereich* name. This means that countless banal wines from no special vineyards can also bear the name. The best example is a wine called Niersteiner Gutes Domtal, which is a fairly characterless quaffing wine that comes from anywhere in the large surrounding area (*grosslage*) known as Gutes Domtal.

There is one other category of Rheinhessen wines; these fall between simple Liebfraumilch and top-class estate wine. They are good, everyday thirst quenchers known as regional/varietal wines (see page 527). They are made by a large number of producers using agreed upon methods and one common label. The best example is Rheinhessen silvaner, a dry QbA wine made by more than fifty producers.

---

*Some of the Best*
*Rheinhessen Producers*

BRÜDER DR. BECKER

BÜRGERMEISTER CARL KOCH

CHRISTIAN-WILHELM BERNHARD

FREIHERR HEYL ZU HERRNSHEIM

GEORG ALBRECHT SCHNEIDER

GUNDERLOCH

HEINRICH BRAUN

HEINRICH SEEBRICH

J. UND H. A. STRUB

LOUIS GUNTRUM

MERZ

ST. ANTONY

WITTMANN

---

# VISITING RHEINHESSEN WINE ESTATES

Compared to the breathtakingly beautiful Mosel, Mittelrhein, and Rheingau, the Rheinhessen is a rather plain-Jane place. Still, it has a simple, quiet beauty of its own, especially along the Rheinterrasse, which is where all of the top producers are located.

The Rheinterrasse is less than a dozen miles south of Mainz, the bustling unofficial wine capital of the Rhineland. (It was in Mainz that Johannes Gutenberg changed the course of history when he invented the movable-type printing press in 1450.)

As is true in most German wine regions, it is best to call ahead and make an appointment before visiting, and after being treated to a tour and tasting, it's a kind gesture to buy a bottle or two of wine. Being able to speak German is helpful. The telephone numbers include the dialing code you'll need when calling from the United States. If you're calling from within Germany, eliminate the 011-49 and add a zero before the next number. Don't worry if you notice that some of the phone numbers are longer than others; German telephone numbers are not standardized the way they are in the United States.

**WEINGUT BRÜDER DR. BECKER**
3 Mainzer Strasse
55278 Ludwigshöhe
011-49-62-49-8430

**WEINGUT BÜRGERMEISTER CARL KOCH**
62 Wormser Strasse
55276 Oppenheim/Rhein
011-49-61-33-2326

**WEINGUT GUNDERLOCH**
1 Carl-Gunderloch-Platz
55299 Nackenheim
011-49-61-35-2341

**WEINGUT J. UND H. A. STRUB**
42 Rheinstrasse
55283 Nierstein/Rhein
011-49-61-33-5649

**WEINGUT MERZ**
43 Mainzer Strasse
55437 Ockenheim
011-49-67-25-2387

**WEINGUT WITTMANN**
19 Mainzer Strasse
67593 Westhofen
011-49-62-44-905036

549

# THE RHEINHESSEN WINES TO KNOW

*You'll find the wines here, all of which are white, listed according to the category of the degree of ripeness of the grapes from which they were made, from* kabinett *up to* trockenbeerenauslese *(for a full description of these categories, see page 522).*

## *Whites*

### BRUDER DR. BECKER

Riesling

Dienheimer Paterhof

kabinett halbtrocken

100% riesling

Brüder Dr. Becker's riesling *kabinetts* are known for their high definition and classy, beautifully balanced flavors. Like a single, small, exquisite piece of jewelry, they can be elegant and refined without being showy. At their best, a subtle peachy, stony, spicy smokyness runs through these wines, as well as the estate's superb dry *(trocken)* rieslings from the neighboring Tafelstein vineyard.

### WEINGUT GUNDERLOCH

Riesling

Nackenheim Rothenberg

spätlese

100% riesling

Gunderloch, like Müller-Catoir in the Pfalz, is an estate that rose to prominence in the last few decades, and *every* wine it makes will leave you awestruck. In great years the atomlike density and laser-sharp focus of Gunderloch's *spätlese* from the Rothenberg vineyard is mind-blowing. Apricot nectar, bergamot, marzipan, and mango flavors fly through the wine, yet it still seems elegant. The dry *(trocken)* version of the *spätlese* has intense stony—no, bouldery—flavors as well. The *auslese* is blindingly delicious.

### J. UND H. A. STRUB

Riesling

Niersteiner Pettenthal

spätlese

100% riesling

If you could whip together peaches, Winesap apples, cantaloupe, nectarines, and vanilla and then drizzle them over stones . . . pure deliciousness! Strub is known for big, expressive, snappy rieslings that always end bone-dry.

## *Sweet Wine*

### WITTMANN

Huxelrebe

Westhofener Rotenstein

trockenbeerenauslese

100% huxelrebe

cles is the right word, for most crosses make good but rarely great wine. Huxelrebe is a cross of chasselas and the French table grape courtillier musqué. What an extraordinary TBA! Absolute pinpoint balance, shimmering energy, a seductive flavor of essence of apricot, and a long rippling finish.

More than any other wine estate in Germany, Wittmann works miracles with crosses. And mira-

# Wine Regions of Note

As some of the most historically significant white-wine regions in all of Europe, the Mosel-Saar-Ruwer, Rheingau, Pfalz, and Rheinhessen are deservedly Germany's best-known and most renowned wine regions. But good—occasionally very good—wines are made in several neighboring districts as well, including the Ahr, Baden, Franken, Mittelrhein, and the Nahe. Many of these wines won't match Germany's best for sheer intensity and brilliance of flavor. The majority are little more than quaffing wines, ready to be downed with abandon at the nearest *weinstube* (wine tavern). Yet, as in France and Italy, less famous wine districts often boast hidden gems. Half the fun is finding them.

## AHR

One of Germany's smallest wine regions, the Ahr is also the most northerly, after Sachsen and Saale-Unstrut in the former East Germany. It is defined by the Ahr River, which flows into the Rhine just south of Bonn in the Mittelrhein. The rough, rocky, forested terrain is beautiful. This region is a favorite wine country getaway for residents of Bonn.

Although counterintuitive, most of the wine made here is red. Specifically, it is pale, light spätburgunder (pinot noir)—decent enough but not usually remarkable. The best producers include Meyer-Näkel, Kreuzberg, Sonnenberg-Görres & Linden, and J. J. Adeneuer.

## BADEN

The wines of Baden do not—and could not—have one single character, for this extremely diverse region is made up of several, large, noncontiguous chunks of land. One part of Baden is in central Germany, not all that far from Würzburg; another, on the Bodensee (Lake Constance) near Switzerland; and the biggest and most important part runs parallel to the Rhine from Heidelberg all the way south to Basel.

The southern part of this stretch—roughly from Basel up to the famous spa town Baden-Baden—is where the very top wines are to be found. Immediately west

*Germany's beautiful old villages are lined with half-timbered houses.*

551

of this district is France's Alsace region, and to the east, the Black Forest. In particular, wines from the area around the Kaiserstuhl (literally emperor's throne), an extinct volcano, are prized.

This is one of the warmest vineyard areas in Germany and the wines taste like it. By German wine standards, they're very bosomy, big-bodied quaffs with lots of alcohol and only modest acidity. They are galaxies away from the Mosel in spirit and style.

The leading grape in Baden is Müller-Thurgau, which makes wines for everyday drinking. You'll also find ruländer (pinot gris), gutedel (chasselas), silvaner, weissburgunder (pinot blanc), gewürztraminer, spätburgunder (pinot noir), and of course, riesling. (Very little of the latter is grown.)

The largest number of Baden wines are made by cooperatives (four out of every five growers sell their grapes to co-ops). The leading co-op is the Badischer Winzerkeller. Even by cooperative standards, it is mammoth, making more than one third of all of Baden's wine.

Baden is more famous for its food than for its wine. The forests of Baden abound with game, berries, and wild mushrooms. In particular, venison, country bacon, and ham from the Black Forest are legendary, as are *preiselbeeren* (a kind of small sweet-tart cranberry) and *heidelbeeren* (huckleberries). Many Baden dishes combine kirsch, cream, and tart cherries, including of course, the sine qua non of Baden cooking: Black Forest chocolate cake.

Among the top producers of Baden wine are Karl Johner, Salwey, Bercher, Staatsweingut Meersburg, Dr. Heger, Freiherr von Gleichenstein, Gräflich Wolff-Metternich, Heinrich Männle, Hermann Dörflinger, and Winzergenossenschaft Sasbachwalden.

# FRANKEN

Just about due east of the Rheingau, beyond the city of Frankfurt, is the W-shaped wine region known as Franken. Here, at the northern edge of Bavaria, the climate is severe, springtime frosts are common, and the size of the harvests fluctuates widely according to the weather.

*By law, only Franken wine is bottled in a squat, plump flagon called a* bocksbeutel *(literally a goat scrotum).*

Franken wines are broad, sharp, and sturdy with little of the elegance, transparency, or brilliant fruit of those of the Rhineland or the Mosel. Nonetheless, they are well loved by the Bavarians who consume most of them (few are exported to the United States).

The top wines in Franken are usually made from silvaner; little riesling is planted there. Common, everyday wines tend to be made (often by cooperatives) from Müller-Thurgau or crosses, such as scheurebe,

Bocksbeutels *are the signature bottles of Franken. On the back of each* bocksbeutel *is a Franken label and special seal.*

bacchus, kerner, or rieslaner. Most are made in a very dry style. *Trockenbeeren-auslesen* and *beerenauslesen* are very rare.

Among the best Franken producers are Staatliche Hofkeller, Burgerspital, Hans Wirsching, and Juliusspital. Of these, Hans Wirsching makes silvaners with unmatched peachy, gingery, vanilla-y zing.

# MITTELRHEIN

The vineyards of the Mittelrhein (Middle Rhine) lie, technically speaking, both north and south of where the Mosel flows into the Rhine. On the northern end, the region stretches almost to Bonn. But virtually all of the important vineyards are located along the southern stretch from Koblenz down to Bingen. At Bingen, where the Rhine makes an abrupt turn, the Mittelrhein ends and the Rheingau begins. The Mittelrhein is a wine region right out of Hänsel and Gretel. Fairy-tale medieval castles are poised above the steep vineyards; there are numerous quaint villages, such as Bacharach and Boppard; the half-timbered houses are postcard perfect. (The opera *Hänsel und Gretel*, based on the Grimm fairy tale, was actually composed in Boppard by Engelbert Humperdinck.)

Many Mittelrhein estates make wines geared to the tourist business. These simple, inexpensive quaffs (mostly based on Müller-Thurgau) are happily drunk up in the region's bustling restaurants and cafés. There are, however, a handful of top estates that make extremely good riesling and *sekt*. The best of these have a mineralness and clarity reminiscent of the Mosel. This is not by chance. Like the Mosel's, the Mittelrhein's vineyards hover over the river on slate slopes that seem to soar skyward.

## CASTLES IN THE RIVER

⟞⟐⟞

Among the most impressive sights along the Mittelrhein are the medieval castles smack in the middle of the narrow river. Though built on tiny islands, the castles appear to rise straight up out of the water. They were once toll posts. Ships that sought to pass by either paid a fee or were sunk by cannonballs.

There are problems here. The vineyards, sadly, are diminishing in number and have been doing so for decades. The terrain is difficult to work, and for a variety of complex reasons, most Mittelrhein wines have never been able to command high enough prices to justify the cost of making good wine. Any vineyard that is not absolutely stellar is eventually abandoned for lack of profit. (And it may never be used as a vineyard again. By EEC law if a vineyard has been abandoned for a period of eight years,

553

*A castle near Kaub, located in the middle of the Rhine River.*

## A PERFECT PARTNER

The high acid in German rieslings coupled with their clean, pure flavors and the absence of obfuscating oak makes this the most exciting and versatile white wine when it comes to pairing with food. And—unusually for a white wine—the range of possibilities begins with meat. In Germany riesling is drunk with every dish imaginable from grilled sausages to pork roast. Talk about brilliant combinations! The wine's penetratingly sharp acid is a dramatic counterpoint to the fat in meat. But riesling is also stunning with salads and simple vegetable dishes. Here, its light body and overall fresh character work to echo the light, fresh flavors of the food. The most inspired pairing of all, however, is that of riesling with complex Asian dishes, where chiles, soy sauce, garlic, and other bold seasonings create vivid contrasting flavors often within the same dish. Many wines simply shut down in such company. But not riesling. Riesling's bracing acidity, pure fruit, and floral aromas and flavors create a delicious juxtaposition.

it must revert to nature and can no longer be used for any commercial purpose.)

All this said, the top wine estates—Adolf Weingart, August Perll, Heinrich Weiler, Jochen Ratzenberger, and Toni Jost produce some stunning wines. In particular, the rieslings that Jochen Ratzenberger makes are almost scary, they can be so intense, minerally, and majestic. Adolf Weingart's rieslings could blind you with their brilliant clarity. And for pure uncomplicated scrumptiousness, the rieslings of Toni Jost are irresistible.

## NAHE

The Nahe River, south of and parallel to the Mosel, flows into the Rhine near Bingen, close to where the Rheingau ends. The region named after it is fairly large, with both decent, nondescript wines and wines that can be exceptionally beautiful and complex. The latter are often described as a little like a cross between Rheingau and Mosel wines. But that doesn't really get to the soul of the matter, for Nahe wines have an essential vividness and gracefulness; they can be exquisitely intense and nearly explosive—all at the same time. Theirs is a fiery elegance.

The Nahe is one of the most geologically diverse of Germany's wine regions, a factor that seems to give the best wines their broad mineral flavors. Riesling, silvaner, and Müller-Thurgau are all grown, although the finest wines are almost always made from riesling.

The best producers include Gänz, Hans Crusius & Sohn, Hehner-Kiltz, Hermann Dönnhoff, Kruger-Rumpf, Paul Anheuser, Schlossgut Diel, and the Nahe State Domaine, a state-owned enterprise created in the early part of the twentieth century and called in German—get ready—Staatliche Weinbaudmänen Niederhausen-Schlossböckelheim. The ravishing Dönnhoff rieslings have flavors so intricate and dense they seem, like a Japanese sword, to be the fusion of hammered layers folded back into themselves. No Nahe estate makes wines that are more mesmerizing. Also captivating are the wines from Hehner-Kiltz. The flavors of even its simplest *kabinetts* drop on the palate and detonate like bombs.

# Austria

## LOWER AUSTRIA
## BURGENLAND
## STYRIA
## VIENNA

Austria makes the raciest, most exciting wines in central-eastern Europe. That might seem to be a pretty big claim, but to taste them is to be easily convinced. These are wines—whites in particular—with an absolutely uncanny synergy between power and elegance. To possess such a character they must be dry, and most of them are, hauntingly so. (The only exceptions are the sweet wines that are deliberately made that way.)

Until the mid-1990s Austrian wines were a total secret. Few—if any—were ever imported into the United States. Today, though the number of Austrian wines available here is still small, those you can find are among the most delicious and compelling.

Austrian viticulture is quite old. The Celts, discoverers of what would eventually become many of the top wine regions of central Europe, planted the first grapes in the fourth century B.C. Later the vineyards fell within the vast arc of the Roman empire. By the Middle Ages, Austrian vineyards, like those of France, Germany, and Italy, were in the painstaking care of

Austria ranks eighteenth in wine-producing countries worldwide. Austrians drink an average of 9.10 gallons of wine per person each year; they're eleventh in world wine consumption.

*Exuberant about life and passionate about wine, Austrians have always loved wine festivals.*

556

## THE QUICK SIP ON AUSTRIA

- Austria makes the most riveting wines in central-eastern Europe.

- Like Germany, Austria is devoted primarily to dry white wines and magnificent sweet wines. In general, however, Austrian wines are fuller bodied than German wines.

- The leading grapes in Austria are riesling and the indigenous white grape variety grüner veltliner, known for spicy, snazzy wines.

monks. But more than any other historical period, the twentieth century—and its tumultuous politics—shaped Austrian wine.

The modern country called Austria, about the size of Maine, dates from 1919 when the sprawling Austro-Hungarian Empire was dissolved by the Treaty of Saint

Germain. In its place, the post-World War I countries of Czechoslovakia, Hungary, Yugoslavia, and (a far smaller) Austria were formed.

The new Austria, economically unstable and enfeebled by war, could no longer afford to make the sort of handcrafted wines that were a hallmark of the empire past. Something serviceable and cheap was the order of the day. Austrian wine merchants began the mass manufacture of rather insipid, slightly sweet, cheap quaffs that sufficed locally, satisfied tourists, and could be exported easily—especially to Germany, which was also financially strapped. The market for such wines, notwithstanding their lack of character, grew. Austrian growers, paid peanuts for their grapes, increasingly planted the highest yielding, most innocuous varieties. Wine merchants and winemakers began taking every production shortcut they could find.

Then, in 1985, the downward spiral hit bottom. A small group of corrupt wine

*The Stift (abbey) Göttweig, perched above the Danube near Krems, transformed many of its land holdings into vineyard in what is now Austria's most famous wine region—the Wachau.*

558

Austria is often wrongly assumed to be a sociocultural subset of Germany. Though they share (more or less) the same language, the two countries have national characters that are quite different. Austria, on the doorstep of Asia, is influenced by Eastern thinking, philosophy, culture, and art. Austrians can seem both more passionate and more melancholy than Germans. Austria is, after all, the homeland of both Sigmund Freud and Wolfgang Amadeus Mozart.

For their part, Austrian wines bear very little resemblance in taste to German wines. Austrian whites are much fuller in body and fruit than German whites and—except for dessert wines—they are always dry *(trocken)*. Compared to the light, low-alcohol, elegant, and mannered white wines of Germany, Austrian whites can be wildly untamed. And though fine red wines don't play a major part in either country, here again the two countries differ considerably.

Austrian reds—juicy, husky, and often streaked with pepper and spice flavors—have almost nothing in common with the gentle, light-bodied, pale reds of Germany.

That said, Austria and Germany do share a few things. Both countries are known for handcrafting some of the most decadent sweet wines in Europe. Both countries designate these wines according to the ripeness of the grapes. Like Germany, Austria is heralded for *eiswein,* a sweet wine of often mesmerizing finesse. In both countries, the extreme difficulty of making legendary dessert wines ensures their rarity. Austrian sweet wines—*eisweins, auslesen, beerenauslesen,* and *trockenbeerenauslesen*—make up just 3 percent of the total production of high-quality wine.

Lastly, we mustn't overlook one more thing Austria and Germany have in common—they both make delicious *sekt,* sparkling wine that is happily popped open at the slightest provocation.

559

brokers, trying to pass off cheap plonk as higher quality, more expensive wine, doctored it with diethylene glycol (a component of antifreeze) to make it taste fuller and sweeter. Though the merchants were caught and no one died from the tainted wine, the news spread around the world. Austrian wines were characterized en masse as shoddy; jokes abounded about drinking them to stay warm.

In the end, this wine scandal proved to be what one winemaker called a cleansing thunderstorm. The mass market for inferior wine collapsed, leaving the few remaining quality producers to build a new Austrian wine industry from the ground up. The turnaround has been dramatic.

For the impassioned, knowledgeable winemakers and viticulturists of today's Austria, top-quality wine is a virtual religion.

## AUSTRIA'S WINE LAWS

Austria's current wine laws are the strictest in Europe. They stipulate precise requirements for every wine, including the minimum sugar content of the grapes at harvest and the maximum alcohol level.

For the highest levels of the six tiers of *Prädikatswein,* the detailed laws regulate where the grapes can be grown, the maximum yield of wine per hectare,

## THE MOST IMPORTANT

### AUSTRIAN WINES

**LEADING WINES**

**Grüner Veltliner** white (dry and sweet)

**Riesling** white (dry and sweet)

**Sauvignon Blanc** white

**Weissburgunder\*** white (dry and sweet)

**Welschriesling** white (dry and sweet)

**WINES OF NOTE**

**Blaufränkisch** red

**Zweigelt** red

*\*pinot blanc*

CUVÉE FALSTAFF
ROSSATZER GRÜNER
VELTLINER SMARAGD
ERNTE
FREIE WEINGÄRTNER WACHAU

whether chaptalization is permissible, what methods of fermentation may be used, and what information must appear on the label. The laws also require that each wine be examined, tasted, and found true to type. Finally, each wine must be scientifically tested and given an official test number.

You may find it useful to refer to Reading a German Wine Label (see page 519) for help in following Austrian wine labels. In many cases Austrian labels present comparable information.

# THE LAND, THE GRAPES, AND THE VINEYARDS

Austria, a landlocked country, is bordered by the Czech Republic, the Slovak Republic, Germany, Hungary, Slovenia, Italy, and Switzerland. Although the western part of the country with its cities, such as Salzburg and Innsbruck, is well known, the vineyards are all in the distant, more exotic eastern half. There, like a backward C, they form a crescent along the country's eastern border.

There are four major wine regions: Lower Austria (which includes the Wachau), Burgenland, Styria, and Vienna. Vienna—tiny as wine regions go—is the only major city in the world considered an actual wine region. Numerous commercial vineyards exist within the city limits. Lower Austria, the largest and most important wine region, is in the north along the Slovakian border. Lower refers to the lower part of the Danube River, which flows through the region. Burgenland is the easternmost Austrian wine region; much of it lies along the Hungarian border. And Styria, the hilliest region, is in the south along the Slovenian border. Each of these wine regions is climatically and geologically distinct.

Austria is mostly a white-wine producer; 80 percent of all its wine is white. In total, there are some thirty-three grape varieties. They range from the internationally recognized, such as chardonnay and pinot blanc, to the local favorites, like grüner veltliner (the leading white grape) and blaufränkisch (the main red). Of all the varieties, about sixteen are considered prominent, and six of these are the most important. Some top producers occasionally blend grape varieties, hoping to achieve a wine greater than the sum of its parts. However, for the most part Austrian wines are made from a single grape.

# THE GRAPES OF
# AUSTRIA

*Thirty-three grape varieties are grown in Austria; these are the most significant.*

## WHITES

**Furmint:** Minor grape but a common component in *ausbruch*, the famous sweet wine of Burgenland.

**Grüner Veltliner:** Austria's most important grape in terms of both quality and the acreage of vineyards devoted to it. The unique flavor of the wines made from it often begins with vanilla-dipped peaches and ends with a rush of white pepper.

**Morillon** or **Chardonnay:** Chardonnay is called by both names in Austria. A minor grape; the best dry wines from it are elegant, almost taut in style. Also made into some good sweet wines in Burgenland. Though plantings are small, they're increasing.

**Muskateller:** Locally also known as gelber muskateller, this is the same as muscat blanc à petits grains and part of the muscat family of grapes. Grown mainly in Styria; muskateller is extremely fragrant and lush; generally drunk as an aperitif.

**Neuburger:** Very simple workhorse grape; a source of pedestrian dry wine and some good sweet wines.

**Pinot Gris:** Minor grape; made into dry wines and sometimes used as part of the blend in sweet wines.

**Riesling:** A major grape even though not widely planted in Austria. The source of lively, vibrant, often stunning wines, generally with more power than German rieslings. Austrian rieslings have an aroma of peaches and roses.

**Riesling X Sylvaner:** Minor grape; although referred to as riesling X sylvaner in Austria, some believe it to be the same as Germany's Müller-Thurgau. Turned into simple quaffing wines.

**Sämling:** Minor grape; another cross between sylvaner and riesling. Sometimes used for *eiswein*.

**Sauvignon Blanc:** Not widely planted except in the region of Styria, but important because of the quality of the exotically smoky and grassy wines made from it.

**Traminer:** The aromatic ancestor of gewürztraminer; extremely expressive; made into dry and sweet wines.

**Weissburgunder:** Major grape; known elsewhere as pinot blanc. Makes well-focused dry wines that range from creamy to racy, as well as sweet wines, a specialty of Burgenland.

**Welschriesling:** Major grape; not a type of riesling despite its name. Makes simple, straightforward dry wines, sometimes with the aroma of fresh hay. Also used for sweet wines in the region of Burgenland.

## REDS

**Blauburgunder:** Known elsewhere as pinot noir. Widely variable in quality depending on the vintage, vineyard, and winemaker; at best it produces light wines with raspberry overtones.

**Blaufränkisch:** Major grape; known in Germany as lemberger. Grown predominantly in Burgenland; the source of bold, spicy wines often with commanding structures.

**Cabernet Sauvignon:** From great vineyards and winemakers can make surprisingly rich, structured wines with good balance and deep flavors.

**St. Laurent:** Produces simple, hearty, and fruity wines.

**Zweigelt:** Cross between blaufränkisch and St. Laurent. Its wines are reminiscent of California's zinfandel: inky, grapey, fruity.

The Austrian philosophy of winemaking closely parallels that of Germany and Alsace—namely, that greatness resides in purity. Austrian winemakers are after the clearest possible expression of the grape's inherent flavors. Techniques that superimpose flavor (such as the barrel fermentation of white wines) are used infrequently and cautiously. Circumspect experimentation is commonplace, yet there is a firm respect for tradition and accumulated knowledge. Many of the extraordinary sweet wines, for example, are painstakingly made according to practices established hundreds of years ago.

These sweet wines notwithstanding, virtually all Austrian wines are dry (*trocken*). In Austria, there's really nothing equivalent to off-dry or semisweet or half-dry. What is meant by dry? As in Germany, a *trocken* wine, by law, is one that contains less than 0.9 percent sugar (in other words, it has less than 9 grams of residual sugar per liter). In reality, most Austrian wines have less than half that amount. There's no mistaking their dryness. The word *trocken*, by the way, does not always appear on an Austrian wine's label. If it does, you can be sure the wine is very dry. If it doesn't, chances are the wine is still very dry (unless, of course, it's a sweet wine that's in question).

A remarkable two thirds of all Austrian wine is sold directly from the winemaker to the consumer. In order to offer something for everyone, the typical winemaker may make ten or more different wines. The amount of each will be extremely limited, for most producers are small; some thirty thousand own less than one hectare (2.47 acres) of grapes.

## RIEDEL GLASSES

〜〜〜

Can a simple glass make a wine smell and taste better or worse? The world's top winemakers—from Bordeaux to the Napa Valley to Vienna—are convinced that it can. They are equally convinced that the wineglasses of choice are Riedel (rhymes with needle).

A tenth generation Austrian firm, Riedel is considered one of the finest crystal works companies in the world. The firm's wineglasses are not simply beautiful but actually engineered so that certain components in the wine are emphasized on the tongue, thereby bringing out the best in the wine's flavor. Skeptics remain so only until they experience the revelatory Riedel glass test in which the same wine is tasted from a standard glass and a Riedel glass. Not only do many leading winemakers use Riedel glasses for their tastings, but the glasses are increasingly found in the most expensive restaurants in Paris, London, and Rome.

Not so in Austria. There, it's impossible to find a winery or restaurant (no matter how humble) that does *not* use Riedel glasses.

# RIPENESS: THE AUSTRIAN HIERARCHY

Most Austrian wines, like German wines, are organized in a hierarchy that depends upon how ripe the grapes were at harvest. The less ripe the grapes, the lighter bodied the wine; the more ripe the grapes, the fuller the wine. Austria's opulent, unctuous, richly sweet wines come from the very ripest grapes of all. Hang on—it's going to take a bit of explanation to get to these.

The yardstick by which Austrians measure ripeness is the Klosterneuburger

*Austrian winemakers leave their best grapes on the vine well past the normal harvest. With luck, these grapes will be attacked by* Botrytis cinerea; *from such grapes, Austria's sensational sweet wines are made.*

Mostwage scale (the KMW). Like the Oechsle in Germany, the KMW is a measure of the weight of the must (the thick, pulpy liquid of crushed grapes) at harvest. The must weight is essentially the weight of all the grape sugar. The categories of ripeness of Austrian wines are usually referred to as "quality categories." This is a bit misleading. From the category of *kabinett* on, what is being stipulated is not quality but ripeness. Ripeness is always a clue to a wine's body but not necessarily a predictor of its quality. A well-made *kabinett* from a top producer may be, in the quality of its flavor, leagues above a poor *spätlese* from a less-conscientious producer. As in most other wine regions, a producer's reputation is paramount. There are four major categories of ripeness. In ascending order

they are: *Tafelwein, Landwein, Qualitätswein,* including the subgroup *kabinett,* and *Prädikatswein,* which includes, among others, the subgroup *spätlese.*

**Tafelwein** and **Landwein** are categories of fairly neutral table wines that are the least costly of all Austrian wines. *Landwein,* the better of the two, must be produced solely from officially recognized grape varieties. Most of these wines stay in Austria (or Europe) where they are sold in supermarkets.

**Qualitätswein:** Literally quality wine, this is the basic level of good everyday drinking wine made from the least ripe grapes. The wine tends to be light and simple. A *Qualitätswein* must come from a single wine region and be made from an authorized grape variety. It must also be tested for typicity and must display a test number. *Qualitätswein* may be chaptalized—that is, sugar may be added to the unfermented grape juice to boost the final alcohol level. There is one subgroup:

*Kabinett:* A *kabinett* must qualify as a *Qualitätswein* but must be made from slightly riper grapes and may not be chaptalized.

**Prädikatswein:** Literally wine with special attributes. Most of the top Austrian wines fall into this stringent category. *Prädikatswein* may not be chaptalized. The grapes are allowed to come from one region only (rather than blending grapes or wines from multiple regions). Any residual sugar in the wine must be present naturally. This means the wine must stop fermenting on its own; fermentation cannot be stopped by the addition of sulfur, nor can sweet concentrated grape juice be added at the end. The wine must be examined and tested for

563

typicity, carry a test number, and bear a vintage date. There are six subgroups:

*Spätlese:* The word literally means late harvest, but in fact this category simply means that the grapes were fully ripe when picked. *Spätlesen* have greater intensity and strength than *kabinett* wines.

*Auslese:* Literally selected harvest. Made from very ripe grapes harvested bunch by bunch, *auslese* represents another step up in richness and intensity. All underripe or faulty grapes must be discarded.

*Eiswein:* Literally ice wine, *eiswein* gets its name because it is made from very ripe frozen grapes that have been picked usually during the night by workers wearing gloves so that their hands don't warm the grapes. As these grapes are pressed, the sweet, high-acid, concentrated juice is separated from the ice (the water in the grape). The wine, made solely from the concentrated juice (the ice is thrown away), is miraculously high in both sweetness and acidity, making drinking it an ethereal sensation. *Eiswein* grapes must freeze naturally on the vine (not in a commercial freezer). On the palate, *eisweins* have a sweetness comparable to *beerenauslese.*

*Beerenauslese:* Literally harvest selected by berry, *beerenauslese* (BA for short) is made from very ripe grapes chosen individually by hand. The grapes may have been affected by the noble rot *Botrytis cinerea*, giving them a deep honeyed richness. BAs are rare and expensive.

## THE WINEMAKER AS CHEF

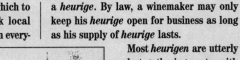

The best places in Austria in which to taste home-style food, drink local wines, and immerse yourself in everyday Austrian life are not cafés or restaurants. They are *heurigen* (HOY-rig-en)—rustic eating and drinking rooms (it would be erroneous to call them dining rooms), which are often attached to winemakers' homes.

Traditionally, all of the food at a *heurige,* including the breads, soups, salads, strudels, and even the sausages, is made from scratch by the winemaker and his family. Similarly, the wine offered is the winemaker's. The word *heurige,* in fact, refers both to the wine of the latest vintage and the place where it's drunk. In other words, you drink *heurige* at a *heurige.* By law, a winemaker may only keep his *heurige* open for business as long as his supply of *heurige* lasts.

Most *heurigen* are utterly modest gathering spots, with communal tables and often a small playground for the children of their patrons. People go as much to socialize as to eat or drink. Though wine is available by the bottle, lots of it is ordered and drunk by the glass or is made into a spritzer and served in a mug. Somewhat more sophisticated *heurigen* serve wine from other winemakers as well as their own. In the countryside outside Vienna *heurigen* are often called *buschenschenken,* named after the swags of fir branches (*buschenschenken*) tied to the doors.

*Since the eighteenth century, Grinzing, outside of Vienna, has been known for its buschenschenken.*

***Ausbruch:*** Slightly more oppulent than *beerenauslese, ausbruch* must be made from overripe, botrytized, and naturally shriveled grapes. *Ausbruch* is the one Austrian category that Germany doesn't share.

***Trockenbeerenauslese:*** Literally dry berry selected harvest, *trockenbeerenauslesen* (TBAs) are the richest, sweetest, rarest, and most costly of all Austrian wines. Produced only in exceptional years, they are made from individual grapes shriveled almost to raisins by botrytis. The intensity of TBAs is absolutely captivating, and you can expect to pay dearly for the experience.

# THE FOODS OF AUSTRIA

No wonder everyone in *The Sound of Music* sang so happily. They'd probably just had a piece of the plum cake called *zwetschkenfleck* (literally plum stain), made with the ripest plums so that the purple juices seep down into the cake as it cooks.

Austria's culinary traditions, along with Hungary's, are the most sophisticated and compelling in central Europe. Essays could be written on the soups alone. The gem of that genre is pumpkin soup. Every top restaurant, every great home cook, has a personalized recipe, including decadent versions in which whipped cream is folded in and roasted pumpkinseed oil is drizzled on top. But there are also extraordinary potato soups that prove just how majestic that tuber can be. In wine country one must also try a frothy *weinsuppe* (wine soup), usually made with riesling or grüner veltliner, beef stock, paprika, and cream.

Strudels are ubiquitous in Austria, as often savory (made with wild mushrooms, root vegetables, ham, shellfish, herbs, cheese, and so on) as sweet (made with

## GOT GRÜNER VELTLINER?

In much of western Europe, the United States, and Australia, red wine accompanies meat dishes so automatically that it's easy to overlook white wine as a possibility. But in Austria, where white wines are usually served with game, beef, pork, poultry, and veal, delicious combinations abound. One of the best is grüner veltliner and Austria's national dish Wiener schnitzel. To make Wiener schnitzel, bread crumb–coated veal cutlets are fried quickly in lard until they are golden brown and almost crunchy on the outside. Nothing tastes better with this than a chilled, supercrisp, bold, peppery white wine, in short grüner veltliner. The same principle holds true for traditional American fried chicken. When it comes to wine, think cold, vibrant white. In fact, when it comes to exciting cross-cultural marriages of food and wine, fried chicken and grüner veltliner are pretty unbeatable.

565

apples, plums, nuts, cherries, apricots). Strudel dough, similar to phyllo dough, is rolled into ultrathin sheets and brushed lightly with butter before it is filled and rolled. At the Heurige Schandl in the village of Rust in the wine region of Burgenland, the juicy baked red cabbage and caraway strudel comes with a pool of dill and sour cream sauce. (Peter Schandl, the owner, is also a winemaker who makes an irresistible pinot blanc.) Strudel is a venue for offal as well. Austrians are quite fond of wrapping the thin dough around lamb and veal tongues, hearts, sweetbreads, and brains.

The breads in Austria, like those in Germany, make bread in western Europe seem about as nutritious as Styrofoam. Austrian breads are usually multigrain and often include herbs, spices, and nuts; you'll find roasted-onion and walnut bread, pumpkinseed bread, and anise and black pepper bread. The best bread I have ever had—anywhere in the world—is made by the Austrian baker Hubert Auer in the city of Graz in Styria. The Auer breads are often made with ancient types of grain, custom cultivated for the company. The breads are available in Auer's shops in Graz as well as in Vienna.

When Austrians themselves are asked to name the quintessential Austrian dish, a majority answer Wiener schnitzel, pounded veal medallions that are coated in coarse whole-grain bread crumbs—to make the schnitzel crunchy—then fried. Even the great American chef Wolfgang Puck, who was born in Austria, moons about what he admits was his favorite food as a child.

The other well-loved meat specialties are venison, game birds, wild boar, all manner of pork, and *tafelspitz* (boiled beef), which tastes much better than it sounds and is usually served with *apfelkren*, fresh horseradish puréed with cooked apples, and roasted potatoes.

Meat and potatoes. Bread and soup. If these do not seem the stuff of culinary dreams, it is because we consider them common, too fundamental to be inspirational. But Austria's position as an Old World crossroads between East and West has meant that the cooking is anything but plebeian. The exotic and the familiar have been intriguingly mingled here for centuries. You can smell it. The aroma wafting out of any kitchen window is not just vegetables or meat, but a mesmerizing collective scent of those plus ginger, paprika,

## ABOUT THOSE "FRENCH" CROISSANTS

For centuries, imperialistic Turkish tribes hoping to invade western Europe considered Austria a militarily strategic foot in the door. Austria usually managed to defend itself against these periodic sieges, but occasionally the Turks prevailed. A brief occupation in the late 1600s had two redeeming results—both culinary. Coffee beans were brought to Vienna, instigating a revolutionary change in Austrian drinking habits, and Viennese bakers created the croissant to commemorate the end of the Turkish siege. The rich dough's shape was modeled after the crescent moon emblem on Turkish banners.

cumin, caraway, dill, garlic, poppy seed, nutmeg, cinnamon, and juniper.

The Austro-Hungarian monarchy left numerous culinary remnants, including the two most famous: dumplings, *knödel*, and goulash, *gulasch*. Dumplings can be made simply from potato flour or from crumbled up bread rolls. But more intriguing are those that are an invention of bread mixed with meat, herbs, and/or cheese or, for sweet dumplings, fruit, jam, and/or sugar. *Knödel* are masterful and irresistible in Austria and are often served with soup, meats, or dessert. As for goulash, it is still traditional in Vienna for friends to go out for this paprika-rich beef ragout after the opera or theater.

Another Austrian custom is wurst snacking. All over Vienna and other major cities small kiosks sell dozens of different grilled sausages served with hot or sweet mustard, crisp pickles, and hot peppers.

## Save Room

Austrian desserts are so good that Austrians often have them for breakfast or with coffee at 10 A.M. or at 4 P.M. There are the classics: *apfelstrudel* (apple strudel) and *topfenstrudel* (strudel made with sweetened fresh cheese and raisins and served with a vanilla custard sauce), *Linzertorte* (a raspberry and nut torte named after the city of Linz), Sacher torte (a dense chocolate torte, after which the Hotel Sacher in Vienna is named), plus countless poppy seed puddings.

In Vienna the most sumptuous spot for dessert—indeed, one of the premier café/pastry shops in the world—is Demel. They bake some ninety-five types of cakes and tortes alone, plus perfect strudels bursting with fruit and dark chocolate desserts that beg you to order them. These are all grandly showcased along antique wooden sideboards and will be served to you by perfectly mannered Viennese waitresses. The accompaniment of choice is rich Viennese coffee served with whipped cream. Demel is on the elegant shopping street called (counterintuitively) Kohlmarkt—cabbage market—at number 14.

As for actual cabbages, the place to see them is Vienna's bustling outdoor market, the Naschmarkt, with its purple figs the size of apples, its wooden barrels of fresh sauerkraut, and the dizzying array of fragrant Turkish breads, olives, and cheeses. First-time visitors can be taken aback by finding Austrian *apfelstrudel* and Turkish baklava sold side by side. But the Naschtmarkt clearly reflects the symbiosis that has existed for centuries (sometimes happily, most times not) between the two countries. Today, Turkish immigrants make up a large part of the Austrian population, and their rich culinary traditions continue to be woven into the Austrian gastronomic mainstream with delicious results. One of the most magnificent examples: the croissant.

567

*The posh café at the Hotel Sacher in Vienna. For decades the hotel was embroiled in a legal battle with Demel, Vienna's most luxurious pastry shop, regarding who makes the authentic Sacher torte.*

# Lower Austria

Of Austria's four wine regions, Lower Austria (*Niederösterreich*) is both the largest and the most important. More than 50 percent of Austria's vineyards are located here. The region is not in the south, as the name would seem to suggest but, rather, tucked up into the northeastern corner of the country, along the lower part of the Danube River.

Lower Austria is made up of five separate wine districts that loop in a grand arc around the city of Vienna. (Curiously, Vienna is not included in one of these districts; it's a separate wine region of its own.) Of these five districts, the Wachau, Donauland-Carnuntum, and the Kamptal-Donauland are considered three of the best areas for elegant dry white wine in Austria. Thermenregion is noteworthy for its unusual grapes, as we'll see, and the Wein-

> ### THE WINE DISTRICTS OF LOWER AUSTRIA
>
> Donauland-Carnuntum
> Kamptal-Donauland
> Thermenregion
> Wachau
> Weinviertel

viertel is largely overshadowed by its better-known neighbors.

The Wachau (Vac-HOW)—the tiniest of the districts—is also the most important. The whites here are unmatched in their sheer clarity of flavor, elegance, and balance. Through the middle of the Wachau, the Danube flows slowly and

*Tranquil and meandering, the Danube flows right through the Wachau, the smallest but most significant wine district in Lower Austria. Here, vineyards ring the village of Spitz.*

silently. Terraced vineyards climb up the banks on either side. This is wine country at its most serene, with storybook villages and country restaurants all along the riverbanks. The soil on the slopes is mostly gneiss, granite, and slate; on the floor of the valley closer to the water, it can be lighter loamy sand. The climate, tempered by the river, is nonetheless cool, with extreme variations in temperature between day and night. Both the soil and the climate are thought to give good structure and acidity to the grapes.

The most important white varieties are grüner veltliner and riesling. Planted in the best sites these make mouthwatering wines with the vinous equivalent of perfect pitch. Grüner veltliner is Austria's most fascinating indigenous white grape. Tasting it blind, wine experts can be fooled into thinking it's an unusual but charming chardonnay, pinot blanc, or even riesling. What finally gives grüner veltliner away is the finish: a subtle but unmistakable rush of white pepper.

------

*Some of the Best Producers of Grüner Veltliner*

**BRÜNDLMAYER**

**EMMERICH KNOLL**

**FRANZ HIRTZBERGER**

**FREIE WEINGÄRTNER WACHAU**

**F. X. PICHLER**

**JOSEF HICK**

**JOSEF HIRSCH**

**LOIMER**

**WINZER KREMS**

------

Riesling accounts for only 2.5 percent of Austria's vineyards; most of these are in Lower Austria, and the best vineyard sites

are in the Wachau. Wachau rieslings are fairly big-bodied and potent wines with lots of grip and "coating action" on the palate. In some cases they can be downright gargantuan—the producer F. X. Pichler's riesling is one such.

The other traditional white grapes in Lower Austria include the oddly named riesling x sylvaner (which some believe to be Müller-Thurgau), welschriesling, weissburgunder (pinot blanc), a small amount of chardonnay, and the slightly fat, somewhat neutral neuberger.

Just below Vienna in the Thermenregion (so named for the many hot springs there), two rare whites can be found: zierfandler and rotgipfler. The Rosencrantz and Guildenstern of the grape world? Both make mostly rough-hewn, sweetish-tasting wines with a sledgehammer of fruit plus aromas and flavors that run from bubble gum to canned fruit salad to diesel oil.

Though red wine is not Lower Austria's strong suit, there are some good

569

*Set against the deep blue-green of the Danube, the medieval monastery at Dürnstein (painted stunningly sky blue) is one of the loveliest sites in the Wachau.*

ones, including a number of simple, spicy blauburgunders (pinot noir) and Zweigelts. One of the very most lip-smacking Zweigelts is that of Josef Jamek, who owns the wonderful restaurant Jamek on the bank of the Danube near the Old World village of Dürnstein (where, for a time, the English king Richard the Lion-Hearted was imprisoned).

One of the most extraordinary wine academies in Austria, the Kloster Und, is located in Lower Austria just outside the historic city of Krems. A seventeenth-century Capuchin monastery, the Kloster Und is not only a school but also a wine library, wine information center, wine museum, and conference center. In the vaulted stone cellar under the nave of the church, 150 Austrian wines are available for tasting. The tasting cellars were designed to evoke both religion and myth. Information about visiting the Kloster Und and several wineries in Lower Austria appears at the end of this section on page 583.

## Ripeness Hierarchy in the Wachau

And now it gets a bit dicey. The Wachau is the only place in all of Austria that departs from the established system of categorizing wines according to the ripeness of the grapes (*spätlese*, *auslese*, and so

### THE BLUE MONASTERY OF DÜRNSTEIN

The medieval village of Dürnstein is one of the prettiest in the Wachau. Along cobblestone streets sit houses outlined in flower boxes. The village itself can be seen from quite far away thanks to the strikingly beautiful blue spire of the monastery's church, said to be the color of the Virgin Mary's robe.

## THE AUSTRIAN WINE ACADEMY

—◦◦◦—

Wine, as much a part of Austria's identity as Mozart or the Alps, is easy to learn about in Austria. The Austrian Wine Academy conducts one-week seminars in English, designed for visitors. Students visit all the Austrian wine-growing regions and hear lectures given by leading experts. The country's best winemakers guide participants through vineyards and cellars and conduct a wide range of tastings. For information, contact the *Austrian Wine Academy, 81 Hauptstrabe, A-7071 Rust; 011-43-2-685-453.*

forth). Instead, with Wachau wines, you'll encounter three words used nowhere else: *steinfeder, federspiel,* and *smaragd.* These terms were created by the Vinea Wachau, an association of the top Wachau producers whose goal was to set their dry white wines apart (even though one might argue that they created confusion in the process). According to the association's laws, the categories (which must be listed on the wine labels) are defined as follows:

*Steinfeder:* Natural unchaptalized wines with no more than 10.7 percent alcohol. (*Steinfeder* is the name of a local strain of grass, and the association poetically describes these wines as "dainty.")

*Federspiel:* Natural unchaptalized wines with no more than 11.9 percent alcohol. *Federspiel* wines are more or less equivalent to a *kabinett.*

*Smaragd:* The word *smaragd* (meaning emerald) is also the name of a bright green lizard that suns itself in the vineyards here. *Smaragd* wines are considered the best because the grapes are the ripest at harvest. The wines must have a minimum of 11.3 percent alcohol; most have higher. A wine labeled *smaragd* will be at least the level of ripeness of a *spätlese* and often more.

*The Wachau is prime territory for Austria's two greatest white varieties, grüner veltliner and riesling. Here grüner veltliner vines grow near the village of Dürnstein.*

# THE LOWER AUSTRIAN WINES TO KNOW

*In Lower Austria, white wines predominate. These wines are all white.*

## Whites

### FREIE WEINGARTNER WACHAU

Grüner Veltliner

*smaragd*

100% grüner veltliner

Grüner veltliner usually does not become a wine one would describe as opulent or decadent, but this style is precisely what the esteemed cooperative Freie Weingärtner Wachau (literally independent winegrowers of Wachau) achieves. In top years the wine is peaches layered over mirabelles, layered over apricots, layered over guavas, with a little ginger-vanilla crème anglaise for good measure.

### F. X. PICHLER

Grüner Veltliner

Loibner Berg

*smaragd, trocken*

100% grüner veltliner

When it's at its best, F. X. Pichler's is, without doubt, one of the most delicious grüner veltliners in Austria—dripping with gorgeous peach and peppery flavors, with mineral notes going off like minifireworks in the glass. The texure is as soft and appealing as a goose down comforter. The finish does not ever quite seem to. Pichler also makes a riesling so masterful and perfectly balanced it's unreal. The firm is considered one of the stars of the Wachau.

### J. HICK

Grüner Veltliner

*smaragd, trocken*

100% grüner veltliner

Josef Hick makes grüner veltliners that come at you like a basketful of apple blossoms and mirabelles. This alone would be fine, but it's the counterpoint of slate and mineral flavors that makes the wine intriguing. Plus the vibrant texture that's almost alive. Imagine stones made of mirabelles in a rushing stream and you've got it.

### WEINGUT BRUNDLMAYER

Riesling

Zöbinger Heiligenstein

*kabinett, trocken*

100% riesling

Willi Bründlmayer typifies the quality-obsessed New Wave generation of Austrian winemakers who inherited some of Austria's best estates. Bründlmayer makes wines in the Kamptal-Donauland district, just north of the Wachau. His rieslings, with their bright, powerful aromas and crystal-clear flavors, are like climbing into a lemon tree. Bründlmayer also makes some of the best grüner veltliners and one of the few chardonnays in Lower Austria—it's big but skillfully balanced.

## Sweet Wine

### WEINGUT PRAGER

Riesling

Ried Steinriegl

*eiswein*

100% riesling

A small producer, Franz Prager is the Wachau's riesling king and days after drinking his incomparable *eiswein,* you still can't stop thinking about it. This nectar of pears, peaches, roses, and litchis is so mesmerizing, so profound, that just about everyone who tastes it is rendered speechless. Prager harvests his *eisweins* well into the bitter cold of winter, often past Christmas. Generally, fewer than 500 bottles are made.

# Burgenland

ustria's second-largest wine region after Lower Austria, Burgenland huddles against Hungary on the far eastern border (Budapest is only some 130 miles away). The vineyards here, along with those in Hungary, formed a vast uninterrupted sea of vines during the Austro-Hungarian monarchy.

1992
Horitschoner
**Blaufränkisch**
Jahrgangsreserve
Mittelburgenland
Qualitätswein E 9424/93
ALK 12,9% VOL. · TROCKEN
ÖSTERREICH

Burgenland is known primarily for its opulent sweet wines, although some remarkable, assertive reds also come from here. Sweet wines have been the glory of this part of central Europe for eons. The most celebrated type—*ausbruch*—is made from grapes infected by *Botrytis cinerea*. For *ausbruch*, these botrytized grapes are then mixed with freshly pressed must from grapes that are partially botrytized. (Reflecting Burgenland's proximity to Hungary, this process is similar to the manner in which Hungary's famous sweet wine Tokay Aszú is made; see page 594.) Both the fully and partially botrytized grapes for *ausbruch* must come from the same vineyard. The grapes are sometimes foot trodden, and the wine is aged in casks. *Ausbruch* is more Amazonian, outrageous, and honeyed than *beerenauslese* but has less residual sugar and more alcohol than *trockenbeerenauslese* (see page 565).

The most famous *ausbruche*, as well as BAs and TBAs, come from the north of Burgenland where there is an almost super-

*Small family wine cellars in Burgenland: Many families make just enough wine for themselves and a tiny following of customers.*

## MUST VISIT: TAUBENKOBEL

Taubenkobel is the kind of country restaurant you usually do not find in the countryside but always wish you could. Here, about a thirty-minute drive south of Vienna, even humble cabbage is raised to high art by Walter Eselböck, the young chef/owner. The restaurant is, by just about everyone's estimation, Burgenland's best.

The name Taubenkobel means dovecote. Its aura is at once simple and sophisticated. Antique fir armoires are draped with lace cloths. The massive stone floor is covered with oriental carpets. Instead of flowers, the room is adorned with pumpkins and other "garden art."

Austrian chefs in general are among the world's great bread bakers: Eselböck's roasted-onion and walnut bread leaves you powerless to resist it. With a glass of wine, this bread could be dinner. But, of course you'll eat much more.

To begin, there's *erdäpfelrahmsuppe*, a silken soup made with celery root broth, special Hungarian potatoes, butter, and whipped cream, lightly dusted with freshly ground nut-meg and topped with thick-cut, garlicky roasted wild mushrooms. For the next course, the "must have" at Taubenkobel is surely the slow-roasted venison. The meat is marinated for a day or more in red wine with juniper berries and then cooked until it is meltingly tender. The venison's perfect partner is *himbeerkraut*—sweet red cabbage marinated in cinnamon and raspberry vinegar, steamed with red wine, and tossed with fresh crushed raspberries and more cinnamon.

Desserts at Taubenkobel can defy imagination. The sweet cheese dumplings with bitter chocolate and green tomatoes represent creativity on the verge of madness. But there are comforting traditional desserts, too.

If great books are judged by their ability to hold your thoughts long after you've finished reading them, should it be surprising that the day after dinner at Taubenkobel, all you can think about is running out to the market to buy cabbages and potatoes and locking yourself in the kitchen? *Taubenkobel, 33 Hauptstrasse, 7081 Schützen/Gebirge; 011-43-2-684-22-97.*

natural lake named Neusiedl (the Austrians call this the Neusiedlersee). More than 186 square miles in size, it is only 2 to 7 feet deep. The shallow lake is threatened by constant evaporation. In fact, twice during the last century it dried up completely. Reeds and grasses love the lake. So many of them grow around it that thatching material developed into a local industry. Birds also love the lake. The population is so diverse that the area has become one of Europe's largest wildlife preserves. But as much as the reeds or the birds, grapes love the lake. They love to rot there.

The moisture-filled air and the mild climate foster the growth of botrytis, which of course, is critical in the making of *ausbruch*. The tempting sweet grapes do not go unnoticed by the birds at the lake. Every last grape would be eaten by them were it not for the programmed gun blasts that thunder through the tranquil vineyards every few minutes, keeping the flocks away.

A number of different grape varieties are used for Burgenland's sweet wines: welschriesling, weissburgunder (pinot blanc), neuberger, chardonnay, traminer, and others, including the principal grape used in Hungarian Tokay Aszú, furmint. The vines are planted in sandy/stony/chalky soil, within half a mile of the water, all around the lake. Pickers generally go into the vineyards three separate times, hand harvesting only perfectly botrytized bunches each time.

The eastern shore of the Neusiedlersee is said to produce a more bosomy, earthy style of sweet wine than the slightly more austere style of the hillier western shore. On the western side, the Neusiedlersee-Hügelland, is the charming village of Rust (pronounced roost), which along with Tokay in Hungary has been one of central Europe's most eminent wine towns since the Middle Ages. In 1681 Rust bought its political independence and religious freedom by paying Leopold I 60,000 gold guilders and 30,000 liters of *ausbruch*.

In addition to *ausbruch*, BA, and TBA, Burgenland also produces another famous sweet wine, this one not influenced by botrytis: *eiswein. Eiswein* is the sweet outcome of grapes left on the vine until frozen. The long hang-time—well into the dead of winter—concentrates the grapes' sugar and acid. In the best *eisweins* voluptuous sweetness is wrapped around an electrifying nucleus of acidity, making for an unparalleled taste sensation.

Then there are the reds. Specializing in ornate sweet white wines and gutsy dry reds only *seems* like enological schizophrenia. Many Burgenland winemakers do both quite successfully. Though decent red wine has a long-established foundation here, superb red wine is rare and a far more recent phenomenon. Quality leapt forward in the mid-1980s as advanced winemaking techniques and improved vineyard practices became the common denominator among young professionals.

*Some of the Best Producers*
*of Blaufränkisch*

**ERNST TRIEBAUMER**

**GESELLMANN**

**HANS IBY**

**HANS IGLER**

**HANS NITTNAUS**

**HERMANN KRUTZLER**

**UMATHUM**

The foremost red grape is blaufränkisch, and when it is good, it can become a daring wine, suffused with the unusual flavor of raspberries dusted with white pepper. In texture, the wine's crushed-velvet softness and juiciness are reminiscent of the best California zinfandels.

The two other well-loved local red grapes are Zweigelt and St. Laurent. Zweigelt, a cross between blaufränkisch and St. Laurent, is grapey and uncomplicated. St. Laurent has flavors that range from simple cherry to a combination of earth, mushrooms, and dry leaves.

---

## AMERICAN BLAUFRÄNKISCH?

The grape variety known as blaufränkisch in Austria is also grown in the United States by wineries in Washington State, New York State, and Colorado. Americans call it by its German name, lemberger. Lemberger is thought to have been brought to the States from central Europe in the early twentieth century by Hungarian growers who first planted it in British Columbia. From there, it was introduced to Washington State in the early 1940s. By the mid-1960s lemberger was considered the third best suited red grape (after cabernet sauvignon and merlot) to Washington State's climate.

In Burgenland some winemakers also make dry whites, including chardonnay. The best are elegant, made entirely without wood, and brimming with creamy flavors balanced by just the right flash of acidity. Look for the producers Wilhelm Mad, Velich, and Helmut Lang. The latter even makes a beautiful *trockenbeeren-auslese* from chardonnay!

The wineries to visit in Austria have all been grouped together. You'll find them at the end of this section on page 583.

---

# THE BURGENLAND WINES TO KNOW

*Burgenland is famous most of all for its sweet wines and, while many terrific examples are produced each year, here are three of the most extraordinary.*

### KRACHER

Chardonnay-Welschriesling
Nouvelle Vague
*beerenauslese*
approximately 70% chardonnay,
30% welschriesling

Austria has numerous immensely talented producers of sweet wines, but Kracher stands above them all, making some of the most hedonistic wines in the world. They are the kind of sensual wines that go beyond poetic description, eliciting contented groans instead. Curiously, the man behind these ultravoluptuous and riveting wines looks like he'd be more likely to be riding a Harley-Davidson than working in a vineyard. This *beerenauslese* is made from the fascinating combination of chardonnay and welschriesling. Pure nectar could not be more nectarlike. Kracher makes several other mindblowing *beerenauslesen,* including ones made from muscat ottonel, traminer, and sämling.

### LANG

Sämling-Welschriesling
*eiswein*
approximately 75% sämling,
25% welschriesling

The aroma of Lang's *eiswein* is like being in an apricot forest during a rain shower. The texture—which is what you notice next—is gossamer. Finally, after you extract yourself from the trance-inducing first impression, you taste wave after wave of pure luxurious fruit. This is a fabulous *eiswein*—not unctuous, not thick, not sugary sweet—instead, rarefied, almost ephemeral. Young, self-taught winemaker Helmut Lang does not send hired workers into his vineyards to harvest; helped by only one or two trusted pickers, he picks the berries himself "because each one must be perfect."

### WENZEL

*ausbruch*
Cuvée Süss
approximately 60% neuberger,
20% pinot gris, 10% furmint,
and 10% sauvignon blanc

If a pure essence could be made from sweet almonds dipped in honey and then drizzled with apricot glaze, and if that essence could then be set to echoing through an opulent sweet wine, one would have come close to achieving what nature and Mr. Wenzel have done. This is a rich, silken *ausbruch* from a producer who understands the platonic ideal better than most.

# Styria

Styria, along Austria's mountainous southern Alpine border, is the second smallest wine region. Yet this is arguably one of the world's top spots for sauvignon blanc as well as Austria's most beautiful wine region.

Behind the small houses with their lace curtains and flower boxes, the vineyards stretch over kelly green hills. Many vineyards have a *klapotez*—a wooden windmill with hammers that make a loud clacking noise to scare off the birds (who, unfooled, sometimes sit right on top of the contraption).

Everywhere in Styria there are pumpkin patches, for this is the home of Austria's famous specialty, pumpkinseed oil. Made from the roasted seeds of a special pumpkin, the dark green oil is hauntingly rich and delicious. In Styria it is drizzled over everything from chewy multigrain breads to savory strudels.

Styrian wines can be dazzling, with bright focused flavors that have a keen edge to them. Most of the top wines are found along the wine route (*weinstrasse*) in the province of south Styria, Südersteiermark, where the lemon yellow daylight is so vivid it almost seems polished.

Southern Styria is fondly called the Tuscany of Austria, but the lush, hilly vineyards also look uncannily like those in

*Vineyards near Riegersburg Castle in southeast Styria produce decent wines, but Riegersburg's real claim to fame is its schnapps. Local distiller Johann Zieser makes quince and raspberry schnapps that are enjoyed throughout Austria.*

# WHAT DO PUMPKINSEEDS AND OLIVES HAVE IN COMMON?

The answer is oil. Pumpkinseed oil is to Austria what olive oil is to Italy—a culinary icon. Pumpkinseed oil comes from the seeds of a particular type of pumpkin grown mainly in the southern province of Styria. The greenish pumpkin, about the size of a honeydew melon, is harvested in September and October. The prized seeds are then removed, roasted, and hydraulically pressed. Far less valued, the pumpkin itself becomes livestock feed.

Pumpkinseed oil is deep emerald green, with an almost hauntingly intense, nutty flavor. Austrians drizzle it over lettuces, vegetables, and breads and pour small puddles into soups, including pumpkin soup (made from a different variety of pumpkin). The best oils are made solely from pumpkinseeds; lesser oils are pumpkinseed-safflower seed blends.

Pumpkinseed oil's high content of unsaturated fatty acids makes it easy to digest. The oil is also rich in vitamins E, A, and D.

Oregon. (Like Oregon, this wine region is also known for its jams.) Vineyards here are among the steepest in the country, with inclines of more than 26 percent. The hilly landscape fosters multiple tiny microclimates tucked into crevices and stretched over sun-catching ribbons of southern-facing slopes. The wines can therefore vary in quality and style quite a bit, depending on whether the small pocket they came from was blessed with a lot of sun. In general, however, the cold air that sweeps down the hillsides and the relatively high altitude of the vineyards lead to wines with kinetic acidity and good focus. The soil in the best vineyards is granitic, and the wines often display a flinty, mineral quality.

Chardonnay (called morillon in Styria) has a long history here, the vines having been brought from the Champagne region of France in the nineteenth century. For the most part, Styrian chardonnay is made in the style of French Chablis—taut and linear, rather than fat and buttery.

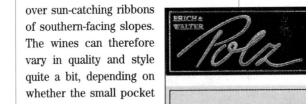

But the biggest surprise—and Austria's best-kept secret—is Styrian sauvignon blanc. These are racy, herbal, lemony wines, with a wild outdoorsy quality and a tanginess not unlike a good French Sancerre.

Though red grape varieties are grown here, Styria is too cool and rain prone to be a great area for red wines. Whites dominate, as they do on the other side of the Alps in northern Italy. In addition to sauvignon blanc and morillon, the varieties of note include weissburgunder (pinot blanc), welschriesling, traminer, and muskateller.

Muskateller (otherwise known as muscat blanc à petits grains) is part of the giant muscat family, a web of related varieties found all over the world. From good sites and skilled producers, Styrian muskateller, locally called gelber muskateller, is a beautifully taut, refreshing wine with compelling musky aromas and delicious, dry, juicy fruit flavors.

Styria is also known for rosés—or rather, a single type of rosé called *schilcher*. Made from the blauer wildbacher grape, which grows almost exclusively in west Styria, *schilcher* is very high in acid. There is no better mate for the smoked, aged bacon that is also a specialty of the region.

Styrian wine estates tend to be very small but often have an adjoining restaurant, *buschenschenk*, or small inn. One not to be missed is Sattler, a wine estate in Gamlitz, known for its extremely delicious sauvignon blanc and chardonnay and its adjoining restaurant, Sattlerhof, considered one of the best restaurants in Styria. You'll find the street address and telephone number in Visiting Austrian Wineries on page 583.

## EAU-DE-AUSTRIA

In Austria schnapps is said to be made from every fruit and berry you have heard of and every fruit and berry you haven't. Schnapps, like eau-de-vie in France and grappa in Italy, is a clear, unaged distillate (about 40 proof) that is drunk after the meal. Often Austrian families proudly make their own schnapps from fruit they (also proudly) grow themselves, and it's frequently a delicious, relatively mild liqueur. In restaurants you'll also find hundreds of handcrafted, limited-production, very expensive versions made by individual winemakers and artisanal distillers. Plum is the most common flavor, but more intriguing perhaps are schnapps made from elderberries, quince, juniper, apricots, cherries, blueberries, blackberries, and rowanberries from the mountain ash tree.

579

*Graz is the only town of any size in Styria. Much of the region is pastoral, perfect for growing vines and the pumpkins that are the source of Austria's unique pumpkinseed oil.*

# THE STYRIAN WINES TO KNOW

*Styria specializes in white wines, so all of the wines here are white.*

### E & M TEMENT

Sauvignon Blanc

Zieregg

100% sauvignon blanc

Sauvignon blanc—generally so lean, so taut, so lithe—here takes on Orson Welles–like proportions and a personality to match. Tement's sauvignon is one huge powerhouse of smoke, minerals, vanilla, and herbs. A take-no-prisoners style of sauvignon blanc.

### GROSS

Morillon

*trocken*

100% morillon

At their best the morillons (more familiarly chardonnays) from Gross have the style, elegance, and definition of thoroughbred racehorses. Lemon and ginger flavors gallop through the wine. Not so the small bit of butteryness; like sun shining on a lace curtain, it dapples through. The effect is charming, a wine that is at the same time creamy but lean.

### GROSS

Weissburgunder

Kittenberg

*trocken*

100% weissburgunder

In many vineyards worldwide, including those in Austria, pinot blanc—weissburgunder to the Austrians— produces a wine that could be described as chardonnay's less exciting younger sister. Gross leaps beyond this parameter with his crisply focused, racy, minerally weissburgunders that manage to hold on to their creamy textures and are both sumptuous and easy to drink.

### SATTLERHOF

Muskateller

Prämiumwein

*trocken*

100% muskateller

One of the most intriguing and complex muskatellers (a kind of muscat) in the country: The ripe, juicy fruit is counterbalanced by bone-dry flint and stone flavors. A stiletto of acidity pierces the belly of the wine. The Falstaffian-looking Mr. Sattler likes bold, pure flavors and ultradry wines. For this muskateller, he uses only hand-selected bunches from a single vineyard.

### WEINGUT WALTER UND EVELYN SKOFF

Sauvignon Blanc

Classique

100% sauvignon blanc

Talk about uninhibited sauvignon blanc! In great years Skoff makes a wild yet sophisticated style of sauvignon that suggests gooseberry, ginger, and lime. As you continue to drink, other flavors and aromas emerge: damp soil, truffles, vanilla beans. Skoff also makes a morillon so elegant, it's gossamer.

### WINKLER-HERMADEN

Sauvignon Blanc

Zwei Rieden

*trocken*

100% sauvignon blanc

Some sauvignon blancs are far more herbal than grassy, and the Winkler-Hermaden is one. It's an exotic tangle of things—fragrant wild herbs, smoke, gunflint, minerals, and lime leaves. All of this rushes at you like the intoxicating aroma of wind in a pine forest. Winkler-Hermaden also makes a scrumptious, creamy/spicy traminer.

# Vienna

There is a vineyard of sorts in Paris. Someone in Rome must have a vine or two planted next to the tomatoes. But Vienna is the only major city in the world that is a commercially significant wine region unto itself. Within the city limits there are 1,738 acres of grapes. The vineyards are even protected by the government lest developers be tempted to put such valuable real estate to more profitable uses.

The name Vienna, or Wien—Veen as the Austrians pronounce it—would seem to derive from wein (wine), but it does not. The word is of Celtic origin and means white or wild river. The city itself is romantic and exhilarating, the kind of place that makes you want to abandon yourself to its beauty. As in Paris, the very air seems to shimmer with the secrets of centuries past. Everywhere, stately buildings glow in the white sunlight. There is a potent aura of mystery and passion. That this also happens to be a wine region makes perfect sense to those for whom wine is mystery, beauty, and romance.

From the Middle Ages on, Viennese vineyards were planted to slake the thirst of the local citizenry. Many plots were in the care of either monks or nobles who studied viticulture and built cellars, some of which are still in use. Vineyards were planted with different varieties of grapes side by side. The grapes would be picked and pressed together as a field blend. This traditional style of wine, called *gemischter satz*—mixed planting— makes up about a third of all Viennese wine today. Such wines are rarely very good, but they are always fasci-

*Majestic and historic, Vienna is the world's only major city that is also a wine region.*

nating. Just try to imagine the flavor of a white wine made from riesling, pinot blanc, neuberger, grüner veltliner, and grapes unfortunately called spätrot and rotgipfler.

During the early period of Viennese viticulture, the foundation was also laid for what can only be described as an Austrian institution, the *heurigen*. These wineries-cum-cafés, usually small, were where Austrian life was played out. People went to drink wine, eat, gossip, argue, and hold hands—sometimes concomitantly. *Heurigen* now exist all over the country, but some of the oldest and most infamous are in Vienna. The Heurige Franz Mayer is a good example. The Mayer family makes wines from one of the best city plots, the

## THE COFFEEHOUSES OF VIENNA

—⟶⟵—

Unlike cafés anywhere in the world from Rome to Seattle, the Viennese coffeehouse is only tangentially about drinking coffee. Here, in the city where psychoanalysis was born, a coffeehouse is home to a complex ritual—more intimate than social, supremely private even within the public domain.

Traditionally, coffeehouses were more or less demarcated by profession or social ranking. There were coffeehouses for politicians, coffeehouses for artists, coffeehouses for scholars, and so on. Every person had a single place to which he or she went exclusively. At a minimum, you spent an hour at a coffeehouse (no quickly downed espressos), but more commonly, you would spend several hours and possibly the entire day there. Coffee would be ordered by color—gold, light gold, blond, dark gold—according to the amount of milk added, and would be served on a small tray with a few sugar cubes and a glass of water. The main activity was, and still is, reading newspapers provided by the house, although you could also write or work in complete solitude, using the café table as a private desk. Since the waiters knew every customer and his or her preferred coffee, you never really had to utter a single word. When people did go to the coffeehouse in pairs, it was either to read in mutual silence or to discuss problems or personal intimacies. Still, private conversations, not social banter, was the custom.

Modern life has changed Viennese coffeehouses but not by much. During the daytime, a respectful solemnity still pervades. People just sit, think, read, and sip coffee. At night, coffeehouses become somewhat more animated, serving goulash and then coffee and strudel to opera and theatergoers.

In the late fall and winter, coffee can become more substantial, including a particularly fortifying rendition called a *fiaker*. Made with liberal amounts of rum and whipped cream, *fiakers* are named after the open horse-drawn carriages that once transported people through the streets of Vienna. Riding in a *fiaker* on a cold Austrian night made you want to stop and sip a *fiaker*.

Among Vienna's best coffeehouses:

**Café Hawelka,** 6 Dorotheergasse, 1. Bezirk; 011-43-1-512-82-30. Café Hawelka is noble and chic.

**Café Landtmann,** 4 Dr. Karl Lueger Ring, 1. Bezirk; 011-43-1-532-06-21. Be sure to sit outside, weather permitting.

**Café Sacher,** 4 Philharmonikerstrasse, 1. Bezirk; 011-43-1-512-14-87. A classic.

**Café Sperl,** 11 Gumpendorferstrasse, 6. Bezirk; 011-43-1-504-73-34. Traditional and a classic.

**Demel Konditorei,** 14 Kohlmarkt, 1. Bezirk; 011-43-1-535-55-16. Also classic.

**Heiner Konditorei,** 21-23 Karntnerstrasse, 1. Bezirk; 011-43-512-68-63. Chic, and Heiner Konditorei has good sweets.

Alsegar vineyard, as well as from other less distinguished urban vineyards. All of these wines, noble and lackluster alike, are cheerfully consumed at the family's boisterous, cacophonous, 800-seat *heurige*, where it is said Beethoven wrote part of his Ninth Symphony.

Most of the better Viennese vineyards are planted with riesling, although there

are decent wines being made from weissburgunder (pinot blanc), gewürztraminer, chardonnay, and among reds, Zweigelt and cabernet sauvignon. Look for the producers Fritz Wieninger and Leopold Breyer. Both also have *heurigen*.

On the outskirts of Vienna is the impressive headquarters of Schlumberger, Austria's largest sparkling wine firm, with a production of 4 million bottles per year. (It's no relation to Domaines Schlumberger in Alsace.) Below Schlumberger's lemon yellow building are 6,000 square meters of labyrinthine underground aging cellars. One of them, the apostles' cellar, has old wooden vats (no longer used) with images of the apostles carved in relief.

Schlumberger's wine is impressive. This is not transfer method *sekt* but, rather, crisp, fresh sparkling wine made by the traditional Champagne method. Robert Schlumberger, who founded the firm in 1842, worked at the Champagne house Ruinart before bringing his dream of making sparkling wine to Vienna.

Schlumberger's golden sparkling wine is made from welschriesling and grüner veltliner grapes grown in Lower Austria. Its rosé sparkler is made from blaufränkisch. Both wines come in brut and demi-sec styles, although the driest wines are the most popular. Austrians appear to drink sparkling wine at the drop of a hat. Everyday life is enough of a special occasion.

# VISITING AUSTRIAN WINERIES

Though most Austrian wineries do not have organized tours, proprietors, most of whom speak English, are accustomed to receiving guests by appointment. It is customary to purchase a bottle or two of wine in return for a tasting. The word for winery in Austrian (which is to say German) is *weingut*.

In addition to wineries, the Kloster Und—once a monastery, now a center for wine and culture—is well worth visiting. The Weinkolleg (wine college) Kloster Und, in Lower Austria, has more than a hundred wines available for tasting in its ancient wine cellars. *Weinkolleg Kloster Und, 6 Undstrasse, A-3504 Krems-Stein; 011-43-2-732-73-074.*

The telephone numbers include the dialing code you'll need when calling from the United States. If you're calling from within Austria, eliminate the 011-43 and add a zero before the next number. Don't worry if you notice that some of the phone numbers are longer than others. Austrian telephone numbers are not standardized the way they are in the United States.

## BURGENLAND

**WEINGUT ALOIS KRACHER**
37 Apetloner Strafle
A-7142 Illmitz
011-43-2-175-33-77

**WEINGUT LANG**
5 Quergasse
A-7142 Illmitz
011-43-2-175-29-23

## LOWER AUSTRIA

**WEINGUT BRÜNDLMAYER**
23 Zwettlerstrasse
A-3550 Langenlois
011-43-2-734-21-72
Winery and *heurige*.

**WEINGUT JOSEF JAMEK**
45 Joching
A-3610 Weisskirchen
011-43-2-715-22-35
Winery and restaurant.

**WEINGUT NIKOLAIHOF**
A-3512 Mautern
011-43-2-732-82-90
Winery and *heurige*.

## STYRIA

**WEINGUT SATTLER**
2 Sernau, A-8462 Gamlitz
011-43-3-453-25-56
Winery and restaurant.

# THE WINES OF SWITZERLAND

～o✺o～

Switzerland is surrounded on all sides by some of Europe's most prominent wine-producing countries, and though its wines are not nearly as renowned (or numerous), they are increasingly worthy of attention. To begin with, Switzerland does not produce nearly as much wine as its latitude might suggest it could. Much of this Alpine country is just simply too high and therefore too cold for grapevines to grow successfully. Switzerland ranks twenty-fifth in the world in wine production, just after Uzbekistan and Mexico. Most of its wines come from the western, predominantly French-speaking part of the country and especially from the important provinces, or cantons as they are known in Switzerland, of Valais, Geneva, Vaud, and Neuchâtel. Wine is also made, however, in the southern, Italian-speaking area known as Ticino and in the more northern, German-speaking Ostschweiz.

As befits a cold-climate country, Switzerland produces mainly white wines, although red wines, especially pinot noir, are gaining in importance and prestige. The major white grape variety is chasselas, known in German as gutedel, which makes light-bodied wines that range from neutral quaffing wines to crisp, minerally whites laced with citrus and almond flavors. So that the acidity and freshness of these wines is accentuated, they virtually never encounter oak barrels of any sort. Chasselas is grown mainly in Valais, Vaud, Neuchâtel, and Geneva. Confusingly, in the Valais, chasselas is known as fendant. Thus bottles labeled either chasselas or fendant will be made with chasselas grapes.

Other Swiss white wines include Müller-Thurgau, sylvaner (also known as Johannisberg), pinot blanc, and pinot gris. And while the Swiss seem anxious to prove they can make reputable chardonnays, most Swiss chardonnays end up tasting lackluster or overoaked. Far more interesting are the intensely floral, exotically fruity, and minerally wines made from the indigenous, ancient variety petite arvine.

As for red wines, Swiss pinot noir, called blauburgunder, is light, spicy, and often quite good, although rarely complex or nuanced in flavor. Some tasty light red wines are also made from gamay and from pinot noir-gamay blends, which are called Dôle. In the southern canton of Ticino, merlot has been growing since the early part of the twentieth century, and again, the wines are light, sleek, fairly high in acid, and sometimes spicy. Though it could make you shudder to think of it, there's even a merlot bianco (white merlot) made in this province, and like white zinfandel in the United States, it's very popular with the local population. But perhaps the most intriguing red variety of all in Switzerland is the indigenous cornalin, which can be the source of superjuicy, spicy wines redolent of black cherries and pomegranates.

The vineyards in Switzerland can be enormously challenging to work because of their steepness. Along with the vineyards of Germany, these are some of the steepest vineyards in the world, some of them appearing to be nearly vertical. As a result, terraces, called *tablars,* are cut into the mountainsides and grapes are often transported up and down the slopes on monorails.

Swiss wines are usually labeled by varietal, making them fairly easy to understand. While Swiss wines are not widely exported, some of the leading producers you might come across include Bon Père Germanier, Robert Gilliard, Imesch Vins Sierre, Domaine E. de Montmollin Fils, Provins Valais, Les Perrières, and Rouvinez Vins.

# Hungary

Of all the countries in the eastern part of Europe, none has had as solid a tradition of producing great wines as Hungary. Its only possible rival might be Austria, and though the wines of Austria are certainly soaring in quality and recognition today, the wines of Hungary were for centuries the more esteemed of the two. In fact, from the seventeenth to the twentieth century, Hungary possessed what was arguably the third most sophisticated wine culture in Europe after France and Germany. Among other distinctions, it was in the 1600s in Hungary's famous Tokaj-Hegyalja region—not in Bordeaux or Burgundy—that the first system for classifying wine on the basis of quality was developed.

Bordered on the north by Slovakia, on the northeast by the Ukraine, on the east by Romania, on the south by the former Yugoslavia, and on the west by Austria, Hungary sits virtually in the middle of eastern Europe. Vineyards have flourished here at least since Roman times. When the Magyars, an ancient tribe from the Ural

Hungary ranks eleventh in wine-producing countries worldwide. Hungarians drink an average of 7.54 gallons of wine per person each year; they're fourteenth in world wine consumption.

*Commonly thirty to sixty feet underground, the small damp cellars in Tokay were dug centuries ago—often as places to hide during Turkish invasions. Everything is covered in a thick blackish mold thought to provide optimal conditions for wines to age.*

Mountains from whom modern Hungarians are descended, arrived in the region in the ninth century, they found vines growing everywhere and well-established viticultural and winemaking practices in place. (The Magyars brought something besides themselves to Hungary—namely their idiosyncratic language. As you're about to experience, trying to read Hungarian, a Finno-Ugric language, can make you feel like you've got a mouth full of marbles.) But in the seventeenth century it was the emergence in Tokaj-Hegyalja of the rare, extraordinary wine known as Tokay, or more formally Tokay Aszú, that put Hungary on the international wine map. Tokay became and remains not only the most stunning wine of eastern Europe, but one of the greatest dessert wines in the

## THE QUICK SIP ON HUNGARY

• Hungary is one of the most important wine regions in eastern Europe. Until recently, however, Hungarian wines were little known outside of the Soviet Union and other Communist bloc countries thanks to forty years of Communist rule, from 1949 to 1989.

• Hungary's leading wine is Tokay Aszú, considered one of the great dessert wines of the world.

• Though small in size, Hungary boasts an enormous number of different grape varieties, including indigenous grapes, such as furmint, and international varieties, such as chardonnay.

world. Today Tokay is certainly the most important Hungarian wine exported to the United States and western Europe, even though it represents only about 4 percent of the country's total wine production.

## THE LAND, THE GRAPES, AND THE VINEYARDS

Hungary is a landlocked country of grassy plains, orchards, forests, and vineyards. The country is divided more or less in half by the Danube River, called the Duna in Hungarian, which runs north to south through the entire country much like the Mississippi River does in the United States. The climate is continental—warm to hot summers and very cold winters. Soil ranges all across the board; several of the best wine regions are spread over a mix of well-drained ones, including volcanic rock.

Of Hungary's twenty-two wine regions, seven are considered the most important based on the historic quality of their wines.

By far, the most prestigious of these is Tokaj-Hegyalja, the region where Tokay is produced, in the northeastern part of the country known as the Northern Massif along the Slovakian border. As for the other six wine zones, Badacsony and Somló are in the central Transdanubia region in the west near Lake Balaton, the largest lake in Europe. Badacsony produces primarily white wines from chardonnay, sauvignon blanc, szürkebarát (pinot gris), and olaszrizling (welschriesling). Somló, one of the smallest and most beautiful wine regions in Hungary, is the source of traditional wood-aged, somewhat oxidized white wines that can be a challenge to appreciate if your palate is accustomed to fresh, light modern-style whites. Nonetheless Hungarians insist Somló whites are a specialty and that they're especially perfect with heavy Hungarian dishes. In the southern part of Transdanubia are two more important wine regions, Szekszárd and Villány-Siklós. These are the two most dynamic wine

*The Tisza River, seen here, and the nearby Bodrog River, provide mists and humidity ideal for the development of* Botrytis cinerea—*indispensable in the creation of Tokay Aszú.*

## BULL'S BLOOD

—⟨ℯ⟩ℯ⟨ℯ⟩—

The most well known dry red wine of Hungary is Egri Bikavér—bull's blood of Eger. It is made primarily from the kékfrankos grape, grown in Eger, which is about halfway between Budapest and Tokaj. The legend behind the wine dates back to the mid-1500s when the fortress of Eger, which belonged to the Magyars (ancestors to modern Hungarians), was besieged by the Turks. The Magyars fought fiercely, drinking huge amounts of red wine in the process. As the story goes, when the Turks encountered the Magyars' ferocious fighting skills and saw their red-stained beards, they retreated, fearing that the Magyars attained their prowess by drinking the blood of bulls.

the other hand, are white wine territory. Here, good-quality wines are made from olaszrizling and muscat, as well as chardonnay, sauvignon blanc, and sémillon.

None of Hungary's most important wine regions are in the Great Alföld, the vast flat plain south of Budapest where nonetheless more than half of the country's vineyards are found. Curiously, most of the simple inexpensive quaffing wines produced here are based on international varieties, such as chardonnay and merlot, which were first planted in Hungary after phylloxera swept the country in the 1870s and then later planted even more extensively in the 1970s and 1980s. In total Hungary has about 324,000 acres of vineyards, making it the fourteenth in the world in terms of acreage under vine.

For a country about the size of the state of Maine, Hungary grows a wide range of grape varieties. These include many varieties that even the most avid wine fans may not recognize, such as furmint, hárslevelű, kadarka, and kékoporto. But Hungary is also home to many varieties, such as the aforementioned olaszrizling, kékfrankos (known in Austria as blaufränkisch), and zweigelt, that are common throughout the eastern part of Europe. Then there's a whole brigade of well-known international varieties—everything from sauvignon blanc, gewürztraminer (known in Hungary as tramini), and pinot gris (known as szürkebarát) to cabernet sauvignon, cabernet franc, and pinot noir. More than 60 percent of total wine production is white, although red wines are growing more popular and their production is increasing. Most of the wines made from these grapes

regions in Hungary and the regions where you are most likely to find producers using modern equipment and new oak barrels. Each of these regions produces some of the country's best red wines. Kadarka, a specialty of Szekszárd, is said to be the ideal red wine for paprika-based dishes. In the warm area known as Villány-Siklós, several top small producers make what are, for Hungary, fairly full-bodied reds from cabernet sauvignon, kékfrankos, kékoporto, merlot, and zweigelt. Finally, there are Eger and the Mátra Foothills, both of which are located, along with Tokaj-Hegyalja, in the Northern Massif. Eger is noted for Hungary's best-known dry red wine, Egri Bikavér (bull's blood), made from kékfrankos. It's also the source of light-bodied reds. The Mátra Foothills, on

## HUNGARIAN WINES

*While very little detailed information is available about Hungarian wines, these appear to be the most important. Most of this chapter concentrates on the Tokays, arguably the most important of the important wines, and the ones you are most likely to want to know about.*

**Cabernet Sauvignon** *red*

**Chardonnay** *white*

**Egri Bikavér** *red*

**Furmint** *white (dry and sweet)*

**Hárslevelü** *white (dry and sweet)*

**Kadarka** *red*

**Kékfrankos** *red*

**Kékoporto** *red*

**Merlot** *red*

**Muscat Lunel** *white*

**Olaszrizling** *white*

**Szamorodni** *white (dry and semisweet)*

**Szürkebarát** *white*

**Tokay Aszú** *white (sweet)*

**Tokay Aszú Eszencia** *white (sweet)*

**Tokay Eszencia** *white (sweet)*

**Zweigelt** *red*

590

Grapes were grown on enormous state-run farms, wines were made in large cooperatives, and all wine exports were controlled by a single large state-owned trading organization. Wines not consumed in Hungary were sold in bulk almost exclusively to the Soviet Union or Eastern Germany. Wine quality was dismal almost without exception. The post-Communist decade brought hope but confusion over vineyard ownership rights, foreign investments, and newly devised governmental regulations. Today, Hungary's wine industry is still in transition but is growing steadily. As the 1990s came to a close, there were an estimated 700 wineries, several of which were large enough to produce more than 40,000 cases a year. If Tokay is any model, the country's wines can be expected to undergo a major revolution in quality as the twenty-first century unfolds.

## HUNGARY'S WINE LAWS

Hungarian wines are governed by a set of national laws last revised in 1997. Roughly similar to the *Appellation d'Origine Contrôlée* laws of France, Hungary's regulations define the boundries of wine regions, stipulate the grape varieties that can be planted, designate allowable winemaking and viticultural processes, and govern how wines are labeled.

## TOKAY

Over the millennia of wine's existence, there have been multiple occasions when politics, war, and/or disease have combined to nearly destroy a wine region and its wines. No more poignant example exists than that of Tokay (toe-KAY in English). Considered (along with France's

are labeled both varietally, as are wines in the United States, and according to place, as is common in western Europe. You'll see a merlot from Szekszárd labeled as just that—Szekszárd merlot.

As for who makes Hungarian wines, for the forty years prior to the fall of Communism in 1989, the Hungarian wine industry was controlled by the state.

Sauternes and the sweet wines of Germany and Austria) one of the greatest sweet wines in the world, as well as the most majestic wine of eastern Europe, today it is nonetheless a wine few of us know or have ever tasted. It's not that Tokay Aszú, as it is formally known, ceased to be produced exactly. But for most of the last century, Tokay has fallen far short of Louis XIV's legendary description of it as *"vinum regum, rex vinorum"*—the wine of kings and the king of wines.

Tokay's long but thankfully temporary demise began with the deadly aphid phylloxera. As the twentieth century dawned, the vineyards of Tokay lay in ruin as a result of the pest. Over the next several decades, vineyards were rebuilt only to be devastated again during World War I and World War II. But the biggest upheaval was yet to come. In 1949 as Hungary collapsed under Communist rule, wineries and vineyards were confiscated and nationalized. The preciously refined and highly individual sweet wines of Tokay were blended en masse in big cooperative cellars run by the

## THE GRAPES OF
# HUNGARY

*There are dozens of grape varieties in Hungary, ranging from indigenous varieties to international ones. The ones here are the most significant.*

## WHITES

**Chardonnay, Pinot Blanc, Sauvignon Blanc,** and **Sémillon:** Important international grapes increasingly grown throughout Hungary.

**Furmint:** The most important grape in Tokay Aszú, Hungary's famous sweet wine. Also makes dry wines. Very high in acid.

**Hárslevelü:** The second most important grape in Tokay Aszú. Contributes a floral and fruity aroma.

**Muscat Lunel:** The same as muscat blanc à petits grains; the third most important grape in Tokay Aszú.

**Olaszrizling:** A specialty in the wines of Transdanubia, west of the Danube River; this is the same grape as the Austrian welschriesling.

**Orémus:** The fourth most important grape in Tokay Aszú; highly susceptible to botrytis.

**Szürkebarát:** Also known as pinot gris; makes well-regarded wines, especially when grown near Lake Balaton.

**Tramini:** The same variety as gewürztraminer; imported from western Europe but now grown all over Hungary.

## REDS

**Cabernet Sauvignon, Cabernet Franc, Merlot,** and **Pinot Noir:** Important international grapes increasingly grown throughout Hungary.

**Kadarka:** Important grape of fairly high quality; a specialty of Szekszárd.

**Kékfrankos:** Same as the Austrian grape blaufränkisch; sometimes blended with merlot and cabernet sauvignon. Kékfrankos is the major grape in the famous Hungarian wine Egri Bikavér—bull's blood.

**Kékoporto:** Important red grape; especially in Villány-Siklós.

**Zweigelt:** Like kékoporto, an important red grape in Villány-Siklós, but perhaps better known in Austria, where it's made into very good red wine.

591

state. Over subsequent years, vineyards were neglected, equipment deteriorated, the quality of grapes declined drastically, old winemaking traditions were abolished in favor of cheaper, easier shortcuts, and winemaking itself was degraded to the point where it was little more than bureaucratic drudgery. By the mid-1980s the innocuous wines called Tokay bore no resemblance to the wines once considered so extraordinarily delicious (not to

---

## SERVING, AGING, AND KEEPING TOKAY ASZÚ

——⟋⟋⟋⟋——

Tokay Aszú is usually served in wineglasses that taper a bit at the rim to concentrate the aroma. The wine should be chilled to about 55°F, which is not icy cold but just slightly cool. Like other dessert wines, a 2-ounce serving is fairly standard. Because Tokay is considered ready to drink upon release, there is no need to age it. That said, you certainly can age it if you want to since the wine's high concentrations of sugar and acid act as preservatives. Eastern European royal families would sometimes age the wine for close to a hundred years. And, because of its sweetness, an opened but unfinished bottle of Tokay will last for many months, especially if you keep it in the refrigerator. I recently discovered a partially finished bottle of Tokay in my cellar that had been opened five years ago. (Proving there are at least some benefits to a less than perfectly organized cellar.) Though some of the freshness was gone, it was surprisingly delicious all the same.

---

mention their purported therapeutic and aphrodisiacal properties) that a detachment of Russian soldiers was regularly stationed in the region to procure sufficient supplies and then escort them to the court of Czar Peter the Great.

Luckily Tokay was not beyond redemption. When Hungary became a democratic republic in 1989, foreign investment swiftly followed. By the fall of that year, a group of prominent investors, including Lord Jacob Rothschild, the British wine authority Hugh Johnson, and the noted Bordeaux winemaker Peter Vinding-Diers, formed the Royal Tokaji Wine Company in conjunction with sixty-three of the best remaining winegrowers. Within three years, a slew of other foreign investors, consultants, winemakers, and businessmen acquired estates and vineyards. These included Jean-Michel Arcaute of Château Clinet in Bordeaux, who helped found Château Pajzos; the owners of Spain's most famous wine estate, Vega-Sicilia, who founded Oremus; and three French multinational insurance companies, one of which, AXA, also owns Bordeaux's Château Pichon-Longueville, Baron and Château Suduiraut as well as the famous Port firm Quinta do Noval. AXA's Tokay firm is called Disznókő. The financial capital these companies brought was formidable. In less than half a decade, Tokay was reborn.

Tokay is the English spelling of Tokaji, meaning wine from the place Tokaj. The Tokay region, known officially as Tokaj-Hegyalja (Tokay Hill), is about 120 miles northeast of Budapest, close to the Slovakian border. It includes twenty-eight villages spread over sloping hills, the remnants of ancient volcanoes. As the 1990s

*The town of Tokaj, in the region known as Tokaj-Hegyalja, gives its name to Hungary's greatest wine—Tokay Aszú. The clock at the railway station in Tokaj (left) is appropriately decorated with grapes.*

came to a close there were only about 12,000 acres of vines in the Tokay region, making it about one third the size of the Napa Valley. (Abandoned and neglected vineyards continue to be reclaimed, and vineyard acreage is expected to grow.) The vineyards belong to about thirty leading producers of Tokay, as well as hundreds of tiny family-run operations, many of which make very small amounts of wine for their own and local consumption.

The Tokay region produces both dry and sweet wines, but it is the lusciously honeyed wine Tokay Aszú for which it is world famous, even though Tokay Aszú represents less than 10 percent of all the wine produced in the region. Tokay Aszú has been called the Sauternes of eastern Europe, but perhaps the phrase should be reversed and Sauternes should be called the Tokay Aszú of France since it was in the Tokay region, not Sauternes, that the world's first lusciously sweet botrytized wines were made. Their creation was

something of an accident. It's well documented that during the Middle Ages wines from the region were highly regarded and many vineyards were owned by members of the royalty. The style of those wines and whether they were sweet or dry remains unknown. As the story goes, in the mid-1600s a priest named Máté Szepsi Laczkó began experimenting with furmint, an indigenous grape still used in Tokay today. The priest's experiments included letting the grapes begin to raisinate on the vine. At this point, history intervened. As the crop was about to be harvested, the Turks swept through in one of their periodic invasions. Hungarians were called to war or fled, leaving the grapes on the vine. When the Hungarians returned late in the fall, the grapes, shriveled completely, had also begun to rot (the Hungarians called the dry, rotting grapes *aszú*). In desperation, Szepsi Laczkó instructed the harvesters to pick the moldy grapes anyway.

593

## How Sweet They Are

ᗣᑐᗢ

Tokay Aszú is one of the most decadent but well-balanced sweet wines in the world thanks to the natural acidity in the grapes. The sweetness of Tokay is measured in *puttonyos*. Below are the legal requirements for the sugar content that wines of the various numbers of *puttonyos* must have. In practice many wineries make Tokay Aszús that exceed the degree of sweetness required for a particular number of *puttonyos*. So a wine labeled 5 *puttonyos* may contain 20 percent residual sugar even though the law only requires between 12 and 15 percent. For comparison's sake, the residual sugar in a French Sauternes is roughly equal to that of a 4 *puttonyos* Tokay Aszú.

**3 Puttonyos**
Sweet: 6 to 9 percent residual sugar

**4 Puttonyos**
Quite sweet: 9 to 12 percent residual sugar

**5 Puttonyos**
Very pronounced sweetness: 12 to 15 percent residual sugar

**6 Puttonyos**
Dramatically sweet: 15 to 18 percent residual sugar

**Tokay Aszú Eszencia**
Outrageously sweet: more than 18 percent residual sugar

**Tokay Eszencia**
Off the charts: 40 to 70 percent residual sugar

Miraculously, the small amount of liquid that oozed from them tasted like honey. When the priest blended this nectar with the regular table wine from the previous year, the prototype of Tokay Aszú was born.

## Making Tokay Aszú

Like all wines made with the help of *Botrytis cinerea*, Tokay Aszú is dependent on a singular set of climatic conditions. For the botrytis fungus to take hold on healthy, ripe grapes, the region must have just the right amount of humidity and warmth (too little *or* too much can produce problems). Tokaj-Hegyalja is well situated. The Carpathian Mountains, which arc around the region, shelter it from cold winds from the east, north, and west, creating prolonged, gently warm autumns. The region, shaped like a check mark, lies along a range of volcanic hills topped with loesses, fine-grained deposits of clay and silt, which warm easily. Following the length of these hills is the Bodrog River, which meets the Tisza River at the bottom point of the check mark, near the village of Tokaj. Mists and humidity rising from these rivers are held in place by the warm hills, creating the perfect environment for botrytis to form.

The four white grapes used in Tokay are ideally suited for this purpose. Furmint, which makes up about 60 percent of all grapes planted in the region, is high in acid, late ripening, thin-skinned, and easily susceptible to botrytis. Hárslevelű—the name means linden leaf—is second in importance, and though slightly less susceptible to botrytis, it too is high in acid, as well as very aromatic and rich tasting. Muscat blanc à petits grains, called muscat lunel in Tokay, is also both highly aromatic and crisply acidic. It is used as a seasoning grape. Since 1993, a fourth grape, orémus, also called zéta, has also been allowed. It's both very susceptible to botrytis and capable of attaining high sugar levels. The fact that three of these grapes naturally possess a bracing level of acidity means that, even at its sweetest, Tokay Aszú tastes beautifully balanced, not saccharine or candied.

The beneficial botrytis mold punctures the grapes' skins in search of water to germinate its spores. This causes water in the grapes to evaporate, and the grapes begin to dehydrate. Inside the shriveled grapes, the sugar and acid in the juice become progressively more concentrated. It is a perfect system to foster sweetness, but it's not without challenges. Botrytis spreads erratically, affecting some grapes and not others, some bunches and not others. It also moves through the vineyards sporadically; in some years, when little or no botrytis takes hold, no Tokay Aszú will be produced.

Producers differ slightly in how they make Tokay Aszú, but generally speaking the process goes like this. First, throughout the fall the shriveled *aszú* grapes are picked one by one from botrytis-affected bunches. These *aszú* grapes are then brought to the winery where they are lightly crushed into a paste. Meanwhile, the rest of the crop (all the grapes and bunches not affected by botrytis) is picked separately and

## TOKAY IN HUNGARY, TOKAY IN ALSACE

——⟶⟿⟿⟿——

The famous Tokay wines of Hungary, made from furmint, hárslevelű, muscat lunel, and orémus are not the same as the tokay wines of Alsace. In Alsace, tokay is a synonym for pinot gris. The confusion arises because pinot gris is thought to have been brought from France to Hungary in the late fourteenth century and then brought back to Alsace two centuries later, rechristened as Hungary's most famous wine Tokay. Neither Hungarian Tokay or Alsace tokay (toe-KAY) is related to tocai (pronounced toe-KI), a popular indigenous white grape of northern Italy.

made into a base wine. The *aszú* paste is added in various proportions to the base wine of the same year. (In the past *aszú* was sometimes added to a base wine held back from the previous year; this practice is now rare.)

595

*The bottle cellars at the Disznókő winery are filled with the majestic nectar Tokay Aszú.*

The proportions of *aszú* added are measured in *puttonyos*. A *puttony* is a basket in which the *aszú* grapes were traditionally gathered. It holds 20 to 25 kilos (44 to 55 pounds) of grapes, equal to about 20 liters (5.2 gallons) of *aszú* paste. The ratio of *puttonyos* to base wine in each barrel determined the sweetness of the wine. The traditional barrels, called *gönci* (after the village of Gönc, known for its barrel makers), hold about 140 liters of wine. Thus a wine labeled Tokay Aszú 2 *puttonyos* would have 40 liters of *aszú* paste and 100 liters of base wine. A wine labeled Tokay Aszú 4 *puttonyos* would be even richer and sweeter, as it would have 80 liters of *aszú* paste and 60 liters of base wine. A 4 or 5 *puttonyos* Tokay would be about as sweet and concentrated as a German *beerenauslese*. The sweetest Tokay Aszús are 6 *puttonyos* and they are technically much sweeter than Sauternes (but don't taste like it because of the wine's acidity). Today Tokay Aszú is more commonly made in stainless steel tanks rather than in barrels, and the number of *puttonyos* assigned is now officially based on the amount of residual sugar the wine contains (see page 594).

Depending on the concentration of sweetness in the *aszú* grapes when they were picked, the *aszú* paste will steep in the base wine for as few as eight hours or as many as three days. At this point the sweetened wine will be drawn off the *aszú* paste and allowed to ferment again in Tokay's small cellars, dug centuries ago as places to hide during Turkish invasions. In these single-vaulted, cold, damp, moldy cellars, the second fermentation can take months, even years, since the cold temperatures coupled with the high sugar content of the wine slow down the process. Under current law, Tokay Aszú must be aged for at least two years in oak barrels and one year in bottle before being sold. The bottles are always the traditional squat 500 milliliter Tokay Aszú bottles, three quarters the size of a standard wine bottle.

In the past, as the wines of Tokay aged, the barrels would not be topped up, leaving air space in each. At the same time, a special strain of natural yeasts, which flourished in Tokay's cool dark cellars, would coat the surface of the wine with a fine film, rather like flor in Sherry. The combination of the yeasts and the partial oxidation of the wine would contribute yet another unique flavor to Tokay Aszú. Today many Tokay Aszús are intentionally made in completely full barrels and tanks so that they are protected from oxygen and their fruity character is preserved, although yeasts (omnipresent in these cellars) still contribute to the flavor.

There are two other categories of rare, superconcentrated Tokay Aszús: Tokay Eszencia (also spelled Essencia, or Essence) and Tokay Aszú Eszencia. Straight Tokay Eszencia is the most luxuri-

## TOKAY AT THE TABLE

While drinking Tokay Aszú by itself can be a perfect exercise in indulgence, the wine's richness and underlying acidity make it a fascinating partner for many dishes. In Hungary it is traditionally served with celebratory desserts, such as crepes (*palacsinták*, literally pancakes) filled with thick chocolate cream or apricot cake, or else paired hedonistically, as Sauternes would be, with foie gras, or a blue cheese like Roquefort or Stilton.

ous, hedonistic Tokay of all. Only a minuscule amount is made and the wine is frighteningly expensive. In exceptionally good years, the *aszú* grapes will be put in a cask and the juice that runs free from these grapes and out of the bottom of the cask (traditionally through a goose quill put in the bunghole of the cask) with no pressure other than the weight of the grapes on top is Tokay Eszencia. At more than 45 percent sugar, this liquid is so syrupy and sweet that the yeasts, slowed to a stupor, barely manage to do their work, and the luscious liquid ferments unbelievably slowly—sometimes barely at all. A Château Pajzos Tokay Eszencia from the legendary great vintage of 1993 took four years to ferment to 4.7 percent alcohol and a Royal Tokaji Company Tokay Eszencia from the same 1993 vintage was still fermenting in 1999! In the end most Tokay Eszencias may only reach an alcohol level of 2 to 5 percent. But simply to say the wine is sweet does not do it justice. The color of honey, velvety rich, and tasting of dried apricots and dried peaches, Tokay Eszencia is one of the world's most penetrating and profound taste sensations, rendering wine lovers (including this one) weak in the knees. It is said to be one of the longest lasting of all wines, capable of aging for centuries. Historically it was reserved for royalty, who sometimes drank it on their deathbeds, hoping to be revived.

Tokay Eszencia is so rare and precious that most of it is not bottled on its own but instead is blended sparingly into 6 *puttonyos* Tokay Aszú to make the highly revered Tokay Aszú Eszencia, itself a rare, superexpensive, extraordinary wine that is also made only in exceptional years. Tokay Aszú Eszencia must be aged five years, of which three must be in the barrel.

## A PASSION FOR PAPRIKA

It's hard to imagine that three centuries ago, one of the (now) defining ingredients of the Hungarian kitchen—paprika—was not yet known in Hungary. But it wasn't. According to George Lang, author of *George Lang's Cuisine of Hungary* and co-owner of Budapest's famous restaurant Gundel, as well as New York City's Café des Artistes, paprika, along with several other Hungarian culinary essentials—tomatoes, sour cherries, coffee, and phyllo (which the Hungarians immortalized by reinventing as strudel)—were all introduced by the Turks during their numerous occupations. Be that as it may, in Hungary, paprika found its true admirers and raison d'être. Fiery and passionate themselves, Hungarians like their dishes to have drama. Even something as simple as paprika chicken (*paprikás csirke*) is a kind of lusty and luscious duel between the tangy richness of sour cream on the one hand and the tantalizing bite of paprika on the other. What wine to serve when paprika's in the pot? Well, it shouldn't be dainty. In Hungary, they'd drink a gutsy cabernet or maybe Bull's Blood (a wine made primarily from kékfrankos grapes), but I love southern French wines like Châteauneuf-du-Pape with paprika-laced, sour-cream-rich dishes, too. Blackish in color and smelling like someone sprinkled exotic spices on the forest floor, Châteauneuf-du-Pape may be French but it has more than enough soulfulness to please any hungry Hungarian.

## The Tokay Classification System

The vineyards of Tokay were the first in the world to be classified according to quality. In 1700, about a century and a half before Bordeaux's 1855 Classification, Prince Rákóczi issued a royal decree assigning the vineyards of Tokay rankings of first, second, and third class, using the Latin designations *primae classis*, *secunde classis*, and so on. In addition, two vineyards, Csarfas and Mézes Mály, were given a special designation, a sort of superfirst-class status called *pro mensa caesaris primus*, or chosen for the royal table. In total 173 vineyards were classified, and others that were not particularly well sited were listed as unclassified. Throughout much of the forty-year Communist regime, with vineyards in poor condition, the classification system was largely meaningless. But in 1995 the top producers of Tokay formed an association called Tokaj Renaissance with the goal of reviving the significance of the old classification system. As of the late 1990s, such vineyard names as Betsek and Szt. Tamás began appearing on bottles along with their rankings; in this case, both are first class.

---

*Some of the Best Producers of Tokay Aszú*

**CHÂTEAU PAJZOS**

**DISZNÓKŐ**

**HÉTSZŐLŐ**

**ISTVÁN SZEPSY**

**ROYAL TOKAJI WINE COMPANY**

**TOKAJ-OREMUS**

---

## Other Wines of the Tokay Region

The vast viticultural and winemaking improvements of the 1990s not only elevated the quality of Tokay Aszú, they also improved the region's dry white wines. Dry furmint bottled as a single variety makes a crisp, slightly citrusy white wine that's an easy partner for all sorts of dishes. Hárslevelű is softer, slightly creamy, and has the added bonus of an appealingly fruity aroma. And muscat lunel often has ripe peach, apricot, and quince flavors. Though these wines represent the majority of all the wines produced in the Tokay region, very few are sold outside of Hungary, Russia, and central Europe. What are catching on in the United States are the sweet late harvest versions of these wines. They contain some botrytized grapes, but the wines are made differently from traditional Tokay Aszú and are usually not aged three years. Two wines to try include Château Pajzos Muskatoly and Oremus Tokaji Furmint Noble Late Harvest.

Yet another type of wine made in the Tokay region is Szamorodni, which means as it is grown or as it comes. When vineyards are not sufficiently affected by botrytis to get enough *aszú* berries to make Tokay Aszú, a blended wine from Tokay's three main grapes is made. The Szamorodni may be dry (*száraz*) or slightly sweet (*édes*). The slightly sweet version is made by arresting the fermentation of the wine before all of the sugar is converted into alcohol. Szamorodni must be aged two years in the barrel, and most often barrels are not topped up, so the wine is slightly oxidized. Thus Szamorodni takes on an intriguing toasted-nut character similar to Sherry.

# THE HUNGARIAN WINES TO KNOW

With the exception of Tokay Aszú, top Hungarian wines are not easy to find in the marketplace. So, we'll focus primarily on Tokay Aszú, which, in any case, no wine lover should miss. The quality of these wines is so stunning across the board that those of any of the top producers listed on the opposite page are well worth seeking out. My descriptions here are of wines made from the 1991 vintage or later. Wines made before this come from the Communist era and therefore predate the vast improvements made in the cellars of the Tokay region. The wines below are listed in ascending order of sweetness.

## TOKAJ-OREMUS

Tokaji Furmint

Late Harvest

100% furmint

This is the new style of lighter, less intensely sweet dessert wine coming out of the Tokay region—a late harvest wine made with both botrytized and extremely ripe grapes but not made with *aszú* paste in the traditional manner of Tokay Aszú. There's a beautiful balance here of honey and dramatic acidity. More sleek than syrupy, Oremus' late harvest Tokaji tastes like a light-bodied Sauternes, and the price is lighter too. Just waiting for a fruit tart.

## CHATEAU PAJZOS

Tokaji Aszú

5 puttonyos

approximately 50% muscat lunel, 45% furmint, and a small amount of hárslevelű

It's hard to imagine a 5 *puttonyos* Tokay that is more sensual than that of Château Pajzos. In great vintages, the wine positively drips with honey, lavender, vanilla, dried apricot, and coconut flavors and radiates an aroma evocative of meadows. Even with a residual sugar that usually hovers around 15 percent, the wine is gorgeously poised in pinpoint balance between sweetness and acidity.

## ROYAL TOKAJI WINE COMPANY

Tokaji Aszú

5 puttonyos

approximately 65% furmint, 35% hárslevelű

One of the first firms founded after Communism, the Royal Tokaji Wine Company was also one of the first to invest heavily in the Tokay region. This is the Royal Tokaji Wine Company's basic, moderately priced Tokay, and its pure, delicate, melt-in-your-mouth honey flavors are irresistible. The aroma hints at *crème caramel* and burnt sugar, yet at the same time, there's a floral or meadowy quality to this wine that's always very attractive. Though usually around an astounding 20 percent residual sugar—much higher than the requirements for a 5 *puttonyos*—the wine is gossamer in its lightness.

## DISZNOKO

Tokaji Aszú

6 puttonyos

approximately 60% furmint, 30% hárslevelű, and 10% orémus

At 6 *puttonyos*, Tokays begin to be so concentrated they are literally syrupy and their aromas have an almost frightening intensity. Disznókő's 6 *puttonyos* is a deeply profound, lush wine with flavors that suggest honey mixed with orange marmalade. A mere thimbleful is exquisite and satisfying, though who could stop at that?

599

### ROYAL TOKAJI WINE COMPANY

Tokaji Aszú

6 puttonyos

Szt. Tamás

primae classis 1700

approximately 70% furmint, 30% hárslevelű

From the *primae classis* (first class) vineyard known as Szt. Tamás (St. Thomas) come wines that stop you in your tracks, they are so luscious and long. Flavors of roasted apricots, roasted peaches, and crème brûlée dance in your mouth with a refinement that is breathtaking. Generally made at around 23 percent residual sugar, this hedonistic wine could actually qualify as a Tokay Aszú Eszencia.

### ROYAL TOKAJI WINE COMPANY

Aszú Essencia

approximately 50% furmint, 50% hárslevelű

This is surely one of the rarest and most exciting wines in the world. Usually made only once or twice in a decade, RTWC's Aszú Essencia is nearly indescribable. It might be more accurate to report taking a bite, rather than a sip, of this wine for it is so dense it could be added to the periodic table as a new element. All of Tokay's lush flavors are here: honey, dried apricots, dried orange peel, and caramel, plus dried figs, baked pears, and even a mesmerizing roasted pumpkin character. Utterly long, supple, and elegant, even at an astounding 30 percent residual sugar or more.

# VISITING HUNGARIAN WINERIES

The most fascinating (and easiest) Hungarian wineries to visit are those of Tokay in northeast Hungary about 120 miles, or a three hour train trip, from Budapest. The majority of Tokay's leading wineries are located in or near the sleepy village of Mád (easy to remember). They are generally open for tastings and tours of their old underground cellars from May through October, and tours can usually be conducted in English on request. It is best to make appointments with individual wineries ahead of time. The organization Tokaj Renaissance will also help set up tours; contact them at 011-36-47-380-765. The telephone numbers include the dialing code you'll need when calling from the United States. If you're calling from within Hungary, eliminate the 011-36 and add the numbers 06 before the next number.

If, on your way to or from wine country, you stop overnight in Budapest, be sure to dine at Gundel, the palatial nineteenth-century restaurant restored in 1992 by international businessman Ronald Lauder and restaurant consultant George Lang. The menu is devoted entirely to traditional Hungarian classics, including legendary Hungarian pastries (Allatkerti 2, Budapest; 011-361–321-3550).

**CHÂTEAU PAJZOS RT.**
Nagy Lajos út 12
H-3950 Sárospatak
011-36-47-312-310

**DISZNÓKŐ RT.**
Disznókő dülö
H-3931 Mezözombor
011-36-47-361-371

**ROYAL TOKAJI BORÁSZATI KFT.**
Rákóczi út 35
H-3909 Mád
011-36-47-348-011

**TOKAJ OREMUS PINCÉSZET**
Bajcsy-Zsilinszky út 45-47
H-3934 Tolcsva
011-36-47-384-504

Greece

The birthplace of Western civilization, Greece is in many ways also the birthplace of our modern wine culture. For the ancient Greeks wine was a gift to man from the god Dionysus, a gift of formidable importance since the recipient actually took the offering into his own body. Dionysus' gift established wine (and not beer, the more common beverage of antiquity) as a symbol of worthiness, a luxurious blessing, and the beverage that would henceforth be inextricably woven into the very fabric of religious celebration. Homer, Plato, Aristotle, and Hippocrates all wrote of wine's virtues and its beneficial effects on

thought, health, and creativity. For the ancient Greek man, the intellectual discussions that arose when drinking wine formed the central core of the symposia, animated get-togethers from which sprang the beginnings of Western philosophy.

Bordered by Bulgaria, Macedonia, and Albania on the north and by Turkey on the east, Greece nonetheless gives the impression of being a country made up as much of water as of land. Three seas—the Aegean, the Mediterranean, and the Ionian—nudge into the mountainous landmass, creating a tumble of islands, inlets, bays, and rugged peninsulas. The dominance and beauty of all this water and the 2,500 miles of coast-

*Ancient storage jars—possibly for wine or olive oil—at the palace at Knossos, Crete.*

Greece ranks thirteenth in wine-producing countries worldwide. Greeks drink an average of 7.46 gallons of wine per person each year; they're fifteenth in world wine consumption.

N

BULGARIA

REPUBLIC OF
MACEDONIA

ALBANIA

*Lake
Prespa*

**MACEDONIA**

CENTRAL
MACEDONIA

*Strymon River*

THRACE

[1]

*Vermion Mts.*

WESTERN
MACEDONIA

[2]

*Aliákmon R.*

• Thessalonika
• Epanomi
*Chalcidice*

*Samothrace*

▲ *Mount
Olympus*

[3]

*Mount
Athos*

*Lemnos*

TURKEY

EPIRUS

*Achelous River*

[4]

*Piniós River*

• Larissa

**THESSALY**

• Vólos

*Northern
Sporades*

*Aegean
Sea*

*Cephisus River*

CENTRAL
GREECE

Patras •
[5]

*Gulf of
Corinth*

WESTERN
GREECE

ATTICA

*Isthmus of
Corinth*

Corinth •

• Athens ✪
Piraeus •

[8]

*Cephalonia*

[6]

**PELOPONNESE**

*Alpheus R.*

[7]

**AEGEAN ISLANDS**

*Cyclades*

*Ionian Sea*

Monemvasia •

[9]

*Mediterranean
Sea*

*Sea of Crete*

Hania •

**CRETE**

Iráklion •

100 mi
100 km
© MapQuest.com

**KEY TO GREECE'S WINE REGIONS**

**MACEDONIA**
1 Goumenissa
2 Naoussa
3 Côtes de Meliton
**THESSALY**
4 Rapsani
**PELOPONNESE**
5 Patras

6 Nemea
7 Mantinia
**AEGEAN
ISLANDS**
8 Samos
9 Santorini
**CRETE**

line are inescapable. No part of Greece, except for a small portion in the northwest, is more than 50 miles from the sea.

Precisely when winemaking began here is not entirely clear. The oldest evidence, an ancient pottery jar containing residue from wine fermentation, dates from between 3500 and 2900 B.C. and comes not from Greece but from Godin Tepe in the Zagros Mountains of western Iran. Whether or not the Godin Tempe jar actually reflects the earliest attempts at winemaking is a question that archaeologists and archaeobotanists cannot answer. Considerable other evidence (grape seeds, amphorae, winemaking scenes painted on drinking vessels, and so on) suggests that winemaking and domesticated grape production were likely to have had multiple origins wherever wild grapevines of the species *Vitis vinifera* subspecies *sylvestris* grew. Wild grapevines of this subspecies are thought to be native to the area stretching from northern Greece to the woodlands south and west of the Caspian Sea. From chardonnay to sangiovese, every European grape variety known today is the progeny of these wild vines.

Despite the lack of a precise date of origin for Greek winemaking, the remains of grape skins, stalks, and primitive wine presses suggest that making wine was a well-established part of Minoan civilization on the Greek island of Crete between 2500 and 2100 B.C. From this period on,

604

## THE QUICK SIP ON GREECE

• The wines of Greece were the most important wines in antiquity. Thanks to Greece's extensive trade and colonization, wine became an integral part of the cultures of western Europe from their earliest beginnings.

• Greece is home to more than 300 indigenous and not very well known grape varieties.

• During the 1990s, the Greek wine industry began to experience a revolution in quality. Finer wines are now being made than at any other time in the country's history.

vines and olives are known to have been cultivated alongside one another. Moreover, Greece's extensive trade with Egypt, which was also recognized for its widespread grape cultivation and winemaking, and evidence from Cretan and Egyptian hieroglyphics have led scholars to theorize that the eastern Mediterranean posessed a thriving wine industry and that wine, along with olive oil, meat, cheese, and honey, was collected at palaces for distribution to the wealthy. It was primarily through trading in wine, and the subsequent social relationships wine encouraged, that ancient Greece's influence on

*An ancient Greek* kylix, *or decorated wine cup, from around 490 B.C.*

everything from ethics to politics spread throughout the Mediterranean world. This proved especially important in the western Mediterranean where the knowledge of winemaking and viticulture turned out to be one of the most pivotal of all Greek legacies. As a result of early Greek colonization, the making and drinking of wine would become an integral part of the cultural identities of France, Spain, and Italy.

The wines drunk in ancient Greece were sometimes flavored—intentionally and unintentionally—by pine resin, which was used to coat the otherwise porous insides of the amphorae, or jars, that wines were stored and transported in (see page 609). Millennia later, the resinated wine known as retsina is still immensely popular in Greece (see page 615). During classical times, wines were also sometimes flavored with flowers and flower oils, giving them what Plato considered to be even more positive odors than they already possessed. In the ancient Greek view, the proper odors were necessary for restoring the body to its natural harmony. The similarity between floral aromas and the aromas of certain wines raised the reputation of those wines for floral smells were thought to be particularly beneficial to the brain and, in addition, were deemed capable of forestalling intoxication.

Intoxication itself was something the Greeks denounced for its harmful effects. Accordingly, wine was always diluted with water in proportions ranging from two parts wine and three parts water to one part wine and three parts water. To the Greeks, only barbarians drank wine straight. Eubulus, the Greek poet of the fourth century B.C. known for his mythological burlesques, summarized the Greek penchant for moderation when he attributed these words to Dionysus:

*Three kraters [bowls used for wine] do I mix for the temperate: one to health, which they empty first, the second to love and pleasure, the third to sleep. When this bowl is drunk up, wise guests go home. The fourth bowl is ours no longer, but belongs to hubris, the fifth to uproar, the sixth to prancing about, the seventh to black eyes, the eighth brings the police, the ninth belongs to vomiting, and the tenth to insanity and the hurling of furniture.*

Reflecting on the Greek wisdom of taking no more than three drinks, Hugh Johnson, the esteemed British wine expert, notes that throughout history three drinks have been considered the model for moderation. Johnson even goes on to suggest that from this historic counsel is derived the wine bottle, which just happens to contain 750 milliliters or about three glasses each for two people.

## THE MODERN GREEK WINE INDUSTRY

For all its hegemony as the single most important wine producer of antiquity, Greece has had an arduous climb into the modern world of fine wine. During the Middle Ages the country was part of the Byzantine Empire, and the best Greek wines were made by monks following monastic traditions. But the fall of Byzantium and the subsequent occupation of Greece by the Ottoman Turks effectively brought an end to Greece's respected place among wine producers. The Turks did not formally forbid winemaking for the Christian population, but the strictures and taxes imposed during nearly four hundred years of Ottoman domination were severe enough to prevent Greece from developing a significant wine industry. While the wine industries of certain parts of western Europe (notably Bordeaux) progressed toward ever greater quality and commercial success, Greek wine remained the work of peasants whose necessary goal was subsistence not sophistication.

Greece's wine industry remained largely undeveloped until the twentieth century. Then, as was true in virtually every other European country, the situation worsened. The devastating plant louse phylloxera, which arrived in Greece in the late 1890s and stayed for several decades, followed by two world wars, and then Greece's own civil war left the coun-

try's wine industry in ruins. Even as of the 1960s most Greek wines were still being sold in bulk directly from barrels to buyers who brought their own jugs to fill. It was not until the mid-1980s, with Greece's newfound political and economic stability and its entry into the European Economic Community, that the country's wine industry began to shift away from very inexpensive serviceable table wines intended for local consumption toward wines of finer quality. This meant lowering grape yields substantially, improving viticultural techniques in the vineyards, employing more modern equipment, and in many cases, using expensive small oak barrels for the first time in the history of Greek winemaking.

Today the country's wine industry is composed of a handful of well-organized large firms, such as Boutari, Achaia-Clauss, D. Kourtakis, and Tsantali, as well as scores of medium-size and small family-run estates. In a country where land own-

## GREEK WINE LABELS

Greek wines are labeled in three different ways: by appellation, by varietal, or by proprietary name. An example of labeling by appellation, which is common throughout Europe, would be Boutari's Naoussa. Some knowledgeable consumers will recognize that Naoussa comes from xynomavro grapes, in the same way they know Sancerre is made from sauvignon blanc grapes. But then there's Boutari's xynomavro-merlot, an example of a wine labeled by variety (in this case two varieties: xynomavro and merlot). And Boutari's Kallisti is an example of a wine labeled with a proprietary name. Kallisti

(the word means fairest of all) is a barrel-fermented white wine from Santorini made with assyrtiko grapes.

ership is fragmented, most of these firms both own their own vineyard land and buy from thousands of small-scale growers. All of these firms—large and small—are more oriented to quality than they've been at any other time, and for the most part very cheap bulk wine is now left to the cooperatives.

## GREECE'S WINE LAWS

Greek wines are governed by a set of national laws implemented by the Ministry of Agriculture in 1971. A decade later, when Greece joined the European Economic Community, the regulations were revised along the lines of the European Economic Community wine legislation, which uses the *Appellation d'Origine Contrôlée* (AOC) laws of France as its base. The laws define the boundries of wine regions, stipulate which grape varieties can be planted, designate allowable winemaking and viticultural processes, and govern how wines are permitted to be labeled.

The Greek laws define three categories of wine. These categories are not necessarily a hierarchy. Very good wines can be found in any of them.

**Appellation of Origin of Superior Quality and Controlled Appellation of Origin:** The designations Appellation of Origin of Superior Quality (its Greek acronym is OPAP) and the Controlled Appellation of Origin (OPE) indicate dry and sweet wines that come from defined areas and are made in prescribed ways similar to French AOC wines. There are a total of twenty-eight wines with appellation status in Greece. Within this category are two levels beyond standard wine, reserve and grand reserve. White

### GREEK WINES

**Archarnes** red
**Goumenissa** red
**Mantinia** white and rosé
**Mavrodaphne of Patras** red (sweet)
**Muscat of Patras** white (sweet)
**Muscat of Samos** white (sweet)
**Naoussa** red
**Nemea** red
**Patras** white
**Rapsani** red
**Retsina** white
**Santorini** white
**Visánto** white (sweet)

607

wine in the reserve category must be aged two years, with a minimum of six months in barrel. A reserve red must be aged three years, with a minimum of six months in barrel. Grand reserve whites must be aged three years, with a minimum of twelve months in barrel, while reds must be aged four years, with a minimum of two years in barrel.

**Topikos Oenos:** Greece's rough equivalent of the French *vin de pays*, or country wine, *topikos oenos* wines (think of them as T.O. wines) do not possess appellations of origin but, instead, may be made in a large number of specified areas from a large number of grape varieties both indigenous and international. The labels of *topikos oenos* wines sometimes also include one of the following terms: *ktima* (estate), *monastiri* (monastery), or *archondiko* (château).

**Epitrapezios Oenos:** Roughly equivalent to France's *vin de table*, or table wine, many *epitrapezios oenos* (E.O. will do) wines, while very popular, do not possess appellations of origin, and in fact they may be blends of grapes from different regions. The top wines in this category are labeled *cava* and are aged longer than the regular wines. *Cava* whites must be aged two years, with a minimum of six months in barrel. *Cava* reds must be aged three years, with a minimum of six months in new oak barrels or one year in old oak barrels.

# THE LAND, THE GRAPES, AND THE VINEYARDS

In square miles, Greece is smaller than the state of Florida, and of its total land area, about 70 percent is mountains and 20 percent islands. Mountainous regions are used primarily for grazing sheep and goats, although some vineyards are planted on the more moderate mountain slopes and high plateaus. The relatively small amount of land that is available for agriculture—some 326,000 acres, an amount only modestly greater than the acreage planted with grapes in Bordeaux—is widely planted with grapevines and olive trees; both do well in Greece's mostly infertile, thin, dry soil.

Greece's climate is well adapted for grape growing. Rains come mainly in the winter when the vines are dormant. There is more than enough sunlight, augmented by sunlight reflected off the sea, to

*This Greek vessel from the second or first century B.C. mimics the shape of a wineskin.*

ripen the grapes fully. If anything, too much sun and heat is a problem, for grapes that ripen too quickly often have simple, monochromatic flavors. For this reason some vineyards are planted on north-facing slopes to slow down the ripening process.

The proximity of Greek vineyards to the sea and cooling maritime breezes is usually an advantage. But even sea breezes can pose problems. To anyone accustomed to vines that stand 6 feet tall or more, as vines can do in California, it's startling to see the vineyards on some of the most windswept Greek islands. There, the vines are trained close to the ground in a circular fashion that, from a distance, makes them look like coiled up ropes or hoses. Trained this way, each vine is called a *stefáni*, or crown. In the center of the *stefáni*, protected from the wind, you find the grapes.

*For the Greeks, the vineyard, the olive tree, and the Aegean Sea have always been powerfully important symbols standing for, respectively: passion and joy in life, peace and noblesse, and new horizons.*

Greece's peculiar geographic configuration, with its 4,000 plus islands, allowed a vast number of different grape varieties to become established. More than 300 ancient indigenous varieties have been identified, although some are disappearing due to the lack of a market for the wines made from them. Several Greek winemakers, however, are determined to protect them from extinction. At the same time, international varieties, such as chardonnay and caber-

## TRANSPORTING WINE IN THE ANCIENT WORLD

Other than goatskin bags, the earliest vessels for transporting wine in the ancient world were amphorae, terra-cotta jars with two looped handles and, usually, a pointed base. Although the exact date and place in the eastern Mediterranean where these distinctive jars originated has often been debated, their history can be traced back to at least 2000 B.C. and the so-called Canaanite jars that were used to ship a variety of goods, including wine, in Canaan's extensive trade with Pharaonic Egypt. By the thirteenth century B.C. such vessels were being shipped as far afield as mainland Greece, where they were found in the tombs of Mycenaean royalty. The hundreds of thousands of amphora fragments that have been uncovered by anthropologists attest to the enormous volume of commerce, including that in wine, that occurred in antiquity.

While some small amphorae held about 2½ gallons, the jars used in transporting wine were generally larger, holding 6½ gallons or more and weighing at least 22 pounds when empty. Filled with wine, an amphora would have been heavy, hence the practicality of two handles, allowing two people to carry the jar. Although the pointed base seems odd, it too was pragmatic, offering a third "handle" when necessary. Such a design was also very functional on ships where the pointed bases could be buried deeply in sand and the handles of the jars tied together for stability. When they weren't being carried, amphorae would be leaned against the wall of a room or placed in special ring stands to hold them erect.

Since different Greek city-states produced their own distinctive styles of amphorae, archaeologists theorize that the various jar shapes would have signaled different kinds of wine in the marketplace. In addition, before they were fired, the handles of many jars were stamped with information about the type, the origin, and often the date of the wine that the amphora contained.

In order to form an airtight seal and thereby prevent bacteria from turning the wine into vinegar, the narrow necks of ancient wine amphorae were sealed in a variety of ways. Frequently the mouths of amphorae would be filled with a clump of fibrous material, such as straw or grass, that had been soaked in pine resin and then capped with clay. Likewise, because the jars were porous, the insides of many amphorae were coated with resin in order to prevent or retard evaporation and oxidation. Since the resinous coating would have been soluble in alcohol, early Greek wines probably tasted as much of pine pitch as of the wine itself, and in this way they were the forerunners of modern retsina, the resinated Greek wine that is nothing if not an acquired taste. Sometime later, certainly by Roman times, lumps of pine pitch were also thrown into wine to help preserve it or to disguise the flavor of a wine gone bad.

From an amphora wine would be poured into a bronze or pottery bowl called a krater. From the krater the wine might then be scooped out with a ladle called a *kythos* into a shallow, two-handled, often beautifully decorated cup known as a *kylix*.

net sauvignon, have also been planted in recent years. Greek winemakers often blend these with indigenous varieties, creating some fascinating, unusually flavored wines in the process.

Since white wines make up from 75 to 80 percent of Greece's total wine production, white grape varieties are very important, yet Greece's native red grapes are the source of some of the country's most memorable and delicious wines, even if red wines account for less than 15 percent of production. Among the top white grapes are assyrtico, muscat blanc à petits grains, robola (thought to be related to the ribolla gialla grape of northern Italy), roditis, savatiano (the grape usually used to make the unforgettable Greek wine retsina), and the well-liked moscofilero grape, which is said to make the best aperitif in all of Greece. The most important red varieties include agiorgitiko (also known as St. George), kotsifali, mandelari, limnio, mavrodaphne, and the bold xynomavro, whose uninviting name means acid black.

Greece is made up of ten distinct regions that have been well known since antiquity. Five of these regions—from north to south, Macedonia, Thessaly, Peloponnese, the Aegean Islands, and the island of Crete—contain one or more smaller subregions that are famous for wine. Macedonia lies along the northern coast of the Aegean Sea. Within Macedonia are the two prestigious wine regions Naoussa and Goumenissa. Of the two, Naoussa, with its vineyards spread over the slopes of the Vermion Mountains, can be the source of sharp, powerful red wines made from xynomavro. Boutari's Grande Reserve Naoussa, in some years one of Greece's top wines, is a dark, brooding, powerful wine with a rich texture. In Goumenissa, xynomavro is blended with negoska, a softer, less dramatic tasting grape.

Macedonia is also home to a third and relatively new wine region: Côtes de Meliton, which is situated on the Chalcidice (or Halkidiki or Khalkidiki) peninsula, which thrusts out into the Aegean like three fingers. (Transliterated Greek words can have multiple spellings, thanks to the lack of universal rules for converting from the phonetically based

610

## AN ANCIENT VINTAGE

＝＠＝

Archaeologists excavating a tomb in China's Henan Province in 1980 unearthed an ornate, bronze wine jug. Unlike many vessels recovered from grave sites dating from the Shang dynasty, this one contained nearly two quarts of wine.

The wine—about 3,000 years old at the time of discovery—was a pale, tealike liquid with a faintly grassy scent. For cultural and religious reasons the archaeologists, both Chinese, did not taste the wine since it had come from a tomb.

According to texts written in 1122 B.C., the upper class in ancient China drank four different alcoholic beverages with meals. Three of these were made from millet, the nation's main crop, and one from fruit and berries. Yeasts for fermentation may have been derived from either sprouted grains or from grasses.

Thus it seems that, for thousands of years, winemaking and wine drinking were woven into the cultures of both China and the eastern Mediterranean, though neither would have known of the other's existence.

Greek alphabet into English, with its Roman alphabet.) Côtes de Meliton was created by the Carras family with the help of the famous French enologist Emile Peynaud. Domaine Carras produces several wines, the most well known of which, also named Domaine Carras, is a blend of cabernet sauvignon and limnio, an ancient grape variety with a delicious full-blown spicy, earthy character.

In Thessaly, on the east coast of mainland Greece, is the wine region Rapsani where xynomavro plus two other minor red grapes, stavroto and krassato, grow on the foothills of Mount Olympus, Greece's highest and best-known mountain. Krassato means wine colored, a description used frequently in antiquity, including by Homer, who, in the *Odyssey*, describes Odysseus' journey on the "wine-dark sea."

The southernmost region of the Greek mainland is the peninsula known as Peloponnese, which in fact is so completely surrounded by water that save for the 4-mile-wide and 20-mile-long Isthmus of Corinth, it would be a large island. Peloponnese has a number of wine regions, the three most important of which are Nemea, Mantinia, and Patras. The wines of Nemea, thought to have been the palace wines of Agamemnon, are made from the highly regarded agiorgitiko, a red grape. Nemea can be almost Port-like in its lushness and can have a fascinating spicy and peppery flavor. The wine from Mantinia is usually a dry, spicy, aromatic white, but it can also be a rosé since the moscofilero grape from which it's made is pink-skinned. And Patras is home to three different wines. In its most straight-forward version, Patras is just a simple, dry white wine made from the roditis grape. More unusual and interesting is muscat of Patras, made from muscat blanc à petits grains, a thickish dessert wine that is sometimes fortified, sometimes not. Most idiosyncratic of all is mavrodaphne of Patras, made primarily from mavrodaphne (the word means black laurel). Amber to mahogany colored, sweet, thick, fortified, complex and slightly oxidized, mavrodaphne of Patras is aged for several years in barrels in a manner somewhat like tawny Port. The most famous mavrodaphne of Patras is made by Achaia-Clauss, the company credited with inventing the wine during the middle of the nineteenth century. Traditionally, Greeks drink mavrodaphne of Patras in the afternoon with a small plate of figs or oranges. It is also the wine most often used in Greek Orthodox churches during Holy Communion.

611

*Along with Nemea, Mantinia, and Patras, many simple quaffing wines are made in the Peloponnese, the southernmost region of the Greek mainland.*

## The Wine of Atlantis

Greece's multiple islands boast numerous intriguing grapes—Cephalonia's robola, for example—but of all the islands, the one most famous for wine is Santorini, considered by some Greeks to be the legendary Atlantis. A spectacular, almost surreal volcanic Aegean Island, Santorini is a giant blackened crater poised between the shockingly blue sky and the equally blue sea, each of which can seem indistinguishable from the other. The soil that makes up many vineyards on the island is little more than eerie-looking, pockmarked, jet black rocks, the remnants of multiple ancient volcanic eruptions. One of these in 1500 B.C. was so catastrophic, it is thought to have destroyed the Minoan civilization on nearby Crete.

Most wine from Santorini is fresh, light, dry, white, and perfectly suited to the island's simple seafood-based cooking. Santorini is made from the assyrtiko grape. However, the island is also famous for *visánto*, a sweet dessert wine reminiscent of the Tuscan dessert wine *vin santo*. Both are made from grapes that have been dried to concentrate their sugar. In the case of Santorini *visánto*, assyrtiko and mandelari grapes are first spread out on mats to dry in the sun for one to two weeks. When they achieve a state referred to as half-baked, the grapes are fermented. Afterward, the wine is aged in barrel for a decade, giving it a mellow, rich flavor. Although less well known than Santorini, Samos, an Aegean island off the coast of Turkey, is also noteworthy for its wines. In particular, the island's muscat of Samos, a sweet, apricotish, lightly fortified wine made from aromatic muscat grapes, is highly regarded by the Greeks.

And, finally, the island of Crete, the largest of all the Greek islands, was one of the first places in the world to develop a systematic approach to grape growing and winemaking, and the varieties that grow there even today are unique to the island. Kotsifali and mandelari, for example, are the two rare grapes that are blended together to make the famous red wines of Archarnes, the most important wine region on the island. Kotsifali in particular is considered a grape of such impressively well-balanced alcohol, acidity, and extract that the wines made principally from it have been compared to Bordeaux.

# THE FOODS OF GREECE

If the French can't wait to impress you with their cooking and the Italians want to romance you with theirs, the Greeks have decided to keep their cuisine—the real stuff, that is—mostly a secret. It's a shame, for the country can legitimately boast one of the most exciting (and healthful) cuisines in Europe. Greece's mountainous, arid terrain has always prohibited large-scale agriculture, and most good products—from cheeses and yogurts to olives and vegetables—are still made largely on an artisanal basis. Even today, working women and men who live in Greek cities often return to their families' villages in the fall to help with the olive and grape harvests and to put up fruits and vegetables.

Greek cuisine is also intrinsically tied to religion. In no other country that I know of is fasting (especially during Lent and Advent) still so much a part of contemporary life. For the typical Greek, fasting and feasting, frugality and wealth, are irrevocably interwoven. Greek cuisine

## THE GRAPES OF
# GREECE

reece is home to some 300 indigenous grape varieties. (If you think pronouncing the names of Greek gods is difficult, you're in for a real treat.) Here are the most important ones. Though international varieties, such as chardonnay and cabernet sauvignon, also grow there, these account for just a fraction of the wine produced and are often blended with native varieties.

## WHITES

**Assyrtiko:** Major grape, native to Santorini and other Aegean Islands. Makes crisp dry wine.

**Moscofilero:** Despite this grape's pinkish-red skin, only white wines and occasionally rosés are made from it. Highly aromatic, with a spicy character and capable of finesse, moscofilero is the source of the Peloponnesian wine Mantinia.

**Muscat Blanc à Petits Grains:** Used in the famous aromatic sweet and often lightly fortified wines muscat of Patras from Peloponnese and muscat of Samos from Samos, an Aegean Island.

**Robola:** A fascinating, but not indigenous, grape variety common on Cephalonia and other Ionian Islands. Robola is thought to have been brought to Greece by the Venetians in the thirteenth century. It is possibly related to the northern Italian grape ribolla gialla.

**Roditis:** Makes the simple, dry white wine of Patras in Peloponnese.

**Savatiano:** Widely planted grape, including in the region of Attica where Athens is located. A source of simple, serviceable wines. Most retsina is made from savatiano.

## REDS

**Agiorgitiko:** One of Greece's two most important red varieties, also known as St. George. Makes the easy-drinking, spicy, dried-cherry flavored wine Nemea.

**Kotsifali:** Unique to the island of Crete. Main grape of Acharnes, the wines of which are structured and well-balanced.

**Limnio:** Ancient unique variety mentioned by Aristotle. Spicy, earthy. Native to the island of Lemnos, now also grown in the Côtes de Meliton.

**Mandelari:** Unique to Crete and the Aegean Islands. Fairly tannic; blended in small amounts with kotsifali to make the Cretan wine Acharnes.

**Mavrodaphne:** Major grape. The leading variety in the most widely known of all wines made in Peloponnese, mavrodaphne of Patras, a sweet fortified aged wine.

**Negoska:** Soft, low-acid variety blended with xynomavro to make Goumenissa.

**Stavroto** and **Krassato:** Minor grapes grown on Mount Olympus. Used in Rapsani.

**Xynomavro:** One of Greece's two most important red varieties. Makes the earthy, sometimes spicy wine Naoussa and is the leading grape in Goumenissa.

613

encompasses both utterly humble dishes based on little more than vegetables and olive oil, and extravagant dishes served at Easter and Christmas, including a whole repertoire of elaborate, rich breads baked for holidays.

A Greek meal is adamantly languorous. Greeks do not plunge straightaway into a main course but rather begin with a deeply ingrained ritual known as the meze (the name refers to both the concept and the foods that make it up). A meze is a nugget of food, smaller than an American appetizer, more like a tapa in Spain. Typically many different *mezedes* are offered for the express purpose of accompanying wine or ouzo, the well-loved local anise-flavored liqueur. (The Greeks, who rarely drink without eating something, all seem to have an opinion on which *mezedes* are *krasomezedes*, those that go better with wine—*krasi*—and which are *ouzomezedes*, those that go better with ouzo.) There might be bite-size golden triangles of crisp phyllo stuffed with cheese (*tyropittakia*) or small mint-and-anise-flavored lamb meatballs (*keftedes*). Always, there's a rich dip like *tzatziki*, a tangy jolt of thick yogurt, garlic, dill, and cucumbers; *taramasalata*, a creamy swirl of carp roe, olive oil, and lemon; or my favorite, *skordalia*, a bracingly garlicky purée of potatoes, olive oil, wine vinegar,

614

## WHAT TO SIP
## WITH SIMPLE
## SEAFOOD

In Greece you are constantly aware of the sea and, by extension, seafood. Nowhere is this more apparent than on the volcanic island of Santorini, where the almost cobalt blue sea is inescapable and where the narrow white-walled streets are lined with tavernas cooking seafood. On summer days, bottles of assyrtiko and platters of crisp calamari and grilled octopus are on every table. The combination couldn't be more perfect. Assyrtiko, Santorini's most popular white wine, is lean, fresh, straightforward, and a satisfying thirst quencher between bites.

and, depending on the cook, enough garlic to beat aioli at its own game. *Dolmadakia*, one of the most traditional *mezedes* (this should win over just about every wine lover) is made from tender grape leaves usually picked in the spring and then rolled and stuffed with lemony, dill-scented rice.

There are a seemingly infinite number of *mezedes*, but the very simplest is one that no Greek would omit: olives. Since the days when it was the cradle of western civilization, Greece has been renowned for the diversity and abundance of its olives, virtually all of which are stronger in flavor and more pungent in aroma than French or Italian olives because of the low-tech, centuries-old ways in which they are still picked and cured.

The meze completed, Greeks may still not yet delve into the main meal, for next comes *pitta* (assuming that tiny *pittas* weren't served as *mezedes*). A *pitta* is not the same as the flatish pocket bread we know as pita but rather is a savory pie with a phyllo crust. The best known is spanakopita, stuffed with spinach, but there are also *melitzanopitta*, eggplant, cheese, and walnuts flavored with ouzo and with oregano wrapped up in a phyllo crust and, perhaps closest to the Greek heart, *hortopitta*, a phyllo pie filled with wild greens for which women forage around their villages. Everything from dandelion greens and sorrel to fennel and lemon balm might be included, making it difficult to put your finger on a *hortopitta*'s flavor, though all Greeks instantly recognize their mothers' versions. The most sensational (and sensuous) *pitta* I ever had was made with homemade phyllo dough stuffed with a creamy purée of a type of pumpkin that grows in the mountains of northern Greece.

## RETSINA

—⟨⟨⟩⟩—

Few visitors to Greece escape without falling in love with or learning to abhor retsina, the pungent, pine-resin-flavored wine, the drinking of which is virtually a baptismal right in Greek tavernas. Today retsina accounts for an impressive 30 percent of Greece's total production of table wine, an indication of the solid role resinated wines play in Greek wine culture. Resinated wines have a long history in Greece. Traces of pine resin have been found in Greek wine amphorae dating back to the thirteenth century B.C. Modern retsina can be made anywhere in Greece, though most of it is made in Attica, the region that surrounds Athens. While many different white grape varieties can be used and are, the most common variety is savatiano, a relatively neutral white grape. Small amounts of resin from the Aleppo pine are added to savatiano grape juice as it ferments, imparting retsina's inimitable piney flavor and unmistakable turpentine-like aroma. Among non-Greeks retsina is often the subject of good-natured jokes. But a number of Greeks take the unique wine quite seriously, suggesting that it is the perfect accompaniment to many Greek meze (small dishes of appetizers served like Spanish tapas) and that it should be drunk when it is at its freshest, during the first several months after it is released, usually around Easter. During the Easter season retsina is served with everything from roast lamb to *tsoureki*, traditional Easter bread. Retsina holds a special appellation status in Greece. Thus, just as no other country except Spain can make true Sherry and no other country except France can make true Champagne, no other country except Greece can make authentic retsina. There are dozens of producers of retsina. Two good ones you are likely to come across in the United States are Kourtakis and Boutari.

615

Phyllo, for its part, is inescapable. Today, the ultrathin dough that turns golden, crisp, and flaky when baked is almost uniformly made commercially in Greece and sold in supermarkets. But there are women—usually old women in remote villages—who continue to make phyllo by hand, rolling the dough out to a seemingly impossible thinness using very thin rolling pins that are several feet long.

The long stretches of poverty that Greeks have experienced throughout their history make this a country where vegetables, salads, and legumes are prized and where they often constitute the main part of the meal.

Markets are piled high with shiny eggplants, tomatoes, cucumbers, zucchini, leeks, cauliflowers, fennel, and carrots, plus dozens of types of wild and cultivated greens. Vegetables like leeks and zucchini are often stuffed with a lemony rice mixture emboldened by fresh mint and dill. But they are also cooked as ragouts or baked and then laced with Greece's one famous and nearly ubiquitous sauce, avgolemono, a delicate, deep yellow sauce made with egg, lemon juice, and broth. When the broth is chicken, the sauce can become the basis for *kotosoupa* avgolemono—chicken soup.

As for salads, the custom of ending a meal with a refreshing green salad probably originated in ancient Greece (sorry, France), but today, salads are more commonly served first. None is better known than the classic Greek salad, a dish that ranges from awesome to appalling. Done right, it has juicy vine-ripened tomatoes, cucumber that is almost crunchy it's so crisp, tangy fresh feta cheese, rich briny kalamata olives, good anchovies, snappy green peppers, pungent oregano, and a dressing of piquant green-gold extra-virgin olive oil, with a splash of spunky red wine vinegar. Lettuce is optional.

Greece's thousands of miles of coastline and numerous islands make it a logical haven for seafood. Sitting in a no-frills harborfront taverna, you can grow faint smelling all the immaculately fresh, delicious whole grilled fish being whisked out of the kitchen. Greece has dozens upon dozens of different fish, and besides being grilled, they are baked in salt, baked in grape leaves, baked with feta cheese, fried in olive oil, and simmered in countless stews that recall bouillabaisse. But the seafood that truly epitomizes Greece is the world's most sumptuous cephalopods—octopus and squid (*htapothi* and *kalamaria*). In particular the delicate, oceanic flavor of salt-crusted octopus grilled over hot coals then dressed with lemon and olive oil is incomparable.

Asked to name the one food they most associate with Greece many people would name lamb, and lamb is indeed revered by the Greeks. The biggest testament to this is at Easter, when all over Greece it is traditional to serve a whole spit-roasted lamb. As it cooks, the lamb is basted using rosemary branches dipped in olive oil. Not that Easter is lamb's fifteen minutes of fame. The meat is everywhere—in tavernas it shows up as souvlaki, chunks of leg of lamb skewered and grilled until they're black and crusty on the outside and juicy within; or baked with preserved lemons in clay; in spicy stews with mint, rice, raisins, and walnuts; and in casseroles with honey (the thyme-scented honey of Crete is

*Going shopping in Greece not only means picking up local specialties like octopus (right), but also buying wine, sometimes directly from the barrel (above).*

*The markets of Greece are packed with dried fruits and Mediterranean herbs like thyme and oregano, plus spices from the nearby Near East.*

honey and nuts, which are supposed to appease any malicious spirits lingering around the household. Lest anyone feel unsatisfied, most Greek homes also have an ample supply of cookies, tarts, and biscuits, often made with sesame seeds, almonds, or walnuts and—what else? honey. It's hard to say where the herculean Greek sweet tooth comes from, but certainly it's an ancient trait. Which I guess rules out my secret hypothesis: Was it really so improbable to think the Greek love of sweet things is just a bit of sweet revenge for all those bad Greek salads?

## HUNTING DOWN THE HOME OF EASTER EGGS

renowned), raisins, cinnamon, vinegar, and capers. Finally, there is moussaka, ground lamb layered with eggplant, tomatoes, cinnamon, and feta, topped with béchamel sauce and baked in clay pots.

Finally there are sweets. Greeks may be able to give up meat for long periods of time, but when it comes to sweets, forget it. The Greek passion for sweet things could give you a toothache just thinking about it. When guests arrive unexpectedly, they are often served syrupy preserves meant to be eaten with a spoon and made from quince, walnuts, pistachios, bergamot (the citrusy tasting herb that flavors Earl Grey tea), figs, or oranges. There are all manner of ultra-sweet phyllo-based pastries soaked with honey—baklava, for example—plus *thiples*, fried pieces of dough dipped in

Devouring a handful of milk-chocolate Easter eggs or hunting aroung the backyard for plastic ones are two behaviors that are, well, all greek to the Greeks. In Greece, where the practice of dying eggs for Easter originated, the custom continues to be a deeply felt religious ritual. The eggs (real ones needless to say) are dyed on Holy Thursday (the Thursday preceding Easter Sunday) and are eaten after midnight mass on Holy Saturday as a way of breaking the Lenten fast. In Greece, Easter eggs are always dyed a deep red, symbolizing the blood of Christ, while the egg itself represents life and regeneration. In some parts of northern Greece the eggs are not just dyed, they are also handpainted with figures, often of birds—a symbol of Christ's resurrection from the dead.

# VISITING GREEK WINERIES

Consistent with its reputation as a generous and welcoming destination for tourists, Greece offers many opportunities for visiting wine lovers. Among the best are two programs, the Wine Roads of Macedonia and the Wine Roads of Peloponnese. Each of these outlines specific routes, with directions to wineries that accept visitors, plus information on local food specialties, restaurants, archaeological sites, monasteries, museums, and churches. Greek wineries are generally open year-round except during holidays. Tours and tastings can be given in English on request. It is best to make individual appointments ahead of time. The telephone numbers include the dialing code you'll need when calling from the United States. If you're calling from within Greece, eliminate the 011-30 and add a zero before the next number. Don't worry if you notice that some of the phone numbers are longer than others. Greek telephone numbers are not standardized the way they are in the United States.

**WINE ROADS OF MACEDONIA**
Macedonia, Helexpo S.A.
154 Egnatias Street
54636 Thessaloniki,
  Macedonia
011-30-31-281-617

**WINE ROADS OF PELOPONNESE**
Athens, care of Arkas S.A.
32 Iroon Politechniou Street
14122 Neo Iraklion, Attica
011-30-12-845-962

**BOUTARI** (Aegean Islands)
Boutari/Santorini
84700 Megalochori, Santorini
011-30-286-81-606
The firm has several wineries but the one on Santorini is wonderful.

**D. KOURTAKIS** (Athens)
19003 Markopoulo, Attica
011-30-12-99-2-2231

**DOMAINE CARRAS** (Macedonia)
63081 Porto Carras, Halkidiki
011-30-375-71184

**OENOFOROS** (Peloponnese)
25100 Selinous, Egio
011-30-691-20791
This is a particularly beautiful winery.

**PAPAIOANNOU**
  **PAPE JOHANNOU** (Peloponnese)
20500 Archaia, Nemea
011-30-746-23138

**TSANTALI** (Macedonia)
63080 Agios Pavlos, Halkidiki
011-30-399-61395
Tsantali has several wineries; this is the main one.

# THE GREEK WINES TO KNOW

*For each wine the specific region from which it comes is noted.*

## *Whites*

### D. KOURTAKIS

| Kouros |
| --- |
| Patras, Peloponnese |
| 100% roditis |

Simple, fresh, and lively, the white wines of Patras are popular every-night dinner wines. Kouros, with its citrus and almond flavors and light herbal notes, is especially good.

### D. KOURTAKIS

| Muscat of Samos |
| --- |
| Samos, Aegean Islands |
| 100% muscat blanc à petits grains |

For several centuries the mountainous island of Samos, off the coast of Turkey, has been one of the most famous islands in the Aegean. The word *samos* is thought to come from the Phoenician word for heights. Here muscat grapes, planted in terraced vineyards, make wines that are stunningly and penetratingly aromatic and redolent of flowers, perfumes, and fruits. Most muscat of Samos is also lightly fortified with grape spirits, giving the wine even more punch.

### TSANTALI

| Ambelonas |
| --- |
| Halkidiki, Macedonia |
| approximately 50% sauvignon blanc, 50% assyrtiko |

As Greek winemakers experiment more with international varieties, we can expect to find such unusual blends as Ambelonas, a combination of sauvignon blanc and the native variety assyrtiko. While lots of these odd combinations never quite work out, this one is a winner. The lean, taut freshness of assyrtiko is augmented by the herbal snappiness of sauvignon blanc. Somehow, Ambelonas manages to taste and smell like mint plus lemons and tangerines—a whole citrus grove. A sensational wine to go with Greek salads and vegetable dishes.

## *Rosé*

### DOMAINE SPIROPOULOS

| Meliasto |
| --- |
| Peloponnese |
| mostly moscofilero |

Many Greek rosé and white wines have a light but exotic floral, spicy, aromatic quality that's intriguing and not quite like

any wine made in the United States. This is especially true of wines made from moscofilero, a pinkish-red-skinned grape used to make rosé and white wines. Meliasto, though a simple wine, is not to be missed for its fascinating amalgam of rose hip tea, strawberry preserves, fruit cocktail, roses, and red licorice.

# *Reds*

## GAIA ESTATE

Nótios

Peloponnese

100% agiorgitiko

Nótios is a good example of the sleek, spicy, sharp red wines served in every taverna and restaurant in Greece. The wine's good grip, more from acid than tannin, and its simple dried-cherry flavors make it easy to drink with just about any food.

## MANOUSAKIS WINERY

Nostos

Crete

35% syrah, 35% grenache, 20% mourvèdre, and 10% roussanne

Manousakis Winery, founded in the late 1990s by Greek-American businessman Theodore Manousakis, is making fabulous wines from a blend of varieties commonly associated with the southern Rhône, but this time grown on the island of Crete. Nostos is an intriguing light-bodied red with vivid forest floor and wild iris aromas and the flavors of menthol, licorice, and chocolate. Delicious with skewers of grilled lamb.

## PAPE JOHANNOU VINEYARDS

Nemea Old Vines

Peloponnese

100% agiorgitiko

With its dense berry fruit and hint of spice, Pape Johannou's old vines Nemea could easily double for an old vine zinfandel from California. While the regular Pape Johannou Nemea is a delicious wine filled with attractive licorice and dark cherry flavors, it's this special bottling that's the superstar. The old vines wine is made from the winery's best vineyards at the highest elevation, where the soil is especially rocky and the vines average fifty-five years old. Unusual for Greece, this Nemea is also aged in 100 percent new French oak, giving it a sophisticated deep flavor that many other Nemeas lack.

## TSANTALI

Merlot

Halkidiki, Macedonia

100% merlot

Tsantali's delicious merlot won't remind you of Bordeaux or the Napa Valley, but it has a charm all its own. Lean, fresh, and a lip smacker, this is a light-bodied red with spicy grenadine flavors. The perfect sort of red wine for a hot, sunny day in Greece.

*The skyphos was a deep, two-handled drinking cup for everyday use. More elaborate versions, like these dating from possibly as early as the first century B.C., were often made of silver or gold.*

620

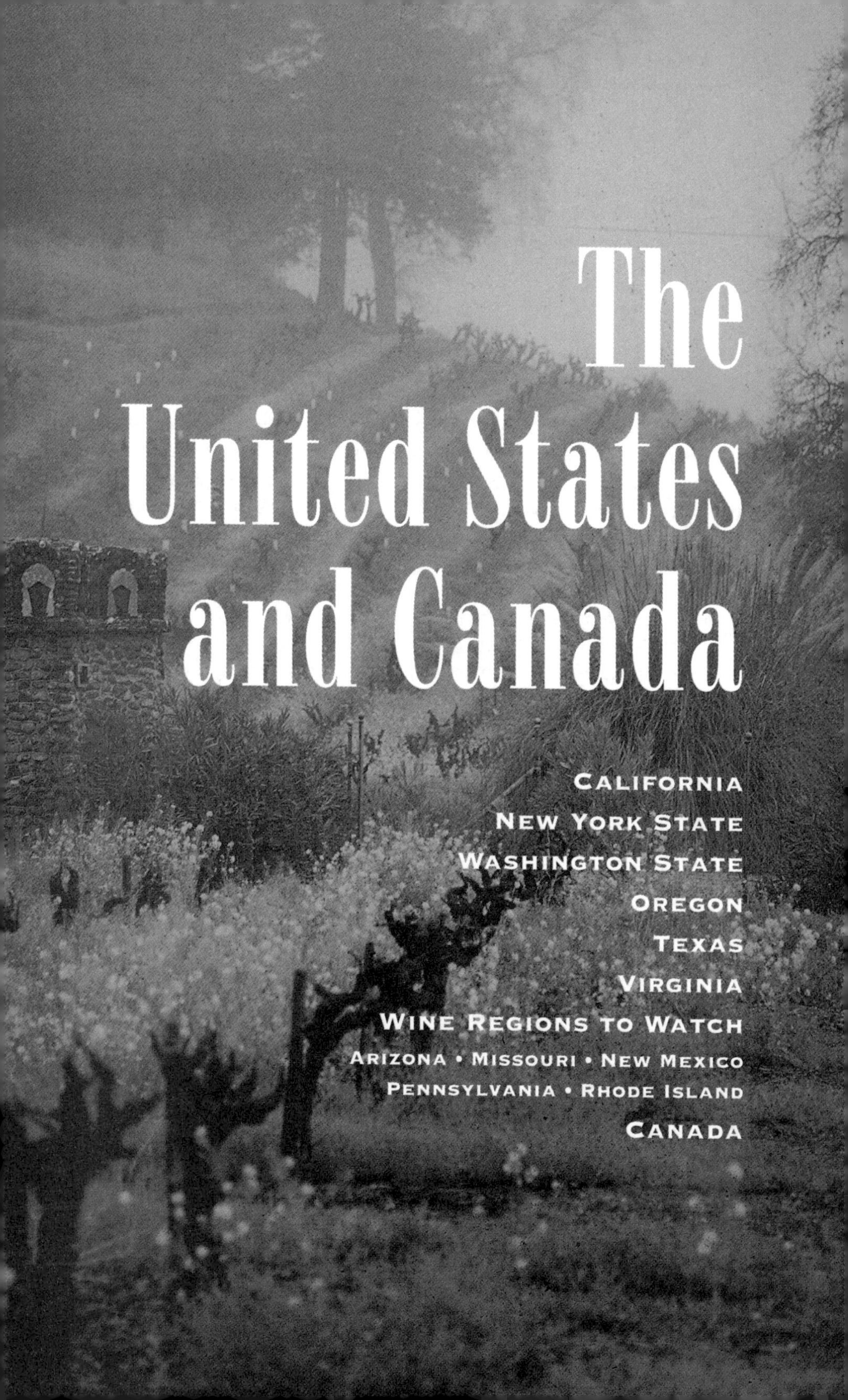

# The United States and Canada

CALIFORNIA
NEW YORK STATE
WASHINGTON STATE
OREGON
TEXAS
VIRGINIA
WINE REGIONS TO WATCH
ARIZONA • MISSOURI • NEW MEXICO
PENNSYLVANIA • RHODE ISLAND
CANADA

It's often said of the United States and Canada that each possesses a pioneering spirit, the vestige of the early days of their beginnings. Nowhere is that pioneering spirit more alive than in the world of wine. These are the two significant wine-producing countries in North America. (Though wine is also being made in the Guadalupe Valley of northern Mexico, the Mexican wine industry is as yet too small to command much attention.) Of course, the United States is the more dominant player. Ranked fourth worldwide in wine production, it makes almost sixty times as much wine as Canada, which ranks thirty-ninth. What the wine industries in both countries share is a palpable sense of excitement. Year after year, the number of new producers in both countries continues to climb, and the quality of wines continues to rise dramatically.

When you think of wine in North America, California probably springs to mind first. But the Pacific Northwest is emerging as a region of equal stature and New York State is producing some of the best wines it ever has in its long history. Plus, some strikingly good wines are beginning to come from places as far-flung as Texas, Virginia, and British Columbia. We'll take a good look at all of these and glance at several even more unexpected locations.

622

*Wines are produced throughout the United States—even in places that might, at first, seem unlikely, such as beside an enormous mesa in the West Texas desert.*

The United States ranks fourth in wine-producing countries worldwide. Americans drink an average of 1.97 gallons of wine per person each year; they're thirty-third in world wine consumption.

# THE UNITED STATES: AN OVERVIEW

The United States is now arguably one of the most dynamic wine-producing countries in the New World. Never before have Americans had so much wine of such high quality to choose from. Yet, sadly, wine drinking has never been an integral part of the culture of the United States. Thanks to the twists and turns of our idiosyncratic history, soft drinks, coffee, milk, and beer are what we drink most. Wine, by comparison, remains the provence and the passion of only a few. As of 1998, just 11 percent of adult Americans consumed 88 percent of the wine sold in the United States.

Changes have begun to take place. Shifting lifestyles and mounting evidence of wine's health benefits caused wine consumption to rise significantly in the mid-1990s. Between 1994 and 1998 wine became the second fastest growing beverage after soft drinks, and the trend is expected to continue. The number of wineries in the United States is greater than ever before—more than 2,338 in forty-seven states. The number of wineries in California alone quadrupled between 1965 and 1995.

Excitement is burgeoning, but just as wines from France can't be categorized as a single thing, neither can wines from the United States. The leading wine-producing states—California, New York State, Washington State, Oregon, Virginia, and Texas—make wines that are as different from one another as Brooklynites are from San Antonians. Contrast and variation also characterize the climates in the United States. The frosty wine regions of upper New York State have more in common with parts of Germany than with Cali-

> ## WHO PRODUCES WINE IN THE UNITED STATES?
>
> Though it seems hard to believe, every state in the United States produces wine except three—Alaska, North Dakota, and Wyoming. No state, however, makes a huge amount of wine except one: California alone produces more than 90 percent of the United States total.

*One of four coveted bottles of 1787 Château Lafite—Lafitte is what you'll see on this bottle, along with the letters Th J. The wine is thought to have belonged to America's third president, Thomas Jefferson.*

623

fornia. Texas' sun-drenched wine regions share more similarities with Portugal than with Oregon, and on it goes. The United States, after all, is a vast country—the fourth largest in the world, spread over more than 3.5 million square miles.

Given the country's size, it comes as little surprise that the history of viticulture in the United States is really two separate histories, each independent of the other and centered on a separate coast. On the East Coast, the first attempts at producing wine from European grapes occurred in the early decades of the seventeenth century. Most ended in failure, including the multiple efforts of Thomas Jefferson, who was convinced that Virginia possessed the perfect environment for making fine wine. For Jefferson and others it was especially frustrating to note that wild native American

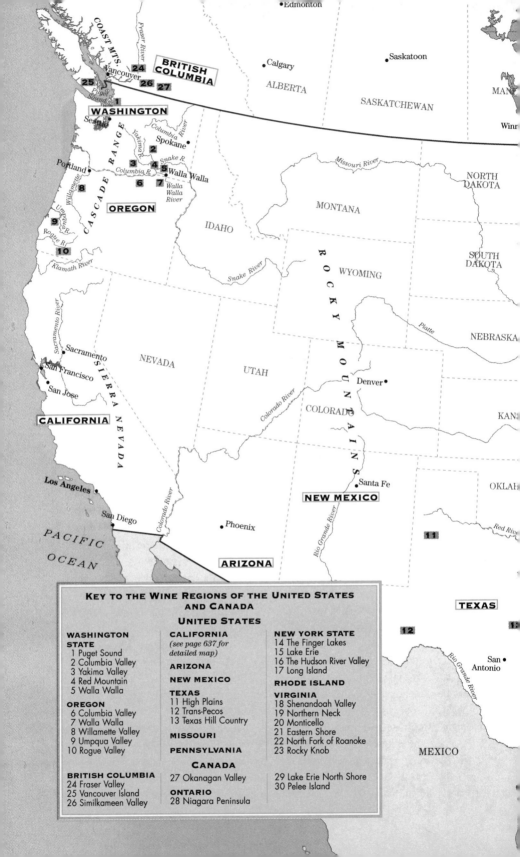

KEY TO THE WINE REGIONS OF THE UNITED STATES
AND CANADA

UNITED STATES

**WASHINGTON
STATE**
1 Puget Sound
2 Columbia Valley
3 Yakima Valley
4 Red Mountain
5 Walla Walla

**OREGON**
6 Columbia Valley
7 Walla Walla
8 Willamette Valley
9 Umpqua Valley
10 Rogue Valley

**BRITISH COLUMBIA**
24 Fraser Valley
25 Vancouver Island
26 Similkameen Valley

**CALIFORNIA**
*(see page 637 for
detailed map)*

**ARIZONA**

**NEW MEXICO**

**TEXAS**
11 High Plains
12 Trans-Pecos
13 Texas Hill Country

**MISSOURI**

**PENNSYLVANIA**

**CANADA**
27 Okanagan Valley

**ONTARIO**
28 Niagara Peninsula

**NEW YORK STATE**
14 The Finger Lakes
15 Lake Erie
16 The Hudson River Valley
17 Long Island

**RHODE ISLAND**

**VIRGINIA**
18 Shenandoah Valley
19 Northern Neck
20 Monticello
21 Eastern Shore
22 North Fork of Roanoke
23 Rocky Knob

29 Lake Erie North Shore
30 Pelee Island

## VIRGINIA DARE

━━◁〜〜▷━━

Thought to be the oldest branded wine in the United States (dating from circa 1835), Virginia Dare was named after the first child born of English parents in America. The wine was made from a grape called scuppernong, a native variety that is still grown in the South. This white Virginia Dare was originally called Minnehaha. There was also a red wine called Pocahontas.

vines grew in hearty profusion all around the colonies. Unfortunately, the wine made from these native vines tasted pretty odd (at least to those who had developed a European palate). And so wave after wave of immigrants persisted in bringing vines with them to the East Coast. And those European vines, for their part, continued

to die of various diseases and pests, including the most virulent pest of all and one the immigrants could not have known about—phylloxera (see page 24).

Undeterred by such setbacks, settlers in New York and Virginia soon began to reexamine native grapes, hoping to come up with ways of making the wine from them taste better. By crossing certain native grapes with others, they succeeded. Later these new crosses were joined by French-American hybrid grapes, created mostly by French scientists and quickly adopted in the United States. By the time of the Civil War, the East Coast had a well-established, if small, wine industry based primarily on native grape varieties, crosses, and hybrids.

Meanwhile, out West, another winemaking culture was emerging. In the early 1700s Spanish explorers and Franciscan fathers, moving north from Mexico into Texas and southern California, established a string of missions, each of which had its own vineyard so that wine might

## AMERICA THINKS BIG

━━◁〜〜▷━━

The largest winery in the United States, E. & J. Gallo, is also the largest winery in the world. Industry estimates peg production at close to 70 million cases a year—about the same amount as the entire country of Portugal.

The Gallo company's beginnings, however, could not have been more humble. In 1933, in the aftermath of the Depression and Prohibition, Ernest and Julio Gallo, aged twenty-four and twenty-three respectively, decided to start a winery in the then dusty farm town of Modesto, in California's Central Valley. There were, they realized, a few problems with their plan. The brothers

had no experience with winemaking, no equipment, no vineyards, no winemaker, and no money.

But by reading pamphlets in the Modesto public library on winemaking, by borrowing equipment, and by taking out loans to buy grapes, Ernest and Julio managed to make their first batch of wine. Today, at any given moment, more people in the United States are drinking a Gallo wine than any other brand. And while most of those will be among Gallo's numerous inexpensive wines, the company now also makes fine wines, most of which come from grapes grown in Sonoma County.

*Built in 1879 by Finnish sea captain Gustave Niebaum, Inglenook (the name means a cozy nook) was one of the first truly majestic wineries in the Napa Valley and the first in the valley to have vineyards planted with all of the red Bordeaux varieties. No less famous today, the winery is now owned by film director Francis Ford Coppola, who renamed it Niebaum-Coppola.*

be made for the Mass. The grapes the fathers planted, known simply as mission grapes, were of Spanish origin, having been brought to Mexico two centuries before by the explorer Cortés. As the nineteenth century dawned, the missions and their tiny vineyards stretched beyond San Francisco as far north as Sonoma.

The next big push came with the discovery of gold in 1849 in the Sierra foothills. The gold rush brought risk-taking, hardworking adventurers, many of whom turned to grape growing and agriculture when the mines dried up. California at the time was already home to a number of rugged individualists from all over the world who had come to America's western frontier to seek their fortunes. Two of the most successful were the Finnish sea

captain Gustave Niebaum and the Hungarian aristocrat Agoston Haraszthy. After founding a prosperous fur trading company, Niebaum went on to build one of the Napa Valley's most impressive wineries—Inglenook (today film director Francis Ford Coppola owns this property). And the dashing Haraszthy not only founded Sonoma's Buena Vista winery but also promoted winegrowing with such fervor that for years he was called the Father of California Wine. In his first year at Buena Vista, Haraszthy is said to have imported 165 different varieties of grapes.

As a result of the efforts of such men as these, viticulture in northern California experienced its first boom. By the 1880s the West Coast had a thriving wine industry, and the United States as a whole

## SHIP CHRISTENINGS

⸺ↂ𝓸𝓸𝓸ↂ⸺

In the third millennium B.C., a Babylonian sailor, hoping to placate the gods and ensure a safe voyage, poured an unknown dark liquid over a newly launched ship. The vessel's enterprise must have proved successful because ship christening not only continued but eventually was taken up by the Egyptians, Greeks, and Romans. As well as the United States Navy.

Over the centuries beverages for christenings have ranged from whiskey to holy water. *Old Ironsides,* the first American warship to be dedicated, was launched with a bottle of fine Madeira. Champagne became particularly popular at the end of the nineteenth century, but Prohibition effectively ended that extravagance, and cider or water were substituted for the duration.

Today wine is once again used in Navy christenings. The wine may be sparkling or still, but it is always domestic. Selection of the brand, however, is left to the discretion of the individual shipbuilder who may (or may not) have an expensive taste in wine.

seemed poised to become a wine-drinking nation, much like the countries of Europe. It was not to be. Over the next half century, the United States wine industry on both coasts crumbled under the cumulative devastation of phylloxera, followed by Prohibition, followed by World War I, the Depression, and World War II. Though a few wineries managed to hang on and a few others began operating, the spirit of wine in America was substantially subdued. Wine production was modest at best. Fairly large wineries controlled most of that production, and most of what they made—huge blends of cheap generic sweet wines—tasted just about the same no matter whose wine it was or what you bought.

A new era was about to dawn, and it would begin in California. In the 1960s and early 1970s a wave of wealthy, well-educated, independent-minded individuals came to northern California with the idealistic notion of starting wineries. In a number of cases these individuals—who typically knew little about grape growing—had other lucrative careers in publishing, medicine, education, technology, or law.

Many wanted a simpler life. Few knew just what kind of life they were in for.

As newcomers, such as the Cakebreads, Shafers, Jordans, and Davies (of Schramsberg), joined the by then established vintners, such as the Martinis, de Latours (of Beaulieu), Mondavis, and Gallos, the California wine industry boomed for the second time. Meanwhile, thanks largely to the financial support provided by Gallo, the enology and viticulture

## BIG CHANGES

⊂⦿⦿⦿⊃

The number of wineries in the United States is increasing dramatically. This is made very clear when you compare the number of wineries in 1960 to that in 2000 for the states below.

| State | 1960 | 2000 |
|---|---|---|
| California | 256 | 1,185 |
| Washington State | 15 | 145 |
| New York State | 15 | 140 |
| Oregon | 0 | 138 |
| Virginia | 0 | 59 |
| Texas | 1 | 34 |

school of the University of California at Davis became one of the leading institutions of its kind anywhere. The quality of California wine soared. By 1980 most wine professionals around the world agreed that California wines could be considered in the same company as the finest wines of Europe.

California's rejuvenation, however, would not stop there. The state's success would ultimately inspire winemakers from New York State to Texas to attempt to rival it. Today more than 90 percent of all the wine produced in the United States is from California. Still, each of the major wine states plays an important, and some-

## WINE CONSUMPTION IN THE UNITED STATES

≈⸨∅∅⸩≈

According to the wine industry accounting and research firm Motto, Kryla, and Fisher, here's how the country stacks up when it comes to wine drinking in 1999. Figures are based on adult per capita consumption measured by case, a case being twelve 750 milliliter bottles. (Keep in mind that tourism plus prices and the selection available sometimes cause residents of one state to buy wine in another.)

| State | Rank | Gallons | State | Rank | Gallons |
|-------|------|---------|-------|------|---------|
| Idaho | 1 | 2.82 | New Mexico | 27 | 1.02 |
| District of Columbia | 2 | 2.81 | Wisconsin | 28 | 1.00 |
| Nevada | 3 | 2.55 | Louisiana | 29 | 0.92 |
| New Hampshire | 4 | 2.09 | Georgia** | 30 | 0.91 |
| Massachusetts | 5 | 1.90 | Michigan | 31 | 0.89 |
| Connecticut | 6 | 1.88 | North Carolina** | 32* | 0.89 |
| California | 7 | 1.82 | Missouri | 33 | 0.87 |
| Delaware | 8 | 1.80 | Texas | 34 | 0.81 |
| Rhode Island | 9 | 1.77 | South Carolina | 35 | 0.78 |
| Vermont | 10 | 1.75 | Pennsylvania | 36 | 0.77 |
| New Jersey | 11 | 1.74 | Ohio | 37* | 0.77 |
| Washington | 12 | 1.66 | Indiana | 38 | 0.75 |
| Oregon | 13 | 1.65 | Wyoming | 39 | 0.69 |
| Alaska | 14 | 1.58 | Nebraska | 40 | 0.65 |
| Florida | 15 | 1.52 | Kansas** | 41 | 0.59 |
| Hawaii | 16 | 1.49 | Tennessee | 42 | 0.58 |
| New York | 17 | 1.43 | North Dakota | 43 | 0.57 |
| Arizona | 18 | 1.38 | South Dakota | 44 | 0.54 |
| Colorado | 19 | 1.36 | Alabama | 45* | 0.54 |
| Maine | 20 | 1.27 | Oklahoma | 46* | 0.54 |
| Illinois | 21 | 1.24 | Kentucky | 47 | 0.51 |
| Arkansas | 22 | 1.23 | Iowa | 48 | 0.48 |
| Virginia | 23 | 1.19 | Utah | 49 | 0.43 |
| Maryland | 24 | 1.14 | Mississippi | 50 | 0.37 |
| Montana | 25 | 1.13 | West Virginia** | 51 | 0.35 |
| Minnesota | 26 | 1.03 | | | |

*When a state's rank appears with an asterisk (*), the amount of wine consumed per person is practically identical to that consumed by residents of the state above it. **1998 figures; 1999 figures not available.

# PROHIBITION

More than any other political event in the history of the United States, the nearly thirteen-year period called Prohibition shaped our current drinking patterns. Prohibition quashed the budding wine culture in America, and we became, almost overnight, a society that found pleasure and solace in hard liquor. The Eighteenth Amendment's constitutional ban on the manufacture, sale, and transport of all beverages containing alcohol officially took effect January 16, 1920 (although various Prohibition laws were on the books of individual states earlier), and ended December 5, 1933. It was enforced by a set of rules known as the Volstead Act, named after its sponsoring Minnesota congressman, Andrew J. Volstead.

At the time the law was enacted, California had roughly the same number of wineries it would have some seventy years later—slightly more than 700. By the end of Prohibition only 140 wineries remained. Most were destitute, having barely survived by making sacramental and kosher wine for priests, ministers, and rabbis (a rash of new religious sects had formed) and nonprescription medicinal wine "tonics" for the infirm and convalescent (whose numbers greatly increased).

The decades before Prohibition had been a golden age for wine in the United States. Founded by ambitious German, Swiss, and Italian immigrants, the wine industry had grown rapidly, unfettered by European laws and land rights. American wine had won awards in dozens of international competitions, including the prestigious Paris Exhibition of 1900. A vibrant culture of wine with food—not unlike Europe's—was just beginning to take hold. But the Prohibitionists had been gaining power for a decade, led, in many cases, by women pleased to use their newfound right to vote. In the face of growing antagonism, vintners remained surprisingly optimistic. Surely wine, the beverage of the Bible and Thomas Jefferson, would be exempt, they rationalized. After all, weren't immoral saloons and public drunkenness, not the moderate consumption of wine with meals, the Prohibitionists' real targets? In what can only be described as naïveté or denial, even after Prohibition was signed into law, many winemakers believed it would be suspended so that the 1920 crop could be harvested. To the architects of Prohibition, of course, alcohol was alcohol.

Ironically, during this time grape production and home winemaking increased. A veiled provision in the Volstead Act

times unique, role in the American wine industry in general.

Oregon has become a region specifically suited and devoted to the difficult but delicious variety pinot noir. Washington State has emerged as one of the country's top spots for ripe, concentrated merlots and cabernet sauvignons. And similarly, New York State is proving to be prime riesling territory. No other rieslings in the country have quite the same clarity, lightness, and elegance as those from New York. These are the kinds of grape-to-ground matches that take decades, if not centuries, to figure out. The United States lags behind Europe in this regard, but the process has decidedly begun.

Of the more than one hundred varieties of grapes grown in the United

allowed citizens to make up to 200 gallons annually of nonintoxicating cider and fruit juices. Nonintoxicating, however, was never actually defined. Brokers and wineries immediately began shipping crates of grapes, grape concentrates (the most famous one, called Vine-Glo, came in eight varieties), and even compressed grape "bricks" to home winemakers around the country. Along with the bricks came the convenient admonition: "Warning. Do not place this brick in a one gallon crock, add sugar and water, cover, and let stand for seven days or else an illegal alcoholic beverage will result."

Meanwhile, the bootlegging of powerful high-proof spirits became a thriving industry, and the local drinking establishment formed a new order for what and how people drank. *Speakeasy* was the name given to the raucous illegal saloons that sprung up during Prohibition. According to John F. Mariani in *The Dictionary of American Food and Drink,* the word derived from the English underworld term "speak softly shop"—a smuggler's house where one could buy cheap liquor. "Designed to shut down all saloons, the Volstead Act instead spurred more illicit ones to open," Mariani writes. "Thanks to a thoroughly entrenched system of graft and police corruption, New York [by the end of Prohibition] had more than thirty-two thousand speakeasies—twice the number of saloons closed."

The hard drinking and notorious behavior carried on inside speakeasies set a new tone for alcohol consumption in the United States. A glass of zinfandel with roast chicken it was not. At the same time, home winemaking, however amusingly clandestine and resourceful, would ultimately prove detrimental to whatever crippled wine industry was left. To provide a quick supply of basic grapes the best California vineyards were torn out and replanted mostly with inferior, tough-skinned varieties that would not rot in the boxcar during the long haul back East. Over time, an affinity for fine wine was lost, supplanted by a taste for sweet, cheap, fortified wine. Even after repeal, the desire for sweet, cheap, and strong remained. It was not until 1967 that fine table wine, rather than inexpensive sweet wine, once again led production in California.

Most sadly, Prohibition eviscerated the soul of winemaking in the United States— the collective knowledge, the techniques, traditions, and passions that are passed down from winemaker to winemaker. When the wine industry was finally able to reinvent itself in the mid-1960s, most of the winemakers had no historical knowledge and no traditions to rely on. Even Robert Mondavi and Ernest and Julio Gallo—three of the most successful vintners of the second half of the twentieth century—had to teach themselves to make wine by reading books.

631

States, five dominate sales: chardonnay, cabernet sauvignon, zinfandel, merlot, and sauvignon blanc. While wines made from these varieties are, in many cases, better than ever before, vintners and winemakers have also looked to other grapes, especially Rhône and Italian varieties. Syrah, grenache, mourvèdre, and sangiovese are now being made into some of the most intriguing wines and

wine blends in the United States, and a number of other grape varieties hold promise.

In the end, of course, part of what makes winemaking in the United States compelling is the freedom winemakers have to create whatever sorts of wine they want. The strict laws that define wine regions in Europe and that govern the grape varieties that can comprise specific

## UNCLE SAM, VINTNER

—⁕⁕⁕—

T he United States government's interest in wine once extended far beyond warning labels. According to Thomas Pinney, author of *A History of Wine in America*, in the eighteenth century Congress actually subsidized winegrowing in Indiana and Alabama, hoping to encourage the production of an inexpensive national beverage. Prohibition put an end to that experiment, but during the Depression the government once again got into the wine business, this time seeing it as an aid to economic recovery. The Department of Agriculture even built two model wineries, replete with shiny, high-tech equipment, that were intended to set the standard for the new American wine industry.

Unfortunately, the Dry forces still had enough congressional clout to shut the USDA wineries down before they ever crushed a grape. The equipment was sold at auction, and Uncle Sam's days as a vintner were over before they'd begun.

European wines have very few parallels in the United States. That said, viticultural areas are legally defined in the United States, and there *are* wine laws. Here's a look at both.

## AMERICAN VITICULTURAL AREAS

D efining a wine by first establishing the area from which the grapes can come is a well-entrenched concept in Europe. In France this is one aspect of the detailed system known as the *Appellation d'Origine Contrôlée*. The wine Sancerre, for instance, can be only made from grapes grown in the appellation Sancerre.

In the United States the process of defining wine regions was begun in 1978 when the Bureau of Alcohol, Tobacco, and Firearms began to draw up requirements for establishing the first American Viticultural Areas or AVAs. An AVA is defined as "a delimited grape growing region, distinguished by geographical features, the boundaries of which have been recog- nized and defined." On United States wine labels such place-names as Napa Valley, Sonoma Valley, Carneros, Finger Lakes, Willamette Valley, and Columbia Valley are all AVAs. There are now more than 140 AVAs in the United States.

At first, it might seem as though American Viticultural Areas and European appellation systems are similar constructs. In fact, they are immensely different in critical ways. The appellation rules in

## WHERE THE VINEYARDS ARE

⦥⦥

| State | Acres of Vineyards (as of 1998) |
| --- | --- |
| California | 427,000 |
| New York State | 31,000* |
| Washington State | 20,000 |
| Oregon | 9,000 |
| Texas | 3,200 |
| Virginia | 1,500 |

*About 20,000 acres of these 31,000 are of Concord grapes, most of which are destined to become grape juice or jelly, not wine.

European countries do not simply define the boundaries of a region. They also legally mandate a sweeping array of details, from which grape varieties can be grown to how the wines must be made. By comparison, winemakers in the United States are free to plant whatever they want and to make wine in almost any way they want. Not surprisingly, two wines made from the same grape grown in different spots within one AVA often taste as though they have little in common (though this can be true within a European appellation as well). Still, "tasting the place" is usually more difficult with an American wine than with a European one since whatever you taste may be the result of something the winemaker did rather than a characteristic of where the grapes were grown.

There's another factor. The unique character of a site can be said to impart a given character to a wine only if that place

---

## WHO CAME FIRST?

~ めめめ ~

The first American Viticultural Area was, curiously enough, Augusta, Missouri, approved in 1980. The largest AVA is the Texas Hill Country. At slightly over 15,000 square miles, it is larger in size than many states, including both Vermont and Massachusetts.

---

is strictly defined viticulturally. In other words, the boundaries of the place have to be drawn according to geography and *terroir*. Wherever the unique geography and *terroir* stop is where the area has to end. Several AVAs do not meet this criterion, for they are spread over areas that are too large and too dissimilar. In addition, for

633

*Vineyards grace Virginia's Blue Ridge Mountains. Although the modern Virginia wine industry is considered mere decades old, the state's first wines were made nearly four centuries ago by the Jamestown colonists.*

## READING A UNITED STATES WINE LABEL

FREEMARK ABBEY

Name of the winery

NAPA VALLEY — Wine region

Grape variety — CABERNET SAUVIGNON

Bosché Vineyard — Vineyard

PRODUCED AND BOTTLED BY FREEMARK ABBEY WINERY, ST. HELENA, CA., USA
ALCOHOL 13.3% BY VOLUME — Name of the producer

Percentage of alcohol by volume

634

some prestigious American Viticultural Areas there have been considerable arguments among vintners over who's inside the territory and who's outside. As a result, some AVAs have been defined as much by political jockeying as by viticulture. (To be fair, politics have influenced European appellations too.) None of this means that the area stated on the label is irrelevant, only that it is an imperfect guide. For the vast majority of wines from the United States, the producer's name is *the* indispensable indicator of that wine's quality and style.

## THE UNITED STATES' WINE LAWS

Though winemakers in the United States have far more creative free-dom to make whatever sorts of wines they want than their European colleagues, there are several important federal rules and regulations wine producers must abide by. These are administered by the Bureau of Alcohol, Tobacco, and Firearms, under whose jurisdiction wine falls. Here is a quick summary of the most important laws.

• When a wine is labeled with an American Viticultural Area, 85 percent of the grapes that make up the wine must come from that AVA.

• In place of an AVA, a wine can also be labeled by county—Sonoma County, Mendocino County, and so on. When a wine is labeled by county, 75 percent of the grapes must come from that county.

• In place of an AVA, a wine may be labeled by state. Wines labeled by state

## LABELS AND POLITICS

——◁◁▷▷——

I n 1989 the Bureau of Alcohol, Tobacco, and Firearms (BATF) issued a controversial regulation requiring wine bottles to carry the warning: "(1) According to the Surgeon General, women should not drink alcoholic beverages during pregnancy because of the risk of birth defects. (2) Consumption of alcoholic beverages impairs your ability to drive a car or operate machinery and may cause health problems." No other country except Mexico mandates a warning label on wine, and the Mexican label stipulates that *abuse* (as opposed to use) is not good for health.

Soon after the United States rule was enacted, a well-known Berkeley wine importer named Kermit Lynch proposed balancing the warning with a statement about wine's benefits. He suggested Louis Pasteur's declaration that wine was the most hygienic beverage known to man. The bureau ruled that the quote was unacceptable. Lynch, a man not easily dissuaded, tried again suggesting a biblical quote about wine's healing properties. Again, the bureau rejected the new text.

Finally, Lynch proposed two quotes from Thomas Jefferson. The first was turned down because, according to the BATF, Jefferson had implied that wine was healthy. The second read, "Good wine is a necessity of life for me." That quote was considered acceptable long enough for Lynch to print 50,000 labels. Upon reconsideration, however, the bureau rescinded their decision, and Lynch was out the printing costs.

When William Jefferson "Bill" Clinton was elected president in 1992, Lynch decided to try one last time. He wrote a letter to the BATF arguing that the phrase "necessity of life" did not imply that wine was healthful, merely that it was pleasurable. He also questioned whether it was the role of a governmental agency to censor Thomas Jefferson. Lynch's persistence paid off. Later that year the BATF finally approved Lynch's request. All bottles of wine imported by Kermit Lynch now carry Jefferson's statement affirming that wine was, for him, a "necessity of life."

must contain at least 75 percent wine from that state. Some states, however, require higher percentages. In California 100 percent of the wine must be from California and in Texas 85 percent of the wine must be from Texas.

• When a grape variety is named on the label (for example, chardonnay), the wine must be composed of at least 75 percent of that variety. Again, some states have stricter rules. In Oregon this percentage has been raised to 90 percent, except for wines made principally from cabernet sauvignon, which still need only be 75 percent cabernet.

• When a vintage is declared on the label, 95 percent of the wine must be from that vintage.

• All bottles of wine made in the United States are required to carry a warning about the dangers of alcohol and to indicate that the wine contains sulfites (see page 34).

# California

California is wine's Camelot—a place of sometimes awesome beauty and high ideals; a wine region where the realm of possibility knows no bounds. The third largest state in the United States and not quite three fourths the size of France, California now produces more than 90 percent of all wine made in the country. The state's wine history goes back more than two centuries to the Spanish explorers and Franciscan fathers who moved north from Mexico and painstakingly built rustic missions, surrounding them with small vineyards that could supply wine for the Mass. From those harsh beginnings the industry progressed, becoming remarkably successful in the decades after the gold rush, only to crumble under the dual devastation of phylloxera and Prohibition. It was not until the late 1960s—in what might be thought of as its second golden age—that California once again became a thriving wine region.

Today the conviction that anything is achievable is as irrepressible as ever in the Golden State. Fine wines are being made from a steadily expanding range of grapes, among them Rhône and Italian varieties, and based on what avant-garde winemakers predict, Spanish varieties promise to be next. At the same time, better and better classics are being made, including some gorgeously rich cabernet sauvignons.

California's nearly 1,200 wine producers range from extremely large (Gallo is in fact the largest wine producer in the world) to tiny (some don't have vineyards or a winery building, but function by buying grapes and occasionally wines to blend). About one hundred grape varieties are grown in the state, but just six lead the pro-

*Rising impressively over a sea of vines, Domaine Carneros' eighteenth-century château-style building was inspired by the Château de la Marquetterie, owned by the Champagne house of Taittinger, a co-owner of the winery.*

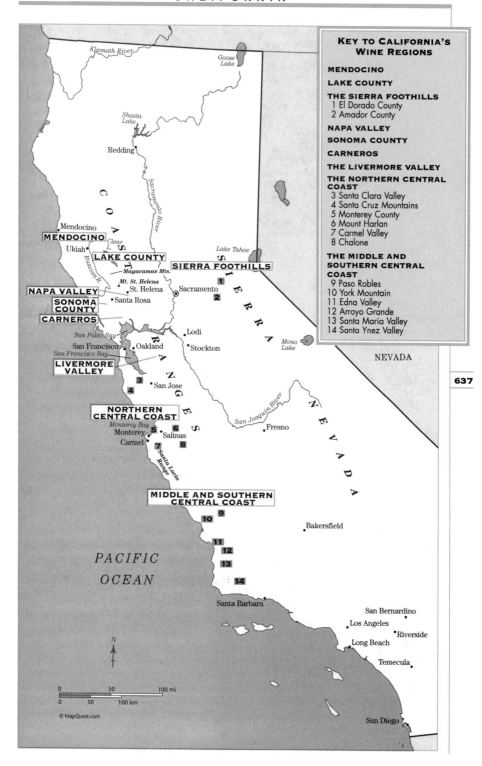

**KEY TO CALIFORNIA'S WINE REGIONS**

**MENDOCINO**

**LAKE COUNTY**

**THE SIERRA FOOTHILLS**
1 El Dorado County
2 Amador County

**NAPA VALLEY**

**SONOMA COUNTY**

**CARNEROS**

**THE LIVERMORE VALLEY**

**THE NORTHERN CENTRAL COAST**
3 Santa Clara Valley
4 Santa Cruz Mountains
5 Monterey County
6 Mount Harlan
7 Carmel Valley
8 Chalone

**THE MIDDLE AND SOUTHERN CENTRAL COAST**
9 Paso Robles
10 York Mountain
11 Edna Valley
12 Arroyo Grande
13 Santa Maria Valley
14 Santa Ynez Valley

637

© MapQuest.com

## THE QUICK SIP ON CALIFORNIA

෴

- More than 90 percent of the wine made in the United States is made in California.

- The state's incredibly diverse yet beneficent climate and geography allow California wines to be made in a profusion of styles from dozens of different grape varieties.

- California's winemakers are among the most innovative and open to experimentation in the world.

rolling forests of Mendocino in the north to the sun-drenched hills of Temecula south of Los Angeles. The climate, soil, and geology over so vast a territory are markedly different. Still, overall California is considered to be the New World's Mediterranean, for the state's vineyards are blessed by such generous, bright sunlight that winemakers almost never worry about whether or not grapes will ripen. Sunlight and ripeness mean that California wines are all about cream, not about skim milk. The wines have a natural plumpness and extroverted fruit. They are, in the words of one winemaker, "Here-I-am wines."

## THE LAND

duction of fine wines: chardonnay, zinfandel, cabernet sauvignon, sauvignon blanc, merlot, and pinot noir. The state's wine regions cover more than 427,000 acres, stretching more than 700 miles from the

Millions of years ago, as large tectonic plates on the earth's crust repeatedly collided with the continent of North America, California was formed. It became

638

*Mount St. Helena, 4,343 feet high, marks the northern boundary of the Napa Valley. The volcano was last active 3 million years ago.*

## CALIFORNIA'S BIGGEST WINE-PRODUCING REGION

⟨≈⟩

The Central Valley, a vast, hot, 300-mile-long expanse extending from the Sacramento Valley in the north to the San Joaquin Valley in the south, is one of the most fertile areas in the United States. The Central Valley produces a full 60 percent of all the agricultural products in California and crushes 75 percent of *all* the wine grapes. Wineries here are huge. And so are the crops.

Blended generic wines are the Central Valley's bread and butter, with such well-established firms as E. & J. Gallo (which makes close to 70 million cases, including some of the most popular inexpensive wines in the world).

Varietal wines are made here too, especially in the area around Lodi where slightly more than 6 million cases of Robert Mondavi Woodbridge wines are made each year. And finally, though their production is comparatively small, some of California's finest dessert wines are made in the Central Valley, notably by Quady Winery, makers of the extraordinary, nectarlike wine known as Essensia.

a place of amazing geologic and climatic diversity. Almost every kind of climate, land formation, vegetation, and animal life that can be found anywhere else in the United States can be found in California. Much of the state, however, is either too bone chillingly cold or too torridly hot to be ideal for wine grapes. Close to the 840-mile-long Pacific coastline people often wear down jackets in the summer. Eighty miles inland the immense, oval cradle of the Central Valley can be as blistering as an oven. None of the top wine regions are either inland or on the coast. All are poised between the ocean on the west and the inland Central Valley on the east. Thus the major wine regions are stacked, one on top of the other, up and down the length of the state, from Santa Barbara County in the south to Mendocino in the north.

But there's more to the story. California's fine wine regions exist only because of a unique climatic phenomenon, itself the result of the state's distinct topography. As the day warms up and the heat in the interior intensifies and rises,

cool winds and fog are sucked in from the Pacific through a series of gaps in the low coastal mountain ranges. The big yawning mouth of the San Francisco Bay, for instance, acts like a funnel for cool winds that are drawn in off the ocean and then are pulled into Carneros and from there up into the Napa and Sonoma Valleys. All along the coast a similar cycle of warming and cooling is at work. Admittedly, this wondrous climatic yin-yang is more dramatic in some wine regions than in others. Still, it is an essential and crucial aspect of California's overall viticulture, for without it the state would be full of areas too hot to produce fine wine.

## BEGINNING AND BEGINNING AGAIN

The California wine industry would seem to owe its beginnings to divine providence. The Spanish explorers who moved north from Mexico in the early 1700s secured their new territory—known as Alta (Upper) California—with a string

## CALIFORNIA DREAMIN'

O ne of the core differences between the wine industry in California and that in Europe is the people who run it. The California wine revolution of the 1960s and 1970s was largely initiated by men and women who were not from winemaking families. Instead, they were investment bankers, professors, pilots, lawyers, doctors, or businessmen whose passion for wine and fascination with the romantic lifestyle making wine seemed to imply superseded everything—including the fact that many had never planted a tomato, never mind a vineyard.

of missions, each a day's journey from the next. Wine was required by the missions for sacramental ceremonies and by the explorers themselves, who needed it both for daily nourishment and as solace amid the harshness of daily life.

*The name California was used officially in Spanish documents as early as 1542.*
*It is believed to come from the description of a fabled island called California in the sixteenth-century Spanish novel*
The Exploits of Esplandián.

Californian wine, however, almost did not come to be. According to the writer and historian Thomas Pinney, the Spanish authorities decided that the California missions would be perfectly well off with Mexican wine, which could be shipped

north. But accidents and difficulties along the supply route ultimately led California's Franciscan fathers to plant vineyards of their own.

The cuttings they brought from Mexico were of Spanish origin and were descended from those brought there nearly two centuries earlier by Hernán Cortés. In California that grape variety was called simply mission, after the missions where it was planted. For the next fifty years, all of the wine made in California was made from the mission grape alone. The missions' success with grape growing inspired secular attempts. California settlers began planting small vineyards as early as 1783, and by the 1830s commercial wineries had begun in Los Angeles.

From the 1850s onward California's future looked bright. The gold rush of 1849 pumped up the local population (in the

*An old, wooden wine press at Franciscan Vineyards recalls earlier times. Today this winery and most others in California have state-of-the-art, computer-controlled pneumatic presses.*

two years from 1848 to 1850 San Francisco alone went from 800 inhabitants to 25,000) and created both a new demand for wine and a pool of potential vintners. The wine industry shifted north first to Sonoma and then to Napa, both valleys being better suited to viticulture than Los Angeles, and some of the great wineries were founded, including Buena Vista, Charles Krug, Ingelnook, and Schramsberg. As if this boom was not enough, California's future soon took on international possibilities, for the mildew odium and the plant louse phylloxera had already begun to destroy the vineyards of Europe.

Excitement over burgeoning markets notwithstanding, winemaking at the time was tough business. The early California vintners had no schools, no technical help, little or no knowledge of exactly what grape varieties they were planting, very little equipment (even bottles were scarce until a bottle-making factory was founded in 1862), and no traditions on which to rely. Ever willful, Californians forged full speed ahead until the mid-1880s when phylloxera finally made its way to California. By 1890 the louse had wreaked havoc throughout the state.

The industry rebuilt itself fairly quickly. At the dawn of the twentieth century, 300 varieties of grapes were being grown in California and there were nearly 800 wineries. To the vintners at that time, the idea that such hard-won success could vanish overnight must have seemed unreal. But on the sixteenth day of January in 1920 when the Volstead Act took effect, Prohibition became the law. Almost fourteen years later when Prohibition finally ended in December of 1933, only 140 wineries remained. Ironically, many had managed to hang on by making what the very first California winemakers had—sacramental wines.

Californian vintners were down but not out. It would take until the late 1960s for winemaking to really get going again, but once it did it soared ahead with startling speed. Within a decade California became one of the most advanced and accomplished wine regions in the world. The enormity of the transformation is captured by the juxtaposition of two facts. In 1966 the best-selling California wines were cheap, sweet "ports," often made primarily from carignan or Thompson seedless, both of which were important grapes at the time. Just ten years later, the state's fine wines were so good that French judges were left reeling when, in the now legendary Paris tasting of 1976, two wines—

641

## CHINESE CONTRIBUTIONS

With the gold rush of 1849, Chinese immigrants began to come to California in large numbers. Many were poor laborers and farmers who immediately went to work for the wealthy new winery owners in Sonoma and Napa. From the 1860s to the 1880s, Chinese vineyard workers cleared fields, planted vineyards, built wineries, harvested grapes, and dug by hand many of northern California's most impressive underground cellars. What is now the golf course of Napa Valley's prestigious Meadowood resort was once a Chinese camp where several hundred Chinese vineyard workers lived in barracks. According to the historian Jack Chen, an economic crisis in the late 1870s resulted in agitation against Chinese labor and ultimately in the Chinese Exclusion Act passed by Congress in 1882. By 1890 most of the Chinese in the wine country had fled.

## MAKING THE MOST OF LOUSY LUCK

—◦◦◦—

After a century of absence, phylloxera once again surfaced in California, in the Napa Valley during the mid-1980s. The plant louse immediately began to destroy some vineyards—those planted on the rootstock AxR1 (see page 24)—at an astonishing clip. Vintners were stunned and, at first, extremely despondent. But many soon recognized a silver lining in phylloxera's black cloud: The destructive pest compelled them to replant. With two decades worth of experience and scientific data behind them, California's vintners could now begin to choose varieties and clones of grapes that might be better suited to their vineyard sites than the varieties and clones previously planted. Over the next several decades, the result, it is to be hoped, will be more and more distinct wines of even higher quality.

Stag's Leap Wine Cellars' cabernet sauvignon and Chateau Montelena's chardonnay—took the first places for red and white wine, respectively, beating out such exalted wines as Château Mouton-Rothschild or Château Haut-Brion and Domaine Roulot Meursault-Charmes. (Chateau Montelena, like a number of wineries in the United States, spells château "New World" style—without the accent on the *a*.)

# THE GRAPES AND THE WINES

Unlike most European winemakers, Californian winemakers have always been free to plant whatever grape varieties they want. Of the approximately one hundred varieties that are planted in the state, the six that dominate fine wine production are well known: chardonnay, cabernet sauvignon, merlot, sauvignon blanc, zinfandel, and pinot noir.

Some of the most exquisite wines in California are made with these grapes, and you'll find portraits of them and recommendations for some of their best producers starting on the next page. But in the late 1980s and 1990s, as wine drinkers increasingly felt they'd been there, done that with cabernet and chardonnay, much of the excitement among winemakers and wine drinkers was generated by a slew of other grapes, most of them Mediterranean in origin. Seemingly overnight, wines were being made from a delicious new galaxy of grapes including viognier, roussanne, pinot gris (some California wineries label their pinot gris by its Italian name, pinot grigio), syrah, petite sirah, mourvèdre, sangiovese, barbera, and grenache. Of these, syrah in particular has proven so successful that it is well on its way to becoming one of the state's most important grapes for fine wines.

The person who, more than any other, unlocked this treasure chest of grapes was Randall Grahm, the madcap owner, winemaker, philosopher, and resident poet of Bonny Doon Vineyard. Grahm was the first winemaker to produce a string of successful fine wines from dozens of obscure or never-before-tried-in-California grape varieties, and his impact on the California wine industry has been profound. Just when things were getting stale, just when the wine industry was drowning in same-

## CALIFORNIA WINES

LEADING WINES

**Cabernet Sauvignon** and **Cabernet Blends** *red*

**Chardonnay** *white*

**Merlot** *red*

**Pinot Noir** *red*

**Riesling** *white (dry and sweet)*

**Sauvignon Blanc** *white (dry and sweet)*

**Sparkling Wines** *white*

**Syrah** and **Rhône Blends*** *red*

**Zinfandel** *red*

WINES OF NOTE

**Barbera** *red*

**Chenin Blanc** *white*

**Gewürztraminer** *white*

**Marsanne** *white*

**Mourvèdre** *red*

**Muscat** *white (sweet)*

**Petite Sirah** *red*

**Pinot Gris** *white*

**Port-Style Wines** *red (fortified; sweet)*

**Roussanne** *white*

**Sangiovese** *red*

**Viognier** *white*

*The number of vineyards planted with syrah is increasing dramatically thanks to the wine's quality and burgeoning popularity. Because I think there's no doubt that syrah is headed toward becoming one of California's most important wines, as is the category of wines known as Rhône blends, most of which are based primarily on syrah, I have included these here in Leading Wines (a subjective decision at the time of writing this book).*

ness, Grahm inspired a whole generation of winemakers to make us more imaginative wines to drink.

Of course, greeting these new wines with "wine blinders" on would be silly of us. Many of the new, up-and-coming Mediterranean varieties being made into wine should probably be called old, up-and-coming. Such grapes as barbera and petite sirah were first planted by Italian immigrants in California as early as the 1880s. Robust and adaptable, these grapes grew happily and made tasty everyday wines seemingly no matter where they were planted. As a result, such grapes were replanted again and again, but an entire century would pass before top winemakers in California would begin making *fine* wines from these grapes and discovering the places they grow best.

## Chardonnay

By all rights, chardonnay—a wine that almost every winery in California makes—should be one of the most exciting wines in the state. The sheer number of them (more than 1,000 produced each year) would lead you to believe that scores are full of personality and character. Nothing could be further from the truth. Many are simply oily, clumsy wines that taste like buttered toast soaked in alcohol. What about elegance?

In fairness, *great* chardonnay is not easy to make, and the sites where the grapes are grown is critical. Generally, the best-balanced chardonnays come from cool regions, or at least cool pockets within a given viticultural area. The clones of chardonnay that were planted in California from the 1960s through 1990 may not be ideal for many vineyard sites. In the mid-1990s, however, new and better clones of chardonnay became available for the first time. As winemakers become experienced with these new clones, the

## THE WHITE GRAPES OF
# CALIFORNIA

*More than one hundred different white and red grape varieties grow in California. These fifteen whites are the most important.*

**Chardonnay:** Most widely planted white grape. The source of wines that range from bland to extraordinary. Most of the best come from cool areas and are made by winemakers who prize balance over oak.

**Chenin Blanc:** Historically used for jug wines. Capable of making very tasty fine wines, although plantings have been in decline for some time.

**French Colombard:** Widely planted in less than ideal locations. Grown at very high yields for jug wines.

**Gewürztraminer:** Minor grape in terms of production, but some surprisingly delicious wines come from it, especially when those grapes are grown in cool areas.

**Marsanne:** Makes good, though somewhat simple wines on its own and is a leading component with roussanne in white Rhône-style blends.

**Muscat Canelli, Black Muscat, and Orange Muscat:** All members of the muscat family of grapes and all used to make delightful sweet wines. Muscat Canelli, the same as muscat blanc à petits grains, is the most frequently used of the three.

**Pinot Blanc:** Minor grape but capable of becoming a tasty wine. Top producers of pinot blanc are few.

**Pinot Gris:** Also known by its Italian name, pinot grigio. Minor grape but growing in importance. Turned into light quaffing wines as well as more serious, creamy wines of substance.

**Riesling:** Makes light, refreshing wines with delicious fruit and floral aromas and flavors; often slightly sweet. Also used for late harvest dessert wines, some of which are stellar.

**Roussanne:** Minor grape in terms of production but prized for the elegance of its wines. Aromatic. Sometimes blended with marsanne in white Rhône-style blends.

**Sauvignon Blanc:** Major grape. Makes dry wines that range from snappy, citrusy, and herbal to creamier, more buttery and toasty versions that can seem almost chardonnay-like in flavor. Sauvignon blanc is also used, often with sémillon, to make botrytized dessert wines.

**Sémillon:** Minor grape. Used primarily for botrytized dessert wines, often in conjunction with sauvignon blanc, although there are some dry examples.

**Viognier:** Very little planted before the mid-1990s; more recently, plantings have increased dramatically. The leading white Rhône variety. Makes opulent, rich, full-bodied whites, evocative of honeysuckle and melons.

*At the southern end of the Napa Valley, The Grape Crusher, a bronze statue by Santa Fe sculptor Gino Miles, looms large on a hilltop.*

644

# THE RED GRAPES OF
## CALIFORNIA

*While the varieties of grapes grown in California, both red and white, number more than one hundred, these fourteen reds are the most significant.*

**Barbera:** Fairly widely planted for use primarily in jug wines. Increasingly harvested at lower yields to make fine wines with good structure and appealing red cherry and red raspberry flavors.

**Cabernet Franc:** Minor grape; generally blended with cabernet sauvignon or merlot in California's Bordeaux-style blends, although cabernet franc is occasionally found as an interesting wine on its own.

**Cabernet Sauvignon:** The most important of all red grape varieties; capable of making powerful, opulent, and complex wines that are also ageworthy. Wines made from cabernet sauvignon were the first to put California on the international wine map. As of the late 1990s, the most widely planted red grape in California.

**Carignane:** The Californian spelling of the French grape carignan, historically used in jug wines. Increasingly harvested at lower yields to make fine wines. Often blended with syrah, mourvèdre, and grenache to make Rhône-style blends.

**Grenache:** Like barbera, fairly widely planted for use primarily in jug wines. Increasingly harvested at lower yields to make high quality, spicy, juicy wines that are often blended with syrah, mourvèdre, and carignane to make Rhône-style blends. Also the source of numerous delicious rosés.

**Malbec:** Not widely planted in California, but small amounts are often blended with cabernet sauvignon, cabernet franc, and merlot to make Bordeaux-style blends.

**Merlot:** Major grape. Many solidly good red wines and occasionally some very expensive sensational wines are made from merlot. Used alone and blended with cabernet sauvignon.

**Mourvèdre:** Minor grape in terms of production but an essential part of the blend in many top Rhône-style wines.

**Petite Sirah:** Makes delicious, robust, highly tannic wines. DNA testing in the late 1990s confirmed that what grape growers and wineries have traditionally called petite sirah could be several different grapes, the most likely of which is Durif, a cross of the Rhône variety peloursin and true syrah. Also spelled petite syrah.

**Petit Verdot:** Minor grape. Like malbec, however, tiny amounts of petit verdot are often blended with cabernet sauvignon, cabernet franc, and merlot to make Bordeaux-style blends.

**Pinot Noir:** Major grape. Capable of making complex, earthy, supple wines especially when grown in cool areas. Also used in sparkling wines.

**Sangiovese:** The leading Italian variety for fine wines, although making these is a challenge. Plantings nonetheless increased dramatically in the 1990s. Usually results in medium-bodied wines with straightforward cherrylike flavors.

**Syrah:** Most prestigious and most successful of the red Rhône varieties. Makes concentrated, deeply colored wines that can be rich and complex. Often blended with mourvèdre, grenache, and carignane to make Rhône-style blends. On its way to becoming one of the most important red grapes in California.

**Zinfandel:** The second most widely planted red grape variety. An enormously versatile grape, used for everything from the sweetish pink wine known as white zinfandel to rich, jammy, robust wines that are almost purple in color.

## A CRITICAL THIRD OF A CENTURY

— ✐✐✐ —

- In 1964 the tonnage of chardonnay grapes was so small that it was not yet tracked by the California Agricultural Service; in 1998 more than 330,000 tons of chardonnay grapes were crushed.

- In 1964 there were some 230 wineries in California; in 1998 there were about 840 in the state.

- In 1964 there were fewer than five women winemakers in California and all were self-taught (none had an enological degree). In 1998 there were more than fifty professionally trained female winemakers in California.

- In 1964 most of the wine served in the White House was from France; in 1998 most was from California.

---

overall quality of chardonnay is expected to rise. Meanwhile, here are the names of some producers whose chardonnays are consistently above average.

*Some of the Best
Chardonnay Producers*

ACACIA WINERY

ARROWOOD VINEYARDS AND WINERY

AU BON CLIMAT

BERINGER VINEYARDS

BYRON VINEYARDS AND WINERY

CAKEBREAD CELLARS

CHALK HILL ESTATE VINEYARDS AND WINERY

CHALONE VINEYARD

CHATEAU MONTELENA WINERY

CHATEAU ST. JEAN WINERY AND VINEYARDS

CUVAISON WINERY

EDNA VALLEY VINEYARD

FAR NIENTE WINERY

FLORA SPRINGS WINE COMPANY

FORMAN VINEYARDS

GRGICH HILLS CELLAR

HANZELL VINEYARDS

HARRISON VINEYARDS

J. ROCHIOLI VINEYARDS AND WINERY

KISTLER VINEYARDS

LIPARITA CELLARS

LITTORAI WINES

LONG VINEYARDS

MARCASSIN VINEYARD

MARIMAR TORRES ESTATE

MATANZAS CREEK WINERY

MERRYVALE VINEYARDS

MORGAN WINERY

MOUNT EDEN VINEYARDS

NAVARRO VINEYARDS

PATZ & HALL WINE COMPANY

PETER MICHAEL WINERY

QUPÉ WINE CELLARS

ROBERT TALBOTT VINEYARDS AND WINERY

PETER MICHAEL
— WINERY —

'POINT ROUGE'

SONOMA COUNTY CHARDONNAY ♦ ALCOHOL 14.1% BY VOLUME
PRODUCED AND BOTTLED BY PETER MICHAEL
CALISTOGA, CA USA

SAINTSBURY

SHAFER VINEYARDS

SONOMA-CUTRER VINEYARDS

STAGS' LEAP WINERY

STONY HILL VINEYARDS

TREFETHEN VINEYARDS

## Sauvignon Blanc

California sauvignon blancs are nothing if not underappreciated. The very good ones can be absolutely exceptional. Racy, keen edged, and refreshing, they are arguably the best California whites for serving with food thanks to their vibrant acidity and clean, fresh flavors. Most such sauvignon blancs are not fermented in oak barrels. The sauvignon blancs that are barrel fermented (or partially so) are a different story. A few of them are delicious, with creamy, round,

long flavors. But too many of this style are manipulated to such an extent and given so much contact with oak that they become washed out shadows of their former selves. I think of these deadened wines as sauvignon blancs on Valium.

Sauvignon Blanc in California is sometimes called fumé blanc. As a group, California sauvignon blancs are not stylistically different from wines labeled fumé blanc. Vintners simply use the name they think you'll like best and want to buy. Both the oaked and unoaked styles of sauvignon blanc are represented by the producers below.

*Some of the Best*
*Sauvignon Blanc and Fumé Blanc*
*Producers*

CAKEBREAD CELLARS

CHALK HILL ESTATE VINEYARDS
AND WINERY

CHATEAU ST. JEAN WINERY
AND VINEYARDS

DRY CREEK VINEYARD

FROG'S LEAP WINERY

GRGICH HILLS CELLAR

GROTH VINEYARDS AND WINERY

HONIG VINEYARD AND WINERY

HUSCH VINEYARDS

KUNDE ESTATE WINERY

LAMBERT BRIDGE WINERY

MARKHAM WINERY

MASON CELLARS

MORGAN WINERY

ROBERT MONDAVI WINERY

ST. SUPÉRY VINEYARDS AND
WINERY

SEGHESIO FAMILY VINEYARDS

SELENE WINES

SPOTTSWOODE WINERY

647

## Cabernet Sauvignon

The grape that put California on the international map as one of the world's top wine regions, cabernet sauvignon today is arguably the state's single most compelling variety, capable of becoming wines of enormous structure and concentration. Since the late 1980s the best California cabernets have gotten lusher, richer, softer, and more complex by the year as winemakers and viticulturists have continued to refine their methods for growing the grape and making the wine. One of the key elements has been a new understanding of ripeness and the necessity of letting grapes high in tannin, such as cabernet sauvignon, hang on the vine long enough for that tannin to mature.

Cabernet sauvignon can also be a team player. It is usually the leading grape in such Bordeaux-style blends as Insignia from Joseph Phelps and Rubicon from Niebaum-Coppola.

*Some of the Best*
*Cabernet Sauvignon and*
*Bordeaux-Style Blend Producers*

ARAUJO ESTATE WINES

BEAULIEU VINEYARD

BERINGER VINEYARDS

CAFARO CELLARS

CAYMUS VINEYARDS

CHATEAU MONTELENA WINERY

CHATEAU POTELLE WINERY

CHATEAU ST. JEAN WINERY AND VINEYARDS

CHIMNEY ROCK WINERY

DALLA VALLE VINEYARDS

DIAMOND CREEK VINEYARDS

DOMINUS ESTATE

DUNN VINEYARDS

E. & J. GALLO

FAR NIENTE WINERY

FIFE VINEYARDS

FLORA SPRINGS WINE COMPANY

FREEMARK ABBEY WINERY

GRACE FAMILY VINEYARDS

HARLAN ESTATE

HARRISON VINEYARDS

JOSEPH PHELPS VINEYARDS

LAUREL GLEN VINEYARDS

LIVINGSTON WINES

MAYACAMAS VINEYARDS

MOUNT VEEDER WINERY

NEWTON VINEYARD

NIEBAUM-COPPOLA ESTATE WINERY

OPUS ONE

PARADIGM

PHILLIP TOGNI VINEYARD

RIDGE VINEYARDS AND WINERY

RISTOW ESTATE

ROBERT CRAIG

ROBERT MONDAVI WINERY

648

JOSEPH PHELPS
VINEYARDS
*Cabernet Sauvignon*
NAPA VALLEY

ROBERT PECOTA WINERY

SCREAMING EAGLE WINERY

SHAFER VINEYARDS

SILVERADO VINEYARDS

SILVER OAK WINE CELLARS

SPOTTSWOODE WINERY

STAGLIN FAMILY VINEYARD

STAG'S LEAP WINE CELLARS

STAGS' LEAP WINERY

SWANSON VINEYARDS AND WINERY

TURNBULL WINE CELLARS

VIADER VINEYARDS

VON STRASSER WINERY

*In Sonoma the Dry Creek General Store, built in 1881, is still the valley's favorite hangout. Within a few miles are dozens of wineries famous for zinfandel.*

## Merlot

The reputation of merlot in California far exceeds the quality of most of the wines. In fact, despite the old saw about merlot being softer than cabernet sauvignon, many California versions are about as soft as stiletto heels. Much of the problem has to do with where the grape is planted. Thanks to high demand from the 1990s on, merlot has often been planted indiscriminately, regardless of the true suitability of the vineyard.

The great merlots from top vineyards, however, are magnificent and hedonistic wines. Densely concentrated and very plush, these wines can be captivating.

*Some of the Best Merlot Producers*

AZALEA SPRINGS

BERINGER VINEYARDS

CAFARO CELLARS

CHATEAU ST. JEAN WINERY AND VINEYARDS

CUVAISON WINERY

DUCKHORN VINEYARDS

DURNEY VINEYARDS

LAMBERT BRIDGE WINERY

LIPARITA CELLARS

MARKHAM WINERY

MATANZAS CREEK WINERY

PARADIGM

PRIDE MOUNTAIN VINEYARDS

ROBERT SINSKEY VINEYARDS

STAGS' LEAP WINERY

SWANSON VINEYARDS AND WINERY

649

## Pinot Noir

California pinot noir has been on a fast learning curve, getting significantly more nuanced and more delicious year by year. This is no small achievement for pinot noir is one of the most sensitive grapes in the world. Everything done or not done to it, every aspect of viticulture and winemaking, seems to show through in the flavor of the final wine.

The styles of California pinot differ considerably from producer to producer.

Still, on the whole, California pinot noirs are fairly dependable, especially in comparison to Burgundies, which are the vinous equivalents of manic-depressives (very high quality or very low; not much stuff in the middle). However, the flavor of pinot noir—no matter where it's grown—can vary considerably from vintage to vintage.

*Some of the Best
Pinot Noir Producers*

ACACIA WINERY

ANCIEN

AU BON CLIMAT

BABCOCK VINEYARDS

CALERA WINE COMPANY

CARNEROS CREEK WINERY

DAVID BRUCE WINERY

DAVIS BYNUM WINERY

DOMAINE CARNEROS

ETUDE WINES

FLOWERS VINEYARD AND WINERY

FOXEN VINEYARD

GARY FARRELL WINES

HANZELL VINEYARDS

HARTLEY OSTINI

IRON HORSE VINEYARDS

JOSEPH SWAN VINEYARDS

J. ROCHIOLI VINEYARDS AND WINERY

LITTORAI WINES

LYNMAR WINERY

ROBERT MONDAVI WINERY

ROBERT MUELLER CELLARS

SAINTSBURY

SANTA BARBARA WINERY

STEELE WINES

TALLEY VINEYARDS

WILLIAMS-SELYEM WINERY

## Zinfandel

Until cabernet sauvignon superseded it in 1998, zinfandel was the most widely planted red grape in California. Although a large percentage of these grapes are turned into slightly sweet, mild tasting, inexpensive white zinfandels, the very best grapes are made into the real stuff: jammy, mouthwatering, big-fruited dry red zinfandels that can be as lovable and irresistible as puppies.

Some of the most prized vineyards in California are those planted with old zinfandel vines. These gnarled, twisted vines have low productivity, but the grapes often make for wines of amazing richness and depth. Though the term old vines has no legal definition, if you see it on a label it generally signifies that the wine came from vineyards in continual production for at least forty years and sometimes more than a hundred.

While zinfandel is often called America's grape (no place in Europe produces a wine by that name), it is of European descent. In the late 1990s DNA testing revealed that zinfandel is the same as the Italian grape primitivo, although curiously, historical records indicate that zinfandel arrived in California before primitivo arrived in Italy. Further DNA testing revealed that zinfandel (primitivo) is closely related to the grape plavac mali and probably originated on the Dalmatian Coast of Croatia.

*Some of the Best
Zinfandel Producers*

A. RAFANELLI WINERY

BALLENTINE VINEYARDS

CHATEAU POTELLE

E. & J. GALLO

EBERLE WINERY

ELYSE WINERY

FIFE VINEYARDS

GRANITE SPRINGS WINERY

GREEN & RED VINEYARD

HARTFORD COURT WINERY

HENDRY

JOSEPH SWAN VINEYARDS

LAVA CAP WINERY

LOLONIS WINERY

MARIAH VINEYARDS

MINER FAMILY VINEYARDS

MONTEVINA WINERY

PEACHY CANYON WINERY

RAVENSWOOD WINERY

RIDGE VINEYARDS AND WINERY

ROSENBLUM CELLARS

ST. FRANCIS VINEYARDS
AND WINERY

STEELE WINES

STORYBOOK MOUNTAIN
VINEYARDS

SUTTER HOME WINERY

TURLEY WINE CELLARS

651

or from a blend of different varieties. Red Rhône blends are generally composed of syrah, grenache, mourvèdre, and/or carignane. White Rhône blends, which are not as common, are most often made up of viognier, marsanne, and roussanne. Blended wines are given proprietary names, such as Le Cigare Volant from Bonny Doon and Le Mistral from Joseph Phelps Vineyards. Rhône-style rosés (some of the most exciting of any rosés made in California) can be blends of several varieties, but grenache usually plays the dominant role.

*Some of the Best Producers of
Rhône-Style Wines*

ALBAN VINEYARDS

ANDREW MURRAY VINEYARDS

BONNY DOON VINEYARD

CALERA WINE COMPANY

DOMAINE DE LA TERRE ROUGE

EBERLE WINERY

EDMUNDS ST. JOHN

FIFE VINEYARDS

JOSEPH PHELPS VINEYARDS

LA JOTA VINEYARD

MCDOWELL VALLEY VINEYARDS

OJAI VINEYARD

QUPÉ WINE CELLARS

THACKERY & CO.

ZACA MESA WINERY

## Rhône-Style Wines

California wines based on grapes native to France's Rhône Valley have become some of the most successful new reds, whites, and rosés in the state. The red and white wines are made from a single grape variety—the red grape syrah or the white grape viognier, for example—

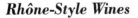

## SPARKLING SIBLINGS AND FIZZY FAMILIES

Here's how California's sparkling wine companies relate to some well-known European houses.

**Domaine Carneros**
Taittinger, France; co-owner

**Domaine Chandon**
Moët Hennessy Louis Vuitton, France; owner (also owns Moët & Chandon and Veuve Clicquot)

**Gloria Ferrer Champagne Caves**
Freixenet, Spain; owner

**Iron Horse Vineyards**
Laurent-Perrier, France; partner

**Pacific Echo**
Moët Hennessy Louis Vuitton, France; owner (also owns Moët & Chandon and Veuve Clicquot)

**Piper Sonoma**
Rémy Martin, France; owner

**Roederer Estate**
Louis Roederer, France; owner

*Some of the Best California Sparkling Wine Houses*

DOMAINE CARNEROS

DOMAINE CHANDON

GLORIA FERRER CHAMPAGNE CAVES

IRON HORSE VINEYARDS

JORDAN J WINE COMPANY

MUMM NAPA VALLEY

PACIFIC ECHO

ROEDERER ESTATE

SCHRAMSBERG VINEYARDS

I'm talking here of the best California sparkling wines made by the *méthode champenoise*, in which the fermentation that causes the bubbles takes place inside each individual bottle. By contrast, inexpensive, basic fizzies, such as André, Tott's, and Cook's are made in large tanks by the easier, faster, cheaper Charmat process. These are definitely not in the same class.

For the best California sparklers the path to excellence was neither simple nor straightforward. The story begins in Sonoma in the mid-1890s when three brothers, Czechoslovakian immigrants named Korbel, made California's first sparkling wines. Old ledgers indicate that the Korbels used several grapes, including chasselas, riesling, traminer, and muscatel, and that they made their sparkling wine by the Champagne method.

Despite this promising beginning, the period from Prohibition to the 1960s was a kind of Dark Ages for California sparkling wine. Most of the sparklers produced were cheap, frothy Charmat method wines. Only Korbel and the Napa Valley winery Hanns Kornell continued to make *méthode champenoise* sparklers. But with the founding of the then tiny Schramsberg

## Sparkling Wines

Many wine drinkers assume that no matter how good a California sparkling wine is, a French Champagne will always be better. On this point, many wine drinkers are wrong. Admittedly, the great Champagnes are masterpieces, and once upon a time no other sparklers came even close to matching them in elegance and appeal. But it's simply no longer true that California sparkling wines are lower-rank substitutes. In fact, the quality of the top California sparkling wines is now so high that one can only think of them as Champagne's peers. Different in flavor, yes, but definitely not second-class.

# CALIFORNIAN SPARKLERS
# AND FRENCH CHAMPAGNE

—◁◈▷—

The temptation to compare California sparkling wines and French Champagnes is inevitable. Here is a look at how the two types of wine are made, the styles in which they are produced, the aging each undergoes, and a host of other factors that influence how each tastes.

With Champagne many of these factors are mandated by law, which is not the case in California. This chart features California's *méthode champenoise* producers; it does not consider wines made by the Charmat (bulk) process, such as those of André, Cook's, or Tott's.

|  | CALIFORNIA | FRANCE |
|---|---|---|
| **Winemaking Technique** | *Méthode champenoise* | *Méthode champenoise* |
| **Grapes** | Chardonnay, pinot noir, and occasionally pinot meunier and pinot blanc* | Chardonnay, pinot noir, and pinot meunier |
| **Types of Sparkling Wine** | Nonvintage with some vintage and prestige *cuvée* wines | Virtually all firms make nonvintage and, in exceptional years, vintage and prestige *cuvée* wines |
| **Styles of Wine** | Golden, *blanc de blancs*, rosé, and *blanc de noirs* | Golden, *blanc de blancs*, and rosé |
| **Degrees of Sweetness** | Levels not regulated by law but most top producers follow the European standard for brut and extra dry. Other levels are rarely made. | Brut: less than 1.5% sugar Extra dry: 1.2 to 2% sugar Sec: 1.7 to 3.5% sugar Demi-sec: 3.35 to 5% sugar Doux: more than 5% sugar |
| **Number of Wines in a Nonvintage Blend** | Approximately 20 to 60 depending on the winery | Generally 30 to 60, depending on the winery |
| **Number of Different Years in a Nonvintage Blend** | Usually 1 to 2 years | Usually 4 to 6 years |
| **Length of Aging on Yeasts Before Release** | 18 months to 6 years, depending on the winery and type of wine | 15 months minimum for nonvintage; 3 years minimum for vintage; prestige *cuvée* are commonly aged for up to 7 years |
| **Yearly Production** | Approximately 2 million cases | Approximately 20.5 million cases |
| **Source of Grapes** | Most firms grow a substantial amount of their grapes | Most firms buy the majority of their grapes from the region's 15,000 growers |
| **Vineyard Climate** | Generally cool | Cool |
| **Soil** | Varies considerably depending on the vineyard | Mainly chalk |

*Korbel, the exception to most other California méthode champenoise winemakers, uses chardonnay, pinot noir, chenin blanc, and French colombard grapes.*

653

winery in the mid-1960s, a new age for California sparkling wine dawned. The first Schramsberg wines were made with chardonnay—a grape that was scarce in the 1960s. Schramsberg's sparklers quickly outclassed every other California sparkling wine being made.

Schramsberg's sparklers and the emerging fine wines of California in general did not go unnoticed by the Champenois themselves. Not only were certain parts of California well suited to chardonnay and pinot noir, but land in California—unlike land in Champagne—was both available and affordable. (Champagne is a delimited area. Virtually all of the best land has already been planted, and vineyards rarely come up for sale.) In 1973 the famous Champagne house Moët & Chandon purchased 200 acres in the Napa Valley and, with an initial 2.5 million dollar investment, established Domaine Chandon. The ball was set in motion. Over the next fifteen years, some half dozen of the top Champagne firms plus the world's two largest sparkling wine firms—the Spanish giants Freixenet and Codorníu—would set up joint ventures or subsidiaries in California. There are now more than thirty wineries in California that make *méthode champenoise* sparkling wine, including many firms that specialize in both sparkling and still wines (examples of the latter include Iron Horse, Jordan, and Wente).

So what makes the best California sparkling wines distinctive, and why did they improve dramatically in quality in the 1980s and 1990s? Their specialness is based on their finesse, clarity, nuance, and focus. Contrary to what is often written, the finest California sparklers are not heavily fruity (considered a fault in a sparkling wine) but instead often have a gossamer lightness and purity of flavor. What you won't find as much of in most California sparklers, however—which you will in Champagne—is an evocative biscuity, bread doughy, yeasty quality.

The rapid improvement in quality was based on two factors. First, a shift in the location of vineyards away from warm areas and toward distinctly cool places, such as Carneros and the Anderson Valley. And second, a move away from using

## THE SPIRITS OF CALIFORNIA

The best of California's brandies, grappas, and eaux-de-vie are made by a small group of distillers known as the Artisan Distillers of California. These distillers handcraft their products in tiny lots, using traditional European methods, alembic stills, and extremely high quality fruit, including heirloom varieties of apples, peaches, pears, and naturally, grapes.

Some examples not to be missed: Germain-Robin brandy (the single finest brandy from the United States and one that could best most Cognacs) and the vividly sensual grappas and eaux-de-vie from Bonny Doon Vineyard and St. George Spirits.

## WHAT'S IN A YEAR?

—⚘⚘⚘—

In general, vintages matter less in California than they do in Europe. The state's benevolent, fairly uniform climate means that California wines are, for the most part, dependably good year after year. This doesn't mean that a producer's wines taste the same every year or that you'll like every vintage of every wine equally well. The point is simply that truly miserable vintages are not something most California wine drinkers have to worry about coming across.

Unlike many wine regions in the Old World, California's wine regions are usually threatened neither by rain during the harvest (potentially waterlogging or rotting the grapes), nor by severe frost during the spring (possibly killing the fragile young shoots), nor by short cool summers (mak-ing full ripening virtually impossible). Nature tends to be on a Californian wine-maker's side.

When a California wine does seem to change a lot from one year to the next, it's often for reasons other than climate. The producer may have lost an important source of grapes. Or, in the most ironic scenario of all, maybe the wine was so successful the producer decided to make more of it, necessitating buying grapes from other, less ideal vineyard areas to blend with the best grapes. (This very phenomenon resulted in a small ocean of mediocre merlot in the late 1990s.) Thus, in any given year, the character of some wines may deteriorate somewhat, though the reverse happens too, and every year some wines prove surprisingly good.

Champagne as a role model for making California sparkling wines. Ironically, once California sparkling winemakers stopped applying precisely the same philosophy and principles used in Champagne and made wines based on their own experience and instincts, the wines improved.

So, what's particular to California sparkling wine?

• California's benevolent climate (unlike the more marginal climate in Champagne) allows vintage sparkling wines to be made every year. As a result, several California sparkling wine firms vintage date all their wines. Other California firms follow the traditional French practice of making nonvintage wines.

• The top California sparkling wines, like the top Champagnes, achieve their nuance and complexity through blending. The best California sparklers are blends of from twenty to sixty separate still wines. The goal of blending this many wines is to marry them in such a way that they do not cancel each other out but, rather, coalesce into a compelling, synergistic whole. It is an amazingly difficult skill, which in California, as in Champagne, requires years of experience to master. (Most of the finest California sparkling wine firms make only brut—very dry—wines. Sweeter styles of sparkling wine, such as extra dry or demi-sec, are made by only a handful of these wineries.)

• In addition to a regular bottling, many California sparkling wine firms also make a *blanc de blancs* (literally, white from whites), made entirely from char-donnay grapes, and/or a *blanc de noirs* (white from blacks; red grapes are often referred to as black in France), made

## Up, Up, and Away

⚬⚬

California vineyards are pastoral from the ground, but from the air, they are striking—often set off against a breathtaking backdrop of coastal mountains, volcanoes, and the sparkling Pacific. There are several companies that offer vineyard tours by air, via plane, helicopter, glider, or balloon. Some have fixed packages and rates, others tailor tours to the customer's interests. Here are a few of them.

**Above the Wine Country Balloons and Tours**
2508 Burnside Road
Sebastopol, CA 95472
(800) 759-5638

**Bravo Helicopters**
3401 Airport Drive
Torrance, CA 90505
(310) 325-9565

**Bridgeford Flying Service**
Napa County Airport
2030 Airport Road
Napa, CA 94558
(707) 224-0887

**Crazy Creek Soaring**
P.O. Box 575
18896 Grange Road
Middletown, CA 95461
(707) 987-9112

entirely from the red grape pinot noir, sometimes with a small amount of the red grape pinot meunier blended in.

• Several California sparkling wine firms also make a top-of-the-line sparkling wine that would be equivalent to a prestige *cuvée* in Champagne. Among these are Roederer Estate's L'Ermitage, Mumm Napa Valley's DVX, Domaine Chandon's Etoile, Schramsberg's J. Schram, and Domaine Carneros' Le Rêve.

## *Dessert and Port-Style Wines*

California's dessert wines and Port-style wines are like gems kept hidden in the jewelry box. Quietly over the last few decades, while seemingly few people were taking notice, some have become simply extraordinary.

**Dessert wines** in California generally fall into one of three broad groups:

• Botrytized wines made from sauvignon blanc and sémillon, and modeled on Sauternes

• Late harvest wines, usually made from riesling

• Wines from the muscat family of grapes, modeled on southern French and Italian dessert wines

**Sauternes-style wines** are rare and very difficult to make in California since the state tends to be either too dry and hot or too cool for the perfect formation of the noble rot, *Botrytis cinerea.* However, in 1957 Beringer's famous winemaker Myron Nightingale made California's first botrytis induced sweet wine by inoculating already harvested grapes with botrytis spores in a laboratory. Today one of California's most devastatingly luscious dessert wines is Beringer Vineyards Nightingale made from botrytis-inoculated sémillon and sauvignon blanc grapes. Because it is still handcrafted much in the way Nightingale himself made the first such wine, only sixty to three hundred cases of half-bottles are made each year.

**Late harvest rieslings** are generally made by letting the grapes hang for an extended period of time on the vine and then stopping the wine's fermentation early, thereby leaving some natural sweetness in the wine. Truly great late harvest

## HOW TO MARRY RICH

From Thanksgiving well into the winter, when much of America is dining on the sort of hearty roasts and hot stews that could easily figure into a Dickens novel, Californians are feasting on a wholly West Coast indulgence: huge Dungeness crabs. Accompanied by crusty loaves of sourdough bread and washed down with glasses of cold chardonnay, Dungeness crab may well be the best use California chardonnay is ever put to. Though there are more than 4,000 species of crabs in the world (and more of these live off the coasts of North America than anyplace else), there are only a few that serious eaters need to know about, and the most delicious among these is arguably the Dungeness, 38 million pounds of which are landed on average every year. More than 20 percent meat by weight and weighing about four pounds each, Dungeness crabs are prized for their pure, succulent, sweet flavor. As a result, they're often served cold with nothing more than warm melted butter as a dipping sauce. Which is where chardonnay comes in. Rich, buttery, and yes, sweet on its own, chardonnay's flavors mirror a lump of butter-drenched crabmeat like no other wine can. The best chardonnays of all in this regard are those that aren't massively oaky. It's hard to taste the ocean if all you can smell is a lumberyard.

rieslings are, like botrytized wines, exceptionally hard to make (many turn out to be dull sweetish wines without verve, grip, real lushness, or complexity). The best are two of the most scrumptious dessert wines in all of California—Navarro Vineyards' Cluster Select Late Harvest White Riesling (made only in exceptional years from grapes grown in the Anderson Valley, which is sometimes humid enough for botrytis to occur) and Chateau St. Jean Special Select Late Harvest Johannisberg Riesling from the renowned Belle Terre Vineyard also in the Alexander Valley.

**Southern French and Italian dessert wines** are the inspiration for the utterly easy to love, wonderfully delicious dessert wines made from muscat grapes. Muscat is actually a large ancient family of grape varieties that were spread throughout the Mediterranean by the Phoenicians and Greeks. In California the leading muscat varieties are muscat canelli, orange muscat, and black muscat. All muscat grapes are known for their captivating aromas.

Muscat wines are usually not quite as syrupy or voluptuous as other dessert wines but, instead, are riotously fresh and full of racy mandarin orange, melon, and apricot flavors. They are some of the most charming (if underappreciated) sweet wines from the state. The leading California wineries for world-class muscats are Quady and Bonny Doon. In 1980 Quady produced a sweet orange muscat called Essensia and then in 1983 a black muscat called Elysium. Each is an epiphany of pleasure. Similarly, Bonny Doon's muscats are so luscious they can make you weak-kneed. Try Bonny Doon's muscat Vin de Glacière, a study in elegance, and Bonny Doon's Ca' del Solo Moscato del Solo, a fizzy geyser of orange blossoms and apricots.

**California Port-style wines** are a mixed bag. In the past, many were simply inexpensive syrupy-sweet wines made from rather poor quality, overripe grapes. While such "ports" still exist, the best California Port-style wines are made by a

657

handful of wineries that generally use traditional Portuguese grape varieties, such as touriga nacional, tinta cão, and tinta roriz. There are also, however, some excellent examples made from zinfandel and petite sirah. Again, Quady is the leader, with a magnificently rich, citrusy, mocha-y Port called—playfully—Starboard. (The United States government allows vintners to use the word Port, even though most other countries refrain from the designation out of respect for Portuguese law which stipulates that true Port can only come from the geographically delimited region of the Douro Valley in Portugal.)

## THE VINEYARDS AND MAJOR WINE REGIONS

Californian vineyards themselves are immensely varied. Many are viticulturally state-of-the-art and equipped with, among other devices, computerized sensors to track such environmental information as the moisture in the soil. Only the high-tech vineyards of Australia and New Zealand can rival California's sophisticated vineyard designs and multiple trellising systems. At the same time, you can go to many California wine regions and

still find vineyards with old zinfandel vines (dating back to the 1940s or earlier) standing—not trellised—looking like solitary Rumpelstiltskins with thick, craggy trunks and long tresses of leaves that sprout from the heads of the vines and fall to the ground. (Though old-vine vineyards can be difficult to care for and usually give smaller crops, many are nonetheless prized because the grapes they do yield usually have a highly concentrated flavor. Thus many old vineyards are not taken out and replanted using modern techniques, even though those techniques are certainly well known and widely used.)

What follows is a look at the major wine regions of California. (California has some 81 American Viticultural Areas. They can be large or tiny, and some AVAs are located within others.) After exploring the familiar regions of Napa Valley, Sonoma County, and Carneros, we'll travel more or less north to south through Mendocino and Lake counties, the Sierra Foothills (Amador and El Dorado counties), Livermore Valley, the northern Central Coast (from the San Francisco Bay south to and including Monterey), and the middle and southern Central Coast (from Paso Robles south to the Santa Ynez Valley).

## NAPA VALLEY

About 55 miles northeast of San Francisco, the Napa Valley is California's best-known and most renowned wine region, even though it is responsible for an astoundingly small amount of all the wine produced in the state—just 4 percent. Its fame (and infamy) is derived from an eventful commingling of history and humanity. For almost a century and a half, the valley has attracted a major-

ity of the most ambitious, dashing, and outspoken vintners in the United States.

Where else but in the Napa Valley would a palatial wine estate (Inglenook) be built by an adventurous Finnish sea captain named Gustave Niebaum and sold more than a hundred years later to a superstar film director named Francis Ford Coppola? Where else but in the Napa Valley would an Olympian monolith called Opus

One be built by two of the world's leading vintners, Robert Mondavi and Baron Philippe de Rothschild? Where else but in the Napa Valley would the first California wine to cost $100 a bottle be made, not to mention the first to cost $200? (The wines are Diamond Creek Cabernet Sauvignon Lake Vineyard 1987 and 1992, respectively.) Where else but in the Napa Valley would the world's largest charity wine auction be held, raising millions of dollars ($9.5 million in 2000) each year?

Critics say Napa Valley has an ego. But what it really has is a gargantuan appetite for life and a palpable hunger for success. You can taste it in the wines. While the Napa Valley is not the only California region to make great wine, it consistently makes a good share of the most polished, classy, and complex wines in the state. The Napa Valley's reputation as the premier wine region in the United States is, however, not due solely to the quality of its wines and the hard-driving will of its vintners. Some of the credit must also be given to the relentless prophesying of a single man—Robert Mondavi, patriarch of the Robert Mondavi Winery and tireless crusader for California's place in the wine empyrean. Mondavi, whose father sold grapes to home winemakers during Prohibition, constantly rejected a second-place status for California behind the great wine regions of Europe. His credo that California wines belong in the company of the greatest wines of the world would eventually become—in the Napa Valley at least—not a goal, but a given.

*The Napa Valley was once home to many thousands of Wappo Indians, even though there is almost no trace of an Indian population in the valley today. The word* napa *comes from the Wappo dialect and means plenty.*

*One of two identical, and often photographed, signs welcoming visitors to the Napa Valley. When the first welcome sign was erected in 1950, it was probably more than a little presumptuous to suggest that the valley was* world famous. *The "bottled poetry" quote comes from Robert Louis Stevenson.*

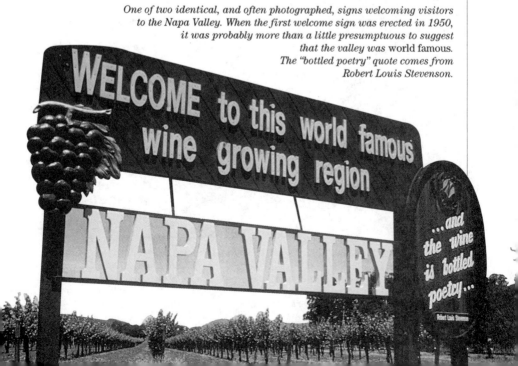

The valley proper is small and neatly framed. Stretching 30 miles long and ranging between 1 and 5 miles wide, it begins at a bay, ends at a volcano (Mount St. Helena), and is flanked on each side by mountain ranges. The Napa Valley wine region, however, extends beyond these borders to incorporate parts of the mountains themselves and smaller valleys nestled high up in the mountains. Though the main valley looks geographically uniform, nothing could be further from the truth. The volcanic eruptions that occurred here two million years ago have left the valley with almost three dozen different soil types belonging to eight of the twelve major soil classifications found worldwide. The ground itself is also subtly irregular, with numerous benches, terraces, canyons, and fans that have been carved out or pushed up from the valley floor. This geologic potpourri coupled with highly independent winemaking styles

## MUD BATHS

—◦◦◦—

Calistoga, the northernmost town in the Napa Valley, is famous for its spas specializing in mud baths. The mud, which is rich in volcanic ash, contains minerals and sea salts reported to detoxify and regenerate the body (a welcome concept for tourists who find they've been a bit overenthusiastic in their visits to the valley's numerous wineries and restaurants). The first Calistoga spa offering mud baths, Indian Springs, opened in 1860 and is still in operation.

means that wine estates next door to one another often make wines that taste totally different.

The valley's geologic diversity is underscored by its variable climate. A person

660

*Born in 1913, Robert Mondavi has been one of Napa Valley's, and California's, most ardent advocates. After a bitter split with his brother Peter in the late 1950s, Mondavi left Charles Krug Winery (which his family owned) and, in 1966, opened the Robert Mondavi Winery (seen above). Designed by California architect Cliff May, it was considered the epitome of modernity in what was then a very rural valley.*

standing at the southern end, which is open to the San Pablo Bay, might be pulling on a sweater at the very same minute someone in the north near Calistoga might be stripping down to a bathing suit. This said, much of the valley experiences the magical combination of days that are hot but not blistering and nights that are cool but not cold.

*Napa Valley was named an American Viticultural Area in 1983, making it the first AVA in California.*

Napa Valley vineyard land is thought to be the most expensive agricultural land in the United States. As of 2000, a single acre of planted vineyards in a prime location might cost as much as $130,000 or more. Vineyards cover roughly 37,000 acres of the 485,000 acres that comprise the valley.

Though the Napa Valley is planted with numerous varieties, no grape captures the soul of the valley better than cabernet sauvignon. Chardonnay, sauvignon blanc, merlot, and zinfandel can all become very good and occasionally brilliant wines in the Napa Valley, but the top cabernets are simply stellar. No other wine region in the country makes as many stunningly rich and complex cabernets year after year.

Some of these top-notch cabernet sauvignons aren't made exclusively from cabernet. Often small amounts of merlot, cabernet franc, petit verdot, and/or malbec—the so-called Bordeaux varieties—are blended in. (By law, the wine can still be called cabernet sauvignon as long as the other varieties make up less than 25 percent of the total wine.) These "not 100 percent" cabernets are often the most complex cabernet sauvignons of all.

## THE THRILL OF THE GRILL

California may not have a full-fledged cuisine of its own, but as any Californian knows, there's a style and sensibility to the local cooking that's unmistakable. Grilled lamb with raspberry-mango relish doesn't exactly have Massachusetts written all over it, any more than grilled avocado salad with pesto is evocative of Arkansas. No, when it comes to culinary personalities, California's is clear. Take, for instance, California's unofficial religion: grilling. From peaches to porterhouses, no food is exempt from this beloved technique. Grilling is also one of the best things that can happen to wine, especially red wine. (Well, not to it exactly.) The sweet, charred flavor and slightly crusty texture grilling imparts make any food more red wine willing. Which is why—warm weather be damned—oceans of red wine are drunk all summer long in California. Three types of reds underscore the flavors of grilled foods best: zinfandel, syrah, and petite sirah. Zinfandel's simple jammy fruitiness is an easygoing match for grilled vegetables, grilled chicken, even grilled cheese sandwiches, which à la California, really are grilled. Then there's syrah with its primal, peppery, earthy flavors just begging for grilled lamb or duck. As for petite sirah (don't be fooled by the name; there's nothing petite about it), the wine's massive structure and brooding, rustic, sensual flavors make it one of the best friends a grilled steak can have.

In 1974 this realization led Joseph Phelps Vineyards to take the concept of a blended cabernet one step further. With the idea of making the very best wine they

*An enduring Napa Valley symbol, Beringer Vineyards' Rhine House, built in 1884, is on the National Register of Historic Places. When it was constructed by German-born vintner and businessman Frederick Beringer, the medieval-inspired seventeen-room mansion with its gabled slate roof cost $28,000. Eight years earlier Frederick and his younger brother Jacob founded Beringer Vineyards, today the oldest continuously operated winery in the valley.*

could—even if that sometimes meant using far less than 75 percent cabernet—Phelps made the first Bordeaux blend. It was called Insignia. Several other top Napa Valley wineries followed suit, each giving their Bordeaux blend its own proprietary name. Today the Napa Valley is famous for such wines, collectively sometimes referred to as Meritage wines. Among the best are Opus One, Dominus, Rubicon, Trilogy, and, of course, Insignia.

## Napa Valley AVAs

In addition to the American Viticultural Area Napa Valley, there are thirteen smaller AVAs within the valley. The most important of these are Stags Leap District, Rutherford, Oakville, Spring Mountain

District, Mount Veeder, Howell Mountain, and Atlas Peak. The AVA Carneros, at the southern tip of the valley, straddles both Napa and Sonoma counties and is covered in the Carneros section (see page 677).

Stags Leap District, a small pocket of land, is named for what looms above it— majestic, sun-dappled outcroppings of tortured rock over which, as fable has it, stags have leapt to escape hunters. The vineyards have a more auspicious existence, sprawled as they are on the rocky foothills below. The district lies in the southern part of the Napa valley along the eastern flank and is known mainly for cabernet sauvignons from such leading wineries as Shafer, Stag's Leap Wine Cellars, Stags' Leap Winery, Silverado Vineyards, Chimney Rock, and Clos du Val.

The two separate AVAs of Rutherford and Oakville are, geologically speaking, large alluvial fans sitting side by side and spreading out north and south from the towns of Rutherford and Oakville, smack in the heart of the valley. An alluvial fan is a sloping mass of sediments deposited by a river where it issues from its canyon onto the valley floor. The Rutherford and Oakville fans are composed of deep gravelly and sandy clay loam soil. Some of the most famous and historic of all Napa wineries are found here, including Beaulieu Vineyard, Niebaum-Coppola (the former Inglenook property), Robert Mondavi, Opus One, Caymus, Cakebread Cellars, and Grgich Hills.

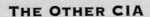

GRGICH HILLS

*Napa Valley*
CHARDONNAY

PRODUCED AND BOTTLED BY GRGICH HILLS CELLAR
RUTHERFORD, CA   ALC. 13.4% BY VOL. • CONTAINS SULFITES

Vines not only carpet the valley floor but are also sprinkled over both the Mayacamas mountain range on the west and the Vaca mountain range on the east. Some of the most famous, small viticultural areas within the Napa Valley are located on these mountains, including Mount Veeder and Spring Mountain on the Mayacamas range and Howell Mountain and Atlas Peak on the Vaca range. Napa's mountain vineyards are highly prized for the wines that come from them can be superbly concentrated yet elegant at the same time. At up to 2,000 feet in elevation, the grapes in these vineyards ripen slowly, yet because they are above the fog line, the vineyards are also drenched in sun for long hours each day.

Examples of quality Napa mountain wines are numerous and include the merlots from Beringer and the cabernet sauvignons from Dunn (both from Howell Mountain); the cabernets from Mayacamas and Mount Veeder Winery (from Mount Veeder); the cabernets from Diamond Creek (from Diamond Mountain, among the Napa Valley's most prestigious AVAs); plus Ridge's York Creek zinfandels and one of the most legendary of all California chardonnays, Stony Hill's (both from Spring Mountain).

663

## THE OTHER CIA

One of the most remarkable of the Napa Valley's many architecturally stunning wineries is Greystone. Built in 1889, it is the largest stone winery in the world and was the first winery in California with electricity.

Greystone was originally a cooperative. It sat vacant during Prohibition and later changed ownership four times before becoming the Christian Brothers winery in 1950. In 1992 it was donated to The Culinary Institute of America, commonly referred to as the CIA, and in 1995, after a 14-million-dollar renovation, became the school's West Coast center for culinary and wine education. The 30-acre campus, just north of the town of St. Helena, includes herb and vegetable gardens, a merlot vineyard, a restaurant, interactive classrooms, and teaching kitchens of unparalleled magnitude where chefs and food and wine experts from all over the world teach throughout the year.

*The Culinary Institute of America, 2555 Main Street, St. Helena, CA 94574; (800) 333-9242.*

## Visiting Napa Valley Wineries

The Napa Valley is a perfect wine region as far as touring is concerned. The wineries love visitors and have great tasting rooms and trained staffs to show you around. There are fabulous restaurants, including the restaurant many consider the single best in the United States: The French Laundry (6640 Washington Street,

CLOS PEGASE

Yountville, CA 94599; [707] 944-2380). The hotels and spas are wonderful for relaxing in after a day of tasting. And the valley itself can be awe inspiring in its beauty. As a result of all this, the Napa Valley is hardly undiscovered. Summertime in general, as well as weekends in September and October when the harvest draws near, means crowds, traffic, and restaurant reservations that can be difficult to come by. On the other hand, the valley is a joy to visit in the spring when the vines are beginning to flower and the number of visitors is far smaller. Since many Napa Valley wineries also have wonderful cultural events, concerts, art exhibits, cooking classes, and slide presentations, you may want to call ahead for a schedule of events. In particular, the art museums at the Hess Collection Winery and at Clos Pegase are not to be missed, and the Wine Discovery Center at St. Supery has terrific interactive educational exhibits. Many wineries now charge a small fee for tasting.

The Napa Valley Chamber of Commerce can provide information on events throughout the valley all year long. Call them at (707) 226-7455.

**BERINGER VINEYARDS**
2000 Main Street
St. Helena, CA 94574
(707) 963-7115

**CLOS PEGASE**
1060 Dunaweal Lane
Calistoga, CA 94515
(707) 942-4981

**DOMAINE CHANDON**
1 California Drive
Yountville, CA 94599
(707) 944-2280

**HESS COLLECTION WINERY**
4411 Redwood Road
Napa, CA 94558
(707) 255-1144

**ROBERT MONDAVI WINERY**
7801 St. Helena Highway
Oakville, CA 94562
(707) 963-9611

**STAG'S LEAP WINE CELLARS**
5766 Silverado Trail
Napa, CA 94558
(707) 944-2020

**ST. SUPÉRY VINEYARDS AND WINERY**
8440 St. Helena Highway
Rutherford, CA 94573
(707) 963-4507

**STERLING VINEYARDS**
1111 Dunaweal Lane
Calistoga, CA 94515
(707) 942-3344
The view from the tram to the winery is scenic.

STERLING VINEYARDS.

ESTATE GROWN & BOTTLED

# THE NAPA VALLEY
# WINES TO KNOW

*For each wine, the specific American Viticultural Area from which it comes is noted.*

## Sparkling Wine

**SCHRAMSBERG VINEYARDS**

J. Schram

prestige *cuvée*, vintage brut

Napa Valley

approximately 80% chardonnay,
20% pinot noir

J. Schram is the prestige *cuvée* (top of the line) of Napa's historic Schramsberg winery, credited with initiating in the mid-1960s California's modern era of sophisticated sparkling wines made by the Champagne method. J. Schram is rich, creamy, and refined, with the hauntingly beautiful aromas of freshly baked apple pies and loaves of bread straight from the oven. The wine is named for Jacob Schram who, in 1862, established Schramsberg, then the first winery on the hillsides of the Napa Valley.

## Whites

**MASON**

Sauvignon Blanc

Napa Valley

100% sauvignon blanc

Drinking this sauvignon blanc is like being in a lime tornado. First you are dazzled by a whirlwind of green flavors (in addition to that lime, there are green pepper, mint, snow peas, green plums, herbs) and then

the wine's exotic tropical flavors kick in. A very small producer, Mason makes wines that are about as bracingly fresh and clean, dramatic, and delicious as California sauvignon blanc gets.

**STONY HILL**

Chardonnay

Napa Valley

100% chardonnay

From Stony Hill's volcanic hillside vineyards come the Napa Valley's most legendary and historic chardonnay. When it was first made by novice winemakers Fred and Eleanor McCrea in the mid-1940s, chardonnay was virtually unknown in the valley. Their wine's reputation rests on its absolutely amazing ability to age. Stories abound of twenty-five- and thirty-year-old Stony Hill chardonnays that still tasted gorgeously bright thanks to the wine's exquisite acidity. Oblivious to fashion, Stony Hill makes its chardonnay not in an oaky, buttery style, but rather in a leaner, purer one.

## TREFETHEN
Chardonnay

Napa Valley

100% chardonnay

This is the Audrey Hepburn of chardonnays—graceful and timelessly classic. The beautifully wrought apple and cream flavors are not big, not fat, and not powerful, just elegant and very, very long. There are, of course, numerous chardonnays made in the Napa Valley that are bigger in style, but Trefethen, founded in 1968, has a long track record of making deliciously refined ones.

*Lunch alfresco in the gardens at Trefethen: Enjoying wine and food together has become an ineluctable part of the wine country lifestyle.*

# Reds

## BEAULIEU VINEYARD
Georges De Latour Private Reserve

Napa Valley

100% cabernet sauvignon

First made in 1936, Georges de Latour Private Reserve comes as close as any wine in the United States to being the equivalent of a Bordeaux First Growth. It is huge, concentrated, and massively structured, yet for all of this intensity, it remains, in most vintages, refined and gorgeously balanced. Rich cassis, plum, chocolate-covered-cherry, tobacco, and eucalyptus aromas and flavors carry over into a long, hedonistic finish.

## BERINGER VINEYARDS
Merlot

Bancroft Ranch

Howell Mountain

approximately 95% merlot, with cabernet sauvignon and cabernet franc

The textures of Beringer's red wines are so lavishly soft they could make you weak-kneed. None more so than the winery's justifiably famous Bancroft Ranch merlot that can feel as seamless and opulent as melted chocolate, even though it's one of the most powerfully structured merlots in California. The dazzling complex flavors change by the second—a mind teaser. Bancroft Ranch, at 1,800 feet atop Howell Mountain, is known for grapes that, like most mountain-grown fruit, have real intensity of flavor.

## JOSEPH PHELPS

Insignia

Napa Valley

usually 70% to 85% cabernet sauvignon, plus cabernet franc, merlot, and petit verdot

Since it was first made in 1974, Insignia has inspired a slew of extraordinary Bordeaux blends. And, when it's in top form, Insignia truly can be inspiring. Thick, black, and almost syrupy in its richness, the wine exudes opulent cassis, menthol, and chocolate flavors. Though it hardly seems possible for a wine this powerfully built, Insignia is also polished and elegant.

## PRIDE MOUNTAIN VINEYARDS

Merlot

Napa Valley

approximately 75% merlot, 25% cabernet sauvignon

The small, family-owned Pride Mountain Vineyards makes atom-dense, massive, black, rich, sassy merlots that are utterly irresistible. At their best, so packed are they with flavor that you feel as though you're drinking the pure essence of merlot. Given the wine's concentration, it's not surprising that the grapes come from vineyards atop Spring Mountain at 2,000 feet, growing in volcanic soil.

## SHAFER

Cabernet Sauvignon

Hillside Select

Stags Leap District

100% cabernet sauvignon

Year after year this is one of the truly extraordinary cabernets in all of California and a wine so impeccably balanced and sensual that it's impossible to resist. The texture is like cashmere; the flavors and aromas, a complex interplay of cassis, chocolate, leather, tobacco, espresso, and licorice. But it's the density and superb concentration of these flavors that's especially winning.

## STAG'S LEAP WINE CELLARS

Cabernet Sauvignon

S.L.V.

Napa Valley

approximately 95% cabernet sauvignon, 5% merlot

Warren Winiarski and his winemakers, including daughter Julia, are adamant about elegance; "power is not beauty." Their cabernets express the philosophy best, for they are restrained, graceful, and quiet. The sort of cabernets that don't shout at you; in fact, you have to listen carefully to hear them. In great years, the S.L.V. (Stag's Leap Vineyard) cabernet is a silky commingling of smoky, sweet cigar box and leather aromas and flavors infused with ripe cassis. The 1974  vintage of this wine was the one that beat out a slew of top Bordeaux in the famous Paris tasting of 1976. Before being planted with grapes in the early 1970s, the vineyard was a prune orchard.

## STAGS' LEAP WINERY

Petite Syrah

Napa Valley

100% petite sirah

Stags' Leap Winery has a cult following for its massive and hugely expressive petite

sirah (or, as they spell it, petite syrah). The rich, concentrated grapes for the wine come in part from a historic plot planted in 1939. Like the villain in a Victorian novel, this wine is dark, brooding, and dangerously delicious. Surrender now.

## SONOMA COUNTY

irectly north of San Francisco and bordering on the Pacific Ocean, Sonoma County has 1 million acres of land, making it more than two times bigger than its somewhat more famous next-door neighbor, the Napa Valley. Sonoma's size means, among other things, that the county is not a single, uniform place but rather, a geographic patchwork quilt of valleys, mountains, riverbeds, plains, and slight uplifts in the terrain known as benchlands. Within this shifting landscape are twelve viticultural areas that can be quite different in their nuances of climate and soil.

From a psychosocial and cultural standpoint, Sonoma County could not be more different from Napa. Vineyards were planted here as the nineteenth century dawned, well before they were planted in Napa, and many vintners and winemakers are members of old established farming families. An easygoing, down-home mentality pervades the region. People drive around in dusty pickups, no one puts on the ritz very much, and when Sonomans do get together, the talk is as likely to be about tractors as wine sales in Tokyo. There's as much cutting-edge wine stuff happening in Sonoma as anywhere. It's just that most Sonomans have never been on a mission to prove it to the world. Theirs is a more kicked-back, country style—and they seem to like it that way.

The county itself is beautifully pastoral and is often called California's Provence. Vineyards alternate with apple orchards, vegetable farms, redwood forests, dairies (cheese is a local specialty), sheep ranches, nurseries (including dozens of Christmas tree farms), and even aquaculture fisheries along the rugged coast. Sonoma boasts one

*Morning sun breaks through the fog in the Alexander Valley, sending temperatures rising. Cabernet sauvignon, seen here, thrives under these conditions.*

of the best bakeries west of the Mississippi (the Downtown Bakery in Healdsburg) and the first commercial shiitake mushroom farm in the United States.

A morning in Sonoma reveals why the region is special climatically. Soft white fog rises in massive banks off the coast and drifts inland, wrapping itself around mountains, filling the valleys and riverbeds with pillows of cool vapor. Sonoma is well known for the daily ebb and flow—almost a yin and yang—of fog and sunshine. Of course, areas closer to the coast tend to be somewhat cooler, while areas farther inland are warmer. But overall, what makes Sonoma Sonoma is its pendulum-like climate of warm days and cool nights, the classic scenario for grapes with the potential to mature evenly and fully.

Sonoma County is not known for one or two grape varieties in the way Napa is renowned for cabernet sauvignon or Amador County is noted for zinfandel. Instead, Sonoma's size and generally propitious climate coupled with its highly variable topography and changes in altitude mean that many different varieties do well here. Virtually every grape variety grown in California is grown someplace in Sonoma. Which place, of course, is the key. Over the last decade Sonoma's viticultural areas—like viticultural areas throughout much of California—have become increasingly specialized as vintners understand the fine points of matching grape variety to site. Today the Alexander Valley,

a warm interior valley, is prized for its soft cabernet sauvignons, and the county's cooler coastal areas, such as the Russian River Valley and Green Valley, are known for what, in great years, can be lusciously complex pinot noirs.

Sonoma County became, in the early 1800s, the first northern county to be planted with vineyards (grape growing having previously been centered around the Spanish missions near today's Los Angeles). According to some, those first Sonoma vineyards were not planted by Spaniards but by Russian fishermen who, around the beginning of the nineteenth century, hunted otters and seals and established a community on the coast near Fort Ross (said to be derived from their name for their homeland—Rossiya).

By the mid-1820s the Spanish were in on the act. Franciscan fathers planted

## TANGLED ROOTS

There are many legends concerning the origin of the name Sonoma. According to Arthur Dawson in *The Stories Behind Sonoma Valley Place Names*, the most frequent of these is that the word *sonoma* means valley of the moon. This was the translation given by General Mariano Vallejo, the Mexican commander of the northern territories in the 1840s when what is now California was conquered by the United States. Vallejo reportedly said that *sono* meant moon in Suisan, the language of a Native American tribe who lived not in Sonoma but in the Napa Valley. It appears that Vallejo may have simply liked the idea of this meaning, since the general wrote admiringly of how full moons seemed to rise and set several times over Sonoma's eastern hills. Then there's the Pinocchio version:

*sono* supposedly also means nose. As this legend goes, an Indian servant in the Vallejo household told of a time long before the Mexicans' arrival in California, when a baby with an especially large nose was born. The baby grew up to be chief of the tribe, and thus *sonoma* came to mean the land of Chief Big Nose. The most likely interpretation, according to Dawson, is based on the work of early-twentieth-century anthropologists who noted that *sonoma* is a common Wappo suffix appearing at the end of village names. The Wappo tribe is thought to have occupied Sonoma before being pushed out by other tribes and relocating in what became known as the Napa Valley. According to Laura Somersal, the last fluent speaker of Wappo, who died in 1990, *sonoma* meant abandoned camping place.

vineyards surrounding their northernmost mission, the Mission San Francisco Solano, which today still stands in the town of Sonoma. The missions were eventually to be appropriated by the Mexican government and soon thereafter, in 1850, the whole of California was annexed by the United States. During this time of political instability, cuttings from Sonoma's vines were planted throughout northern California.

*Buena Vista, founded in 1857, is one of Sonoma's oldest wineries.*

But Sonoma's role as the cradle of northern viticulture was to be even more solidly established once Agoston Haraszthy, the "Father of the California Wine Industry," arrived on the scene, the region having returned to political stability. Haraszthy —a cross between Indiana Jones, James Bond, and Thomas Jefferson—was a Hungarian wheeler-dealer who made and lost his fortune multiple times. Haraszthy thought big, and in 1857 he established Buena Vista, which with 300 acres of vineyards was the largest winery in the state at the time. One of Haraszthy's other coups

was to convince the nascent California legislature to send him to Europe, where he studied viticulture, ultimately returning to Sonoma in 1861 with 100,000 French, German, Spanish, and Italian vines. Haraszthy considered Sonoma a viticultural paradise, and his promotion of it was so effective that within a few years, land prices jumped from $6 to $150 an acre as waves of French, German, and Italian winemakers moved into the region.

Among the Italians who ultimately moved into Sonoma were a couple of brothers who, after reading a book on winemaking borrowed from the public library, went on to build America's best-known and largest wine brand—E. & J. Gallo. As poor, hardworking young men coming of age at the end of Prohibition, Ernest and Julio Gallo began their winery in the farm town of Modesto in California's hot Central Valley. Early on, however, the brothers became convinced that Sonoma was where the state's best wines would eventually be made. Year by year they bought increasing amounts of Sonoma grapes to use as top-flight blending material in their regular wines. By the time the Gallos launched their expensive, ultra-premium, small production wines in 1993 (a $60 cabernet and a $30 chardonnay), they owned 4,000 acres in Sonoma.

Sonoma County's long history lives on today in the old vineyards to be found there. Sonoma, along with the Sierra Foothills, is home to more old vineyards than any other wine region in California. Such vineyards are extremely special and historically important for they were planted with clones of grapes—especially clones of zinfandel—that have, as a result of more than a century's worth of natural adaptation, developed their own personalities and unique flavors.

*The Russian River winds through
numerous appellations in Sonoma County.*

## Sonoma County AVAs

Of the twelve AVAs within Sonoma County, the most important are the Alexander Valley, the Russian River Valley (within which are the smaller AVAs Green Valley and Chalk Hill), Dry Creek Valley, and Sonoma Valley (with its smaller AVA Sonoma Mountain). The AVA Carneros, which straddles both Sonoma and Napa counties, is included in a separate section later in this chapter (see page 677).

The Alexander Valley at the northern end of Sonoma County is a long, warm, inland corridor of vines. If you arrived there for the first time around 3 P.M. on a summer afternoon, you'd swear the valley was one of the hotter places in northern California. But you'd only be right until twilight. As night approaches, the valley cools down considerably thanks

to the Russian River (which runs through the valley) and the fog that snakes its way up and down the river's basin. Generally, the fog wallows along the river until it is burned off by the strong morning sun. This is cabernet sauvignon territory, although some powerful full-bodied chardonnays are also made here, including Marcassin's Gauer Vineyard Upper Barn chardonnay, Peter Michael's Mon Plaisir chardonnay, and Chateau St. Jean's Robert Young Vineyard chardonnay. Among the wineries that make top cabernet sauvignon from the Alexander Valley are Silver Oak and Geyser Peak.

After flowing down through the Alexander Valley, the Russian River makes a few hairpin turns and then starts flowing westward through the valley that takes its name. Most of the Russian River Valley and the smaller viticultural area inside it, Green Valley, is the opposite of the Alexander Valley. Generally speaking, these regions are quite cool (parts of both are less than 10 miles from the Pacific Ocean) and as a result, pinot noir and chardonnay are the prominent grape varieties, with chardonnay being capable of producing a more balanced, less fat style of wine here than in the warmer Alexander Valley.

Pinot noir, of course, is the bad boy of grapes—difficult, moody, generally inclined to get into trouble. But despite the grape's irascible nature, the pinots from this part of Sonoma can have real richness and complexity, as one sip of Williams-Selyem or J. Rochioli—pinots to die for—will attest. As for chardonnay, very good versions abound here, and those from Kistler can be spellbinding (the winery makes chardonnays from several AVAs within Sonoma County).

Given so much high-quality pinot noir and chardonnay, plus the region's cool temperature, it comes as no surprise that some of Sonoma County's finest sparkling wines, including the two best, those from Iron Horse and Jordan's J, are also made from Russian River or Green Valley grapes.

*Chateau St. Jean, established in 1973, was one of the first wineries in Sonoma to market wines from individual vineyards separately. By the late 1970s Chateau St. Jean was making seven chardonnays, each from a different vineyard.*

Though it seems entirely illogical, the cool Russian River Valley is also known for zinfandel, a warm-climate grape that grows in warm pockets that dot the valley. And cabernet sauvignon, another warm-climate grape, grows here too, especially in the small AVA of Chalk Hill, which is about 20 miles from the ocean.

Among the top wineries making wines from the Russian River Valley, Green Valley, and Chalk Hill areas are Chalk Hill Estate Vineyards and Winery, Chateau St. Jean, Davis Bynum, Gary Farrell, Hartford Court, Iron Horse, Joseph Swan, J. Rochioli, Kistler, Marimar Torres Estate, and Williams-Selyem.

Perhaps the most charming viticultural area of all in Sonoma County is Dry Creek Valley. Time seems to have stood still here. The gently rolling blond hills are dotted with old gnarled vines (there are many old vineyards) that lift their twisted black arms skyward as though they were imploring heaven. Due west of Alexander Valley, Dry Creek Valley is a zinfandel paradise. Other wines are made here—including some good cabernets and Rhône blends—but zinfandel is the variety through which the earth speaks most compellingly. Some Dry Creek zinfandels are big and meaty; others, soft and graceful. What the best of them share is a sensual richness of flavor that can be irresistible. Among the Dry Creek producers to look for: A. Rafanelli, Ferrari-Carano, Mazzocco, and Ridge.

• • •

"I can no more think of my own life without thinking of wine and wines and where they grew for me and why I drank them when I did and why I picked the grapes and where I opened the oldest procurable bottles, and all that, than I can remember living before I breathed."

—*M. F. K. Fisher*, Wine Is Life

*The writer M. F. K. Fisher lived in Glen Ellen, in a small house surrounded by vineyards, in the later part of her life.*

• • •

Finally, the AVA Sonoma Valley and its smaller AVA Sonoma Mountain are in the southern part of Sonoma County edged up against the Mayacamas Mountains. This is where viticulture in northern California began. Sonoma Valley is anything but your conventional valley. The topography, much of it spread over the foothills of the Mayacamas Mountains, rises and dips over knolls and glens with such fanciful names as Valley of the Moon and Glen Ellen (the winery Glen Ellen is named after the place). Sonoma Valley is a wonderful mishmash both geographically and climatically. Given the total variability of the region, many different varieties of grapes are grown here and made into a scrumptious grab bag of wines. Among the best things to taste are the cabernets from Laurel Glen, the zinfandels from Ravenswood, the pinot noirs from Hanzell, and the chardonnays from Kistler and Matanzas Creek.

*Modest-looking Arrowood Vineyards and Winery was begun in 1987 by superstar winemaker Richard Arrowood.*

## Visiting Sonoma Wineries

The wineries of Sonoma are not neatly lined up along a main road but, instead, are spread all over the county. Count on following lots of twisting country roads, and bring a good map. Often thought of as California's Provence, Sonoma County is also full of small towns that sell local cheeses, olive oils, honey, fruits, and vegetables. In particular, don't miss both Healdsburg and Sonoma, wonderful historic towns built around charming squares. And if you are interested in understanding the impact of viticulture on wine flavor, be sure to visit the Benziger Family Winery, which has what is possibly the state's best tour geared specifically to viticulture. In addition to the wineries listed, the California Welcome Center near Santa Rosa (easy to find since it's right off Highway 101) is well worth a visit. There you can get armfuls of information, watch videos on the vineyards, and taste lots of Sonoma County wines. *California Welcome Center, 5000 Roberts Lake Road, Rohnert Park, CA 94928; (707) 586-3795.*

**ARROWOOD VINEYARDS AND WINERY**
14347 Sonoma Highway
Glen Ellen, CA 95442
(707) 938-5170

**BENZIGER FAMILY WINERY**
1883 London Ranch Road
Glen Ellen, CA 95442
(707) 935-3000

**FERRARI-CARANO WINERY**
8761 Dry Creek Road
Healdsburg, CA 95448
(707) 433-6700

**IRON HORSE VINEYARDS**
9786 Ross Station Road
Sebastopol, CA 95472
(707) 887-1507

**MATANZAS CREEK WINERY**
6097 Bennett Valley Road
Santa Rosa, CA 95404
(707) 528-6464

*Ferrari-Carano's visitor's center: The winery, owned by lawyer-turned-casino-owner-turned-vintner Don Carano and his wife, Rhonda, was named in part for Carano's maternal grandmother, Amelia Ferrari.*

# THE SONOMA COUNTY WINES TO KNOW

*For each wine, the specific American Viticultural Area from which it comes is noted.*

## Sparkling Wine

**IRON HORSE**

Wedding Cuvée

vintage brut

Green Valley

mostly pinot noir

Look to Iron Horse for some of the snappiest sparkling wines in

California, including their delicious Wedding Cuvée. Originally created in 1980 for the marriage of one of the owners, Wedding Cuvée has become a favorite sparkler for couples all over the United States. In most years it is made entirely from pinot noir.

## Whites

**ARROWOOD**

Viognier

Saralee's Vineyard

Russian River Valley

100% viognier

Viognier—more sensual and more feminine than chardonnay—is relatively new on the

scene in California and it's proving compelling. Arrowood gives you one of the finest examples. At its finest this wine has the poise and elegance of Katharine Hepburn. Its flavors are a tropical symphony of honeysuckle, muscat, guava, litchi, and lime. Arrowood is owned by the Robert Mondavi Winery.

**674**

**LITTORAI**

Chardonnay

Mays Canyon

Russian River Valley

100% chardonnay

After years spent in Burgundy working as a winemaker at such prestigious estates as Domaine Dujac and Domaine Georges Roumier, Littorai owner and winemaker Ted Lemmon comes as close as anyone in California to making chardonnays with the refinement and richness of white Burgundies. In particular, the Mays Canyon chardonnay, from a cool-climate vineyard just 8 miles from the Pacific Coast, has a lush creaminess that you can't say no to. Most amazing though is the wine's beautiful and seamless integration. Unlike many California chardonnays, the oak and alcohol are never obvious. The word *littorai* is derived from the Latin word *litor,* coast.

**PETER MICHAEL WINERY**

Chardonnay

Mon Plaisir

Sonoma County

100% chardonnay

Peter Michael has a stellar reputation for its four separate chardonnays, each from a different vineyard, the most lovely of which is often the Mon Plaisir (my pleasure). The grapes for this wine come from a small mountain vineyard on the well-regarded Gauer Ranch high above the Alexander Valley. In top years it is hauntingly elegant and seamless, with rich, high-definition fruit. A chardonnay of exquisite style.

# *Reds*

## A. RAFANELLI
Zinfandel

Dry Creek Valley

mostly zinfandel with a touch of petite sirah

The Rafanelli family's zinfandels have a way, over time, of making you crave them. The best are deep, generous, totally alive with flavor, and have a sensual softness that you could lose yourself in. The Rafanellis own zinfandel vineyards that have been in existence for close to a century.

## CHATEAU ST. JEAN
Cabernet Sauvignon

Cinq Cépages

Sonoma County

approximately 75% cabernet sauvignon plus small amounts of merlot, cabernet franc, malbec, and petit verdot

Massive and dense, Chateau St. Jean's Cinq Cépages (French for five grape varieties) is a powerful, penetrating wine with deep cassis flavors and leathery aromas. At top form Cinq Cépages can be so concentrated and have such forceful tannin that it needs several years of aging before it tastes harmonious. Ah, but then . . .

## ERNEST AND JULIO GALLO
Cabernet Sauvignon

Northern Sonoma

Sonoma County

approximately 80% cabernet sauvignon, 10% cabernet franc, and 10% merlot

The family-owned firm of E. & J. Gallo, the best-known and largest wine company in the United States, made its reputation on easy-drinking jug wines. But in the 1980s the company also began to make relatively small quantities of fine wines from their best vineyards in Sonoma. This estate cabernet sauvignon from northern Sonoma is the star in the Gallo galaxy. Saturated and rich, with dense earthy-leathery fruit, it's a wine with terrific power and focus. The texture, rustically supple, is winning. This is also Gallo's most expensive wine. As of the late 1990s, it cost $65 a bottle.

## FOPPIANO VINEYARDS
Petite Sirah

Russian River Valley

100% petite sirah

One of the most intense petite sirahs in Sonoma is made by the Foppianos, a historic Italian winemaking family that has been making this wine since 1896, when the winery was founded. The Foppiano petites are often proportioned like a sumo wrestler—big powerhouses with loads of muscular tannin and a well-endowed body. Think steak.

## GEYSER PEAK
Shiraz

reserve

Alexander Valley

approximately 90% syrah, with small amounts of petite sirah

In great years this is one howling fruit bomb of a wine. A purple-black concatenation of berries—totally teeth staining. Geyser Peak could have called this wine syrah but decided instead to call it by the grape's Australian name—shiraz (two of the winery's winemakers are Australian). It was a good choice, for this lip-smacking wine is every bit as saturated and supple as a top Aussie shiraz.

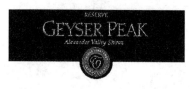

675

## J. ROCHIOLI

Pinot Noir

West Block;

reserve

Russian River Valley

100% pinot noir

Generally one of the most massive, saturated, and intense pinot noirs in Sonoma, Rochioli's reserve, with its opulent, dark, almost brooding berry flavors and utterly supple texture, can be a mindblower. The Rochioli family has been growing grapes in Sonoma since the 1930s, but it wasn't until the 1980s that they began making their own wines. The West Block of their estate vineyard—about 500 yards from the Russian River—is where the most concentrated lots of their pinot noir come from.

## RIDGE

Zinfandel

Geyserville

Sonoma County

approximately 75% zinfandel, with small amounts of carignan, petite sirah, and mourvèdre

Year after year, Ridge makes some of the most polished, refined, and beautifully balanced zinfandels in California. There are five different designations of them: Geyserville (Anderson Valley), Lytton Springs (Dry Creek Valley), Paso Robles (Paso Robles), Pagani Ranch (Sonoma Valley), and York Creek (Napa Valley). Of the five, the Geyserville—packed with sweet brambly boysenberry fruit—is often the most captivating, and the Pagani Ranch—soaring with violets and rich black raspberries and cherries—the most seductive.

## SILVER OAK

Cabernet Sauvignon

Alexander Valley

100% cabernet sauvignon

Though the winery itself is located in the Napa Valley, Silver Oak Cellars makes two different famous cabernet sauvignons, one from the winery's vineyards in the Napa Valley (the more structured) and the other from its vineyards in Sonoma's Alexander Valley (possibly a shade more hedonistic). Immensely popular, the Alexander Valley cabernet is captivating, full of energy, and easy to love. Berry, plum, and vanilla flavors are overlaid with a hint of pine and dill, the signature flavors of wines matured in American oak. Year in and year out, the texture of this cabernet is as irresistible as homemade jam that's just been taken off the stove.

*Old zinfandel vines can be found all over northern California. Many of these vineyards were planted 60 to 80 years ago and some are thought to be 120 years old or more. Despite their gnarly, rugged appearance, old vines generally produce wines that are elegant, concentrated, and rich.*

# CARNEROS

E arly on in the modern era of California winemaking when most wines were known by their producers—but not by where they came from—Carneros was already considered a special spot. As the 1960s dawned, while other wine regions were still discovering themselves, the wind-stroked hills of Carneros were considered ideal for producing chardonnays and pinot noirs of beauty and elegance. It is a serene place. No towns, just softly loping hills that, now vine-covered, were once the exclusive domain of sheep. The region begins about 40 miles north of San Francisco (it is the first wine region you encounter) and straddles the lower ends of both Napa and Sonoma counties. It's a small place; Carneros has only about a fourth as many vines as the Napa Valley, itself a small place.

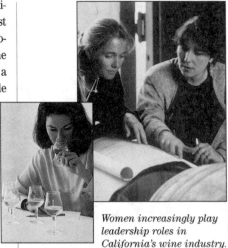

*Women increasingly play leadership roles in California's wine industry. Judy Matulich-Weitz (above right), Buena Vista's winemaker, consults with Anne Moller-Racke, director of vineyard operations. Winemaker Eileen Crane (left) is the managing director of Domaine Carneros. Both wineries are in Carneros.*

677

*The word carneros is Spanish for ram.*

What makes Carneros special is its proximity to the San Pablo Bay, which is the most northern part of the San Francisco Bay. It acts as a giant funnel for the cool ocean air and fog that surge through Carneros as they are pulled up into the warmer Napa and Sonoma Valleys. The effect on the region's vineyards is profound. The grapes, while getting plenty of sun, never become scorched. Because of the constant caress of cool air, the risk of flavors being baked out of the grapes (a definite danger in some parts of California) is nonexistent. They ripen in a slow, even manner over a long period of time. The wines, as a result, often have gorgeous balance. They are rarely fat, flaccid, or overwrought. They are not behemoths but instead have a proclivity for that all too rare commodity: elegance. Which is not to say that they always achieve it; poor winemaking, after all, can ruin even the best grapes.

The greatest number of the grapes grown in Carneros are either chardonnay (about 50 percent) or pinot noir (about 35 percent), although merlot is on the rise, especially in warmer pockets. Two other wine regions in the world are famous for the same chardonnay-pinot combination: Champagne and Burgundy. This is not a coincidence for in all three regions the cool climate dictates which grapes will work best. Although chardonnay seems as though it can be grown anywhere on the planet, the grape in many places tends to make clumsy, one-dimensional wines. Distinct chardonnays—chardonnays with nuance and grace—generally come from cool areas. For its part, pinot noir, the

*Until the 1970s the bucolic rolling hills of Carneros were considered suitable for nothing much more than sheep. Today this cool region, fronting on the San Pablo Bay, is a virtual carpet of chardonnay and pinot noir vines.*

enfant terrible of grapes, provokes a labor of love. More genetically fragile than other grapes, it will not taste pinot-noir-like *unless* it is grown in well-suited cool areas. The world's best sparkling wines—and Champagnes—are the marriage of these two grapes, and again, the region must be cool if the wines are to be elegant. The top Carneros sparkling wines have such a clarity and refinement that many of the leading California sparkling wine firms (Domaine Carneros, Mumm Napa Valley, Gloria Ferrer, Domaine Chandon) are located in or buy grapes from the region.

The fact that virtually every one of the thirty or so wineries in Carneros makes pinot noir and chardonnay, each viticulturally challenging, says something about the character of the place. Wine people in Carneros are forced to be on their toes, and one senses that they like that.

Individually and collectively, the wineries and grape growers of Carneros undertake and underwrite an ambitious amount of research. Clonal research in this region has been considerable. To backtrack for a minute, worldwide it's always been assumed that the grapes of a given area would share certain characteristics of flavor. However, this has been difficult to demonstrate in California where winemakers often treat wines in vastly different ways, altering flavors in the process. So in California it can be very hard to determine exactly what is contributing to any given flavor: something the winemaker did or some characteristic of the *terroir?* What the Carneros research shows is that even despite different winemaking styles, certain flavor characteristics can still show through in the wines. And in fact, a 1986 investigation into Carneros pinot noirs revealed that they shared specific flavor characteristics, namely those of fresh berries, cherries, berry jam, and spice. A more recent and more complex study of regional *terroir* revealed that Carneros chardonnays, too, share characteristics, namely citrus, muscat, and apple-pear flavors.

# Visiting Carneros Wineries

Carneros, which straddles Napa Valley and Sonoma County, is made up almost exclusively of wineries and vineyards. (There is no small town; there are no restaurants and no shops.) Artesa, owned by the giant Spanish sparkling wine firm Codorníu, is architecturally an exceptionally stunning northern California winery, and Buena Vista—one of the oldest wineries in the state—is well worth visiting for its rich history. Besides visiting wineries, however, you won't want to miss the di Rosa Preserve, a celebrated and eclectic collection of contemporary art (5200 Carneros Highway, Napa, CA 94559; [707] 226-5991).

When you want to make plans to visit several wineries consecutively, you'll be able to tell from their addresses which are in the Napa part of Carneros and which are in the Sonoma part.

**ACACIA WINERY**
2750 Las Amigas Road
Napa, CA 94559
(707) 226-9991
By appointment only.

**ARTESA**
1345 Henry Road
Napa, CA 94559
(707) 224-1668

*Larry Brooks (left), Acacia's first winemaker and now a consultant, talks with legendary grape grower Angelo Sangiacomo. The Sangiacomo family owns hundreds of acres of prime vineyard land.*

**BUENA VISTA WINERY**
18000 Old Winery Road
Sonoma, CA 95476
(707) 252-7117

**CARNEROS CREEK WINERY**
1285 Dealy Lane
Napa, CA 94559
(707) 253-9463

*In 1972 winemaker Francis Mahoney founded Carneros Creek, the first winery to open in Carneros after Prohibition.*

**DOMAINE CARNEROS**
1240 Duhig Road
Napa, CA 94559
(707) 257-0101

679

*Standing by the French doors in the entrance hall, visitors have a sweeping view of the vineyards of Domaine Carneros. The winery, renowned for its sparkling wine, is owned in part by the Champagne house Taittinger.*

**GLORIA FERRER CHAMPAGNE CAVES**
23555 Highway 121
Sonoma, CA 95476
(707) 996-7256

# THE CARNEROS WINES TO KNOW

*Each of the following wines carries the American Viticultural Area designation Carneros.*

## Sparkling Wines

### DOMAINE CARNEROS

Le Rêve

prestige *cuvée*, vintage brut

approximately 95% chardonnay, with a small amount of pinot blanc

Jointly owned by the Champagne firm Taittinger and the United States importer Kobrand, Domaine Carneros makes what are possibly the most strikingly graceful sparklers from Carneros. They shimmer with elegance. In particular, Domaine Carneros' prestige *cuvée* Le Rêve (the dream) has beautiful creamy-appley flavors and crystalline clarity.

### MUMM CUVEE NAPA

Winery Lake

vintage brut

approximately 80% pinot noir, 20% chardonnay

At 175 acres, Winery Lake is the best-known single vineyard in Carneros. Each year, from its prized grapes, Mumm Cuvée Napa makes a beautifully elegant, creamy yet jazzy sparkler with balance and energy. Also not to be missed is DVX, the winery's prestige *cuvée*.

*For all the fame of its wines, Carneros is about as modest a wine region as you can find. There are no restaurants, no hotels, no fancy homes, and virtually no shops except for the one at the gas station that, this being California, sells fine wine and cappuccino.*

# *Whites*

### ETUDE
Pinot Blanc

100% pinot blanc

Drop-dead sophistication, dripping with elegance. In great years this wine is Lauren Bacall, Grace Kelly, and Katharine Hepburn rolled into one (and it dances like Ginger Rogers). The flavors glitter—slow notes of passion fruit, jasmine, honeysuckle, Key lime pie. Etude is best known for its pinot noir (see below), this pinot blanc being a well-kept secret.

### SHAFER
Chardonnay

Red Shoulder Ranch

100% chardonnay

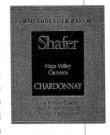

The Shafer Vineyards winery in the Napa Valley makes two chardonnays—a very good one from Napa Valley vineyards and a positively stellar one from Carneros grapes grown on the Red Shoulder Ranch. Its totally lavish honeysuckle and tropical fruit flavors are drizzled with honey and exotic spices.

# *Reds*

### ACACIA
Pinot Noir

reserve

100% pinot noir

As sensual and evocative as a good massage, year after year, the pinot noirs from Acacia—especially the reserves—are known for being utterly primal, earthy, and full of sweet ripe fruit. These wines are charmingly Old World in style.

### CARNEROS CREEK
Pinot Noir

Signature Reserve

100% pinot noir

When Carneros Creek was founded in 1972, it became the first winery to be built in Carneros since Prohibition. Shortly thereafter the winery pioneered the groundbreaking research on clones of pinot noir in California. Simply put, no winery could be more committed to Carneros or pinot noir than Carneros Creek. The winery's very hedonistic Signature Reserve is a testament. In great years the richness and depth of this wine are striking.

### ETUDE
Pinot Noir

100% pinot noir

A small wine firm specializing in pinot noir, Etude came on the scene in the mid-1980s with wines so full of personality they became famous almost overnight. In the best vintages Etude's pinot noir can be flashy with aromas and flavors of cigar box, leather, baked plums, black currants, exotic spices, and smoked meats that are so vibrant they seem to levitate out of the glass. The word *étude* is French for study, a reference to the idea that for the winemaker, working with pinot noir is a lifelong study that is never completely mastered.

681

### SAINTSBURY
Pinot Noir

100% pinot noir

Saintsbury makes some of the most scrumptious, easiest to love pinot noirs in California. When they're in top form, enchanted forest aromas open up into a dizzying array of flavors—a delicious fusion of spiced cherries, dried orange, chocolate, mocha, and ripe plums. The way the wine's richness balloons in your mouth is heavenly.

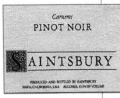

# MENDOCINO AND LAKE COUNTY

California's two most northern wine regions, Mendocino and Lake County, are just north of Sonoma and Napa counties, but they are light-years away in temperament. Their vast, ravishing wilderness is the California of a century ago. Rolling mountains covered in golden grasses and wild oats alternate with immense stands of giant redwoods. Mendocino's jagged, almost menacing coastline has been carved out over eons by icy dark blue waters. Farther inland, in the middle of Lake County, the grand body of water known as Clear Lake is the largest natural lake in California. On any given day in these two regions you're more likely to see a whale, mountain lion, or rattlesnake than someone in a business suit. Everywhere you turn, Nature's presence is thunderous, even intimidating.

*The word* mendocino *is a diminutive of de Mendoza, the name of one of the earliest Spanish explorers to come ashore in Mendocino in the late sixteenth century.*

The first small wineries in Mendocino and Lake County were established in the 1850s by failed prospectors turned farmers in the wake of the gold rush. But by the end of Prohibition, virtually every winery had disappeared, and pear orchards or nut trees stood where vineyards had once flourished. The two counties, so rugged and remote, were not quick to be reborn as wine regions. As of 1967 there was only one winery in Mendocino (Parducci), even though the wine business was begin-

*Founded in 1858, the secluded town of Mendocino is the most picturesque in Mendocino County. An artist's colony, it sits on a bluff poised above the Pacific Ocean. Getting to the town means driving through forests of giant redwoods and some of Mendocino County's most beautiful vineyards.*

ning to take off in both Napa and Sonoma. The next year, however, proved to be a turning point. In 1968 Mendocino's Fetzer Vineyards was founded by lumber executive Barney Fetzer. Fetzer's growth was meteoric. During the decade of the 1980s, ten of Barney Fetzer's eleven children built the family winery into one of the largest in California. Although Fetzer Vineyards is now owned by the Brown-Forman Corporation, the Fetzer family continues to hold prime vineyard land in Mendocino.

In Lake County, Fetzer's counterpart was Kendall-Jackson. Kendall-Jackson began with one small vineyard there in the mid-1970s. Today it owns vineyards throughout California and is one of the ten largest wineries in the state (see The Rise of Kendall-Jackson, on page 686).

Thus Mendocino and Lake County became home to two of California's most technologically sophisticated large wineries. Surrounding these are some fifty smaller wineries, plus about 260 grape growers who range from modern, large-scale operators to tiny one-man operations where the last technological innovation might well have been replacing the horse with a tractor. Today there are some 15,000 acres of vineyards in Mendocino and almost 5,000 in Lake County. The leading grape variety in both regions is chardonnay, although some terrific sauvignon blancs and gewürztraminers are made here too. Above all, however, it's the scrumptious zinfandels, petite sirahs, Rhône blends, and wines from other Mediterranean varieties that rivet your attention. Mendocino may well become a leading area for these wines. Already experiments are underway with exciting but little-known Mediterranean varieties, such as fiano, montepulciano, and arneis.

Mendocino is also where you'll find one of the producers of California's most stunning, complex sparkling wines—Roederer Estate—plus Germain-Robin brandy, considered the finest brandy made in the United States.

*Winemaker Dennis Patton instructs me on the finer points of enjoying Mendocino wines.*

## Mendocino

L ogging is the main industry in Mendocino, a place of tranquility and almost reckless beauty. More than a million acres of forest stand majestically amid the vine-covered sun-dappled hills. Orchards and ranches are sprinkled over the landscape. On the coast, the windswept town of Mendocino is an artists' hamlet.

*Mendocino has the largest percentage of organic vineyards of any county in California— more than 20 percent. Many are certified by the California Certified Organic Farmers.*

Mendocino is known for a wide variety of outstanding wines, but it's also noteworthy as the place that organic viticulture and sustainable agriculture—practices now embraced by top wineries throughout the

## AMERICA'S FINEST BRANDY

===⟨∂∕∂⟩===

In 1982 American Ansley Coale and Frenchman Hubert Germain-Robin founded the artisanal distillery Germain-Robin/Alambic near the town of Ukiah in Mendocino. Today Germain-Robin's brandies are considered the best brandies made in the United States and have, in multiple blind tastings, repeatedly bested a host of Cognacs.

To make these brandies, Hubert Germain-Robin, a master Cognac distiller, whose family has produced Cognac since 1782, uses an antique alembic still. Each year, he hand-distills eighty barrels of brandy from such premium grapes as pinot noir and sauvignon blanc (in Cognac and elsewhere in Europe, brandies are usually distilled from lesser grape varieties). Of the five brandies Germain-Robin makes, the most stunning is the XO Reserve, a brandy so smooth, elegant, and lush it can leave you speechless.

*Germain-Robin/Alambic, 3001 South State Street, No. 35, Ukiah, CA 95482; (707) 462-0314.*

state—were pioneered. One winery that led the way was Fetzer Vineyards, which by the late 1980s was already farming several hundred acres of grapes without the use of any artificial fertilizers or synthetic chemicals. However, you won't see many Mendocino wines (or, for that matter, wines from other regions of California) labeled with the word *organic*. For many vintners, farming in a way that respects and protects the land is a matter of principle. They do it for moral reasons, not as a marketing tool.

The American Viticultural Area Mendocino stretches from the cool Pacific coast inland to several warmer valleys tucked between the coastal mountain range and the Mayacamas. The headwaters of the powerful Russian River are located here and flow down through Mendocino and much of Sonoma County before curving abruptly and spilling into the Pacific Ocean. Within Mendocino are several smaller AVAs, the most important of which are Anderson Valley, Redwood Valley, and McDowell Valley.

Anderson Valley is distinctly different from the others. Slicing like a fjord inland from the cold sea, the valley, especially its northwestern end, is one of the chilliest grape-growing areas in California. Chardonnay and pinot noir are the leading grapes, and not surprisingly, they are blended by Roederer Estate (owned by the Champagne house of Louis Roederer) to make some of the raciest sparkling wines in California.

Before it bought land in Anderson Valley in 1981, the house of Louis Roederer searched for several years for the perfect sparkling wine site in California. Roederer was so convinced that Anderson Valley was that place that it waited seven years—until its own vineyards matured—before making its first sparkler, instead of buying grapes from someplace else.

Anderson Valley's dramatic coolness means the region is also ideal for two grapes other parts of California have largely given up on, gewürztraminer and riesling. The most complex, hedonistic, and exciting gewürztraminers and rieslings in California are made here by Navarro Vineyards.

Like Sonoma's Russian River Valley, Mendocino's cool Anderson Valley has some warm spots. High above the chilly and often foggy valley are mountain ridges directly exposed to the warm sun. The grapes for some of Mendocino's top berry-and-spice zinfandels come from vineyards here. Though they were recently part of Anderson Valley, many of these vineyards are now part of Mendocino's newest AVA, Mendocino Ridge, which because it is composed of disparate mountain areas is the first noncontiguous AVA in California.

The other significant AVAs in Mendocino are Redwood Valley (once so thick with redwoods that, legend has it, you couldn't see the sky) and McDowell Valley. Both can experience remarkable climatic seesaws of temperature, with hot days but very cold nights.

The Redwood Valley, bordered on the south by a geologic uplift in the ground known as the Ricetti bench, which has trademark crimson red soil, is where Mendocino's first vineyards were planted. Today the top wines here are, well, red—specifically, zinfandels, many of which are full of pepper, berry, and spice. The two wineries that are best known are Lolonis and Fife Vineyards (the latter also has a winery in the Napa Valley).

McDowell Valley, not really a valley but a small, elevated, sloping plateau, is home to a single winery, McDowell Valley Vineyards, one of the first wineries in California to make Rhône-style wines. With its century-old syrah and grenache vines, the winery continues to make some of the best Rhône-style wines in the state, including one of the most lip-smacking rosés ever.

685

*In Mendocino County rolling vineyards alternate with majestic forests, making the county one of the most attractive and most rural wine regions in California.*

Guenoc

PETITE SIRAH
NORTH COAST

LILLIE LANGTRY
PROPRIETOR 1888-1906

*Lake County's Guenoc winery pays homage to the English actress Lillie Langtry by picturing her on many of its wine labels. In the 1850s Langtry owned the property and was the first to plant grapevines there.*

est and rarest of these varieties (Langtry would have approved). The owner of Guenoc, Orville Magoon, has a fascinating story himself. Of Irish, French, Hawaiian, and Chinese ancestry, Magoon is a descendant of Hawaiian royalty. When, in order to build the University of Hawaii, the United States government appropriated 21 acres of prime Hawaiian land that Magoon owned, it gave him in return a choice of several parcels of land in California. In what turned out to be an auspicious trade, Magoon acquired 23,000 acres of land in Lake County.

The other notable Lake County winery, Steele Wines, is owned by Jed Steele, a well-known and highly respected winemaker who, as the winemaker at Kendall-

## Lake County

Taking its name from the immense and beautiful Clear Lake, Lake County is smaller, drier, and less diverse than Mendocino. The county is primarily a provider of grapes to a number of large wineries, including Beringer, Sutter Home, and Kendall-Jackson. There are only four actual wineries here, the two most important of which are Guenoc Estate Vineyards and Steele Wines.

The first vineyards at Guenoc (Celtic for good rock) were cultivated by the enterprising English actress Lillie Langtry. Langtry planted the hillsides of her remote estate in the 1850s, intending to make what she hoped would become "the greatest claret in California" (a goal she may have thought she achieved, but history doesn't record). Today the Magoon family owns the original Langtry vineyards and is recultivating them with Bordeaux varieties, including carmenère, one of the old-

## THE RISE OF KENDALL-JACKSON

━━◦ᴠᴠᴠᴠ━━

In 1974 San Francisco lawyer Jess Jackson bought some lake property in Lake County as a country retreat. A few years later, he decided to grow grapes "for fun." By 1995 Kendall-Jackson's Vintner's Reserve chardonnay, at 2 million cases, had become one of the best-selling chardonnays in the country. Like many Kendall-Jackson wines, it was made from grapes grown not just in Lake County but all over California. Since planting the initial vineyard, Jess Jackson has amassed a vineyard and winery empire, making Kendall-Jackson one of the largest wine companies in California. Among the wineries that members of the Jackson family own are Cambria, Pepi, Cardinale, La Crema, and Matanzas Creek.

Jackson in the 1980s and early 1990s, established the Kendall-Jackson style of soft, round, easy-drinking wines. Steele makes some twenty-four different wines, each from a different vineyard, which is designated on the label, from vineyards all over California, including eight different chardonnays, four different pinot noirs, and three different zinfandels (many of these wines are outstanding).

## Visiting Mendocino and Lake County Wineries

Mendocino and Lake County are beautifully pastoral regions that are wonderful to visit. Wineries are scattered throughout the area, so count on a good amount of meandering to and fro. As always in rural regions, it's best to call ahead for an appointment.

Besides being home to a slew of terrific wineries, Mendocino in particular is full of zany things to do. You may want to attend the whale festival (usually in March, when the whales are running off the coast) or taste your way through the self-proclaimed world's largest salmon barbecue (in July) or take in the Paul Bunyan parade (on Labor Day) or go for a vegetarian lunch at the City of Ten Thousand Buddhas, the largest Buddhist monastery in California. For a full calendar of events, contact the Fort Bragg-Mendocino Coast Chamber of Commerce at (800) 726-2780.

Every visit to Mendocino, however, should absolutely include a stopover in the charming town of Mendocino itself (have breakfast at Cafe Beaujolais) and a visit to Fetzer's Valley Oaks Center in Hopland, which in addition to vineyards, includes spectacular organic vegetable and fruit gardens.

**FETZER VINEYARDS**
13601 Eastside Road
Hopland, CA 95449
(707) 744-1737

**GUENOC ESTATE VINEYARDS**
21000 Butts Canyon
Middletown, CA 95461
(707) 987-2385

**MCDOWELL VALLEY VINEYARDS**
13380 South Highway 101
Hopland, CA 95449
(707) 744-1053
This is the address of McDowell's tasting room. Stop by there to arrange for a tour of the winery.

**NAVARRO VINEYARDS**
5601 Highway 128
Philo, CA 95466
(707) 895-3686

**ROEDERER ESTATE**
4501 Highway 128
Philo, CA 95466
(707) 895-2288

687

*Roederer Estate, owned by the Champagne house Roederer, makes some of California's most sensational sparkling wines. The Champagne house spent years searching California for a site that would be ideal for growing chardonnay and pinot noir, the two primary grapes in the world's best sparkling wines. In 1981 they settled on the cool Anderson Valley.*

# THE MENDOCINO AND LAKE COUNTY WINES TO KNOW

*These wines have the American Viticultural Area designation of either Mendocino or Lake County, and subappellations, where applicable, are also given.*

## *Sparkling Wine*

### ROEDERER ESTATE
L'Ermitage
prestige *cuvée*, vintage brut
Anderson Valley, Mendocino
approximately 55% chardonnay,
45% pinot noir

L'Ermitage is Roederer Estate's prestige *cuvée*, and it's always one of the most profoundly complex sparkling wines made in California. The wonderful play of silky yet prickly textures, the rich layers of custard, vanilla, and woodsy flavors, the impeccable focus and clarity of the wine, plus the mesmerizingly long finish all add up to a completely luxurious experience.

## *Whites*

### GUENOC
Chardonnay
Genevieve Magoon Vineyard
reserve
Guenoc Valley, Lake County
100% chardonnay

Guenoc Valley was the first American Viticultural Area in California to have a single proprietor—the Magoon family, owners of the Guenoc winery. From their Genevieve Magoon Vineyard comes this rich dynamo of a chardonnay. The beautifully delineated flavors are laced with butterscotch, honey, and spice, all bracketed by a keen citrusy edge.

### MONTE VOLPE
Pinot Bianco
Mendocino
100% pinot blanc

When Gregory Graziano's grandfather came to Mendocino from Italy in 1910 he planted two grapes Italians love, moscato and barbera. Today the younger Graziano tends vineyards planted with a dozen different Italian varieties and from them makes some of the most personality-driven wines in the region. A favorite: the Monte Volpe (mountain of the foxes) pinot bianco (pinot blanc)—a tantalizing swirl of pure peach, honeysuckle, and ginger flavors, all without a whit of oak.

### NAVARRO VINEYARDS
Gewürztraminer
Anderson Valley, Mendocino
100% gewürztraminer

Navarro makes the most sophisticated, complex, and delicious dry gewürztraminers in California. Vintage after vintage, they are wines of remarkable clarity, precision, and pizzazz. Pears, stones, minerals, and litchi come at you in what can only be described as a driving rainstorm of flavor. Navarro first planted gewürztraminer grapes in 1974 and has since developed a cult following for the wine it produces.

# *Reds*

## HIDDEN CELLARS

Mendocino Heritage Sorcery

Mendocino

approximately 75% zinfandel, with small amounts of syrah and petite sirah

Hidden Cellars is known for gutsy wines that march to their own drummer. Especially its zinfandels. Sorcery is massive but beautifully integrated. With its spicy, chocolaty, boysenberry flavors and jammy texture, it could easily cast a spell over anyone who drinks it.

## LOLONIS

Zinfandel

Redwood Valley, Mendocino

100% zinfandel

Wonderfully and stubbornly Greek in temperament, the Lolonis family has been growing grapes in Mendocino since 1920. Their zinfandel shows their commitment and passion. A supple, dense, opulent wine, it's packed with the kind of jammy boysenberry flavors that make zinfandel so captivating, yet it's never so big and overripe as to seem like pseudo-Port.

## MCDOWELL

Syrah

Mendocino

approximately 95% syrah, with a tiny amount of grenache and viognier

Unsubtle but delicious, this syrah is slightly roguish—like a guy with a perpetual 5 o'clock shadow. McDowell's syrah has a wonderful spiciness and a texture that's almost syrupy. McDowell was one of the wineries that pioneered Rhône varieties in California in the early 1980s. Like many producers in the Rhône, and an increasing number of producers in California, McDowell adds a little white viognier wine to this red to give it a small but intriguing boost in aroma.

## STEELE

Zinfandel

Catfish Vineyard

Clear Lake, Lake County

100% zinfandel

Jed Steele makes several zins, but the one from the Catfish Vineyard (named after a local bookstore, plus there are a lot of really big catfish in Clear Lake) is always a favorite. With a sledgehammer of powerful boysenberry fruit, the wine is often drenched with gunsmoke, mint, and spices.

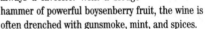

689

# *Sweet Wine*

## NAVARRO VINEYARDS

White Riesling

Cluster Select Late Harvest

Anderson Valley, Mendocino

100% riesling

This may well be the most opulent yet elegant dessert wine made in the United States. Every year the Bennett-Cahn family, which owns Navarro, takes a gamble and lets the grapes in

a portion of their vineyard hang on the vine well beyond the normal harvest. Their hope is that these grapes will be attacked by *Botrytis cinerea*, the noble rot that makes French Sauternes. Some years nothing develops and birds eventually eat the grapes. But in years when their luck holds, a wine of majestic honeyed apricot richness is the result.

# THE SIERRA FOOTHILLS

Until the mid-nineteenth century, California's wine industry was centered around Los Angeles. Only a few wineries existed in the northern counties, most of them tiny, noncommercial ventures. But in 1849, with the discovery of gold near the town of Coloma in the Sierra Nevada foothills, the wine industry took off in a new direction. Mining camps sprang up everywhere, and in their wake, so did vineyards and small wineries begun mostly by Italian immigrants seeking their fortunes. By the 1860s there were nearly 200,000 vines growing in the "gold counties" of northern California and wineries there outnumbered those in other parts of the north. These were the first wineries in the state to forgo the common mission grape in favor of better varieties, such as zinfandel.

In time the gold supply diminished and eventually dried up. The population shrank. Winemaking and grape growing slowed considerably and then, following the double blows of phylloxera and Prohibition, virtually disappeared in some areas. By the end of World War II, the Sierra Foothills were home mostly to ghost wineries and abandoned vineyards. Only one winery managed to remain continuously in operation, the D'Agostini Winery, now the Sobon Estate in Amador County.

A renaissance came in the early 1970s with the establishment of Montevina, Boeger Winery, and Stevenot. Today, there are some forty wineries in the Sierra Foothills and in this American Viticultural Area, more than 3,500 acres are planted with vines.

*The view from Madroña Vineyards looking east at the Sierras: At 3,000 feet in elevation, this is considered to be the highest vineyard in California.*

The Sierra Foothills is a strip of eight remote counties roughly stacked one on top of the next. California's capital, Sacramento is to the west; the Nevada border to the east. Of the eight counties, the two most important are El Dorado and Amador. Both are ruggedly beautiful regions where the spirit of the Old West and a strong sense of individualism live on. Wineries there are generally small and usually family owned.

For numerous and complex reasons, the wineries of the Sierra Foothills are not yet as well known as they deserve to be, given the quality and distinct personality of the best wines. This is changing quickly, however. Montevina and Boeger, as well as Domaine de la Terre Rouge, have already developed followings nationally, and there are a half dozen more wineries poised to join them.

A remarkable number of grape varieties (more than thirty) are planted in the Sierra Foothills, but the best wines are almost invariably from red Mediterranean varieties. In particular, the zinfandels (usually from very old vineyards), barberas, syrahs, mourvèdres, and Rhône blends have a robust boldness that can be irresistible. In the midst of all this "redness," there are two types of white wine made in the Sierra Foothills that should not be missed: slightly sweet and dessert wines. Totally scrumptious examples are Lava Cap's off-dry Muscat Canelli and Madroña's Select Late Harvest Riesling, a dessert wine.

## El Dorado County

Flanked by Nevada on its eastern border, El Dorado County is ruggedly mountainous, with volcanic and granitic soils derived from ancient volcanoes and streambeds lined with granite and (once upon a time) gold. It is said of El Dorado County that the mountains are in the wines, and indeed, some of the wineries at the highest elevations in the entire state are here, including what is thought to be the highest of all, Madroña Vineyards, at

an elevation of 3,000 feet. Thanks to the breezes that sweep down off the 10,000-foot peaks of the Sierra Nevada, nights here are very cool. The grapes in these mountain vineyards remain small in size, producing concentrated wines with distinct richness buttressed by firm structures. In particular, El Dorado syrahs, zinfandels, and petite sirahs can be excellent.

*El Dorado County took its name*
*from a mythical being—*
*El Dorado, the golden one—who,*
*according to legend, was searched*
*for by the conquistadores.*

El Dorado's leading wineries are Boeger, Lava Cap, Madroña, Sierra Vista, Granite Springs, and Perry Creek. The region's main town, Placerville, is the unofficial center of winemaking, just as it was once the center of mining. During the gold rush, it was known as Hangtown—a name that lives on in Hangtown Red, an easy-drinking zinfandel-cabernet blend made by Boeger Winery.

## Amador County

A mador first came onto the scene in the 1970s with gutsy, teeth-staining, King Kong-size zinfandels that lots of red wine drinkers immediately fell in love with. The intensely flavored grapes came from very old (often pre-Prohibition) vineyards that had been kept in production as a source of fruit for home winemakers. One of the first wineries to realize the true value of these old Amador vineyards was Sutter Home in the Napa Valley. In 1971 the winery released its first Amador County zinfandel, a stunning wine made from grapes from the now highly regarded Deaver Ranch in the Shenandoah Valley. Amador's big break had arrived. Within a few years, zinfandel producers in other parts of California were scrambling to get Amador grapes.

Amador County, warmer than El Dorado, is spread over lower foothills composed of granite with some sandy loam. Overall, this is a softer, gentler landscape; for some wine drinkers the region is reminiscent of Tuscany.

Amador's leading winery is Montevina, owned by Sutter Home. In 1996

Montevina released its Terra d'Oro (Italian for land of gold) wines—a special line of reserve wines based on Italian varieties. Montevina's experimental vineyard now has more than forty Italian varieties, including some heirloom grapes no longer grown in Italy. Other leading wineries include Shenandoah Vineyards, Sobon Estate, Amador Foothill Winery, Renwood, Easton, and Domaine de la Terre Rouge.

## Visiting Sierra Foothills Wineries

T he historic gold towns of the Sierra Foothills are dotted with wineries, many of which are nestled along ridges of the Rocky Mountains. Because the wineries are generally small and family owned, it's best to call ahead for an appointment.

**BOEGER WINERY**
1709 Carson Road
Placerville, CA 95667
(530) 622-8094

**DOMAINE DE LA TERRE ROUGE**
10801 Dickson Road
Plymouth, CA 95669
(209) 245-4277

**LAVA CAP WINERY**
2221 Fruitridge Road
Placerville, CA 95667
(530) 621-0175

**MADROÑA VINEYARDS**
2560 High Hill Road
Camino, CA 95707
(530) 644-5948

**MONTEVINA WINERY**
20680 Shenandoah School Road
Plymouth, CA 95669
(209) 245-6942

**SOBON ESTATE**
14430 Shenandoah Road
Plymouth, CA 95669
(209) 245-6554

*The distinctive etched bottles of Terra d'Oro, a brand owned by Montevina.*

# THE SIERRA FOOTHILLS WINES TO KNOW

*Though white wines are made in the Sierra Foothills, the region's reputation rests solidly on its reds. That's what you'll find here, and the American Viticultural Area of each is indicated.*

## BOEGER

Barbera

El Dorado

approximately 90% barbera, 10% zinfandel

Boeger's barbera can often be a primal, spicy, tar-black wine just loaded with pepper and sweet cherry flavors. The Italian region of Piedmont (the translation is foot of the mountain) may be barbera's first home, but it's not the only hilly place where the grape loves to grow. At its best keen-edged and almost spiky in your mouth, this Sierra Foothills wine is just waiting for spicy dishes.

## DOMAINE DE LA TERRE ROUGE

Terre Rouge Noir

Sierra Foothills

approximately 50% grenache, 30% mourvèdre, and 20% syrah

Not for the fainthearted. Domaine de la Terre Rouge, a small family winery specializing in Rhône-style wines, takes as its inspiration the wines of Châteauneuf-du-Pape, but its Terre Rouge Noir, the domaine's best wine, is thicker, fleshier, and darker. At its core it possesses that classic irresistibly ripe flavor that the French call *confiture* (a hallmark of excellent grenache). With a hunk of great cheese, this would be a killer.

## LAVA CAP

Zinfandel

El Dorado

100% zinfandel

One of the best in a crowded field of terrific Sierra Foothills zinfandels, Lava Cap's zin requires total surrender. Its gargantuan sweet-spicy brambly fruit can have the density of steak (with which it would be great). The winery's volcanic ash vineyards at 2,600 feet are known for yielding grapes full of personality.

## MONTEVINA

Terra d'Oro

Sangiovese

Amador County

approximately 95% sangiovese, 5% barbera

In top vintages, Montevina's Terra d'Oro sangiovese is deliciously soft and comforting as a lullaby. Like Old World sangioveses in Tuscany, it exudes gentle plummy flavors suffused with hints of dried orange, mocha, and sweet, meaty prosciutto and, at the same time, has good, bright acidity. Neither massive nor meager, it is a wine with silky gracefulness.

693

## RENWOOD

Zinfandel

Old Vine

Amador County

100% zinfandel

Muscular, full-blooded, gutsy zins are Amador County's trademark, and in great years Renwood's hits the mark. The wine's black raspberry, mocha, and plum pudding flavors are about as restrained as a bull in a china shop, and the wine's texture can broach chocolate syrup. From vineyards more than half a century old.

## THE LIVERMORE VALLEY

East and slightly south of San Francisco is one of California's most historically influential wine regions, the small Livermore Valley. Some of the state's most important wineries were begun here over a century ago, including Wente, Concannon, and Cresta Blanca (now gone). Wente, in particular, has made remarkable contributions not solely to Livermore Valley but to the California wine industry as a whole. Many of the chardonnay grapes grown in the state today are so-called Wente selections, the result of painstaking genetic research Ernest Wente conducted over his lifetime. Ernest, son of the founder C. H. Wente, began experimenting with chardonnay in 1912 when the grape was all but unheard of in California and only minuscule amounts were planted, most of them in Livermore. Today Wente not only makes wonderful still chardonnays but also crisp, lively sparkling wines based largely on chardonnay.

Early on, the Livermore Valley thrived not only because of the dynamism of its first vintners and its suitability for viticulture but also because of its close proximity to San Francisco and the bay. Sadly, the latter would also prove—almost—to be the valley's undoing. Housing divisions, industrial parks, and an endless stream of urban development throughout the 1960s, 1970s, and 1980s gobbled up Livermore's vineyards with frightening finality. By the late 1980s thousands of acres of grapes had simply disappeared.

The valley has initiated a comeback. An innovative land-use plan begun in 1993 protects the region's existing vineyards and encourages the development of new ones.

*Overhead sprinklers irrigate an older vineyard in the Livermore Valley. New vineyards, and there are many here, are equipped with drip irrigation, which though costly to install is far more effective and uses much less water.*

Livermore now has sixteen wineries (there were fifty before the turn of the century), with new ones planned.

The Livermore Valley is about 15 miles long and, atypically, runs east-west. Though it can be brightly sunny and as hot as blazes during the day, the valley becomes an enormous wind tunnel by late afternoon. Temperatures can drop a full 50°F at night. The combination of bright light, heat, and strong winds, followed by nighttime cooling, plus the valley's shallow soil, is reminiscent of parts of southern France. Many of the best Livermore wines have a kind of wild herb, resiny, garigue character similar to the wines of Provence and the Languedoc-Roussillon.

Livermore's other leading historic winery is Concannon, built in 1883 (the same year as Wente) by Irish immigrant and devout Catholic James Concannon. During his lifetime, James Concannon's son Joseph sent a barrel of the Concannon muscat de Frontignan to the pope every five years. Concannon is now owned by Wente.

The Wentes and Concannons were helped significantly by the ambitions of another prominent Livermore figure, newspaper journalist turned winemaker Charles Wetmore. Just before founding Cresta Blanca in 1882, Wetmore persuaded the California legislature to establish the state viticultural commission. As the commission's first president and CEO, Wetmore headed straight for Europe where he obtained cuttings from prestigious sources, including cuttings of sauvignon blanc, sémillon, and muscadelle from no less than Château d'Yquem. Those cuttings became the mother plant material for Livermore vineyards, which in turn, provided cuttings for vineyards all over the state.

In addition to Wente and Concannon, the valley boasts a number of up-and-coming small wine producers including Chouinard, Murrieta's Well, Retzlaff Vineyards, and Cedar Mountain.

## Visiting Livermore Wineries

As mentioned, thanks to new land-use legislation, Livermore's wine country is expanding. There are now numerous small family-owned wineries, such as Elliston Vineyards and Fenestra Winery, that are fun to visit, and most are no more than 40 miles from the city of San Francisco. But no visit would be complete without a stop at Wente Vineyards Visitors Center, with its beautiful gardens, golf course, tasting room, and top-notch restaurant.

**CEDAR MOUNTAIN WINERY**
7000 Tesla Road
Livermore, CA 94550
(925) 373-6636

**CONCANNON VINEYARD**
4590 Tesla Road
Livermore, CA 94550
(925) 456-2505

**ELLISTON VINEYARDS**
463 Kilkare Road
Sunol, CA 94586
(925) 862-2377

**FENESTRA WINERY**
83 Vallecitos Road
Livermore, CA 94550
(925) 447-5246

**WENTE VINEYARDS VISITORS CENTER**
5050 Arroyo Road
Livermore, CA 94550
(925) 456-2405

# THE LIVERMORE VALLEY
# WINES TO KNOW

*Each of the following wines carries the American Viticultural Area designation Livermore Valley.*

## *Whites*

**MURRIETA'S WELL**

Vendimia

approximately 50% sémillon, 40% sauvignon blanc, and a small amount of muscat

MURRIETA'S WELL

LIVERMORE VALLEY
VENDIMIA

One of the most personality-driven sémillon-based wines in California is the white Vendimia, from Murrieta's Well (named after the well where Joaquin Murrieta, a California bandit, watered his horse). At its best the wine oozes with beautiful light honey flavors. The vines that produce Vendimia are likely descended from the first Livermore sémillon, which came from the vineyards of Château d'Yquem.

**WENTE VINEYARDS**

Chardonnay

Herman Wente Reserve

100% chardonnay

Beautifully crafted and, when in top form, extremely elegant, Wente's head-of-the-line chardonnay from the famed Herman Wente vineyard is more gentle and subtle than most California chardonnays. The 300-acre Herman Wente vineyard was acquired circa 1915 and is one of Wente's original chardonnay "mother" vineyards, cuttings from which have been taken to plant numerous other vineyards throughout California.

## *Reds*

**CEDAR MOUNTAIN**

Cabernet Sauvignon

Blanches Vineyard

100% cabernet sauvignon

Cedar Mountain makes smooth smoky-juicy cabernets full of sweet brambly, boysenberry, and tobacco flavors. The winery was established in 1990 by a husband and wife team, Earl and Linda Ault, who—with no experience in agriculture—taught themselves how to grow grapes and make wine. Curiously, the property was once owned by Bing Crosby.

**CHOUINARD**

Zinfandel

100% zinfandel

Bright and intensely flavored but not bulky, Chouinard's tasty zinfandel is dependably full of raspberry and the wild, resinous flavors that the French call garigue.

**CONCANNON VINEYARD**

Petite Sirah

reserve

approximately 80% petite sirah, with 20% zinfandel or syrah

This wine tastes like it's right out of the southern French countryside. At its best it's soft, full of wild herbs and garigue, with back flips of black pepper on the end. Concannon is thought to be the first winery in California to bottle a petite sirah (in around 1960).

# THE NORTHERN CENTRAL COAST

While there is no official definition of the northern Central Coast, I am using the term to encompass Monterey County and those American Viticultural Areas north of it up to the San Francisco Bay, including the Santa Cruz Mountains, Santa Clara Valley, Chalone, Mount Harlan, and the Carmel Valley. These AVAs range in size from quite large (Monterey has about 40,000 acres of grapevines) to diminutive (Chalone has 300 acres of grapevines), and each has a distinct personality.

## *Santa Cruz Mountains*

The Santa Cruz Mountains seem to exude "Californianess." The mountain air so close to the sea has a thrillingly sharp freshness to it. Ancient redwood forests soar up into a cerulean sky. The mountains themselves have been torn and thrust into beautifully rugged formations by the perilous San Andreas Fault, which lies below them.

Thanks to the tangle of mountain crevices, canyons, hilltops, craggy slopes, knolls, and valleys, plus varying altitudes and orientations to the sun, the vineyards of the Santa Cruz Mountains can have widely different microclimates. In general, the higher vineyards (some are more than 2,000 feet in elevation) and those facing toward the Pacific Ocean are considerably cooler than lower vineyards and those facing east toward the warmer interior valleys.

The individuality of the vineyards explains why the region is known, seeming paradoxically, not only for pinot noir and chardonnay (cool-climate varieties) but also for zinfandel and cabernet sauvignon (warm-climate varieties), plus such

*Paul Draper, one of the most influential winemakers of the twentieth century, started at Ridge Vineyards in the Santa Cruz Mountains in 1969. Today he is Ridge's chief executive officer as well as chief winemaker—and many might add, chief philosopher.*

varieties as syrah and marsanne that fall in between. What all vines here do share is the beneficial struggle of growing in the region's thin, stony mountain soil.

Because the vineyards of the Santa Cruz Mountains are neither easy to farm nor do they give high yields, it's mostly top vintners and winemakers dedicated to making small-production, personality-driven wines who tend to settle here. There are forty-five wineries in the Santa Cruz Mountains, including some that are among the most dynamic in the state, such as Ridge Vineyards, Mount Eden Vineyards, and David Bruce Winery.

Ridge would probably be on most wine collectors' A lists. Year in and year out, the wines (cabernet sauvignon, zinfandel, chardonnay, and Rhône blends) are nothing short of majestic. They possess the utterly fascinating ability to be refined yet powerful in the same split second. No wine illustrates the idea better than Ridge's Monte Bello cabernet sauvi-

697

gnon. A hauntingly, explosively rich cabernet, it is the voice and soul of the Monte Bello vineyard on Monte Bello ridge in the Santa Cruz Mountains.

David Bruce Winery has a cult following for its pinot noirs, which are pinots to the core—unpredictable (sometimes great, sometimes not so) but always full of character. And the estate chardonnays from Mount Eden Vineyards have almost mythic stature. The vineyards, on the crest of a mountain, were planted with chardonnay in 1948.

The supercreative and wonderfully wacky winery Bonny Doon Vineyard is also located in Santa Cruz. Bonny Doon's highly talented winemaker/owner Randall Grahm, a character right out of Dr. Seuss, works with dozens of obscure or overlooked (in California) grape varieties, ultimately making from them some of the most exciting wines in California.

## Santa Clara Valley

The American Viticultural Area Santa Clara Valley begins on the eastern-facing slopes of the Santa Cruz Mountains and then spreads down and outward,

encompassing the valley. Confusingly, several wineries are entitled to use either the Santa Clara Valley or Santa Cruz Mountain appellation.

Like the Livermore Valley, Santa Clara was prime wine country before the turn of the century when it had more than a hundred wineries. But again like Livermore, its easy access to San Francisco and the bay (this is California's Silicon Valley) proved irresistible to developers. What was once a great agricultural valley full of vineyards is now largely covered with housing tracts and industrial parks, although about twenty wineries are to be found. Most are small, but the two largest— J. Lohr and Mirassou—have solid reputations for easy-drinking, inexpensive wines, the grapes for which often come from Monterey.

## Monterey County

Descending southeast from the vast arc of Monterey Bay lies Monterey County, the largest appellation within the northern part of the Central Coast. There are about 40,000 acres of vines here, plus thousands upon thousands of acres of vegetables in the fertile garden known as the Salinas Valley.

Although there were Franciscan missions in Monterey in the eighteenth century, the area did not really emerge as a wine region until the 1960s and 1970s,

*With his unstoppable wit, whimsy, and wisdom, Randall Grahm, winemaker and president (or as he puts it: "president for life") of Bonny Doon Vineyards, has helped change the course of winemaking in California.*

when extensive urban development in Livermore and Santa Clara, plus rising land prices in Sonoma and Napa, caused many wineries to look elsewhere for suitable vineyard land. Monterey, an easily accessible, agricultural coastal region, was just waiting to be tapped.

*Besides growing grapes, Monterey's Salinas Valley is the so-called lettuce capital of the world. In addition to lettuce, more than 50 percent of the United States' broccoli, strawberries, mushrooms, spinach, artichokes, and chile peppers are grown here.*

The southern part of Monterey can be extremely hot, but the northern part of the county is a chilly tunnel for cold winds that whip in off the whitecapped waters of Monterey Bay (home to otters, seals, and migrating whales). The severity of the winds can be seen in the permanently bowed trees, many of which are stripped of growth on their ocean-facing side. While a little bit of wind is generally good for vines (it cools them and helps guard against mildew and rot), extreme wind can cause the cells responsible for photosynthesis to shut down, inhibiting the ripening of the grapes. In a region that's already cool, anything that further constrains ripening is no blessing. Thus the top vintners have had to be extremely careful in selecting protected vineyard sites, as well as in choosing appropriate farming and trellising methods. Monterey vintners who have not been diligent in these two areas or who have pushed their vineyards to produce high yields have

often made wines with a "green" herbaceous streak running through them.

There are about thirty wineries in Monterey, and a considerable number of wineries located elsewhere buy Monterey grapes. Chardonnay is the dominant grape in the county, especially in the cooler northern part where wines of real character can be made. Caymus and Morgan are just two of the best producers making lively Monterey chardonnays.

One of the most delicious varietals made in Monterey is riesling, which, while it rarely shows up on restaurant wine lists, positively flies out of the door of tasting rooms, since just about every wine drinker who samples a Monterey riesling can't help but buy a few bottles.

Cabernet sauvignon and merlot are the leading red grape varieties; both are planted mostly in small selected warm pockets in the north or in the warmer southern part of the county.

699

## Chalone, Mount Harlan, and the Carmel Valley

Within Monterey County and its neighbor San Benito County are several small appellations, the most significant of which are Chalone, Mount Harlan, and the Carmel Valley. Chalone and Mount Harlan, the two most prestigious, each have only a single winery. The Chalone appellation (the name comes from the Native Americans who lived there) is home to Chalone Vineyard; Mount Harlan is home to the Calera Wine Company. Both Chalone Vineyard and the Calera Wine Company were founded by individuals maniacally possessed by the conviction that chalky limestone (a major component in the best soils of Burgundy) was essential for world-class pinot noir and chardonnay.

In the case of Chalone Vineyard, that individual was Curtis Tamm, a Burgundian who, in 1919, found limestone in the Gavilan mountain range and planted a vineyard. This first Chalone vineyard is the oldest still producing in Monterey County. Chalone Vineyard was later bought by Harvard University music graduate Dick Graff, who initially made wine in an old chicken coop. Today the publicly traded Chalone Wine Group (owners of Chalone Vineyard, Acacia Winery, Carmenet Vineyard, and Edna Valley Vineyard) has more than 10,000 shareholders, with 50 percent of the stock being held by Domaines Barons de Rothschild, which, among other properties, owns Château Lafite-Rothschild.

In the late 1960s and early 1970s, Yale- and Oxford-educated Josh Jensen also went looking for limestone in California. He, too, found it in the Gavilan mountain range where, on Mount Harlan, he established the Calera Wine Company in 1975. Calera's four pinot noirs—Jensen, Mills, Reed, and Selleck—are handcrafted from single vineyards and are made in what can only be described as a purist's manner. Like most of the best pinots, they are variable and capricious: Sometimes they're stunning; sometimes not quite so. Calera also makes a lip-smackingly rich viognier.

The Carmel Valley is named for the postcard-quaint tourist town of Carmel nearby and the Carmel River watershed. There are only a handful of wineries spread over this mountainous area, including Bernardus, Galante, and Durney. Most of the better vineyards sit on warm east-facing benches and ridges.

Unlike the rest of Monterey, which is known for white wine, this is prime cabernet sauvignon and merlot territory.

## Visiting the Wineries of the Northern Central Coast

The wineries of the northern Central Coast are spread out over a large and diverse area. Several of the most beautiful are tucked into remote enclaves in the coastal mountains. Because the wineries here are generally not on a tourist route, it's best to call ahead for an appointment. Above all, don't miss an overnight stay, or at least dinner, at either the Highlands Inn on Highland Drive in Carmel ([831] 620-1234) or the Ventana Inn on Highway 1 in Big Sur ([831] 667-2331). Two of the most spectacular, secluded hotels on California's coast, each has stunning views of the Pacific Ocean.

**BONNY DOON VINEYARD**
10 Pine Flat Road
Santa Cruz, CA 95060
(831) 425-3625

**CHALONE VINEYARD**
Stonewall Canyon Road
(Highway 146)
Soledad, CA 93960
(831) 678-1717

**DAVID BRUCE WINERY**
21439 Bear Creek Road
Los Gatos, CA 95033
(408) 354-4214

**MIRASSOU VINEYARDS**
3000 Aborn Road
San Jose, CA 95135
(408) 274-4000

**RIDGE VINEYARDS AND WINERY**
17100 Monte Bello Road
Cupertino, CA 95014
(408) 867-3233

# THE NORTHERN CENTRAL COAST
# WINES TO KNOW

*For each wine below, the specific American Viticultural Area from which it comes is noted.*

## *Whites*

### CHALONE VINEYARD
Chardonnay
Chalone
100% chardonnay

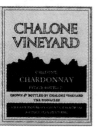

Chalone Vineyard's chardonnays are among the most elegant, graceful, and complex made in California. Their opulent, nutty, honeyed flavors fairly vibrate with intensity, and their textures could not be more hedonistically silky. The best part, however, is in store for those who wait—with age, Chalone's chardonnays seem to melt into a state of total sumptuousness. Also not to be missed: Chalone pinot blanc, one of the top pinot blancs in California and a gorgeous wine. Chalone is located high (at 2,000 feet) in the remote Gavilan Mountains on limestone-rich soil, reminiscent of that in Burgundy.

### MER SOLEIL
Chardonnay
Central Coast
100% chardonnay

For more than a decade, Chuck Wagner, a proprietor of Napa Valley's famous Caymus Vineyards, studied the soil of California, looking for a cool, well-drained slope on which to plant chardonnay. He settled on a site in Monterey where in 1992 he produced the first Mer et Soleil (sea and sun, now called just Mer Soleil). At its best this is a wonderfully honeyed chardonnay shot through with the flavors of wild herbs and new-mown hay.

### MIRASSOU
Riesling
Monterey
100% riesling

A family-owned winery, Mirassou was begun in the early 1850s and is thought by some historians to be the oldest winery in continual operation in California. Its rieslings are not only delicious but a steal. The flavors of very ripe sweet apricots and peaches are overlaid with a touch of minerals and spice—a terrific match with Asian dishes.

### MORGAN
Chardonnay
reserve
Monterey
100% chardonnay

Morgan is well known for big rich chardonnays packed with style. At its best, the reserve in particular exudes baked apple, brioche, and butterscotch flavors, and the wine's creamy roundness is very seductive. While many big chardonnays are overwrought with oak and toast, the Morgan chardonnays manage to achieve a balanced elegance.

# Reds

### BONNY DOON VINEYARD
Le Cigare Volant

California

approximately 40% grenache,
30% mourvèdre, 25% syrah, and a bit of cinsaut

LE CIGARE VOLANT
RED WINE
CALIFORNIA

Randall Grahm's first and leading Rhône wine, Le Cigare Volant, is modeled after the wines of Châteauneuf-du-Pape and takes its name from a law on that city's books prohibiting flying saucers—or flying cigars as they're called in France—from landing in the region's vineyards (true). Juicy, spicy, and meaty, Le Cigare Volant is also something of a zany wine, hopping up and down with rushes of pepper and berryocity. You'll see. Grahm gets grapes from up and down the state, though a good share come from vineyards in the northern Central Coast.

### CALERA
Pinot Noir

Selleck

Mt. Harlan

100% pinot noir

CALERA
SELLECK
Mt. Harlan Pinot Noir

GROWN, PRODUCED & BOTTLED
BY CALERA WINE COMPANY.
HOLLISTER, CALIFORNIA
TABLE WINE

Calera makes four single-vineyard pinot noirs (Selleck, Reed, Mills, and Jensen) from vineyards on limestone soil in the heart of the Gavilan Mountains. Each year they are some of the most complex and refined pinots in California. Picking a favorite is next to impossible; these are handcrafted wines that are always changing and evolving. What they all possess is the seamless expression of rich fruit and elegant texture that drives pinot noir lovers mad.

### DURNEY VINEYARDS
Merlot

Carmel Valley

100% merlot

Durney makes merlots that are full of *umph*. The best examples are packed with thick mocha and black currant fruit drizzled with hints of smoke, pepper, and licorice. The winery's vineyards in the Carmel Valley run almost to the edge of the rugged Ventana Wilderness area of the Los Padres National Forest.

### RIDGE
Monte Bello

Santa Cruz Mountains

approximately 80% cabernet sauvignon,
10% merlot, and 10% petit verdot

As classic, structured, and concentrated as First Growth Bordeaux, the Ridge Monte Bello cabernet sauvignons are mighty and majestic wines. Opening one from a great vintage when it's young is almost criminal, for the wine will be as firmly closed as a steel trap. But in ten years or so a stunningly rich superstar saturated with black currant fruit will emerge. Ridge was founded in 1959 by three Stanford Research Institute engineers.

RIDGE
CALIFORNIA
MONTE BELLO

# Sweet Wine

### BONNY DOON VINEYARD
Muscat

Vin de Glacière

California

approximately 70% muscat canelli,
25% orange muscat, and a small amount of malvasia bianca

Randall Grahm of Bonny Doon Vineyards makes a slew of ethereal dessert potions (a more apt word than *wines* in his case), including this outrageous muscat from grapes grown in several parts of the northern Central Coast (hence the AVA California). It's utterly and totally gossamer elegance, without a whit of sagging sweetness. Essence of apricot coalesces with essence of litchi, plus a few mango, lime, and spice notes thrown in for good measure. *Vin de glacière* translates as wine of the icebox, a playful takeoff on Germany's extraordinary *eiswein*, the grapes for which are left to freeze on the vine. This muscat is modeled after them, only Grahm freezes his grapes in a fridge.

# THE MIDDLE
# AND SOUTHERN CENTRAL COAST

lthough the viticultural areas of the middle and southern Central Coast are (at the moment) less well known than the Napa Valley or Sonoma County, they are among the most exciting in the state. Some of California's dynamic Rhône-style wines are made here, including viogniers and roussannes dripping with sensuality, plus syrahs that, like a cowboy in a tuxedo, seem rugged yet polished at the same time. Rhône varieties show so much promise here that the ultraprestigious winery Château de Beaucastel from France's Rhône Valley, chose Paso Robles as the site for its California nursery, vineyard, and winery. Much of the syrah planted in California is thought to be descended from the origi-

nal syrah vines planted by Paso Robles' Eberle Winery in 1975.

While there is no official ruling on where the northern, middle, and southern parts of the Central Coast begin and end, Paso Robles—being more or less smack midway between San Francisco and Los Angeles—is definitely middle Central Coast. For that reason, I've chosen to define the middle and southern Central Coast as those AVAs from Paso Robles south, including not only Paso Robles and just to its west, York Mountain, but also Edna Valley and Arroyo Grande (both in San Luis Obispo County) and Santa Maria Valley and Santa Ynez Valley (both in Santa Barbara County).

*Lying over a 1,500-foot-high plateau, the vineyards of Zaca Mesa exude serenity. A former Chumash Indian meeting place, the site was settled by the Spanish, who called it La Zaca Mesa—the restful place.*

Paradoxically, the middle and southern parts of the Central Coast are among the oldest wine regions in California—and, at the same time, among the newest. Spanish missions and vineyards were strung like beads on a necklace here in the eighteenth century. Yet neither area came into its own as a contemporary wine region until the 1980s with the national recognition of such wineries as Edna Valley, Zaca Mesa, Sanford, Au Bon Climat, Qupé, Eberle, Peachy Canyon, and Wild Horse.

Speaking of just the southern Central Coast for a minute (farther north is more variable), the most salient fact is this: It's a cool place (thermally). Despite its southerly latitude, the southern Central Coast is by far one of the coolest wine areas in the state. The reason has to do with the way the valleys lie. Thanks to California's tumultuous geologic past, most of the valleys in the state were formed in an essentially north to south direction (think of Napa and Sonoma as well as the huge Central Valley, for example). Unusually for California, however, the wine valleys of the southern Central Coast were formed so that they run basically east to west, enabling them to become direct conduits for fog and cold offshore breezes that barrel inland from the Pacific Ocean. Summer in the Santa Maria Valley is goose bump season; the *average* summer temperature is only 75°F.

Not surprisingly, this is chardonnay and pinot noir country, for while it is possible to make either wine in a warm region, top-class chardonnays and pinots—the kind that have character, focus, and complexity—are almost exclusively the provenance of cool places (consider Champagne, Burgundy, Oregon, Carneros).

As for the wineries themselves, early on the middle and southern Central Coast was a haven for tiny, creative wine companies on shoestring budgets headed by maverick winemakers who intuitively understood the region's potential. (One of the best and a typical example is Jim Clendenen of Au Bon Climat, often described as looking more like a Hell's Angel than a vintner.) By the late 1980s, however, so many delicious wines were coming out of the region that big companies moved in and snapped up vineyard land at comparatively rock-bottom prices. Among the large wineries that now own extensive vineyards in the middle and southern Central Coast are Robert Mondavi, Kendall-Jackson, and Beringer Blass Wine Estates (the latter owns Meridian Vineyards in Paso Robles and in the Napa Valley, Beringer Vineyards).

Here are capsulizations of the different viticultural areas, starting in the north and moving south.

## Paso Robles and York Mountain

Paso Robles is the most dramatic exception to the generally cool climates of the middle and southern Central Coast. A warm expanse of sun-baked, oak-studded hills (the original name, El Paso de Robles means the pass of oaks), Paso Robles is shielded from the cool, maritime influence of the Pacific Ocean by the almost solid curtain of the Santa Lucia Range on its western side. In Paso Robles the nights are chilly but the days are long, dry, and quite hot—exactly what's needed for ripe cabernet sauvignon and zinfandel, as well as syrah. Ridge Vineyards makes one of its four exquisite zinfandels from Paso Robles grapes; Peachy Canyon and Eberle also make knockout zins; and Meridian Vineyards, the largest winery in the area, makes a slew of very good, well-priced, every night dinner wines.

Just west of Paso Robles, the York Mountain viticultural area—the smallest in the mid-Central Coast—sits more than 1,500 feet high in the mountains near a deep gash in the range known as the Templeton Gap. Although there are a few vineyards, there is just one winery here, York Mountain Winery, which dates from the late nineteenth century.

## Edna Valley and Arroyo Grande

At 35 square miles and 67 square miles respectively, Edna Valley and Arroyo Grande may be small viticultural areas, but they are chardonnay and pinot noir Edens. Both areas are close to the sea and profoundly influenced by its cool, damp breezes. The most well-known chardonnays are made by Edna Valley Vineyards and Talley Vineyards, though chardonnays full of personality are also made by the minuscule Salamandre Wine Cellars. In addition, using grapes from Edna Valley, tiny Alban Vineyards makes one of the most sensual viogniers in California.

## Santa Maria Valley and Santa Ynez Valley

Two extremely dynamic wine regions, Santa Maria Valley and Santa Ynez Valley, fall within Santa Barbara County (although a small part of the Santa Maria Valley is partly in San Luis Obispo County). Viticulture and winemaking exploded here in the 1980s. By way of an example, in 1970 there were 171 acres of grapes in Santa Barbara County and they accounted for very little revenue. By 1998, there were 16,500 acres generating over 59 million dollars in revenue.

The Santa Maria and Santa Ynez Valleys are, again, very cool places. Santa Maria, closest to the ocean, is the coolest, with dense banks of morning fog that can take many hours to burn off, only to be replaced by chilly afternoon breezes. Santa Ynez, south and east of Santa Maria, is slightly more sheltered by surrounding hills and mountains and is, as a result, more temperate.

Chardonnay represents more than 60 percent of all the grapes grown in these two regions, although in warm pockets some snappy sauvignon blancs are made. The red grapes of renown (deservedly) are pinot noir and syrah, which in the hands of great producers here can make very delicious wines full of personality.

While lots of wineries located elsewhere buy Santa Maria and Santa Ynez grapes and make good wines from them, some of the very top wines are made by local producers. On the "don't miss" list are the wines from Au Bon Climat, Byron, Foxen, Qupé, Zaca Mesa, Cambria, and Santa Barbara Winery.

705

# THE MIDDLE AND SOUTHERN CENTRAL COAST WINES TO KNOW

*For each wine below, the specific American Viticultural Area from which it comes is noted.*

## *Whites*

### ALBAN VINEYARDS

Viognier
Alban Estate Vineyard
Edna Valley
100% viognier

Exotic, elegant, and endlessly captivating—that's what the Alban viogniers are year after year. With ballet-like balance, the flavors of honeysuckle, lime, ginger, jasmine, and crenshaw melon coalesce to become something indescribably and deliciously complex. Alban Vineyards, one of California's top wineries for Rhône varieties, makes two viogniers—this one, the premier estate viognier from the Edna Valley, and a less expensive Central Coast viognier. Both are produced in tiny quantities and both have developed cult followings.

### BYRON

Chardonnay
Santa Barbara County
100% chardonnay

Byron's chardonnays are exceptionally refined yet lively, with peach, pear, and apricot flavors that fairly glitter. No chubbiness here. No flab. Nothing overwrought. Just beautiful precision, balance, and chardonnayness. The estate chardonnay in particular is laced with gorgeous nutty, brioche flavors and an ultra-creamy texture. Byron is owned by the Robert Mondavi Winery.

## *Reds*

### AU BON CLIMAT

Pinot Noir
La Bauge Au-dessus
Santa Barbara County
100% pinot noir

From the day the winery was founded in 1982, Au Bon Climat has made some of the most compelling and controversial wines (people either love them or hate them) in southern California. Supertalented owner Jim Clendenen is an unconventional wild man whose passion for great Burgundy shows through in his own pinots, which are about as primal, sensual, and earthy as they come. *La bauge au-dessus* is French slang for the (illicit) party upstairs.

### EBERLE

Zinfandel
Sauret Vineyard
Paso Robles
100% zinfandel

This wine could do justice to a medieval feast of roasted meats. In most years, it's a big, masculine bear of a wine, richly suffused with leather, chocolate, raspberry, and cigar box aromas and flavors. Best of all, the flavors are fascinatingly complex, changing ever so slightly minute by minute. Eberle (the name means little wild boar in Low German) was founded by Gary Eberle, a former defensive tackle for Penn State who holds degrees in zoology and fermentation science and who was one of the pioneers of viticulture in Paso Robles.

## PEACHY CANYON WINERY

Zinfandel

Dusi Ranch

Paso Robles

100% zinfandel

Peachy Canyon makes several zinfandels, each one of which is usually loaded with personality. The zin from the old, unirrigated and untrellised vineyards of Dusi Ranch, considered perhaps the single best zinfandel vineyard in the middle Central Coast, is especially fine. The wine's structure is profound; the balance is perfect; and you can't say no to flavors that seem to have been lifted right out of a homemade boysenberry pie.

## QUPE

Los Olivos Cuvée

Santa Barbara County

approximately 50% syrah, 40% mourvèdre, and 10% grenache

*Owner/winemaker Dick Dore (left) and winemaker Bill Wathan have a magic touch when it comes to turning syrah grapes into sensational wine. The winery building, like the two men, is humble.*

The owner/winemaker of Qupé, Bob Lindquist, is one of the most talented small producers of Rhône-style wines. Year after year, Qupé's syrahs and Rhône blends are astonishing in their complexity and richness. And none more so than the Los Olivos Cuvée, a cashmere-soft, supple wine full of super-concentrated blackberry fruit. In great years, this wine achieves an opulence and power that few other Rhône blends match. *Qupé* is the Chumash Indian word for the California golden poppy.

707

## FOXEN

Syrah

Morehouse Vineyard

Santa Ynez Valley

100% syrah

In every vintage the wines from Foxen, a small family-owned winery, come out among the best being made in the southern Central Coast. In particular Foxen's sweetly ripe and meaty syrahs are winning. Often infused with exotic spice flavors, they are impeccably balanced, rich in flavor, and extremely satisfying.

## ZACA MESA

Z Cuvee

Santa Barbara County

approximately 50% grenache, 30% mourvèdre, 15% syrah, and small amounts of cinsaut and counoise

A leading candidate for the perfect every-night house wine, Z Cuvee is juicy, fleshy, and packed with boysenberry and raspberry flavors. When it's at its best, there's just enough tannin here to give the wine grip and just enough acidity to make the flavors bright.

## Visiting the Wineries of the Middle and Southern Central Coast

The Santa Maria and Santa Ynez Valleys can be stunningly beautiful, with vast stretches of vineyards covering mesas and plateaus. This part of the southern Central Coast is only 90 miles from Los Angeles and makes a great day trip.

Wineries of the middle and southern Central Coast are mostly unpretentious and down-to-earth. Many are small family operations with simple tasting rooms and picnic facilities. It's best to call ahead for hours and/or an appointment.

The restaurant *not* to be missed in this part of wine country is The Hitching Post in Buellton, a no-frills local hangout (usually full of winemakers) where the specialty is grilled red meats.

Both the Paso Robles Vintners and Growers Association, (805) 239-8463, and the Santa Barbara County Vintners' Association, (805) 688-0881, can be counted on for maps, information, and schedules of yearly events.

**CAMBRIA WINERY AND VINEYARD**
5475 Chardonnay Lane
Santa Maria, CA 93454
(805) 937-8091
This is one of the larger wineries.

**EBERLE WINERY**
3810 Highway 46 East
(3.8 miles east of Highway 101)
Paso Robles, CA 93446
(805) 238-9607

**MERIDIAN VINEYARDS**
7000 Highway 46 East
(7 miles east of Highway 101)
Paso Robles, CA 93446
(805) 237-6000

**PEACHY CANYON WINERY**
2025 Nacimiento Drive
Paso Robles, CA 93446
(805) 237-1577

**SANTA BARBARA WINERY**
202 Anacapa Street
Santa Barbara, CA 93101
(805) 963-3633

**ZACA MESA WINERY**
6905 Foxen Canyon Road
Los Olivos, CA 93441
(805) 688-9339

# New York State

The name *New York* usually sparks glamorous images of one of the world's most high-powered cities. But there is another New York as well, the New York of cornfields and potato barns, of rolling farmland and flowing rivers, of sapphire blue lakes and graceful mountains. Much of New York State is, in fact, utterly and magnificently rural.

What would become New York State was formed during the Ice Age as receding glaciers gouged out the Adirondack and Catskill Mountains and carved deep passageways that would become the Hudson and Mohawk river valleys. As the glaciers retreated north, more than 8,000 lakes and ponds were created in the state. Eventually, these same glaciers would hollow out the five massive Great Lakes, including Lake Erie and Lake Ontario, which form parts of the northern and western borders of the state. In their wake, the glaciers not only left behind bodies of water but also deep, well-drained soil. By the time the colonists arrived, the area, already full of wild indigenous vines, seemed naturally poised to become an important place for grapes. And so it would become; by the latter part of the twentieth century, New York State would have four major wine regions: the Hudson River Valley, the Finger Lakes, the Lake Erie region, and Long Island.

Although Dutch colonists attempted to grow grapes on Manhattan Island as early as 1647, viticulture and winemaking did not take serious hold until the nineteenth century when French, Dutch, and English immigrants began planting vine-

709

*Quaint barns and farmhouses are home to wineries in the Finger Lakes district of upper New York State.*

NEW YORK STATE'S WINE REGIONS

The Hudson River Valley
The Finger Lakes
Lake Erie
Long Island

## THE QUICK SIP ON NEW YORK STATE

* New York State is one of the most diversified wine regions in the United States, growing *vinifera* grape varieties as well as native American grapes, crosses, and hybrids.

* New York's cool northern climate makes it well suited to producing not only dry still table wines but also lively sparkling wines plus some excellent late harvest and ice wines.

* Of New York's four major wine regions, Long Island is the newest; the Finger Lakes has the most wineries and is the fastest growing.

yards on the rolling hills of the Hudson River Valley. From there the immigrants pushed westward into the state's stunning, remote, lake-clad interior.

As was true in California, New York's wine industry blossomed in the decades before Prohibition. In particular, the Finger Lakes benefited from waves of German, French, and Swiss immigrants who were experienced at both grape growing and winemaking. Riding on their skills and ambitions, by the 1870s the Finger Lakes had become the heart of the New York wine industry. Steamboats laden with grapes and wine cruised back and forth doing a brisk business among the wineries that ringed the lakes. With the founding of the Geneva Experiment Station in the early 1880s, significant advances in grape breeding and viticulture led to leaps in quality among Finger Lakes wines. According to the grandfather of American wine writing, Leon Adams, New York wines were so highly regarded in the years just

before Prohibition that menus for important banquets and events often included as many Finger Lakes and Hudson Valley wines as California wines.

The southern shores of Lake Erie, now one of the largest grape belts in the United States, were also planted with grapes around this time. The region, however, soon became a political stronghold for America's nascent temperance movement. All too soon, growers who might have planted wine grapes were focusing on juice and table grapes instead.

From the end of Prohibition until the mid-1970s the New York wine industry was controlled by a few powerful companies. As of 1976 there were only nineteen wineries in the state, most of them specializing in native American grapes, crosses, and hybrids. Small growers, their hands tied by exorbitant New York State licensing fees and bureaucratic red tape, grew and sold the sorts of grapes the big wineries wanted rather than creating wine

## POLITICAL BEGINNINGS

Two of the most culturally significant political movements in the history of the United States began in the wine regions of New York State: the temperance movement and the women's rights movement. The temperance movement began in Saratoga Springs and quickly spread to the Lake Erie region as early as 1808, eventually culminating in national Prohibition in 1920. The women's rights movement began in Seneca Falls in the Finger Lakes with the first Women's Rights Convention in 1848.

brands of their own. At the same time, the big wineries began buying inexpensive bulk wine from California and blending it into their own wines to make cheap New York-California jug wine blends. By the middle of the 1970s, New York's reputation as a producer of fine wines seemed to be sliding downhill fast.

In 1976 the critical turnaround came with the passage of the Farm Winery Act, which substantially reduced fees and made operating a small winery economically feasible by permitting direct sales to restaurants, wine stores, and consumers. Within seven years, nearly fifty small farm wineries had opened for business. Today, with the exception of the state's sole very large winery, Canandaigua Wine Company (the second-largest wine company in the United States after E. & J. Gallo), the majority of New York's 140 wineries are small to medium in size and grow most, if not all, of their own grapes.

The Farm Winery Act also opened the doors for the growth of New York's fourth major wine region, Long Island, born more than a century after the first vineyards were planted in the Finger Lakes. Many of Long Island's vineyards, though today among the most prestigious in the state, were humble potato farms just two to three decades ago.

One of the most fascinating aspects of New York viticulture is how diverse it is. Most of the world's wine regions make wine from grapes that belong to a single species, the European *Vitis vinifera*. New York, however, not only grows *Vitis vinifera* but also boasts more acreage of native American grapes than anyplace else in the world. Native American grapes belong to a number of species including, *Vitis labrusca*, *Vitis riparia*, and others. In addition, wine here is made from at least a dozen hybrids and crosses (see page 715). Given such biological scope, it is not surprising that the range of flavors in New York State wines is enormous.

711

*It's no surprise for the vineyards of Gristina on Long Island to be covered in snow during cold winter months. The grapevines don't mind—they are dormant during this season. Come early spring, each vine will need to be individually pruned (left).*

A total of about fifty different grape varieties is planted in the state, ten to fifteen of which are grown in commercially significant amounts. Of these, chardonnay, riesling, cabernet sauvignon, and merlot lead among *vinifera* varieties; more Concord is grown than any other native grape, although most of these grapes become juice and jelly, not wine; catawba is the leading American cross; and top French-American hybrids include seyval blanc, vidal blanc, vignoles, and cayuga.

## THE GRAPES AND THE WINES

As you can imagine, the wines creating the most excitement in New York State today are chardonnays, rieslings, merlots, and cabernets, but there are a number of other delicious wines, many of which are both fascinating and rare. A case in point is Dr. Konstantin Frank's rkatsiteli (ar-kat-si-TEL-lee), a light, refreshing, and floral wine. Though rarely planted in western Europe or the New World, rkatsiteli is the most widely planted grape in Russia and was brought to New York in the 1950s by the late Dr. Frank.

But with all due respect to such wonderfully oddball varieties, New York State, like virtually every other wine region in the United States, has become smitten with something far more familiar: chardonnay. The chardonnays of New York, however, usually bear only a faint resemblance to their big buttery sisters in California. Generally leaner and more brisk, they seem perfectly built for the myriad of seafood caught off Long Island. A great vintage of Palmer chardonnay, with its boltingly fresh

## THE GRAPES OF (WELCH'S) WRATH

Approximately 50 percent of the grapes harvested in New York State become not wine, but rich, purply, aromatic grape juice. New York produces more grape juice than any other state. That juice includes the famous brand Welch's Concord grape juice, invented by Dr. Thomas Welch in 1869. Like most other grape juices, Welch's is made from native Concord grapes grown along the banks of Lake Erie, a huge viticultural region that New York shares with Ohio and Pennsylvania. Were it not for Dr. Welch, an ardent Prohibitionist, the Lake Erie region might have developed as an important producer of wine grapes rather than juice grapes. Today 95 percent of the grapes grown in the Lake Erie region are still Concords destined for juice.

flavors of just picked apples, juicy lemons, and mandarin oranges is a good example.

New York's rieslings are possibly the most evanescent rieslings coming out of the United States. Utterly light in both body and flavor, they have what the Germans (riesling specialists, after all) would approvingly call clarity and transparency. Modern wine drinkers accustomed to full-bodied powerhouse wines may be quick to dismiss New York rieslings as intangible. That would be a mistake. Just as music isn't better because it's louder, wine isn't better because it's more robust.

New York's rieslings (a few of which are still labeled with the old-fashioned

**Dr. Konstantin Frank**
1995
*Rkatsiteli*
NEW YORK FINGER LAKES
PRODUCED & BOTTLED BY
KONSTANTIN D. FRANK & SONS VINIFERA WINE CELLARS, LTD.
HAMMONDSPORT, N.Y. 14840  ALCOHOL 13% BY VOLUME

## THE GRAPES OF
## NEW YORK STATE

### WHITES

**Cayuga:** Major French-American hybrid. Cayuga is often used in off-dry blends and for dessert wines.

**Chardonnay:** Major grape. The good to very good wines it becomes are leaner in style than California chardonnays.

**Gewürztraminer:** One of New York's best-kept secrets. Can be turned into stupendous wines reminiscent of the gewürztraminers of Alsace.

**Niagara:** American cross. Often made into off-dry and dessert wines.

**Riesling:** Major grape. Makes many dynamic, vibrant dry wines, as well as delicious off-dry and dessert wines. Most of the best examples of riesling come from the Finger Lakes.

**Seyval Blanc:** Major French-American hybrid. Used on its own and in blends. Can make good-tasting, dry wines.

**Vidal Blanc:** Major French-American hybrid. A source of dry wines and some exceptional ice wines.

**Vignoles:** Major French-American hybrid also known as Ravat blanc. Used for dry wines and some tasty ice wines.

### REDS

**Baco Noir:** French-American hybrid grape. Makes simple fruity red wines.

**Cabernet Franc:** Major grape. Often blended with merlot and cabernet sauvignon for Bordeaux-style reds.

**Cabernet Sauvignon:** Major grape. Often blended with merlot to create Bordeaux-style reds. Only a modest number of producers, notably on Long Island, use it as a single varietal.

**Catawba:** An American cross; not truly red skinned but more pinkish. Makes fruity, light red and rosé wines.

**Concord:** Native grape belonging to the *labrusca* species. The most widely planted grape in New York State, although 80 percent of production is used for grape juice (and a little jelly), not wine. The remainder is used to make sweet kosher wines and fortified wines.

**Merlot:** Major grape. Merlot can become sleek, berried wines that range from good to delicious, especially those produced on Long Island.

**Pinot Noir:** Generally used for New York's numerous sparkling wines.

713

name Johannisberg riesling) come in all styles, from dry to off-dry to sweet late harvest and ice wines. The dry versions can be crisp, even austere, especially in less sunny years. Though purists often love such wines, other wine drinkers may prefer off-dry rieslings, which can taste a bit more harmonious and mellow. (As with a teaspoon of sugar in a cup of coffee, a tiny bit of natural sweetness tempers the wine without making it sweet per se.) There are numerous New York rieslings that shouldn't be missed, including those from Standing Stone, Fox Run, Swedish Hill, Wagner, and Hermann J. Wiemer.

As of the late 1990s, about 60 percent of all the wine produced in New York State was white, but red wines are on the rise. In particular, the Bordeaux varieties cabernet sauvignon, merlot, and cabernet franc are being planted at a pace that reflects their surging popularity. Many of the new plantings are on Long Island, which has the longest growing season in the state and a climate warm and sunny enough to bring these red varieties to ripeness. Even so, Long Island's cabernets and merlots tend to be sleek and medium bodied, not richly fruity and lush. Many can be angular and tight upon first opening. A grilled steak will help the situation nicely, as will aerating the wine by simply pouring it from the bottle into a decanter. For reds, Lenz, Gristina, Palmer, and Millbrook are the producers to watch.

Besides dry still wines, New York State is also known for dependably good sparkling wines and some delicious dessert wines, especially late harvest rieslings and riesling ice wines that have become, in a word, famous. Both sparklers and dessert wines are, of course, generally at their best when made in cool climates such as New York's. More than twenty-five wineries now make two or more different sparkling wines. With the exception of the big brands, such as Canandaigua's Great Western, these sparklers are virtually all made from chardonnay, pinot noir, pinot meunier, and pinot blanc, using the traditional Champagne method.

New York's sweet wines are without a doubt some of the best in the country, each year racking up gold medals in competitions nationwide. Mostly made in the Finger Lakes, they come in two styles: late harvest wines and ice wines. The late harvest wines are usually made with the help of *Botrytis cinerea*, the noble rot that contributes richness and depth of flavor. (It is botrytis that gives French Sauternes its character.) Most of the state's ice wines are, like the magnificent *eisweins* of Germany, made naturally from frozen grapes that have been left on the vines until well into winter. Along with riesling, many of these late harvest and ice wines are made from French-American hybrids, such as vidal blanc and vignoles. Drinking them with (or as) dessert is one delicious way to go, but there's another possibility. New York State also happens to be famous for foie gras, and there is no appetizer in the world more sensuous than warm sautéed foie gras and a small glass of chilled ice wine.

## L'CHAIM

Wine is central to the religious rites of Jews and especially to such profoundly important Jewish holidays as Passover. Historically in the United States, most of the wine used in Jewish ceremonies was made in New York State relatively near large urban centers of Jewish populations, including New York City. Much of this wine was, and continues to be, made in a very sweet style from native American varieties, particularly Concord grapes. Today the leading brands of sweet kosher wine are Manischewitz, Kedem, and Mogen David.

## FOIE GRAS AND ICE WINE

Foie Gras (literally, fat liver) is the lusciously rich fattened liver of a duck or goose. A specialty in France for centuries, foie gras arrived on the scene in the United States in the 1990s when two American companies finally perfected the technique for raising ducks and fattening their livers (geese have thus far proven too susceptible to disease). The biggest and best known of these companies is New York State's Hudson Valley Foie Gras, which every week produces 8,500 pounds of the stuff, and still, top restaurants around the country can't seem to get enough. Foie gras can be poached, baked, or made into a pâté or mousse, but the most classic and easiest way to prepare it is to simply sauté slices until they are seared on the outside and opulently creamy within. And what to drink with something that is so delicate and so off-the-charts in richness? The French often head straight for Sauternes, a rich-on-rich match that comes perilously close to maxing out the human tolerance for pleasure. An even more seductive match, however, may well be foie gras and ice wine. An ice wine's sweetness is counterbalanced by its penetrating acidity, and that acidity cuts through the unctuousness of foie gras like a hot knife through cold butter. Which ice wine? Perhaps the French had the right idea when they invented the concept of chauvinism. There are dozens of delicious New York State ice wines. If the foie gras is from New York State, why not the wine?

## The Vast Grab Bag of Grapes

Grape culture in New York State is a real embodiment of the American ideal; immigrants and natives live side by side. New York's wines are based on grapes from several species of vines, some indigenous, one European. By contrast, most wine regions worldwide grow just one vine species. Depending upon the derivation of the grapes, the wines of New York fall into three different camps.

### WINES FROM VINIFERA VARIETIES

*Vitis vinifera*, the only vine species that originated in Europe, includes such grapes as chardonnay, riesling, merlot, and cabernet sauvignon. Although *vinifera* is a relative newcomer to New York State, most of the top wines coming up are made with grapes that belong to this species. The majority of the new wineries of Long Island and the Finger Lakes, for example, focus primarily on *vinifera* grapes.

### WINES FROM NATIVE GRAPES AND AMERICAN CROSSES

Most of the world's grapevine species originated in North America, and several of these indigenous species are still grown in New York State. The best known and most popular of New York's native grapes, Concord, belongs to the hardy American species *Vitis labrusca*. New York grows more Concord grapes than any other state—on average, more than 100,000 tons each year, the vast majority of which is grown in the Lake Erie region. These grapes mostly get turned into grape juice, jelly, and jam, although a small percentage is also used to make wine, especially

715

# NEW YORK STATE WINES

LEADING WINES

**Cabernet Franc** red
**Cabernet Sauvignon** red
**Chardonnay** white
**Gewürztraminer** white
**Merlot** red
**Riesling** white (dry and sweet)
**Sparkling Wines** white

WINES OF NOTE

*Several of the wines below are made from native grapes, American crosses, or French-American hybrid grapes.*

**Baco Noir** red
**Catawba** red and rosé
**Cayuga** white
**Niagara** white
**Rkatsiteli** white
**Seyval Blanc** white
**Vidal Blanc** white (dry and sweet)
**Vignoles** white (dry and sweet)

716

enough, is also grown in Japan, although it's not clear how and why this came to be.) Like Concord, each of these grapes has an unusual grapey, soda-popish aroma and flavor generally referred to as foxy. Niagara, Delaware, and catawba are often used to make low-alcohol, wine cooler-type wines. Most of New York State's American cross grapes are grown in the Lake Erie region, with a small number found in the Finger Lakes.

## WINES FROM FRENCH-AMERICAN HYBRIDS

From 1880 to 1950 French scientists and horticulturists attempted to develop grape varieties that would taste similar to *vinifera* varieties yet be hardy and disease resistant like native varieties. To come up with these new "super" grape varieties, hundreds, if not thousands, of hybrids of *vinifera* and native American varieties were bred. The word *hybrid* is important here: technically a hybrid is not the same as a cross. A hybrid is a grape variety created by breeding a European (*vinifera*) vine species with one or more American species. A cross is a grape created by breeding two varieties from the *same* species, like the Niagara, catawba, and Delaware grapes just discussed.

Many of the hybrids created by the French scientists turned out to be fairly successful. Their flavors, while

sweet kosher wine and fortified dessert wines, such as New York Port- and Sherry-style wines.

In the 1800s grapes from such American species as *Vitis labrusca* were crossed with other American species, such as *Vitis riparia* and *Vitis rupestris*, resulting in what are known as American crosses. Niagara, catawba, and Delaware are all American crosses grown in New York State. (Delaware, curiously

*Lenz Merlot was one of the first merlots to put Long Island on the map as prime merlot-growing territory.*

not absolutely *vinifera*-like, were not completely foxy either, and the hybrids were indeed hardy in the vineyard. Among the French-American hybrids grown in New York State today are seyval blanc, vignoles, vidal blanc, and Baco noir. These hybrids make wines that are, in a sense, comparable to French *vins de pays*—pleasant, affordable, unique to the region, and usually consumed there. Most of New York's French-American hybrids are grown in the Finger Lakes, with some in the Hudson Valley.

The story of how New York's vineyards came to be so genetically diversified revolves around an assumption that later proved to be false. For centuries European grapes were wrongly presumed too fragile to withstand New York's cold winters. As late as 1980 there were just 324 acres of *vinifera* grapes in all New York. Native varieties, crosses, and hybrids became the stalwart, dependable grapes upon which the industry was founded. But as the 1970s and 1980s progressed, New York's winemakers grew increasingly worried and dissatisfied. Tastes had changed. For many wine drinkers familiar with Californian and European wines, native varieties, American crosses, and French-American hybrids made wines that were, by modern standards, an acquired taste. Some possessed that hard-to-describe pungent grapey flavor, the infamous foxy character. By the mid-1980s, many wine drinkers had begun to eschew such wines as being too peculiar.

Two prescient European immigrants had long sensed the impending plight. Charles Fournier, a French Champagne master and later the head of New York's Gold Seal Wine Company, and Dr. Konstantin Frank, a Russian-born professor of plant science, ultimately changed the course of New York viticultural history by initiating in the 1950s what would become a mini *vinifera* revolution. Frank came to New York as an immigrant in 1951 at the age of fifty-four and took the only job he could find—hoeing blueberries. Later, Charles Fournier hired him and allowed him to plant *vinifera* varieties. Frank knew that *vinifera* grew in the Ukraine, where winter temperatures were well below those in the Finger Lakes. By employing some careful and, at the time, sophisticated viticultural techniques, Frank was successful at growing the species and Fournier at making it into good wine. By the early 1960s Frank had established his own winery and was growing chardonnay, riesling, and some sixty other European grapes theretofore considered impossible to cultivate in New York State.

This triumph inspired other leading-edge winemakers. By 1996 there were 4,000 acres of *vinifera* grapes in New York State, a 1,200 percent rise over the acreage of 1980, and such wines as chardonnay, riesling, merlot, and cabernet sauvignon were breathing new life into New York's wine industry. Each year the trend continues as more *vinifera* is planted. I do hope that *vinifera* varieties will never fully replace all others, for while it is true that such grapes as merlot, chardonnay, and cabernet sauvignon are acknowledged to make the most refined wines in the world, for anyone with a shred of vinous curiosity, New York State wines are fascinating precisely because they offer dozens of flavors that can't be had almost anyplace else. Moreover, because native grapes and hybrids are now becoming increasingly scarce, they are all the more fun to taste and important to preserve.

# THE LAND

Of New York's approximately 31,000 acres of grapes, the vast majority are Concords grown primarily for grape juice plus a small amount for jelly. That leaves about 12,000 acres of wine grapes, a tiny amount compared to California's 427,000 acres.

These grapes grow in what is arguably a cool-climate wine-producing region. Winter generally comes soon after Thanksgiving and can last until April, well after vines in California are already budding. Long months of continuous sunshine and long hours of sun each day are, needless to say, not the norm. Instead, vines must work harder to ripen their grapes. Of course, there is a blessing buried within this imperfect situation. New York State, like other areas with cool climates, has the potential to make some truly lovely, elegant wines.

*Brotherhood Winery, founded in 1839, began as a producer of sacramental wine.*

The state's four major wine regions are fairly distant from one another. While all are relatively cool, they also share another critically important common denominator. All are adjacent to large bodies of water that have stabilizing effects on the environments around them. The presence of water helps moderate extremes of temperature, protecting the vines from severe cold snaps in spring and fall and fanning them with refreshing breezes during hot summers. The Finger Lakes region is dominated by four major (and numerous smaller) long, skinny lakes that look like the fingers of a hand. The Hudson River region is close by the river that gave it its name, just as the Lake Erie region is near the shores of Lake Erie. Long Island, of course, is surrounded by water on all sides. Were it not for these large bodies of water, grape growing might often prove unfeasible.

During the Ice Age the glaciers that created New York's myriad lakes also left behind an amalgam of soil. Upstate, there is deep, well-drained soil—principally shale, schist, and limestone. On Long Island, silt and loam dominate. Taken together, the combination of a cool but water-moderated climate, a variety of soil types, and individual sites that, geographically, can deviate considerably, means that New York State wines are highly influenced by the specific place where the grapes were grown. Place, in fact, is everything here. Or to put it another way, *terroir* reigns. (*Terroir*, once again, is the sum entity and effect—no single word exists in English—of soil, slope, orientation to the sun, and elevation, plus every nuance of climate: rainfall, wind velocity, frequency of fog, cumulative hours of sunshine, average high temperature, average low temperature, and so on.)

# THE HUDSON RIVER VALLEY

The Hudson River, the first great passageway into the New World, was explored in 1609 by the Englishman Henry Hudson who, on behalf of the Dutch East India Company, was searching for a water route across the North American continent to the Pacific. The deep, navigable river quickly became so important to trade that the harbor at its mouth is credited with helping New York City become one of the world's most prominent cities.

The vineyards of the Hudson River Valley, first planted in 1677 by French Huguenots, are the oldest in New York State. They begin just forty miles north of New York City. Most of the notable wineries, such as Benmarl and Cascade Mountain, are small or medium size, and production focuses on *vinifera* and hybrid varieties. Perhaps the most avant-garde winery in the region is Millbrook, owned by John Dyson, the former state commissioner of Agriculture and Markets. Millbrook grows twenty-five different *vinifera* grapes, from chardonnay to sangiovese, though many of these are grown on an experimental basis.

## BROTHERHOOD: THE OLDEST WINERY IN THE UNITED STATES

Brotherhood Winery, located in the rolling Catskill foothills of the Hudson River Valley, fifty miles northwest of New York City, has been in continuous operation longer than any other winery in the United States. Known today for its holiday spice wines and *eiswein*, Brotherhood began in 1839 as a producer of sacramental wines.

The inspiration behind the winery was a Huguenot immigrant shoemaker named Jean Jaques, who settled in the area in 1809 and bought land with the intention of growing fine table grapes to sell to city markets. He was successful in this venture until the early 1830s, when difficult economic times made grapes too costly to ship. It was then that Jaques decided to try his hand at winemaking. Naming the nascent winery Blooming Cove, he sold his first product, a sacramental wine, to his own church in 1839.

During the 1870s Jesse and Edward Emerson bought wines from Blooming Cove and blended them with wines made from grapes grown by a local commune called the Brotherhood of New Life. Cultlike, the colony behaved with uncompromising obedience to a leader who, among other things, decided where husbands and wives should sleep, which was usually not with each other. The commune eventually disbanded, but in 1885, when Jesse Emerson bought Blooming Cove, he decided to rename the winery Brotherhood.

For most of its history Brotherhood produced sweet fruit and dessert wines. And although chardonnay, cabernet sauvignon, and Johannisberg riesling were added in the 1980s, it's the winery's *eiswein*, a sweet wine made from grapes left on the vine until the winter cold freezes them, that continues to make converts.

*The Brotherhood Winery, 35 North Street, Washingtonville, NY 10992; (914) 496-3661.*

*The vineyards of the Finger Lakes ring the long, beautiful lakes. The Iroquois nation, which once reigned here, considered the lakes the imprint of the Great Spirit's hand. Wineries in the Finger Lakes (inset) are often converted old barns.*

# THE FINGER LAKES

Upstate New York's Finger Lakes region has been the center and soul of the New York wine industry since the Civil War. As of the late 1990s, it was still the fastest-growing wine region in the state, with more than sixty-seven wineries and several more in development. (Though its wines are very popular, Long Island has fewer wineries—twenty-four—and a slower rate of growth.)

The region fans out from eleven finger-shaped lakes. Of these, the four major ones are Seneca, Cayuga, Canandaigua, and Keuka, all Native American Indian names. These deep, narrow lakes were considered by the Iroquois to be formed by the hand of the Great Spirit. Many wineries are within sight of the lakes, which are considered some of the most beautiful in New York State.

The Finger Lakes are where both French-American hybrids and *vinifera* varieties got their start in New York. Originally, the vineyards here were planted with *labrusca* varieties and American crosses to make sweet wines. But after Prohibition, as the newly created hybrids became available, these too were planted. The first to do so was Charles Fournier, winemaker for the Urbana Wine Company (later known as Gold Seal) and a former Champagne master at the Champagne house Veuve Clicquot.

In 1936 Fournier planted French-American hybrids at Gold Seal. Seventeen years later, Fournier hired Dr. Konstantin Frank and the two decided to plant *vinifera* varieties as well. In 1961 the first *vinifera* wines in New York State were produced at Gold Seal.

Today the Finger Lakes region is abuzz with activity. All types of wine are made here from tasty chardonnays, rieslings, and gewürztraminers to Concord-based wines, such as Manischewitz, the leading brand of kosher wine in the United States. Not to be missed are the region's excellent late harvest and ice wines, generally based on French-American hybrids.

Among the Finger Lakes most famous historic wineries are Dr. Frank's Vinifera Wine Cellars, Glenora Wine Cellars, Wagner Vineyards, and Bully Hill Vineyards, the latter being a highly personalized, almost idio-

syncratic winery founded by Walter Taylor and owned by his family. Bully Hill is ardently devoted to hybrids and makes some very unusual, fascinating wines from them. The Finger Lakes is also home to a number of newer wineries, including such rising stars as Standing Stone Vineyards, Swedish Hill Vineyard, Lamoreaux Landing Wine Cellars, Knapp Vineyards, Fox Run, Lakewood Vineyard, and Hunt Country Vineyards.

*Wagner Vineyards, a historic Finger Lakes winery, frequently makes as many as thirty wines from* vinifera *and native varieties and hybrids.*

**721**

## LAKE ERIE

The vast Lake Erie region (also known as Chautauqua) is spread over 20,000 acres along the southern shore of that Great Lake. The region actually spans three states, New York, Ohio, and Pennsylvania. Though the largest of all the New York grape-growing districts, Lake Erie produces only a small amount of wine and is home to just a handful of wineries. Native American Concord grapes destined to become not wine, but juice, cover 19,000 of the region's 20,000 acres.

Among the small- and medium-size Lake Erie producers focusing on hybrid and/or *vinifera* grapes are Woodbury Vineyards, Merritt Estate Winery, and Schloss Doepken.

*Merritt Estate is one of the few wineries in the huge grape-growing region of Lake Erie.*

# LONG ISLAND

About ninety-five miles from New York City, the eastern end of Long Island is New York State's newest wine region. The wine boom began here in earnest in the late 1970s and early 1980s, after John Wickham, a farmer in the small hamlet of Cutchogue, successfully grew *vinifera* grapes in the mid-1960s. Though Wickham never made a commercial wine, it was only a matter of a decade before someone did.

In 1973 Louisa and Alex Hargrave founded Hargrave Vineyard in a former Cutchogue potato field. Several years later, the Hargraves' cabernets were generating waves of surprise and excitement throughout the state. Other would-be Long Island vintners soon followed. By the late 1990s, Long Island had twenty-four wineries.

Shaped like a lobster claw, Long Island begins close to the mainland of New York State and then thrusts out into the sea on a northeast angle, roughly

*Louisa and Alex Hargrave pioneered grape growing and winemaking on Long Island. Their winery Hargrave was sold to Marco and Ann Marie Borghese in 1999 and is now known as Castello di Borghese-Hargrave.*

*At SagPond Vineyards, in Sagaponack, visitors are offered Wolffer, the winery's top wine, which is named after the owner, Christian Wolffer.*

paralleling the Connecticut coast. The end of the island splits into two slivers of land, called the North Fork and the South Fork. The North Fork was historically known for its orchards, potato fields, and small farms; the South Fork for its white-duned beaches and whaling ports. Today the South Fork is probably best known for the Hamptons, a string of chic small villages where well-to-do Manhattanites spend summer weekends.

Although there are a sprinkling of wineries in the Hamptons, notably Channing Daughters and SagPond Vineyards, most of Long Island's vineyards are on the more protected and less populated North Fork. The North Fork is surrounded by water (Long Island Sound to the north, Peconic Bay to the south, and the Atlantic Ocean to the east), but it is not exposed broadside to the ocean as are the Hamptons on the South Fork. Thus the North Fork benefits from the moderating influences of

*The shingled tower of Pellegrini Vineyards in Cutchogue: The winery specializes in chardonnay, merlot, cabernet sauvignon, and dessert wines.*

the waters around it yet, at the same time, remains fairly well sheltered from severe saltwater storms and the area's not infrequent hurricanes. As an additional boon, the North Fork of Long Island is the sunniest part of New York State, an obvious advantage for ripening grapes.

A viticultural threat both forks share, however, is birds. Long Island is on the Atlantic flyway, a migratory route for numerous species of birds who can decimate a vineyard within days. Many Long Island vineyards must be netted at considerable expense to vintners.

Long Island's Atlantic maritime climate led early vintners to look at another Atlantic maritime climate for inspiration and guidance: Bordeaux. As a result, Long Island is now heavily planted with the Bordeaux red varieties merlot, cabernet sauvignon, and cabernet franc.

Many Long Island wineries are among the most expensively and technically well equipped in the state. A number were begun by wealthy individuals whose passions for wine superseded their lack of experience with grape growing or winemaking. The island's proximity to Manhattan also means that vineyard land here is the most expensive in New York, as much as ten times more expensive than that in the Finger Lakes, for example. Top Long Island wineries include Palmer Vineyards, Lenz Winery, Bedell Cellars, Pellegrini Vineyards, and Gristina Vineyards.

723

*Palmer Vineyards, in Aquebogue, is housed in a collection of wood frame buildings, one dating from Colonial times. The winery is one of the older and larger wineries on Long Island.*

# THE NEW YORK STATE WINES TO KNOW

*For each wine below, the specific American Viticultural Area from which it comes is noted.*

## Sparkling Wine

### CHATEAU FRANK

Blanc de Blancs

vintage

Finger Lakes

approximately 90% chardonnay,
10% pinot blanc

Willy Frank, son of Dr. Konstantin Frank, founded Chateau Frank in the mid-1980s. Devoted entirely to sparklers, the winery produces some of the best

bubblies in New York State today. Principal among them is the winery's *blanc de blancs,* a delicious shower of light, creamy, gingery flavors. In addition, don't miss Célèbre, a fresh, gentle peachy sparkler (inexpensive to boot) made from riesling blended with a touch of chardonnay. Célèbre is a *crémant*—that is, the wine is under only half as much pressure as a typical sparkling wine and so is less bubbly.

## Whites

### BULLY HILL VINEYARDS

White Wine

Finger Lakes

approximately 90% seyval blanc, 10% aurore

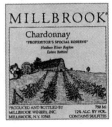

New York's most eccentric winery, Bully Hill is owned by the infamous and unsinkable Walter Taylor who, after losing control of the Taylor Wine Company, promptly began Bully Hill. Bully Hill makes no fewer than fifty wines, all based on hybrids and most with curious names, including Bulldog Baco Noir, Miss Love White, Goat White, and Mother Ship Over Paris Champagne Rouge. Of all the wines, the light and refreshing estate-bottled white is a top pick. This is the wine to try if you've never tasted a French-American hybrid before.

### DR. KONSTANTIN FRANK

Gewürztraminer

New York

100% gewürztraminer

Dr. Frank's Vinifera Wine Cellars markets wines under the brand name Dr. Konstantin Frank, which makes one of the best, snappiest gewürztraminers in the United States. At its best, it's bone-dry, rich, full-bodied, and solidly in the Alsace style. Intense pear and litchi flavors are laced with a haunting faint taste of crushed minerals. The wine's texture, again harkening to Alsace, is pure lanolin. Gewürztraminer is a strong suit for many wineries in New York State, but year in and year out, no one tops Dr. Frank and you can't beat the price.

### MILLBROOK

Chardonnay

Proprietor's Special Reserve

Hudson River Region

100% chardonnay

Millbrook's chardonnay exemplifies New York State chardonnay at its

fleshiest. Laced with vanilla crème brûlée flavors, it is supple, creamy, and lovely but not overwrought. As with all fine New York State chardonnays, in the best years there is a focus and clarity here that comes, in part, from fruit that has matured slowly in a cool climate.

## PALMER VINEYARDS

Select Reserve

North Fork of Long Island

approximately 55% chardonnay,
20% sauvignon blanc, 10% pinot blanc, and
15% gewürztraminer

When at its finest, this is quite possibly the most exciting white wine made on Long Island. A whirlwind of blazing flavor, Palmer's Select Reserve tastes of mint, straw, and litchi, which all come forward brilliantly. The blend, which changes each year, is a synergistic fusion of some of Long Island's leading white grapes: chardonnay, pinot blanc, sauvignon blanc, and gewürztraminer. Palmer, in Aquebogue, is considered one of Long Island's leading wineries.

## STANDING STONE VINEYARDS

Riesling

Finger Lakes

100% riesling

Here's another Finger Lakes riesling that's so scrumptious it sells out within months of release. The wine's bright, peachy flavors and gossamer lightness are simply irresistible. Even though there's a touch of residual sugar, the wine is balanced and focused thanks to its forthright acidity. And don't miss Standing Stone's sensational gewürztraminers. They are some of the most exciting gewürztraminers made in the United States.

## Reds

## GRISTINA

Merlot

Andy's Field

North Fork of Long Island

100% merlot

Merlot is Long Island's best-loved red variety, and the Gristina proves why. Smoky and chocolaty in good years, it's layered with delicious raspberry, menthol, and spiced tea flavors, all ensconced in a taut, fairly tannic body. Like many Long Island merlots, the Gristina opens up once it's poured into a carafe to breathe. Andy's Field is the winery's top vineyard.

## LENZ WINERY

Merlot

North Fork of Long Island

100% merlot

725

Year in and year out, the Lenz merlot is one of the (if not *the*) most supple and deeply flavored merlots made on Long Island. The ripe red currant, leather, and pine forest aromas and flavors, the smooth texture, and the strong internal core of fruit are reminiscent of a young St.-Emilion. Serve this with lamb chops and watch the wine really come alive.

## MILLBROOK

Cabernet Franc

New York State

approximately 90% cabernet franc,
10% cabernet sauvignon

Some of the world's most tasty cabernet francs come from Chinon and

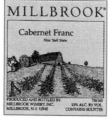

Bourgeuil in France's Loire Valley, and while these terrific wines are not well known in the United States, they are an archetype for New York's cabernet francs. Millbrook's is a great example. Juicy, chocolaty, and full of raspberry and cassis flavors, it is lively, mouthwatering, and very sleek.

## *Sweet Wine*

**WAGNER VINEYARDS**

Ravat Blanc

Ice Wine

Finger Lakes

100% vignoles

Upstate New York is famous for its ice wines, dessert wines made by allowing the grapes to remain on the vine well into the winter. When the frozen grapes are finally picked, the juice that slowly oozes from them is concentrated and luscious. Wagner's languorous, rich ice wine, with its delicious lemon custard flavor, is made from the hybrid grape Ravat blanc, more commonly known as vignoles. Drink it *as* dessert or as a fantastic match with blue-veined cheeses.

# VISITING NEW YORK STATE WINERIES

The wineries of New York are set into some of the most charming rural landscapes in the United States. Many are housed in converted barns or colonial farmhouses. Others have panoramic views of stunning lakes or bays and picnic areas where you can relax, sip some wine, and take in the pastoral beauty. To complete the picture nicely, New York State's wine districts are full of old-fashioned inns, bed-and-breakfasts, and country restaurants.

Most New York State wineries are well set up for tastings and tours since many sell a considerable amount of the wine they produce directly from their own tasting rooms. There is a real spirit of conviviality in these tastings; many are conducted by the winery owners themselves.

Keep in mind that even a trip to New York City can easily include a day visiting wineries. Long Island's are roughly 100 miles away from the city, and the wineries of the Hudson River Valley are about 50 miles away.

Each year the New York Wine & Grape Foundation publishes a guide to all of the wineries of New York State, complete with maps, addresses, phone numbers, and hours of operation. The foundation also publishes a wine country calendar that lists all of the festivals and celebrations (there are hundreds) that New York wineries host each year. For a copy, contact the foundation at 350 Elm Street, Penn Yan, New York 14527; (315) 536-7442.

### THE FINGER LAKES

**DR. KONSTANTIN FRANK'S VINIFERA WINE CELLARS**
9749 Middle Road
Hammondsport, NY 14840
(607) 868-4884

**GLENORA WINE CELLARS**
5435 Route 14
Dundee, NY 14837
(607) 243-5511

**HUNT COUNTRY VINEYARDS**
4021 Italy Hill Road
Branchport, NY 14418
(315) 595-2812

**KNAPP VINEYARDS**
2770 County Road 128
Romulus, NY 14541
(607) 869-9271
Restaurant on site.

**LAMOREAUX LANDING
WINE CELLARS**
9224 Route 414
Lodi, NY 14860
(607) 582-6011

**WAGNER VINEYARDS**
9322 Route 414
Lodi, NY 14860
(607) 582-6450

**THE HUDSON RIVER VALLEY**

**BENMARL WINE COMPANY LTD.**
156 Highland Avenue
Marlboro, NY 12542
(845) 236-4265

**CASCADE MOUNTAIN WINERY**
835 Cascade Mountain Road
Amenia, NY 12501
(914) 373-9021

**MILLBROOK VINEYARDS AND
WINERY**
26 Wing Road
Millbrook, NY 12545
(845) 677-8383

*Woodbury Vineyards, in New York's Lake
Erie district, sells most of its wine from its
tasting room.*

**LAKE ERIE**

**MERRITT ESTATE WINERY**
2264 King Road
Forestville, NY 14062
(716) 965-4800

**WOODBURY VINEYARDS**
3230 South Roberts Road
Fredonia, NY 14063
(716) 679-9463

*Bedell Cellars on Long Island was founded
in Cutchogue in 1979. The winery is
celebrated for its merlots and cabernet
sauvignons, which are always among the
best produced in the state.*

**727**

**LONG ISLAND**

**BEDELL CELLARS**
36225 Route 25 (Main Road)
Cutchogue, NY 11935
(631) 734-7537

**GRISTINA VINEYARDS**
24385 Route 25 (Main Road)
Cutchogue, NY 11935
(631) 734-7089

**PALMER VINEYARDS**
108 Sound Avenue
Aquebogue, NY 11931
(631) 722-9463

**PELLEGRINI VINEYARDS**
23005 Route 25 (Main Road)
Cutchogue, NY 11935
(631) 734-4111

# Washington State

Most of the world's classic grapes can grow lots of places. But each has a kind of spiritual home—a place (or sometimes places) where that grape can ascend beyond what is merely good and be transformed into stunning wine. In the 1990s Washington State, much to most wine drinkers' surprise, emerged as one of the great spiritual homes of merlot and cabernet sauvignon. The phenomenon was startling, for only a dozen or so years before most winemakers' hopes were pinned on the riesling, gewürztraminer, chardonnay, and other "northern" white grapes that filled the vineyards. As it turns out, these grapes

728

> ## THE QUICK SIP ON WASHINGTON STATE
>
> ❧
>
> • Washington State is considered one of the top producers in the United States of merlot and cabernet sauvignon.
>
> • Washington State merlots and cabernet sauvignons can have powerful structures and a deep saturated berryness.
>
> • Virtually all of Washington's vineyards are in the dry, warm eastern part of the state, separated from the rainy western part by the Cascade Range.

**WASHINGTON STATE'S WINE REGIONS**

Columbia Valley
Puget Sound
Red Mountain
Walla Walla
Yakima Valley

*Canoe Ridge Vineyard is part of the vast 10.7-million-acre Columbia Valley viticultural area. The valley, carved deeply into the land, was formed 12,000 to 15,000 years ago by a series of floods—equal to the flows of all the world's modern rivers combined—the result of the breakup of northern ice dams.*

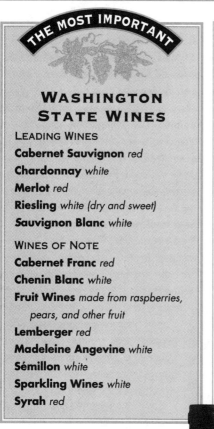

## THE MOST IMPORTANT

# WASHINGTON STATE WINES

**LEADING WINES**

**Cabernet Sauvignon** red

**Chardonnay** white

**Merlot** red

**Riesling** white (dry and sweet)

**Sauvignon Blanc** white

**WINES OF NOTE**

**Cabernet Franc** red

**Chenin Blanc** white

**Fruit Wines** made from raspberries, pears, and other fruit

**Lemberger** red

**Madeleine Angevine** white

**Sémillon** white

**Sparkling Wines** white

**Syrah** red

The idea that Washington—a state renowned for its rain—can produce great wine seems, at first, nonsensical. However, virtually all of the state's grapes (there are more than twenty varieties) are grown not in the west near Seattle but in the arid, almost desertlike eastern part of the state. The massive Cascade mountain range, which divides the two areas, is so effective as a rain shield that eastern and western Washington are about as similar in appearance as Montana and Vermont. There are five appellations in Washington State: Columbia Valley, Yakima Valley, Red Mountain, Walla Walla, and finally, the smallest one (and the only appellation on the western side of the Cascades), Puget Sound. Although the first wine grapes were planted in Washington State by Italian and German immigrants in the 1860s and 1870s, the modern wine industry was born 100 years later. The number of wineries in the state is increasing rapidly. In 1960, Washington State had 15 wineries; in 1995, it had 88. By 2000, there were 145.

729

The forerunners of Washington's striking merlots and cabernets were three wines, pinot noir, grenache, and gewürztraminer, made in 1951 by a psychology professor in his basement. Humble as those wines must have been, they held a promise. Indeed, a little more than a decade

(which are still widely grown in Washington) make good wine there. But *nothing* like the top tier of merlots and cabernets.

What you notice immediately about the greatest Washington State merlots and cabernet sauvignons (or blends of the two) is the mind-boggling concentration of the wines. It almost seems as though, by some magical osmosis, they've been infused with the primal, lush berryness of wild Northwest blackberries, boysenberries, raspberries, and cherries. That lushness carries over into the texture of the wines, which is at once supple and seamless.

*Chaleur Estate, a Bordeaux-style blend from DeLille Cellars, is one of Washington's most structured and impressive red wines.*

## WINE AND ONIONS

—❧—

It's not every county that can claim they're famous for wine and . . . onions. But Walla Walla—the tiny wine region in southeastern Washington—can. Walla Walla produces some of the state's most delicious merlots and cabernet sauvignons and some of the world's most delicious onions, 35 million pounds of which are harvested each year. Like the Vidalia from Georgia and the Maui from Hawaii, Walla Walla onions are so sweet they can be eaten out of hand, like apples. And while onions may not immediately spring to mind as a partner for powerful red wines, they certainly can be. Each year Canoe Ridge Vineyard asks chefs from around the country to create Walla Walla onion dishes that marry perfectly with the winery's merlot. Among the favorites: merlot-filled barbecued Walla Walla onions, Walla Walla sweet onion tart with mushrooms and bacon, and roasted Walla Walla onion salad with blue cheese and toasted hazelnuts.

one of the first of two Washington State wineries devoted to premium wines.

Meanwhile, other wines were being produced in Washington, just as they had been for decades. Mostly they were cheap, sweet, and fortified. After Prohibition, for example, the Pommerelle and Nawico wine companies made millions of gallons of such stuff from Concord and other native varieties. Pommerelle and Nawico are now unknown names, but the company that they became after they merged is the most well-known and largest winery in Washington State: Chateau Ste. Michelle, founded in 1965 under the name Ste. Michelle Vintners. Chateau Ste. Michelle immediately left its legacy of plonk behind and hired the most famous United States wine consultant of the postwar era, André Tchelistcheff. Cabernet sauvignon, pinot noir, sémillon, and grenache were the first varieties the winery produced.

For the next twenty years, the Washington State wine industry moved steadily along the quality track. Every winery, from Chateau Ste. Michelle to the smallest family-run operation, was on a steep learning curve, for Washington had almost nothing in common—climatically or geographically—with its neighbors to the south, Oregon and California. What it did share with California and Oregon was the discovery that the best teacher was trial and error.

If Washington was once considered a curious outpost, 800 miles north of (but light-years behind) California's Napa Valley, that is not true today. Leonetti Cellar, the state's most prestigious small winery, makes merlots and cabernets that are now deemed by some to be *the* best red wines in the United States. Leonetti Cellar is not an anomaly. Quilceda Creek, Woodward

later, the modern Washington wine industry began to take form. The professor, Dr. Lloyd Woodburne, was a home winemaker who was soon joined in his hobby by several of his university colleagues. They named themselves Associated Vintners and began making wine together. As their skills and production increased, the hobby turned serious. A commercial winery was built, and in 1967 the first wines—cabernet sauvignon, gewürztraminer, pinot noir, and Johannisberg riesling—were produced. In 1984 Associated Vintners became Columbia Winery,

Canyon, Andrew Will, Hedges Cellars, DeLille Cellars, and several other Washington State wineries have carved out national reputations for their fine wines. And for simple, every night drinking, the affordable merlots and cabernets of Columbia Crest, Arbor Crest, and Hogue Cellars are, dollar for dollar, among the best in the country.

*Some of the Best Producers of Washington State Merlot and Cabernet Sauvignon*

**ANDREW WILL WINERY**

**CANOE RIDGE VINEYARD**

**CHATEAU STE. MICHELLE**

**CHINOOK**

**COLUMBIA WINERY**

**DELILLE CELLARS**

**HEDGES CELLARS**

**THE HOGUE CELLARS**

**KIONA VINEYARDS**

**LEONETTI CELLAR**

**MATTHEWS CELLARS**

**PEPPER BRIDGE WINERY**

**QUILCEDA CREEK VINTNERS**

**SNOQUALMIE WINERY**

**WATERBROOK WINERY**

**WILRIDGE WINERY**

**WOODWARD CANYON**

## ONE PLACE PHYLLOXERA HASN'T HARMED

Though the phylloxera scourge of the late nineteenth century damaged most of the vineyards in the world, including those in California and Oregon (where it has since appeared again), the deadly aphid has never destroyed vineyards in Washington State, even though it probably exists there. The state's sandy soils, cold winters, and broad dispersal of wineries are thought to have prevented the pest's movement and to have significantly limited its overall population.

## THE LAND, THE GRAPES, AND THE VINEYARDS

Were it not for several cold mountain rivers—the Columbia, the Yakima, the Snake, and the Walla Walla—eastern Washington would be a virtual desert. Rainfall here can be as little as 6 inches per year. But the river valleys and the irrigation they make possible have transformed the vast expanse into hauntingly beautiful rangeland, wheat fields, and orchards. Plus patches of prime vineyards.

The dryness of the climate is only one of the factors that give Washington its distinct viticultural personality. Because of its northern latitude, the vineyards here get an average of two more hours of sun a day than vineyards in the Napa Valley. Temperatures are very warm but, again because of the latitude, not excessively hot. The extended hours of light and

731

warmth (but not severe heat) help ripening progress evenly. This, in turn, contributes to a wine's elegance and finesse.

The day to night temperature contrast in eastern Washington can be remarkable—a difference of 50 degrees or more in a single day is not uncommon. Cool nights mean that grapevines can temporarily shut down and rest, thereby preserving acidity in the grapes. The potential for brutal winters with fast-moving, subzero Arctic winds is one of the most severe threats in eastern Washington. Temperatures may go from a mild 40°F to well below zero in a matter of a few hours. Water in the plants' systems freezes so quickly the vines can literally explode. In most years, however, the vines are not damaged, but they do go into a deep, long

*Wind machines churn up the air and help protect against frost.*

dormancy. Dormancy is as critical for a plant as sleep is for a human being. Without a full and long dormancy, the vine goes into the growing season in a feeble condition, rendering it less capable of producing good grapes.

Soil in Washington tends to be sandy loam or volcanic, both of which are poor in nutrients and provide good drainage. As for grapes, Washington's winemakers have always had a soft spot in their hearts for the unconventional and obscure. While well-known grapes, such as chardonnay, riesling, merlot, and cabernet sauvignon, clearly lead production, winemakers here also grow grapes that almost no one has ever heard of, such as Madeleine angevine (grown mostly in England) and lemberger (grown mostly in Germany and Austria).

*About once every ten years some grape vines freeze and die during eastern Washington's severely cold winters.*

## THE GRAPES OF
# WASHINGTON STATE

### WHITES

**Chardonnay:** Major grape. A source of wines that are dependably good but rarely extraordinary.

**Chenin Blanc:** Minor grape. Can become a delicious or merely decent wine.

**Gewürztraminer:** Minor grape. Its quality is generally disappointing in Washington State.

**Madeleine Angevine:** Minor variety but appealing for its pleasing off beat floral character. Most of what is grown in the world is found in England.

**Muscat Canelli:** Minor variety, the same as muscat blanc à petits grains. Can turn into simple but delightful sweet wines.

**Riesling:** Commonly planted grape. Wines made from it can be very attractive, snappy, peachy, and minerally. Made into dry, off-dry, and sweet wines.

**Sauvignon Blanc:** Minor grape. The top wines are appealingly fresh, clean, and herbal tasting.

**Sémillon:** Minor but important grape. Its quality shows promise. Used alone and blended with sauvignon blanc or chardonnay.

### REDS

**Cabernet Franc:** Minor grape. Shows potential, especially in blends with merlot and/or cabernet sauvignon.

**Cabernet Sauvignon:** Major grape. Capable of making powerful, tannic wines with structure and depth. Used alone and blended with merlot.

**Lemberger:** Minor but important grape, traditionally grown in Germany and Austria. Washington State has the only significant plantings in the United States.

**Merlot:** Major grape. The source of a majority of the state's most lush, concentrated, beautifully balanced wines. Used alone and blended with cabernet sauvignon.

**Syrah:** Minor grape. Current wines made from it demonstrate a lot of promise.

Both Madeleine angevine and lemberger—despite having names that make marketing executives wince (especially lemberger)—have been great successes in Washington. Madeleine angevine can make easy to like, very floral white wines. Lemberger can make rich, dark, spicy reds—Washington's equivalent of California zinfandels. There are also notable plantings of other grape varieties, especially syrah, cabernet franc, sauvignon blanc, chenin blanc, and sémillon. The last appears promising in Washington. There are a number of delicious sémillon-chardonnay blends, and several vintners are attempting dessert sémillons, in the manner of French Sauternes, made with the help of the noble rot, *Botrytis cinerea.*

*Some of the Best Producers of*
*Washington State Lemberger*

**THE HOGUE CELLARS**

**KIONA VINEYARDS**

**LATAH CREEK WINE CELLARS**

With 25,000 acres of grapevines, Washington State is a far smaller wine producer than California, where there are 427,000 acres of vines. Of Washington's five appellations, the Columbia Valley is the largest. It extends over 18,000 square miles, from the Okanogan wilderness in the north, south into Oregon (the appellation is actually shared by the two states although few Oregon grapes are grown within it), and east along the Snake River to the Idaho border. Almost 60 percent of the state's total production comes from this single appellation. Like large appellations in premium winegrowing areas everywhere, the Columbia Valley contains smaller appellations, including the Yakima Valley, which itself contains Red Mountain.

The Yakima Valley is generally considered the heart of Washington wine country. Here some of the state's top wineries, including Hogue Cellars and Covey Run, are clustered fairly close together, and many other wineries buy Yakima grapes. On the northern edge of the Yakima Valley are the Rattlesnake Hills; to the south are the Horse Heaven Hills; to the west are the foothills of the Cascade mountains; the eastern border is formed by Red Mountain. In 2001 Red Mountain was named as an appellation of its own. Known as one of the best places for red grapes in particular, Red Mountain is home to several of the state's best vineyards, including Hedges Estate and Klipsun.

Walla Walla, an appellation also shared with Oregon, is tiny in comparison to the Columbia Valley, yet some of the best wineries, including Leonetti Cellar, are located here or buy its grapes.

Puget Sound, the fourth appellation, is more of a curiosity than a great wine region. It spreads over the islands and lands adjoining the sound itself. The climate is very wet when compared to those of the other regions. Only a few wineries are located here.

## FRUIT WINES

Washington State has a long tradition of delicious fruit wines. Though fewer of these are made today, the Paul Thomas winery still specializes in delicious raspberry and Bartlett pear wines that have gorgeous fruit flavors and are very winelike at the same time. Another Washington specialty is Whidbey's loganberry liqueur made from the state's famed loganberries (a hybrid of raspberries and blackberries).

# VISITING THE WINERIES OF WASHINGTON STATE

Visiting Washington State's wineries requires time and a spirit of adventure. Most of them are in rural eastern Washington. It's about a two-and-a-half-hour drive from Seattle to the Yakima Valley, for example, four hours to Spokane, and almost five hours to Walla Walla. That said, the drive over the Cascade mountains can in itself be an exhilarating part of the journey. Wineries out here are often quite a distance from one another and restaurants are few. Packing a picnic lunch is a good idea.

Several wineries, however, are less than an hour from Seattle. The two lead-

## SLURP AND SIP

T he icy bays and estuaries around the Puget Sound are home to a wide variety of Pacific Northwest oysters, from the thumbnail-size Olympias to those named after the bays from which they come, such as Penncove Bay, Westcott Bay, and Shoalwater Bay. Pacific Northwest oysters, generally more briny and minerally than East Coast or Southern varieties, are a perfect match for Washington State's crisp, minerally rieslings, as well as its zesty, dry, herb-scented sémillons and sauvignon blancs. Some favorites: Columbia Winery sémillon, Covey Run fumé blanc, Hogue Cellars Johannisberg riesling, Paul Thomas Winery riesling, and Waterbrook Winery sauvignon blanc.

ing wineries, Columbia Winery and Chateau Ste. Michelle, are both in Woodinville (about 20 miles northeast of Seattle), and both have terrific tasting rooms, usually jammed with visitors. No appointments are necessary at either place. In addition, several of the wineries on the islands in Puget Sound are also less than an hour's drive from Seattle.

You'll find a couple of wineries here that weren't highlighted earlier; they are particularly interesting to visit. In general, with the exception of Chateau Ste. Michelle and Columbia Winery, it is best to call ahead and make an appointment.

Finally, each year the Washington Wine Commission publishes a helpful guide called "Touring the Washington Wine Country." It's available by calling (206) 667-9463.

PUGET SOUND

**QUILCEDA CREEK VINTNERS**
11306 52nd Street Southeast
Snohomish, WA 98290
(360) 568-2389

**WHIDBEY ISLAND GREENBANK FARM**
765 East Wonn Road (off Highway 525)
Greenbank, WA 98253
(360) 678-7700
You'll find all kinds of fruit wines here.

SEATTLE AREA

**CHATEAU STE. MICHELLE**
1 Stimson Lane
Woodinville, WA 98072
(425) 488-1133

**COLUMBIA WINERY**
14030 North East 145th Street
Woodinville, WA 98072
(425) 488-2776

SPOKANE AREA

**ARBOR CREST WINE CELLARS**
4705 North Fruithill Road
Spokane, WA 99217
(509) 927-9463

WALLA WALLA

**CANOE RIDGE VINEYARD**
1102 West Cherry Street
Walla Walla, WA 99362
(509) 527-0885

**WATERBROOK WINERY**
31 East Main Street
Walla Walla, WA 99362
(509) 522-1262

YAKIMA VALLEY

**COVEY RUN VINTNERS**
1500 Vintage Road
Zillah, WA 98953
(509) 829-6235

**HEDGES CELLARS**
53511 North Sunset Road
Benton City, WA 99320
(509) 588-3155

**THE HOGUE CELLARS**
2800 Lee Road
Prosser, WA 99350
(509) 786-4557

735

# THE WASHINGTON STATE
# WINES TO KNOW

*For each wine below, the specific American Viticultural Area from which it comes is noted.*

## Whites

### ARBOR CREST WINE CELLARS

Sauvignon Blanc

Bacchus Vineyard

Columbia Valley

approximately 85% sauvignon blanc, 15% sémillon

Wine drinkers who like uninhibited sauvignon blanc that has not gone through the wine equivalent of plastic surgery will love this. Wild, sharp, and herbal (but not vegetal), Arbor Crest's sauvignon has lots of gooseberry and newly mown hay aromas and flavors. The winery, one of the most beautiful in Washington State and a national historic monument, sits high on a cliff above the winding Spokane River.

### CHATEAU STE. MICHELLE

Chardonnay

Indian Wells Vineyard

Columbia Valley

100% chardonnay

The largest winery in Washington State, Chateau Ste. Michelle has been a benevolent godfather to smaller wineries and, as such, has been responsible for much of the state's success. Ste. Michelle's wines are some of the most lovely and dependable in the state, but its special single-vineyard chardonnay, Indian Wells, along with its sister, another single-vineyard chardonnay called Cold Creek, are knockouts. When at their best, these are beautifully delineated chardonnays with creamy pear, peach, and tropical fruit flavors.

### CHATEAU STE. MICHELLE AND DR. LOOSEN

Riesling

Eroica

Columbia Valley

100% riesling

*Eroica*, the name Beethoven gave to his passionate Third Symphony, means heroic in Italian, and it certainly took some courage (and passion) to create this, the first "global" riesling. Eroica is a joint venture between Washington State's Chateau Ste. Michelle and Germany's Weingut Dr. Loosen and the first such wine of the kind made from riesling. Stunning nectarine and peach aromas lure you into a flavor that's minerally and beautifully refined. Though the grapes were grown in Washington State's Columbia Valley, Eroica has the German Mosel region's exquisite clarity, lightness, and freshness written all over it. Joint-venture wines sometimes end up neither fish nor fowl. Eroica is the best of two great worlds.

## Reds

### ANDREW WILL

Merlot

Klipsun

Washington State

approximately 95% merlot, 5% cabernet franc

Headquartered on Vashon Island, the small, family winery Andrew Will is known for formidably structured merlots with vivid, plush fruit flavors and thick, almost syrupy textures. In top vintages, the powerful Klipsun Vineyard merlot, from the Yakima Valley, oozes with sweet black cherry flavors and a massive amount of tannin that only a few years of cellaring can tame. The Klipsun vineyard is on Red Mountain in the Yakima Valley.

## DELILLE CELLARS

Chaleur Estate

Yakima Valley

approximately 65% cabernet sauvignon, 25% merlot, and 10% cabernet franc

A spare-no-expense, small, family winery, DeLille Cellars is emerging as one of the leading producers in Washington State. In the best vintages, every molecule of Chaleur Estate has the lush, velvety density of melted chocolate and saturated flavors reminiscent of boysenberry, menthol, and roasted coffee. DeLille also makes a less expensive, but delicious, wine called D2, packed with juicy black cherry and raspberry flavors.

## HEDGES CELLARS

Red Mountain Reserve

Columbia Valley

approximately 65% cabernet sauvignon, 35% merlot

As of the mid-1990s, several of the best wine estates in Washington State began making Bordeaux-style blends, including Hedges Cellars, which makes one of the most scrumptious. In top vintages this wine is smoky, tarry, spicy, minty, and vibrantly berrylike, with rich fruit wrapped up in an elegant texture. The Red Mountain area of the Yakima Valley, with its hot, dry, breezy climate and sandy, high-carbonate soil, is one of the best places in the state for red grape varieties. As of the 2001 vintage Red Mountain will be the appellation appearing on this wine.

## LEONETTI CELLAR

Cabernet Sauvignon

Columbia Valley

approximately 85% cabernet sauvignon, 10% merlot, and 5% cabernet franc

The greatest wine estate in Washington State, Leonetti Cellar is one of the best in the United States. The density and richness of its cabernets and merlots is mesmerizing. The cabernet grips the palate with bold splashes of flavor—red licorice, cherry pie, and red currants, plus a tantalizing cedary, cigar box aroma. Amazingly, the wine is both mighty and elegant at the same time, rather like a Gothic arch that can both be exquisitely graceful and hold up the cathedral.

## SNOQUALMIE

Merlot

reserve

Columbia Valley

100% merlot

The tiny Snoqualmie Winery makes very intense, juicy merlots and cabernet sauvignons. In great vintages, the winery's reserve merlot in particular is a powerhouse of muscular cassis and berry fruit laced with hints of vanilla. Often hemmed in by tannin when young, this merlot will unfurl and grow more complex if it's poured into a decanter and left to aerate before serving (preferably with a big roast).

## *Sweet Wine*

## PAUL THOMAS

Razz

Raspberry Dessert Wine

Washington State

100% raspberries

Razz, a luscious, fresh, vibrant, sweet wine made from raspberries, is not to be believed. Intensely raspberryish and almost syrupy but not sugary sweet, it is sensational after dinner with a slice of chocolate cake or just pour it straight over French vanilla ice cream. Paul Thomas also makes a dry Bartlett pear wine that is the essence of pear with a light, gossamer body (not at all syrupy) and a long crisp finish. Just waiting for Thai food or curry.

# Oregon

If Oregon had been established as a wine region during the Middle Ages, it would undoubtedly have been the work of monks, for only those with an ascetic temperament could find joy in the nail-biting, nerve-racking reality of Oregon viticulture. Growing grapes here is fraught with problems. Sunlight and heat are often in short supply, making ripening a challenge for the grapes. Rain (about 40 inches a year) and frost are threats during spring and fall—the two times grapes are most vulnerable. Weather patterns can be erratic year to year, a stressful scenario for vines, which like all plants, love constancy and stability. In short, Oregon grapes have it tough.

And Oregon winemakers wouldn't have it any other way. The dicey climate, after all, is the key to the wines' success. Grapes here cannot burst into ripeness but instead must make their way slowly and methodically toward maturity. Each year is a gamble with Nature, but when the grapes do win, a wine of utter beauty, focus, and finesse can emerge.

Although a number of small wineries struggled along prior to Prohibition, the modern Oregon wine industry takes 1961 as the date of its birth. In that year, Richard Sommer, a graduate in agronomy from the University of California at Davis,

**OREGON'S WINE REGIONS**

Columbia Valley
Rogue Valley
Umpqua Valley
Walla Walla
Willamette Valley

*The verdant Willamette Valley is Oregon's most prestigious viticultural area and home to virtually all of its top wineries. Abundant rainfall (most, but not all, of it in the winter when the vines are dormant) and cool temperatures (thanks to air blowing in from the Pacific Ocean) make for a climate often compared to Burgundy, France.*

Willamette Valley, a corridor of soft, green hills, which runs for a hundred miles due south of Portland. Here, more than two thirds of the state's wines, including most of the best, are made.

Oregon winemakers are a story in themselves. Almost all of them are renegade dropouts or exes. Dropouts from college. Ex-professors. Dropouts from big city life. Ex-doctors. Dropouts from the counterculture. Ex-hippies. Even ex-theologians. Some have degrees in enology; others do not. But it doesn't seem to matter, for in Oregon, the greatest (and cruelest) teacher is Nature herself.

planted riesling and other grapes at Hillcrest Vineyard in the Umpqua Valley. Five years later, David Lett, another UC Davis graduate, planted the state's first pinot noir at The Eyrie Vineyards in the Willamette (pronounced Will-AM-ette) Valley. Both were warned by university professors that *vinifera* grapes would not fare well in Oregon. And with that piece of advice unheeded, the Oregon wine industry was born.

Today there are more than 138 wineries in the state. Virtually all of them grow pinot noir, the great red grape of Burgundy and one of the world's most fragile. Oregon is the only major region outside of Burgundy that specializes in this variety.

The leading white (in terms of production) is chardonnay, although Oregon winemakers are far more smitten with pinot gris, an ancestral sister of pinot noir. Pinot gris' skyrocketing popularity is based on the wine's irresistible freshness. Another pinot noir relative, pinot blanc, is also on the rise.

Oregon is divided into five appellations, but the most important is the

## OREGON'S WINE LAWS

By state law, Oregon wines must contain 90 percent of whatever grape variety is named on the label (except for Oregon cabernet sauvignons, which must be 75 percent cabernet sauvignon). All California wines, by comparison, must consist of 75 percent of the grape named on the label.

**THE MOST IMPORTANT**

### OREGON WINES

LEADING WINES
**Chardonnay** white
**Pinot Gris** white
**Pinot Noir** red

WINES OF NOTE
**Pinot Blanc** white
**Riesling** white

# THE LAND, THE GRAPES, AND THE VINEYARDS

In the spring, the 100-mile-long Willamette Valley is ablaze in emerald. The sky alone is exempted from being green. Curiously, it's possible to drive for long periods without seeing a single grapevine. The filbert orchards are endless; forests of fir, oak, and maple blanket the hills; and there are fields of Christmas trees. The vineyards are slightly hidden, situated up on gentle slopes and plateaus above the valley floor to better protect them from frost. These hills are covered with remarkably red soils known as Jory and Nekia, which are nutrient deficient and usually well drained.

The Willamette Valley is Oregon's preeminent appellation and has the coolest climate. The valley follows the Willamette River, which extends like a long, wagging tail south from Portland. On the eastern side of the valley, the Cascade mountains form a north-south spine. If the geographic picture stopped there, then swollen clouds lumbering in off the Pacific 50 miles away would eventually hit the Cascades and buckets of rain would shower Willamette and its vineyards. But on the western side of the valley, separating it from the Pacific, is another, smaller range of mountains called the Coast Range. These help block the worst of the rain and cold. If it were not for the Coast Range, Willamette would probably, like Seattle, be known for coffeehouses instead of wineries.

There are two other fairly important appellations due south of Willamette, the Umpqua Valley and south of that, the Rogue Valley. Warmer than the Willamette Valley, both have more varied soil and microclimates. Certain pockets of land in

## THE GRAPES OF OREGON

### WHITES

**Chardonnay:** Leading white grape in terms of production. Wines made from it range in quality from merely decent to classically elegant and focused.

**Pinot Blanc:** Minor grape but growing in importance. A genetic variant of pinot noir. Can make good creamy wines.

**Pinot Gris:** Major grape; the same as pinot grigio. Like pinot blanc, a genetic variant of pinot noir; it can be turned into popular, usually delicious wines. Considered the emerging star among Oregon's white wines.

**Riesling:** On the decline. Mostly made into light, easy-drinking wines although there are some stunning examples.

### REDS

**Cabernet Sauvignon** and **Merlot:** Minor grapes. Their success is highly dependent on microclimates and producers. Most of the best wines made from them come from the warmer Rogue Valley and Walla Walla.

**Pinot Noir:** Most prestigious grape. Virtually every winery grows it. In good years it makes supple, earthy wines.

both these appellations are warm enough for such grapes as cabernet sauvignon and merlot, neither of which do well in the cool Willamette.

Oregon's two smallest appellations, Columbia Valley and Walla Walla, straddle the border with Washington State. But while the appellation Columbia Valley is quite large in Washington State, it's pretty small in Oregon. Oregon's Columbia Valley appellation follows a short stretch of the Columbia River, where the climates of eastern Oregon and western Oregon collide, creating both wet and dry, warm and cool climates. Many grape varieties grow there. Walla Walla, which isn't all that big in Washington State, is absolutely tiny in Oregon. In Walla Walla the long, warm, dry growing season is well suited to cabernet sauvignon and merlot, just as it is in Washington.

As for grape varieties in Oregon, nothing is more important—qualitatively or quantitatively—than pinot noir. Among white varieties pinot gris continues to stir up excitement, and chardonnay, the leading white in terms of production, may have an even brighter future ahead. Let's look closer at these three grapes.

## Pinot Noir

Pinot noir is more than just the leading red grape of Oregon; it is also the soul of winemaking here. It was pinot noir that put Oregon on the map internationally, and despite its fragility and persnicketiness, it is still the best wine made by most wineries. Pinot noir is also the passion of another place with a marginal climate—its homeland, Burgundy.

741

### THE BIG BREAK

In Paris in 1979 the French publisher Gault Millau sponsored a wine Olympiad. Nearly six hundred wines from thirty-three different wine regions in the world competed. When The Eyrie Vineyards 1975 pinot noir placed third, beating a number of famous Burgundies, the French wine industry was stunned. And hardly convinced. In 1980 Robert Drouhin, a leading Burgundy vintner, decided to set up a rematch, this time in Burgundy itself. Eyrie came in second. Subsequently, in 1987, Drouhin bought land near The Eyrie Vineyards and set up the first French venture in Oregon: Domaine Drouhin Oregon.

*Some of the Best Producers of Oregon Pinot Noir*

ADELSHEIM VINEYARD

AMITY VINEYARDS

ARCHERY SUMMIT

BEAUX FRÈRES

BETHEL HEIGHTS VINEYARD

BROADLEY VINEYARDS

CHEHALEM

CRISTOM VINEYARDS

DOMAINE DROUHIN OREGON

ERATH VINEYARDS

THE EYRIE VINEYARDS

KING ESTATE

PONZI VINEYARDS

REX HILL VINEYARDS

WILLAKENZIE ESTATE

YAMHILL VALLEY VINEYARDS

## PAPA PINOT

A photo in the February 16, 1967, *Newberg Graphic Farm News* shows a smiling young couple in heavy jackets and work boots, standing behind a wheelbarrow heaped with roots. The caption reads, "David and Diana Lett, who recently purchased the John Marner place in Dundee, pause with their European wine grape rootings. The Letts plan to remove prunes from the 20 acre farm and put in quality wine grapes."

The town's farmers thought David Lett was crazy, of course. And, in a way, he *was* possessed—by an idea. Namely, that finesse and complexity in wine were related to the marginality of the climate where the grapes were grown. In other words, grapes that had it easy, that ripened effortlessly thanks to unmitigating sun, would never make elegant wine. On the other hand, grapes that lived on the edge, that received barely enough sun to help them cross the finish line of ripeness, had at least a chance of making graceful wine.

Lett had earned a degree in viticulture at the University of California at Davis, but his thinking had been shaped even more pivotally by wandering around French vineyards for a year. The lesson out there, among the vines, seemed to be that grapes were sort of like life: No pain, no gain.

As it turns out, some grapes are more dependent on this angst than others. Pinot

*Prescient David Lett, the first person to plant pinot noir in Oregon.*

noir—the great red grape of Burgundy and the grape responsible for some of the most sensual wines in the world—is at the top of the list. And pinot noir was what Lett had his mind set on.

He planted it along with several other grapes that do well in cool, marginal climates—pinot gris, gewürztraminer, pinot meunier, riesling, muscat ottonel, and chardonnay. Other winemakers understood the logic of being on the periphery of ripeness and followed suit. In the process, Oregon established itself as a wine region built not on trends, not on marketing strategies, not on the personal wine preferences of the vintner, but on the simple reality of its own *terroir*.

Today David Lett, whose nickname is Papa Pinot, is considered the father of Oregon pinot noir.

---

Graphs published in the French journal *Progrès Agricole et Viticole* compared rainfall, daily temperatures, and hours of sunlight in the town of McMinnville in the Willamette Valley and the city of Beaune in Burgundy. The curves plotted for sunlight and temperature are virtually identical, while the rainfall graph shows that McMinnville gets most of its rain in the winter (when the vines are dormant), and Beaune's rainfall is spaced throughout the year. While not implying that Oregon pinot noir and Burgundy taste the same, the graphs underscore the coolness of both climates. History—at least in Burgundy's case—suggests just how necessary a cool ripening period is for great pinot noir. Grown where they are bathed in the hot sun, the grapes end up as a wine that tastes something like puréed prunes mixed with flat cola.

In Oregon the vineyards begin to settle down into summer around the Fourth of July (some Texas *harvests* happen the same month). Oregon harvests are usually around mid-October, although some occur during cold snaps in November.

Good pinot noir is obviously not solely a matter of cool growing conditions, however. Lots of places are cool; not many make exceptional pinot. The age of the vines appears to be extremely important, as do the clones (see page 22) found in the vineyard. Exactly how these factors fit together in Oregon is not wholly understood and, in any case, the picture is constantly changing. New French clones are being planted, creating a greater diversity of flavors within vineyards. As for the age of the vineyards, it's not necessarily true that an older vineyard will produce higher quality grapes than a younger vineyard, but there is a point when a vineyard seems to come into its own. In Oregon, as the vineyards have truly matured (by the beginning of the twenty-first century, some were around thirty years old), many of the wines have taken on greater depth, concentration, and complexity.

The most compelling Oregon pinots seem to mirror the land itself with their forest floor, wild mushroom, brambles, and pine characteristics—characteristics that taken together are sometimes described as duff. Circling this earthy core are the aromas and flavors of blackberries, blueberries, lilacs, and a kind of sweet meatiness. But pinot noir is so sensitive to its site that flavor generalizations are hard to make.

A generalization *can* be made when it comes to winemaking, however. The top Oregon winemakers are convinced that

pinot noir requires an ultragentle touch during harvesting and in the cellar. Grapes that have been handled a fraction too much can end up making wines that seem denuded, bitter, or simply out of whack. Winemakers adopt a minimalist approach, and often a percentage of the grapes is not crushed. Instead, whole grapes are put directly into the fermenting tank, which also helps maximize fruity flavors in the wine. To keep those fruit flavors dominant, many winemakers are also extremely careful and sparing in their use of new oak for aging.

## WHEN RED WEDS RED

~~~

In the United States the sumptuous combination of grilled salmon and Oregon pinot noir was the first well-known food and wine marriage to forsake the old chestnut: White wine with fish; red wine with meat. And that it did brilliantly, for as anyone who has tasted grilled salmon and Oregon pinot noir together knows, the two are a consummate match. The rich fattiness and light char of the grilled salmon could have no better partner than an earthy Oregon pinot noir, with its relatively high (for red wine) acidity. Also critical to the partnership is the fact that pinot noir is very low in tannin and thus doesn't interfere with the beautiful flavors of the fish. (By contrast, wines that are high in tannin, such as cabernet sauvignon, often make fish taste dry or metallic.) The biggest testament to the success of Oregon pinot noir and salmon happens each year on the final night of the International Pinot Noir Celebration (see the next page) when 600 pounds of king salmon are consumed with no one knows how many bottles of pinot noir.

743

744

As is true in Burgundy, Oregon pinot noir is always made as a single varietal, never blended. One of the grape's great attributes is its ability to make on its own a complex and complete wine. And in any case, pinot noir simply doesn't blend well. When mixed with other varieties it regresses so much it can barely be perceived. The only blends made anywhere that successfully incorporate pinot noir are Champagne and certain other sparkling wines.

Oregon pinot noir falls into three unofficial categories: regular bottlings, reserve bottlings, and vineyard-designated bottlings. Virtually every winery makes a regular bottling. Most also make a more expensive reserve. This can either be a wine that has been aged longer or a special selection of the best lots or both. Don't assume that the reserve wine is always better, however. If it's a reserve

solely by virtue of having spent more time in oak, it may not be. Some wineries also make separate vineyard-designated wines. These, too, are more expensive but again, they are not necessarily better. Blending from different vineyards and different lots has historically been the way Oregon pinot noir has achieved complexity. The idea is a good one, and it works.

## Pinot Gris

Oregon's identity with pinot noir is so strong it seems as though white wine couldn't possibly come close in importance. Yet Oregon's pioneering winemakers suspected that a number of northern European whites might do well here. They planted riesling, gewürztraminer, sylvaner, chardonnay, pinot gris, and muscat, among others. Mostly being farmers, they didn't consider fashion—until sales forced them to. Sadly enough, varieties considered "unfashionable" in the 1980s and 1990s, such as riesling and gewürztraminer, sold so poorly that many wineries eventually stopped making them. Others cut produc-

## GRIS AREA

—⊷*ↄ/ↄ/ↄ*⊶—

Pinot gris is not the same as *vin gris*. The French term *vin gris* (literally, gray wine) refers to any number of slightly pinkish-tinted white wines made from red grapes. *Vins gris* are usually not as deeply colored as rosé or blush wines. While there are dozens of pinot gris in the United States, there are only a few *vins gris*. In California Bonny Doon Vineyard makes a tasty and fascinating one called Vin Gris de Cigare, a blend of seven or more different red grape varieties, depending on the year.

tion to a minimum. When muscat sales began to decline, too, winemaker David Lett figured it was because no one could imagine what food it was good with. He began telling people the wine was good with sex. Muscat ottonel now has a small established market.

One white grape, however, seemed as effortlessly likeable as the girl next door: pinot gris. By the mid-1990s most of the top Oregon wineries were not only making it but increasing their production every year and still selling out within six months.

According to researchers at the University of California at Davis' Department of Viticulture and Enology, pinot gris (gray pinot) has the same general DNA profile as pinot noir, however as a result of a genetic mutation that took place centuries ago, the grapes are a different color. Were it not for the color of the grapes, pinot gris and pinot noir vines

would be impossible to tell apart. Not surprisingly, pinot gris, like pinot noir, needs a cool climate and is highly sensitive to *terroir*. Though the grape *can* grow in several places, it makes engaging wine in only a few. Alsace is one of them. Alsace pinot gris are among the richest and most compactly flavored in the world. In northern Italy pinot gris, called pinot grigio, can be racy and thirst quenching or—if planted in a spot too warm or cropped at high yields—blander than water.

David Lett planted Oregon's first pinot gris in 1966 at The Eyrie Vineyards. Originally lacking a strong market for the wine, he traded much of it with salmon fishermen. And thus began what is still considered a delicious Oregon food and wine marriage: salmon and pinot gris (though salmon and pinot noir is an even more famous match). Few wine drinkers stop with salmon, however. Pinot gris is one of the two white wines made in the United States that are the most versatile with food (the other is sauvignon blanc). Oregon pinot gris in particular has an inherent slightly creamy yet slightly crisp character that begs for all kinds of food. Most winemakers have preferred to keep the winemaking simple; only a few ferment or age pinot gris in new oak.

Some of Oregon's most intriguing new white wines are blends based in large part on pinot gris. Sokol Blosser's Evolution No. 9 is a zesty, superdelicious wine based on pinot gris, sémillon, Müller-Thurgau, and six other grape varieties. Archery Summit's Vireton combines pinot gris with chardonnay and pinot blanc to make a delightful wine with a creamy body and marzipan-like aroma.

---

*Some of the Best Producers of
Oregon Pinot Gris*

**CHEHALEM**

**THE EYRIE VINEYARDS**

**KING ESTATE**

**PONZI VINEYARDS**

**WESTREY WINE COMPANY**

**WILLAKENZIE ESTATE**

**YAMHILL VALLEY VINEYARDS**

---

## Chardonnay

Until recently, the story of Oregon chardonnay was that of a soap opera, replete with promises, dashed hopes, and even villains. Villain number one was the nondiscriminating chardonnay drinker who only bought what he'd always had (à la facial tissue) and would have rather (for unspecified reasons) drunk California chardonnay anyway.

Villain number two was the particular chardonnay clone planted in Oregon. Named 108, it was propagated in California because it performed well in warm regions there. It was also planted early on in Oregon before clonal research was advanced or even customary. Unfortunately, in a cool climate, the 108 clone often makes a blowsy, diffuse wine with little character. As new Burgundy clones of chardonnay became available in the mid-1990s, many Oregon vintners planted them. Over time these French clones are expected to improve the state's chardonnays considerably.

Imperfect as the clone 108 may be, some wineries make beautiful wine from it anyway—elegant, graceful, finely etched chardonnays. They are thrilling because of what they are not: not fleshy, not powerful,

not high in alcohol, and not woody-sweet. Imagine an American chardonnay that doesn't scream at you. Among the best producers are Bethel Heights, Chehalem, St. Innocent, Hamacher, and Ponzi, and, one using grapes not from the 108 clone, The Eyrie Vineyards.

## VISITING OREGON WINERIES

Most Oregon wineries are as welcoming, unpretentious, and down-to-earth as they come. Often the owner is also the winemaker, tour guide, tractor operator, and chief wineglass washer. Although a number of wineries do offer tours and tastings, others are just too small to be open to the public. It's best to call ahead.

The majority of Oregon's wineries are in the verdant Willamette Valley, an easy drive from Portland. However, both the Umpqua and Rogue Valleys have important wineries and are well worth visiting.

Twice a year—over the Memorial Day and Thanksgiving weekends—Oregon wineries host massive open houses. Virtually every winery, no matter how tiny, is open for tastings and tours and, in the spirit of rural hospitality, there are usually heaps of food and sometimes there is music to boot. No appointments are necessary at the wineries, although nearby bed-and-breakfasts are quickly booked.

Whenever you visit, however, don't miss a dinner at the Joel Palmer House in the Willamette Valley. Owned by Jack and Heidi Czarnecki, two of the leading wild-mushroom experts in the United States and authors of several mushroom cookbooks, the Joel Palmer House specializes in (what else?) mushroom dishes (cooked by Jack) paired with Oregon pinot noirs (selected by Heidi and Jack). The Czarneckis themselves forage for many of the mushrooms they serve. The Joel Palmer House was built in 1857 as the residence of an Oregon pioneer by the same name. Now listed on both the national and Oregon registers of historic places, it is located at 600 Ferry Street in Dayton and can be reached at (503) 864-2995.

The Oregon Wine Advisory Board, (503) 228-0713 or (800) 242-2363, provides a full list and description of the state's wineries, plus maps and a guide to local bed-and-breakfasts. The wineries listed below are all in the Willamette Valley.

**ARCHERY SUMMIT**
18599 Northeast Archery Summit Road
Dayton, OR 97114
(503) 864-4300

**BETHEL HEIGHTS VINEYARD**
6060 Bethel Heights Road Northwest
Salem, OR 97304
(503) 581-2262

**CHEHALEM**
31190 North East Veritas Lane
Newberg, OR 97312
(503) 538-4700

**ERATH VINEYARDS**
9409 Northeast Worden
Hill Road
Dundee, OR 97115
(503) 538-3318

**KING ESTATE**
80854 Territorial Road
Eugene, OR 97405
(541) 942-9874 or
(800) 884-4441

**PONZI VINEYARDS**
14665 Southwest
Winery Lane
Beaverton, OR 97007
(503) 628-1227

**YAMHILL VALLEY VINEYARDS**
16250 Oldsville Road
McMinnville, OR 97128
(800) 825-4845

## PEAR EXCELLENCE

—◁🍐▷—

Though traditional in Europe for centuries, the making of hand-crafted eaux-de-vie and fruit brandies is rare in the United States. Only a handful of tiny American distillers now practice the craft; among these is Clear Creek Distillery in Portland, Oregon. Clear Creek makes a pear brandy and an *eau-de-vie de poire Williams* that are two of the most extraordinary eaux-de-vie in America, indeed, in the world. To make them, perfectly ripe Williams pears (as the French call them; they're Bartletts in the United States) from orchards in Oregon's Hood river valley are fermented and then distilled in an alembic or pot still. Although the process sounds straightforward, enormous skill is required to achieve an eau-de-vie with intense fruit concentration that is smooth and elegant at the same time. Clear Creek's *eau-de-vie de poire Williams* is especially renowned (and difficult to make) since it has an actual pear inside each bottle. To achieve this, empty bottles are carefully attached to tree limbs just after flowering. The pears actually grow inside the glass. After being rinsed with a special citric solution to sterilize the pears, the bottles are then filled with 80-proof pear eau-de-vie. *Clear Creek Distillery, 1430 Northwest 23rd Avenue, Portland, OR 97210; (503) 248-9470.*

# THE OREGON WINES TO KNOW

❦

*For each wine below, the specific American Viticultural Area from which it comes is noted.*

## Whites

### CHEHALEM
Dry Riesling
reserve
Willamette Valley
100% riesling

Chehalem makes such complex pinot noirs and lovely, creamy chardonnays that it might seem unusual to write about its riesling, which in comparison to the other two wines is the winery's best-kept secret. But the riesling is just too good to ignore. At its finest, it has the same kind of thrilling purity, clarity, and minerality that makes German riesling so intriguing. Light in body, with penetrating acidity, and beautiful peachy notes, it's a wine riesling lovers should not miss.

### THE EYRIE VINEYARDS
Pinot Gris
Willamette Valley
100% pinot gris

Owner and winemaker David Lett is considered the father of both pinot gris and pinot noir in Oregon, and he continues to make stunning examples of both. When it's in top form, his pinot gris could dance in the Bolshoi; it's graceful and powerful in the same split second. Wonderful surges of almond and spice flavors flow through the wine like a current.

### KING ESTATE
Pinot Gris
Oregon
100% pinot gris

The largest winery in Oregon, King Estate produces more pinot gris than any other winery in the state. The style of the wine is so gentle and round, it's impossible not to be seduced. You may find that this pinot gris reminds you of an old-fashioned honey cake topped with caramelized pears.

### WILLAKENZIE ESTATE
Pinot Blanc
Willamette Valley
100% pinot blanc

When the weather cooperates, WillaKenzie Estate makes the finest pinot blanc in Oregon. A dramatic wine with very pure flavors of pears, apricots, peaches, and apples, it has just the right tension between acidity and creaminess. For a wine so suffused with fruit flavors, it is also surprisingly elegant.

### YAMHILL VALLEY VINEYARDS
Pinot Gris
Willamette Valley
100% pinot gris

This pinot gris can be as bracingly refreshing as falling into a mountain lake. In great vintages, the snappy, racy aromas and flavors are all about limes, pine forests, and ripe melons. Yet a solid core of creaminess means the wine never tastes sharp.

# *Reds*

## ARCHERY SUMMIT

Pinot Noir

Arcus Estate

Oregon

100% pinot noir

A relative newcomer (its first vintage was 1993), Archery Summit makes powerful stylized pinot noirs that at their best have warm spiced berry aromas and smoky grenadine and pomegranate flavors. The winery uses more new oak than most and, as a result, when the wines are first opened, their flavors are often hidden behind that oak's curtain. But pour the wine into a decanter and watch the flavors bloom. Archery Summit, which makes four different pinot noirs (most of them expensive), is owned by the Napa Valley winery Pine Ridge.

## BEAUX FRERES

Pinot Noir

Yamhill County

100% pinot noir

While all Oregon winemakers seem intense in their own way, there's something fervent, maniacal, and untamed about Michael Etzel, the co-owner and winemaker of Beaux Frères. This guy's veins must run with pinot noir. And what pinots he makes! Sweetly ripe, meaty, massive, and thickly textured, they border on losing the refinement pinot noir is known for. Still it's hard to resist such hedonism.

## BROADLEY VINEYARDS

Pinot Noir

Claudia's Choice

Willamette Valley

100% pinot noir

Broadley Vineyards makes some of the lushest, thickest, most intense pinot noirs in Oregon. In warm years, when the grapes get really ripe, the wines can border on seeming like something other than

pinot noir, they are so dense. That said, these can be totally irresistible pinots in which the aromas and flavors of chocolate, cherries, tangerines, prosciutto, earth, and smoke mingle beautifully. Compared to many other wineries, Broadley uses a considerable amount of new oak.

## DOMAINE DROUHIN OREGON

Pinot Noir

Oregon

100% pinot noir

Burgundy vintner Robert Drouhin planted a vineyard in the Willamette Valley in 1988 and put his daughter, Veronique, an enologist, in charge of making the wine. Most years she has an extremely elegant hand, making a sumptuous blackberry, black cherry pinot that makes you think of fresh berry pies. The wine starts out softly and then balloons in your mouth. The texture can be utterly silky.

749

## THE EYRIE VINEYARDS

Pinot Noir

Willamette Valley

100% pinot noir

The Eyrie pinots are always among the most elegant and understated (Burgundian?) in Oregon. The aromas and flavors seep softly out of the wine: damp earth, raspberries, sweet pipe tobacco, smoke, blackberries, mushrooms, and a wonderful suggestion of the forest floor. One after another, they keep coming in a very delicate manner. Eyrie's pinot noirs have come to define what is meant by a traditional, Old World style of Oregon pinot noir.

# Texas

Some wine drinkers may find it surprising that fine wine—or any wine at all, for that matter—can be eked out of lands that even the cowboys found trying. Those same wine drinkers will find it even more surprising that Texas was one of the earliest places in the United States to produce wine. But Texas vintners maintain that stereotypical images of dusty cattle trails overblown with sagebrush do not depict the current viticultural reality. Certain parts of Texas have now established themselves as among the most serious winegrowing regions in America.

Texas is the largest of the forty-eight contiguous states. In land mass, it is bigger than France, though all of the vineyard acreage in the state, some 3,200 acres, could easily fit into the confines of the small French appellation of Sancerre.

## THE QUICK SIP ON TEXAS

• Texas is one of the oldest wine regions in the United States.

• No one grape variety dominates, although chardonnay and cabernet sauvignon are by both critics and winemakers considered to be the leading grapes in the state.

• Texas' thirty-four wineries are scattered across thousands of miles with differing microclimates.

There are three broad grape-growing areas—the Texas Hill Country in the center of the state, the High Plains, covering much of the Texas Panhandle, and the vast

**TEXAS' WINE REGIONS**

High Plains
Texas Hill Country
Trans-Pecos

*After a trip to Burgundy, France, in the 1970s (ostensibly to buy cattle), Susan and Ed Auler fell in love with wine and ultimately founded Fall Creek Vineyards on their ranch in the Texas Hill Country in the early 1980s.*

Trans-Pecos region in the high southwest desert, bordering on Mexico. Within each region wineries are not grouped closely together but scattered across hundreds of miles of differing microclimates and terrains. Neighboring wineries are often more than an hour's drive apart.

Although Texas is still in its infancy in terms of grape growing and winemaking, several white grapes have already proven adaptable and suitable to the rigors of the climate. Lone Star sauvignon blanc can be full of personality. Fruity chenin blanc and a soft, floral type of riesling are also successful. For popularity, however, chardonnay takes the cake, just as it does in California. The jury is still out on which red will ultimately become Texas' most successful, though cabernet sauvignon shows the most promise.

# A Texas Tradition

Wine has been made in Texas for centuries. Historians theorize that Franciscan priests may have planted vineyards as early as 1660 in what is now far west Texas. The grapes they planted were mission, a variety closely related to Chile's pais and Argentina's criolla. The parent grapes of all three had been brought to Mexico more than a century earlier by Spanish conquistadores. Several historians have documented how serious the missionaries and conquistadores were about wine. In *Dionysus: A Social History of the Wine Vine*, Edward Hyams writes that "one of the problems which faced the conquistadores in their conquests and colonizations in America was that of providing a supply of wine for the Mass. It should not be thought of as a minor problem; to the Spaniard of the sixteenth century, it was of the very first importance." As the

conquistadores moved deeper into the Americas and as the trail of Spanish missions grew, viticulture spread from Mexico north into Texas and California and south into Latin and South America.

For the early settlers of Texas, wine was more than simply a necessity of the soul, it was a staple, as essential to daily life as bread. Settlers planted European (*vinifera*) vines along with other European crops, hoping to recreate the culture and food of their homeland. Many of the crops—and most of the vines—perished as a result of pests, foreign diseases, and the harshness of the climate. Only the mission grape proved tough enough to endure.

However serviceable mission wine might have been, it was apparently not particularly tasty. In the nineteenth century, as new immigrants from Germany, Italy, and

## SPAIN'S GIFT

No alcoholic beverage made from grapes appears to have been produced in the Americas before the arrival of the Spanish conquistadores in the sixteenth century, according to Tim Unwin in *Wine and the Vine: An Historical Geography of Viticulture and the Wine Trade*. Instead, the indigenous peoples of Meso-America made such alcoholic drinks as *pulque*, the forerunner of mescal, from the maguey or agave plant; *tesgüino* from the sprouted kernels of maize; and balche from mead, flavored with the leaves of the *Lonchocarpus*, a tropical tree or climbing shrub with colorful flowers. What makes this all the more fascinating is that numerous native species of the grape genus *Vitis* were to be found in the Americas.

751

## A TEXAS HERO

If Texas' long history of grape growing comes as a surprise, there's an even bigger one in the story of the Texas horticulturist T. V. Munson, whose research virtually saved the vineyards of Europe from total phylloxera devastation in the nineteenth century. In 1876 Munson began studying grapes. According to his journals, he traveled—often on horseback—from his home north of Dallas in Denison some 75,000 miles throughout the United States and Mexico, collecting native American grape varieties as he went. Using these as parents, Munson developed more than three hundred disease-resistant varieties of grapes. Based on his research, he wrote the classic text *Foundation of American Grape Culture* in 1909.

When phylloxera struck the vineyards of Europe, it was Munson who shipped supplies of native rootstocks to European vintners. By grafting their vines onto the Texas-grown rootstocks, Europeans were ultimately able to salvage what remained of their vineyards. According to Frank Giordano in *Texas Wines and Wineries*, "Under the ground, vines in Bordeaux and Burgundy are, to this day, of the same lineal rootstock as those in Denison and throughout Texas." Munson was awarded the French Legion of Honor Cross of Mérite Agricole in 1888.

France came to Texas, they brought more European grape varieties. Again, the vines succumbed to the severities of the climate and disease. Texas' immigrant winemakers were undeterred. When their European vines failed, they made wine from native Texas grapes, including one called mustang.

While there were at least sixteen commercial wineries operating in Texas prior to Prohibition, after it only Val Verde Winery, near the border city of Del Rio on the Rio Grande, remained. Almost four decades passed. Then in the 1970s the modern wine boom boomed. It did so in a peculiarly Texan way.

In 1973 Ed Auler, a Texas cattle rancher and lawyer, went to France with his wife, Susan, to further his knowledge of cattle breeds. A few days of looking at cattle metamorphosed into several weeks of looking at vineyards and tasting wine. When the Aulers stood outside Clos de Vougeot, one of Burgundy's most famous vineyards, they noticed how much the topography and the granite-limestone soil reminded them of their ranch in the Hill Country. The Aulers thought the Texas thought: We can do that. Fall Creek Vineyards was born ten years later.

*In Italy, wine, bread, and olive oil are called the* Santa Trinità Mediterrananea—*the Mediterranean Holy Trinity. The Texas Holy Trinity is only slightly different: wine, cattle, and oil (no, not olive).*

Meanwhile, out on the High Plains, other vineyards were being planted. In 1974, after noticing how exuberantly the grape trellis over his patio was growing, Texas Tech professor Bob Reed teamed up with another professor, Clinton McPherson, and the two decided to plant grapes. The one hundred varieties they planted outside of Lubbock were intended merely as a fun

## STE. GENEVIEVE

〜᪣〜

he largest winery in Texas, Ste. Genevieve, is owned jointly by the French wine giant Domaines Cordier and the University of Texas. Reflecting the winery's partial French parentage, it is named after a fifth-century nun who ultimately became the patron saint of Paris.

science project for their students. Within a few years the science project had become the highly successful Llano Estacado Winery, currently the second-largest winery in the state.

Segue to 1976. The University of Texas began to ponder the future of its 2.1 million acres of land scattered across nineteen counties in the West Texas desert. Early in 1921 the Santa Rita oil well struck lucky, helping the university to become one of the richest in the world. But oil was a limited resource. The university's manager of lands and property, Billy Carr, proposed a mind-blowing idea: plant vineyards. In 1981 the first vines belonging to what would later become Ste. Genevieve winery were planted beside a giant mesa in the middle of the West Texas desert. By 1992 the winery was producing several hundred thousand cases of wine each year and was the largest winery in the state. And so the stories went. Texans thinking about cattle, about land, about oil, about fun things to do, found their way to wine grapes. The movement had begun.

# THE LAND AND THE GRAPES

here is a Texas spirit, a Texas accent, a Texas sense of propriety, a Texas cuisine, a Texas way of thinking about things, maybe even a Texas ego—but

753

*The vineyards of Ste. Genevieve in western Texas sprawl out from a giant mesa.*

STE GENEVIEVE

TEXAS
CHARDONNAY

## THE GRAPES OF

# TEXAS

### WHITES

**Chardonnay:** Major white grape. The styles and quality of the wines made from it are in flux.

**Chenin Blanc:** Major grape. Often made into off-dry wines as a counterpoint to the region's chile-rich cuisine.

**Riesling:** Minor grape. The quality of its wines varies, but the best are appealing, soft, and floral.

**Sauvignon Blanc:** Major grape. Can be the source of surprisingly delicious, often peachy-herbal-flavored wines.

### REDS

**Cabernet Sauvignon:** Leading red grape. Makes simple good wines.

**Merlot:** A small amount is grown; it's mostly blended into cabernet-sauvignon-based wines.

there is not *a* Texas land. Texas covers more than 267,000 square miles. Geologically and climatically, the state is enormously varied.

It is broadly divided into three grape-growing regions: the Texas Hill Country, an AVA in the center of the state; the High Plains, an AVA on the Texas Panhandle; and the Trans-Pecos, not an appellation but a commonly used name for the large winegrowing area in the southwest. Within these areas are several other American Viticultural Areas. In the Texas Hill Country are Bell Mountain and Fredericksburg. In the Trans-Pecos you find Escondido Valley and Texas Davis Mountains. A tiny portion of the AVA known

as the Mesilla Valley is also in Texas, but most of this appellation is in southern New Mexico.

The Texas Hill Country is a concatenation of rolling hills and color. The white limestone and pink granite soil stares out from the rough rock faces it clings to. In the spring these hills are covered with scratchy olive-green mesquite and awash in bluebonnets and wagon-red Indian paintbrushes. By comparison, the High Plains are precisely that: majestic flat plains some 3,600 feet above sea level, carpeted with wild grasses as far as the eye can see. The Trans-Pecos, in the West Texas desert, is yet again different, full of awe-inspiring, isolated mountainscapes; vast, barren red mesas; canyons; and, occasionally, fertile river valleys. Within the Trans-Pecos region, the Escondido Valley viticultural area is made up of limestone-laced hills and mountains full of marine sedimentary rock.

What is viticulturally critical in each of these regions is the geologic complexity of the soil, the high altitude of the best vineyards, and the fact that hot days end in cool nights. Without those cool nights, Texas would not be able to produce wines with character. From a global perspective, however, Texas is still a comparatively warm place for grapes. The vines wake up from their winter dormancy early in the year. As a result, grapes are sometimes ready to be harvested by the end of July—a full two months before California and three months earlier than most European wine regions.

Most of the wineries that began in the 1970s, including Fall Creek and Llano Estacado, planted hardy French-American hybrids, such as villard blanc and cham-

## THE MOST IMPORTANT

### TEXAS WINES

LEADING WINES
**Cabernet Sauvignon** red
**Chardonnay** white
**Chenin Blanc** white
**Sauvignon Blanc** white

WINE OF NOTE
**Riesling** white

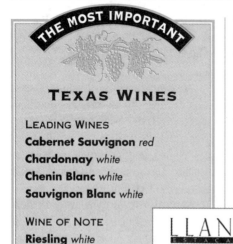

LLANO
ESTACADO

TEXAS HIGH PLAINS
CHENIN BLANC

PRODUCED AND BOTTLED BY LLANO ESTACADO WINERY
LUBBOCK, TEXAS
ALCOHOL 11.0% BY VOLUME

# THE FOODS OF TEXAS

For most of its history Texas was better known for its cowboy boots than for its cooking. That changed radically in the 1980s when a handful of dynamic young chefs began exploring Texas' rich and varied culinary heritage. In the process, a maverick new style of cooking called Southwestern cuisine was born.

Southwestern cuisine has no tidy parameters, but it does have deep historical roots. They begin with the native Hopi and Pueblo Indians who roasted corn to bring out its sweetness, used chiles to heighten flavor, grilled fish over hot-burning Texas woods, and smoked game.

Cowboys, too, left their culinary mark. With only a sack of pinto beans, a bucket of lard, a dozen eggs, chiles, garlic, a sack of *masa harina* (ground corn), a sack of flour, and coffee as provisions, cowboys set off to uninhabited ranch lands for weeks at a time. They hunted and grilled wild turkey, quail, venison, and baby goat and made rough, homemade biscuits or camp bread cooked over coals in black cast-iron pots. Biscuits, in fact, were a cowboy's silverware.

Though both are Texas specialties, grilling is not the same as barbecuing. Grilled food is cooked quickly over an open flame. The American word barbecue comes from *barbacoa*, the word Spanish explorers used to describe meats cooked extremely slowly in a pit so that the meat was cooked by smoke as much, if not more, than by flame. In the end, the meat would be so tender and succulent it would fall off the bone. Pit barbecue restaurants are still found all over the state.

bourcin. Small amounts of such *vinifera* varieties as chardonnay, sauvignon blanc, and cabernet sauvignon were planted experimentally, even though no one had much hope for them. Historical experience plus research at Texas A&M University had suggested that *vinifera* would always prove too fragile to stand up to Texas frost, heat, and diseases, such as cotton root rot. Not surprisingly, by the late 1970s, small grape growers in the west, central, and north of Texas had all had phenomenal success growing the robust hybrids. What was surprising, however, was that they'd also had success with many *vinifera* varieties.

The wine made from hybrids can be decent enough, but it is never what every winemaker hopes to make: wine that is complex and nuanced; wine that aims for greatness. After the false start with hybrids, Texas vintners replanted a whole laundry list of *vinifera* grapes, including everything from zinfandel to riesling. Today a half dozen varieties have proven most successful.

755

## SALSAS
## AND WINE

In both Southwestern and Mexican cooking, a major consideration in pairing food and wine is not only the food itself but also the accompanying sauce, or salsa as it's known in Mexico. Most of these salsas are vegetable based and do not contain meat, cream, or butter. But they do have very piquant and often intense flavors thanks to chiles, roasted garlic, lime, cilantro, and other bold seasonings. Which sorts of wine work best with such high-powered seasonings? Three kinds. First, wines that are high in acid, such as sauvignon blanc. High-acid wines stay alive and vibrant in the mouth. Like a sharp knife, the acidity cuts through even the most extroverted spicy flavors. Second, extremely fruity wines that have a touch of sweetness. An off-dry chenin blanc or riesling (such as those made by the Texas winery Fall Creek) has just enough sweetness to nicely counterbalance the heat of chiles. And third, wines that have a plush, thick, jammy texture, such as zinfandels from California and shirazes from Australia. Here, the concentrated, supple, superberried flavors of the wine act like a soft cushion for the robust seasonings to dance upon.

Texas shares 1,240 miles of border with Mexico. From the Mexicans, Texans learned how to cook with avocados, tomatoes, vanilla, and chocolate. Texas salsas (rough, uncooked sauces made from diced tomatoes, other vegetables, tropical fruits, and spices) are Mexican inspired, as are flan desserts. Mexican home cooks taught Texans how to make food refreshing by using lime juice in marinades and as a seasoning. (Today, many Texans still drink beer as Mexicans do, with fresh lime squeezed in.)

Mexican tortillas—thin, unleavened corn or flour disks—are the unofficial Texas bread. In Texas, hand-formed tortillas are made fresh in tiny tortilla factories owned and operated by Mexican families. About one hundred such tortilla factories still exist in Texas.

The greatest commingling of Mexican and Texan cooking has been the development of Tex-Mex cuisine. Gutsy, homey, and inexpensive, Tex-Mex was created by Mexican-Americans living in Texas and working with limited ingredients and a limited budget. The most famous Tex-Mex dishes (tacos, burritos, *chile rellenos*, fajitas) are all based on tortillas, usually wrapped around some combination of beans, melted cheese, and ground or sliced beef or pork, all spiked up with a fiery-hot dipping sauce. Texans say if your forehead does not break out in beads of sweat, you are in the wrong Tex-Mex restaurant.

Texas, however, is as much the South as it is the West. Chicken-fried steak with cream gravy—a Southern dish—could almost be called the official Texas state dish. The name makes no sense, for the dish has nothing to do with chicken, and there is no cream in the gravy. To make it, an inexpensive cut of beef is ground up, seasoned with black pepper, flattened into a thin patty, coated in a flour, milk, and egg batter, and then deep-fried until it is crunchy. Over it, Texans pour the cream gravy, a mass of dense, gray-brown sauce made by mixing flour with nutmeg, black pepper, and a little milk and then cooking the mixture until it is thick and lumpy. If anything begs for a glass of Texas cabernet, it's chicken-fried steak.

# THE TEXAS WINES TO KNOW

*For each wine below, the specific American Viticultural Area from which it comes is noted.*

## Sparkling Wine

### CAP ROCK

Sparkling Wine

vintage brut

Texas

approximately 90% pinot noir,
10% chardonnay

What could be better than a mouthful of cold, clean bubbles on a scorching

Texas summer afternoon? Cap Rock's sparkling wine won't threaten French Champagne sales, but it is vibrantly fresh with just the right crisp bite. It's made by the traditional *méthode champenoise* and aged on the lees for sixteen months. The winery's chardonnay, equally excellent, has the same sort of peachy, citrusy zip.

## Whites

### FALL CREEK VINEYARDS

Chenin Blanc

Texas

100% chenin blanc

Fall Creek's chenin blanc makes you immediately want to have a picnic in some exquisite meadow. The wine has a gentle, creamy texture and is packed with peachy-appley fruit. Its slightly off-dry character stands right up to spicy, chile-laced Texas dishes.

### LLANO ESTACADO

Johannisberg Riesling

Texas

100% riesling

The winery's name, Llano Estacado, means staked plains, which is what the area was called by Francisco Coronado, the early explorer who marked his way across the High Plains searching for the legendary cities of gold. Startling as the thought of riesling from Texas may be, Llano Estacado's can be a delicious wine, as intensely fruity, lively, and apricoty as an apricot sorbet. Its good streak of acidity is balanced by a touch of natural sweetness.

**757**

### STE. GENEVIEVE

Sauvignon Blanc

Texas

100% sauvignon blanc

Poised beside mammoth red mesas in the West Texas desert, the winery Ste. Genevieve is owned by Cordier Estates, a joint venture between the University

of Texas and the French wine giant Domaines Cordier. It is the Lone Star State's largest winery, producing more than 350,000 cases each year, but makes wines full of surprising character. The sauvignon blanc, a great example, has a bold flash of peach, smoke, and citrus flavors, and the fresh peachiness also shows up in the winery's chardonnay.

# *Reds*

### CAP ROCK

Cabernet Sauvignon

Texas

approximately 80% cabernet sauvignon, 10% merlot, and 10% cabernet franc

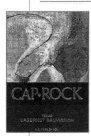

Cabernet sauvignon is emerging as one of the most successful red grapes in Texas. Cap Rock's regular cabernet (a small amount of reserve is also made) is simple but just plain good—a big splash of juicy cranberry and black cherry fruit.

### LLANO ESTACADO

Cabernet Sauvignon

Texas

100% cabernet sauvignon

This cabernet sauvignon is anything but a tough-guy red. The wine's juicy, tobacco aromas and flavors remind you of a simple, inexpensive Bordeaux, except the Llano has softer tannin. The wine's more expensive sibling, Cabernet Sauvignon Cellar Select, is a bigger wine that's been aged longer, but the regular cab is just fine, too.

## VISITING TEXAS WINERIES

There's something indescribably charming about watching winemakers wearing cowboy boots as they explain the intricacies of their "why-ine . . ." (a multisyllabic word in the Lone Star State). Many Texas wineries welcome visitors, although it's necessary to call ahead to check the tour and tasting schedule, or make an appointment, and ask for more specific driving instructions, since most wineries are deep in the countryside. It's often the owners themselves who will take you around.

PHEASANT RIDGE

PROPRIETOR'S RESERVE

CABERNET SAUVIGNON 54%, MERLOT 32%, CABERNET FRANC 14%
TEXAS HIGH PLAINS

Produced & Bottled by Pheasant Ridge Winery, Lubbock, Texas  Alc. 12.7% by Vol

### CAP ROCK WINERY
4 miles south of Lubbock
Tahoka Highway, on the High Plains
(mailing address:
Route 6, Box 713K,
Lubbock, TX 79423)
(806) 863-2704

### FALL CREEK VINEYARDS
2.2 miles northeast of Tow, on the shores
of Lake Buchanan in the Hill Country
(mailing address:
1820 County Road 222,
Tow, TX 78672)
(512) 476-4477 or (915) 379-5361

### LLANO ESTACADO WINERY
3.2 miles east of US 87
south on FM 1585, on the High Plains
(mailing address:
P.O. Box 697,
Lubbock, TX 79452)
(806) 745-2258

### PHEASANT RIDGE WINERY
2 miles east and 1 mile south
of New Deal on the High Plains
(mailing address:
Route 3, Box 181,
Lubbock, TX 79401)
(806) 746-6033

### STE. GENEVIEVE WINES
west on IH 10, near Fort Stockton,
amid the mesas of West Texas
(mailing address:
P.O. Box 697,
Fort Stockton, TX 79735)
(915) 395-2417

# Virginia

Among the first wines produced in America were those made around 1607 by Jamestown colonists from wild, musky-tasting scuppernong grapes. The wines were so poor—even by Colonial standards—that in 1619 the Virginia Company sent French vine cuttings and eight French winemakers to Jamestown to help establish proper vineyards and make decent wine. That same year, by legislative act, each colonist was required to plant at least ten grapevines. French help proved futile. The maiden vineyards soon died from fungal diseases and pests.

Remarkably, the early Virginians were undeterred. For almost two centuries they

## THE QUICK SIP ON VIRGINIA

- Attempts to make wine in Virginia began in 1607—the earliest record of wine production in the United States.

- Diseases, pests, and difficult weather destroyed most of the early vineyards, including those that were planted by Thomas Jefferson.

- The modern era of Virginia winemaking started in the 1970s with the planting of chardonnay, riesling, cabernet sauvignon, and such French-American hybrid grapes as seyval blanc and vidal blanc.

759

**VIRGINIA'S WINE REGIONS**

Eastern Shore
Monticello
Northern Neck
North Fork of Roanoke
Rocky Knob
Shenandoah Valley

*Linden Vineyards is cradled in Virginia's Blue Ridge Mountains.*

continued to plant vines, and the vines, for their part, continued to perish. By Thomas Jefferson's time, the prospects for a Virginia wine industry appeared nonexistent. Not that this stopped Jefferson. In 1787 he visited the best vineyards of Europe, taking detailed notes on viticulture and winemaking. His own quarter-acre vineyard was planted in 1807 with about twenty vines each of twenty-four different varieties of European and native grapes. There is no record of a harvest. Jefferson's grapes, too, probably died of diseases and pests.

*"I expect to be gratified with the great desideratum of making at home a good wine."*

—Thomas Jefferson writing to a friend in 1816

Then in the late nineteenth and early twentieth centuries, the picture changed radically. The devastation wrought by phylloxera and vine diseases caused French and American plant breeders to develop a number of new crosses and hybrid grapes hardy enough to withstand many pests and diseases, as well as colder temperatures. American grapes such as Norton were crosses of grape varieties that belonged to American vine species (*labrusca*, *aestivalis*, and so on). The wines made from these new crosses usually tasted better than the wines made from native grapes. Thus American wines based on crosses, such as Virginia Claret, made from the Norton grape, became quite successful even though, in comparison to European wines, they were still something of an acquired taste.

A step up in quality came with the French-American hybrids, such as seyval

760

*For centuries, problems with humidity and pests curtailed any success the Virginian wine industry might have had. Today, with more sophisticated viticultural techniques, healthy vines are thriving.*

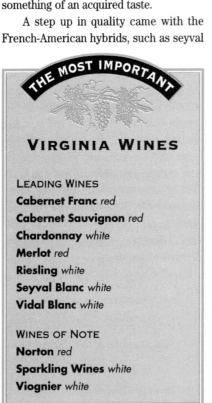

## THE MOST IMPORTANT

## VIRGINIA WINES

LEADING WINES
**Cabernet Franc** red
**Cabernet Sauvignon** red
**Chardonnay** white
**Merlot** red
**Riesling** white
**Seyval Blanc** white
**Vidal Blanc** white

WINES OF NOTE
**Norton** red
**Sparkling Wines** white
**Viognier** white

blanc, vidal blanc, Maréchal Foch, and chambourcin. These were hybridizations of American vine species with the European vine species *vinifera*. French-American hybrids are still grown and the wines made from them continue to be popular in Virginia today.

Prohibition brought the collapse of Virginia's wine industry, which wasn't revived until the 1970s when wineries like Meredyth and Farfelu once again began making wine from French-American hybrids. But it was with the widespread planting of *vinifera* grapes, such as chardonnay and cabernet sauvignon, in the late seventies and early eighties that Virginia became one of the two most dynamic wine regions on the East Coast (the other is New York State). Between 1979 and 1986 the hard-won success of Virginia's chardonnays, cabernets, and

# AMERICA'S FIRST WINE EXPERT

Thomas Jefferson, third president of the United States and author of the Declaration of Independence, was an accomplished architect, scientist, musician, philosopher, scholar, and farmer in addition to being a politician. He was also America's first wine expert.

Born in Albermarle County, Virginia, on April 13, 1743, Jefferson was appointed ambassador to France at the age of forty-one and moved to Paris. There he became deeply impressed by the French—especially their love of food and wine. He was so fascinated with the way the French prepared and presented their meals that he took extensive notes on both. He even arranged for his slave James Hemings to take lessons from a French chef. He promised Hemings his freedom when they returned to the United States if Hemings, in turn, would teach French cooking to the other slaves at Monticello.

*Monticello*

It was during his time in Europe that Jefferson became profoundly curious about wine, and with his interest grew his expertise. In 1787 and 1788 he toured the wine regions of France, Germany, and northern Italy, visiting the top producers, documenting the best vintages, and taking detailed notes in hopes of growing *vinifera* (European) grapes and making wine at Monticello. Sadly for Jefferson, his numerous attempts at growing *vinifera* grapes in Virginia repeatedly failed.

When Jefferson returned from France in 1789, wines from the most prestigious vineyards of Europe were included in his eighty-six packing cases. He also came back zealously enthusiastic, convinced that, in moderation, wine was an integral part of healthful living.

The White House cellar was amply stocked during the Jefferson presidency. One historian estimates that during his two four-year terms, Jefferson personally spent a total of $10,000 on wine. (His presidential salary was $2,500 a year in 1800s dollars.)

Jefferson was also greatly responsible for what lay in the White House cellar well before and long after his terms. From Washington's presidency through Monroe's, Jefferson positioned himself as the unofficial presidential wine adviser, always ready with recommendations, even when none were requested. When James Monroe was elected, for example, he received a long letter from Jefferson—two sentences of congratulations and the rest a list suggesting European wines Monroe should order for the White House.

Among collectors, one of the most sought after wines in the world is a 1787 Château Lafite bearing the initials Th J. Four bottles of the Lafite, thought to have been bottled for Jefferson, are currently known to exist. In December 1985 Christopher Forbes, the son of the late publishing magnate Malcolm Forbes, paid $156,450—then the highest price ever paid for a single bottle of wine— for one of the Jefferson bottles.

Since the presidency of Ronald Reagan, most of the wines served at the White House have come from the United States. In 1993 the first official dinner hosted by President William Jefferson "Bill" Clinton included wines chosen in tribute to Jefferson. The first, Oakencroft chardonnay, came from vineyards near Monticello. This was followed by the Jefferson Cuvee cabernet sauvignon from Monticello Vineyards in the Napa Valley. The winery was named for the residence of the third president.

rieslings caused vineyard acreage in the state to jump 420 percent.

Today there are some fifty-nine wineries in Virginia, most of which are small and family owned. They grow a vast array of grapes, all in small quantities. These include not only chardonnay, cabernet sauvignon, and riesling, and the hybrids and crosses, but also several Rhône varieties that show promise, especially viognier.

Virginia's six viticultural areas are scattered across the state. They include Virginia's Eastern Shore, the Shenandoah Valley, Monticello (named after the nearby home of Thomas Jefferson), Northern Neck (George Washington's birthplace), North Fork of Roanoke, and Rocky Knob.

# THE LAND, THE GRAPES, AND THE VINEYARDS

Although the vineyards of Virginia are scattered across the state, they share a dramatic continental climate. Winters can be so bitingly cold that the trunks of the vines can freeze and split open. Springtime frosts can kill new buds. In summer excessive heat can make the grapes ripen too quickly, which detracts from the elegance of the final wine, and humidity can lead to rot, mildew, and other diseases. Initially only hardy hybrids proved indestructible. By the late 1970s, however, viticultural research, including that on site selection and trellising systems, had progressed far enough that vintners tried planting *vinifera* grapes once again. The first significant commercial planting of chardonnay was at Barboursville Vineyards near Charlottesville in 1976. Today more than three fourths of Virginia's approximately 1,500 acres of

## THE GRAPES OF VIRGINIA

### WHITES

**Chardonnay:** Leading grape. Virtually every winery makes a chardonnay.

**Riesling:** Major grape. A source of good, generally inexpensive quaffing wines, often slightly sweet.

**Seyval Blanc:** Major French-American hybrid. Can be turned into light, refreshing wines.

**Vidal Blanc:** Major French-American hybrid. Can make delicious wines.

**Viognier:** Famous Rhône (French) variety. Only a tiny amount of wine from this grape comes from Virginia, but the quality can be very good.

### REDS

**Cabernet Franc:** Shows promise. Makes lean reds that at their best are smoky and slightly spicy.

**Cabernet Sauvignon:** Leading red grape. The wines from it vary in quality, depending on the producer and location of the vineyards.

**Merlot:** Like cabernet franc, merlot shows promise. Most examples are fairly light and lean.

**Norton:** American cross; makes zinfandel-like wines. Though only a tiny amount is planted, the quality of the wines is surprisingly high.

vineyards is planted with *vinifera* grapes.

Virtually every winery in the state now produces a chardonnay, and riesling is the second most widely planted white grape. Cabernet sauvignon, cabernet franc, and merlot are very popular, and there are minuscule plantings of numerous other grapes, including sauvignon blanc, gewürztraminer, and pinot noir. A small number of experiments with Rhône varieties, especially viognier, have proven successful, and the cross known as Norton makes surprisingly tasty wines that could easily pass for zinfandel. At the same time, such French-American hybrid grapes as seyval blanc and vidal blanc remain well liked—and justifiably so. Virginia is one of the few states that has managed to make tasty wine from such hybrids. But, as of the late 1990s, hybrids represented less than a quarter of vineyard acreage in Virginia.

Many wineries also make unique blends of hybrid and *vinifera* grapes, such as Ingleside Plantation's Chesapeake Blanc, which contains seyval blanc, vidal blanc, chardonnay, and sauvignon blanc or The Williamsburg Winery's Governor's White, made from riesling, vidal blanc, and mus-

*In 1983 Felicia Warburg Rogan founded Oakencroft Vineyard. Prior to that, with the help of noted Virginia ampelographer Lucie Morton, Rogan had been a successful home winemaker, making chardonnay, merlot, and seyval blanc in a converted toolshed.*

## HORTON'S NORTON

—◦◦◦◦◦—

The Norton grape—Virginia's most famous American cross—was nearly extinct in the state when Horton Vineyards decided in 1991 to bring it back into commercial production because of its historical significance. Before Prohibition Norton was the prized grape in the wildly popular wine called Virginia Claret. Norton was first propagated in 1835 in Richmond by D. N. Norton, who wanted to develop a grape suited to Virginia's climate. Horton's modern Norton is a remarkably delicious, spicy, zinfandel-like wine that has been blended with a drop of mourvèdre and cabernet franc to give it added structure and body.

cat. Finally, a small number of wineries make very creditable sparkling wine.

Virginia's wineries are scattered all over the state from the Shenandoah Valley in the northwest, between the Allegheny and Blue Ridge Mountains, to Monticello, near Charlottesville in the center of the state, to the eastern seaboard. Soil varies considerably from clay and sandy loam to silty loam. Officially there are six appellations in the state, but because the differences among them are not yet well established, many of the state's top winemakers prefer to simply label their wine Virginia.

Most Virginia wineries are small family-run operations. In many cases they are headed by self-taught winemakers who are former profes-

## FRENCH-AMERICAN HYBRIDS

—◁⟁▷—

Virginia's popular seyval blanc and vidal blanc are both French-American hybrids, grape varieties created by hybridizing one or more American vine species with the European vine species *vinifera*. Such varieties were created in the nineteenth and early twentieth centuries by French plant breeders who hoped to combine the disease resistance of American vines with the flavor of European vines. In the United States hybrids are planted almost exclusively in cold, eastern wine regions, such as Virginia and New York State. A hybrid is different from a cross, which is a grape created by breeding two varieties from the *same* species. Within the European species *Vitis vinifera*, two of the most famous crosses are pinotage (pinot noir x cinsaut) and scheurebe (silvaner x riesling).

conducts tours and tastings. Virginia wine country is among the most beautiful in the United States, and many wineries have pick-your-own apple orchards, picnic facilities, and wine festivals. You'll find a couple of wineries here that haven't been highlighted; they are interesting to visit and their wines are certainly worth trying.

Three wineries, Prince Michel de Virginia, Chateau Morrisette, and Barboursville have very good restaurants. In addition, one of the top restaurant/inns in the United States, the Inn at Little Washington (no, not D.C.—Middle and Main Streets, Washington; [540] 675-3800), is just a short ride from many northern Virginia wineries.

The Virginia Wine Marketing Program publishes a complete guide to the wineries of Virginia, including tour and festival information. Contact the Virginia Wine Marketing Program at P.O. Box 1163, Richmond, Virginia 23218; (800) 828-4637.

sors, physicists, investment bankers— even former Marines. There are also a handful of medium and large estates. Among these Prince Michel de Virginia and Rapidan River wineries are owned by a French industrialist, and Barboursville Vineyards is owned by the giant Italian wine producer Zonin.

## VISITING VIRGINIA WINERIES

More than 90 percent of Virginian wine is sold in state and much of that is sold directly from the wineries themselves. As a result, even the tiniest of Virginia wineries welcomes (with considerable Southern hospitality) visitors and

CENTRAL VIRGINIA

**BARBOURSVILLE VINEYARDS**
17655 Winery Road
Barboursville, VA 22923
(540) 832-3824

**HORTON VINEYARDS**
6399 Spotswood Trail
Gordonsville, VA 22942
(540) 832-7440

**OAKENCROFT VINEYARD AND WINERY**
1486 Oakencroft Road
Charlottesville, VA 22901
(804) 296-4188

**PRINCE MICHEL DE VIRGINIA AND RAPIDAN RIVER VINEYARDS**
Route 29
Leon, VA 22725
(540) 547-3707

*Prince Michel de Virginia, one of the largest wineries in Virginia, was founded in 1982 by Jean Leducq, chairman of a multinational industrial French laundry.*

# VIRGINIA COUNTRY HAM

Arguably the quintessential Southern food, country ham has been produced in Virginia and its neighboring states from the earliest Colonial times. As the number of artisanal producers has declined, however, production of true country ham has diminished sharply.

Unlike the thick-slab baked ham often eaten at Easter, Virginia country ham has a very dramatic sweet, meaty flavor and can be quite salty. Like Italian prosciutto, it's meant to be sliced paper thin.

The best country hams—such as those produced near the town of Smithfield—come from peanut-fed hogs. The hams are dry-cured for five weeks or longer with sugar, which tenderizes and sweetens the meat, plus other seasonings. They are then smoked over hickory wood and aged from three months to up to one year. The longer the aging, the saltier the meat.

Saltiness in food can be hard on wine (possibly the best worst marriage going is cabernet and caviar), so Virginia ham takes some consideration in the wine department. Generally, high-acid wines like sauvignon blanc work magically, and if you're up for an adventure, try a juicy, not very tannic red that's uniquely Virginian: Norton.

Dry-cured country hams are shipped via UPS around the United States. Here are three top Virginia producers.

- *Gwaltney of Smithfield, (800) 292-2773*
- *Smithfield Packing Co., (800) 926-8448*
- *S. Wallace Edwards & Sons, (800) 222-4267*

# THE VIRGINIA WINES TO KNOW

*For each wine below, the specific American Viticultural Area from which it comes is noted.*

## *Sparkling Wine*

### OASIS
Cuvée d'Or
nonvintage brut
Virginia
approximately 60% chardonnay,
40% pinot noir

Virginia boasts a small number of very good sparkling wines, among them the Oasis brut. Made according to the traditional Champagne method, this is a crisp, light sparkler with hints of vanilla—just waiting for grilled seafood.

## *Whites*

### HORTON VINEYARDS
Viognier
Orange County, Virginia
100% viognier

Horton's viognier is one of Virginia's most surprising success stories, for it ranks among the top viogniers made in the United States. At its best, loads of honeysuckle, melon, litchi, lime, and white pepper flavors race through the wine. The lush, creamy body is elegant and sophisticated. Horton Vineyards specializes in growing Rhône varietals in Virginia, and these wines are remarkably scrumptious.

### LINDEN
Sauvignon Blanc
Virginia
100% sauvignon blanc

Of the tiny number of sauvignon blancs made in Virginia, the best is Linden's. Zesty and bright in top years, it's got a perfect keen-honed edge to it, plus beautifully focused melon, gooseberry, and lime flavors. This is the sort of wine that fills your mouth with a snappy sensation of herbs and meadows.

### PRINCE MICHEL DE VIRGINIA
Chardonnay
Virginia
100% chardonnay

The largest premium winery in the state, Prince Michel de Virginia was established in 1982 by a French industrialist. A French hand is clearly evident in the chardonnay. This is no toasty blob of butter and alcohol but rather a refined, classically structured chardonnay with fine honey and lime flavors.

### STONEWALL VINEYARDS
Cayuga White
Virginia
100% cayuga

Cayuga, an American hybrid, is probably not on anyone's list of chic grape varieties, but this wine is a charmer anyway. Lively, citrusy, and slightly peppery, it has a floral hint reminiscent of muscat. Nothing could be better on a Virginia summer afternoon.

## THE WILLIAMSBURG WINERY

Chardonnay

Acte 12 of Sixteen Nineteen

Virginia

100% chardonnay

Chardonnay, the leading grape in Virginia, can turn into lovely wines—wines that are creamy but not overwrought, full-bodied but not monstrous. The Williamsburg Winery's Acte 12 is often one of the best. The wine is named after an act passed in 1619 by the Jamestown colonists requiring each of them to plant at least ten grapevines.

## THE WILLIAMSBURG WINERY

Governor's White

America

approximately 50% riesling, 45% vidal blanc, plus a small amount of muscat

This wine is perfectly named for, in the best diplomatic sense, it could please anyone and everyone (not surprisingly, it's one of the best-selling wines in Virginia). When at its finest, there's a peachy, floral aroma and then a light, easy to love flavor. And though it's fairly unusual, the grapes for this wine come not just from Virginia, but from New York State and California as well, hence the AVA America.

## *Reds*

## BARBOURSVILLE VINEYARDS

Barbera

reserve

Monticello

100% barbera

Barbera is a fairly rare grape in Virginia, but the tight, lean, sharp smokiness of Barboursville's barbera is appealingly reminiscent of the red wines of the Loire Valley in France. The best examples have just the right subtle suggestion of roasted meats and boysenberries. While taut reds are not everyone's cup of tea, this wine can be very convincing.

## HORTON VINEYARDS

Norton

Orange County, Virgina

mostly Norton, with a little cabernet franc and mourvèdre

Made from the American cross called Norton, Horton's Norton would make any red-wine drinker positively gleeful—especially a zinfandel lover. Its psychedelic ruby-purple color is right out of the 1960s, and the wine's mouth-filling black cherry flavor bursts on the scene like a thunderstorm.

## LINDEN VINEYARDS

Cabernet

Virginia

approximately 60% cabernet sauvignon, 40% cabernet franc

After the first sip of this juicy, spicy blend of cabernet sauvignon and cabernet franc, called simply Cabernet, it's hard to put the glass down. In top years, the flavor is all about black: ripe blackberries, black cherries, black pepper, and black licorice, plus a zing of menthol and a hint of vanilla from American oak barrels. Linden is a small winery in the Blue Ridge Mountains about an hour's drive west of Washington, D.C.

## OAKENCROFT

Merlot

Monticello

100% merlot

Oakencroft's delicious, light, zesty merlot is simple and straightforward, but purely from the standpoint of pleasure, it can be a winner. Its tobacco, spice, and black currant aromas and flavors beg for a slice of Virginia ham.

# Wine Regions to Watch

While California, with its near-perfect wine-growing climate, will undoubtedly always lead wine production in the United States, the fact is that wines from unexpected states are getting more exciting and more numerous year by year. A wine from Arizona with dinner? It's no longer a far-fetched idea. Of the forty-one states that now make wine, but have not been covered earlier in this section, here are five to watch.

## ARIZONA

Whatever the Apache warrior chief Cochise envisioned as the destiny of his homeland, it probably wasn't as wine country. But on the parched, blindingly bright high desert of southeast Arizona where Cochise once reigned, that's exactly what has happened. Just 20 miles from the Mexican border, the cactus-ringed villages of Sonoita, Patagonia, and Elgin (John Wayne westerns were filmed here) have sprouted the improbable: small green vines that clutch the earth with true grit.

Although Arizona's scorchingly hot desert climate would seem to preclude grape growing, ten wineries now exist thanks to irrigation. All is not quite perfect however. As it turns out, the state's large population of coyotes not only adores grapes but also possesses a special fondness for the flavor of irrigation hoses without which no Arizonan winery could survive.

The first attempts to grow grapes in Arizona were made by Franciscan missionaries in the late seventeenth century, but the state's modern wine industry didn't emerge until the 1980s, when Gordon Dutt, who has a Ph.D. in soil science from the University of Arizona, planted grapes near Sonoita. Today the leading winery by far is Callaghan Vineyards, which makes exciting cabernet blends and Rhône-style wines.

## MISSOURI

If Missouri's place in the history of great American winemaking has been neglected (and it has), then the wrong is about to be righted. With thirty-five wineries, Missouri is now one of the most promising up-and-coming wine regions in the United States. Until relatively recently, Missouri's was a riches to rags story. In 1866 George Husmann, a professor at the University of Missouri, prophesied that the United States would one day be the world's greatest wine-producing country. At the time, it seemed as if his home state might lead the way; it ranked second in the nation in grape growing, and wines from Missouri quite frankly stunned critics in wine exhibitions in Paris, Vienna, and elsewhere in Europe. The grape variety Norton, an American cross, was especially highly regarded, being compared by one British wine expert to no less than French Burgundy "without the finesse." (As descriptions go, this was probably a bit fanciful; Norton can be delicious, but its deep color, full body, lip-smackingly jammy fruit flavors, and all-around meatiness are more reminiscent of zinfandel or Rhône varieties than pinot noir.) Ultimately and unfortunately, a combination of disease (especially mildew and rot), overproduction, and local prohibition laws took their toll on Missouri's wine industry. By the 1880s most vineyards were dying or abandoned. Those that survived national Prohibition did so by reinventing themselves as juice and jelly manufacturers.

A rebirth came in the 1970s and 1980s, with new laws that helped jump-start a modern wine industry. Today the quality of the top Missouri wines is downright astonishing. Anyone possessed of a sort of vinous prejudice against the Midwest should taste Augusta Winery's spicy, lively vignoles (a French-American hybrid) or juicy, chocolaty cynthiana (the local name for Norton).

# NEW MEXICO

I n the 1990s a sparkling wine named Gruet developed a cult following in knowledgeable wine circles around the United States. On the face of it, there was nothing remarkable about this fact; there were many terrific California sparkling wines made according to the traditional Champagne method. But Gruet wasn't from Napa or Sonoma or anyplace else in California for that matter. Gruet was from Truth or Consequences, a small town in New Mexico, and as surprising as that was, when you called the winery looking for the owner, a French woman got on the line.

In 1983, Nathalie Gruet, her brother Laurent Gruet, and her husband, Farid Himeur, moved from France to Truth or Consequences, a stark plateau 150 miles south of Albuquerque, with the intention of making a sparkling wine. Strange as this seemed, they'd fallen in love with the American Southwest and instinctively felt that it was wine country waiting to be discovered. Land prices were cheap. They figured that if the wine they made turned out bad, they wouldn't be out a lot of capital; and if it turned out good, well, the notoriety would launch them. And that's exactly what happened. The first Gruet brut was released in 1989 to amazing press reviews. Crisp, frothy, and elegant, it's easily the equal of many California sparklers.

Like Arizona, New Mexico's first grapes were planted in the seventeenth century by Franciscan fathers who required wine for the Mass. But as with so many other states, disease, severe weather, and national Prohibition proved the New Mexican wine industry's undoing. At least until the 1980s. Today New Mexico boasts nineteen wineries, most of them smaller than Gruet, which proved that truth, consequences, and wine can be a formidable combination.

# PENNSYLVANIA

W ith more than 800 chardonnays made in California, you don't expect to find one of your favorites in Pennsylvania, but many wine lovers have. Pennsylvania has more wineries than most of us would guess—fifty-five—but none is more renowned than the Chaddsford Winery in Chadds Ford, in the southeastern corner of the state. The winery is owned by Eric and Lee Miller and is a direct result

*In 1982 Eric and Lee Miller founded Chaddsford, now considered the best winery in Pennsylvania.*

## RHODE ISLAND

With the exception of Newport's mansions, most things in Rhode Island have a humble New England character, including the state's four wineries. Four wineries isn't very many of course, but then the state isn't a very big place. More than 149 Rhode Islands could fit into California, for example. Rhode Island is included here because of the success of one winery, Sakonnet (sa-KON-et). Located thirty-five miles southeast of Providence in Little Compton, Sakonnet was founded in 1975 by Jim and Lolly Mitchell on the premise that southeastern New England possessed a climate similar to that of many wine regions in northern Europe, wine regions which the Mitchells had visited and simply fallen in love with. In 1987 the winery was purchased by Earl and Susan Samson, a venture capitalist and theatrical producer respectively, who wanted a simpler lifestyle and who ended up turning Sakonnet into the most highly regarded and largest winery in New England. Sakonnet's vidal blanc (a French-American hybrid) has even gone where no hybrid has gone before: onto wine lists in chic California restaurants. Sakonnet also produces award-winning gewürztraminer, chardonnay, and pinot noir.

of Eric's year spent in Burgundy, France, drinking what else? Great Burgundies. The son of Mark Miller, who owns New York's Benmarl Winery, Eric went out on his own, determined to make world-class chardonnay and pinot noir. That he achieved the former seems at least possible, but making a great pinot noir, from one of the world's most difficult grapes, has been a remarkable achievement.

Not surprisingly, Pennsylvania was the location of one of the first successful commercial winegrowing ventures in the United States, the Pennsylvania Wine Company, which began in 1793 but closed soon thereafter, its vineyards decimated by disease. Today more advanced viticultural knowledge promises a brighter future for the state.

*Rhode Island's top winery, Sakonnet, has New England charm.*

# Canada

Although Canada is probably still better known for hockey than wine, the country represents one of the newest wine regions in the New World. From seemingly out of nowhere, a tiny wine industry has sprung, and some Canadian wines—especially sweet ones—are now turning heads in competitions internationally. That said, as the twenty-first century gets under way, Canadian dry wines (with a few exceptions) still have quite a way to go before they can compete successfully on the world wine stage.

Many in the United States and, indeed, many Canadians may never have tasted a Canadian wine, but grape growing here dates from the 1860s when

## THE QUICK SIP ON CANADA

• Canada's tiny wine industry is one of the newest in the New World.

• The country's most famous wine is ice wine, a sweet wine made from frozen grapes that are harvested in the middle of winter.

• Canada's two most important wine regions are on opposite sides of the country—British Columbia in the west, Ontario in the east.

grapes, intended for sacramental wine, were planted near the Okanagan Mission

**771**

Canada ranks thirty-eighth in wine-producing countries worldwide. Canadians drink an average of 2.19 gallons of wine per person each year; they're thirty-second in world wine consumption.

*The 100-mile-long Okanagan Valley, wedged between the foothills of the Rocky Mountains to the east and the Cascade Range to the west, forms the heart of the wine industry of British Columbia.*

## THE GRAPES OF

# CANADA

Most wine regions ultimately become known—if not renowned—for just a few grape varieties (Bordeaux for cabernet sauvignon and merlot, for example; Burgundy for pinot noir and chardonnay; and so on). The process of discovering which grapes grow best in a given location, however, takes decades—sometimes centuries—plus considerable experimentation with many different varieties. It's precisely in this sorting-out stage in its wine evolution that Canada finds itself. As a result, definitive conclusions about the merits of various grapes are hard to make. The many familiar white grapes being planted include chardonnay, riesling, gewürztraminer, pinot gris, pinot blanc, and sauvignon blanc, with the first four showing the most promise. Well-known reds include cabernet franc, cabernet sauvignon, merlot, pinot noir, and a tiny bit of gamay (Canada is one of the rare places outside France where you find this grape). Although red wines haven't been as successful as whites in Canada, winemakers have high hopes for them in the future.

Grape varieties that are less familiar overall but nonetheless successful include the white French-American hybrid vidal blanc (sometimes called simply vidal) and the red French-American hybrids Baco noir and Maréchal Foch. Vidal blanc, in particular, is transformed into some stellar ice wines.

in British Columbia, as well as on Lake Erie's Pelee Island. Yet for more than a century the development of a prosperous wine industry was hampered by a complex series of political and economic barriers, including the creation of government monopolies that control the sale and distribution of alcoholic beverages. It was not until the 1990s, after legal changes made owning a winery and selling wine more economically viable and after Canadians too began to experience the excitement and optimism that was pervading wine regions throughout much of the New World, that the wine industry finally began to take hold and thrive.

It is still a minuscule industry by world standards. As of the late 1990s, there were slightly more than 17,000 acres of vineyards in Canada (the Napa Valley alone has more than two times as much land planted with grapes). Most of these vineyards are planted with white grapes, including such *vinifera* varieties as riesling, pinot gris, and chardonnay, as well as crosses and French-American hybrids.

A handful of Canada's approximately 140 wineries are large producers, but the

# VQA

Most top Canadian wines carry a seal with the letters VQA, which stand for Vintner's Quality Alliance. The VQA stamp means that the wine has been tasted and adheres to standards set forth by a board of Canadian vintners and growers. The VQA also stipulates how and when appellation names such as Okanagan Valley or Niagara Peninsula can be used.

vast majority are tiny. Often family run, these small wineries can be divided into two camps: professional producers who make creditable fine wines and what might be called amateur producers whose wines reflect enthusiasm more than they do skill. Despite their size, many wineries make six to twelve different wines. It's quite common for the lion's share of these wines to be sold from the wineries' own tasting rooms.

## CANADIAN WINES

**Ice Wine** white (sweet)
**Late Harvest Wine** white (sweet)

Canada's two most important wine-producing regions, Ontario and British Columbia, are 2,000 miles apart on opposite sides of the country (wine is also made in Nova Scotia and Quebec, though not in commercially significant amounts). Of the two, Ontario, with some sixty wineries, is the larger producer, accounting for about 75 percent of all the wine made in the country. Ontario's three wine districts—Niagara Peninsula, Lake Erie North Shore, and Pelee Island—lie along the shores (or just offshore) of two of the Great Lakes, Lake Ontario and Lake Erie. These wine districts are Canada's most southerly, but the icy Arctic winds that sweep across the region would render viticulture nearly impossible were it not for the warming and moderating effect of the lakes. Like the lakes themselves, the wine districts of Ontario were carved out by

## FROZEN ASSETS

The sometimes icy relationship between the New World and the Old World holds no sway in at least one area: ice wine, or *eiswein* as it is spelled in Europe. As of 2000, Canada, Austria, and Germany forged what is thought to be the first international agreement concerning a dessert wine. Under the agreement, all three countries have pledged to make ice wine only in the traditional centuries-old manner by allowing the grapes to freeze naturally on the vine, picking them by hand one frozen grape at a time, then gently pressing them to yield tiny amounts of superconcentrated juice. Fraught with numerous difficulties, from the exigencies of harvesting in subzero degree weather to hungry animals and birds who can quickly strip the vines of every last sweet frozen grape, the painstaking technique is quite different from the shortcut sometimes used elsewhere: freezing grapes in huge industrial freezers.

773

retreating ancient glaciers that left behind a variety of deep, well-drained soils.

British Columbia, at the 50th parallel in latitude, is one of the most northern wine regions in the world, commensurate with the Mosel region of Germany. It is made up of four wine districts—the Okanagan Valley, Similkameen Valley, Fraser Valley, and Vancouver Island. Of these, the 150-mile-long Okanagan Valley is where most of British Columbia's sixty-one wineries are located.

Though British Columbia is considerably farther north than Ontario, the temperatures in the region are often warmer thanks to its unique microclimate and

*Grapes frozen naturally on the vine will soon be picked by hand, crushed extremely gently, and made into one of the world's most miraculous and decadent beverages—ice wine. Canada produces more ice wine than other country in the world.*

**774**

geography. This is especially true of the Okanagan Valley, which while quite close to the Pacific Ocean as the crow flies, hides behind the curtain of the Coastal mountain range. Rainfall here is scant, and the southern end of the valley is officially classified as Canada's only desert. Days are consistently sunny and arid; nights, very cool—a viticulturist's dream scenario.

As for the grapes, white *vinifera* varieties, such as riesling, chardonnay, and pinot gris, are on the rise, however a significant amount of Canadian production is made up of wines produced from hardy French-American hybrids, such as vidal blanc, Baco noir, and

*Inniskillin is one of Canada's leading producers of ice wine.*

Maréchal Foch, as well as a smaller number of crosses, such as the very obscure ehrenfelser (a cross of riesling and silvaner). As in upstate New York, these hybrids and crosses were originally planted out of the fear that *vinifera* varieties would not be able to withstand the extremes of the climate. Experience has proven otherwise and, again as in New York, hybrids and crosses continue to be pulled out and replaced with *vinifera* grapes.

White grapes are made not only into dry still wines but also into sparkling wines and into Canada's superstar specialty, sweet wines. These delicious sweet wines have begun

## ICE WINES AND DESSERT

When you compare them to top dessert wines made elsewhere in the world, Canada's top ice wines are steals, making them good choices for entertaining. Most Canadian ice wines are fairly light bodied, not particularly syrupy in texture, and have flavors reminiscent of ripe peaches, apricots, pineapples, and citrus fruits. A Canadian ice wine's moderate amount of natural sugar, about 13 percent, is balanced by fairly high acidity, so the wines rarely come off as cloying. Great matches for these fairly delicate wines include poached fruit, fruit tarts, crème brûlée, and simple shortbread or sugar cookies. Chocolate, alas, clashes horribly and makes ice wines taste thin.

no higher than 17.6°F; Canadian law requires that it be at least this cold before grapes for ice wine can be picked. As the frozen grapes are pressed, the sweet, high-acid, concentrated juice is separated from the ice. The ice is thrown away and the resulting wine is made solely from the superintense juice. As a result, the greatest ice wines possess an almost otherworldly contrapuntal tension between acidity and sweetness, making drinking them an ethereal sensation.

You may not come across many Canadian wines, but if you do, give them a try—especially if they are late harvest or ice wines. You could be in for a rare treat.

---

*Some of Canada's Best Small Producers*

**775**

### BRITISH COLUMBIA

BLUE MOUNTAIN VINEYARD AND CELLARS

BURROWING OWL VINEYARDS

HAWTHORNE MOUNTAIN VINEYARDS

QUAILS' GATE ESTATE WINERY

SUMAC RIDGE ESTATE

TINHORN CREEK VINEYARDS

### ONTARIO

CAVE SPRING CELLARS

CHÂTEAU DES CHARMES

HENRY OF PELHAM ESTATE

INNISKILLIN

PILLITTERI ESTATES WINERY

THIRTY BENCH VINEYARD AND WINERY

VINELAND ESTATES WINERY

---

to give Canada an international reputation as a serious wine producer. There are two types: late harvest wines that have often been affected by the noble rot *Botrytis cinerea* (the mold also responsible for Sauternes) and the rare, treasured ice wines. Because Canada has reliably cold winters, ice wines can be produced every year, making Canada the world's leading producer of ice wine.

Canadian ice wines have almost mythic status. Virtually every top producer in the country tries to make one. Like the extraordinary *eisweins* of Germany, Canadian ice wines are made from frozen grapes, usually riesling or vidal blanc. These are picked in the dead of winter (assuming bears, deer, or coyotes don't eat them first) at temperatures

*With three other independent-minded partners, Dr. Thomas Muckle, a physician, established Ontario's Thirty Bench Vineyard on the Niagara Peninsula in 1994.*

## VISITING CANADIAN WINERIES

B ecause so much Canadian wine is bought directly from wineries, wineries here are well set up for visitors. Many offer not only tastings and tours but also breathtakingly beautiful scenery, and some have cafés or restaurants. In addition, numerous festivals and special events are held throughout the year. For a complete guide to these, as well as information and maps contact the British Columbia Wine Institute, Suite 400, 601 West Broadway, Vancouver, British Columbia V5Z 4C2; (604) 664-7744, and the Vintner's Quality Alliance of Canada, 110 Hannover Drive, Suite B205, St. Catherines, Ontario L2W 1A4; (905) 684-8070.

### BRITISH COLUMBIA

**BLUE MOUNTAIN VINEYARD AND CELLARS**
R.R. #1, Site 3, Comp 4
Allendale Road
Okanagan Falls, BC V0H 1R0
(250) 497-8244

**QUAILS' GATE ESTATE WINERY**
3303 Boucherie Road
Kelowna, BC V1Z 2H3
(250) 769-4451

**SUMAC RIDGE ESTATE WINERY**
17403 Highway 97, Box 307
Summerland, BC V0H 1Z0
(250) 494-0451

### ONTARIO

**CAVE SPRING CELLARS**
3836 Main Street
Jordan, ON L0R 1S0
(905) 562-3581

**HENRY OF PELHAM ESTATE WINERY**
1469 Pelham Road
St. Catharines, ON L2R 6P7
(905) 684-8423

**INNISKILLIN WINES**
Line 3 at the Niagara Parkway
R.R. #1, Niagara-on-the-Lake
ON L0S 1J0
(905) 468-3554

776

# Australia

SOUTH AUSTRALIA
NEW SOUTH WALES
VICTORIA
WESTERN AUSTRALIA

Covering a landmass of 3 million square miles, Australia is almost as large as the United States and possesses a wine industry that is quite possibly the most dynamic and cutting edge in the world. Though France produced seven and a half times the wine that Australia did in 2000, the volume of Australian wine is growing so fast that Australia is now poised to unseat France as the second leading wine exporter to the United States, after Italy.

High tech could be the Australian wine industry's middle name. Most winer-

778

### KEY TO AUSTRALIA'S WINE REGIONS

**SOUTH AUSTRALIA**
1 Clare Valley
2 Barossa Valley
3 Eden Valley
4 Adelaide Hills
5 McLaren Vale
6 Padthaway
7 Coonawarra

**NEW SOUTH WALES**
8 Mudgee
9 Hunter Valley
10 Riverina

**VICTORIA**
11 Murray Darling
12 Rutherglen
13 Glenrowan
14 Goulburn Valley

15 Bendigo
16 Pyrenees
17 Macedon
18 Grampians
19 Yarra Valley
20 Geelong
21 Mornington Peninsula

**TASMANIA**

**WESTERN AUSTRALIA**
22 Swan Valley
23 Perth Hills
24 Margaret River
25 Great Southern Region
26 Pemberton

Australia ranks eighth in wine-producing countries worldwide. Australians drink an average of 5.25 gallons of wine per person each year; they're eighteenth in world wine consumption.

*Australia's wine industry is one of the most technologically advanced. Here, fermentation takes place in large fermenters that lie on their sides and can be rotated.*

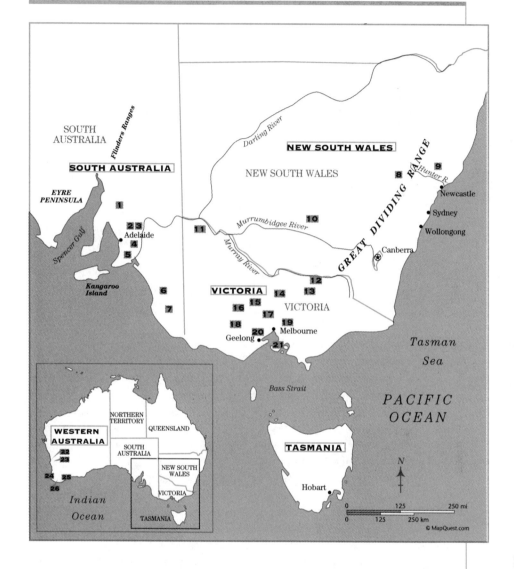

ies use state-of-the-art equipment and employ winemakers trained in the most advanced techniques. Virtually every vineyard task from pruning to harvesting is automated. Yet, for all this industrial sophistication, most Australian wines are rather like the Australians themselves: outgoing and unpretentious. Fittingly, most are also easy on the wallet. Even Australia's greatest wines are comparatively very good values.

For a large part of the twentieth century, the majority of the wine made in Australia was either cheap and sweet or had whopping levels of alcohol. But the industry changed radically in the 1960s as high-quality dry wines became the focus. By the mid-1980s Australian wines—especially the country's fruit-packed chardonnays, honeyed sémillons, and ripe, plummy shirazes—were known throughout the world, and some countries,

## THE QUICK SIP ON AUSTRALIA

• Australia is known for big, supple, mouthfilling white and red wines, many of which are terrific values.

• The most renowned and best-loved red grape is shiraz (the same as the French grape syrah), which is turned into irresistible wines saturated with deep berry flavors.

• The majority of Australia's vineyards are clustered in the southeastern part of the continent, relatively near the major cities of Sydney, Melbourne, and Adelaide.

other parts of the New World, including Colonial Virginia in the United States and Cape Town in South Africa. The men who planted them were Australia's first European settlers, mainly Englishmen who knew a lot about drinking wine but little about growing grapes. The vines they planted were cuttings of European (*vinifera*) varieties, generally brought from the South African Cape of Good Hope, where ships stopped for provisions en route to Australia.

*Australia has the highest per capita wine consumption of any English-speaking country. Australians in fact consume about two and a half times as much wine per capita as Americans do.*

Unfortunately, the area where the first tiny vineyards were planted—part of a penal colony—was so hot and humid the grapes rotted and the vines died. Today, ironically, Sydney's botanical gardens are just across the road from that same spot. The Australian settlers were undeterred. They moved slightly inland to what is now the Hunter Valley and, with practice, grew more adept at grape growing. Between the 1850s and 1870s, as new, more viticulturally savvy immigrants arrived, vineyards began to thrive.

Australia soon found itself capable of producing far more wine than its tiny population could consume. Exporting was the logical answer, and Great Britain, to which Australia belonged until 1901 (it remains part of the Commonwealth), was the most economically advantageous market even if it was half the world away.

In 1877 phylloxera was discovered in Australia, specifically in the state of Victoria. Although the pest did not spread to every other wine region, it effectively crip-

notably Great Britain, were absolutely smitten with them.

Hollywood's portrayal of Australia as an untamed outback populated mainly by sheep, crocodiles, and kangaroos doesn't quite square with most people's idea of a top-class wine region. Of course, serious vineyards are not planted in the desertlike center of the country nor in the steamy, tropically hot north. The greatest number are located in the cooler southern part of the continent within a few hours' drive of the coast.

There are some 1,115 wineries in Australia, and they make every style of wine: dry, sweet, still, sparkling, and fortified. About seventy varieties of grapes are grown, the five most important of which are chardonnay, riesling, sémillon, cabernet sauvignon, and the most eminent of all, shiraz.

The first Australian vineyards were planted in New South Wales at the end of the eighteenth century, more than 100 years after the first vineyards were planted in

pled some important vineyards—especially in Victoria—before the vines could be replanted on tolerant American rootstocks. Replanting resulted in the production of fine wines by some producers, but others rebounded by doing the opposite—making cheap, sweet fortified wines of passable quality. To make even more of them, large tracts of hot, fertile, irrigated valley land, potentially one of the worst possible habitats for grapes, were planted with vines.

With the 1960s a new era dawned. Changing tastes, changing economic forces, and the development of new wine technologies all propelled Australia toward a modern wine industry focused on dry table wines. In 1960 only a million cases of dry table wine were produced. By 1999 the amount had shot up to approximately 85 million cases. In the process, an Australian style of wine emerged: creamy whites and soft reds packed with fruit. The style stuck. Today's Australian wines are renowned for their concentrated flavor and easy approachability.

Although Australia has many wonderful tiny producers, such as Chain of Ponds, Clarendon Hills, and Jasper Hill, the industry is dominated by medium-size producers as well as by four very large, influential companies that together are responsible for well more than 50 percent of all Australian wine. They are Southcorp Wines, BRL Hardy, Orlando Wyndham, and Mildara Blass. Each of these firms owns multiple wine brands. Southcorp, for one, owns Penfolds, Lindemans, Rosemount, Wynns, and numerous others. And Mildara Blass' parent company, Foster's Brewing Group, owns California's prominent Beringer Wine Estates as well as several Australian wineries.

## AUSTRALIA'S WINE LAWS

Australia, like the United States, does not have a strict system of laws regulating grape growing and winemaking. There are no rules similar to the French *Appellation d'Origine Contrôlée* laws, which govern the varieties of grapes that can be planted in specific areas, the yield produced from those grapes, how the grapes are vinified, how long the wines are aged, and so on.

*All of Australia's major cities (and wine areas) are near the coast, hundreds of miles away from the country's vast, remote, arid inland outback.*

However, there are regulations that define viticultural regions and govern labeling (some of these laws are in the process of revision). The regulations are set forth by the Australian Wine and Brandy Corporation. They stipulate the following:

• If a grape variety is named on the label, 85 percent of the wine must be composed of the grape named.

• If two wines are used in a blend and neither represents 85 percent of the total, both grapes must be listed on the label in order of importance. Thus, a wine labeled Cabernet-Shiraz has more cabernet than shiraz; a wine labeled Shiraz-Cabernet, just the opposite.

• Blended wines must also state the percentage of each grape used in the blend.

• If an area, district, or region is named on the label, 85 precent of the wine must come from that place.

## THE AUSTRALIAN PHILOSOPHY OF WINEMAKING

Conventional European wisdom holds that good wine comes from specific sites that have distinctive *terroir*. In Australia, however, many winemakers believe there is another principle for producing good wines, namely, by selection and blending.

The grapes for many Australian wines do not come from a single place but instead may be grown over vast stretches of territory. Wines labeled South Eastern Australia may be made with grapes grown anywhere within the entire southeastern part of the continent. Such grapes will be made into separate lots of wine, then depending on the quality level, certain lots will be selected and blended together. (This philosophy is not at work quite as

### READING AN AUSTRALIAN WINE LABEL

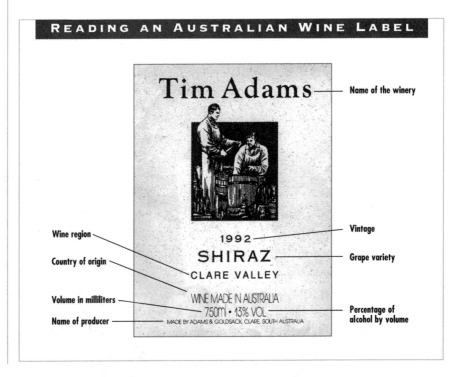

Name of the winery

Wine region

Country of origin

Volume in milliliters

Name of producer

Vintage

Grape variety

Percentage of alcohol by volume

Tim Adams

1992

SHIRAZ

CLARE VALLEY

WINE MADE IN AUSTRALIA
750ml • 13% VOL
MADE BY ADAMS & GOLDSACK, CLARE, SOUTH AUSTRALIA

much in the United States, where it would be unheard of to blend, say, a batch of chardonnay from southern California with a batch from Washington State and then label it Western U.S.A. Chardonnay.)

It had to happen somewhere, and in keeping with Australia's reputation for being avant-garde, it happened here first. As of the 2000 vintage virtually every riesling in Australia's Clare Valley is now stoppered with a screw cap, making them the first upscale wines in the world to shun tradition and forsake cork.

The goal of the selecting and blending process is to make brands of wine that have fairly consistent flavors year after year. Which doesn't mean the wine will lack excitement. A good example is Hardys Nottage Hill Cabernet Sauvignon-Shiraz, which is a very delicious wine and a steal to boot.

Even some of the most prestigious wines in the country are made by the same process of selecting and blending. Australia's most legendary and expensive wine, Penfolds' Grange, is a blend of shiraz grapes (sometimes with small amounts of cabernet sauvignon) grown in various vineyards as many as 300 miles apart. To make Grange, winemakers at Penfolds start out with the equivalent of 40,000 cases of wine. After selecting the best lots and blending them together, fewer than a total of 7,000 cases of Grange are made. The remainder of the lots go to make other Penfolds wines.

Grange and a few other expensive wines notwithstanding, multiregional blending is mostly practiced for the production of lower and moderately priced wines. The majority of Australia's top wines come from a single renowned wine district, such as Coonawarra, the Barossa Valley, or Margaret River.

**THE MOST IMPORTANT**

## AUSTRALIAN WINES

LEADING WINES

**Cabernet Sauvignon** red
**Cabernet-Shiraz Blends** red
**Cabernet-Merlot Blends** red
**Chardonnay** white
**Muscat** white (fortified; sweet)
**Port-Style Wines** red (fortified; sweet)
**Riesling** white (dry and sweet)
**Rhône-Style Blends** red
**Sémillon** white (dry and sweet)
**Shiraz** red
**Tokay** white (fortified; sweet)

WINES OF NOTE

**Chardonnay-Sémillon Blends** white
**Sparkling Wines** white and red

783

## Combination Wines, Bin Numbers, and Special Designations

A ustralian wines seem straightforward enough, but there are a few idiosyncracies that will be helpful for a wine drinker to know about, including combination wines, bin numbers, and designations such as Show Reserve.

**Combination wines** are made by blending two grape varieties, such as shiraz with cabernet or sémillon with chardonnay. Any combination of varieties is possible. Both names are put on the label to maximize the wine's appeal and also because the winemaker's goal is to reflect a little of the character and flavor

## AUSTRALIA'S WINE MATE: CALIFORNIA

Over the last few decades, the wine industries in Australia and California have had a number of things in common:

• Before 1960, most of the wine made in both places was sweet and fairly cheap.

• In the 1960s and 1970s, a wave of inventive, independent producers in Australia and California began making finer wines based mostly on chardonnay and cabernet sauvignon.

• Flexible wine laws encourage creativity in both places. (Neither Australia nor California has the equivalent of the strict French AOC or Italian DOC laws.)

• Both have been world leaders in viticultural and enological research.

• Sunny, Mediterranean-like climates bless winegrowing areas in both places, making the production of good wines possible virtually every year.

of each variety. As mentioned earlier, by law the variety named first must make up the largest part of the blend. The exact numerical percentage must be listed; often, it's on a back label.

There are also numerous wines made from a blend of more than two varieties. Sometimes the wine is named after all the varieties, as with Clancy's Shiraz-Cabernet Sauvignon-Cabernet Franc-Merlot (*whew*). Other times, the wine may be given a proprietary name like Henschke's Keyneton Estate, a blend of shiraz, cabernet sauvignon, and malbec. And sometimes the wine may be labeled both ways, as is the case with d'Arenberg's The Ironstone Pressings Grenache-Shiraz. These multivarietal blends are often packed with personality and can be among the best wines made in the country. In addition to the three wines above, two others deserve to be singled out: Yeringberg's Yeringberg Red, a blend of cabernet sauvignon, cabernet franc, merlot, and malbec, and Mitchelton Shiraz-Mourvèdre-Grenache.

**Bin numbers** are used by many Australian wine companies as the names

of various wines. Penfolds, for example, makes three wines based on cabernet sauvignon. The wine named Bin 407 is the company's moderately priced cabernet; Bin 707, made in smaller lots, is their most expensive cabernet. And Penfolds' superplummy cabernet-shiraz is named Bin 389. Probably the most recognized bin number is Lindeman's Bin 65 chardonnay. A remarkably inexpensive wine for its quality, Bin 65 is one of the biggest selling brands of

*Irreverence seems to be in an Australian's genes. Here a group of prominent Aussies, including winemaker/owners (from left) Ron Laughton, of Jasper Hill; Kym Tolley, of Penley Estate; and Chester Osborn, of d'Arenberg, have fun at a wine dinner.*

784

chardonnay in the world—more than 1½ million cases are made each year.

Bin numbers were being put on Australian wine labels as early as the 1930s, although it's not clear exactly when the practice began. Originally the numbers were either a winemaker's way of tracking the wines through blending and aging or else they signified the place or bin in the winery where a given wine was typically stored year after year. The shorthand stuck, and now countless Australian wines are known by their numbers.

**Special designations,** such as Show Reserve, frequently appear on wine labels, but such terms have no legal definition. Rather, they refer to the fact that the wine has won an award in one of Australia's many wine shows or competitions. More than wine drinkers elsewhere in the world, Australians take wine competitions seriously and have a good deal of faith in their results.

# THE LAND, THE GRAPES, AND THE VINEYARDS

Australia is the oldest of the continents. Its landmass is believed to have existed for more than one billion years. The ancient, weathered soil here is impoverished and, in many places, highly eroded. The continent is completely surrounded by water—by the Timor and Arafura Seas and the Gulf of Carpentaria to the north, the Coral Sea and the Tasman Sea to the east, and the Indian Ocean to the west and south. Antarctica is about 2,380 miles away.

Virtually all of the vineyard land (and most of the population) is clustered in the southeast corner of the country, specifically in the three states of New South Wales, Victoria, and South Australia. The

other thriving, though smaller, wine region is the state of Western Australia, near Perth in the southwestern corner of the continent. These southern regions have a sunny, fairly stable, Mediterranean-like climate. The harvest takes place during the Southern Hemisphere's summer, February through May, at which point the grapes have ripened fully, leading to the sort of soft, juicy-jammy wines for which Australia is known.

*The historic, barnlike Yeringberg winery was built around 1885 in the beautiful Yarra Valley.*

Still, there are challenges. Rot, frost, and strong, salt-laden winds all take their toll in various districts. Not to mention kangaroos, which jump (really) at the chance to feed on the soft leaves and buds of young vines. High fences topped with barbed wire surround some vineyards to keep the herbivorous marsupials out.

Given its fairly limited population, Australia lacks a ready supply of harvest workers. As a result, viticulture here is the most mechanized in the world. While some small, prestigious vineyards are cared for by hand, in most Australian vineyards

# THE GRAPES OF AUSTRALIA

## WHITES

**Chardonnay:** The leading white grape, made into wines that span all levels of quality from simple, fruity quaffers to lush, complex powerhouses.

**Muscadelle:** Makes Victoria's rare but renowned sweet fortified wine known as tokay. Australian tokay is not the same as the famous Hungarian sweet wine Tokay made in the Hungarian wine region Tokaj-Hegyalja principally from the furmint and hárslevelű grape varieties.

**Muscat Blanc à Petits Grains:** One of the leading grapes in the large muscat family of grapes. Makes the rare but well-loved sweet, fortified muscat wines of Australia.

**Muscat Gordo Blanco:** Declining in importance but still widely used in inexpensive bag-in-the-box wines; the same as muscat of Alexandria. Sometimes blended with Palomino and Pedro Ximénez to make inexpensive Sherry-type wines.

**Palomino** and **Pedro Ximénez:** Minor grapes used mostly for inexpensive Sherry-type wines of rather low quality.

**Riesling:** Major grape. Makes dry, floral wines that can be quite racy and capable of aging, as well as delicious late harvest and botrytized sweet wines.

**Sauvignon Blanc:** Minor grape. Generally blended with sémillon.

**Sémillon:** Major grape. Makes everything from ordinary blending wines to extraordinary dry whites, the best of which, when aged, become honeyed with rich lanolin textures. Also made into sweet wines.

**Verdelho:** Minor grape. Grown mostly in Western Australia. Makes good, tasty wines with soft, fruity flavors.

## REDS

**Cabernet Sauvignon:** Major grape. Can make delicious, powerfully structured, but supple wines. Sometimes considered more sophisticated than shiraz, with which it is often blended. Cabernet sauvignon is also commonly blended with merlot.

**Grenache:** Important grape. On its own, can make rich, concentrated, superfruity red wines, especially when they're made from grapes grown in older vineyards. Also commonly blended with shiraz and mourvèdre to make Rhône-style blends. In addition, used as part of the blend in many of Australia's top Port-style wines.

*John Duval, chief winemaker at Penfolds*

**Merlot:** Grown mostly for use in cabernet sauvignon-merlot blends.

**Mourvèdre:** Increasingly important grape, especially for Rhône-style blends in which it's combined with shiraz and grenache. Also used along with grenache as part of the blend in Australia's Port-style wines.

**Pinot Noir:** On the rise. Used mostly for sparkling wines, although some good still wines are made in cool areas.

**Shiraz:** The leading red grape, the same as the French syrah. Can make seductive, jammy, mouthfilling wines with loads of personality and packed with fruit flavors. Sometimes blended with cabernet sauvignon or grenache. Also used in Australia's top Port-type wines.

machines perform almost every critical task, including picking the grapes, pruning the vines, spraying for disease, trimming leaves during the growing season, and so on.

Pioneers and iconoclasts that they are, the Australians have also been the first to challenge many of the generally held truths about the best way to grow grapes. In a few of their most futuristic vineyards, vines are spaced more closely than previously thought possible, and sophisticated trellis systems are used to open the vines to maximum sunlight and air. Most remarkably—and contrary to the wisdom of grape growers for the last 2,000 years—some vines are not pruned but allowed to grow at will and regulate themselves. Whether or not these methods make for better wine is a complex question, but it seems significant that creative vintners elsewhere in the world (especially California) are adopting certain Australian techniques.

White wine makes up a little more than 60 percent of Australian wine; about 30 percent is red. The leading high-quality white grape is chardonnay, followed by riesling and sémillon; the leading reds are shiraz and cabernet sauvignon. Inexpensive Australian bag-in-the-box wines—which comprise about 58 percent of all wine sold locally—are made from a number of varieties, including chardonnay and muscat gordo blanco, the Australian name for muscat of Alexandria, as well as such less prestigious grapes as French colombard and trebbiano. While mostly humble in quality, these wines, conveniently packaged in boxes outfitted with spigots, make wine drinking an easy, accessible, everyday enjoyment for many Australians.

---

*Three of the Most Extraordinary Australian Chardonnays*

**LEEUWIN ESTATE ART SERIES**

**PENFOLDS YATTARNA**

**ROSEMOUNT ESTATE ROXBURGH**

---

Chardonnay is so popular in Australia (a 500 percent increase in production occurred between 1986 and 1996 alone), you'd think the Aussies invented it. Virtually every firm now makes the wine, yet as late as 1967 there were only a minuscule number of chardonnay vines in the entire country. (Tyrrell's in the Hunter Valley made the first chardonnay in 1971, calling it Vat 47 Pinot Chardonnay.)

When Australian chardonnays first burst on the international scene in the early 1980s, there were few white wines like them anywhere. They were so creamy and dense, it seemed like a spoon would stand up in them. Their rich flavors poured out of the glass. Chardonnay lovers went mad.

Today Australia's greatest chardonnays not only possess opulent fruit flavors, but they are refined, elegant, and beautifully complex as well. Among the very best of these are Leeuwin Estate's Art Series, Penfolds' Yattarna, and Rosemount Estate's Roxburgh, all phenomenal wines absolutely suffused with flavor.

After chardonnay, the next most widely planted premium white grape is riesling. In fact, Australia and its neighbor New Zealand are the only wine regions in the New World to take this noble grape seriously. The best Australian rieslings are dry wines with power and grace. Although

787

a small ocean of them is drunk locally, these snappy wines have only recently been imported into the United States in any number. Sweet late harvest rieslings are also made, usually with the help of the noble rot *Botrytis cinerea*.

The most novel white grape in Australia, however, is sémillon (which the Australians pronounce SEM-eh-lawn and spell semillon—without the accent used in France; for consistency's sake, I've kept the accent here). Australia is sémillon's second most famous home after Bordeaux (the dry whites of Bordeaux as well as sweet Sauternes and Barsac are traditionally made by blending sémillon with sauvignon blanc). Sémillon has a split personality. When grown in good but not great vineyard sites, it turns into simple wines usually used in low or moderately priced blends. But when grown in top vineyards in South Australia, the Hunter Valley, and Western Australia, sémillon can be made into remarkable naturally creamy dry whites (often produced without a smidgen of oak) laced with hints of citrus. But for the sémillon grown in these top vineyards, the catch is this: They have to be aged. For reasons that remain mysterious, great sémillon changes rather radically (and wonderfully) with age. After five years or more, the best take on honey and roasted nut flavors plus a wonderful lanolinlike texture. Sémillon alone can be magnificent (try the Henschke sémillon or the Tim Adams sémillon!), but it is usually blended into good combination wines, such as chardonnay-sémillon and sémillon-sauvignon blanc. Aided by *Botrytis cinerea*, it's also made, like riesling, into wonderful sweet wines.

Cabernet sauvignon is the elite red grape in Australia, although shiraz may be closer to many Australians' hearts. The simplest cabernets are blackberry-fruit-

packed bargains. And the very top cabernets are, in a word, mindblowers. Wines such as Henschke Cyril Henschke, Hardys Thomas Hardy Coonawarra, and Parker Coonawarra Estate Terra Rossa First Growth bring together the gripping structure of a good Bordeaux with all the rich, copious, palate-coating fruit of grapes grown under generous sun. Many of these top cabs come from Coonawarra, a small region in South Australia famous for its red, limestone-laced soil and the cabernets grown in it.

*Some of the Top Australian Cabernet Sauvignons*

**HARDYS THOMAS HARDY COONAWARRA**

**HENSCHKE CYRIL HENSCHKE**

**LEEUWIN ESTATE ART SERIES**

**NOON LANGHORNE CREEK**

**PARKER COONAWARRA ESTATE TERRA ROSSA FIRST GROWTH**

**PENFOLDS BIN 707**

**WYNNS JOHN RIDDOCH**

**YARRA YERING DRY RED #1**

And finally there's shiraz, which is to Australia what cabernet sauvignon is to Bordeaux—an icon. Australians are chauvinistically crazy about it, and not surprisingly, it's the leading variety in terms of production. The Australian wine expert James Halliday calls it Australia's Rock of Gibraltar. The derivation of the name shiraz is a mystery. There is a well-worn fable about the grape originating in the Persian city of Shiraz. But among other things, this doesn't explain why the grape is called shiraz only in Australia and South Africa. After all, those two countries got it from France, where it's called syrah.

The rich, sappy, berry taste, seductive aromas, and thick, soft texture of shiraz helped establish Australia as one of the world's top wine-producing countries. The best of these wines have almost syrupy plum, boysenberry, mocha, and violet flavors, with hints of spice and black pepper. By comparison, they are much more saturated with fruit than their parents, the syrahs of the Rhône.

*Winemaker Max Schubert, the creator of Grange, the wine that inspired a revolution in Australian winemaking. The wine is named after the stone cottage (behind Schubert), known as the grange, where it was first made.*

The most legendary—and expensive—Australian shiraz is Grange (formerly called Grange Hermitage), made by the powerful wine firm Penfolds. Like Château Mouton-Rothschild in France, Grange is a national symbol. The wine was first made in 1952 by Penfolds' then winemaker Max Schubert, who after a trip to Bordeaux during which he tasted the wines of several great châteaux, wanted to make a wine of similar intensity, structure, depth, and ageability. Though it is now the most renowned wine in Australia, Grange was belittled by the critics the first few years it was made. One described it as

"a concoction of wild fruits and sundry berries with crushed ants predominating."

Apparently no critic today feels the same way. Grange is widely praised for its power, concentration, and beautiful flavors and aromas of leather and tobacco mingled with boysenberries and mint. To make Grange, Penfolds winemakers taste blind hundreds of different shirazes from vineyards Penfolds owns or has contracts with all over Australia. In the end, fewer than 7,000 cases of Grange are made each year. And while the wine may be 100 percent shiraz in some years, it isn't always so. Depending on the character of the shirazes in any given year, small amounts of cabernet sauvignon may be added to the final blend.

*Some of the Best
Producers of Australian Shiraz
and Shiraz Blends*

CAPE MENTELLE

CLARENDON HILLS

CRAIGLEE

D'ARENBERG

FOX CREEK

HARDYS

HENSCHKE

JASPER HILL

JIM BARRY

LEASINGHAM

MITCHELTON

NORMANS

PENFOLDS

PETER LEHMANN

RICHARD HAMILTON

ROSEMOUNT ESTATE

TYRRELL'S

VASSE FELIX

WYNNS

## WHAT TO THROW ON THE BARBIE

In contemplating all the wonderful foods you could pair with shiraz, I decided to see what the Australians themselves might consider the perfect match. From a book written by one of Australia's top winemakers comes this suggestion: "char-grilled kangaroo fillet with wild mint polenta and quandong chilli sauce." Most of us will just have to trust them on that. As for more familiar possibilities, a thick grilled peppered steak is outrageously good with a top shiraz. The wine's imposing structure and rich, saturated, berried fruit makes for a powerful juxtaposition to the richness and char of grilled steak. And by seasoning the steak with cracked black pepper, you can bring out the spicy pepperyness in many shirazes. But grilled steak is just the beginning. Shiraz is a top bet with almost any substantial meat—lamb, duck, venison—grilled until it's nicely charred on the outside and still juicy in the middle.

## SPARKLING WINES AND STICKIES

Of all Australian wine sold in bottles (that is, not including bag-in-the-boxes), about 20 percent is sparkling. The top Aussie sparklers are made by the Champagne method from pinot noir and chardonnay and are brut in style. In character they can be either fresh, clean, and unfussy or richer and biscuity along the lines of Champagne. It's easy to imagine oceans of such bubblies being downed at Australian barbecues. Among the best producers making a whole range of sparklers from *blanc de blancs* to rosé is the French Champagne house of Moët & Chandon, whose subsidiary, Domaine Chandon Australia, also makes sparklers under the label Green Point.

Then there are the spunky, wonderfully fruity, vividly colored *red* sparkling wines. Australia, like northern Italy, has a tradition of making red sparklers, although most of them, unfortunately, never get exported. The best are made from shiraz. Seppelt is considered the leading producer.

As for sweet wines, Australia has a long history of making wickedly delicious stickies, as the Australians call them. There are several types. The most sensational, mouthwatering, and rare of the stickies are Australia's dark, sweet fortified muscats and tokays made in the hot northeast corner of Victoria. The muscats are made from a brownish-colored version of the grape muscat blanc à petits grains; the tokays, from the muscadelle grape. The best are usually made in relatively small quantities and are rarely exported. To make the wines, the grapes are left on the vine long after the normal harvest until they begin to shrivel and their sugar intensifies. During fermentation, the soupy mass of crushed grapes is fortified with neutral grape spirits, which stop the fermentation, leaving a wine with natural residual sugar and high alcohol. The wine is then aged for ten to twenty years in small oak barrels (not brand new) until it takes on luscious and incomparable but hard to describe flavors reminiscent of toffee, brown sugar, vanilla, chocolate, and honey. Among the best sweet fortified muscats and tokays are those produced by Chambers Rosewood Vineyards, Baileys of Glenrowan, and Morris.

Don't confuse (even though it's completely logical to do so) sweet, fortified Australian tokay with the great Hungarian wine Tokay—Tokaji in Hungarian. Hungarian Tokay is made from hárslevelű and furmint grapes and is not fortified. Also, Hungarian Tokay depends on the noble rot botrytis, which is not a factor in the making of Australian tokay. Nor is Australian tokay related to the Alsace wine sometimes called tokay, which is really made from pinot gris.

In addition to tokays and muscats, Australia also boasts numerous nonfortified sweet wines made from late-harvested grapes, usually riesling or sémillon, that have been affected by *Botrytis cinerea* (just the way Sauternes is).

Next are Australian Port-style wines (by agreement with the European Community, Australia will eventually stop using such traditional geographically defined European designations such as Port and Sherry, although new Australian names for these types of wines have not yet been invented). Aus-

*Yalumba's Heggies Vineyard in the high country of South Australia.*

tralian Port-style wines are made in a way roughly approximate to that used for Portuguese tawny Ports, although they are a touch sweeter, and shiraz, mourvèdre, and grenache are used instead of native Portuguese grapes. The finest Australian Port-style wines are aged ten to twenty-five years in wood and are surging with dramatic, rich, nutty, caramelly flavors. Among the best are Penfolds Grandfather tawny Port, Yalumba Clocktower tawny Port, Chateau Reynella Old Cave tawny Port, and d'Arenberg Nostalgia twelve-year-old tawny Port.

As for Australian Sherry-style wines, they can be either fairly cheap and ordinary or remarkably good. Though they are made using two native Spanish grapes, Palomino and Pedro Ximénez, sometimes with muscat gordo blanco blended in, only the best come close to having the finesse, complexity, and flavor of true Spanish Sherry, and those that do are made in tiny quantities.

791

# THE WINE REGIONS

Here are thumbnail sketches of Australia's major wine regions. Like California's fine wine regions, those of Australia are relatively young, at least compared to Europe where many fine wine regions have been well established for several centuries. In Australia, however, winemakers have only just begun to understand the viticultural nuances of each location. Remember that for multiregional blends labeled South Eastern Australia, the grapes will probably have come from disparate regions possibly quite far apart. For such wines the most important guide to quality is the producer's name.

## SOUTH AUSTRALIA

The wine districts of South Australia form a ring around the city of Adelaide and include Adelaide Hills, Barossa Valley, Eden Valley, Clare Valley, Coonawarra, Padthaway, and McLaren Vale. These top districts were founded by men whose names have become synonymous with Australian wine: Hamilton, Seppelt, Penfold, and so on. Today, more than half of all Australian wine is produced in this state, including many of the country's best cabernet sauvignons, shirazes, chardonnays, rieslings, and sémillons.

Two of these districts—the Barossa Valley and Coonawarra—are among the most renowned grape-growing areas on the whole continent. The Barossa is known for full-blooded shiraz and lively riesling, while Coonawarra is revered as the best place in the country for structured, rich cabernet sauvignons. Coonawarra's most prestigious vineyards are crowded onto a single, narrow, 9-mile-long strip of porous reddish soil overlaying limestone called terra rossa.

*David Wynn's historic winery was built in 1891 in Coonawarra, originally (and mistakenly) assumed to be a second-rate wine region at best but now considered one of the top areas in Australia for red wine.*

A Who's Who of large Australian wine companies is located in South Australia, including Hardys, Orlando, Penfolds, Peter Lehmann, Seppelt, Wolf Blass, Wynns, and Yalumba. But the region is also a hotbed of small and medium-size avant-garde producers such as Henschke, Mountadam, Petaluma, and Tim Adams.

A considerable amount of simple, inexpensive bag-in-the-box wine is also made in South Australia from huge tracts of irrigated vineyards along Australia's Murray River. These vineyards, often called the Riverland, extend from South Australia into Victoria and New South Wales.

## NEW SOUTH WALES

New South Wales, including the Hunter Valley, Mudgee, and Riverina, is Australia's second-leading state in wine production after South Australia. The most famous wine district in the state is the relatively small Hunter Valley, 75 miles north of Australia's oldest and largest city, Sydney. The Hunter Valley was the first wine area in Australia, vineyards having been planted here at the beginning of the nineteenth century by the country's earliest European settlers. Around 1960 Penfolds moved to an area slightly north of the original vineyards, initiating the distinction between what are now known as the Upper Hunter and the Lower Hunter.

The whole Hunter Valley region is something of an anomaly. It has less than ideal clay soil and, being one of the most northerly of Australia's wine districts, is hot and almost too humid for grapes. Nonetheless, and almost against all odds, several top chardonnays come from here,

*In 1971 Tyrrell's winery in the Hunter Valley of New South Wales produced Australia's first chardonnay, called Vat 47 Pinot Chardonnay.*

among them one of the most voluptuous chardonnays of all, Rosemount Estate's Roxburgh.

But if the Hunter Valley has an ace in the hole it's sémillon, a wine that starts out rather plain-Janelike and turns into a princess. When young, sémillon can seem nice enough, yet unexciting. But with age—five to ten years or more—something startling happens: the wine turns into a honey pot of rich, nutty, buttery fruit. Great examples are found from Tyrrell's, McWilliam's Mount Pleasant, Lindemans, and Brokenwood.

Across the Great Dividing Range and 60 miles to the west of the Hunter Valley is Mudgee, the other leading wine district in the state. Mudgee is warmer still but higher in altitude and less rainy than the Hunter Valley. Some of the best structured cabernet sauvignons in New South Wales are made here, including those from Huntington Estate.

In the south central part of New South Wales is Riverina, a vast, flat expanse of vineyards created just after the turn of the century when large-scale irrigation systems became possible. Medium-quality dry wines and fortified wines are made here, along with cheap, generic bag-in-the-box wines.

## VICTORIA

Just as northern California's wine industry was jump-started by the gold rush of 1849, the discovery of gold in Victoria in 1851 paved the way for a fledgling wine industry in the state. As Victoria's economy and population boomed, the ambitions of vintners soared every bit as high as those of gold diggers. Eventually, as the supply of gold dwindled, vintners were known to hire out-of-work miners to dig underground wine cellars.

But when the gold ran out completely, Victoria's fortunes began to spiral downward. The picture grew especially gloomy for wineries as phylloxera, economic decline, competitive wines from South Australia, and changing land use all took a toll. By the 1960s Victoria's wine industry was a shadow of its former self. When the Australian wine industry as a whole began to take off in the 1970s and 1980s, however, a new period of growth ensued for

Victoria and today the wine region is Australia's third most important.

Of all mainland Australia's wine regions, Victoria is the smallest and most southern (only the island of Tasmania, off the Victorian coast, is smaller and farther south). The region includes Bendigo, Geelong, Glenrowan, Goulburn Valley, Grampians, Macedon, Mornington Penninsula, Murray Darling, Pyrenees, Rutherglen, and the Yarra Valley. More than 200 producers are located in Victoria, spread mostly over those wine districts that fan out directly from the city of Melbourne.

Victoria's wine districts vary considerably in climate, terrain, and soil. Several of the most renowned—the Yarra Valley, Geelong, and Mornington Penninsula, for example—are close to the sea and sufficiently cool for chardonnay and pinot noir to thrive. Farther inland, in warmer pockets, Victoria is known for cabernet sauvignon and shiraz, with some producers—

such as Mitchelton—making ravishing reds.

One of Victoria's specialties is the captivating sweet muscats and tokays made in northeastern Victoria, primarily in the districts of Rutherglen and Glenrowan. These unctuous wines—throwbacks to times past when Australia made oceans of powerful sweet stuff—are rare today but remain wonderfully and deliciously unique.

Finally, Victoria has always been associated with Australian sparkling wine because Seppelt, one of Australia's largest and most important sparkling producers, is located in the district of Grampians (known in the recent past as Great Western). Although the grapes for Seppelt's sparklers now come from many regions outside Victoria, the link remains.

# WESTERN AUSTRALIA

Far on the other side of the Australian continent, 3,000 miles away from the power centers of winemaking in the southeast, is the remote state of Western Australia. The first known sighting of the western coastline was in 1622 by the Dutch vessel Leeuwin, meaning lioness. The name would later be adopted by one of the state's most prominent wineries.

Western Australia's several wine districts, which include Margaret River, Great Southern Region, Pemberton, Perth Hills, and Swan Valley, stretch out from the coastal city of Perth. Vines were planted in this area in 1829, some years before the first plantings in either South Australia or Victoria. But the state's isolation and limited population hampered the industry's growth and scope until the 1970s.

The Swan Valley, north of Perth, was Western Australia's first wine district. It became known for table grapes as well as

## ABEL'S ISLAND

Tasmania, the smallest state of the Commonwealth of Australia, is a triangular-shaped island about 150 miles south of Victoria. The island, with its mild, sunny, maritime climate, is considered to have very good potential as a wine region, even though most of its 56 wineries are minuscule. The three leading producers are Pipers Brook, Moorilla Estate, and Heemskerk.

Tasmania is named for the Dutch explorer Abel Tasman, who discovered it in 1642. The island's vast array of plant and animal life includes the Tasmanian devil, a not very devilish, doglike creature, which like the kangaroo, is a marsupial.

## THE ABORIGINES

━━━━━✑⌢✑━━━━━

Many of Australia's wine districts have Aboriginal names, such as Coonawarra—honeysuckle—and Mudgee—nest in the hills. The Aborigines, Australia's native inhabitants, are a distinct race that has no close affinity with any other people. They have lived in Australia for more than 30,000 years and are the oldest race on the earth today.

wine grapes, and the leading wines were mostly sweet and/or fortified and sold in bulk. It was here that Houghton White Burgundy, once Australia's most recognized white wine, was born in the years just before World War II. Though it is slightly more polished now, Houghton's White Burgundy was originally a rustic, powerfully alcoholic wine made from chenin blanc, muscadelle, and chardonnay.

Of all the wine districts in Western Australia, the most renowned and ambitious is Margaret River, a windswept district jutting out like an elbow into the Indian Ocean. Originally known for its timber, Margaret River came to world attention in the 1980s for the elegance, richness, and clarity of its cabernet sauvignons—especially those from three of the leading wineries, Cape Mentelle, Leeuwin Estate, and Cullens.

The combination of the district's maritime location and gravelly soil reminded several vintners of Bordeaux and inspired them to plant not only red Bordeaux grapes, such as cabernet sauvignon and merlot, but also the Bordeaux whites, sémillon and sauvignon blanc. Both white grapes, which are often blended, turned out to make wines chock-full of personality.

On the other hand, when chardonnay was first planted in Margaret River, it seemed to be something of a gamble. As it turned out, chardonnay has an almost magical affinity for the region. Leeuwin Estate, in particular, makes chardonnays of breathtaking elegance that, with several years aging, grow even richer and more expansive. They are among the best produced in all of Australia.

One of the most curious grapes grown in Western Australia is verdelho. It was originally brought to the Swan Valley in 1829 by one of Western Australia's first colonists, a botanist named Thomas Waters, who took cuttings from the island of Madeira off the African coast (a stopping point to pick up provisions on the long voyage out). Two of the best verdelhos to try are Moondah Brook and Willespie.

Today much of the excitement in Western Australia centers around the cool subdistricts within Great Southern Region and the southwest coast. Wineries to watch from these areas include Howard Park, Plantagenet, Goundrey, and Capel Vale, known in the United States as Sheldrake.

795

# THE AUSTRALIAN WINES TO KNOW

*For each of the wines that follow, the specific growing region from which it comes is noted.*

## Sparkling Wine

### SALINGER

vintage

Southeastern Australia

approximately 50% chardonnay,
50% pinot noir and pinot meunier

No firm has done more to make exciting Australian sparkling wines than Seppelt, the winery force behind Salinger. It is one of the most delicious, elegant sparklers produced on the continent. Its high-toned biscuity flavors are almost swordlike in their precision. First created in 1983, the wine is a blend of top selected lots from cool vineyards and is made by the Champagne method in a brut style.

## Whites

### HOWARD PARK

Riesling

Western Australia

100% riesling

Riesling's potential for purity and precision is completely realized in this stunning wine from Howard Park. At its best, the penetrating acidity is wrapped up in flamboyant tropical fruit, apricot, and mineral flavors, resulting in a wine that has more power than most German rieslings and more complexity than virtually every California riesling. It's utterly dry and explosive on the palate with a long persistent finish. Any wine with this kind of dramatic flavor and acidity is just begging for food.

### LEEUWIN ESTATE

Chardonnay

Art Series

Margaret River

100% chardonnay

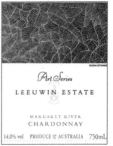

Seemingly at the end of the world in far Western Australia, Leeuwin Estate makes chardonnays so extraordinary and ageworthy they can come perilously close to rivaling the finest white Burgundies of France. Unlike most New World chardonnays, which have conspicuous—even clumsy—flavors, the Leeuwin chardonnays can be absolutely unbelievable in their clarity and pristine elegance. In top vintages, they are suffused with complex and mysterious nuances. Sip after sip, they draw you into them, revealing something new each time. Leeuwin's Art Series wines (so called to distinguish them from the regular Leeuwin wines) are blends of the top lots. Each year labels for the Art Series are commissioned from leading Australian artists.

## PENFOLDS

Chardonnay

Yattarna

Adelaide Hills

100% chardonnay

Australia produces dozens if not hundreds of well-made, creamy, delightful chardonnays, but Yattarna is much more than creamy and delightful. In a class by itself, Yattarna (which in the Aboriginal language means little by little) is simply stunning. At its finest, the wine exudes elegance and is impeccably well integrated. The irresistible flavors and aromas are reminiscent of honey, peaches, gardenias, and crème brûlée. As with Leeuwin's Art Series chardonnay, comparisons between Yattarna and the best French white Burgundies are inevitable.

## TIM ADAMS

Semillon

Clare Valley

100% sémillon

Sémillon (or as the Australians write it, semillon) is one of Australia's treasures. In the hands of a top winemaker and in a good year, it evolves into white wines of great beauty and strength—wines that are rich and silky yet rarely overdone. The Tim Adams is a favorite. Its butteriness and vibrancy are like oppositely charged molecules in total attraction. For Tim Adams, the owner/winemaker, sémillon is so much more compelling than chardonnay that he doesn't event make the latter.

# *Reds*

*Australian shiraz is the same grape as the French syrah.*

## D'ARENBERG

Grenache

The Custodian

McLaren Vale

100% grenache

Packed with sweet jammy boysenberry and cherry flavors, The Custodian is quite possibly one of the best grenaches in the world. In great vintages the concentration and explosiveness of flavor in the wine are not to be believed. The name The Custodian refers to the fact that the grapes come from extremely old, very low-yielding vineyards that the Osborne family, owners of d'Arenberg, have preserved rather than replant.

## HARDYS

Cabernet Sauvignon

Thomas Hardy

Coonawarra

100% cabernet sauvignon

Hardys' top-of-the-line cabernet sauvignon (named after the founder of the company, Thomas Hardy) is an utterly beautiful, voluptuous wine with dazzling streaks of menthol running through its earthy flavors.

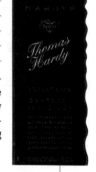

### HENSCHKE

Shiraz

Hill of Grace

Eden Valley

100% shiraz

Year in and year out, Hill of Grace, as it is known, is one of Australia's most voluptuous and impressive shirazes. Made from vines that, amazingly, are over 130 years old, it is a rich, aromatic wine with aromas and flavors suggestive of black raspberry, bitter chocolate, boysenberry pie, cedar, leather, and cigar boxes. The density and power behind this wine is incredible. And though it can be drunk upon release, a wine this massive will certainly benefit from several years of aging.

### MITCHELTON

Shiraz

Goulburn Valley

100% shiraz

Pure hedonism in a bottle. In top years Mitchelton's shiraz has loads of velvety, minty black cherry fruit plus soft, chewy prune and fig flavors and saturated, seamless texture. The winery also makes a wonderful spicy blend of shiraz, mourvèdre, and grenache. Mitchelton's vineyards are in the temperate Goulburn Valley just north of Melbourne.

### NORMANS

Shiraz

Chais Clarendon

South Australia

100% shiraz

The intensity of this wine can be almost surreal. In most years you could drown in all the soft, saturated blackberry, black cherry, and black raspberry fruit that engulfs you. Tinges of sweet marzipan and rich vanilla add delicious nuances. The winery, in the Adelaide Hills of South Australia, was founded by Englishman Jesse Norman in 1851 and has been one of Australia's best-kept secrets.

### PENFOLDS

Grange

South Australia

mostly shiraz, occasionally with a tiny bit of cabernet sauvignon

Grange is Australia's most famous shiraz and the country's most famous wine, comparable in stature to a First Growth Bordeaux. Depending on the vintage, it can be either classically structured with lush ripe boysenberry and plum fruit or an absolute powerhouse of a shiraz with mighty cedar, leather, licorice, chocolate, berry, and game aromas and flavors. The texture is always seductive. Grange is made by Australia's largest wine company—Penfolds.

### PETER LEHMANN

Cabernet Sauvignon

Barossa Valley

100% cabernet sauvignon

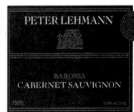

A wine to fall in love with (or over). All of Peter Lehmann's wines are outrageously delicious in good vintages, but his cabernet sauvignons can be miraculous. With gymnastic precision, they exude perfect elegance, strength, and balance—all in the same millisecond. The lingering complex flavors are a swirl of blackberry fruit, menthol, and exotic spices. Although competitions aren't always reliable, it's pretty remarkable that the Peter Lehmann 1993 cabernet sauvignon was named best cabernet worldwide in the prestigious U.K. International Wine & Spirits Competition.

## ROSEMOUNT ESTATE
Syrah
Balmoral
McLaren Vale
100% shiraz

Although Rosemount is widely known for its inexpensive wines (the chardonnay, shiraz, and cabernet sauvignon are all unbeatable at the price), the winery also produces several wines that are among the best in Australia. Their Balmoral syrah is one of them. Superfleshy and almost syrupy in texture, Balmoral has intense, rich berry, chocolate, spice, and menthol aromas and flavors. For such a massively structured wine Balmoral is nonetheless beautifully balanced and integrated. Rosemount decided to call Balmoral syrah rather than shiraz as a way of suggesting that it is more Old World in style and as a tribute to the great rich syrahs of France's Rhône Valley.

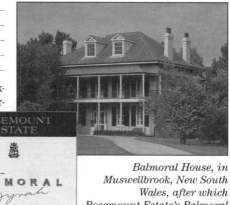

*Balmoral House, in Muswellbrook, New South Wales, after which Rosemount Estate's Balmoral wines are named.*

# Sweet Wine

## PENFOLDS
Grandfather Port
Barossa Valley
mostly shiraz with some mourvèdre

A luscious, enticing, deeply satisfying Australian Port-style wine, Grandfather Port is infused with complex, rich, buttery roasted nut, caramel, maple syrup, and orange peel flavors. Deeply amber in color, the wine is reminiscent of a twenty-year-old Portuguese tawny Port, although it's made more in the manner of a Spanish Sherry. To make the wine, a soleralike system of barrels is stacked in a pyramid with the oldest barrels of wine, originally filled with a 1915 Australian "port," on the bottom. Every few years a small amount of wine is taken out of the bottom barrels. This is the Grandfather Port. The bottom barrels are then topped up with wine from the barrels above them. The process continues until the uppermost barrel is topped up with wine from the current vintage. In this slow and painstaking manner an after-dinner wine of beautiful lushness is made.

*The Barossa Valley in South Australia is lauded for its lip-smacking shirazes. Some of the grapes from these shiraz vines go into Penfolds' sensational Grandfather Port.*

# VISITING AUSTRALIAN WINE ESTATES

M any of Australia's wineries are well set up for visitors who come to tour, taste, and buy. The larger wineries often have multiple facilities and attractions, including restaurants, galleries, concerts, and so forth—all in addition to the winery itself. The small wineries are, of course, far more humble, but chances are you'll have the opportunity to taste with the owners themselves, which is always exciting and eminently educational. Many wineries are within easy driving distance of Australia's major cities, Sydney, Melbourne, Adelaide, and Perth. You'll find a couple of wineries here that weren't highlighted earlier; they're interesting to visit and their wines are certainly worth trying. The telephone numbers include the dialing code you'll need when calling from the United States. If you're calling from within Australia, eliminate the 011-61 and add a zero before the next number.

## NEW SOUTH WALES

**ROSEMOUNT ESTATE**
18 Herbert Street
Artamon, NSW 2064
011-61-2-9902-2100

**ROTHBURY ESTATE**
Broke Road
Pokolbin, NSW 2321
011-61-2-4-998-7555

## SOUTH AUSTRALIA

**D'ARENBERG WINES**
Osborn Road
McLaren Vale, SA 5171
011-61-8-8323-8315
Restaurant on-site.

**HARDYS**
Reynell Road
Reynella, SA 5161
011-61-8-8392-2222

**PENFOLDS WINES**
Tanunda Road
Nuriootpa, SA 5355
011-61-8-8563-2500

**PETER LEHMANN WINES**
Samuel Road off Para Road
Tanunda, SA 5352
011-61-8-8563-2500

## VICTORIA

**MITCHELTON**
Mitchellstown
Nagambie, VIC 3608
011-61-3-5794-2710
Art gallery, wine museum, and restaurant on-site.

**SEPPELT GREAT WESTERN WINERY**
Moyston Road
Great Western, VIC 3377
011-61-3-5361-2239

**YARRA RIDGE VINEYARD**
Glenview Road
Yarra Glen, VIC 3775
011-61-3-9730-1022

## WESTERN AUSTRALIA

**EVANS & TATE**
Lionel's Vineyard
Payne Road
Jindong, WA 6280
011-61-8-9755-8855

**LEEUWIN ESTATE**
Stevens Road
Margaret River, WA 6285
011-61-8-9757-6253
Has a restaurant featuring specialties of southwestern Australia on-site, as well as picnic grounds and an outdoor amphitheater for concerts.

New Zealand

Located roughly midway between the equator and the South Pole, New Zealand lies isolated in the middle of the South Pacific. The nearest landmass, Australia, is 1,000 miles to the northwest. The country is composed of two long main islands, called simply the North Island and the South Island, plus numerous small offshore islands. New Zealand's vineyards are the southernmost in the world. They are also the first vineyards on earth to see the sun each day thanks to New Zealand's location close by the international date line.

Until recently, few wine drinkers, other than New Zealanders themselves, had ever tried a New Zealand wine. That changed abruptly in the mid-1980s, when a single wine, sauvignon blanc, put New Zealand on the international wine map—and deservedly so. New Zealand's top sauvignons are among the most exotic, vibrant, intensely flavored sauvignon blancs in the world. Quite simply, they taste like no other sauvignons made.

The remote islands of New Zealand were unknown to the western world until Abel Tasman, the Dutch sea captain after

802

New Zealand ranks thirty-third in wine-producing countries world-wide. New Zealanders drink an average of 2.96 gallons of wine per person each year; they're twenty-eighth in world wine consumption.

*The spectacular maze of mountaintops and waterways known as the Marlborough Sounds lies at the northern end of the South Island. Inland and south from the sounds are vast plains covered in vineyards, many of them growing sauvignon blanc.*

Three Kings Islands

North Cape

•Kaitaia

Great Barrier Island

**AUCKLAND**

Coromandel
Peninsula

**KEY TO
NEW ZEALAND'S
WINE REGIONS**

**AUCKLAND**
1 Kumeu/Huapai
2 Waiheke Island
3 Henderson
**GISBORNE**
**HAWKE'S BAY**
**WAIRARAPA/
MARTINBOROUGH**
**NELSON**
**MARLBOROUGH**
**CANTERBURY**
**CENTRAL OTAGO**

*NORTH
ISLAND*

1
2
3
•Auckland
•Manukau

*Bay of
Plenty*

Hamilton•

*Waikato River*

*North
Taranaki
Bight*

*Lake
Taupo*

*East
Cape*

**GISBORNE**

•Gisborne

*Cape
Egmont*

**HAWKE'S
BAY**

*Hawke
Bay*

*South Taranaki
Bight*

*Rangitikei R.*

•Napier

Hastings•

*Tasman

Sea*

Cape Farewell

*Tasman
Bay*

*Cook Strait*

**NELSON**

**WAIRARAPA/
MARTINBOROUGH**

•Martinborough

Nelson•

*Wairau R.*

•Wellington

•Blenheim

*Cape Palliser*

**MARLBOROUGH**

*SOUTH
ISLAND*

*SOUTHERN ALPS*

*Pegasus Bay*

**PACIFIC

OCEAN**

Mt.
Cook

*L. Tekapo*

•Christchurch

**CANTERBURY**

*Banks
Peninsula*

*Lake
Wanaka*

*Lake
Hawea*

*Waitaki R.*

*Canterbury
Bight*

•Queenstown

*Lake
Te Anau*

**CENTRAL
OTAGO**

*Clutha River*

•Dunedin

*Puysegur
Point* *Foveaux Strait*

*Stewart
Island*

*South West
Cape*

N

0          150          300 mi
0      150      300 km

© MapQuest.com

## THE QUICK SIP ON NEW ZEALAND

• New Zealand is best known for its white wines and, in particular, for its racy, vibrant sauvignon blancs and elegant chardonnays.

• New Zealand's wine industry, while infused with excitement and growing quickly, remains tiny by world standards.

• The vineyards of New Zealand are the most southerly in the world.

whom Tasmania was named, landed on the northern tip of the South Island in 1642. There, Tasman encountered a violent group of native peoples—the Maori—and promptly left. More than a century would pass before the next westerner ventured onto New Zealand's shores. In 1769 the English explorer Captain James Cook circumnavigated the islands. His explorations resulted in the British colonization of New Zealand and in the bond between the two countries that still exists today.

Almost fifty years later, in 1819, the first New Zealand vines were planted by an Anglican missionary named Samuel Marsden, though there is no record of wine being produced from the grapes. Then in 1839 Scotsman James Busby successfully made the country's first wines. Both Marsden and Busby had written of New Zealand's promise as a wine producer, for the climate and terrain appeared exceptionally well suited to grapevines.

Despite this auspicious beginning, it would be a century and a half before a solid wine industry would take hold. From the 1840s to the 1980s the obstacles to success were pervasive. To begin with, many of the pioneering New Zealand winemak-

ers were English immigrants who had no history of experience with grape growing. To make matters worse, for decades before and after the turn of the twentieth century, New Zealand came under the influence of a relentless temperance movement, which severely handicapped the establishment of any sort of wine culture. For most of the 1800s wineries could not sell wine to consumers; they could only sell to hotels for banquets and only then if certain conditions were met. It wasn't until after World War II that wine was permitted to be sold by the bottle from wine shops, and selling wine in restaurants became legal only in the 1960s! Even then there was a 10 P.M. curfew after which no wine or alcohol could be sold.

None of this fully deterred the young country's would-be winemakers. In the late 1800s immigrants from the Dalmatian coast, now in Croatia, intending to make their fortunes in New Zealand's gum fields, eventually turned to farming and grape growing instead. Though many of these immigrants were experienced winemakers, they were powerless against oidium (powdery mildew) and phylloxera (a root-eating aphid), which soon decimated their young vineyards.

In the wake of these diseases and in the face of continued social hostility, New Zealand's downtrodden vintners looked for hearty, prolific grapes that could be sold as table grapes in the event that wine was banned completely. The grapes they chose would, in the long run, prove unwise. Instead of *Vitis vinifera* varieties, such as chardonnay and cabernet sauvignon, New Zealand vintners decided to plant French-American hybrids, such as Isabella and Baco noir. These grapes were good at resisting disease, but often the wines made from them either tasted like cheap jelly or they were poor quality, sugary, fortified concoctions roughly modeled on inferior brandy and ersatz Sherry. Isabella, it should be noted, remained the most widely planted grape variety in New Zealand right up until 1960.

As if all of this weren't bad enough, from the 1920s to the 1960s New Zealand wines were often stretched or adulterated with water by as much as 25 percent. Although unethical, this practice was nonetheless quite legal.

Today New Zealand is a vastly different place. Thanks to new laws, new attitudes, considerable investments of capital, and a new generation of talented, trained viticulturists and winemakers, a small but innovative premium wine industry is flourishing. Hybrids are now virtually nonexistent, having been pulled out and replaced with classic *vinifera* vari-

eties. And instead of cheap, sweet, fortified wines, dry table wines now dominate production.

*Between 1994 and 1998 the New Zealand wine industry grew so much that the number of winemakers in the country jumped from 31 to 293.*

In many ways New Zealand remains a wine frontier. The number of wineries (293 as of 1998) nearly tripled in the decade 1988 to 1998. In just the five years between 1993 and 1998, vineyard land grew by more than 40 percent, and new developments in winemaking and viticulture are being made with lightning speed. Yet given all its recent growth, the coun-

*Within a matter of hours, birds can strip a vineyard bare of its grapes. As a result, many vineyards, including these at Kumeu River near Auckland, must be netted (at considerable expense to the grower).*

## MIGHTY MONTANA

⊂⦿⊃

Around half of New Zealand's wines are made by a single large producer: Montana. Under a slew of brands, the firm makes dozens of wines, ranging from simple quaffers to some of New Zealand's finest. Among these brands is Corbans, which produced New Zealand's first chardonnays and cabernet sauvignons. Montana's most impressive accomplishment, however, was pioneering the planting of sauvignon blanc in Marlborough, today one of the most renowned regions for that varietal.

try's wine industry is still small. New Zealand makes about one twelfth as much wine as Australia, which itself has a modest output. The United States, for example, produces about two and three quarters as much wine as Australia.

New Zealand's wine producers range from tiny to gigantic. Approximately 50 percent of the wine produced, including some of the best, is made by one large company, Montana. As in Australia, grapes are mostly machine harvested, although grapes for the country's very top wines are often picked by hand. While a few small producers do grow all their own grapes, the majority of New Zealand wineries buy grapes from the country's 500 or so independent grape growers. Increasingly, these grape growers are making wine and coming out with their own brands.

Of the twenty or so grape varieties grown in New Zealand today, sauvignon blanc and chardonnay are the most renowned and the most widely planted. Riesling—both as a dry wine and as a late harvest dessert wine—is creating a great

deal of new excitement as well. And, while it's true that as of the late 1990s, about 75 percent of the vineyards were planted with white grape varieties, the grape mix is expected to change a bit as the twenty-first century gets under way. Among the most promising varieties is pinot noir, already New Zealand's leading red grape and a variety that is being planted more extensively year by year.

# NEW ZEALAND'S WINE LAWS

There is no strict system of laws regulating grape growing and winemaking for New Zealand—nothing comparable to the French *Appellation d'Origine Contrôlée* laws, governing such matters as the varieties of grapes that can be planted in specific areas, the yield produced from those grapes, how the grapes are vinified, or how long the wines are aged.

New Zealand does have regulations that govern labeling and certain aspects of wine production. These rules are part of the country's official Food Act and Food Regulations and they mandate that:

• If a grape variety or varieties are named on a label, 75 percent of the wine must be composed of the variety or varieties named. In practice, most New Zealand wines are composed of 85 to 100 percent of the variety or varieties named.

• If two grapes are named on the label, they must be listed in order of importance. When you see a wine labeled cabernet-merlot it contains more cabernet than merlot; a wine labeled merlot-cabernet, has just the opposite.

• When an area, district, or region appears on a label, 75 percent of the wine must come from that place.

# THE LAND, THE GRAPES, AND THE VINEYARDS

The factor that most influences New Zealand's grapes, and hence its wines, is the chilliness of the climate. New Zealand has some of the coolest maritime wine regions in the New World. Because of the long narrow shape of the two main islands, no vineyard is more than 80 miles from the sea. This cool, steady climate allows the grapes to ripen evenly and gently over the course of a long growing season, culminating in a harvest that can take place anywhere from March to May (this is afterall the Southern Hemisphere). In the best of circumstances the length of the growing season can lead to elegant wines with wonderfully pure flavors. It's often said that New Zealand vegetables and fruits, including grapes, have an intensity of flavor rarely found in produce grown elsewhere. Of course, a cool climate also means that, generally speaking, the grapes boast a good amount of natural acidity. For the best New Zealand whites, this can translate into dazzling—and sometimes searing—crispness.

All of this said, New Zealand is not without viticultural hurdles. Principal among these is rain. In the past, rainy weather often led to moldy grape bunches, dense vine canopies, and wines that tasted unripe and vegetative. In the 1980s, however, top viticulturists—including the internationally famous Australian Dr. Richard Smart—developed trellising systems and viticultural techniques that help promote ripeness and maturity. Many of these techniques have been copied around the world.

## THE GRAPES OF NEW ZEALAND

### WHITES

**Chardonnay:** The most widely planted grape in New Zealand, chardonnay is the source of wines of great character. The wines can be found in a variety of styles from lush to lean and Chablis-like. Also used for sparkling wine.

**Müller-Thurgau:** Fairly widely planted grape in New Zealand, but minor in importance. Used to make neutral-tasting, inexpensive jug wines.

**Pinot Gris:** Only a tiny amount is grown, but a few top producers have made very promising wines from it; could be an important grape variety in the future.

**Riesling:** Can make delicious dry wines and sensational botrytized dessert wines.

**Sauvignon Blanc:** The grape that focused world attention on New Zealand wines. Sauvignon blanc makes outrageously good ones with full-throttle green and lightly tropical fruit flavors.

### REDS

**Cabernet Sauvignon:** Planted in the warmest pockets around the country. Often blended with merlot and other varieties to make Bordeaux-style blends.

**Merlot:** Almost always blended with cabernet sauvignon.

**Pinot Noir:** The most widely planted red grape in New Zealand and the country's red specialty. Pinot noir can make delicious earthy still wines; it is also used for sparkling wines.

**THE MOST IMPORTANT**

# NEW ZEALAND WINES

LEADING WINES

**Chardonnay** white

**Pinot Noir** red

**Sauvignon Blanc** white

**Sparkling Wines** white

WINES OF NOTE

**Cabernet Sauvignon** and

**Bordeaux-Style Blends** red

**Riesling** white (dry and sweet)

New Zealand's two main islands stretch more than 900 miles in length, but the amount of land planted with vineyards is tiny—as of 1998, it was approximately 22,000 acres (the Napa Valley alone has almost twice as much vineyard land, even though it's only about 30 miles long). Although New Zealand has extensive and beautiful mountain ranges (the glacier-laced Southern Alps are located here), the slopes are so steep and erosion is such a problem that the country's vineyards are mostly planted on flat plains or gently rolling hills. Soil varies considerably from clays interspersed with particles of volcanic rock to fertile river-basin types. Such diversity is the result of New Zealand's tumultuous geologic past. The country lies at the active juncture of two of the world's great tectonic plates, the Indo-Australian Plate and the South Pacific Plate.

More than 40 percent of New Zealand's vineyards are located on the North Island in the two largest and most important wine districts, Gisborne and Hawke's Bay. Gisborne, near the East Cape and the international date line, is the site of the world's easternmost grapes and is known for numerous delicious chardonnays, often with light honey and tropical-fruit flavors. Hawke's Bay, with its very complex soil pat-

*The rolling green hills of Henderson, near Auckland, are perfectly suited to grapevines. Opposite page: The elaborately carved entrance gate of a Maori village.*

terns and long hours of sunshine, is considered one of New Zealand's best wine regions. This is where many of the country's first-rate sauvignon blancs and chardonnays are to be found, as well as fine cabernet sauvignons and cabernet-merlot blends.

The third major wine district on the North Island is often called simply Auckland, though what is really meant is the territory around Auckland, New Zealand's largest city. Far smaller than Gisborne or Hawke's Bay in terms of wine production and vineyard acreage, Auckland nonetheless boasts the greatest number of wineries. Many of New Zealand's top wine companies are headquartered here, even though their vineyards are located elsewhere in the country. Auckland encompasses several smaller well-known wine districts including Kumeu/Huapai, Henderson, and Waiheke Island.

Finally, in the southeast corner of the North Island, relatively near New Zealand's capital, Wellington, is the small wine region Wairarapa/Martinborough. The two dozen or so high-quality producers here make a variety of good wines. However, their most noteworthy—and hard won—successes have been with pinot noir, possibly the most demanding, difficult grape in the world. In just a few short years, Ata Rangi Vineyard, Martinborough Vineyard, Dry River Wines, Te Kairanga Wines, and others have begun to make such promising pinot noirs that Wairarapa/Martinborough is rapidly becoming New Zealand's prime area for this grape.

The generally cooler South Island had no commercial vineyards until 1973. In that year, Montana Wines planted vines in Marlborough on the northeastern tip of

## THE MAORI

ew Zealand was originally inhabited by the Maori, a Polynesian people who over centuries migrated from subtropical Pacific islands. Although the Maori had no written language, Christian missionaries in the nineteenth century recorded the words the Maori spoke. Today many towns, wineries, and even vineyards have Maori names. The Maori name for New Zealand, Aotearoa, means land of the long white cloud.

the South Island and pioneered what was to become one of the most prestigious wine districts in the country. Other top wine firms followed Montana's lead, including, in 1985, one of New Zealand's most famous wineries, Cloudy Bay. Today, Marlborough is New Zealand's largest wine district, with almost 40 percent of the country's vineyards. (Together, Marlborough plus Gisborne and Hawke's Bay account for more than 80 percent of all the vineyards in New Zealand.) Marlborough is quintessential sauvignon blanc territory. More sauvignon is planted here than any other grape variety.

Other wine districts on the South Island include Nelson, a small but beautiful wine region about 40 miles west of Marlborough; Canterbury, a cool region midway down the length of the island; and most southerly and cool of all, Central Otago, a fast-growing region showing considerable promise especially for those varieties that when grown in cool climates

## THE OTHER KIWI

———⟨≈/≈⟩———

Because of New Zealand's prolonged isolation, which lasted until the eighteenth century, it has both unusual vegetation and a high proportion of species found nowhere else. The only native mammals are two species of bats. In the absence of predatory mammals, New Zealand became home to several rare species of flightless birds. One of these, the kiwi (about the size of a large hen), is also the nickname for a New Zealander.

wines are made in conjunction with French Champagne houses. The New Zealand sparkler Pelorus is a joint effort between Veuve Clicquot and Cloudy Bay, and Deutz Marlborough Cuvée is backed by the Champagne house Deutz and Montana Wines.

Among red varieties, even cabernet sauvignon and merlot are on the rise, especially for making Bordeaux-style blends. These are often served with another New Zealand specialty, venison. The wine to try here is most certainly Providence Vineyard's red wine, a sensational, beautifully structured and concentrated Bordeaux blend that is so Bordeauxlike it's beguiling.

Still, among all the varieties planted in New Zealand, nothing comes close in importance to chardonnay and sauvignon blanc. Chardonnay, the most widely planted grape, is found along nearly the entire length of the country, from Kaitaia, at not quite the top of the North Island, to Central Otago, near the bottom of the South Island. Not surprisingly, the styles of chardonnay vary greatly, ranging from round, lightly honeyed wines with tropical fruit and nutty flavors to leaner versions reminiscent of French Chablis. Among the top labels to look for are Ata Rangi Craighall, Church Road Reserve, Cottage Block Marlborough, Kumeu River Mate's

are capable of making wines of real elegance: riesling, pinot noir, and chardonnay.

Overall, New Zealand is primarily a white-wine producer. More than 75 percent of all the wine produced is white although, as I said, pinot noir is rapidly growing in popularity. While much of this is used for still wines, New Zealand's crisp sparkling wines (made from pinot noir and chardonnay) are also extremely popular, as Sunday brunch in just about any Auckland restaurant will testify to (very few of these are exported to the United States). As in California, several sparkling

*Larnach Castle, built in the 1870s on the Otago Peninsula, at the southern tip of the South Island, has been called New Zealand's most princely residence.*

Vineyard, Matua Valley Ararimu, Mills Reef Elspeth, and Sacred Hill Riflemans.

## Sauvignon Blanc

While sauvignon blanc may rank second in terms of acreage planted, no grape produces wines about which New Zealanders are more proud. If any grape is central to New Zealand's wine identity, it's sauvignon blanc. New Zealand sauvignon blancs have no parallel anywhere in the world. Though they are sometimes compared to the vibrant wines of Sancerre in France's Loire Valley, New Zealand sauvignons taste quite different. Explosive yet taut, they evoke a spectrum of greens: fresh limes, wild herbs, watercress, cardoons, gooseberries, green olives, green figs, green tea, green melons, plus a host of green vegetables from snow peas to green beans. This does not mean the wines are necessarily vegetal. (The term *vegetal* is generally used pejoratively to describe flavors and aromas reminiscent of boiled cabbage or the water left-over from boiled artichokes.) Clean herbal flavors are something else again and can be zingingly refreshing.

But greenness isn't all. New Zealand sauvignons also have an exotic tropical backdrop. They often hint at mango or passion fruit. The combination can be dynamite, making for untamed, unruly, un-leashed wines that are true to their name—sauvignon, from the French *sauvage*, means wild. Then, too, the flavors of most New Zealand sauvignon blancs are not disguised or mollified by wood. Like French Sancerres, the majority of New Zealand sauvignon blancs are

Here I'm with Kevin Judd, the winemaker at Cloudy Bay (seen above), tasting wines in his laboratory.

made in stainless steel tanks rather than in oak barrels. As a result, they possess a clarity, crispness, and razor-sharp focus for which they are rightly loved.

811

*Some of the Best Producers of New Zealand Sauvignon Blanc*

**BABICH**

**BRANCOTT**

**CLOUDY BAY**

**COOPERS CREEK VINEYARD**

**LAKE CHALICE WINES**

**MATUA VALLEY**

**MILLS REEF WINERY**

**NAUTILUS ESTATE**

**SACRED HILL**

**SAINT CLAIR**

**TRINITY HILL**

**VAVASOUR**

**VILLA MARIA**

**WAIRAU RIVER**

**WITHER HILLS**

# THE NEW ZEALAND WINES TO KNOW

*For each of the wines that follow, the specific growing region from which it comes is noted.*

## Sparkling Wine

**DEUTZ**
Marlborough Cuvée
nonvintage brut
Marlborough
approximately 60% chardonnay,
40% pinot noir

New Zealand makes deliciously lively, pure-tasting sparkling wines, and the Deutz Marlborough Cuvée is a terrific example. It is both

creamy yet penetrating in the same second—a mouthwatering achievement that makes you want to drink more and more. Fresh apples, warm biscuits, and the lightest hint of lime are all subtly woven into the flavor, and the finish is beautifully sheer. Deutz Marlborough Cuvée is made by New Zealand's leading wine company, Montana, through a licensing arrangement with the French Champagne house Deutz.

## Whites

**BRANCOTT VINEYARDS**
Sauvignon Blanc
reserve
Marlborough
100% sauvignon blanc

Depending on the year, Brancott's reserve sauvignon blanc can be a huge gripping wine with a penetrating herbal green edge or fatter and richer with tangerine, tropical fruit, and floral flavors. The Brancott winemaker, drinking this sauvignon blanc away from home, calls it a cure for homesickness. You may find it provokes wanderlust. Brancott is one of the leading brands owned by Montana.

**CLOUDY BAY**
Sauvignon Blanc
Marlborough
100% sauvignon blanc

When Cloudy Bay sauvignon blanc was first released in 1985, it became an overnight sensation in Australia and Britain and, for the first time, focused world attention on the wines of New Zealand. The wine is a torpedo of intensity. Lime zest, new mown hay, grapefruit, mint, and smoke

go off like flavor grenades in your mouth, followed by fireworks of spice and citrus. Best of all, these wild exuberant flavors have a long, brilliant finish. Sauvignon blanc is not Cloudy Bay's only success, however. The winery makes a delicious pinot noir and a devastating late harvest riesling. Cloudy Bay is co-owned by the French firm Veuve Clicquot and David Hohnen, founder of Cape Mentelle Vineyards in the Margaret River region of Western Australia.

## GROVE MILL

Riesling

Marlborough

100% riesling

With all the attention on sauvignon blanc and chardonnay, riesling is New Zealand's best-kept secret. But in a cool country like this, it's no surprise that riesling can produce some stellar wines. Grove Mill's is one of the best. It is hugely perfumed, spicy, mineraly, and laced with such intriguing flavors as tangerine and lime leaf—all of this, plus riesling's beautiful purity and focus. Here's a wine just begging for southeast Asian–inspired dishes (which are very common in New Zealand).

## KUMEU RIVER

Chardonnay

Kumeu

100% chardonnay

Year in and year out, Kumeu River makes two of the most impressive chardonnays in New Zealand—the regular Kumeu River and the vineyard-designated Mate's Vineyard. Both rise far above the ranks of typical New World chardonnay. Most amazing are the grip, clarity, precision, and balance the wines possess. They are, each in their own way, smoky, lime tinged, honeyed, and creamy, with bolts of vanilla surging through the middle. Of the two, the Mate's Vineyard is both the more powerful and the more expensive.

## NAUTILUS ESTATE

Sauvignon Blanc

Marlborough

100% sauvignon blanc

In top vintages the wild, explosive green fruit of Nautilus' terrific sauvignon blanc is quintessential New Zealand. With lots of green peas, green tea, green peppercorns, and lime, this wine is an unstoppable bullet of fresh flavor. Yet it's also beautifully balanced and refined.

## SAINT CLAIR

Sauvignon Blanc

Marlborough

100% sauvignon blanc

A great example of New Zealand's exotic herbal and tropical fruit sauvignons, Saint Clair's wine is packed with personality. At its best, fresh lime, litchi, and tarragon flavors are laced with pineapple, mineral, and peach notes. Like a ribbon, the wine's brisk acidity ties up the flavors and makes the whole package utterly mouthwatering. The family-owned winery was among the first to plant grapes in the Marlborough region.

## VILLA MARIA

Sauvignon Blanc

Marlborough

100% sauvignon blanc

Villa Maria has a track record of producing top-quality wines at terrific prices. In good vintages, this beautifully expressive sauvignon is a rush of melon, guava, kiwi, papaya, green tea, snow pea, and sage flavors—a perfect illustration of the pure, green, tropical freshness that New Zealand sauvignon is all about.

# Reds

## CHURCH ROAD-
## THE MCDONALD WINERY
Cabernet Sauvignon-Merlot

Hawke's Bay

approximately 90% cabernet sauvignon,
10% merlot

Cabernet and merlot aren't easy to grow in New Zealand's cool climate, but with consulting help from Bordeaux (another fairly cool climate region), Church Road has been making some of the best wines from these two grapes. In top years this sleek, scrumptious cabernet sauvignon-merlot blend has a sweet-smoky character with intriguing mocha, plum, and leather aromas and flavors. The McDonald Winery, founded in 1897, is one of the three oldest wineries in Hawke's Bay and was the first in the region to make serious red wines.

## DRY RIVER
Pinot Noir

Martinborough

100% pinot noir

With its tiny production, Dry River has nonetheless established a cult following for its soft, beautiful pinot noirs. These are pinots with aromas and flavors reminiscent of dried leaves, dried fruit, and damp earth. Lovers of Burgundy and Oregon pinot noir will feel right at home. Dry River was founded by Dr. Neil McCallum, who holds an Oxford Ph.D. in chemistry and was one of the pioneers of pinot noir in the Martinborough region.

## TE KAIRANGA
Pinot Noir

reserve

Martinborough

100% pinot noir

One of the largest wineries in Martinborough, Te Kairanga (Maori for the land where the soil is rich and the food plentiful) makes big-style pinot noirs with bold earthy aromas, loads of cherry and pomegranate

fruit flavors, and a sweet, toasty smokiness from considerable aging in new oak. The wine is only made in the best vintages.

# Sweet Wine

## PALLISER ESTATE
Botrytis Riesling

Martinborough

100% riesling

If riesling is New Zealand's best-kept secret, late harvest dessert wines based on riesling are an even bigger secret. But again, the success of these wines comes as no surprise. The juxtapositioning of the acidity that comes from a cool climate with the rich sweetness of grapes harvested well into the season can be spectacular. Take Palliser Estate's botrytized riesling, made only when perfect weather conditions allow. The opulent flavor of sweet caramelized pears is set off against a core of taut acidity, making for a simply delicious finale to any meal.

## FUSING FUSION WITH WINE

Once known culinarily as the land of mutton, lamb, and little else, New Zealand now boasts some of the most exciting food in the Pacific. Auckland alone has dozens of wildly creative restaurants where the dramatic, boldly seasoned dishes are a spin on European ideas infused with the complex flavors of Southeast Asia, Polynesia, and the South Pacific islands. And on every restaurant table it seems is a bottle of New Zealand wine. But then, not just any wine will work when it comes to fusion dishes uninhibitedly laced with chiles, lime, and tropical fruits. What does work? The sassy, dagger-sharp, herbal, and tropical flavors of New Zealand sauvignon blancs. Fusion checkmate.

*New Zealand's most lively city, Auckland, has a vibrant restaurant scene. And just about every restaurant-goer drinks wine, or so it seems.*

## VISITING NEW ZEALAND WINERIES

New Zealand wineries range from tiny to very large, and it's fascinating to visit several of different sizes. The two areas best suited for extensive visiting and tasting are Hawke's Bay and Marlborough, where there are a number of wineries in close proximity. Many are well set up with tasting rooms where you can both sample wines and purchase them. In addition, a number of wineries have restaurants and picnic facilities. You'll find a few wineries here that weren't highlighted earlier; their wines are certainly worth trying. It's always wise to call ahead to determine hours of operation. The telephone numbers include the dialing code you'll need when calling from the United States. If you're calling from within New Zealand, eliminate the 011-64 and add a zero before the next number.

New Zealand's wineries and vineyards are often surrounded by beautifully pastoral rolling hills, majestic mountains, and unspoiled coastlines. Don't miss one of the country's most breathtaking features, the Southern Alps on the South Island, with nineteen peaks that are more than 10,000 feet in height, including Mount Cook.

### NORTH ISLAND

**BABICH WINES**
10 Babich Road
Henderson, Auckland
011-64-9-833-7859

**CHURCH ROAD-
THE MCDONALD WINERY**
150 Church Road
Taradale, Napier, Hawke's Bay
011-64-6-844-2053

**KUMEU RIVER WINES**
550 State Highway 16
Kumeu, Auckland
011-64-9-412-8415

**MATUA VALLEY**
Waikoukou Road
Waimauku, Kumeu, Auckland
011-64-9-411-8301

**PINOT NOIR**

Produced and bottled by Palliser Estate Wines
Kitchener Street, Martinborough

alc. 13.0% by Vol 750ml

**PALLISER ESTATE**
Kitchener Street
Martinborough, Wairarapa
011-64-6-306-9019

**STONYRIDGE VINEYARD**
80 Onetangi Road
Ostend, Waiheke Island
011-64-9-372-8822

**SOUTH ISLAND**

**ALLAN SCOTT WINES
AND ESTATES**
Jacksons Road, R.D. 3
Blenheim, Marlborough
011-64-3-572-9054

**CLOUDY BAY**
Jacksons Road
Blenheim, Marlborough
011-64-3-520-9140

**GIBBSTON VALLEY WINES**
Main Queenstown-Cromwell Highway
Queenstown, Central Otago
011-64-3-442-6910

**GROVE MILL**
Waihopai Valley Road
Renwick, Blenheim, Marlborough
011-64-3-572-8200

**PEGASUS BAY**
Stockgrove Road, R.D. 2
Waipara, North Canterbury, Amberley
011-64-3-314-6869
Restaurant on-site.

**WAIRAU RIVER WINES**
Corner of Rapaura Road and
State Highway 6, R.D. 3
Blenheim, Marlborough
011-64-3-572-9800
Restaurant on-site.

*Despite its rather humble winery, Cloudy Bay is nothing short of a sensation. In the late 1980s and early 1990s its sauvignon blanc won raves from wine circles in London and New York.*

# South Africa

Of the more than fifty countries on the African continent, only eight are wine producers: South Africa, Morocco, Algeria, Tunisia, Egypt, Libya, Zimbabwe, and Kenya. Most make only minuscule amounts of bland wine. South Africa, by comparison, is both a leading wine producer (seventh in the world) and the source of the continent's finest wines. Startlingly, however, half of the grapes grown in the country are not made into wine but rather are distilled into brandy and cheap spirits.

Not quite twice as large as Texas, South Africa is bordered on the north by Namibia, Botswana, and Zimbabwe and on the east by Mozambique and Swaziland. With about 1,800 miles of coastline, it is the only wine region in the world sandwiched between two oceans, the Atlantic and the Indian.

The first South African wines were made more than three centuries ago by Dutch colonists who vinified the wild grapes they found growing on the southwestern tip (known as the Cape) of the African

South Africa ranks seventh in wine-producing countries worldwide. South Africans drink an average of 2.27 gallons of wine per person each year; they're thirtieth in world wine consumption.

*The impressive, new, French-inspired cellars of Morgenhof, a three-hundred-year-old estate in Stellenbosch; and workers (inset).*

continent. The colonists, employees of the Dutch East India Company, planned to establish the Cape as a restocking station for food and provisions halfway between Europe and the spice-rich East Indies.

*In South Africa wineries are referred to as wine farms.*

Though the presence of native grapes was encouraging to the colonists, the wine made from them was not. The commander of the small settlement, Jan van Riebeeck,

immediately sent word back to Holland, imploring his employers to send European vine cuttings on the next ship out. Within a decade, French vine cuttings—most probably chenin blanc and muscat of Alexandria—were thriving in Cape soil.

The closely spaced vineyards were too narrow to be worked by animal-drawn ploughs and too extensive to be worked by the colonists and their Malayan slaves alone. In 1658 Dutch ships brought 200 slaves from Madagascar and Mozambique to the settlement. The very next year, on

## THE QUICK SIP ON SOUTH AFRICA

• South Africa has a more than three-hundred-year-old history of grape growing.

• Most South African wine is made by large cooperatives. The best South African wine, however, comes from several dozen small private estates.

• Though the majority of South African wines are white, the growing excitement is for red wines, such as cabernet sauvignon, shiraz, and pinotage, a South African crossing of cinsaut and pinot noir.

the first day of the harvest, February 2, 1659, van Riebeeck recorded in his journal: "Today, God be praised, wine was pressed for the first time from Cape grapes."

Despite the long history of Cape winemaking, South African wines were virtually unknown in the United States before the 1990s. Cape wine producers traditionally sold their wines—often in bulk—to Europeans. United States trade sanctions imposed in response to the South African policy of racial apartheid kept Cape wines out of America. When the ban on South African goods was lifted in 1991, however, the doors of commerce inched open. By mid-decade, Cape wines had begun to turn up in restaurants and wine shops.

## A Glance Back

All of the country's top wine districts fan out from the old port city of Cape Town, which is dominated by a 3,500-foot flat-topped mountain called Table Mountain. (Clouds on the mountain are called a tablecloth.) One of the smallest of these districts, Constantia, was already so well established by the mid-1700s that a sweet muscat-based wine named simply Constantia was renowned throughout Europe and was reportedly a favorite of Napoleon.

*Founded in 1652 as a depot for Dutch East Indian Company ships, Cape Town is South Africa's oldest European settlement and second largest city (after Johannesburg).*

## THE CAPE OF GOOD HOPE

—◈◈◈—

In 1487 the Portuguese navigator Bartholomeu Dias sailed through tempestuous seas to round the southern tip of Africa. He named it Cabo Tormentoso, the Cape of Storms. Later, Portugal's king, fearing that mariners would refuse to sail around the cape, renamed it Cabo de Boa Esperança, the Cape of Good Hope.

If there is one factor that more than any other has shaped the current state of South African wine, it was the establishment of extremely powerful cooperatives at the turn of the twentieth century. The cooperative movement began after the combined devastation of the Anglo-Boer War and phylloxera, a root-killing aphid, left the country's vineyards in near ruin. In the aftermath of these destructive forces, South African vineyards were replanted with a vengeance. Overproduction ensued, and grape prices hit rock bottom. In 1905 the South African government appointed a commission to examine the widespread financial depression in the wine industry. The result was the formation of the first South African co-op funded with huge government grants. The stage was set.

Almost a dozen co-ops sprung up over the next several years, but many of these were unsuccessful. Grape prices plummeted again after World War I. In desperation, ten million vines were uprooted, and farmers planted alfalfa fields to feed ostriches—ostrich feathers being highly fashionable in Europe at the time. But when the feather fad faded and farmers went back to planting grapes, overproduction loomed yet again.

In 1918 one of the most massive, mighty cooperatives in the world was formed—the KWV or Ko-operatieve Wijnbouwers Vereniging van Zuid-Afrika (the Cooperative Wine Growers Association of South Africa). Over the next few decades the KWV became omnipotent. No wine could be made, sold, or bought in South Africa except through the KWV. Today, although the KWV is not as all-powerful as it once was and has been restructured as a group of private companies rather than a cooperative, it still controls 25 percent of all South African wine and spirits exports. KWV wine in cork-sealed bottles is usually decent and drinkable but rarely has anything more going for it. Screw-top bottles contain extremely neutral wine. Several dozen types of wine are made, including sparkling and still wines, "ports," "sherries," muscadels, and botrytis-infected noble late harvest wines (the last two can be fairly good).

Though the KWV helped to stabilize prices, its dominance proved to be a noose around the neck of the Cape wine

## NELSON MANDELA

—◈◈◈—

Elected in 1994, Nelson Mandela was South Africa's first black president and the first to be elected with voter participation from all races. Mandela's release from prison in 1990, after more than twenty-seven years in confinement, signaled a new era in South African politics and paved the way for the lifting of trade sanctions and the importation of South African wine into the United States.

821

*The vineyards at Klein Constantia were first planted around 1700. The wines made from their grapes had numerous noteworthy customers, including Napoleon, Frederick the Great, and Bismarck.*

industry for nearly a century. While creativity, technological invention, and viticultural advances swept through Europe, Australia, and the United States, South Africa's wine industry remained largely static. The small but growing movement toward quality did not begin until the mid-1980s. In 1976 there were seventy wine cooperatives in South Africa and just thirty-five private firms making fine wine from estate-grown grapes. Today, the number of small estates has grown by more than sevenfold, while the number of co-ops has remained about the same.

At the top level, estates are moving away from the varieties that yield oceans of cheap wine and concentrating instead on more flavor-packed varieties like pinotage (South Africa's signature red) plus such classics as cabernet sauvignon, shiraz (syrah), sauvignon blanc, riesling, and the like. The white to red and sweet to dry ratios are also shifting. South Africa is no longer a country where nearly every still wine is sweet and white. That said, the best sweet white wines remain one of the country's strong suits. Riesling (sometimes called Rhine riesling or weisser riesling), for example, is the source of some gorgeous late harvest dessert wines.

Sparkling wines, too, have gotten a fresh start. South Africa now produces a small quantity of tasty sparkling wines made by the Champagne process, as opposed to the cheaper tank method. These Champagne-method sparklers are called Cap Classique. They are sometimes made from a blend that includes sauvignon blanc and chenin blanc, although increasingly, chardonnay and pinot noir are used.

Today, much Cape wine is still bland and simplistic or downright poor in quality, but small estates are forging a new direction. The higher-quality international-style wines from these producers have a long way to go on the road to excellence, but the South African wine revolution has indisputably begun.

## SOUTH AFRICA'S WINE LAWS

I n 1972 South Africa's Wine of Origin legislation was enacted. This established designated areas as having distinctive viticultural qualities. Further legislation in the mid-1990s defined the term *estate*. An estate wine may come from one or more parcels of land that share the same "ecological conditions" within the same district of origin. The parcels do not need to be contiguous.

Most wines in South Africa are labeled by grape type. A varietally labeled wine must contain 75 percent of those grapes; in other words, a Saxenburg sauvignon blanc must be at least 75 percent sauvignon blanc.

## THE LAND, THE GRAPES, AND THE VINEYARDS

G rape growing and winemaking are concentrated in the southwestern part of South Africa bordered on the west by the Atlantic Ocean and on the south by the Indian Ocean. Farther north toward the center of the country, deserts make viticulture virtually impossible. But even within the southwestern section of the country, there are big differences among wine regions. Those that are inland and removed from the direct influence of the sea—Worcester and Klein Karoo for example—are so hot that a majority of the wines produced are either heavy and fairly

823

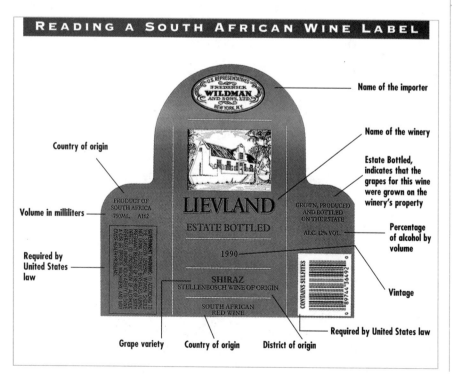

READING A SOUTH AFRICAN WINE LABEL

Name of the importer

Name of the winery

Country of origin

Estate Bottled, indicates that the grapes for this wine were grown on the winery's property

Volume in milliliters

Percentage of alcohol by volume

Required by United States law

Vintage

Required by United States law

Grape variety    Country of origin    District of origin

## THE GRAPES OF

# SOUTH AFRICA

## WHITES

**Cape Riesling:** Minor grape when it comes to the production of fine wines. Cape riesling makes mundane, common whites. It is thought to be related to the French grape crouchen blanc.

**Chardonnay:** Important and very popular up-and-coming grape. Usually made in an "international" style with lots of oak.

**Chenin Blanc:** Major grape; nearly a quarter of all South African vineyards are planted with chenin blanc, although production is in decline. Locally, it's often called steen. It is made (mostly by co-ops) into dry and sweet still wines as well as into sparkling wines.

**Hanepoot:** Very popular ancient grape, also known as muscat of Alexandria. Makes sweet fortified wines of modest quality.

**Muscadel:** A member of the muscat family; thought to be the same as muscat ottonel. Muscadel is used for sweet fortified wines, some of which can have an appealing raisiny character.

**Riesling:** Sometimes called Rhine riesling or weisser riesling in South Africa. Can make impressive late harvest sweet wines, although the dry white wines made from it are merely decent.

**Sauvignon Blanc:** South Africa's "Great White Hope." Sauvignon blanc makes grassy, herbal, bone-dry wines with high acidity and lots of personality.

## REDS

**Cabernet Franc:** Minor blending grape. Generally used with cabernet sauvignon.

**Cabernet Sauvignon:** Prestigious red grape planted in the best regions. Often made into Bordeaux-style blends.

**Cinsaut:** French Rhône grape; in South Africa it's often called hermitage. Here, it's the source of light, grapey reds. Cinsaut is often used in blending.

**Merlot:** Gaining in popularity, though not yet as successful as cabernet sauvignon. Merlot is made as a varietal and used for blending.

**Pinotage:** Unique and popular South African cross of cinsaut and pinot noir. Makes rustic, simple, appealing reds.

**Pinot Noir:** Minor grape; historically not very successful in South Africa, but its quality is improving. Used primarily for sparkling wines.

**Shiraz:** The same as the French grape syrah. Shiraz is the source of popular, big-fruit wines with lots of smoky-chocolate flavors. It is used for varietal wines, as well as for blending.

coarse or fortified. By contrast, higher-quality wines are mostly made in a handful of small wine regions on or near the coast. The most important and established of these—Constantia, Franschhoek Valley, Paarl, and Stellenbosch—ring Cape Town and share a climate that mirrors the hotter parts of the Mediterranean. Frost and rain are rarely problems. What occasionally could be scorching heat is kept at bay by the commingling of maritime breezes off the Atlantic and Indian Oceans. The best vineyard sites in these regions are often on high slopes, sheltered from the piercing late afternoon sun. Soil varies considerably; some of the most prominent types include gravel, granite, clay, sand, shale, and hutton, a deep, rich red soil also known as Cape sandstone. As is always true in the Southern Hemisphere, the harvest occurs between the end of January and mid-April.

In addition to the well-established regions, several new wine regions are emerging in South Africa and these, too, benefit from close proximity to the sea. Mossel Bay, right on the Indian Ocean, is a relatively isolated wine region far east of Cape Town, on the southeastern side of the continent's tip. Walker Bay and Elgin, also on the coast, are closer to Cape Town. Each of these regions has produced promising sauvignon blancs in particular.

The most popular of the forty different South African grape varieties, accounting for about a quarter of all planted vines, is white: chenin blanc, or steen, as it is often called locally. South African chenin blanc can be delicious, but many of the top small producers believe it lacks a sophisticated image and are pulling it out. Although chenin blanc is in decline, white

*Blessed with sunshine throughout the long summer, South Africa's wine regions have no trouble ripening grapes. The harvest takes place from the end of January to mid-April.*

grapes still far outnumber red. Sauvignon blanc and chardonnay are on the rise, and there are huge plantings of not very prestigious grape varieties such as hanepoot (muscat of Alexandria), Cape riesling, colombar (French colombard), Thompson seedless, and Palomino (the grape that makes Spanish Sherry).

*South Africa's centuries-old wine industry notwithstanding, beer—not wine—is the leading alcoholic beverage. Per ounce, it costs less than soft drinks do.*

The leading red grape is cabernet sauvignon, which is made into wines labeled by that name as well as used in Bordeaux-style blends. Second in importance is cinsaut (an average-quality blending grape sometimes used in wines from southern France). Cape cinsaut is a lightish red and is usually blended. Confusingly, Cape cinsaut is locally sometimes called hermitage, an allusion to its Rhône heritage.

825

## RICH BEYOND GRAPES

⟶⟨∘∕∘∕∘⟩⟵

South Africa has the largest known reserves of gold in the world and is the foremost supplier (accounting for about 35 percent of total world production). Johannesburg began as a gold mining camp in the 1800s. South Africa also has the largest known reserves of chromium, platinum, vanadium, manganese, andalusite, and fluorspar, as well as substantial deposits of many other minerals, such as coal, uranium, diamonds, iron ore, antimony, asbestos, nickel, and phosphates.

## SOUTH AFRICAN WINES

LEADING WINES
**Cabernet Sauvignon** red
**Chardonnay** white
**Chenin Blanc** aka **Steen** white (dry and sweet)
**Pinotage** red
**Riesling** white (sweet)
**Sauvignon Blanc** white
**Shiraz** red

WINES OF NOTE
**Hanepoot** white (fortified; sweet)
**Sparkling Wines** white

In 1925 Cape cinsaut was genetically crossed with pinot noir in a South African laboratory, creating pinotage, the basis for a rustic red wine produced almost nowhere else in the world. Pinotage was first bottled by the Stellenbosch Farmer's Winery in 1959. With its current popularity and cult status, pinotage could be thought of as South Africa's zinfandel. However, among reds, shiraz (syrah) shows the most promise of becoming South Africa's star variety.

Planting high-quality grape varieties is one thing; however, making fine wine is another. In this regard, South Africa faces numerous challenges. Many cooperatives have no viticulturist and no modern sensibility or expertise when it comes to grape growing, harvesting, and handling. In order to make fine wines, grapes must be picked in that narrow band of time when they are perfectly ripe but not overripe. Unfortunately, South African grape pickers tradi-

tionally harvest the grapes only on weekdays, not on weekends, which are reserved for leisure and religious activities. If the grapes sit in the hot sun for two extra days, becoming overripe, so be it. Moreover, grapes are picked in a fairly rough manner throughout the day, not just during the coolest hours (which would help to preserve the fruit's flavor). It's not uncommon to see a dozen or more farmers with large, grape-laden trucks waiting in line for hours outside a co-op's crushers. Meanwhile, as time ticks by, the fiery South African sun bakes the flavor out of the grapes.

Thankfully, wines from small private estates and some wines from the better co-ops are often another story. These wines of higher quality are made from grapes that are more carefully handled than are grapes at the average co-op. But there's still a lot of room for improvement. In the mid-1990s even many of the more expensive South African red wines possessed an oxidized, roasted character as a result of less than ideal harvesting and handling. And many white wines had a flat, highly alcoholic flavor.

*Some of the Best Producers of
South African Sauvignon Blanc*

**BOSCHENDAL**

**L'ORMARINS**

**NEIL ELLIS**

**SAXENBURG**

**THELEMA MOUNTAIN VINEYARDS**

**VILLIERA ESTATE**

**ZONNEBLOEM**

All this said, in the best winemakers' hands, and especially with such heat-loving grapes as sauvignon blanc, shiraz, and cabernet sauvignon, Cape wines can be delicious. Cape sauvignon blancs can be as wildly herbal, smoky, gunflinty, and gooseberryish as sauvignon gets anywhere in the world. The best South African sauvignon blancs are fermented in stainless steel so that they retain their zestiness. Those that are fermented in wood are sometimes referred to as blanc fumé; as a group these tend to be less successful.

At a basic level, Cape shiraz and cabernet sauvignon often have the classic South African soft texture plus smoky flavors. These are not big, power-packed reds but rather unfussy, straightforward wines. The best Cape shiraz and cabernet, however, do broach complexity. Their smokiness is balanced by bright cherry, plum, and coffee flavors. Increasingly, top producers are aging shiraz and cabernet sauvignon in American oak, giving these wines expanded richness, depth, and length.

*Some of the
Best Producers of Pinotage*

**BEYERSKLOOF**

**CLOS MALVERNE**

**FAIRVIEW**

**KANONKOP**

**SIMONSIG**

827

*The Stellenbosch countryside is dotted with farms and whitewashed, fancifully gabled, thatch-roofed Cape Dutch homesteads.*

## THE NEDERBURG AUCTION

—◆◇◆—

Held each April in Paarl, the Neder-burg Auction of rare Cape wines is one of the leading wine auctions in the world, along with Burgundy's Hospices de Beaune, Germany's Kloster Eberbach, and the Napa Valley Wine Auction. The first Nederburg Auction, which was held in 1975, was intended both as a showcase for South African wine and as an incentive for vintners to produce higher-quality wine. Every wine producer in South Africa is invited to participate. Judges taste the wines blind and then choose about a hundred to be auctioned during a day of festivities and feasting. The auction proceeds benefit the Hospice Association of Southern Africa. For information, call 011-27-21-770-2482.

# THE FOODS OF SOUTH AFRICA

Once, as a young child, I saw a vivid photo in *National Geographic* of a South African ostrich egg. It was frighteningly large. Around it were even more frightening looking tribesmen. On my first trip to South Africa's wine regions, I wondered if I'd be eating anything other than ostrich omelets. In fact, Cape cooking goes far beyond egg dishes. The culinary bold strokes are a curious blend of Dutch, English, and Malay cookery, Malayans having been brought to the earliest Cape settlements as slaves.

Well-loved dishes include *bredie*, a humble Malay stew often made with lamb neck bones and *waterblommetjie*, water lilies. These are a popular South African vegetable and taste like a cross between artichokes and green beans. They grow wild on the surface of roadside ponds. Somewhat more exciting than *bredie* is *bobotie*, best described as Malayan shepherd's pie. In the tastiest *booties*, the chopped meat is spiked with cinnamon, curry, and raisins and frequently served with a chutney of dried peaches and apricots.

South Africa is, not surprisingly, a land of extraordinary game. All sorts of deer and antelope are roasted and made into pies. During the famous South African *braai* (rhymes with cry), a traditional outdoor Sunday barbecue, an amazing number of meats are grilled—guinea fowl, several types of antelope and deer, plus pork, Karoo lamb, beef, and ostrich, which tastes remarkably like sirloin steak but is leaner and lower in fat than chicken. (The Cape alone has almost 300 ostrich farms.) In the wine regions, the meats are grilled over a fire fueled with the pruned branches of grapevines. A *braai* may also include *potjiekos* (pot food)—layers of vegetables, onions, and beef, cooked all afternoon in a pot over the fire, and *potbrood*, bread baked in a cast-iron pot over the fire.

In restaurants, the bread that is virtually always served is a sprouted-wheat bread that harkens back to the Cape's Dutch heritage. Any number of dishes will be accompanied by chips—potato chips— or slap chips—French fries.

Poised as it is between two oceans, South Africa is famed for its seafood, including what we call South African lobster tails, which the South Africans call

## BARBECUE AND PINOTAGE

A South African *braai*—outdoor barbecue—is a carnivorous feast that can include grilled antelope, deer, lamb, sausages, and beef. Several grills are set up at the same time, and the meats are cooked without any seasonings so that in the end, their rich, smoky flavors dominate. What do the South Africans consider the perfect barbecue wines? Pinotage and shiraz, both of which are gutsy, rustic, smoky reds that easily match the flavors of grilled foods.

Since a *braai* is not all that different from countless backyard barbecues in the United States (except perhaps for the antelope and deer), a South African pinotage or shiraz can be a fascinating change of pace from that ever so ubiquitous barbecue beverage in the United States: beer.

# VISITING SOUTH AFRICAN WINE FARMS

The top wine estates in South Africa are all in easy driving distance from Cape Town. Many of them have beautifully restored buildings in the whitewashed Cape Dutch–style of architecture. There's usually a tasting room where, for a nominal fee, you can sample and learn about the estate's wines. English is always spoken.

If you have time to visit just a few wineries, consider making Groot Constantia and The Bergkelder two of them. Groot (Large) Constantia, with its beautiful Cape Dutch architecture, embodies South Africa of the past, while its sister winery next door Klein (Little) Constantia is a good example of the modern New World winemaking now taking place in South Africa. The impressive Cape Dutch homestead known as The Bergkelder is both a winery and a co-owner of more than fifteen other small top-notch wineries including, Meerlust, Stellenryck, and L'Ormarins, each of which make their wines at The Bergkelder.

crayfish. Both are incorrect. It's actually a type of spiny lobster with a wide tail but no claws. Then there are *perlemoen* (abalone), mussels, calamari, clams, oysters, and several kinds of deep-sea fish, such as *snoek* (pronounced snook), a large fish related to the barracuda family. Smoked *snoek* pâté shows up everywhere.

South African desserts are humble—even now in keeping with the customs of the earliest settlers for whom things like cream, chocolate, and fresh fruit were rarities. The two homiest desserts are *koeksusters* (a dish that definitely requires careful pronunciation)—deep-fried dough, recooked in sugar syrup—and milk tarts, essentially rich pastry tarts filled with cinnamon-spiked milk custard.

*The cellars of The Bergkelder (meaning mountain cellar) are tunneled into the slopes of Papegaaiberg (Parrot Mountain) in Stellenbosch.*

*An avenue of pines (called Pine Avenue) forms the entrance to Neethlingshof Estate in Stellenbosch. The estate, with its Cape Dutch–designed winery and restaurant, is built on the site of a farm established in 1692.*

Several South African wineries have restaurants; in fact, some of the best restaurants in the Cape region are part of wineries. Reservations are recommended but not always necessary.

The telephone numbers include the dialing code you'll need when calling from the United States. If you're calling from within South Africa, eliminate the 011-27 and add a zero before the next number.

### CONSTANTIA

**GROOT CONSTANTIA ESTATE**
Private Bag, Constantia 7848
011-27-21-794-5128
Wonderful casual restaurant on-site.

**KLEIN CONSTANTIA ESTATE**
P. O. Box 375, Constantia 7848
011-27-21-794-5188

### PAARL

**BOSCHENDAL ESTATE**
Groot Drakenstein 7680
011-27-21-114-1031

**NEDERBURG WINES**
P. O. Box 46, Huguenot 7645
011-27-22-116-2310

### STELLENBOSCH

**THE BERGKELDER**
P. O. Box 5001,
Stellenbosch 7600
011-27-21-887-2440

**KANONKOP ESTATE**
P. O. Box 19,
Muldersvlei 7606
011-27-22-319-4656

**NEETHLINGSHOF ESTATE**
P. O. Box 104, Stellenbosch 7599
011-27-21-883-8988
The Lord Neethling Restaurant, on-site, is charming in an Old World fashion.

**SAXENBURG**
P. O. Box 171, Kuils River 7580
011-27-21-903-6113
The winery's restaurant, called The Guinea Fowl, is one of the best and most creative in South Africa.

# THE SOUTH AFRICAN WINES TO KNOW

South African winemaking is changing rapidly. Besides the specific wines here and wines from the producers listed on page 827, look for wines from the following estates: Buiten-verwachting, Glen Carlou, Klein Constantia, Lievland, Meerlust, Mulderbosch, Rustenberg, and Rust en Vrede. For each wine below the specific region from which it comes is noted.

## *Whites*

### BOSCHENDAL
Sauvignon Blanc

Paarl

approximately 90% sauvignon blanc, 10% sémillon

Boschendal made a name for itself with its modern, quite correct

chardonnay. But it's the estate's take-no-prisoners, wild-as-Tarzan sauvignon blanc that can really capture a wine lover's heart. Smoke, gunflint, and hay come shooting out of this sauvignon like a cannonball. The vineyards are more than 1,200 feet above sea level.

### L'ORMARINS
Chardonnay

Franschhoek Valley

100% chardonnay

Chardonnay is hugely popular in South Africa, but most examples are so heavily oaked they end up tasting more like toast dusted with vanilla and sugar than wine. At its best, L'Ormarins is a stunning exception. Here's a fresh, snappy chardonnay with grip, focus, and jazzy nuances of lime, peach, and smoke.

### SAXENBURG
Sauvignon Blanc

Stellenbosch

100% sauvignon blanc

Tasting like a lime-coated chunk of flint, Saxenburg's outrageously expressive and extremely smoky, crisp sauvignon blanc is a dead ringer for a great Sancerre. The grapes are picked only in the cool early morning hours, as you can tell by the wine's vibrant zestiness.

831

## *Reds*

*As in Australia, the French grape syrah is called shiraz in South Africa.*

### CHATEAU LIBERTAS
Stellenbosch

approximately 60% cabernet sauvignon, 20% cinsaut, with the remainder shiraz and merlot

Libertas, one of South Africa's most famous red blends, has comprised, at

different times, a combination of just about every good red grape grown in the country. The aromas and flavors are classic South African: smoky, dusty, bacony, tarry, and plummy. In great years there's also an intriguing suggestion of peaches on the end. The wine is very light bodied and almost silky in texture.

## KANONKOP

Pinotage

Stellenbosch

100% pinotage

Pinotage wants to be a heavy-metal gulper red—in a word: *coarse*. But every now and then it turns out like this Kanonkop—zesty, classy, vibrant, and intriguing. The wine gushes with smoky, roasted coffee flavors, and at the same time, it's packed with sweet cherries and pierced with a lemony zing. The name Kanonkop refers to the series of cannons poised on the hills above Cape Town, which were once used to signal inland farmers that ships had arrived in the port. It's a good name for an estate that makes wines with explosive fruit.

## NEDERBURG

Cabernet Sauvignon

Paarl

100% cabernet sauvignon

Nederburg is both a winery (where Bordeaux winemaker Paul Pontallier of Château Margaux is a consultant) and the organization that runs the prestigious Nederburg Auction (see page 828). Nederburg cabernets are (not surprisingly) among the most sought after wines at the Nederburg wine auction. Older vintages often take on a deep, smoky, chocolate-mocha flavor, while young vintages can be sharp, with piney, cassis flavors. Invariably, these are cabernets with lots of personality.

# *Sweet Wines*

## NEDERBURG

Special Late Harvest

Paarl

100% riesling

Of all of the Nederburg wines, this one—called simply Special Late Harvest—is especially appealing, with its texture and flavor reminiscent of melted peach-apricot ice cream. Like the Neethlingshof that follows, the Nederburg late harvest wine is made from botrytis-affected grapes. It's undoubtedly most often drunk as a dessert wine, but the actual sweetness level is so modest (only about 3 percent residual sugar) and the fruit is so expressive, the wine could easily be drunk on a picnic with a bowl of peaches.

## NEETHLINGSHOF

Weisser Riesling

Noble Late Harvest

Stellenbosch

100% riesling

Sweet late harvest wines are a Cape specialty, and this is one of the best. Like the great Sauternes, Neethlingshof's weisser riesling (a South African name for riesling) is infected with the noble rot botrytis. The wine just seethes with the flavors of ripe apricots and wild honey. This is a wine to curl up on the couch with.

# Chile

Chile exists in near perfect seclusion. On the west is the Pacific Ocean; on the east, the massive Andes Mountains; to the north, the Atacama Desert; and to the south about 400 miles across the water, frozen masses of Antarctic ice. The country, squeezed in between these barriers, is roughly 2,700 miles long but at its narrowest point only 96 miles wide. Within these formidable natural boundaries exists an almost Eden-like environment for grapes and other fruits. The warm, dry, brightly sunny days recall the Mediterranean. Snow melting on the Andes creates roaring rivers for irrigation. And thanks to the country's physical isolation, there are very few vine diseases and pests, obviating the need for almost all sprays and chemical treatments. In short, grape-growing conditions are so ideal, the cost of vineyard land and labor is so reasonable, and good wines are, relatively speaking, so easy to make that Chile has become one of the world's leading producers of wines with an extremely high ratio of value to price. This remains true even as prices for Chilean wines continue to increase and even though many Chilean

**834**

Chile ranks ninth in wine-producing countries world-wide. Chileans drink an average of 4.29 gallons of wine per person each year; they're twenty-first in world wine consumption.

*Chile's sunny vineyards are enviably free from major pests and diseases. The harvest begins at the end of February and often continues through the end of April.*

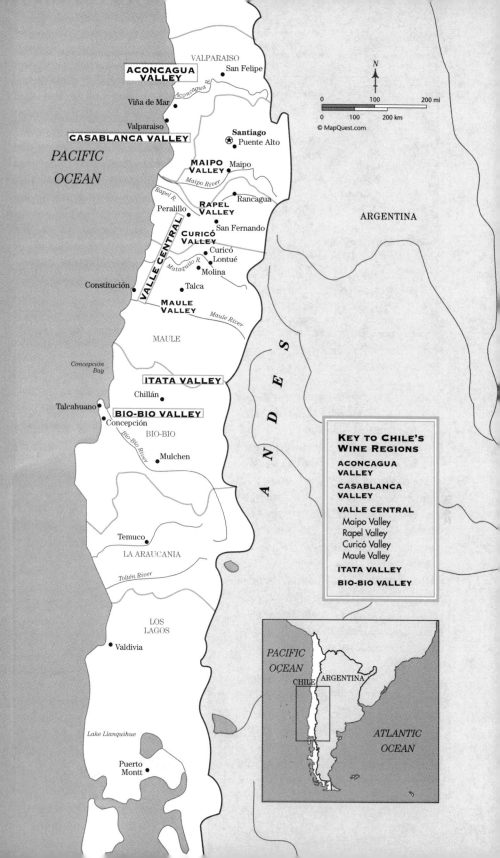

VALPARAISO

**ACONCAGUA VALLEY**

San Felipe

*Aconcagua R.*

Viña de Mar

Valparaiso

**CASABLANCA VALLEY**

*PACIFIC OCEAN*

**Santiago**
Puente Alto

**MAIPO VALLEY**
Maipo

*Maipo River*

*Rapel R.*

Rancagua

Peralillo

**RAPEL VALLEY**

San Fernando

**CURICÓ VALLEY**

Curicó
Lontué

*Mataquito R.*

Molina

Constitución

Talca

**VALLE CENTRAL**

**MAULE VALLEY**

*Maule River*

MAULE

*Concepción Bay*

**ITATA VALLEY**

Chillán

Talcahuano

**BIO-BIO VALLEY**

Concepción

BIO-BIO

*Bio-Bio River*

Mulchen

Temuco

LA ARAUCANIA

*Toltén River*

LOS LAGOS

Valdivia

*Lake Llanquihue*

Puerto Montt

ARGENTINA

A N D E S

N

| 0 | 100 | 200 mi |
| 0 | 100 | 200 km |

© MapQuest.com

**KEY TO CHILE'S WINE REGIONS**

**ACONCAGUA VALLEY**

**CASABLANCA VALLEY**

**VALLE CENTRAL**
Maipo Valley
Rapel Valley
Curicó Valley
Maule Valley

**ITATA VALLEY**

**BIO-BIO VALLEY**

*PACIFIC OCEAN*

CHILE

ARGENTINA

*ATLANTIC OCEAN*

## THE QUICK SIP ON CHILE

- Chile makes the most consistently good wines from the South American continent. In particular, Chilean cabernet sauvignons stand out for their quality.

- The large part of the best Chilean wine is sold outside of Chile—especially in the United States, Chile's leading export market.

- Though Chile built its wine reputation on good values, the number of bargains has begun to decrease while the number of moderate and expensive wines continues to rise.

wines are no longer the great bargains they were in the 1980s and most of the 1990s.

The first European vines (*Vitis vinifera*) in Chile were Spanish varieties planted in the mid-sixteenth century by conquistadores and missionaries who brought them from Peru, probably via Mexico. Grapevines had been brought to Mexico originally by Hernán Cortés around 1520. Among the varieties Cortés introduced was the one referred to simply as the common black grape, thought to be the Spanish parent of the first European grape varieties to become prevalent in the Americas—the pais grape in Chile, the criolla grape in Argentina, and the (now no longer abundant) mission grape in California.

Despite Spain's historic and political hegemony in Chile, France, not Spain, has had the greatest influence on the country's wines. In the mid-nineteenth century, rich Chilean landowners and mining barons showcased their wealth by building wine estates modeled after Bordeaux châteaux. They planted vineyards with imported

French grapes, most notably cabernet sauvignon. And whenever possible they hired French winemakers, who, by the latter part of the century, were easy to lure from their homeland, thanks to a twist of fate. The deadly aphid phylloxera had just begun its sweep through France. As vineyard after vineyard was destroyed, unemployed winemakers looked to other wine regions, including the wine frontiers of the New World. (Though phylloxera ultimately ravaged vineyards in virtually every wine-producing country, Chile and Argentina have never been affected.)

For much of the twentieth century, Chilean wine was unexceptional and serviceable, rarely more. The combined impact of political instability, bureaucratic red tape, high taxes, and a local market that seemed perfectly satisfied with cheap, ordinary wine, effectively handcuffed Chilean winemakers and limited the scope of their ambitions. Then in the

## THE CURIOUS ABSENCE OF PHYLLOXERA

As of the late 1990s, Chilean vineyards had never been victims of the lethal aphid phylloxera, which devastated most of the world's vineyards in the mid- and late nineteenth century. Although Chile's physical isolation, dry soil, and use of flood irrigation may have all helped to protect the country, phylloxera's absence is not fully understood. Some scientists speculate that it's only a matter of time before the pest finds a route in, despite the Chilean government's strict quarantine requirements for plant materials.

## THE ANDES

━━━━━━ ◈◈◈ ━━━━━━

Rising up behind many of Chile's vineyards are the majestic Andes, the longest mountain chain in the world. The Andean peaks reach 22,000 feet and are exceeded in elevation only by the Himalayas. When the mountain chain was formed, sedimentary rocks were folded and bent into ridges, creating many of the sheltered valleys in which Chile's vineyards lie.

late 1980s, vast changes in the country's political, economic, and social climate led to considerable domestic and foreign investment in the wine industry. In less than a decade Chile went from being a Third World wine producer to being dubbed the Bordeaux of South America. Among the first leading European wine families to invest were the Torres from Spain and the Rothschilds from Château Lafite-Rothschild in Bordeaux. Within a few years, Paul Pontallier, director of Bordeaux's Château Margaux, and Bruno Prats, the former owner of Château Cos d'Estournel, founded a Chilean winery called Domaine Paul Bruno. And from the United States, Agustin Huneeus, former president of Franciscan Estates, bought and developed some of the first vineyards in Casablanca, now considered Chile's top white wine region. Simultaneously, Chile's historic grand wine firms, such as Cousiño-Macul, Concha y Toro, Canepa, Viña Errázuriz, Santa Rita, Undurraga, and Santa Carolina, spent millions modernizing their wineries and buying state-of-the-art equipment and new French and American oak barrels. At the same time, a new type of winery was emerging in Chile—the small wine estate owned by a grower who, instead of selling his grapes, decided to market his own brand.

**837**

*The Andes loom above every vineyard, as the grapes flourish in the bright sun.*

Remarkably, the success of Chile's wine revolution hinged on a bet that the United States would become the major market for the new, better-quality Chilean wines that nonetheless remained bargains when compared to many California and European wines. To help ensure this would be the case, Chilean producers focused their exports on wines already extremely popular in the United States, especially chardonnay, sauvignon blanc, merlot, and cabernet sauvignon. As it turned out, the United States has not only become the leading export market for Chilean wine, but many of the more expensive, premium wines are sold almost exclusively there or in Great Britain. A case in point is Seña, an expensive blend of cabernet sauvignon, merlot, and carmenère produced by Caliterra, a joint venture between California's Robert Mondavi Winery and Viña Errázuriz. When the 1995 vintage was first released in 1998, it cost $55 a bottle, about seven times the cost of most other Chilean wines being sold in the United States at the time (admittedly, it

was a more sophisticated and better structured wine). Not surprisingly, Seña was created for the affluent American market, and most of the production continues to be sold there. Seña is not alone. In 1999 the 1996 vintage of Almaviva, a joint venture between Château Mouton-Rothschild and Concha y Toro, debuted at $70 a bottle. There are now several more noteworthy Chilean cabernet sauvignons and cabernet blends that are expensive by any country's standards. Luckily, however, Chile's good-value wines show no sign of disappearing, even if they no longer carry the rock-bottom prices they once did. Indeed, thanks to the continuing quality and value of Chilean wines, they now rank a remarkable third in volume among all imports into the United States, behind Italian and French wines.

## CHILE'S WINE LAWS

Like the United States, Chile does not have a strict system of laws that regulate grape growing and winemaking—

*Not far from the Maipo Valley, the lookout on top of Santa Lucía was established in 1541.*

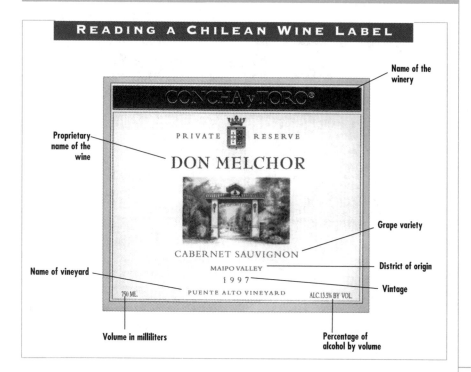

## READING A CHILEAN WINE LABEL

Name of the winery

Proprietary name of the wine

PRIVATE RESERVE

DON MELCHOR

CABERNET SAUVIGNON

MAIPO VALLEY

Grape variety

District of origin

Name of vineyard

1 9 9 7

750 ML

PUENTE ALTO VINEYARD

ALC 13.5% BY VOL

Vintage

Volume in milliliters

Percentage of alcohol by volume

839

nothing comparable to the French *Appellation d'Origine Contrôlée* laws, which govern not only what grapes can be planted in specific areas but also details of harvesting and vinification. In 1995, for the first time, however, new laws went into effect governing viticultural regions and labeling. These were established jointly by the Servicio Agricola Ganadero, the Ministerio de Agricultura, and the wineries themselves. The laws define appellations and subregions and zones within those regions.

The 1995 laws also mandate that:

If a wine is labeled with a viticultural region, at least 75 percent of the wine must come from that region.

If a grape variety is named on the label, the wine must be composed of at least 75 percent of the grape named.

In wines with labels specifying a vintage, at least 75 percent of the wine must come from that vintage.

## THE LAND, THE GRAPES, AND THE VINEYARDS

If you flipped Chile over into the Northern Hemisphere, the best vineyards would fall roughly at the latitude of North Africa or southern Spain. Thanks to the moderating effect of the Pacific Ocean and the Andes Mountains, however, temperatures in Chile's wine country rarely rise above 90°F and summertime nights are cool.

The vineyards are located in numerous valleys. The most important of these are the Aconcagua and Casablanca valleys in the northern part of the country and the Maipo, Rapel, Curicó, and Maule valleys, all in the center. These central valleys, collectively known as the Valle Central, are separated by rivers that begin high in the Andes and flow to the Pacific Ocean. Of much lesser importance are Bío-Bío and Itata,

## THE GRAPES OF CHILE

### WHITES

**Chardonnay:** An important grape. Plantings have increased, mostly to slake the thirst in the United States for inexpensive chardonnay.

**Sauvignon Blanc:** Makes light, fresh, and agreeable wines. Some wines bottled under this name are actually made from sauvignon vert, a less prestigious grape.

**Sauvignon Vert:** Also known as sauvignonasse. Makes a decent but unexceptional wine with floral notes. Some Chilean wines labeled sauvignon blanc may in fact be sauvignon vert.

### REDS

**Cabernet Sauvignon:** Chile's star grape. Makes a full range of styles, from quaffing wines to fine wines.

**Carmenère:** A variety brought to Chile in the late nineteenth century from Bordeaux where it is no longer prominent. The source of good, medium-bodied reds. Some Chilean wines labeled merlot may in fact be carmenère.

**Merlot:** An important grape. Makes good to very good wines. However, many wines labeled merlot may actually be carmenère.

**Pais:** Major grape. Chile's first grape (brought by Spanish conquistadores) and still the most widely planted. Turned into rustic jug wines.

two valleys in the cooler, wetter, swampy southern part of the country where historically, simple jug wines based primarily on pais have been made.

Of all of the central valleys, the Maipo, known primarily for cabernet sauvignon, is the most famous. Edged up against the city limits of Santiago, the Maipo Valley is one of Chile's oldest wine regions and, because of its proximity to the capital, many wineries are headquartered there.

The Maipo Valley, along with the other three central valleys, is directly across the Andes from Argentina's most famous wine region, Mendoza. Unlike the arid, extremely high-altitude vineyards of Mendoza, however, the vineyards in Chile's central valleys are low in altitude and relatively close to the sea. Although these valleys do experience cooling effects from the Pacific Ocean, they are largely protected from extreme maritime weather by a low-lying range of mountains just inland from the coast.

If the Maipo Valley is Chile's most prestigious wine region and one of the most historic, the Casablanca Valley is the most avant-garde and one of the newest. The closest to the ocean of any of Chile's wine-growing valleys, Casablanca has, in the view of many winemakers, the potential to be the source of some of Chile's greatest wines. In the 1990s the valley became the site of the wine equivalent of a gold rush as virtually every top winery in Chile swooped in, bought land, and began planting chardonnay and sauvignon blanc.

North of the Casablanca Valley, the Aconcagua Valley is the hottest of all of Chile's winegrowing regions, with temperatures warm enough to dictate that such heat-loving red grape varieties as cabernet sauvignon and merlot be grown.

Although vineyards could be planted on the hillsides flanking Chile's winegrowing valleys (an advantageous scenario for the production of fine wine), in reality, most Chilean vineyards are planted on the flat valley floors in fairly fertile soil, which along with steady water and sun, makes life easy for the vines. In the Aconcagua and Maipo regions, the soil is often partially alluvial, the product of ancient river beds. Farther south, the soil contains more loam and clay.

As in Argentina, one of Chile's leading viticultural assets—the easy availability of water—is also the country's downfall as far as the quality of the wine is concerned. Snow melting on the Andes provides a steady supply of water that is channeled to the vineyards through a system of dikes and canals. Growers who want huge crops have no problem achieving them by literally flooding the vineyards. When the yield is high enough, the outcome is thin, bland wine. Only since the early 1990s have some of the top growers replaced flood irrigation with more controlled and expensive drip irrigation in their best vineyards.

More than twenty varieties of wine grapes are grown in Chile. The most widely planted, pais (about 20 percent of all vines), is the source of very basic, largely forget-table red wines. There are also limited plantings of everything from riesling and pinot noir to zinfandel and barbera. But most fine wines are based on just four major grapes: cabernet sauvignon, chardonnay, merlot, and sauvignon blanc. That said, the story behind Chilean merlot and sauvignon blanc is, as we'll see, a bit more complicated.

Of all the grapes grown in Chile, cabernet sauvignon is by every account the star. Moderately priced Chilean cabernets are usually very easy to drink, with soft, minty, black-currant and olive flavors and a ribbon of smoke floating through them. The newer high-priced cabernets are polished wines with much more concentrated and complex flavors and firmer structures.

Most Chilean chardonnay is generally good and straightforward but, with few exceptions, it's not the sort of wine that makes you sit up and take notice. In the 1990s chardonnay was extensively planted in

841

*The aging cellars of the Santa Carolina winery and (inset) some of the winery's workers.*

## CHILEAN WINES

**Cabernet Sauvignon** *red*
**Chardonnay** *white*
**Merlot** *red*
**Sauvignon Blanc** *white*

response to the seemingly bottomless demand for inexpensive ones in the United States. Today, many of these wines are simple, light, clean, and tasty. Good examples include the chardonnays from Calina, Caliterra, Viña Errázuriz, J. & F. Lurton, Santa Rita, Veramonte, and Viña Santa Carolina. Among richer, more concentrated, and pricier chardonnays, Casa Lapostolle and Montes make two of the best.

Chilean sauvignon blanc is fairly understated, with none of the dramatic, penetrating green flavors of the sauvignon blancs from New Zealand or France's Loire Valley. And in any case, what is called sauvignon blanc in Chile is only sometimes true sauvignon blanc. Often the wine is actually made from sauvignon vert, also called sauvignonasse (there's no way to tell this from the label). Sauvignon vert, slightly floral and, if picked late, high in alcohol, lacks sauvignon blanc's jazzy herbal tones.

As for merlot, Chile's examples keep getting better and some, such as those from Viña Tarapaca and Cousiño-Macul, are concentrated, compelling wines with good power behind their flavors. As with sauvignon blanc, however, what is called

*The nineteenth-century Don Melchor estate of Concha y Toro is the crown jewel of the winery's holdings. The winery estate is named for Don Melchor de Concha y Toro, the winery's founder.*

## THE SPIRIT OF THE DESERT

—∽∿∾—

hile's famous and traditional distilled spirit, Pisco, is made from grapes that by law can only be grown in the desertlike, high-altitude regions of Atacama and Coquimbo in the northern part of the country. In some parts of the Atacama no measurable rainfall has ever been recorded.

Pisco can be made from any one or a combination of muscat, torontel, and Pedro Giménez grapes, which can grow only because snowmelt from the Andes creates small rivers that can be tapped for irrigation. The wine is aged for a few months in wood and then distilled with mountain water. Although in Chile Pisco is often drunk straight, in the United States it is most often consumed in mixed drinks, including Pisco sours, Pisco margaritas, and Chilean manhattans. To make a manhattan, mix two parts Pisco with one-half part sweet vermouth.

merlot may not be true merlot. Many such wines are actually made from carmenère, a Bordeaux variety brought to Chile in the late nineteenth century and now virtually extinct in Bordeaux itself. Again, there is no way to determine if a Chilean wine labeled merlot is in fact merlot or carmenère, and in many cases, even wineries are unsure of what is actually planted in their vineyards. As more Chilean vines are correctly identified based on their DNA, however, more producers may choose to label their wines accordingly and in fact, a few already have.

## QUALITY AND COST

Many Chilean wineries make four or more different versions of the same wine, each costing somewhat more as the level of quality rises (at least this is the theory). There are no official regulations for these tiers. Consumers simply guess at what they're buying based on the price and the sophistication (or lack thereof) of the packaging. Terms such as *reserve* have no legal definition, although they're generally used on the labels of more expensive wines.

While it's certainly possible to prefer a winery's simplest, least expensive wine, the most expensive wines, often still good values, usually come from the best, low-yielding vineyards and are aged in French and/or American oak barrels.

### GOOD-VALUE CHILEAN MERLOTS

ompared to most French and American merlots, those from Chile are a good deal and some remain a downright steal. Among the best producers of good-value merlot:

| | |
|---|---|
| Canepa | Cousiño-Macul |
| Carmen | La Playa |
| Carta Vieja | Montes |
| Casa Lapostolle | Santa Rita |
| Chateau La Joya | Viña Tarapaca |
| Concha y Toro | |

# VISITING CHILEAN WINERIES

A number of Chile's top wineries, including the palatial Cousiño-Macul, are in the Maipo Valley, just minutes from the capital, Santiago. Other wineries well worth visiting are within a few hours' drive south from Santiago in the Rapel region or north of the city in Casablanca. It is best to make an appointment in advance. While some English is spoken, it's helpful if you can speak Spanish. The telephone numbers include the dialing code you'll need when calling from the United States. If you're calling from within Chile, eliminate the 011-56. Don't worry that some of the phone numbers are longer than others. Chilean telephone numbers are not standardized the way they are in the States.

**CANEPA WINERY**
1500 Camino Lo Sierra
Santiago
011-56-2-557-9121

**CASA LAPOSTOLLE**
Kilometer 36
Camino San Fernando-Pichilemu
Cunaco
011-56-72-858-281

*Arturo Cousiño (above left), managing director of Cousiño-Macul, is of the sixth generation to run the historic estate that dates from the sixteenth century. Beside him is winemaker Jaime Rios; below, the winery's impressive and extensive aging cellars.*

**VIÑA COUSIÑO-MACUL**
7-100 Av Quilin
Penalolen, Santiago
011-56-2-284-1011

**VIÑA SANTA CAROLINA**
1431 Rodrigo de Araya
Santiago
011-56-2-238-2855

**VIÑA SANTA RITA**
60 Hendaya
Las Condes, Santiago
011-56-2-331-5222

*Alexandra Marnier-Lapostolle of France and her Chilean partner, José Rabat Gorchs, heads of Casa Lapostolle, one of Chile's newer premium wineries.*

# THE CHILEAN WINES TO KNOW

*For each wine below, the specific region from which it comes is noted.*

## Whites

### CASA LAPOSTOLLE
Chardonnay
Colchagua
100% chardonnay

At its best, Casa Lapostolle's chardonnay is a big, rich powerhouse of ripe tropical fruit overlaid with notes of honey and butter plus plenty of toasty oak.

Compared to most other Chilean chardonnays, this one has real force and personality. The French Marnier-Lapostolle family, makers of Grand Marnier, built a winery in the Colchagua district of Chile's Rapel region in 1994 and hired the renowned French consulting enologist Michel Roland to supervise the winemaking.

### SANTA CAROLINA
Chardonnay
*gran reserva*
Maipo Valley
100% chardonnay

A good, bold, juicy chardonnay with refreshing lime and lively tropical fruit flavors, plus a nice creamy texture. Effortless to drink. The grapes for this wine come from eighty-year-old vines planted in the Maipo Valley on the foothills of the Andes. Santa Carolina's beautiful cellars, within the city limits of Santiago, date from 1875 and are a national monument.

### SANTA RITA
Sauvignon Blanc
*reserva*
Maule Valley
100% sauvignon blanc

The best Chilean sauvignon blancs—and this is usually one of them—have a style that is totally unlike sauvignon blancs from California, France, or New Zealand. Sweet herbs and wildflowers dance in the glass, and though the flavors are fresh and bright, the texture is soft. Santa Rita is one of the most dependable Chilean wineries for good-value wines with considerable flavor.

845

## Reds

### CALITERRA
Cabernet Sauvignon
Maipo Valley
100% cabernet sauvignon

Here's an inexpensive cabernet sauvignon that is generally loaded with personality. Dynamic earthy mushroom and truffle flavors are underscored by notes of chalk and menthol. The bright fruit soars out of the glass.

### CASA LAPOSTOLLE
Merlot
Cuvée Alexandre
Rapel Valley
approximately 90% merlot, 10% malbec

Lively, focused, and concentrated, top vintages of Casa Lapostolle's merlot are pretty unbeatable for balance and power. The rush of ripe, bright blackberry and boysenberry flavors is irresistible and the texture is soft and inviting.

## CONCHA Y TORO

Cabernet Sauvignon

Don Melchor

Maipo Valley

100% cabernet sauvignon

Concha y Toro, one of the largest wineries in Chile, makes oceans of good basic wine. But it's the winery's top wine—Don Melchor— that's exciting. One of the first premium cabernet sauvignons made in the country, Don Melchor is, when at its best, a masculine, smoky, meaty cabernet with lots of Old World soft, earthy flavors. The wine is named after Don Melchor de Concha y Toro, who founded the wine estate in 1883.

## COUSINO-MACUL

Cabernet Sauvignon

Antiguas Reservas

Maipo Valley

100% cabernet sauvignon

One of Chile's historic grand estates, Cousiño-Macul makes Old World-style cabernet sauvignons that recall a different era. In top vintages, the estate's Antiguas Reservas can be an expansive earthy wine with aromas that hint of saddle leather, minerals, mint, and spice. Cousiño-Macul, which was founded in 1870, owns some of the most beautiful and prized vineyard land in Chile—more than 700 acres that are now encircled by the city of Santiago, which has grown and expanded around them.

## MONT GRAS

Merlot

reserva

Colchagua

100% merlot

This big, juicy, satisfying merlot is one of Chile's incredible buys. You can expect the best vintages of the Mont Gras to have the density and concentration of a wine twice its price, plus attractive, spicy, cherry and vanilla flavors and a solidly long finish.

## DOMUS AUREA

Cabernet Sauvignon

Clos Quebrada de Macul

Maipo Valley

100% cabernet sauvignon

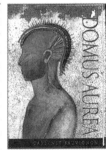

Ignacio Recabarren, one of Chile's top winemakers, is at the helm of this relatively new winery, which produced its first cabernet sauvignon in 1996. Powerful, fleshy, and packed with thick blackberry, black cherry, and cedar flavors, Domus Aurea is a delicious example of the more concentrated, sophisticated, and expensive cabernets now coming out of Chile.

Argentina

Of all the wine-producing countries of South America, Argentina seems the most perplexing. How does a country manage to be the fifth-largest wine producer in the world and at the same time make wines that very few people, other than the Argentinians themselves, have ever tasted? The immediate answer is that until recently the country consumed almost all the wine it produced. Just a few decades ago the annual wine consumption per person was 26 gallons—a figure well befitting the country's reputation for knowing how to live the good life. (To put this in some perspective, annual wine consumption in the United States has ranged between a little more than 1 gallon and a little more than 2 gallons per person for several decades.)

Argentina's healthy thirst was just one factor behind the anonymity of its wines. Another and perhaps more significant reason had to do with quality. For most of its history, Argentina produced rough and tumble wines. They were simple, even mundane, but they were also incredibly cheap. And Argentinians seemed to like them that way. The story might have ended there, but

Argentina ranks fifth in wine-producing countries worldwide. Argentinians drink an average of 10.4 gallons of wine per person each year; they're eighth in world wine consumption.

*Soaring 22,000 feet above sea level, the snowcapped Andes form a stunning backdrop for Argentina's vineyards.*

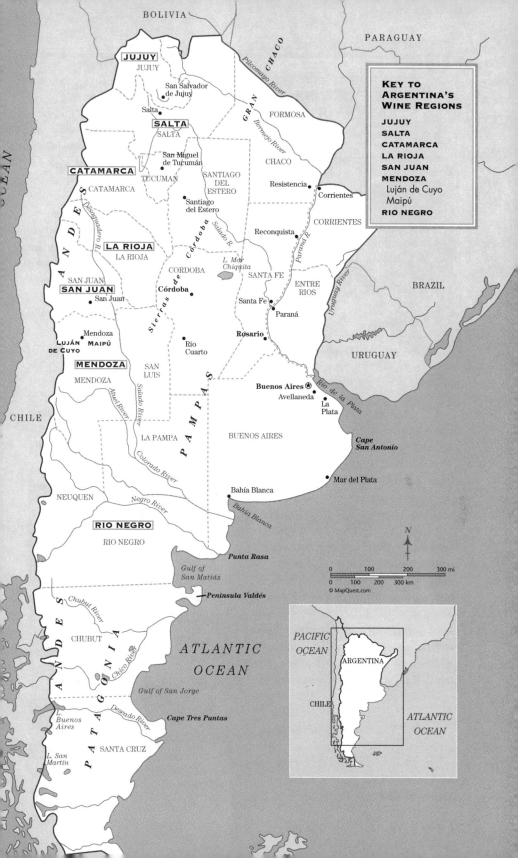

◦⊗◦

• Argentina's considerable wine production (it's fifth in the world) has in the past centered almost exclusively on fairly neutral, inexpensive table wines that were blends of many different grapes. Only since the mid-1990s has Argentina begun to develop a fine-wine industry.

• Argentina's most interesting wine is malbec, a red wine that is far more delicious when made in Argentina than in its native Bordeaux.

• Such international varieties as chardonnay and cabernet sauvignon represent the most rapidly growing segment of the Argentinian wine industry and are intended almost exclusively for export.

late in the twentieth century, fate, politics, and changing societal mores intervened. As it did virtually everywhere else in the world, wine consumption in Argentina began to drop. By 1997 Argentinians were drinking dramatically less wine than they once did—a comparatively modest 10.4 gallons per person per year. At the same time, Argentina found itself at the end of nearly a century's worth of political instability and economic depression, during which time inflation often soared over 1,000 percent and the country wobbled under a series of power-hungry military governments. By the 1990s, despite the fact that Argentina was economically and politically stable for the first time in decades, leading wineries, like many Argentinian businesses, found themselves in dire need of capital and new markets.

In Chile, its neighbor across the Andes, Argentina found the blueprint for a solution. Chile had virtually reinvented

its wine industry by improving the quality of its wines, recrafting some of them to fit international tastes, pricing those wines higher, and then exporting them, especially to the United States and Great Britain. Argentina's most progressive wineries decided to do the same. Since then, the changes within the Argentinian wine industry have been slow but steady. Large foreign wine companies, mostly from France and the United States, are beginning to invest in Argentina. French and American consultants are being hired to help modernize Argentinian wines. New-oak barrels and temperature-controlled stainless steel tanks (the indispensable tools of modern winemaking) are being purchased. Thus, while many Argentinian wines remain utterly basic and rustic, or even tired and dried out as a result of poor winemaking and inferior equipment, the emergence of a group of modern, higher quality, higher

*Tens of thousands of bottles of malbec rest in the caves of Trapiche, a huge winery owned by Argentina's wine giant, Peñaflor.*

*Harvesting in Argentina has been done in essentially the same way for centuries, although trucks rather than horses now haul the grapes to the winery.*

priced wines represents a whole new world of possibility. Of course, the success of these modern wines means that even more of them are being made. And exported—in 1994, Argentina exported 389,000 gallons of wine to the United States. Just four years later that figure was 3.3 million gallons. (This is still considerably behind Chile, which in the same year exported 12.6 million gallons to the United States.) As is true in Chile, many of these modern wines are aimed almost entirely at affluent export markets, principally the United States. The most striking example of one of these wines is Iscay, a malbec-merlot blend made by Bodegas Trapiche with the help of renowned Bordeaux consultant Michel Rolland. In 1999 the first Iscay was released at a price of $50 a bottle, even though most other Trapiche wines sold at the time for less than $10 a bottle. Argentina has often been called the wine

world's sleeping giant. It appears the sleeping giant has woken up.

At more than a million square miles, Argentina is the second-largest country in South America, after Brazil. From the Tropic of Capricorn in the north, the country extends southward to the tip of the continent, just 600 miles from Antarctica. Argentina's western border with Chile lies along the crest of the Andes. From these majestic peaks, the highest in the Americas, the country slopes downward until it meets the Atlantic Ocean in the east.

Winemaking began here, as it did in Chile, in the latter part of the sixteenth century with Spanish missionaries and conquistadores who brought vines with them from Spain. While some of these vines came directly from the Old World, others were brought to Argentina on expeditions from Peru and Chile, which in turn received some of their grapevines via Mexico. Numerous types of vines were

*The stately facade of Bodega y Cavas de Weinert, considered by many people to be Argentina's best winery.*

imported, but ironically the one that would have lasting importance was the one referred to by the Spanish fathers as simply the common black grape. From the common black grape evolved three closely related grape varieties, all of which made relatively crude wine: Argentina's criolla, Chile's pais, and California's mission. While criolla and pais went on to form the foundation of South American wine production for the next 300 years, mission was a leading red grape in California only until phylloxera arrived in the 1890s, after which most mission grapes were never replanted.

Though the early Spanish settlers planted vines on the Argentinian coast as well as inland, it soon became apparent that the sunny, dry foothills of the Andes were an ideal location. Employing a system of dams and canals begun hundreds of years before by the Incas and other native Indians, the early missionaries learned to use snowmelt from the mountains to irrigate what otherwise would have been a virtual desert. With a constant supply of water, vineyards flourished.

In the 1820s, with the ending of Spanish colonial rule, waves of European immigrants—mostly from Italy, France, and Spain—came to Argentina bringing vines with them. They were followed in the 1890s by a second wave of French, Italians, and Spaniards, many of whom were from wine-producing regions and were escaping the phylloxera epidemic, which had ravaged the vineyards of the Old World. For all of these immigrants, wine was an integral part of daily life. In Argentina, they found a place where wine could play a similar role. In 1885 the first railway linking Argentina's premier wine region, Mendoza, with Buenos Aires was finished, opening access to a huge new market of wine drinkers. By 1900 Argentina had the beginnings of a massive wine industry.

There are now some 1,500 wineries, including hundreds of small producers that sell only bulk wine for blending. Despite this number, the industry is dominated by two large companies: Peñaflor and Bodegas Esmeralda. With a production of 13 million cases annually, Peñaflor is one of the largest wine companies in the world. More than 40 percent of all basic Argentinian table wine, most of it sold in cartons, not bottles, is made by the company under several different brand names. Peñaflor also owns the higher-quality brand Bodegas Trapiche, known in the United States mostly for good-value wines. Bodegas Esmeralda, more focused on premium wine, is the parent company of Catena, widely considered one of the most progres-

*The large wooden casks, like this one, at Valentin Bianchi are carved with the words El Vino es Vida—Wine Is Life.*

sive wineries in the country, and its modern-style wines are consistently some of Argentina's best. But when it comes to producing truly extraordinary wines, one bodega above all stands out—Bodegas y Cavas de Weinert. No other bodega comes close to consistently producing wines of such nuance, complexity, and richness. When aged, these cedary, leathery, utterly supple wines are easily mistaken for older vintages of top Bordeaux. Weinert's best wine, Cavas de Weinert, a blend of cabernet sauvignon, malbec, and merlot, can be nothing short of stunning.

In addition to modernizing winemaking techniques and viticultural practices, the top wineries in Argentina are also beginning to focus more heavily on certain grape varieties. Though criolla and cereza are still the grapes that lead in acreage, their popularity is declining, and Argentinian wineries are moving steadily into the world of international varieties, including chardonnay, cabernet sauvignon, and merlot. Each of these grapes can produce good, and sometimes very good, wine in Argentina, but the country's real star is malbec, a variety that, in its home Bordeaux, ranks well below cabernet sauvignon and merlot in quality. In Argentina, however, malbec can broach magic.

## ARGENTINA'S WINE LAWS

Although wine exports and grape production in general are monitored by its Instituto Nacionale de Vitivinicultura, Argentina, like the United States, does not have a strict system of laws regulating grape growing and winemaking. There are no rules similar to the French *Appellation d'Origine Contrôlée* laws, governing what grapes may be planted in which regions with details for their cultivation and how wine should be made from them. There have, however, been a few industry-sponsored attempts to define specific viticultural regions and these attempts will probably continue. As for labeling regulations, if a grape variety is named on the label, 80 percent of the wine must be composed of that grape.

# THE LAND, THE GRAPES, AND THE VINEYARDS

Argentina's wine regions are in the west central part of the country, scattered across the foothills of the Andes at elevations ranging up to 4,900 feet above sea level, making these some of the highest-altitude wine regions in the world. (Chile's major wine regions are directly across the Andes; close to the Pacific Coast, they are therefore considerably lower in elevation.) With the exception of Río Negro in southern Patagonia, Argentina's wine regions all have a semidesert-like climate, with copious amounts of intense sunlight—some 320 days per year on average—and rainfall that rarely exceeds 8 to 10 inches per year. The bone-dry air means that Argentinian vineyards are mostly free of fungal diseases, virtually eliminating the need to spray preventive chemicals. The flip side, of course, is that Argentinian vineyards rely heavily on irrigation, a fact that has been both a blessing and a curse.

Irrigation can be a blessing because, unlike rainfall, the amount of water the vines receive can be limited and timed so that the vines only get water during certain critical phases in their growth cycles. But in Argentina, as in Chile, irrigation has mostly been used in a different way, to lit-erally flood the vineyards, thereby supplying the vines with so much water that huge yields can be achieved. In the 1970s, when Argentinian consumption was still high and dirt cheap wine still reigned, there were reports of yields surpassing 22 tons per acre, an astounding amount that surely strained the realm of possibility for grapevines. (Yields in top wine-producing regions, such as Bordeaux or the Napa Valley, have historically been the equivalent of 2 to 5 tons per acre.) No wonder the wines were thin, bland, and rustic. Many Argentinian wines are still the product of high yields, but all of the wineries making the best wines in the country now limit the extent to which they irrigate.

Like Chile, Argentina has never been the victim of phylloxera, the plant aphid that devastated many of the world's vineyards in the mid- and late-nineteenth century and showed up again in the 1980s and 1990s, destroying many vineyards in the western United States. It's not entirely clear why Argentina and Chile have been

*A religious niche in the vineyards of Valentin Bianchi.*

## THE GRAPES OF
# ARGENTINA

## WHITES

**Chardonnay:** Major grape especially for exported wines. Wine styles range from simple to toasty, oaky imitations of California chardonnays.

**Chenin Blanc:** Used as a blending grape or as the base for inexpensive sparkling wines.

**Criolla** and **Cereza:** Argentina's most widely planted grapes, descended from the grapes brought by Spanish conquistadores and missionaries in the sixteenth century. Both of these are actually pink-skinned varieties used to make coarse, bland white wines blended with other varieties and sold in jugs or cardboard cartons or in bulk.

**Moscatel de Alejandria:** Also known as muscat of Alexandria. Widely planted for use in cheap blends.

**Torrontés:** Argentinian specialty. Makes delightful, spicy, perfumed wines.

## REDS

**Barbera, Bonarda, Sangiovese,** and **Tempranilla:** Varieties planted by early Italian and Spanish immigrants. These are used mainly in inexpensive blends that are sold in jugs and cartons, though sometimes they are made into varietal wines. Tempranilla is the Argentinian spelling of the Spanish tempranillo.

**Cabernet Sauvignon:** Important red mainly intended for the export market. Its wines can range from simple to powerful and sleek.

**Malbec:** Argentina's most important and impressive red. Can makes wines of surprising grip, depth, and velvety texture.

**Merlot:** While less prestigious and less successful than cabernet sauvignon, merlot still a source of good-value wines mainly for the export market.

855

spared, though both countries are relatively well isolated, bordered as each is by ocean, desert, and the soaring Andes. Even the phylloxera that do manage to get in have a difficult time thriving in soil that is routinely flooded for irrigation. In addition, Argentina's extremely dry climate and fairly sandy and gravelly soil may have helped impede the pest. Because phylloxera has never been a factor in Argentinian viticulture, most vines still have their own roots; they have not been grafted onto American rootstocks as are most other vines worldwide. Nonetheless, most vintners are not keen on taking any more chances. New vineyards, as a result, are often planted on rootstocks.

Argentina has four major wine regions, the most important of which is Mendoza, followed by San Juan, La Rioja, and Salta. Minor regions include two small districts, Jujuy and Catamarca near Salta in the north and Río Negro, the farthest south. Because Argentina is in the Southern Hemisphere, Río Negro is the coolest of the country's wine regions.

Mendoza is more than just the leading wine region, it is the heartbeat of the Argentinian wine industry. Virtually all of the wineries of any importance are to be found here. The region lies directly east of Buenos Aires, upon the foothills of the Andes roughly 1,000 miles inland from the Atlantic Ocean. The vineyards, some of the highest in the country, are stunningly framed by the mountains, snowcapped year round. Given the region's size, it's not surprising that 70 percent of all Argentinian wine is made in Mendoza. With more than 360,000 acres planted with grapes, Mendoza is quite a bit larger than Bordeaux, itself a fairly large wine region. Australia and New Zealand combined have considerably fewer vines than Mendoza. In fact, the vineyard acreage of this one Argentinian region alone is equal to a bit less than half of all the vineyard land in the United States. Within Mendoza, the two most important subregions are Luján de Cuyo and Maipú.

The most famous grape in Mendoza is malbec. Why the grape is so much more successful here than in Bordeaux is not entirely understood, but the wines made from Mendoza malbec have a grip, struc-

### THE MOST IMPORTANT

## ARGENTINIAN WINES

**Cabernet Sauvignon** red
**Chardonnay** white
**Malbec** red
**Torrontés** white

ture, and density rarely found in wines made from malbec in Bordeaux. For this reason, the percentage of malbec in most Bordeaux wines is small, usually well under 10 percent, while in Argentina, malbec is compelling enough to be made into a wine on its own or blended with small amounts of cabernet sauvignon. (Malbec

*Vines grow profusely in Argentina's climate, where it's sunny, the air is dry, and the water available for irrigation is plentiful. Here, harvest workers in the vineyards of Bodega y Cavas de Weinert load a truck with small crates of just-picked grapes.*

is also the most important grape in the southwestern French region of Cahors, where it is usually blended with tannat, a darkly colored, very tannic grape variety, as well as with merlot.)

Argentina's second most important wine region, at least in terms of volume, is San Juan. Farther north than Mendoza, San Juan is considerably hotter, with summertime temperatures that can approach 110°F. Because of the heat, most of the grapes planted here are of lower quality and are planted for high yields. Many of them ultimately end up not as Argentinian wine but as grape concentrate sent to Japan or as base material for distilling into brandy. As for the other regions, La Rioja is Argentina's oldest wine-producing region. It specializes in white wines made from the torrontés grape. Of Salta, Jujuy, and Catamarca, Salta is the most important, again specializing in wines made from torrontés as well as cabernet sauvignon. And Río Negro in the much cooler south is a fruit-growing area that is known mostly for white wines and many of Argentina's sparkling wines.

The staff of Bodega la Rural standing in front of the bodega's wine museum.

857

Argentina is primarily a red wine country. About 60 percent of the total production of fine wine is red, and red wines in general are more compelling and flavorful than whites. There is also a fairly significant sparkling wine industry, with such prestigious Champagne houses as Moët & Chandon, Piper-Heidsieck, and Mumm having Argentinian subsidiaries.

Argentina is home to about twenty grape varieties. Besides malbec and the abundant criolla and cereza, a handful of Italian and Spanish varieties brought by immigrants in the nineteenth century grow there. These include moscatel de Alejandría, barbera, bonarda, sangiovese, and tempranillo, spelled tempranilla in Argentina, most of which are used as components in inexpensive jug blends, although sangiovese is beginning to be made into a varietal wine on its own. Among white grapes, the most fascinating by far is torrontés, a grape that the Argentinians feel chauvinistically proud of since it grows almost no place else in the world. Torrontés makes flowery aromatic wines reminiscent of gewürztraminer, only lighter. As for the international varieties, many of the top Argentinian wineries are focusing heavily on good-value chardonnays and these wines can be very attractive. Cabernet sauvignon is also promising, with the best wines having an almost Bordeaux-like structure. As elsewhere in the New World, Argentinian wines are labeled according to their variety.

## VISITING ARGENTINIAN WINERIES

Most of Argentina's wineries are located in the province of Mendoza, approximately 600 miles west of the capital, Buenos Aires. You'll find a couple of wineries here that weren't highlighted earlier; they are interesting to visit and their wines are certainly worth trying. Appointments for tours and tastings should be made in advance. While some English is spoken, knowledge of Spanish is helpful. The telephone numbers include the dialing code you'll need when calling from the United States. If you're calling from within Argentina, eliminate the 011-54 and add a zero before the next number.

**BODEGA NORTON**
Kilometer 23.5 Ruta Provincial 15
Perdriel, Luján de Cuyo, Mendoza
011-54-261-488-0480

**BODEGAS ESMERALDA**
4565 Guatemala, Buenos Aires
011-54-148-332-2080
in Mendoza, 011-54-262-342-9437

**BODEGAS TRAPICHE**
Nueva Mayorga s/n
Coquimbito, Maipú, Mendoza
011-54-261-497-2388

**ESCORIHUELA-GASCON**
1188 Belgrano
Godoy Cruz 5501, Mendoza
011-54-261-424-2282
The winery also has a famous restaurant on-site.

**ETCHART**
Kilometer 12.5 Ruta 40
Luján de Cuyo, Mendoza
011-54-261-488-0223

**FINCA FLICHMAN**
800 Munives, Barranca
Maipú, Mendoza
011-54-261-497-2039

## PERFECTING THE RED WINE WITH MEAT RULE

In no other country in the world is beef as celebrated, or as much a part of daily life, as it is in Argentina. Argentinians eat beef in every form—breaded, fried, rolled, stuffed, chopped, combined with raisins, olives, and eggs in empanadas, and perhaps most irresistibly of all, right off the *parilla*, or grill, as part of the Argentine *asado*. The word *asado* means roast meat, but everyone agrees that *asado* is really a no-holds-barred barbecue. Beef in fact is so much a part of Argentine cuisine that Argentinians have the highest beef consumption in the world—in 1999, 103 pounds per person (the United States was third highest with 69 pounds per person). Argentine beef is relatively lean, with a pronounced flavor that Argentinians say is the true beef flavor, attributable to the fact that the cattle feed on grasses as they roam over enormous expanses of land rather than being fattened in feed lots and fed growth hormones. And what do the Argentinians drink with their national culinary treasure? Their national vinous treasure: malbec.

*In Argentina, grilling meat for an asado (barbecue) is serious business.*

# THE ARGENTINIAN WINES TO KNOW

*For each wine below, the specific region from which it comes is noted.*

## *White*

### BODEGA LURTON
Torrontés
Mendoza
100% torrontés

One of the most exciting new wine companies in Argentina, Bodega Lurton is owned by Jacques and François Lurton, sons of one of Bordeaux's highly respected château owners, André Lurton. Bodega Lurton is now making some of Argentina's boldest, freshest,

and most intriguing wines, including this beautiful, light, floral torrontés, with its fresh litchi and tangerine flavors. Look, too, for the Bodega Lurton chardonnay, which at its best, is Argentina's most elegant chardonnay, with lovely baked pear and crème brûlée flavors. Unbelievably, in 2000 the cost of these terrific wines was $5 and $6 per bottle, respectively.

## *Reds*

### BODEGA NORTON
Malbec
Mendoza
100% malbec

### BODEGA Y CAVAS DE WEINERT
Cavas de Weinert
Mendoza
approximately 70% cabernet sauvignon, 20% malbec, and 10% merlot

859

Among all of Argentina's moderate- to low-priced wines, those of Bodega Norton stand out for being consistently satisfying. Though simple and rustic, the malbec is full of the flavor of juicy red berries and aromas that suggest smoked meats. Equally good is the winery's cabernet sauvignon, with its dried cherry character. And it's hard to beat the winery's soft, smoky merlot. These are wines for pizza, not pâté.

Weinert, as it is simply known, makes the best wines in Argentina. These include a very fine merlot and cabernet sauvignon plus Carrascal, a sensational malbec, merlot, and cabernet sauvignon blend that must rank as one of the great bargains worldwide. But Weinert's most impressive wine of all is Cavas de Weinert, an enormously complex wine with mesmerizingly sweet, voluptuous blackberry fruit flavors permeated by vanilla, cigar box, and saddle leather aromas. Other than older wines from Weinert's library (which are released from time to time), Cavas de Weinert is the bodega's most expensive wine. Even so, if it were from France or California, it would undoubtedly sell for three to five times as much.

## BODEGAS TRAPICHE

Iscay

Mendoza

50% malbec, 50% merlot

When the very large and well-respected Bodegas Trapiche released its first Iscay in 1999, eyebrows rose and heads turned. Iscay (which means two in Quechua, the language of the Incas; a reference to the two grapes that make it up) was priced at $50 a bottle, considerably more than most other Argentinian wines, many of which cost $6 to $10 at the time. But Iscay comes with more star power than most wines. The grapes are grown in Trapiche's two best vineyards, and the wine is made under the guidance of consulting winemaker Michel Roland, one of Bordeaux's most famous enologists. As for quality, Iscay is beautifully structured, with classic cassis and leather aromas and flavors and fairly massive tannin. Its plump core of soft fruit is reminiscent of a topflight California merlot.

**860**

## FELIPE RUTINI

Malbec

reserva

Mendoza

100% malbec

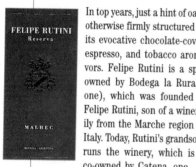

In top years, just a hint of oak graces this otherwise firmly structured malbec with its evocative chocolate-covered cherry, espresso, and tobacco aromas and flavors. Felipe Rutini is a special brand owned by Bodega la Rural (the rural one), which was founded in 1885 by Felipe Rutini, son of a winemaking family from the Marche region of Italy. Today, Rutini's grandson runs the winery, which is co-owned by Catena, one of Argentina's most progressive and modern wine companies.

## TAPIZ

Malbec

reserve

Mendoza

100% malbec

Owned by the large United States wine firm Kendall-Jackson, the brand Tapiz was created in the early 1990s to supply export markets with tasty moderately priced wines. The spicy blackberryish malbec reserve definitely fits the bill. Boldly flavored and more concentrated than many wines costing twice the price, it is made from malbec grapes that come from vines 75 to 120 years old.

## VALENTIN BIANCHI

Cabernet Sauvignon

San Rafael

approximately 80% cabernet sauvignon, 20% malbec and merlot

One of the older family-run wineries of Argentina, Valentin Bianchi makes extremely well-priced reds, the best of which, like this cabernet sauvignon, can have firm structures and good-tasting fruit. The cabernet in particular tastes more expensive than it is and has satisfying blackberry and black cherry flavors laced with leather and spice aromas. San Rafael, a subdistrict in the southern part of Mendoza, is a fairly large wine-producing area.

*In many wineries, carved statues of saints watch over the winemaking, providing a little divine help. These antique statues are part of Bodega la Rural's museum collection.*

# Appendixes

# Glossaries

I've provided here a main glossary with a comprehensive set of definitions for common English wine words and extensive glossaries for French, Italian, Spanish, and German and Austrian wine terms. You'll also find glossaries for the most important Portuguese, Hungarian, and Greek terms. Words appearing in all CAPITAL LET-TERS are cross-referenced within the main glossary or the glossaries for the individual countries. The French glossary begins on page 875, the Italian on page 878, the Spanish on page 880, the Portuguese on page 881, the German and Austrian on page 881, the Hungarian on page 884, and the Greek on page 884.

## *Main Glossary*

### A

**Acetaldehyde:** Produced naturally during FERMENTATION, acetaldehyde is a colorless volatile substance with a pungent odor. It is an asset in slightly oxidized (see OXIDATION) wines, such as Sherry, but a detectable amount in table wine is considered a flaw.

**Acetic:** A negative description for a wine with an unpleasant, sharp, vinegar-like smell and taste. A wine becomes acetic as a result of the presence of acetobacter, a bacteria that causes the natural conversion of wine to vinegar by producing acetic acid in the presence of air. See VOLATILE ACIDITY.

**Acid:** A natural component of wine; responsible for the zesty, refreshing qualities of some, acidity also helps wine to age. Wines with the proper amount of acid relative to their ALCOHOL content are vibrant and lively to drink. Wines with little acid relative to the alcohol are the opposite: FLAT and blowsy. Wines with excess acid taste sharp and biting. There are multiple acids in wine, the three most important of which—tartaric, malic, and citric—all come from the grapes. Other acids may be produced during FERMENTATION.

**Acidification:** A process practiced in warm wine regions whereby a winemaker adds ACID to grape MUST before FERMENTATION in order to boost a naturally low level of acidity, in hopes of creating a more balanced wine. Acidification is legal and widely practiced in many parts of the world, including California. Also called acidulation.

**Acidity:** See ACID.

**Aeration:** The process of intentionally exposing wine to oxygen to "open up" and soften it. Aeration occurs during the winemaking process, as when wine is poured or racked (see RACKING) from barrel to barrel, but it may also take place at serving time, as when a young wine is poured into a carafe or decanter or even just swirled in the glass.

**Aftertaste:** See FINISH.

**Aging:** The process of intentionally holding a wine for a period of time so that the components in it can integrate and the wine can grow softer and possibly more COMPLEX. Wines are generally aged first in a barrel and later in bottles, since wines evolve differently in each vessel. The length of time any wine is aged is initially up to the producer, though many of the top European wines by law must be aged a certain minimum number of months or years. Most wines worldwide are not aged at all.

**Alcohol:** During FERMENTATION, yeasts convert the natural sugar in grapes to alcohol (also known as ETHANOL or ETHYL ALCOHOL) and CARBON DIOXIDE. The riper the grapes, the more sugar they contain and the higher the potential alcohol content of the wine will be (see How Wine Is Made, page 30). Wines with low alcohol (German rieslings, for example) are LIGHT-BODIED; wines with high alcohol (many California chardonnays) are FULL-BODIED and almost CHEWY. When a high alcohol wine has too little FRUIT and a low ACID content, it tastes out of BALANCE and gives off a HOT or slightly burning sensation in your mouth.

**Alcohol by Volume:** The percentage of the ALCOHOL content by volume in a wine must, by United States law, appear on every wine label. However, because alcohol can be difficult to measure precisely and because wineries often need to print their labels before they know the exact alcohol content, the percentage stated on the label need only be accurate within 1.5 percent as long as the amount is not more than 14 percent. If greater than 14 percent, it must be accurate to within 1 percent. For example, a wine labeled 12 percent alcohol by volume may contain anywhere from 10.5 to 13.5 percent alcohol.

862

**Aldehydes:** Produced as FERMENTATION converts sugar to ALCOHOL, aldehydes contribute to the flavor and quality of wine but in excess are undesirable.

**Ampelography:** The science of the identification and classification of grapevines according to their physical properties, such as the size and shape of their leaves and grape clusters. Increasingly, grapevines are also being identified by DNA fingerprinting.

**Anthocyanins:** The red pigments in grape skins and wine.

**Appearance:** One of the categories by which a wine can be judged by sensory evaluation, generally including an assessment of clarity and COLOR.

**Appellation:** In general conversation the word *appellation* is often used simply to indicate the place where the grapes for a given wine were grown and subsequently made into wine. Technically, however, the word has much broader significance and importance. For this we must understand the historical underpinnings of the appellation concept. Let's consider, for example, the French system known as *Appellation d'Origine Contrôlée*, often abbreviated as AOC (see page 116). France's AOC regulations have become the world's model for laws that define and protect geographically named wines, spirits, and even certain foods. For any given wine the AOC laws stipulate, among other things, the precise area where the grapes that make the wine can be grown, the grape varieties that the wine can be made from, the permissible YIELD, aspects of VITICULTURE, such as PRUNING and irrigation, the minimum alcoholic strength of the wine, plus various details of how the wine can be made. For a given French wine to carry an appellation, it must meet all of the criteria set down in the AOC laws. Multiple appellations can exist within a larger appellation. For example, Margaux is an AOC within the AOC Haut-Médoc, which itself is an AOC within the larger AOC Bordeaux. The AOC laws evolved progressively, beginning in the 1930s. Today, most European wine-producing countries have similar, fairly stringent systems that define and govern the wines produced. In the NEW WORLD, including the United States, regulations defining the geographic boundaries of wine-producing areas are more recent. While New World regulations may specify the boundaries of a given place, such as the Napa Valley, they rarely stipulate or regulate details, such as grape varieties, permissible yields, or how the wine can be made. See also AVA.

**Aroma:** A term broadly used to describe a wine's smell. Technically, however, the smell of any wine is divided into the aroma, the smell that derives from the grapes, and the BOUQUET, a more complex smell that a wine acquires after AGING.

**Aromatic:** A positive description, indicating that a wine has a pronounced AROMA. Some VARIETAL wines, such as muscat and gewürztraminer, are well known for being especially aromatic, often having SPICY and/or floral (see FLOWERY) scents.

**Astringent:** A term describing the MOUTHFEEL of a wine with a considerable amount of TANNIN; a dry sensation provoked by some wines and certain foods, such as walnuts. Often used negatively to describe red wines with a lot of green or unripe tannin. Excess astringency is unpleasant and causes the mouth to pucker.

**Autolysis:** The decomposition of spent yeast cells by enzymes they contain. When a wine is SUR LIE, or on the LEES, it is left in contact with the spent yeasts that performed the FERMENTATION. As the yeast cells break down, they impart, for reasons not fully understood, an extra dimension of flavor, VISCOSITY, and complexity to the wine.

**AVA:** The acronym for American Viticultural Area. An AVA is defined as "a delimited grape-growing region, distinguished by geographical features, boundaries of which have been recognized and defined." On United States wine labels such place names as Napa Valley, Sonoma Valley, Columbia Valley, and so on are all AVAs. There are now more than 140 AVAs in the United States.

**B**

**Baked:** Negative term used when a table wine's AROMA and/or flavor seems overripe, caramel-like, or even burnt. Poorly made table wines allowed to get too warm or to become oxidized often taste baked (see OXIDATION). For certain wines, such as Sherry and Madeira, however, some "bakedness" is considered appropriate and positive, especially when combined with the wines' tangy nuttiness.

**Balance:** An equilibrium among the components of a wine (ACID, ALCOHOL, FRUIT, TANNIN, and so on) such that no one characteristic stands out like a sore thumb. Great wines have balance. Also referred to as integration.

**Barrel-Fermented:** Used to describe a wine—usually a white—that has undergone FERMENTATION in small oak barrels as opposed to in more neutral large casks, cement vats, or stainless steel tanks. Fermentation in a small barrel can impart a richer flavor and creamier texture to some wines, though these characteristics may be acquired at the expense of the wines' FRUIT. To mitigate against too intense a barrel-fermented character, wine-

863

makers can use older barrels, larger barrels, and/or ferment only a portion of the wine in barrels and then BLEND this portion with wine that has not been barrel-fermented.

**Bentonite:** A type of light clay, usually from the United States, mixed into wine to fine or clarify it (see FINING). As the bentonite settles, it absorbs and carries particles suspended in the wine along with it to the bottom of the vessel.

**Big:** A descriptive term used for FULL-BODIED, robust wines that are usually high in ALCOHOL.

**Bitter:** A harsh flavor in wine, often derived from stems and seeds that have been carelessly or inadvertently crushed along with the grapes. Bitterness can also be caused by unripe grapes or unripe TANNIN. In certain big, SMOKY red wines, a slight bitterness is considered a positive nuance, just as it would be in a good espresso.

**Blend:** To combine two or more lots of wine in hopes of enhancing flavor, BALANCE, and/or complexity. Often these are wines from different grape varieties, cabernet sauvignon and merlot, for example. However, blends may also be made up of wines that come from grapes grown in different soil or microclimates, wines that come from vines of different ages, wines from different CLONES, or wines made by different winemaking methods (some aged in one kind of oak, some in another, for instance). Virtually all Bordeaux wines and Champagnes are blends, as are wines from the southern Rhône and numerous other wines from elsewhere around the world.

**Body:** The perceived weight of a wine in your mouth. The perception is dependent on ALCOHOL—the higher the alcohol content, the more FULL-BODIED the wine. As a point of reference, consider the relative weights of skim milk, whole milk, and half-and-half. Light-bodied wines feel like skim milk, medium-bodied ones like whole milk, and full-bodied ones like half-and-half.

**Botrytis Cinerea:** A beneficial fungus, also known as noble rot, which is necessary to produce many of the world's great sweet wines, including Sauternes. In certain years, when the degree of humidity is just right, *Botrytis cinerea* will attack grapes, covering them with a gray mold. The mold lives by penetrating the grapes' skins and using up the available water in the juice. This concentrates the sugar, flavor, and ACID so that a COMPLEX wine of exceptional sweetness can be made. Botrytis is unique in that, unlike other molds, it produces flavors that harmonize with the flavors of particular grapes.

**Botrytized:** Affected by BOTRYTIS CINEREA.

**Bottle Aging:** The process of allowing a wine to rest for a considerable period of time (often years) in a bottle. Wines that have been bottle aged taste more mature, and their flavors can become so integrated that it's no longer easy to identify such specific fruit flavors as lemon, raspberry, or cherry. Bottle aging makes a wine more COMPLEX (see AGING).

**Bottle Sickness:** A temporary condition that occurs following the bottling process, when after months or years in an undisturbed environment (usually a barrel), a wine is suddenly pumped, possibly undergoes FINING and/or filtration (see FILTER), and then is run through a bottling machine. The shock of all this activity causes what is called bottle sickness. A wine with bottle sickness can temporarily taste FLAT, dull, or out of BALANCE. The condition usually goes away in a few weeks, occasionally after months.

**Bouquet:** Technically, bouquet refers specifically to the aspects of a wine's scent derived from the winemaking processes and BOTTLE AGING (see AROMA).

**Briary:** A term used to describe a briar patch, peppery taste in a wine. Often briary wines have a slightly scratchy texture, rather than being soft and round.

**Brilliant:** When applied to a wine's color, it means the wine is absolutely clear.

**Brix:** A measure of the sugar content of grapes before they are harvested. Used to estimate the ALCOHOL content of the resulting wine.

**Brut:** French term indicating a Champagne or sparkling wine that is dry to very dry, with less than 1.5 percent residual sugar.

**Bulk Process:** An inexpensive and quick way of making SPARKLING WINE. The bulk process, also called the Charmat method, involves placing wine in large, pressurized tanks for its SECONDARY FERMENTATION. In an alternative, and far more expensive, method, known as the MÉTHODE CHAMPENOISE (see French glossary), the secondary fermentation takes place inside individual bottles.

**Bulk Wine:** Literally, wine not in a bottle. Wineries of all types, sizes, and levels of quality buy and sell wines in bulk. Some sell all of their production that way. Most large producers buy significant amounts of bulk wines from other wineries and then BLEND, bottle, and distribute those wines under their own labels. Small prestigious wineries, however, may also sell small amounts of high-quality wine in bulk to producers who will use it to enhance their own wines.

**Bung:** A plug for stoppering a wine barrel.

**Buttery:** Used to describe a wine that has an AROMA and flavor reminiscent of butter, often applied to chardonnay that has been put through MALOLACTIC FERMENTATION.

C

**Cane:** A SHOOT (stem) that has turned from green to tannish brown and has become hard and fibrous. Shoots turn to canes in the fall in order to withstand the oncoming winter. The canes will ultimately be pruned back, usually in the late winter. See PRUNING.

**Canopy:** The "umbrella" formed by the leaves and SHOOTS of the grapevine.

**Cap:** The crusty layer, up to two feet or more deep, of grape skins, pulp, stems, and seeds that rises and floats on top of the juice during a red wine's FERMENTATION. The cap must be kept in contact with the juice by one of several methods. It may be PUNCHED DOWN into the juice, or the juice can be PUMPED OVER, that is, drawn up from the bottom of the tank and then showered over the cap. Only if the cap is thoroughly in contact with the ALCOHOL in the fermenting juice can COLOR, AROMA, flavor, and TANNIN be extracted. In addition, if the cap is not broken up and kept wet with the juice, it dries out and becomes a haven for bacteria that will ultimately mar the wine.

**Capsule:** The molded plastic, bimetal, or aluminum sheath that fits over the cork and top part of the neck of a wine bottle. Historically capsules were made of lead to keep animals and bugs away from the cork. Today lead is banned because of potential health risks.

**Carbon Dioxide:** Along with ALCOHOL, the gas carbon dioxide ($CO_2$) is a by-product of FERMENTATION. Sometimes the small amounts of $CO_2$ remaining in a wine make it slightly SPRITZY. In making a SPARKLING WINE, when a second fermentation occurs in a closed vessel, such as a bottle, the $CO_2$ becomes trapped in the wine and will ultimately form bubbles.

**Carbonic Maceration:** More accurately called semicarbonic maceration, carbonic maceration is a type of FERMENTATION in which bunches of uncrushed grapes are placed whole inside a closed tank. The weight of the bunches on top crushes those on the bottom, releasing juice that ferments in the standard manner. For the intact bunches on top however, fermentation takes place inside each grape, leading to an extremely juicy style of wine. Carbonic maceration is used exten-sively in Beaujolais, where it heightens the wine's already soft grapey flavor.

**Chaptalization:** The addition of cane or beet sugar to wine MUST before or during FERMENTATION in order to increase the total amount of sugar and hence raise the potential ALCOHOL content. Chaptalization is legal and widely practiced in many cooler northern European wine regions, where colder temperatures in some years lead to grapes that aren't fully ripe and, in turn, to wines that are thin and lacking in BODY. By increasing the alcohol content of such wines, the winemaker can make them fuller bodied and therefore make them seem more substantial. Chaptalization is not permitted in many warm wine regions, including California, where it is not needed but could be used to produce cheap wines high in alcohol but with virtually no flavor.

**Charmat Method:** See BULK PROCESS.

**Chewy:** A term for mouthfilling, FULL-BODIED wines, chunky and viscous enough to seem almost chewable. Certain grape varieties such as zinfandel produced in very warm areas like Amador County, California, often take on a chewy character.

**Clone:** The verb to clone means to propagate a group of vines from a "mother" vine that has desirable characteristics. The noun clone refers to plants of the same species that have identical physical characteristics and hence probably can be traced to a common "mother" plant. For example, pinot noir, a variety of grape, has many clones thanks to natural genetic mutations that have occurred over hundreds, possibly thousands, of years. Clones are critical in VITICULTURE because two clones of the same grape variety can taste remarkably different. There is no way of knowing how many clones of a given variety exist at any one time.

**Closed In:** Refers to a wine that seems to have considerable potential, yet its AROMAS and flavors are temporarily muted. A wine can be closed in for a variety of reasons. Two common ones: It's young or it's densely concentrated and needs time and/or oxygen to open up. In the first instance, the closed in wine may need additional BOTTLE AGING before it opens up; in the second case, pouring the wine into a carafe or decanter and giving it an hour or so to breathe will help.

**Cloudy:** Descriptive term, not necessarily negative, for a wine that looks hazy rather than brilliantly clear. A wine can be slightly cloudy because it has not undergone FINING or filtration (see FILTER). Some wines, however, are cloudy as the result of faulty winemaking.

865

**Cloying:** Describes a wine with unbearable, candy-like sweetness that often sticks to your tongue in an unpleasant way. Dessert wines should not be cloying.

**Coarse:** Descriptive term for a harsh, unsophisticated, bull in a china shop sort of wine, lacking in FINESSE.

**Cold Fermentation:** A type of FERMENTATION that takes place in a vessel that can be cooled, usually a stainless steel tank. Because cool fermentations are slower and more gentle than those that occur at warm temperatures, they help preserve the wine's fresh FRUIT AROMAS and flavors. Many light- and medium-bodied white wines are cold fermented.

**Cold Stabilization:** A common winemaking technique whereby harmless TARTRATE crystals and small protein molecules are intentionally precipitated out of the wine. This is done by quickly chilling it. Unstabilized wines sometimes become hazy or form snowflakelike crystals, which are odorless and tasteless but look a bit unnerving.

**Color:** One of the distinguishing characteristics of wine, color is derived primarily from grape skins. White wines vary from pale straw to greenish-yellow to yellow-gold to amber; reds from garnet to crimson to brick red to lipstick red to purple. While the color of a wine is a tip-off to its variety (zinfandel will be purplish, for example) and an indication of its age (white wines get darker as they get older; red wines get lighter), color is not a predictor of a wine's flavor or quality.

**Complex:** Describes a multifaceted wine with compelling nuances and character. All great wines are complex.

**Cooperage:** Containers a winery uses for storing wine, usually barrels or wood casks, though the term cooperage can also apply to concrete or stainless steel vessels.

**Corked:** A term used to describe a wine that smells like a wet dog in a basement or, sometimes, like wet cardboard. Wines become corked or corky when certain bacteria in the cork cells interact with minute amounts of chemical residues that may remain in corks or wine bottles after they are cleaned. A corked wine has a defective AROMA and flavor, although it will not harm the drinker. Corked wine cannot be predicted. Any wine regardless of its quality or price can be corky.

**Cross:** A grape created by fertilizing one variety of grape with another variety from the same species. While a cross may be the result of breeding, most

crosses occur spontaneously in nature. Most modern grape varieties, for example, are natural crosses. Within the European species VITIS *vinifera* two highly regarded man-made crosses are scheurebe (riesling x silvaner) and pinotage (pinot noir x cinsaut). A cross is not the same as a HYBRID.

**Crush:** Used as a verb, to crush means to break the grape skins so that FERMENTATION can more easily begin. As a noun, crush is the general term used for all of the steps (harvesting, and so on) that take place just prior to fermentation.

**Cutting:** A segment of a CANE or SHOOT that is cut off a growing vine and used to propagate a new plant through grafting or direct planting.

**D**

**Decant:** The act of pouring a wine (generally an older wine) off any SEDIMENT or deposits that may have precipitated out and settled in the bottle. Sometimes the term is used to describe the action of pouring a young wine into a decanter to mix it with oxygen and open it up, but this is more correctly called AERATION.

**Declassify:** With European wines, the decision to place a wine in a category that is lower in status than seems appropriate given the quality of the wine. European wines may be declassified for a variety of reasons. In France, for example, wines that do not meet the strict requirements of AOC laws are declassified, usually to TABLE WINE.

**Demi-Sec:** Literally half-dry in French. Term used for a SPARKLING WINE or Champagne that is moderately sweet.

**Depth:** Intensity and concentration. An especially intense and concentrated cabernet sauvignon, for example, might be described as having depth.

**Dessert Wine:** General term for a wine that is sweet and, as such, could accompany, or be, dessert. In the United States, such wines often fall into the category of LATE HARVEST. There are many ways of making dessert wines (see page 46). Two of the world's most famous dessert wines, French Sauternes and German *trockenbeerenauslesen*, come from grapes that are infected with the noble rot BOTRYTIS CINEREA.

**Destemmer:** A machine that separates the stems from the grapes. When combined with a crusher, it is called a crusher-destemmer.

**Dirty:** A negative description of wines with off flavors and odors resulting from faulty winemaking. The implication is that something is present in the wine that shouldn't be.

**Disgorging:** Referred to in French as DÉGORGE-MENT (see French glossary), this is the process used in the making of Champagne or Champagne-method SPARKLING WINE by which yeasty sediment is removed from the bottle after the second bubble-forming FERMENTATION.

**Dry:** Used to describe any wine that doesn't contain significant grape sugar. Commonly a dry wine is one fermented until less than 0.2 percent of natural (RESIDUAL) sugar remains. A wine can be dry and taste FRUITY at the same time.

**Dumb:** Describes a wine that temporarily has little taste. This can be a wine, usually white, that is served so cold that it tastes as though it's not altogether there. Or it can be a wine, usually red, in an awkward stage of its development when it tastes neither full of FRUIT and young nor mature. In this strange state, sometimes called adolescence, the wine seems dull, ungenerous, almost mute. Why some wines go through dumb phases and others do not is not fully understood.

**E**

**Earthy:** Used to describe a wine, the AROMA or flavor of which is reminiscent of the earth. It refers to flavors that evoke soil or things that grow in it—moss, truffles, and the like. The term is sometimes extrapolated to include the pleasant, sensual aromas of the human body.

**Elegant:** A descriptive term for a wine with such FINESSE and BALANCE that it tastes refined rather than rustic.

**Enology:** The science and study of winemaking, differentiated from VITICULTURE, the study of grape growing. Also spelled oenology.

**Estate Bottled:** Exact definitions of estate bottled differ depending on the country from which the wine comes. In the United States the term may be used by a winery only if its wine is entitled to use a viticultural area or appellation of origin on its label and only if the winery is located in that area; grew all of the grapes used in the wine on land owned or controlled by the winery within that area; and completely produced the wine, aged it, and bottled it at the winery.

**Esters:** Aromatic compounds produced by yeasts and bacteria primarily during FERMENTATION. Esters may be complementary or deleterious to the wine.

**Ethanol** or **Ethyl Alcohol:** The ALCOHOL that results when yeasts convert the natural sugar in ripe grapes during FERMENTATION. Commonly referred to simply as alcohol.

**Extract:** The soluble particles in wine that would remain if all the liquid were drawn off.

**Extra Dry:** A confusing designation, extra dry actually refers to Champagne or SPARKLING WINE that is slightly sweet, containing 1.2 to 2.0 percent residual sugar.

**F**

**Fat:** A descriptive term for the texture of a FULL-BODIED wine with saturated fruit. Although being fat is generally considered a positive wine trait, being flabby is not. A flabby wine is a fat wine that lacks acidity so that it seems gross and unfocused.

**Fermentation:** The process during grape fermentation whereby yeasts convert the natural sugar in the grapes into ALCOHOL and CARBON DIOXIDE. The alcohol will remain a constituent of the wine that results, but in most cases, the carbon dioxide will be allowed to escape as a by-product.

**Filter:** A filter is a porous membrane or other device used to remove selected particles from a liquid. In winemaking, a filter can be used to remove yeast cells and bacteria from the wine. Winemakers may filter a wine extensively, not at all, or to any degree in between. Some critics contend that too often, in an effort to produce "clean" wine, some winemakers filter wines excessively, thereby stripping them of positive flavors and textures.

**Finesse:** Used to describe a wine with elegance and BALANCE. The term implies that the wine is polished and sophisticated. Hearty, rustic country wines would not be described as having finesse, while a well-made Champagne or top white Burgundy might be.

**Fining:** A process of clarifying wine by adding one or more agents, such as gelatin, egg whites, BENTONITE, or ISINGLASS, to the wine. As the clarifying agent slowly settles to the bottom of the container, it carries along with it unwanted particles suspended in the wine. Like filtering (see FILTER), severe fining can strip a wine of flavor and texture.

**Finish:** The impression that a wine leaves in your mouth even after you have swallowed it. A finish may be almost nonexistent, fairly short, or extremely long. It may be smooth and lingering or rough and choppy. A finish may also be dominated by one component in the wine, such as ALCOHOL (a HOT finish), ACID (a tart finish), or TANNIN (an ASTRINGENT finish). A great wine, as opposed to a good wine, always has a pronounced, very long, lingering, well-balanced finish. In some judgings, officials actually measure the length of time that the wine can still be tasted after it has been swallowed.

867

**Flat:** Refers to wines that taste dull and uninteresting. Often, this is because the wine lacks ACIDITY.

**Flowery:** Used to describe AROMAS and flavors, usually present in white wines, that are reminiscent of flowers.

**Fortified:** A wine, such as Sherry or Port, that has had its ALCOHOL content increased by the addition of distilled grape spirits (clear brandy). Most fortified wines contain 16 to 20 percent ALCOHOL BY VOLUME.

**Foxy:** An odd descriptive term (having nothing to do with foxes, or sex appeal, for that matter) for the wild, grapey flavor associated with wines that come from native American grapes of the VITIS *labrusca* species, such as Concord. The flavor is derived from an ESTER, methyl anthranilate.

**Free Run:** The juice that runs—freely—simply as the result of the weight of the grapes, before any mechanical pressure is applied in a PRESS.

**Fruit:** The part of a wine's AROMA and flavor that comes from grapes. The fruit in a wine is distinguished from the wine's ALCOHOL or ACIDITY.

**Fruity:** A catchall term for the pronounced flavor or AROMA that comes from the wine grapes themselves. Wines are generally most fruity when they are young. In addition, certain VARIETAL wines (gewürztraminer, gamay, zinfandel) seem more fruity than others.

**Full-Bodied:** Having pronounced weight on the palate. Full-bodied wines are to LIGHT-BODIED wines as half-and-half is to skim milk. All other things being equal, the higher a wine's ALCOHOL content, the more full-bodied it will seem.

**Futures:** See EN PRIMEUR in the French glossary.

**G**

**Generic:** A category of inexpensive wine that has been given a general generic name that is not controlled by law. In the United States, terms such as "chablis," "rhine," "sherry," and "burgundy" are all considered generic terms because they are not controlled by United States law. The fact that these are stringently defined terms in Europe is, sadly enough, beside the point. Thus, any inexpensive blended wine in the United States may be called "chablis" even though the wine itself will bear little if any resemblance to its namesake.

**Glycerol:** One of the minor by-products of FERMENTATION, glycerol, or glycerine, has no COLOR, no AROMA, and a light, faintly sweet taste. Its thick, syrupy quality is thought to contribute to a wine's texture and VISCOSITY.

**Graft:** To splice one grape variety (say, chardonnay) onto another variety (say, Concord). Grafting also makes it possible to splice a given variety, such as chardonnay, onto a disease-resistant variety of ROOTSTOCK. Without the ability to graft, many of the great vineyards of the world would have long ago succumbed to PHYLLOXERA.

**Grassy:** A descriptive term for flavors and AROMAS reminiscent of those of just-cut grass, meadows, fields of hay, and the like, often overlaid with a GREEN or VEGETAL note. Grassiness can be positive or negative depending on its degree and on the preferences of the taster. The VARIETAL most often described as grassy is sauvignon blanc.

**Green:** A flavor in wine generally associated with those of grass, moss, or vegetables. Also a flavor found in wines made from underripe grapes. A certain amount of greenness can be characteristic of and therefore positive in some varietals like sauvignon blanc. With most red varietals, however, obvious greenness is considered a fault.

**Gunflint:** The taste or smell suggested by wet metal. Often used to describe sauvignon blanc, particularly French ones.

**H**

**Herbal:** When used to describe a wine with flavors or AROMAS slightly reminiscent of herbs, herbal is positive. Good sauvignon blanc, for example, is considered slightly herbal. When herbal flavors become extreme, they are often described as herbaceous, a quality some wine drinkers like and others don't. Herbal is different than VEGETAL, a term used negatively to describe a wine with a dank green OFF ODOR.

**Hot:** Refers to a wine with a level of ALCOHOL that is out of BALANCE with its ACID and FRUIT. The impression of excessive alcohol produces a slight burning "hit" at the top of the nasal passages and on the palate.

**Hybrid:** As distinguished from a CROSS, a hybrid is a new grape variety developed by breeding two or more varieties from different species or subgenera. The most common hybrids are part European species (VITIS *vinifera*) and part any one of several American species. These are commonly referred to as French-American hybrids since they were developed by French plant breeders after the massive PHYLLOXERA infestation in the late nineteenth century. Well-known hybrids include Baco noir, villard blanc, and seyval blanc.

**I**

**Isinglass:** A gelatinous material, obtained from the air bladders of sturgeons and other fish, that is used in clarifying wine and that, happily enough, is not left in it (see FINING).

## J

**Jammy:** Having the thick, concentrated berry AROMA or flavor of jam. Also, the thick, rich, mouthfilling texture of jam. Full-bodied, ripe, red zinfandel is often described as jammy.

**Jug Wines:** Inexpensive wines sold in large bottles. Jug wines can be GENERIC blends or made from one variety of grape.

## L

**Labrusca:** See VITIS.

**Late Harvest:** As the term suggests, a wine that comes from grapes picked after the normal harvest and therefore containing a greater percentage of sugar. Late-harvested wines may also be infected with the noble rot, BOTRYTIS CINEREA. DESSERT WINES are usually late harvested.

**Lees:** The remnants of yeast cells that settle to the bottom of the container after FERMENTATION is complete. Leaving the fermented wine in contact with its lees (SUR LIE), rather than removing the lees right away, often adds complexity and nuance. See AUTOLYSIS.

**Legs:** Also known as tears in Spain and cathedral windows in Germany, legs are the rivulets of wine that have inched up the inside surface of the glass above the wine, then run slowly back down. Myth has it that the fatter the legs, the better the wine. This is not true. The width of legs is determined by the interrelationship of a number of complex factors, including the amount of alcohol, the amount of GLYCEROL, and the rate of evaporation of the alcohol. But the most important point is this: Legs have nothing to do with quality. It is irresistible to point out that wines—like women—should not be judged by their legs.

**Light-Bodied:** The term that describes a wine that has very little weight on the palate. A light-bodied wine literally feels light in your mouth, while a FULL-BODIED wine feels just the opposite. Light-bodied wines are low in ALCOHOL.

## M

**Maderized:** A term for a wine that has been subject to a long period of OXIDATION and, usually, heat. The best-known example is Madeira, from which the term *maderized* comes. Table wines should not be maderized.

**Magnum:** A 1.5-liter bottle, which contains the equivalent of two normal (750 milliliter) bottles.

**Malolactic Fermentation:** This process has nothing to do with regular FERMENTATION since it does not involve yeasts or the production of ALCOHOL. Rather, malolactic fermentation is a chemical con-

version of ACID instigated by beneficial bacteria. During the process, the strident, sharp malic acid in grapes is converted to softer lactic acid. This has the effect of softening the overall impression of acid when the wine is drunk. Malolactic fermentation may also contribute a buttery character to the wine and may add complexity—white Burgundies are a good example. Malolactic fermentation can either occur naturally or be prompted by the winemaker. All red wines go through malolactic fermentation. White wines may or may not. If the winemaker wants to achieve a soft MOUTHFEEL in the white wine, then malolactic fermentation is induced. If he or she prefers to retain dramatic, snappy acidity, then malolactic fermentation is prevented, usually by the use of SULFUR.

**Mercaptans:** Offensive-smelling compounds that result when hydrogen sulfide combines with the components of the wine—due to poor winemaking. The AROMAS can include putrid food, skunk, sweat, and burnt rubber.

**Meritage:** A United States trademarked designation, adopted in 1988 by the Meritage Association, for California wines that are a blend of the varieties of grapes used in Bordeaux. A red Meritage might be made up of cabernet sauvignon, merlot, and cabernet franc. A white Meritage would be a blend of sauvignon blanc and sémillon. Meritage wines are usually expensive and are often given fanciful proprietary names. Such wines as Opus One, Rubicon, Insignia, Cain Five, and Soliloquy would all qualify as Meritage if their producers chose to have them so designated. Producers may choose not to use the term Meritage even if their wine meets the qualifications.

**Mouthfeel:** The tactile impression of a wine in your mouth. Like clothing, wine can feel soft, rough, velvety, and so on.

**Must:** The juice and liquidy pulp produced by crushing or pressing grapes before FERMENTATION.

**Musty:** A dank, old-attic smell in a wine, attributed to unclean storage containers and sometimes to grapes processed when moldy.

## N

**Négociant:** See the French glossary.

**New World:** A descriptive term encompassing all of those wine-producing countries that do not belong to the OLD WORLD. The most important New World wine producers are the United States, Australia, New Zealand, South Africa, Argentina, and Chile. By extension, New World techniques generally refer to modern viticultural and wine-making methods that rely heavily on science. Avant-garde, Old World wine producers are often said to use New World techniques.

**Noble Rot:** See BOTRYTIS CINEREA.

**Nonvintage:** When applied to Champagne, a more correct term would be multivintage, for this type is made by blending the wines of several complementary years' harvests. The majority of Champagnes are nonvintage. Most table wines today carry a vintage.

**Nose:** The smell of a wine, including both the AROMA from the grape and the BOUQUET from AGING.

**O**

**Oaky:** A descriptive term for the toasty, woody, and vanilla smells and flavors contributed to wine during its FERMENTATION or AGING in oak barrels. The newer the oak barrel, the greater the potential for the wine to have a pronounced oaky character. And, the longer the wine is left in oak, the greater the oaky influence. A wine that has an oak flavor that dominates all natural fruit flavors is considered over oaked and, hence, flawed.

**Oenology:** See ENOLOGY.

**Off-Dry:** Ever so slightly sweet.

**Off Odors:** Unpleasant smells (chemicals, dankness, moldiness, rotten eggs, burnt rubber, sauerkraut, and so on) that suggest that the wine was stored in unclean containers or poorly made.

**Oidium:** A vine disease also known as powdery mildew.

**Old World:** As applied to wine, Old World refers to those countries where wine first flourished, namely European ones and others ringing the Mediterranean basin. Old World techniques, by extension, refer to ways of growing grapes and making wines that rely more on tradition and less on science. The Old World is usually talked about in contrast to the NEW WORLD. Wine producers in the New World, however, are often fond of saying that they employ Old World techniques as a way of establishing that their wines are made at least in part by traditional methods.

**Oxidation:** The process of exposing wine to air, which changes it. A little oxidation can be positive; it can help to soften and open up a wine, for example. Too much exposure to air, however, is deleterious. It can make a wine turn brown and take on a tired flavor reminiscent of poor-quality Sherry. When too much exposure to air occurs, the wine is described as oxidized.

**P**

**PH:** A measure of the degree of the relative acidity versus the relative alkalinity of wine (or any liquid) on a scale of 0 to 14. The lower the number is below 7 (neutral), the greater the relative acidity. Winemakers consider the pH of a wine in relationship to other factors (ALCOHOL, TANNIN, EXTRACT, and the like) to determine if the wine is in BALANCE. As grapes mature, plotting the change in the pH of their pulp is a way of determining ripeness.

**Phenols:** A group of chemical compounds occurring naturally in all plants. In wine, phenols are derived from grape skins, stems, and seeds, as well as from oak barrels. Among the most important phenols are TANNIN, COLOR pigments, and some flavor compounds, such as VANILLIN.

**Phylloxera:** A highly destructive, small aphid that attacks a vine's roots and slowly destroys the vine by preventing the roots from absorbing nutrients and water. Native American vines, such as those belonging to the species VITIS *labrusca* or *Vitis riparia*, tolerate the insect without adverse consequences. In the latter part of the nineteenth century, a phylloxera epidemic swept through Europe and eventually around the world. By the time a remedy was discovered, millions of acres of vines had been destroyed. That remedy, still the only known solution, was to replant each vineyard, vine by vine, with native American ROOTSTOCKS, then graft *Vitis vinifera* vines on top.

**Pomace:** The mashed-up solid residue (skins, stems, seeds, pulp) that is left after grapes are pressed. When pomace is distilled, it can be made into grappa (Italy), MARC (France), or EAU-DE-VIE (France and the United States).

**Press:** To press means to exert pressure on grapes to extract their juices. A press is a device used to do that. There are many kinds; one of the simplest and oldest is the hand-operated wooden basket press. One of the most modern presses—the bladder press—is essentially a horizontal tank with an inflatable membrane running through its middle. As the membrane swells, it gently squeezes the grapes against the side of the revolving tank. Grape bunches can be put whole into a press, but more often, they are crushed and the stems are removed first.

**Private Reserve:** A term found on some NEW WORLD wine labels for which there is no legal definition. Sometimes a wine labeled private reserve is truly special and of high quality (such as Beaulieu Vineyards' Georges de Latour Private Reserve, considered one of the best cabernet sauvignons from California). Other times, however, the phrase is simply a now hackneyed way of marketing an ordinary wine. Similar terms include proprietor's reserve and special select.

**Pruning:** Cutting back the CANES of the vine when it is dormant. Because pruning affects how the vine will grow, it can be used to regulate the size and quality of the next year's crop. Pruning is usually done by hand with shears, but mechanical pruners do exist to speed up pruning in large vineyards.

**Puckery:** Used to describe a wine that is so high in TANNIN that it causes your mouth to pucker from the astringency. Most often the wine will have been made from insufficiently ripe grapes.

**Pulp:** The soft, fleshy part of the grape, which is infused with juice.

**Pump Over:** A process during the FERMENTATION of red wine in which the juice is pumped from the bottom of the container to the top and then sprayed over the CAP of skins to keep it wet. By trickling through this mass of skins, the juice picks up even more COLOR, flavor, and TANNIN. Pumping over also helps prevent the growth of undesirable bacteria that might spoil the wine or create off flavors.

**Punch Down:** The opposite of to PUMP OVER, this process accomplishes the same goals. During punching down, the CAP is pushed down with a paddle into the fermenting grape juice.

**Puncheon:** A large wooden cask for storing wine, roughly equal to the size of two standard barrels, though as with barrels, puncheons come in different sizes.

**Punt:** The indentation found in the bottom of many wine bottles. The punt may be shallow or, as in the case of Champagne bottles, quite pronounced. The punt adds stability by weighting the bottom of the bottle and strengthens the glass at its weakest point.

**R**

**Racking:** A method of clarifying a wine that has SETTLED by siphoning or pumping off solids and particulate matter, such as yeast cells and bits of grape skins, and pouring it into a different clean barrel. Racking also aerates a wine.

**Raisiny:** A descriptive term for a wine (generally a red) that tastes slightly like raisins because the grapes were overripe when picked. A small bit of this quality can add an interesting nuance to the wine, but too much is a flaw.

**Reserve:** Many producers the world over make a reserve wine in addition to their regular offering, the reserve being of higher quality (theoretically) and higher price (dependably). In the United States, a reserve wine may be a selection of the best lots of wine from grapes grown in the best vineyards, and/or it may be a wine that has been allowed to age longer before release. But since the term reserve is not actually defined by United States law, an embarrassing number of producers use it purely as a marketing ploy to get you to buy wine that is in fact of cheap quality and pretty pedestrian. The one exception to this is Washington State, where in 1999, an industry group, the Washington Wine Quality Alliance, set forth its own stipulations regarding the term. Members of the alliance—virtually all of the top wine producers in the state—agreed to use the term reserve only for 10 percent of a winery's production or 3,000 cases, whichever is greater. Additionally, a wine labeled reserve must be among the higher priced wines the winery produces and all of the grapes for the wine must be grown in Washington State. In contrast to the United States, most European countries strictly define the terms *riserva* (Italy), *reserva* (Spain), and the like.

**Residual Sugar:** Natural grape sugar that remains in wine because it has not been converted into ALCOHOL during FERMENTATION. Wines that taste dry can nonetheless have a tiny amount of residual sugar in them. Winemakers often leave small amounts of sugar in wine to make it seem rounder and more appealing (sweetness has a slight fat feeling to it). Wine producers are not required to list residual sugar contents on labels.

**Riddling:** Called RÉMUAGE in French, riddling is the process during the making of Champagne or SPARKLING WINE whereby the bottles are individually rotated and tilted a small bit day after day in order to concentrate the yeast sediment in the necks prior to DISGORGING. In the past bottles held in A-shape frames called *pupitres* were riddled by hand. Today it may also be done by a computerized machine called a gyropalette.

**Rootstock:** The part of the grapevine that is planted directly in the soil. Rootstocks from different varieties have different tolerances to disease and climatic stress, and will be more or less suitable to a given type of soil. The variety of rootstock also affects how slowly or quickly the vine itself will grow. A vine need not grow from its own roots. In fact, most vines are not grown from their own roots but instead are grafted onto select rootstocks well known for their disease-resistant properties (see PHYLLOXERA).

871

**Rotten Egg:** The term most often used to describe a wine that exhibits the fault of having excessive hydrogen sulfide.

**Rough:** Used to describe the coarse texture of a (usually young) tannic red wine. AGING can sometimes soften a rough wine.

S

**Sec:** French for DRY. In wine, however, the opposite is usually true. Champagne that is labeled sec, for example, is medium sweet to sweet.

**Secondary Fermentation:** A FERMENTATION that takes place after the first fermentation, either spontaneously or by intention. In the making of top Champagnes and SPARKLING WINES, the secondary fermentation takes place inside the bottle and produces the gas that eventually becomes the wines' bubbles (see CARBON DIOXIDE). In table wine a secondary fermentation is undesirable.

**Second Crop:** Fruit that matures after the first crop has been picked. This is usually not picked because the quantity is too small to be economically viable, and the grapes may not be sufficiently ripe.

**Second Wine:** The term for a secondary and usually less expensive wine made by a winery. In California, for example, Stag's Leap Wine Cellars has a second label called Hawk Crest. In Bordeaux, Château Latour's second label is Les Forts de Latour. Most wineries that make a second label are highly respected for their primary label and may not want to actively market (or be known for) their second label. The wine that is sold under the second label is never as high in quality as wine of the primary label. The grapes may come from younger vines and/or lesser vineyards.

**Sediment:** The particulate matter (usually harmless) and color pigments that may precipitate out of a wine as it ages. The presence of sediment is not negative; many of the best wines in the world throw off sediment as they age.

**Settling:** The precipitation (settling out) of solid matter in wine. SEDIMENT, for example, settles out of a mature wine.

**Shoot:** A new green stem that springs from the vine as it begins to grow in the spring. Shoots will ultimately sprout leaves and clusters of grapes.

**Skin Contact:** In a sense, all red wines experience skin contact since in red wine FERMENTATION the juice and skins of the grapes are in contact. But in contemporary winemaking, the term *skin contact* generally refers to the process of letting crushed white grapes sit with the skins and the juice together, rather than immediately separating

them. This process helps add flavor and AROMA to the final wine. A white wine may be given anywhere from a few hours to a couple of days of skin-contact time.

**Smoky:** A smoky smell and taste found in both white and red wines. Though wines can take on smoky characters from the barrels in which they are aged, certain wines just have a naturally smoky character as a result of their TERROIR (see the French glossary). Many Pouilly-Fumés and Sancerres from France's Loire Valley are smoky, for example.

**Sommelier:** The French term for a wine steward, which has been appropriated by English speakers. In the United States, many sommeliers prefer the title wine steward, as a reaction against a certain type of sommelier who was as skilled at making people feel inadequate as he was at wine.

**Sour:** A descriptive term, generally used negatively, for a wine with a flavor that, as far as the taster is concerned, is too sharp and acidic.

**Sparkling Wine:** A wine with bubbles. The most famous sparkling wine is Champagne, made in the region of the same name in France. Other types of sparkling wine include CAVA (from Spain), SEKT (from Germany), and SPUMANTE (from Italy).

**Spicy:** A descriptive term for a wine with an AROMA or flavor suggestive of aromatic spices. Spicy wines are also often peppery and can have a slight pleasantly scratchy texture.

**Split:** A small wine bottle containing 6.4 ounces (187.5 milliliters), one fourth of a standard 750 milliliter bottle.

**Spritzy:** Wines with a small amount of sparkle from carbonation left or trapped in the wine. In a still wine, this is usually undesirable.

**Starter:** Commercial yeasts used to initiate and ensure fermentation.

**Stemmy:** A descriptive term for a wine with the green odor of stems or, sometimes, wet grain.

**Still Wines:** All wines that are not SPARKLING.

**Sulfur:** A natural chemical element that has been used as a wine preservative since antiquity. Sulfur in all its forms is harmless to people except for the tiny number of individuals who are severely allergic to it. The most common form of sulfur used in winemaking is sulfur dioxide ($SO_2$), which is formed when elemental sulfur is burned in air. Added to wine (usually as a gas), sulfur dioxide prevents OXIDATION as well as bacterial spoilage, and it inhibits the growth of yeasts. As a result of this, sulfur dioxide can be used to stop FERMENTA-TION in order to produce a sweet wine, and it can be used to prevent MALOLACTIC FERMENTATION. A form of sulfur dioxide known as metabisulfite is often added to freshly picked grapes (and fruit juices in general) as a preservative. Sulfur dioxide's disadvantage is that it has an unpleasant odor, which can be smelled at low concentrations, although people vary widely in the thresholds at which they can detect it. The detectability of sulfur dioxide also varies based on the type of wine, since in some wines the compound reacts to or combines with other compounds, rendering it more difficult to perceive. In any case, during the last few decades, winemakers the world over have sought to minimize the amount of sulfur dioxide they use in winemaking, mostly in response to health concerns voiced by wine drinkers. Nonetheless, it's virtually impossible to produce a wine that is entirely sulfur free because a small amount of sulfur dioxide is a by-product of the metabolic action of yeasts during fermentation (this is why bread, too, contains sulfur dioxide). As a result, United States law mandates that the term *contains sulfites* appear on all labels of wines that contain more than 10 parts per million of sulphur dioxide (and most do), even when the wine has been produced without the addition of any sulfur dioxide. The word *sulfites* in the warning is a catchall term for sulfur in all its various forms, including sulfur dioxide, sulfurous acid, bisulfite ion, and sulfite ion, as well as other complex forms.

**T**

**Table Wine:** The term used around the world to describe wines of moderate alcoholic strength (usually 9 to 15 percent ALCOHOL BY VOLUME) as opposed to FORTIFIED wines, which have grape spirits added to them and thus have a greater alcoholic strength (usually between 16 and 20 percent alcohol by volume). In common speech, however, the term *table wine* is often used to indicate dry, STILL WINES served to accompany dinner, rather than sweet wines intended for dessert or SPARKLING WINES.

**Tannin:** A PHENOL (a kind of compound) derived from the skins, seeds, and stems of grapes and from barrels. The presence of tannin is beneficial, for it gives certain red wines a firm structure as well as the potential for long aging. Tannin is not tasted as much as it is felt. Highly tannic wines can have a slight PUCKERY quality when young. If the wine has been made from mature, ripe grapes, however, this puckery quality will mellow and soften over time. Excessively dry, harsh, scratchy tannin is a negative and may never ameliorate. Harsh tannin, often called green or unripe tannin, most often results when grapes have been picked before they are completely physiologically mature. Most white wines have only tiny amounts of tannin because they are not fermented on their skins nor are they barrel aged for long periods.

**Tartrates:** Tasteless, odorless, harmless salts of tartaric ACID that can precipitate out of a wine that has not been COLD STABILIZED. Tartrates look like small white snowflakes.

**Tastevin:** See the French glossary.

**Terroir:** See the French glossary.

**Thin:** Used to describe a wine lacking body, because it is low in ALCOHOL, as well as lacking fruit flavors, possibly because it was made from grapes produced at a very high YIELD. An extremely thin wine is called watery.

**Toasting:** Charring the inside of new or relatively new barrels over an open flame. Charring caramelizes the staves of the wood. Wine stored in barrels treated this way will pick up a VANILLIN, toasty character.

**Topping Up:** To add more wine to a barrel or container to replace any wine lost through evaporation and thereby prevent the wine from experiencing OXIDATION. The term is also used in more general circumstances to mean adding wine to a glass in which there's only a sip or two left.

**Transfer Process:** A less expensive way of making SPARKLING WINE than the traditional MÉTHODE CHAMPENOISE. In the transfer process the secondary fermentation takes place in the individual bottles (as it does in Champagne), but then instead of RIDDLING and DISGORGING each bottle, the wine is emptied into large tanks where these two processes take place under pressure. Finally, the wine is filtered, a DOSAGE (see the French glossary) is added, and the wine is rebottled.

**Typicity:** A quality that a wine possesses if it is typical of its region and reflects the characteristics of the grape variety from which it came. Whether or not a wine demonstrates typicity is pretty subjective. It also has nothing to do with how good the wine tastes. A wine can be quite delicious and nonetheless show no typicity. A rich, full-bodied, buttery, oaky Sancerre, for example, would not have typicity, since Sancerres are typically lean, minerally, zesty, and have grassy flavors. In certain OLD WORLD countries, an evaluation of typicity, even though it's subjective, is required by law in order for a wine to obtain APPELLATION status.

873

## U

**Ullage:** The space that develops at the top of bottles or containers when wine is lost by leakage or evaporation. When ullage is significant, the wine often experiences OXIDATION and becomes spoiled.

**Unfiltered:** Used to describe a wine that has not been FILTERED to clarify it. Winemakers who believe that filtering strips wine of some flavors and texture may leave their wines unfiltered and may even label them as such. An unfiltered wine often still undergoes FINING to remove large particles in suspension. Unfiltered wines are sometimes less than brilliantly clear.

**Unfined:** A wine that has not gone through FINING to clarify it. As with FILTERING, many winemakers believe fining can harm the flavor and texture of the wine. An unfined wine may still be filtered.

## V

**Vanillin:** A compound in oak barrels that is ultimately imparted to wine as a flavor and smell reminiscent of vanilla. New barrels have more vanillin than older barrels and hence wine stored in new barrels has a more pronounced vanilla character.

**Varietal:** Wine made from a particular variety of grape. Chardonnay, riesling, pinot noir, cabernet sauvignon, and so on are all varietal wines. In general, each varietal has a unique flavor, distinct from other varietals. When a wine has a pronounced varietal flavor it is said to have varietal character. On January 1, 1983, United States law established that a wine named after a grape—a varietal—must contain 75 percent or more of that grape variety. Prior to that date, a varietally labeled wine had to contain 51 percent or more of the named grape.

**Vegetal:** Used to describe a wine with off-putting AROMAS and flavors reminiscent of stewed vegetables: bell peppers, green beans, asparagus, artichokes, and the like.

**Vinegary:** Describes a wine with the harsh aroma of vinegar, usually produced by ACETIC acid. Considered a major fault in a wine.

**Viniculture:** The science of winemaking. The term is used much less frequently than ENOLOGY.

**Vinifera:** See VITIS.

**Vinous:** Winelike. Europeans sometimes criticize California wines as being too fruity and so not vinous enough.

**Vintage:** The year the grapes were grown and harvested. A vintage year appears on the labels of most wines, though some famous wines—nonvintage Champagne, Sherry, and many styles of Port, for example—never carry a vintage date because they are blends of wines from several different years. In the United States, most wines bottled with a vintage date are made up entirely of grapes from that year. Technically, however, United States law requires only that 95 percent of the wine come from grapes harvested in the year appearing on the label.

**Vintage Champagne:** Champagne made from a single year's harvest. Aged a minimum of three years and often four or five. Called MILLÉSIME in French.

**Vintner:** A person who makes or sells wine. Often used to describe the owner of a winery who may also employ a winemaker.

**Viscosity:** The character some wines possess of being somewhat syrupy and slow to move around in the mouth. A spoonful of honey, for example, is more viscous than a spoonful of water, and ALCOHOL, by its nature, is viscous. Thus both sweet wines and wines with high alcohol are more viscous than dry wines and wines low in alcohol.

**Viticulture:** The science of growing grapes.

**Vitis:** The genus of the plant kingdom to which grapevines belong. Within the genus *Vitis* there are some sixty separate species. The most famous species—and the only one to have originated in Europe—is *Vitis vinifera*, which includes all of the well-known wine grapes, chardonnay, pinot noir, cabernet sauvignon, and so on, and accounts for virtually all of the wines made today. Most species of vines, however, originated in North America. These include *Vitis labrusca, Vitis riparia, Vitis rupestris, Vitis rotundifolia,* and *Vitis berlandieri,* among others. Only a small percentage of American wines are made from indigenous species, which generally produce wines that are far less sophisticated and complex than those made from *vinifera* varieties. *Labrusca* grapes, such as Concord, are easily recognizable by their pungent, candylike aroma and flavor, usually described as FOXY. Although no well-known wines are made from *Vitis riparia, Vitis rupestris, Vitis berlandieri,* and *Vitis rotundifolia,* they are very resistant to PHYLLOXERA and so are frequently used for ROOTSTOCKS. Over centuries, many American species have hybridized by chance, and from 1880 to 1950 scientists in both France and the United States intentionally created HYBRIDS by crossing *vinifera* varieties with hardier, more disease- and pest-resistant American varieties. While their use for wine is declining, hybrids remain critically important as rootstocks.

**Volatile Acidity:** All wines have a tiny amount of volatile acidity, usually, with any luck, imperceptible. In excess, V.A., as it is known, causes a wine to have an unpleasant sharp vinegary aroma. Volatile acidity occurs because unwanted bacteria have produced ACETIC acid, the result of poor winemaking.

**Y**

**Yeasty:** In STILL WINES, yeasty describes an AROMA suggestive of the yeasts used in FERMENTATION. The quality should not be pronounced. In Champagne and SPARKLING WINES, it refers to the aroma of bread dough, considered positive and often the result of long aging on the LEES.

**Yield:** The measure of how much a vineyard produces. In general, very high yields are associated with low-quality wine, and low yields are associated with high-quality wine. However, the relationship of yield of grapes to wine quality is extremely complex and not linear. Thus, a yield of 2 tons per acre does not necessarily produce better wine than a yield of 3 tons per acre, which doesn't necessarily portend better wine than if the yield were 4 tons per acre. Every vineyard is different, and yield must always be considered in light of multiple other factors, including the variety of grape, the type of CLONE, the age of the vine, the particular ROOTSTOCK, and the TERROIR. In Europe yield is measured in hectoliters per hectare (one hectoliter equals 26.4 gallons; one hectare equals 2.47 acres). The unofficial French dictum is that great red wine cannot be made from yields of more than 50 hectoliters per hectare. In the United States yield is generally measured in tons of grapes per acre. Roughly speaking, 1 ton per acre equals 15 hectoliters per hectare. Yields in the United States can range from less than 1 ton per acre to 10 or more. This said, the way yield is thought about in the United States is changing as a result of new vineyards, many of which are now planted so that the vines are much more closely spaced than they were in the past. With such vineyards, viticulturists talk of pounds of grapes per vine rather than tons per acre.

# French Wine Terms

**A**

**Appellation d'Origine Contrôlée (AOC):** See page 116.

**Assemblage:** A Champagne or SPARKLING WINE term that refers to the blending, or assembling, of STILL WINES before the SECONDARY FERMENTATION, which creates the bubbles.

**B**

**Baumé:** The scale used in France and much of the rest of Europe for measuring sugar in grapes and, hence, their ripeness. Other scales for measuring sugar include BRIX (used in the United States) and OECHSLE (used in Germany).

**Blanc de Blancs:** Literally white from whites. A golden Champagne or SPARKLING WINE made entirely from chardonnay grapes.

**Blanc de Noirs:** Literally white from blacks. A golden Champagne or SPARKLING WINE made from black (*noir*) grapes. (The French refer to red grapes as black.) It is possible to make a white wine from red grapes because the juice and PULP of red-skinned grapes is white. *Blanc de noirs* are usually made from pinot noir, but pinot meunier may be used in some cases. Very few Champagne houses produce *blanc de noirs* Champagnes. The practice is more common among makers of Californian sparkling wines.

**Brut:** A DRY to very dry Champagne or SPARKLING WINE. EXTRA BRUT is slightly drier than brut.

**C**

**Cépage Noble:** *Cépage* means grape variety. The so-called noble grape varieties—*cépages nobles*— are those that consistently make fine wine, such as cabernet sauvignon, pinot noir, or chardonnay.

**Chai(s):** Above-ground facilities that are used to store wine.

**Château:** A building where wine is made and around which vines grow. Despite the images most of us have of palatial estates, such as Bordeaux's regal Château Margaux, a château can be as humble as a garage. The names of most Bordeaux estates are preceded by the word *château*, though the word is used infrequently elsewhere in France and never in Burgundy, where the roughly equivalent term would be DOMAINE.

**Climat:** The term used especially in Burgundy to mean a specific field or plot. Each *climat* is distinguished by its own soil, climate, orientation to the sun, slope, drainage capacity, and so on.

**Clos:** A term used especially in Burgundy to indicate a vineyard enclosed by a wall. One of Burgundy's largest and most famous walled vineyards is Clos Vougeot.

**Commune:** A small village that is often an APPELLATION. In Bordeaux the communes of Margaux, Pauillac, St.-Julien, and St.-Estèphe are famous appellations.

**Crémant:** Today the word *crémant* is reserved for French SPARKLING WINES made outside the Champagne region using the MÉTHODE CHAMPENOISE. Important examples include Crémant d'Alsace, Crémant de Bourgogne, and Crémant de Loire. Since 1994 the term has not been permitted to be used in Champagne. It was once used to describe a Champagne with about half the usual effervescence, often called a creaming wine. These half-sparkling Champagnes are still made, but today they are given proprietary names.

**Cru:** Translated in English as growth, the word *cru* can mean a vineyard or an estate, usually a superior one, that has been classified geographically or by reputation. A classified *cru* is known as a *cru classé*. Within any given classification (such as those in Bordeaux and Burgundy), there are *Premiers Crus* (first growths), *Grands Crus* (great growths), and so on.

**Cuvée:** The wine from a selected barrel or vat (the term is derived from the French *cuve*, meaning vat). In Champagne, however, the word *cuvée* is used to describe a blend of wines. A Champagne *cuvée* is often made up of different varieties of grapes, or grapes from different vineyard plots, or both. The term prestige *cuvée* is used in Champagne to refer to a house's most expensive and prestigious wine. Dom Pérignon, for example, is the prestige *cuvée* of Moët & Chandon.

**Cuverie:** The building that houses FERMENTATION tanks or vats. The place where the wine ferments.

**D**

**Dégorgement:** Disgorgement (see DISGORGING)— the process of removing the yeasty sediments from a Champagne bottle after the second, bubble-forming FERMENTATION.

**Demi-Sec:** A sweet Champagne or SPARKLING WINE. Demi-sec is sweeter than EXTRA DRY, which is sweeter than BRUT.

**De Primeur:** Wines that are sold and drunk very young. The most famous of these is Beaujolais Nouveau, although more than fifty French wines are allowed by law to be sold the year the grapes were harvested. Not to be confused with EN PRIMEUR.

**Domaine:** A wine-producing estate. Many wineries throughout France incorporate the word in their names, especially Burgundian estates, the most famous of which is the Domaine de la Romanée-Conti.

**Dosage:** The degree of sweetness of the LIQUEUR D'EXPÉDITION, which is used to TOP UP Champagne

before its final corking. The *dosage* is what determines whether a Champagne will be BRUT, EXTRA DRY, DEMI-SEC, and so on.

**E**

**Eau-de-Vie:** Literally, water of life. *Eaux-de-vie* (the plural) are grape spirits, or clear brandies, that have been made by distilling wine or POMACE.

**Encépagement:** The various grape varieties used in any given wine.

**En Coteaux:** Vines planted on slopes, usually making superior wine.

**En Primeur:** A method of buying, wherein the wine is bought before it is released. Also known as buying futures. Buying wine *en primeur* allows collectors to be more certain of securing given wines. The wines most likely to be sold *en primeur* are Bordeaux wines from top châteaux.

**Extra Brut:** A very DRY Champagne or SPARKLING WINE, with minimal (less than 0.6 percent) added sweetness or DOSAGE. Drier than BRUT.

**Extra Dry:** Easily confused with EXTRA BRUT, its meaning is the opposite. Extra dry Champagne or SPARKLING WINE is slightly sweeter than BRUT.

**G**

**Garigue:** A word used to describe the arid landscape of Provence and the southern Rhône, which is covered with dry scrub and tough, resiny wild herbs, such as rosemary, thyme, and lavender. The wines of Provence and the southern Rhône are said to smell and taste of garigue, *garrigue* in French.

**Goût de Terroir:** The distinctive taste imparted by the combination of a given grape variety grown in a specific TERROIR.

**Grande Marque:** A member of a particular association of about thirty of the longest-established Champagne HOUSES. The Syndicat de Grandes Marques is devoted to upholding a written charter of high standards in the production of Champagne.

**H**

**House:** As used in the Champagne region, house refers to a producer selling Champagne under its brand name. The grapes may come from its own vineyards, from independent growers, or most often from a combination of the two. Such firms as Veuve Clicquot, Moët & Chandon, and Taittinger are all referred to as houses.

**L**

**Liqueur de Tirage:** The mixture of wine and sugar added along with yeasts to the blend of still wines in a Champagne bottle in order to induce the second, bubble-forming fermentation.

**Liqueur d'Expédition:** The wine added to the Champagne bottle after DISGORGING to top it up and, usually, to add some sweetness (see DOSAGE). The *liqueur d'expédition* is often made up of wines reserved from previous years.

**M**

**Macération Carbonique:** CARBONIC MACERATION, as it is referred to in English, is a type of FERMENTATION in which uncrushed grapes are placed whole into vats that are then closed. As the weight of the grapes on top crushes grapes on the bottom, juice is released and fermentation begins. This in turn releases the gas CARBON DIOXIDE ($CO_2$), which causes other grapes to ferment, in effect, within their skins. Carbonic maceration is commonly used to ferment fruity red wines for early drinking, typically in Beaujolais and sometimes in the Loire and Languedoc-Roussillon.

**Marc:** The French term for an EAU-DE-VIE made specifically by distilling the POMACE (grape skins, stems, and seeds) left over after pressing, not by distilling wine. *Marc* is generally a slightly more powerfully flavored spirit than *eau-de-vie*.

**Mas:** The southern French term for a DOMAINE, sometimes translated as farm.

**Méthode Champenoise:** The labor-intensive method used to make Champagne and other fine SPARKLING WINES: The wine undergoes a SECONDARY FERMENTATION, which creates the bubbles, in individual bottles rather than in one large cask or vat.

**Millésime:** A VINTAGE CHAMPAGNE.

**Moelleux:** A term commonly used in the Loire for very sweet, luscious white wines that can be almost syrupy.

**Monopole:** Used most frequently in Burgundy and to a lesser extent in Champagne, a *monopole* is a vineyard owned entirely by one estate.

**Mousse:** The French term for the actual effervescence, froth, foam, or sparkle of Champagne or SPARKLING WINES.

**Mousseux:** French for sparkling. Some VIN MOUSSEUX are made by the MÉTHODE CHAMPENOISE (with SECONDARY FERMENTATION taking place in the bottle); other less expensive *mousseux* are made in large tanks.

**Muselet:** The wire cage holding a Champagne cork onto the bottle.

**N**

**Négociant:** An individual or firm that buys grapes and/or ready-made wine from growers and/or cooperatives. The *négociant* then blends, bottles, labels, and sells the wine under its own brand or name. The first *négociant* houses were established in France around the time of the French Revolution. The sudden profusion of peasant growers who were inexperienced in sales created the need for firms that could bottle and sell the production from many small properties.

**Nouveau:** A young wine meant for immediate drinking, usually seven to ten weeks after being made. The most famous wine made in a nouveau style is Beaujolais Nouveau.

**O**

**Oeil de Perdrix:** Literally partridge eye, *oeil de perdrix* is the term used to describe the color of a pale rosé.

**R**

**Rémuage:** The RIDDLING (rotating and tilting) of Champagne bottles to concentrate yeast sediments in their necks. Riddling is done by hand in A-shape frames called *pupitres* or by a computerized machine called a gyropalette.

**S**

**Saignée:** A process used to make rosé by drawing pink-colored juice off fermenting red grapes. This process also results in concentrating the remaining red wine since the ratio of skins to juice in the tank is increased when some juice is drawn off.

**Sec:** DRY. However, when sec appears on a Champagne or SPARKLING WINE label, the wine inside will be medium sweet to sweet.

**Sélection de Grains Nobles:** In Alsace the term for wines made from very late picked berries that have been affected by BOTRYTIS CINEREA.

**Sur Lie:** Literally on the LEES. For a period of time after fermentation is complete some white wines, notably white Burgundies, are left in contact with the lees (spent yeasts). Wines that have been left *sur lie* take on a creamy, rounder MOUTHFEEL and generally display more COMPLEX flavors.

**T**

**Tastevin:** A shallow, silver tasting cup used by a SOMMELIER. The cup was designed with dimpled sides that would reflect candlelight in dark cellars and thereby allow the sommelier to see the color of the wine.

**Terroir:** French term for the sum entity and effect (no single word exists in English) of a vineyard's soil, slope, orientation to the sun, and elevation, plus every nuance of climate: rainfall, wind velocity, frequency of fog, cumulative hours of sunshine, average high temperatures, average low temperatures, and so on. Each vineyard is said to have its own *terroir*.

**V**

**Vendange Tardive:** In Alsace, the term for wines made from late-picked, very ripe grapes.

**Vin de Garde:** A wine to save—in other words, a wine that can and should receive AGING.

**Vin de Pays:** Country wine—an everyday wine from a specific region, but less rigorously controlled than an APPELLATION D'ORIGINE CONTRÔLÉE or VIN DÉLIMITÉ DE QUALITÉ SUPÉRIEURE wine.

**Vin de Table:** Table wine. Generally used to indicate a simple wine without APPELLATION D'ORIGINE CONTRÔLÉE status.

**Vin Délimité de Qualité Supérieure (VDQS):** See page 117.

**Vin Gris:** A very pale rosé wine, sometimes light gray in color.

**Vin Liquoreux:** A very sweet, syrupy white wine, generally made from grapes affected by BOTRYTIS CINEREA.

**Vin Mousseux:** Sparkling wine, made either by SECONDARY FERMENTATION in bottle or in tank, or for inexpensive wines, the addition of carbon dioxide.

**Vin Ordinaire:** Literally ordinary wine—a plain wine with no regional or VARIETAL characteristics. An everyday drinking wine, *vin ordinaire* is the opposite of VIN DE GARDE, a wine to save, that is, a wine with aging potential.

## Italian Wine Terms

**A**

**Abbadia:** The term for abbey, sometimes shortened to just *badia*. Buildings that were once abbeys have often been converted into renowned Italian wine estates, such as Tuscany's Badia a Coltibuono.

**Abboccato:** Slightly sweet.

**Amabile:** A little sweeter than ABBOCCATO.

**Amaro:** Bitter. Many Italian wines, both white and red, have a slight *amaro* character, which is considered a positive attribute by Italians.

**Annata:** The year of the vintage.

**Asciutto:** Totally DRY.

**Azienda Agricola:** Wine estate—this term, sometimes abbreviated Az. Ag., often appears on wine labels, along with the actual name of the wine estate, when the grapes were grown on that estate and the wine was produced there as well.

**Azienda Vinicola:** The term for a winery. It often appears on wine labels.

**Azienda Vitivinicola:** Grape-growing and winemaking company. Like AZIENDA AGRICOLA and AZIENDA VINICOLA, the term often appears on wine labels.

**B**

**Bianco:** White, as in *vino bianco*, white wine.

**Botte:** Cask or barrel.

**Bottiglia:** Bottle.

**C**

**Cantina:** Wine cellar or yet another term for a winery.

**Cantina Sociale:** A growers' cooperative cellar. Italy, like France and Spain, has hundreds of wine co-ops, some of which make good but rarely great wine. Also referred to as a Cooperativa.

**Casa Vinicola:** A wine firm, usually making wine from wine or grapes it has purchased (as opposed to grapes grown on its own estate). The word *casa* itself means house.

**Cascina:** Northern Italian term for a farmhouse or estate.

**Castello:** The word for castle. Several famous Italian wine estates are housed in what were once castles—Castello dei Rampolla in Tuscany, for example.

**Chiaretto:** A very light red or even a rosé wine.

**Classico:** An official designation, referring to the heart of a DOC zone—by implication the classic or best part. In Chianti, the *classico* zone is so highly regarded that it has a DOC of its own—Chianti Classico.

**Consorzio:** A consortium of producers of a certain wine, who join forces to control and promote it.

**Cooperativa:** See CANTINA SOCIALE.

**D**

**Denominazione di Origine Controllata (DOC):** See page 323.

**Denominazione di Origine Controllata e Garantita (DOCG):** See page 323.

**Dolce:** Fully sweet. Italy produces countless sweet wines from many different grape varieties.

**E**

**Enoteca:** Wine library; a place where bottles of wine from different regions are displayed. Often these wines are also available for tasting. The most famous *enoteca* in Italy is in Siena.

**Etichetta:** Label.

## F

**Fattoria:** Tuscan term for a farm or wine estate. Many top Chianti producers use this term as part of their names—Fattoria di Felsina, for example.

**Fiasco:** Literally, a flask; more often used for the straw-encased Chianti bottle that was a fixture of the bohemian lifestyle in the 1960s in the United States. Chiantis sold in *fiaschi* (the plural) were usually pretty thin and quite cheap. Today very few Chiantis are sold in straw-covered bottles.

**Frizzante:** Slightly fizzy, but less so than SPARKLING WINE. The Veneto's prosecco is *frizzante*.

## G

**Gradazione Alcoolica:** Percentage of ALCOHOL BY VOLUME.

**Grappa:** A clear brandy (EAU-DE-VIE in French) made by distilling the POMACE left over after MUST or wine is pressed. *Grappa di monovitigno* is a grappa from a single grape variety, such as moscato or picolit. Because grappas made this way have a subtle suggestion of the aroma and flavor of the original grapes, they are considered superior.

## I

**Imbottigliato all'Origine:** Bottled at the source; the term may be used only by estates that produce and bottle the wine on the property where the grapes were grown.

**Imbottigliato da:** Bottled by, which will be followed by the producer's name; does not denote an ESTATE BOTTLED wine.

**Imbottigliato dal Viticoltore:** Bottled by the grower; may be used only by growers bottling their own wines.

**Indicazione Geografica Tipica (IGT):** See page 323.

## L

**Liquoroso:** Strong, often but not necessarily FORTIFIED, wine, which can be sweet or not.

## M

**Metodo Tradizionale:** The Champagne method (MÉTHODE CHAMPENOISE) for making SPARKLING WINE; also referred to as *metodo classico*. Most top Italian sparkling wines are made this way.

## N

**Nero:** Black or very dark red; said of both grapes and wines.

## P

**Passito:** An intensely flavored, usually sweet wine made from grapes half-dried to concentrate them.

**Pastoso:** Medium (not very) dry.

**Podere:** A farm, often turned into a wine estate.

These often use the word *podere* in their names, as in the Tuscan Podere Il Palazzino.

**Produttore:** Producer.

## R

**Riserva:** A wine that has been matured for a specific number of years, according to DENOMINAZIONE DI ORIGINE CONTROLLATA regulations.

**Rosato:** Rosé.

**Rosso:** Red. *Vino rosso* is distinguished from *vino bianco* (white wine) and *vino rosato* (rosé wine).

## S

**Secco:** DRY.

**Semisecco:** Semidry; in reality, medium sweet.

**Spumante:** Sparkling; literally, foaming.

**Stravecchio:** Very old, a term more frequently applied to spirits than wine.

**Superiore:** Generally indicates a wine of higher quality, often because it has more alcohol than the minimum required and/or it has been aged longer than regulations stipulate. Valpolicella Superiore, for example, is a Valpolicella with at least one year of aging in contrast to basic Valpolicella, which has no minimum.

## T

**Tenuta:** Holding or estate. Wine estates often incorporate the word tenuta into their names, as in the Tuscan estate Tenuta San Guido.

## U

**Ue:** A softer, lighter type of GRAPPA achieved by distilling actual grapes rather than POMACE.

**Uva:** Grape.

## V

**Vecchio:** Old; said of mature wines.

**Vendemmia:** The vintage, can be used in place of ANNATA on labels.

**Vigna:** Vineyard, also referred to as a *vigneto*.

**Vignaiolo:** Grape grower, also called a *viticoltore*.

**Villa:** Country manor, often one where wine is produced.

**Vino da Arrosto:** Wine for a roast, implying a red that is FULL-BODIED and has a deep COLOR.

**Vino da Pasto:** Everyday wine.

**Vino da Tavola:** Table wine—the regulation term for non-DOC wines.

**Vino Novello:** The wine of the current year, now used in the same sense as Beaujolais Nouveau, though Italy's *vino novellos* are not as highly promoted as France's Beaujolais Nouveau.

**Vite:** Vine.

**Vitigno:** Grape variety.

# Spanish Wine Terms

**A**

**Añada:** See VENDIMIA.

**Año:** Year.

**B**

**Bodega:** Wine cellar or wine-producing company. Curiously, a single wine company may nonetheless use the plural form bodegas in its name, as in Bodegas Ismael Arroyo.

**C**

**Cava:** The name for Spanish SPARKLING WINE made by the Champagne method (MÉTHODE CHAMPENOISE). *Cava* is a specialty of the Penedès region of north central Spain near Barcelona. The two largest *cava* producers, Freixenet and Codorníu, each produce far more sparkling wine by the Champagne method than any Champagne house makes.

**Consejo Regulador:** Local governing body that enforces wine policy for a given area, including the boundaries of the area, the grape varieties permitted, maximum YIELD, and so forth. Every Spanish wine region with a DENOMINACIÓN DE ORIGEN has a *Consejo Regulador.*

**Cosecha:** Year of harvest, or vintage.

**Criadera:** Literally nursery, *criadera* refers to a layer of Sherry casks, all of which contain wine of approximately the same age and blend. Multiple *criaderas*—sometimes more than a dozen—make up a SOLERA.

**Crianza:** The basic-quality wine produced by each BODEGA. *Crianzas* are considered every-night drinking wines. They are less prestigious, less costly, and aged for shorter periods than RESERVAS or GRAN RESERVAS. While national law stipulates that *crianzas* must be aged for a minimum of six months in oak barrels, each DENOMINACIÓN DE ORIGEN or DENOMINACIÓN DE ORIGEN CALIFICADA can set higher standards. In Rioja, for example, a *crianza* must be aged for at least two years, one of which must be in oak barrels.

**D**

**Denominación de Origen (DO):** See page 413.

**Denominación de Origen Calificada (DOC):** See page 413.

**Dulce:** Sweet. Spain has less of a reputation for making top-quality sweet wines than France, Italy, or Germany, although several styles of Sherry, Spain's extraordinary FORTIFIED wine, can be sweet.

**E**

**Elaborado por:** Produced by.

**Embotellado por:** Bottled by.

**Extra Seco:** SPARKLING WINE that is not quite as dry as BRUT (SECO).

**F**

**Flor:** Literally flower, a layer of yeast cells that forms naturally on top of manzanilla and fino Sherries as they age in the cask. Flor acts to prevent OXIDATION and also contributes a unique flavor to the wine.

**G**

**Gran Reserva:** A BODEGA's top wine, produced only in excellent years and then subject to lengthy AGING. Though national law stipulates that red *gran reservas* must be aged two years in oak barrels, each DENOMINACIÓN DE ORIGEN or DENOMINACIÓN DE ORIGEN CALIFICADA can set higher standards. In Rioja, for example, red *gran reservas* must be aged for two years in barrel followed by three years in bottle, and in practice, many Rioja producers exceed even that.

**L**

**Lágrima:** Literally, tears; *lágrima* also refers to a wine made from free-run juice without any mechanical pressing.

**M**

**Método Tradicional:** Spanish term denoting SPARKLING WINE made by the Champagne method (MÉTHODE CHAMPENOISE). CAVA must be made this way.

**P**

**Pasada:** Term used to describe a well-aged Sherry.

**R**

**Reserva:** A wine produced only in excellent years. Though national law stipulates that red *reservas* must be aged for one year in oak barrels, each DENOMINACIÓN DE ORIGEN or DENOMINACIÓN DE ORIGEN CALIFICADA can set higher standards. Red *reservas* from Rioja, for example, must be aged for a minimum of three years, one of which must be in barrel. Many Rioja producers nonetheless exceed these requirements.

**Roble:** Oak. Despite Spain's proximity to France, many Spanish producers age their wines in American oak.

**Rosado:** Rosé. It's still a well-kept secret that Spain makes some of the best rosés in Europe. The rosés from Navarra are especially well thought of.

**S**

**Seco:** Dry.

**Semiseco:** Medium dry.

**Solera:** Complex network of barrels used for aging Sherry by progressively blending younger wines into older wines. Since the barrels are not completely filled, the wine is allowed to be gently subjected to OXIDIZATION during the process. Wine held in a solera is said to undergo the solera process.

**V**

**Vendimia:** Vintage.

**Viejo:** Old.

**Viña:** Literally means vineyard, but the word *viña* is often used as part of a brand name as, for example, in Viña Arana.

**Vino de Mesa:** Table wine.

**Vino Espumoso:** General term for SPARKLING WINE.

**Vino Generoso:** FORTIFIED wine developed under FLOR.

## Portuguese Wine Terms

**C**

**Colheita:** Literally, harvest. However, *colheita* is also the name for an aged tawny Port from a single harvest. *Colheita* Ports are rare.

**D**

**Denominação de Origem Controlada (DOC):** See page 483.

**E**

**Estufagem:** The step in the process of making Madeira that involves heating the wine. Depending on the quality of the Madeira being produced, there are several *estufagem* methods. The most basic involves placing the FORTIFIED base wines in containers that are then heated to an average temperature of 105°F for three to six months. To make the very finest Madeiras, however, the containers may be placed in a warehouse attic, which builds up tremendous heat thanks to the intense Madeiran sun. There the Madeira-to-be may be left for twenty years or more.

**G**

**Garrafeira:** Used in reference to Portuguese still wines, the word *garrafeira* indicates a wine of especially high quality. But the word also means

wine cellar or bottle cellar (from the Portuguese *garrafa*—bottle). In addition *garrafeira* is a style of Port, albeit a rare one. Rich and supple, *garrafeira* Ports are usually from a single outstanding year and are aged briefly in wood and then a long time—as many as twenty to forty years—in large glass bottles. After aging, the *garrafeira* is decanted and transferred into standard 750 milliliter bottles and sold.

**L**

**Lagar:** A shallow stone or cement trough in which grapes are trodden by foot (usually for several hours) in order to crush them and mix the skins with the juice. Tredding grapes by foot, an ancient practice, is still widely practiced in Portugal and thus many wineries have *lagares*.

**Q**

**Quinta:** Literally farm. In Portugal, the word *quinta* is used to refer both to a specific vineyard and to a wine estate. Quinta do Noval, for example, is the name of a highly regarded wine estate in the Douro region. Ports known as single vintage *quinta* Ports come from grapes grown on a single estate in a single year.

881

## German and Austrian Wine Terms

**A**

**Amtliche Prüfungsnummer:** A quality-control test number (the AP number) signifying that a wine has passed official analytical and taste tests. It appears on every bottle of quality German wine in the category of QUALITÄTSWEIN BESTIMMTER ANBAUGEBIETE or QUALITÄTSWEIN MIT PRÄDIKAT.

**Anbaugebiet:** One of thirteen specified wine-growing regions in Germany. Plural *anbaugebiete*.

**Ausbruch:** A category of wine made in Austria, in Burgenland. *Ausbruche* (the plural) are slightly more opulent than BEERENAUSLESEN, and must be made from overripe, BOTRYTIZED grapes.

**Auslese:** Plural *auslesen*. See page 523 for the German definition, page 564 for the Austrian.

**B**

**Beerenauslese (BA):** Plural *beerenauslesen*. See page 523 for the German definition, page 564 for the Austrian.

**Bereich:** One of forty official districts. Germany's thirteen wine regions (ANBAUGEBIETE) are officially broken down into forty *bereiche* (the plural of *bereich*), which in turn are broken down into GROSS-LAGEN, which are broken down into EINZELLAGEN.

**Berg:** Hill or mountain.

**Blau:** Blue; when used to describe grapes, it means red.

**Bocksbeutel:** Flagon-shaped bottle used for the wines of Germany's Franken region.

**Burg:** Fortress.

**Buschenschenk:** In the southern Austrian countryside this is the name for a rustic restaurant that elsewhere is called a HEURIGE. A *buschenschenk* is easily identified by the *buschenschenk* (also the name for a swag of fir branches) tied to its doors.

**C**

**Classic:** A term sometimes used on the labels of Germany's regional/varietal wines (e.g., Rheinhessen riesling) to indicate that the wine is dry. To be considered classic, the wine must have less than 1.5 percent RESIDUAL SUGAR. The term, which can be used or not at the producer's discretion, first appeared on German wine labels as of the 2000 vintage.

**E**

**Edelfäule:** BOTRYTIS CINEREA; Germany's and Austria's luscious DESSERT WINES BEERENAUSLESEN and TROCKENBEERENAUSLESEN are made with the help of *edelfäule*.

**Einzellage:** The official name for an individual vineyard site. There are more than 2,500 of them in Germany. Germany's 13 wine regions are officially broken down into 40 BEREICHE, which in turn are broken down into 163 GROSSLAGEN, which are broken down into *einzellagen*, the plural of *einzellage*.

**Eiswein:** A rare and especially intense DESSERT WINE made by pressing frozen grapes that have been left hanging on the vine into midwinter (sometimes February). These are gently pressed while still frozen, so that the ice is separated from the remaining concentrated, very sweet, high-acid juice. Because of their ACIDITY, *eiswein* are usually less unctuous but more vibrant than BEERENAUSLESEN or TROCKENBEERENAUSLESEN. *Eiswein* age for decades and are extremely expensive.

**Erstes Gewachs:** Literally, first growth. A designation used in the Rheingau (but not in other German wine regions) for vineyards considered exemplary. Only vineyards planted with riesling or spätburgunder are eligible to be classified *Erstes Gewachs*. For the term to appear on a wine label, the wine made from the *Erstes Gewachs* vineyard must itself be produced in a way that meets exacting standards and it must pass a sensory examination.

**Erzeugerabfüllung:** Wines produced and bottled by a grower or a cooperative. You won't see *erzeugerabfüllung* on the labels of well-known estates.

**F**

**Federspiel:** A term used only in the Wachau region of Lower Austria to indicate natural unchaptalized wines with no more than 11.9 percent ALCOHOL. *Federspiel* wines are more or less equivalent to wines that in other Austrian regions are known as KABINETTS.

**Flasche:** Bottle—the English word *flask* is derived from *flasche.*

**G**

**Grosslage:** One of approximately 163 collections of vineyards. Germany's 13 wine regions are officially broken down into 40 BEREICHE, which in turn are broken down into 163 *grosslagen* (the plural of *grosslage*), which are broken down into more than 2,500 EINZELLAGEN.

**Gutsabfüllung:** Estate bottled.

**H**

**Halbtrocken:** Literally, half-dry, this term is used in Germany, but rarely in Austria, where most wines are very dry. Wines labeled *halbtrocken* usually still taste extremely DRY because of the high corresponding ACIDITY in German wines. A wine of KABINETT, SPÄTLESE, or AUSLESE ripeness levels can be *halbtrocken* or TROCKEN.

**Heurige:** In Austria, a rustic type of restaurant often attached to a winemaker's home. Traditionally, all of the food at a *heurige* is made from scratch by the winemaker and his family. Similarly, the wine offered (which is also referred to as *heurige*) is the winemaker's.

**K**

**Kabinett:** See page 522 for the German definition, page 563 for the Austrian.

**Keller:** Cellar.

**KMW:** Acronym for Klosterneuburger Mostwaage. In Austria the KMW scale is used to measure sugar in grapes and hence their ripeness. In Germany, sugar is measured in OECHSLE; in France, in BAUMÉ; and in the United States, in BRIX.

**L**

**Landwein:** A category of simple, neutral TABLE WINE above TAFELWEIN in quality but below QUALITÄTSWEIN BESTIMMTER ANBAUGEBIETE in Germany and below QUALITÄTSWEIN in Austria.

**Lese:** Harvest—harvest dates range from September to December, according to the variety of grape, weather conditions, and the kind of wine being produced (KABINETT, SPÄTLESE, AUSLESE, and so forth).

**O**

**Oechsle:** Scale used in Germany to indicate the ripeness of grapes. Developed in the nineteenth century by the physicist Ferdinand Oechsle, Oechsle measures the weight of the grape juice or MUST. Since the contents of the must are primarily sugar and ACIDS, the must weight is an indication of ripeness. According to German law, ripeness categories are based on Oechsle levels that are specified according to the grape variety and wine region. For example, in order for a riesling wine in the Mosel to be considered a SPÄTLESE, it must have 76 degrees Oechsle; in the Rheingau, a riesling must have 85 degrees Oechsle to be a *spätlese*.

**P**

**Prädikat:** Special attribute of ripeness. In Germany, there are six *prädikat* levels, from KABINETT to TROCKENBEERENAUSLESE. See PAGE 521.

**Prädikatswein:** Wine with special attributes. In Austria, there are six *prädikatswein* levels, from SPÄTLESE to TROCKENBEERENAUSLESE. See page 563.

**Q**

**Qualitätswein:** An Austrian wine category; see page 563.

**Qualitätswein bestimmter Anbaugebiete (QbA):** A German wine category; see page 521.

**Qualitätswein mit Prädikat (QmP):** A German wine category; see page 521.

**R**

**Rotwein:** Red wine; Germany and Austria are famous for their whites, but a good deal of red wine is made in each and consumed locally.

**S**

**Schilcher:** Austrian name for a high-acid rosé made from the blauer wildbacher grape, which grows almost exclusively in west Styria.

**Schloss:** Castle—many German wine estates are housed in what were once medieval castles.

**Sekt:** SPARKLING WINE.

**Selection:** A term indicating that the wine contains less than 1.2 percent RESIDUAL SUGAR and therefore is DRY. The word selection may be used only on German wine labels that site the specific village and vineyard where the grapes were grown. However, use of the term *selection* is at the producer's discretion. Some producers prefer the term TROCKEN, which stipulates an even lower percentage of allowable residual sugar.

**Smaragd:** Austrian term used exclusively in the Wachau region of Lower Austria for the ripest grapes and hence fullest bodied wines. *Smaragd* wines must have a minimum of 11.3 percent alcohol. They are roughly equivalent to wines that elsewhere in Austria would be labeled SPÄTLESE. The

word *smaragd* is also the name of a bright green lizard that suns itself in the Wachau vineyards.

**Spätlese:** Plural *spätlesen*. See page 522 for the German definition, page 564 for the Austrian.

**Steinfeder:** In the Wachau region of Lower Austria, natural unchaptalized wines with no more than 10.7 percent alcohol are referred to as *steinfeders*. These come from the least ripe grapes and hence are the lightest bodied of Wachau wines.

**Strausswirtschaft:** German wine pubs, often attached to growers' homes, where they can sell their own wines and light foods for a total of only four months of the year, so as not to take business away from full-fledged restaurants open twelve months a year. A *strauss*—wreath—is usually hung over the door.

**Süssreserve:** Grape juice that has been held back from the harvest and left unfermented so that it has all of its natural sweetness. In Germany, small amounts of *süssreserve* may be added to very high ACID wines in order to BALANCE them.

**T**

**Tafelwein:** TABLE WINE, the humblest category of wine. Although the ALCOHOL content, grape varieties, and origin of grapes are all controlled by law, *tafelwein* is usually so light, it's often just a step above water. In Germany, when the word *Deutsche* (German) appears before *tafelwein*, it means the grapes were grown in Germany. Absent that designation, the grapes may come from one of several other EEC countries.

**Trocken:** Dry. Wines labeled *trocken* from both Germany and Austria must have less than 0.9 percent RESIDUAL SUGAR.

**Trockenbeerenauslese:** Plural *trockenbeerensauslesen*, but usually referred to as TBA. See page 523 for the German definition, 565 for the Austrian.

**W**

**Weingut:** Wine estate.

**Weinkellerei:** Winery that buys grape MUST or wine from a grower, then bottles and markets the wine.

**Weinstube:** German for wine tavern; a comfortable, casual restaurant where Germans go for simple food and a bottle of wine.

**Weissherbst:** In Germany, a rosé wine of at least QUALITÄTSWEIN BESTIMMTER ANBAUGEBIETE status made from red grapes of a single variety. A specialty of Baden.

**Winzer:** Grape farmer.

# Hungarian Wine Terms

### A

**Aszú:** This is literally the term for shriveled grapes that have been attacked by the beneficial mold BOTRYTIS CINEREA. More commonly, however, you'll encounter *aszú* as part of the name of Hungary's most famous wine: Tokay Aszú. Luscious and honeyed, Tokay Aszú is to Hungary what Sauternes is to France—a renowned sweet wine that is both difficult and expensive to make.

### E

**Edes:** Slightly sweet, a term usually applied to Szamorodni, the type of wine made in Tokay from vineyards where the grapes have not been sufficiently affected by BOTRYTIS CINEREA to make Tokay Aszú. Szamorodni may be slightly sweet or dry (SZÁRAZ).

### G

**Gönci:** The traditional barrels, which hold about 140 liters of wine, used to make Tokay Aszú (named after the village of Gönc, known for its barrel makers).

### P

**Primae Classis:** Literally, first class. A Latin designation used by the Hungarians since around 1700 to indicate a Tokay vineyard of first-class stature. The Tokay Aszú wines produced from grapes grown in such a vineyard would by extension be considered topflight.

**Pro Mensa Caesaris Primus:** Around 1700 two Tokay vineyards were given this designation, which means chosen for the royal table. These vineyards, Csarfas and Mézes Mály, ranked above those designated PRIMAE CLASSIS.

**Puttony:** The traditional basket in which ASZÚ grapes were gathered. The word *puttony* has given rise to *puttonyos*, the manner by which the sweetness of Tokay Aszú is measured. Tokay Aszú wines are labeled from 2 to 6 *puttonyos*; the more *puttonyos*, the sweeter the wine.

### S

**Secundo Classis:** Second class in Latin, first used in Hungary around 1700 to indicate a Tokay vineyard considered second best and hence a Tokay Aszú wine that was second in quality compared to wines made from grapes grown in PRIMAE CLASSIS vineyards but still well above most other vineyards.

**Száraz:** Dry. The term is usually applied to Szamorodni, the type of wine made in the Tokay region from vineyards where the grapes are not sufficiently affected by BOTRYTIS CINEREA to make Tokay Aszú.

884

# Greek Wine Terms

### A

**Amphora:** An earthenware vessel used by the ancient Greeks and Romans to store and ship wine. An amphora was oval in shape, with two large handles at the top for carrying and a pointed bottom so that the vessel could be pushed into the soft earth where it would remain upright. Amphorae range in size from that of a milk can to a refrigerator.

**Archondiko:** A word appearing on the labels of TOPIKOS OENOS wines, *archondiko* roughly translates as CHÂTEAU.

### E

**Epitrapezios Oenos (E.O.):** The simplest category of Greek wine, equivalent to VIN DE TABLE, or TABLE WINE, in France.

### K

**Krater:** A shallow bronze or pottery bowl used in antiquity to hold wine; wine would be poured from an AMPHORA into a krater to be served.

**Ktima:** Estate; can appear on the labels of TOPIKOS OENOS wines.

**Kylix:** A shallow, two-handled, often beautifully decorated cup from which wine was drunk in antiquity.

**Kythos:** In antiquity, a ladle used to scoop wine from the KRATER and transfer it into a KYLIX.

### M

**Monastiri:** Monastery; several Greek wine estates are located in former monasteries, and several Greek monasteries still produce wine. The word *monastiri* sometimes appears on the labels of TOPIKOS OENOS wines.

### S

**Stefáni:** A way of training grapevines that is especially common on windswept Greek islands. The vines are trained in a circle low to the ground (*stefáni* means crown), so that the grapes grow in the center protected from the wind.

### T

**Topikos Oenos (T.O.):** One of the simpler categories of Greek wine, equivalent to that of VIN DE PAYS, or country wine, in France.

# THE 1855 CLASSIFICATION OF BORDEAUX

## THE MÉDOC

The Médoc classification was based on the châteaux and did not take into account whether they produced red or white wines. In point of fact, virtually all of these châteaux make red wines exclusively.

| Premiers Crus (First Growths) | Appellation |
|---|---|
| Château Haut-Brion | Pessac-Léognan, in Graves not the Médoc |
| Château Lafite-Rothschild | Pauillac |
| Château Latour | Pauillac |
| Château Margaux | Margaux |
| Château Mouton-Rothschild* | Pauillac |

| Deuxièmes Crus (Second Growths) | Appellation |
|---|---|
| Château Brane-Cantenac | Margaux |
| Château Cos d'Estournel | St.-Estèphe |
| Château Ducru-Beaucaillou | St.-Julien |
| Château Durfort-Vivens | Margaux |
| Château Gruaud-Larose | St.-Julien |
| Château Lascombes | Margaux |
| Château Léoville-Barton | St.-Julien |
| Château Léoville-Las Cases | St.-Julien |
| Château Léoville-Poyferré | St.-Julien |
| Château Montrose | St.-Estèphe |
| Château Pichon-Longueville, Baron | Pauillac |
| Château Pichon-Longueville, Comtesse de Lalande | Pauillac |
| Château Rausan-Ségla | Margaux |
| Château Rauzan-Gassies | Margaux |

| Troisièmes Crus (Third Growths) | Appellation |
|---|---|
| Château Boyd-Cantenac | Margaux |
| Château Calon-Ségur | St.-Estèphe |
| Château Cantenac-Brown | Margaux |
| Château Desmirail | Margaux |
| Château d'Issan | Margaux |
| Château Ferrière | Margaux |
| Château Giscours | Margaux |
| Château Kirwan | Margaux |
| Château Lagrange | St.-Julien |
| Château la Lagune | Haut-Médoc |
| Château Langoa-Barton | St.-Julien |
| Château Malescot St.-Exupéry | Margaux |
| Château Marquis d'Alesme-Becker | Margaux |
| Château Palmer | Margaux |

| Quatrièmes Crus (Fourth Growths) | Appellation |
|---|---|
| Château Beychevelle | St.-Julien |
| Château Branaire-Ducru | St.-Julien |
| Château Duhart-Milon-Rothschild | Pauillac |
| Château Lafon Rochet | St.-Estèphe |
| Château la Tour-Carnet | Haut-Médoc |
| Château Marquis-de-Terme | Margaux |
| Château Pouget | Margaux |
| Château Prieuré-Lichine | Margaux |
| Château St.-Pierre | St.-Julien |
| Château Talbot | St.-Julien |

| Cinquièmes Crus (Fifth Growths) | Appellation |
|---|---|
| Château Batailley | Pauillac |
| Château Belgrave | Haut-Médoc |
| Château Cantermerle | Haut-Médoc |
| Château Clerc-Milon | Pauillac |
| Château Cos Labory | St.-Estèphe |
| Château Croizet-Bages | Pauillac |
| Château d'Armailhac | Pauillac |
| Château Dauzac | Margaux |

*In 1855 Mouton-Rothschild was ranked a Second Growth. In 1973 it was elevated to First Growth status.

(continued)

*(continued)*

# THE 1855 CLASSIFICATION OF BORDEAUX

### *Cinquièmes Crus*
**(Fifth Growths)** *continued*

| | |
|---|---|
| Château de Camensac | Haut-Médoc |
| Château du Tertre | Margaux |
| Château Grand-Puy-Ducasse | Pauillac |
| Château Grand-Puy-Lacoste | Pauillac |

| | |
|---|---|
| Château Haut-Bages-Liberal | Pauillac |
| Château Haut-Batailley | Pauillac |
| Château Lynch-Bages | Pauillac |
| Château Lynch-Moussas | Pauillac |
| Château Pédesclaux | Pauillac |
| Château Pontet-Canet | Pauillac |

## SAUTERNES AND BARSAC

*These châteaux in Sauternes and Barsac make mainly sweet white wines.*

### *Premier Cru Supérieur*
**(First Great Growth)**

Château d'Yquem

### *Premiers Crus*
**(First Growths)**

Château Climens
Château Coutet
Château Clos Haut-Peyraguey
Château de Rayne-Vigneau
Château Guiraud
Château Lafaurie-Peyraguey
Château La Tour Blanche
Château Rabaud-Promis
Château Rieussec
Château Sigalas-Rabaud
Château Suduiraut

### *Deuxièmes Crus* *
**(Second Growths)**

Château Broustet
Château Caillou
Château d'Arche
Château de Malle
Château de Myrat
Château Doisy-Daëne
Château Doisy-Dubroca
Château Doisy-Védrines
Château Filhot
Château Lamothe-Despujols
Château Lamothe-Guignard
Château Nairac
Château Romer
Château Romer-du-Hayot
Château Suau

*When Sauternes and Barsac were classified in 1855, twelve *Deuxièmes Crus Classés* were designated. Since then, some of these have split into more than one château. The *Deuxièmes Crus Classés* now number fifteen.

# Bibliography

The following reference materials have been invaluable in writing this book. If an asterisk (*) appears at the end of an entry, a more recent edition is available. Readers should be aware, however, that most of the research for *The Wine Bible* was conducted on site, in wine-producing countries around the world. This research was augmented by hundreds of lengthy interviews with individual experts on specific topics and on particular wine-producing regions. My gratitude to all of these individuals is inestimable. Finally, nothing supplants thousands of hours spent tasting and thinking hard about many thousands of wines each year (research does have its rewards).

## GENERAL REFERENCE

Ackerman, Diane. *A Natural History of the Senses.* New York: Random House, 1990.

Amerine, Maynard A., and Vernon L. Singleton. *Wine: An Introduction for Americans.* Berkeley: University of California Press, 1965.

Bespaloff, Alexis. *Alexis Bespaloff New Signet Book of Wine.* New York: Signet, 1971.

———. *The New Frank Schoonmaker Encyclopedia of Wine,* 8th ed. New York: William Morrow, 1988.

Clarke, Oz. *Oz Clarke's New Classic Wines.* New York: Simon & Schuster, 1991.

———. *Oz Clarke's 1993 Wine Handbook.* New York: Simon & Schuster, 1992.

———. *Oz Clarke's Wine Atlas.* Boston: Little, Brown and Company, 1995.

Dovaz, Michel, and Steven Spurrier. *Académie du Vin Wine Course: The Complete Course in Wine Appreciation, Tasting, and Study of the Paris Académie du Vin,* 2nd ed. London: Mitchell Beazley, 1990.

Hyams, Edward. *Dionysus: A Social History of the Wine Vine.* New York: Macmillan, 1965.

Johnson, Hugh. *Hugh Johnson's Modern Encyclopedia of Wine.* New York: Simon & Schuster, 1991, and 4th ed., 1998.

———. *The Story of Wine.* London: Mitchell Beazley, 1989.

———. *The World Atlas of Wine: A Complete Guide to the Wines and Spirits of the World.* New York: Simon & Schuster, 1971.*

Johnson, Hugh, and James Halliday. *The Vintner's Art: How Great Wines Are Made.* New York: Simon & Schuster, 1992.

Johnson, Hugh, Dora Jane Janson, and David Revere McFadden. *Wine: Celebration and Ceremony.* New York: Cooper-Hewitt Museum, 1985.

Kolpan, Steven, Brian H. Smith, and Michael A. Weiss. *Exploring Wine: The Culinary Institute of America's Complete Guide to Wines of the World.* New York: Van Nostrand Reinhold, 1996.

McGovern, Patrick E., Stuart J. Fleming, and Solomon H. Katz, editors. *The Origins and Ancient History of Wine.* Philadelphia: Gordon and Breach Publishers, 1995.

Peynaud, Emile. *The Taste of Wine: The Art and Science of Wine Appreciation.* Translated by Michael Schuster. London: Macdonald Orbis, 1987.

Robinson, Jancis, editor. *The Oxford Companion to Wine.* Oxford: Oxford University Press, 1994, and 2nd ed., 1999.

Robinson, Jancis. *Vines, Grapes and Wines.* New York: Alfred A. Knopf, 1986.

Siegel, Ronald K. *Intoxication: Life in Pursuit of Artificial Paradise.* London: Simon & Schuster, 1989.

Unwin, Tim. *Wine and the Vine: An Historical Geography of Viticulture and the Wine Trade.* London: Routledge, 1991.

Watney, Bernard M., and Homer D. Babbidge. *Corkscrews for Collectors.* London: Sotheby Parke Bernet, 1981.

## FRANCE

Atkin, Tim. *Vin de Pays d'Oc.* Bailly, France: Editions Gilbert & Gaillard, 1994.

Coates, Clive. *The Wines of France.* South San Francisco: The Wine Appreciation Guild, 1999.

Faith, Nicholas. *The Story of Champagne.* New York: Facts On File, 1989.

Fried, Eunice. *Burgundy: The Country, the Wines, the People.* New York: Harper and Row, 1986.

Friedrich, Jacqueline. *A Wine and Food Guide to the Loire.* New York: Henry Holt and Company, 1996.

George, Rosemary. *The Wines of Chablis.* London: Sotheby Publications, 1984.

Hanson, Anthony. *Burgundy.* London: Faber and Faber, 1982.*

Jacquemont, Guy, and Paul Mereaud. *Beaujolais: The Complete Guide*. Boston: Little, Brown and Company, 1986.

Kramer, Matt. *Making Sense of Burgundy*. New York: William Morrow, 1990.

Livingstone-Learmonth, John, and Melvyn C. H. Master. *The Wines of the Rhône*. London: Faber and Faber, 1983.

Lynch, Kermit. *Adventures on the Wine Route: A Wine Buyer's Tour of France*. New York: Farrar, Straus and Giroux, 1988.

Markham, Dewey, Jr. *1855: A History of the Bordeaux Classification*. New York: John Wiley & Sons, 1998.

Mayberry, Robert W. *Wines of the Rhône Valley: A Guide to Origins*. Totowa, New Jersey: Rowman & Littlefield, 1987.

Norman, Remington. *Rhône Renaissance*. San Francisco: Wine Appreciation Guild, 1996.

Olney, Richard. *Romanée-Conti: The World's Most Fabled Wine*. New York: Rizzoli, 1995.

Parker, Robert M., Jr. *Bordeaux: The Definitive Guide for the Wines Produced Since 1961*, 2nd ed. New York: Simon & Schuster, 1991, and 3rd ed., 1998.

————. *Burgundy: A Comprehensive Guide to the Producers, Appellations, and Wines*. New York: Simon & Schuster, 1990.

————. *The Wines of the Rhône Valley*, 2nd ed. New York: Simon & Schuster, 1997.

Penning-Rowsell, Edmund. *The Wines of Bordeaux*, 6th ed. London: Penguin Books, 1989.

Peppercorn, David. *Bordeaux*, 2nd ed. London: Faber and Faber, 1991.

Seely, James. *Great Bordeaux Wines*. Boston: Little, Brown and Company, 1986.

Simon, André L. *The History of Champagne*. London: Octopus Books Limited, 1971.

Stevenson, Tom. *The Wines of Alsace*. London: Faber and Faber, 1993.

Style, Sue. *A Taste of Alsace*. New York: William Morrow, 1990.

Sutcliffe, Serena. *Champagne: The History and Character of the World's Most Celebrated Wine*. New York: Simon & Schuster, 1988.

Voss, Roger. *Wines of the Loire*. London: Faber and Faber, 1995.

## ITALY

Anderson, Burton. *The Simon & Schuster Guide to the Wines of Italy*. New York: Simon & Schuster, 1992.

————. *The Wine Atlas of Italy and Traveller's Guide to the Vineyards*. New York: Simon & Schuster, 1990.

————. *Vino: The Wines and Winemakers of Italy*. Boston: Little, Brown and Company, 1980.

Flower, Raymond. *Chianti: The Land, the People, and the Wine*. New York: Universe Books, 1979.*

Hazan, Victor. *Italian Wine*. New York: Alfred A. Knopf, 1982.

Steinberg, Edward. *The Vines of San Lorenzo: The Making of a Great Wine in the New Tradition*. Hopwell, New Jersey: Ecco Press, 1992.

Wasserman, Sheldon, and Pauline Wasserman. *Italy's Noble Red Wines*, 2nd ed. New York: Macmillan Publishing, 1991.

## SPAIN AND PORTUGAL

Begg, Desmond. *Travellers Wine Guide: Spain*. New York: Sterling Publishing Company, 1990.

Bradford, Sarah. *The Story of Port*. London: Christie's Wine Publications, 1983.

Cossart, Noël. *Madeira: The Island Vineyard*. London: Christie's Wine Publications, 1984.

Delaforce, John. *The Factory House at Oporto*, bicentenary ed. Bromley, Kent, England: Christopher Helm, 1990.

Duijker, Hubrecht. *The Wine Atlas of Spain and Traveller's Guide to the Vineyards*. New York: Simon & Schuster, 1992.

Galhano, A., A. Moreira da Fonseca, J. R.-P. Rosas, and E. Serpa Pimentel. *Port Wine: Notes on Its History, Production and Technology*, 4th ed. Oporto: Instituto do Vinho Porto, 1991.

Jeffs, Julian. *The Wines of Spain*. London: Faber and Faber, 1999.

McWhirter, Kathryn, and Charles Metcalfe. *Encyclopedia of Spanish and Portuguese Wines*. New York: Simon & Schuster, 1991.

Read, Jan. *The Simon & Schuster Guide to the Wines of Spain*. New York: Simon & Schuster, 1992.

Suckling, James. *Vintage Port: The Wine Spectator's Ultimate Guide for Consumers, Collectors, and Investors*. San Francisco: Wine Spectator Press, 1990.

Walker, Ann, and Larry Walker. *A Season in Spain*. New York: Simon & Schuster, 1992.

## GERMANY

Ambrosi, Hans, and Kerry Brady Stewart. *Travellers Wine Guide: Germany*. New York: Sterling Publishing Company, Inc., 1990.

Anderson, Jean, and Hedy Würz. *The New German Cookbook: More than 230 Contemporary and Traditional Recipes*. New York: HarperCollins Publishers, Inc., 1993.

BIBLIOGRAPHY

Jamieson, Ian. *German Wines*. London: Faber and Faber, 1991.

———. *The Simon & Schuster Guide to the Wines of Germany*. New York: Simon & Schuster, 1992.

Johnson, Hugh. *The Atlas of German Wines and Traveller's Guide to the Vineyards*. London: Mitchell Beazley, 1986.

Pigott, Stuart. *Life Beyond Liebfraumilch*. London: Sidgwick & Jackson, Limited, 1988.

## AUSTRIA

MacDonogh, Giles. *The Wine and Food of Austria*. London: Mitchell Beazley, 1992.

## GREECE

Lambert-Gocs, Miles. *The Wines of Greece*. Boston: Faber and Faber, 1990.

## UNITED STATES AND CANADA

### GENERAL

Adams, Leon D. *The Wines of America*. New York: McGraw-Hill, 1985.

Cass, Bruce, editor, and Jancis Robinson, consulting editor. *The Oxford Companion to the Wines of North America*. Oxford: Oxford University Press, 2000.

De Villiers, Marq. *The Heartbreak Grape: A Journey in Search of the Perfect Pinot Noir*. Toronto: HarperCollins Publishers Ltd., 1993.

Gabler, James M. *Passions: The Wines and Travels of Thomas Jefferson*. Baltimore: Bacchus Press, 1995.

Kramer, Matt. *Making Sense of California Wine*. New York: William Morrow, 1992.

Mariani, John F. *The Dictionary of American Food and Drink*. New Haven: Ticknor & Fields, 1983.*

Pinney, Thomas. *A History of Wine in America from the Beginnings to Prohibition*. Berkeley: University of California Press, 1989.

Thomas, Marguerite. *Wineries of the Eastern States*. Lee, Massachusetts: Berkshire House, 1996.

Wagner, Philip M. *Grapes into Wine: A Guide to Winemaking*. New York: Alfred A. Knopf, 1987.

### CALIFORNIA

Halliday, James. *Wine Atlas of California*. New York: Viking, 1993.

Muscatine, Doris, Maynard A. Amerine, and Bob Thompson, editors. *The University of California/ Sotheby Book of California Wine*. Berkeley: University of California Press, 1984.

Sullivan, Charles L. *A Companion to California Wine: An Encyclopedia of Wine and Winemaking from the Mission Period to the Present*. Berkeley: University of California Press, 1998.

### TEXAS

English, Sarah Jane. *The Wines of Texas: A Guide and a History*. Austin: Eakin Press, 1989.*

Giordano, Frank. *Texas Wines and Wineries*. Austin: Texas Monthly Press, 1984.

### WASHINGTON STATE AND OREGON

Casteel, Ted, editor. *Oregon Winegrape Grower's Guide*, 4th ed. Portland: Oregon Winegrowers' Association Publishers, 1992.

Clark, Corbet. *American Wines of the Northwest*. New York: William Morrow, 1989.

Gregutt, Paul, and Jeff Prather. *Northwest Wines: A Pocket Guide to the Wines of Washington, Oregon, and Idaho*. Seattle: Sasquatch Books, 1994.

Hill, Chuck. *The Northwest Winery Guide*. Seattle: Speed Graphics, 1988.

## AUSTRALIA AND NEW ZEALAND

Cooper, Michael. *The Wines and Vineyards of New Zealand*. Auckland: Hodder and Stoughton, 1984.*

Halliday, James. *A History of the Australian Wine Industry, 1949–1994*. Cowandilla, South Australia: Winetitles Publishers, 1994.

———. *Wine Atlas of Australia and New Zealand*. Sydney: HarperCollins Australia, 1991.*

Iland, Patrick, and Peter Gago. *Australian Wine from the Vine to the Glass*. Adelaide: Patrick Iland Wine Promotions Publishers, 1997.

Mayo, Oliver. *The Wines of Australia*. London: Faber and Faber, 1991.

## SOUTH AFRICA

Platter, John. *John Platter's South African Wine Guide*. Edited by Erica Platter. Stellenbosch, South Africa: J. & E. Platter, 1992, and 2nd ed., 1997.

## CHILE

Hernandez, Alejandro, and Gonzales Contreras. *Wine and Vineyards of Chile*. Santiago: Ediciones Copygraph Publishers, 1993.

## ARGENTINA

Young, Alan. *Wine Routes of Argentina*. San Francisco: International Wine Academy, 1998.

## NEWSPAPERS AND PERIODICALS

The following publications specialize in wine or regularly run informative articles about it:

*Decanter, International Wine Cellar, San Francisco Chronicle, The New York Times, The New York Wine Cellar, The Underground Wine Journal, The Wine News, Wine Enthusiast Magazine,* and *Wine Spectator*

889

# Photo Credits

All photographs are by Karen MacNeil unless noted below.

**Action Photo:** p. 660 (inset); **a.g.e. fotostock:** p. 37 (bottom left); **Antinori Vineyard:** p. 379; **Argentina Wine Board:** p. 856 (both); **John Bean:** p. 9; **Bildagentur Buenos Dias, Vienna:** pp. 567, 573, 861; **B.I.V.B.:** pp. 187, 208; **B.I.V.B./Gaudillere:** p. 206; **B.I.V.B./Muzard:** p. 200; **B.I.V.B./Office of Tourism:** p. 211; **Black Star/Tim Hart:** p. 445; **Bonny Doon Vineyards:** p. 698; **Brotherhood Winery:** p. 718; **David Browne:** p. 747; **California Division of Tourism:** pp. 670, 703; **California Office of Tourism:** p. 678; **Canoe Ridge:** p. 728 (bottom); **Castarede Cellars:** p. 229 (top); **Castello Banfi's Glass Museum:** p. 366 (top); **CEPHAS/Rock:** pp. 585, 586, 588, 593 (both), 595; **Chile Tourism Board:** p. 834; **Christie's Images:** p. 623; **C.I.V.B. Bordeaux:** p. 50 (bottom left); **C.I.V.C.:** pp. 162, 165 (both), 167, 168; **Cognac Board:** pp. 43 (bottom right), 158; **Collection, Gloria Ferrer:** pp. 97, 366 (bottom); **Collection, The Rare Wine Company:** p. 94; **CORBIS:** pp. 466, 761; **CORBIS/Baldizzo:** p. 48; **CORBIS/Lees:** pp. 30, 379 (top left); **CORBIS/Listri:** p. 386; **CORBIS/Spiegel:** p. 10; **Cordoniu:** pp. 3, 458 (both); **Court of the Master Sommeliers:** p. 314; **Distillerie Poli:** p. 367; **Rod Dresser:** p. 205 (inset); **ENVISION:** p. 338 (center); **ENVISION/Agence Top:** pp. 255, 423, 474; **ENVISION/Asen:** pp. 380, 406 (both); **ENVISION/Needham:** pp. 212, 399, 449; **Eyrie vineyards:** p. 742; **Dennis Fife:** p. 383; **Peter Finger:** pp. 720 (all), 721 (both), 727 (bottom left); **F.I.V.A.L.:** pp. 260, 263 (inset), 264, 267 (inset), 270, 271; **FPG:** pp. 37 (bottom right), 81, 105, 106, 427, 556, 568, 570, 571, 577, 602, 682, 781; **FPG/Barone:** p. 353; **FPG/Bartuff:** p. 809; **FPG/Bibikow:** p. 579; **FPG/Castro:** p. 611; **FPG/Cooper:** pp. 50, 640, 662; **FPG/Cundy:** p. 822; **FPG/Grehan:** pp. 360, 558, 563; **FPG/Marche:** p. 306; **FPG/Ross:** p. 830; **FPG/Sacks:** p. 342 (center); **FPG/VCG:** p. 409; **FPG/Zalon:** p. 403; **Owen Franken:** p. 750; **French Tourist:** pp. 154 (both), 155; **French Wine Board:** pp. 284, 303; **German Information Center:** pp. 538, 543, 551, 553; **German Wine Insititute:** pp. 60, 516, 521, 522 (both), 523, 532, 541 (bottom); **Richard Gillette:** p. 687; **Dan Gustafson:** p. 464; **House of Sandeman:** p. 495; **ICEP:** p. 486 (both); **The Image Bank/Becker:** pp. 827, 829; **The Image Bank/Berglund:** p. 114; **The Image Bank/Lockyer:** p. 2; **The Image Bank/Pistolesi:** p. 817; **The Image Bank/Veiga:** p. 479; **Inniskillin:** p. 774 (top); **Kirk Irwin:** p. 707 (both); **Jadot Archive:** pp. 195 (both), 214; **Jordan Vineyard:** p. 668 (both); **Joseph Phelps Vineyards:** p. 34; **Krug:** pp. 170 (inset),172, 175; **LaPoja:** p. 368; **David Lett:** p. 742; **Liaison International:** p. 480; **Liaison International/Bazin:** p. 437; **Liaison International/Chib:** p. 601; **Liaison International/Francolon:** p. 450; **Liaison International/Guerrini:** p. 715; **Liaison International/Kaehler:** p. 833; **Liaison International/Nes:** p. 259; **Liaison International/Ramon:** p. 315; **Liaison International/Rapho:** p. 295; **Tom Liden:** p. 683; **Loire Tourism:** p. 265; **Anthony Loew:** pp. xi, 52, 90, 91, 178, 248, 405, 441, 443, 545, 552, 615, 859; **Fred Lyon:** pp. 621, 649; **MacNeil Collection:** pp. 3, 97, 334, 366, 690, 697; **Martini Vermouth:** p. 334; **Sara Mathews:** pp. 5, 11, 12, 17, 23 (both), 26, 27, 36, 41, 44, 50 (center bottom, left center), 55, 57, 62, 63, 75, 76, 78, 103, 118, 122, 123, 128, 131, 132, 133, 136, 140, 141, 143, 149, 153, 181, 202, 205, 219, 224, 226, 251, 263 (left and right), 267, 268, 274, 286, 288, 289, 291, 292, 318, 324, 325, 326, 329, 336, 337, 338 (bottom), 350, 417, 431 (both), 435, 711 (both), 722 (both), 723 (all), 727, 732 (top), 759, 765, 770 (top left), 774 (bottom), 776, 837, 838, 841 (both), 842 (all), 844 (all), 848, 850, 851, 853, 854, 857 (both), 860; **Steve Murez:** p. 379 (center); **Napa Valley Grape Growers:** pp. 8, 644, 659; **National Bureau of Calvados:** p. 186 (both); **New Zealand Board:** pp. 801, 802; **New Zealand Postal Service:** p. 53; **New Zealand Tourism:** pp. 810, 811 (top right), 815, 816; **New Zealand Wine Guild:** p. 808; **Oregon Tourism:** p. 738 (bottom); **Peter Arnold, Inc./Auscape:** p. 793; **Peter Arnold, Inc./Greenberg:** p. 32; **Peter Arnold, Inc./Lade:** p. 512; **Peter Arnold, Inc./Schafer:** p. 518; **PhotoDisc:** pp. xii, 84 (top left), 85, 86, 180, 389, 530, 732 (bottom); **photonica:** p. 564; **photonica/Hiraga:** p. 581; **photonica/Plummer:** p. 777; **photonica/Robbins:** pp. 373, 385; **Pintos:** p. 488 (both); **Private Collections:** pp. 604, 608, 618, 620; **Terry Reise:** p. 548; **Rhône Tourism:** pp. 234, 237, 252; **Ribera del Duera:** p. 428; **Riedel Stemware:** p. 95; **Ridge Vineyards:** p. 697; **Rioja Wines:** pp. 412, 418; **Roederer Estates:** p. 169; **George Rose:** p. 685; **Rubin/Hunter Communication, Inc.:** pp. 677, 679 (all), 680, 786, 789, 792, 799 (bottom left); **SABA/Boisseaux-Chical:** p. 220; **SABA/Decout:** pp. 818 (both), 825; **SABA/Knight:** p. 467; **SABA/Moschetti:** p. 170 (bottom); **SABA/Visum:** p. 820; **SABA/Wallis:** pp. 410, 414; **SAMA/Menuez:** p. 656; **Franco Biondi Santo:** p. 98; **Shremp Institute:** p. 444; **Gail Skoff:** pp. 20, 308 (both); **Sonoma County Grape Growers:** p. 638; **Sonoma County Wine Growers:** p. 676; **Sopexa:** pp. 222, 277 (both); **St. Genevieve:** pp. 622, 753; **StockFood America:** pp. 58 (center), 92, 270 (top right), 293, 322, 395, 425, 633, 694 (bottom), 791; **StockFood America/Christodolo:** pp. 785, 799 (top right); **StockFood America/Fleming:** p. 673 (bottom right); **StockFood America/Rock:** pp. 54, 155 (bottom right), 192, 241, 296, 300, 387, 407, 455, 476, 511, 672, 709; **StockFood America/Stefanski:** p. 673 (top left); **The Stock Market:** pp. 354, 391; **The Stock Market/Fisher:** p. 778; **The Stock Market/Geirsperger:** p. 555; **The Stock Market/Raga:** p. 454; **The Stock Market/Rossotto:** p. 396; **STONE:** p. 858; **STONE/Alexander:** pp. ii–iii, 7; **STONE/Ford:** p. 30 (top left); **STONE/Franken:** p. 111; **STONE/Gunderson:** p. 398; **STONE/Hiser:** p. 320, 321 (both); **STONE/Ivaldi:** p. 147; **Stone/McClymont:** p. 1; **STONE/Salaverry:** p. 84; **STONE/Shaw:** p. iii (inset); **STONE/Streano:** p. 372; **Superstock:** pp. 14, 299, 420, 627, 660 (bottom), 671, 771; **Symington Port & Madeira Shippers:** pp. 491 (both), 497 (both), 500, 501 (both), 502, 503; **Trefethen Vineyards:** p. 666; **Janet Vicario:** p. 134; **Tony Vicario:** p. 342 (bottom); **Virginia Tourism:** pp. 760, 763; **Veuve Clicquot:** pp. 161, 179 (both), 185; **Vinexpo:** p. 135; **Vinos USA, Inc.:** pp. 39, 40, 847, 852; **The Wine Museum:** pp. 93, 401; **Wines from Spain:** p. 439.

# Indexes

## INDEX OF PRODUCERS FOUND IN WINES TO KNOW

**893**

## GENERAL INDEX